The Broadview Antholo

SEVENTEENTH-CENTURY VERSE & PROSE

VOLUME II: PROSE

The Broadview Anthology of
Seventeenth-Century
Verse & Prose

VOLUME II: PROSE

EDITED BY

ALAN RUDRUM, JOSEPH BLACK, & HOLLY FAITH NELSON

BROADVIEW ANTHOLOGIES OF ENGLISH LITERATURE

broadview press

Canadian Cataloguing in Publication Data

Main entry under title:
    The Broadview anthology of seventeenth-century verse and prose

(Broadview anthologies of English literature)
Includes bibliographical references and indexes.
Contents: v. 1. Verse — v. 2. Prose.
ISBN 1-55111-462-3 (v. 1)   ISBN 1-55111-463-1 (v. 2)

1. English poetry – Early modern, 1500-1700. 2. English prose literature – Early modern, 1500-1700. I. Rudrum, Alan, 1932- . II. Black, Joseph Laurence, 1962- . III. Nelson, Holly Faith, 1966- . IV. Series.

PR1127.B76 2001   820.8'004   B2001-930370-X

Broadview Press Ltd., is an independent, international publishing house, incorporated in 1985.

North America:
P.O. Box 1243, Peterborough, Ontario, Canada K9J 7H5
3576 California Road, Orchard Park, NY 14127
TEL: (705) 743-8990; FAX: (705) 743-8353;
E-MAIL: customerservice@broadviewpress.com

United Kingdom:
Turpin Distribution Services Ltd.,
Blackhorse Rd., Letchworth, Hertfordshire SG6 1HN
TEL: (1462) 672555; FAX (1462) 480947; E-MAIL: turpin@rsc.org

Australia:
St. Clair Press, P.O. Box 287, Rozelle, NSW 2039
TEL: (02) 818-1942; FAX: (02) 418-1923

www.broadviewpress.com

Broadview Press gratefully acknowledges the financial support of the Book Publishing Industry Development Program, Ministry of Canadian Heritage, Government of Canada.

Cover design by George Kirkpatrick

PRINTED IN CANADA

Copyrights

Editorial Preface

Regular church-goers have sometimes remarked on an oddity of modern preaching: many sermons are delivered in apparent unawareness of the last two centuries of biblical scholarship and theological discussion. To a less dramatic extent, there has been a similar situation in the resources available to students of seventeenth-century literature. For many years now, no teaching anthology has been available which reflects current scholarship and criticism. As long ago as 1986 I wrote to a major American publisher, drawing attention to this situation. They were not interested, and there the matter rested until several years later a publisher's representative came to my office, and I suggested that his firm might consider the relationship between scholarly discussion and available classroom texts. No longer thinking of compiling such an anthology myself, and unaware that I was talking to Broadview's president, I had no idea what this brief conversation was to lead to.

One more piece of history. On accepting the commission I suggested that, while I take responsibility for male-authored verse, two editors be appointed to take overall responsibility for male-authored prose and for women's writing. The assumption was that both would be senior scholars. However, shortly after Professor David Wootton joined the project he accepted a chair in England with administrative responsibilities, and thereafter lacked time to contribute. He did, however, make a number of useful suggestions for which we are grateful. I eventually suggested that Holly Nelson, then a Ph.D. candidate at Simon Fraser University, should take responsibility for women's writing. Later, Joseph Black, then of the University of Toronto, took responsibility for prose; he also suggested and prepared several verse selections.

Literature used to be taught as *belles-lettres*. Texts were valued for their aesthetic qualities, and studied for the most part with little reference to the historical moment into which they were published. Milton, for example, was taught, and treated in histories of literature, as a pre-Restoration author, though his major poems were published, and almost certainly mainly written, after 1660. The aim of this anthology is certainly not to suggest that readers should forget about aesthetic quality. If we did not enjoy literature, there would be small point in reading it. However, if we feel the need to understand what we enjoy, we may well find ourselves taken out of "literature" and into "life," which is rarely aesthetically shaped. We shall find ourselves thinking of the historical context of what we read, of what the author hoped his or her work might accomplish in the furtherance of a particular project. We shall want to set ourselves at an author's own viewpoint, to learn, so far as we can, of the formative influences that turned the person into the writer. What about their families, their schools or their tutors? Why did Westminster School, for example, produce so many poets? Were the parents or grandparents of a given writer Catholic or Protestant? What did such choices mean to a family's security or hope of prosperity? What sort of influence might family background have at the point when minds had to be made up as political and religious tensions broke into civil war? What social forces operated to bring it about that people of similar religious views found themselves on opposite sides in that conflict? How did censorship, implicit or official, operate through that author's writing lifetime? How did education, personality, impoverishment or the possibility of enrichment combine to lead people into this choice or that? How did the social networks in which given authors lived and wrote influence their work? How was the meaning of texts shaped by the material conditions of their publication and distribution?

This anthology has been compiled in order to suggest the importance of such questions, and to provide some of the materials that students of seventeenth-century literature will need in their own explorations. What James VI/I thought about kingship might not be great literature; set out in his own words, it suggests vividly the atmosphere in which those who sought influence had to operate. Lawrence Clarkson's autobiographical *The Lost Sheep Found* and Thomas Edwards's *Gangraena* might not be the finest examples of the period's prose, but one illustrates the variety of religious choices briefly available, and the other the virulence of anti-tolerationist sentiment that such choices gave rise to in those (and they were the majority) who thought that their way was the only way. These are three examples of works which have not formerly been anthologized along with "canonical" literature. Most of the women's writing, of course, also falls into that category.

Analysis and comparison have been said to be the tools of criticism, and we have tried to make comparison possible, for example by including more than one "country house" poem, more than one poem on Jonson's response to the disastrous reception of *The New Inn*, more than one translation of Horace's "Beatus ille" ode. We have also tried, in headnotes and footnotes, to cross-refer from one such work to another to facilitate such comparisons. Some of our headnotes are longer than is customary. If we seem to be following Samuel Johnson's enjoyment of "the biographical part of literature" it is in the hope that a knowledge of the life will promote interest in and understanding of the work. In the early stages a good deal of thought was given to footnotes, and I liked the suggestion of one correspondent, who shares my view that annotating a poem is perhaps the best way to discipline oneself to a careful reading, that some poems should be printed "blank" and then again with notes. The question had to be faced as to whether detailed annotation is likely to facilitate learning, or to impede it. In the end, habit, custom, and the realization that very few undergraduates are likely to have the time and resources to deal on their own with poets such as Cleveland or Vaughan led me to think that we should annotate as thoroughly as possible. One pitfall of working in this period is that many words were spelled as they are today, and appear in contexts in which today's meanings look plausible, but may not represent the author's intentions: "horrid," "nice," and "conscience" readily spring to mind. When we are reading *Sir Gawain and the Green Knight*, we know that we are on unfamiliar linguistic territory; early modern English, in its apparent similarity to our own language, is more insidious; and we have tried to bear this too in mind when annotating. Of course, experience suggests that full accuracy in editing is difficult.

Numerous queries about our progress, in the last two years or so, suggest that university and college teachers were anxious to see the anthology in print. I am sorry for what must have seemed a slow march to completion. All three of us have experienced periods when work on the anthology had to give way to other priorities. We all hope that the result of our labours will be found at least provisionally satisfactory: a benefit of modern printing technology is the comparative ease with which improvements can be incorporated, and we shall be glad to receive comments and suggestions.

Alan Rudrum
Vancouver, April 23, 2000

A NOTE ON MODERNIZATION

With one or two brief exceptions, our texts are modernized. However, through much of the verse we have retained the italics so frequent in early modern printing; they do not impede understanding, and in fact quite often help us to hear an author's emphases. Most initial capitals have been removed, but we have sometimes introduced them where the early texts did not, to indicate personification.

ACKNOWLEDGEMENTS

This anthology is to a high degree a collective enterprise. At the outset, university teachers were asked, on electronic discussion groups such as Ficino and Milton-L, what they would like to see in an anthology of seventeenth-century verse and prose. So long ago was this, and so fickle the computer, that the following list is likely to be deficient. If so, we shall be glad to hear from those who wrote to us so that we can rectify omissions in the future. The anonymous reviewers who commented on the penultimate draft made a great many useful suggestions. In addition, we should like to thank Sharon Achinstein, Jonquil Bevan, David Boocker, Lisa Celovsky, Anne Coldiron, Tabitha Driver, Joseph Holtgen, Alan Howard, Ana Kothe, John Leonard, Michael Lofaro, Diane McColley, Mark McDayter, the denizens of Ficino and Milton-L, David Northrup, Hugh de Quehen, Sheila Roberts, Peggy Samuels, Paul Stanwood, June Sturrock, Stefano Villani, Germaine Warkentin, John Watkins, Thomas Wheeler, Samuel Wong, David Wootton, and James D. Young. Sharon Alker, Hannah Calder, Jim Daems, and Jasmine McAdam gave valuable help as research assistants. Holly Nelson wishes to thank for proof-reading: Juliet Henderson, Marion Henderson and Russell Nelson. Joseph Black wishes to thank the Northrop Frye Centre (Victoria College, University of Toronto); Trinity College, University of Toronto; the Department of English, University of Edinburgh; the Centre for the History of the Book, University of Edinburgh; the Department of English, University of Tennessee; and the Graduate School, University of Tennessee. Alan Rudrum wishes to thank the staff of Simon Fraser University Library, of the Newberry Library, and of four research libraries which have been happy hunting grounds for many years: the Bodleian Library, Oxford; the British Library; the Clark Library, Los Angeles; and the Henry E. Huntington Library, San Marino, California. Finally, at Broadview Press, it has been a pleasure to work with Don LePan; and Eileen Eckert as proofreader and Kathryn Brownsey as production coordinator have worked miracles of observation, endurance and patience.

In the notes we have used the following abbreviations:

OED   *The Oxford English Dictionary*
OCD   *The Oxford Classical Dictionary*
OCCL   *The Oxford Companion to Classical Literature*
ODCC   *The Oxford Dictionary of the Christian Church*

Contents

A MISCELLANY

INDEXES

John Chamberlain
1553 – 1627

John Chamberlain's letters, generally considered the finest of the Jacobean age, provide a continuous commentary on political and social life in London from the late sixteenth century through to the first years of the reign of Charles I. The son of a wealthy ironmonger who left him with an independent income, Chamberlain attended Trinity College, Cambridge, and Gray's Inn in the 1570s, though he appears not to have taken a degree nor to have been called to the bar. Little is known of his activities until 1597, the year he wrote the earliest of his nearly five hundred extant letters. While his wealth relieved him of the necessity of working, Chamberlain was in effect a professional supplier of information: except for a few trips abroad, he never lived more than a short walk from St. Paul's Cathedral, London's general meeting place and the centre of the trade in both books and gossip. Like Samuel Pepys, Chamberlain was well connected, with an unusual number of friends prominent in the city and court; these included Lancelot Andrewes, antiquary William Camden, scientist William Gilbert, diplomat Sir Ralph Winwood, and his most frequent correspondent, Sir Dudley Carleton, ambassador to Venice (1610–15) and Secretary of State (1628–32). Twenty years older than Carleton, Chamberlain was a trusted advisor and discreet friend who kept the diplomat informed of all the news during his stays abroad. Carleton's sister Alice, a recipient of several of the letters included here, was also a life-long friend, and there are hints in the letters that they might have contemplated marriage, though both died unmarried.

えンベつ

Letters

The Death of Queen Elizabeth

March 30, 1603, to Dudley Carleton in Paris: I have not written since I received yours of the 8th of this present, after your style,[1] for we were held in suspense and know not how nor what to write, the passages being stopped, and all conveyance so dangerous and suspicious.[2] I make no question but you have heard of our great loss before this come at you; and no doubt but you shall hear her Majesty's sickness and manner of death diversely related, for even here the papists do tell strange stories, as utterly void of truth as of all civil honesty or humanity.

I had a good means to understand how the world went,[3] and find her disease to be nothing but a settled and unremovable melancholy, insomuch that she could not be won or persuaded, neither by the Council, divines, physicians, nor the women about her, once to taste or touch any physic; though ten or twelve physicians that were continually about her did assure her with all manner of asseverations of perfect and easy recovery if she would follow their advice....

Here was some whispering that her brain was somewhat distempered, but there was no such matter, only she held an obstinate silence for the most part; and because she had a persuasion that if

---

[1] *after your style* Because he was living in Europe, Carleton used the Gregorian calendar, which was ten days ahead of the Julian calendar used in England until the eighteenth century:

[2] The Queen died on March 24, and shipping and travel were restricted to prevent the possibility of anyone organizing a coup during the transition from one monarch to another (a standard early modern practice).

[3] Chamberlain's inside source was his friend William Gilbert, the Queen's physician.

she once lay down she should never rise, could not be gotten to bed in a whole week till three days before her death. So that after three weeks' languishing, she departed the 24 of this present, being Our Lady's eve, between two and three in the morning....

The Archbishop of Canterbury, the Bishop of London, the Almoner,[1] and other her chaplains and divines had access to her in her sickness diverse times, to whom she gave good testimony of her faith by word, but specially towards her end by signs when she was speechless, and would not suffer the Archbishop to depart as long as she had sense, but held him twice or thrice when he was going and could no longer endure, both by reason of his own weakness and compassion of hers.

She made no will, nor gave anything away, so that they which come after shall find a well-stored jewel house and a rich wardrobe of more than 2000 gowns with all things else answerable.

The nobility and Council came from Richmond that morning, and before ten o'clock had proclaimed King James at Whitehall, Temple Bar, and so forward in Cheapside and other places. Sir Robert Carey was the first that of his own motion carried news of her death into Scotland.[2] The next day the Lords sent Sir Charles Percy and Thomas Somerset, with the proclamation and letters to the King; and yesterday Master [George] Carew, a Mastery of the Chancery, and Master [Thomas] Lake were dispatched about other business. There is much posting that way and many run thither of their own errand, as if it were nothing else but first come first served, or that preferment were a goal to be got by footmanship....

We attend him here with great devotion and begin to think long till we have him.[3] The Lords have sent to know his pleasure whether he will come by land or sea, for which purpose there be eight or ten ships ready that were going for the coast of Spain but do now tarry to keep the Narrow Seas. Surely the Council dealt very providently and beyond that that was to be expected or hoped for in so sudden an accident; and no doubt but God did direct them, seeing all things passed so quietly and in good order....

The Marriage of Princess Elizabeth and Prince Frederick, Elector Palatine[4]

February 4, 1613, to Alice Carleton in Venice: Here is extraordinary preparation for fireworks and fights upon the water, with three castles built upon eight western barges, and one great castle upon the land over against the Court. One or two of the King's pinnaces are come already from Rochester,[5] and diverse other vessels to the number of six and thirty are provided,...and above five hundred watermen already pressed, and a thousand musketeers of the trained bands in the Shires hereabout made ready for this service, which in all computation cannot stand the king in so little as five thousand pounds...

February 11, 1613, to Sir Dudley Carleton: The marriage draws near and all things are ready. On Sunday was their last time of asking openly in the

---

[1] respectively John Whitgift, Richard Bancroft, and Anthony Watson, Bishop of Chichester.

[2] Carey made the almost four-hundred-mile journey to Edinburgh on horse in a remarkable three days; he was knighted for being the first to arrive with the news.

[3] *attend* look out for, await (*OED* attend 13).

[4] Elizabeth (1596–1662), eldest daughter of James I and for one year Queen of Bohemia (the brevity of her reign gave rise to the name "the Winter Queen"); Frederick V, Elector Palatine (1596–1632). His acceptance of the crown of Bohemia in 1619 helped initiate the Thirty Years' War. His forces were soon routed, and the couple fled to The Hague, where Elizabeth lived until returning to England after the Restoration. Prince Rupert, Royalist General of Horse during the Civil War, was their son. The Act of Succession (1701) vested the English throne in her descendants (George I was her grandson).

[5] *pinnaces* small boats.

chapel. The Queen grows every day more favorable, and there is hope she will grace it with her presence. Here is a band of 500 musketeers made ready by the City to guard the Court during these triumphs, and we have extraordinary watches of substantial householders every night, and an alderman in person to oversee them. Many searches are made, and much listening there is, which gives occasion to suspect that there is intelligence of some intended treachery....The preparations for fireworks and fights upon the water are very great, and have already consumed 6000 pounds....

February 18, 1613, to Alice Carleton: On Thursday night the fireworks were reasonably well performed, all save the last castle of five, which bred most expectation and had most devices, but when it came to execution had worst success. On Saturday likewise, the fight upon the water came short of that show and brags had been made of it, but they pretend the best to be behind and left for another day, which was the winning of the castle on land: but the King and indeed all the company took so little delight to see no other activity but shooting and potting of guns that it is quite given over and the navy unrigged and the castle pulled down, the rather for that there were diverse hurt in the former fight (as one lost both his eyes, another both his hands, another one hand, with diverse others maimed and hurt), so that to avoid further harm, it was thought best to let all alone, and this is the conclusion of all the preparation with so much expense of powder and money which amounted to no less than 9000 pounds.

On Sunday I was fetched from Paul's (where I was set at the sermon) to see the bride go to church, and though it were past ten o'clock before we came there, yet we found a whole window reserved in the jewel-house, which was over against her coming down a pair stairs out of the gallery in the preaching place to a long stage or gallery made along the court into the hall,[1] so that we had as much view as a short passage could give. But the excess of bravery and the continued succession of new company did so dazzle me that I could not observe the tenth part of that I wished. The bridegroom and bride were both in a suit of cloth of silver, richly embroidered with silver, her train carried up by thirteen young Ladies (or Lord's daughters at least) besides five or six more that could not come near it; these were all in the same livery with the bride, though not so rich. The bride was married in her hair that hung down long,[2] with an exceeding rich coronet on her head which the King valued the next day at a million of crowns. Her two bridemen were the young Prince and the Earl of Northampton.

The King and Queen both followed, the Queen all in white but not very rich saving in jewels. The King methought was somewhat strangely attired in a cap and a feather, with a Spanish cape and a long stocking. The chapel was very straitly kept,[3] none suffered to enter under the degree of a baron, but the three Lords Chief Justices: in the midst there was a handsome stage or scaffold made, on the one side whereof sat the King, Prince, Count Palatine and Count Henry of Nassau, on the other side the Queen with the bride and one or two more....It was done all in English, and the Prince Palatine had learned as much as concerned his part reasonable perfectly. The French, Venetian and [Dutch] States ambassadors dined that day with the bride. The Spanish ambassador was sick and the Archduke's was invited for the next day but would not come. That night was the Lord's masque whereof I hear no great commendation save only for the riches,

---

[1] *pair stairs* a flight of stairs (*OED* pair 6b).

[2] *hair that hung down long* as a sign of her virginity.

[3] *straitly* strictly, rigorously (*OED* straitly 6).

their devices being long and tedious and more like a play than a masque.[1]

The next morning the King went to visit these young turtles that were coupled on St. Valentine's day, and did strictly examine him whether he were his true son-in-law, and was sufficiently assured.[2] That afternoon the King, Prince, Count Palatine, with diverse others, ran at the ring, and when that was ended and the King and Prince gone, the Palsgrave mounted upon a high-bounding horse which he managed so like a horseman that he was exceedingly commended and had many shouts and acclamations of the beholders, and indeed I never saw any of his age come near him in that exercise.

It were long and tedious to tell you all the particularities of the excessive bravery both of men and women,[3] but you may conceive the rest by one or two. The Lady Wotton had a gown that cost fifty pound a yard the embroidering…and the Lord Montague (that hath paid reasonably well for recusancy) bestowed fifteen hundred pound in apparel for his two daughters.…But this extreme of cost and riches makes us all poor.

On Monday night was the Middle Temple and Lincoln's Inn masque,[4] presented in the Hall at Court, whereas the Lord's was in the banqueting room. It went from the Rolls all up Fleet Street and the Strand,[5] and made such a gallant and glorious show that it is highly commended. They had forty gentlemen of best choice out of both houses ride before them in their best array, upon the King's horses. And the twelve maskers with their torch-bearers and pages rode likewise upon horses exceedingly well trapped and furnished, besides a dozen little boys dressed like baboons that served for an antimasque (and they say performed it exceedingly well when they came to it), and three open chariots drawn with four horses apiece that carried their musicians and other personages that had parts to speak. All which, together with their trumpeters and other attendants, were so well set out that it is generally held for the best show that hath been seen many a day.…

On Tuesday it came to Gray's Inn and the Inner Temple's turn to come with their masque, whereof Sir Francis Bacon was the chief contriver. And because the former came on horseback and open chariots, they made choice to come by water from Winchester Place in Southwark, which suited well enough with their device, which was the marriage of the river of Thames to the Rhine; and their show by water was very gallant by reason of infinite store of lights very curiously set and placed, and many boats and barges with devices of light and lamps, with three peals of ordnance: one at their taking water, another in the Temple garden, and the last at their landing; which passage by water cost them better than three hundred pounds.…

One thing I had almost forgotten for haste, that all this time there was a course taken and so notified, that no Lady or gentlewoman should be admitted to any of these sights with a farthingale, which was to gain the more room, and I hope may serve to make them quite left off in time. Any yet there were more scaffolds and more provision made for room than ever I saw, both in the Hall and Banqueting Room, besides a new room built to dine, sup, and dance in.

—(1603, 1613)

---

[1] The masque was by Thomas Campion, and was printed with *A Relation of the Late Royall Entertainment given by the Lord Knowles* (1613).

[2] *turtles* turtle-doves, a traditional image for young lovers; *did strictly examine him* probably a verbal examination to assure himself that the marriage had been consummated.

[3] *bravery* finery, fine clothes (*OED* bravery 3b).

[4] by George Chapman, printed as *The Memorable Maske of the Middle Temple, and Lyncolns Inne* (1613).

[5] *Rolls* Rolls Chapel, in Chancery Lane.

Lancelot Andrewes

1555 – 1626

Lancelot Andrewes' father was a merchant who became master of Trinity House, the corporation responsible for overseeing the lighthouses around the British coast. Andrewes' teachers, seeing his great promise as a pupil, persuaded his parents to give him the opportunity to become a scholar, an opportunity of which he took full advantage. He learned to read many languages, and his interest in the meanings of words is the basis of his style as a writer of sermons. Andrewes was successively Bishop of Chichester, of Ely, and of Winchester; many were surprised that he was not made Archbishop of Canterbury. He was in 1607 appointed as one of the translators of the Authorized (or King James) Version of the Bible, published in 1611.

Andrewes was politically conservative and accepted the view of royalty promulgated by the Tudors and pushed to an extreme by James; but he was a politic rather than a political person. There is a story that James asked Bishop Neale of Durham and Andrewes, then Bishop of Winchester, whether he could not take his subjects' money without "all this formality in Parliament." Neale replied that indeed he could, for "you are the breath of our nostrils." Andrewes replied that he had no skill in Parliamentary cases, but when pressed for a further comment replied, "I think it lawful for you to take my brother Neale's money, because he offers it."

Though he wrote some polemical works against Roman Catholicism, Andrewes is now best remembered for a volume of prayers, first published in 1648 in translation from the Greek and Latin of Andrewes' manuscript, and republished in various formats through the centuries; and for his sermons, ninety-six of which were published in 1628. In his sermons some readers will miss Donne's wonderful rhythms and uninhibited emotionalism. Others will find, in the meticulous and imaginative attention Andrewes brings to his biblical texts, the authentic passion of a great scholar and a genuinely spiritual man. For a seventeenth-century life of Andrewes, see John Aubrey's *Brief Lives*.

❦

A Sermon Preached Before The King's Majesty at Whitehall,
on the Sixteenth of April, A.D. MDCIX, Being Easter-Day

JOHN 20:19

Cum ergo sero esset die illo, una sabbatorum, et fores essent clausæ, ubi erant Discipuli congregati propter metum Judæorum, venit Jesus, et stetit in medio, et dixit eis, Pax vobis.

The same day then, at night, which was the first day of the week, and when the doors were shut, where the Disciples were assembled for fear of the Jews, came Jesus and stood in the midst, and said to them, Peace be unto you.

This is the interview of Christ and his Disciples, and this his first speech at his first interview; both this day, the very first day of his rising.

Five sundry times appeared he this day. To Mary Magdalene, to the women coming from the sepulchre, to the two that went to Emmaus, to St. Peter, and here now to the Eleven and those that were with them. The two first to women, the three last to men; so both sexes. To Peter and to Mary Magdalene, so to sinners of both sexes. To the Eleven as the Clergy, to those with them, as the Laity; so, to both estates. Abroad at Emmaus, at home here. Betimes, and now late. When they were scattered severally, and now jointly when they were gathered together. That no sex, sort, estate, place or time excepted, but as *visitavit nos oriens ab alto*, so *visitavit occidens ab imo*; "rising from above at his birth, rising from beneath at his resurrection, he visited all." [1]

But of all the five, this is the chief. Those were to one, as Peter; or two, as those of Emmaus; or three, as the women. This to all; the more, the more witnesses, the better for faith. Those when they were scattered; this here when they were all together. The more together, the more meet for this salutation here, Peace be to you.

Which salutation is the very substance of the text, the rest but appendant all.

In it, two things give forth themselves: 1. The persons to whom, *vobis*. 2. The matter of the wish itself, "peace." The persons are thus set down: *Discipuli, congregati, conclusi*. 1. His "Disciples" they were, 2. "gathered," 3. and "the doors shut" on them "for fear of the Jews."

There will fall out besides four other points. 1. Christ's site; that he stood, when he wished it. 2. His place; that in the midst he stood. 3. The time; all this, the same day, the first day of the week, Sunday, Easter-day: 4. and the very time of the day, that it was late.

The speech of itself is a salutation; any will so conceive it at the first hearing. And if it were but so, and no more, that were enough. Christ's salutations are not, as ours be, formal, but good matter in them.

But it is more than a salutation, say the Fathers, for this reason. At meeting men use to salute but once: within a verse, he repeateth it again. So it keeps not the law of a salutation, but it is certainly somewhat besides. *Votum Christi*, they call it. *Votum pacis, votum Christi*; "Christ's vow, or wish"; his vow, and his first vow.

Now every vow implieth an advice at the least. What Christ wisheth to us, he wisheth us to. Every wish so. But if it be the wish of a superior in his optative, there is an imperative; his wish is a command, if he have wit that hears it. So that these words, rightly understood, are both an advice, and an injunction to it, of the nature of an edict. *Pax vobis* is as much as *Pacem habete in vobis*, "be at peace among yourselves." [2]

We are then to join with Christ, to follow him in his wish. To whom he wisheth it; to all Christ's Disciples together, even to his whole Christian Church; and even to them that, it may be, as little deserve it, as these here did. 1. To make it *caput voti*, "our first vow"; yea, first and second, as Christ here did. 2. *Oportet stantem optare*, "to wish it standing." 3. And standing where Christ stood, that is material, "in the midst." 4. This day to do it, and think it pertinent to the time; it is *votum paschale*. [3] As for *sero*, [4] we shall never need to take thought for it, it is never too soon; late enough always if it be not too late, that is all the fear.

The chief point first: *Pax vobis*. The words are but two, yet even between them there seemeth to be no peace, but one in a manner opposite to the other. Looking to *vobis*, the persons, this should not be a salutation for them, *pax*. Looking to the salutation, "peace," it should not be to those persons, *vobis*, "to you." So that our first work will be, to make peace between the two words.

Vobis, "to you." Will you know who they be? "To you," Peter, and John, and the rest. "To you," of whom none stood by Me. "To you," of whom some ran away, some denied, yea forsware me. "To you," of whom all, every one shrunk away and forsook me. How evil doth this greeting agree with

---

[1] Luke 1:78.

[2] Mark 9:50.

[3] "the Easter prayer."

[4] "at a late hour."

this *vobis*! Yet even to these, *venit, et stetit, et dixit*; "He came, stood, and said, Peace be to you."

Used by them as he had been, no cause he should come, or stand, or speak at all; or if speak, not thus. Not come to them that went from him, nor stand amongst them that had not stood to him, nor speak to them that had renounced him. It is said, "they feared the Jews." All things considered, they had more cause to fear him, and to look for some real revenge at his hands. If not that, some verbal reproof, a salutation of another style or tenor; and well, if they might scape so. *Confitemini Domino, quia bonus:*[1]—it is not so, no evil deed for all this, no, not so much as an unkind word. Above that they could look for, far above that they deserved it is; *Pax vobis*. You and I are at peace, you and I are friends; "Peace be unto you." This is his first goodness, his making a peace between *pax* and *vobis*.

This speech to these persons is much mended by adding the time in the text, that it was *illo die*, the day of his rising. *Pax vobis* is a good speech for Good-Friday; then men grow charitable, when ready to die. But on their Easter-day, at their rising, the day when *exultavit Eum Deus*, "the day of their exaltation," they use to take other manner spirits, and remember former disgraces, with a far other congé.[2] *Haec est lex hominis*; men do thus, but not Christ. Neither their indignity, *vobis*; nor his own dignity changeth him. Rising, exalted, the very day of his exaltation, *illo die*, he saith, "Peace be unto you."

Another yet: that it was *primâ sabbati*, the very "first day of the week"; took no long day for it, nay, no day at all, but the very first day. Joseph exalted dealt well with his brethren, but not the first day; it

was some time first. He kept them in fear a while, but showed himself at the last. Christ doth not so hold them in suspense: *illo die, primo die*, "the same day, the first day," he came, and showed himself and said, "Peace be unto you."

Yea, not so much as *dixit* here but, as it falls out, will bear a note. Even that it is *dixit*, and not *respondit*; a speech, not an answer. That he spake it, unspoken to; he to them first, ere they to him. He might well have stayed till then, and reason would they should first have sued for it. Ere they ask it he giveth it, and "prevents them with the blessing of peace." They first in falling out, he first at making friends.

A great comfort for poor sinners, when the many indignities we have offered Christ shall present themselves before us, to think of this *vobis*. That when the Disciples had done the like, yet he forgat all, and spake thus kindly to them this day; that he will vouchsafe us the like, specially if we seek it he will, and say to us, *Pax vobis*.

Will ye remember now to extend your wish of peace 1. to them that, it may be, deserve it as evil as these here, even *his qui longe*.[3] 2. To do it at our rising, at our high day, when it is Easter with us; 3. not to make their hearts to pant, and eyes to fail first, but even *primâ sabbati* to do it. 4. And not to take state upon us, and be content to answer Peace, and not speak; be moved for it, but not move it; yes, even move it first. If we do, we join with Christ in his first part, the personal part of the wish.

Illis, and *illo die*, and *primo die*, what they were we see, and in what sort. Yet not to grate on this point altogether, some smoke yet was there in the flax, some small remainders, *illices misericordiae* as Tertullian, to move his mercy. In these words, 1. *Discipuli*, 2. *congregati*, 3. *conclusi*, 4. *propter ti-*

---

[1] rendered "O give thanks unto the Lord; for he is good" in *AV* (Psalm 106:1).

[2] *congé* a bow or other formal gesture of salutation or leave-taking; Andrewes' point is that Christ's greeting, even in his exaltation, was humble. See *OED* congee *sb*.

[3] "to those [who are] far off." See Ephesians 2:17.

morem Judæorum: that his "Disciples" yet they were; and "together" they were; and "in fear of the Jews" they were "shut up."

Whatsoever, or howsoever they were else, yet they were his Disciples; "unprofitable servants," yet servants; "lost" sons, yet sons; forgetful Disciples, yet Disciples. His Disciples they were, and howsoever they had made a fault, as it seemeth, so meant to hold themselves still, and hereafter to learn their lesson better.

And I like well their fear, that they were afraid of the Jews. It shows there were no good terms betwixt them, and that they shut their doors upon them; therefore they meant not to go out to them, or seek *Pax vobis* of the Jews. They had no meaning it seemeth to give over Christ. If they had, what need they fear the Jews? The Jews would have done them no harm, they might have set open their doors well enough.

And *congregatis*, I take it well, is no evil sign. It would have been *ex aliâ causâ*, for love rather than fear; and again, for fear of God, rather than of the Jews. Yet even thus I mislike it not, and much better this fear, than that at the Passion. That scattered them one from another, every man shift for one. This makes them draw together, and keep together, as if they meant to stand out afresh. Which very *congregatis* makes them fit for this salutation. It cannot well be said, *disgregatis*, "to them that are in sunder." *Una* is a disposition to unity; and gathering, to the binding up in the band of peace. Christ that said, *Quoties volui congregare?*[1] liked it well, to find them thus together; and his coming was, as to take away their fear, so to continue their gathering still.

And shall we learn this of the Disciples? 1. If a fault fall out, not to give over school, but to continue our discipleship still. 2. And not to go over, to seek our *Pax vobis* at the hands of his enemies; to shut out both them, and their peace too. 3. And lastly, not to forsake the fellowship, to keep together still. For being so together, we are nearer our peace. This shall make Christ come and say it to us the sooner, and the more willingly.

The real part, *voti summa*, that which he wisheth, is "peace." First, why peace? then, what peace?

Why peace? Is there nothing more worth the wishing? Nothing more, of itself; nothing more fit for these persons, this place, and this time.

Of itself, *votum pacis summa votorum*. "It is all wishes in one," nothing more to be wished. For *in brevi voce breviarium*, "this little word is a breviary of all" that good is.

To show how, a little; *quam bonum*, "how good," how worth the wishing it is. It is *tam bonum*, "so good," as without it nothing is good. With it, saith Solomon, "an handful of herbs"; without it, "an house full of sacrifices is not good."[2] With trouble and vexation nothing is good, nothing is to be wished.

And as without it nothing is to be wished, so all that is to be wished, all good, is within it. *Evangelizantium pacem, evangelizantium bona, quia in pace omnia bona*: "to bring news of peace, is to bring news of all good things," "for all good things are in peace."[3] *Bona* is the true gloss or exposition of peace.

Quam bonum, you know, and *quam jucundum* too. But good and pleasant; and pleasant, not only as Aaron's ointment which was only pleasant, but as Hermon dew which brings profit with it.[4] *Abundantia pacis*, saith the Psalm, "peace and plenty" go together.[5]

---

[1] quoted from the Vulgate. See Matthew 23:37.

[2] Proverbs 15:16–17.

[3] Romans 10:15.

[4] *Hermon dew*   See Psalm 133.

[5] probably a reference to Psalm 37:11: "But the meek shall inherit the earth; and shall delight themselves in the abundance of peace."

And yet, how much it is to be wished, this showeth, *pacem te poscimus omnes.* All wish it. Angels wish it, Heaven to earth, *pax in terris*; and men wish it, earth to Heaven, *pax in Cælis.* God wisheth it, most kindly for him; *Deus pacis, pacem Dei*; "the God of peace," "the peace of God." Yea the enemy of all peace wisheth it, for he complains, *Venisti nos inquietare,* "Are ye come to trouble us?" So he would not be troubled that troubles all, but set all together by the ears, and sit quiet himself.

But it is much for the honour of peace, that *cum bellum geritur, pax quaeritur.* Even military persons, with sword in one hand and fire in the other, give this for their emblem, *sic quaerimus pacem,* "thus, with sword and fire, seek we peace." As seek it at last they must; we must all. Best *primâ sabbati*, but *sero,* "sooner or later," come to it we must: if it be not the first, it must be our last.

But if there were nothing else, this only were enough, and though there be many, this chiefly doth show it; that our Saviour Christ so often, so divers ways, so earnestly wisheth it. Going he did it, *Pacem meam do vobis.*[1] And now coming, he doth it. Sitting, he did it; and now, standing. Living, when he was born, *Pax in terris*; *Xenium Christi,* "it was Christ's New-year's gift." Dying, when he was to suffer, *Pacem meam relinquo vobis,* it was *legatum Christi,* "Christ's legacy." And now here rising again, it is his wish still. To show, not only the good of this life, but of the next, to be in peace. Prayed for it, paid for it, wept for it; "O if thou hadst known the things that pertain to thy peace!" Wept for it, and bled for it: therefore immediately, the very next words, he showeth them his hands and his side, as much to say; See what I have suffered to procure your peace. Your peace cost me this, *Pax vobis* cost *Crux mihi*;—see you hold it dear. Now sure, if there were any one thing better than other, those hands would not have withheld it, and that

heart would wish it. And peace it doth wish, therefore nothing more to be wished. Complete it is, *Votum pacis summa votorum.*[2]

There need no other sign be given but that of the Prophet Jonas,[3] that Christ wished his wish: so the tempest may cease, and peace as a calm ensue, spare me not, "take me, cast me into the sea,"[4] make me a peace-offering and kill me. This is enough to show it is to be wished, to make it precious in our eyes. For we undervalue it at too low a rate, when that which cost so dear, for every trifling ceremony we are ready to lose it. Our faint persuasion in this point is the cause we are faint in all the rest.

Well, though this be thus good, yet good itself is not good, unless it be in season, come fitly. Doth this so? Every way fitly. 1. For the *Persons*; 2. For the *Place*; 3. And for the *Time.*

The persons; both 1. Christ by whom, and 2. they to whom it is wished. 1. Christ, by whom; *decet largitorem pacis haec salutatio,* saith Cyril. "It is meet for him to give peace that made peace"; nay, *ipse est pax nostra,*[5] saith the Apostle, and for peace, what fitter salutation than peace?

2. They to whom, for they needed it. With God they had no peace, whom they had provoked; nor peace with men, nor with the Jews about them; nor peace with themselves, for they were in fear, and night-fear, which is the worst of all others. Fit for them, and they for it, for together they were, and so not unfit to entertain it.

And with the place it suiteth well. For they were shut up, as men environed and beleaguered with

---

[1] "My peace I give unto you."

[2] "The prayer for peace is the highest of prayers."

[3] See Matthew 12:39.

[4] Jonah 1:12.

[5] Ephesians 2:14.

their enemies, *conclusi et derelicti*, "shut up and forsaken"; and to such peace is ever welcome.

And for the time, seasonable. For after a falling out, peace is so; and after a victory, peace is so. Fit therefore for this day, the day of the Resurrection; for till then it was not in kind. The great battle was not fought, "the last enemy, death," was not overcome.[1] Never till now, but now the last enemy is conquered, now it is in season.

And for the thing itself, peace is a kind of resurrection. When Christ was risen, his Disciples were dead. Those dead affections of sorrow and fear, when they seize thoroughly upon men, what are they but *mors ante mortem?* Upon good news of Joseph, Jacob is said to "revive," as if before he had been given for dead.[2] It was their case here. The house was to them as their grave, and the door as the gravestone, and they buried in fear. When they saw him, in the next verse, and were thus saluted by him, they gat hope, were glad, that is, revived again. For if those were the pangs of death, peace after a sort is a resurrection; and so a fit wish for the time.

And to say truth, peace is never kindly till then. They define felicity shortly, to be nothing else but *pax desiderii*. For give the desire perfect peace, and no more needs to make us happy. Desire hath no rest, and will let us have none, till it have what it would, and till the Resurrection that will not be.

1. *Pax et pressura*, our Saviour opposeth.[3] If we be pinched with any want, desire hath no peace. 2. Let us want nothing if it were possible. No peace yet; *pax et scandalum* the Psalmist opposeth.[4] When we have what we would, somewhat cometh to us we would not, somewhat thwarts us. Till *non est eis*

scandalum, till that be had away, desire hath no peace. 3. Let that be had away, yet a new war there cometh. Peace and fear are here opposed. We are well; neither *pressura* nor *scandalum*, but we fear *tolletur a vobis*, that it will not hold, or we shall not hold. "The last enemy" will not let us be quiet. Till he "be overcome," our desire hath no perfect peace. That will not be till the Resurrection. But then it is *pax plena, pura, perpetua*; "full" without want, "pure" without mixture of offensive matter, and "perpetual" without all fear of foregoing, of *tolletur a vobis*. And that is *pax desiderii*, and that is perfect felicity; the state of the Resurrection, and the wish of the Resurrection day.

Thus we see good it is, and fit it is. It remains we see what it is, what peace. When we speak of peace, the nature of the word leadeth us to ask, With whom? And they be diverse. But as diverse as they be, it must be understood of all, though of some one more especially than the rest.

There is a peace above us in Heaven with God; that first. They were wrong here, their fear ran all upon the Jews, it should have looked higher. The Jews they kept out with shutting their doors; against God no door can be shut. First, peace with him; and with him they have peace, to whom Christ saith *Pax vobis*.

There is another peace within us, *in sinu*, "with our heart." For between our spirit and our flesh there is in manner of a war. "The lusts of the flesh" ever militant, "wage war," saith St. Peter, "against the soul;" and where there is a war, there is a peace too.[5] This is peace with fear, here. Which war is sometime so fearful, as men to rid themselves of it, rid themselves of life and all, conclude a peace there. This followeth of the first; if all be well above, all is well within.

---

[1] I Corinthians 15:26.

[2] Genesis 45:27.

[3] In the Vulgate, the second part of John 16:33 reads: "*In mundo pressuram habebitis: sed confidite, ego vici mundum.*" *AV* reads: "In the world ye shall have tribulation: but be of good cheer; I have overcome the world."

[4] Psalm 119:165.

[5] I Peter 2:11.

There is a peace without us, in earth with men, with all men. The Apostle warrants it; peace with the Jews here and all. I will never fear to make civil peace a part of Christ's wish, nor of his *beati pacifici* neither.[1] He will be no worse at Easter, than at Christmas he was; at this his second, than at that his first birth. Then Janus was shut, and peace over all the world. *Orbem pacatum* was ever a clause in the prayers of the Primitive Church, that the world might be quiet.

Yet is not this the peace of Christ's principal intendment, but their peace to whom Christ spake, *Pax discipulorum, Pax vobis inter vos*; "Peace among them, or between themselves." It was "the ointment on Aaron's head," Aaron that had the care of the Church.[2] It was "the dew" that fell upon Sion, Sion the place where the Temple stood.[3] "The peace of Jerusalem," that it may be once "as a city at unity within itself." The primitive peace, that "the multitude of believers" may be "of one heart and one mind." All the rest depend upon our peace with God, and our peace with him upon this; *pacem habete inter vos*, and *Deus pacis erit vobiscum*. "The peace of Jerusalem," "they shall prosper that love it," saith David.[4] "Joy shall be to them that counsel it," saith Solomon.[5] "Blessed" shall they be that make it, saith Christ.[6] How great a reward should he find in Heaven, how glorious a name should he leave on earth, that could bring this to pass!

This is Christ's wish, and what is become of it? If we look upon the Christian world, we see it not, it is gone as if Christ had never wished it. Between Jehu and Jeroboam, Solomon's seed went to rack. Jehu's proceedings, like his chariot-wheels, headlong and violent. But Jehu is but a brunt, too violent to last long. Jeroboam is more dangerous, who makes it his wisdom to keep up a schism in religion; they shall sway both parts more easily. God forbid we should ever think Jeroboam wiser than Solomon! If peace were not a wise thing, the wisest man's name should not have been Solomon. "A greater than Solomon" would never have said *Habete salem et pacem*; "if you have any salt, you will have peace." Sure, when the Disciples lost their peace, they lost their wisdom; their wisdom and their strength both. They were stronger by *congregatis*, than by *clausis foribus*; "more safe by their being together, than any door could make them."

It is as Christ told us (Luke 10, where he prescribes this form of salutation[7]): it speeds or it misses thereafter, as it meets with "the Son of peace"; speeds if it find him, if not, comes back again, and takes no place.

Well, though it do not, we must still hold us to Christ's wish, and when all fails, still there must be *Votum pacis in corde*; though enmity in the act, yet "peace in the heart still." Still it must hold, *amicus et non alter, inimicus ut non idem*; "friends as if never otherwise, enemies as if not ever so." *Quasi torrens, bellum*; "war, like a land-flood," that will be dry again. *Quasi fluvius, pax*; "peace, as a river," never dry, but to run still and ever.

But yet, many times "we ask and have not, because we ask not aright," saith St. James; "we know not the things that belong to our peace"; we err in the order, manner, site, place, or time.[8]

The order, which helpeth much, first it is; first, *primum et ante omnia, caput fidei*, "the prime of his wishes." No sooner born, but *pax in terris*; no sooner risen, but *pax vobis. Apertio labiorum*, "the

---

[1] Matthew 5:9.

[2] See Psalm 133 and Exodus 28.

[3] See Psalm 133; "Zion was the citadel of Jerusalem...probably situated...south of the site of the Temple. The name came to signify God's holy hill at Jerusalem; see Psalm 2:6" (*ODCC*).

[4] Psalm 122:6.

[5] Proverbs 12:20.

[6] Matthew 5:9.

[7] See Luke 10:5–6.

[8] James 4:3.

very opening of his lips" was with these words; the first words at the first meeting, on the very first day. It is a sign it is so in his heart. That which most grieveth us, we first complain of; and that which most affecteth us, ever soonest speak of. This is the first error. That which was first with Christ, is last with Christians, and I would it were so last; for then it were some, now scarce any at all as it seemeth.

In the manner; for first is but first, that is but once. This is first and second. Here he saith it, and within a verse he is at it again. Nay first, second, and third, 1. in this, 2. the twenty-first, and 3. the twenty-sixth verses; as if like *actio* in Rhetoric, all in all.[1]

All Christ's vows are to be esteemed, specially his solemn vows; and his speeches, chiefly those he goeth over and over again. That which by him is double and treble said, would not by us be singly regarded. He would have it better marked; therefore he speaketh it the second time. He would have it yet sink deeper; therefore the third also. We faulty in the manner. Once we do it, it may be, but upon any repulse we give over; if it come not at first, we go not to it *secundo et tertio, repetitis vicibus.*[2] We must not leave at once, that Christ did so oft.

The second error is; we ask it sitting, I fear, and Christ stood; his standing imports something. Standing is the site of them that are ready to go about a matter, as they to take their journey in the twelfth of Exodus. That site is the site of them that wish for peace; *oportet stantem optare.*[3] A sedentary desire it may be we have, but loath to leave our cushion. We would it were well, but not willing to dis-ease ourselves. *Utinam hoc esset laborare,*[4] said he, that lay along and stretched himself. So say we; peace we would, but standing is painful. Our wish hath lips, but no legs.

But it could not be said, "beautiful are the feet of them that bring peace," if the feet had nothing to do in this business. With sitting and wishing it will not be had. Peace will hide itself, it must be sought out; it will fly away, it must be pursued. This then is a point wherein we are to conform ourselves to Christ; as well to use our legs, as to open our lips for it. To stand, is *situs voventis;*[5] to hold up the hands, *habitus orantis.*[6] The meaning of which ceremony of lifting up the hands with prayer is, *ut pro quo quis orat pro eo laboret,* "what we pray for we should labour for"; what we wish for, stand for. We see Christ showeth his hands and his feet, to show what must be done with both for it. If we should be put to do the like, I doubt our wish hath never a good leg to stand on.

To stand then, but to stand in a certain place. Every where to stand will not serve the turn. *Stetit in medio,* that standing place is assigned for it, thus "guiding our feet into the way of peace." And the place is material for peace. All bodies natural never leave moving, are never quiet, till they recover their proper places; and there they find peace. The midst is Christ's place by nature; he is the second person *in Divinis,* and so the middlemost of the other two. And on earth, follow him if you will, you shall not lightly find him out of it; not according to the letter, speaking of the material place. At his birth, *in medio animalium,* in the stable. After, a child, *in medio doctorum,* in the Temple. After, a man, *medius vestrûm stetit,* saith John Baptist, "in the

---

[1] *actio* in rhetoric is the combination of voice and bodily gesture. Cicero writes, "He had great splendor in his voice, and high dignity in his motion" (*Brutus sive de Claris Oratoribus,* quoted in Lewis and Short, *A Latin Dictionary*).

[2] "a second and a third time, repeating it by turns."

[3] See Exodus 12:11.

[4] "If only working were [like] this."

[5] "the manner of making a solemn promise."

[6] "the deportment proper to prayer."

midst of the people";[1] saith he of himself, *Ecce ego in medio vestri,* "in the midst of his Apostles."[2] At his death it fell to his turn likewise, that place; even then, he was in the midst. And now rising, there he is, we see. They in the midst of the Jews, and he in the midst of them. After this, in Patmos, St. John saw him in Heaven, "in the midst of the throne";[3] in earth, walking "in the midst of the candlesticks."[4] And at the last day he shall be in the midst of "the sheep on his right hand, and the goats on his left." All which show, the place and he sort very well.

But were it not natural for him, as the case standeth, there he is to stand, being to give peace? No place so fit for that purpose, none so kindly as it. His office being to be "a Mediator," *Medius* "between God and man," where should a Mediator stand but *in Medio*?

Besides, the two qualities of good, being to be *diffusivum* and *unitivum,* that is the fittest place for both. To distribute, best done from the centre. To unite likewise, soonest meet there. The place itself hath a virtue specially to unite, which is never done but by some middle thing. If we will conclude, we must have a *medius terminus;* else we shall never get *majus* and *minus extremum* to come together. Nor in things natural either combine two elements disagreeing in both qualities, without a middle symbolizing with both; nor flesh and bone, without a cartilage between both. As for things moral, there the middle is all in all. No virtue without it. In justice, incline the balance one way or other, the even poise is lost, *et opus justitiae pax,* "peace is the very work of justice." And the way to peace is the mid-way; neither to the right hand too much, nor to the left hand too little. In a word, all analogy, symmetry, harmony, in the world, goeth by it.

It cometh all to this; the manner of the place doth teach us what manner of affection is to be in them, that wish for or stand for peace. The place is indifferent, equally distant, alike near to all. There pitch the ark, that is the place for it. Indifferency in carriage preserveth peace; by foregoing that, and leaning to extremities, it is lost. Thither we must get again, and there stand, if ever we shall recover it. *Discessit a medio* lost it, *stetit in medio* must restore it.[5]

Therefore, when you hear men talk of peace, mark whether they stand where they should. If with the Pharisee to the corners, either by partiality one way, or prejudice another, no good will be done. When God will have it brought to pass, such minds he will give unto men, and make them meet to wish it, seek it, and find it.

A little now of the time. This was Christ's wish at this time, and Christ never speaks out of season. Therefore a special interest hath this feast in it. It is *votum paschale,* and this is *festum pacis.*[6]

And sure, *Habemus talem consuetudinem, et Ecclesia Dei;* "such a custom we have, and so the Church of God hath used it," to take these words of Christ in the nature of an edict for pacification, ever at this time. That whatsoever become of it all the year beside, this time should be kept a time of peace; we should seek it and offer it—seek it of God, and offer it, each to other.

There hath not, these sixteen hundred years, this day passed without a peace-offering. And the law of a peace-offering is; he that offers it must take his part of it, eat of it, or it doth him no good. This day therefore the Church never fails, but sets forth her peace-offering;—the Body whose hands were here showed, and the side whence issued *Sanguis crucis,*[7]

---

[1] John 1:26.

[2] Luke 22:27.

[3] Revelation 7:17.

[4] Revelation 1:13.

---

[5] *Discessit a medio* "He left the centre"; *stetit in medio* "He stood in the centre."

[6] *votum paschale* "the Easter prayer"; *festum pacis* "the feast of peace."

[7] "the blood of the Cross."

"the Blood that pacifieth all things in earth and Heaven," that we, in and by it, may this day renew the covenant of our peace. Then can it not be but a great grief to a Christian heart, to see many this day give Christ's peace the hearing, and there is all; hear it, and then turn their backs on it; every man go his way, and forsake his peace; instead of seeking it shun it, and of pursuing, turn away from it.

We "have not so learned Christ,"[1] St. Paul hath not so taught us. his rule it is, "Is Christ our Passover offered for us" as now he was? *Epulemur itaque*—that is his conclusion, "Let us then keep a feast," a feast of sweet bread without any sour leaven, that is, of peace without any malice.[2]

So to do, and even then this day when we have the peace-offering in our hands, then, then, to remember always, but then specially to join with Christ in his wish; to put into our hearts, and the hearts of all that profess his name, theirs specially that are of all others most likely to effect it, that Christ may have his wish, and there may be peace through the Christian world; that we may once all partake together of one peace-offering, and "with one mouth and one mind glorify God, the Father of our Lord Jesus Christ."

—1628 (1609)

---

[1] Ephesians 4:20.

[2] I Corinthians 5:7–8.

Nicholas Breton
?1555 – 1626

The son of a London merchant, the Oxford-educated Breton was a professional writer who published more than fifty books of poetry and prose in a wide variety of genres, including satires, religious meditations, pastorals, dialogues, essays, letter books, anthologies, and political pamphlets. The following selections are from *The Good and the Badde, or Descriptions of the Worthies and Unworthies of this Age* (1616), a collection of literary "characters" or descriptions of classes, occupations, or types of people. Breton presents his characters in twenty-five contrasting pairs (e.g. he juxtaposes the selections below with "A Good Man," "A Virgin," "An Unquiet Woman," and "A Worthy Lawyer"). The ostensible point of the genre—a popular one in the period—was didactic. "You will find your description in one place or the other," Breton tells his readers; "if among the Worthies, hold you where you are…if among the other, mend that [which] is amiss and all will be well." But style was equally important: like sonneteering, character-writing provided a forum for virtuoso displays of concision, wit, and rhetorical effect. The rhetorical trope Breton employs so relentlessly in the first three selections is isocolon, the repetition of phrases identical in length and structure. This pattern breaks down in the fourth, the "Unworthy Lawyer," a character much less abstract than the others. For other examples of character-writing, see the selections from the Overburian Character, Owen Felltham, John Earle, and Samuel Butler.

એજ્જ

An Atheist or Most Bad Man

An atheist is a figure of desperation, who dare do anything even to his soul's damnation. He is in nature a dog, in wit an ass, in passion a bedlam,[1] and in action a devil. He makes sin a jest, grace a humour, truth a fable, and peace a cowardice. His horse is his pride, his sword is his castle, his apparel his riches, and his punk his paradise.[2] He makes robbery his purchase, lechery his solace, mirth his exercise, and drunkenness his glory. He is the danger of society, the love of vanity, the hate of charity, and the shame of humanity. He is God's enemy, his parents' grief, his country's plague, and his own confusion. He spoils that is necessary and spends that is needless. He spits at the gracious and spurns the godly. The tavern is his palace and his belly is his god; a whore is his mistress and the devil is his master. Oaths are his graces, wounds his badges, shifts are his practices, and beggary his payments. He knows not God, nor thinks of heaven, but walks through the world as a devil towards hell. Virtue knows him not, honesty finds him not, wisdom loves him not, and honour regards him not. He is but the cutler's friend and the chirurgeon's agent,[3] the thief's companion and the hangman's benefactor. He was begotten untimely and born unhappily, lives ungraciously and dies unchristianly. He is of no religion nor good fashion, hardly good complexion, and most vile in condition. In sum, he is a monster among men, a Jew among Christians, a fool among wise men, and a devil among saints.

—1616

---

[1] *bedlam* madman (*OED* bedlam 3).

[2] *punk* prostitute or mistress (*OED* punk *sb*[1]).

[3] since he uses knives (made by cutlers) to create business for the surgeon.

A Wanton Woman

A wanton woman is the figure of imperfection; in nature an ape, in quality a wagtail, in countenance a witch, and in condition a kind of devil. Her beck is a net,[1] her word a charm, her look an illusion, and her company a confusion. Her life is the play of idleness, her diet the excess of dainties, her love the change of vanities, and her exercise the invention of follies. Her pleasures are fancies, her studies fashions, her delight colours, and her wealth her clothes. Her care is to deceive, her comfort her company, her house is vanity, and her bed is ruin. Her discourses are fables, her vows dissimulation, her conceits subtleties, and her contents varieties. She would she knows not what, and spends she cares not what, she spoils she sees not what, and doth she thinks not what. She is youth's plague and age's purgatory, time's abuse and reason's trouble. In sum, she is a spice of madness, a spark of mischief, a touch of poison, and a fear of destruction.
—1616

A Quiet Woman

A quiet woman is like a still wind, which neither chills the body, nor blows dust in the face. Her patience is a virtue that wins the heart of love and her wisdom makes her will well worthy regard. She fears God and flyeth sin, showeth kindness and loveth peace. Her tongue is tied to discretion and her heart is the harbour of goodness. She is a comfort of calamity and in prosperity a companion; a physician in sickness and a musician in help. Her ways are the walk toward heaven and her guide is the grace of the Almighty. She is her husband's down-bed where his heart lies at rest, and her children's glass in the notes of her grace; her servants' honour in the keeping of her house and her

neighbours' example in the notes of a good nature. She scorns fortune and loves virtue and out of thrift gathereth charity. She is a turtle in her love, a lamb in her meekness, a saint in her heart, and an angel in her soul. In sum, she is a jewel unprizeable and a joy unspeakable, a comfort in nature incomparable and a wife in the world unmatchable.
—1616

An Unworthy Lawyer

An unlearned and unworthily called a lawyer is the figure of a foot-post, who carries letters but knows not what is in them, only can read the superscriptions to direct them to their right owners. So trudgeth this simple clerk, that can scarce read a case when it is written, with his handful of papers from one court to another and from one counsellor's chamber to another, when by his good payment for his pains he will be so saucy as to call himself a solicitor. But what a taking are poor clients in when this too much trusted cunning companion, better read in *Piers Plowman* than in Ploydon and in the play of *Richard the Third* than in the pleas of Edward the Fourth,[2] persuades them all is sure when he is sure of all! And in what a misery are the poor men when upon a *Nihil dicit*, because indeed this poor fellow *Nihil potest dicere*, they are in danger of an execution before they know wherefore they are condemned.[3] But I wish all such, more wicked than witty, unlearned in the Law and abusers of the same, to look a little better into their consciences and to leave their crafty courses, lest when the Law indeed lays them open, instead of

---

[1] *beck* inviting look or signal (*OED* beck *sb*[2] 1).

[2] that is, better read in popular literature (William Langland's fourteenth-century poem *Piers Plowman* or Shakespeare's *Richard the Third*) than in legal texts (Edmund Plowden's commentaries or medieval legal precedents).

[3] *Nihil dicit* "he says nothing": a judgment rendered against a defendant who fails to plead; *Nihil potest dicere* "lacks the ability to say anything."

carrying their papers in their hands they wear not papers on their heads,[1] and instead of giving ear to their clients' causes, or rather else into their purses, they have ne'er an ear left to hear withal, nor good eye to see withal, or at least honest face to look out withal; but, as the grasshoppers of Egypt, be counted the caterpillars of England,[2] and not the fox that stole the goose but the great fox that stole the farm from the gander.

—1616

---

[1] *papers* bandages.

[2] *caterpillars* a common Renaissance metaphor for social parasites.

Francis Bacon
1561 – 1626

The younger son of the Lord Keeper of the Privy Seal, Bacon attended Trinity College, Cambridge, studied law at Gray's Inn, and spent three years in Paris with the English ambassador before completing his law studies in 1582. Despite his legal brilliance and high-ranking connections, Bacon failed to win office under Queen Elizabeth, though he did play a key role in the prosecution of his former friend Robert Devereux, Earl of Essex. His rise began with the accession of James I: between 1603 and 1621, Bacon was successively knighted (1603), made Solicitor-General (1607), Attorney-General (1613), Lord Keeper (1617), Lord High Chancellor and Baron Verulam (1618), and Viscount St. Albans (1621). In 1621 Bacon was brought before Parliament for accepting bribes; he pleaded guilty, was deprived of office, and retired to private life. Bacon appears to have been no more corrupt than any other office holder of the period: the real cause of his fall from power was Parliament's hostility to the King and the royal favourite, the Duke of Buckingham. They were untouchable, but Bacon, a leading royal minister, was not. According to John Aubrey, Bacon died of pneumonia contracted while experimenting with the refrigerating qualities of snow.

Throughout his busy political and legal career, Bacon actively pursued his literary and philosophical interests. In 1597 he published the first version of his *Essays*, containing ten short, aphoristic pieces. Bacon revised and expanded the collection for the remainder of his life, publishing enlarged versions in 1612 and 1625; eventually, the collection grew to 58 essays (the 1597 and 1625 versions of "Of Studies" are both printed here for comparison). The *Essays* provided seventeenth-century writers with an important model of both genre and prose style. But the bulk of Bacon's work was in the philosophy of science. Bacon sought to provide science with a new method, one based on evidence and observation, and he thought big: "I have taken all knowledge to be my province," he wrote in a letter to Lord Burghley. The following excerpts from *Novum Organum* (published in Latin in 1620) include Bacon's influential discussion of scientific method and of the intellectual, psychological, and linguistic obstacles we continue to face in the pursuit of knowledge. Bacon has been criticized for downplaying the real scientific achievements of his time, such as Copernican astronomy and William Gilbert's work on magnetism. More recently, he has been read unfavourably (and not always fairly) as a founding voice in the discourses of scientific progress and of humanity's domination over nature. But he was also a writer of immense intellectual achievement whose perception, originality, and style would prove quite influential, particularly in the Restoration (see the selection from Thomas Sprat's *History of the Royal Society*). In addition to pamphlets on legal, religious, and political issues, Bacon's other works include *The Advancement of Learning* (1605); *De sapientia veterum* (1609), which discusses classical myths as symbolic expressions of scientific truths; a biography, *The Historie of the Raigne of King Henry the Seventh* (1622); *The New Atlantis* (1627), a utopian tale of a futuristic community devoted to science; *Sylva Sylvarum* (1627), an encyclopedic natural history; as well as court masques, a translation of the Psalms, apophthegms, and other studies of natural history.

CଦେCଦ

Essays
(excerpts)

OF TRUTH

"What is Truth?" said jesting Pilate, and would not stay for an answer.[1] Certainly there be that delight in giddiness, and count it a bondage to fix a belief; affecting free-will in thinking, as well as in acting. And though the sects of philosophers of that kind be gone,[2] yet there remain certain discoursing wits which are of the same veins, though there be not so much blood in them as was in those of the ancients. But it is not only the difficulty and labour which men take in finding out of truth, nor again that when it is found it imposeth upon men's thoughts, that doth bring lies in favour; but a natural though corrupt love of the lie itself. One of the latter school of the Grecians examineth the matter,[3] and is at a stand to think what should be in it, that men should love lies, where neither they make for pleasure, as with poets, nor for advantage, as with the merchant; but for the lie's sake. But I cannot tell: this same truth is a naked and open daylight, that doth not show the masks and mummeries and triumphs of the world half so stately and daintily as candle-lights. Truth may perhaps come to the price of a pearl, that showeth best by day; but it will not rise to the price of a diamond or carbuncle, that showeth best in varied lights. A mixture of a lie doth ever add pleasure.

Doth any man doubt, that if there were taken out of men's minds vain opinions, flattering hopes, false valuations, imaginations as one would, and the like, but it would leave the minds of a number of men poor shrunken things, full of melancholy and indisposition, and unpleasing to themselves? One of the Fathers, in great severity, called poesy *vinum daemonum* [wine of devils] because it filleth the imagination;[4] and yet it is but with the shadow of a lie. But it is not the lie that passeth through the mind, but the lie that sinketh in and settleth in it, that doth the hurt; such as we spake of before. But howsoever these things are thus in men's depraved judgements and affections, yet truth, which only doth judge itself, teacheth that the inquiry of truth, which is the love-making or wooing of it, the knowledge of truth, which is the presence of it, and the belief of truth, which is the enjoying of it, is the sovereign good of human nature.

The first creature of God, in the works of the days, was the light of the sense; the last was the light of reason; and his sabbath work ever since, is the illumination of his Spirit. First he breathed light upon the face of the matter or chaos; then he breathed light into the face of man; and still he breatheth and inspireth light into the face of his chosen. The poet that beautified the sect that was otherwise inferior to the rest saith yet excellently well: "It is a pleasure to stand upon the shore, and to see ships tossed upon the sea; a pleasure to stand in the window of a castle, and to see a battle and the adventures thereof below: but no pleasure is comparable to the standing upon the vantage ground of Truth" (a hill not to be commanded, and where the air is always clear and serene), "and to see the errors, and wanderings, and mists, and tempests, in the vale below";[5] so always that this prospect be with pity, and not with swelling or pride. Certainly, it is heaven upon earth to have a man's mind move in

---

[1] John 18:38.

[2] *philosophers of that kind* the Sceptics, who asserted the impossibility of knowledge.

[3] *One of the latter school* Lucian of Samosata (ca. 120–180 C.E.), in his satiric dialogue *Philopseudes* ("The Lover of Lies").

[4] *One of the Fathers* Bacon appears to conflate passages from St. Augustine (*Confessions* I.xvi.26) and St. Jerome (Epistle 146).

[5] Lucretius, *De rerum natura*, II.1–13; *the sect that was otherwise inferior* the Epicureans, often dismissed as irreligious hedonists because they taught that the universe came into existence by chance and that the criterion for a good life was pleasure.

charity, rest in providence, and turn upon the poles of truth.

To pass from theological and philosophical truth to the truth of civil business; it will be acknowledged even by those that practise it not that clear and round dealing is the honour of man's nature; and that mixture of falsehood is like alloy in coin of gold and silver, which may make the metal work the better, but it embaseth it. For these winding and crooked courses are the goings of the serpent, which goeth basely upon the belly, and not upon the feet. There is no vice that doth so cover a man with shame as to be found false and perfidious. And therefore Montaigne saith prettily, when he inquired the reason, why the word of the lie should be such a disgrace and such an odious charge? Saith he, "If it be well weighed, to say that a man lieth, is as much to say, as that he is brave towards God and a coward towards men."[1] For a lie faces God, and shrinks from man. Surely the wickedness of falsehood and breach of faith cannot possibly be so highly expressed, as in that it shall be the last peal to call the judgements of God upon the generations of men; it being foretold, that when Christ cometh, "he shall not find faith upon the earth."[2]
—1625

OF SIMULATION AND DISSIMULATION

Dissimulation is but a faint kind of policy or wisdom; for it asketh a strong wit and a strong heart to know when to tell truth, and to do it. Therefore it is the weaker sort of politiques that are the great dissemblers.[3]

Tacitus saith, "Livia sorted well with the arts of her husband and dissimulation of her son"; attributing arts or policy to Augustus, and dissimulation to Tiberius. And again, when Mucianus encourageth Vespasian to take arms against Vitellius, he saith, "We rise not against the piercing judgment of Augustus, nor the extreme caution or closeness of Tiberius." These properties, of arts or policy and dissimulation or closeness, are indeed habits and faculties several, and to be distinguished. For if a man have that penetration of judgment as he can discern what things are to be laid open, and what to be secreted, and what to be showed at half lights, and to whom and when (which indeed are arts of state and arts of life, as Tacitus well calleth them), to him a habit of dissimulation is a hindrance and a poorness. But if a man cannot obtain to that judgment, then it is left to him generally to be close, and a dissembler. For where a man cannot choose or vary in particulars, there it is good to take the safest and wariest way in general; like the going softly, by one that cannot well see. Certainly the ablest men that ever were have had all an openness and frankness of dealing; and a name of certainty and veracity;[4] but then they were like horses well managed; for they could tell passing well when to stop or turn; and at such times when they thought the case indeed required dissimulation, if then they used it, it came to pass that the former opinion spread abroad of their good faith and clearness of dealing made them almost invisible.

There be three degrees of this hiding and veiling of a man's self. The first, closeness, reservation, and secrecy; when a man leaveth himself without observation, or without hold to be taken, what he is. The second, dissimulation, in the negative; when a man lets fall signs and arguments, that he is not that he is. And the third, simulation, in the affirmative; when a man industriously and expressly feigns and pretends to be that he is not.

For the first of these, secrecy; it is indeed the virtue of a confessor. And assuredly the secret man heareth many confessions. For who will open

---

[1] Montaigne, *Essays*, II.18, "Of Giving the Lie."

[2] Luke 18:8.

[3] *politiques* men of public life; politicians.

[4] *name of certainty* reputation for reliability.

himself to a blab or babbler? But if a man be thought secret, it inviteth discovery; as the more close air sucketh in the more open; and as in confession the revealing is not for worldly use, but for the ease of a man's heart, so secret men come to the knowledge of many things in that kind; while men rather discharge their minds than impart their minds. In few words, mysteries are due to secrecy. Besides (to say truth) nakedness is uncomely, as well in mind as body; and it addeth no small reverence to men's manners and actions, if they be not altogether open. As for talkers and futile persons,[1] they are commonly vain and credulous withal. For he that talketh what he knoweth, will also talk what he knoweth not. Therefore set it down, that an habit of secrecy is both politic and moral. And in this part, it is good that a man's face give his tongue leave to speak. For the discovery of a man's self by the tracts of his countenance is a great weakness and betraying; by how much it is many times more marked and believed than a man's words.

For the second, which is dissimulation; it followeth many times upon secrecy by a necessity; so that he that will be secret must be a dissembler in some degree. For men are too cunning to suffer a man to keep an indifferent carriage between both, and to be secret, without swaying the balance on either side. They will so beset a man with questions, and draw him on, and pick it out of him, that, without an absurd silence, he must show an inclination one way; or if he do not, they will gather as much by his silence as by his speech. As for equivocations, or oraculous speeches, they cannot hold out long. So that no man can be secret, except he give himself a little scope of dissimulation; which is, as it were, but the skirts or train of secrecy.

But for the third degree, which is simulation and false profession; that I hold more culpable, and less politic; except it be in great and rare matters. And

therefore a general custom of simulation (which is this last degree) is a vice, rising either of a natural falseness or fearfulness, or of a mind that hath some main faults, which because a man must needs disguise, it maketh him practice simulation in other things, lest his hand should be out of ure.[2]

The great advantages of simulation and dissimulation are three. First, to lay asleep opposition, and to surprise. For where a man's intentions are published, it is an alarum to call up all that are against them. The second is, to reserve to a man's self a fair retreat. For if a man engage himself by a manifest declaration, he must go through or take a fall. The third is, the better to discover the mind of another. For to him that opens himself men will hardly show themselves adverse; but will (fair) let him go on, and turn their freedom of speech to freedom of thought. And therefore it is a good shrewd proverb of the Spaniard, "Tell a lie and find a truth." As if there were no way of discovery but by simulation. There be also three disadvantages, to set it even. The first, that simulation and dissimulation commonly carry with them a show of fearfulness, which in any business doth spoil the feathers of round flying up to the mark.[3] The second, that it puzzleth and perplexeth the conceits of many, that perhaps would otherwise cooperate with him; and makes a man walk almost alone to his own ends. The third and greatest, is, that it depriveth a man of one of the most principal instruments for action; which is trust and belief. The best composition and temperature is to have openness in fame and opinion;[4] secrecy in habit; dissimulation in seasonable use; and a power to feign, if there be no remedy.

—1625

---

[1] *futile* talkative; Bacon's usage retains the Latin sense of *futilis*, "leaky" (*OED* futile *a* 3).

[2] *ure* use, practice (*OED* ure *sb*[1] 1).

[3] spoil the arrow's direct ("round") flight to its target.

[4] *temperature* temperament.

Of Marriage and Single Life

He that hath wife and children hath given hostages to fortune; for they are impediments to great enterprises, either of virtue or mischief. Certainly the best works, and of greatest merit for the public, have proceeded from the unmarried or childless men; which both in affection and means have married and endowed the public. Yet it were great reason that those that have children should have greatest care of future times; unto which they know they must transmit their dearest pledges. Some there are, who though they lead a single life, yet their thoughts do end with themselves, and account future times impertinences. Nay, there are some other that account wife and children but as bills of charges. Nay more, there are some foolish rich covetous men, that take a pride in having no children, because they may be thought so much the richer. For perhaps they have heard some talk, "Such an one is a great rich man," and another except to it, "Yea, but he hath a great charge of children"; as if it were an abatement to his riches. But the most ordinary cause of a single life is liberty, especially in certain self-pleasing and humorous minds,[1] which are so sensible of every restraint, as they will go near to think their girdles and garters to be bonds and shackles.

Unmarried men are best friends, best masters, best servants; but not always best subjects; for they are light to run away; and almost all fugitives are of that condition. A single life doth well with churchmen; for charity will hardly water the ground where it must first fill a pool. It is indifferent for judges and magistrates; for if they be facile and corrupt,[2] you shall have a servant five times worse than a wife. For soldiers, I find the generals commonly in their hortatives put men in mind of their wives and children; and I think the despising of marriage amongst the Turks maketh the vulgar soldier more base. Certainly wife and children are a kind of discipline of humanity; and single men, though they may be many times more charitable, because their means are less exhaust, yet, on the other side, they are more cruel and hardhearted (good to make severe inquisitors), because their tenderness is not so oft called upon. Grave natures, led by custom, and therefore constant, are commonly loving husbands; as was said of Ulysses, *vetulam suam praetulit immortalitati.*[3] Chaste women are often proud and froward, as presuming upon the merit of their chastity. It is one of the best bonds both of chastity and obedience in the wife, if she think her husband wise; which she will never do if she find him jealous. Wives are young men's mistresses; companions for middle age; and old men's nurses. So as a man may have a quarrel to marry when he will. But yet he was reputed one of the wise men, that made answer to the question, when a man should marry?– "A young man not yet, an elder man not at all."[4] It is often seen that bad husbands have very good wives; whether it be that it raiseth the price of their husband's kindness when it comes; or that the wives take a pride in their patience. But this never fails, if the bad husbands were of their own choosing, against their friends' consent; for then they will be sure to make good their own folly.

—1612, REVISED 1625

Of Love

The stage is more beholding to Love, than the life of man. For as to the stage, love is ever matter of comedies, and now and then of tragedies; but in life it doth much mischief; sometimes like a

---

[1] *humorous* whimsical.

[2] *facile* easily swayed, compliant (*OED* facile *a* 5).

[3] a Latin version of *Odyssey* v.135: "He preferred his old wife to immortality."

[4] Thales (b. seventh century B.C.E.), one of the Seven Sages of ancient Greece; the story is told in several classical sources.

siren, sometimes like a fury. You may observe, that amongst all the great and worthy persons whereof the memory remaineth, either ancient or recent, there is not one that hath been transported to the mad degree of love: which shows that great spirits and great business do keep out this weak passion. You must except nevertheless Marcus Antonius, the half-partner of the empire of Rome,[1] and Appius Claudius, the decemvir and lawgiver;[2] whereof the former was indeed a voluptuous man, and inordinate; but the latter was an austere and wise man: and therefore it seems (though rarely) that love can find entrance not only into an open heart, but also into a heart well fortified, if watch be not well kept. It is a poor saying of Epicurus, *Satis magnum alter alteri theatrum sumus;*[3] as if man, made for the contemplation of heaven and all noble objects, should do nothing but kneel before a little idol, and make himself a subject, though not of the mouth (as beasts are), yet of the eye; which was given him for higher purposes.

It is a strange thing to note the excess of this passion, and how it braves the nature and value of things, by this: that the speaking in a perpetual hyperbole is comely in nothing but in love. Neither is it merely in the phrase; for whereas it hath been well said that the arch-flatterer, with whom all the petty flatterers have intelligence, is a man's self; certainly the lover is more. For there was never proud man thought so absurdly well of himself as the lover doth of the person loved; and therefore it was well said, that "it is impossible to love and to be wise."[4] Neither doth this weakness appear to others only, and not to the party loved; but to the loved most of all, except the love be reciproque. For it is a true rule, that love is ever rewarded either with the reciproque or with an inward and secret contempt. By how much the more men ought to beware of this passion, which loseth not only other things, but itself. As for the other losses, the poet's relation doth well figure them; that he that preferred Helena, quitted the gifts of Juno and Pallas.[5] For whosoever esteemeth too much of amorous affection quitteth both riches and wisdom.

This passion hath his floods in the very times of weakness, which are great prosperity and great adversity, though this latter hath been less observed: both which times kindle love, and make it more fervent, and therefore show it to be the child of folly. They do best, who if they cannot but admit love, yet make it keep quarter, and sever it wholly from their serious affairs and actions of life; for if it check once with business, it troubleth men's fortunes, and maketh men that they can no ways be true to their own ends. I know not how, but martial men are given to love: I think it is but as they are given to wine; for perils commonly ask to be paid in pleasures. There is in man's nature a secret inclination and motion towards love of others, which if it be not spent upon some one or a few, doth naturally spread itself towards many, and maketh men become humane and charitable; as it is seen sometime in friars. Nuptial love maketh mankind; friendly love perfecteth it; but wanton love corrupteth and embaseth it.

—1612, REVISED 1625

---

[1] Marcus Antonius (ca. 83–30 B.C.E.), joint ruler with Octavius Caesar of the Empire, who loved Cleopatra.

[2] Appius Claudius (fl. 450 B.C.E.), judge and leader of the decemvirs, ten men responsible for administering Rome; traditionally, his lust for Verginia led to her murder (by her father), an act that precipitated a plebian revolt.

[3] Quoted in Seneca, *Epistles,* vii.2: "Each of us is enough of an audience for the other."

[4] A saying found in classical sources, but best known in the period by its inclusion in Erasmus' *Adagia.*

[5] *he that preferred Helena* Paris, who chose Helen of Troy (offered him by Venus) over the gifts offered by Juno (power) and Pallas Athena (wisdom).

OF SEDITIONS AND TROUBLES

Shepherds of people had need know the calendars of tempests in state;[1] which are commonly greatest when things grow to equality; as natural tempests are greatest about the *Equinoctia*.[2] And as there are certain hollow blasts of wind and secret swellings of seas before a tempest, so are there in states:

> ————*Ille etiam caecos instare tumultus*
> *Saepe monet, fraudesque et operta tumescere bella.*[3]

Libels and licentious discourses against the state, when they are frequent and open; and in like sort, false news often running up and down to the disadvantage of the state and hastily embraced; are amongst the signs of troubles. Virgil giving the pedigree of fame, saith she was sister to the Giants:

> *Illam Terra parens, ira irritata Deorum,*
> *Extremam (ut perhibent) Coeo Enceladoque sororem*
> *Progenuit.*[4]

As if fames were the relics of seditions past; but they are no less indeed the preludes of seditions to come. Howsoever he noteth it right, that seditious tumults and seditious fames differ no more but as brother and sister, masculine and feminine; especially if it come to that, that the best actions of a state, and the most plausible, and which ought to give greatest contentment, are taken in ill sense, and traduced: for that shows the envy great, as Tacitus saith, *conflata magna invidia, seu bene seu male gesta*

premunt.[5] Neither doth it follow, that because these fames are a sign of troubles, that the suppressing of them with too much severity should be a remedy of troubles. For the despising of them many times checks them best; and the going about to stop them doth but make a wonder long-lived. Also that kind of obedience which Tacitus speaketh of, is to be held suspected: *Erant in officio, sed tamen qui mallent mandata imperantium interpretari quam exequi*;[6] disputing, excusing, cavilling upon mandates and directions, is a kind of shaking off the yoke, and assay of disobedience; especially if in those disputings they which are for the direction speak fearfully and tenderly, and those that are against it audaciously.

Also, as Machiavel noteth well, when princes, that ought to be common parents, make themselves as a party, and lean to a side, it is as a boat that is overthrown by uneven weight on the one side; as was well seen in the time of Henry the Third of France; for first himself entered league for the extirpation of the Protestants; and presently after the same league was turned upon himself. For when the authority of princes is made but an accessary to a cause, and that there be other bands that tie faster than the band of sovereignty, kings begin to be put almost out of possession.

Also, when discords, and quarrels, and factions, are carried openly and audaciously, it is a sign the reverence of government is lost. For the motions of the greatest persons in a government ought to be as the motions of the planets under *primum mobile* (according to the old opinion),[7] which is, that every of them is carried swiftly by the highest motion,

---

[1] *calendars* predictable times.

[2] *Equinoctia* spring and autumn equinoxes.

[3] Virgil, *Georgics*, i.464–65: the sun "often warns us that dark tumults threaten, and deceits and hidden wars are swelling."

[4] *Aeneid*, iv.178–80: "Mother earth (as they relate), irritated by anger against the gods, brought forth [Rumour] last as sister to Coeus and Enceladus."

[5] *Histories*, i.7: "when envy is once roused, good actions are as much assailed as bad."

[6] *Histories*, ii.39: "they were on duty, but none the less preferred to interpret the orders of their generals rather than follow them."

[7] *primum mobile* the prime or first mover; in Ptolemaic astronomy, the outermost of the heavenly spheres, from which the other spheres all derived their motion.

and softly in their own motion. And therefore, when great ones in their own particular motion move violently, and, as Tacitus expresseth it well, *liberius quam ut imperantium meminissent*,[1] it is a sign the orbs are out of frame. For reverence is that wherewith princes are girt from God; who threateneth the dissolving thereof: *Solvam cingula regum.*[2]

So when any of the four pillars of government are mainly shaken or weakened (which are Religion, Justice, Counsel, and Treasure), men had need to pray for fair weather. But let us pass from this part of predictions (concerning which, nevertheless, more light may be taken from that which followeth); and let us speak first of the materials of seditions; then of the motives of them; and thirdly of the remedies.

Concerning the materials of seditions. It is a thing well to be considered; for the surest way to prevent seditions (if the times do bear it) is to take away the matter of them. For if there be fuel prepared, it is hard to tell whence the spark shall come that shall set it on fire. The matter of seditions is of two kinds; much poverty and much discontentment. It is certain, so many overthrown estates, so many votes for troubles. Lucan noteth well the state of Rome before the civil war,

Hinc usura vorax, rapidumque in tempore foenus,
Hinc concussa fides, et multis utile bellum.[3]

This same *multis utile bellum*, is an assured and infallible sign of a state disposed to seditions and troubles. And if this poverty and broken estate in the better sort be joined with a want and necessity in the mean people, the danger is imminent and great. For the rebellions of the belly are the worst. As for discontentments, they are in the politic body like to humours in the natural, which are apt to gather a preternatural heat and to inflame. And let no prince measure the danger of them by this, whether they be just or unjust: for that were to imagine people to be too reasonable; who do often spurn at their own good: nor yet by this, whether the griefs whereupon they rise be in fact great or small: for they are the most dangerous discontentments where the fear is greater than the feeling: *Dolendi modus, timendi non item.*[4] Besides, in great oppressions, the same things that provoke the patience, do withal mate the courage;[5] but in fears it is not so. Neither let any prince or state be secure concerning discontentments, because they have been often, or have been long, and yet no peril hath ensued: for as it is true that every vapour or fume doth not turn into a storm; so it is nevertheless true that storms, though they blow over divers times, yet may fall at last; and, as the Spanish proverb noteth well, "The cord breaketh at the last by the weakest pull."

The causes and motives of seditions are, innovation in religion; taxes; alteration of laws and customs; breaking of privileges; general oppression; advancement of unworthy persons; strangers; dearths; disbanded soldiers; factions grown desperate; and whatsoever, in offending people, joineth and knitteth them in a common cause.

For the remedies; there may be some general preservatives, whereof we will speak: as for the just cure, it must answer to the particular disease; and so be left to counsel rather than rule.

The first remedy or prevention is to remove by all means possible that material cause of sedition

---

[1] *Annals*, iii.4: "more freely than if they had remembered their governors."

[2] "I will loosen the girdles of kings," a combination of Job 12:18 and Isaiah 45:1. That is, loss of reverence is the first stage in a king's loss of authority.

[3] *Pharsalia*, i.181–82: "Hence devouring usury and interest rapidly compounded, hence shaken credit, and war profitable to many."

[4] Pliny, *Epistles*, viii.17: "There is an end to suffering, but not to fearing."

[5] *mate* abate, daunt, subdue (*OED* mate *v*[1] 2–5).

whereof we spake; which is, want and poverty in the estate. To which purpose serveth, the opening and well-balancing of trade; the cherishing of manufactures; the banishing of idleness; the repressing of waste and excess by sumptuary laws; the improvement and husbanding of the soil; the regulating of prices of things vendible; the moderating of taxes and tributes, and the like. Generally, it is to be foreseen that the population of a kingdom (especially if it be not mown down by wars) do not exceed the stock of the kingdom which should maintain them. Neither is the population to be reckoned only by number; for a smaller number that spend more and earn less, do wear out an estate sooner than a greater number that live lower and gather more. Therefore the multiplying of nobility and other degrees of quality in an over-proportion to the common people, doth speedily bring a state to necessity; and so doth likewise an overgrown clergy; for they bring nothing to the stock; and in like manner, when more are bred scholars than preferments can take off.

It is likewise to be remembered, that forasmuch as the increase of any estate must be upon the foreigner (for whatsoever is somewhere gotten is somewhere lost), there be but three things which one nation selleth unto another: the commodity as nature yieldeth it; the manufacture; and the vecture, or carriage. So that if these three wheels go, wealth will flow as in a spring tide. And it cometh many times to pass, that *materiam superabit opus*;[1] that the work and carriage is more worth than the material, and enricheth a state more; as is notably seen in Low-Countrymen, who have the best mines above ground in the world.[2]

Above all things, good policy is to be used that the treasure and monies in a state be not gathered into few hands. For otherwise a state may have a great stock, and yet starve. And money is like muck, not good except it be spread. This is done chiefly by suppressing, or at least keeping a straight hand upon the devouring trades of usury, engrossing,[3] great pasturages,[4] and the like.

For removing discontentments, or at least the danger of them; there is in every state (as we know) two portions of subjects; the nobility and the commonality. When one of these is discontent, the danger is not great; for common people are of slow motion, if they be not excited by the greater sort; and the greater sort are of small strength, except the multitude be apt and ready to move of themselves. Then is the danger, when the greater sort do but wait for the troubling of the waters amongst the meaner, that then they may declare themselves. The poets feign, that the rest of the gods would have bound Jupiter; which he hearing of, by the counsel of Pallas, sent for Briareus, with his hundred hands, to come in to his aid. An emblem, no doubt, to show how safe it is for monarchs to make sure of the good will of common people.

To give moderate liberty for griefs and discontentments to evaporate (so it be without too great insolency or bravery), is a safe way. For he that turneth the humours back, and maketh the wound bleed inwards, endangereth malign ulcers and pernicious imposthumations.[5]

The part of Epimetheus might well become Prometheus, in the case of discontentments; for there is not a better provision against them.[6] Epime-

---

[1] Ovid, *Metamorphoses*, ii.5: "the workmanship will surpass the material."

[2] *mines above ground* figurative: despite a lack of natural resources, the Dutch built a commercial empire on their skills in manufacturing and transportation.

[3] *engrossing* buying in bulk to create a monopoly.

[4] *great pasturages* enclosures, which denied small landowners access to lands once used in common.

[5] *imposthumations* tumours.

[6] *Epimetheus* the name means "afterthought"; his use of hope would be an appropriate precaution or "forethought" (the meaning of Prometheus's name) in dealing with discontentments.

theus, when griefs and evils flew abroad, at last shut the lid, and kept hope in the bottom of the vessel. Certainly, the politic and artificial nourishing and entertaining of hopes,[1] and carrying men from hopes to hopes, is one of the best antidotes against the poison of discontentments. And it is a certain sign of a wise government and proceeding, when it can hold men's hearts by hopes, when it cannot by satisfaction; and when it can handle things in such manner, as no evil shall appear so peremptory but that it hath some outlet of hope: which is the less hard to do, because both particular persons and factions are apt enough to flatter themselves, or at least to brave that, which they believe not.

Also the foresight and prevention, that there be no likely or fit head whereunto discontented persons may resort, and under whom they may join, is a known, but an excellent point of caution. I understand a fit head to be one that hath greatness and reputation; that hath confidence with the discontented party, and upon whom they turn their eyes; and that is thought discontented in his own particular: which kind of persons are either to be won and reconciled to the state, and that in a fast and true manner; or to be fronted with some other of the same party, that may oppose them, and so divide the reputation. Generally, the dividing and breaking of all factions and combinations that are adverse to the state, and setting them at distance, or at least distrust, amongst themselves, is not one of the worst remedies. For it is a desperate case, if those that hold with the proceeding of the state be full of discord and faction, and those that are against it be entire and united.

I have noted that some witty and sharp speeches which have fallen from princes have given fire to seditions. Caesar did himself infinite hurt in that speech, *Sulla nescivit literas, non potuit dictare*;[2] for

it did utterly cut off that hope which men had entertained, that he would at one time or other give over his dictatorship. Galba undid himself by that speech, *legi a se militem, non emi*; for it put the soldiers out of hope of the donative.[3] Probus likewise, by that speech, *si vixero, non opus erit amplius Romano imperio militibus*;[4] a speech of great despair for the soldiers. And many the like. Surely princes had need, in tender matters and ticklish times, to beware what they say; especially in these short speeches, which fly abroad like darts, and are thought to be shot out of their secret intentions. For as for large discourses, they are flat things, and not so much noted.

Lastly, let princes, against all events, not be without some great person, one or rather more, of military valour, near unto them, for the repressing of seditions in their beginnings. For without that, there useth to be more trepidation in court upon the first breaking out of troubles than were fit. And the state runneth the danger of that which Tacitus saith: *Atque is habitus animorum fuit, ut pessimum facinus auderent pauci, plures vellent, omnes paterentur.*[5] But let such military persons be assured, and well reputed of, rather than factious and popular; holding also good correspondence with the other great men in the state; or else the remedy is worse than the disease.

—1625

Of Travel

Travel, in the younger sort, is a part of education; in the elder, a part of experience. He that travelleth into a country before he hath some

---

[1] *artificial* skillful.

[2] "Sulla did not know his letters, he could not dictate" [punning on "act the dictator"].

[3] "He selected his soldiers, and did not buy them"; *donative* bonus payment.

[4] "If I live, the Roman empire shall have no more need of soldiers."

[5] Tacitus, *Histories*, I:28: "And such was the condition of their minds, that a few dared the most evil deeds, more desired them, all permitted them."

entrance into the language, goeth to school,[1] and not to travel. That young men travel under some tutor, or grave servant, I allow well; so he be such a one that hath the language, and hath been in the country before; whereby he may be able to tell them what things are worthy to be seen in the country where they go; what acquaintances they are to seek; what exercises or discipline the place yieldeth. For else young men shall go hooded, and look abroad little. It is a strange thing, that in sea voyages, where there is nothing to be seen but sky and sea, men should make diaries; but in land-travel, wherein so much is to be observed, for the most part they omit it; as if chance were fitter to be registered than observation. Let diaries therefore be brought in use.

The things to be seen and observed are: the courts of princes, specially when they give audience to ambassadors; the courts of justice, while they sit and hear causes; and so of consistories ecclesiastic; the churches and monasteries, with the monuments which are therein extant; the walls and fortifications of cities and towns, and so the havens and harbours; antiquities and ruins; libraries; colleges, disputations, and lectures, where any are; shipping and navies; houses and gardens of state and pleasure, near great cities; armories; arsenals; magazines; exchanges; bourses; warehouses; exercises of horsemanship, fencing, training of soldiers, and the like; comedies, such whereunto the better sort of persons do resort; treasuries of jewels and robes; cabinets and rarities; and, to conclude, whatsoever is memorable in the places where they go. After all which the tutors or servants ought to make diligent inquiry. As for triumphs, masques, feasts, weddings, funerals, capital executions, and such shows, men need not to be put in mind of them; yet are they not to be neglected.

If you will have a young man to put his travel into a little room, and in short time to gather much,

this you must do. First as was said, he must have some entrance into the language before he goeth. Then he must have such a servant or tutor as knoweth the country, as was likewise said. Let him carry with him also some card or book describing the country where he travelleth;[2] which will be a good key to his inquiry. Let him keep also a diary. Let him not stay long in one city or town; more or less as the place deserveth, but not long; nay, when he stayeth in one city or town, let him change his lodging from one end and part of the town to another; which is a great adamant of acquaintance.[3] Let him sequester himself from the company of his countrymen, and diet in such places where there is good company of the nation where he travelleth. Let him upon his removes from one place to another, procure recommendation to some person of quality residing in the place whither he removeth; that he may use his favour in those things he desireth to see or know. Thus he may abridge his travel with much profit.

As for the acquaintance which is to be sought in travel; that which is most of all profitable, is acquaintance with the secretaries and employed men of ambassadors: for so in travelling in one country, he shall suck the experience of many. Let him also see and visit eminent persons in all kinds, which are of great name abroad; that he may be able to tell how the life agreeth with the fame. For quarrels, they are with care and discretion to be avoided. They are commonly for mistresses, healths, place, and words. And let a man beware how he keepeth company with choleric and quarrelsome persons; for they will engage him into their own quarrels. When a traveller returneth home, let him not leave the countries where he hath travelled altogether behind him; but maintain a correspondence by letters with those of his acquaintance which are of

---

[1] *goes to school* goes to learn the language.

[2] *card* map.

[3] *adamant* magnet.

most worth. And let his travel appear rather in his discourse than in his apparel or gesture; and in his discourse let him be rather advised in his answers, than forward to tell stories; and let it appear that he doth not change his country manners for those of foreign parts; but only prick in some flowers of that he hath learned abroad into the customs of his own country.[1]

—1625

OF EMPIRE

It is a miserable state of mind to have few things to desire, and many things to fear: and yet that commonly is the case of kings; who, being at the highest, want matter of desire, which makes their minds more languishing; and have many representations of perils and shadows, which makes their minds the less clear. And this is one reason also of that effect which the Scripture speaketh of, that "the king's heart is inscrutable" [Proverbs 25:3]. For multitude of jealousies, and lack of some predominant desire that should marshal and put in order all the rest, maketh any man's heart hard to find or sound. Hence it comes likewise, that princes many times make themselves desires, and set their hearts upon toys; sometimes upon a building; sometimes upon erecting of an order; sometimes upon the advancing of a person; sometimes upon obtaining excellency in some art or feat of the hand; as Nero for playing on the harp, Domitian for certainty of the hand with the arrow, Commodus for playing at fence, Caracalla for driving chariots, and the like.[2] This seemeth incredible unto those that know not the principle, that *the mind of man is more cheered and refreshed by profiting in small things, than by standing at a stay in great.* We see also that kings

that have been fortunate conquerors in their first years, it being not possible for them to go forward infinitely, but that they must have some check or arrest in their fortunes, turn in their latter years to be superstitious and melancholy; as did Alexander the Great; Diocletian; and in our memory, Charles the Fifth;[3] and others. For he that is used to go forward, and findeth a stop, falleth out of his own favour, and is not the thing he was.

To speak now of the true temper of empire; it is a thing rare and hard to keep; for both temper and distemper consist of contraries. But it is one thing to mingle contraries, another to interchange them. The answer of Apollonius to Vespasian is full of excellent instruction. Vespasian asked him, "what was Nero's overthrow?" He answered, "Nero could touch and tune the harp well; but in government sometimes he used to wind the pins too high, sometimes to let them down too low." And certain it is that nothing destroyeth authority so much as the unequal and untimely interchange of power pressed too far, and relaxed too much.

This is true, that the wisdom of all these latter times in princes' affairs is rather fine deliveries and shiftings of dangers and mischiefs when they are near, than solid and grounded courses to keep them aloof. But this is but to try masteries with fortune. And let men beware how they neglect and suffer matter of trouble to be prepared; for no man can forbid the spark, nor tell whence it may come. The difficulties in princes' business are many and great; but the greatest difficulty is often in their own mind. For it is common with princes (saith Tacitus) to will contradictories: *Sunt plerumque regum voluntates vehementes, et inter se contrariae.*[4] For it is

---

[1] *prick in some flowers* transplant or copy the choicest parts.

[2] Nero, Domitian, Commodus, and Caracalla were all Roman emperors; *playing at fence* fencing or swordplay: Commodus (emperor 180–192 C.E.) performed frequently as a gladiator.

[3] Charles the Fifth (Holy Roman Emperor 1519–1558) abdicated after a long and successful reign, though more likely because of illness and old age than melancholy.

[4] Not Tacitus, but Sallust, *Bellum Jugurthinum*, cxiii.1: "The desires of kings are commonly vehement and contradictory."

the solecism of power, to think to command the end, and yet not to endure the mean.

Kings have to deal with their neighbours, their wives, their children, their prelates or clergy, their nobles, their second-nobles or gentlemen, their merchants, their commons, and their men of war; and from all these arise dangers, if care and circumspection be not used.

First for their neighbours: there can no general rule be given (the occasions are so variable), save one, which ever holdeth; which is, that princes do keep due sentinel, that none of their neighbours do overgrow so (by increase of territory, by embracing of trade, by approaches, or the like), as they become more able to annoy them than they were. And this is generally the work of standing counsels to foresee and to hinder it. During that triumvirate of kings, King Henry the Eighth of England, Francis the First King of France, and Charles the Fifth Emperor, there was such a watch kept, that none of the three could win a palm of ground, but the other two would straightways balance it, either by confederation, or, if need were, by a war; and would not in any wise take up peace at interest.[1] And the like was done by that league (which Guicciardine saith was the security of Italy) made between Ferdinando King of Naples, Lorenzius Medices, and Ludovicus Sforza, potentates, the one of Florence, the other of Milan.[2] Neither is the opinion of some of the schoolmen to be received, that *a war cannot justly be made but upon a precedent injury or provocation.*[3] For there is no question but a just fear of an immi-

nent danger, though there be no blow given, is a lawful cause of a war.

For their wives: there are cruel examples of them. Livia is infamed for the poisoning of her husband;[4] Roxalana, Solyman's wife, was the destruction of that renowned prince Sultan Mustapha, and otherwise troubled his house and succession;[5] Edward the Second of England his queen had the principal hand in the deposing and murder of her husband.[6] This kind of danger is then to be feared chiefly, when the wives have plots for the raising of their own children; or else that they be advoutresses.[7]

For their children: the tragedies likewise of dangers from them have been many. And generally, the entering of fathers into suspicion of their children hath been ever unfortunate. The destruction of Mustapha (that we named before) was so fatal to Solyman's line, as the succession of the Turks from Solyman until this day is suspected to be untrue, and of strange blood; for that Selymus the Second was thought to be supposititious.[8] The destruction of Crispus, a young prince of rare towardness, by Constantinus the Great, his father, was in like manner fatal to his house; for both Constantinus and Constance, his sons, died violent deaths; and Constantius, his other son, did little better; who died indeed of sickness, but after that Julianus had taken arms against him. The destruction of Demetrius, son to Philip the Second of Macedon, turned upon the father, who died of repentance. And many like examples there are; but few or none where the fathers had good by such distrust; except

---

[1] Henry (ruled 1509–1547), Francis (ruled 1515–1547), and Charles (ruled 1519–1558) maintained a balance of power for much of the first half of the sixteenth century; *would not...take up peace at interest* would not buy peace if it could cost them in the future.

[2] The league was made in 1480; discussed by Italian historian Francesco Guicciardini (1483–1540) in his *Storia d'Italia*, I.i.

[3] Bacon elsewhere cites Thomas Aquinas, *Summa Theologica*, II.ii.40.i in a similar context, though the idea was commonplace.

[4] *her husband* the Roman Emperor Augustus (63 B.C.E.–14 C.E.).

[5] *his house* the ruling house in mid sixteenth-century Turkey. Bacon is drawing on Richard Knolles' *The Generall Historie of the Turkes* (1603), a book that had a great deal of influence on the British literary imagination in the seventeenth and later centuries.

[6] *his queen* Isabel of France (1292–1358).

[7] *advoutresses* adulteresses (*OED* avouter).

[8] *supposititious* illegitimate (*OED* supposititious 1b).

it were where the sons were up in open arms against them; as was Selymus the First against Bajazet;[1] and the three sons of Henry the Second, King of England.[2]

For their prelates: when they are proud and great, there is also danger from them; as it was in the time of Anselmus and Thomas Becket, Archbishops of Canterbury; who with their crosiers did almost try it with the king's sword;[3] and yet they had to deal with stout and haughty kings: William Rufus, Henry the First, and Henry the Second. The danger is not from that state, but where it hath a dependence of foreign authority; or where the churchmen come in and are elected, not by the collation of the king, or particular patrons, but by the people.[4]

For their nobles: to keep them at a distance, it is not amiss; but to depress them, may make a king more absolute, but less safe; and less able to perform any thing that he desires. I have noted it in my *History of King Henry the Seventh of England*, who depressed his nobility; whereupon it came to pass that his times were full of difficulties and troubles; for the nobility, though they continued loyal unto him, yet did they not co-operate with him in his business. So that in effect he was fain to do all things himself.

For their second nobles: there is not much danger from them, being a body dispersed. They may sometimes discourse high, but that doth little hurt; besides, they are a counterpoise to the higher nobility, that they grow not too potent; and, lastly, being the most immediate in authority with the common people, they do best temper popular commotions.

For their merchants: they are *vena porta*;[5] and if they flourish not, a kingdom may have good limbs, but will have empty veins, and nourish little. Taxes and imposts upon them do seldom good to the king's revenue;[6] for that that he wins in the hundred he leaseth in the shire;[7] the particular rates being increased, but the total bulk of trading rather decreased.

For their commons: there is little danger from them, except it be where they have great and potent heads; or where you meddle with the point of religion, or their customs, or means of life.

For their men of war: it is a dangerous state where they live and remain in a body, and are used to donatives;[8] whereof we see examples in the janizaries,[9] and praetorian bands of Rome; but trainings of men, and arming them in several places, and under several commanders, and without donatives, are things of defence, and no danger.

Princes are like to heavenly bodies, which cause good or evil times; and which have much veneration, but no rest. All precepts concerning kings are in effect comprehended in those two remembrances: *memento quod es homo*; and *momento quod es Deus*, or *vice Dei*;[10] the one bridleth their power, and the other their will.

—1612, REVISED 1625

---

[1] *Selymus* who had his father poisoned.

[2] *three sons* Henry, Geoffrey, and Richard, who rebelled against their father in 1173–1174.

[3] St. Anselm (1033?–1109) and Thomas Becket (1118?–1170) both challenged royal authority in ecclesiastical matters; *crosier* shepherd's crook, emblem of the episcopal office.

[4] *collation* the presentation of a benefice to a clergyman (*OED* collation *sb* 11).

[5] *vena porta* the gate vein, thought to feed the liver, as merchants circulated wealth through the body politic.

[6] *imposts* import duties (*OED* impost *sb*[1] 1).

[7] What he gains in a small matter he loses in a larger; *hundred* English counties were divided into "hundreds," originally supposed to be the number of families they contained.

[8] *donatives* bonus payments.

[9] *janizaries* elite fighting bands in the Turkish army.

[10] "Remember that you are a man" and "remember that you are a God" or "God's lieutenant."

OF THE TRUE GREATNESS OF KINGDOMS AND ESTATES

The speech of Themistocles the Athenian, which was haughty and arrogant in taking so much to himself, had been a grave and wise observation and censure, applied at large to others. Desired at a feast to touch a lute, he said, "He could not fiddle, but yet he could make a small town a great city." These words (holpen a little with a metaphor) may express two differing abilities in those that deal in business of estate.[1] For if a true survey be taken of counsellors and statesmen, there may be found (though rarely) those which can make a small state great, and yet cannot fiddle:[2] as on the other side, there will be found a great many that can fiddle very cunningly, but yet are so far from being able to make a small state great, as their gift lieth the other way; to bring a great and flourishing estate to ruin and decay. And, certainly those degenerate arts and shifts, whereby many counsellors and governors gain both favour with their masters and estimation with the vulgar, deserve no better name than fiddling; being things rather pleasing for the time, and graceful to themselves only, than tending to the weal and advancement of the state which they serve. There are also (no doubt) counsellors and governors which may be held sufficient (*negotiis pares* [equal to the business]), able to manage affairs, and to keep them from precipices and manifest inconveniences; which nevertheless are far from the ability to raise and amplify an estate in power, means, and fortune. But be the workmen what they may be, let us speak of the work; that is, the true greatness of Kingdoms and Estates, and the means thereof. An argument fit for great and mighty princes to have in their hand; to the end that neither by over-measuring their forces, they lease themselves in vain enterprises; nor

on the other side, by undervaluing them, they descend to fearful and pusillanimous counsels.

The greatness of an estate in bulk and territory, doth fall under measure; and the greatness of finances and revenue doth fall under computation. The population may appear by musters; and the number and greatness of cities and towns by cards and maps. But yet there is not anything amongst civil affairs more subject to error, than the right valuation and true judgment concerning the power and forces of an estate. The kingdom of heaven is compared, not to any great kernel or nut, but to a grain of mustard-seed; which is one of the least grains, but hath in it a property and spirit hastily to get up and spread. So are there states great in territory, and yet not apt to enlarge or command; and some that have but a small dimension of stem, and yet apt to be the foundations of great monarchies.[3]

Walled towns, stored arsenals and armories, goodly races of horse, chariots of war, elephants, ordnance, artillery, and the like; all this is but a sheep in a lion's skin, except the breed and disposition of the people be stout and warlike. Nay, number (itself) in armies importeth not much, where the people is of weak courage; for (as Virgil saith) "It never troubles a wolf how many the sheep be." The army of the Persians in the plains of Arbela was such a vast sea of people, as it did somewhat astonish the commanders in Alexander's army; who came to him therefore, and wished him to set upon them by night; but he answered, "He would not pilfer the victory." And the defeat was easy. When Tigranes the Armenian, being encamped upon a hill with four hundred thousand men, discovered the army of the Romans, being not above fourteen thousand, marching towards him, he made himself merry with it, and said, "Yonder men are too many for an ambassage, and too few for a fight." But, before the

---

[1] *holpen* helped.

[2] *fiddle* dissimulate, cheat.

[3] *a small dimension of stem* one of many analogies Bacon draws between states and plants in this essay.

sun set, he found them enough to give him the chase with infinite slaughter. Many are the examples of the great odds between number and courage: so that a man may truly make a judgment, that the principal point of greatness in any state is to have a race of military men. Neither is money the sinews of war (as it is trivially said), where the sinews of men's arms, in base and effeminate people, are failing. For Solon said well to Croesus (when in ostentation he showed him his gold), "Sir, if any other come that hath better iron than you, he will be master of all this gold." Therefore let any prince or state think soberly of his forces, except his militia of natives be of good and valiant soldiers. And let princes, on the other side, that have subjects of martial disposition, know their own strength; unless they be otherwise wanting unto themselves. As for mercenary forces (which is the help in this case), all examples show that whatsoever estate or prince doth rest upon them, he may spread his feathers for a time, but he will mew them soon after.[1]

The blessing of Judah and Issachar will never meet; that "the same people or nation should be both the lion's whelp and the ass between burthens" [Genesis 49:9, 14]; neither will it be, that a people overlaid with taxes should ever become valiant and martial. It is true that taxes levied by consent of the estate do abate men's courage less: as it hath been seen notably in the excises of the Low Countries; and, in some degree, in the subsidies of England. For you must note that we speak now of the heart and not of the purse. So that although the same tribute and tax, laid by consent or by imposing, be all one to the purse, yet it works diversely upon the courage. So that you may conclude, that no people over-charged with tribute is fit for empire.

Let states that aim at greatness, take heed how their nobility and gentlemen do multiply too fast. For that maketh the common subject grow to be a peasant and base swain, driven out of heart, and in effect but the gentleman's labourer. Even as you may see in coppice woods; if you leave your staddles too thick, you shall never have clean underwood, but shrubs and bushes.[2] So in countries, if the gentlemen be too many, the commons will be base; and you will bring it to that, that not the hundred poll will be fit for an helmet;[3] especially as to the infantry, which is the nerve of an army; and so there will be great population and little strength. This which I speak of hath been no where better seen than by comparing of England and France; whereof England, though far less in territory and population, hath been (nevertheless) an over-match; in regard the middle people of England make good soldiers, which the peasants of France do not. And herein the device of king Henry the Seventh (whereof I have spoken largely in the history of his life) was profound and admirable; in making farms and houses of husbandry of a standard; that is, maintained with such a proportion of land unto them, as may breed a subject to live in convenient plenty and no servile condition; and to keep the plough in the hands of the owners, and not mere hirelings. And thus indeed you shall attain to Virgil's character which he gives to ancient Italy:

Terra potens armis atque ubere glebae.[4]

Neither is that state (which, for anything I know, is almost peculiar to England, and hardly to be found anywhere else, except it be perhaps in Poland) to be passed over; I mean the state of free servants and attendants upon noblemen and gentlemen; which are no ways inferior unto the yeomanry for arms. And therefore out of all question, the splendour and magnificence and great retinues and hospitality of

---

[1] *mew* moult, shed (*OED* mew *v*[1] 1).

[2] *coppice* small-growth woods intended for periodic clearing (*OED*); *staddles* young trees left standing after clearing (*OED* staddle *sb* 2).

[3] That is, only one man in a hundred would be fit to be a soldier.

[4] *Aeneid*, i.531: "a land powerful in arms and richness of soil."

noblemen and gentlemen, received into custom, doth much conduce unto martial greatness. Whereas, contrariwise, the close and reserved living of noblemen and gentlemen causeth a penury of military forces.

By all means it is to be procured, that the trunk of Nebuchadnezzar's tree of monarchy be great enough to bear the branches and the boughs [Daniel 4:10-26]; that is, that the natural subjects of the crown or state bear a sufficient proportion to the stranger subjects that they govern.[1] Therefore all states that are liberal of naturalisation towards strangers are fit for empire. For to think that an handful of people can, with the greatest courage and policy in the world, embrace too large extent of dominion, it may hold for a time, but it will fail suddenly. The Spartans were a nice people in point of naturalisation;[2] whereby, while they kept their compass, they stood firm; but when they did spread, and their boughs were becoming too great for their stem, they became a windfall upon the sudden. Never any state was in this point so open to receive strangers into their body as were the Romans. Therefore it sorted with them accordingly; for they grew to the greatest monarchy. Their manner was to grant naturalisation (which they called *jus civitatis*), and to grant it in the highest degree; that is, not only *jus commercii*, *jus connubii*, *jus haereditatis*; but also *jus suffragii*, and *jus honorum*.[3] And this not to singular persons alone, but likewise to whole families; yea to cities, and sometimes to nations. Add to this their custom of plantation of colonies; whereby the Roman plant was removed into the soil of other nations. And putting both constitutions together, you will say that it was not the Romans that spread upon the world, but it was the world that spread upon the Romans; and that was the sure way of greatness. I have marvelled sometimes at Spain, how they clasp and contain so large dominions with so few natural Spaniards; but sure the whole compass of Spain is a very great body of a tree; far above Rome and Sparta at the first. And besides, though they have not had that usage to naturalise liberally, yet they have that which is next to it; that is, to employ almost indifferently all nations in their militia of ordinary soldiers; yea and sometimes in their highest commands. Nay it seemeth at this instant they are sensible of this want of natives; as by the Pragmatical Sanction, now published, appeareth.[4]

It is certain, that sedentary and within-door arts, and delicate manufactures (that require rather the finger than the arm), have in their nature a contrariety to a military disposition. And generally, all warlike people are a little idle, and love danger better than travail.[5] Neither must they be too much broken of it, if they shall be preserved in vigour. Therefore it was great advantage in the ancient states of Sparta, Athens, Rome, and others, that they had the use of slaves, which commonly did rid those manufactures. But that is abolished, in greatest part, by the Christian law. That which cometh nearest to it, is to leave those arts chiefly to strangers (which for that purpose are the more easily to be received), and to contain the principal bulk of the vulgar natives within those three kinds,—tillers of the ground; free servants; and handicraftsmen of strong and manly arts, as smiths, masons, carpenters, &c: not reckoning professed soldiers.

But above all, for empire and greatness, it importeth most that a nation do profess arms as their principal honour, study, and occupation. For the things which we formerly have spoken of are

---

[1] *natural* native; *stranger* foreign or naturalized.

[2] *nice* particular, choosy (*OED* nice *a* 7).

[3] the legal rights respectively of citizenship, commerce, marriage, inheritance, voting, and office-holding.

[4] *Pragmatical Sanction* a Spanish royal proclamation (1622), which offered tax incentives to those who married and bore many children. Spain controlled large parts of the New World.

[5] *travail* labour (*OED* travail *sb*[1] 1).

but habilitations towards arms;[1] and what is habilitation without intention and act? Romulus, after his death (as they report or feign), sent a present to the Romans, that above all they should intend arms; and then they should prove the greatest empire of the world. The fabric of the state of Sparta was wholly (though not wisely) framed and composed to that scope and end. The Persians and Macedonians had it for a flash. The Gauls, Germans, Goths, Saxons, Normans, and others, had it for a time. The Turks have it at this day, though in great declination. Of Christian Europe, they that have it are, in effect, only the Spaniards. But it is so plain that every man profiteth in that he most intendeth, that it needeth not to be stood upon. It is enough to point at it; that no nation which doth not directly profess arms, may look to have greatness fall into their mouths. And on the other side, it is a most certain oracle of time, that those states that continue long in that profession (as the Romans and Turks principally have done) do wonders. And those that have professed arms but for an age, have notwithstanding commonly attained that greatness in that age which maintained them long after, when their profession and exercise of arms hath grown to decay.

Incident to this point is, for a state to have those laws or customs which may reach forth unto them just occasions (as may be pretended) of war. For there is that justice imprinted in the nature of men, that they enter not upon wars (whereof so many calamities do ensue) but upon some, at the least specious,[2] grounds and quarrels. The Turk hath at hand, for cause of war, the propagation of his law or sect;[3] a quarrel that he may always command. The Romans, though they esteemed the extending the limits of their empire to be great honour to their generals when it was done, yet they never rested upon that alone to begin a war. First therefore, let nations that pretend to greatness have this; that they be sensible of wrongs, either upon borderers, merchants, or politique ministers; and that they sit not too long upon a provocation. Secondly, let them be prest and ready to give aids and succours to their confederates;[4] as it ever was with the Romans; insomuch as, if the confederates had leagues defensive with divers other states, and, upon invasion offered, did implore their aids severally, yet the Romans would ever be the foremost, and leave it to none other to have the honour. As for the wars which were anciently made on the behalf of a kind of party, or tacit conformity of estate, I do not see how they may be well justified: as when the Romans made a war for the liberty of Graecia; or when the Lacedaemonians and Athenians made wars to set up or pull down democracies and oligarchies; or when wars were made by foreigners, under the pretence of justice or protection, to deliver the subjects of others from tyranny and oppression; and the like. Let it suffice, that no estate expect to be great, that is not awake upon any just occasion of arming.

No body can be healthful without exercise, neither natural body nor politic; and certainly to a kingdom or estate, a just and honourable war is the true exercise. A civil war indeed is like the heat of a fever; but a foreign war is like the heat of exercise, and serveth to keep the body in health; for in a slothful peace, both courages will effeminate and manners corrupt. But howsoever it be for happiness, without all question, for greatness it maketh, to be still for the most part in arms; and the strength of a veteran army (though it be a chargeable business) always on foot, is that which commonly giveth the law, or at least the reputation, amongst all neighbour states; as may well be seen in Spain, which hath had, in one part or other, a

---

[1] *habilitations* trainings, preparations (*OED*).

[2] *specious* plausible.

[3] *his law or sect* Islam.

[4] *prest* prepared (*OED* prest *a* A).

veteran army almost continually, now by the space of six score years.

To be master of the sea is an abridgment of a monarchy.[1] Cicero, writing to Atticus of Pompey his preparation against Caesar, saith, *Consilium Pompeii plane Themistocleum est; putat enim, qui mari potitur, eum rerum potiri.*[2] And, without doubt, Pompey had tired out Caesar, if upon vain confidence he had not left that way. We see the great effects of battles by sea. The battle of Actium decided the empire of the world.[3] The battle of Lepanto arrested the greatness of the Turk.[4] There be many examples where sea-fights have been final to the war; but this is when princes or states have set up their rest upon the battles. But thus much is certain, that he that commands the sea is at great liberty, and may take as much and as little of the war as he will. Whereas those that be strongest by land are many times nevertheless in great straits. Surely, at this day, with us of Europe, the vantage of strength at sea (which is one of the principal dowries of the kingdom of Great Britain) is great; both because most of the kingdoms of Europe are not merely inland, but girt with the sea most part of their compass; and because the wealth of both Indies seems in great part but an accessary to the command of the seas.

The wars of latter ages seem to be made in the dark, in respect of the glory and honour which reflected upon men from the wars in ancient time. There be now, for martial encouragement, some degrees and orders of chivalry; which nevertheless are conferred promiscuously upon soldiers and no soldiers; and some remembrance perhaps upon the scutcheon;[5] and some hospitals for maimed soldiers; and such like things. But in ancient times, the trophies erected upon the place of the victory; the funeral laudatives and monuments for those that died in the wars; the crown and garlands personal; the style of Emperor, which the great kings of the world after borrowed; the triumphs of the generals upon their return; the great donatives and largesses upon the disbanding of the armies; were things able to inflame all men's courages. But above all, that of the Triumph, amongst the Romans, was not pageants or gaudery, but one of the wisest and noblest institutions that ever was. For it contained three things; honour to the general; riches to the treasury out of the spoils; and donatives to the army. But that honour perhaps were not fit for monarchies; except it be in the person of the monarch himself, or his sons, as it came to pass in the times of the Roman emperors, who did impropriate the actual triumphs to themselves and their sons, for such wars as they did achieve in person; and left only, for wars achieved by subjects, some triumphal garments and ensigns to the general.

To conclude: no man can "by care taking" (as the Scripture saith) "add a cubit to his stature" [Matthew 6:27, Luke 12:25], in this little model of a man's body; but in the great frame of kingdoms and commonwealths, it is in the power of princes or estates to add amplitude and greatness to their kingdoms; for by introducing such ordinances, constitutions, and customs, as we have now touched, they may sow greatness to their posterity and succession. But these things are commonly not observed, but left to take their chance.

—1612, REVISED 1625

---

[1] *abridgement* not a lessening, but a short cut to power for a monarchy.

[2] *Ad Atticum*, x.8: "Pompey's plan is quite Themistoclean; for he thinks that the mastery of the sea means the mastery of the war."

[3] *battle of Actium* where Augustus defeated Antony, in 31 B.C.E.

[4] *battle of Lepanto* where in 1571 the combined navies of Venice, Spain, and the Papacy defeated the fleet of the Ottoman empire, bringing to a close Turkish dominance of the Mediterranean.

[5] *scutcheon* coat of arms or shield, on which could be recorded military achievements (*OED* escutcheon 1).

Of Plantations [1]

Plantations are amongst ancient, primitive, and heroical works. When the world was young it begat more children; but now it is old it begets fewer: for I may justly account new plantations to be the children of former kingdoms. I like a plantation in a pure soil; that is, where people are not displanted to the end to plant in others. For else it is rather an extirpation than a plantation. Planting of countries is like planting of woods; for you must make account to lease almost twenty years' profit, and expect your recompense in the end. For the principal thing that hath been the destruction of most plantations, hath been the base and hasty drawing of profit in the first years. It is true, speedy profit is not to be neglected, as far as may stand with the good of the plantation, but no further.

It is a shameful and unblessed thing to take the scum of people, and wicked condemned men, to be the people with whom you plant; and not only so, but it spoileth the plantation; for they will ever live like rogues, and not fall to work, but be lazy, and do mischief, and spend victuals, and be quickly weary, and then certify over to their country to the discredit of the plantation.[2] The people wherewith you plant ought to be gardeners, ploughmen, labourers, smiths, carpenters, joiners, fishermen, fowlers, with some few apothecaries, surgeons, cooks, and bakers.

In a country of plantation, first look about what kind of victual the country yields of itself to hand; as chestnuts, walnuts, pine-apples,[3] olives, dates, plums, cherries, wild honey, and the like; and make use of them. Then consider what victual or esculent things there are,[4] which grow speedily, and within the year; as parsnips, carrots, turnips, onions, radish, artichokes of Jerusalem, maize, and the like. For wheat, barley, and oats, they ask too much labour; but with peas and beans you may begin, both because they ask less labour, and because they serve for meat as well as for bread. And of rice likewise cometh a great increase, and it is a kind of meat. Above all, there ought to be brought store of biscuit, oatmeal, flour, meal, and the like, in the beginning, till bread may be had. For beasts, or birds, take chiefly such as are least subject to diseases, and multiply fastest; as swine, goats, cocks, hens, turkeys, geese, housedoves, and the like. The victual in plantations ought to be expended almost as in a besieged town; that is, with certain allowance. And let the main part of the ground employed to gardens or corn, be to a common stock; and to be laid in, and stored up, and then delivered out in proportion; besides some spots of ground that any particular person will manure for his own private [use].

Consider likewise what commodities the soil where the plantation is doth naturally yield, that they may some way help to defray the charge of the plantation (so it be not, as was said, to the untimely prejudice of the main business), as it hath fared with tobacco in Virginia. Wood commonly aboundeth but too much; and therefore timber is fit to be one. If there be iron ore, and streams whereupon to set the mills, iron is a brave commodity where wood aboundeth. Making of bay-salt,[5] if the climate be proper for it, would be put in experience. Growing silk likewise, if any be, is a likely commodity. Pitch and tar, where store of firs and pines are, will not fail. So drugs and sweet woods, where they are, cannot but yield great profit. Soap-ashes likewise, and other things that may be thought of. But moil not too much under ground; for the hope of mines

---

[1] *Plantations* colonies.

[2] *certify over* send reports.

[3] *pine-apples* pine-cones, here particularly the edible kernel or pine-nut.

[4] *esculent* edible.

---

[5] *bay-salt* coarse salt extracted from salt-water ponds.

is very uncertain, and useth to make the planters lazy in other things.

For government, let it be in the hands of one, assisted with some counsel; and let them have commission to exercise martial laws, with some limitation. And above all, let men make that profit of being in the wilderness, as they have God always, and his service, before their eyes. Let not the government of the plantation depend upon too many counsellors and undertakers in the country that planteth,[1] but upon a temperate number; and let those be rather noblemen and gentlemen, than merchants; for they look ever to the present gain. Let there be freedoms from custom till the plantation be of strength;[2] and not only freedom from custom, but freedom to carry their commodities where they may make their best of them, except there be some special cause of caution.

Cram not in people, by sending too fast company after company; but rather hearken how they waste and send supplies proportionably; but so as the number may live well in the plantation, and not by surcharge be in penury.

It hath been a great endangering to the health of some plantations, that they have built along the sea and rivers, in marish and unwholesome grounds.[3] Therefore, though you begin there, to avoid carriage and other like discommodities, yet build still rather upwards from the streams, than along. It concerneth likewise the health of the plantation that they have good store of salt with them, that they may use it in their victuals when it shall be necessary.

If you plant where savages are, do not only entertain them with trifles and gingles; but use them justly and graciously, with sufficient guard nevertheless; and do not win their favour by helping them to invade their enemies, but for their defence

it is not amiss; and send oft of them over to the country that plants, that they may see a better condition than their own, and commend it when they return. When the plantation grows to strength, then it is time to plant with women as well as with men; that the plantation may spread into generations, and not be ever pieced from without. It is the sinfullest thing in the world to forsake or destitute a plantation once in forwardness; for besides the dishonour, it is the guiltiness of blood of many commiserable persons.

—1625

OF MASQUES AND TRIUMPHS

These things are but toys, to come amongst such serious observations.[4] But yet, since princes will have such things, it is better they should be graced with elegancy than daubed with cost.

Dancing to song is a thing of great state and pleasure. I understand it, that the song be in choir, placed aloft, and accompanied with some broken music,[5] and the ditty fitted to the device. Acting in song, especially in dialogues, hath an extreme good grace; I say acting, not dancing (for that is a mean and vulgar thing);[6] and the voices of the dialogue would be strong and manly (a bass and a tenor, no treble); and the ditty high and tragical, not nice or dainty. Several choirs, placed one over against another and taking the voice by catches, anthemwise, give great pleasure. Turning dances into figure

---

[4] While Bacon appears to dismiss these court entertainments (which combined theatrical spectacle, music, song, and dance), the essay reveals his first-hand knowledge of the genre: Bacon wrote several masque-like "devices" in the 1590s, and organized two magnificently expensive entertainments in 1613–14 (see the letters of John Chamberlain for a description of one).

[5] *broken music* a small consort containing both wind and string instruments.

[6] *acting, not dancing* singing recitative, as in opera, as opposed to dancing in song, as in a jig; the "dancing to song" with which Bacon begins the paragraph refers to the graceful dancing to music of the main masque.

---

[1] *undertakers* shareholders.

[2] *custom* custom duties.

[3] *marish* marshy.

is a childish curiosity. And generally let it be noted, that those things which I here set down are such as do naturally take the sense, and not respect petty wonderments. It is true, the alterations of scenes, so it be quietly and without noise, are things of great beauty and pleasure; for they feed and relieve the eye, before it be full of the same object.[1]

Let the scenes abound with light, specially coloured and varied; and let the masquers, or any other, that are to come down from the scene,[2] have some motions upon the scene itself before their coming down; for it draws the eye strangely, and makes it with great pleasure to desire to see that [which] it cannot perfectly discern. Let the songs be loud and cheerful, and not chirpings or pulings. Let the music likewise be sharp and loud, and well placed. The colours that show best by candlelight are white, carnation, and a kind of sea-water-green; and oes, or spangs, as they are of no great cost, so they are of most glory.[3] As for rich embroidery, it is lost and not discerned. Let the suits of the masquers be graceful, and such as become the person when the vizards are off;[4] not after examples of known attires, Turks, soldiers, mariners, and the like.

Let anti-masques not be long;[5] they have been commonly of fools, satyrs, baboons, wild-men, antics, beasts, sprites, witches, Ethiops, pygmies, turquets,[6] nymphs, rustics, cupids, statues moving, and the like. As for angels, it is not comical enough to put them in anti-masques; and any thing that is hideous, as devils, giants, is on the other side as unfit. But chiefly, let the music of them be recreative, and with some strange changes. Some sweet odours suddenly coming forth, without any drops falling, are, in such a company as there is steam and heat, things of great pleasure and refreshment. Double masques, one of men, another of ladies, addeth state and variety. But all is nothing except the room be kept clear and neat.

For jousts, and tourneys, and barriers:[7] the glories of them are chiefly in the chariots, wherein the challengers make their entry; especially if they be drawn with strange beasts, as lions, bears, camels, and the like; or in the devices of their entrance;[8] or in the bravery of their liveries; or in the goodly furniture of their horses and armour. But enough of these toys.

—1625

OF STUDIES

(1597 version, not modernized)

Studies serve for pastimes, for ornaments and for abilities. Their chiefe use for pastime is in privateness and retiring; for ornamente is in discourse, and for abilitie is in judgement. For expert men can execute, but learned men are fittest to judge or censure.

¶ To spend too much time in them is slouth, to use them too much for ornament is affectation: to make judgement wholly by their rules, is the humour of a Scholler. ¶ They perfect *Nature*, and are perfected by experience. ¶ Craftie men contemn them, simple men admire them, wise men use them:

---

[1] *alterations of scenes* scene or set changes, possible only in private halls fitted with custom-built stage machinery; the public theatre did not use sets.

[2] *come down from the scene* descend from the stage to the hall, for a dance that could include leading members of the audience.

[3] *oes, or spangs* sequins ("oes" is the plural of the letter "o").

[4] *vizards* masks.

[5] *anti-masques* comic or grotesque episodes that contrasted with the main masque; they often represented the forces of disorder over which the qualities celebrated in the main masque triumph.

[6] *turquets* little Turks.

[7] *jousts, and tourneys, and barriers* the traditional chivalric competitions of martial prowess, respectively tilts on horseback with lances; combat on horseback with swords; and combat on foot with swords and axes, usually across a barrier.

[8] *devices* Each knight created a persona and an elaborate fiction to explain his presence at a tournament; "device" refers collectively to the various means through which this narrative was conveyed (costume, emblematic shield, cryptic mottoes, songs).

For they teach not their owne use, but that is a wisedome without them: and above them wonne by observation. ¶ Reade not to contradict, nor to believe, but to waigh and consider. ¶ Some bookes are to bee tasted, others to bee swallowed, and some few to bee chewed and disgested: That is, some bookes are to be read only in partes; others to be read, but cursorily, and some few to be read wholly and with diligence and attention. ¶ Reading maketh a full man, conference a readye man, and writing an exacte man. And therefore if a man write little, he had neede have a great memorie, if he conferre little, he had neede have a present wit, and if he reade little, hee had neede have much cunning, to seeme to know that he doth not. ¶ Histories make men wise, Poets wittie: the Mathematickes subtle, naturall Phylosophie deepe: Morall grave, Logicke and Rhetoricke able to contend.

—1597

OF STUDIES

(1625 version, modernized)

Studies serve for delight, for ornament, and for ability. Their chief use for delight, is in privateness and retiring; for ornament, is in discourse; and for ability, is in the judgment and disposition of business. For expert men can execute, and perhaps judge of particulars, one by one; but the general counsels, and the plots and marshalling of affairs, come best from those that are learned. To spend too much time in studies is sloth; to use them too much for ornament, is affectation; to make judgment wholly by their rules, is the humour of a scholar. They perfect nature, and are perfected by experience: for natural abilities are like natural plants, that need pruning by study; and studies themselves do give forth directions too much at large, except they be bounded in by experience. Crafty men contemn studies, simple men admire them, and wise men use them; for they teach not their own use; but that is

a wisdom without them, and above them, won by observation. Read not to contradict and confute; nor to believe and take for granted; nor to find talk and discourse; but to weigh and consider. Some books are to be tasted, others to be swallowed, and some few to be chewed and digested; that is, some books are to be read only in parts; others to be read but not curiously;[1] and some few to be read wholly, and with diligence and attention. Some books also may be read by deputy, and extracts made of them by others; but that would be only in the less important arguments, and the meaner sort of books; else distilled books are like common distilled waters, flashy things.[2] Reading maketh a full man; conference a ready man; and writing an exact man. And therefore, if a man write little, he had need have a great memory; if he confer little, he had need have a present wit: and if he read little, he had need have much cunning, to seem to know that he doth not. Histories make men wise; poets witty; the mathematics subtle; natural philosophy deep; moral grave; logic and rhetoric able to contend. *Abeunt studia in mores.*[3] Nay there is no stond or impediment in the wit,[4] but may be wrought out by fit studies; like as diseases of the body may have appropriate exercises. Bowling is good for the stone and reins;[5] shooting for the lungs and breast; gentle walking for the stomach; riding for the head; and the like. So if a man's wit be wandering, let him study the mathematics; for in demonstrations, if his wit be called away never so little, he must begin again. If his wit be not apt to distinguish or find differences, let him study the schoolmen; for they are *cymini sectores*

---

[1] *curiously* carefully, with attention (*OED* curiously *adv* 1).

[2] *distilled waters* juices made from distilled plants and vegetables for medicinal purposes; *flashy* insipid, tasteless (*OED* flashy *a* 2b; this place cited).

[3] Ovid, *Heroides*, xv.83: "Studies shape our behaviour."

[4] *stond* obstacle (*OED* stond 2; this place cited).

[5] *stone and reins* kidney or gall-bladder stones, and kidney disorders.

[splitters of hairs]. If he be not apt to beat over matters, and to call up one thing to prove and illustrate another, let him study the lawyers' cases. So every defect of the mind may have a special receipt.[1]

—1625

Aphorisms Concerning the Interpretation of Nature and the Kingdom of Man
(excerpts)

(from *Novum Organum*)

I

Man, being the servant and interpreter of Nature, can do and understand so much and so much only as he has observed in fact or in thought of the course of nature: beyond this he neither knows anything nor can do anything.

II

Neither the naked hand nor the understanding left to itself can effect much. It is by instruments and helps that the work is done, which are as much wanted for the understanding as for the hand. And as the instruments of the hand either give motion or guide it, so the instruments of the mind supply either suggestions for the understanding or cautions.

III

Human knowledge and human power meet in one; for where the cause is not known the effect cannot be produced. Nature to be commanded must be obeyed; and that which in contemplation is as the cause is in operation as the rule.

IV

Towards the effecting of works, all that man can do is to put together or put asunder natural bodies. The rest is done by nature working within.

V

The study of nature with a view to works is engaged in by the mechanic, the mathematician, the physician, the alchemist, and the magician; but by all (as things now are) with slight endeavour and scanty success.

VI

It would be an unsound fancy and self-contradictory to expect that things which have never yet been done can be done except by means which have never yet been tried.

VII

The productions of the mind and hand seem very numerous in books and manufactures. But all this variety lies in an exquisite subtlety and derivations from a few things already known; not in the number of axioms.

VIII

Moreover the works already known are due to chance and experiment rather than to sciences; for the sciences we now possess are merely systems for the nice ordering and setting forth of things already invented; not methods of invention or directions for new works.

IX

The cause and root of nearly all evils in the sciences is this—that while we falsely admire and extol the powers of the human mind we neglect to seek for its true helps.

X

The subtlety of nature is greater many times over than the subtlety of the senses and understanding; so that all those specious meditations, speculations, and glosses in which men indulge are quite from the purpose, only there is no one by to observe it.

---

[1] *receipt* recipe.

XI

As the sciences which we now have do not help us in finding out new works, so neither does the logic which we now have help us in finding out new sciences.

XII

The logic now in use serves rather to fix and give stability to the errors which have their foundation in commonly received notions than to help the search after truth. So it does more harm than good.

XIII

The syllogism is not applied to the first principles of sciences, and is applied in vain to intermediate axioms; being no match for the subtlety of nature. It commands assent therefore to the proposition, but does not take hold of the thing.

XIV

The syllogism consists of propositions, propositions consist of words, words are symbols of notions. Therefore if the notions themselves (which is the root of the matter) are confused and over-hastily abstracted from the facts, there can be no firmness in the superstructure. Our only hope therefore lies in a true induction.[1]

XV

There is no soundness in our notions whether logical or physical. Substance, quality, action, passion, essence itself, are not sound notions: much less are heavy, light, dense, rare, moist, dry, generation, corruption, attraction, repulsion, element, matter, form, and the like; but all are fantastical and ill defined.

---

[1] *induction* the building up of arguments based on the collection and observation of particulars. Bacon was arguing against deduction, which begins with general principles and proceeds to particulars; in modern usage "deduction" tends to be used for both processes. See aphorisms XIX forward.

XVIII

The discoveries which have hitherto been made in the sciences are such as lie close to vulgar notions, scarcely beneath the surface. In order to penetrate into the inner and further recesses of nature, it is necessary that both notions and axioms be derived from things by a more sure and guarded way; and that a method of intellectual operation be introduced altogether better and more certain.

XIX

There are and can be only two ways of searching into and discovering truth. The one flies from the senses and particulars to the most general axioms, and from these principles, the truth of which it takes for settled and immoveable, proceeds to judgment and to the discovery of middle axioms. And this way is now in fashion. The other derives axioms from the senses and particulars, rising by a gradual and unbroken ascent, so that it arrives at the most general axioms last of all. This is the true way, but as yet untried.

XX

The understanding left to itself takes the same course (namely, the former) which it takes in accordance with logical order. For the mind longs to spring up to positions of higher generality, that it may find rest there; and so after a little while wearies of experiment. But this evil is increased by logic, because of the order and solemnity of its disputations.

XXII

Both ways set out from the sense and particulars, and rest in the highest generalities; but the difference between them is infinite. For the one just glances at experiment and particulars in passing, the other dwells duly and orderly among them. The one, again, begins at once by establishing certain abstract and useless generalities, the other rises by gradual steps to that which is prior and better known in the order of nature.

XXIII

There is a great difference between the idols of the human mind and the ideas of the divine. That is to say, between certain empty dogmas, and the true signatures and marks set upon the works of creation as they are found in nature.

XXVI

The conclusions of human reason as ordinarily applied in matter of nature, I call for the sake of distinction *Anticipations of Nature* (as a thing rash or premature). That reason which is elicited from facts by a just and methodical process, I call *Interpretation of Nature*.

XXXI

It is idle to expect any great advancement in science from the superinducing and engrafting of new things upon old. We must begin anew from the very foundations, unless we would revolve for ever in a circle with mean and contemptible progress.

XXXII

The honour of the ancient authors, and indeed of all, remains untouched; since the comparison I challenge is not of wits or faculties, but of ways and methods, and the part I take upon myself is not that of a judge, but of a guide.

XXXIII

This must be plainly avowed: no judgment can be rightly formed either of my method or of the discoveries to which it leads, by means of anticipations (that is to say, of the reasoning which is now in use); since I cannot be called on to abide by the sentence of a tribunal which is itself on its trial.

XXXVI

One method of delivery alone remains to us; which is simply this: we must lead men to the particulars themselves, and their series and order; while men on their side must force themselves for awhile to lay their notions by and begin to familiarise themselves with facts.

XXXVII

The doctrine of those who have denied that certainty could be attained at all, has some agreement with my way of proceeding at the first setting out; but they end in being infinitely separated and opposed. For the holders of that doctrine assert simply that nothing can be known; I also assert that not much can be known in nature by the way which is now in use. But then they go on to destroy the authority of the senses and understanding; whereas I proceed to devise and supply helps for the same.

THE IDOLS

XXXVIII

The idols and false notions that are now in possession of the human understanding, and have taken deep root therein, not only so beset men's minds that truth can hardly find entrance, but even after entrance obtained, they will again in the very instauration of the sciences meet and trouble us,[1] unless men being forewarned of the danger fortify themselves as far as may be against their assaults.

XXXIX

There are four classes of idols which beset men's minds. To these for distinction's sake I have assigned names,—calling the first class *Idols of the Tribe*; the second, *Idols of the Cave*; the third, *Idols of the Market-place*; the fourth, *Idols of the Theatre*.

---

[1] *instauration* restoration, renewal, renovation (*OED*).

XL

The formation of ideas and axioms by true induction is no doubt the proper remedy to be applied for the keeping off and clearing away of idols. To point them out, however, is of great use; for the doctrine of idols is to the interpretation of nature what the doctrine of the refutation of sophisms is to common logic.

XLI

The Idols of the Tribe have their foundation in human nature itself, and in the tribe or race of men. For it is a false assertion that the sense of man is the measure of things. On the contrary, all perceptions as well of the sense as of the mind are according to the measure of the individual and not according to the measure of the universe. And the human understanding is like a false mirror, which, receiving rays irregularly, distorts and discolours the nature of things by mingling its own nature with it.

XLII

The Idols of the Cave are the idols of the individual man. For every one (besides the errors common to human nature in general) has a cave or den of his own, which refracts and discolours the light of nature; owing either to his own proper and peculiar nature; or to his education and conversation with others; or to the reading of books, and the authority of those whom he esteems and admires; or the differences of impressions, accordingly as they take place in a mind preoccupied and predisposed or in a mind indifferent and settled; or the like. So that the spirit of man (according as it is meted out to different individuals) is in fact a thing variable and full of perturbation, and governed as it were by chance. Whence it was well observed by Heraclitus that men look for sciences in their own lesser worlds, and not in the greater or common world.

XLIII

There are also idols formed by the intercourse and association of men with each other, which I call Idols of the Market-place, on account of the commerce and consort of men there. For it is by discourse that men associate; and words are imposed according to the apprehension of the vulgar. And therefore the ill and unfit choice of words wonderfully obstructs the understanding. Nor do the definitions or explanations wherewith in some things learned men are wont to guard and defend themselves, by any means set the matter right. But words plainly force and overrule the understanding, and throw all into confusion, and lead men away into numberless empty controversies and idle fancies.

XLIV

Lastly, there are idols which have immigrated into men's minds from the various dogmas of philosophies, and also from wrong laws of demonstration. These I call Idols of the Theatre; because in my judgment all the received systems are but so many stage-plays, representing worlds of their own creation after an unreal and scenic fashion. Nor is it only of the systems now in vogue, or only of the ancient sects and philosophies, that I speak; for many more plays of the same kind may yet be composed and in like artificial manner set forth; seeing that errors the most widely different have nevertheless causes for the most part alike. Neither again do I mean this only of entire systems, but also of many principles and axioms in science, which by tradition, credulity, and negligence have come to be received.

But of these several kinds of idols I must speak more largely and exactly, that the understanding may be duly cautioned.

IDOLS OF THE TRIBE

XLV

The human understanding is of its own nature prone to suppose the existence of more order and regularity in the world than it finds. And though there be many things in nature which are singular and unmatched, yet it devises for them parallels and conjugates and relatives which do not exist. Hence the fiction that all celestial bodies move in perfect circles; spirals and dragons being (except in name) utterly rejected. Hence too the element of fire with its orb is brought in, to make up the square with the other three which the sense perceives. Hence also the ratio of density of the so-called elements is arbitrarily fixed at ten to one. And so on of other dreams. And these fancies affect not dogmas only, but simple notions also.

XLVI

The human understanding when it has once adopted an opinion (either as being the received opinion or as being agreeable to itself) draws all things else to support and agree with it. And though there be a greater number and weight of instances to be found on the other side, yet these it either neglects and despises, or else by some distinction sets aside and rejects; in order that by this great and pernicious predetermination the authority of its former conclusions may remain inviolate. And therefore it was a good answer that was made by one who when they showed him hanging in a temple a picture of those who had paid their vows as having escaped shipwreck, and would have him say whether he did not now acknowledge the power of the gods, "Aye," asked he again, "but where are they painted that were drowned after their vows?" And such is the way of all superstition, whether in astrology, dreams, omens, divine judgments, or the like; wherein men, having a delight in such vanities, mark the events where they are fulfilled, but where they fail, though this happen much oftener, neglect

and pass them by. But with far more subtlety does this mischief insinuate itself into philosophy and the sciences; in which the first conclusion colours and brings into conformity with itself all that come after, though far sounder and better. Besides, independently of that delight and vanity which I have described, it is the peculiar and perpetual error of the human intellect to be more moved and excited by affirmatives than by negatives; whereas it ought properly to hold itself indifferently disposed towards both alike. Indeed in the establishment of any true axiom, the negative instance is the more forcible of the two.

XLVII

The human understanding is moved by those things most which strike and enter the mind simultaneously and suddenly, and so fill the imagination; and then it feigns and supposes all other things to be somehow, though it cannot see how, similar to those few things by which it is surrounded. But for that going to and fro to remote and heterogeneous instances, by which axioms are tried as in the fire, the intellect is altogether slow and unfit, unless it be forced thereto by severe laws and overruling authority.

XLIX

The human understanding is no dry light, but receives an infusion from the will and affections;[1] whence proceed sciences which may be called "sciences as one would." For what a man had rather were true he more readily believes. Therefore he rejects difficult things from impatience of research; sober things, because they narrow hope; the deeper things of nature, from superstition; the light of experience, from arrogance and pride, lest his mind should seem to be occupied with things mean and transitory; things not commonly believed, out of

---

[1] *dry light* reason or intellect untinged by personal predilection or fancy.

deference to the opinion of the vulgar. Numberless in short are the ways, and sometimes imperceptible, in which the affections colour and infect the understanding.

L

But by far the greatest hindrance and aberration of the human understanding proceeds from the dullness, incompetency, and deceptions of the senses; in that things which strike the sense outweigh things which do not immediately strike it, though they be more important. Hence it is that speculation commonly ceases where sight ceases; insomuch that of things invisible there is little or no observation. Hence all the working of the spirits inclosed in tangible bodies lies hid and unobserved of men. So also all the more subtle changes of form in the parts of coarser substances (which they commonly call alteration, though it is in truth local motion through exceedingly small spaces) is in like manner unobserved. And yet unless these two things just mentioned be searched out and brought to light, nothing great can be achieved in nature, as far as the production of works is concerned. So again the essential nature of our common air, and of all bodies less dense than air (which are very many), is almost unknown. For the sense by itself is a thing infirm and erring; neither can instruments for enlarging or sharpening the senses do much; but all the truer kind of interpretation of nature is effected by instances and experiments fit and apposite; wherein the sense decides touching the experiment only, and the experiment touching the point in nature and the thing itself.

LI

The human understanding is of its own nature prone to abstractions and gives a substance and reality to things which are fleeting. But to resolve nature into abstractions is less to our purpose than to dissect her into parts; as did the school of Democritus, which went further into nature than the rest.[1] Matter rather than forms should be the object of our attention, its configurations and changes of configuration, and simple action, and law of action or motion; for forms are figments of the human mind, unless you will call those laws of action forms.

LII

Such then are the idols which I call Idols of the Tribe; and which take their rise either from the homogeneity of the substance of the human spirit, or from its preoccupation, or from its narrowness, or from its restless motion, or from an infusion of the affections, or from the incompetency of the senses, or from the mode of impression.

IDOLS OF THE CAVE

LIII

The Idols of the Cave take their rise in the peculiar constitution, mental or bodily, of each individual; and also in education, habit, and accident. Of this kind there is a great number and variety; but I will instance those the pointing out of which contains the most important caution, and which have most effect in disturbing the clearness of the understanding.

LIV

Men become attached to certain particular sciences and speculations, either because they fancy themselves the authors and inventors thereof, or because they have bestowed the greatest pains upon them and become most habituated to them. But men of this kind, if they betake themselves to philosophy and contemplations of a general character, distort and colour them in obedience to their former fancies; a thing especially to be noticed in Aristotle, who made his natural philosophy a mere bond-servant to his logic, thereby rendering it

---

[1] *the school of Democritus* They held that matter was composed of atoms.

contentious and well nigh useless. The race of chemists again out of a few experiments of the furnace have built up a fantastic philosophy, framed with reference to a few things; and Gilbert also, after he had employed himself most laboriously in the study and observation of the loadstone, proceeded at once to construct an entire system in accordance with his favourite subject.[1]

LV

There is one principal and as it were radical distinction between different minds, in respect of philosophy and the sciences; which is this: that some minds are stronger and apter to mark the differences of things, others to mark their resemblances. The steady and acute mind can fix its contemplations and dwell and fasten on the subtlest distinctions: the lofty and discursive mind recognises and puts together the finest and most general resemblances. Both kinds however easily err in excess, by catching the one at gradations, the other at shadows.

LVII

Contemplations of nature and of bodies in their simple form break up and distract the understanding, while contemplations of nature and bodies in their composition and configuration overpower and dissolve the understanding: a distinction well seen in the school of Leucippus and Democritus as compared with the other philosophies. For that school is so busied with the particles that it hardly attends to the structure; while the others are so lost in admiration of the structure that they do not penetrate to the simplicity of nature. These kinds of contemplation should therefore be alternated and taken by turns; that so the understanding may be rendered at once penetrating and comprehensive,

and the inconveniences above mentioned, with the idols which proceed from them, may be avoided.

LVIII

Let such then be our provision and contemplative prudence for keeping off and dislodging the Idols of the Cave, which grow for the most part either out of the predominance of a favourite subject, or out of an excessive tendency to compare or to distinguish, or out of partiality for particular ages, or out of the largeness or minuteness of the objects contemplated. And generally let every student of nature take this as a rule,— that whatever his mind seizes and dwells upon with peculiar satisfaction is to be held in suspicion, and that so much the more care is to be taken in dealing with such questions to keep the understanding even and clear.

IDOLS OF THE MARKET-PLACE

LIX

But the Idols of the Market-place are the most troublesome of all: idols which have crept into the understanding through the alliances of words and names.[2] For men believe that their reason governs words; but it is also true that words react on the understanding; and this it is that has rendered philosophy and the sciences sophistical and inactive. Now words, being commonly framed and applied according to the capacity of the vulgar, follow those lines of division which are most obvious to the vulgar understanding. And whenever an understanding of greater acuteness or a more diligent observation would alter those lines to suit the true divisions of nature, words stand in the way and resist the change. Whence it comes to pass that the high and formal discussions of learned men end oftentimes in disputes about words and names; with

---

[1] *Gilbert* William Gilbert (1540–1603), physician to Elizabeth and James I. His book on magnetism, *De Magnete* (1600), was in fact one of the great scientific achievements of the era.

[2] *alliances of words and names* For a Restoration elaboration of this idea, see the selection from Thomas Sprat's *History of the Royal Society* (1667).

which (according to the use and wisdom of the mathematicians) it would be more prudent to begin, and so by means of definitions reduce them to order. Yet even definitions cannot cure this evil in dealing with natural and material things; since the definitions themselves consist of words, and those words beget others: so that it is necessary to recur to individual instances, and those in due series and order; as I shall say presently when I come to the method and scheme for the formation of notions and axioms.

LX

The idols imposed by words on the understanding are of two kinds. They are either names of things which do not exist (for as there are things left unnamed through lack of observation, so likewise are there names which result from fantastic suppositions and to which nothing in reality corresponds), or they are names of things which exist, but yet confused and ill-defined, and hastily and irregularly derived from realities. Of the former kind are fortune, the prime mover,[1] planetary orbits,[2] element of fire, and like fictions which owe their origin to false and idle theories. And this class of idols is more easily expelled, because to get rid of them it is only necessary that all theories should be steadily rejected and dismissed as obsolete.

But the other class, which springs out of a faulty and unskilful abstraction, is intricate and deeply rooted. Let us take for example such a word as *humid*; and see how far the several things which the word is used to signify agree with each other; and we shall find the word *humid* to be nothing else than a mark loosely and confusedly applied to denote a variety of actions which will not bear to be reduced to any constant meaning. For it both signifies that which easily spreads itself round any other body; and that which in itself is indeterminate and cannot solidise; and that which readily yields in every direction; and that which easily divides and scatters itself; and that which easily unites and collects itself; and that which readily flows and is put in motion; and that which readily clings to another body and wets it; and that which is easily reduced to a liquid, or being solid easily melts. Accordingly when you come to apply the word—if you take it in one sense, flame is humid; if in another, air is not humid; if in another, fine dust is humid; if in another, glass is humid. So that it is easy to see that the notion is taken by abstraction only from water and common and ordinary liquids, without any due verification.

There are however in words certain degrees of distortion and error. One of the least faulty kinds is that of names of substances, especially of lowest species and well-deduced (for the notion of *chalk* and of *mud* is good, of *earth* bad); a more faulty kind is that of actions, as *to generate, to corrupt, to alter*; the most faulty is of qualities (except such as are the immediate objects of the sense) as *heavy, light, rare, dense*, and the like. Yet in all these cases some notions are of necessity a little better than others, in proportion to the greater variety of subjects that fall within the range of the human sense.

IDOLS OF THE THEATRE

LXI

But the Idols of the Theatre are not innate, nor do they steal into the understanding secretly, but are plainly impressed and received into the mind from the play-books of philosophical systems and the perverted rules of demonstration. To attempt refutations in this case would be merely inconsistent with what I have already said: for since we agree

---

[1] *prime mover* the *primum mobile*, in Ptolemaic astronomy the outermost of the planetary spheres, from which the other spheres all derived their motion.

[2] *planetary orbits* Bacon may be referring to the Ptolemaic theory of planetary spheres.

neither upon principles nor upon demonstrations there is no place for argument. And this is so far well, inasmuch as it leaves the honour of the ancients untouched. For they are no wise disparaged—the question between them and me being only as to the way. For as the saying is, the lame man who keeps the right road outstrips the runner who takes a wrong one. Nay it is obvious that when a man runs the wrong way, the more active and swift he is the further he will go astray.

But the course I propose for the discovery of sciences is such as leaves but little to the acuteness and strength of wits, but places all wits and understandings nearly on a level. For as in the drawing of a straight line or a perfect circle, much depends on the steadiness and practice of the hand, if it be done by aim of hand only, but if with the aid of rule or compass, little or nothing; so is it exactly with my plan. But though particular confutations would be of no avail, yet touching the sects and general divisions of such systems I must say something; something also touching the external signs which show that they are unsound; and finally something touching the causes of such great infelicity and of such lasting and general agreement in error; that so the access to truth may be made less difficult, and the human understanding may the more willingly submit to its purgation and dismiss its idols.

LXII

Idols of the Theatre, or of Systems, are many, and there can be and perhaps will be yet many more. For were it not that now for many ages men's minds have been busied with religion and theology; and were it not that civil governments, especially monarchies, have been averse to such novelties, even in matters speculative; so that men labour therein to the peril and harming of their fortunes,—not only unrewarded, but exposed also to contempt and envy; doubtless there would have arisen many other philosophical sects like to those which in great

variety flourished once among the Greeks. For as on the phenomena of the heavens many hypotheses may be constructed, so likewise (and more also) many various dogmas may be set up and established on the phenomena of philosophy. And in the plays of this philosophical theatre you may observe the same thing which is found in the theatre of the poets, that stories invented for the stage are more compact and elegant, and more as one would wish them to be, than true stories out of history.

In general however there is taken for the material of philosophy either a great deal out of a few things, or a very little out of many things; so that on both sides philosophy is based on too narrow a foundation of experiment and natural history, and decides on the authority of too few cases. For the Rational School of philosophers snatches from experience a variety of common instances, neither duly ascertained nor diligently examined and weighed, and leaves all the rest to meditation and agitation of wit.[1]

There is also another class of philosophers, who having bestowed much diligent and careful labour on a few experiments, have thence made bold to educe and construct systems; wresting all other facts in a strange fashion to conformity therewith.

And there is yet a third class, consisting of those who out of faith and veneration mix their philosophy with theology and traditions; among whom the vanity of some has gone so far aside as to seek the origin of sciences among spirits and genii. So that this parent stock of errors—this false philosophy—is of three kinds: the sophistical, the empirical, and the superstitious.

LXIII

The most conspicuous example of the first class was Aristotle, who corrupted natural philosophy by his logic: fashioning the world out of categories;

---

[1] Bacon's target here is scholastic philosophy, with its confidence in logical reasoning unsupported by empirical experiment.

assigning to the human soul, the noblest of substances, a genus from words of the second intention;[1] doing the business of density and rarity (which is to make bodies of greater or less dimensions, that is, occupy greater or less spaces), by the frigid distinction of act and power; asserting that single bodies have each a single and proper motion, and that if they participate in any other, then this results from an external cause; and imposing countless other arbitrary restrictions on the nature of things; being always more solicitous to provide an answer to the question and affirm something positive in words, than about the inner truth of things; a failing best shown when his philosophy is compared with other systems of note among the Greeks. For the Homœomera of Anaxagoras; the atoms of Leucippus and Democritus; the Heaven and Earth of Parmenides; the strife and friendship of Empedocles; Heraclitus's doctrine how bodies are resolved into the indifferent nature of fire, and remoulded into solids; have all of them some taste of the natural philosopher—some savour of the nature of things, and experience, and bodies; whereas in the physics of Aristotle you hear hardly anything but the words of logic; which in his metaphysics also, under a more imposing name, and more forsooth as a realist than a nominalist, he has handled over again. Nor let any weight be given to the fact, that in his books on animals and his problems, and other of his treatises, there is frequent dealing with experiments. For he had come to his conclusion before; he did not consult experience, as he should have done, in order to the framing of his decisions and axioms; but having first determined the question according to his will, he then resorts to experience, and bending her into conformity with his placets leads her about like a captive in a procession;[2] so that even on this count he is more guilty than his modern followers, the schoolmen, who have abandoned experience altogether.

LXIV

But the Empirical school of philosophy gives birth to dogmas more deformed and more monstrous than the Sophistical or Rational school. For it has its foundations not in the light of common notions (which though it be a faint and superficial light, is yet in a manner universal, and has reference to many things), but in the narrowness and darkness of a few experiments. To those therefore who are daily busied with these experiments, and have infected their imagination with them, such a philosophy seems probable and all but certain; to all men else incredible and vain. Of this there is a notable instance in the alchemists and their dogmas; though it is hardly to be found elsewhere in these times, except perhaps in the philosophy of [William] Gilbert. Nevertheless with regard to philosophies of this kind there is one caution not to be omitted; for I foresee that if ever men are roused by my admonitions to betake themselves seriously to experiment and bid farewell to sophistical doctrines, then indeed through the premature hurry of the understanding to leap or fly to universals and principles of things, great danger may be apprehended from philosophies of this kind; against which evil we ought even now to prepare.

LXV

But the corruption of philosophy by superstition and an admixture of theology is far more widely spread, and does the greatest harm, whether to entire systems or to their parts. For the human understanding is obnoxious to the influence of the imagination no less than to the influence of common notions. For the contentious and sophistical

---

[1] *words of the second intention* secondary conceptions (e.g. genus, species, variety) formed by application of thought to first intentions, or primary conceptions (e.g. tree).

[2] *placets* expressions of assent (*OED* placet 2).

kind of philosophy ensnares the understanding; but this kind, being fanciful and tumid and half poetical, misleads it more by flattery. For there is in man an ambition of the understanding, no less than of the will, especially in high and lofty spirits.

Of this kind we have among the Greeks a striking example in Pythagoras, though he united with it a coarser and more cumbrous superstition; another in Plato and his school, more dangerous and subtle. It shows itself likewise in parts of other philosophies, in the introduction of abstract forms and final causes and first causes, with the omission in most cases of causes intermediate, and the like. Upon this point the greatest caution should be used. For nothing is so mischievous as the apotheosis of error; and it is a very plague of the understanding for vanity to become the object of veneration. Yet in this vanity some of the moderns have with extreme levity indulged so far as to attempt to found a system of natural philosophy on the first chapter of Genesis, on the book of Job, and other parts of the sacred writings; seeking for the dead among the living: which also makes the inhibition and repression of it the more important, because from this unwholesome mixture of things human and divine there arises not only a fantastic philosophy but also an heretical religion. Very meet it is therefore that we be sober-minded, and give to faith that only which is faith's.

LXVIII

So much concerning the several classes of idols, and their equipage: all of which must be renounced and put away with a fixed and solemn determination, and the understanding thoroughly freed and cleansed; the entrance into the kingdom of man, founded on the sciences, being not much other than the entrance into the kingdom of heaven, whereinto none may enter except as a little child [Mark 10:15, Luke 18:17].

APPLICATION OF THE METHOD

LXIX

But vicious demonstrations are as the strongholds and defences of idols; and those we have in logic do little else than make the world the bond-slave of human thought, and human thought the bond-slave of words. Demonstrations truly are in effect the philosophies themselves and the sciences. For such as *they* are, well or ill established, such are the systems of philosophy and the contemplations which follow. Now in the whole of the process which leads from the sense and objects to axioms and conclusions, the demonstrations which we use are deceptive and incompetent. This process consists of four parts, and has as many faults. In the first place, the impressions of the sense itself are faulty; for the sense both fails us and deceives us. But its shortcomings are to be supplied, and its deceptions to be corrected. Secondly, notions are ill drawn from the impressions of the senses, and are indefinite and confused, whereas they should be definite and distinctly bounded. Thirdly, the induction is amiss which infers the principles of sciences by simple enumeration, and does not, as it ought, employ exclusions and solutions (or separations) of nature. Lastly, that method of discovery and proof according to which the most general principles are first established, and then intermediate axioms are tried and proved by them, is the parent of error and the curse of all science. Of these things however, which now I do but touch upon, I will speak more largely, when, having performed these expiations and purgings of the mind, I come to set forth the true way for the interpretation of nature.

LXX

But the best demonstration by far is experience, if it go not beyond the actual experiment. For if it be transferred to other cases which are deemed similar, unless such transfer be made by a just and orderly process, it is a fallacious thing. But the manner of making experiments which men now use is blind and stupid. And therefore, wandering and straying as they do with no settled course, and taking counsel only from things as they fall out, they fetch a wide circuit and meet with many matters, but make little progress; and sometimes are full of hope, sometimes are distracted; and always find that there is something beyond to be sought. For it generally happens that men make their trials carelessly, and as it were in play; slightly varying experiments already known, and, if the thing does not answer, growing weary and abandoning the attempt. And even if they apply themselves to experiments more seriously and earnestly and laboriously, still they spend their labour in working out some one experiment, as Gilbert with the magnet, and the chemists with gold; a course of proceeding not less unskilful in the design than small in the attempt. For no one successfully investigates the nature of a thing in the thing itself; the inquiry must be enlarged, so as to become more general.

And even when they seek to educe some science or theory from their experiments, they nevertheless almost always turn aside with overhasty and unseasonable eagerness to practice; not only for the sake of the uses and fruits of the practice, but from impatience to obtain in the shape of some new work an assurance for themselves that it is worth their while to go on; and also to show themselves off to the world, and so raise the credit of the business in which they are engaged. Thus, like Atalanta, they go aside to pick up the golden apple, but meanwhile they interrupt their course, and let the victory escape them.[1] But in the true course of experience, and in carrying it on to the effecting of new works, the divine wisdom and order must be our pattern. Now God on the first day of creation created light only, giving to that work an entire day, in which no material substance was created. So must we likewise from experience of every kind first endeavour to discover true causes and axioms; and seek for experiments of light, not for experiments of fruit. For axioms rightly discovered and established supply practice with its instruments, not one by one, but in clusters, and draw after them trains and troops of works. Of the paths however of experience, which no less than the paths of judgment are impeded and beset, I will speak hereafter; here I have only mentioned ordinary experimental research as a bad kind of demonstration. But now the order of the matter in hand leads me to add something both as to those *signs* which I lately mentioned,—(signs that the systems of philosophy and contemplation in use are in a bad condition)—and also as to the *causes* of what seems at first so strange and incredible. For a knowledge of the signs prepares assent; an explanation of the causes removes the marvel: which two things will do much to render the extirpation of idols from the understanding more easy and gentle.

LXXXIX

Neither is it to be forgotten that in every age Natural Philosophy has had a troublesome adversary and hard to deal with; namely, superstition, and the blind and immoderate zeal of religion. For we see among the Greeks that those who first proposed to men's then uninitiated ears the natural causes for thunder and for storms, were thereupon found guilty of impiety. Nor was much more forbearance shown by some of the ancient fathers of the Christian church to those who on most convincing grounds (such as no one in his senses would now think of contradicting) maintained that the earth was round, and of consequence asserted the existence of the antipodes.

---

[1] In mythology, Atalanta vowed to marry only if a suitor could defeat her in a footrace; Hippomenes won her hand by dropping three golden apples during the race, distracting Atalanta, who stopped to pick them up.

Moreover, as things now are, to discourse of nature is made harder and more perilous by the summaries and systems of the schoolmen; who having reduced theology into regular order as well as they were able, and fashioned it into the shape of an art, ended in incorporating the contentious and thorny philosophy of Aristotle, more than was fit, with the body of religion.

To the same result, though in a different way, tend the speculations of those who have taken upon them to deduce the truth of the Christian religion from the principles of philosophers, and to confirm it by their authority; pompously solemnising this union of the sense and faith as a lawful marriage, and entertaining men's minds with a pleasing variety of matter, but all the while disparaging things divine by mingling them with things human. Now in such mixtures of theology with philosophy only the received doctrines of philosophy are included; while new ones, albeit changes for the better, are all but expelled and exterminated.

Lastly, you will find that by the simpleness of certain divines, access to any philosophy, however pure, is well nigh closed. Some are weakly afraid lest a deeper search into nature should transgress the permitted limits of sobermindedness; wrongfully wresting and transferring what is said in holy writ against those who pry into sacred mysteries, to the hidden things of nature, which are barred by no prohibition. Others with more subtlety surmise and reflect that if second causes are unknown everything can more readily be referred to the divine hand and rod; a point in which they think religion greatly concerned; which is in fact nothing else but to seek to gratify God with a lie. Others fear from past example that movements and changes in philosophy will end in assaults on religion. And others again appear apprehensive that in the investigation of nature something may be found to subvert or at least shake the authority of religion, especially with the unlearned. But these two last fears seem to me

to savour utterly of carnal wisdom; as if men in the recesses and secret thoughts of their hearts doubted and distrusted the strength of religion and the empire of faith over the sense, and therefore feared that the investigation of truth in nature might be dangerous to them. But if the matter be truly considered, natural philosophy is after the word of God at once the surest medicine against superstition, and the most approved nourishment for faith, and therefore she is rightly given to religion as her most faithful handmaid, since the one displays the will of God, the other his power. For he did not err who said "Ye err in that ye know not the Scriptures and the power of God" [Matthew 22:29, Mark 12:24], thus coupling and blending in an indissoluble bond information concerning his will and meditation concerning his power. Meanwhile it is not surprising if the growth of Natural Philosophy is checked, when religion, the thing which has most power over men's minds, has by the simpleness and incautious zeal of certain persons been drawn to take part against her.

XC

Again, in the customs and institutions of schools, academies, colleges, and similar bodies destined for the abode of learned men and the cultivation of learning, everything is found adverse to the progress of science. For the lectures and exercises there are so ordered, that to think or speculate on anything out of the common way can hardly occur to any man. And if one or two have the boldness to use any liberty of judgment, they must undertake the task all by themselves; they can have no advantage from the company of others. And if they can endure this also, they will find their industry and largeness of mind no slight hindrance to their fortune. For the studies of men in these places are confined and as it were imprisoned in the writings of certain authors, from whom if any man dissent he is straightway arraigned as a turbulent person and an innovator. But surely there is a great distinction between matters of state and the arts; for the danger from new motion and from new light is not the same. In matters of state a change even for the better is distrusted, because it unsettles what is established; these things resting on authority, consent, fame and opinion, not on demonstration. But arts and sciences should be like mines, where the noise of new works and further advances is heard on every side. But though the matter be so according to right reason, it is not so acted on in practice; and the points above mentioned in the administration and government of learning put a severe restraint upon the advancement of the sciences.

XCII

But by far the greatest obstacle to the progress of science and to the undertaking of new tasks and provinces therein, is found in this—that men despair and think things impossible. For wise and serious men are wont in these matters to be altogether distrustful; considering with themselves the obscurity of nature, the shortness of life, the deceitfulness of the senses, the weakness of the judgment, the difficulty of experiment and the like; and so supposing that in the revolution of time and of the ages of the world the sciences have their ebbs and flows; that at one season they grow and flourish, at another wither and decay, yet in such sort that when they have reached a certain point and condition they can advance no further. If therefore any one believes or promises more, they think this comes of an ungoverned and unripened mind, and that such attempts have prosperous beginnings, become difficult as they go on, and end in confusion. Now since these are thoughts which naturally present themselves to grave men and of great judgment, we must take good heed that we be not led away by our love for a most fair and excellent object to relax or diminish the severity of our judgment;

we must observe diligently what encouragement dawns upon us and from what quarter; and, putting aside the lighter breezes of hope, we must thoroughly sift and examine those which promise greater steadiness and constancy. Nay, and we must take state-prudence too into our counsels, whose rule is to distrust, and to take the less favourable view of human affairs. I am now therefore to speak touching Hope; especially as I am not a dealer in promises, and wish neither to force nor to ensnare men's judgments, but to lead them by the hand with their good will. And though the strongest means of inspiring hope will be to bring men to particulars; especially to particulars digested and arranged in my Tables of Discovery (the subject partly of the second, but much more of the fourth part of my *Instauration*),[1] since this is not merely the promise of the thing but the thing itself; nevertheless that everything may be done with gentleness, I will proceed with my plan of preparing men's minds; of which preparation to give hope is no unimportant part. For without it the rest tends rather to make men sad (by giving them a worse and a meaner opinion of things as they are than they now have, and making them more fully to feel and know the unhappiness of their own condition) than to induce any alacrity or to whet their industry in making trial. And therefore it is fit that I publish and set forth those conjectures of mine which make hope in this matter reasonable; just as Columbus did, before that wonderful voyage of his across the Atlantic, when he gave the reasons for his conviction that new lands and continents might be discovered besides those which were known before; which

---

[1] *Tables of Discovery* Bacon's proposed method for organizing data, described in more detail in aphorism CV. His example later in *Novum Organum* (the incomplete second part of his *Instauratio magna*) is heat: he compiles a list of objects that display the quality of heat, another of related objects that do not, and a third in which heat is associated in varying degrees within the same object, as a prelude to inductive reasoning. The planned fourth part of the *Instauratio* was to offer more examples of his experimental method in action.

reasons, though rejected at first, were afterwards made good by experience, and were the causes and beginnings of great events.

CV

In establishing axioms, another form of induction must be devised than has hitherto been employed; and it must be used for proving and discovering not first principles (as they are called) only, but also the lesser axioms, and the middle, and indeed all. For the induction which proceeds by simple enumeration is childish; its conclusions are precarious, and exposed to peril from a contradictory instance; and it generally decides on too small a number of facts, and on those only which are at hand. But the induction which is to be available for the discovery and demonstration of sciences and arts, must analyze nature by proper rejections and exclusions; and then, after a sufficient number of negatives, come to a conclusion on the affirmative instances: which has not yet been done or even attempted, save only by Plato, who does indeed employ this form of induction to a certain extent for the purpose of discussing definitions and ideas. But in order to furnish this induction or demonstration well and duly for its work, very many things are to be provided which no mortal has yet thought of; insomuch that greater labour will have to be spent in it than has hitherto been spent on the syllogism. And this induction must be used not only to discover axioms, but also in the formation of notions. And it is in this induction that our chief hope lies.

CXIII

Moreover I think that men may take some hope from my own example. And this I say not by way of boasting, but because it is useful to say it. If there be any that despond, let them look at me, that being of all men of my time the most busied in affairs of state, and a man of health not very strong (whereby much time is lost), and in this course altogether a pioneer, following in no man's track, nor sharing these counsels with any one, have nevertheless by resolutely entering on the true road, and submitting my mind to *things*, advanced these matters, as I suppose, some little way. And then let them consider what may be expected (after the way has been thus indicated) from men abounding in leisure, and from association of labours, and from successions of ages: the rather because it is not a way over which only one man can pass at a time (as is the case with that of reasoning), but one in which the labours and industries of men (especially as regards the collecting of experience) may with the best effect be first distributed and then combined. For then only will men begin to know their strength, when instead of great numbers doing all the same things, one shall take charge of one thing and another of another.

CXIV

Lastly, even if the breath of hope which blows on us from the New Continent were fainter than it is and harder to perceive; yet the trial (if we would not bear a spirit altogether abject) must by all means be made. For there is no comparison between that which we may lose by not trying and by not succeeding; since by not trying we throw away the chance of an immense good; by not succeeding we only incur the loss of a little human labour. But as it is, it appears to me from what has been said, and also from what has been left unsaid, that there is hope enough and to spare, not only to make a bold man try, but also to make a sober-minded and wise man believe.

CXXX

And now it is time for me to propound the art itself of interpreting nature; in which, although I conceive that I have given true and most useful precepts, yet I do not say either that it is absolutely necessary (as if nothing could be done without it) or that it is perfect. For I am of opinion that if men had ready at hand a just history of nature and experience, and laboured diligently thereon; and if they could bind themselves to two rules,—the first, to lay aside received opinions and notions; and the second, to refrain the mind for a time from the highest generalisations, and those next to them,— they would be able by the native and genuine force of the mind, without any other art, to fall into my form of interpretation. For interpretation is the true and natural work of the mind when freed from impediments. It is true however that by my precepts everything will be in more readiness, and much more sure.

Nor again do I mean to say that no improvement can be made upon these. On the contrary, regard the mind not only in its own faculties, but in its connection with things, must needs hold that the art of discovery may advance as discoveries advance. —1620

King James VI/I
1566 – 1625

James was already an experienced king when he succeeded Elizabeth in 1603: King of Scotland at the age of one, he had been educated for the role since childhood and had successfully ruled his northern kingdom since 1585 (and in some respects even earlier). His ideas about monarchy, however, developed in opposition to those of his tutor, the classicist George Buchanan, who argued that a people had the right to rebel against a wicked ruler. In his political treatise *The Trew Law of Free Monarchies* (1598) and in *Basilicon Doron* (1599), an influential book on the art of government addressed to his son Henry, James argued for a monarch's divinely ordained power over his subjects. At the same time, James conceded that a monarch had a duty to rule by law and for the subjects' common good: his was a moderated absolutism.

Both facets of James's political thinking are evident in this extract from a speech he made to Parliament in 1610. The occasion was the negotiation over the "Great Contract," a proposal to establish an annual royal income in exchange for the abandonment of some much-resented royal prerogatives. The plan would eventually founder, but was still an option when this speech was delivered.

James's purpose was conciliatory. He argues that monarchs were accountable only to God, and that even to debate the limits of royal power was treason. But he assures his listeners of his reasonableness, of his respect for the common law and for the "ancient form of this State," that is, government through the two Houses of Parliament. The remainder of the speech addresses practical matters—James justifies his spending against complaints of royal extravagance, encourages support for legislation against recusants and on the preservation of forests and game, and even proposes the translation of the common laws from the "law French" in which they were written to English (an idea resurrected in the 1640s, also unsuccessfully, by the Levellers).

Like several of James's other speeches, this one was published soon after it was delivered, and was included in his folio of collected *Workes* (1616). James was an unusually prolific writer for an early modern monarch. In addition to his widely circulated and often translated political treatises, he wrote theological works; a book on witchcraft, *Daemonologie* (1598); *A Counterblaste to Tobacco* (1604); a treatise on writing poetry in Scots; and poetry in Scots, Latin, and English.

೧೩೮೩

A Speech to the Lords and Commons of the Parliament at White-Hall

.   .   .   .

The state of monarchy is the supremest thing upon earth: For Kings are not only God's lieutenants upon earth, and sit upon God's throne, but even by God himself they are called gods.[1] There be three principal similitudes that illustrate the state of monarchy: One taken out of the word of God; and the two other out of the grounds of policy and philosophy. In the Scriptures kings are called gods, and so their power after a certain relation compared to the divine power. Kings are also compared to fathers of families: for a king is truly *parens patriae* [the parent of the fatherland], the politic father of his people. And lastly, kings are compared to the head of this microcosm of the body of man.

Kings are justly called gods, for that they exercise a manner or resemblance of divine power upon earth. For if you will consider the attributes to God,

---

[1] Psalm 82:6.

you shall see how they agree in the person of a king. God hath power to create, or destroy, make, or unmake at his pleasure, to give life, or send death, to judge all, and to be judged nor accountable to none: To raise low things, and to make high things low at his pleasure, and to God are both soul and body due. And the like power have kings: they make and unmake their subjects; they have power of raising and casting down; of life and of death; judges over all their subjects and in all causes, and yet accountable to none but God only. They have power to exalt low things, and abase high things, and make of their subjects like men at the chess: a pawn to take a bishop or a knight, and to cry up or down any of their subjects, as they do their money. And to the king is due both the affection of the soul, and the service of the body of his subjects....

As for the father of a family, they had of old under the law of nature *patriam potestatem* [fatherly power], which was *potestatem vitae et necis* [the power of life and death], over their children or family. I mean such fathers of families as were the lineal heirs of those families whereof kings did originally come: For kings had their first original from them who planted and spread themselves in colonies through the world. Now a father may dispose of his inheritance to his children at his pleasure: yea, even disinherit the eldest upon just occasions, and prefer the youngest, according to his liking; make them beggars, or rich at his pleasure; restrain, or banish out of his presence, as he finds them give cause of offence, or restore them in favour again with the penitent sinner: So may the king deal with his subjects.

And lastly, as for the head of the natural body, the head hath the power of directing all the members of the body to that use which the judgement in the head thinks most convenient. It may apply sharp cures, or cut off corrupt members, let blood in what proportion it thinks fit, and as the body may spare, but yet is all this power ordained by God

ad aedificationem, non ad destructionem [for edification, not destruction].[1] For although God have power as well of destruction as of creation or maintenance, yet will it not agree with the wisdom of God to exercise his power in the destruction of nature and overturning the whole frame of things, since his creatures were made that his glory might thereby be the better expressed: So were he a foolish father that would disinherit or destroy his children without a cause, or leave off the careful education of them; And it were an idle head that would in place of physic so poison or phlebotomize the body as might breed a dangerous distemper or destruction thereof.[2]

But now in these our times we are to distinguish between the state of kings in their first original, and between the state of settled kings and monarchs, that do at this time govern in civil kingdoms: For even as God, during the time of the Old Testament, spake by oracles, and wrought by miracles; yet how soon it pleased him to settle a Church which was bought and redeemed by the blood of his only Son, Christ, then was there a cessation of both;[3] He ever after governing his people and Church within the limits of his revealed will. So in the first original of kings, whereof some had their beginning by conquest, and some by election of the people, their wills at that time served for law; Yet how soon kingdoms began to be settled in civility and policy, then did kings set down their minds by laws, which are properly made by the king only, but at the rogation of the people,[4] the king's grant being obtained thereunto. And so the king became to be *lex loquens* [a speaking law], after a sort, binding himself by a double oath to the observation of the

---

[1] See II Corinthians 10:8, 13:10.

[2] *phlebotomize* to let blood (*OED*).

[3] Milton devotes eight stanzas of his poem "On the Morning of Christ's Nativity" (1629) to the cessation of the oracles.

[4] *rogation* a formal request (*OED* rogation 3).

fundamental laws of his kingdom: tacitly, as by being a king, and so bound to protect as well the people as the laws of his kingdom; and expressly, by his oath at his coronation. So as every just king in a settled kingdom is bound to observe that paction made to his people by his laws,[1] in framing his government agreeable thereunto, according to that paction which God made with Noah after the deluge: *Hereafter seed-time and harvest, cold and heat, summer and winter, and day and night shall not cease, so long as the earth remains.*[2] And therefore a king governing in a settled kingdom leaves to be a king, and degenerates into a tyrant, as soon as he leaves off to rule according to his laws. In which case the king's conscience may speak unto him as the poor widow said to Philip of Macedon: "Either govern according to your law, *aut ne rex sis* [or may you be no king]." And though no Christian man ought to allow any rebellion of people against their Prince, yet doeth God never leave kings unpunished when they transgress these limits: For in that same psalm where God saith to kings, *vos dii estis* [you are gods], he immediately thereafter concludes, *But ye shall die like men.*[3] The higher we are placed, the greater shall our fall be. *Ut casus sic dolor* [the greater the fall, the greater the pain]: the taller the trees be, the more in danger of the wind; and the tempest beats sorest upon the highest mountains. Therefore all kings that are not tyrants, or perjured,

will be glad to bound themselves within the limits of their laws; and they that persuade them the contrary, are vipers and pests, both against them and the commonwealth. For it is a great difference between a king's government in a settled state and what kings in their original power might do in *individuo vago* [as unrestricted individuals].[4] As for my part, I thank God, I have ever given good proof that I never had intention to the contrary: And I am sure to go to my grave with that reputation and comfort, that never king was in all his time more careful to have his laws duly observed, and himself to govern thereafter, than I.

I conclude then this point touching the power of kings, with this axiom of divinity, that as to dispute what God may do is blasphemy, but *quid vult deus* [what God wants], that divines may lawfully, and do ordinarily, dispute and discuss; for to dispute *a posse ad esse* [from what may be to what is] is both against logic and divinity: So is it sedition in subjects to dispute what a king may do in the height of his power. But just kings will ever be willing to declare what they will do, if they will not incur the curse of God. I will not be content that my power be disputed upon: but I shall ever be willing to make the reason appear of all my doings, and rule my actions according to my laws.

—1610

---

[1] *paction* pact, agreement (*OED*).

[2] Genesis 8:22.

[3] Psalm 82:6–7.

[4] that is, before their powers had been defined or regulated.

Aemilia Lanyer
1569 – 1645

Aemilia Lanyer was the daughter of Baptist Bassano, an Italian musician at the English court, and his mistress Margaret Johnson. She was baptised in the parish church of St. Botolph, Bishopsgate. It is thought that she was brought up for a time in the household of Lady Susan, Countess Dowager of Kent. Her father, who died in 1576 after some financial difficulties, nevertheless left her £100. Her mother died nine years later. For a time, Lanyer was the mistress of Henry Carey, first Lord Hunsdon, who was forty-five years her senior. When, in 1592, she became pregnant by him, she was hastily married to one of the Queen's musicians, Captain Alfonso Lanyer, with an annuity of £40. Her son, Henry, was born the following year. Most of the details of Lanyer's life come from the diary and casebooks of the astrologer Simon Forman, whom she consulted on several occasions in 1597. Forman notes that Lanyer told him that "her husband hath dealt hardly with her and spent and consumed her goods and she is now...in debt." Lanyer, whose husband had set off on a sea voyage in hopes of being knighted, wished to know about the possibility of financial and social improvement. Forman's assurance of good fortune was not especially accurate. In 1604, Lanyer's husband was granted a patent by King James which provided him with the income from weighing of hay and grain, thereby improving their financial situation. It appears that in or about the same year, Lanyer accompanied Margaret, Countess of Cumberland, and Anne Clifford, her daughter, to Cookeham, the royal country house estate, a visit that may have inspired Lanyer to write *Salve Deus Rex Judaeorum*, published in 1611. While the purported subject of *Salve Deus* is the Passion of Christ, its broader aim is to praise female spiritual and cognitive virtues within the broader cultural practice of patronage. Diane Purkiss has argued that *Salve Deus* is "a carefully-structured and organised attempt to put together the discourses of patronage, encomium, religious verse, defences of women, and the evocation of nature," "to create new ways of celebrating the female and to endorse a female (or feminist) interpretation of the biblical text and the material world." *The Description of Cooke-ham*, published with this work appears to be the first English country house poem, predating Jonson's *To Penshurst*. When her husband died in 1613, Lanyer engaged in litigation with his relations over the legacy of the patent granted him in 1604. Her legal battles continued after she opened a school in the wealthy district of St. Giles-in-the-Field in 1617, as disputes with her landlord over repairs and rent led to lengthy litigation. In 1633, Lanyer undertook to assist her son's widow and two children financially, petitioning for a patent in 1635. She died ten years later and was buried at St. James, Clerkenwell.

ᚄᚄᚄ

To the Virtuous Reader

Often have I heard, that it is the property of some women, not only to emulate the virtues and perfections of the rest, but also by all their powers of ill speaking, to eclipse the brightness of their deserved fame:[1] now contrary to this custom, which men I hope unjustly lay to their charge, I have written this small volume, or little book, for the general use of all virtuous ladies and gentlewomen of this kingdom; and in commendation of some particular persons of our own sex, such as for the most part, are so well known to myself, and others, that I dare undertake fame dares not to call any better. And this have I done, to make known to

---

[1] *emulate*   strive to equal or rival (*OED* emulate *v* 1).

the world, that all women deserve not to be blamed though some forgetting they are women themselves, and in danger to be condemned by the words of their own mouths, fall into so great an error, as to speak unadvisedly against the rest of their sex; which if it be true, I am persuaded they can show their own imperfection in nothing more: and therefore could wish (for their own ease, modesties, and credit) they would refer such points of folly, to be practised by evil-disposed men, who forgetting they were born of women, nourished of women, and that if it were not by the means of women, they would be quite extinguished out of the world, and a final end of them all, do like vipers deface the wombs wherein they were bred, only to give way and utterance to their want of discretion and goodness. Such as these, were they that dishonoured Christ, his apostles and prophets, putting them to shameful deaths. Therefore we are not to regard any imputations, that they undeservedly lay upon us, no otherwise than to make use of them to our own benefits, as spurs to virtue, making us fly all occasions that may colour their unjust speeches to pass current.[1] Especially considering that they have tempted even the patience of God himself, who gave power to wise and virtuous women, to bring down their pride and arrogancy. As was cruel Cesarus by the discreet counsel of noble Deborah, judge and prophetess of Israel: and resolution of Jael, wife of Heber the Kenite: wicked Haman, by the divine prayers and prudent proceedings of beautiful Esther: blasphemous Holofernes, by the invincible courage, rare wisdom, and confident carriage of Judith: and the unjust judges, by the innocency of chaste Susanna:[2] with infinite others,

which for brevity sake I will omit. As also in respect it pleased our Lord and Saviour Jesus Christ, without the assistance of man, being free from original and all other sins, from the time of his conception, till the hour of his death, to be begotten of a woman, born of a woman, nourished of a woman, obedient to a woman; and that he healed woman, pardoned women, comforted women: yea, even when he was in his greatest agony and bloody sweat, going to be crucified, and also in the last hour of his death, took care to dispose of a woman: after his resurrection, appeared first to a woman, sent a woman to declare his most glorious resurrection to the rest of his disciples.[3] Many other examples I could allege of divers faithful and virtuous women, who have in all ages, not only been confessors, but also endured most cruel martyrdom for their faith in Jesus Christ. All which is sufficient to enforce all good Christians and honourable minded men to speak reverently of our sex, and especially of all virtuous and good women. To the modest censures of both which, I refer these my imperfect endeavours, knowing that according to their own excellent dispositions, they will rather, cherish, nourish, and increase the least spark of virtue where they find it, by their favourable and best interpretations, than quench it by wrong constructions. To whom I wish all increase of virtue, and desire their best opinions.
—1611

---

[1] *pass current* pass for authentic currency.

[2] *cruel Cesarus...Susanna* Deborah called the warriors led by Barak to attack the Canaanite general Cesarus ("Sisera"). Jael lured Sisera into her quarters after the Canaanite defeat and hammered a tent peg through his skull (Judges 4:12–31); Esther, queen consort to King Ahasuerus, persuaded her husband to save the Israelites from the

---

genocide planned by Haman (Esther 5–7); Judith entered the camp of her Assyrian enemies and beheaded Holofernes, their leader, ensuring an Israelite military victory (Judith 8–13). Susanna rejected the advances of two elders who subsequently falsely accused her of adultery. Daniel exposed their false testimony and saved Susanna from stoning (the apocryphal Daniel 13).

[3] *to be begotten...his disciples* For a detailed account of Jesus's interaction with women see Margaret Fell's *Women's Speaking Justified* (1667) included in this volume.

Lady Margaret Hoby
1571 – 1633

Lady Margaret Hoby was the only child of Arthur Dakins, gentleman and Justice of the Peace of Linton in the East Riding of Yorkshire, and his wife Tomasine Gye. As a child, she was educated in the Puritan household of Henry Hastings, third Earl of Huntingdon, where she learned the habits of daily self-examination recorded so often in her *Diary*. As the heir of Arthur Dakins, a substantial land owner, Margaret was much in demand on the marriage market. Her first two marriages were brief. In 1588, she married Walter, the younger son of Walter Devereux, first Earl of Essex. The manor and parsonage of Hackness were provided for the couple and given to Margaret when her first husband died in 1591 at the siege of Rouen. As her father and Walter Devereux did not pay their entire portion of the purchase price of Hackness, lengthy litigation ensued, but Margaret eventually retained possession of the estate. In 1591, a year before her father's death, Margaret married Thomas Sidney, Sir Philip Sidney's brother. Thomas died four years later. Margaret was only twenty-five years old when she married her third husband Thomas Posthumous Hoby, who had wooed her unsuccessfully in 1591. Margaret had no children from any of her marriages. The *Diary* of Lady Hoby records her activities from 1599 to 1605. She is the earliest known Englishwomen to write such a diary. We read little of the emotion or sentiment commonly associated with the genre. Margaret Hoby is more concerned to record her daily religious observances, the medical, social and religious duties involved in running a country estate, and the occasional account of significant people and events of her day. She refused to settle her property on her husband and his heirs until one year before her death. She was buried in the chancel of Hackness Church.

☙☙☙

The Diary of Lady Margaret Hoby
1599–1605
(excerpts) [1]

1599

[Friday August 17]

After private prayers I went about the house and read of the bible and wrought till dinner time:[2] and after dinner it pleased for a just punishment to correct my sins to send me feebleness of stomach and pain of my head that kept me upon my bed til 5 o'clock: at which time I arose, having release of my sickness, according to the wonted kindness of the Lord who after he had let me see how I had offended, that so I might take better heed to my body and soul hereafter, with a gentle correction let me feel he was reconciled to me: at which time I went to private prayer and praises, examination, and so to work till supper time:[3] which done I heard the Lecture and after I had walked an hour with Mr. Hoby I went to bed.[4]

---

[1] The extracts from this *Diary* were chosen and modernized by Holly Nelson, using Dorothy M. Meads' edition, before the 1998 edition of Joanna Moody was available. Alan Rudrum, seeing that neither edition was wholly accurate, subsequently checked the selections against the British Library manuscript (Egerton MS 2614). He corrected some errors, restored some of the diarist's capitals (to give a hint of the flavour of the manuscript), and lightened the punctuation. The reader should imagine a manuscript chaotic in spelling and scarcely punctuated at all. In most cases, dates have been standardized for convenience and do not represent the diarist's own notations.

[2] *wrought* worked at needlework, or more generally performed tasks (*OED* work B.I.5a).

[3] *examination* that is, she examined or tested herself according to the Christian standard or rule (*OED* examine *v* 2a).

[4] *Lecture* either the reading of a passage aloud or a brief exhortation.

[Monday September 10]

After private prayers I went about the house, an[d] then ate my breakfast: then I walked to the church with Mr. Hoby: after that I wrought a little and neglected my custom of prayer for which as for many other sins it pleased the Lord to punish me with an inward assault: But I know the Lord hath pardoned it because he is true of his promise, and if I had not taken this course of examination I think I had forgotten it: after dinner I walked with Mr. Hoby and after he was gone I went to get tithe apples[1]: After I came home, I prayed with Mr. Rhodes,[2] and after that privately by myself and took examination of myself: and so after I had walked a while I went to supper, after that to the Lecture and so to bed.

[The Lord's day September 16]

After I had prayed privately I went to church and from thence returning I praised God both for the enabling the minister so profitably to declare the word as he had, and my self to hear with that Comfort and understanding I did: after dinner I walked with Mr. Hoby till Catechizing was done and then I went to church[3]: after the sermon I looked upon a poor man's Leg and after that I walked and read a sermon of Gifford upon the Song of Solomon:[4] then I examined myself and prayed: after supper I was busy with Mr. Hoby till prayer time after which I went to bed.

[Monday September 17]

After private prayer I saw a man's Leg dressed, took order for things in the house and wrought till dinner time: after dinner I went about the house, and read of the herbal:[5] then I took my Coach and came to Linton, where after I had talked a while with my mother examined myself and prayed I went to supper and then prayed publicly and so to bed.

[Thursday December 20]

After private prayers, I did eat my breakfast then I writ in my sermon book: after I prayed then I dined, and almost I writ in my bible all the afternoon: then I dispatched some business in the house and then prayed and examined myself: then I went about the house and in talk with Mr. Rhodes I understood thus much, that, whereas graces are of 2 sorts some general belonging to every Christian others special as continency and [[6]] for the better prevailing against a temptation, it is not sufficient only to have faith, whereby I know that I shall neither yield unto it, nor be overcome by it:[7] but I must likewise pray especially for that virtue which is opposed to that vice where unto I am then tempted, because, though faith be the Fundamental Cause of overcoming sin, yet the several graces of God work operatively: after, I supped, then I heard the Lecture, and then prayed, and so went to bed.

---

[1] *tithe apples* A tenth part of the produce of agriculture was a due or payment for the support of the church or clergy (*OED* tithe *sb¹ B* 1).

[2] *Mr. Rhodes* Lady Hoby's chaplain.

[3] *catechizing* the oral instruction by which the elements of religion are taught (*OED* catechizing *vbl sb* a).

[4] *looked upon a poor man's leg* The lady of the manor often knew more of surgery and medicine than other members of the village as no doctor was generally available in the country; *sermon of Gifford* Master George Gifford published *Sermons upon the Songe of Salomon* in 1598. Gifford was a Puritan divine who had refused to subscribe to the Thirty-Nine Articles of the Established Church and was deprived of his living as a result.

[5] *herbal* possibly an allusion to the *New Herball* of the reformer William Turner who indulged in botany. His *Herball*, first published in 1551, is considered to mark the onset of the study of botany in England. Alternatively, it may be an allusion to John Gerard's *Herbal or General History of Plants* (1597).

[6] This word is illegible. Dorothy M. Meads thought it might be "pretching" (i.e. preaching), but the final letters appear to be "ie" and the word intended probably refers to an inner quality, analogous to "constancy," dear to Puritan moral theology.

[7] *where as graces are of two sorts....others special* General or common grace is so named because its benefits are experienced by the whole human race. Special grace is the grace by which God redeems, sanctifies and glorifies particular individuals, those elected to have eternal life.

1600

[The 5 day of the week February 1]
After I was ready I went about the house and then prayed brake my fast, dressed a poor boy's leg that was hurt, and Jurden's hand:[1] after took a lecture, read of the bible, prayed and so went to dinner: after, I went down a while, then wrought till 4 o'clock and took order for supper, and then talked a while with Mr. Hoby and after went to private prayer and meditation: after to supper then to public prayers and lastly to bed.

[The 4 day after the Lord's Day, April 10]
After private prayers I went to the minister where I heard Mr. Smith defend the truth against the papist: The question being whether the regenerate do sin: after I came home I went to dinner: I went to the church where I heard Mr. Stuart handle this question between the papists and us—whether we were Justified by faith or work:[2] after I came to my lodging and after I had prayed I went and talked with my cousin Bouser: then I went to Mr. Doctor Benets and after supper I prayed publicly with Mr. Rhodes, and so went to bed.

[July 15]
After I was ready and had prayed I went about the house and did eat: after I heard news of the Death of my Sister Elizabeth Russell:[3] after I prayed then dined; and after I talked with a cousin of mine and after a Goldsmith: then I heard Mr. Rhodes read, and so I went to private examination and prayer: after I went to supper and after I went to the Lec-

ture: then I walked and prayed privately, and so went to bed.

[November 29]
After I had prayed I read and went to dinner: In the afternoon I was visited by Mr. Genkins who told me that young Goodericke for his Drawing of his Dagger and striking one before the Readers was fined £200 expulsed the house imprisoned bound to the good behaviour and enjoined to confess his fault and ask pardon in all the Courts: and, furthermore, he told us of the like punishment of another that quarrelled in the street: after he was gone I went to private examination and prayer: after to supper then I prayed some after and so went to bed.

1601

[April 1]
This day for praying reading, and working I continued my ordinary exercises,[4] with much Comfort and peace of Conscience, I thank god, having learned some thing from Mr. Rhodes his reading unto me as first that no calling is lawful without a ground for it in God's word:[5] 2. that the title of Lord Archbishops are unlawful: 3. that no minister should be made without a ministry and charge unto which he should be ordained.

[The 5 day of May 1601]
After prayers I went to the church where I heard a sermon: after I came home and heard Mr. Rhodes read: after dinner I went abroad and when I was come home I dressed some sores: after I heard Mr. Rhodes read and wrought with in a while: after I went to see a calf at Munckman's which had 2 great heads, 4 ears, and had to either head a throat pipe besides: the heads had long hairs like bristles about the mouths, such as n' other cow hath: the hinder

---

[1] Jurden was one of the manservants.

[2] *justified by faith or work* Protestant reformers held that individuals could achieve salvation by the grace of God through faith not by works. Catholics were seen to rely on good works as a means to earn salvation.

[3] *my sister, Elizabeth Russell* Lady Elizabeth Russell was the mother-in-law of Margaret Hoby. The Elizabeth Russell to whom she refers in this entry is her mother-in-law's daughter by her second marriage.

[4] *exercises* private religious exercises (*OED* exercise *sb* 10a).

[5] *calling* that is, to a spiritual office (*OED* calling *vbl sb* I.3b).

legs had no parting from the rump, but grew backward, and were no longer but from the first joint: also the back bone was parted about the midest of the back, and a round hole was in the midst in to the body of the Calf: but one would have thought that to have comed of some stroke it might get in the cow's belly: after this I came in to private meditation and prayer.

[August 26]
This day in the afternoon I had had a child brought to see that was born at Silpho, one Talliour son who had no fundament, and had no passage for excrements but at the Mouth: I was earnestly entreated to cut the place to see if any passage could be made, but although I cut deep and searched there was none to be found.

[December 5]
All this week following I was well, I praise god, being visited by divers that came to see Mr. Hoby: by whom we heard some news, as by Mr. Pollard, that the Wednesday fortnight, before which was the 4 of November died of Drunkenness one Sir Hunter Adam, minister of the Betheme of York:[1] we heard also of Mr. Bishop['s] marriage to Mr. Cholmleys' Daughter, being about 14 years old and himself fifty: besides we heard of Woodruff's hurt by young George Dakins with some other things of less moment.

[December 26]
Was young Farley slain by his father's man one that the young man had before threatened to kill and for that end prosecuting him: the man, having a pike staff in his hand, run him into the eye and so into the brain: he never spoke after: this Judgment is worth noting, this young man being extraordinary profane, as once causing a horse to be brought into the church of god and there christening him with a name which horrible blasphemy the Lord did not leave unrevenged, even in this world, for example t'others.

1602

[May 6]
I praise god I had health of body: howsoever justly god hath suffered Satan to afflict my mind, yet my hope is that my redeemer will bring my soul out of troubles, that it may praise his name: and so I will wait with patience for deliverance.

From the 6th unto the 20th I praise god I continued well, and found God's mercy in vouchsafing me comfort every way: and now I beseech thee o Lord give me power to render unto thee the calves of my Lips and with my whole heart to follow righteousness.[2]

[The Lords day June 27]
Until this day I have continued in bodily health notwithstanding Satan hath not ceased to cast his malice upon [me]: but temptations hath exercised me, and it hath pleased my god to deliver me from all: Mrs. Girlington with her daughter and son-in-law came but after the sermon: & so, when the Communion was ended and after dinner, we all heard the afternoon exercises together.

---

[1] *Mr. Pollard* Mr. Pollard, High Constable of Pickering Lythe, would have been privy to a wealth of information; he was entitled to be informed by the Constables of each parish, so that he could pass on intelligence to both the central government and the local Court of Quarter Sessions; *Betheme* that is, Bedlam, a hospital or asylum for the mentally ill (*OED* bedlam 3a).

[2] *calves of my Lips* "Take with you words, and turn to the Lord: say unto him, Take away all iniquity and receive us graciously: so we will render the calves of our lips" (Hosea 14:2). The Geneva Bible provides a note for "calves": "Declaring, that this is the true sacrifice, that the faithful can offer, even thanks & praise, Ebr. 13,15."

1603

[The 23 of March: which day the Queen departed this life][1]

Mr. Hoby received Letters which came from the Privy Council to the Lord President and all the Justices of Peace that our Queen was sick which wrought great sorrow and dread in all good subjects' hearts: these Letters were dated the 16 of March.

[March 26]

This day being the Lord's day was the death of the Queen published and our now King James of Scotland proclaimed king to succeed her: god send him a Long and Happy Reign, Amen.

[October 23]

This day I heard the plague was so great at Whitby that those which were clear shut themselves up, and the infected that escaped did go abroad: Likewise it was reported that, at London, the number was taken of the Living and not of the Dead: Lord grant that these Judgments may cause England with speed to turn to the Lord.

—1930 (1599–1603)

---

[1] *The 23 of March....Queen departed this life* Queen Elizabeth I actually died on March 24, 1603.

John Donne
1572 — 1631

Donne was, as a recent biographer has noted, a Londoner born and bred. He was born in Bread Street, in the City of London, the third of six children; his father was of Welsh descent, his mother a lifelong Catholic, daughter of the writer John Heywood, and great-niece of Sir Thomas More. Her brothers, Ellis and Jasper Heywood, lived in exile as Jesuits. Donne's brother Henry died of plague in Newgate Prison, where he had been held for harbouring a Catholic priest. As he was born and raised in a Catholic family at a time when Catholicism was equated with disloyalty to the English crown, the question of religious allegiance was of paramount spiritual and practical importance to Donne, and one he addressed in several works. From 1591 to 1594 he studied law, and was for most of that time a member of Lincoln's Inn, following a tradition in his mother's family. In 1596, like many other young adventurers wishing to recommend themselves for service, he sailed in the expedition to Cadiz led by Essex and Raleigh, and in 1597 went on another expedition to the Azores. This second expedition was the occasion of two verse letters, "The Storm" and "The Calm," with its famous couplet "No use for lanthorns; and in one place lay / Feathers and dust, today and yesterday." Donne remained fascinated by travel and exploration, as his many metaphors drawn from voyages of discovery attest. After these expeditions he was in the service of Sir Thomas Egerton, the Lord Keeper of England; in 1601 he secretly married Ann More, the daughter of Egerton's brother-in-law, and was dismissed from his post. For some years thereafter, as his wife produced child after child, he sought employment. The precise date of Donne's conversion to Protestantism is unknown, but towards the end of the first decade of the new century he was interesting himself in the work of the Dean of Gloucester, Thomas Morton, who was writing anti-Catholic propaganda. However, in spite of many well-placed friends, he did not find regular employment until he was ordained deacon and priest at St. Paul's Cathedral in 1615. King James is said to have declared that he would get no employment from him, except in the church. Donne became perhaps the most famous preacher of his age; his sermons have dramatic intensity and, as one realizes when reading them aloud, are very skilfully written for the human voice. He was also the most celebrated poet of his time, copied into commonplace books and circulated more frequently in manuscript collections than any other poet of the age. He seems to have been ambivalent about print culture, writing for educated coteries and the social elite, and little of his work was published in his lifetime. In 1617 his wife died after giving birth to a stillborn child. In the years that followed he went as chaplain on Doncaster's embassy to Germany and Bohemia; he preached at the most prestigious venues available: at Court, in the House of Lords, at the Inns of Court, before the Countess of Bedford, and so on. In 1621 he was elected Dean of St. Paul's. In 1625 he preached to Charles I, a few days after the death of James, and again shortly after Charles's coronation. Self-dramatization is an essential part of his literary persona, as preacher and as poet; in 1631 he posed for a portrait of himself in his shroud, a few weeks before his death.

᭞᭞᭞

Devotions: Upon Emergent Occasions
(excerpts)

IV. EXPOSTULATION

I have not the righteousness of Job, but I have the desire of Job: "I would speak to the Almighty, and I would reason with God" [Job 13:3]. My God, my God, how soon wouldst thou have me go to the physician, and how far wouldst thou have me go with the physician? I know thou hast made the matter, and the man, and the art; and I go not from thee when I go to the physician. Thou didst not make clothes before there was a shame of the nakedness of the body, but thou didst make physic before there was any grudging of any sickness; for thou didst imprint a medicinal virtue in many simples,[1] even from the beginning; didst thou mean that we should be sick when thou didst so? when thou madest them? No more than thou didst mean, that we should sin, when thou madest us: thou foresawest both, but causedst neither. Thou, Lord, promisest here trees, "whose fruit shall be for meat, and their leaves for medicine" [Ezek. 47:12]. It is the voice of thy Son, "Wilt thou be made whole?" [John 5:6] that draws from the patient a confession that he was ill, and could not make himself well. And it is thine own voice, "Is there no physician?" [Jer. 8:22] that inclines us, disposes us, to accept thine ordinance. And it is the voice of the wise man, both for the matter, physic itself, "The Lord hath created medicines out of the earth, and he that is wise shall not abhor them" [Ecclesiasticus 38:4], and for the art, and the person, the physician cutteth off a long disease. In all these voices thou sendest us to those helps which thou hast afforded us in that. But wilt not thou avow that voice too, "He that hath sinned against his Maker, let him fall into the hands of the physician" [Ecclesiasticus 38:15]; and wilt not thou afford me an understand-

ing of those words? Thou, who sendest us for a blessing to the physician, dost not make it a curse to us to go when thou sendest. Is not the curse rather in this, that only he falls into the hands of the physician, that casts himself wholly, entirely upon the physician, confides in him, relies upon him, attends all from him, and neglects that spiritual physic which thou also hast instituted in thy church. So to fall into the hands of the physician is a sin, and a punishment of former sins; so, as Asa fell, who in his disease "sought not to the Lord, but to the physician" [I Chron. 16:12]. Reveal therefore to me thy method, O Lord, and see whether I have followed it; that thou mayest have glory, if I have, and I pardon, if I have not, and help that I may. Thy method is, "In time of thy sickness, be not negligent": wherein wilt thou have my diligence expressed? "Pray unto the Lord, and he will make thee whole" [Ecclesiasticus 38:9]. O Lord, I do; I pray, and pray thy servant David's prayer, "Have mercy upon me, O Lord, for I am weak; heal me, O Lord, for my bones are vexed" [Psalm 6:2]: I know that even my weakness is a reason, a motive, to induce thy mercy, and my sickness an occasion of thy sending health. When art thou so ready, when is it so seasonable to thee, to commiserate, as in misery? But is prayer for health in season, as soon as I am sick? Thy method goes further: "Leave off from sin, and order thy hands aright, and cleanse thy heart from all wickedness" [Ecclesiasticus 38:10]. Have I, O Lord, done so? O Lord, I have; by thy grace, I am come to a holy detestation of my former sin. Is there anymore? In thy method there is more: "Give a sweet savour, and a memorial of fine flour, and make a fat offering, as not being" [Ecclesiasticus 38:11]. And, Lord, by thy grace, I have done that, sacrificed a little of that little which thou lentest me, to them for whom thou lentest it: and now in thy method, and by thy steps, I am come to that, "Then give place to the physician, for the Lord hath created him; let him not go from

---

[1] *simples* herbs or other plants used for medicinal purposes.

thee, for thou hast need of him" [Ecclesiasticus 38:12]. I send for the physician, but I will hear him enter with those words of Peter, "Jesus Christ maketh thee whole" [Acts 9:34]; I long for his presence, but I look "that the power of the Lord should be present to heal me" [Luke 5:17].

V. MEDITATION

SOLUS ADEST
The physician comes

As sickness is the greatest misery, so the greatest misery of sickness is solitude; when the infectiousness of the disease deters them who should assist from coming; even the physician dares scarce come. Solitude is a torment which is not threatened in hell itself. Mere vacuity, the first agent, God, the first instrument of God, nature, will not admit; nothing can be utterly empty, but so near a degree towards vacuity as solitude, to be but one, they love not. When I am dead, and my body might infect, they have a remedy, they may bury me; but when I am but sick, and might infect, they have no remedy but their absence, and my solitude. It is an excuse to them that are great, and pretend, and yet are loath to come; it is an inhibition to those who would truly come, because they may be made instruments, and pestiducts,[1] to the infection of others, by their coming. And it is an outlawry, an excommunication upon the patient, and separates him from all offices, not only of civility but of working charity. A long sickness will weary friends at last, but a pestilential sickness averts them from the beginning. God himself would admit a figure of society, as there is a plurality of persons in God, though there be but one God; and all his external actions testify a love of society, and communion. In heaven there are orders of angels, and armies of martyrs, and in that house many mansions; in earth, families, cities, churches,

colleges, all plural things; and lest either of these should not be company enough alone, there is an association of both, a communion of saints which makes the militant and triumphant church one parish; so that Christ was not out of his diocese when he was upon the earth, nor out of his temple when he was in our flesh. God, who saw that all that he made was good, came not so near seeing a defect in any of his works, as when he saw that it was not good for man to be alone, therefore he made him a helper; and one that should help him so as to increase the number, and give him her own, and more society. Angels, who do not propagate nor multiply, were made at first in an abundant number, and so were stars; but for the things of this world, their blessing was, Increase; for I think, I need not ask leave to think, that there is no phoenix; nothing singular, nothing alone. Men that inhere upon nature only, are so far from thinking that there is any thing singular in this world, as that they will scarce think that this world itself is singular, but that every planet, and every star, is another world like this; they find reason to conceive not only a plurality in every species in the world, but a plurality of worlds; so that the abhorrers of solitude are not solitary, for God, and Nature, and Reason concur against it. Now a man may counterfeit the plague in a vow, and mistake a disease for religion, by such a retiring and recluding of himself from all men as to do good to no man, to converse with no man. God hath two testaments, two wills; but this is a schedule, and not of his, a codicil, and not of his, not in the body of his testaments, but interlined and postscribed by others, that the way to the communion of saints should be by such a solitude as excludes all doing of good here. That is a disease of the mind, as the height of an infectious disease of the body is solitude, to be left alone: for this makes an infectious bed equal, nay, worse than a grave, that though in both I be equally alone, in my bed I know it, and feel it, and shall not in my grave: and

---

[1] *pestiducts* conveyers of pestilence.

this too, that in my bed my soul is still in an infectious body, and shall not in my grave be so.

XVII. Meditation

NUNC LENTO SONITU DICUNT, MORIERIS
Now, this bell tolling softly for another, says to me:
Thou must die

Perchance he for whom this bell tolls may be so ill, as that he knows not it tolls for him; and perchance I may think myself so much better than I am, as that they who are about me, and see my state, may have caused it to toll for me, and I know not that. The church is Catholic, universal, so are all her actions; all that she does belongs to all. When she baptizes a child, that action concerns me; for that child is thereby connected to that body which is my head too, and ingrafted into that body whereof I am a member. And when she buries a man, that action concerns me: all mankind is of one author, and is one volume; when one man dies, one chapter is not torn out of the book, but translated into a better language; and every chapter must be so translated; God employs several translators; some pieces are translated by age, some by sickness, some by war, some by justice; but God's hand is in every translation, and his hand shall bind up all our scattered leaves again for that library where every book shall lie open to one another. As therefore the bell that rings to a sermon calls not upon the preacher only, but upon the congregation to come, so this bell calls us all; but how much more me, who am brought so near the door by this sickness. There was a contention as far as a suit (in which both piety and dignity, religion and estimation, were mingled), which of the religious orders should ring to prayers first in the morning; and it was determined, that they should ring first that rose earliest. If we understand aright the dignity of this bell that tolls for our evening prayer, we would be glad to make it ours by rising early, in that application, that it might be ours as well as his, whose indeed it is. The bell doth toll for him that thinks it doth; and though it intermit again, yet from that minute that that occasion wrought upon him, he is united to God. Who casts not up his eye to the sun when it rises? but who takes off his eye from a comet when that breaks out? Who bends not his ear to any bell which upon any occasion rings? but who can remove it from that bell which is passing a piece of himself out of this world? No man is an island, entire of itself; every man is a piece of the continent, a part of the main. If a clod be washed away by the sea, Europe is the less, as well as if a promontory were, as well as if a manor of thy friend's or of thine own were: any man's death diminishes me, because I am involved in mankind, and therefore never send to know for whom the bells tolls; it tolls for thee. Neither can we call this a begging of misery, or a borrowing of misery, as though we were not miserable enough of ourselves, but must fetch in more from the next house, in taking upon us the misery of our neighbours. Truly it were an excusable covetousness if we did, for affliction is a treasure, and scarce any man hath enough of it. No man hath affliction enough that is not matured and ripened by it, and made fit for God by that affliction. If a man carry treasure in bullion, or in a wedge of gold, and have none coined into current money, his treasure will not defray him as he travels. Tribulation is treasure in the nature of it, but it is not current money in the use of it, except we get nearer and nearer our home, heaven, by it. Another man may be sick too, and sick to death, and this affliction may lie in his bowels, as gold in a mine, and be of no use to him; but this bell, that tells me of his affliction, digs out and applies that gold to me: if by this consideration of another's danger I take mine own into contemplation, and so secure myself, by making my recourse to my God, who is our only security.

XXI. MEDITATION

ATQUE ANNUIT ILLE, QUI, PER EOS,
CLAMAT, LINQUAS JAM, LAZARE, LECTUM
God prospers their practice, and he, by them, calls
Lazarus out of his tomb, me out of my bed

If man had been left alone in this world at first, shall I think that he would not have fallen? If there had been no woman, would not man have served to have been his own tempter? When I see him now subject to infinite weaknesses, fall into infinite sin without any foreign temptations, shall I think he would have had none, if he had been alone? God saw that man needed a helper, if he should be well; but to make woman ill, the devil saw that there needed no third. When God and we were alone in Adam, that was not enough; when the devil and we were alone in Eve, it was enough. O what a giant is man when he fights against himself, and what a dwarf when he needs or exercises his own assistance for himself? I cannot rise out of my bed till the physician enable me, nay, I cannot tell that I am able to rise till he tell me so. I do nothing, I know nothing of myself; how little and how impotent a piece of the world is any man alone? And how much less a piece of himself is that man? So little as that when it falls out (as it falls out in some cases) that more misery and more oppression would be an ease to a man, he cannot give himself that miserable addition of more misery. A man that is pressed to death, and might be eased by more weights, cannot lay those more weights upon himself: he can sin alone, and suffer alone, but not repent, not be absolved, without another. Another tells me, I may rise; and I do so. But is every raising a preferment? or is every present preferment a station? I am readier to fall to the earth, now I am up, than I was when I lay in the bed. O perverse way, irregular motion of man; even rising itself is the way to ruin! How many men are raised, and then do not fill the place they are raised to? No corner of any place can be empty; there can be no vacuity. If that man do not fill the place, other men will; complaints of his insufficiency will fill it; nay, such an abhorring is there in nature of vacuity, that if there be but an imagination of not filling, in any man, that which is but imagination, neither will fill it, that is, rumour and voice, and it will be given out (upon no ground but imagination, and no man knows whose imagination), that he is corrupt in his place, or insufficient in his place, and another prepared to succeed him in his place. A man rises sometimes and stands not, because he doth not or is not believed to fill his place; and sometimes he stands not because he overfills his place. He may bring so much virtue, so much justice, so much integrity to the place, as shall spoil the place, burthen the place; his integrity may be a libel upon his predecessor and cast an infamy upon him, and a burthen upon his successor to proceed by example, and to bring the place itself to an undervalue and the market to an uncertainty. I am up, and I seem to stand, and I go round, and I am a new argument of the new philosophy, that the earth moves round; why may I not believe that the whole earth moves, in a round motion, though that seem to me to stand, when as I seem to stand to my company, and yet am carried in a giddy and circular motion as I stand? Man hath no centre but misery; there, and only there, he is fixed, and sure to find himself. How little soever he be raised, he moves, and moves in a circle giddily; and as in the heavens there are but a few circles that go about the whole world, but many epicycles, and other lesser circles, but yet circles; so of those men which are raised and put into circles, few of them move from place to place, and pass through many and beneficial places, but fall into little circles, and, within a step or two, are at their end, and not so well as they were in the centre, from which they were raised. Every thing serves to exemplify, to illustrate man's misery. But I need go no farther than myself: for a long time I was not able to rise; at last I must be raised by others; and now I am up, I am ready to sink lower than before.

—1624

The second of my Prebend Sermons upon my five Psalms. Preached at S. Paul's, January 29, 1626

PSAL. 63:7 *Because thou hast been my help, therefore in the shadow of thy wings will I rejoice.*

The Psalms are the manna of the church. As manna tasted to every man like that that he liked best,[1] so do the Psalms minister instructions, and satisfaction, to every man, in every emergency and occasion. David was not only a clear prophet of Christ himself, but a prophet of every particular Christian; he foretells what I, what any shall do, and suffer, and say. And as the whole book of Psalms is *Oleum effusum* (as the spouse speaks of the name of Christ),[2] an ointment poured out upon all sorts of sores, a cerecloth that supples all bruises, a balm that searches all wounds; so are there some certain Psalms, that are imperial Psalms, that command over all affections, and spread themselves over all occasions, Catholic, universal Psalms, that apply themselves to all necessities. This is one of those; for, of those constitutions which are called apostolical, one is, that the church should meet every day, to sing this Psalm.[3] And accordingly, S. Chryso-

stome testifies,[4] that it was decreed, and ordained by the primitive fathers, that no day should pass without the public singing of this Psalm. Under both these obligations (those ancient constitutions, called the Apostles, and those ancient decrees made by the primitive fathers) belongs to me, who have my part in the service of God's church, the especial meditation, and recommendation of this Psalm. And under a third obligation too, that it is one of those five Psalms, the daily rehearsing whereof, is enjoined to me, by the constitutions of this church, as five other are to every other person of our body. As the whole book is manna, so these five Psalms are my Gomer, which I am to fill and empty every day of this manna.[5]

Now as the spirit and soul of the whole book of Psalms is contracted into this Psalm, so is the spirit and soul of this whole Psalm contracted into this verse. The key of the psalm (as S. Jerome calls the titles of the Psalms) tells us, that David uttered this Psalm, "when he was in the wilderness of Judah"; there we see the present occasion that moved him; and we see what was passed between God and him before, in the first clause of our text ("Because thou hast been my help"); and then we see what was to come, by the rest ("Therefore in the shadow of thy wings will I rejoice"). So that we have here the whole compass of time, past, present, and future; and these three parts of time, shall be at this time, the three parts of this exercise; first, what David's distress put him upon for the present; and that lies in the context; secondly, how David built his assurance upon that which was past ("Because thou hast been my help"); and thirdly, what he established to himself for the future ("Therefore in the shadow of thy wings will I rejoice"). First, his distress in the wilderness, his present estate carried him upon the memory of that which God had done

---

[1] "thou…didst send them from heaven bread prepared without their labour, able to content every man's delight and agreeable to every taste" (Wisdom of Solomon 16:20). For "manna" see Exodus 16:11–15. See also *ODCC* "Psalms, Book of." This records that the whole Psalter was recited every week in the Roman Catholic Church, and every month in the Church of England .

[2] "thy name is as ointment poured forth" (Song of Solomon 1:3). This work was interpreted as referring to Christ's love for the Church.

[3] The *Apostolic Constitutions*: a work of the late fourth century, dealing with, among other matters, the official responsibilities of the clergy. See *ODCC*, "Apostolic Canons."

[4] St. John Chrysostom (ca. 347–407) has been described as the greatest of Christian expositors.

[5] Exodus 16:16. The Vulgate has "gomor," AV "omer."

for him before, and the remembrance of that carried him upon that, of which he assured himself after. Fix upon God any where, and you shall find him a circle; he is with you now, when you fix upon him; he was with you before, for he brought you to this fixation; and he will be with you hereafter, for "He is yesterday, and today, and the same for ever."

For David's present condition, who was now in a banishment, in a persecution in the wilderness of Judah, (which is our first part) we shall only insist upon that (which is indeed spread over all the Psalm to the text, and ratified in the text) that in all those temporal calamities David was only sensible of his spiritual loss; it grieved him not that he was kept from Saul's court, but that he was kept from God's church.[1] For when he says, by way of lamentation, "That he was in a dry and thirsty land, where no water was,"[2] he expresses what penury, what barrenness, what drought and what thirst he meant; "To see thy power, and thy glory, so as I have seen thee in the sanctuary." For there, "my soul shall be satisfied as with marrow, and with fatness," and there, "my mouth shall praise thee with joyful lips." And in some few considerations conducing to this, that spiritual losses are incomparably heavier than temporal, and that therefore, the restitution to our spiritual happiness, or the continuation of it, is rather to be made the subject of our prayers to God, in all pressures and distresses, than of temporal, we shall determine that first part. And for the particular branches of both the other parts (the remembering of God's benefits past, and the building of an assurance for the future, upon that remembrance), it may be fitter to open them to you anon when we come to handle them, than now.

Proceed we now to our first part, the comparing of temporal and spiritual afflictions.

In the way of this comparison, falls first the consideration of the universality of afflictions in general, and the inevitableness thereof. It is a blessed metaphor, that the Holy Ghost hath put into the mouth of the Apostle, *Pondus Gloriae*, that our afflictions are but light, because there is an exceeding, and an eternal weight of glory attending them.[3] If it were not for that exceeding weight of glory, no other weight in this world could turn the scale, or weigh down those infinite weights of afflictions that oppress us here. There is not only *Pestis valde gravis* ("the pestilence grows heavy upon the land"), but there is *Musca valde gravis*, God calls in but the fly, to vex Egypt, and even the fly is a heavy burden unto them. It is not only Job that complains, "That he was a burden to himself," but even Absalom's hair was a burden to him, till it was pulled. It is not only Jeremy that complains, *Aggravavit compedes*, that God had made their fetters and their chains heavy to them, but the workmen in harvest complain, that God had made a fair day heavy unto them ("We have borne the heat, and the burden of the day").[4] "Sand is heavy," says Solomon; and how many suffer so? under a sand-hill of crosses, daily, hourly afflictions, that are heavy by their number, if not by their single weight? And "a stone is heavy" (says he in the same place); and how many suffer so?[5] How many, without any former preparatory cross, or comminatory, or commonitory cross, even in the midst of prosperity, and security, fall under some one stone, some grind-stone, some mill-stone, some one insupportable cross that ruins them? But then (says Solomon there), "A fool's anger is heavier than both"; and how many children, and servants, and wives suffer

---

[1] Donne is relying on Psalm 63, rather than on the story of David in I and II Samuel. Apart from St. Jerome and, in the Reformation, Calvin, most authorities until after Donne's time thought of David as the author of all the Psalms.

[2] Psalm 63:1.

[3] II Corinthians 4:17.

[4] See Lamentations 3:7 and Matthew 20:12.

[5] Proverbs 27:3.

under the anger, and morosity, and peevishness, and jealousy of foolish masters, and parents, and husbands, though they must not say so? David and Solomon have cried out, that all this world is vanity, and levity; and (God knows) all is weight, and burden, and heaviness, and oppression; and if there were not a weight of future glory to counterpose it, we should all sink into nothing.

I ask not Mary Magdalen, whether lightness were not a burden (for sin is certainly, sensibly a burden); but I ask Susanna whether even chaste beauty were not a burden to her; and I ask Joseph whether personal comeliness were not a burden to him.[1] I ask not Dives, who perished in the next world, the question; but I ask them who are made examples of Solomon's rule, of that "sore evil" (as he calls it), "Riches kept to the owners thereof for their hurt," whether riches be not a burden.[2]

All our life is a continual burden, yet we must not groan; a continual squeezing, yet we must not pant; and as in the tenderness of our childhood, we suffer, and yet are whipped if we cry, so we are complained of, if we complain, and made delinquents if we call the times ill. And that which adds weight to weight, and multiplies the sadness of this consideration, is this, that still the best men have had most laid upon them. As soon as I hear God say, that he hath found "an upright man, that fears God, and eschews evil," in the next lines I find a commission to Satan, to bring in Sabians and Chaldeans upon his cattle, and servants, and fire and tempest upon his children, and loathsome diseases upon himself.[3] As soon as I hear God say,

that he hath found "a man according to his own heart," I see his sons ravish his daughters, and then murder one another, and then rebel against the father, and put him into straits for his life. As soon as I hear God testify of Christ at his baptism, "This is my beloved Son in whom I am well pleased," I find that Son of his "led up by the spirit, to be tempted of the Devil." And after I hear God ratify the same testimony again, at his Transfiguration ("This is my beloved Son, in whom I am well pleased"), I find that beloved Son of his, deserted, abandoned, and given over to scribes, and Pharisees, and publicans, and Herodians, and priests, and soldiers, and people, and judges, and witnesses, and executioners, and he that was called the beloved Son of God, and made partaker of the glory of Heaven, in this world, in his Transfiguration, is made now the sower of all the corruption, of all the sins of this world, as no Son of God, but a mere man, as no man, but a contemptible worm. As though the greatest weakness in this world, were man, and the greatest fault in man were to be good, man is more miserable than other creatures, and good men more miserable than any other men.

But then there is *Pondus Gloriae*, "An exceeding weight of eternal glory," and that turns the scale; for as it makes all worldly prosperity as dung, so it makes all worldly adversity as feathers. And so it had need; for in the scale against it, there are not only put temporal afflictions, but spiritual too; and to these two kinds, we may accommodate those words, "He that falls upon this stone" (upon temporal afflictions), may be bruised, broken, "But he upon whom that stone falls" (spiritual afflictions), "is in danger to be ground to powder." And then, the great, and yet ordinary danger is, that these spiritual afflictions grow out of temporal; murmuring, and diffidence in God, and obduration, out of worldly calamities; and so against nature, the fruit is greater and heavier than the tree, spiritual heavier than temporal afflictions.

---

[1] St. Mary Magdalen, on the basis of Luke 7:37, has been thought of through Christian history as a reformed prostitute. For Susanna, see the Story of Susanna in the Apocrypha (an early detective story, incidentally); for Joseph's resistance to the blandishments of Potiphar's wife, see Genesis 39.

[2] *Dives* a Latin adjective meaning "rich." It came to be used as the name of the rich man; see Luke 16:19–31. For the quotation from Solomon see Ecclesiastes 5:13.

[3] See Job 1.

They who write of natural story,[1] propose that plant for the greatest wonder in nature, which being no firmer then a bull-rush, or a reed, produces and bears for the fruit thereof no other but an entire, and very hard stone. That temporal affliction should produce spiritual stoniness, and obduration, is unnatural, yet ordinary. Therefore doth God propose it, as one of those greatest blessings, which he multiplies upon his people, "I will take away your stony hearts, and give you hearts of flesh"; and, Lord let me have a fleshly heart in any sense, rather than a stony heart.[2] We find mention amongst the observers of rarities in nature, of hairy hearts, hearts of men, that have been overgrown with hair; but of petrified hearts, hearts of men grown into stone, we read not; for this petrifaction of the heart, this stupefaction of a man, is the last blow of God's hand upon the heart of man in this world. Those great afflictions which are poured out of the vials of the seven Angels upon the world, are still accompanied with that heavy effect, that that affliction hardened them. "They were scorched with heats and plagues," by the fourth Angel, and it follows, "They blasphemed the name of God, and repented not, to give him glory." Darkness was induced upon them by the fifth Angel, and it follows, "They blasphemed the God of Heaven, and repented not of their deeds." And from the seventh Angel there fell hailstones of the weight of talents (perchance four pound weight), upon men; and yet these men had so much life left, as to blaspheme God, out of that respect, which alone should have brought them to glorify God, "Because the plague thereof was exceeding great."[3] And when a great plague brings them to blaspheme, how great shall that second plague be, that comes upon them for blaspheming?

Let me wither and wear out mine age in a discomfortable, in an unwholesome, in a penurious prison, and so pay my debts with my bones, and recompense the wastefulness of my youth, with the beggary of mine age; let me wither in a spittle under sharp, and foul, and infamous diseases, and so recompense the wantonness of my youth, with that loathsomeness in mine age; yet, if God withdraw not his spiritual blessings, his grace, his patience, if I can call my suffering his doing, my passion his action, all this that is temporal, is but a caterpillar got into one corner of my garden, but a mildew fallen upon one acre of my corn; the body of all, the substance of all is safe, as long as the soul is safe.[4] But when I shall trust to that, which we call a good spirit, and God shall deject, and impoverish, and evacuate that spirit, when I shall rely upon a moral constancy, and God shall shake, and enfeeble, and enervate, destroy and demolish that constancy; when I shall think to refresh my self in the serenity and sweet air of a good conscience, and God shall call up the damps and vapors of Hell itself, and spread a cloud of diffidence, and an impenetrable crust of desperation upon my conscience; when health shall fly from me, and I shall lay hold upon riches to succor me, and comfort me in my sickness, and riches shall fly from me, and I shall snatch after favor, and good opinion, to comfort me in my poverty; when even this good opinion shall leave me, and calumnies and misinformations shall prevail against me; when I shall need peace, because there is none but thou, O Lord, that should stand for me, and then shall find, that all the wounds that I have, come from thy hand, all the arrows that stick in me, from thy quiver; when I shall see, that because I have given my self to my corrupt nature, thou hast changed thine; and because I am all evil towards thee, therefore thou hast given over being good towards me; when it comes to this height, that

---

[1] *natural story* natural history. Donne has taken this story of the "lithospermus" from Pliny.

[2] See Ezekiel 11:19, a highly significant text in early modern religious writing.

[3] See Revelation 16, especially verses 1, 9, 11, and 21.

[4] This whole paragraph, from "Let me wither" to "irremediably," should be read aloud if its beauty is to be fully appreciated.

the fever is not in the humors, but in the spirits, that mine enemy is not an imaginary enemy, fortune, nor a transitory enemy, malice in great persons, but a real, and an irresistible, and an inexorable, and an everlasting enemy, the Lord of Hosts himself, the Almighty God himself, the Almighty God himself only knows the weight of this affliction, and except he put in that *pondus gloriae*, that exceeding weight of an eternal glory, with his own hand, into the other scale, we are weighed down, we are swallowed up, irreparably, irrevocably, irrecoverably, irremediably.

This is the fearful depth, this is spiritual misery, to be thus fallen from God. But was this David's case? was he fallen thus far, into a diffidence in God? No. But the danger, the precipice, the slippery sliding into that bottomless depth, is, to be excluded from the means of coming to God, or staying with God; and this is that that David laments here, that by being banished, and driven into the wilderness of Judah, he had not access to the Sanctuary of the Lord, to sacrifice his part in the praise, and to receive his part in the prayers of the congregation; for Angels pass not to ends, but by ways and means, nor men to the glory of the triumphant Church, but by participation of the Communion of the Militant. To this note David sets his harp, in many, many Psalms: Sometimes, that God had suffered his enemies to possess his tabernacle ("He forsook the Tabernacle of Shiloh, he delivered his strength into captivity, and his glory into the enemies' hands"), but most commonly he complains, that God disabled him from coming to the Sanctuary. In which one thing he had summed up all his desires, all his prayers ("One thing have I desired of the Lord, that will I look after; that I may dwell in the house of the Lord, all the days of my life, to behold the beauty of the Lord, and to enquire in his Temple"), his vehement desire of this, he expresses again ("My soul thirsteth for God, for the living God; when shall I come and appear before God?"), he expresses a holy jealousy, a religious envy, even to the sparrows and swallows (yea, "the sparrow hath found a house, and the swallow a nest for her self, and where she may lay her young, even thine altars, O Lord of Hosts, my King and my God"). Thou art my King, and my God, and yet excludest me from that, which thou affordest to sparrows, "And are not we of more value than many sparrows?"

And as though David felt some false ease, some half-tentation,[1] some whispering that way, that God is in the wilderness of Judah, in every place, as well as in his Sanctuary, there is in the original in that place, a pathetical, a vehement, a broken expressing expressed, "O thine altars"; it is true (says David), thou art here in the wilderness, and I may see thee here, and serve thee here, but, "O thine altars, O Lord of hosts, my King and my God." When David could not come in person to that place, yet he bent towards the Temple ("In thy fear will I worship towards thy holy Temple"). Which was also Daniel's devotion; when he prayed, "his chamber windows were open towards Jerusalem"; and so is Hezekiah's turning to the wall to weep, and to pray in his sick bed, understood to be to that purpose, to conform, and compose himself towards the Temple. In the place consecrated for that use, God by Moses fixes the service, and fixes the reward; and towards that place (when they could not come to it), doth Solomon direct their devotion in the consecration of the Temple ("when they are in the wars, when they are in captivity, and pray towards this house, do thou hear them"). For, as in private prayer, when (according to Christ's command) we are shut in our chamber, there is exercised *Modestia fidei*, the modesty and bashfulness of our faith, not pressing upon God in his house: so in the public prayers of the congregation, there is exercised the fervor, and holy courage of our faith, for *Agmine facto obside-*

---

[1] *tentation* temptation (*OED*).

mus Deum, it is a mustering of our forces, and a besieging of God. Therefore does David so much magnify their blessedness, that are in this house of God ("Blessed are they that dwell in thy house, for they will be still praising thee"); those that look towards it, may praise thee sometimes, but those men who dwell in the Church, and whose whole service lies in the Church, have certainly an advantage of all other men (who are necessarily withdrawn by worldly business) in making themselves acceptable to almighty God, if they do their duties, and observe their church-services aright.

Man being therefore thus subject naturally to manifold calamities, and spiritual calamities being incomparably heavier than temporal, and the greatest danger of falling into such spiritual calamities being in our absence from God's Church, where only the outward means of happiness are ministered unto us, certainly there is much tenderness and deliberation to be used, before the Church doors be shut against any man. If I would not direct a prayer to God, to excommunicate any man from the Triumphant Church (which were to damn him), I would not oil the key, I would not make the way too slippery for excommunications in the Militant Church; for, that is to endanger him. I know how distasteful a sin to God, contumacy, and contempt, and disobedience to order and authority is; and I know (and all men, that choose not ignorance, may know), that our excommunications (though calumniators impute them to small things, because, many times, the first complaint is of some small matter) never issue but upon contumacies, contempts, disobediences to the Church. But they are real contumacies, not interpretative, apparent contumacies, not presumptive, that excommunicate a man in Heaven; and much circumspection is required, and (I am far from doubting it) exercised in those cases upon earth; for, though every excommunication upon earth be not sealed in Heaven, though it damn not the man, yet it damns up that man's way, by shutting him out of that Church, through which he must go to the other; which being so great a danger, let every man take heed of excommunicating himself. The impersuasible recusant does so; the negligent libertine does; the fantastic separatist does so; the half-present man, he, whose body is here, and mind away, does so; and he, whose body is but half here, his limbs are here upon a cushion, but his eyes, his ears are not here, does so: All these are self-excommunicators, and keep themselves from hence. Only he enjoys that blessing, the want whereof David deplores, that is here entirely, and is glad he is here, and glad to find this kind of service here, that he does, and wishes no other.

And so we have done with our first part, David's aspect, his present condition, and his danger of falling into spiritual miseries, because his persecution, and banishment amounted to an excommunication, to an excluding of him from the service of God, in the church. And we pass, in our order proposed at first, to the second, his retrospect, the consideration what God had done for him before, "Because thou hast been my help."

Through this second part, we shall pass by these three steps. First, that it behoves us, in all our purposes, and actions, to propose to ourselves a copy to write by, a pattern to work by, a rule, or an example to proceed by. Because it hath been thus heretofore, says David, I will resolve upon this course for the future.[1] And secondly, that the copy, the pattern, the precedent which we are to propose to ourselves, is, the observation of God's former ways and proceedings upon us, because God hath already gone this way, this way I will await his going still. And then, thirdly and lastly, in this second part, the way that God had formerly gone with David, which was, that he had been his help ("Because thou hast been my help").

---

[1] In effect, Donne is here presenting the text of his sermon, Psalm 63:7, in a more abstract form that has general application.

First then, from the meanest artificer, through the wisest philosopher, to God himself, all that is well done, or wisely undertaken, is undertaken and done according to ourselves beforehand. A carpenter builds not a house, but that he first sets up a frame in his own mind, what kind of house he will build. The little great philosopher Epictetus, would undertake no action, but he would first propose to himself, what Socrates, or Plato, what a wise man would do in that case, and according to that, he would proceed. Of God himself, it is safely resolved in the School, that he never did any thing in any part of time, of which he had not an eternal preconception, an eternal idea, in himself before. Of which ideas, that is, preconceptions, predeterminations in God, S. Augustine pronounces, *Tanta vis in Ideis constituitur*, there is so much truth, and so much power in these ideas, as that without acknowledging them, no man can acknowledge God, for he does not allow God counsel, and wisdom, and deliberation in his actions, but sets God on work, before he have thought what he will do. And therefore he, and others of the Fathers read that place (which we read otherwise), *Quod factum est, in ipso vita erat*; that is, in all their expositions, whatsoever is made, in time, was alive in God, before it was made, that is, in that eternal idea, and pattern which was in him. So also do divers of those fathers read those words to the Hebrews (which we read, "the things that are seen, are not made of things that do appear"), *Ex invisibilibus visibilia facta sunt*, "Things formerly invisible, were made visible"; that is, we see then not till now, till they are made, but they had an invisible being, in that idea, in that prenotion, in that purpose of God before, for ever before. Of all things in Heaven, and earth, but of himself, God had an idea, a pattern in himself, before he made it.

And therefore let him be our pattern for that, to work after patterns; to propose to ourselves rules and examples for all our actions; and the more, the more immediately, the more directly our actions concern the service of God. If I ask God, by what idea he made me, God produces his *Faciamus hominem ad Imaginem nostram*,[1] that there was a concurrence of the whole Trinity, to make me in Adam, according to that image which they were, and according to that idea, which they had predetermined. If I pretend to serve God, and he ask me for my idea, how I mean to serve him, shall I be able to produce none? If he ask me an idea of my religion, and my opinions, shall I not be able to say, it is that which thy word, and thy Catholic Church hath imprinted in me? If he ask me an idea of my prayers, shall I not be able to say, it is that which my particular necessities, that which the form prescribed by thy Son, that which the care, and piety of the Church, in conceiving fit prayers, hath imprinted in me? If he ask me an idea of my sermons, shall I not be able to say, it is that which the analogy of faith, the edification of the congregation, the zeal of thy work, the meditations of my heart have imprinted in me? But if I come to pray or to preach without this kind of idea, if I come to extemporal prayer, and extemporal preaching, I shall come to an extemporal faith, and extemporal religion; and then I must look for an extemporal Heaven, a Heaven to be made for me; for to that Heaven which belongs to the Catholic Church, I shall never come, except I go by the way of the Catholic Church, by former ideas, former examples, former patterns, to believe according to ancient beliefs, to pray according to ancient forms, to preach according to former meditations. God does nothing, man does nothing well, without these ideas, these retrospects, this recourse to preconceptions, pre-deliberations.

Something then I must propose to myself, to be the rule, and the reason of my present and future actions; which was our first branch in this second

---

[1] "Let us make man in our own image" (Genesis 1:26).

part; and then the second is, that I can propose nothing more availably, than the contemplation of the history of God's former proceeding with me; which is David's way here, because this was God's way before, I will look for God in this way still. That language in which God spake to man, the Hebrew, hath no present tense; they form not their verbs as our Western languages do, in the present, "I hear," or "I see," or "I read," but they begin at that which is past, "I have seen" and "heard," and "read." God carries us in his language, in his speaking, upon that which is past, upon that which he hath done already; I cannot have better security for present, nor future, than God's former mercies exhibited to me. *Quis non gaudeat*, says S. Augustine, who does not triumph with joy, when he considers what God hath done? *Quis non & ea, quae nondum venerunt, ventura sperat, propter illa, quæ jam tanta impleta sunt?* Who can doubt of the performance of all, that sees the greatest part of a prophecy performed? If I have found that true that God hath said, of the person of Antichrist, why should I doubt of that which he says of the ruin of Antichrist? *Credamus modicum quod restat*, says the same Father, it is much that we have seen done, and it is but little that God hath reserved to our faith, to believe that it shall be done.

There is no state, no church, no man, that hath not this tie upon God, that hath not God in these bands, that God by having done much for them already, hath bound himself to do more. Men proceed in their former ways, sometimes, lest they should confess an error, and acknowledge that they had been in a wrong way. God is obnoxious to no error, and therefore he does still, as he did before. Every one of you can say now to God, Lord, thou broughtest me hither, therefore enable me to hear; Lord, thou dost that, therefore make me understand; and that, therefore let me believe; and that too, therefore strengthen me to the practice; and all that, therefore continue me to a perseverance. Carry

it up to the first sense and apprehension that ever thou hadst of God's working upon thee, either in thy self, when thou camest first to the use of reason, or in others in thy behalf, in thy baptism, yet when thou thinkest thou art at the first, God had done something for thee before all that; before that, he had elected thee, in that election which S. Augustine speaks of, *Habet electos, quos creaturus est eligendos*, God hath elected certain men, whom he intends to create, that he may elect them; that is, that he may declare his election upon them. God had thee, before he made thee; He loved thee first, and then created thee, that thou loving him, he might continue his love to thee. The surest way, and the nearest way to lay hold upon God, is the consideration of that which he had done already. So David does; and that which he takes knowledge of, in particular, in God's former proceedings towards him, is, because God had been his help, which is our last branch in this part, "Because thou hast been my help."

From this one word, that God hath been my "Help," I make account that we have both these notions; first, that God hath not left me to myself, He hath come to my succor, He hath helped me; and then, that God hath not left out myself; He hath been my Help, but he hath left some thing for me to do with him, and by his help. My security for the future, in this consideration of that which is past, lies not only in this, that God hath delivered me, but in this also, that he hath delivered me by way of a Help, and Help always presumes an endeavour and co-operation in him that is helped. God did not elect me as a helper, nor create me, nor redeem me, nor convert me, by way of helping me; for he alone did all, and he had no use at all of me. God infuses his first grace, the first way, merely as a Giver; entirely, all himself; but his subsequent graces, as a helper; therefore we call them auxiliary graces, helping graces; and we always receive them, when we endeavour to make use of his former grace.

"Lord, I believe" (says the man in the Gospel to Christ), "Help mine unbelief." If there had not been unbelief, weakness, imperfectness in that faith, there had needed no help; but if there had not been a belief, a faith, it had not been capable of help and assistance, but it must have been an entire act, without any concurrence on the man's part.

So that if I have truly the testimony of a rectified conscience, that God hath helped me, it is in both respects; first, that he hath never forsaken me, and then, that he hath never suffered me to forsake my self; He hath blessed me with that grace, that I trust in no help but his, and with this grace too, that I cannot look for his help, except I help myself also. God did not help Heaven and earth to proceed out of nothing in the Creation, for they had no possibility of any disposition towards it; for they had no being: But God did help the earth to produce grass, and herbs; for, for that, God had infused a seminal disposition into the earth, which, for all that, it could not have perfected without his farther help. As in the making of Woman, there is the very word of our text, Gnazar, God made him a helper, one that was to do much for him, but not without him. So that then, if I will make God's former working upon me, an argument of his future gracious purposes, as I must acknowledge that God hath done much for me, so I must find, that I have done what I could, by the benefit of that grace with him; for God promises to be but a helper. "Lord open thou my lips," says David; that is God's work entirely; and then, "My mouth, my mouth shall show forth thy praise"; there enters David into the work with God. And then, says God to him, *Dilata os tuum*, "Open thy mouth" (it is now made "Thy mouth," and therefore do thou open it) "and I will fill it"; all inchoations and consummations, beginnings and perfectings are of God, of God alone; but in the way there is a concurrence on our part (by a successive continuation of God's grace), in which God proceeds as a helper; and I put him to more than

that, if I do nothing. But if I pray for his help, and apprehend and husband his graces well, when they come, then he is truly, properly my helper; and upon that security, that testimony of a rectified conscience, I can proceed to David's confidence for the future, "Because thou hast been my Help, therefore in the shadow of thy wings will I rejoice"; which is our third, and last general part.

In this last part, which is (after David's aspect, and consideration of his present condition, which was, in the effect, an exclusion from God's Temple, and his retrospect, his consideration of God's former mercies to him, that he had been his help), his prospect, his confidence for the future, we shall stay a little upon these two steps; first, that that which he promises himself, is not an immunity from all powerful enemies, nor a sword of revenge upon those enemies; it is not that he shall have no adversary, nor that that adversary shall be able to do him no harm, but that he should have a refreshing, a respiration, *In velamento alarum*, under the shadow of God's wings. And then (in the second place), that this way which God shall be pleased to take, this manner, this measure of refreshing, which God shall vouchsafe to afford (though it amount not to a full deliverance), must produce a joy, a rejoicing in us; we must not only not decline to a murmuring, that we have no more, no nor rest upon a patience for that which remains, but we must ascend to a holy joy, as if all were done and accomplished, "In the shadow of thy wings will I rejoice."

First then, lest any man in his dejection of spirit, or of fortune, should stray into a jealousy or suspicion of God's power to deliver him, as God hath spangled the firmament with stars, so hath he his Scriptures with names, and metaphors, and denotations of power. Sometimes he shines out in the name of a Sword, and of a Target, and of a Wall, and of a Tower, and of a Rock, and of a Hill; and sometimes in that glorious and manifold constellation of all together, *Dominum exercituum*, "the Lord of Hosts." God, as God, is never represented to us, with defensive arms; He needs then not. When the poets present their great heroes, and their worthies, they always insist upon their arms, they spend much of their invention upon the description of their arms; both because the greatest valour and strength needs arms (Goliah himself was armed), and because to expose one's self to danger unarmed, is not valour, but rashness. But God is invulnerable in himself, and is never represented armed; you find no shirts of mail, no helmets, no cuirasses in God's armory. In that one place of Esay, where it may seem to be otherwise, where God is said "to have put on righteousness as a breastplate, and a helmet of salvation upon his head"; in that prophecy God is Christ, and is therefore in that place, called the Redeemer. Christ needed defensive arms, God does not. God's word does; his Scriptures do; and therefore S. Jerome hath armed them, and set before every book his *Prologum galeatum*, that prologue that arms and defends every book from calumny. But though God need not, nor receive not defensive arms for himself, yet God is to us a helmet, a breastplate, a strong tower, a rock, everything that may give us assurance and defense; and as often as he will, he can refresh that Proclamation, *Nolite tangere Christos meos*, our enemies shall not so much as touch us.

But here, by occasion of his metaphor in this text (*Sub umbra alarum*, "In the shadow of thy wings"), we do not so much consider an absolute immunity, that we shall not be touched, as a refreshing and consolation, when we are touched, though we be pinched and wounded. The names of God, which are most frequent in the Scriptures, are these three, Elohim, and Adonai, and Jehovah; and to assure us of his power to deliver us, two of these three are names of power. Elohim is *Deus fortis*, the mighty, the powerful God: and (which deserves a particular consideration) Elohim is a plural name;

it is not *Deus fortis*, but *Dii fortes*, powerful Gods. God is all kind of Gods; all kinds, which either idolaters and gentiles can imagine (as riches, or justice, or wisdom, or valour, or such), and all kinds which God himself hath called gods (as princes, and magistrates, and prelates, and all that assist and help one another), God is Elohim, all these Gods, and all these in their height and best of their power; for Elohim is *Dii fortes*, Gods in the plural, and those plural Gods in their exaltation.

The second name of God is a name of power too, Adonai. For, Adonai is *Dominus*, the Lord, such a Lord, as is Lord and proprietary of all his creatures, and all creatures are his creatures; and then, *Dominium est potestas tum utendi, tum abutendi*, says the law; to be absolute Lord of any thing, gives that Lord a power to do what he will with that thing. God, as he is Adonai, the Lord, may give and take, quicken and kill, build and throw down, where and whom he will. So then two of God's three names are names of absolute power, to imprint, and re-imprint an assurance in us, that he can absolutely deliver us, and fully revenge us, if he will. But then, his third name, and that name which he chooses to himself, and in the signification of which name, he employs Moses, for the relief of his people under Pharaoh, that name Jehovah, is not a name of power, but only of essence, of being, of subsistence, and yet in the virtue of that name, God relieved his people. And if, in my afflictions, God vouchsafe to visit me in that name, to preserve me in my being, in my subsistence in him, that I be not shaked out of him, disinherited in him, excommunicate from him, divested of him, annihilated towards him, let him, at his good pleasure, reserve his Elohim, and his Adonai, the exercises and declarations of his mighty power, to those great public causes, that more concern his glory, than any thing that can befall me; but if he impart his Jehovah, enlarge himself so far towards me, as that I may live, and move, and have my being in him, though I be not instantly delivered, nor mine enemies absolutely destroyed, yet this is as much as I could promise myself, this is as much as the Holy Ghost intends in this metaphor, *Sub umbra alarum*, "Under the shadow of thy wings," that is a refreshing, a respiration, a conservation, a consolation in all afflictions that are inflicted upon me.

Yet, is not this metaphor of wings without a denotation of power. As no act of Gods, though it seem to imply but spiritual comfort, is without a denotation of power (for it is the power of God that comforts me; to overcome that sadness of soul, and that dejection of spirit, which the adversary by temporal afflictions would induce upon me, is an act of his power), so this metaphor, "The shadow of his wings" (which in this place expresses no more, than consolation and refreshing in misery, and not a powerful deliverance out of it), is so often in the Scriptures made a denotation of power too, as that we can doubt of no act of power, if we have this shadow of his wings. For, in this metaphor of wings, doth the Holy Ghost express the Maritime power, the power of some nations at sea, in navies ("Woe to the land shadowing with wings"), that is, that hovers over the world, and intimidates it with her sails and ships. In this metaphor doth God remember his people, of his powerful deliverance of them ("You have seen what I did unto the Egyptians, and how I bare you on eagle's wings and brought you to myself"). In this metaphor doth God threaten his and their enemies, what he can do ("The noise of the wings of his cherubims, are as the noise of great waters, and of an army"). So also, what he will do ("He shall spread his wings over Bozrah, and at that day shall the hearts of the mighty men of Edom, be as the heart of a woman in her pangs"). So that, if I have the shadow of his wings, I have the earnest of the power of them too; if I have refreshing, and respiration from them, I am able to say (as those three confessors did to Nebuchadnezzar), "My God is able to deliver me,"

I am sure he hath power; "And my God will deliver me," when it conduces to his glory, I know he will; "But, if he do not, be it known unto thee, O King, we will not serve thy Gods"; be it known unto thee, O Satan, how long soever God defer my deliverance, I will not seek false comforts, the miserable comforts of this world. I will not, for I need not; for I can subsist under this shadow of these wings, though I have no more.

The Mercy-seat itself was covered with the cherubims' wings; and who would have more than Mercy? and a Mercy-seat; that is, established, resident Mercy, permanent and perpetual Mercy; present and familiar Mercy; a Mercy-seat. Our Saviour Christ intends as much as would have served their turn, if they had laid hold upon it, when he says, "That he would have gathered Jerusalem, as a hen gathers her chickens under her wings." And though the other prophets do (as ye have heard) mingle the signification of Power, and actual deliverance, in this metaphor of wings, yet our Prophet, whom we have now in especial consideration, David, never doth so; but in every place where he uses this metaphor of wings (which are in five or six several Psalms) still he rests and determines in that sense, which is his meaning here; that though God do not actually deliver us, nor actually destroy our enemies, yet if he refresh us in the shadow of his wings, if he maintain our subsistence (which is a religious constancy) in him, this should not only establish our patience (for that is but half the work), but it should also produce a joy, and rise to an exultation, which is our last circumstance, "Therefore in the shadow of thy wings, I will rejoice."

I would always raise your hearts, and dilate your hearts, to a holy joy, to a joy in the Holy Ghost. There may be a just fear, that men do not grieve enough for their sins; but there may be a just jealousy, and suspicion too, that they may fall into inordinate grief, and diffidence of God's mercy; and

God hath reserved us to such times, as being the later times, give us even the dregs and lees of misery to drink. For, God hath not only let loose into the world a new spiritual disease; which is, an equality, and an indifferency, which religion our children, or our servants, or our companions profess (I would not keep company with a man that thought me a knave, or a traitor; with him that thought I loved not my Prince, or were a faithless man, not to be believed, I would not associate myself; and yet I will make him my bosom companion, that thinks I do not love God, that thinks I cannot be saved); but God hath accompanied, and complicated almost all our bodily diseases of these times, with an extraordinary sadness, a predominant melancholy, a faintness of heart, a cheerlessness, a joylessness of spirit, and therefore I return often to this endeavour of raising your hearts, dilating your hearts with a holy joy, joy in the Holy Ghost, for "Under the shadow of his wings," you may, you should, "rejoice."

If you look upon this world in a map, you find two hemispheres, two half worlds.[1] If you crush Heaven into a map, you may find two hemispheres too, two half Heavens; half will be joy, and half will be glory; for in these two, the joy of Heaven, and the glory of Heaven, is all Heaven often represented unto us. And as of those two hemispheres of the world, the first hath been known long before, but the other (that of America, which is the richer in treasure), God reserved for later discoveries; so though he reserve that hemisphere of Heaven, which is the glory thereof, to the Resurrection, yet the other hemisphere, the joy of Heaven, God opens to our discovery, and delivers for our habitation even whilst we dwell in this world. As God hath cast upon the unrepentant sinner two deaths, a temporal, and a spiritual death, so hath he breathed into us two lives; for so, as the word for

death is doubled, *Morte morieris,*[2] "Thou shalt die the death," so is the word for life expressed in the plural, *Chaiim, vitarum,* "God breathed into his nostrils the breath of lives," of divers lives. Though our natural life were no life, but rather a continual dying, yet we have two lives besides that, an eternal life reserved for Heaven, but yet a heavenly life too, a spiritual life, even in this world; and as God doth thus inflict two deaths, and infuse two lives, so doth he also pass two judgements upon man, or rather repeats the same judgement twice. For, that which Christ shall say to thy soul then at the last Judgement, "Enter into thy Master's joy," He says to thy conscience now, "Enter into thy Master's joy." The everlastingness of the joy is the blessedness of the next life, but the entering, the inchoation is afforded here. For that which Christ shall say then to us, *Venite benedicti,* "Come ye blessed," are words intended to persons that are coming, that are upon the way, though not at home; here in this world he bids us "Come," there in the next, he shall bid us "Welcome." The Angels of Heaven have joy in thy conversion, and canst thou be without that joy in thy self? If thou desire revenge upon thine enemies, as they are God's enemies, that God would be pleased to remove, and root out all such as oppose him, that affection appertains to glory; let that alone till thou come to the hemisphere of glory; there join with those martyrs under the altar, *Usquequo Domine,* how long O Lord, dost thou defer judgement? and thou shalt have thine answer there for that. Whilst thou art here, here join with David, and the other Saints of God, in that holy increpation of a dangerous sadness, "Why art thou cast down O my soul? why art thou disquieted in me?" That soul that is dissected and anatomized to God, in a sincere confession, washed in the tears of true contrition, embalmed in the blood of reconciliation, the blood of Christ Jesus, can assign no rea-

---

[1] Donne's interest in geography and map-making is also apparent in a number of poems.

[2] literally, "by death you will die." The Latin is from the Vulgate, Genesis 2:17.

son, can give no just answer to that interrogatory, "Why art thou cast down O my soul? why art thou disquieted in me?" No man is so little, as that he can be lost under these wings, no man so great, as that they cannot reach to him; *Semper ille major est, quantumcumque creverimus,* to what temporal, to what spiritual greatness soever we grow, still pray we him to shadow us under his wings; for the poor need those wings against oppression, and the rich against envy. The Holy Ghost, who is a dove, shadowed the whole world under his wings; *Incubabat aquis,* he hovered over the waters, he sat upon the waters, and he hatched all that was produced, and all that was produced so, was good. Be thou a Mother where the Holy Ghost would be a Father; conceive by him; and be content that he produce joy in thy heart here. First think, that as a man must have some land, or else he cannot be in wardship, so a man must have some of the love of God, or else he could not fall under God's correction; God would not give him his physic, God would not study his cure, if he cared not for him. And then think also, that if God afford thee the shadow of his wings, that is, consolation, respiration, refreshing, though not a present, and plenary deliverance, in thy afflictions, not to thank God, is a murmuring, and not to rejoice in God's ways, is an unthankfulness. Howling is the noise of Hell, singing the voice of Heaven; sadness the damp of Hell, rejoicing the serenity of Heaven. And he that hath not this joy here, lacks one of the best pieces of his evidence for the joys of Heaven; and hath neglected or refused that earnest, by which God uses to bind his bargain, that true joy in this world shall flow into the joy of Heaven, as a river flows into the sea; this joy shall not be put out in death, and a new joy kindled in me in Heaven; but as my soul, as soon as it is out of my body, is in Heaven, and does not stay for the possession of Heaven, nor for the fruition of the sight of God, till it be ascended through air, and fire, and moon, and sun, and planets, and firmament, to that place which we conceive to be Heaven, but without the thousandth part of a minute's stop, as soon as it issues, is in a glorious light, which is Heaven (for all the way to Heaven is Heaven; and as those Angels, which came from Heaven hither, bring Heaven with them, and are in Heaven here, so that soul that goes to Heaven, meets Heaven here; and as those Angels do not divest Heaven by coming, so these souls invest Heaven, in their going). As my soul shall not go towards Heaven, but go by Heaven to Heaven, to the Heaven of Heavens, so the true joy of a good soul in this world is the very joy of Heaven; and we go thither, not that being without joy, we might have joy infused into us, but that as Christ says, "Our joy might be full," perfected, sealed with an everlastingness; for, as he promises, "That no man shall take our joy from us," so neither shall Death itself take it away, nor so much as interrupt it, or discontinue it, but as in the face of Death, when he lays hold upon me, and in the face of the Devil, when he attempts me, I shall see the face of God (for, everything shall be a glass, to reflect God upon me), so in the agonies of Death, in the anguish of that dissolution, in the sorrows of that valediction, in the irreversibleness of that transmigration, I shall have a joy, which shall no more evaporate, than my soul shall evaporate, a joy, that shall pass up, and put on a more glorious garment above, and be joy super-invested in glory. *Amen*

—1626

William Laud
1573 – 1645

Born in Reading, the son of a clothier, Laud entered St. John's College, Oxford in 1589 and remained there for more than two decades, as scholar, Fellow, and eventually College President (1611). His early career in the church was slowed by the hostility of George Abbot, the puritan Archbishop of Canterbury, and the suspicions of James I, who distrusted what he called Laud's "restless spirit." Laud eventually caught the attention of the Duke of Buckingham, with whose help he was made Bishop of St. David's, in Wales, in 1621. But it was the accession of Charles I that marked the beginning of Laud's rapid rise to national prominence: he was made Dean of the Chapel Royal (1626), Bishop of Bath and Wells (1626), Privy Councillor (1627), Bishop of London (1628), Chancellor of the University of Oxford (1629), and finally Archbishop of Canterbury (1633).

Laud and King Charles shared a strong belief in the need for uniformity of worship within the church, in the value and dignity of ceremony, and in the necessity of obedience to religious and political superiors. Laud's dislike of opposition and of religious debate mirrored the King's dislike of unruly and questioning parliaments. His Arminian or "high church" emphasis on ceremony and ritual in worship led to accusations that Laud was seeking to reintro-

duce Catholic practices into the English church. Some historians have argued that it was Laud's insistence on compulsory uniformity that divided into hostile camps a church that had previously tolerated a measure of diversity. Eventually, an increasingly radicalized puritan opposition blamed Laud for the "Bishops' wars" that followed the attempt to introduce a new service book in Scotland; he was impeached of high treason by Parliament in 1640, committed to the Tower in 1641, tried in 1644, and beheaded in January 1645.

The history of the following diary is sketched in the preface by Henry Wharton, the text's seventeenth-century editor. It was first published, with some deliberate inaccuracies, by Laud's political enemies in the 1640s. Wharton published a corrected version as an introduction to his edition of Laud's self-defence, *The History of the Troubles and Tryal of... William Laud* (1695). While not as detailed or personal (except for the records of his dreams) as the diaries kept by Samuel Pepys and John Evelyn, Laud's diary provides a capsule summary of major events from the 1620s to the 1640s by a person who was intimately involved in them. For a contemporary view of Laud, see Clarendon's "character" of the Archbishop in the selection from *The History of the Rebellion*.

⟡⟡⟡

The Diary of... William Laud
(selections)

THE PREFACE

That the reader may be satisfied how it came to pass, that an history wrote of, and by, a person of so great a character in this nation, and by him designed for the public, hath lain hid, and been suppressed for near fifty years; through whose hands it hath passed; and by what means, and by whose

labour it is at last published; he may be pleased to take the following account.[1]

The Most Reverend Archbishop, the author and subject of this history, was very exact and careful in keeping all papers, which concerned himself, or any affairs of Church and State, passing through his hands; not only kept a journal of his own actions, but from time to time took minutes of whatsoever

---

[1] *an history* referring to the autobiographical *History of the Troubles and Tryal of... William Laud* (1695), with which this *Diary* was published.

passed at Council Table, Star Chamber, High Commission Court,[1] etc.; digested all his papers in most exact order; wrote with his own hand on the back or top of every one, what it concerned, when it was received, when wrote or answered, etc.

This his enemies knew full well; and therefore, when after they had caused him to be impeached of High Treason, of endeavouring to introduce Popery and arbitrary government, and to be imprisoned upon the impeachment in the end of the year 1640, and had now in vain laboured for two years and an half, to find out evidence to prove this their accusation; but the more they sought, they found to their confusion, so much the greater evidence of the contrary: After they had in vain ransacked all papers left by the Archbishop in his study at Lambeth, and examined all his intimate friends and subaltern agents upon oath; when nothing did appear, they hoped to find somewhat against him, either in his private journal of his life, which they knew to be kept by him, or in those papers, which he had carried with him from Lambeth at his first commitment, in order to his future defence. Upon these hopes, they with great privacy framed an order, for the searching his chamber and pockets in the Tower, in May 1643, and committed the execution of it, to his inveterate enemy, William Prynne;[2] who thereupon took from the Archbishop twenty-one bundles of papers, which he had prepared for his defence; his Diary, his book of private devotions,

the Scotch Service-Book,[3] and directions accompanying it, &c. And although he then faithfully promised restitution of them within three or four days, yet never restored any more than three bundles; employed such against the Archbishop at his trial, as might seem prejudicial to his cause; suppressed those, which might be advantageous to him; published many, embezzled some; and kept the rest to the day of his death.

As soon as Prynne was possessed of the Archbishop's papers, he set himself with eager malice to make use of them to his defamation, and to prove the charge of Popery and abetting arbitrary government, by the publication of many of them. His first specimen in this kind was a pamphlet, which came out in August following, entitled *Rome's Masterpiece*, in five sheets in quarto, containing the papers and letters relating to the plot contrived by Papists against the Church and State then established in England, and discovered by Andreas ab Habernfeild.[4] But never did malice appear so gross and ridiculous together, as in this case. For from this plot, if there were any truth in it, it appeared that the life of the Archbishop was chiefly aim'd at by the plotters, as the grand obstacle of their design, and one who could by no arts be wrought to any connivance of them, much less concurrence with them. This pamphlet being, after the publication of it, carried to the Archbishop in the Tower, he made several marginal annotations on it, in answer to Prynne's falsifications and malicious calumnies intermixed therein. Which copy, coming afterwards into the hands of Dr. Baily, the Archbishop's

---

[1] That is, Laud took notes during the deliberations of the Privy Council (the governing body of the realm), and at proceedings at the courts of Star Chamber (associated with the maintenance of royal authority) and High Commission (an ecclesiastical court).

[2] *Prynne* A prolific controversialist, the Presbyterian William Prynne (1600–69) had spent much of the 1630s in prison (and had had his ears cut off) for writing pamphlets that attacked the church, particularly Laud and episcopacy, and the theatre, particularly court entertainments.

[3] *Scotch Service-Book* a revised liturgy that Laud and the King attempted to introduce in Scotland, with disastrous results, in 1637 (see the King's *Proclamation* against the Scots).

[4] Prynne, *Rome's Master-peece; or, the Grand Conspiracy of the Pope and his Jesuited Instruments to Extirpate the Protestant Religion* (1643). In 1640, Habernfeld brought English authorities in The Hague a fantastic story about an elaborate Catholic plot to promote a civil war.

executor,[1] was by him given to the learned anti-quary, Mr. Anthony Wood, and by him transmitted to me, in order to be placed among the other papers and memorials which are to follow this history, according to the Archbishop's own direction.

But Prynne's malice could not be abated by the shame of one miscarriage. In the next place, he bethought himself of publishing the Archbishop's Diary, as soon as his trial ended, wherein it had been often produced as evidence against him. This then he published in the beginning of September, 1644, in nine sheets in folio, with this title, *A Breviat of the Life of*, &c. (intending it, as he saith, for a prologue to the much desired history of his trial) but neither the entire, nor faithfully, as far as he did publish it; but altered, mangled, corrupted, and glossed in a most shameful manner; accompanied with desperate untruths, as the Archbishop complains in this history; and therefore addeth: "For this *Breviat* of his, if God lend me life and strength to end this [the history] first; I shall discover to the world, the base and malicious slanders, with which it is fraught." This the Archbishop wrote, when he despaired that ever his Diary should be recovered out of those vile hands, in which it then was; and be published faithfully and entirely, which would be the most effectual discovery of the baseness and malice of Prynne therein.

Yet notwithstanding so vile and corrupt an edition of it, all those who have wrote any thing of this excellent prelate, have been forced to make use of it; not being able to gain the sight of the original, nor perhaps so much as suspecting any such fraud in the edition of it. Particularly, it is much to be lamented, that Dr. Heylin, who wrote the *History* of the Archbishop's life with great care and elegance,[2] was forced, in most things, to borrow his account from this corrupted edition of his Diary, and hath thereby been led into many and great errors. Others also have, since him, taken up and divulged many false opinions concerning the Diary itself; as that it was wholly wrote in Latin by the Archbishop, that it was by himself entitled *A Breviat of his Life*, and that it was translated and published entire by Prynne.

The true and faithful publication of it, which I have made from the original, now in my hands, will not only supply the defect of what the Archbishop intended in the words before related, but never effected; but will also undeniably assert his innocence from those greater accusations formerly brought against him, and will farther clear him from many later aspersions of lesser moment....

HENRY WHARTON

. . . . . .

Anno 1624

January 25. It was Sunday. I was alone, and languishing with I know not what sadness. I was much concerned at the envy and undeserved hatred born to me by the Lord Keeper.[3] I took into my hands the Greek Testament; that I might read the portion of the day. I lighted upon the XIII Chapter to the Hebrews; wherein that of David, Psalm 56 occurred to me then grieving and fearing: *The Lord is my helper: I will not fear, what man can do unto me.* I thought an example was set to me; and who is not safe under that shield? Protect me O Lord my God.

. . . .

February 1. I stood by the most illustrious Prince Charles at dinner. He was then very merry; and talked occasionally of many things with his

---

[1] Dr. Richard Baylie, Laud's protégé and executor of his estate.

[2] Peter Heylyn, *Cyprianus Anglicus; or, the History of the Life and Death of ... William ... Lord Archbishop of Canterbury* (1668).

[3] John Williams (1582–1650), at the time Lord Keeper and Bishop of Lincoln, eventually Archbishop of York; Laud's temperamental opposite and life-long political rival. The two competed for the patronage of the Duke of Buckingham throughout the 1620s.

attendants. Among other things, he said, that if he were necessitated to take any particular profession of life, he could not be a lawyer; adding his reasons. *I cannot* (saith he) *defend a bad, nor yield in a good cause.* May you ever hold this resolution and succeed (most Serene Prince) in matters of greater moment, for ever prosperous.

.   .   .   .

Anno 1625

January 30. Sunday night, my dream of my Blessed Lord and Saviour Jesus Christ. One of the most comfortable passages that ever I had in my life.

.   .   .   .   .   .

March 27. Midlent Sunday, I preached at White-Hall. I ascended the pulpit, much troubled, and in a very melancholy moment, the report then spreading, that his Majesty King James, of most sacred memory to me, was dead. Being interrupted with the dolours of the Duke of Buckingham, I broke off my sermon in the middle. The King died at Theobalds, about three quarters of an hour past eleven in the forenoon. He breathed forth his blessed soul most religiously, and with great constancy of faith, and courage. That day, about five o'clock, Prince Charles was solemnly proclaimed King. God grant to him a prosperous and happy reign. The King fell sick, March 4 on Friday. The disease appeared to be a tertian ague. But I fear it was the gout, which by the wrong application of medicines, was driven from his feet to his inward vital parts.

April 1. I received letters from the Earl of Pembroke, Lord Chamberlain to the King, and therein a command from his Majesty King Charles, to preach a sermon before himself and the House of Peers in the session of Parliament, to be held on the 17 day of May next following.

April 3. I delivered into the Duke of Buckingham's hands, my short Annotations upon the Life and Death of the most august King James; which he had commanded me to put in writing.

April 5. I exhibited a schedule, in which were wrote the names of many churchmen, marked with the letters "O" and "P".[1] The Duke of Buckingham had commanded to digest their names in that method; that (as himself said) he might deliver them to King Charles.

.   .   .   .   .   .

May 1. The marriage was celebrated at Paris, between his Majesty King Charles, and the most illustrious Princess Henrietta Maria of France, daughter of Henry IV.[2]

May 7, Saturday. We celebrated the funeral of King James.

May 11. Early in the morning the Duke of Buckingham went towards the sea-side, to pass over into France to meet Queen Mary. I wrote letters to the Duke that day; which might follow after him. For he went in great haste.

May 17. The Parliament was put off till the last day of May.

May 18. I took a short journey with my brother to Hammersmith, that we might there see our common friends. It was Wednesday.

May 19. I sent letters the second time to the Duke of Buckingham, then staying for a while at Paris.

May 29. I gave a third letter into the hands of the Bishop of Durham, who was to attend the King; that he might deliver them to the Duke of Buckingham at his first landing.

May 30. I went to Chelsea, to wait upon the Duchess of Buckingham.

---

[1] for "orthodox" (meaning sympathetic to the high church or "Arminian" ceremonialism later associated with Laud) and "puritan."

[2] The two were married by proxy; the Queen arrived in England the following month.

May 31. The Parliament was a second time put off, till Monday the 13 of June. King Charles set forward toward Canterbury, to meet the Queen.

June 5, Whitsunday. In the morning, just as I was going to prayers, I received letters from France, from the most illustrious Duke of Buckingham.

June 6. I wrote an answer next morning. After I had finished my answer, the Right Reverend Lancelot Lord Bishop of Winchester and I went together to the country house which John Lord Bishop of Rochester hath by Bromley. We dined there; and returned in the evening.

June 8. I went to Chelsea, but returned with my labour lost.

June 12. It was Trinity Sunday, Queen Mary crossing the seas, landed upon our shore about seven o'clock in the evening. God grant, that she may be an evening and an happy star to our orb.

.   .   .   .

July 3, Sunday. In my sleep his Majesty King James appeared to me. I saw him only passing by swiftly. He was of a pleasant and serene countenance. In passing he saw me, beckoned to me, smiled, and was immediately withdrawn from my sight.

July 7. Richard Montague was brought into the Lower House of Parliament,[1] &c.

July 9. It pleased his Majesty King Charles, to intimate to the House of Commons that what had been there said and resolved, without consulting him, in Montague's cause, was not pleasing to him.

July 11. The Parliament was prorogued to Oxford, against the first day of August.

July 13. There having died in the former week at London 1222 persons, I went in to the country, to the house of my good friend Francis Windebank.

In going thither, Richard Montague met me by chance. I was the first, who certified him of the King's favour to him.

.   .   .   .

August 21, Sunday. I preached at Brecknock; where I stayed two days, very busy in performing some business. That night, in my sleep, it seemed to me, that the Duke of Buckingham came into bed to me; where he behaved himself with great kindness towards me, after that rest, wherewith wearied persons are wont to solace themselves. Many also seemed to me to enter the chamber, who saw this. Not long before, I dreamed that I saw the Duchess of Buckingham, that excellent Lady, at first very much perplexed about her husband, but afterwards cheerful, and rejoycing, that she was freed from the fear of abortion, so that in due time she might be again a mother.

August 24, Wednesday, and the Festival of St. Bartholomew. I came safely (thanks be to God) to my own house at Aberguilly.[2] Although my coach had been twice that day overturned between Aber-Markes and my house. The first time I was in it; but the latter time it was empty.

August 28, Sunday. I consecrated the Chapel or Oratory, which I had built at my own charge in my house, commonly called Aberguilly-House. I named it the Chapel of St. John Baptist, in grateful remembrance of St. John Baptist's College in Oxford, of which I had been first Fellow, and afterwards President. And this I had determined to do. But another thing intervened (of no ill omen as I hope) of which I had never thought. It was this. On Saturday, the evening immediately preceding the consecration, while I was intent at prayer, I know not how, it came strongly into my mind, that the day of the beheading of St. John Baptist was very near. When prayers were finished, I consulted the calendar. I found that day to fall upon Monday, to

---

[1] *Montague* Richard Montague (1577–1641) scandalized Parliament with publications that appeared to minimize the differences between the Church of England and Catholicism; he was examined before the Commons and placed in custody, but released by the King. He was later made Bishop of Chichester (1628) and Norwich (1638).

[2] Abergwili, in Wales; Laud at the time was Bishop of St. David's.

wit, the 29th of August, not upon Sunday. I could have wished, it had fallen upon that same day, when I consecrated the Chapel. However, I was pleased, that I should perform that solemn consecration at least on the eve of that Festival. For upon that day, his Majesty King James heard my cause about the election to the Presidentship of St. John's College in Oxford, for three hours together at least; and with great justice delivered me out of the hands of my powerful enemies.[1]

September 4, Sunday. The night following I was very much troubled in my dreams. My imagination ran altogether upon the Duke of Buckingham, his servants, and family. All seemed to be out of order: that the Duchess was ill, called for her maids, and took her bed. God grant better things.

. . . .

September 26, Sunday. That night I dreamed of the marriage of I know not whom at Oxford. All that were present, were clothed with flourishing green garments.

. . . .

Anno 1626

January 29. I understood what D.B. [Duke of Buckingham] had collected concerning the cause, book, and opinions of Richard Montague, and what R.C. [King Charles] had determined with himself therein. Methinks, I see a cloud arising, and threatening the Church of England. God of his mercy dissipate it.

January 31. The Bishops and other peers before nominated by the King to consult of the ceremonies of the coronation, that the ancient manner might be observed, by his Majesty's command went together to him. The King viewed all the regalia; put on St. Edward's tunics; commanded me to read the rubrics of direction. All being read, we carried back the regalia to the church of Westminster, and laid them up in their place.

February 2, Thursday and Candlemas day. His Majesty King Charles was crowned. I then officiated in the place of the Dean of Westminster. The King entered the Abby Church a little before ten o'clock; and it was past three, before he went out of it. It was a very bright sun-shining day. The solemnity being ended, in the great Hall at Westminster, when the King delivered into my hands the regalia, which are kept in the Abby Church of Westminster, he did (which had not before been done) deliver to me the sword called *Curtana*, and two others, which had been carried before the King that day, to be kept in the Church, together with the other regalia. I returned, and offered them solemnly at the altar in the name of the King, and laid them up with the rest. In so great a ceremony, and amidst an incredible concourse of people, nothing was lost, or broke, or disordered. The theatre was clear, and free for the King, the Peers, and the business in hand; and I heard some of the nobility saying to the King in their return, that they never had seen any solemnity, although much less, performed with so little noise, and so great order.

February 6, Monday. I preached before King Charles and the House of Peers, at the opening of the Parliament.

February 11, Saturday. At the desire of the Earl of Warwick, a conference was held concerning the cause of Richard Montague, in the Duke of Buckingham's house [between Dr. Morton and Dr. Preston on the one side, and Dr. White on the other].[2]

. . . .

May 8, Monday. At two o'clock in the afternoon, the House of Commons brought up to the

---

[1] Laud won the College Presidency in a contested election in 1611.

[2] The material in square brackets was supplied in a note by Henry Wharton; the debaters were Thomas Morton, then Bishop of Lichfield; John Preston, Master of Emmanuel College, Cambridge; and Francis White, Dean of Carlisle.

House of Peers a charge against the Duke of Buckingham, consisting of thirteen articles.[1]

May 11. King Charles came into the Parliament House, and made a short speech to the Lords, concerning preserving the honour of the nobility against the vile and malicious calumnies of those in the House of Commons, who had accused the Duke, &c.[2] They were eight, who in this matter chiefly appeared. The prologue, Sir Dudley Digges, the epilogue, John Elliot, were this day by the King's command committed to the Tower. They were both dismissed thence within few days.

. . . .

June 15, Thursday. After many debates and strugglings, private malice against the Duke of Buckingham prevailed, and stopped all business. Nothing was done; but the Parliament was dissolved.

. . . .

August 25, Friday. Two robin red-breasts flew together through the door into my study, as if one pursued the other. That sudden motion almost startled me. I was then preparing a sermon on Ephes. 4:30 and studying.

September 14. Thursday evening, the Duke of Buckingham willed me to form certain Instructions, partly political, partly ecclesiastical, in the cause of the King of Denmark, a little before brought into great straits by General Tilly, to be sent through all parishes.[3] Certain heads were delivered to me. He would have them made ready by Saturday following.

September 16, Saturday. I made them ready, and brought them at the appointed hour. I read them to the Duke. He brought me to the King. I being so commanded, read them again. Each of them approved them.

September 17, Sunday. They were read (having been left with the Duke) before the Lords of the Privy Council; and were (thanks be to God) approved by them all.

. . . .

September 21, Monday. About four o'clock in the morning, died Lancelot Andrewes, the most worthy Bishop of Winchester, the great light of the Christian world.

September 30, Saturday. The Duke of Buckingham signified to me the King's resolution, that I should succeed the Bishop of Winchester in the office of Dean of the Chapel-Royal.

October 2, Monday. The Duke related to me, what the King had farther resolved concerning me, in case the Archbishop of Canterbury should die, &c.

. . . .

Anno 1627

January 5, Epiphany-Eve, and Friday. In the night I dreamed that my mother, long since dead, stood by my bed, and drawing aside the clothes a little, looked pleasantly upon me; and that I was glad to see her with so merry an aspect. She then show'd to me a certain old man, long since deceased; whom, while alive, I both knew and loved. He seem'd to lie upon the ground; merry enough, but with a wrinkled countenance. His name was Grove. While I prepared to salute him, I awoke....

January 14, Sunday. Towards morning, I dreamed that the Bishop of Lincoln came,[4] I know not whither, with iron chains. But returning loosed

---

[1] For Buckingham, see the selection of "Poems on the Duke of Buckingham."

[2] This speech was written by Laud.

[3] An exercise in "tuning the pulpits." Having dissolved Parliament before it voted him the usual subsidies, Charles was forced to look for alternative sources of funds. These instructions encouraged public contributions to a loan, ostensibly to aid the King's (Protestant) uncle, Christian IV of Denmark, in his battle against the (Catholic) Holy Roman Emperor.

[4] *Bishop of Lincoln* John Williams, Laud's rival.

from them, leaped on horseback, went away; neither could I overtake him.

January 16, Tuesday. I dreamed that the King went out to hunt; and that when he was hungry, I brought him on the sudden into the house of my friend Francis Windebank. While he prepareth to eat, I, in the absence of others, presented the cup to him after the usual manner. I carried drink to him; but it pleased him not. I carried it again, but in a silver cup. Thereupon his Majesty said: You know, that I always drink out of glass. I go away again; and awoke.

January 17, Wednesday. I show my reasons to the King, why the papers of the late Bishop of Winchester, concerning Bishops, that they are *jure divino*,[1] should be printed; contrary to what the Bishop of Lincoln had pitifully, and to the great detriment of the Church of England, signified to the King; as the King himself had before related to me.

February 7, Ash-Wednesday. I preached at Court, at White-Hall.

February 9, Friday. The following night I dreamed, that I was troubled with the scurvy; and that on the sudden all my teeth became loose; that one of them especially in the lower jaw, I could scarce hold in with my finger, till I called out for help, &c.

. . . .

March 8. I came to London. The night following I dreamed, that I was reconciled to the Church of Rome. This troubled me much; and I wondered exceedingly, how it should happen. Nor was I aggrieved with myself, [only by reason of the errors of that Church, but also][2] upon account of the scandal, which from that my fall, would be cast upon many eminent and learned men in the Church of England. So being troubled at my dream, I said with myself, that I would go immediately, and, confessing my fault, would beg pardon of the Church of England. Going with this resolution, a certain Priest met me, and would have stopped me. But moved with indignation, I went on my way. And while I wearied myself with these troublesome thoughts, I awoke. Herein I felt such strong impressions ; that I could scarce believe it to be a dream.

. . . .

Anno 1628

June 1, Whitsunday. I preached at White-Hall.

June 11. My Lord Duke of Buckingham voted in the House of Commons to be the cause, or causes, of all grievances in the Kingdom.

June 12. I was complained of by the House of Commons for warranting Doctor Manwaring's sermons to the press.[3]

June 13. Dr. Manwaring answered for himself before the Lords; and the next day.

June 14, being Saturday, was censured. After his censure my cause was called to the report. And by God's goodness towards me, I was fully cleared in the House. The same day the House of Commons were making their Remonstrance to the King: one head was innovation of religion. Therein they named my Lord the Bishop of Winchester and myself. One in the House stood up, and said: Now we have named these persons, let us think of some causes why we did it. Sir Edward Coke answered, Have we not named my Lord of Buckingham without showing a cause, and may we not be as bold with them?

. . . .

---

[1] *jure divino*   the doctrine that episcopacy was by "divine right."

[2] These words are most maliciously omitted by Prynne [note by Wharton, referring to the material in square brackets].

[3] Roger Manwaring (1590–1653), at the time chaplain to the King; Laud had facilitated the publication of two sermons he made that argued the duty of subjects to submit to their superiors on issues of religion.

August 23, Saturday, St. Bartholomew's Eve. The Duke of Buckingham slain at Portsmouth by one Lieutenant Felton, about nine in the morning.

August 24. The news of his death came to Croydon; where it found myself and the bishops of Winchester, Ely, and Carlisle, at the consecration of Bishop Montague for Chichester, with my Lord's Grace.

.   .   .   .   .   .

October 20. I was forced to put on a truss for a rupture. I know not how occasioned, unless it were with swinging of a book for my exercise in private.

November 29. Felton was executed at Tyburn for killing the Duke; and afterwards his body was sent to be hanged in chains at Portsmouth. It was Saturday and St. Andrew's even; and he killed the Duke upon Saturday St. Bartholomew's even.

.   .   .   .   .   .

Anno 1629

January 26. The 240 Greek manuscripts were sent to London House. These I got my Lord of Pembroke to buy and give to Oxford.[1]

January 31, Saturday night. I lay in Court. I dreamed, that I put off my rochet,[2] all save one sleeve; and when I would have put it on again, I could not find it.

February 6. Sir Thomas Roe sent to London House 28 manuscripts in Greek, to have a catalogue drawn, and the books to be for Oxford.

March 2. The Parliament to be dissolved declared by proclamation, upon some disobedient passages to his Majesty that day in the House of Commons.

March 10. The Parliament dissolved, the King present. The Parliament, which was broken up this March 10, laboured my ruin; but, God be ever blessed for it, found nothing against me.

March 29. Two papers were found in the Dean of Paul's his yard before his house. The one was to this effect concerning myself: Laud, look to thy self; be assured thy life is sought. As thou art the fountain of all wickedness, repent thee of thy monstrous sins, before thou be taken out of the world, &c. And assure thy self, neither God nor the world can endure such a vile counsellor to live, or such a whisperer; or to this effect. The other was as bad as this, against the Lord Treasurer. Mr. Dean delivered both papers to the King that night. Lord, I am a grievous sinner; but I beseech thee, deliver my soul from them that hate me without a cause.

.   .   .   .   .   .

Anno 1630

May 29, Saturday. Prince Charles was born at St. James's. *Paulo ante horam primam post meridiem* [just before one o'clock in the afternoon], I was in the house 3 hours before, and had the honour and the happiness to see the Prince, before he was full one hour old.

June 27, Sunday. I had the honour, as Dean of the Chapel, my Lord's Grace of Canterbury being infirm, to christen Prince Charles at St. James's, *horâ ferè quintâ pomeridianâ* [at nearly five o'clock in the afternoon].

.   .   .   .   .   .

Anno 1633

August 4, Sunday. News came to court of the Lord Archbishop of Canterbury's death;[3] and the King resolved presently to give it me. Which he did

---

[1] The Baroccian collection of Greek manuscripts, which Laud persuaded the Chancellor of the University, the Earl of Pembroke, to purchase and present to the Bodleian library.

[2] *rochet* a white linen vestment worn by bishops (*OED* rochet[1] 2).

[3] George Abbot (1562–1633), whose puritan sympathies had made him a long-time opponent of Laud's.

August 6. That very morning, at Greenwich, there came one to me, seriously, and that avowed ability to perform it, and offered me to be a Cardinal: I went presently to the King, and acquainted him both with the thing and the person.

. . . .

August 14. A report brought to me, that I was poisoned.

August 17. I had a serious offer made me again to be a Cardinal: I was then from court, but so soon as I came thither (which was Wednesday August 21) I acquainted his Majesty with it. But my answer again was, that somewhat dwelt within me, which would not suffer that, till Rome were other than it is.

. . . .

September 19. I was translated to the Archbishopric of Canterbury. The Lord make me able, &c. The day before, *viz.* September 18, when I first went to Lambeth,[1] my coach, horses and men sunk to the bottom of the Thames in the ferry-boat, which was over-laden, but I praise God for it, I lost neither man, nor horse. A wet summer, and by it a casual harvest. The rainy weather continuing till November 14 which made a marvellous ill seed-time. There was barley abroad this year, within 30 miles of London, at the end of October.

November 13. Richard Boyer, who had formerly named himself Lodowick, was brought into the Star Chamber, for most grossly misusing me, and accusing me of no less than treason, &c. He had broken prison for felony, when he did this. His censure is upon record. And God forgive him.

About the beginning of this month the Lady Davis prophesied against me,[2] that I should very few days out-live the fifth of November.

. . . .

Anno 1634

January 1. The way to do the town of Reading good for their poor;[3] which may be compassed by God's blessing upon me, though my wealth be small. And I hope God will bless me in it, because it was his own motion in me. For this way never came into my thoughts (though I had much beaten them about it) till this night, as I was at my prayers. *Amen* Lord.

March 30, Palm-Sunday. I preached to the King at White-Hall.

May 13. I received the seals of my being chose Chancellor of the University of Dublin in Ireland. To which office I was chosen September 14, 1633. There were now, and somewhat before, great fractions in Court: And I doubt, many private ends followed to the prejudice of public service. Good Lord preserve me.

June 11. Mr. Prynne sent me a very libellous letter, about his censure in the Star Chamber for his *Histriomastix*,[4] and what I said at that censure; in which he hath many ways mistaken me, and spoken untruth of me.

June 16. I showed this letter to the King; and by his command sent it to Mr. Attorney Noye.

June 17. Mr. Attorney sent for Mr. Prynne to his chamber; showed him the letter, asked him whether it were his hand. Mr. Prynne said, he could not tell, unless he might read it. The letter being given into his hand, he tore it into small pieces, threw it out at the window, and said, that should never rise in judgement against him: Fearing, it seems, an *Ore tenus* for this.[5]

---

[1] *Lambeth* the palace of the Archbishops of Canterbury.

[2] Lady Eleanor Davies (d. 1652) would publish numerous works of mysticism and prophecy in the 1640s; one is included in this anthology.

[3] See number 16 in Laud's list of his projects at the end of this text.

[4] Prynne's *Histriomastix* (1632) attacked the theatre, and by implication the King and Queen for participating in court masques; Prynne was censured in Star Chamber in 1634.

[5] *Ore tenus* "by word of mouth" or oral pleading; here a form of legal action.

June 18. Mr. Attorney brought him for this into the Star-Chamber; where all this appear'd with shame enough to Mr. Prynne. I there forgave him, &c.

June 26. I received word from Oxford, that the Statutes were accepted and published, according to my letters, in the Convocation-House that week.[1]

. . . . . .

Anno 1635

September 29. The Earl of Arundel brought an old man out of Shropshire. He was this present Michaelmas-day showed to the King and the other Lords, for a man of 152 or 153 years of age.

October 26, Monday. This morning between four and five of the clock, lying at Hampton Court: I dreamed, that I was going out in haste, and that when I came into my outer chamber, there was my servant William Pennell in the same riding suit, which he had on that day sevennight at Hampton Court with me. Methoughts I wondered to see him (for I left him sick at home) and asked him, how he did, and what he made there. And that he answered me, he came to receive my blessing; and with that fell on his knees. That hereupon I laid my hand on his head, and prayed over him, and therewith awaked. When I was up, I told this to them of my chamber; and added, that I should find Pennell dead or dying. My coach came; and when I came home, I found him past sense, and giving up the ghost. So my prayers (as they had frequently before) commended him to God.

. . . . . .

Anno 1636

October 14, Friday night. I dreamed marvellously, that the King was offended with me, and would cast me off, and tell me no cause why.

Avertat Deus [may God prevent it]. For cause I have given none.

. . . . . .

Anno 1637

June 14. This day John Bastwick Dr. of Physick, Henry Burton Batch. of Divinity, and William Prynne Barrister at Law, were censured for their libels against the hierarchy of the Church, &c.[2]

June 16. The Speech I then spake in the Star-Chamber, was commanded by the King to be printed. And it came out June the 25.

June 26. This day, Monday, the Prince Elector and his brother Prince Rupert,[3] began their journey toward the sea side, to return for Holland.

June 30. Friday, the above named three Libellers lost their ears.

July 7. A note was brought to me of a short libel pasted on the cross in Cheapside: that the archwolf of Canterbury had his hand in persecuting the saints, and shedding the blood of the martyrs: Memento, for the last of June.

July 11. Dr. Williams Lord Bishop of Lincoln was censured in the Star Chamber for tampering, and corrupting of witnesses, in the King's cause.

. . . . . .

August 25. The same day at night, my Lord Mayor sent me another libel, hanged upon the standard in Cheapside. My speech in the Star-Chamber, set in a kind of pillory, &c.

August 29. Another short libel against me, in verse.

October 22. A great noise about the perverting of the Lady Newport: Speech of it at the Council: My free speech there to the King, concerning the

---

[1] See number 8 in Laud's list of his projects.

[2] Burton, Bastwick, and Prynne were all fined, punished, and imprisoned for publishing anti-episcopal works; many contemporaries considered them martyred heroes for their opposition to the Laudian church (see the entry for July 7 below).

[3] *Prince Elector…Prince Rupert* respectively, the King's brother-in-law and nephew.

increasing of the Roman party, the freedom at Denmark-house, the carriage of Mr. Walter Montague and Sir Toby Matthews. The Queen acquainted with all I said that very night, and highly displeased with me; and so continues.[1]

November 22. The extreme and unnatural hot winter weather began, and continued till December 8.

. . . .

Anno 1638

April 29. The tumults in Scotland, about the Service-Book offered to be brought in, began July 23, 1637, and continued increasing by fits, and hath now brought that Kingdom in danger. No question, but there is a great concurrence between them, and the Puritan party in England. A great aim there to destroy me in the King's opinion, &c.[2]

. . . .

October 26. A most extreme tempest upon the Thames. I was in it, going from the Star-Chamber home, between six and seven at night. I was never upon the water in the like storm. And was in great danger at my landing at Lambeth Bridge.

. . . .

Anno 1639

March 27, Wednesday, Coronation-day. King Charles took his journey northward, against the Scottish Covenanting rebels. God of his infinite mercy bless him with health and success.

. . . .

June 4, Whitsun-Tuesday. As I was going to do my duty to the Queen, an officer of the Lord Mayor's met me, and delivered to me two very seditious papers, the one to the Lord Mayor and aldermen, the other to excite the apprentices, &c. Both subscribed by John Lilburne,[3] a prisoner in the Fleet, sentenced in the Star-Chamber, &c.

June 5. I delivered both these to the Lords of the Council.

June 15 & 17, Saturday and Monday. The peace concluded between the King and the Scottish rebels.[4] God make it safe and honourable to the King and Kingdom.

June 28. I sent the remainder of my manuscripts to Oxford, being in number 576. And about an hundred of them were Hebrew, Arabic, and Persian. I had formerly sent them above 700 volumes.

. . . .

Anno 1640

January 24. At night I dreamed, that my father (who died 46 years since) came to me; and, to my thinking, he was as well and as cheerful, as ever I saw him. He asked me, what I did here? And after some speech, I asked him, how long he would stay with me? He answered, he would stay, till he had me away with him. I am not moved with dreams; yet I thought fit to remember this.

. . . .

May 9. A paper posted upon the Old-Exchange, animating apprentices to sack my house upon the Monday following, May 11, early.

May 11, Monday night. At midnight, my house at Lambeth was beset with 500 of these rascal routers. I had notice, and strengthened the house as

---

[1] This entry refers to the conversion to Catholicism of Anne, Countess of Newport. Mountjoy Blount, Earl of Newport, asked Laud for help in punishing those responsible for encouraging his wife, a group rumoured to include the Catholic converts Montague and Matthews; Laud's efforts in this case led to a quarrel with the Catholic Queen.

[2] For more detail on the "tumults in Scotland," see Charles I's *Proclamation* against the Scots (1639) and *Information from the Scottish Nation* (1640).

[3] *John Lilburne* political radical, a leader of the Leveller party.

[4] *The peace concluded* The Pacification of Berwick (1639) humbled the English and ended the first Bishops' war, but proved a temporary respite.

well I could; and God be thanked, I had no harm, they continued there full two hours: Since I have fortified my house as well as I can; and hope all may be safe. But yet libels are continually set up in all places of note in the city. My deliverance was great; God make me thankful for it.

May 21. One of the chief being taken, was condemned at Southwark, and hanged and quartered on Saturday morning following, May 23. But before this, May 15, some of these mutinous people came in the day time, and brake the White-Lyon prison; and let loose their fellows, both out of that prison, and the King's-Bench, and the other prisoners also out of the White-Lyon.

.   .   .   .   .   .

August 20. His Majesty took his journey towards the North in haste, upon information that the Scots were entered the Monday before into England, and meant to be at Newcastle by Saturday: The Scots entered August 20.

August 22. A vile libel brought me, found in Covent-Garden; animating the apprentices and soldiers to fall upon me in the King's absence.

September 21. I received a letter from John Rockel, a man both by name and person unknown to me. He was among the Scots, as he travelled through the Bishoprick of Durham he heard them inveigh and rail at me exceedingly, and that they hoped shortly to see me, as the Duke was, slain by one least suspected. His letter was to advise me to look to my self.

September 24. A great Council of the Lords were called by the King to York, to consider what way was best to be taken to get out the Scots; and this day the meeting began at York, and continued till October 28.

October 22. The High Commission sitting at St. Paul's, because of the troubles of the times: very near 2000 Brownists made a tumult at the end of the Court, tore down all the benches in the consistory; and cried out, they would have no Bishop, nor no High Commission.[1]

October 27, Tuesday, Simon and Jude's Eve. I went into my upper study, to see some manuscripts, which I was sending to Oxford. In that study hung my picture, taken by the life; and coming in, I found it fallen down upon the face, lying on the floor, the string being broken, by which it was hanged against the wall. I am almost every day threatened with my ruin in Parliament. God grant this be no omen.

.   .   .   .   .   .

November 11. Thomas Viscount Wentworth, Earl of Strafford, accused to the Lords by the House of Commons, for High Treason, and restrained to the Usher of the House.[2]

November 25. He was sent to the Tower.

December 2. A great debate in the House, that no bishop should be so much as of the Committee for Preparatory Examinations in this cause, as accounted *causa sanguinis* [a blood case]; put off till the next day.

December 3. The debate declined.

December 4. The King gave way, that his Council should be examined upon oath in the Earl of Strafford's case. I was examined this day.

December 16. The canons condemned in the House of Commons, as being against the King's prerogative, the fundamental laws of the realm, the liberty and propriety of the subject, and containing divers other things tending to sedition, and of dangerous consequence. Upon this I was made the author of them, and a committee put upon me to enquire into all my actions, and to prepare a charge.

---

[1] *Brownists* technically, Separatists who followed the teachings of Robert Browne (ca. 1550–1633), but used here as a general term for radicalized groups opposed to episcopacy.

[2] The King's most formidable minister, Wentworth (1593–1641) was Lord Deputy of Ireland and a close friend of Laud's, with whom he shared an unswerving loyalty to the crown and a ruthlessness toward opponents.

The same morning, in the Upper House, I was named as an incendiary by the Scottish commissioners; and a complaint promised to be drawn up tomorrow.

December 18. I was accused by the House of Commons for High Treason, without any particular charge laid against me; which they said, should be prepared in convenient time. Mr. Denzill Hollis was the man that brought up the message to the Lords. Soon after, the charge was brought into the Upper House by the Scottish commissioners, tending to prove me an incendiary. I was presently committed to the Gentleman Usher; but was permitted to go in his company to my house at Lambeth, for a book or two to read in, and such papers, as pertained to my defence against the Scots. I stayed at Lambeth till the evening, to avoid the gazing of the people. I went to Evening Prayer in my chapel. The psalms of the day (93 and 94), and Chapter 50 of Esai, gave me great comfort. God make me worthy of it, and fit to receive it. As I went to my barge, hundreds of my poor neighbours stood there, and prayed for my safety, and return to my house. For which I bless God and them.

December 21. I was fined £500 in the Parliament House, and Sir John Lambe and Sir Henry Martin £250 a piece, for keeping Sir Robert Howard close prisoner in the case of the escape of the Lady Viscountess Purbecke out of the Gate-House; which Lady he kept avowedly, and had children by her. In such a case, say the imprisonment were more than the law allow; what may be done for honour and religion sake? This was not a fine to the King, but damage to the party.

December 23. The Lords ordered me to pay the money presently; which was done.

Anno 1641

January 21. A Parliament man of good note, and interest with diverse Lords, sent me word, that by reason of my patient and moderate carriage since my commitment, four Earls of great power in the Upper House of the Lords were not now so sharp against me as at first. And that now they were resolved only to sequester me from the King's Council, and to put me from my Archbishopric. So I see, what justice I may expect; since here is a resolution taken, not only before my answer, but before my charge was brought up against me.

February 14, Saturday, A.R. And this, if I live, and continue Archbishop of Canterbury, till after Michaelmas-day come twelve-month, *Anno* 1642. God bless me in this.[1]

February 26. This day I had been full ten weeks in restraint at Mr. Maxwell's house. And this day, being St. Augustine's day, my charge was brought up from the House of Commons to the Lords, by Sir Henry Vane the Younger. It consisted of fourteen articles. These generals they craved time to prove in particular. The copy of this general charge is among my papers. I spake something to it. And the copy of that also is among my papers. I had favour from the Lords not to go to the Tower till the Monday following.

March 1. I went in Mr. Maxwell's coach to the Tower. No noise, till I came into Cheapside. But from thence to the Tower, I was followed and railed at by the apprentices and the rabble, in great numbers to the very Tower gates, where I left them; and I thank God, he made me patient.

.   .   .   .   .   .

March 15. A Committee for Religion settled in the Upper House of Parliament. Ten Earls, ten Bishops, ten Barons. So the lay votes shall be double to the clergy. This committee will meddle with doctrines as well as ceremonies; and will call some divines to them to consider of the business. As appears by a letter hereto annexed, sent by the Lord Bishop of Lincoln, to some divines to attend this

---

[1] The meaning of this entry is uncertain.

service. Upon the whole matter, I believe this Committee will prove the National Synod of England, to the great dishonour of this Church. And what else may follow upon it, God knoweth.

March 22. The Earl of Strafford's trial began in Westminster Hall; and it continued till the end of April, taking in the variation of the House of Commons, who after a long hearing drew a Bill of Attainder against him.[1]

.   .   .   .

May 1. The King came into the Upper House; and there declared before both Houses, how diligently he had hearkened to all the proceedings with the Earl of Strafford; and found that his fault, whatever it was, could not amount to High Treason: That if it went by Bill it must pass by him; and that he could not with his conscience find him guilty, nor would wrong his conscience so far. But advised them to proceed by way of misdemeanor; and he would concur with them. The same day, after the King was gone, a letter was read in the Upper House from the Scots; in which, they did earnestly desire to be gone. It was moved for a present conference with the House of Commons about it. The debate about it was very short; yet the Commons were risen beforehand.

May 12. The Earl of Strafford beheaded upon Tower Hill.

June 23. I acquainted the King by my Lord of London, that I would resign my Chancellorship of Oxford, and why.

June 25. I sent down my resignation of the Chancellorship of Oxford, to be published in Convocation.

July 1. This was done; and the Earl of Pembroke chosen Chancellor by joint consent.

August 10. The King went post into Scotland, the Parliament sitting, and the armies not yet dissolved.

September 23. Mr. Adam Torles, my ancient, loving and faithful servant, then my steward, after he had served me full forty-two years, died, to my great loss and grief.

October 23. The Lords in Parliament sequestered my jurisdiction to my inferior officers; and ordered, that I should give no benefice, without acquainting them first, to whom I would give it; that so they might approve. This order was sent to me on Tuesday, November 2, in the afternoon.

November 1. News came to the Parliament of the troubles in Ireland,[2] the King being then in Scotland, where there were troubles enough also.

November 25. The King at his return from Scotland, was sumptuously entertained in London; and great joy on all hands. God prosper it.

December 30. The Archbishop of York, and eleven Bishops more, sent to the Tower for High Treason, for delivering a petition and a protestation into the House, that this was not a free Parliament, since they could not come to vote there, as they are bound, without danger of their lives.

Anno 1642

January 4. His Majesty went into the House of Commons; and demanded the persons of Mr. Denzill Hollis, Sir Arthur Haslerig, Mr. John Pym, Mr. John Hampden, and Mr. William Stroude; whom his attorney had the day before, together with the Lord Kimbolton, accused of High Treason, upon seven articles. They had information; and were not then in the House: they came in after, and

---

[1] A Bill of Attainder marked the extinction of the legal rights (to inherit or pass on land, for example) of a person convicted of a felony or sentenced to death.

[2] *troubles in Ireland* the Irish rebellion, which began with the massacre of thousands of English settlers.

great stir was made about this breach of the privileges of Parliament.[1]

February 6. Voted in the Lord's House, that the Bishops shall have no votes there in Parliament. The Commons had passed that Bill before. Great ringing for joy, and bonfires in some parishes.

February 11. The Queen went from Greenwich toward Dover, to go into Holland with her daughter the Princess Mary, who was lately married to the Prince of Orange his son. But the true cause was, the present discontents here. The King accompanied her to the sea.

February 14. His Majesty's message to both Houses, printed, by which he puts all into their hands; God bless us.

. . . . . .

February 20. There came a tall man to me, under the name of Mr. Hunt. He professed he was unknown to me; but came (he said) to do me service in a great particular; and prefaced it, that he was not set on by any statesman, or any of the Parliament. So he drew a paper out of his pocket, and showed me four articles drawn against me to the Parliament, all touching my near conversation with priests, and by my endeavours by them to subvert religion in England. He told me, the articles were not yet put into the House: they were subscribed by one Willoughby, who (he said) was a priest, but now come from them. I asked him, what service it was he could do me. He said, he looked for no advantage to himself. I conceived hereupon, this was a piece of villainy: And bade him tell Willoughby, he was a villain; and bid him put his articles into the Parliament, when he will. So I went presently into my inner chamber; and told Mr. Edward Hyde, and Mr. Richard Cobb, what had befallen me. But after I was sorry at my heart, that my indignation at this base villainy made me so

hasty, to send Hunt away; and that I had not desired Mr. Lieutenant to seize on him, till he brought forth this Willoughby.

. . . . . .

March 6, Sunday. After sermon, as I was walking up and down my chamber before dinner, without any slip or treading awry, the sinew of my right leg gave a great crack, and brake asunder in the same place where I had broken it before.

It was two months, before I could go out of my chamber. On Sunday (May 15) I made shift between my man and my staff to go to church. There one Mr. Joslin preached, with vehemency becoming Bedlam, with treason sufficient to hang him in any other state, and with such particular abuse to me, that women and boys stood up in church, to see how I could bear it. I humbly thank God for my patience.

All along things grew higher between the King and the Parliament. God send a good issue.

May 29. Four ships came into the river, with part of the ammunition from Hull.

August 22, Monday. The King set up his Standard at Nottingham.[2]

. . . . . .

October 15. Resolved upon the question, that the fines, rents, and profits of Archbishops, Bishops, Deans and Chapters, and of such notorious delinquents who have taken up arms against the Parliament, or have been active in the Commission of Array,[3] shall be sequestered for the use and service of the Commonwealth.

. . . . . .

Anno 1643

January 26. The Bill passed the Lord's House for abolishing episcopacy, &c.

. . . . . .

---

[1] The King's unsuccessful attempt to arrest the "Five Members" served only to unite the Lords and Commons against him, and proved one of the precipitating events of the Civil War.

[2] The official beginning of the Civil War.

[3] *Commission of Array* the muster of soldiers to fight for the King.

March 2, Thursday, St. Cedd's day. The Lord Brooke shot in the left eye, and killed in the place, at Lichfield, going to give the onset upon the close of the church; he having ever been fierce against Bishops and Cathedrals: His beaver up,[1] and armed to the knees; so that a musket at that distance could have done him but little harm. Thus was his eye put out, who about two years since said, he hoped to live to see at St. Paul's not one stone left upon another.

.　　.　　.　　.　　.　　.

March 24. One Mr. Foord told me (he is a Suffolk man) that there was a plot to send me and Bishop Wren as delinquents to New England, within fourteen days. And that Wells, a minister that came thence, offered wagers of it. The meeting was at Mr. Barks, a merchant's house in Friday Street, being this Foord's son-in-law. I never saw Mr. Foord before.

.　　.　　.　　.　　.　　.

April 25. It was moved in the House of Commons to send me to New England. But it was rejected. The plot was laid by Peters, Wells, and others.

May 1. My chapel windows at Lambeth defaced, and the steps torn up.

May 2. The cross in Cheapside taken down.

May 9. All my goods seized upon, books and all. The seizers were Captain Guest, Layton, and Dickins. The same day an order for further restraint of me, not to go out of it without my keeper. This order was brought to me May 10.

May 16. An order of both houses for the disposing of my benefices, &c. void, or to be void. This order was brought to me Wednesday, May 17 at night. Methinks, I see a cloud rising over me, about Chartham business:[2] There having been a rumour twice, that I shall be removed to a prison lodging.

May 23. I sent my petition for maintenance. This day the Queen was voted a traitor in the Commons House.

.　　.　　.　　.　　.　　.

H[enry]W[harton]: Thus far the Archbishop had proceeded in his Diary; when it was violently seized, and taken out of his pockets by William Prynne, on the last day of May 1643. The seizure of it is related by Prynne himself (*Breviat of the Arch-Bishop's Life*, p. 28) and gloried in, as a most worthy action. But the barbarous manner of it is more largely described by the Archbishop himself in the following history. After the book came into his enemy's hands, it was frequently urged against him as evidence at his trial; and when the trial was near finished, Prynne caused it to be printed, and published it in the beginning of September 1644 but corrupted, and in part only; of which see before in the Preface. The Archbishop had almost filled up his paper book (where he wrote this Diary) when it was taken from him. But in the last leaf of it are found certain projects wrote with his own hand (at what time, or in what year, is uncertain) which I have subjoined.

Things which I have projected to do, if God bless me in them.

I. [Blotted out.]

II. To build at St. John's in Oxford, where I was bred up, for the good and safety of that College. Done.

---

[1] *beaver* the lower portion of the face-guard of a helmet (*OED* beaver²).

[2] *Chartham* a rectory in Laud's gift; he had received conflicting requests from the King and the House of Lords (among others) as to a recipient.

III. To overthrow the Feoffment, dangerous both to Church and State, going under the specious pretence of buying in impropriations.[1] Done.

IV. To procure King Charles to give all the impropriations, yet remaining in the Crown, within the Realm of Ireland, to that poor Church. Done, and settled there.

V. To set upon the repair of St. Paul's Church in London. Done.

VI. To collect and perfect the broken, crossing,[2] and imperfect statutes of the University of Oxford; which had lain in a confused heap some hundred of years. Done.

VII. [Blotted out.]

VIII. To settle the statutes of all the Cathedral Churches of the new foundations; whose statutes are imperfect, and not confirmed. Done for Canterbury.

IX. To annex for ever some settled *commendams*, and those, if it may be, *sine curâ*, to all the small bishoprics.[3] Done for Bristol, Peterborough, St. Asaph, Chester, Oxford.

X. To find a way to increase the stipends of poor vicars.

XI. To see the tithes of London settled, between the clergy and the city.

XII. To set up a Greek press in London and Oxford, for printing of the library manuscripts; and to get both letters and matrices. Done for London.

XIII. To settle eighty pounds a year for ever, out of Dr. Fryar's Lands, (after the death of Dr. John Fryar the son) upon the fabric of St. Paul's, to the repair till that be finished, and to keep it in good state after.

XIV. To procure a large charter for Oxford, to confirm their ancient privileges, and obtain new for them, as large as those of Cambridge, which they had gotten since Hen. 8 which Oxford had not. Done.

XV. To open the great square at Oxford between St. Marys and the Schools, Brasen-nose and All-Souls.

XVI. To settle an hospital of land in Reading, of one hundred pounds a year, in a new way. I have acquainted Mr. Barnard, the Vicar of Croydon, with my project. He is to call upon my executors to do it; if the surplusage of my goods (after debts and legacies paid) come to three thousand pounds. Done to the value of two hundred pounds *per annum*.

XVII. To erect an Arabic Lecture in Oxford, at least for my lifetime, my estate not being able for more: That this may lead the way, &c. Done. I have now settled it for ever. The lecture began to be read August 10, 1636.

---

[1] Impropriation was the transference (after the English Reformation) to a lay patron of the right to collect tithes from a parish. The result was that in many parishes, only a small percentage of the tithe income went to the clerical incumbent. Laud planned to transfer or buy up impropriations whenever possible to return the full income to the church. The feoffees were a group of puritan laymen and clerics who purchased impropriations in order to place sympathetic clerics in the livings they thereby controlled.

[2] *crossing* contradictory.

[3] *commendams* benefices (with income attached) which a bishop could hold along with his bishopric, preferably *sine curâ*, "without cure," that is, without duties. Laud was trying to increase the income of the smaller bishoprics.

XVIII. The impropriation of the vicarage of Cuddesden to the Bishop of Oxford, finally sentenced Wednesday April 19, 1637. And so the House built by the now Bishop of Oxford Dr. John Bancroft, settled for ever to that Bishopric. Done.

XIX. A book in vellum fair written, containing the records which are in the Tower, and concern the clergy. This book I got done at my own charge, and have left it in my study at Lambeth for posterity, June 10, 1637. *Ab Anno* 20 *Ed.* 1 *ad Annum* 24 *Ed.* 4. [from the 20th year of the reign of Edward I to the 24th year of the reign of Edward IV]. Done.

XX. A new charter for the College near Dublin to be procured of his Majesty; and a body of new statutes made, to rectify that government. Done.

XXI. A charter for the Town of Reading, and a mortmain of &c.[1] Done.

XXII. If I live to see the repair of St. Paul's near an end, to move his Majesty for the like grant from the High Commission, for the buying in of impropriations, as I have now for St. Paul's. And then I hope to buy in two a year at least.

XXIII. I have procured for St. John Baptist's College in Oxford the perpetual inheritance and patronage of &c.
—(1624–43)

---

[1] *mortmain* a legal condition which would give the corporation inalienable control over (here unspecified) lands (*OED*).

Elizabeth Clinton, Countess of Lincoln
ca. 1574 – ca. 1630

Elizabeth Clinton, Countess of Lincoln, was the daughter of Sir Henry Knyvet, of Charlton, Wiltshire. She married Thomas Clinton who was to become the third Earl of Lincoln and the eleventh Baron Clinton. During their marriage, Elizabeth Clinton bore eighteen children, many of whom did not survive infancy. In 1618, Thomas Clinton died, and his son Theophilus succeeded him as Earl. Anne Bradstreet's father, Thomas Dudley, arranged Theophilus's marriage to Bridget Fiennes.

It is to her daughter-in-law Bridget that the Countess dedicated her advice manual on the virtue of breast-feeding, *The Countess of Lincoln's Nursery* (1622). Clinton's advice book should be read in light of a broad cultural dialogue on motherhood in early modern culture. Reformers and humanists alike championed breast-feeding by the natural mother on functional, medical and ethical grounds. However, it is clear from Clinton's treatise that it was the general practice of the wealthy to employ wet-nurses. While there is no record of her death, it is believed that Elizabeth Clinton died in 1630.

❧❧❧

The Countess of Lincoln's Nursery
(excerpts)

Because it hath pleased God to bless me with many children, and so caused me to observe many things falling out to mothers, and to their children; I thought good to open my mind concerning a special matter belonging to all child-bearing women, seriously to consider of: and to manifest my mind the better, even to write of this matter, so far as God shall please to direct me; in sum, the matter I mean, is the duty of nursing due by mothers to their own children.

In setting down whereof, I will first show that every woman ought to nurse her own child; and secondly, I will endeavour to answer such objections as are used to be cast out against this duty to disgrace the same.

The first point is easily performed. For it is the express ordinance of God that mothers should nurse their own children, and being his ordinance they are bound to it in conscience. This should stop the mouths of all repliers, for *God is most wise*, and therefore must needs know what is fittest and best

for us to do:[1] and to prevent all foolish fears, or shifts, we are given to understand that he is also *all sufficient*, and therefore infinitely able to bless his own ordinance, and to afford us means in ourselves (as continual experience confirmeth) toward the observance thereof.[2]

If this (as it ought) be granted, then how venturous are those women that dare venture to do otherwise, and so to refuse, and by refusing to despise that order, which the most wise and almighty God hath appointed, and instead thereof to choose their own pleasures? Oh what peace can there be to these women's consciences, unless through the darkness of their understanding they judge it no disobedience?

And then they will drive me to prove that this nursing, and nourishing of their own children in their own bosoms is God's ordinance; they are very wilful, or very ignorant, if they make a question of it. For it is proved sufficiently to be their duty, both by God's word, and also by his works.

---

[1] *God is most wise* "Isaiah 31.2" (original marginalia).

[2] *shifts* evasions (OED shift *sb* III.4a); *all sufficient* "Gen. 17.1" (original marginalia).

By his word it is proved, first by examples, namely the example of Eve. For who suckled her sons Cain, Abel, Seth, etc. but herself? Which she did not only of mere necessity, because yet no other woman was created; but especially because she was their mother, and so saw it was her duty: and because she had a true natural affection, which moved her to do it gladly. Next the example of Sarah the wife of Abraham; for she both gave her son Isaac suck, as doing the duty commanded of God: and also took great comfort, and delight therein, as in a duty well pleasing to her self;[1] whence she spake of it, as of an action worthy to be named in her holy rejoicing. Now if Sarah, so great a princess, did nurse her own child, why should any of us neglect to do the like, except (which God forbid) we think scorn to follow her, whose daughters it is our glory to be, and which we be only upon this condition, that we imitate her well doing.[2] Let us look therefore to our worthy pattern, noting withal, that she put herself to this work when she was very old, and so might the better have excused herself, than we younger women can: being also more able to hire, and keep a nurse, than any of us.[3] But why is she not followed by most in the practise of this duty? Even because they want her virtue, and piety.[4] This want is the common hindrance to this point of the woman's obedience; for this want makes them want love to God's precepts, want love to his doctrine, and like stepmothers, want due love to their own children.

. . . .

And so much for proof of this office, and duty to be God's ordinance, by his own word according to the argument of examples: I hope I shall likewise prove it by the same word from plain precepts.[5] First from that precept, which willeth the younger women to marry, and to bear children, that is, not only to bear them in the womb, and to bring them forth; but also to bear them on their knee, in their arms, and at their breasts:[6] for this bearing a little before is called nourishing, and bringing up: and to enforce it the better upon women's consciences, it is numbered as the first of the good works, for which godly women should be well reported of. And well it may be the first, because if holy ministers, or other Christians do hear of a good woman to be brought to bed, and her child to be living; their first question usually is, whether she herself give it suck, yea, or no? If the answer be she doth, then they commend her: if the answer be she doth not, then they are sorry for her.

And thus I come to a second precept. I pray you, who that judges aright; doth not hold the suckling of her own child the part of a true mother, of an honest mother, of a just mother, of a sincere mother, of a mother worthy of love, of a mother deserving good report, of a virtuous mother, of a mother winning praise for it? All this is assented to by any of good understanding. Therefore this is also a precept, as for other duties, so for this of mothers to their children; which saith, whatsoever things are true, whatsoever things are honest, whatsoever things are just, whatsoever things are pure, whatsoever things be worthy of love, whatsoever things be of good report, if there be any virtue, if there be any praise, think on these things, these things do and the God of peace shall be with you.[7]

---

[1] *Isaac suck* "Gen. 21.7" (original marginalia).

[2] *that we imitate her well doing* "I Pet. 3.6" (original marginalia).

[3] *she was very old* In Genesis 18:11, Sarah is described as "old" and "stricken in age" when she is informed that she will bear a child. She was also post-menopausal ("and it ceased to be with Sarah after the manner of women"). While her precise age is not given, we are told that "Abraham was an hundred years old, when his son Isaac was born unto him" (Genesis 21:5); *nurse* wet-nurse.

[4] *want* lack (*OED* want *v* 2a).

[5] *plain precepts* "I Tim. 5.14" (original marginalia).

[6] *but also to bear...at their breasts* "ver. 10" (original marginalia); that is, I Timothy 5:10.

[7] *whatsoever things are true...be with you* "Philip. 4.8" (original marginalia).

So far for my promise, to prove by the word of God, that it is his ordinance that women should nurse their own children: now I will endeavour to prove it by his works: First by his works of judgment; if it were not his ordinance for mothers to give their children suck, it were no judgment to bereave them of their milk, but it is specified to be a great judgment to bereave them hereof, and to give them dry breasts, therefore it is to be gathered, even from hence, that it is his ordinance, since to deprive them of means to do it, is a punishment of them.[1]

I add to this the work that God worketh in the very nature of mothers, which proveth also that he hath ordained that they should nurse their own children: for by his secret operation, the mother's affection is so knit by nature's law to her tender babe, as she finds no power to deny to suckle it, no not when she is in hazard to lose her own life, by attending on it; for in such a case it is not said, let the mother fly, and leave her infant to the peril, as if she were dispensed with: but only it is said woe to her, as if she were to be pitied, that for nature to her child, she must be unnatural to herself; now if any then being even at liberty, and in peace, with all plenty, shall deny to give suck to their own children, they go against nature and show that God hath not done so much for them as to work any good, no not in their nature, but left them more savage than the dragons, and as cruel to their little ones as the ostriches.[2]

.   .   .   .

Oh consider, how comes our milk? Is it not by the direct providence of God? Why provides he it, but for the child? The mothers then that refuse to nurse their own children, do they not despise God's providence? Do they not deny God's will? Do they not as it were say, *I see, O God, by the means thou hast put into me, that thou wouldst have me nurse the child thou hast given me, but I will not do so much for thee.* Oh impious, and impudent unthankfulness; yea monstrous unnaturalness, both to their own natural fruit born so near their breasts, and fed in their own wombs, and yet may not be suffered to suck their own milk.

And this unthankfulness, and unnaturalness is oftener the sin of the higher, and the richer sort, than of the meaner, and poorer, except some nice and proud idle dames, who will imitate their betters, till they make their poor husbands beggars. And this is one hurt which the better rank do by their ill example; egg, and embolden the lower ones to follow them to their loss: were it not better for us greater persons to keep God's ordinance, and to show the meaner their duty in our good example? I am sure we have more helps to perform it, and have fewer probable reasons to allege against it, than women that live by hard labour, and painful toil. If such mothers as refuse this office of love, and of nature to their children, should hereafter be refused, despised, and neglected of those their children, were they not justly requited according to their own unkind dealing?

.   .   .   .

And so I come to the last part of my promise; which is to answer objections made by divers against this duty of mothers to their children.[3]

.   .   .   .

....It is objected, that it is troublesome; that it is noisome to one's clothes; that it makes one look old, &c.[4] All such reasons are uncomely, and unchristian to be objected: and therefore unworthy to be answered; they argue unmotherly affection,

---

[1] *But it is specified...dry breasts* "Give them, O LORD: what wilt thou give? give them a miscarrying womb and dry breasts" (Hosea 9:14).

[2] ll. 100–105 "Lam. 7.3" (original marginalia); actually Lamentations 4:3.

[3] *divers* sundry (people) (*OED* divers *a* 3).

[4] *noisome* harmful, injurious, ill-smelling (*OED* noisome *a* 1, 2).

idleness, desire to have liberty to gad from home, pride, foolish fineness, lust, wantonness, and the like evils. Ask Sarah, Hannah, the blessed Virgin, and any modest loving mother, what trouble they accounted it to give their little ones suck: behold most nursing mothers, and they be as clean and sweet in their clothes, and carry their age, and hold their beauty, as well as those that suckle not: and most likely are they so to do; because keeping God's ordinance, they are sure of God's blessing: and it hath been observed in some women that they grew more beautiful, and better favoured, by very nursing their own children.

But there are some women that object fear: saying that they are so weak, and so tender, that they are afraid to venture to give their children suck, lest they endanger their health thereby. Of these, I demand, why then they did venture to marry, and so to bear children; and if they say they could not choose, and that they thought not that marriage would impair their health: I answer, that for the same reasons they should set themselves to nurse their own children, because they should not choose but do what God would have them to do: and they should believe that this work will be for their health also, seeing it is ordinary with the Lord to give good stomach, health, and strength to almost all mothers that take this pains with their children.[1]

. . . .

Now if any reading these few lines return against me, that it may be I myself have given my own children suck: and therefore am bolder, and more busy to meddle in urging this point, to the end to insult over, and to make them to be blamed that have not done it. I answer, that whether I have, or have not performed this my bounden duty, I will not deny to tell my own practice. I know and acknowledge that I should have done it, and having

not done it, it was not for want of will in myself, but partly I was overruled by another's authority, and partly deceived by some's ill counsel, and partly I had not so well considered of my duty in this motherly office, as since I did, when it was too late for me to put it in execution.[2] Wherefore being pricked in heart for my undutifulness, this way I study to redeem my peace; first by repentance towards God, humbly and often craving his pardon for this my offence: secondly by studying how to show double love to my children to make them amends for neglect of this part of love to them, when they should have hung on my breasts, and have been nourished in mine own bosom: thirdly by doing my endeavour to prevent many Christian mothers from sinning in the same kind, against our most loving and gracious God.

. . . .

Do you submit yourselves, to the pain and trouble of this ordinance of God, trust not other women, whom wages hires to do it, better than yourselves, whom God, and nature ties to do it. I have found by grievous experience, such dissembling in nurses, pretending sufficiency of milk, when indeed they had too much scarcity, pretending willingness, towardness, wakefulness, when indeed they have been most wilful, most froward, and most slothful, as I fear the death of one or two of my little babes came by the default of their nurses. Of all those which I had for eighteen children, I had but two which were thoroughly willing, and careful: divers have had their children miscarry in the nurse's hands, and are such mothers (if it were by the nurse's carelessness) guiltless? I know not how they should, since they will shut them out

---

[1] *good stomach* spirit, courage (*OED* stomach *sb* 8).

[2] *overruled by another's authority* Clinton may be alluding to her husband. As King notes, husbands often discouraged lactation because it had a known contraceptive effect and because "sexual intercourse was both forbidden and feared during lactation because it was universally thought that the milk would become corrupted by intercourse or a new conception and kill the child" (*Women of the Renaissance*, 1991:14).

of the arms of nature, and leave them to the will of a stranger; yea to one that will seem to estrange herself from her own child, to give suck to the nurse-child. This she may fain to do upon a covetous composition, but she frets at it in her mind, if she have any natural affection.

Therefore be no longer at the trouble, and at the care to hire others to do your own work: be not so unnatural to thrust away your own children: be not so hardy as to venture a tender babe to a less tender heart: be not accessory to that disorder of causing a poorer woman to banish her own infant, for the entertaining of a richer woman's child, as it were, bidding her unlove her own to love yours. We have followed Eve in transgression, let us follow her in obedience. When God laid the sorrows of conception, of breeding, of bringing forth, and of bringing up her children upon her, and so upon us in her loins, did she reply any word against? Not a word; so I pray you all mine own daughters, and others that are still childbearing reply not against the duty of suckling them, when God has sent you them.

Indeed I see some, if the weather be wet, or cold; if the way be foul; if the church be far off, I see they are so coy, so nice, so lukewarm, they will not take pains for their own souls: alas, no marvel if these will not be at trouble, and pain to nourish their children's bodies, but fear God, be diligent to serve him; approve all his ordinances; seek to please him; account it no trouble, or pain to do anything that hath the promise of his blessing: and then you will, no doubt, do this good, laudable, natural, loving duty to your children. If yet you be not satisfied, inquire not of such as refuse to do this: consult not with your own conceit: advise not with flatterers: but ask counsel of sincere, and faithful preachers. If you be satisfied; then take this with you, to make you do it cheerfully. Think always, that having the child at your breast, and having it in your arms, you have God's blessing there. For children are God's blessings. Think again how your babe crying for your breast, sucking heartily the milk out of it, and growing by it, is the Lord's own instruction, every hour, and every day, that you are suckling it, instructing you to show that you are his *new born babes*, by your earnest desire after his word; and the sincere doctrine thereof, and by your daily growing in grace and goodness thereby, so shall you reap pleasure, and profit.[1] Again, you may consider, that when your child is at your breast, it is a fit occasion to move your heart to pray for a blessing upon that work; and to give thanks for your child, and for ability and freedom unto that, which many a mother would have done and could not; who have tried and ventured their health, and taken much pains, and yet have not obtained their desire. But they that are fitted every way for this commendable act, have certainly great cause to be thankful: and I much desire that God may have glory and praise for every good work, and you much comfort, that do seek to honour God in all things. *Amen*
—1622

---

[1] *new born babes* "As newborn babes, desire the sincere milk of the word, that ye may grow thereby: If so be ye have tasted that the Lord is gracious" (I Peter 2:2–3).

Robert Burton

1577 – 1640

"I have been brought up a student in the most flourishing college of Europe," writes Burton of himself in *The Anatomy*; "for thirty years I have continued…a scholar." This is an accurate biographical summary. Burton was born in Lindley, Leicestershire, and educated at Nuneaton and Sutton Coldfield schools; he entered Brasenose College, Oxford in 1593, and transferred to Christ Church, Oxford (his "most flourishing college of Europe") in 1599. He proceeded to MA in 1605 and took the Bachelor of Divinity degree in 1614. Burton then stayed at Christ Church, as tutor and librarian, for the remainder of his life. He was given several ecclesiastical benefices, but did not perform any duties in these parishes.

Burton had a hand in a now lost pastoral play, and his Latin comedy *Philosophaster* was performed at his college. But after *The Anatomy of Melancholy* was published in 1621, he continued rewriting it for the rest of his life, enlarging it to almost half a million words in six successive editions through to 1651 (the changes in the final edition were based on an annotated copy Burton left at his death). Ostensibly a medical treatise, *The Anatomy of Melancholy* is a learned, affectionately satiric meditation on human learning and endeavour: the pseudonym he chose to publish under, Democritus Junior, hints at the kind of text that follows (his namesake Democritus was known as "the laughing philosopher"). Burton was an omnivorous reader, and he builds his argument on a foundation of citations from a remarkably wide range of authorities; only some are identified in the following selections. He also uses a great deal of Latin, most of which he either translates or paraphrases within his text. Translations are supplied within square brackets for any Latin Burton left without an explanatory gloss; most of these translations are from the edition of the *Anatomy* edited by A. R. Shilleto (London, 1893).

భారత

The Anatomy of Melancholy
(excerpts)

DEMOCRITUS JUNIOR
TO THE READER

Gentle Reader, I presume thou wilt be very inquisitive to know what antic or personate actor this is, that so insolently intrudes upon this common theatre, to the world's view, arrogating another man's name, whence he is, why he doth it, and what he hath to say? Although, as he [Seneca] said, *Primum si noluero, non respondebo, quis coacturus est?* I am a free man born, and may choose whether I will tell, who can compel me? If I be urged I will as readily reply as that Egyptian in Plutarch, when a curious fellow would needs know what he had in his basket, *Quum vides velatam, quid inquiris in rem absconditam?* It was therefore covered, because he should not know what was in it. Seek not after that which is hid, if the contents please thee, and be for thy use, suppose the Man in the Moon, or whom thou wilt to be the author; I would not willingly be known. Yet in some sort to give thee satisfaction, which is more than I need, I will show a reason, both of this usurped name, title, and subject. And first of the name of Democritus; lest any man by reason of it should be deceived, expecting a pasquil,[1] a satire, some ridiculous treatise (as I myself should have done), some prodigious tenet, or paradox of the earth's motion, of

---

[1] *pasquil* a libel or satire, named after a statue in Rome on which abusive verses were posted.

infinite worlds *in infinito vacuo, ex fortuitâ ato-morum collisione,* in an infinite waste, so caused by an accidental collision of motes in the sun, all which Democritus held, Epicurus and their Master Leucippus of old maintained, and are lately revived by Copernicus, Brunus, and some others. Besides it hath been always an ordinary custom, as Gellius observes, for later writers and impostors to broach many absurd and insolent fictions, under the name of so noble a philosopher as Democritus, to get themselves credit, and by that means the more to be respected, as artificers usually do, *Novo qui marmori ascribunt Praxitelem suo* [who put Praxiteles' name on their new marble statue]. 'Tis not so with me.

> *Non hic Centauros, non Gorgonas, Harpyasque*
> *Invenies, hominem pagina nostra sapit.*
> No centaurs here, or gorgons look to find,
> My subject is of Man, and humane kind.

Thou thy self art the subject of my discourse.

> *Quicquid agunt homines, votum, timor, ira,*
> *   voluptas,*
> *Gaudia, discursus, nostri farrago libelli.*
> What e're men do, vows, fears, in ire, in sport,
> Joys, wanderings, are the sum of my report.

My intent is no otherwise to use his name, than *Mercurius Gallobelgicus, Mercurius Britannicus,* use the name of Mercury,[1] *Democritus Christianus,* &c. Although there be some other circumstances, for which I have masked my self under this visard, and some peculiar respects, which I cannot so well express, until I have set down a brief character of this our Democritus, what he was, with an epitome of his life.

Democritus, as he is described by Hippocrates & Laertius, was a little wearish old man,[2] very melancholy by nature, averse from company in his latter days, and much given to solitariness, a famous philosopher in his age, *coævus* with Socrates,[3] wholly addicted to his studies at the last, and to a private life, writ many excellent works. A great divine, according to the divinity of those times, an expert physician, a politician, an excellent mathematician, as Diacosmus, and the rest of his works do witness. He was much delighted with the studies of husbandry, saith Columella, and often I find him cited by Constantinus and others treating of that subject. He knew the natures, differences of all beasts, plants, fishes, birds, and as some say, could understand the tunes and voices of them. In a word he was *omnifariàm doctus,* a general scholar, a great student; and to the intent he might better contemplate, I find it related by some, that he put out his eyes, and was in his old age voluntarily blind, yet saw more than all Greece besides, and writ of every subject, *Nihil in toto opificio naturæ, de quo non scripsit.* A man of an excellent wit, profound conceit; and to attain knowledge the better in his younger years he travelled to Egypt and Athens, to confer with learned men, admired of some, despised of others. After a wandering life he settled at Abdera a town in Thrace, and was sent for thither to be their lawmaker, recorder or town clerk, as some will, or as others, he was there bred and born. Howsoever it was, there he lived at last in a garden in the suburbs, wholly betaking himself to his studies, and a private life. Saving that sometimes he would walk down to the haven,[4] and laugh heartily at such variety of ridiculous objects, which there he saw. Such a one was Democritus.

---

[1] Burton cites the titles of contemporary newsbooks, which adopted these names because they, like Mercury, were messengers, delivering news of latest events.

[2] *wearish* sickly in health or appearance (*OED* wearish 2).

[3] *coævus* coeval, contemporary with. Socrates lived ca. 470–ca. 399 B.C.E.; Democritus, ca. 460–370 B.C.E.

[4] *haven* harbour.

But in the meantime, how doth this concern me, or upon what reference do I usurp his habit? I confess indeed that to compare myself unto him for ought I have yet said, were both impudency and arrogancy. I do not presume to make any parallel, *Antistat mihi millibus trecentis, parvus sum, nullus sum, altum nec spiro, nec spero* [He excels me in 300,000 ways, I am an insignificant person, a nobody, I have neither high aims nor hopes]. Yet thus much I will say of myself, and that I hope without all suspicion of pride, or self-conceit, I have lived a silent, sedentary, solitary, private life, *mihi & musis* [to myself and letters], in the University as long almost as Xenocrates in Athens, *ad senectam ferè* [to old age almost], to learn wisdom as he did, penned up most part in my study. For I have been brought up a student in the most flourishing college of Europe,[1] *augustissimo collegio*, and can brag with Jovius, almost, *in eâ luce domicilii Vacicani, totius orbis celeberrimi, per 37 annos multa opportunaque didici*; for 30 years I have continued (having the use of as good libraries as ever he had) a scholar, and would be therefore loath, either by living as a drone, to be an unprofitable or unworthy member of so learned and noble a society, or to write that which should be any way dishonourable to such a royal and ample foundation. Something I have done, though by my profession a divine, yet *turbine raptus ingenii*, as he [Scaliger] said, out of a running wit, an unconstant, unsettled mind, I had a great desire (not able to attain to a superficial skill in any) to have some smattering in all, to be *aliquis in omnibus, nullus in singulis* [something in everything, no authority in anything], which Plato commends, out of him Lipsius approves and furthers, as fit to be imprinted in all curious wits, not be a slave of one science, or dwell altogether in one subject, as most do, but to rove abroad, *centum puer artium*, to have an oar in every man's boat, to taste of every dish,

and sip of every cup, which saith Montaigne, was well performed by Aristotle and his learned countryman Adrian Turnebus. This roving humor (though not with like success) I have ever had, and like a ranging spaniel, that barks at every bird he sees, leaving his game, I have followed all, saving that which I should, and may justly complain, and truly, *qui ubique est, nusquam est* [he who is everywhere is nowhere], which Gesner did in modesty, that I have read many books, but to little purpose, for want of good method, I have confusedly tumbled over divers authors in our libraries, with small profit, for want of art, order, memory, judgement. I never travelled but in map or card,[2] in which mine unconfined thoughts have freely expatiated, as having ever been especially delighted with the study of cosmography. Saturn was Lord of my geniture, culminating, &c. and Mars principal significator of manners, in partial conjunction with mine ascendent; both fortunate in their houses, &c. I am not poor, I am nor rich; *nihil est, nihil deest*, I have little, I want nothing: all my treasure is in Minerva's tower.[3] Greater preferment as I could never get, so am I not in debt for it, I have a competency (*Laus Deo* [God be praised]) from my noble and munificent patrons, though I live still a collegiate student, as Democritus in his garden, and lead a monastic life, *ipse mihi Theatrum* [a theatre to myself], sequestered from those tumults and troubles of the world, *Et tanquam in speculâ positus* (as he [Heinsius] said) in some high place above you all, like Stoicus Sapiens, *omnia sæcula, præterita presentiaque videns, uno velut intuitu* [seeing all ages, past and present, as at one glance], I hear and see what is done abroad, how others run, ride, turmoil, & macerate themselves in court and country,[4] far from

---

[2] *card* chart.

[3] Minerva was the Roman goddess of the arts and professions.

[4] *macerate* to cause the body to waste away, especially through fasting; more generally, to fret, vex or worry (*OED* macerate *v* 2, 3).

those wrangling law suits, *aulæ vanitatem, fori ambitionem, ridere mecum soleo*: I laugh at all, only secure, lest my suit go amiss, my ships perish, corn and cattle miscarry, trade decay, I have no wife nor children, good or bad to provide for. A mere spectator of other men's fortunes and adventures, and how they act their parts, which me thinks are diversely presented unto me, as from a common theatre or scene. I hear new news every day, and those ordinary rumors of war, plagues, fires, inundations, thefts, murders, massacres, meteors, comets, spectrums, prodigies, apparitions, of towns taken, cities besieged in France, Germany, Turkey, Persia, Poland, &c. daily musters and preparations, and such like, which these tempestuous times afford, battles fought, so many men slain, monomachies,[1] shipwrecks, piracies, and sea-fights, peace, leagues, stratagems, and fresh alarums. A vast confusion of vows, wishes, actions, edicts, petitions, lawsuits, pleas, laws, proclamations, complaints, grievances, are daily brought to our ears. New books every day, pamphlets, currantoes,[2] stories, whole catalogues of volumes of all sorts, new paradoxes, opinions, schisms, heresies, controversies in philosophy, religion, &c. Now come tidings of weddings, maskings, mummeries,[3] entertainments, jubilees, embassies, tilts and tournaments, trophies, triumphs, revels, sports, plays: Then again, as in a new shifted scene, treasons, cheating tricks, robberies, enormous villainies in all kinds, funerals, burials, death of princes, new discoveries, expeditions; now comical, then tragical matters. Today we hear of new lords and officers created, tomorrow of some great men deposed, and then again of fresh honours conferred; one is let loose, another imprisoned; one purchaseth, another breaketh: he thrives, his neighbour turns bankrupt; now plenty, then again dearth and famine; one runs, another rides, wrangles, laughs, weeps, &c. Thus I daily hear, and suchlike, both private, and public news, amidst the gallantry and misery of the world; jollity, pride, perplexities and cares, simplicity and villainy; subtlety, knavery, candor and integrity, mutually mixed and offering themselves, I rub on *privus privatus* [in a strictly private life], as I have still lived, so I now continue, *statu quo priùs*, left to a solitary life, and mine own domestic discontents: Saving that sometimes, *ne quid mentiar* [not to tell a lie], as Diogenes went into the city, and Democritus to the haven to see fashions, I did for my recreation now and then walk abroad, look into the world, and could not choose but make some little observation, *non tam sagax observator, ac simplex recitator* [not so sagacious an observer as a simple narrator], not as they did to scoff or laugh at all, but with a mixed passion.

> *Bilem sæpè, jocum vestri movêre tumultus.*
> [Oft have your passions raised my rage or mirth.]

I did sometime laugh and scoff with Lucian, and satirically tax with Menippus, lament with Heraclitus, sometimes again I was *petulanti splene cachinno* [a laugher with a petulant spleen], and then again, *urere bilis jecur*, I was much moved to see that abuse which I could not amend. In which passion howsoever I may sympathise with him or them, 'tis for no such respect I shroud myself under his name, but either in an unknown habit, to assume a little more liberty and freedom of speech, or if you will needs know, for that reason and only respect, which Hippocrates relates at large in his Epistle to Damagetus, wherein he doth express, how coming to visit him one day, he found Democritus in his garden at Abdera, in the suburbs, under a shady bower, with a book on his knees, busy at his study, sometimes writing, sometime walking. The subject of his book was melancholy and madness, about

---

[1] *monomachies* duels or combats between two people (*OED*).

[2] *currantoes* also corantos; short pamphlets containing current news (*OED* coranto[2]).

[3] *mummeries* traditional masked mime shows; also a pejorative term for ceremonies thought ridiculous or hypocritical.

him lay the carcasses of many several beasts, newly by him cut up and anatomized, not that he did contemn God's creatures, as he told Hippocrates, but to find out the seat of this *atra bilis* or melancholy, whence it proceeds, and how it was engendered in men's bodies, to the intent he might better cure it in himself, by his writings and observations, teach others how to prevent and avoid it. Which good intent of his, Hippocrates highly commended: Democritus Junior is therefore bold to imitate, and because he left it imperfect, and it is now lost, *quasi succenturiator Democriti* [as a substitute for Democritus], to revive again, prosecute and finish in this treatise.

You have had a reason of the name, if the title and inscription offend your gravity, were it a sufficient justification to accuse others, I could produce many sober treatises, even sermons themselves, which in their fronts carry more fantastical names. Howsoever it is a kind of policy in these days, to prefix a fantastical title to a book which is to be sold: For as larks come down to a day-net, many vain readers will tarry and stand gazing like silly passengers, at an antic picture in a painter's shop, that will not look at a judicious piece. And indeed, as Scaliger observes, nothing more invites a reader than an argument unlooked for, unthought of, and sells better than a scurrile pamphlet, *tum maximè cùm novitas excitat palatum* [especially when its novelty whets the palate]. Many men, saith Gellius, are very conceited in their inscriptions, and able (as Pliny quotes out of Seneca) to make him loiter by the way, that went in haste to fetch a midwife for his daughter, now ready to lie down. For my part I have honourable precedents for this which I have done:[1] I will cite one for all, Anthony Zara Pap. Episc. his Anatomy of Wit, in four sections, members, subsections, &c. to be read in our libraries.

---

[1] Anatomy of Popery, Anatomy of Immortality, Angelus Scalas, Anatomy of Antimony, etc. [Burton's note].

If any man except against the matter or manner of treating of this my subject, and will demand a reason of it, I can allege more than one, I write of melancholy, by being busy to avoid melancholy. There is no greater cause of melancholy than idleness, "no better cure than business," as Rhasis holds: and howbeit, *stultus labor est ineptiarum*, to be busied in toys is to small purpose, yet hear that divine Seneca, better *aliud agere quàm nihil*, better do to no end than nothing. I writ therefore, and busied myself in this playing labor, *otiosâque diligentiâ ut vitarem torporem feriandi* [that I might avoid the torpor of laziness], with Vectius in Macrobius, *atque otium in utile verterem negotium* [and turn my leisure to useful purposes].

> ———— *Simul & jucunda & idonea dicere vitæ,*
> *Lectorem delectando simul atque monendo.*
> [At once to say both useful things and pleasant so as to please the reader, and instruct.]

To this end I write, like them, saith Lucian, "that recite to trees, and declaim to pillars for want of auditors": as Paulus Ægineta ingeniously confesseth, "not that anything was unknown or omitted, but to exercise myself," which course if some took, I think it would be good for their bodies, and much better for their souls, or peradventure as others do for fame, to show myself (*Scire tuum nihil est, nisi te scire hoc sciat alter*). I might be of Thucydides' opinion, "to know a thing and not express it, is all one as if he knew it not." When I first took this task in hand, and *quod ait ille, impellente Genio negotium suscepi* [and, as he says, undertook the work, my genius impelling me], this I aimed at; *vel ut lenirem animum scribendo*, to ease my mind by writing, for I had *gravidum cor, fœtum caput*, a kind of impostume in my head, which I was very desirous to be unladen of, and could imagine no fitter evacuation than this. Besides I might not well refrain, for *ubi dolor, ibi digitus*, one must needs scratch where it itcheth. I was not a little offended with this malady, shall I say my Mistress Melancholy, my *Ægeria*,[1] or my *malus Genius* [evil genius], and for that cause as he that is stung with a scorpion, I would expel *clavum clavo*, comfort one sorrow with another, idleness with idleness, *ut ex viperâ Theriacum*, make an antidote out of that which was the prime cause of my disease. Or as he did, of whom Felix Plater speaks, that thought he had some of Aristophanes' frogs in his belly, still crying *Brecec'ekex, coax, coax, oop, oop, oop*, and for that cause studied physic seven years, and travelled over most part of Europe to ease himself: To do myself good I turned over such physicians as our libraries would afford, or my private friends impart, and have taken this pains. And why not? Cardan professeth he writ his book *De Consolatione* after his son's death, to comfort himself,[2] so did Tully write of the same subject with like intent, after his daughter's departure, if it be his at least, or some impostor's put out in his name, which Lipsius probably suspects. Concerning myself, I can peradventure affirm with Marius in Salust, "That which others hear or read of, I felt and practised myself, they get their knowledge by books, I mine by melancholizing," *experto crede* ROBERTO [believe Robert, who speaks from experience].[3] Something I can speak out of experience *ærumnabilis experientia me docuit* [painful experience has taught me], and with her in the poet, *Haud ignara mali miseris succurrere disco* [It is my acquaintance with evil that teaches me to help the miserable]. I would help others out of a fellow-feeling, and as

that virtuous lady did of old, being a leper herself, bestow all her portion to build an hospital for lepers, I will spend my time and knowledge, which are my greatest fortunes, for the common good of all.

Yea but you will infer, that this is *actum agere*, an unnecessary work, *cramben bis coctam apponere*, the same again and again in other words: To what purpose? "Nothing is omitted that may well be said," so thought Lucian in the like theme. How many excellent physicians have written just volumes and elaborate tracts of this subject? No news here, that which I have is stolen from others, *Dicitque mihi mea pagina fur es* [and my page says to me, you are a thief]. If that severe doom of Synesius be true, "It is a greater offence, to steal dead men's labours, than their clothes," what shall become of most writers? I hold up my hand at the bar amongst others, and am guilty of felony in this kind, *habes confitentem reum*, I am content to be pressed with the rest. 'Tis most true, *tenet insanabile multos scribendi cacoëthes* [many are possessed by an incurable itch to write], and "there is no end of writing of books,"[4] as the Wise-man found of old, in this scribbling age, especially wherein "the number of books is without number" (as a worthy man saith), presses be oppressed, and out of an itching humor, that every man hath to show himself, desirous of fame and honour (*scribimus indocti doctique*—[we write, learned and unlearned]) he will write no matter what, and scrape together it boots not whence. Bewitched with this desire of fame, *etiam mediis in morbis*, to the disparagement of their health, and scarce able to hold a pen, they must say something, have it out, "and get themselves a name," saith Scaliger, "though it be to the downfall and ruin of many others." To be counted writers, *scriptores ut salutentur*, to be thought and held Polymaths and Polyhistors, *apud imperitum vulgus*

---

[1] *Ægeria* tutelary divinity; a patroness and advisor.

[2] *Cardan* Girolamo Cardano, a sixteenth-century Italian mathematician, physician, and natural philosopher who wrote numerous books; Burton frequently cites his work.

[3] *believe Robert* a hint by Burton as to his identity, which he reveals in an epilogue to the first edition (not reprinted in any subsequent issue, though much of the material this epilogue contains was transferred to the prefatory "Democritus to the Reader").

[4] Ecclesiastes 12:12.

ob ventosæ nomen artis, to get a paper-kingdom: *nulla spe quæstus sed amplâ famæ* [from no hope of gain but great hope of fame], in this precipitate, ambitious age, *nunc ut est sæculum, inter immaturam eruditionem ambitiosum & præceps*, ('tis Scaliger's censure) and they that are scarce auditors, *vix auditores*, must be masters and teachers, before they be capable and fit hearers. They will rush into all learning, *togatam, armatam*, divine, humane authors, rake over all indexes and pamphlets for notes, as our merchants do strange havens for traffic, write great tomes, *Cum non sint revera doctiores, sed loquaciores*, when as they are not thereby better scholars, but greater praters. They commonly pretend public good, but as Gesner observes, 'tis pride and vanity that eggs them on, no news or ought worthy of note but the same in other terms. *Ne feriarentur fortasse typographi, vel ideo scribendum est aliquid ut se vixisse testentur* [they turn authors lest peradventure the printers should have a holiday, or they must write something to prove they have lived]. As apothecaries we make new mixtures every day, pour out of one vessel into another, and as those old Romans robbed all the cities of the world, to set out their bad sited Rome, we skim off the cream of other men's wits, pick the choice flowers of their tiled gardens to set out our own sterile plots. *Castrant alios ut libros suos per se graciles alieno adipe suffarciant* (so Jovius inveighs). They lard their lean books with the fat of other works. *Ineruditi fures, &c* [unskilful thieves]. A fault that every writer finds, as I do now, and yet faulty themselves, *Trium literarum homines*, all thieves, they pilfer out of old writers to stuff up their new comments, scrape Ennius's dung-hills, and out of Democritus' pit, as I have done. By which means it comes to pass, that not only libraries and shops are full of our putrid papers, but every close-stool and jakes, *Scribunt carmina quæ legunt cacantes*; they serve to put under pies, to lap spice in, and keep roast meat from burning. With us in France, saith Scaliger, "every man hath liberty to write, but few ability, heretofore learning was graced by judicious scholars, but now noble sciences are vilified by base and illiterate scribblers," that either write for vain-glory, need, to get money, or as parasites to flatter and collogue with some great men, they put out *burras, quisqualiasque ineptiasque* [trifles, rubbish, and trash]. "Amongst so many thousand authors you shall scarce find one by reading of whom you shall be any whit better, but rather much worse," *quibus inficitur potius, quam perficitur*, by which he is rather infected than anyway perfected.

> ——— *Qui talia legit,*
> *Quid didicit tandem, quid scit nisi somnia, nugas?*
> [What has anyone who reads such works learned, what does he know but dreams and trifling things?]

So that oftentimes it falls out (which Callimachus taxed of old) a great book is a great mischief. Cardan finds fault with Frenchmen and Germans, for their scribbling to no purpose, *non inquit ab edendo deterreo, modo novum aliquid inveniant*, he doth not bar them to write, so that it be some new invention of their own; but we weave the same web still, twist the same rope again and again, or if it be a new invention, 'tis but some bauble or toy, which idle fellows write, for as idle fellows to read, and who so cannot invent? "He must have a barren wit, that in this scribbling age can forge nothing." "Princes show their armies, rich men vaunt their buildings, soldiers their manhood, and scholars vent their toys," they must read, they must hear whether they will or no.

> *Et quodcunque semel chartis illeverit, omnes*
> *Gestiet à furno redeuntes scire lacuque,*
> *Et pueros & anus———*
> What once is said and writ, all men must know,
> Old wives and children as they come and go.

"What a company of poets hath this year brought out," as Pliny complains to Sossius Sinesius; "This April every day some or other have recited." What a catalogue of new books all this year, all this age (I say) have our Frankfurt marts,[1] our domestic marts brought out? Twice a year, *Proferunt se nova ingenia & ostentant*, we stretch our wits out and set them to sale, *magno conatu nihil agimus* [with mighty effort we attain nothing]. So that which Gesner much desires, if a speedy reformation be not had, by some prince's edicts and grave supervisors, to restrain this liberty, it will run on *in infinitum. Quis tam avidus librorum helluo* [what a glut of books!], Who can read them? As already, we shall have a vast chaos and confusion of books, we are oppressed with them, our eyes ache with reading, our fingers with turning. For my part I am one of the number, *nos numerus sumus*, I do not deny it, I have only this of Macrobius to say for myself, *Omne meum, nihil meum*, 'tis all mine and none mine. As a good housewife out of divers fleeces weaves one piece of cloth, a bee gathers wax and honey out of many flowers, and makes a new bundle of all,

Floriferis ut apes in saltibus omnia libant,

I have laboriously collected this *cento* out of diverse writers,[2] and that *sine injuriâ*, I have wronged no authors, but given every man his own,[3] which Hierom so much commends in Nepotian, he stole not whole verses, pages, tracts, as some do nowadays, concealing their authors' names, but still said this was Cyprian's, that Lactantius, that Hilarius, so said Minutius Felix, so Victorinus, thus far Arnobius: I cite and quote mine authors (which howso-

ever some illiterate scribblers accompt pedantical, as a cloak of ignorance, and opposite to their affected fine style, I must and will use), *sumpsi, non surripui* [I have borrowed, not stolen], and what Varro lib. 6 *De re rust.* speaks of bees, *minimè maleficæ nullius opus vellicantes faciunt deterius* [that they are by no means malicious, because they injure nothing they extract honey from], I can say of myself, whom have I injured? The matter is theirs most part, and yet mine, *apparet unde sumptum sit* (which Seneca approves) *aliud tamen quàm unde sumptum sit apparet* [whence it is taken appears, yet it appears as something different from what it is taken from], which nature doth with the aliment of our bodies, incorporate, digest, assimilate, I do *conquoquere quod hausi*, dispose of what I take. I make them pay tribute, to set out this my *Maceronicon*,[4] the method only is mine own, I must usurp that of Wecker *è Terentio, nihil dictum quod non dictum priùs, methodus sola artificem ostendit*, we can say nothing but what hath been said, the composition and method is ours only, and shows a scholar. Oribasius, Ætius, Avicenna, have all out of Galen, but to their own method, *diverso stylo, non diversa fide*, our poets steal from Homer, he spews, saith Ælian, they lick it up. Divines use Austin's words verbatim still, and our story-dressers do as much, he that comes last is commonly best,

—— *donec quid grandius ætas*
Postera, sorsque ferat melior. ——
[Until a later age and a happier lot produce something more truly grand]

Though there were many giants of old in physic and philosophy, yet I say with Didacus Stella, "A dwarf standing on the shoulders of a giant may see farther than a giant himself"; I may likely add, alter, and see farther than my predecessors; and it is no greater

---

[1] The annual book fair ("mart" or market) in Frankfurt was the largest in Europe.

[2] *cento* a composition formed by joining scraps from other authors (*OED* cento 2); originally, any patchwork material.

[3] In the original editions, Burton provided the names of the authors he cites in marginal notes.

[4] *Maceronicon* a jumble or medley, particularly used of works which consistently introduce words from other languages (especially Latin).

prejudice for me to indite after others, than for Ælianus Montaltus that famous physician, to write *De morbis capitis* [about diseases of the head] after Jason Pratensis, Heurnius, Hildesheim, &c. Many horses to run in a race, one logician, one rhetorician, after another. Oppose then what thou wilt,

> *Allatres licet usque nos & usque,*
> *Et gannitibus improbis lacessas.*
> [Bark and snarl at me as wantonly as you choose]

I solve it thus. And for those other faults of barbarism, Doric dialect, extemporanean style, tautologies, apish imitation, a rhapsody of rags gathered together from several dung-hills, excrements of authors, toys and fopperies, confusedly tumbled out, without art, invention, judgement, wit, learning, harsh, raw, rude, fantastical, absurd, insolent, indiscreet, ill-composed, indigested, vain, scurrile, idle, dull and dry; I confess all ('tis partly affected) thou canst not think worse of me than I do of myself. 'Tis not worth the reading, I yield it, I desire thee not to lose time in perusing so vain a subject, I should be peradventure loath myself to read him or thee, so writing, 'tis not *operæ pretium* [worthwhile]. All I say, is this, that I have precedents for it, which Isocrates calls *perfugium iis qui peccant* [a windfall for sinners], others as absurd, vain, idle, illiterate, &c. *Nonnulli alii idem fecerunt*, others have done as much, it may be more, and perhaps thou thyself, *Novimus & qui te, &c.* we have all our faults, *scimus & hanc veniam, &c.* thou censurest me, so have I done others, and may do thee, *Cædimus inque vicem, &c.* 'tis *lex talionis, quid pro quo*. Go now censure, criticize, scoff, and rail.

> *Nasutus sis usque licet, sis denique nasus:*
> *Non potes in nugas dicere plura meas,*
> *Ipse ego quam dixi, &c.*
> Wer'st thou all scoffs and flouts, a very Momus,
> Then we ourselves, thou canst not say worse of us.

Thus as when women scold have I cried whore first, and in some men's censures, I am afraid I have over-shot myself, *Laudare se vani, vituperare sulti* [the vain praise themselves, the foolish blame themselves], as I do not arrogate, I will not derogate. *Primus vestrûm non sum, nec imus*, I am none of the best, I am none of the meanest of you. As I am an inch, or so many feet, so many parasangs,[1] after him or him, I may be peradventure an ace before thee. Be it therefore as it is, well or ill, I have assayed, put myself upon the stage, I must abide the censure, I may not escape it. It is most true, *stylus virum arguit*, our style bewrays us, and as hunters find their game by the trace, so is a man's genius descried by his works, *Multò meliùs ex sermone quàm lineamentis, de moribus hominum judicamus* [we judge better of a man's character by his conversation than his features]; 'twas old Cato's rule. I have laid myself open (I know it) in this treatise, turned mine inside outward, I shall be censured, I doubt not, for to say truth with Erasmus, *nihil morosius hominum judiciis*, there's naught so peevish as men's judgements, yet this is some comfort, *ut palata, sic judicia*, our censures are as various as our palates.

> *Tres mihi convivæ prope dissentire videntur*
> *Poscentes vario multum diversa palato, &c.*
> [They seem to me to differ like three guests
> Whose palates each require different food]

Our writings are as so many dishes, our readers guests; our books like beauty, that which one admires another rejects; so are we approved as men's fancies are inclined.

> *Pro captu lectoris habent sua fata libelli*
> [The reader's fancy makes the fate of books],

---

[1] *parasangs* A parasang was a Persian unit of length equal to about five kilometres.

That which is most pleasing to one is *amaracum sui* [marjoram to a sow], most harsh to another. *Quot homines, tot sententiæ*, so many men, so many minds: that which thou condemnest he commends.

> *Quod petis, id sane est invisum acidumque duobus* [What you wish, that the other two detest].

He respects matter, thou art wholly for words, he loves a loose and free style, thou art all for neat composition, strong lines, hyperboles, allegories; he desires a fine frontispiece, enticing pictures, such as Hieron: Natali the Jesuit hath cut to the Dominicals,[1] to draw on the reader's attention, which thou rejectest, that which one admires, another explodes as most absurd and ridiculous. If it be not point blank to his humour, his method, his conceit, *Si quid forsan omissum, quod is animo conceperit, si quæ dictio, &c.* If ought be omitted or added, which he likes or dislikes, thou art *mancipium paucæ lectionis* [a sorry fellow of little reading], an idiot, an ass, *nullus es*, or *plagiarius* [not worth reading, or a plagiarist], a trifler, a trivant,[2] thou art an idle fellow; or else 'tis a thing of mere industry, a collection without wit or invention, a very toy. *Facilia sic putant omnes quæ jam facta, nec de salebris cogitant, ubi via strata* [All people think things so easy that are already done, nor do they think of the trouble the road has taken to make when it is made], so men are valued, their labours vilified by fellows of no worth themselves; as things of nought, who could not have done as much: *Unusquisque abundat sensu suo*, every man abounds in his own sense, and whilst each particular party is so affected, how should one please all?

Quid dem, quid non dem? Renuis tu quod jubet ille?
[What shall I give my guests? For you refuse what he demands.]

How shall I hope to express myself to each man's humour and conceit, or to give satisfaction to all? Some understand too little, some too much, *Qui similitèr in legendos libros, atque in salutandos homines irruunt, non cogitantes quales, sed quibus vestibus induti sint* [who value books by the authors as people judge of men by their clothes], as Austin observes, not regarding what, but who write, *orexin habet Authoris celebritas* [the author's fame sells the book], not valuing the metal, but stamp that is upon it, *Cantharum aspiciunt, non quid in eo* [they look at the tankard, and not the liquor in it]. If he be not rich, in great place, polite and brave, a great doctor, or full fraught with grand titles, though never so well qualified, he is a dunce, but as Baronius hath it of Cardinal Caraffa's works, he is a mere hog that rejects any man for his poverty. Some are too partial, as friends to overween, others come with a prejudice to carp, vilify, detract, and scoff (*qui de me forsan, quicquid est omni contemptu contemptiùs judicant* [who judge perhaps whatever I produce as unworthy of anything but contempt]); some as bees for honey, some as spiders to gather poison; What shall I do in this case? As a Dutch host, if you come to an inn in Germany, and dislike your fare, diet, lodging, &c. replies in a surly tone, *aliud tibi quæras diversorium*, if you like not this, get you to another inn; I resolve, if you like not my writing, go read something else. I do not much esteem thy censure, take thy course, 'tis not as thou wilt, nor as I will, but when we have both done, that of Plinius Secundus to Trajan, will prove true, "Every man's witty labour takes not, except the matter, subject, occasion, and some commending favourite happen to it." If I be taxed, exploded by thee and some such, I shall haply be approved and

---

[1] In liturgical books, dominical letters were letters printed in a distinctive fashion (usually in red ink or in a larger type) to denote Sundays; Burton is referring to a folio published in Antwerp in 1607 with "cut" (engraved) illustrations.

[2] *trivant* a dialect variant of "truant," an idler (*OED*).

commended by others, and so have been (*Expertus loquor* [I speak from experience]) and may truly say with Jovius in like case *(absit verbo jactantia) heroum quorundam, pontificum, & vivorum nobilium familiaritatem & amicitiam, gratasque gratias, & multorum benè laudatorum laudes sum indè promeritus* [(let me not speak boastfully) I have had the intimacy and friendship of some eminent men, pontiffs, and noblemen, and had pleasant favours from them, and been praised by many who themselves were highly esteemed], as I have been honoured by some worthy men, so have I been vilified by others, and shall be. At the first publishing of this book (which Probus of Persius satires), *editum librum continuò mirari homines, atque avidè deripere cœperunt* [men began both to admire and eagerly carp at it], I may in some sort apply to this my work, the first, second, and third edition were suddenly gone, eagerly read, and as I have said, not so much approved by some, as scornfully rejected by others. But it was Democritus his fortune, *Idem admirationi & irrisioni habitus* [he was both admired and jeered at]. 'Twas Seneca's fate, that superintendent of wit, learning, judgement, *ad stuporem doctus* [learned to a marvel], the best of Greek and Latin writers, in Plutarch's opinion, that "renowned corrector of vice," as Fabius terms him, "and painful omniscious philosopher, that writ so excellently and admirably well," could not please all parties, or escape censure: How is he vilified by Caligula, Agellius, Fabius, and Lipsius himself, his chief propugner?[1] *In eo pleraque pernitiosa*, saith the same Fabius, many childish tracts and sentences he hath, *sermo illaboratus*, too negligent often, and remiss, as Agellius observes, *oratio vulgaris & protrita, dicaces & ineptæ sententiæ, eruditio plebeia*, an homely shallow writer as he is, *In partibus spinas & fastidia habet* [in some of his works he has difficulties and inspires disgust], saith Lipsius, and as in all

---

[1] *propugner* defender (*OED* propugner).

his other works, so especially in his epistles, *aliæ in argutiis & ineptiis occupantur, intricatus alicubi, & parum compositus, sine copiâ rerum hoc fecit*, he jumbles up many things together immethodically, after the Stoics' fashion, *parum ordinavit, multa accumulavit, &c.* If Seneca be thus lashed, and many famous men that I could name, what shall I expect? How shall I that am *vix umbra tanti Philosphi* [scarce a shadow of so great a philosopher], hope to please? "No man so absolute," Erasmus holds, "to satisfy all, except antiquity, prescription, &c. set a bar." But as I have proved in Seneca, this will not always take place, how shall I evade? 'Tis the common doom of all writers, I must (I say) abide it, I seek not applause; *Non ego ventosæ venor suffragià plebis* [I court not the approval of the common people], again *non sum adeò informis* [I am not so ugly], I would not be vilified:

> —— *laudatus abundè,*
> *Non fastiditus si tibi lector ero.*
> [I shall have praise enough if, gentle reader, you not despise me]

I fear good men's censures, and to their favourite acceptance I submit my labours,

> —— *& linguas Mancipiorum*
> *Contemno,* ——
> [But I despise the tongues of slaves]

As the barking of a dog, I securely contemn those malicious and scurrile obloquies, flouts, calumnies, of railers and detractors, I scorn the rest. What therefore I have said, *pro tenuitate meâ* [in my poor fashion], I have said.

One or two things yet I was desirous to have amended if I could, concerning the manner of handling this my subject, for which I must apologize, *depracari*, and upon better advice give the friendly reader notice. It was not mine intent to prostitute my Muse in English, or to divulge *secreta*

Minervæ [the secrets of Minerva], but to have exposed this more contract in Latin,[1] if I could have got it printed. Any scurrile pamphlet is welcome to our mercenary stationers in English, they print all,

> —— *cuduntque libellos*
> *In quorum foliis vix simia nada cacaret.*
> [and they print books upon whose pages a
> naked ape would hardly shit.]

But in Latin they will not deal; which is one of the reasons Nicholas Car in his oration of the paucity of English writers, gives; that so many flourishing wits are smothered in oblivion, lie dead and buried in this our nation. Another main fault is, that I have not revised the copy, and amended the style, which now flows remissly, as it was first conceived, but my leisure would not permit, *Feci nec quod potui, nec quod volui*, I confess it is neither as I would, or as it should be.

> *Cùm relego scripsisse pudet, quia plurima cerno*
> *Me quoque quæ fuerant judice digna lini.*
> When I peruse this tract which I have writ,
> I am abash'd, and much I hold unfit.

Et quod gravissimum [and what is most important], in the matter itself, many things I disallow at this present, which then I writ, *Non eadem est ætas non mens* ['twas in my salad days, when I was green, not ripe in judgement], I would willingly retract much, &c. but 'tis too late, I can only crave pardon now for what is amiss.

I might indeed (had I wisely done) observed that precept of the poet,

> —— *nomunque prematur in annum,*
> [let a book wait nine years before it is printed]

And have taken more care: Or as Alexander the physician would have done by lapis lazuli, fifty times washed before it be used, I should have revised, corrected, and amended this tract; but I had not (as I said) that happy leisure, no amanuenses or assistants. Pancrates in Lucian, wanting a servant as he went from Memphis to Coptus in Egypt, took a door bar, and after some superstitious words pronounced (Eucrates the relator was then present) made it stand up like a serving-man, fetch him water, turn the spit, serve in supper, and what work he would besides; and when he had done that service he desired, turned his man to a stick again. I have no such skill to make new men at my pleasure, or means to hire them; no whistle to call like the master of a ship, and bid them run, &c. I have no such authority, no such benefactors as that noble Ambrosius was to Origen, allowing him six or seven amanuenses to write out his dictates, I must for that cause do my business myself, and was therefore enforced, as a bear doth her whelps, to bring forth this confused lump, I had not time to lick it into form, as she doth her young ones,[2] but even so to publish it, as it was first written *quicquid in buccam venit* [whatever came uppermost], in an extemporean style, as I do commonly all other exercises, *effudi quicquid dictavit Genius meus* [I poured forth whatever my genius dictated], out of a confused company of notes, and writ with as small deliberation as I do ordinarily speak, without all affectation of big words, fustian phrases, jingling terms, tropes, strong lines, that like Acestes' arrows caught fire as they flew; strains of wit, brave heats, elegies, hyperbolical exhortations, elegancies, &c. which many so much affect. I am *aquæ potor* [a water drinker], drink no wine at all, which so much improves our modern wits, a loose, plain, rude wri-ter, *ficum voco ficum, & ligonem ligonem* [I call a fig a fig and a spade a spade], and as free, as loose, *idem calamo quod in mente*, I call a spade a spade, *animis hæc scribo, non auribus*, I respect matter not words;

---

[1] *more contract* more briefly.

[2] According to classical and Renaissance natural history lore, bear cubs were born without form and licked into shape by their mother.

remembering that of Cardan, *verba propter res, non res propter verba* [words exist for things, not things for words]: and seeking with Seneca, *quid scribam non quemadmodum*, rather what, than how to write. For as Philo thinks, "he that is conversant about matter, neglects words, and those that excel in this art of speaking, have no profound learning,"

> *Verba nitent phaleris, at nullas verba medullas*
> *Intus habent* ———
> [Words may sound fine, but have no inner meaning]

Besides, it was the observation of that wise Seneca, "when you see a fellow careful about his words, and neat in his speech, know this for a certainty, that man's mind is busied about toys, there's no solidity in him." *Non est ornamentum virile concinnitas* [prettiness of style is not a manly distinction], as he said of a nightingale,

> ——— *vox es præterea nihil, &c.*
> [you are a voice, and nothing else].

I am therefore in this point a professed disciple of Apollonius, a scholar of Socrates, I neglect phrases, and labour wholly to inform my readers' understanding, not to please his ear; 'tis not my study or intent to compose neatly, which an orator requires, but to express myself readily and plainly as it happens. So that as a river runs sometimes precipitate and swift, then dull and slow; now direct, then *per ambages* [windingly]; now deep, then shallow; now muddy, then clear; now broad, then narrow; doth my style flow: now serious, then light; now comical, then satirical; now more elaborate, then remiss, as the present subject required, or as at that time I was affected. And if thou vouchsafe to read this treatise, it shall seem no otherwise to thee, than the way to an ordinary traveller, sometimes fair, sometimes

foul; here champaign,[1] there enclosed; barren in one place, better soil in another: by woods, groves, hills, dales, plains, &c. I shall lead thee *per ardua montium, & lubrica vallium, & roscida cespitum, & glebosa camporum*, through variety of objects, that which thou shalt like and surely dislike...

The last and greatest exception is, that I being a divine, have meddled with physic,

> ——— *tantumne est ab re tuâ otii tibi,*
> *Aliena ut cures, eaque nihil quæ ad te attinent?*

Which Menedemus objected to Chremes, have I so much leisure, or little business of mine own, as to look after other men's matters which concern me not? What have I to do with physic? *quod mediocorum est promittant medici* [let doctors attend to what concerns doctors]. The Lacedemonians were once in counsel about state matters, a debauched fellow spake excellent well, and to the purpose, his speech was generally approved. A grave senator steps up, and by all means would have it repealed, though good, because *dehonestabatur pessimo Authore*, it had no better an author; let some good man relate the same, and then it should pass. This counsel was embraced, *factum est*, and it was registered forthwith, *Et sic bona sententia mansit, Malus Author mutatus est* [and so the good advice was taken, the bad advisor was changed]. Thou sayest as much of me, stomachosus as thou art,[2] and grantest peradventure this which I have written in physic, not to be amiss, had another done it, a professed physician, or so; but why should I meddle with this tract? Hear me speak: There be many other subjects, I do easily grant, both in humanity and divinity, fit to be treated of, of which had I written *ad ostentationem* only, to show myself, I should have rather chosen, and in which I have been more conversant, I could

---

[1] *champaign*   level open country.

[2] *stomachosus*   resentful, bitter, irascible (*OED* stomachous b).

have more willingly luxuriated, and better satisfied myself and others; but that at this time I was fatally driven upon this rock of melancholy, and carried away by this by-stream, which as a rillet, is deducted from the main channel of my studies, in which I have pleased and busied myself at idle hours, as a subject more necessary and commodious. Not that I prefer it before divinity, which I do acknowledge to be the queen of professions, and to which all the rest are as handmaids, but that in divinity I saw no such great need. For had I written positively, there be so many books in that kind, so many commentators, treatises, pamphlets, expositions, sermons, that whole teams of oxen cannot draw them; and had I been as forward and ambitious as some others, I might have haply printed a sermon at Paul's Cross, a sermon in St Maries Oxon[iensis], a sermon in Christ Church, or a sermon before the right Honorable, right Reverend, a sermon before the right Worshipful, a sermon in Latin, in English, a sermon with a name, a sermon without, a sermon, a sermon, &c. But I have ever been as desirous to suppress my labours in this kind, as others have been to press and publish theirs. To have written in controversy, had been to cut off an hydra's head, *lis litem generat* [litigation begets litigation], one begets another, so many duplications, triplications, and swarms of questions, *In sacro bello hoc quod stili mucrone agitur* [in this sacred war which is fought with the point of the pen], that having once begun, I should never make an end.

. . . .

LOVE OF LEARNING, OR OVERMUCH STUDY.
WITH A DIGRESSION OF THE MISERY OF SCHOLARS,
AND WHY THE MUSES ARE MELANCHOLY
(pt. 1, sect. 2, memb. 3, subs. 15)

Leonartus Fuchsius *Instit*. lib. 3 sect. 1 cap. 1, Fælix Plater lib. 3 *de mentis alienat.*, Herc. de Saxonia *tract. post. de melanch.* cap. 3 speak of a peculiar

fury, which comes by overmuch study. Fernelius lib. 1 cap. 18 puts study, contemplation, and continual meditation, as an especial cause of madness: and in his 86 *consul.* cites the same words. Jo: Arculanus in lib. 9, Rhasis *ad Almansorem* cap. 16, amongst other causes, reckons up *studium vehemens* [overmuch study]: so doth Levinus Lemnius, *lib. de occul. nat. mirac.* lib. 1 cap. 16. "Many men" (saith he) "come to this malady by continual study, and night-waking, and of all other men, scholars are most subject to it": and such Rhasis adds, "that have commonly the finest wits," *cont.* lib. 1 tract. 9. Marsilius Ficinus *de sanit. tuenda*, lib. 1 cap. 7 puts melancholy amongst one of those five principal plagues of students, 'tis a common maul unto them all, and almost in some measure an inseparable companion. Varro belike for that cause calls *Tristes Philosophos & severos* [philosophers sad and severe], severe, sad, dry, tetrick,[1] are common epithets to scholars: And Patritius therefore in the *Institution of Princes*, would not have them to be great students. For (as Machiavel holds) study weakens their bodies, dulls the spirits, abates their strength and courage; and good scholars are never good soldiers; which a certain Goth well perceived, for when his countrymen came into Greece, and would have burned all their books, he cried out against it, by all means they should not do it, "leave them that plague, which in time will consume all their vigor, and martial spirits." The Turks abdicated Cornutus the next heir, from the Empire, because he was so much given to his books: and 'tis the common tenet of the world, that learning dulls and diminisheth the spirits, and so *per consequens* [consequently] produceth melancholy.

Two main reasons may be given of it, why students should be more subject to this malady than others. The one is, they live a sedentary, solitary life, *sibi & musis* [to themselves and letters], free from

---

[1] *tetrick* austere, harsh, morose (*OED* tetric *a* 1).

bodily exercise, and those ordinary disports which other men use: and many times if discontent and idleness concur with it, which is too frequent, they are precipitated into this gulf on a sudden: but the common cause is overmuch study; too much learning (as Festus told Paul) hath made thee mad; 'tis that other extreme which effects it. So did Trincavellius lib. 1 consil. 12 & 13 find by his experience, in two of his patients, a young baron, and another, that contracted this malady by too vehement study. So Forestus *observat.* lib. 10 observ. 13 in a young divine in Louvain, that was mad, and said, "he had a Bible in his head." Marsilius Ficinus *de sanit. tuend.* lib. 1 cap. 1, 3, 4 & lib. 2 cap. 16 gives many reasons, "why students dote more often than others." The first is their negligence: "Other men look to their tools, a painter will wash his pencils, a smith will look to his hammer, anvil, forge: an husbandman will mend his plough-irons, and grind his hatchet if it be dull; a falconer or huntsman will have an especial care of his hawks, hounds, horses, dogs, &c. a musician will string and unstring his lute, &c. only scholars neglect that instrument, their brain and spirits (I mean) which they daily use, and by which they range over all the world, which by much study is consumed." *Vide* (saith Lucian) *ne funiculum nimis intendeno, aliquandò abrumpas*: See thou twist not the rope so hard, till at length it break. Ficinus in his fourth cap. gives some other reasons; Saturn and Mercury, the patrons of learning, are both dry planets: and Origanus assigns the same cause, why Mercurialists are so poor, and most part beggars; for that their president Mercury had not better fortune himself. The destinies of old, put poverty upon him as a punishment; since when, poetry and beggary, are *Gemelli*, twin-born brats, inseparable companions:

And to this day is every scholar poor,
Gross gold from them runs headlong to the boor:[1]

Mercury can help them to knowledge but not to money.

The second is contemplation, which dries the brain, and extinguisheth natural heat; for whilst the spirits are intent to meditation above in the head, the stomach and liver are left destitute, and thence come black blood and crudities by defect of concoction, and for want of exercise, the superfluous vapours cannot exhale, &c. The same reasons are repeated by Gomesius lib. 4. cap. 1. *de sale*, Nymannus *orat. de Imag.* Jo. Voschius lib. 2. cap. 5. *de peste*: and something more they add, that hard students are commonly troubled with gouts, catarrhs, rheums, *cachexia, bradiopepsia*, bad eyes, stone and colic, crudities, oppilations, vertigo, winds, cramps, consumptions, and all such diseases as come by overmuch sitting;[2] they are most part lean, dry, ill coloured, spend their fortunes, lose their wits, and many times their lives, and all through immoderate pains, and extraordinary studies. If you will not believe the truth of this, look upon great Tostatus and Thomas Aquinas works, and tell me whether those men took pains? peruse Austin, Hierom, &c. and many thousands besides.

> *Qui cupit optatam cursu contingere metam,*
> *Multa tulit, fecitque puer, sudavit & alsit.*
> He that desires this wished goal to gain,
> Must sweat and freeze, before he can attain,

and labour hard for it. So did Seneca, by his own confession ep. 8. "Not a day that I spend idle, part

---

[1] from Christopher Marlowe, *Hero and Leander*, first sestiad, ll. 471–72.

[2] *cachexia* a condition of weakness or mental debilitation due to chronic illness; *bradiopepsia* slowness of digestion; *crudities* indigestion; *oppilations* obstructions or stoppages.

of the night I keep mine eyes open tired with waking, and now slumbering to their continual task." Hear Tully *pro Archia Poeta*: "whilst others loitered, and took their pleasures, he was continually at his book": so they do that will be scholars, and that to the hazard (I say) of their healths, fortunes, wits, and lives. How much did Aristotle and Ptolemy spend? *unius regni precium* they say, more than a King's ransom, how many crowns *per annum* [per year], to perfect arts, the one about his history of creatures, the other on his *Almagest*? How much time did Thebet Benchorat employ, to find out the motion of the eighth sphere, 40 years and more, some write, how many poor scholars have lost their wits, or become dizards, neglecting all worldly affairs, and their own health, wealth, *esse* and *benè esse*, to gain knowledge? for which, after all their pains in the world's esteem they are accounted ridiculous and silly fools, idiots, asses, and (as oft they are) rejected, contemned, derided, doting, and mad. Look for examples in Hildesheim *spicel. 2 de mania & delirio*: read Trincavellius lib. 3 consil. 36 & consil. 17, Montanus consil. 233, Garcæus *de Judic. genit.* cap. 33, Mercurialis consil. 86 consil. 25, Prosper Calenus in his book *de atrâ bile*: Go to Bedlam and ask. Or if they keep their wits, yet they are esteemed scrubs and fools by reason of their carriage: after seven years study

> ——— *statua taciturnius exit,*
> *Plerumque & risum populi quatit.* ———
> [In general he's more silent than a statue,
> And makes the people shake their sides with laughter.]

Because they cannot ride an horse, which every clown can do; salute and court a gentlewoman, carve at table, cringe and make congies,[1] which every common swasher can do, *hos populus ridet &c.* they are laughed to scorn, and accounted silly fools

by our gallants. Yea many times, such is their misery, they deserve it: a mere scholar, a mere ass.

> *Obstipo capite, & figentes lumine terram,*
> *Murmura cùm secum, & rabiosa silentia rodunt,*
> *Atque exporrecto trutinantur verba labello,*
> *Ægroti veteris meditantes somnia, gigni*
> *De nihilo nihilum; in nihilum nil posse reverti.*
> ——— who do lean awry
> Their heads, piercing the earth with a fixed eye:
> When by themselves they gnaw their murmuring,
> And furious silence, as 'twere balancing,
> Each word upon their outstretched lip, and when
> They meditate the dreams of old sick men,
> As, *Out of nothing, nothing can be brought,*
> *And that which is; can ne're be turn'd to naught.*

Thus they go commonly meditating unto themselves, thus they sit, such is their action and gesture. Fulgosus lib. 8 cap. 7 makes mention how Th. Aquinas supping with King Lewis of France, upon a sudden knocked his fist upon the table, and cried, *conclusum est contra Manichæos* [the Manichees are proved wrong], his wits were a woolgathering, as they say, and his head busied about other matters; when he perceived his error, he was much abashed. Such a story there is of Archimedes in Vitruvius, that having found out the means to know how much gold was mingled with the silver in King Hieron's crown, ran naked forth of the bath and cried εὕρηκα [eureka], I have found: "and was commonly so intent to his studies, that he never perceived what was done about him, when the city was taken, and the soldiers now ready to rifle his house, he took no notice of it." S. Bernard rode all day long by the Leman lake, and asked at last where he was, Marulus lib. 2. cap. 4. It was Democritus' carriage alone that made the Abderites suppose him to have been mad,[2] and send for Hippocrates to cure him: if he had been in any solemn company,

---

[1] *congies* ceremonial leave-takings, obeisances (*OED* congee *sb* 2).

[2] *carriage* habitual conduct or behaviour (*OED* carriage 14).

he would upon all occasions fall a laughing. Theophrastus saith as much of Heraclitus, for that he continually wept, & Laertius of Menedemus Lampsacus, because he ran about like a mad man, "saying he came from hell as a spy, to tell the devils what mortal men did." Your greatest students are commonly no better, silly, soft fellows in their outward behaviour, absurd, ridiculous to others, and no whit experienced in worldly business; they can measure the heavens, range over the world, teach others wisdom, and yet in bargains and contracts they are circumvented by every base tradesman. Are not these men fools? and how should they be otherwise? "but as so many sots in schools, when (as he [Petronius] well observed), they neither hear nor see such things as are commonly practised abroad," how should they get experience, by what means? "I knew in my time many scholars," saith Æneas Sylvius (in an Epistle of his to Gaspar Schlick, Chancellor to the Emperor) "excellent well learned, but so rude, so silly, that they had no common civility, nor knew how to manage their domestic or public affairs. Paglarensis was amazed, and said his farmer had surely cozened him, when he heard him tell that his sow had eleven pigs, and his ass had but one foal." To say the best of this profession, I can give no other testimony of them in general, than that of Pliny of Isæus; "He is yet a scholar, than which kind of men there is nothing so simple," so sincere none better, they are most part harmless, honest, upright, innocent, plain dealing men.

Now because they are commonly subject to such hazards and inconveniences, as dotage, madness, simplicity, &c. Jo. Voschius would have good scholars to be highly rewarded, and had in some extraordinary respect above other men, "to have greater privileges than the rest, that adventure themselves and abbreviate their lives for the public good." But our patrons of learning are so far nowadays, from respecting the Muses, and giving that honour to scholars, or reward which they deserve, and are allowed by those indulgent privileges of many noble princes, that after all their pains taken in the universities, cost and charge, expenses, irksome hours, laborious tasks, wearisome days, dangers, hazards (barred interim from all pleasures which other men have, mewed up like hawks all their lives) if they chance to wade through them, they shall in the end be rejected, contemned, & which is their greatest misery, driven to their shifts, exposed to want, poverty and beggary.[1] Their familiar attendants are,

> *Pallentes morbi, luctus, curæque laborque*
> *Et metus, & malesuada fames, & turpis egestas,*
> *Terribiles visu formæ* ———
> Grief, labour, care, pale sickness, miseries,
> Fear, filthy poverty, hunger that cries,
> Terrible monsters to be seen with eyes.

If there were nothing else to trouble them, the conceit of this alone were enough to make them all melancholy. Most other trades and professions after some seven years prenticeship, are enabled by their craft to live of themselves. A merchant adventures his goods at sea, and though his hazard be great, yet if one ship return of four, he likely makes a saving voyage. An husbandman's gains are almost certain; *quibus ipse Jupiter nocere non potest* ('tis Cato's hyperbole, a great husband[man] himself) only scholars, methinks are most uncertain, unrespected, subject to all casualties, and hazards. For first, not one of a many proves to be a scholar, all are not capable and docile,[2] *ex omni ligno non fit Mercurius*: we can make Mayors and officers every year, but not scholars: Kings can invest Knights and Barons, as Sigismond the Emperor confessed; universities can give degrees; and *Tu quod es, è populo quilibet*

---

[1] For a similar argument, see the latter part of the 1660 sermon by Robert South.

[2] *docile* teachable (*OED* docile 1).

esse potest [what you are, anyone in the world can be]; but he nor they, nor all the world can give learning, make philosophers, artists, orators, poets: we can soon say, as Seneca well notes, *O virum bonum, ô divitem*, point at a rich man, a good, an happy man, a proper man, *sumptuosè vestitum, Calamistratum, bene olentem, magno temporis impendio constat hæc laudatio, ô virum literatum*, but 'tis not so easily performed to find out a learned man. Learning is not so quickly got, though they may be willing to take pains, to that end sufficiently informed and liberally maintained by their patrons and parents, yet few can compass it. Or if they be docile, yet all men's wills are not answerable to their wits, they can apprehend, but will not take pains; they are either seduced by bad companions, *vel in puellam impingunt, vel in poculum* [they come to grief with women or wine], and so spend their time to their friends' grief and their own undoings. Or put case they be studious, industrious, of ripe wits, and perhaps good capacities, then how many diseases of body and mind must they encounter? No labour in the world like unto study. It may be, their temperature will not endure it,[1] but striving to be excellent to know all, they lose health, wealth, wit, life and all. Let him yet happily escape all these hazards, *æneis intestinis*, with a body of brass, and is now consummate and ripe, he hath profited in his studies, and proceeded with all applause: after many expenses, he is fit for preferment, where shall he have it? he is as far to seek it as he was (after twenty years standing) at the first day of his coming to the university. For what course shall he take, being now capable and ready? The most parable and easy,[2] and about which many are employed, is to teach a school, turn lecturer or curate, and for that he shall have falconer's wages, ten [pounds] *per annum*, and his diet, or some small stipend, so long as he can please his patron or the parish; if they approve him not (for usually they do but a year or two) as inconstant, as they that cried "Hosanna" one day, and "Crucify him" the other; serving-man like, he must go look a new master: if they do what is his reward?

> *Hoc quoque te manet ut pueros elementa docentem*
> *Occupet extremis in vicis alba senectus.*
> [This fate, too, awaits you, that stammering age will come upon you as you teach boys their ABC in the city's outskirts]

Like an ass, he wears out his time for provender, and can show a stump rod,[3] *togam tritam & laceram*, saith Hædus, an old torn gown, an ensign of his infelicity, he hath his labour for his pain, a modicum to keep him till he be decrepit, and that is all. *Grammaticus non est fælix, &c.* [a scholar is not a happy man]. If he be a trencher chaplain in a gentleman's house,[4] as it befell Euphormio, after some seven years service, he may perchance have a living to the halves,[5] or some small rectory with the mother of the maids at length, a poor kinswoman, or a cracked chamber-maid, to have and to hold during the time of his life. But if he offend his good patron, or displease his lady mistress in the meantime,

> *Ducetur Plantâ velut ictus ab Hercule Cacus,*
> *Poneturque foras, si quid tentaverit unquam*
> *Hiscere* ———

as Hercules did by Cacus, he shall be dragged forth of doors by the heels, away with him. If he bend his

---

[1] *temperature* bodily constitution (*OED* temperature 5).

[2] *parable* procurable (*OED* parable *a*).

[3] *stump rod* probably a rod worn to a stump by its use to punish the boys whom the impoverished old teacher is compelled to teach (*OED* stump *a* 1; this place cited).

[4] *trencher chaplain* a contemptuous term for a domestic chaplain, one who eats at his patron's table (*OED* trencher-chaplain).

[5] *living to the halves* receiving only half the income belonging to the position, with the other half being kept by the patron (see the note on the buying and selling of livings below).

forces to some other studies, with an intent to be *à secretis* [a secretary] to some nobleman, or in such a place with an ambassador, he shall find that these persons rise like prentices one under another, as in so many trademen's shops, when the master is dead, the foreman of the shop commonly steps in his place. Now for poets, rhetoricians, historians, philosophers, mathematicians, sophisters, &c. they are like grasshoppers, sing they must in summer, and pine in the winter, for there is no preferment for them. Even so they were at first, if you will believe that pleasant tale of Socrates, which he told fair Phaedrus under a plane-tree, at the banks of the river Ilissus; about noon when it was hot, and the grasshoppers made a noise, he took that sweet occasion to tell him a tale, how grasshoppers were once scholars, musicians, poets, &c. before the Muses were born, and lived without meat and drink, and for that cause were turned by Jupiter into grasshoppers. And may be turned again, *In Tythoni Cicadas, aut Lyciorum ranas* [into Tithonius' grasshoppers, or frogs of the Lycians], for any reward I see they are like to have: or else in the meantime, I would they could live as they did without any viaticum,[1] like so many *Manucodiatæ,* those Indian birds of paradise, as we commonly call them, those I mean that live with the air, and dew of heaven and need no other food: for being as they are, their Rhetoric only serves them, to curse their bad fortunes, and many of them for want of means are driven to hard shifts, from grasshoppers they turn humblebees and wasps, plain parasites, and make the Muses, mules, to satisfy their hunger-starved paunches, and get a meal's meat. To say truth, 'tis the common fortune of most scholars, to be servile and poor, to complain pitifully, and lay open their wants to their respectless patrons, as Cardan doth, as Xilander, and many others: And which is too common in those dedicatory epistles,

for hope of gain, to lie, flatter, and with hyperbolical elogiums and commendations, to magnify and extol an illiterate and unworthy idiot, for his excellent virtues, whom they should rather as Machiavel observes, vilify, and rail at downright for his most notorious villainies and vices. So they prostitute themselves as fiddlers, or mercenary tradesmen, to serve great men's turns for a small reward. They are like Indians, they have store of gold; but know not the worth of it, for I am of Synesius' opinion, "King Hieron got more by Simonides' acquaintance, than Simonides did by his": they have their best education, good institution, sole qualification from us, and when they have done well, their honour and immortality from us, we are the living tombs, registers, and as so many trumpeters of their fames: what was Achilles without Homer; Alexander without Arrian and Curtius; who had known the Cæsars, but for Suetonius and Dion?

> *Vixerunt fortes ante Agamemnona*
> *Multi: sed omnes illachrimabiles*
> *Urgentur, ignotique longâ*
> *Nocte, carent quia vate sacro.*
> [Many brave persons lived ere Agamemnon
> But all are buried in night's long obscurity
> Unwept, unknown, because they lacked a bard.]

They are more beholden to scholars, than scholars to them; but they undervalue themselves, and so by those great men are kept down. Let them have that *Encyclopædian,* all the learning in the world, they must keep it to themselves, "live in base esteem, and starve, except they will submit," as Budæus well hath it, "so many good parts, so many ensigns of arts, virtues, be slavishly obnoxious to some illiterate potentate, and live under his insolent worship, or honour, like parasites, *qui tanquam mures alienum panem comedunt*" [who like mice devour another man's bread]. For to say truth, *artes hæ non sunt Lucrativæ,* as Guido Bonat that great astrologer

---

[1] *viaticum* a supply of food, money or other necessaries for a journey (*OED* viaticum 2, 2c).

could foresee, they be not gainful arts these, *sed esurientes & famelicæ*, but poor and hungry.

> *Dat Galenus opes, dat Justinianus honores,*
> *Sed genus & species cogitur ire pedes*:
> The rich physician, honour'd lawyers ride,
> Whil'st the poor scholar foots it by their side.

Poverty is the Muses' patrimony, and as that poetical divinity teacheth us, when Jupiter's daughters were each of them married to the Gods, the Muses alone were left solitary, Helicon forsaken of all suitors, and I believe it was, because they had no portion.

> *Calliope longum cælebs cur vixit in ævum?*
> *Nempe nihil dotis, quod numeraret, erat.*
> Why did Calliope live so long a maid?
> Because she had no dowry to be paid.

Ever since all their followers are poor, forsaken, and left unto themselves. In so much, that as Petronius argues, you shall likely know them by their clothes. "There came," saith he, "by chance into my company, a fellow not very spruce to look on, that I could perceive by that note alone he was a scholar, whom commonly rich men hate: I asked him what he was, he answered; a poet; I demanded again why he was so ragged, he told me this kind of learning never made any man rich."

> *Qui Pelago credit, magno se fænore tollit,*
> *Qui pugnas & rostra petit, præcingitur auro:*
> *Vilis adulator picto jacet ebrius ostro,*
> *Sola pruinosis horret facundia pannis.*
> A merchant's gain is great that goes to sea,
>   A soldier embossed all in gold:
> A flatterer lies fox'd in brave array,
>   A scholar only ragged to behold.

All which our ordinary students, right well perceiving in the universities how unprofitable these poetical, mathematical, and philosophical studies are, how little respected, how few patrons; apply themselves in all haste to those three commodious professions of law, physic, and divinity, sharing themselves between them, rejecting these arts in the meantime, history, philosophy, philology, or lightly passing them over, as pleasant toys, fitting only table talk, and to furnish them with discourse. They are not so behoveful: he that can tell his money hath arithmetic enough: He is a true geometrician, can measure out a good fortune to himself; A perfect astrologer, that can cast the rise and fall of others, and mark their errant motions to his own use. The best optics are, to reflect the beams of some great men's favour and grace to shine upon him. He is a good engineer that alone can make an instrument to get preferment. This was the common tenet and practise of Poland, as Cromerus observed not long since, in the first book of his history, their universities were generally base, not a philosopher, a mathematician, an antiquary, &c. to be found of any note amongst them, because they had no set reward or stipend, but every man betook himself to divinity, *hoc solum in votis habens, optimum sacerdotium*, a good parsonage was their aim. This was the practise of some of our near neighbors, as Lipsius inveighs, "they thrust their children to the study of law and divinity, before they be informed aright, or capable of such studies." *Scilicet omnibus artibus antistat spes lucri, & formosior est cumulus auri, quam quicquid Græci Latinique delirantes scripserunt. Ex hoc numero deinde veniunt ad gubernacula reipub. intersunt & præsunt consiliis regum o pater o patria!* [in fact the hope of gain stands before all the arts, and a load of gold is more beautiful than all that Greek and Latin fools have written. Such monied men come to govern the helm of state, and are present and prominent at kings' councils. O my father! O my country!] so he [Ennius] complained, and so may others. For even so we find, to serve a great man, to get an office in some Bishop's court (to practise in some good town) or compass a benefice, is the mark we shoot at, as being so advantageous, the highway to preferment.

Although many times, for ought I can see, these men fail as often as the rest in their projects, and are as usually frustrate of their hopes. For let him be a doctor of the law, an excellent civilian of good worth, where shall he practise and expatiate? Their fields are so scant, the civil law with us so contracted with prohibitions, so few causes, by reason of those all devouring municipal laws, *quibus nihil illiteratius*, saith Erasmus, an illiterate and a barbarous study (for though they be never so well learned in it, I can hardly vouchsafe them the name of scholars, except they be otherwise qualified), and so few courts are left to that profession, such slender offices, and those commonly to be compassed at such dear rates, that I know not how an ingenuous man should thrive amongst them.[1] Now for physicians, there are in every village so many mountebanks, empirics, quacksalvers, Paracelsians,[2] as they call themselves, *Causifici & sanicidæ* [pretenders and killers of persons in good health], so Clenard terms them, wizards, alchemists, poor vicars, cast apothecaries, physicians' men, barbers, and goodwives, professing great skill, that I make great doubt how they shall be maintained, or who shall be their patients. Besides, there are so many of both sorts, and some of them such harpies, so covetous, so clamorous, so impudent; and as he said, litigious idiots,

Quibus loquacis affatim arrogantiæ est,
Peritiæ parùm aut nihil,
Nec ulla mica literariis salis,
Crumeni-mulga natio:

Loquuteleia turba, litium strophæ,
Maligna litigantium cohors, togati vultures,
Lavernæ alumni, Agyrtæ, &c.
Which have no skill but prating arrogance,
No learning, such a purse-milking nation:
Gown'd vultures, thieves, and a litigious rout
Of cozeners, that haunt this occupation,

that they cannot well tell how to live one by another, but as he jested in the comedy of clocks,[3] they were so many, *major pars populi aridâ reptant fame*: they are almost starved a great part of them, and ready to devour their fellows, *et noxiâ calliditate se corripere*; such a multitude of pettifoggers and empirics; such impostors, that an honest man knows not in what sort to compose and behave himself in their society, to carry himself with credit in so vile a rout, *scientiæ nomen, tot sumptibus partum & vigiliis profiteri dispudeat, postquam &c.*

Last of all to come to our divines, the most noble profession and worthy of double honour, but of all others the most distressed and miserable. If you will not believe me, hear a brief of it, as it was not many years since, publicly preached at Paul's Cross, by a grave Minister then, and now a reverend Bishop of this land.[4] "We that are bred up in learning, and destinated by our parents to this end, we suffer our childhood in the Grammar school, which Austin calls *magnam tyrannidem, & grave malum*, and compares it to the torments of martyrdom, when we come to the university, if we live of the college allowance, as Phalaris objected to the Leontines πάντων ἐνδεεῖς πλὴν λιμοῦ καὶ φόβου, needy of all things but hunger and fear; or if we be maintained but partly by our parent's cost, do expend in unnecessary maintenance, books and degrees, before we come to any perfection, five

---

[1] *ingenuous* probably ingenious, that is, talented or clever; but possibly also ingenuous in the sense of noble or high-minded (*OED* ingenuous *a* 2, 6).

[2] *Paracelsians* followers of the Swiss physician, chemist, natural philosopher, and mage Paracelsus (ca. 1493–1541).

[3] by Plautus; a lost play of which only fragments survive.

[4] John Howson, bishop of Oxford (1619–28) and Durham (1628–32).

hundred pounds, or a thousand marks.[1] If by this price of the expense of time, our bodies and spirits, our substance and patrimonies, we cannot purchase those small rewards, which are ours by law, and the right of inheritance, a poor parsonage, or a vicarage of fifty [pounds] per annum but we must pay to the patron for the lease of a life (a spent and outworn life) either in annual pension, or above the rate of a copy hold, and that with the hazard and loss of our souls, by simony and perjury, and the forfeiture of all our spiritual preferments, in *esse* and *posse*, both present and to come.[2] What father after awhile will be so improvident, to bring up his son to his great charge, to this necessary beggary? What Christian will be so irreligious, to bring up his son in that course of life, which by all probability and necessity, *cogit ad turpia*, enforcing to sin, will entangle him in simony and perjury, when as the poet saith, *Invitatus ad hæc aliquis de ponte negabit*: a beggar's brat taken from the bridge where he sits a begging, if he knew the inconvenience, had cause to refuse it." This being thus, have not we fished fair all this while, that are initiate divines, to find no better fruits of our labours, *hoc est cur palles, cur quis non prandeat hoc est?* do we macerate ourselves for this? Is it for this we rise so early all the year long? "Leaping" (as he saith) "out of our beds, when we hear the bell ring, as if we had heard a thunder clap." If this be all the respect, reward and honour we shall have, *frange leves calamos, & scinde Thalia libellos*: let us give over our books, and betake ourselves to some other course of life. To what end should we study? *Quid me litterulas stulti docuere parentes*, what did our parents mean to make us scholars, to be as far to seek of preferment after

---

[1] *marks* monetary units used to keep track of accounts; one mark was equivalent to about two-thirds of a pound.

[2] *copy hold* a kind of land tenure in which tenants paid rent on manor lands according to manorial custom and the will of the lord of the manor (*OED* copyhold 2, copy *sb* 5b); *simony* the buying and selling of ecclesiastical privileges, in this case, of benefices (*OED*).

twenty years study, as we were at first: why do we take such pains? *Quid tantum insanis juvat impallescere chartis?* If there be no more hope of reward, no better encouragement. I say again; *Frange leves calamos, & scinde Thalia libellos*; let's turn soldiers, sell our books, and buy swords, guns, and pikes, or stop bottles with them, turn our philosophers' gowns, as Cleanthes once did into millers' coats, leave all, and rather betake ourselves to any other course of life, than to continue longer in this misery. *Præstat dentiscalpia radere, quàm literariis monumentis magnatum favorem emendicare* [it would be better to make toothpicks, than by literary labours to try and get the favour of the great].

Yea, but me thinks I hear some man except at these words, that though this be true which I have said of the estate of scholars, and especially of divines, that it is miserable and distressed at this time, that the church suffers shipwreck of her goods, and that they have just cause to complain; there is a fault, but whence proceeds it? If the cause were justly examined, it would be retorted upon ourselves, if we were cited at that tribunal of truth, we should be found guilty, and not able to excuse it. That there is a fault among us, I confess, and were there not a buyer, there would not be a seller: but to him that will consider better of it, it will more than manifestly appear, that the fountain of these miseries proceeds from these griping patrons. In accusing them, I do not altogether excuse us; both are faulty, they and we: yet in my judgement, theirs is the greater fault, more apparent causes, and much to be condemned. For my part, if it be not with me as I would, or as it should, I do ascribe the cause, as Cardan did in the like case; *meo infortunio potiùs quam illorum sceleri*, to mine own infelicity, rather than their naughtiness: Although I have been baffled in my time by some of them, and have as just cause to complain as another: or rather indeed to mine own negligence; for I was ever like that Alexander in Plutarch, Crassus his tutor in philosophy,[1] who though he lived many years familiarly with rich Crassus, was even as poor when from[2] (which many wondered at), as when he came first to him; he never asked, the other never gave him anything; when he travelled with Crassus he borrowed an hat of him, at his return restored it again; I have had some such noble friends' acquaintance and scholars, but most part (common courtesies and ordinary respects excepted), they and I parted as we met; they gave me as much as I requested, and that was— .[3] And as Alexander ab Alexandro Genial. *Dier.* lib. 6 cap. 16 made answer to Hieronimus Massainus, that wondered, *quum plures ignavos & ignobiles ad dignitates & sacerdotia promotos quotidiè videret,* when other men rose, still he was in the same state, *eodem tenore & fortunâ cui mercedem laborum studiorumque deberi putaret,* whom he thought to deserve as well as the rest. He made answer that he was content with his present estate, was not ambitious, and although *objurgabundus suam segnitiem accusaret, cum obscuræ sortis homines ad sacerdotia & pontificatus evectos &c.* he chid him for his backwardness, yet he was still the same, and for my part (though I be not worthy perhaps to carry Alexander's books) yet by some overweening and well-wishing friends, the like speeches have been used to me, but I replied still with Alexander that I had enough, and more peradventure than I deserved; and with Libanius Sophista that rather chose (when honours and offices by the Emperor were offered unto him) to be *talis Sophista, quam talis magistratus,* I had as lief be still Democritus Junior, and *privus privatus, si mihi jam daretur optio, quam talis fortasse Doctor, talis Dominus.—Sed quorsum hæc?* [And a private person, if I had the choice now, than a Doctor of Divinity or Lord Bishop. But to what purpose do I say all this?] For the rest, 'tis on both sides *facinus detestandum* [an abominable deed], to buy and sell livings,[4] to detain from the Church, that which God's and men's laws have bestowed on it;[5] but in them most, and that from the covetousness and ignorance of such as are interested in this business; I name covetousness in the first place, as the root of all these mischiefs, which Achan like,[6] compels them to commit sacrilege, and to make simoniacal compacts (and what not), to their own ends, that kindles God's wrath, brings a plague, vengeance, and an heavy visitation upon themselves and others. Some out of that insatiable desire of filthy lucre, to be enriched, care not how they come by it, *per fas & nefas,* hook or crook, so they have it. And others when they have with riot and prodigality, embezzled their estates, to recover themselves, make a prey of the Church, robbing it, as Julian the Apostate did,[7] spoil parsons of their revenues (in "keeping half back," as a great man amongst us observes, "and that maintenance on which they should live"[8]): by means whereof, barbarism is increased, and a great decay of Christian professors, for who will apply himself to these divine studies, his son, or friend, when after great pains taken, they shall have nothing whereupon to live? But with what event do they these things?

---

[1] that is, like that Alexander who was tutor to Crassus in philosophy.

[2] that is, was even as poor when he left Crassus.

[3] I had no money, I wanted impudence, I could not scamble, temporize, dissemble [Burton's note].

---

[4] *livings* A living was a position as church officer (vicar or rector usually) with income or property or both.

[5] As a result of the Reformation, many livings were "impropriate": tithes or other income that belonged to the living went to the lay patron who had bought or inherited the right; the patron then passed on only a percentage of that income to the incumbent.

[6] For the covetousness of Achan, see Joshua 7:19-25.

[7] Julian the Apostate (Roman Emperor 361–363 C.E.) instituted a vigorous anti-Christian policy as part of his efforts to re-establish pagan worship.

[8] *a great man* Sir Edward Coke (1552–1634), the most prominent legal expert of the era.

Opesque totis viribus venamini,
At inde messis accidit miserrima.
[You pursue wealth with all your might,
  but the result is miserable]

They toil and moil, but what reap they? They are commonly unfortunate families that use it, accursed in their progeny, and as common experience evinceth, accursed themselves in all their proceedings. "With what face" (as he [Sir Henry Spelman] quotes out of Austin) "can they expect a blessing or inheritance from Christ in Heaven, that defraud Christ of his inheritance here on earth?" I would all our simoniacal patrons, and such as detain tithes, would read those judicious tracts of Sir Henry Spelman, and Sir James Sempill Knights; those late elaborate and learned treatises of Dr Tilslye, and Mr Montague, which they have written of that subject.[1] But though they should read, it would be to small purpose, *clames licet & mare cœlo Confundas*; thunder, lighten, preach hell and damnation, tell them 'tis a sin, they will not believe it; denounce and terrify, they have "cauterized consciences," they do not attend, as the enchanted adder, they stop their ears. Call them base, irreligious, profane, barbarous, pagans, atheists, epicures (as some of them surely are), with the bawd in Plautus, *Euge, optimè,* they cry and applaud themselves, with that miser, *simulac nummos contemplor in arcâ*: say what you will, *quocunque modo rem*: as a dog barks at the moon, to no purpose are your sayings: Take you Heaven, let them have money. A base, profane, epicurean, hypocritical rout; for my part, let them pretend what zeal they will, counterfeit religion, blear the world's eyes, bombast themselves, and stuff out their greatness with Church spoils, shine like so many peacocks; so cold is my charity, so defective

in this behalf, that I shall never think better of them, than that they are rotten at core, their bones are full of epicurean hypocrisy, and atheistical marrow, that they are worse than heathens. For as Dionysius Halicarnasseus observes *antiq. Rom.* lib. 7 *Primum locum &c* "Greeks and barbarians observe all religious rites, and dare not break them for fear of offending their Gods"; but our simoniacal contractors, our senseless Achans, our stupefied patrons, fear neither God nor devil, they have evasions for it, it is no sin, or not due *jure divino* [by divine right], or if a sin, no great sin, &c. And though they be daily punished for it, and they do manifestly perceive, that as he said, frost and fraud come to foul ends; yet as Chrysostome follows it, *Nulla ex pœnâ sit correctio, & quasi adversis malitia hominum provocetur, crescit quotidiè quod puniatur.* they are rather worse than better,—*iram atque animos à crimine sumunt,* and the more they are corrected, the more they offend: but let them take their course, *Rode caper vites* [gnaw, goat, the vines], go on still as they begin, 'tis no sin, let them rejoice secure, God's vengeance will overtake them in the end, and these ill gotten goods as an eagle's feathers, will consume the rest of their substance: It is *aurum Tholosanum* [the gold of Toulouse],[2] and will produce no better effects. "Let them lay it up safe, and make their conveyances never so close, lock and shut door," saith Chrysostome, "yet fraud and covetousness, two most violent thieves, are still included, and a little gain evil gotten, will subvert the rest of their goods." The eagle in Aesop, seeing a piece of flesh, now ready to be sacrificed, swept it away with her claws, and carried it to her nest; but there was a burning coal stuck to it by chance, which unawares consumed her, young ones, nest and all together. Let our simoniacal church-chop-

---

[1] Spelman, *A Tract of the Rights and Respect Due to Churches* (1613); Sempill, *Sacrilege Sacredly Handled* (1619); Richard Tillesley, *Animadversions upon M. Selden's History of Tithes* (1619); Richard Montagu, *Diatribae upon the First Part of the Late History of Tithes* (1621).

[2] Referring to the pillaging of a temple in Toulouse by the commander of a Roman force in 106 B.C.E.; the phrase was proverbial for ill-gotten gains.

ping patrons, and sacrilegious harpies, look for no better success.

A second cause is ignorance, and from thence contempt, *successit odium in literas ab ignorantiâ vulgi*; which [Franciscus] Junius well perceived: this hatred and contempt of learning, proceeds out of ignorance, as they are themselves barbarous, idiots, dull, illiterate, and proud, so they esteem of others.

Sint Mecænates, non deerunt Flacce Marones:

Let there be bountiful patrons; and there will be painful scholars in all sciences. But when they contemn learning, and think themselves sufficiently qualified, if they can write and read, scamble at a piece of evidence,[1] or have so much Latin as that Emperor [Frederick Barbarossa] had, *qui nescit dissimulare, nescit vivere* [he that cannot dissemble, cannot live], they are unfit to do their country service, to perform or undertake any action or employment, which may tend to the good of a Commonwealth, except it be to fight, or to do country justice, with common sense, which every yeoman can likewise do. And so they bring up their children, rude as they are themselves, unqualified, untaught, uncivil most part. *Quis è nostrâ juventute legitimè instituitur literis? Quis oratores aut Philosophos tangit? quis historiam legit, illam rerum agendarum quasi animam? præcipitant parentes vota sua, &c.* [which of our youths is sufficiently instructed in letters? Who handles the orators or philosophers? Who reads history, the soul as it were of actions? Parents are in too great a hurry for their own views] 'twas Lipsius' complaint to his illiterate countrymen, it may be ours. Now shall these men judge of a scholar's worth, that have no worth, that know not what belongs to a student's labours, that cannot distinguish between a true scholar, and a drone? or him that by reason of a voluble tongue, a strong

voice, a pleasing tone, and some trivantly polyanthean helps,[2] steals and gleans a few notes from other men's harvests, and so makes a fair show, and him that is truly learned indeed: that thinks it no more to preach, than to speak, "or to run away with an empty cart"; as a grave man [Dr John King] said; and thereupon vilify us, and our pains; scorn us, and all learning. Because they are rich, and have other means to live, they think it concerns them not to know, or to trouble themselves with it; a fitter task for younger brothers, or poor men's sons, to be pen and inkhorn men, pedantical slaves, and no whit beseeming the calling of a gentleman, as Frenchmen and Germans commonly do, neglect therefore all humane learning, what have they to do with it? Let mariners learn astronomy; merchant's factors study arithmetic; surveyors get them geometry; spectacle-makers optics; land-leapers geography;[3] town clerks rhetoric; what should he do with a spade, that hath no ground to dig; or they with learning, that have no use of it? Thus they reason, and are not ashamed to let mariners, prentices, and the basest servants be better qualified than themselves. In former times, Kings, Princes, and Emperors were the only scholars, excellent in all faculties. Julius Caesar mended the year, and writ his own commentaries,

> —— *media inter prælia semper,*
> *Stellarum cœlique plagis, superisque vacavit.*
> [And, though for ever fighting, yet found time
> To study the heavenly bodies.]

Antoninus, Adrian, Nero, Severus, Julian, &c. Michael the Emperor, and Isacius, were so much

---

[1] *scamble* make way as best one can, stumble along (*OED* scamble *v* 4; this place cited).

[2] *trivantly* truant or idle (see previous note on "trivant"). A polyanthea was a collection of literary "flowers" or choice extracts. Burton is contrasting true scholars with those who give themselves an air of learning by culling quotations from collections of extracts from learned works.

[3] *land-leaper* land-loper, a vagabond or adventurer (*OED* land leaper; this place cited).

given to their studies, that no base fellow would take so much pains: Orion, Perseus, Alphonsus, Ptolomeus, famous astronomers: Sabor, Mithridates, Lysimachus, admired physicians: Plato's kings all: Evax that Arabian Prince, a most expert jeweller, and an exquisite philosopher; the kings of Egypt were priests of old, and chosen from thence,—*Idem rex hominum, Phœbique sacerdos*: but those heroical times are past; the Muses are now banished in this bastard age, *ad sordida tuguriola*, to meaner persons and confined alone almost to universities. In those days, scholars were highly beloved, honoured, esteemed; as old Ennius by Scipio Africanus, Virgil by Augustus; Horace by Mecænas: Princes' companions; dear to them as Anacreon to Polycrates; Philoxenus to Dionysius, and highly rewarded. Alexander sent Xenocrates the philosopher fifty talents, because he was poor, *visu rerum aut eruditione præstantes viri, mensis olim regum adhibiti*, as Philostratus relates of Adrian and Lampridius of Alexander Severus, famous clerks came to these Princes' courts,[1] *velut in Lycæum*, as to an university, and were admitted to their tables, *quasi divûm epulis accumbentes*; Archelaus that Macedonian King would not willingly sup without Euripides (amongst the rest he drank to him at supper one night and gave him a cup of gold for his pains), *delectatus poetæ suavi sermone* [being delighted with the agreeable conversation of the poet], and it was fit it should be so: Because as Plato in his *Protagoras* well saith, a good philosopher as much excels other men, as a great king doth the commons of his country; and again, *quoniam illis nihil deest, & minimè egere solent, & disciplinas quas profitentur, soli à contemptu vindicare possunt*, they needed not to beg so basely, as they compel scholars in our times to complain of poverty, or crouch to a rich chuff for a meal's meat,[2] but could vindicate themselves, and those arts which they professed. Now they would, and cannot: for it is held by some of them, as an axiom, that to keep them poor, will make them study; they must be dieted, as horses to a race, not pampered, *Alendos volunt, non saginandos, ne melioris mentis flammula extinguatur*, a fat bird will not sing, a fat dog cannot hunt; and so by this depression of theirs, some want means, others will, all want encouragement, as being forsaken almost: and generally contemned. 'Tis an old saying *Sint Mæcenates non deerunt Flacce Marones* [let there be Maecenases, Flaccus, and Virgils will not be wanting] and 'tis a true saying still.[3] Yet oftentimes I may not deny it the main fault is in ourselves. Our academics too frequently offend in neglecting patrons, as Erasmus well taxeth, or making ill choice of them *negligimus oblatos aut amplectimur parum aptos*, or if we get a good one, *non studemus mutuis officiis favorem ejus alere*, we do not ply and follow him as we should. *Idem mihi accidit Adolescenti* [the same happened to myself when I was a young man] (saith Erasmus) acknowledging his fault, *& gravissimè peccavi*, and so may I say myself, I have offended in this,[4] and so peradventure have many others. We did not *spondere magnatum favoribus, qui ceperunt nos amplecti*, apply ourselves with that readiness we should, idleness, love of liberty, *immodicus amor libertatis effecit ut diù cum perfidis amicis*, as he confesseth, *& pertinaci paupertate colluctarer*, bashfulness, melancholy, timorousness cause many of us to be too backward and remiss. So some offend in one extreme, but too many on the other, we are most part too forward, too solicitous, too ambitious; too impudent; we

---

[2] *chuff* any disliked person, usually with implications of boorishness or miserliness (*OED* chuff *sb* 12).

[3] Gaius Maecenas (died 8 B.C.E.) was a great patron of Latin poets, including both Horace ("Flaccus") and Virgil.

[4] Had I done as others did, put myself forward, I might have haply been as great a man as many of my equals [Burton's note].

---

[1] *clerks* scholars (see headnote to *OED* clerk *sb*).

commonly complain *deesse Mæcenates* [that Maecenases are wanting], want of encouragement, want of means, when as the true defect is in our own want of worth, our insufficiency, did Mæcenas take notice of Horace or Virgil till they had showed themselves first, or had Bavius and Mevius any patrons? *Egregium specimen dent*, saith Erasmus, let them approve themselves worthy first, sufficiently qualified for learning and manners, before they presume or impudently intrude and put themselves on great men as too many do, with such base flattery, parasitical colloguing, such hyperbolical elogies they do usually insinuate,[1] that it is a shame to hear and see. *Immodicæ laudes conciliant invidiam, potius quam laudem* [immoderate panegyric raises envy rather than praise], and vain commendations derogate from truth, and we think in conclusion, *non melius de laudato, pejus de laudante*, ill of both, the commender and commended. So we offend, but the main fault is in their harshness, defect of patrons. How beloved of old, and how much respected was Plato to Dionysius? How dear to Alexander was Aristotle, Demeratus to Philip, Solon to Cræsus, Anaxarchus and Trebatius to Augustus, Cassius to Vespatian, Plutarch to Trajan? Seneca to Nero? Simonides to Hieron? how honoured?

> *Sed hæc priùs fuere, nunc recondita*
> *Senent quiete,*

those days are gone:

> *Et spec, & ratio studiorum in Cæsare tantùm:*
> [All our hope and motive in study turns on
>   Caesar only]

as he [Juvenal] said of old, we may truly say now, he [King James I] is our amulet, our sun, our sole comfort and refuge, our Ptolemy, our common Mæcenas, *Jacobus munificus, Jacobus pacificus, mysta Musarum, Rex Platonicus: Grande decus, columenque nostrum* [James the munificent, James the peace-loving, the priest of the muses, the platonic king]. A famous scholar himself, and the sole patron, pillar, and sustainer of learning: but his worth in this kind is so well known, that as Paterculus of Cato, *Jam ipsum laudare nefas sit* [it would be monstrous to praise him]: and which Pliny to Trajan. *Seria te carmina, honorque æternus annalium, non hæc brevis & pudenda prædicatio colet* [thus serious poetry and the everlasting glory of our historic past pay you tribute in place of a moment's disgraceful publicity]. But he is now gone, the sun of ours set, and yet no night follows,

> —— *Sol occubuit, nox nulla sequuta est.*

We have such an other in his room

> —— *aureus alter*
> *Avulsus, simili frondescit virga metallo,*
> [Another golden one does not fail when the first
>   is removed; the new king is a chip off the old
>   block]

and long may he [King Charles I] reign and flourish amongst us.

Let me not be malicious, and lie against my genius; I may not deny, but that we have a sprinkling of our gentry, here and there one, excellently well learned, like those Fuggeri in Germany, Du Bartas, Du Plessis, Sadael in France, Picus Mirandula, Schottus, Barotius in Italy;

> *Apparent rari nantes in gurgite vasto.*
> [Here and there, in the vast abyss, a swimmer
>   is seen.]

But they are but few in respect of the multitude, the major part (and some again excepted, that are

---

[1] *elogies* eulogies; brief, usually favourable, summaries of a person's character (*OED* elogy 2).

indifferent) are wholly bent for hawks and hounds, and carried away many times with intemperate lust, gaming, and drinking. If they read a book at any time (*si quid est interim otii à venatu, poculis, aleâ, scortis* [if they have any leisure from hunting, drinking, dicing, drabbing]) 'tis an English chronicle, Sir Huon of Burdeaux, Amadis de Gaule, &c. a play-book, or some pamphlet of news, and that at such seasons only, when they cannot stir abroad, to drive away time, their sole discourse is dogs, hawks, horses, and what news? If someone have been a traveller in Italy, or as far as the Emperor's court, wintered in Orleans, and can court his mistress in broken French, wear his clothes neatly in the newest fashion, sing some choice outlandish tunes, discourse of lords, ladies, towns, palaces, and cities, he is complete and to be admired: Otherwise he and they are much at one; no difference betwixt the master and the man, but worshipful titles: wink and choose betwixt him that sits down (clothes excepted) and him that holds the trencher behind him: yet these men must be our patrons, our governors too sometimes, statesmen, magistrates, noble, great, and wise by inheritance.

Mistake me not (I say again) *Vos ô Patritius sanguis*, you that are worthy Senators, Gentlemen, I honour your names and persons, and with all submissiveness, prostrate myself to your censure and service. There are amongst you, I do ingeniously confess, many well deserving patrons, and true patriots, of my knowledge, besides many hundreds which I never saw, no doubt, or heard of, pillars of our commonwealth, whose worth, bounty, learning, forwardness, true zeal in religion, and good esteem of all scholars, ought to be consecrated to all posterity: but of your rank there are a debauched, corrupt, covetous, illiterate crew again, no better than stocks,[1] *merum pecus (testor Deum, non mihi videri dignos ingenui hominis appellatione)*

[mere cattle (I call God to witness, that they do not seem to me to deserve the name of free men)], barbarous Thracians, *& quis ille Thrax qui hoc neget?* [and what Thracian would deny this?], a sordid, profane, pernicious company, irreligious, impudent and stupid, I know not what epithets to give them, enemies to learning, confounders of the Church, and the ruin of a commonwealth: Patrons they are by right of inheritance, and put in trust freely to dispose of such livings to the Church's good; but (hard task-masters they prove) they take away their straw, and compel them to make their number of brick: they commonly respect their own ends, commodity is the steer of all their actions, and him they present in conclusion, as a man of greatest gifts, that will give most; no penny, no *Pater noster*,[2] as the saying is: *Nisi preces auro fulcias ampliùs irritas: ut Cerberus offa*, their attendants and officers must be bribed, fed and made, as Cerberus is with a sop by him that goes to hell. It was an old saying, *Omnia Romæ venalia* [all things are for sale at Rome], 'tis a rag of popery, which will never be rooted out, there is no hope, no good to be done without money. A clerk may offer himself, approve his worth, learning, honesty, religion, zeal, they will commend him for it; but—*probitas laudatur & alget* [virtue is commended, but not rewarded]. If he be a man of extraordinary parts, they will flock a far off to hear him, as they did in Apuleius, to see Psyche: *multi mortales confluebant ad videndum sæculi decus, speculum gloriosum: laudatur ab omnibus, spectatur ab omnibus, nec quisquam non rex, non regius, cupidus ejus nuptiarum petitor accedit, mirantur quidem divinam formam omnes, sed ut simulacrum fabrè politum mirantur*; many mortal men came to see fair Psyche the glory of her age, they did admire her, commend, desire her for her divine beauty, and gaze upon her; but as on a picture; none would

---

[1] *stocks* tree stumps or blocks of wood; hence, senseless or stupid people (*OED* stock *sb* 1 1a,b,c).

[2] No "Our Father," that is, no payment, no prayer.

marry her, *quòd indotata* [because without dowry], fair Psyche had no money. So they do by learning;

> —— *didicit jam dives avarus*
> *Tantùm admirari, tantùm laudare disertos,*
> *Ut pueri Junonis avem* ——
> Your rich men have now learn'd of latter days
>   T'admire, commend, and come together
> To hear and see a worthy scholar speak,
>   As children do a peacock's feather.

He shall have all the good words that may be given, a proper man, and 'tis pity he hath no preferment, all good wishes, but inexorable, indurate as he is, he will not prefer him, though it be in his power, because he is *indotatus*, he hath no money. Or if he do give him entertainment, let him be never so well qualified, plead affinity, consanguinity, sufficiency, he shall serve 7 years, as Jacob did for Rachel,[1] before he shall have it. If he will enter at first, he must get in at that simoniacal gate, come off soundly, and put in good security to perform all covenants, else he will not deal with, or admit him. But if some poor scholar, some parson chuff will offer himself; some trencher chaplain, that will take it to the halves, thirds, or accept of what he will give, he is welcome, be conformable, preach as he will have him, he likes him before a million of others; for the best is always best cheap: and then as Hierom said to Cromatius, *patellâ dignum operculum* [a worthy cover is added to the pan], such a patron, such a clerk; the cure is well supplied, and all parties pleased. So that is still verified in our age, which Chrysostome complained of in his time, *Qui opulentiores sunt in ordinem parasitorum cogunt eos, & ipsos tanquam canes ad mensas suas enutriunt, eorumque impudentes Ventres iniquarum cœnarum reliquiis differtiunt, iisdem pro arbitrio abutentes:* Rich men keep these lecturers, and fawning parasites, like so many dogs at their tables, and filling

their hungry guts with the offals of their meat, they abuse them at their pleasure, and make them say what they propose. "As children do by a bird or a butterfly in a string, pull in and let him out as they list, do they by their trencher chaplains, prescribe, command their wits, let in and out as to them it seems best." If the patron be precise, so must his chaplain be; if he be papistical, his clerk must be so too, or else be turned out. These are those clerks which serve the turn, whom they commonly entertain, and present to church livings, whilst in the meantime we that are university men, like so many hide-bound calves in a pasture, tarry out our time, wither away as a flower ungathered in a garden, and are never used: or as so many candles, illuminate ourselves alone, obscuring one another's light, and are not discerned here at all; the least of which, translated to a dark room, or to some country benefice, where it might shine apart, would give a fair light, and be seen over all. Whilst we lie waiting here as those sick men did at the pool of Bethesda,[2] till the Angel stirred the water, expecting a good hour, they step between, and beguile us of our preferment. I have not yet said, if after long expectation, much expense, travel, earnest suit of ourselves and friends, we obtain a small benefice at last: our misery begins afresh, we are suddenly encountered with the flesh, world, and devil, with a new onset, we change a quiet life for an ocean of troubles, we come to a ruinous house, which before it be habitable, must be necessarily to our great damage repaired, we are compelled to sue for dilapidations,[3] or else sued ourselves, and scarce yet settled, we are called upon for our predecessor's arrearages; first fruits, tenths, subsidies, are instantly to be paid, benevolence, procurations, &c. and which is most to be feared, we light upon a cracked title, as it befell Clenard of Brabant, for his rectory and charge

---

[1] For the story of Jacob and Rachel, see Genesis 29:16–20.

[2] John 5:2.

[3] *sue for dilapidations*   that is, to sue in an attempt to get money from the previous incumbent for damage to the property.

of his [the town of] Beginæ, he was no sooner inducted, but instantly sued, *cepimusque* (saith he) *strenuè litigare, & implacabili bello confligere*: at length after ten years suit, as long as Troy's siege, when he had tired himself, and spent his money, he was fain to leave all for quietness sake, and give it up to his adversary. Or else we are insulted over, and trampled on by domineering officers, fleeced by those greedy harpies to get more fees, we stand in fear of some precedent lapse; we fall amongst refractory, seditious sectaries, peevish puritans, perverse papists, a lascivious rout of atheistical epicures, that will not be reformed, or some litigious people ("those wild beasts of Ephesus," must be fought with), that will not pay their dues without much repining, or compelled by long suit; for *Laici clericis oppido infesti* [the laity hate the clergy], an old axiom, all they think well gotten that is had from the Church, and by such uncivil, harsh dealings, they make their poor minister weary of his place, if not his life: and put case they be quiet, honest men, make the best of it, as often it falls out, from a polite and terse academic, he must turn rustic, rude, melancholize alone, learn to forget, or else, as many do become maltsters, graziers, chapmen, &c. (now banished from the academy, all commerce of the Muses, and confined to a country village, as Ovid was from Rome to Pontus), and daily converse with a company of idiots and clowns.

—1621–51

The Overburian Character

A poet and courtier educated at Queen's College, Oxford and the Middle Temple, Sir Thomas Overbury (1581–1613) is best known in political history for being the victim of the most infamous scandal of the Jacobean court. His patron was the royal favourite Robert Carr (later Earl of Somerset); Overbury encouraged an intrigue between Carr and Frances Howard, the Countess of Essex, but opposed the marriage projected between the two after the Countess won a controversial divorce. On the pretext of his refusal of a diplomatic post, Overbury was imprisoned in the Tower and slowly poisoned to death by agents employed by Lady Essex. When the plot was discovered, four agents were hanged, and Carr and Lady Essex were both convicted of murder (Francis Bacon was the prosecutor) but pardoned.

The literary "characters" associated with Overbury first appeared in the second edition of Overbury's posthumously published poem "A Wife" (1614), where they are described as by Overbury and "other learned Gentlemen his friends." A year later, more than forty characters were added to this initial collection of twenty-two; by 1622 the collection totalled more than eighty. While not the first set of characters in English (the genre was introduced by Joseph Hall), the "Overburian" character inspired a succession of imitators through much of the seventeenth century. Depicting a social type with his or her habits, manners, and affectations, the Overburian character initiated the witty, playful, "conceited" language that became the hallmark of the genre. The authorship of individual characters is difficult to determine: they would have circulated in anonymous manuscript as a kind of literary parlour game. Of the selections below, "A Good Woman" is very likely by Overbury himself; "A Fair and Happy Milkmaid" and "A Waterman" are probably by the dramatist John Webster; and "A Prisoner" (part of a series of six characters dealing with the life of a debtor) is likely the work of dramatist and pamphleteer Thomas Dekker. For other examples of character-writing, see works by John Earle, Nicholas Breton, Owen Felltham, and Samuel Butler.

✧✧✧

A Good Woman

A good woman is a comfort, like a man. She lacks of him nothing but heat. Thence is her sweetness of disposition, which meets his stoutness more pleasingly; so wool meets iron easier than iron, and turns resisting into embracing. Her greatest learning is religion, and her thoughts are on her own sex, or on men, without casting the difference. Dishonesty never comes nearer than her ears, and then wonder stops it out, and saves virtue the labour. She leaves the neat youth telling his luscious tales, and puts back the serving-man's putting forward with a frown: yet her kindness is free enough to be seen, for it hath no guilt about it; and her mirth is clear, that you may look through it into virtue, but not beyond. She hath not behaviour at a certain, but makes it to her occasion.[1] She hath so much knowledge as to love it; and if she have it not at home, she will fetch it, for this sometimes in a pleasant discontent she dares chide her sex, though she use it never the worse. She is much within, and frames outward things to her mind, not her mind to them. She wears good clothes, but never better; for she finds no degree beyond decency. She hath a content of her own, and so seeks not an husband, but finds him. She is indeed most, but not much of description, for she is direct and one, and hath not the

---

[1] She has not learned the behaviour appropriate to a situation by rote from a book of manners, but relies on natural discretion.

variety of ill. Now she is given fresh and alive to a husband, and she doth nothing more than love him, for she takes him to that purpose. So his good becomes the business of her actions, and she doth herself kindness upon him. After his, her chiefest virtue is a good husband, for she is he.

—1614

A Fair and Happy Milkmaid

Is a country wench, that is so far from making herself beautiful by art, that one look of hers is able to put all face-physic out of countenance.[1] She knows a fair look is but a dumb orator to commend virtue, therefore minds it not. All her excellences stand in her so silently, as if they had stolen upon her without her knowledge. The lining of her apparel (which is herself) is far better than outsides of tissue; for though she be not arrayed in the spoil of the silk-worm, she is decked in innocency, a far better wearing. She doth not, with lying long a-bed, spoil both her complexion and conditions; Nature hath taught her too immoderate sleep is rust to the soul; she rises therefore with chanticleer, her dame's cock, and at night makes lamb her curfew. In milking a cow and straining the teats through her fingers, it seems that so sweet a milk-press makes the milk the whiter or sweeter; for never came almond glove or aromatic ointment off her palm to taint it.[2] The golden ears of corn fall and kiss her feet when she reaps them, as if they wished to be bound and led prisoners by the same hand that felled them. Her breath is her own, which scents all the year long of June, like a new made haycock. She makes her hand hard with labour, and her heart soft with pity; and when winter's evenings fall early (sitting at her merry wheel) she sings a defiance to the giddy wheel of fortune. She doth all things with

so sweet a grace, it seems ignorance will not suffer her to do ill, because her mind is to do well. She bestows her year's wages at next fair; and, in choosing her garments, counts no bravery in the world like decency. The garden and beehive are all her physic and chirurgery, and she lives the longer for it. She dares go alone and unfold sheep in the night,[3] and fears no manner of ill because she means none; yet, to say truth, she is never alone, for she is still accompanied with old songs, honest thoughts, and prayers, but short ones;[4] yet they have their efficacy, in that they are not palled with ensuing idle cogitations. Lastly, her dreams are so chaste that she dare tell them: only a Friday's dream is all her superstition;[5] that she conceals for fear of anger. Thus lives she, and all her care is that she may die in the springtime, to have store of flowers stuck upon her winding-sheet.

—1615

A Waterman [6]

Is one that hath learnt to speak well of himself, for always he names himself "the first man."[7] If he had betaken himself to some richer trade, he could not have choosed but done well; for in this, though a mean one, he is still plying it, and putting himself forward. He is evermore telling strange news, most commonly lies. If he be a sculler, ask him if he be married; he'll equivocate, and swear he's a single man. Little trust is to be given to him, for he thinks that day he does best when he fetches most men

---

[1] *face-physic* cosmetics.

[2] *almond glove* a perfumed glove.

[3] *unfold* let sheep out of their fold or pen.

[4] *prayers, but short ones* as opposed to the long, extemporized prayers associated with puritan worship.

[5] *a Friday's dream* probably a dream foretelling whom she will love or marry.

[6] *Waterman* a boatman who rowed people to and from points on the Thames.

[7] *the first man* an expression used to claim the right to the next customer.

over.[1] His daily labour teaches him the art of dissembling, for, like a fellow that rides to the pillory,[2] he goes not that way he looks. He keeps such a bawling at Westminster, that, if the lawyers were not acquainted with it,[3] an order would be taken with him. When he is upon the water he is fair company; when he comes ashore he mutinies, and, contrary to all other trades, is most surly to gentlemen when they tender payment. The playhouses only keep him sober,[4] and as it doth many other gallants, make him an afternoon's man. London Bridge is the most terrible eyesore to him that can be.[5] And, to conclude, nothing but a great press makes him fly from the river, nor anything but a great frost can teach him any good manners.[6]
—1615

A Prisoner

Is one that hath been a monied man, and is still a very close fellow;[7] whosoever is of his acquaintance, let them make much of him, for they shall find him as fast a friend as any in England: he is a sure man, and you know where to find him. The corruption of a bankrupt is commonly the generation of this creature. He dwells on the back side of the world, or in the suburbs of society, and lives in a tenement which he is sure none will go about to take over his head. To a man that walks abroad, he is one of the antipodes; that goes on the top of the world, and this under it. At his first coming in, he is a piece of new coin, all sharking old prisoners lie sucking at his purse. An old man and he are much alike, neither of them both go far. They are still angry and peevish, and they sleep little. He was born at the fall of Babel, the confusion of languages is only in his mouth. All the vacations he speaks as good English as any man in England, but in term times he breaks out of that hopping one-legged pace into a racking trot of issues, bills, replications, rejoinders, demures, querelles, subpoenas,[8] etc., able to fright a simple country fellow, and make him believe he conjures. Whatsoever his complexion was before, it turns in this place to choler or deep melancholy, so that he needs every hour to take physic to loose his body; for that, like his estate, is very foul and corrupt, and extremely hard bound. The taking of an execution off his stomach gives him five or six stools, and leaves his body very soluble. The withdrawing of an action is a vomit. He is no sound man, and yet an utter barrister, nay, a sergeant of the case, will feed heartily upon him; he is very good picking meat for a lawyer. The barber-surgeons may, if they will, beg him for an anatomy after he hath suffered an execution. An excellent lecture may be made upon his body; for he is a kind of dead carcase—creditors, lawyers, and jailors devour it: creditors peck out his eyes with his own tears; lawyers flay off his own skin, and lap him in parchment; and jailors are the Promethean vultures that gnaw his very heart.[9] He is a bondslave to the law, and, albeit he were a shopkeeper in London, yet he cannot with safe conscience write

---

[1] *fetches* to transport, but also to cheat.

[2] *like a fellow that rides to the pillory* like a rider who faces the tail of the horse.

[3] that is, if the lawyers were not accustomed to hearing such harangues from one another.

[4] Most playhouses were in Southwark, across the Thames; the implication is that the business they provided kept him busy in the afternoons (performances began at about two o'clock) and out of the pubs.

[5] The narrow passages between the arches of London Bridge created a potentially dangerous rapid; to pass through, watermen had to ship oars and "shoot the bridge."

[6] *a great press* impressing of men for the army or, more likely in this case, navy.

[7] *close* stingy, but also confined.

[8] All legal terms; their individual meanings are less important than their opposition, as a group, to "good English."

[9] In mythology, Prometheus was condemned to have a vulture (or eagle) eat his (ever-renewing) liver each day.

himself a freeman. His religion is of five or six colours: this day he prays that God would turn the hearts of his creditors, and tomorrow he curseth the time that ever he saw them. His apparel is daubed commonly with statute lace, the suit itself of durance, and the hose full of long pains.[1] He hath many other lasting suits which he himself is never able to wear out, for they wear out him. The zodiac of his life is like that of the sun, marry not half so glorious. It begins in Aries and ends in Pisces.[2] Both head and feet are, all the year long, in troublesome and laborious motions, and Westminster Hall is his sphere. He lives between the two tropics of Cancer and Capricorn, and by that means is in double danger of crabbed creditors for his purse, and horns for his head, if his wife's heels be light. If he be a gentleman, he alters his arms so soon as he comes in. Few here carry fields or argent, but whatsoever they bear before, here they give only sables.[3] Whiles he lies by it, he is travelling over the Alps, and the hearts of his creditors are the snows that lie unmelted in the middle of summer. He is an almanac out of date; none of his days speak of fair weather. Of all the files of men, he marcheth in the last, and comes limping, for he is shot, and is no man of this world. He hath lost his way, and being benighted, strayed into a wood full of wolves, and nothing so hard as to get away without being devoured. He that walks from six to six in Paul's goes still but a quoit's cast before this man.[4]

—1618

---

[1] Three puns play on the legal resonances of terms from fashion: Statute lace refers to the quality or quantity of lace prescribed by an Act of Apparel (frequently passed in the period); durance was a durable cloth but also imprisonment (*OED* durance 3, 5); hose of long pains were breeches with small panes or squares of silk or velvet.

[2] Aries was associated with the head, Pisces with the feet.

[3] Playing on terms from heraldry: field was the surface of a heraldic shield, argent the silver or white colour of the devices on it, sable the black. The prisoner of course lacks access to open spaces or money, and lives in the dark.

[4] St. Paul's churchyard, the information hub of London, was a popular place to meet and discuss business or news; the implication is that the possibility of imprisonment followed close on the heels of all.

Thomas Hobbes
1588 – 1679

Educated in his home town of Malmesbury and at Magdalen Hall, Oxford, Hobbes in 1608 became tutor and secretary in the household of William Cavendish, the Earl of Devonshire, and would remain associated with the Cavendish family for more than thirty years. Hobbes spent eight years abroad during this period, accompanying his noble pupils on their grand tours; during these trips he met many of Europe's most important political and intellectual figures, including Descartes and Galileo. At one point, Hobbes acted as an amanuensis for Francis Bacon, helping translate some of the *Essays* into Latin. In addition to Bacon, other friends and admirers included Ben Jonson, John Aubrey, William Harvey, John Dryden, Lucius Carey, and Abraham Cowley. Hobbes spent the civil war decade in Paris, leaving England at the prospect of hostilities in 1640 and returning in 1652; in the later 1640s he acted as mathematical tutor to the exiled Charles II. It was while in Paris, hearing news of the wars at home, that Hobbes wrote *Leviathan* (published in London in 1651), the century's classic work of political philosophy. On his return to England Hobbes engaged in political, religious, philosophical, and mathematical controversy; his ideas usually managed to outrage representatives on all sides of most issues. After the Restoration he was awarded a pension from Charles II, and continued to write until the end of his long life, completing a translation of Homer at the age of 86.

In addition to *Leviathan*, Hobbes' writings include a translation of Thucydides (1629); *De Cive* (1642, in English 1651), treating ethics and politics; *The Elements of Law* (1650); *De Corpore* (1655), on metaphysics and physics; *De Homine* (1658), on human sensation and emotion; his own Latin translation of *Leviathan* (1668); *Behemoth, or the Long Parliament* (1679), a dialogue about the civil war; and works on politics, law, religion, rhetoric, geometry, ballistics, and other subjects. For a contemporary biography, see the "brief life" by John Aubrey.

ඥ

Leviathan, or The Matter, Form, and Power of a Commonwealth
(excerpts)

THE INTRODUCTION

Nature (the art whereby God hath made and governs the world) is by the art of man, as in many other things, so in this also imitated, that it can make an artificial animal. For seeing life is but a motion of limbs, the beginning whereof is in some principal part within; why may we not say, that all *automata* (engines that move themselves by springs and wheels as doth a watch) have an artificial life? For what is the heart, but a spring; and the nerves, but so many strings; and the joints, but so many wheels, giving motion to the whole body, such as was intended by the artificer? Art goes yet further, imitating that rational and most excellent work of nature, Man. For by art is created that great Leviathan called a Commonwealth, or state (in Latin *civitas*), which is but an artificial man; though of greater stature and strength than the natural, for whose protection and defence it was intended; and in which, the sovereignty is an artificial soul, as giving life and motion to the whole body; the magistrates, and other officers of judicature and execution, artificial joints; reward and punishment (by which fastened to the seat of the sovereignty, every joint and member is moved to perform his duty) are the nerves, that do the same in the body natural; the wealth and riches of all the particular members, are the strength; *salus populi* (the people's safety) its business; counsellors, by whom all things needful for it to know, are suggested unto it, are the memory; equity and laws, an artificial reason and will; concord, health; sedition, sickness; and civil war, death. Lastly, the pacts and covenants, by which the parts of this body politic were at first made, set together, and united, resemble that *fiat*, or the "Let us make man," pronounced by God in the Creation [Genesis 1:26].

To describe the nature of this artificial man, I will consider

First, the matter thereof, and the artificer; both which is Man.
Secondly, how, and by what covenants it is made; what are the rights and just power or authority of a sovereign; and what it is that preserveth and dissolveth it.
Thirdly, what is a Christian Commonwealth.
Lastly, what is the Kingdom of Darkness.

Concerning the first, there is a saying much usurped of late, that wisdom is acquired not by reading of books, but of men. Consequently whereunto, those persons, that for the most part can give no other proof of being wise, take great delight to show what they think they have read in men, by uncharitable censures of one another behind their backs. But there is another saying not of late understood, by which they might learn truly to read one another, if they would take the pains; and that is, *Nosce teipsum,* "read thy self": which was not meant, as it is now used, to countenance either the barbarous state of men in power towards their inferiors; or to encourage men of low degree to a saucy behaviour towards their betters; but to teach us, that for the similitude of the thoughts and passions of one man, to the thoughts and passions of another, whosoever looketh into himself and considereth what he doth, when he does think, opine, reason, hope, fear, &c., and upon what grounds; he

shall thereby read and know, what are the thoughts, and passions of all other men, upon the like occasions. I say the similitude of passions, which are the same in all men, desire, fear, hope, &c; not the similitude of the objects of the passions, which are the things desired, feared, hoped, &c: for these the constitution individual, and particular education do so vary, and they are so easy to be kept from our knowledge, that the characters of man's heart, blotted and confounded as they are, with dissembling, lying, counterfeiting, and erroneous doctrines, are legible only to him that searcheth hearts. And though by men's actions we do discover their design sometimes; yet to do it without comparing them with our own, and distinguishing all circumstances, by which the case may come to be altered, is to decipher without a key, and be for the most part deceived, by too much trust, or by too much diffidence; as he that reads, is himself a good or evil man.

But let one man read another by his actions never so perfectly, it serves him only with his acquaintance, which are but few. He that is to govern a whole nation, must read in himself, not this, or that particular man; but mankind: which though it be hard to do, harder than to learn any language, or science; yet, when I shall have set down my own reading orderly, and perspicuously, the pains left another, will be only to consider, if he also find not the same in himself. For this kind of doctrine, admitteth no other demonstration.

.   .   .   .   .   .

Chapter XIII
Of the Natural Condition of Mankind, as Concerning their Felicity, and Misery

Nature hath made men so equal, in the faculties of body, and mind; as that though there be found one man sometimes manifestly stronger in body, or of quicker mind than another; yet when all is reckoned together, the difference between man and man is not so considerable, as that one man can thereupon claim to himself any benefit, to which another may not pretend as well as he. For as to the strength of body, the weakest has strength enough to kill the strongest, either by secret machination, or by confederacy with others that are in the same danger with himself.

And as to the faculties of the mind (setting aside the arts grounded upon words, and especially that skill of proceeding upon general and infallible rules, called science; which very few have, and but in few things; as being not a native faculty, born with us; nor attained (as prudence), while we look after somewhat else), I find yet a greater equality amongst men, than that of strength. For prudence is but experience; which equal time, equally bestows on all men in those things they equally apply themselves unto. That which may perhaps make such equality incredible, is but a vain conceit of one's own wisdom, which almost all men think they have in a greater degree than the vulgar; that is, than all men but themselves, and a few others, whom by fame, or for concurring with themselves, they approve. For such is the nature of man, that howsoever they may acknowledge many others to be more witty, or more eloquent, or more learned; yet they will hardly believe there be many so wise as themselves: For they see their own wit at hand, and other men's at a distance. But this proveth rather that men are in that point equal, than unequal. For there is not ordinarily a greater sign of the equal distribution of any thing, than that every man is contented with his share.

From this equality of ability, ariseth equality of hope in the attaining of our ends. And therefore if any two men desire the same thing, which nevertheless they cannot both enjoy, they become enemies; and in the way to their end (which is principally their own conservation, and sometimes their delectation only), endeavour to destroy, or subdue one another. And from hence it comes to pass, that where an invader hath no more to fear, than another man's single power; if one plant, sow, build, or possess a convenient seat, others may probably be expected to come prepared with forces united, to dispossess and deprive him, not only of the fruit of his labour, but also of his life, or liberty. And the invader again is in the like danger of another.

And from this diffidence of one another, there is no way for any man to secure himself, so reasonable, as anticipation; that is, by force, or wiles, to master the persons of all men he can, so long, till he see no other power great enough to endanger him: And this is no more than his own conservation requireth, and is generally allowed. Also because there be some, that taking pleasure in contemplating their own power in the acts of conquest, which they pursue farther than their security requires; if others, that otherwise would be glad to be at ease within modest bounds, should not by invasion increase their power, they would not be able, long time, by standing only on their defence, to subsist. And by consequence, such augmentation of dominion over men, being necessary to a man's conservation, it ought to be allowed him.

Again, men have no pleasure (but on the contrary a great deal of grief), in keeping company, where there is no power able to overawe them all. For every man looketh that his companion should value him at the same rate he sets upon himself: And upon all signs of contempt, or undervaluing, naturally endeavours, as far as he dares (which amongst them that have no common power to keep them in quiet, is far enough to make them destroy each other) to extort a greater value from his contemnors, by damage; and from others, by the example.

So that in the nature of man, we find three principal causes of quarrel. First, competition; secondly, diffidence; thirdly, glory.

The first, maketh men invade for gain; the second, for safety; and the third, for reputation. The first use violence, to make themselves masters of other men's persons, wives, children, and chattel; the second, to defend them; the third, for trifles, as a word, a smile, a different opinion, and any other sign of undervalue, either direct in their persons, or by reflexion in their kindred, their friends, their nation, their profession, or their name.

Hereby it is manifest, that during the time men live without a common power to keep them all in awe, they are in that condition which is called war; and such a war, as is of every man against every man. For war consisteth not in battle only, or the act of fighting; but in a tract of time, wherein the will to contend by battle is sufficiently known: and therefore the notion of time is to be considered in the nature of war; as it is in the nature of weather. For as the nature of foul weather lieth not in a shower or two of rain, but in an inclination thereto of many days together: So the nature of war, consisteth not in actual fighting, but in the known disposition thereto, during all the time there is no assurance to the contrary. All other time is peace.

Whatsoever therefore is consequent to a time of war, where every man is enemy to every man; the same is consequent to the time, wherein men live without other security than what their own strength and their own invention shall furnish them withal. In such condition, there is no place for industry; because the fruit thereof is uncertain: and consequently no culture of the earth; no navigation, nor use of the commodities that may be imported by sea; no commodious building; no instruments of moving, and removing such things as require much force; no knowledge of the face of the earth; no account of time; no arts; no letters; no society; and which is worst of all, continual fear, and danger of violent death; and the life of man, solitary, poor, nasty, brutish, and short.

It may seem strange to some man, that has not well weighed these things, that nature should thus dissociate, and render men apt to invade, and destroy one another: and he may therefore, not trusting to this inference, made from the passions, desire perhaps to have the same confirmed by experience. Let him therefore consider with himself, when taking a journey, he arms himself, and seeks to go well accompanied; when going to sleep, he locks his doors; when even in his house he locks his chests; and this when he knows there be laws, and public officers, armed, to revenge all injuries shall be done him; what opinion he has of his fellow subjects, when he rides armed; of his fellow citizens, when he locks his doors; and of his children, and servants, when he locks his chests. Does he not there as much accuse mankind by his actions, as I do by my words? But neither of us accuse man's nature in it. The desires and other passions of man are in themselves no sin. No more are the actions that proceed from those passions, till they know a law that forbids them: which till laws be made they cannot know: nor can any law be made, till they have agreed upon the person that shall make it.

It may peradventure be thought, there was never such a time, nor condition of war as this; and I believe it was never generally so, over all the world: but there are many places where they live so now. For the savage people in many places of America, except the government of small families, the concord whereof dependeth on natural lust, have no government at all; and live at this day in that brutish manner, as I said before. Howsoever, it may be perceived what manner of life there would be, where there were no common power to fear, by the manner of life which men that have formerly lived under a peaceful government, use to degenerate into, in a civil war.

But though there had never been any time wherein particular men were in a condition of war one against another; yet in all times, kings, and persons of sovereign authority, because of their independency, are in continual jealousies, and in the state and posture of gladiators; having their weapons pointing, and their eyes fixed on one another; that is, their forts, garrisons, and guns upon the frontiers of their kingdoms; and continual spies upon their neighbours, which is a posture of war. But because they uphold thereby the industry of their subjects; there does not follow from it that misery which accompanies the liberty of particular men.

To this war of every man against every man, this also is consequent; that nothing can be unjust. The notions of right and wrong, justice and injustice have there no place. Where there is no common power, there is no law: where no law, no injustice. Force and fraud are in war the two cardinal virtues. Justice and injustice are none of the faculties neither of the body, nor mind. If they were, they might be in a man that were alone in the world, as well as his senses, and passions. They are qualities that relate to men in society, not in solitude. It is consequent also to the same condition, that there be no propriety, no dominion, no *mine* and *thine* distinct; but only that to be every man's, that he can get; and for so long, as he can keep it. And thus much for the ill condition which man by mere nature is actually placed in; though with a possibility to come out of it, consisting partly in the passions, partly in his reason.

The passions that incline men to peace are fear of death; desire of such things as are necessary to commodious living; and a hope by their industry to obtain them. And reason suggesteth convenient articles of peace, upon which men may be drawn to agreement. These articles are they which otherwise are called the Laws of Nature: whereof I shall speak more particularly in the two following chapters.[1]

---

[1] not included in this selection, but summarized in the second paragraph of Chapter 17 below. For Hobbes, self-preservation is the fundamental right of nature; the laws of nature are those rules or

CHAPTER XVII
Of the Causes, Generation, and Definition of a Commonwealth

The final cause, end, or design of men (who naturally love liberty, and dominion over others), in the introduction of that restraint upon themselves (in which we see them live in Commonwealths), is the foresight of their own preservation, and of a more contented life thereby; that is to say, of getting themselves out from that miserable condition of war, which is necessarily consequent (as hath been shown) to the natural passions of men, when there is no visible power to keep them in awe, and tie them by fear of punishment to the performance of their covenants, and observation of those Laws of Nature set down in the fourteen and fifteenth chapters.

For the Laws of Nature (as justice, equity, modesty, mercy, and (in sum), *doing to others, as we would be done to*) of themselves, without the terror of some power, to cause them to be observed, are contrary to our natural passions, that carry us to partiality, pride, revenge, and the like. And covenants, without the sword, are but words, and of no strength to secure a man at all. Therefore notwithstanding the Laws of Nature (which everyone hath then kept, when he has the will to keep them, when he can do it safely), if there be no power erected, or not great enough for our security; every man will and may lawfully rely on his own strength and art, for caution against all other men. And in all places where men have lived by small families, to rob and spoil one another, has been a trade, and so far from being reputed against the Law of Nature, that the

---

precepts conducive to this right of self-preservation. The primary law of nature is to seek peace, as a safer alternative to the war of all against all. Other laws, such as willingness to make contracts or covenants, justice, gratitude, mutual accommodation, equity, and mercy, all contribute to the maintenance of peace.

greater spoils they gained, the greater was their honour; and men observed no other laws therein, but the laws of honour; that is, to abstain from cruelty, leaving to men their lives, and instruments of husbandry. And as small families did then; so now do cities and kingdoms which are but greater families (for their own security) enlarge their dominions, upon all pretences of danger, and fear of invasion, or assistance that may be given to invaders, endeavour as much as they can, to subdue, or weaken their neighbours, by open force, and secret arts, for want of other caution, justly; and are remembered for it in after ages with honour.

Nor is it the joining together of a final number of men that gives them this security; because in small numbers, small additions on the one side or the other, make the advantage of strength so great, as is sufficient to carry the victory; and therefore gives encouragement to an invasion. The multitude sufficient to confide in for our security is not determined by any certain number, but by comparison with the enemy we fear; and is then sufficient, when the odds of the enemy is not of so visible and conspicuous moment, to determine the event of war, as to move him to attempt.

And be there never so great a multitude; yet if their actions be directed according to their particular judgments, and particular appetites, they can expect thereby no defence, nor protection, neither against a common enemy, nor against the injuries of one another. For being distracted in opinions concerning the best use and application of their strength, they do not help, but hinder one another; and reduce their strength by mutual opposition to nothing: whereby they are easily not only subdued by a very few that agree together; but also when there is no common enemy, they make war upon each other, for their particular interests. For if we could suppose a great multitude of men to consent in the observation of justice, and other Laws of Nature, without a common power to keep them all

in awe; we might as well suppose all mankind to do the same; and then there neither would be, or need to be any civil government, or Commonwealth at all; because there would be peace without subjection.

Nor is it enough for the security, which men desire should last all the time of their life, that they be governed, and directed by one judgment, for a limited time; as in one battle, or one war. For though they obtain a victory by their unanimous endeavour against a foreign enemy; yet afterwards, when either they have no common enemy, or he that by one part is held for an enemy, is by another part held for a friend, they must needs by the difference of their interests dissolve, and fall again into a war amongst themselves.

It is true that certain living creatures, as bees, and ants, live sociably one with another (which are therefore by Aristotle numbered amongst political creatures), and yet have no other direction, than their particular judgments and appetites; nor speech, whereby one of them can signify to another, what he thinks expedient for the common benefit: and therefore some man may perhaps desire to know, why mankind cannot do the same. To which I answer,

First, that men are continually in competition for honour and dignity, which these creatures are not; and consequently amongst men there ariseth on that ground, envy and hatred, and finally war; but amongst these not so.

Secondly, that amongst these creatures, the common good differeth not from the private; and being by nature inclined to their private, they procure thereby the common benefit. But man, whose joy consisteth in comparing himself with other men, can relish nothing but what is eminent.

Thirdly, that these creatures, having not (as man) the use of reason, do not see, nor think they see any fault, in the administration of their common business: whereas amongst men, there are very many that think themselves wiser, and abler to govern the public, better than the rest; and these strive to reform and innovate, one this way, another that way; and thereby bring it into distraction and civil war.

Fourthly, that these creatures, though they have some use of voice, in making known to one another their desires and other affections; yet they want that art of words, by which some men can represent to others that which is good, in the likeness of evil; and evil, in the likeness of good; and augment, or diminish the apparent greatness of good and evil; discontenting men, and troubling their peace at their pleasure.

Fifthly, irrational creatures cannot distinguish between injury, and damage; and therefore as long as they be at ease, they are not offended with their fellows: whereas man is then most troublesome, when he is most at ease: for then it is that he loves to show his wisdom, and control the actions of them that govern the Commonwealth.

Lastly, the agreement of these creatures is natural; that of men, is by covenant only, which is artificial: and therefore it is no wonder if there be somewhat else required (besides covenant) to make their agreement constant and lasting; which is a common power, to keep them in awe, and to direct their actions to the common benefit.

The only way to erect such a common power, as may be able to defend them from the invasion of foreigners, and the injuries of one another, and thereby to secure them in such sort, as that by their own industry and by the fruits of the earth, they may nourish themselves and live contentedly; is, to confer all their power and strength upon one man, or upon one assembly of men, that may reduce all their wills, by plurality of voices, unto one will: which is as much as to say, to appoint one man, or

assembly of men, to bear their person;[1] and everyone to own, and acknowledge himself to be author of whatsoever he that so beareth their person, shall act, or cause to be acted, in those things which concern the common peace and safety; and therein to submit their wills, everyone to his will, and their judgments, to his judgment. This is more than consent, or concord; it is a real unity of them all, in one and the same person, made by covenant of every man with every man, in such manner, as if every man should say to every man, "I authorize and give up my right of governing myself, to this man, or to this assembly of men, on this condition, that thou give up thy right to him, and authorize all his actions in like manner." This done, the multitude so united in one person is called a Commonwealth, in Latin *Civitas*. This is the generation of that great Leviathan, or rather (to speak more reverently) of that mortal God, to which we owe under the immortal God, our peace and defence. For by this authority, given him by every particular man in the Commonwealth, he hath the use of so much power and strength conferred on him, that by terror thereof, he is enabled to conform the wills of them all, to peace at home, and mutual aid against their enemies abroad. And in him consisteth the essence of the Commonwealth; which (to define it) is *one person, of whose acts a great multitude, by mutual covenants one with another, have made themselves every one the author, to the end he may use the strength and means of them all, as he shall think expedient, for their peace and common defence.*

And he that carryeth this person, is called *sovereign*, and said to have *sovereign power*; and everyone besides, his *subject*.

The attaining to this sovereign power, is by two ways. One, by natural force; as when a man maketh

---

[1] an allusion to a passage in Cicero, *De Officiis* (I.124), where the elected magistrate is said to "bear the person" of the Commonwealth— an example of Hobbes' use of republican political theory to define the role of a king.

his children to submit themselves and their children to his government, as being able to destroy them if they refuse; or by war subdueth his enemies to his will, giving them their lives on that condition. The other, is when men agree amongst themselves, to submit to some man, or assembly of men, voluntarily, on confidence to be protected by him against all others. This latter, may be called a political Commonwealth, or Commonwealth by institution; and the former, a Commonwealth by acquisition. And first, I shall speak of a Commonwealth by institution.

Chapter XVIII
Of the Rights of Sovereigns by Institution

A Commonwealth is said to be instituted, when a multitude of men do agree, and covenant, everyone, with everyone, that to whatsoever man, or assembly of men, shall be given by the major part the right to present the person of them all (that is to say, to be their representative), every one, as well he that voted for it, as he that voted against it, shall authorize all the actions and judgments of that man, or assembly of men, in the same manner, as if they were his own, to the end, to live peaceably amongst themselves, and be protected against other men.

From this institution of a Commonwealth are derived all the rights and faculties of him, or them, on whom the sovereign power is conferred by the consent of the people assembled.

First, because they covenant, it is to be understood, they are not obliged by former covenant to anything repugnant hereunto. And consequently they that have already instituted a Commonwealth, being thereby bound by covenant, to own the actions and judgments of one, cannot lawfully make a new covenant amongst themselves, to be obedient to any other, in anything whatsoever, without his permission. And therefore, they that are subjects to a monarch, cannot without his leave cast off monar-

chy, and return to the confusion of a disunited multitude; nor transfer their person from him that beareth it, to another man, or other assembly of men: for they are bound, every man to every man, to own, and be reputed author of all, that he that already is their sovereign, shall do, and judge fit to be done: so that any one man dissenting, all the rest should break their covenant made to that man, which is injustice: and they have also every man given the sovereignty to him that beareth their person; and therefore if they depose him, they take from him that which is his own, and so again it is injustice. Besides, if he that attempteth to depose his sovereign be killed, or punished by him for such attempt, he is author of his own punishment, as being by the institution, author of all his sovereign shall do: And because it is injustice for a man to do anything for which he may be punished by his own authority, he is also upon that title, unjust. And whereas some men have pretended for their disobedience to their sovereign, a new covenant, made, not with men, but with God; this also is unjust: for there is no covenant with God, but by mediation of somebody that representeth God's person; which none doth but God's Lieutenant, who hath the sovereignty under God. But this pretence of covenant with God is so evident a lie, even in the pretenders' own consciences, that it is not only an act of an unjust, but also of a vile, and unmanly disposition.

Secondly, because the right of bearing the person of them all is given to him they make sovereign, by covenant only of one to another, and not of him to any of them; there can happen no breach of covenant on the part of the sovereign; and consequently none of his subjects, by any pretence of forfeiture, can be freed from his subjection. That he which is made sovereign maketh no covenant with his subjects beforehand, is manifest; because either he must make it with the whole multitude, as one party to the covenant; or he must make a several covenant with every man. With the whole, as one party, it is impossible; because as yet they are not one person: and if he make so many several covenants as there be men, those covenants after he hath the sovereignty are void, because what act soever can be pretended by anyone of them for breach thereof, is the act both of himself, and of all the rest, because done in the person, and by the right of everyone of them in particular. Besides, if any one, or more of them, pretend a breach of the covenant made by the sovereign at his institution; and others, or one other of his subjects, or himself alone, pretend there was no such breach, there is in this case, no judge to decide the controversy: it returns therefore to the sword again; and every man recovereth the right of protecting himself by his own strength, contrary to the design they had in the institution. It is therefore in vain to grant sovereignty by way of precedent covenant. The opinion that any monarch receiveth his power by covenant, that is to say on condition, proceedeth from want of understanding this easy truth, that covenants being but words, and breath, have no force to oblige, contain, constrain, or protect any man, but what it has from the public sword; that is, from the untied hands of that man, or assembly of men that hath the sovereignty, and whose actions are avouched by them all, and performed by the strength of them all, in him united. But when an assembly of men is made sovereign; then no man imagineth any such covenant to have passed in the institution; for no man is so dull as to say, for example, the people of Rome made a covenant with the Romans, to hold the sovereignty on such or such conditions; which not performed, the Romans might lawfully depose the Roman people. That people see not the reason to be alike in a monarchy, and in a popular government, proceedeth from the ambition of some, that are kinder to the government of an assembly, whereof they may hope to participate, than of monarchy, which they despair to enjoy.

Thirdly, because the major part hath by consenting voices declared a sovereign; he that dissented must now consent with the rest; that is, be contented to avow all the actions he shall do, or else justly be destroyed by the rest. For if he voluntarily entered into the congregation of them that were assembled, he sufficiently declared thereby his will (and therefore tacitly covenanted) to stand to what the major part should ordain: and therefore if he refuse to stand thereto, or make protestation against any of their decrees, he does contrary to his covenant, and therefore unjustly. And whether he be of the congregation, or not; and whether his consent be asked, or not, he must either submit to their decrees, or be left in the condition of war he was in before; wherein he might without injustice be destroyed by any man whatsoever.

Fourthly, because every subject is by this institution author of all the actions, and judgments of the sovereign instituted; it follows, that whatsoever he doth, it can be no injury to any of his subjects; nor ought he to be by any of them accused of injustice. For he that doth anything by authority from another, doth therein no injury to him by whose authority he acteth: But by this institution of a Commonwealth, every particular man is author of all the sovereign doth; and consequently he that complaineth of injury from his sovereign, complaineth of that whereof he himself is author; and therefore ought not to accuse any man but himself; no nor himself of injury; because to do injury to one's self, is impossible. It is true that they that have sovereign power, may commit iniquity; but not injustice, or injury in the proper signification.

Fifthly, and consequently to that which was said last, no man that hath sovereign power can justly be put to death, or otherwise in any manner by his subjects punished. For seeing every subject is author of the actions of his sovereign; he punisheth another, for the actions committed by himself.

And because the end of this institution is the peace and defence of them all; and whosoever has right to the end, has right to the means; it belongeth of right, to whatsoever man, or assembly that hath the sovereignty, to be judge both of the means of peace and defence; and also of the hindrances, and disturbances of the same; and to do whatsoever he shall think necessary to be done, both before hand, for the preserving of peace and security, by prevention of discord at home, and hostility from abroad; and, when peace and security are lost, for the recovery of the same. And therefore,

Sixthly, it is annexed to the sovereignty to be judge of what opinions and doctrines are averse, and what conducing to peace; and consequently, on what occasions, how far, and what, men are to be trusted withal, in speaking to multitudes of people; and who shall examine the doctrines of all books before they be published. For the actions of men proceed from their opinions; and in the well governing of opinions, consisteth the well governing of men's actions, in order to their peace, and concord. And though in matter of doctrine, nothing ought to be regarded but the truth; yet this is not repugnant to regulating of the same by peace. For doctrine repugnant to peace can no more be true, than peace and concord can be against the Law of Nature. It is true, that in a Commonwealth, where by the negligence, or unskilfulness of governors, and teachers, false doctrines are by time generally received; the contrary truths may be generally offensive: Yet the most sudden, and rough bustling in of a new truth, that can be, does never break the peace, but only sometimes awake the war. For those men that are so remissly governed that they dare take up arms, to defend, or introduce an opinion, are still in war; and their condition not peace, but only a cessation of arms for fear of one another; and they live as it were, in the precincts of battle continually. It belongeth therefore to him that hath the sovereign power, to be judge, or constitute all judges of opinions and doctrines, as a thing necessary to peace; thereby to prevent discord and civil war.

Seventhly, is annexed to the sovereign the whole power of prescribing the rules, whereby every man may know what goods he may enjoy, and what actions he may do, without being molested by any of his fellow subjects: And this is it men call *propriety*. For before constitution of sovereign power (as hath already been shown) all men had right to all things; which necessarily causeth war: and therefore this propriety, being necessary to peace, and depending on sovereign power, is the act of that power, in order to the public peace. These rules of propriety (or *Meum* and *Tuum* [mine and thine]) and of good, evil, lawful, and unlawful in the actions of subjects, are the civil laws; that is to say, the laws of each Commonwealth in particular; though the name of civil law be now restrained to the ancient civil laws of the city of Rome; which being the head of a great part of the world, her laws at that time were in these parts the civil law.

Eighthly, is annexed to the sovereignty the right of judicature; that is to say, of hearing and deciding all controversies which may arise concerning law, either civil, or natural, or concerning fact. For without the decision of controversies, there is no protection of one subject against the injuries of another; the laws concerning *Meum* and *Tuum* are in vain; and to every man remaineth, from the natural and necessary appetite of his own conservation, the right of protecting himself by his private strength, which is the condition of war; and contrary to the end for which every Commonwealth is instituted.

Ninthly, is annexed to the sovereignty the right of making war and peace with other nations, and Commonwealths; that is to say, of judging when it is for the public good, and how great forces are to be assembled, armed, and paid for that end; and to levy money upon the subjects, to defray the expenses thereof. For the power by which the people are to be defended consisteth in their armies; and the strength of an army, in the union of their strength under one command; which command the sovereign instituted, therefore hath; because the command of the militia, without other institution, maketh him that hath it sovereign. And therefore whosoever is made general of an army, he that hath the sovereign power is always generalissimo.

Tenthly, is annexed to the sovereignty the choosing of all counsellors, ministers, magistrates, and officers, both in peace, and war. For seeing the sovereign is charged with the end, which is the common peace and defence; he is understood to have power to use such means, as he shall think most fit for his discharge.

Eleventhly, to the sovereign is committed the power of rewarding with riches, or honour; and of punishing with corporal, or pecuniary punishment, or with ignominy every subject according to the law he hath formerly made; or if there be no law made, according as he shall judge most to conduce to the encouraging of men to serve the Commonwealth, or deterring of them from doing disservice to the same.

Lastly, considering what values men are naturally apt to set upon themselves; what respect they look for from others; and how little they value other men; from whence continually arise amongst them emulation, quarrels, factions, and at last war, to the destroying of one another, and diminution of their strength against a common enemy; it is necessary that there be laws of honour, and a public rate of the worth of such men as have deserved, or are able to deserve well of the Commonwealth; and that there be force in the hands of some or other, to put those laws in execution. But it hath already been shown, that not only the whole militia, or forces of the Commonwealth; but also the judicature of all controversies is annexed to the sovereignty. To the sovereign therefore it belongeth also to give titles of honour; and to appoint what order of place and dignity each man shall hold; and what signs of respect, in public or private meetings, they shall give to one another.

These are the rights which make the essence of sovereignty; and which are the marks whereby a man may discern in what man, or assembly of men, the sovereign power is placed, and resideth. For these are incommunicable, and inseparable. The power to coin money; to dispose of the estate and persons of infant heirs; to have preemption in markets; and all other statute prerogatives, may be transferred by the sovereign; and yet the power to protect his subjects be retained. But if he transfer the militia, he retains the judicature in vain, for want of execution of the laws: Or if he grant away the power of raising money, the militia is in vain: or if he give away the government of doctrines, men will be frighted into rebellion with the fear of spirits. And so if we consider any one of the said rights, we shall presently see that the holding of all the rest will produce no effect in the conservation of peace and justice, the end for which all Commonwealths are instituted. And this division is it, whereof it is said, "a Kingdom divided in itself cannot stand":[1] For unless this division precede, division into opposite armies can never happen. If there had not first been an opinion received of the greatest part of England, that these powers were divided between the King, and the Lords, and the House of Commons, the people had never been divided, and fallen into this civil war; first between those that disagreed in politics; and after between the dissenters about the liberty of religion; which have so instructed men in this point of sovereign right, that there be few now (in England) that do not see, that these rights are inseparable, and will be so generally acknowledged, at the next return of peace; and so continue, till their miseries are forgotten; and no longer, except the vulgar be better taught than they have hitherto been.

---

[1] Matthew 12:25; Mark 3:24; Luke 11:17.

And because they are essential and inseparable rights, it follows necessarily, that in whatsoever words any of them seem to be granted away, yet if the sovereign power itself be not in direct terms renounced, and the name of sovereign no more given by the grantees to him that grants them, the grant is void: for when he has granted all he can, if we grant back the sovereignty, all is restored, as inseparably annexed thereunto.

This great authority being indivisible, and inseparably annexed to the sovereignty, there is little ground for the opinion of them, that say of sovereign kings, though they be *singulis majores*, of greater power than every one of their subjects, yet they be *universis minores*, of less power than them all together. For if by *all together*, they mean not the collective body as one person, then *all together*, and *every one*, signify the same; and the speech is absurd. But if by *all together*, they understand them as one person (whose person the sovereign bears), then the power of all together is the same with the sovereign's power; and so again the speech is absurd: which absurdity they see well enough, when the sovereignty is in an assembly of the people; but in a monarch they see it not; and yet the power of sovereignty is the same in whomsoever it be placed.

And as the power, so also the honour of the sovereign, ought to be greater, than that of any, or all the subjects. For in the sovereignty is the fountain of honour. The dignities of Lord, Earl, Duke, and Prince are his creatures. As in the presence of the master, the servants are equal, and without any honour at all; so are the subjects, in the presence of the sovereign. And though they shine some more, some less, when they are out of his sight; yet in his presence, they shine no more than the stars in presence of the sun.

But a man may here object, that the condition of subjects is very miserable; as being obnoxious to the lusts, and other irregular passions of him, or them that have so unlimited a power in their hands.

And commonly they that live under a monarch, think it the fault of monarchy; and they that live under the government of democracy, or other sovereign assembly, attribute all the inconvenience to that form of Commonwealth; whereas the power in all forms, if they be perfect enough to protect them, is the same; not considering that the estate of man can never be without some incommodity or other; and that the greatest, that in any form of government can possibly happen to the people in general, is scarce sensible, in respect of the miseries, and horrible calamities, that accompany a civil war; or that dissolute condition of masterless men, without subjection to laws, and a coercive power to tie their hands from rapine, and revenge: nor considering that the greatest pressure of sovereign governors proceedeth not from any delight, or profit they can expect in the damage, or weakening of their subjects, in whose vigor consisteth their own strength and glory; but in the restiveness of themselves, that unwillingly contributing to their own defence, make it necessary for their governors to draw from them what they can in time of peace, that they may have means on any emergent occasion, or sudden need, to resist, or take advantage of their enemies. For all men are by nature provided of notable multiplying glasses (that is their passions and self-love), through which every little payment appeareth a great grievance; but are destitute of those prospective glasses (namely moral and civil science), to see afar off the miseries that hang over them, and cannot without such payments be avoided.

CHAPTER XIX
Of the Several Kinds of Commonwealth by Institution, and of Succession to the Sovereign Power

The difference of Commonwealths consisteth in the difference of the sovereign, or the person representative of all and every one of the multitude. And because the sovereignty is either in one man, or in an assembly of more than one; and into that assembly either every man hath right to enter, or not every one, but certain men distinguished from the rest; it is manifest, there can be but three kinds of Commonwealth. For the representative must needs be one man, or more: and if more, then it is the assembly of all, or but of a part. When the representative is one man, then is the Commonwealth a monarchy: when an assembly of all that will come together, then it is a democracy, or popular Commonwealth: when an assembly of a part only, then it is called an aristocracy. Other kind of Commonwealth there can be none: for either one, or more, or all, must have the sovereign power (which I have shown to be indivisible) entire.

There be other names of government in the histories, and books of policy, as tyranny, and oligarchy: But they are not the names of other forms of government, but of the same forms misliked. For they that are discontented under monarchy, call it tyranny; and they that are displeased with aristocracy, called it oligarchy: So also, they which find themselves grieved under a democracy, call it anarchy (which signifies want of government), and yet I think no man believes that want of government is any new kind of government: nor by the same reason ought they to believe, that the government is of one kind, when they like it, and another, when they mislike it, or are oppressed by the governors.

It is manifest, that men who are in absolute liberty, may, if they please, give authority to one man, to represent them every one; as well as give such authority to any assembly of men whatsoever; and consequently may subject themselves, if they think good, to a monarch, as absolutely, as to any other representative. Therefore, where there is already erected a sovereign power, there can be no other representative of the same people, but only to certain particular ends, by the sovereign limited. For that were to erect two sovereigns; and every

man to have his person represented by two actors, that by opposing one another must needs divide that power, which (if men will live in peace) is indivisible; and thereby reduce the multitude into the condition of war, contrary to the end for which all sovereignty is instituted. And therefore as it is absurd to think that a sovereign assembly, inviting the people of their dominion, to send up their deputies, with power to make known their advice, or desires, should therefore hold such deputies, rather than themselves, for the absolute representative of the people: so it is absurd also, to think the same in a monarchy. And I know not how this so manifest a truth, should of late be so little observed; that in a monarchy, he that had the sovereignty from a descent of 600 years, was alone called sovereign, had the title of majesty from every one of his subjects, and was unquestionably taken by them for their king, was notwithstanding never considered as their representative; that name without contradiction passing for the title of those men, which at his command were sent up by the people to carry their petitions, and give him (if he permitted it) their advice. Which may serve as an admonition, for those that are the true, and absolute representative of a people, to instruct men in the nature of that office, and to take heed how they admit of any other general representation upon any occasion whatsoever, if they mean to discharge the trust committed to them.

The difference between these three kinds of Commonwealth consisteth not in the difference of power; but in the difference of convenience, or aptitude to produce the peace, and security of the people; for which end they were instituted. And to compare monarchy with the other two, we may observe; first, that whosoever beareth the person of the people, or is one of that assembly that bears it, beareth also his own natural person. And though he be careful in his politic person to procure the common interest; yet he is more, or no less careful to procure the private good of himself, his family, kindred and friends; and for the most part, if the public interest chance to cross the private, he prefers the private: for the passions of men are commonly more potent than their reason. From whence it follows, that where the public and private interest are most closely united, there is the public most advanced. Now in monarchy, the private interest is the same with the public. The riches, power, and honour of a monarch arise only from the riches, strength and reputation of his subjects. For no king can be rich, nor glorious, nor secure; whose subjects are either poor, or contemptible, or too weak through want, or dissension, to maintain a war against their enemies: Whereas in a democracy, or aristocracy, the public prosperity confers not so much to the private fortune of one that is corrupt, or ambitious, as doth many times a perfidious advice, a treacherous action, or a civil war.

Secondly, that a monarch receiveth counsel of whom, when, and where he pleaseth; and consequently may hear the opinion of men versed in the matter about which he deliberates, of what rank or quality soever, and as long before the time of action, and with as much secrecy, as he will. But when a sovereign assembly has need of counsel, none are admitted but such as have a right thereto from the beginning; which for the most part are of those who have been versed more in the acquisition of wealth than of knowledge; and are to give their advice in long discourses, which may, and do commonly excite men to action, but not govern them in it. For the understanding is by the flame of the passions, never enlightened, but dazzled: Nor is there any place, or time, wherein an assembly can receive counsel with secrecy, because of their own multitude.

Thirdly, that the resolutions of a monarch, are subject to no other inconstancy, than that of human nature; but in assemblies, besides that of nature, there ariseth an inconstancy from the number. For

the absence of a few, that would have the resolution once taken, continue firm (which may happen by security, negligence, or private impediments), or the diligent appearance of a few of the contrary opinion, undoes today, all that was concluded yesterday.

Fourthly, that a monarch cannot disagree with himself, out of envy, or interest; but an assembly may; and that to such a height, as may produce a civil war.

Fifthly, that in monarchy there is this inconvenience; that any subject, by the power of one man, for the enriching of a favourite or flatterer, may be deprived of all he possesseth; which I confess is a great and inevitable inconvenience. But the same may as well happen, where the sovereign power is in an assembly: For their power is the same; and they are as subject to evil counsel, and to be seduced by orators, as a monarch by flatterers; and becoming one another's flatterers, serve one another's covetousness and ambition by turns. And whereas the favourites of monarchs, are few, and they have none else to advance but their own kindred; the favourites of an assembly, are many; and the kindred much more numerous, than of any monarch. Besides, there is no favourite of a monarch, which cannot as well succour his friends, as hurt his enemies: But orators, that is to say, favourites of sovereign assemblies, though they have great power to hurt, have little to save. For to accuse, requires less eloquence (such is man's nature) than to excuse; and condemnation, than absolution more resembles justice.

Sixthly, that it is an inconvenience in monarchy, that the sovereignty may descend upon an infant, or one that cannot discern between good and evil: and consisteth in this, that the use of his power, must be in the hand of another man, or of some assembly of men, which are to govern by his right, and in his name; as curators, and protectors of his person, and authority. But to say there is inconvenience, in putting the use of the sovereign power, into the hand of a man, or an assembly of men; is to say that all government is more inconvenient, than confusion, and civil war. And therefore all the danger that can be pretended, must arise from the contention of those, that for an office of so great honour, and profit, may become competitors. To make it appear, that this inconvenience, proceedeth not from that form of government we call monarchy, we are to consider, that the precedent monarch, hath appointed who shall have the tuition of his infant successor, either expressly by testament, or tacitly, by not controlling the custom in that case received: And then such inconvenience (if it happen) is to be attributed, not to the monarchy, but to the ambition, and injustice of the subjects; which in all kinds of government, where the people are not well instructed in their duty, and the rights of sovereignty, is the same. Or else the precedent monarch, hath not at all taken order for such tuition; and then the Law of Nature hath provided this sufficient rule, That the tuition shall be in him, that hath by nature most interest in the preservation of the authority of the infant, and to whom least benefit can accrue by his death, or diminution. For seeing every man by nature seeketh his own benefit, and promotion; to put an infant into the power of those, that can promote themselves by his destruction, or damage, is not tuition, but treachery. So that sufficient provision being taken, against all just quarrel, about the government under a child, if any contention arise to the disturbance of the public peace, it is not to be attributed to the form of monarchy, but to the ambition of subjects, and ignorance of their duty. On the other side, there is no great Commonwealth, the sovereignty whereof is in a great assembly, which is not, as to consultations of peace, and war, and making of laws, in the same condition, as if the government were in a child. For as a child wants the judgment to dissent from counsel given him, and is thereby necessitated to take the advice of them, or him, to whom he is committed: So an assembly wanteth the liberty, to dissent from the counsel of the major part, be it good, or bad. And as a child has need of a tutor, or protector, to preserve his person, and authority: So also (in great Commonwealths) the sovereign assembly, in all great dangers and troubles, have need of *Custodes libertatis*; that is of dictators, or protectors of their authority; which are as much as temporary monarchs; to whom for a time, they may commit the entire exercise of their power; and have (at the end of that time) been oftener deprived thereof, than infant kings, by their protectors, regents, or any other tutors.

Though the kinds of sovereignty be, as I have now shown, but three; that is to say, monarchy, where one man has it; or democracy, where the general assembly of subjects hath it; or aristocracy, where it is an assembly of certain persons nominated, or otherwise distinguished from the rest: Yet he that shall consider the particular Commonwealths that have been, and are in the world, will not perhaps easily reduce them to three, and may thereby be inclined to think there be other forms, arising from these mingled together. As for example, elective kingdoms; where kings have the sovereign power put into their hands for a time; or kingdoms, wherein the king hath a power limited: which governments, are nevertheless by most writers called monarchy. Likewise if a popular, or aristocratical Commonwealth, subdue an enemy's country, and govern the same, by a president, procurator, or other magistrate; this may seem perhaps at first sight, to be a democratical, or aristocratical government. But it is not so. For elective kings are not sovereigns, but ministers of the sovereign; not limited kings, sovereigns, but ministers of them that have the sovereign power: Nor are those provinces which are in subjection to a democracy, or aristocracy of another Commonwealth, democratically or aristocratically governed, but monarchically.

And first, concerning an elective king, whose power is limited to his life, as it is in many places of Christendom at this day; or to certain years or months, as the dictator's power amongst the Romans; if he have right to appoint his successor, he is no more elective but hereditary. But if he have no power to elect his successor, then there is some other man, or assembly known, which after his decease may elect a new, or else the Commonwealth dieth, and dissolveth with him, and returneth to the condition of war. If it be known who have the power to give the sovereignty after his death, it is known also that the sovereignty was in them before: For none have right to give that which they have not right to possess, and keep to themselves, if they think good. But if there be none that can give the sovereignty, after the decease of him that was first elected; then has he power, nay he is obliged by the Law of Nature, to provide, by establishing his successor, to keep those that had trusted him with the government, from relapsing into the miserable condition of civil war. And consequently he was, when elected, a sovereign absolute.

Secondly, that king whose power is limited, is not superior to him, or them that have the power to limit it; and he that is not superior, is not supreme; that is to say not sovereign. The sovereignty therefore was always in that assembly which had the right to limit him; and by consequence the government not monarchy, but either democracy, or aristocracy; as of old time in Sparta; where the kings had a privilege to lead their armies; but the sovereignty was in the *Ephori*.[1]

Thirdly, whereas heretofore the Roman people, governed the land of Judea (for example) by a president; yet was not Judea therefore a democracy; because they were not governed by an assembly, into the which, any of them, had right to enter; nor by an aristocracy; because they were not governed

by any assembly, into which, any man could enter by their election: but they were governed by one person, which though as to the people of Rome was an assembly of the people, or democracy; yet as to people of Judea, which had no right at all of participating in the government, was a monarch. For though where the people are governed by an assembly, chosen by themselves out of their own number, the government is called a democracy, or aristocracy; yet when they are governed by an assembly, not of their own choosing, 'tis a monarchy; not of one man, over another man; but of one people, over another people.

Of all these forms of government, the matter being mortal, so that not only monarchs, but also whole assemblies die, it is necessary for the conservation of the peace of men, that as there was order taken for an artificial man, so there be order also taken, for an artificial eternity of life; without which, men that are governed by an assembly, should return into the condition of war in every age; and they that are governed by one man, as soon as their governor dieth. This artificial eternity, is that which men call the Right of Succession.

There is no perfect form of government, where the disposing of the succession is not in the present sovereign. For if it be in any other particular man, or private assembly, it is in a person subject, and may be assumed by the sovereign at his pleasure; and consequently the right is in himself. And if it be in no particular man, but left to a new choice; then is the Commonwealth dissolved; and the right is in him that can get it; contrary to the intention of them that did institute the Commonwealth, for their perpetual, and not temporary security.

In a democracy, the whole assembly cannot fail, unless the multitude that are to be governed fail. And therefore questions of the right of succession, have in that form of government no place at all.

In an aristocracy, when any of the assembly dieth, the election of another into his room belong-

[1] *Ephori*   the Spartan magistrates, who had the power to restrain the authority of the kings.

158

eth to the assembly, as the sovereign, to whom belongeth the choosing of all counsellors, and officers. For that which the representative doth, as actor, every one of the subjects doth, as author. And though the sovereign assembly, may give power to others, to elect new men, for supply of their court; yet it is still by their authority, that the election is made; and by the same it may (when the public shall require it) be recalled.

The greatest difficulty about the right of succession, is in monarchy: And the difficulty ariseth from this, that at first sight, it is not manifest who is to appoint the successor; nor many times, who it is whom he hath appointed. For in both these cases, there is required a more exact ratiocination, than every man is accustomed to use. As to the question, who shall appoint the successor, of a monarch that hath the sovereign authority; that is to say, who shall determine of the right of inheritance (for elective kings and princes have not the sovereign power in propriety, but in use only), we are to consider, that either he that is in possession, has right to dispose of the succession, or else that right is again in the dissolved multitude. For the death of him that hath the sovereign power in propriety, leaves the multitude without any sovereign at all; that is, without any representative in whom they should be united, and be capable of doing any one action at all: And therefore they are incapable of election of any new monarch; every man having equal right to submit himself to such as he thinks best able to protect him; or if he can, protect himself by his own sword; which is a return to confusion, and to the condition of a war of every man against every man, contrary to the end for which monarchy had its first institution. Therefore it is manifest, that by the institution of monarchy, the disposing of the successor, is always left to the judgment and will of the present possessor.

And for the question (which may arise sometimes) who it is that the monarch in possession, hath designed to the succession and inheritance of his power; it is determined by his express words, and testament; or by other tacit signs sufficient.

By express words, or testament, which it is declared by him in his life time, *viva voce* [with the living voice; orally], or by writing; as the first emperors of Rome declared who should be their heirs. For the word heir does not of itself imply the children, or nearest kindred of a man; but whomsoever a man shall any way declare, he would have to succeed him in his estate. If therefore a monarch declare expressly, that such a man shall be his heir, either by word or writing, then is that man immediately after the decease of his predecessor, invested in the right of being monarch.

But where testament, and express words are wanting, other natural signs of the will are to be allowed: whereof the one is custom. And therefore where the custom is, that the next of kindred absolutely succeedeth, there also the next of kindred hath right to the succession; for that, if the will of him that was in possession had been otherwise, he might easily have declared the same in his life time. And likewise where the custom is, that the next of the male kindred succeedeth, there also the right of succession is in the next of the kindred male, for the same reason. And so it is if the custom were to advance the female. For whatsoever custom a man may by a word control, and does not, it is a natural sign he would have that custom stand.

But where neither custom, nor testament hath preceded, there it is to be understood, first, that a monarch's will is, that the government remain monarchical; because he hath approved that government in himself. Secondly, that a child of his own, male, or female, be preferred before any other; because men are presumed to be more inclined by nature, to advance their own children, than the children of other men; and of their own, rather a male than a female; because men, are naturally fitter than women, for actions of labour and danger.

Thirdly, where his own issue faileth, rather a brother than a stranger; and so still the nearer in blood, rather than the more remote; because it is always presumed that the nearer of kin, is the nearer in affection; and 'tis evident that a man receives always, by reflection, the most honour from the greatness of his nearest kindred.

But if it be lawful for a monarch to dispose of the succession by words of contract, or testament, men may perhaps object a great inconvenience: for he may sell, or give his right of governing to a stranger; which, because strangers (that is, men not used to live under the same government, nor speaking the same language) do commonly undervalue one another, may turn to the oppression of his subjects; which is indeed a great inconvenience: but it proceedeth not necessarily from the subjection to a stranger's government, but from the unskilfulness of the governors, ignorant of the true rules of politics. And therefore the Romans when they had subdued many nations, to make their government digestible, were wont to take away that grievance, as much as they thought necessary, by giving sometimes to whole nations, and sometimes to principal men of every nation they conquered, not only the privileges, but also the name of Romans; and took many of them into the Senate, and offices of charge, in the Roman city. And this was it our most wise King James aimed at, in endeavouring the union of his two realms of England and Scotland. Which if he could have obtained, had in all likelihood prevented the civil wars, which make both those kingdoms, at this present, miserable. It is not therefore any injury to the people, for a monarch to dispose of the succession by will; though by the fault of many princes, it hath been sometimes found inconvenient. Of the lawfulness of it, this also is an argument, that whatsoever inconvenience can arrive by giving a kingdom to a stranger, may arrive also by so marrying with strangers, as the Right of

Succession may descend upon them: yet this by all men is accounted lawful.

CHAPTER XX
Of Dominion Paternal, and Despotical

Dominion is acquired two ways; by generation, and by conquest. The right of dominion by generation, is that, which the parent hath over his children; and is called paternal. And is not so derived from the generation, as if therefore the parent had dominion over his child because he begat him; but from the child's consent, either express, or by other sufficient argument declared. For as to the generation, God hath ordained to man a helper; and there be always two that are equally parents: the dominion therefore over the child, should belong equally to both; and he be equally subject to both, which is impossible; for no man can obey two masters. And whereas some have attributed the dominion to the man only, as being of the more excellent sex; they misreckon in it. For there is not always that difference of strength, or prudence between the man and the woman, as that the right can be determined without war. In Commonwealths, this controversy is decided by the civil law: and for the most part (but not always), the sentence is in favour of the father; because for the most part Commonwealths have been erected by the fathers, not by the mothers of families. But the question lieth now in the state of mere nature; where there are supposed no laws of matrimony; no laws for the education of children; but the Law of Nature, and the natural inclination of the sexes one to another, and to their children. In this condition of mere nature, either the parents between themselves dispose of the dominion over the child by contract; or do not dispose thereof at all. If they dispose thereof, the right passeth according to the contract. We find in history that the Amazons contracted with the men of the neighbouring countries, to whom they had recourse for issue, that the issue male should be sent back, but the female remain with themselves: so that the dominion of the females was in the mother.

If there be no contract, the dominion is in the mother. For in the condition of mere nature, where there are no matrimonial laws, it cannot be known who is the father, unless it be declared by the mother: and therefore the right of dominion over the child dependeth on her will, and is consequently hers. Again, seeing the infant is first in the power of the mother, so as she may either nourish, or expose it; if she nourish it, it oweth its life to the mother; and is therefore obliged to obey her, rather than any other; and by consequence the dominion over it is hers. But if she expose it, and another find, and nourish it, the dominion is in him that nourisheth it. For it ought to obey him by whom it is preserved; because preservation of life being the end, for which one man becomes subject to another, every man is supposed to promise obedience, to him, in whose power it is to save, or destroy him.

. . . .

Dominion acquired by conquest, or victory in war, is that which some writers call despotical, from Δεσπότης, which signifieth a lord, or master; and is the dominion of the master over his servant. And this dominion is then acquired to the victor, when the vanquished, to avoid the present stroke of death, covenanteth either in express words, or by other sufficient signs of the will, that so long as his life, and the liberty of his body is allowed him, the victor shall have the use thereof, at his pleasure. And after such covenant made, the vanquished is a servant, and not before: for by the word *servant* (whether it be derived from *servire*, to serve, or from *servare*, to save, which I leave to grammarians to dispute) is not meant a captive, which is kept in prison, or bonds, till the owner of him that took him, or bought him of one that did, shall consider

what to do with him (for such men (commonly called slaves), have no obligation at all; but may break their bonds, or the prison; and kill, or carry away captive their master, justly): but one, that being taken, hath corporal liberty allowed him; and upon promise not to run away, nor to do violence to his master, is trusted by him.

It is not therefore the victory that giveth the right of dominion over the vanquished, but his own covenant. Nor is he obliged because he is conquered; that is to say, beaten, and taken, or put to flight; but because he cometh in, and submitteth to the victor; nor is the victor obliged by an enemy's rendering himself (without promise of life), to spare him for this his yielding to discretion; which obliges not the victor longer, than in his own discretion he shall think fit.

. . . .

The master of the servant, is master also of all he hath; and may exact the use thereof; that is to say, of his goods, of his labour, of his servants, and of his children, as often as he shall think fit. For he holdeth his life of his master, by the convenant of obedience; that is, of owning, and authorising whatsoever the master shall do. And in case the master, if he refuse, kill him, or cast him into bonds, or otherwise punish him for his disobedience, he is himself the author of the same; and cannot accuse him of injury.

In sum, the rights and consequences of both paternal and despotical dominion, are the very same with those of a sovereign by institution; and for the same reasons: which reasons are set down in the precedent chapter. So that for a man that is monarch of divers nations, whereof he hath, in one the sovereignty by institution of the people assembled, and in another by conquest, that is by the submission of each particular, to avoid death or bonds; to demand of one nation more than of the other, from the title of conquest, or as being a conquered nation, is an act of ignorance of the rights of sovereignty. For the sovereign is absolute over both alike; or else there is no sovereignty at all; and so every man may lawfully protect himself, if he can, with his own sword, which is the condition of war.

By this it appears, that a great family if it be not part of some Commonwealth, is of itself, as to the rights of sovereignty, a little monarchy; whether that family consist of a man and his children; or of a man and his servants; or of a man, and his children, and servants together: wherein the father or master is the sovereign. But yet a family is not properly a Commonwealth; unless it be of that power by its own number, or by other opportunities, as not to be subdued without the hazard of war. For where a number of men are manifestly too weak to defend themselves united, every one may use his own reason in time of danger, to save his own life, either by flight, or by submission to the enemy, as he shall think best; in the same manner as a very small company of soldiers, surprised by an army, may cast down their armies, and demand quarter, or run away, rather than be put to the sword. And thus much shall suffice; concerning what I find by speculation, and deduction, of sovereign rights, from the nature, need, and designs of men, in erecting of Commonwealths, and putting themselves under monarchs, or assemblies, entrusted with power enough for their protection.

.   .   .   .

So that it appeareth plainly, to my understanding, both from reason, and Scripture, that the sovereign power, whether placed in one man, as in monarchy, or in one assembly of men, as in popular, and aristocratical Commonwealths, is as great, as possibly men can be imagined to make it. And though of so unlimited a power, men may fancy many evil consequences, yet the consequences of the want of it, which is perpetual war of every man against his neighbour, are much worse. The condition of man in this life shall never be without inconveniences; but there happeneth in no Commonwealth any great inconvenience, but what proceeds from the subject's disobedience, and breach of those covenants, from which the Commonwealth hath its being. And whosoever thinking sovereign power too great, will seek to make it less; must subject himself, to the power, that can limit it; that is to say, to a greater.

The greatest objection is, that of the practise; when men ask, where, and when, such power has by subjects been acknowledged. But one may ask them again, when, or where has there been a kingdom long free from sedition and civil war. In those nations, whose Commonwealths have been long-lived, and not been destroyed, but by foreign war, the subjects never did dispute of the sovereign power. But howsoever, an argument from the practise of men, that have not sifted to the bottom, and with exact reason weighed the causes and nature of Commonwealths, and suffer daily those miseries that proceed from the ignorance thereof, is invalid. For though in all places of the world, men should lay the foundation of their houses on the sand, it could not thence be inferred, that so it ought to be. The skill of making and maintaining Commonwealths consisteth in certain rules, as doth arithmetic and geometry; not (as tennis-play) on practise only: which rules, neither poor men have the leisure, nor men that have had the leisure, have hitherto had the curiosity, or the method to find out.

CHAPTER XXI
Of the Liberty of Subjects

Liberty, or freedom, signifieth (properly) the absence of opposition (by opposition, I mean external impediments of motion); and may be applied no less to irrational, and inanimate creatures, than to rational. For whatsoever is so tied, or environed, as it cannot move, but within a certain space, which space is determined by the opposition of some external body, we say it hath not liberty to go further. And so of all living creatures, whilst they are imprisoned, or restrained, with walls, or chains; and of the water whilst it is kept in by banks, or vessels, that otherwise would spread itself into a larger space, we use to say, they are not at liberty, to move in such manner, as without those external impediments they would. But when the impediment of motion, is the constitution of the thing itself, we use not to say, it wants the liberty; but the power to move; as when a stone lieth still, or a man is fastened to his bed by sickness.

And according to this proper, and generally receiving meaning of the word, *a free man, is he, that in those things, which by his strength and wit he is able to do, is not hindered to do what he has a will to.*

.   .   .   .

But as men, for the attaining of peace, and conservation of themselves thereby, have made an artificial man, which we call a Commonwealth; so also have they made artificial chains, called Civil Laws, which they themselves, by mutual covenants, have fastened at one end, to the lips of that man, or assembly, to whom they have given the sovereign power; and at the other end to their own ears. These bonds in their own nature but weak, may nevertheless be made to hold, by the danger, though not by the difficulty of breaking them.

In relation to these bonds only it is, that I am to speak now, of the liberty of subjects. For seeing there is no Commonwealth in the world, wherein there be rules enough set down, for the regulating of all the actions, and words of men (as being a thing impossible), it followeth necessarily, that in all kinds of actions, by the laws pretermitted,[1] men have the liberty, of doing what their own reasons

shall suggest, for the most profitable to themselves. For if we take liberty in the proper sense, for corporal liberty; that is to say, freedom from chains, and prison, it were very absurd for men to clamor as they do, for the liberty they so manifestly enjoy. Again, if we take liberty, for an exemption from laws, it is no less absurd, for men to demand as they do, that liberty, by which all other men may be masters of their lives. And yet as absurd as it is, this is it they demand; not knowing that the laws are of no power to protect them, without a sword in the hands of a man, or men, to cause those laws to be put in execution. The liberty of a subject, lieth therefore only in those things, which in regulating their actions, the sovereign hath pretermitted: such as is the liberty to buy, and sell, and otherwise contract with one another; to choose their own abode, their own diet, their own trade of life, and institute their children as they themselves think fit; and the like.

Nevertheless we are not to understand, that by such liberty, the sovereign power of life, and death, is either abolished, or limited. For it has been already shown, that nothing the sovereign representative can do to a subject, on what pretence soever, can properly be called injustice, or injury; because every subject is author of every act the sovereign doth; so that he never wanted right to anything, otherwise, than as he himself is the subject of God, and bound thereby to observe the laws of nature. And therefore it may, and doth often happen in Commonwealths, that a subject may be put to death, by the command of the sovereign power; and yet neither do the other wrong: As when Jeptha caused his daughter to be sacrificed [Judges 11:30–39]: In which, and the like cases, he that so dieth, had liberty to do the action, for which he is nevertheless, without injury put to death. And the same holdeth also in a sovereign prince, that putteth to death an innocent subject. For though the action be against the law of nature, as being contrary to

---

[1] *pretermitted* passed over, omitted, not mentioned (*OED*).

equity (as was the killing of Uriah, by David), yet it was not an injury to Uriah; but to God. Not to Uriah, because the right to do what he pleased, was given him by Uriah himself: And yet to God, because David was God's subject; and prohibited all iniquity by the law of nature. Which distinction, David himself, when he repented the fact, evidently confirmed, saying, "To thee only have I sinned" [II Samuel 11:1–27, 12:1–13].

. . . .

But it is an easy thing, for men to be deceived, by the specious name of liberty; and for want of judgment to distinguish, mistake that for their private inheritance, and birthright, which is the right of the public only. And when the same error is confirmed by the authority of men in reputation for their writings in this subject, it is no wonder if it produce sedition, and change of government. In these western parts of the world, we are made to receive our opinions concerning the institution, and rights of Commonwealths, from Aristotle, Cicero, and other men, Greeks and Romans, that living under popular states, derived those rights, not from the principles of nature, but transcribed them into their books, out of the practise of their own Commonwealths, which were popular; as the grammarians describe the rules of language, out of the practise of the time; or the rules of poetry, out of the poems of Homer and Virgil. And because the Athenians were taught (to keep them from desire of changing their government), that they were free men, and all that lived under monarchy were slaves; therefore Aristotle puts it down in his *Politics* (lib.6, cap.2 [actually VI.i.6]), "In democracy, liberty is to be supposed: for 'tis commonly held, that no man is free in any other government." And as Aristotle; so Cicero, and other writers have grounded their civil doctrine, on the opinions of the Romans, who were taught to hate monarchy, at first, by them that having deposed their sovereign, shared amongst

them the sovereignty of Rome; and afterwards by their successors. And by reading of these Greek, and Latin authors, men from their childhood have gotten a habit (under a false show of liberty) of favouring tumults, and of licentious controlling the actions of their sovereigns; and again of controlling those controllers, with the effusion of so much blood; as I think I may truly say, there was never anything so dearly bought, as these western parts have bought the learning of the Greek and Latin tongues.

To come now to the particulars of the true liberty of a subject; that is to say, what are the things, which though commanded by the sovereign, he may nevertheless, without injustice, refuse to do; we are to consider, what rights we pass away, when we make a Commonwealth; or (which is all one), what liberty we deny ourselves, by owning all the actions (without exception) of the man, or assembly we make our sovereign....

First therefore, seeing sovereignty by institution, is by covenant of everyone to everyone; and sovereignty by acquisition, by covenants of the vanquished to the victor, or child to the parent; it is manifest, that every subject has liberty in all those things, the right whereof cannot by covenant be transferred. I have shown before in the 14th Chapter, that covenants, not to defend a man's own body, are void. Therefore,

If the sovereign command a man (though justly condemned) to kill, wound, or maim himself; or not to resist those that assault him; or to abstain from the use of food, air, medicine, or any other thing, without which he cannot live; yet hath that man the liberty to disobey.

If a man be interrogated by the sovereign, or his authority, concerning a crime done by himself, he is not bound (without assurance of pardon) to confess it; because no man (as I have shown in the same Chapter) can be obliged by covenant to accuse himself.

．　．　．　．　．　．　．

To resist the sword of the Commonwealth, in defence of another man, guilty, or innocent, no man hath liberty; because such liberty, takes away from the sovereign, the means of protecting us; and is therefore destructive of the very essence of government. But in case a great many men together, have already resisted the sovereign power unjustly, or committed some capital crime, for which everyone of them expecteth death, whether have they not the liberty then to join together, and assist, and defend one another? Certainly they have: For they but defend their lives, which the guilty man may as well do, as the innocent. There was indeed injustice in the first breach of their duty; their bearing of arms subsequent to it, though it be to maintain what they have done, is no new unjust act. And if it be only to defend their persons, it is not unjust at all. But the offer of pardon taketh from them, to whom it is offered, the plea of self-defence, and maketh their perseverance in assisting, or defending the rest, unlawful.

As for other liberties, they depend on the silence of the law. In cases where the sovereign has prescribed no rule, there the subject hath the liberty to do, or forbear, according to his own discretion. And therefore such liberty is in some places more, and in some less; and in some times more, in other times less, according as they that have the sovereignty shall think most convenient. As for example, there was a time, when in England a man might enter in to his own land (and dispossess such as wrongfully possessed it), by force. But in after-times, that liberty of forcible entry, was taken away by a statute made (by the King) in Parliament. And in some places of the world, men have the liberty of many wives: in other places, such liberty is not allowed.

．　．　．　．　．　．　．

The obligation of subjects to the sovereign, is understood to last as long, and no longer, than the power lasteth, by which he is able to protect them. For the right men have by nature to protect themselves, when none else can protect them, can by no covenant be relinquished. The sovereignty is the soul of the Commonwealth; which once departed from the body, the members do no more receive their motion from it. The end of obedience is protection; which, wheresoever a man seeth it, either in his own, or in another's sword, nature applieth his obedience to it, and his endeavour to maintain it. And though sovereignty, in the intention of them that make it, be immortal; yet is it in its own nature, not only subject to violent death, by foreign war; but also through the ignorance, and passions of men, it hath in it, from the very institution, many seeds of natural mortality, by intestine discord.

．　．　．　．　．　．　．

CHAPTER XLVII
Of the Benefit that Proceedeth from such Darkness,[1]
and to Whom it Accrueth.

Cicero maketh honorable mention of one of the Cassii, a severe judge amongst the Romans, for a custom he had in criminal causes (when the testimony of the witnesses was not sufficient), to ask the accusers, *Cui bono* [who stands to gain]; that is to say, what profit, honor, or other contentment, the accused obtained, or expected by the fact. For amongst presumptions, there is none that so evidently declareth the author, as doth the benefit of the action. By the same rule I intend in this place to examine, who they may be, that have possessed the people so long in this part of Christendom, with these doctrines, contrary to the peaceable societies of mankind.

And first, to this error, *that the present Church now militant on earth, is the Kingdom of God* (that is,

---

[1] The previous chapter is entitled "Of Darkness from Vain Philosophy, and Fabulous Traditions."

the kingdom of glory, or the land of promise; not the kingdom of grace, which is but a promise of the land), are annexed these worldly benefits; first, that the pastors, and teachers of the church, are entitled thereby, as God's public ministers, to a right of governing the church; and consequently (because the church, and Commonwealth are the same persons) to be rectors, and governors of the Commonwealth. By this title it is, that the Pope prevailed with the subjects of all Christian princes, to believe, that to disobey him was to disobey Christ himself; and in all differences between him and other princes (charmed with the word *Power Spiritual*), to abandon their lawful sovereigns; which is in effect an universal monarch over all Christendom. For though they were first invested in the right of being supreme teachers of Christian doctrine, by, and under Christian emperors, within the limits of the Roman Empire (as it is acknowledged by themselves) by the title of *Pontifex Maximus* [supreme pontiff], who was an officer subject to the civil state; yet after the Empire was divided, and dissolved, it was not hard to obtrude upon the people already subject to them, under title, namely, the right of St. Peter; not only to save entire their pretended power; but also to extend the same over the same Christian provinces, though no more united in the Empire of Rome. This benefit of an universal monarch (considering the desire of men to bear rule), is a sufficient presumption, that the Popes that pretended to it, and for a long time enjoyed it, were the authors of the doctrine, by which it was obtained; namely, that the church now on earth, is the Kingdom of Christ. For that granted, it must be understood, that Christ hath some lieutenant amongst us, by whom we are to be told what are his commandments.

After that certain churches had renounced this universal power of the Pope, one would expect in reason, that the civil sovereigns in all those churches, should have recovered so much of it, as (before they had unadvisedly let it go), was their own right, and in their own hands. And in England it was so in effect; saving that they, by whom the kings administered the government of religion, by maintaining their employment to be in God's right, seemed to usurp, if not a supremacy, yet an independency on the civil power: and they but seemed to usurp it, in as much as they acknowledged a right in the king, to deprive them of the exercise of their functions at his pleasure.

But in those places where the presbytery took that office, though many other doctrines of the Church of Rome were forbidden to be taught; yet this doctrine, that the Kingdom of Christ is already come, and that it began at the Resurrection of our Saviour, was still retained. But *cui bono*? What profit did they expect from it? The same which the Popes expected: to have a sovereign power over the people. For what is it for men to excommunicate their lawful king, but to keep him from all places of God's public service in his own kingdom? and with force to resist him, when he with force endeavoureth to correct them? Or what is it, without authority from the civil sovereign, to excommunicate any person, but to take from him his lawful liberty, that is, to usurp an unlawful power over their brethren? The authors therefore of this darkness in religion, are the Roman, and the Presbyterian clergy.

To this head, I refer also all those doctrines, that serve them to keep the possession of this spiritual sovereignty after it is gotten. As first, that the *Pope in his public capacity cannot err*. For who is there, that believing this to be true, will not readily obey him in whatsoever he commands?

Secondly, that all other bishops, in what Commonwealth soever, have not their right, neither immediately from God, nor mediately from their civil sovereigns, but from the Pope, is a doctrine, by which there comes to be in every Christian Commonwealth many potent men (for so are bishops), that have their dependence on the Pope, and owe obedience to him, though he be a foreign prince; by which means he is able (as he hath done many times), to raise a civil war against the state that submits not itself to be governed according to his pleasure and interest.

Thirdly, the exemption of these, and of all other priests, and of all monks, and friars, from the power of the civil laws. For by this means, there is a great part of every Commonwealth, that enjoy the benefit of the laws, and are protected by the power of the civil state, which nevertheless pay no part of the public expense; nor are liable to the penalties, as other subjects, due to their crimes; and consequently, stand not in fear of any man, but the Pope; and adhere to him only, to uphold his universal monarchy.

Fourthly, the giving to their priests (which is no more in the New Testament but presbyters, that is, elders) the name of *Sacerdotes*, that is, sacrificers, which was the title of the civil sovereign, and his public ministers, amongst the Jews, whilst God was their King. Also, the making the Lord's supper a sacrifice, serveth to make the people believe the Pope hath the same power over all Christians, that Moses and Aaron had over the Jews; that is to say, all power, both civil and ecclesiastical, as the high priest then had.

Fifthly, the teaching that matrimony is a sacrament, giveth to the clergy the judging of the lawfulness of marriages; and thereby, of what children are legitimate; and consequently, of the right of succession to hereditary kingdoms.

Sixthly, the denial of marriage to priests, serveth to assure this power of the Pope over kings. For if a king be a priest, he cannot marry, and transmit his kingdom to his posterity; if he be not a priest then the Pope pretendeth this authority ecclesiastical over him, and over his people.

Seventhly, from auricular confession, they obtain, for the assurance of their power, better intelligence of the designs of princes, and great persons in the civil state, than these can have of the designs of the state ecclesiastical.

Eighthly, by the canonization of saints, and declaring who are martyrs, they assure their power, in that they induce simple men into an obstinacy against the laws and commands of their civil sovereigns even to death, if by the Pope's excommunication, they be declared heretics or enemies to the church; that is (as they interpret it), to the Pope.

Ninthly, they assure the same, by the power they ascribe to every priest, of making Christ; and by the power of ordaining penance; and of remitting, and retaining of sins.

Tenthly, by the doctrine of purgatory, of justification by external works, and of indulgences, the clergy is enriched.

Eleventhly, by their demonology, and the use of exorcism, and other things appertaining thereto, they keep (or think they keep) the people more in awe of their power.

Lastly, the metaphysics, ethics, and politics of Aristotle, the frivolous distinctions, barbarous terms, and obscure language of the schoolmen, taught in the universities (which have been all erected and regulated by the Pope's authority), serve them to keep these errors from being detected, and to make men mistake the *ignis fatuus* of vain philosophy, for the light of the gospel.

To these, if they sufficed not, might be added other of their dark doctrines, the profit whereof redoundeth manifestly, to the setting up of an unlawful power over the lawful sovereigns of Christian people; or for the sustaining of the same, when it is set up; or to the worldly riches, honour and authority of those that sustain it. And therefore by the aforesaid rule, of *Cui bono*, we may justly pronounce for the authors of all this spiritual darkness, the Pope, and Roman clergy; and all those besides that endeavour to settle in the minds of men this erroneous doctrine, that the church now on earth, is that Kingdom of God mentioned in the Old and New Testament.

But the emperors, and other Christian sovereigns, under whose government these errors, and the like encroachments of ecclesiastics upon their office, at first crept in, to the disturbance of their possessions, and of the tranquillity of their subjects, though they suffered the same for want of foresight of the sequel, and of insight into the designs of their teachers, may nevertheless be esteemed accessaries to their own, and the public damage: For without their authority there could at first no seditious doctrine have been publicly preached. I say they might have hindered the same in the beginning: But when the people were once possessed by those spiritual men, there was no human remedy to be applied, that any man could invent: And for the remedies that God should provide, who never faileth in his good time to destroy all the machinations of men against the truth, we are to attend his good pleasure, that suffereth many times the prosperity of his enemies, together with their ambition, to grow to such a height, as the violence thereof openeth the eyes, which the wariness of their predecessors had before sealed up, and makes men by too much grasping let go all, as Peter's net was broken, by the struggling of too great a multitude of fishes; whereas the impatience of those, that strive to resist such encroachment, before their subject's eyes were opened, did but increase the power they resisted. I do not therefore blame the Emperor Frederick for holding the stirrup to our countryman Pope Adrian;[1] for such was the disposition of his subjects then, as if he had not done it, he was not likely to have succeeded in the Empire: But I blame those, that in the beginning, when their power was entire, by suffering such doctrines to be forged in the

universities of their own dominions, have holden the stirrup to all the succeeding Popes, whilst they mounted into the thrones of all Christian sovereigns, to ride, and tire, both them, and their people, at their pleasure.

But as the inventions of men are woven, so also are they ravelled out; the way is the same, but the order is inverted: The web begins at the first elements of power, which are wisdom, humility, sincerity, and other virtues of the Apostles, whom the people converted, obeyed, out of reverence, not by obligation: Their consciences were free, and their words and actions subject to none but the civil power. Afterwards the presbyters (as the flocks of Christ increased) assembling to consider what they should teach, and thereby obliging themselves to teach nothing against the decrees of their assemblies, made it to be thought the people were thereby obliged to follow their doctrine, and when they refused, refused to keep them company (that was then called excommunication), not as being infidels, but as being disobedient: And this was the first knot upon their liberty. And the number of presbyters increasing, the presbyters of the chief city of a province, got themselves an authority over the parochial presbyters, and appropriated to themselves the names of bishops: And this was a second knot on Christian liberty. Lastly, the Bishop of Rome, in regard of the imperial city, took upon him an authority (partly by the wills of the emperors themselves, and by the title of *Pontifex Maximus*, and at last when the emperors were grown weak, by the privileges of St. Peter) over all other bishops of the Empire: Which was the third and last knot, and the whole synthesis and construction of the pontifical power.

And therefore the analysis, or resolution is by the same way; but beginneth with the knot that was last tied; as we may see in the dissolution of the

---

[1] Frederick I (ca. 1123–1190), German King and Holy Roman Emperor; Pope Adrian IV (ca. 1100–1159), the only English Pope, crowned Frederick Emperor on the condition that he maintain the superiority of Popes over Emperors.

praetorpolitical church government in England.[1] First, the power of the Popes was dissolved totally by Queen Elizabeth; and the bishops, who before exercised their functions in right of the Pope, did afterwards exercise the same in right of the Queen and her successors; though by retaining the phrase of *Jure Divino* [divine right], they were thought to demand it by immediate right from God: And so was untied the first knot. After this, the Presbyterians lately in England obtained the putting down of Episcopacy: And so was the second knot dissolved: And almost at the same time, the power was taken also from the Presbyterians: And so we are reduced to the independency of the primitive Christians to follow Paul, or Cephas, or Apollos, every man as he liketh best: Which, if it be without contention, and without measuring the doctrine of Christ, by our affection to the person of his minister (the fault which the Apostle reprehended in the Corinthians),[2] is perhaps the best: First, because there ought to be no power over the consciences of men, but of the word itself, working faith in every one, not always according to the purpose of them that plant and water, but of God himself, that giveth the increase: and secondly, because it is unreasonable in them, who teach there is such danger in every little error, to require of a man endued with reason of his own, to follow the reason of any other man, or of the most voices of many other men; which is little better, than to venture his salvation at cross and pile.[3] Nor ought those teachers to be displeased with this loss of their ancient authority: For there is none should know better than they, that power is preserved by the same virtues by which it is acquired; that is to say, by wisdom, humility, clearness of doctrine, and sincerity of conversation; and not by suppression of the natural sciences, and of the morality of natural reason; nor by obscure language; nor by arrogating to themselves more knowledge than they make appear; nor by pious frauds; nor by such other faults, as in the pastors of God's church are not only faults, but also scandals, apt to make men stumble one time or other upon the suppression of their authority.

But after this doctrine, *that the church now militant, is the Kingdom of God spoken of in the Old and New Testament*, was received in the world; the ambition, and canvassing for the offices that belong thereunto, and especially for that great office of being Christ's lieutenant, and the pomp of them that obtained therein the principal public charges, became by degrees so evident, that they lost the inward reverence due to the pastoral function: in so much as the wisest men, of them that had any power in the civil state, needed nothing but the authority of the princes, to deny them any further obedience. For, from the time that the Bishop of Rome had gotten to be acknowledged for Bishop Universal, by pretence of succession to St. Peter, their whole hierarchy, or kingdom of darkness, may be compared not unfitly to the kingdom of fairies; that is, to the old wives' fables in England, concerning ghosts and spirits, and the feats they play in the night. And if a man consider the original of this great ecclesiastical dominion, he will easily perceive, that the papacy is no other than the ghost of the deceased Roman Empire, sitting crowned upon the grave thereof: For so did the papacy start up on a sudden out of the ruins of that heathen power.

The language also, which they use, both in the churches, and in their public acts, being Latin, which is not commonly used by any nation now in the world, what is it but the ghost of the old Roman language?

The fairies in what nation soever they converse, have but one universal king, which some poets of

---

[1] *praetorpolitical* "hierarchical-political" (a word possibly invented by Hobbes).

[2] the apostle Paul, in I Corinthians 1:11 ff.

[3] *cross and pile* the obverse and reverse sides of a coin (*OED* pile *sb*[4] 2); by "heads or tails."

ours call King Oberon; but the Scripture calls Beelzebub, prince of demons. The ecclesiastics likewise, in whose dominions soever they be found, acknowledge but one universal king, the Pope.

The ecclesiastics are spiritual men, and ghostly fathers. The fairies are spirits, and ghosts. Fairies and ghosts inhabit darkness, solitudes, and graves. The ecclesiastics walk in obscurity of doctrine, in monasteries, churches, and churchyards.

The ecclesiastics have their cathedral churches; which, in what town soever they be erected, by virtue of holy water, and certain charms called exorcisms, have the power to make those towns, cities, that is to say, seats of empire. The fairies also have their enchanted castles, and certain gigantic ghosts, that domineer over the regions round about them.

The fairies are not to be seized on; and brought to answer for the hurt they do. So also the ecclesiastics vanish away from the tribunals of civil justice.

The ecclesiastics take from young men the use of reason, by certain charms compounded of metaphysics, and miracles, and traditions, and abused Scripture, whereby they are good for nothing else, but to execute what they command them. The fairies likewise are said to take young children out of their cradles, and to change them into natural fools, which common people do therefore call elves, and are apt to mischief.

In what shop, or operatory the fairies make their enchantment, the old wives have not determined. But the operatories of the clergy are well enough known to be the universities, that received their discipline from authority pontifical.

When the fairies are displeased with anybody, they are said to send their elves to pinch them. The ecclesiastics, when they are displeased with any civil state, make also their elves, that is, superstitious, enchanted subjects, to pinch their princes, by preaching sedition; or one prince enchanted with promises, to pinch another.

The fairies marry not; but there be amongst them incubi, that have copulation with flesh and blood. The priests also marry not.

The ecclesiastics take the cream of the land, by donations of ignorant men, that stand in awe of them, and by tithes: So also it is in the fable of fairies, that they enter into the dairies, and feast upon the cream, which they skim from the milk.

What kind of money is current in the kingdom of fairies, is not recorded in the story. But the ecclesiastics in their receipts accept of the same money that we do; though when they are to make any payment, it is in canonizations, indulgences, and masses.

To this, and such like resemblances between the papacy, and the kingdom of fairies, may be added this, that as the fairies have no existence, but in the fancies of ignorant people, rising from the traditions of old wives, or old poets: so the spiritual power of the Pope (without the bounds of his own civil dominion) consisteth only in the fear that seduced people stand in, of their excommunication; upon hearing of false miracles, false traditions, and false interpretations of the Scripture.

It was not therefore a very difficult matter, for Henry 8th by his exorcism; nor for Queen Elizabeth by hers, to cast them out. But who knows that this spirit of Rome, now gone out, and walking by missions through the dry places of China, Japan, and the Indies, that yield him little fruit, may not return, or rather an assembly of spirits worse than he, enter, and inhabit this clean swept house, and make the end thereof worse than the beginning? For it is not the Roman clergy only, that pretends the Kingdom of God to be of this world, and thereby to have a power therein, distinct from that of the civil state. And this is all I had a design to say, concerning the doctrine of the politics. Which when I have reviewed, I shall willingly expose it to the censure of my country.

A REVIEW, AND CONCLUSION

From the contrariety of some of the natural faculties of the mind, one to another, as also of one passion to another, and from their reference to conversation, there has been an argument taken, to infer an impossibility that any one man should be sufficiently disposed to all sorts of civil duty. The severity of judgment, they say, makes men censorious, and unapt to pardon the errors and infirmities of other men: and on the other side, celerity of fancy, makes the thoughts less steady than is necessary, to discern exactly between right and wrong. Again, in all deliberations, and in all pleadings, the faculty of solid reasoning, is necessary: for without it, the resolutions of men are rash, and their sentences unjust: and yet if there be not powerful eloquence, which procureth attention and consent, the effect of reason will be little. But these are contrary faculties; the former being grounded upon principles of truth; the other upon opinions already received, true, or false; and upon the passions and interests of men, which are different, and mutable.

And amongst the passions, courage (by which I mean the contempt of wounds, and violent death), inclineth men to private revenges, and sometimes to endeavour the unsettling of the public peace: And timorousness, many times disposeth to the desertion of the public defence. Both these they say cannot stand together in the same person.

And to consider the contrariety of men's opinions, and manners in general, it is they say, impossible to entertain a constant civil amity with all those, with whom the business of the world constrains us to converse: Which business, consisteth almost in nothing else but a perpetual contention for honor, riches, and authority.

To which I answer, that these are indeed great difficulties, but not impossibilities: For by education, and discipline, they may be, and are sometimes reconciled. Judgment, and fancy may have place in the same man; but by turns; as the end which he aimeth at requireth. As the Israelites in Egypt, were sometimes fastened to their labour of making bricks, and other times were ranging abroad to gather straw: So also may the judgment sometimes be fixed upon one certain consideration, and the fancy at another time wandering about the world. So also reason, and eloquence (though not perhaps in the natural sciences, yet in the moral) may stand very well together. For wheresoever there is place for adorning and preferring of error, there is much more place for adorning and preferring of truth, if they have it to adorn. Nor is there any repugnancy between fearing the laws, and not fearing a public enemy; nor between abstaining from injury, and pardoning it in others. There is therefore no such inconsistence of human nature, with civil duties, as some think. I have known clearness of judgment, and largeness of fancy; strength of reason, and graceful elocution; a courage for the war, and a fear for the laws, and all eminently in one man; and that was my most noble and honoured friend Mr. Sidney Godolphin; who hating no man, nor hated of any, was unfortunately slain in the beginning of the late civil war, in the public quarrel, by an undiscerned, and an undiscerning hand.

To the laws of nature, declared in the 15th Chapter, I would have this added, *That every man is bound by nature, as much as in him lieth, to protect in war, the authority, by which he is himself protected in time of peace.* For he that pretendeth a right of nature to preserve his own body, cannot pretend a right of nature to destroy him, by whose strength he is preserved: It is a manifest contradiction of himself. And though this law may be drawn by consequence, from some of those that are there already mentioned; yet the times require to have it inculcated, and remembered.

And because I find by divers English books lately printed, that the civil wars have not yet sufficiently taught men, in what point of time it is, that a subject becomes obliged to the conqueror; nor what is conquest; nor how it comes about, that it obliges men to obey his laws: Therefore for farther satisfaction of men therein, I say, the point of time, wherein a man becomes subject to a conqueror, is that point, wherein having liberty to submit to him, he consenteth, either by express words, or by other sufficient sign, to be his subject. When it is that a man hath the liberty to submit, I have showed before in the end of the 21ˢᵗ Chapter; namely, that for him that hath no obligation to his former sovereign but that of an ordinary subject, it is then, when the means of his life is within the guards and garrisons of the enemy; for it is then, that he hath no longer protection from him, but is protected by the adverse party for his contribution. Seeing therefore such contribution is everywhere, as a thing inevitable (not withstanding it be an assistance to the enemy), esteemed lawful; a total submission, which is but an assistance to the enemy, cannot be esteemed unlawful. Besides, if a man consider that they who submit, assist the enemy but with part of their estates, whereas they that refuse, assist him with the whole, there is no reason to call their submission, or composition an assistance; but rather a detriment to the enemy. But if a man, besides the obligation of a subject, hath taken upon him a new obligation of a soldier, then he hath not the liberty to submit to a new power, as long as the old one keeps the field, and giveth him means of subsistence, either in his armies, or garrisons: for in this case, he cannot complain of want of protection, and means to live as a soldier: But when that also fails, a soldier also may seek his protection wheresoever he has most hope to have it; and may lawfully submit himself to his new master. And so much for the time when he may do it lawfully, if he will. If therefore he do it, he is undoubtedly bound to be a true subject: For a contract lawfully made, cannot lawfully be broken.

By this also a man may understand, when it is, that men may be said to be conquered; and in what the nature of conquest, and the right of a conqueror consisteth: For this submission is it that implieth them all. Conquest, is not the victory itself; but the acquisition by victory, of a right, over the persons of men. He therefore that is slain, is overcome, but not conquered: He that is taken, and put into prison, or chains, is not conquered, though overcome; for he is still an enemy, and may save himself if he can: But he that upon promise of obedience, hath his life and liberty allowed him, is then conquered, and a subject; and not before. The Romans used to say, that their general had pacified such a province, that is to say, in English, conquered it; and that the country was pacified by victory, when the people of it had promised *Imperata facere*, that is, *To do what the Roman people commanded them*: this was to be conquered. But this promise may be either express, or tacit: Express, by promise: Tacit, by other signs. As for example, a man that hath not been called to make such an express promise (because he is one whose power perhaps is not considerable); yet if he live under their protection openly, he is understood to submit himself to the government: But if he live there secretly, he is liable to anything that may be done to a spy, and enemy of the state. I say not, he does any injustice (for acts of open hostility bear not that name); but that he may be justly put to death. Likewise, if a man, when his country is conquered, be out of it, he is not conquered, nor subject: but if at his return, he submit to the government, he is bound to obey it. So that conquest (to define it) is the acquiring of the right of sovereignty by victory. Which right, is acquired, in the people's submission, by which they contract with the victor, promising obedience, for life and liberty.

In the 29ᵗʰ Chapter I have set down for one of the causes of the dissolutions of Commonwealths, their imperfect generation, consisting in the want of an absolute and arbitrary legislative power; for want whereof, the civil sovereign is fain to handle the sword of justice unconstantly, and as if it were too hot for him to hold: One reason whereof (which I have not there mentioned) is this, That they will all of them justify the war, by which their power was at first gotten, and whereon (as they think) their right dependeth, and not on the possession. As if, for example, the right of the Kings of England did depend on the goodness of the cause of William the Conqueror, and upon their lineal, and directest descent from him; by which means, there would perhaps be no tie of the subject's obedience to their sovereign at this day in all the world: wherein whilst they needlessly think to justify themselves, they justify all the successful rebellions that ambition shall at any time after raise against them, and their successors. Therefore I put down for one of the most effectual seeds of the death of any state, that the conquerors require not only a submission of men's actions to them for the future, but also an approbation of all their actions past; when there is scarce a Commonwealth in the world, whose beginnings can in conscience be justified.

And because the name of tyranny, signifieth nothing more, nor less, than the name of sovereignty, be it in one, or many men, saving that they that use the former word, are understood to be angry with them they call tyrants; I think the toleration of a professed hatred of tyranny, is a toleration of hatred to Commonwealth in general, and another evil seed, not differing much from the former. For to the justification of the cause of a conqueror, the reproach of the cause of the conquered, is for the most part necessary: but neither of them necessary for the obligation of the conquered. And thus much I have thought fit to say upon the review of the first and second part of this discourse.

In the 35th Chapter, I have sufficiently declared out of the Scripture, that in the Commonwealth of the Jews, God himself was made the sovereign, by pact with the people; who were therefore called his

Peculiar People,[1] to distinguish them from the rest of the world, over whom God reigned not by their consent, but by his own power: And that in this kingdom Moses was God's lieutenant on earth; and that it was he that told them what laws God appointed them to be ruled by. But I have omitted to set down who were the officers appointed to do execution; especially in capital punishments; not then thinking it a matter of so necessary consideration, as I find it since. We know that generally in all Commonwealths, the execution of corporeal punishments, was either put upon the guards, or other soldiers of the sovereign power; or given to those, in whom want of means, contempt of honour, and hardness of heart, concurred, to make them sue for such an office. But amongst the Israelites it was a positive law of God their sovereign, that he that was convicted of a capital crime, should be stoned to death by the people; and that the witnesses should cast the first stone, and after the witnesses, then the rest of the people. This was a law that designed who were to be the executioners; but not that any one should throw a stone at him before conviction and sentence, where the congregation was judge. The witnesses were nevertheless to be heard before they proceeded to execution, unless the fact were committed in the presence of the congregation itself, or in sight of the lawful judges; for then there needed no other witnesses but the judges themselves. Nevertheless, this manner of proceeding being not thoroughly understood, hath given occasion to a dangerous opinion, that any man may kill another, in some cases, by a right of zeal; as if the executions done upon offenders in the Kingdom of God in old time, proceeded not from the sovereign command, but from the authority of private zeal: which, if we consider the texts that seem to favour it, is quite contrary....

---

[1] *his Peculiar People* his particular or chosen people; see Deuteronomy 14:2, 26:18.

In the 36th Chapter I have said, that it is not declared in what manner God spake supernaturally to Moses: Not that he spake not to him sometimes by dreams and vision, and by a supernatural voice, as to other prophets: For the manner how he spake unto him from the mercy-seat, is expressly set down Numbers 7:89 in these words, "From that time forward, when Moses entered into the tabernacle of the congregation to speak with God, he heard a voice which spake unto him from over the mercy-seat, which is over the ark of the testimony, from between the cherubims he spake unto him." But it is not declared in what consisted the preeminence of the manner of God's speaking to Moses, above that of his speaking to other prophets, as to Samuel, and to Abraham, to whom he also spake by a voice (that is, by vision), unless the difference consist in the clearness of the vision. For face to face, and mouth to mouth, cannot be literally understood of the infiniteness, and incomprehensibility of the divine nature.

And as to the whole doctrine, I see not yet, but the principles of it are true and proper; and the ratiocination solid. For I ground the civil right of sovereigns, and both the duty and liberty of subjects, upon the known natural inclinations of mankind, and upon the articles of the Law of Nature; of which no man, that pretends but reason enough to govern his private family, ought to be ignorant. And for the power ecclesiastical of the same sovereigns, I ground it on such texts, as are both evident in themselves, and consonant to the scope of the whole Scripture. And therefore am persuaded, that he that shall read it with a purpose only to be informed, shall be informed by it. But for those that by writing, or public discourse, or by their eminent actions, have already engaged themselves to the maintaining of contrary opinions, they will not be so easily satisfied. For in such cases, it is natural for men, at one and the same time, both to proceed in reading, and to lose their attention, in the search of objections to that they had read before: Of which, in a time wherein the interests of men are changed (seeing much of that doctrine, which serveth to the establishing of a new government, must needs be contrary to that which conduced to the dissolution of the old), there cannot choose but be very many.

In that part which treateth of a Christian Commonwealth, there are some new doctrines, which, it may be, in a state where the contrary were already fully determined, were a fault for a subject without leave to divulge, as being an usurpation of the place of a teacher. But in this time, that men call not only for peace, but also for truth, to offer such doctrine as I think true, and that manifestly tend to peace and loyalty, to the consideration of those that are yet in deliberation, is no more, but to offer new wine, to be put into new cask, that both may be preserved together. And I suppose, that then, when novelty can breed no trouble, nor disorder in a state, men are not generally so much inclined to the reverence of antiquity, as to prefer ancient errors, before new and well proved truth.

There is nothing I distrust more than my elocution; which nevertheless I am confident (excepting the mischances of the press) is not obscure. That I have neglected the ornament of quoting ancient poets, orators, and philosophers, contrary to the custom of late time (whether I have done well or ill in it), proceedeth from my judgment, grounded on many reasons. For first, all truth of doctrine dependeth either upon reason, or upon Scripture; both which give credit to many, but never receive it from any writer. Secondly, the matters in question are not of fact, but of right, wherein there is no place for witnesses. There is scarce any of those old writers, that contradicteth not sometimes both himself, and others; which makes their testimonies insufficient. Fourthly, such opinions as are taken only upon credit of antiquity, are not intrinsically the judgment of those that cite them, but words that pass (like gaping) from mouth to mouth. Fifthly, it is many times with a fraudulent design that men stick their corrupt doctrine with the cloves of other men's wit. Sixthly, I find not that the ancients they cite, took it for an ornament, to do the like with those that wrote before them. Seventhly, it is an argument of indigestion, when Greek and Latin sentences unchewed come up again, as they use to do, unchanged. Lastly, though I reverence those men of ancient time, that either have written truth perspicuously, or set us in a better way to find it out ourselves; yet to the antiquity itself I think nothing due: For if we will reverence the age, the present is the oldest. If the antiquity of the writer, I am not sure, that generally they to whom such honor is given, were more ancient when they wrote, than I am that am writing: But if it be well considered, the praise of ancient authors, proceeds not from the reverence of the dead, but from the competition, and mutual envy of the living.

To conclude, there is nothing in this whole discourse, nor in that I writ before of the same subject in Latin,[1] as far as I can perceive, contrary either to the word of God, or to good manners; or tending to the disturbance of the public tranquillity. Therefore I think it may be profitably printed, and more profitably taught in the universities, in case they also think so, to whom the judgment of the same belongeth. For seeing the universities are the fountains of civil, and moral doctrine, from whence the preachers, and the gentry, drawing such water as they find, use to sprinkle the same (both from the pulpit, and in their conversation) upon the people, there ought certainly to be great care taken, to have it pure, both from the venom of heathen politicians, and from the incantation of deceiving spirits. And by that means the most men, knowing their duties,

will be the less subject to serve the ambition of a few discontented persons, in their purposes against the state; and be the less grieved with the contributions necessary for their peace, and defence; and the governors themselves have the lesser cause, to maintain at the common charge any greater army, than is necessary to make good the public liberty, against the invasions and encroachments of foreign enemies.

And thus I have brought to an end my discourse of civil and ecclesiastical government, occasioned by the disorders of the present time, without partiality, without application, and without other design, than to set before men's eyes the mutual relation between protection and obedience; of which the condition of human nature, and the laws divine (both natural and positive), require an inviolable observation. And though in the revolution of states, there can be no very good constellation for truths of this nature to be born under (as having an angry aspect from the dissolvers of an old government, and seeking but the backs of them that erect a new), yet I cannot think it will be condemned at this time, either by the public judge of doctrine, or by any that desires the continuance of public peace. And in this hope I return to my interrupted speculation of bodies natural;[2] wherein (if God give me health to finish it), I hope the novelty will as much please, as in the doctrine of this artificial body it useth to offend. For such truth, as opposeth no man's profit, nor pleasure, is to all men welcome.

—1651

---

[1] in his *De Cive* (Paris, 1642).

[2] Hobbes believed that varieties of motion were the underlying cause of all things; his most extended development of this idea was in *De Corpore* (1655), which treated such subjects as geometry, physics, physiology, and animal psychology.

Lady Eleanor Davies
1590 – 1652

The prophetess Lady Eleanor Davies was the fifth daughter of Lucy Mervin and George Touchet, eleventh Baron Audeley and first Earl of Castlehaven. In 1609, she married Sir John Davies, the Attorney General for Ireland, by whom she bore three children. In 1623, Sir John purchased Englefield, a country estate in Berkshire. It was here on July 28, 1625 that Lady Eleanor first heard the voice of the prophet Daniel speaking to her "as through a trumpet." Soon after, she travelled to Oxford to deliver to Archbishop Abbot a tract in which she interpreted the book of Daniel. Thus began her career as the "Handmaid of the Holy Spirit." Lady Eleanor saw her maiden name as significant, since it lent itself to the prophetic anagram, "Eleanor Audelie: reveal o Daniel."

When her husband burned her prophetic writings, Lady Eleanor predicted that he would die within three years and began wearing mourning for him at dinner. When he died in 1626, Lady Eleanor married Sir Archibald Douglas, a Scottish captain who claimed to be the elder half-brother of Charles I. During the early years of their marriage, Lady Eleanor circulated at Court and proffered advice to the royal family on the Queen's fertility. She achieved national recognition when she correctly predicted the death in 1628 of the Duke of Buckingham.

Lady Eleanor's marriage to Douglas eventually proved unhappy. She believed that Douglas burned her papers to win royal favour and warned him that his act would not go unpunished. He was subsequently debilitated with a serious mental illness. Lady Eleanor also found herself at odds with the Court. When in 1633, she undertook to publish her political writings illicitly in Holland, she was harshly penalized. Officials did not take kindly to her comparison of Charles I to the biblical tyrant Belshazzar. Lady Eleanor was called before the Court of High Commission, fined £3000 and imprisoned for two and a half years in the Gatehouse at Westminster for venturing to interpret Scripture. Within months of her release in 1635, she vandalized the church hangings at Lichfield Cathedral, and was committed to Bedlam until 1638. She was transferred to the Tower of London thereafter and finally released in 1640.

Though she was imprisoned briefly on two other occasions, Lady Eleanor spent the remainder of her life writing apocalyptic tracts which she delivered to Members of Parliament. When her predictions that Charles I would be executed and London destroyed by fire were fulfilled, her reputation revived for a time. Many of her writings are obscure and disjointed, but Lady Eleanor poignantly describes her spiritual calling and the vigorous private and public opposition to her vocation in *Her Appeal* (1646).

For another prophetic text, see Abiezer Coppe.

⁊⁊⁊

The Lady Eleanor Her Appeal

*From the Lady Eleanor the Handmaid of the Holy Spirit,
To our beloved brother Mr. Mace,
the anointed of our Lord.*[1]

Having in the burden of his precious Word been myself a partaker, made a public example, no mean one, concerning the way before the Lord's coming to be prepared, have thought it not unnecessary by what means it came to pass, to impart and publish the same unto yourself, in making known some passages, the truth of which unknown not unto the whole world, almost ever since the year 1625.

---

[1] *Mr. Mace* Probably Thomas May, secretary to the Parliament; the mace is the symbol of authority of the Speaker of the House. In effect, the tract is addressed to Parliament, as the venue for public complaints and petitions, which this tract in effect is.

Showing withal about a few days before the former king's departure [from] this life, how first of all there came a Scottish lad to this city, about the age of thirteen, one George Carr by name, otherwise called the dumb boy or fortuneteller, so termed, that spake not for some space of time, with whom it was my hap, upon a visit, to meet where some of them would needs send for this boy, although few more jealous of such acquaintance or sparing, yet able to discern between such a one and impostures, making bold before my departure thence, to direct him the way to my house, where care should be taken of him, not the less because a stranger, accordingly who there abode, where no simple people, but expert and learned as any, tried no few conclusions; some instanced as here:[1]

Sometimes who would take the Bible or a Chronicle, and open it, and close it again, then cause the aforesaid youth to show by signs and such like dumb demonstrations, what was contained therein;[2] which things he so to the life expressed and acted, as were it a psalm or verse, then feigned to sing, though saw not a letter of the book;[3] and sometime that suddenly behind him would blow a horn, whereat never so much as changed his look, seemed so hard of hearing. And again thus, to sound him farther, one must stop his ears fast, and then what [one] whispered at the other end of the gallery, he must declare what they spake in the ear, as often as they pleased several times.[4]

Having by that time gotten a whistling voice, as plain as any can speak, like a bird; before that [he[had used signs for the space of three months, then [was] no longer dumb or deaf.

To conclude, whatsoever it were he [was] able to manifest it, whether contained in letters, enclosed in cabinets, or by numbering how many pence or peppercorns in a bag or box before it was opened, or anything of that kind fit for the vulgar capacity too;[5] or when he was brought into any place amongst strangers, one should write in several papers everyone's name, and he must give them accordingly to each his own name, at first making as though he were in some doubt which way to bestow himself, where the chief divines of the city present, some of them bestowing a shilling on him, without farther consideration thought it sufficient, etc. whilst others of that calling as liberal of their slanderous tongues; that no longer might be harbored in our house, [he was] likened to Friar Rush; servants had so incensed their masters, setting all on fire, with justices of peace and churchmen, giving out he was a vagrant, a counterfeit, or a witch.[6] Immediately upon which the Spirit of Prophecy falling likewise upon me, then were all vexed worse than ever, ready to turn the house upside down, laying this to his charge too: when laying aside household cares all, and no conversation with any but the Word of God, first by conference with the prophet Daniel, cap. 8, ver. 13, I found out this place, *Then I heard ONE saint speaking unto another saint, said unto that certain saint which SPAKE* (in the ori[gi]nal (to wit) *The Numberer of Secrets, or the wonderful Numberer* (Hebr. *Palmoni*) *How long the vision concerning the daily, and the transgression making desolate, to give the host, etc. And he said unto me, unto two thousand three hundred days, then shall the sanctuary be cleansed.*[7]

---

[1] *a few days…this life* James I died on March 27, 1625; *hap* fortune (*OED* hap *sb*[1] 1); *conclusions* examinations (*OED* conclusion 8).

[2] *Chronicle* historical record (*OED* chronicle *sb* 1a).

[3] *feigned* mimed, as he was dumb.

[4] *stop his ears* obstruct his hearing (*stop v* I.8a).

[5] *for the vulgar capacity* for the knowledge or tastes of the common people.

[6] *Friar Rush* the proper name of a demon who poses as a friar to deceive people (*The History of Friar Rush*, 1620).

[7] *Palmoni* palmowniy ("that certain one"), that is to say, "that certain saint."

The sum of it this, as much to say, inquired of such a one that spake not at first, how long from the vision before this prophesy shall be revealed, or whether I should be able, etc. as now about two thousand two hundred years complete since the captivity,[1] as here answered, *O Son of Man, for at the time of the end it shall be: Behold, I will make thee know in the last end of the indignation, for at the time appointed shall be the end, Daniel, cap. 8.*

And thus not only providing for that aforesaid admired guest, but adored him almost; how it afterward came to pass, like that least of all seeds, how it sprang up, as follows:[2] Here following the prophets their order in these circumstances, time, persons, and place observed: Showing,

In the aforesaid year, 1625. the first of his reign, the first of his name, in the month of July, so called after the Roman Emperor, in Berks, the first of shires, myself whose father the prime peer, or first baron, being at my house in Englesfield, then heard early in the morning a voice from heaven, speaking as through a trumpet these words;[3]

There is nineteen years and an half to the judgement day, and be you as the meek Virgin.

When occasioned through the plague, that heavy hand, like the Wisemen's coming from the East, the term came down to Reading our next market town;[4] and that first Parliament following it posting down to Oxford, not far off either:[5] And sometime as in *Augustus's* days, so in this of Great Britain's second monarch, taxed likewise with no ordinary taxes levied;[6] when this morning star, this second babe born, ruling the nations with an iron rod, no light judgements foreshowing at hand:[7] which words in a manuscript annexed to an interpretation of the prophet Daniel's visions, a few days finished afore, was then immediately for to be published, carried to Oxford's Parliament, that ancientest of universities, this golden number heard, extending to the year 1644. January.[8]

Which book perfected about the first of August, was with mine own hand delivered and presented to Abbot, Archbishop, where the babe signed in the presence of no few witnesses, with this token, that the great plague should presently cease;[9] that curse so furiously poured out on the desolate city, where grass grew in her chief streets [which] should be inhabited.

At which time the weekly Bill amounted to five thousand;[10] but because the next week it increased six hundred, this token of such deliverance was utterly cast out of remembrance: Howbeit before the end of August, scarce five hundred of the plague deceased, in such an instant vanished, which sometime was grown up to that height as the age of the world, five thousand six hundred.

---

[1] *the captivity* the captivity of the Israelites in Babylon.

[2] *aforesaid admired guest* George Carr; *like that…sprang up* "The kingdom of heaven is like to a grain of mustard seed…which indeed is the least of all seeds: but when it is grown, it is the greatest among herbs" (Matthew 13:31–32).

[3] *his reign* the reign of Charles I; *July…Emperor* so named after Julius Caesar; *father…first baron* Baron Audeley claimed that he was first among the barons when James I began his reign in 1603; *speaking…trumpet* "After this I looked, and, behold, a door was opened in heaven: and the first voice which I heard was as it were of a trumpet talking with me; which said, Come up hither, and I will show thee things which must be hereafter" (Revelation 4:1).

[4] *term* law term; because of the plague, the session of the law courts in London was adjourned and cases were heard in Reading.

[5] *posting* travelling with haste (*OED* post *v*[1] I.2).

[6] *Augustus's days* Caesar Augustus, Roman Emperor at the time of Christ's birth; *Great Britain's second monarch* Charles I.

[7] *this morning star…with an iron rod* See Revelation 2:27–28; also 12:5 and 19:15.

[8] *golden number* so called for its importance in calculating the date of Easter.

[9] *Abbot, Archbishop* emended from "Abbots Archbishop"; George Abbot, Archbishop of Canterbury; *the babe* Lady Eleanor's prophetic tract.

[10] *Bill* the Bill of Mortality, a weekly report of the deaths for 109 parishes in and around London (*OED* bill *sb*[3] 10).

Concerning which aforesaid judgement or blow, foreshowed no other than the day of judgment's express forerunner, the world's final blow at hand; upon farther consult with the Scriptures, the Book of the Revelation, understood how with the 7th Chapter it accorded, saying, *And I saw four angels standing at the four corners of the earth, holding the four winds that they should not blow*, until expired such a time, such a year.[1]

. . . .

And since prophesy's thundering reign began,[2] what judgments since the year 1625 July, [I] shall give you a list of some of them; beginning at home first, where this book of mine was sacrificed by my first husband's hand, thrown into the fire, whose doom I gave him in letters of his own name (*John Daves*, Jove's hand) within three years to expect the mortal blow;[3] so put on my mourning garment from that time: when about three days before his sudden decease, before all his servants and friends at the table, gave him pass to take his long sleep,[4] by him thus put off, *I pray weep not while I am alive, and I will give you leave to laugh when I am dead.*

Accordingly which too soon came to pass, for contrary to a solemn vow within three months [I was] married to another husband, who escaped not scot-free: he likewise burning my book, another manuscript, a remembrance to the king for beware Great Britain's blow at hand, showed him thus, *Dan. 12. And at that time shall Michael the great prince stand up, and there shall be a time of trouble, such as never was since a nation*, with the resurrection in his time to be prophesied: and for a token of the time, *At that time the people shall be delivered,*

their oppressors put to flight; where very parliament-stars shining forever, as by such a solemn oath taken there sworn, etc. the contents of that last chap. verily concluding with the first year of the present reign, 1625. signified in those no obscure characters, *Blessed is he that waits*: And comes to three hundred thirty-five; which being added unto the former reckoning of two hundred and ninety, amounts to 1625. to wit, when this sealed vision before the end shall be revealed, witness the troublesome time.

. . . .

And not thus resting, shall give you a passage or two more; showing the Holy Spirit besides speaking with other tongues, able to speak without a tongue sometime, as by the prophet Ezekiel to that rebellious age, growing downward, by his portraying and the like: Showing a few days before my deserting the aforesaid house, coming home, having been forth, and meeting with one seeming dumb, that came along with me, soldier like, with a long garment or russet coat, a red cross on the sleeve, by signs uttering his mind; where leaving him at [the] door, without other notice, cold welcome, that had watched about the house all day, as they told me, calling to mind what trouble such a one befell: presently after comes in Sir Archibald Douglas my husband from Whitehall, followed with a chaplain and some six servants, affrighted all, protested he had met with an angel, whose custom always to give something to the poor, saying, he was come with him, a young man very handsome, about his age, praying me to come forth; the servants vowing he came out of heaven, otherwise [they] might (in the open fields) [have] seen him afore suddenly who caught their master by the arm.

Which man applying himself wholly to Sir Archibald Douglas by such discoursing signs, of his late marriage, and former course of his life; would not a look vouchsafe me, till at last by locking, as it

---

[1] *And I…not blow* Revelation 7:1.

[2] *thundering reign* "And I heard a voice from heaven, as the voice of many waters, and as the voice of a great thunder" (Revelation 14:2).

[3] *whose doom…mortal blow* Davies died a year and a half after her prediction.

[4] *gave him…long sleep* gave him permission to die.

were, and unlocking a door, which I interpreting to presage prison, he assented unto this token bestowed on me;[1] and Sir Archibald's back turned, then stepped within the door as none should see him but myself, by pointing at him, and bending the fist, looking up as it were to heaven, as though some heavy hand toward: About a month after that [he] lost both reason and speech, by [the] like signs feign to learn his meaning, as he [was] able to impart his mind, formerly showed.

When the messenger departing, as though had far to go, as swift as an arrow, having taken a shilling in good part, though promised as many pounds would he come again, by spreading the hands which he seemed to understand; where like conference to have, many of the Court sending after him, standing at St. James's gate to staid him; but no more of him heard, amongst the poor though inquired, whether knew any such.

. . . .

As this for another then blazed, being invited by the Lady of Berkshire to her child's christening, sent word I might not, nor would not come; howbeit a fortnight after went, being neighbours, finding there the Lord Goring and the Lady Carlisle, the Lady Berkshire's aspect somewhat sad, relating my denial to her, saying, She knew it boded something to her child: The Lady Carlisle saying, *He is well, is he not? Yes, I praise God*, said she, *as any of the rest*: Then quoth the Lord Goring, *I pray let us know what thundering thumping thing it is about my Lady Berkshire's son*: To which only thus before I went, enquired of her the name of the other born before this last, as I take it she said was Philip, *Then he must be again the youngest*, I again replied, as after a few hours the same night the child suddenly was gone and died, etc.

And though these things [were] not done in corner or remote place, [they] restrained neither city

nor court from such violent doings, vain laughter, like the crack of thorns, as the wiseman, *cap. etc.*[2] shows to be regarded as much, of whose high presumption on record, such a blast from Whitehall, bearing date October, 1633 etc.

From the Court of Whitehall, etc.[3]
His Majesty does expressly command the Lord Archbishop's Grace and his Commissioners, for causes ecclesiastical, That the petitioner be forthwith called before them for presuming to imprint the said books, and for preferring this detestable petition.

Sidney Montague.

Which blasphemous accursed reference thus occasioned was upon their taking away of my books printed at Amsterdam: But pressing to have them restored passages taken out of Scripture concerning great Babylon's blow, Dan. 5 *And the beast ascended out of the bottomless pit,* Rev. 11.[4] Applied to Great Britain, with the handwriting (cap. 5) *Thou art found wanting,* etc. extended from that marriage feast, ever since 1625 into the year 1645 or from the abomination, etc. Dan. 12.[5]

And of the aforesaid reference, thus; save reverence His Grace the foreman of the jury, 1633 Octob. 23 commanding first a candle, he that would not be warned;[6] but said, *No more of that;* burnt the book, saying, *My Lords, I have made you a smoother of doomsday, to be in such a year about*

---

[2] *crack of thorns* "For as the crackling of thorns under a pot, so is the laughter of the fool: this also is vanity" (Ecclesiastes 7:6).

[3] *From the Court…Montague* Lady Eleanor sets forth the text of the warrant summoning her to appear before the Court of High Commission.

[4] *the beast…pit* Revelation 11:7.

[5] *Thou art…wanting* Daniel 5:27; *extended…Dan. 12.* Daniel 12:1.

[6] *His Grace* William Laud, Archbishop of Canterbury, the head of the Court of High Commission. Lady Eleanor refers to him as "Arch BB" (Arch Blaspheming Beast) in several tracts, associating him with the Beast of Revelation.

---

[1] *vouchsafe* bestow on (*OED* vouchsafe *v* I.1).

Candlemas, till then she takes time enough:[1] *What shall we do next?* When with one voice, *Let her be fined three thousand pounds, excommunicated, no Bible allowed her, or pen and ink, or woman servant; carry her away*, as by a warrant under twelve hands, confined to the Gatehouse forever,[2] where kept a close prisoner for two years, the Lord's day unknown from another, the rest for brevity and modesty['s] sake dismissed.

To this day which sentence and remains of the smoked book remain extant in the office, trophies of his triumph, buried by this Achan, this golden wedge or tongue, he surnamed the Beast, from Oxford deriving his name, smothered as other things.[3]

—1646

---

[1] *smoother* smouldering state (*OED* smother *sb* 1b); *Candlemas* the Feast of the Purification of the Virgin Mary, Feb. 2.

[2] *Gatehouse* the apartment over the palace of Westminster, used as a prison.

---

[3] *Achan* After the Israelite defeat of Jericho, Achan stole from the enemy treasures intended for destruction before God; as a result, he and his family were stoned to death (Joshua 7:1–26).

Sir Robert Filmer

ca. 1590 – 1653

The eldest son of a prosperous gentry family in Kent, Filmer attended Trinity College, Cambridge, trained for the law at Lincoln's Inn, and married the daughter of a bishop; he inherited his family's estate in 1629. He started writing on legal and political issues in the 1620s, circulating his treatises in manuscript among gentry circles. Staunchly Royalist, Filmer was imprisoned by Parliament for at least some months in 1643, and in the late 1640s he began to publish pro-monarchical and other pamphlets. In the early 1650s he published commentaries on the political writings of Thomas Hobbes, John Milton, and Aristotle, as well as *Directions for Obedience to Government in Dangerous or Doubtful Times*, a short essay included here on the topical question of how much obedience was due to a usurping government (limited, Filmer concludes).

Patriarcha, Filmer's longest and best known political treatise, was not published in his lifetime, though several of his shorter published pamphlets summarize its arguments. Filmer likely began to write *Patriarcha* in the late 1620s and revised the text until the beginning of the civil wars. The original context of his Scripture-based patriarchalist theory was late sixteenth- and early seventeenth-century political debates about the foundation and extent of royal authority. But as a forceful argument for a monarch's absolute paternal authority, *Patriarcha* attracted attention throughout the civil wars and into the Restoration. It was first published in 1680 during the Exclusion crisis, and John Locke devoted the first of his *Two Treatises of Government* (1689) to criticizing Filmer's ideas. For other discussions of royal or paternal authority, see the selections from James VI/I, Thomas Hobbes, and Charles I; for texts that challenge patriarchal arguments, see the selections from Lady Anne Clifford, Elizabeth Johnson, and Rachel Speght.

❧❧❧

Patriarcha:
The Natural Power of Kings Defended against the Unnatural Liberty of the People
(excerpt)

Chapter One (1) The tenet of the natural liberty of mankind new, plausible and dangerous;[1] (2) the question stated out of Bellarmine; some contradictions of his noted; (3) Bellarmine's argument answered out of Bellarmine himself; (4) the royal authority of the patriarchs before the Flood; (5) the dispersion of nations over the world after the confusion of Babel, was by entire families over which the fathers were kings; (6) and from them all kings are descended; (7) all kings are either fathers of their people; (8) or heirs of such fathers or usurpers of the right of such fathers; (9) of the escheating of kingdoms;[2] (10) of regal and paternal power and of their agreement.

(1) Since the time that school divinity began to flourish, there hath been a common opinion maintained as well by divines as by divers other learned men which affirms: "Mankind is naturally endowed and born with freedom from all subjection, and at liberty to choose what form of government it please, and that the power which any one man hath over others was at the first by human right bestowed according to the discretion of the multitude."

---

[1] *plausible* having the appearance (only) of reasonableness; specious (*OED* plausible *a* 3).

[2] *escheating* the reverting of property or office to the crown when there is no legally qualified heir (*OED* escheat *sb* 1).

This tenet was first hatched in the schools, and hath been fostered by all succeeding papists for good divinity. The divines also of the reformed churches have entertained it, and the common people everywhere tenderly embrace it as being most plausible to flesh and blood, for that it prodigally distributes a portion of liberty to the meanest of the multitude, who magnify liberty as if the height of human felicity were only to be found in it—never remembering that the desire of liberty was the cause of the fall of Adam.

But howsoever this vulgar opinion hath of late obtained great reputation, yet it is not to be found in the ancient Fathers and doctors of the primitive church. It contradicts the doctrine and history of the Holy Scriptures, the constant practice of all ancient monarchies, and the very principles of the law of nature. It is hard to say whether it be more erroneous in divinity or dangerous in policy.

Yet upon the grounds of this doctrine both Jesuits and some overzealous favourers of the Geneva discipline have built a perilous conclusion, which is "that the people or multitude have power to punish or deprive the prince if he transgress the laws of the kingdom". Witness Parsons and Buchanan.[1] The first, under the name of Doleman, in the third chapter of his first book labours to prove that kings have been lawfully chastised by their commonwealths.[2] The latter in his book *De Jure Regni apud Scotos* maintains a liberty of the people to depose their prince. Cardinal Bellarmine (*De Laicis,* book 3, chapter 6) and Mr Calvin (*Institutes,* book 4, chapter 10) both look asquint this way.[3]

This desperate assertion, whereby kings are made subject to the censures and deprivations of their subjects, follows (as the authors of it conceive) as a necessary consequence of that former position of the supposed natural equality and freedom of mankind, and liberty to choose what form of government it please.

And though Sir John Hayward, Adam Blackwood, John Barclay and some others have learnedly confuted both Buchanan and Parsons, and bravely vindicated the right of kings in most points, yet all of them, when they come to the argument drawn from the natural liberty and equality of mankind, do with one consent admit it for a truth unquestionable, not so much as once denying or opposing it.[4] Whereas if they did but confute this first erroneous principle, the whole fabric of this vast engine of popular sedition would drop down of itself.

The rebellious consequence which follows this prime article of the natural freedom of mankind may be my sufficient warrant for a modest examination of the original truth of it. Much hath been said, and by many, for the affirmative. Equity requires that an ear be reserved a little for the negative.

In this discourse I shall give myself these cautions:

First, I have nothing to do to meddle with mysteries of the present state. Such *arcana imperii* [state secrets], or cabinet councils, the vulgar may not pry into. An implicit faith is given to the meanest artificer in his own craft. How much more is it, then, due to a prince in the profound secrets of government. The causes and the ends of the greatest politic actions and motions of state dazzle the eyes and exceed the capacities of all men, save only those

---

[1] *Parsons and Buchanan*   Robert Parsons (1546–1610), the leading Elizabethan Jesuit; George Buchanan (1506–1582), a Protestant Scottish historian.

[2] Robert Parsons (under the pseudonym R. Doleman), *A Conference about the Next Succession to the Crown of Ingland* (1594), pp. 37–63.

[3] *Bellarmine...Calvin*   Robert Bellarmine (1542–1621), Italian Jesuit theologian; John Calvin (1509–1564), French Protestant theologian.

[4] *Hayward...Blackwood...Barclay*   Sir John Hayward (1564?–1627), civil lawyer and historian; Adam Blackwood (1539–1613), a Scottish lawyer and philosopher; John Barclay (1582–1621), Scottish writer (possibly confused by Filmer with his father, the Scottish lawyer William Barclay). All published works that defended the rights of monarchs.

that are hourly versed in managing public affairs. Yet since the rule for each man to know in what to obey his prince cannot be learnt without a relative knowledge of those points wherein a sovereign may command, it is necessary when the commands and pleasures of superiors come abroad and call for an obedience that every man inform himself how to regulate his actions or his sufferings. For according to the quality of the thing commanded an active or passive obedience is to be yielded, and this is not to limit the prince's power, but the extent of the subject's obedience, by giving to Caesar the things that are Caesar's etc. [Matthew 22:21].

Secondly, I am not to question or quarrel at the rights or liberties of this or any other nation. My task is chiefly to enquire from whom these first came, not to dispute what or how many they are, but whether they are derived from the law of natural liberty or from the grace and bounty of princes. My desire and hope is that the people of England may and do enjoy as ample privileges as any nation under heaven. The greatest liberty in the world (if it be duly considered) is for people to live under a monarch. It is the Magna Carta of this kingdom. All other shows or pretexts of liberty are but several degrees of slavery, and a liberty only to destroy liberty.

If such as maintain the natural liberty of mankind take offence at the liberty I take to examine it, they must take heed that they do not deny by retail that liberty which they affirm by wholesale. For if their thesis be true, the hypothesis will follow, that all men may examine their own charters, deeds, or evidences by which they claim and hold the inheritance or freehold of their liberties.

Thirdly, I must not detract from the worth of all those learned men who are of a contrary judgment in the point of natural liberty. The profoundest scholar that ever was known hath not been able to search out every truth that is discoverable: neither Aristotle in natural philosophy, nor Hooker in

divinity.[1] They were but men, yet I reverence their judgments in most points, and confess myself beholding even to their errors in this. Something that I found amiss in their opinions guided me in the discovery of that truth which (I persuade myself) they missed. A dwarf sometimes may see that which a giant looks over, for whilst one truth is curiously searched after, another must necessarily be neglected. Late writers have taken up too much upon trust from the subtle schoolmen,[2] who to be sure to thrust down the king below the pope, thought it the safest course to advance the people above the king, that so the papal power may more easily take place of the regal. Thus many an ignorant subject hath been fooled into this faith, that a man may become a martyr for his country by being a traitor to his prince; whereas the new coined distinction of subjects into royalists and patriots is most unnatural,[3] since the relation between king and people is so great that their well-being is reciprocal.

(2) To make evident the grounds of this question about the natural liberty of mankind, I will lay down some passages of Cardinal Bellarmine, that may best unfold the state of this controversy. "Secular or civil power," saith he

> is instituted by men. It is in the people unless they bestow it on a prince. This power is immediately in the whole multitude, as in the subject of it. For this power is by the divine law, but the divine law hath given this power to no particular man. If the positive law be taken away, there is left no reason why amongst a multitude (who are

---

[1] *Hooker* Richard Hooker (1554?–1600), whose *Of the Lawes of Ecclesiasticall Politie* (1593) was the most famous Elizabethan defence of the Church of England.

[2] *schoolmen* medieval theologians.

[3] *new coined distinction* The word "royalist" first appeared in the 1620s, though the earliest reference in the *OED* is from the early 1640s.

equal) one rather than another should bear rule over the rest. Power is given by the multitude to one man, or to more by the same law of nature, for the commonwealth of itself cannot exercise this power, therefore it is bound to bestow it upon some one man, or some few. It depends upon the consent of the multitude to ordain over themselves a king, or consul, or other magistrate; and if there be a lawful cause, the multitude may change the kingdom into an aristocracy or democracy. (*De Laicis*, book 3, chapter 4 [actually 6])

Thus far Bellarmine, in which passages are comprised the strength of all that ever I have read or heard produced for the natural liberty of the subject.

Before I examine or refute these doctrines, I must a little make some observations upon his words.

First, he saith that by the law of God power is immediately in the people. Hereby he makes God to be the immediate author of a democratical estate. For a democracy is nothing else but the power of the multitude. If this be true, not only aristocracies but all monarchies are altogether unlawful, as being ordained (as he thinks) by men, whenas God himself hath chosen a democracy.

Secondly, he holds that although a democracy be the ordinance of God, yet the people have no power to use the power which God hath given them, but only power to give away their power; whereby it follows that there can be no democratical government, because the people, he saith, "must give their power to one man, or to some few"; which maketh either a regal or aristocratical estate, which the multitude is tied to do, even by the same law of nature which originally gave them the power. And why then doth he say the multitude may change the kingdom into a democracy?

Thirdly, he concludes that "if there be a lawful cause the multitude may change the kingdom into an aristocracy or democracy." Here I would fain know who shall judge of this lawful cause? If the multitude (for I see nobody else can) then this is a pestilent and dangerous conclusion.

(3) I come now to examine that argument which is used by Bellarmine, and is the one and only argument I can find produced by any author for the proof of the natural liberty of the people. It is thus framed: that God hath given or ordained power is evident by Scripture; but God hath given it to no particular man, because by nature all men are equal; therefore he hath given power to the people or multitude.

To answer this reason, drawn from the equality of mankind by nature, I will first use the help of Bellarmine himself, whose very words are these: "if many men had been together created out of the earth, all they ought to have been princes over their posterity" (*De Romano Pontifice*, book 1, chapter 2). In these words we have an evident confession that creation made man prince of his posterity. And indeed not only Adam but the succeeding patriarchs had, by right of fatherhood, royal authority over their children. Nor dares Bellarmine deny this also. "That the patriarchs," saith he, "were endowed with kingly power, their deeds do testify." For as Adam was lord of his children, so his children under him had a command and power over their own children, but still with subordination to the first parent, who is lord paramount over his children's children to all generations, as being the grandfather of his people.

I see not then how the children of Adam, or of any man else, can be free from subjection to their parents. And this subjection of children is the only fountain of all regal authority, by the ordination of God himself. It follows that civil power not only in general is by divine institution, but even the assignment of it specifically to the eldest parent, which quite takes away that new and common distinction which refers only power universal as absolute to

God, but power respective in regard of the special form of government to the choice of the people. Nor leaves it any place for such imaginary pactions between kings and their people as many dream of.[1]

(4) This lordship which Adam by creation had over the whole world, and by right descending from him the patriarchs did enjoy, was as large and ample as the absolutest dominion of any monarch which hath been since the creation. For power of life and death we find that Judah, the father, pronounced sentence of death against Thamar, his daughter-in-law, for playing the harlot. "Bring her forth," saith he, "that she may be burnt" [Genesis 38:24]. Touching war, we see that Abraham commanded an army of 318 soldiers of his own family [Genesis 14:14]; and Esau met his brother Jacob with 400 men at arms [Genesis 33:1]. For matter of peace, Abraham made a league with Abimelech, and ratified the articles by an oath [Genesis 21:23–4]. These acts of judging in capital causes, of making war, and concluding peace, are the chiefest marks of sovereignty that are found in any monarch.

(5) Not only until the Flood, but after it, this patriarchal power did continue—as the very name of patriarch doth in part prove. The three sons of Noah had the whole world divided amongst them by their father, for of them was the whole world overspread, according to the benediction given to him and his sons: "Be fruitful and multiply and replenish the earth" (Genesis 9:[1]). Most of the civillest nations in the world labour to fetch their original from some one of the sons or nephews of Noah, which were scattered abroad after the confusion of Babel. In this dispersion we must certainly find the establishment of regal power throughout the kingdoms of the world.

It is a common opinion that at the confusion of tongues there were seventy-two distinct nations erected. All which were not confused multitudes, without heads or governors, and at liberty to choose what governors or government they pleased, but they were distinct families, which had fathers for rulers over them. Whereby it appears that even in the confusion, God was careful to preserve the fatherly authority by distributing the diversity of languages according to the diversity of families. For so it plainly appears by the text. First, after the enumeration of the sons of Japhet, the conclusion is: "By these were the isles of the gentiles divided in their lands; every one after his tongue, after their families, in their nations" (Genesis 10:5). So it is said: "These are the sons of Ham after their families, after their tongues, in their countries, and in their nations" [Genesis 10:20]. The like we read: "These are the sons of Shem after their families, after their tongues, in their lands, after their nations. These are the families of the sons of Noah after their generations in their nations, and by these were the nations divided in the earth after the Flood" [Genesis 10:31–2].

In this division of the world, some are of opinion that Noah used lots for the distribution of it. Others affirm that he sailed about the Mediterranean sea in ten years and as he went about, pointed to each son his part, and so made the division of the then known world into Asia, Africa, and Europe, according to the number of his sons, the limits of which three parts are all found in that midland sea.

(6) But howsoever the manner of the division be uncertain, yet it is most certain the division itself was by families from Noah and his children, over which the parents were heads and princes.

Amongst these was Nimrod, who no doubt (as Sir Walter Raleigh affirms) was by good right lord

---

[1] *pactions* compacts, contracts, agreements (*OED*).

or king over his family.[1] Yet against right did he enlarge his empire by seizing violently on the rights of other lords of families, and in this sense he may be said to be the author and first founder of monarchy. And all those that do attribute unto him the original of regal power do hold he got it by tyranny or usurpation, and not by any due election of the people or multitude, nor by any paction with them.

As this patriarchal power continued in Abraham, Isaac and Jacob, even until the Egyptian bondage, so we find it amongst the sons of Ishmael and Esau. It is said: "These are the sons of Ishmael, and these are their names by their castles and towns, twelve princes of their tribes or families" (Genesis 25:16), "And these are the names of the dukes that came of Esau, according to their families and their places by their nations" (Genesis 36:40).

(7) Some, perhaps, may think that these princes and dukes of families were but some petty lords under some greater kings, because the number of them are so many that their particular territories could be but small, and not worthy the title of kingdoms. But they must consider that at first kings had no such large dominions as they have nowadays. We find in the time of Abraham, which was about 300 years after the Flood, that in a little corner of Asia nine kings at once met in battle, most of which were but kings of cities apiece, with the adjacent territories, as of Sodom, Gomorrha, Shinar, etc. In the same chapter is mention of Melchisedek, king of Salem, which was but the city of Jerusalem (Genesis 14). And in the catalogue of the kings of Edom, the name of each king's city is recorded as the only mark to distinguish their dominions (Genesis 36). In the land of Canaan, which was but of a small circuit, Joshua destroyed thirty-one kings [Joshua 12:24], and about the same time Adonibezek had seventy kings whose fingers

and toes he had cut off, and made them feed under his table [Judges 1:7]. A few ages after this, thirty-two kings came to Benhadad [I Kings 20:16], king of Syria, and about seventy kings of Greece went to the wars of Troy. Caesar found more kings in France than there be now provinces there, and at his sailing over into this island he found four kings in our county of Kent. These heaps of kings in each nation are an argument that their territories were but small, and strongly confirm our assertion that erection of kingdoms came at first only by distinction of families.

By manifest footsteps we may trace this paternal government unto the Israelites coming into Egypt, where the exercise of supreme patriarchal jurisdiction was intermitted because they were in subjection to a stronger prince. After the return of these Israelites out of bondage, God, out of a special care of them, chose Moses and Joshua successively to govern as princes in the place and stead of the supreme fathers, and after them likewise for a time. He raised up Judges to defend His people in times of peril. But when God gave the Israelites kings, He re-established the ancient and prime right of lineal succession to paternal government. And whensoever He made choice of any special person to be king, He intended that the issue also should have benefit thereof, as being comprehended sufficiently in the person of the father—although the father only were named in the grant.

(8) It may seem absurd to maintain that kings now are the fathers of their people, since experience shows the contrary. It is true, all kings be not the natural parents of their subjects, yet they all either are, or are to be reputed as the next heirs to those progenitors who were at first the natural parents of the whole people, and in their right succeed to the exercise of supreme jurisdiction. And such heirs are not only lords of their own children, but also of

---

[1] *as...Raleigh affirms* Sir Walter Raleigh, *The History of the World* (1614), 1.10.i.

their brethren, and all others that were subject to their fathers.

And therefore we find that God told Cain of his brother Abel: "His desires shall be subject unto thee, and thou shalt rule over him" (Genesis 4:7). Accordingly, when Jacob had bought his brother's birthright, Isaac blessed him thus: "Be lord over thy brethren, and let the sons of thy mother bow before thee" (Genesis 27:29). As long as the first fathers of families lived, the name of patriarchs did aptly belong unto them. But after a few descents, when the true fatherhood itself was extinct and only the right of the father descended to the true heir, then the title of prince or king was more significant to express the power of him who succeeds only to the right of that fatherhood which his ancestors did naturally enjoy. By this means it comes to pass that many a child, by succeeding a king, hath the right of a father over many a grey-headed multitude, and hath the title of *pater patriae* [father of the fatherland].

(9) It may be demanded what becomes of the right of fatherhood in case the crown do escheat for want of an heir, whether doth it not then devolve to the people? The answer is:

1. It is but the negligence or ignorance of the people to lose the knowledge of the true heir, for an heir there always is. If Adam himself were still living, and now ready to die, it is certain that there is one man, and but one in the world, who is next heir, although the knowledge who should be that one man be quite lost.

2. This ignorance of the people being admitted, it doth not by any means follow that for want of heirs the supreme power devolves to the multitude, and that they have power to rule, or choose what rulers they please. No: the kingly power escheats in such cases to the prime and independent heads of families, for every kingdom is resolved into those parts whereof at first it was made. By the uniting of

great families or petty princedoms, we find the greater monarchies were at the first erected, and into such again—as into their first matter—many times they return. And because the dependency of ancient families is oft obscure or worn out of knowledge, therefore the wisdom of all or most princes hath thought fit to adopt many times those for heads of families and princes of provinces whose merits, abilities, or fortunes have enabled them, or made them fit and capable of such royal favours. All such prime heads and fathers have power to consent in the uniting or conferring of their fatherly right of sovereign authority on whom they please. And he that is so elected claims not his power as a donative from the people, but as being substituted properly by God, from whom he receives his royal charter of an universal father, though testified by the ministry of the heads of the people.

If it please God, for the correction of the prince or punishment of the people to suffer princes to be removed and others placed in their rooms, either by the factions of the nobility or rebellion of the people, in all such cases the judgment of God—who hath power to give and to take away kingdoms—is most just. Yet the ministry of men who execute God's judgments without commission is sinful and damnable. God doth but use and turn men's unrighteous acts to the performance of His righteous decrees.

(10) In all kingdoms or commonwealths in the world, whether the prince be the supreme father of the people or but the true heir of such a father, or whether he come to the crown by usurpation, or by election of the nobles or of the people, or by any other way whatsoever, or whether some few or a multitude govern the commonwealth, yet still the authority that is in any one, or in many, or in all of these, is the only right and natural authority of a supreme father. There is, and always shall be continued to the end of the world, a natural right of a

supreme father over every multitude, although, by the secret will of God, many at first do most unjustly obtain the exercise of it.

To confirm this natural right of regal power, we find in the decalogue that the law which enjoins obedience to kings is delivered in the terms of "honour thy father" [Exodus 20:12] as if all power were originally in the father. If obedience to parents be immediately due by a natural law, and subjection to princes but by the mediation of an human ordinance, what reason is there that the law of nature should give place to the laws of men, as we see the power of the father over his child gives place and is subordinate to the power of the magistrate?

If we compare the natural duties of a father with those of a king, we find them to be all one, without any difference at all but only in the latitude or extent of them. As the father over one family, so the king, as father over many families, extends his care to preserve, feed, clothe, instruct and defend the whole commonwealth. His wars, his peace, his courts of justice and all his acts of sovereignty tend only to preserve and distribute to every subordinate and inferior father, and to their children, their rights and privileges, so that all the duties of a king are summed up in an universal fatherly care of his people.

—1680 (CA. 1628?–1642?)

Directions for Obedience to Government in Dangerous or Doubtful Times

All those who in these times so eagerly strive for an original power to be in the people do with one consent acknowledge that originally the supreme power was in the fatherhood; and that the first kings were fathers of families. This is not only evident, and affirmed by Aristotle, but yielded unto by Grotius, Mr Selden, Mr Hobbes, Mr Ascham and all others of that party,[1] not one excepted, that I know of.

Now for those that confess an original subjection in children to be governed by their parents, to dream of an original freedom in mankind is to contradict themselves. And to make subjects to be free, and kings to be limited; to imagine such pactions and contracts between kings and people as cannot be proved ever to have been made, or can ever be described or fancied how it is possible for such contracts ever to have been, is a boldness to be wondered at.

Mr Selden confesseth that Adam

by donation from God was made the general lord of all things, not without such a private dominion to himself as (without his grant) did exclude his children. And by donation or assignation, or some kind of cession (before he was dead or left any heir to succeed him) his children had their distinct territories by right of private dominion. Abel had his flocks, and pastures for them. Cain had his fields for corn, and the land of Nod where he built himself a city.[2]

It is confessed that in the infancy of the world the paternal government was monarchical. But when the world was replenished with multitude of people, then the paternal government ceased and was lost, and an elective kind of government by the people was brought into the world. To this it may be answered that the paternal power cannot be lost. It may either be transferred or usurped, but never lost, or ceaseth. God, who is the giver of power, may transfer it from the father to some other. He

---

[1] *Grotius…Selden…Hobbes…Ascham* Hugo Grotius (1583–1645), Dutch lawyer and scholar; John Selden (1584–1654), lawyer and historian; Thomas Hobbes (1588–1679), philosopher; Antony Ascham (d. 1650), a Parliamentarian ambassador and author of a treatise on the basis for transferring allegiance to a conquering power.

[2] translated by Filmer from John Selden, *Mare Clausum* (1635), book 1, chapter 4.

gave to Saul a fatherly power over his father Kish. God also hath given to the father a right or liberty to alien his power over his children to any other, whence we find the sale and gift of children to have been much in use in the beginning of the world, when men had their servants for a possession and an inheritance as well as other goods. Whereupon we find the power of castrating and making eunuchs much in use in old times. As the power of the father may be lawfully transferred or aliened so it may be unjustly usurped, and in usurpation the title of an usurper is before and better than the title of any other than of him that had a former right. For he hath a possession by the permissive will of God, which permission how long it may endure no man ordinarily knows. Every man is to preserve his own life for the service of God and of his king or father, and is so far to obey an usurper as may tend not only to the preservation of his king and father, but sometimes even to the preservation of the usurper himself when probably he may thereby be reserved to the correction or mercy of his true superior. Though by human laws a long prescription may take away right, yet divine right never dies nor can be lost or taken away.

Every man that is born is so far from being free-born that by his very birth he becomes a subject to him that begets him. Under which subjection he is always to live unless by immediate appointment from God or by the grant or death of his father he become possessed of that power to which he was subject.

The right of fatherly government was ordained by God for the preservation of mankind. If it be usurped, the usurper may be so far obeyed as may tend to the preservation of the subjects, who may thereby be enabled to perform their duty to their true and right sovereign when time shall serve. In such cases to obey an usurper is properly to obey the first and right governor, who must be presumed to desire the safety of his subjects. The command of

an usurper is not to be obeyed in anything tending to the destruction of the person of the governor, whose being in the first place is to be looked after.

It hath been said that there have been so many usurpations by conquest in all kingdoms that all kings are usurpers, or the heirs or successors of usurpers; and therefore any usurper if he can but get the possession of a kingdom hath as good a title as any other. Answer: The first usurper hath the best title, being, as was said, in possession by the permission of God; and where an usurper hath continued so long that the knowledge of the right heir be lost by all the subjects, in such a case an usurper in possession is to be taken and reputed by such subjects for the true heir, and is to be obeyed by them as their father. As no man hath an infallible certitude but only a moral knowledge, which is no other than a probable persuasion grounded upon a peaceable possession, which is a warrant for subjection to parents and governors. For we may not say, because children have no infallible or necessary certainty who are their true parents, that therefore they need not obey, because they are uncertain. It is sufficient, and as much as human nature is capable of, for children to rely upon a credible persuasion. For otherwise the commandment of "honour thy father" would be a vain commandment, and not possible to be observed.

By human positive laws a possession time out of mind takes away or bars a former right—to avoid a general mischief of bringing all right into a disputation not decidable by proof and consequently to the overthrow of all civil government—in grants, gifts and contracts between man and man. But in grants and gifts that have their original from God or nature, as the power of the father hath, no inferior power of man can limit nor make any law of prescription against them. Upon this ground is built that common maxim, that *nullum tempus occurrit regi*, no time bars a king.

All power on earth is either derived or usurped from the fatherly power, there being no other original to be found of any power whatsoever. For if there should be granted two sorts of power without any subordination of one to the other, they would be in perpetual strife which should be supreme—for two supremes cannot agree. If the fatherly power be supreme, then the power of the people must be subordinate, and depend on it. If the power of the people be supreme, then the fatherly power must submit to it, and cannot be exercised without the licence of the people—which must quite destroy the frame and course of nature. Even the power which God himself exerciseth over mankind is by right of fatherhood: he is both the king and father of us all. As God hath exalted the dignity of earthly kings, by communicating to them his own title by saying they "are gods" [Psalm 82:6]; so on the other side he hath been pleased as it were to humble himself by assuming the title of a king to express his power, and not the title of any popular government. We find it is a punishment to have "no king", Hosea 3:4, and promised as a blessing to Abraham, Genesis 17:6, "that kings shall come out of thee."

Every man hath a part or share in the preservation of mankind in general. He that usurps the power of a superior thereby puts upon himself a necessity of acting the duty of a superior in the preservation of them over whom he hath usurped, unless he will aggravate one heinous crime by committing another more horrid. He that takes upon him the power of a superior sins sufficiently, and to the purpose; but he that proceeds to destroy both his superior and those under the superior's protection goeth a strain higher, by adding murder to robbery. If government be hindered, mankind perisheth. An usurper by hindering the government of another brings a necessity upon himself to govern. His duty before usurpation was only to be ministerial or instrumental in the preservation of others by his obedience. But when he denies his own and hinders the obedience of others, he doth not only not help but is the cause of the distraction in hindering his superior to perform his duty. He makes the duty his own. If a superior cannot protect it is his part to desire to be able to do it, which he cannot do in the future if in the present they be destroyed for want of government. Therefore it is to be presumed that the superior desires the preservation of them that should be subject to him, and so likewise it may be presumed that an usurper in general doth the will of his superior by preserving the people by government. And it is not improper to say that in obeying an usurper we may obey primarily the true superior, so long as our obedience aims at the preservation of those in subjection and not at the destruction of the true governor. Not only the usurper but those also over whom power is usurped may join in the preservation of themselves, yea, and in the preservation sometimes of the usurper himself.

Thus there may be a conditional duty or right in an usurper to govern. That is to say, supposing him to be so wicked as to usurp, and not willing to surrender or forgo his usurpation, he is then bound to protect by government, or else he increaseth and multiplieth his sin.

Though an usurper can never gain a right from the true superior, yet from those that are subjects he may. For if they know no other hath a better title than the usurper, then as to them the usurper in possession hath a true right.

Such a qualified right is found at first in all usurpers, as is in thieves who have stolen goods and during the time they are possessed of them have a title in law against all others but the true owners. And such usurpers to divers intents and purposes may be obeyed.

Neither is he only an usurper who obtains the government, but all they are partakers in the usurpation who have either failed to give assistance to their lawful sovereign, or have given aid either by their persons, estates or counsels for the destroying of that governor under whose protection they have been born and preserved. For although it should be granted that *protection* and *subjection* are reciprocal, so that where the first fails the latter ceaseth, yet it must be remembered that where a man hath been born under the protection of a long and peaceable government, he owes an assistance for the preservation of that government that hath protected him, and is the author of his own disobedience.

It is said by some that an usurped power may be obeyed in things that are lawful. But it may be obeyed not only in lawful things but also in things indifferent.[1] Obedience in things indifferent is necessary, not indifferent. For in things necessarily good God is immediately obeyed, superiors only by consequence. If men command things evil, obedience is due only by *tolerating* what they inflict, not by *performing* what they require. In the first, they declare what God commands to be *done*, in the latter what to be *suffered*. So it remains that things indifferent only are the proper object of human laws. Actions are to be considered simply and alone, and so are good as being motions depending on the first mover; or jointly with circumstances, and that in a double manner: 1. In regard of the *ability* or *possibility*, whilst they may be done. 2. In the *act* when they be performed. Before they be done they be indifferent, but once breaking out into act they become distinctly good or evil according to the circumstances which determine the same. Now an action commanded is supposed as not yet done

(whereupon the Hebrews call the imperative mood the first future) and so remaineth many times indifferent.

Some may be of opinion that if obedience may be given to an usurper in things indifferent, as well as to a lawful power, that then there is as much obedience due to an usurped power as to a lawful. But it is a mistake, for though it be granted that in things indifferent an usurper may be obeyed as well as a lawful governor, yet herein lieth a main difference—that some things are indifferent for a lawful superior, which are not indifferent but unlawful to an usurper to enjoin. Usurpation is the resisting and taking away the power from him who hath such a former right to govern the usurper as cannot be lawfully taken away. So that it cannot be just for an usurper to take advantage of his own unlawful act or create himself a title by continuation of his own injustice, which aggravates and never extenuates his crime. And if it never can be an act indifferent for the usurper himself to disobey his lawful sovereign, much less can it be indifferent for him to command another to do that to which he hath no right himself. It is only then a matter indifferent for an usurper to command, when the actions enjoined are such as the lawful superior is commanded by the law of God to provide for the benefit of his subjects by the same or other like restriction of such indifferent things, and it is to be presumed, if he had not been hindered, would have commanded the same, or the like laws.

—1652

---

[1] *things indifferent* things neither explicitly commanded nor forbidden by Scripture.

William Bradford
1590 – 1657

Born in Yorkshire to prosperous farmers, Bradford opposed his family's wishes by joining a Separatist congregation in Nottinghamshire in 1606. Three years later he followed the community into religious exile in Holland, working as a weaver in Leiden until 1620, when he sailed in the *Mayflower* to New England. In 1621 Bradford was elected governor of the Plymouth colony, a position he would hold for thirty of the next thirty-five years. With dedication and skill he helped ensure that the colony survived, at first physically and later financially. By the time he died in 1657, Plymouth had grown from the fifty-two settlers who survived the first winter (out of the 102 who had sailed in the *Mayflower*) to a community of more than a thousand people. "He was a person for study as well as action," wrote Cotton Mather, skilled in languages and well read in history and theology; at his death Bradford left a library of almost four hundred volumes. Bradford began his *History* in 1630 as a journal, but over two decades of writing it gradually became the first official history of the "Pilgrims" (a word he uses) and their colony.

❧❧❧

History of Plymouth Plantation
(excerpts)

BOOK I
CHAPTER 9

Of their voyage, and how they passed the sea; and of their safe arrival at Cape Cod

September 6, 1620. These troubles being blown over, and now all being compact together in one ship,[1] they [the Pilgrims] put to sea again with a prosperous wind, which continued diverse days together, which was some encouragement unto them; yet according to the usual manner many were afflicted with sea-sickness. And I may not omit here a special work of God's providence. There was a proud and very profane young man, one of the seamen, of a lusty, able body, which made him the more haughty; he would always be condemning the poor people in their sickness, and cursing them daily with grievous execrations, and did not let to tell them, that he hoped to help to cast half of them overboard before they came to their journey's end, and to make merry with what they had; and if he were by any gently reproved, he would curse and swear most bitterly. But it pleased God before they came half seas over, to smite this young man with a grievous disease, of which he died in a desperate manner, and so was himself the first that was thrown overboard. Thus his curses light on his own head; and it was an astonishment to all his fellows, for they noted it to be the just hand of God upon him.

After they had enjoyed fair winds and weather for a season, they were encountered many times with cross winds, and met with many fierce storms, with which the ship was shrewdly shaken,[2] and her upper works made very leaky; and one of the main beams in the midships was bowed and cracked, which put them in some fear that the ship could not be able to perform the voyage. So some of the chief of the company, perceiving the mariners to fear the sufficiency of the ship, as appeared by their mutterings, they entered into serious consultation with the master and other officers of the ship, to consider in time of the danger; and rather to return than to cast

---

[1] The colonists initially set sail in two ships, but one was found unseaworthy and everyone was transferred to the *Mayflower*.

[2] *shrewdly* severely, intensely (*OED* shrewdly *adv* 5).

themselves into a desperate and inevitable peril. And truly there was great distraction and difference of opinion amongst the mariners themselves; fain would they do what could be done for their wages' sake (being now near half the seas over), and on the other hand they were loath to hazard their lives too desperately. But in examining of all opinions, the master and others affirmed they knew the ship to be strong and firm underwater; and for the buckling of the main beam, there was a great iron screw the passengers brought out of Holland, which would raise the beam into his place; the which being done, the carpenter and master affirmed that with a post put under it, set firm in the lower deck, and other ways bound, he would make it sufficient. And as for the decks and upper works they would caulk them as well as they could, and though with the working of the ship they would not long keep staunch, yet there would otherwise be no great danger, if they did not overpress her with sails. So they committed themselves to the will of God, and resolved to proceed.

In sundry of these storms the winds were so fierce, and the seas so high, as they could not bear a knot of sail, but were forced to hull,[1] for divers days together. And in one of them, as they thus lay at hull, in a mighty storm, a lusty young man (called John Howland) coming upon some occasion above the gratings, was, with a seele of the ship thrown into the sea;[2] but it pleased God that he caught hold of the topsail halyards, which hung overboard, and ran out at length; yet he held his hold (though he was sundry fathoms underwater) till he was held up by the same rope to the brim of the water, and then with a boat hook and other means got into the ship again, and his life saved; and though he was something ill with it, yet he lived many years after, and became a profitable

member both in church and commonwealth. In all this voyage there died but one of the passengers, which was William Butten, a youth, servant to Samuel Fuller, when they drew near the coast.

But to omit other things (that I may be brief), after long beating at sea they fell with that land which is called Cape Cod; the which being made and certainly known to be it, they were not a little joyful. After some deliberation had amongst themselves and with the master of the ship, they tacked about and resolved to stand for the southward (the wind and weather being fair) to find some place about Hudson's river for their habitation. But after they had sailed that course about half the day, they fell amongst dangerous shoals and roaring breakers, and they were so far entangled there with as they conceived themselves in great danger; and the wind shrinking upon them withal, they resolved to bear up again for the Cape, and thought themselves happy to get out of those dangers before night overtook them, as by God's providence they did. And the next day they got into the Cape Harbour where they rode in safety.[3] A word or two by the way of this Cape; it was thus first named by Captain Gosnold and his company, Anno 1602,[4] and after by Captain Smith was called Cape James;[5] but it retains the former name amongst seamen. Also that point which first showed those dangerous shoals unto them, they called Point Care, and Tucker's Terror; but the French and Dutch to this day call it Malabar,[6] by reason of those perilous shoals, and the losses they have suffered there.

---

[1] *hull* to drift with the wind under short sail.

[2] *above the gratings* above deck; *seele* roll (*OED* seel *sb*).

---

[3] now Provincetown Harbor. They anchored on November 11, 1620, after sixty-five days at sea.

[4] because they took much of that fish there [note by Bradford]. Bartholomew Gosnold (d. 1607) also led the expedition that founded Jamestown in 1607.

[5] Captain John Smith (1580–1631), head of the Virginia Colony, had tried to name the cape after the king.

[6] Bradford's anglicizing of "Mallebarre," meaning bad or dangerous sandbar.

Being thus arrived in a good harbour and brought safe to land, they fell upon their knees and blessed the God of heaven, who had brought them over the vast and furious ocean, and delivered them from all the perils and miseries thereof, again to set their feet on the firm and stable earth, their proper element. And no marvel if they were thus joyful, seeing wise Seneca was so affected with sailing a few miles on the coast of his own Italy, as he affirmed, that he had rather remain twenty years on his way by land, than pass by sea to any place in a short time, so tedious and dreadful was the same unto him.[1]

But here I cannot but stay and make a pause, and stand half amazed at this poor people's present condition; and so I think will the reader too, when he well considers the same. Being thus passed the vast ocean, and a sea of troubles before in their preparation (as may be remembered by that which went before), they had now no friends to welcome them, nor inns to entertain or refresh their weather-beaten bodies, no houses or much less towns to repair to, to seek for succour. It is recorded in scripture as a mercy to the apostle and his ship-wrecked company, that the barbarians showed them no small kindness in refreshing them,[2] but these savage barbarians, when they met with them (as after will appear) were readier to fill their sides full of arrows than otherwise. And for the season it was winter, and they that know the winters of that country know them to be sharp and violent, and subject to cruel and fierce storms, dangerous to travel to known places, much more to search an unknown coast. Besides, what could they see but a hideous and desolate wilderness, full of wild beasts and wild men? and what multitudes there might be of them they knew not. Neither could they, as it were, go up to the top of Pisgah,[3] to view from this wilderness a more goodly country to feed their hopes; for which way soever they turned their eyes (save upward to the heavens) they could have little solace or content in respect of any outward objects. For summer being done, all things stand upon them with a weatherbeaten face; and the whole country, full of woods and thickets, represented a wild and savage hue.[4] If they looked behind them, there was the mighty ocean which they had passed, and was now as a main bar and gulf to separate them from all the civil parts of the world. If it be said they had a ship to succour them, it is true; but what heard they daily from the master and company? But that with speed they should look out a place with their shallop,[5] where they would be at some near distance; for the season was such as he would not stir from thence till a safe harbour was discovered by them where they would be, and he might go without danger; and that victuals consumed apace, but he must and would keep sufficient for themselves and their return. Yea, it was muttered by some, that if they got not a place in time, they would turn them and their goods ashore and leave them. Let it also be considered what weak hopes of supply and succour they left behind them, that might bear up their minds in this sad condition and trials they were under; and they could not but be very small. It is true, indeed, the affections and love of their brethren at Leyden was cordial and entire towards them,[6] but they had little power to help them, or

[1] from Seneca, *Epistulae Morales*, 53.

[2] Acts 28:2.

[3] *Pisgah* the mountain from which Moses saw the Promised Land (Deuteronomy 34:1–4).

[4] After six weeks anchored off this apparently desolate coast, Bradford's first wife, Dorothy, drowned after either falling or (some have speculated) jumping overboard.

[5] *shallop* the ship's boat, in which a small group of the colonists (including Bradford) explored the coast and first entered Plymouth Bay on December 11.

[6] the remaining members of John Robinson's Separatist congregation in Holland.

themselves; and how the case stood between them and the merchants at their coming away,[1] hath already been declared. What could now sustain them but the spirit of God and his grace? May not and ought not the children of these fathers rightly say: "Our fathers were Englishmen which came over this great ocean, and were ready to perish in this wilderness; but they cried unto the Lord, and he heard their voice, and looked on their adversity,"[2] etc. "Let them therefore praise the Lord, because he is good, and his mercies endure for ever. Yea, let them which have been redeemed of the Lord, show how he hath delivered them from the hand of the oppressor. When they wandered in the desert wilderness out of the way, and found no city to dwell in, both hungry, and thirsty, their soul was overwhelmed in them. Let them confess before the Lord his loving kindness, and his wonderful works before the sons of men."[3]

BOOK II
CHAPTER 19
(excerpt)

A nno 1628: Thomas Morton of Merrymount
About some three or four years before this time, there came over one Captain Wollaston (a man of pretty parts),[4] and with him three or four more of some eminence, who brought with them a great many servants, with provisions and other implements for to begin a plantation; and pitched themselves in a place within the Massachusetts, which they called, after their Captain's name, Mount Wollaston. Amongst whom was one Mr. Morton, who, it should seem, had some small

adventure (of his own or other men's) amongst them; but had little respect amongst them, and was slighted by the meanest servants. Having continued there some time, and not finding things to answer their expectations, nor profit to arise as they looked for, Captain Wollaston takes a great part of the servants, and transports them to Virginia, where he puts them off at good rates, selling their time to other men; and writes back to one Mr. Rasdall, one of his chief partners, and accounted their merchant, to bring another part of them to Virginia likewise, intending to put them off there as he had done the rest. And he, with the consent of the said Rasdall, appointed one Fitcher to be his Lieutenant, and govern the remains of the plantation, till he or Rasdall returned to take further order thereabout. But this Morton abovesaid, having more craft than honesty (who had been a kind of pettifogger, of Furnival's Inn),[5] in the other's absence, watches an opportunity (commons being but hard amongst them),[6] and got some strong drink and other junkets, and made them a feast; and after they were merry, began to tell them, he would give them good counsel. "You see (saith he) that many of your fellows are carried to Virginia; and if you stay till this Rasdall return, you will also be carried away and sold for slaves with the rest. Therefore I would advise you to thrust out this Lieutenant Fitcher; and I, having a part in the plantation, will receive you as my partners and consociates; so may you be free from service, and we will converse, trade, plant, and live together as equals, and support and protect one another," or to like effect. This counsel was easily received; so they took opportunity, and thrust Lieutenant Fitcher out of doors, and would suffer him to come no more amongst them, but forced him to seek bread to eat, and other relief from his neighbours, till he could get passage for England.

---

[1] *the merchants* the merchants who financed the expedition. The colony's relations with its "London partners" had been and would long continue to be vexed.

[2] an adaptation of Deuteronomy 26:5, 7.

[3] Psalm 107:1–5, 8.

[4] *pretty* clever and skillful, or brave and gallant (*OED* pretty *a* 2a, 3).

[5] one of the Inns of Chancery in London, where lawyers were trained. Morton in fact attended not Furnival's but Clifford's Inn.

[6] That is, provisions were scarce among them.

After this they fell to great licentiousness, and led a dissolute life, pouring out themselves into all profaneness. And Morton became lord of misrule, and maintained (as it were) a school of atheism. And after they had got some goods into their hands, and got much by trading with the Indians, they spent it as vainly, in quaffing and drinking both wine and strong waters in great excess, and, as some reported, £10 worth in a morning. They also set up a Maypole, drinking and dancing about it many days together, inviting the Indian women for their consorts, dancing and frisking together (like so many fairies, or furies rather), and worse practises. As if they had anew revived and celebrated the feasts of the Roman goddess Flora, or the beastly practices of the mad Bacchanalians. Morton likewise (to show his poetry) composed sundry rhymes and verses, some tending to lasciviousness, and others to the distraction and scandal of some persons, which he affixed to this idle or idol Maypole.[1] They changed also the name of their place, and instead of calling it Mount Wollaston they call it Merrymount, as if this jollity would have lasted ever. But this continued not long, for after Morton was sent for England (as follows to be declared), shortly after came over that worthy gentleman, Mr. John Endecott, who brought over a patent under the broad seal, for the government of the Massachusetts, who visiting these parts caused the Maypole to be cut down, and rebuked them for their profaneness, and admonished them to look there should be better walking; so they now, or others, changed the name of their place again, and called it Mount Dagon.[2]

Now to maintain this riotous prodigality and profuse excess, Morton, thinking himself lawless, and hearing what gain the French and fishermen made by trading of pieces,[3] powder, and shot to the Indians, he, as the head of this consortship, began the practise of the same in these parts. And first he taught them how to use them, to charge, and discharge, and what proportion of powder to give the piece, according to the size or bigness of the same; and what shot to use for fowl, and what for deer. And having thus instructed them, he employed some of them to hunt and fowl for him, so as they became far more active in that employment than any of the English, by reason of their swiftness of foot, and nimbleness of body, being also quick sighted, and by continual exercise well knowing the haunts of all sorts of game. So as when they saw the execution that a piece would do, and the benefit that might come by the same, they became mad, as it were, after them, and would not stick to give any prize they could attain too for them; accounting their bows and arrows but baubles in comparison of them.

And here I may take occasion to bewail the mischief that this wicked man began in these parts, and which since base covetousness prevailing in men that should know better, has now at length got the upper hand, and made this thing common, notwithstanding any laws to the contrary; so as the Indians are full of pieces all over, both fowling pieces, muskets, pistols, &c. They have also their moulds to make shot, of all sorts, as musket bullets, pistol bullets, swan and goose shot, and of smaller sorts; yea, some have seen them have their screwplates to make screw-pins themselves, when they want them, with sundry other implements, wherewith they are ordinarily better fitted and furnished than the English themselves. Yea, it is well known that they will have powder and shot, when the English want it, nor cannot get it; and that in a time of war or danger, as experience hath manifested, that when lead hath been scarce, and men for their

---

[1] Morton published some of these verses in *New English Canaan* (1637), a book he wrote to get even with the Pilgrims.

[2] *Mount Dagon* after the god of the Philistines (Judges 16:23).

[3] *pieces* guns.

own defence would gladly have given a groat a pound, which is dear enough, yet hath it been bought up and sent to other places, and sold to such as trade it with the Indians, at 12 pence the pound; and it is like they give 3 or 4 shillings the pound, for they will have it at any rate.[1] And these things have been done in the same times, when some of their neighbours and friends are daily killed by the Indians, or are in danger thereof, and live but at the Indian's mercy. Yea, some (as they have acquainted them with all other things) have told them how gunpowder is made, and all the materials in it, and that they are to be had in their own land; and I am confident, could they attain to make saltpeter, they would teach them to make powder. Oh the horribleness of this villainy! how many both Dutch and English have been lately slain by those Indians, thus furnished; and no remedy provided, nay, the evil more increased, and the blood of their brethren sold for gain, as is to be feared; and in what danger all these colonies are in is too well known. Oh! that princes and parliaments would take some timely order to prevent this mischief, and at length to suppress it, by some exemplary punishment upon some of these gain-thirsty murderers (for they deserve no better title), before their colonies in these parts be overthrown by these barbarous savages, thus armed with their own weapons, by these evil instruments, and traitors to their neighbours and country.

But I have forgot myself, and have been too long in this digression; but now to return. This Morton having thus taught them the use of pieces, he sold them all he could spare; and he and his consorts determined to send for many out of England, and had by some of the ships sent for above a score. The which being known, and his neighbours meeting the Indians in the woods armed with guns in this sort, it was a terror unto them, who lived stragglingly, and were of no strength in any place. And other places (though more remote) saw this mischief would quickly spread over all, if not prevented. Besides, they saw they should keep no servants, for Morton would entertain any, how vile soever, and all the scum of the country, or any discontents, would flock to him from all places, if this nest was not broken; and they should stand in more fear of their lives and goods (in short time) from this wicked and debased crew, than from the savages themselves.

So sundry of the chief of the straggling plantations, meeting together, agreed by mutual consent to solicit those of Plymouth (who were then of more strength than them all) to join with them, to prevent the further growth of this mischief, and suppress Morton and his consorts before they grew to further head and strength. Those that joined in this action (and after contributed to the charge of sending him for England) were from Pascataway, Namkeake, Winisimett, Weesagascusett, Natasco, and other places where any English were seated. Those of Plymouth being thus sought too by their messengers and letters, and weighing both their reasons, and the common danger, were willing to afford them their help; though themselves had least cause of fear or hurt. So, to be short, they first resolved jointly to write to him, and in a friendly and neighbourly way to admonish him to forbear these courses, and sent a messenger with their letters to bring his answer. But he was so high as he scorned all advice, and asked who had to do with him; he had and would trade pieces with the Indians in despite of all, with many other scurrilous terms full of disdain. They sent to him a second time, and bade him be better advised, and more temperate in his terms, for the country could not bear the injury he did; it was against their common safety, and against the king's proclamation. He answered in high terms as before, and that the

---

[1] With four pence to a groat and twelve pence to a shilling, traders were buying lead at three times the normal rate and selling it to the Indians for three or four times what they had paid.

king's proclamation was no law; demanding what penalty was upon it. It was answered, more than he could bear, his majesty's displeasure. But insolently he persisted, and said the king was dead and his displeasure with him, and many the like things; and threatened withal that if any came to molest him, let them look to themselves, for he would prepare for them.

Upon which they saw there was no way but to take him by force; and having so far proceeded, now to give over would make him far more haughty and insolent. So they mutually resolved to proceed, and obtained of the Governor of Plymouth to send Captain Standish,[1] and some other aide with him, to take Morton by force. The which accordingly was done; but they found him to stand stiffly in his defence, having made fast his doors, armed his consorts, set diverse dishes of powder and bullets ready on the table; and if they had not been over armed with drink, more hurt might have been done. They summoned him to yield, but he kept his house, and they could get nothing but scoffs and scorns from him; but at length, fearing they would do some violence to the house, he and some of his crew came out, but not to yield, but to shoot; but they were so steeled with drink as their pieces were too heavy for them; himself with a carbine (over-charged and almost half filled with powder and shot, as was after found) had thought to have shot Captain Standish; but he stepped to him, and put by his piece, and took him. Neither was there any hurt done to any of either side, save that one was so drunk that he ran his own nose upon the point of a sword that one held before him as he entered the house; but he lost but a little of his hot blood.

Morton they brought away to Plymouth, where he was kept, till a ship went from the Isle of Shoals for England, with which he was sent to the Council of New England; and letters written to give them information of his course and carriage; and also one was sent at their common charge to inform their Honours more particularly, and to prosecute against him. But he fooled of the messenger, after he was gone from hence, and though he went for England, yet nothing was done to him, not so much as rebuked, for ought was heard; but returned the next year. Some of the worst of the company were dispersed, and some of the more modest kept the house till he should be heard from. But I have been too long about so unworthy a person, and bad a cause.

—(1630–50)

---

[1] Captain Myles Standish (1584–1656), military captain of the colony.

Anne Clifford
1590 – 1676

The diarist Lady Anne Clifford was the daughter and only surviving child of George Clifford, third Earl of Cumberland, and his wife Margaret Russell. Later in life, Lady Anne reflected on her youthful physical and mental attributes: "I was very happy in my first constitution, both in my mind and body…The hair of mine head was brown and thick, and so long as that it reached to the calf of my legs when I stood upright, with a peak of hair on my forehead and a dimple in my chin like my father, full cheeks and round face like my mother, and an exquisite shape of body resembling my father." Her beauty in form was matched by agility of mind: "I had a strong and copious memory, a sound judgment and a discerning spirit, and so much of a strong imagination in me as that many times even my dreams and apprehensions before hand, proved to be true." Her natural inclinations were fostered by a sound education, which was formally commenced at the age of eleven. Her tutor, the poet Samuel Daniel, encouraged her scholarly interests, and her diaries record her life-long enjoyment of reading. John Donne later remarked that "she knew well how to discourse of all things, from predestination to slea-silk."[1] After the death of Queen Elizabeth, Lady Anne became a friend and lady-in-waiting to James I's Queen, Anne of Denmark. During the early years of Lady Anne's life, her parents became estranged and lived for much of the time in separate homes, mainly because of her father's habits as spendthrift, gambler and unfaithful husband. Although he appeared repentant on his deathbed, George Clifford illegally bequeathed certain of his properties to his brother Francis and then to his nephew Henry, both of whom succeeded him in the earldom. While the titles and properties pertaining to the Cumberland earldom legally reverted to his brother Francis, other estates, castles, titles and country offices were strictly entailed upon heirs (male or female) "of the body,

lawfully begotten" of Robert de Clifford and were, therefore, legally entailed to Lady Anne. Inspired by her mother, she spent more than thirty years attempting to obtain possession of her estates, despite threats by both of her husbands and King James I. Lady Anne's first husband was Richard Sackville, Earl of Dorset, by whom she had five children, three of whom died in infancy. In the Knole diary, we find a record of the struggles that surface in this marriage because of Lady Anne's refusal to comply with her husband's instructions to yield up her claim to her property. Shortly after the death of Margaret Clifford in 1616, James I procured an order against Lady Anne, Dorset signed away his claim to her estates, and royal letters patent were issued completing her disinheritance. Dorset died in March 1624, and Clifford married Philip Herbert, fourth Earl of Pembroke and Montgomery, in June 1630. In her second marriage Lady Anne fared no better; after the death of two premature sons, she and Herbert rarely lived together for the remaining sixteen years of their marriage. Despite the King's "resolution" of the Clifford land dispute in favour of her uncle, Lady Anne records her ongoing battle to vindicate her right and interest in the lands of her inheritance in Westmoreland and Craven. In 1644, her cousin Henry Clifford, the fifth Earl, died at York without male issue. At last, Lady Anne assumed possession of her inheritance without adversary, although she could not claim her estates until after the Civil War, when it was safe to travel the countryside. Lady Anne dedicated the remainder of her life to the restoration and administration of her properties in the North. She restored five castles (Skipton, Appleby, Brougham, Brough, Pendragon), Barden Tower, and seven churches on her estate and undertook a family history (*Great Books of the Records of Skipton Castle*), continuing to write her diary until the month before her death in April, 1676.

---

[1] *slea-silk* "silk thread capable of being separated into smaller filaments for use in embroidery etc." (*OED* sleave-silk).

CʃƆCʃƆ

The Knole Diary (1603–1619) [1]
(excerpts)

1603

In Christmas I used to go much to the Court and sometimes I did lie at my Aunt Warwick's chamber on a pallet, to whom I was much bound for her continual care and love of me, insomuch as if Queen Elizabeth had lived she intended to prefer me to be of the Privy Chamber for at that time there was much hope and expectation of me as of any other young lady whatsoever.[2] A little after the Queen removed to Richmond she began to grow sickly.[3] My lady used to go often thither and carry me with her in the coach and using to wait in the coffee chamber, and many times we came home very late.[4]

About the 21st or 22nd of March my Aunt of Warwick sent my mother word about 9 o'clock at night—she living then at Clerkenwell—that she should remove to Austin Friars her house for fear of some commotions, then God in his mercy did deliver us from it.[5] The 20th [of] March Mr. Flocknall, my Aunt Warwick's man, brought us word from his lady that the Queen died about 2:30 o'clock in the morning.[6] This message was delivered to my mother and me in the same chamber where afterwards I was married.[7]

About 10 o'clock King James was proclaimed in Cheapside by all the Council with great joy and triumph.[8] I went to see and hear. This peaceable coming in of the King was unexpected of all parts of the people. Within 2 or 3 days we returned to Clerkenwell again.

A little after this Q.E.'s corpse came by night in a barge from Richmond to Whitehall, my mother and a great company of ladies attending it where it continued a great while standing in the drawing chamber, where it was watched all night by several lords and ladies. My mother sitting up with it two or three nights, but my lady would not give me leave to watch by reason I was held too young.

At this time we used very much to go to Whitehall and walked much in the garden which was frequented by lords and ladies. My mother being all full of hopes every man expecting mountains and finding molehills, excepting Sir R. Cecil and the

---

[1] The manuscript of the Knole diary originated during Lady Anne's first marriage, to Richard Sackville, Earl of Dorset. It is the first of four biographical documents dating from separate periods of her life.

[2] *Aunt Warwick* Anne Russell Dudley, Countess of Warwick, sister of Margaret Russell Clifford.

[3] *A little after…grow sickly* After Christmas, 1602, Queen Elizabeth began to feel frail and six weeks later she fell ill at Richmond.

[4] *coffee chamber* thus in D.J.H. Clifford's edition, without notes; but at this date it makes very dubious sense. Evelyn wrote, "There came in my time [i.e. 1636] to the College, one Nathanial Conopios, out of Greece…He was the first I ever saw drink coffee; which custom came not into England until thirty years after" (*OED* coffee 1); "coffer chamber" seems rather more likely, in the sense of a room in which chests (for linen, etc.) were kept.

[5] *Clerkenwell* Lady Cumberland had inherited Clerkenwell Green, a country house in the fields near to London, from the Countess of Derby in 1596; *Austin Friars* Lady Cumberland had possession of a house in Austin Friars in the very heart of London.

[6] *Queen died…in the morning* Queen Elizabeth I died on March 24, 1603.

[7] I was at Q. Elizabeth's death 13 yrs and 2 months old, and Mr R. Sackville was 14 yrs old, he being then at Dorset House with his grandfather and that great family. At the death of this worthy Queen my mother and I lay at Austin Friars in the same chamber [Clifford's note].

[8] The first time that the K. sent to the Lds in England he gave command that the Earls of Northumberland, Cumbd. Ld Thos Howard and Ld Mountjoy should be bidden to the Council [Clifford's note].

House of the Howards who hated my mother and did not much love my Aunt Warwick.[1]

About this time my Lord Southampton was enlarged of his imprisonment out of the Tower.[2]

When the corpse of Q.E. had continued at Whitehall as the Council thought fit, it was carried with great solemnity to Westminster, the lords and ladies going on foot to attend it. My mother and my Aunt Warwick being mourners, but I was not allowed to be one because I was not high enough, which did much trouble me then, but yet I stood in the church at Westminster to see the solemnities performed.[3]

A little after this my lady and a great deal of other company as Mrs. Elizabeth Bridges, Lady Newton and her daughter Lady Finch went down with my Aunt Warwick to North Hall and from thence we all went to Tibbalds to see the King who used my mother and aunt very graciously.[4] But we all saw a great change between the fashion of the Court as it is now and that in the Queen's time, for we were all lousy by sitting in the chamber of Sir Thomas Erskine.[5]

As the King came out of Scotland when he lay at York, there was a strife between my father and Lord Burleigh, who was the President and who should carry the sword, but it was adjudged on my father's side because it was an office by inheritance, and so is lineally descended to me.[6]

From Tibbalds the King went to Charter House where Lord T. Howard was created Earl of Suffolk and Lord Mountjoy Earl of Devonshire, and restored Lords Southampton and Essex who stood attainted. Likewise he created many Barons among which my Uncle Russell was made Lord Russell of Thorney, and for knights, they were innumerable. All this spring I had my health very well. My father used to come to us sometimes at Clerkenwell but not often, for he had at this time as it were wholly left my mother, yet the house was kept still at her charge.

About this time my Aunt of Bath and her lord came to London and brought them my Lord Fitz-Warren and my cousin Frances Bourchier, whom I met at Bagshot where I lay all night with my cousin, and Mrs. Mary Carey, which was the first beginning of the greatness between us.[7] About 5 miles from London there met my mother, my Lord of Bedford and his lady, my Uncle Russell and much other company so that we were in number about 300 which did all accompany them to Bath House, where they continued most of that summer. Whither I went daily and visited them and grew daily more inward with my cousin Frances and Mrs. Carey.[8]

About this time my Aunt Warwick went to meet the Queen, having Mrs. Bridges with her and my Aunt Vavasour.[9] My mother and I should have gone

---

[1] *Sir Robert Cecil* Robert Cecil, first Earl of Salisbury and first Viscount of Cranborne (ca. 1563–1612), statesman, was the son of William Cecil, Lord Burghley. He was a favourite of Queen Elizabeth I. He remained Secretary of State under James I, and continued to have political power until his death.

[2] *Lord Southampton* Henry Wriothesley, third Earl of Southampton (1573–1624), Shakespeare's patron and friend of the Earl of Essex. His secret marriage to his pregnant mistress Elizabeth Vernon angered the Queen and the couple were briefly imprisoned. When the Queen imprisoned Essex, Southampton conspired with him to regain their place at Court by violence. The scheme of rebellion was carried out February 8, 1601. On February 25th Essex was executed. The first act of James I on his accession was to free Southampton (April 10, 1603).

[3] Q.E.'s funeral was on Thursday, April 8th [Clifford's note].

[4] *Tibbalds* Theobalds, a royal lodge.

[5] *lousy* infested by lice (*OED* lousy *a*1a).

[6] *Lord Burleigh* William Cecil, Lord Burghley (1521–1598).

[7] *Frances Bourchier* Frances Bourchier was first cousin and close friend to Lady Anne. Greatly pained by Frances's death in 1612, Lady Anne erected a tomb at Chenies in her memory; *greatness* intimacy (*OED* greatness 6).

[8] *inward* intimate (*OED* inward A.I.3a).

[9] *Queen* Anne of Denmark (1575–1619) had married James in 1589 when he was King of the Scots; *Aunt Vavasour* In her youth Anne Vavasour had served as a maid of honour to Queen Elizabeth.

with them, but that her horse (which she borrowed from Mr. Elmes) and old Mr. Stickley were not ready. Yet I went the same night and overtook my aunt at Tittinhanger, Lady Blunt's house where my mother came the next day to me at noon—my aunt being gone before. Then my mother and I went on our journey to overtake her, and killed three horses that day with extremities of heat, and came to Wrest, my Lord of Kent's, where we found the doors shut and none in the house, but one servant who only had the keys of the hall, so that we were forced to lie in the hall all night till towards morning, at which time came a man and let us into the higher rooms where we slept 3 or 4 hours.[1]

This morning we hasted away betimes and came that night to Rockingham Castle where we overtook my Aunt Warwick and her company where we continued a day or two with old Sir Edward Watson and his lady. Then we went to Lady Needham's who once served my Aunt of Warwick, and from thence to a sister of hers whose name I have forgotten.

Thither came my Lady of Bedford who was so great a woman with the Queen as everybody much respected her, she having attended the Queen out of Scotland.[2] The next day we went to Mr. Griffin's at Dingleys which was the first time I ever saw the Queen and Prince Henry when she kissed us all and used us kindly.[3] Hither also came my Lady of Suffolk, my young Lady Derby and Lady Walsingham, which three ladies were the great favourites of

Sir Robert Cecil.[4] That night we went along with the Queen's train, there being an infinite number of coaches, and, as I take it, my aunt and my mother and I lay at Sir Rd. Knightley's, where Lady Elizabeth Knightley made exceedingly much of us.[5] The same night my mother and I and only Aunt Vavasour rid on horseback through country and went to a gentleman's house where the Lady Elizabeth, Her Grace, lay, which was the first time I ever saw her;[6] my Lady Kildare and the Lady Harrington being her governesses. The same night we returned to Sir Rd. Knightley's.[7]

The next day we went along with the Queen to Althorp, Lord Spencer's House, where my mother saw my cousin Henry Clifford, my uncle's son, which was the first time we ever saw him.[8] From thence, the 27th being Monday, the Queen went to Hatton, where the King met her, where there were

---

[1] *Lord of Kent* Sir Henry Grey, sixth Earl of Kent.

[2] *Lady of Bedford* Lucy Harrington Russell (1581–1627), wife of Edward, third Earl of Bedford, was the most powerful patron of the Jacobean court, excepting Queen Anne and perhaps Mary Sidney Herbert, Countess of Pembroke.

[3] *Prince Henry* Henry Stuart, the eldest son of James I and Anne, died in 1612 at the age of eighteen.

[4] *Lady of Suffolk...Lady Walsingham* Catherine (Knevet) Howard, Countess of Suffolk, was the daughter of Sir Henry Knevet and widow of Richard, eldest son of Robert Lord Rich. She married Lord Admiral Thomas Howard in 1583. Elizabeth (de Vere) Stanley, Countess of Derby, was the daughter of the Earl of Oxford. Ethelreda, Lady Walsingham, and her husband were appointed the Chief Keepers of the Queen's Wardrobe.

[5] *Sir Rd. Knightley's...Elizabeth Knightley* Richard Knightly's home was in Fawsley Park, Northampton. Elizabeth Knightly was the daughter of Edward, Duke of Somerset, Lord Protector.

[6] *Lady Elizabeth* Princess Elizabeth Stuart (1596–1662), eldest daughter of James I, afterwards Queen of Bohemia.

[7] *Lady Kildare...Lady Harrington* Despite King James I's promotion of Lady Kildare, it was reported that Queen Anne had no such affinity for her: in a letter, Sir Thomas Edmonds reported that "she [Queen Anne] hath hitherto refused to admit my Lady of Kildare or the Lady Walsingham, to be of her privy chamber, and has only as yet sworn my Lady of Bedford to that place." Lady Anne Harrington, mother of the Countess of Bedford, and her husband were chosen as tutor-guardians for Princess Elizabeth.

[8] The Queen and Prince came to Althorp the 25th June on Saturday. My mother, A. Warwick and I not till the next day, which Sunday was kept with great solemnity, there being an infinite number of lords and ladies. There we saw the Queen's favour to Ly Hatton and Ly Cecil, for she showed no favour to the elderly ladies but to Ly Rich and such like company [Clifford's note].

an infinite number of lords and ladies and other people that the country could scarce lodge them.

From thence the Court removed and were banqueted with great royalty by my father at Grafton where the King and Queen were entertained with speeches and delicate presents at which time my lord and the Alexanders did run a course at the field where he hurt Henry Alexander very dangerously.[1] Where the Court lay this night I am uncertain. At this time of the King's being at Grafton my mother was there, but not held as mistress of the house by reason of the difference between my lord and her which was grown to a great height.

The night after, my Aunt of Warwick, my mother and I, as I take it, lay at Dr. Challoner's, where my Aunt of Bath and my Uncle Russell met us, which house my G. Father of Bedford used to lie much at, being in Amersham. The next day the Queen went to a gentleman's house whose name I cannot remember, where there met her many great ladies to kiss her hand, as the Marchioness of Winchester, my Lady of Northumberland, my Lady Southampton etc.

From thence the Sovereign removed to Windsor where the Feast of St. George was solemnized though it should have been done before. There I stood with my Lady Elizabeth's Grace in the shrine of the Great Hall at Windsor to see the King and all the knights sit at dinner. Thither came the Archduke's ambassador, who was received by the King and Queen in the Great Hall where there was an infinite company of lords and ladies and so great a Court as I think I shall never see the like again.

From Windsor the Court removed to Hampton Court, where my mother and I lay at Hampton Court in one of the round towers, round which

were tents where they died 2 or 3 in a day of the plague. There I fell extremely sick of a fever, so as my mother was in some doubt it might turn to the plague, but within 2 or 3 days I grew reasonably well and was sent away to my cousin Stiddolph's for Mrs. Taylor was newly put away from me, her husband dying of the plague shortly after.

A little before this my mother and I, my Aunt of Bath and my cousin Frances went to North Hall, my mother being extreme angry with me for riding before with Mr. Mene, where my mother in her anger commanded that I should lie in a chamber alone, which I could not endure. But my cousin Frances got the key of my chamber and lay with me which was the first time I loved her so well. The next day Mr. Minerill as he went abroad fell down suddenly and died, so as most thought it was the plague which was then very rife; it put us all in great fear and amazement, for my aunt had then a suit to follow in Court and my mother to attend the king about the business between my father and her.

My Aunt of Warwick sent us medicines from a house near Hampton Court where she then lay with Sir Moyle Finch and his lady. Now was the Master of Orkney and the Lord Tilliburne much in love with Mrs. Carey, and came there to see us with George Murray in their company, who was of the King's bed chamber.

Within 9 or ten days we were allowed to come to the Court again, which was before I went to my cousin Stiddolph's. Upon the 25th of July the King and Queen were crowned at Westminster. My father and mother both attended in their robes, and my Aunt of Bath and my Uncle Russell, which solemn sight my mother would not let me see because the plague was hot in London. Therefore I continued at Norbury where my cousin did so feed me with breakfasts and pear pies and such things as shortly after I fell into sickness.

After the coronation the Court returned to Hampton Court, where my mother fetched me

---

[1] *Grafton* The house was known as Grafton Regis and was located in Northamptonshire. Henry VIII, Elizabeth I and James I all stayed at Grafton during their reigns. The home was destroyed during the civil wars.

from Norbury and so we lay at a little house near Hampton Court about a fortnight, and my Aunt of Bath lay in Huggins' lodgings where my cousin Frances and I and Mary Carey did use to walk much about the house and gardens when the King and Queen were gone.[1] About this time my cousin Anne Vavasour was married to Sir Richard Warburton.

From Hampton Court my mother went to Lancilwell, Sir Francis Palmer's house, with my Aunt of Bath, myself and all our company, where we continued as long as the Court lay at Basingstoke and I went often to the Queen and my Lady Arabella.[2] Now was my Lady Rich grown great with the Queen, in so much as my Lady of Bedford was something out with her, and when she came to Hampton Court was entertained but even indifferently, and yet continued to be of the bed chamber. One day the Queen went from Basingstoke and dined at Sir Hy. Wallop's where my lady, my aunt and I had lain 2 or 3 nights before and did help to entertain her.[3] As we rode from my Lady Wallop's to Lancilwell, riding late by reason of our stay at Basingstoke, we saw a strange comet in the night like a canopy in the air which was a thing observed all over England.

From Lancilwell we went to Mr. Dutton's where we continued a week and had great entertainments, and at that time kept a fast by reason of the plague

which was generally observed all over England. From Mr. Dutton's we went to Barton, one Mr. Dormer's, where Mrs. Humphry, her mother and she entertained us with great kindness—from thence we went often to the Court at Woodstock where my Aunt of Bath followed her suit to the King and my mother wrote letters to the King, and her means were by my Lord of —— [blank in manuscript] and to the Q. by my Lady of Bedford.

My father at this time followed his suit to the King about the border lands so that sometimes my mother and he did meet, when their countenance did show the dislike they had one of the other, yet he would speak to me in a slight fashion and give me his blessing. While we lay there we rid through Oxford once or twice but whither we went I remember not. There we saw the Spanish ambassador who was then new come to England about the peace.[4]

While we lay at Barton I kept so ill a diet with Mrs. Carey and Mrs. Kinson on eating fruit so that I shortly fell into the same sickness. From this place my Aunt of Bath, having little hope of her suit, took her leave of my mother and returned into the West Country. While they lay at Barton, my mother and my aunt paid for charge of the house equally.

Some week or a fortnight after my aunt was gone—which was about Michaelmas—my lady went from Barton to Green's Norton and lay one night at my cousin Thomas Sellinger's where we saw old Mr. Hicklin, where he and his daughter proffered Wm. Pond to serve my lady at this place, where we came about 10 o'clock at night, and I was

---

[1] My cousin Frances Bourchier stood to see the coronation though she had not robes and went not among the company [Clifford's note].

[2] *Lady Arabella* Arabella Stuart (1575–1615), a plausible claimant to the English throne, was viewed with suspicion by Elizabeth I and James I. She was kept in seclusion for ten years (1592–1602) after an unsuccessful plot by English recusants and Spanish agents to kidnap and marry her to a suitable Catholic. James I invited her to reside at Court in July, 1603. Later that month another plot surfaced to assassinate James I and crown Arabella. For the next several years, Arabella was a member of Queen Anne's entourage. After a secret marriage to William Seymour (1610), she was imprisoned in the Tower and there remained until her death.

[3] *Sir Hy. Wallop* Henry Wallop was the son of Queen Elizabeth's treasurer.

[4] Not long before this Michaelmas myself, my cousin Frances, Mrs. Goodwin and Mrs. Howbridge waiting on us, went in my mother's coach from Barton to Cookham where my Uncle Russell, his wife and son then lay. The next day we went to Nonsuch where Prince Henry and Her Grace lay where I stayed for a week, and left my cousin there who was proposed to continue with Her Grace, but I came back by Cookham and came to Barton where my A. of Bath went into the country [Clifford's note].

so weary as I could not tell whether I should eat or sleep first.

The next day we went to North Hall where we found my A. of Warwick something ill and melancholy. She herself had not been there passing a month, but lay at Sir Moyle Finch's in Kent by reason of the great plague which was then much about North Hall.

Not long after Michaelmas my Uncle and Aunt Russell and their son, my Lady Bedford, my mother and I gave ale allowance to Mr. Chambers my aunt's steward, in which sort the house was kept. During our being there I used to wear my hair colored velvet every day and learned to sing and play on the bass viol of Jack Jenkins my aunt's boy. Before Christmas my cousin Frances was sent for from Nonsuch to North Hall by reason that Her Grace was to go from thence to be brought up with the Lady Harrington in the country. All this time we were merry at North Hall. My cousin Frances Bourchier and my cousin Francis Russell and I did use to walk much in the garden and were great one with another. Now there was much talk of a masque which the Queen had at Winchester, and how all the ladies about the Court had gotten such ill names that it was grown a scandalous place, and the Queen herself was much fallen from her former greatness and reputation she had in the world.

1616[1]

MAY

Upon the 1st, Rivers came from London in the afternoon and brought me word that I should neither live at Knole or Bolebrooke.[2]

Upon the 2nd came Mr. Legge and told divers of the servants that my Lord would come down and see me once more, which would be the last time that I should see him again.[3]

Upon the 3rd came Baskett down from London and brought me a letter from my lord by which I might see it was his pleasure that the child should go the next day to London, which at first was somewhat grievous to me, but when I considered that it would both make my lord more angry with me and be worse for the child, I resolved to let her go.[4] After, I had sent for Mr. Legge and talked with him about that and other matters and wept bitterly.[5]

Upon the 4th being Saturday, between 10 and 11 the child went into the litter to go to London, Mrs. Bathurst and her two maids with Mr. Legge and a good company of the servants going with her.[6] In the afternoon came a man called Hilton, born in Craven, from my Lady Willoughby to see me which I took as a great argument of her love being in the midst of all my misery.[7]

Upon the 8th I dispatched a letter to my mother.

Upon the 9th I received a letter from Mr. Bellasis how extreme ill my mother had been, and in the afternoon came Humphrey Godding's son with

[1] By 1616, Lady Anne had been married to Richard Sackville, third Earl of Dorset, for seven years, having married him on February 25, 1609. Dorset attempted by a series of stratagems to compel Lady Anne to relinquish claims to her property so that he could receive a cash settlement as her husband.

[2] *Knole* The Sackville family seat was at Knole, Sevenoaks, Kent. Sackville also had a house in Bollbrooke, Sussex (amongst others).

[3] *Mr. Legge* Edward Legge, steward to the Earl of Dorset.

[4] *Baskett* Peter Baskett, Gentleman of the Horse to the Earl of Dorset; *the child* Lady Margaret Sackville (1614–1676), the daughter of Lady Anne and Richard Sackville.

[5] My Lady Margaret lay in the Great Dorset House, for now my lord and his whole company was removed from the Lesser Dorset House where I lay when I was first married [Clifford's note].

[6] *litter* a vehicle containing a couch shut in by curtains and carried on men's shoulders or by beasts of burden (*OED* litter sb2a); *Mrs. Bathurst* Mrs. Bathurst appears to be a Gentlewoman in Waiting to Lady Margaret. In June, Lady Anne and her husband determined that Mrs. Bathurst should "go away from the child" and that Lady Willoughby should have charge of her.

[7] About this time my Lord Shrewsbury died at his house in Broad Street [Clifford's note]; *Lady Willoughby* the wife of William, the third Lord Willoughby.

letters that my mother was exceeding ill, and as they thought, in some danger of death, so as I sent Rivers presently to London with letters to be sent to her and certain cordials and conserves.[1]

At night was brought to me a letter from my lord to let me know his determination was [that] the child should live at Horsley, and not come hither any more, so as this was a very grievous and sorrowful day to me.[2]

Upon the 10th Rivers came from London and brought me word from Lord William that she was not in such danger as I feared; the same day came the stewards from London whom I expected would have given warning to many of the servants to go away because the audits was newly come up.[3]

Upon the 11th being Sunday, before Mr. Legge went away I talked with him an hour or two about all this business and matters between me and my lord, so as I gave him better satisfaction and made him conceive a better opinion of me than ever he did.

A little before dinner came Matthew down from London, my lord sending me by him the wedding ring that my Lord Treasurer and my old lady were married withal, and a message that my lord would be here the next week, and that the child would not as yet go down to Horsley, and I sent my lord the wedding ring that my Lord and I was married with.[4] The same day came Mr. Marsh from London and persuaded me much consent to this agreement.[5]

The 12th at night, Grosvenor came hither and told me how my lord had won £200 at the cocking match, and that my Lord of Essex and Lord Willoughby who was on my lord's side won a great deal and how there were some unkind words between my lord and his side, and Sir William Herbert and his side.[6] This day my Lady Grantham sent me a letter about these businesses between my Uncle Cumberland and me, and returned me an answer.[7]

All this time my lord was in London where he had all and infinite great resort coming to him. He went much abroad to cocking, to bowling alleys, to plays and horse races, and [was] commended by all the world. I stayed in the country having many times a sorrowful and heavy heart and being condemned by most folks because I would not consent to the agreement, so as I may truly say, I am like an owl in the desert.[8]

Upon the 13th being Monday, my lady's footman Thomas Petty brought me letters out of Westmoreland by which I perceived how very sick and full of grievous pains my dear mother was, so as she was not able to write herself to me, and most of her people about her feared she would hardly recover this sickness. At night I went out and prayed to God my only helper that she might not die in this pitiful case.

The 14th. Richard Jones came from London to me and brought a letter with him from Matthew, the effect whereof was to persuade me to yield to my lord's desire in this business at this time, or else I was undone forever.

---

[1] *conserves* confections (*OED* conserve *sb* 4b).

[2] *Horsley* West Horsley, Surrey.

[3] Upon the 10th, early in the morning I wrote a very earnest letter to beseech him that I might not go to the little house that was appointed for me, but that I might go to Horsley and sojourn with my child, and to the same effect I wrote to my sister Beauchamp [Clifford's note].

[4] *Matthew* Matthew Caldicott, secretary and confidant to the Earl of Dorset.

[5] *Mr. Marsh* Christopher Marsh, Lady Anne's attendant or secretary. She later appointed him principal steward and secretary of her Westmoreland estates.

---

[6] *Grosvenor* Gentleman Usher to the Earl of Dorset; *cocking* cockfighting; *Lord of Essex* Robert Devereux, third Earl of Essex. He was eventually to lead the main Parliamentary army against the forces of Charles I in 1643; *Sir William Herbert* afterwards Lord Powis of Powis Castle (Wales).

[7] *Lady Grantham* the wife of Sir Thomas Grantham of Lincoln.

[8] *like an owl in the desert* "I am like a pelican of the wilderness: I am like an owl of the desert" (Psalm 102:6); there is much in the psalm that is relevant to Lady Anne's distress.

Upon the 15th my lord came down from London and my cousin Cecily Neville;[1] my lord lying in Leslie Chamber and I in my own.

Upon the 17th my lord and I after supper had some talk about these businesses, Matthew being in the room, where we all fell out and so parted for that night.

Upon the 18th, being Saturday, in the morning my lord and I having much talk about these businesses, we agreed that Mr. Marsh should go presently down to my mother and that by him I should write a letter to persuade her to give over her jointure presently to my lord, and that he would give her yearly as it was worth.

This day my lord went from Knole to London.[2] Upon the 20th being Monday I dispatched Mr. Marsh with letters to my mother about the business aforesaid. I sent them unsealed because my lord might see them.

My brother Compton and his wife kept the house at West Horsley, and my brother and my sister his wife sojourned with them, so as the child was with both her aunts.[3]

Upon the 22nd Mr. Davy came down from London and brought me word that my mother was very well recovered from her dangerous sickness; by him I writ a letter to my lord that Mr. Amherst and Mr. Davy might confer together about my jointure to free it from the payment of debts and all other encumbrances.[4]

Upon the 24th my Lady Somerset was arraigned and condemned at Westminster Hall where she confessed her fault and asked the King's mercy, and was much pitied by all beholders.[5]

Upon the 25th my Lord of Somerset was arraigned and condemned in the same place and stood much upon his innocency.[6]

Upon the 27th being Monday, my lord came down to Buckhurst. My Lord Vaux and his uncle Sir Henry Neville and divers others came with him, but the lords that promised to go with him stayed behind agreeing to meet him the next day at Lewes.[7]

Upon the 28th my Lady Selby came hither to see me and told me that she had heard some folks say that I have done well in not consenting to the composition.[8]

Upon the 29th Kendal came and brought me the heavy news of my mother's death, which I held as

---

[1] *Cecily Neville* the daughter of Lady Frances Abergavenny, who was the sister of the second Earl of Dorset, Lady Anne's father-in-law.

[2] My lord was at London when my mother died, but he went to Lewes before he heard of her death [Clifford's note].

[3] Upon the 20th my child went to W. Horsley with Mary Neville and Mrs. Bathurst from London. Mary Hicken was with her, for she still lain [lay?] in bed with Lady Margaret [Clifford's note]; *My brother Compton and his wife* Sir Henry Compton of Brambletye House, Sussex, was married to Lady Cecily Sackville.

[4] *Mr. Amherst and Mr. Davy* Mr. Amherst, Bencher of Gray's Inn, was the Queen's Sergeant-at-law and Mr. Davy was another lawyer.

[5] Upon the 24th, being Friday, between the hours of 6 and 9 at night died my dear mother at Brougham, in the same chamber where my father was born, 13 years and 2 months after the death of Queen Elizabeth and ten years and 7 months after the death of my father. I being 26 years and five months, and the child 2 years wanting a month [Clifford's note].

[6] *My Lady Somerset…his innocency* Frances Howard, cousin to Richard Sackville, and wife of Robert Carr, Earl of Somerset, a favourite of James I. She had divorced Robert Devereux, Earl of Essex, in 1613 on the grounds that she loved Carr. She took a strong dislike to Carr's friend Sir Thomas Overbury who had advised against the marriage. James I had Overbury imprisoned in the Tower of London for refusing a diplomatic appointment, and Lady Somerset arranged his murder by poison. When the murder of Overbury was exposed, Somerset was deprived of his office as Lord Chamberlain and both he and his wife were confined for their crimes.

[7] At this great meeting at Lewes, my Lord Compton, my Lord Mordaunt and all that crew with Wat. Raleigh, Jack Laurie and a multitude of such company were there. There was much bull baiting, bowling, cards and dice, with suchlike sports to entertain [Clifford's note].

[8] *composition* an agreement or arrangement between two parties (*OED* composition III.22); or, an agreement for submission on particular terms; capitulation (*OED* composition III.23b). Clifford will not consent to the terms of any agreement which will affect her disinheritance.

the greatest and most lamentable cross that could have befallen me.

Also he brought her will along with him, wherein she appointed her body should be buried in the parish church of Alnwick, which was a double grief to me when I considered her body should be carried away and not interred at Skipton; so as I took that as a sign that I should be dispossessed of the inheritance of my forefathers.

The same night I sent Hamon away with the will to my lord who was then at Lewes.

Upon the 30th the Bishop of St David's came to me in the morning to comfort me in these afflictions, and in the afternoon I sent for Sir William Selby to speak to him about the conveyance of my dear mother's body into Northumberland, and about the building of a little chapel.[1]

Upon the 31st came Mr. Amherst from my lord and brought me word that my lord would be here on Saturday. The same day Mr. James brought me a letter from Mr. Woolrich wherein it seemed it was my mother's pleasure her body should be conveyed to what place I appointed which was some contentment to my aggrieved soul.

1617

JANUARY

Upon New Year's Day, presently after dinner, I went to the Savoy to my Lady Carey [and] from thence she and I went to Somerset House to the Queen where I met Lady Derby, my Lady Bedford, my Lady Montgomery and a great deal of company that came along with the King and the Prince.[2] My Lady Arundel had much talk with me about the business and persuaded me to yield to the King in all things.[3] From Somerset House we went to Essex House to see my Lady of Northumberland. From thence I went to see my Lady Rich and so came home. After supper I went to see my sister Beauchamp and stayed with her an hour or two for my lord was at the play at Whitehall that night.[4]

Upon the 2nd I went to the Tower to see my Lord and my Lady Somerset. This was the first time I saw them since the arraignment.

Upon the 5th I went into the Court. We went up into the King's chamber where my Lord Villiers was created Earl of Buckingham. My lord, my Lord of Buckingham and divers other lords bringing him up to the King. I supped with my Lord and Lady Arundel, and after supper I saw the play of the Mad Lover in the hall.

Upon the 6th being Twelfth Day, I went about 4 o'clock to the Court with my lord. I went up with my Lady Arundel and ate a scrambling supper with her and my Lady Pembroke at my Lord Duke's lodgings.[5] We stood to see the masque in the box with my Lady Ruthven.[6]

Upon the 8th we came from London to Knole. This night my lord and I had a falling out about the land.

Upon the 9th I went up to see the things in the closet and began to have Mr. Sandys' book read to me about the government of the Turks, my lord

---

[1] On the 30th at night or the 31st my lord was told the news of my mother's death, he being then at Lewes [Clifford's note].

[2] *Lady Montgomery* Susan de Vere, Countess of Montgomery, to whom Lady Mary Wroth dedicated *Urania*.

[3] *Lady Arundel* Alatheia Howard, Countess of Arundel.

[4] As the King passed by he kissed me. Afterwards the Queen came out into the drawing chamber when she kissed me and used me very kindly. This was the 1st time I ever saw the King, Queen or Prince since they came out of the north [Clifford's note]; *Sister Beauchamp* Frances Devereux, first cousin of Richard Sackville, was the second wife of William Seymour, Lord Beauchamp;

[5] *scrambling supper* a meal at which partakers help themselves to what they can get.

[6] *Lady Ruthven* Though the identity of Lady Ruthven is unclear, she was probably a daughter of William Ruthven, first Earl of Gowrie. Queen Anne was devoted to the Ruthvens, but James disliked them strongly.

sitting the most part of the day reading in his closet.[1]

Upon the 10th my lord went up to London upon the sudden, we not knowing it till the afternoon.

Upon the 16th I received a letter from my lord that I should come up to London the next day because I was to go before the King on Monday next. Upon the 17th when I came up, my lord told me I must resolve to go to the King the next day.

Upon the 18th being Saturday, I went presently after dinner to the Queen to the drawing chamber where my Lady Derby told the Queen how my business stood, and that I was to go to the King; so she promised me she would do all the good in it she could. When I had stayed but a little while there I was sent for out, my lord and I going through my Lord Buckingham's chamber, who brought us into the King, being in the drawing chamber. He put out all that were there, and my lord and I kneeled by his chair side, when he persuaded us both to peace, and to put the whole matter wholly into his hands. Which my lord consented to, but I beseeched His Majesty to pardon me for that I would never part with Westmoreland while I lived upon any condition whatsoever.

Sometimes he used fair means and persuasions, and sometimes foul means, but I was resolved before so as nothing would move me.

From the King we went to the Queen's side and brought my Lady St John to her lodgings, and so we went home. At this time I was much bound to my lord for he was far kinder to me in all these businesses than I expected, and was very unwilling that the King should do me any public disgrace.[2]

Upon the 19th my Lord and I went to the Court in the morning thinking the Queen would have gone to the chapel, but she did not, so my Lady Ruthven and I and many others stood in the closet to hear the sermon.[3] I dined with my Lady Ruthven. Presently after dinner she and I went up to the drawing chamber where my Lady D., my Lady Montgomery, my Lady Burleigh, persuaded me to refer these businesses to the King.

About 6 o'clock my lord came for me, so he and I and Lady St John went home in her coach. This night the masque was danced at the Court, but I would not stay to see it because I had seen it already.

Upon the 20th, I and my lord went presently after dinner to the Court; he went up to the King's side about his business, I went to my Aunt Bedford in her lodging where I stayed in Lady Ruthven's chamber till towards 8 o'clock, about which time I was sent for up to the King in his drawing chamber, when the door was locked and nobody suffered to stay here but my lord and I, my uncle Cumberland, my cousin Clifford, my Lords Arundel, Pembroke, Montgomery and Sir John Digby.[4]

For lawyers there were my Lord Chief Justice Montagu and Hobart Yelverton, the King's solicitor

---

[2] The Queen gave me a warning not to trust my matters absolutely to the King lest he should deceive me. For lawyers, there were my Lord Chief Justice Montague and Hobart Yelverton the King's Solicitor and Sir Randal Crewe that was to speak for my lord and I [Clifford's note].

[3] *closet* a room in a palace used by the sovereign for private or household devotions (*OED* closet sb 2a).

[4] *Lords Arundel…Sir John Digby* Thomas Howard, Earl of Arundel. William, third Earl of Pembroke, was the brother of Philip Herbert, Lady Anne's second husband. Philip Herbert inherited the earldom of Pembroke on the death of William, was created Earl of Montgomery in 1605, and married Lady Anne in 1630. Of Sir John Digby, the first Lord Digby, Lady Anne writes in the margins of her April 1616 entry: "Sir John Digby, late ambassador to Spain was made Vice-Chamberlain and sworn of the Privy Council."

---

[1] *closet* a room for privacy or retirement; an inner chamber (*OED* closet sb 1a); *Mr. Sandys…of the Turks* George Sandys (1578–1644) left England on a foreign tour in 1610. He passed through France, Italy, Venice, Turkey, Egypt and Palestine. In 1615, he published an account of his travels, *The Relation of a Journey*.

Sir Randal Crewe that was to speak for my lord and I.[1]

The King asked us all if we would submit to his judgment in this case. My uncle Cumberland, my cousin Clifford and my Lord answered they would, but I would never agree to it without Westmoreland, at which the King grew in a great chafe, my Lord of Pembroke and the King's solicitor speaking much against me. At last when they saw there was no remedy, my lord fearing the King would do me some public disgrace, desired Sir John Digby would open the door, who went out with me and persuaded me much to yield to the King. My Lord Hay came to me to whom I told in brief how this business stood.[2] Presently, after my lord came from the King when it was resolved that if I would not come to an agreement, there should be an agreement made without me. We went down, Sir Robert Douglas, and Sir George Chaworth bringing us to the coach. By the way my lord and I went in at Worcester House to see my lord and lady and so came home.

This day I may say I was led miraculously by God's providence, and next to that I trust all my good to the worth and nobleness of my lord's disposition for neither I nor anybody else thought I should have passed over this day so well as I have done.

Upon the 22nd the child had her 6th fit of the ague in the morning. Mr. Smith went up in the coach to London to my lord to whom I wrote a letter to let him know in what case the child was, and to give him humble thanks for his noble usage towards me in London. The same day my lord came down to Knole to see the child.

Upon the 23rd my lord went up betimes to London again. The same day the child put on her red baize coats.[3]

Upon the 25th I spent most of my time in working and in going up and down to see the child. About 5 or 6 o'clock the fit took her which lasted 6 or 7 hours.

Upon the 28th at this time I wore a plain green flannel gown that William Punn made me, and my yellow taffety waistcoat.[4] Rivers used to read to me in Montaigne's *Plays* and Moll Neville in *The Fairy Queen*.[5]

Upon the 30th Mr. Amherst the preacher came hither to see me with whom I had much talk.[6] He told me that now they began to think at London that I had done well in not referring this business to the King, and that everybody said God had a hand in it.[7]

—1923 (1603–17)

---

[3] *baize* a coarse woollen stuff…formerly when made of lighter and finer texture, used as a clothing material in Britain (*OED* baize *sb*1).

[4] *taffety* taffeta.

[5] *Plays* In an earlier entry (November 9, 1616), Clifford writes that she "heard Rivers and Marsh read Montaigne's *Essays*, which book they have read almost this fortnight." So when she writes two months later that "Rivers used to read to me in Montaigne's *Plays*," one suspects a slip of the pen or a mistranscription of *Essays*.

[6] *Mr. Amherst* Dr. Jeffrey Amherst, Rector of Horsmonden, Kent.

[7] All this time of my being in the country there was much ado in London about my business, in so much that my lord, my Uncle Cumberland, my cousin Clifford with the Chief Justice and the Council of both sides, on divers times with the King about it, and then the King hearing it go so directly for me he said there was a law in England to keep me from the land. There was during this time much cock-fighting at the Court where my lord's cocks did fight against the King's. Although this business was somewhat chargeable to my lord, yet it brought him into great grace and favour with the King, so as he useth him very kindly and speaketh very often and better of him than of any other man. My lord grew very great with my Lord of Arundel [Clifford's note].

---

[1] *Sir Randal Crewe* afterwards Lord Chief Justice of the King's Bench.

[2] *Lord Hay* James Hay, later Viscount Doncaster and Earl of Carlisle.

Benjamin Laney
1591 – 1675

The Restoration Bishop successively of Peter-borough, Lincoln, and Ely, Laney was educated at Christ's College, Cambridge, and Pembroke Hall, Oxford. During the 1630s he served as Master of Pembroke Hall, Vice-Chancellor of Oxford, and chaplain to Charles I. Richard Crashaw dedicated the first edition of his *Epigrammata Sacra* (1634) to Laney, praising him for restoring ceremony and adornment to the college chapel. As a Royalist and representative of the Laudian church, Laney was deprived of his offices in the 1640s, and subsequently served as chaplain to both Charles I and the exiled Charles II. At the Restoration he received the first of the three bishoprics he would hold. Despite the apparent hard line he takes in the sermons printed here, Laney was known as a moderate, treating the Nonconformists in his diocese with lenience, in his own words "looking through his fingers at them." He also contributed generously to rebuilding several cathedrals and other church buildings that had suffered damage during the wars. The following two sermons were preached before the King and published, at first separately and then as a linked pair, by royal demand. Laney addresses a central concern of Restoration discourse: how to find ways of living, believing, and thinking that would minimize the chances of the renewal of war. His theme is (religious and political) quietness, a quality "fitted to give an allay to the Heats of these Unquiet Distemper'd times."

ꙮ

The Study of Quiet, in Two Sermons

A Sermon Preached Before His Majesty at Whitehall, March 12, 1665

1 THESSALONIANS 4:11
And that ye study to be quiet

And is a word that takes hold of something that went before, without which the sense of that which follows is not full. That which went next before is, *We beseech you to increase more and more.* *We beseech you*, is that we are to take into the text, and then it runs thus, *We beseech you to study to be quiet.*

But all the use I shall make of it, now we have it here, is but to give you a taste beforehand of the nature and quality of this duty. 1. That it is no trivial thing little to be regarded, but that which obliged St. Paul, Sylvanus, and Timotheus, for they all joined in it, to be so earnest, as to beseech them to study to be quiet. 2. And that which commends this duty the more is (as we use to say, men are best known by the company they keep), "And" brings in this duty in the company of the best of virtues, charity, for that place, St. Paul gives it above all: *Above all things put on Charity, which is the bond of perfection* [Colossians 3:14]. To study to be quiet, and to increase in brotherly love and charity, for that led the way before, are two duties bound together in the same exhortation. 3. Quiet is not only a fit companion for charity, but an ally to it, and grows out of it, as the branch out of the stock; for where brotherly love is, there will be always quiet too. 4. To make all suit the better with charity, the exhortation is advanced by a dialect of love, *We beseech you*. Paul, Sylvanus, and Timotheus were all apostolical men, and might command, as St. Paul of himself in another case to Philemon, *Though I might be bold to enjoin thee, yet for love's sake I rather beseech you.* And lastly, that which might very well set this edge upon their affections, was, that which happened to the Thessalonians at their first conversion; for this Epistle was written immediately after. The story we have in the 17 chap. of the Acts: When St. Paul had preached the Gospel to them, and with good success; for v. 4: *Some of them believed, and consorted with Paul and Silas, and of the devout Greeks a great multitude, and of the chief women not a few.* But v. 5: *The Jews who believed not, moved with envy, took unto them certain lewd fellows of the baser sort, and gathered a company, and set all the City in an uproar, and assaulted the house of Jason, and sought to bring them out to the people*; mad enough of themselves; but the more to ferment and enrage them, they charge the Apostles with the fault that they themselves were acting; *These are they that turn the world upside down.* St. Paul having escaped this fury by going to Athens, and there considering in what a case he left his new converts, both them and their doctrine; them in a furious tumult, and their doctrine under the reproach of troubling the world; out of a zeal, no doubt, and desire to remove that scandal from the faith, of all things begs and beseecheth them to *study to be quiet.*

But how will this concern us? I wish we never had, and had not still the same occasion. It is not so long since, that we should forget how our late troubles first brake in upon our quiet: We had unbelieving Jews then amongst us too, and some, as was thought, in the literal sense; who moved with envy of the times, took unto them likewise a company of lewd fellows of the baser sort, set the city in an uproar; and we may remember whose houses they beset (as the Jews did Jason's) none of the meanest, and cried out for that justice which themselves deserved. And there were religions in the world then too many, to the scandal of the true, who led on, and blew up those tumults: And even now, though (God be thanked) they dare not be so bold to assault us in the streets, and beset our houses as they did then; yet still keep their quarters

and leaguers within doors, with more secrecy, but no less danger.

It will not therefore be unseasonable for us now, who have the same cause the Thessalonians had, with the same affection the Apostle did, to beseech you to *study to be quiet.* We have all need of quiet, and quiet it seems hath need of study, and study hath need of God's blessing, and therefore before we proceed further, Let us pray, &c.

The parts of the text are two; What we are to study, And that we are to study.

First, What? *That ye study to be quiet.*

Quiet is here commended under the notion and quality of an art or science; for we are enjoined to study it. And in them we are to look, first, to the object, the nature and quality of it; and then to the principles and theorems whereon the art is grounded.

.   .   .   .

The quiet we are here to study is not properly with us, but without us; it is not simply a quiet from motion, but commotion, a troubling of others.

And that I may contract my argument and bring it into as narrow a compass as may be, I shall not take in every of the disturbances of the quiet of others: No not that which is the greatest of all, and most contrary to peace and quiet, civil wars and broils. The mischiefs of that we have learned so lately to our cost, and so perfectly, that I hope we need not be set to study that now: when every good man was put to his study how to live, and when vile and contemptible wretches ranted in plenty and power.

The horrid fruits and consequences of that great disturber of quiet, *war*, have induced some learned men, as well as others, to think all wars unlawful; I should have been much inclined to that opinion upon the strictest rules of Christianity, if war were not sometimes necessary to peace. A foreign war for that reason may be lawful, but a civil and domestic, never. And the reason of this difference is, because for the composing of all quarrels that may arise between subjects, God hath by his ordinance provided a remedy in Princes and Magistrates, from whom alone we are to seek for revenge or defence. But for such differences as arise between free Princes and States, because there is no judge on earth to whom they may have recourse for their relief, being destitute of the common remedy, they may, without question, make use of that sword which God hath put into their hands to defend their subjects from the injuries as well of strangers as their own.[1] Nor are they in this judges in their own cause, which hath some appearance of injustice; for a foreign war, for defect of a competent judge on Earth, is but an appeal to the supreme judge of Heaven and Earth. And when they go into the field, it is but to plead their cause before God, with whom are the issues of war. Only they had need be careful, that the cause they bring before him be good. For shall not the judge of all the world do right? But we must leave this to Princes and their ministers, who are the only proper students of that quiet, which is disturbed by war, and come to that which may and must be the study of us all: that is, *a quiet from troubles that arise from different judgments and persuasions in matters of religion*, which cause sects and divisions in it, though they break not out into an open war. Not that war be quite left out of the sectaries' reckoning. For though civil wars and rebellions have their beginning for the most part from the ambition or discontent of a few, yet because the people, who are the necessary instruments of that mischief, be not apt to serve the ambition of others, if it comes

barefaced to them, the mask of religion is always put on, wherein all people are concerned, which makes it a common and popular interest. And therefore you shall scarce hear of a rebellion of late times, in which religion did not carry the colours at least, if not command in chief.

But I shall nevertheless at this time forbear to make that any part of the schismatics' charge, but treat them upon their own terms, that they are as great enemies to war as any that object it to them: Yet I must charge them all to be guilty of the breach of peace and quiet in the Church, and that not accidentally, which may sometimes bear excuse, but necessarily; it is connatural and incident to the very nature of schism, which is a rent or division, so the word signifies. It is the worst disturbance that can be to any body, to be torn in pieces. It dissolves the bonds by which the parts are joined together, especially that which unites them to the head; for schism in the Church's notion is properly a separation from the head and authority, and is the same in the Church that rebellion or treason is in the state. Now as every disobedience to the King and the laws is not treason, though against the King, but the disclaiming the right and power the King hath to govern, and the practice of such things, by which his regalia and rights are usurped by others, as to make war, to make laws, to thrust officers upon him, to order the coin, these and of the like kind are only treason. So every error or disobedience in religion makes not a schism, but the disclaiming the right and power the Church hath to govern them, and a usurpation of a right to themselves, to order and frame points of belief, and forms how to serve and worship God, apart from the Church, for so went the style of the ancient Church for schism, *altare contra altare*, which in our modern dialect is a conventicle against the Church. For though schism be formally a separation from the head, yet consequently it works upon the members; for that which was at first but difference of opinion, soon

---

[1] Spurred primarily by commercial rivalry, England and Holland formally declared war on one another in March 1665, the month Laney delivered this sermon; he takes care to assure his listeners that he does not oppose *this* war.

begets a disaffection, and from that grows to hatred and contempt, and so falls into the practice of such things as destroy the very being and power of religion, which consists in the mutual offices of charity; and though this mischief breaks not out into an actual war, yet is always accompanied with most unnatural and unchristian practices, as St. James long since observed, Jam. 3:16, *Where envy and strife is, there is confusion, and every evil work.* Now to avoid all this, it will highly concern us to *study to be quiet.*

Having cleared the first point, the object of our study, *quiet* ... and how it comes to be disturbed by schism. The next point is, to enquire into the principles whereon we are to ground our study; for if there should be an error or mistake in them, all our labour and study is lost, or worse; for an inveterate, grounded, studied error is so much the harder to be reclaimed. It was no unreasonable demand therefore of the philosopher, who asked a double reward for those scholars that had been already entered into the study of philosophy, because his pains would be double with them, to undo first, and cast out those false prejudices which they had already learned.

Now if it should happen, that they which are otherwise studious and desirous of peace, should not do the things that make for peace, as the Apostle requires, our study will grow upon us, first to unlearn those false deceitful principles of peace, before we enquire into the true: Of some of the chief of these therefore I shall give you an account in the first place. It will conduce much to the peace of the Church, they say, first,

1. *If religion were free, and all compulsory means forborne,*

2. *If mere errors in judgment howsoever were not punished as crimes, which is not in the power of any to help.*

3. *Or if that, yet* (thirdly) *that omission of forms and ceremonies were not more severely and frequently punished, than notorious and scandalous crimes.*

4. *If fewer articles and points of religion were defined, it would make more room in the Church for those that dissent.*

5. Another is, *If men of moderate opinions were only employed in the Church.*

6. The last, and most importunate pretender to peace, is, *Liberty of conscience.*

But that none of all these are things that make for peace, I shall show with as much brevity as the matter is capable of; as first,

I. Not the forbearance of all compulsory means by punishments, which, they say, is repugnant to that freeness with which religion should be entertained, and only forces men to an hypocritical obedience to that which in their judgments they detest.

Religion, I grant, should be free; it is no religion which is not so: But it is as true, that every other act of virtue, and obedience to the laws should be free likewise; but therefore not to punish them that transgress, were to proclaim a perpetual jubilee, and set open all prison doors: God would never have enjoined the magistrate to punish temporally, nor himself threatened to punish eternally, if the fear of that did corrupt our obedience: For our Saviour in the parable, when the guests came not to the banquet at his invitation, commanded his servants to compel them to come in [Luke 14:23]. And where they say, the fruit of that is but hypocrisy; hypocrites they are like enough to be, but from a worse cause, not from the punishment, but their own frailties, because they prefer their temporal safety before the eternal blessing which Christ hath promised to all that suffer for his sake and the truth. Secondly, it is true, that punishments reach not directly the inward man, nor do they teach or inform the judgment, that is, they do not perfect the work; but are nevertheless a good beginning to it: For, *fear is the beginning of wisdom*, which love must perfect. Though the needle stays not in the garment, yet it must lead the thread that makes it up. The rod indeed doth not teach the child, yet scares him to his book where he may learn: So though punishments do not perfect and accomplish our duty, yet they set us to our studies, to consider that we do not rashly cast ourselves upon danger, which otherwise possibly we would never think of, but run on whither our wild vain fancies and groundless persuasions led us....

II. The next is, *That howsoever it be in other matters of religion, it would make much for the quiet of the Church, if errors in judgment were not punished as crimes, because no man can be abler and wiser than God hath made him.*

It is true, that an error, so long as it stays in the understanding, and goes no further, is not properly a sin; for the understanding is not *agens liberum* [a free or active agent], but passive. In that the eye of the mind is as the eye of the body; if that be naturally short-sighted, it is no fault that it sees not so far as another: But if the weakness of the understanding participate with the will, which is *agens liberum*, and so the error comes within our power, then it may be properly a sin. This is the case of all that dissent in sects; for though in speculation the understanding is distinct from the will, yet in practise they are seldom severed. For it is morally impossible, that after a man hath conceived an opinion, he should not be well pleased with it, and have a will as occasion is to defend and propagate it too. And when it is *voluntarium* [voluntary], no doubt but it is *peccatum* [a sin or crime], and when error grows to be a sin, I know no reason why it may not be punished; for *interest reipublicæ peccata puniri* [it is in the interest of the state that crimes/sins be punished]. But for all that it is, they say, a great disturbance of quiet to be tied to assent to that

we cannot know nor comprehend. That's a great mistake. I know there is much exception taken to the too punctual definitions of some mysteries of the faith, and particularly in the Creed commonly called by *Athanasius*, where there are many particulars which they cannot know nor comprehend.[1] Whereas in truth it is not required of them, they are not bound to know them, but to believe them; for it is the mercy of God, that the defect of our knowledge may be supplied by the knowledge of others; for to believe is to see with other men's eyes, as knowledge is with our own.

But may we safely trust others in that which so nearly concerns as a creed? Yes sure, and it is as well the mercy, as the command of God, that we should trust those that watch over our souls; yet still that must be to supply the defect of our knowledge, not otherwise; for the Church is not Lord of our faith, but helper of our ignorance. It supplies the defect of our sight, it doth not put it out: for if a man knows the contrary, he is not bound to believe others; for if he can see with his own eyes, why shall he be tied to see with other men's?....

III. Though errors may be punished, yet it troubles the quiet of many, that *the omission of forms and ceremonies is more severely punished than some foul and scandalous crimes.*

To this I answer, first, That they who object this, are not to be trusted with the balance of sins, for we know how the market went for them when they held the scale: Obedience to the King and the laws, and serving God according to them, were the great scandalous crimes.

2. Allowing it to be true as they say, That omission of forms and ceremonies is by the Church more frequently and severely punished than greater faults. But how greater? It may be in their proper and natural guilt and obliquity, according to which sentence shall be given at the day of Judgment, and

---

[1] the Athanasian Creed, a profession of faith widely used in Western Christendom, and included in the Anglican Book of Common Prayer.

to death eternal. But our earthly tribunals are not erected to anticipate the day of Judgment, to bring all sinners to trial for whatsoever they have committed in the flesh, and according to the proper measure of their guilt; but for a particular end and use; that people, while they live here in the world, and in society, may be kept in good order and quiet, from doing or receiving injuries. And to this end is the degree of their punishments commensurate. Treason and rebellion are more severely punished in the state than many other heinous crimes, because they destroy the very foundation of government and society. And for the same reason, a schismatical disobedience, though but in matters of form and ceremony, is pursued with more care and strictness, because it destroys the very end for which the power is given the Church to punish, which is, the preservation of peace and unity....

For though they are ever telling us, it is for trifles, ceremonies, or indifferent things, it is but the same quarrel the atheists have against God himself, for being so much offended for an apple, a trifle which scarce any man that hath an orchard would have been troubled with; and one answer will serve both in effect. In that forbidden fruit, God's authority in commanding, and Adam's duty in obeying, were symbolically engaged for him and his, and there was venom enough in that to infect both. The rites and ceremonies of the Church, in like manner, though not in like degree, though in their opinion as inconsiderable as the paring of Adam's apple, yet when discord and disobedience is found with them there is poison enough in that for the strongest antidote the Church doth at any time make use of. Let not that therefore mislead or disturb our student of quiet.

IV. Nor that which, in the fourth place, they look at as another expedient for peace, *if fewer points and articles of religion were defined*, that so the Church door may be wider open to let in those whose dissent now troubles the peace of the Church.

It is fit, I grant, the Church door should stand always open, but for such as shall be fit to enter; for it would be a dangerous thing to set any door so wide open to let in an enemy upon us. But to what purpose would we have the Church door so wide, when the Gate of Heaven is straight? why should they be taken in here, if they shall be turned back there? The Church is a city, as Jerusalem, a city that is at unity in itself; so it is a city too that hath gates and walls to shut out others.

He that came to a little city, where there was a great gate, merrily warned the citizens to take heed lest their city went not out at the gate, may soberly be said to those that would have the Church doors so wide to let in all sects, to take heed lest the Church gets not out at the door: For where so many religions are, it may be feared, that soon there will be none at all. If we be not, as the Apostle commands, built up in the same faith, it will avail us little to be found within the same walls.

It is therefore a perverse remedy for peace, to abate or diminish the articles and definitions of the Church, which were made of purpose to take away controversies; it would be a strange course to end controversies, to take away the definitions. Our student must read his books backward, if he seek for peace from hence. We might as well say, all the world would be quiet, if there were no judges nor laws to determine differences.

V. There is another expedient for peace, which I hear much spoken of, and highly set by as a great point of prudence, *If men of moderate opinions were only taken into employment in the Church.*

Moderation, I confess, is an excellent virtue, and much to be desired; *Let your moderation be known unto all men*, Phil. 4:5. But then it must be in a subject capable of it, wherein there are extremes and excesses to be moderated, as there is certainly in our passions, there it is proper. St. Paul gives it for a lesson to all students in religion, Ephes. 4:31: *Let all bitterness, and wrath, and anger, and clamour, and evil speaking, be put away from you, with all malice; and be ye kind one to another, and tender-hearted, forgiving one another, even as God for Christ's sake hath forgiven you.* This no doubt is a very fit temper for quiet, and none more unfit than angry, waspish, and domineering spirits.

Only this caution is to be observed in lenity. That it be such as may win men into the Church, not such as may secure and encourage them to stay without. Yet lenity and gentleness is so good a virtue, that I am loth to cast water upon it, or seem to temper it.

But for men of moderate opinions, I am at a loss to know what they should be; for moderation there cannot be, but between extremes. Now what extremes are there of opinions in a settled Church, unless the Church be one extreme, and the schismatic another? and then the man of moderate opinions is he that is part Church-man, and part schismatic. I hope none are so unkind to their Mother the Church, to charge extremities upon her doctrine or laws. If there be any such, they are but hybrids in religion, and make a new sect in the Church, as pernicious to the peace of it as any of the rest. The truth is, moderate opinions are a chimaera, a fancy; either nothing, or somewhat worse than nothing: for possibly they may bestow that good word (moderation) upon such as care little either to observe the law themselves, or to require it of others. If these be the men of moderate opinions, I wonder how they will be able to give account of their justice and fidelity to the trust committed to them. Yes, they say, very well: it is rather prudence than injustice, to mitigate and sweeten the sharpness and rigour of the law. But if the law itself be too rigorous, in God's name let it be amended, and not left to the arbitrary power of others to do it, for that's known to be a remedy ten

times worse than the disease. It is said in physic, I know not how truly, that an error in the first concoction, is not mended in the second: It is certainly true here, an error or excess in the law, which is the first concoction of justice, will be ill cured afterward by an arbitrary partiality in the execution. I hope therefore no wise student of quiet, will take such moderators for the best ministers of peace. But I leave them, and come to the most popular, and therefore most dangerous principle in the study of quiet; that is, *liberty of conscience.*

VI. I have spoken to this point heretofore in this place; yet because of late our new philosophical divines, as well as others, press hard for it, knowing without a free market, they cannot vend their bold speculations; I shall resume the point again a little more largely, yet within the compass of these two particulars.

First, That there is a great deal of reason to *restrain* the *conscience,* and secondly, That there is no reason to give it *liberty.*

1. There is reason enough to restrain the conscience, for the mischief it doth to quiet when it is at liberty; for all the discord and divisions of the Church grow from hence, and that is a mischief we have reason to avoid. *Mark them* (saith St. Paul) *which cause divisions among you, and avoid them* [Romans 16:17]. There is reason then to mark that which causeth them to make divisions, and that's the *conscience.* It is no quieter in the Commonwealth, where it destroys the very foundation of Government, and frustrates the ordinance of God for it in Princes and Magistrates; for what is left for them to do, if everyone must follow the dictate of his own conscience, that is, in plain terms, be bound only to obey himself.

This is no slander to the pretenders of conscience; they will say as much themselves, if we ask them. Ask the schismatic why he joins not with the congregation of God's people? and he will tell you, His conscience will not suffer him. Ask the rebel in the state, why he takes up arms to the ruin of his King and country? and his conscience will answer for him, That it is God's cause, and it is to do him service. Ask him again, why he doth not repent of the mischief done by it? (for that they seldom do) and the conscience will serve that turn too, It is God's cause, and the conscience will not suffer them to repent of that. Thus we see, the conscience, as it is used, doth not only open a door to sin, but shuts the very door to mercy, that is repentance.

If St. John said true, as no doubt he did, *That there were many Antichrists*, then possibly the *conscience* thus improved may be one of them. For, it sets itself in the Church above all that is called God, yea, and God himself too, in a sense; for his laws are not to be obeyed, unless the *conscience* first allows them to be his: and thus all is resolved into the *conscience*, as the *dernier* [last] resort and last appeal.

While the King and the Pope are contending for supremacy, the conscience without scruple puts in for it against both, and takes it for her rights to be supreme in all causes as well ecclesiastical as civil. There is great complaint in the world of domineering over the conscience; but have we not rather cause to complain of the domineering of the conscience? And if any list to see the conscience acting all this, we need go no further than our late times, when the conscience was loose for a while; one would think Hell had broke loose, so filled was on a sudden the Church with sects, and the Commonwealth with confusion. There is reason enough therefore to restrain the conscience that acts all this, if we knew how.

The next thing I undertook to show, is, That there is no reason why it should have liberty; and particularly, not that which gives the fairest colour to it: Neither the duty we owe to truth, which seems to have some right to liberty; nor that we owe to the will of God, that nothing be done against the conscience. For the first.

Truth is that (I confess) which no consideration of peace may warrant us to desert; for I could never be of that opinion, That truth in smaller matters may for peace sake be either denied or prejudiced.... Truth in that first reference to the thing, admits no qualification; things must be taken as they are, be they never so small: but as the things come to be represented to, and entertained by the understanding, by reason of the mistakes and errors that may happen in that, though truth itself, or truth in the thing cannot, yet my apprehension of it may both yield to better, and may sometimes be waived for peace sake. To argue from truth in the thing, to truth in the apprehension only, is a fallacy against the rules of reasoning, we call it *petitio principii*, or a begging of the question.[1] If a sectary should beg an alms, I wish he may have it; but he shall beg long ere it be granted him, that he hath the truth. How then can he presume upon that truth, to which he hath no other title but his own persuasion, which can be no better than any man's else, who is as strongly persuaded to the contrary? And this is all the service that truth can do the conscience for liberty.

2. The second thing whereupon the conscience especially bears itself so high, is the will of God that nothing be done against the conscience. That no doubt is a great offence, and made so by the greatest authority: Yet the same God that requires our obedience to the conscience, commands us likewise to obey our parents, our Princes and Governors, and all these stand upon as good authority as the conscience. If we cannot reconcile our obedience to that with our obedience to these, we may sin against God, when we do not sin against the conscience. For though God hath erected a tribunal in every man's breast, and there set the conscience to be a judge of all our actions, there be other tribunals of justice besides, of God's erection

---

[1] *petitio principii* "begging the question," the logical fallacy of taking for granted that which remains to be proved.

too, and to which he hath subjected the very conscience. *Ye must needs be subject* (Rom. 13) *not only for wrath, but also for conscience.* And after both these, there is another tribunal in Heaven, to which all judges, conscience and all must give an account one day. For the conscience is no Court of Record; the decrees and acts passed there, will be no good evidence at that bar; there all must be re-examined, and tried over again. *Though I know nothing by myself,* (saith St. Paul) *yet am I not thereby justified.* Though he could not charge his conscience with any offence, he knew a further trial must pass upon him before he could be absolved. My conscience indeed may be pleaded there in evidence against me as a witness to condemn me, but not as a judge to absolve me. It is a great mistake in the power and operation of the conscience: That it will condemn us, if we do any thing against it, the text is clear for that; but that it will absolve us for that we do according to it, there is no text, I am sure, for that we must then be tried by the law, and not by the conscience.

.   .   .   .

If they that stand so much upon their consciences did seriously consider this, they would find as little cause to desire that liberty, as there is to grant it, seeing it stands them in so little stead when they have most need of it; for when they think their conscience shall answer for them, they must then answer for their conscience, and upon trial, the conscience may prove the great offender. Thus have I hitherto given you an account of some of the vulgar mistaken principles of quiet, which our student is first to unlearn....

But I fear I have run out all my time almost in these mistaken ways of peace: I presume it will be a greater offence to leave you here now, than to beg a little more time to set you in the right way, though I shall not go beyond the office of a Mercury, to point the hand where it lies.

There is the King's highway to peace, and the student's private way, and both good in their kind. With the King's way I shall not meddle, as being fitter matter for our thankfulness than instruction, who hath already paved the way for us by wholesome laws for that purpose. But because ofttimes…the compulsory way by law, though always necessary, is not always effectual; to the King's way we must add the student's also: That every one in his particular makes it his care and business to contribute to it, that it be an artificial studied peace, to which not fear only, but conscience of duty and religion obligeth us.

Now every good student of any science searches into the true and proper cause of things.... If the cause of all division in the Church be differing in judgment, nothing can cure that but a consent. St. Paul therefore prescribes that for the remedy, I Cor. 5:10: *That there be no divisions among you*; how may that be helped? it follows, *But that ye be perfectly joined together in the same mind, and in the same judgment.* This is the true Apostolical Principle, whereon we are to ground our study of quiet: For all the fine things and sentences that are spoken for peace and quiet, will little move those that are, and may very well be confident, they ought not howsoever have peace with sin, or error. Unless therefore we can be first persuaded that we ought not to charge the Church with either, we do nothing for peace. This I confess is the great difficulty, yet if this be not done, there can be no hope of peace.

And to do this, I shall not send our student to the polemic school, to convince him out of speculative principles of reason and divinity; for to that study, some have not capacity, others not leisure: I shall only commend to him some practical principles of religion, obvious to all, and denied by none, that out of them he may learn not to dissent from, or condemn the Church of, error.

To prevent the passing that sentence, let the student 1. Study himself, his own condition. 2. Let him study the Church against which he passeth sentence. 3. Let him study the nature and quality of the things whereupon judgment is given. 4. Let him consider well the manner of proceeding in judgment. In all which we shall find some known principle of religion to direct us.

1. First, In the study of ourselves, and our own condition: Religion teacheth us to have an humble, lowly, mean opinion of ourselves; and not without cause, whether we respect our understandings, or our affections: Our understandings are naturally weak, imperfect, short-sighted, we know but in part, the best of us; and our affections too are disloyal to our understandings, *The heart of man*, saith the Prophet, *is deceitful above all things.* We have little reason then to trust ourselves much in either. He that is truly conscious of his own weakness or lameness, will be content to be supported by others. If we study this point well, our own infirmities, we should learn more willingly to assent to, and take support from the Church.

Especially, if in the second place, we study that too whose governors' religion likewise teaches us to obey, *For they watch over our souls*, Heb. 13:17. If it be a good point of religion, *in lowliness of mind to esteem others better than ourselves*, Phil. 2:3, it is religion and reason both, to think our governors wiser too; for there is a presumption always in favour of them. St. Paul gives it for a rule to Timothy, *Not to receive an accusation against an Elder, but before two or three witnesses* [I Timothy 5:19], because it is to be presumed on the part of age and authority, to know more, and offend less. But when it comes to be the whole eldership, all our governors jointly, the presumption is so much the stronger. If we add this study to the former, how little reason we have to trust ourselves, and how much we have to trust our governors, we will not rashly pass sentence against them, if we have either reason or religion in us.

3. And yet we have more work for our student; Let him, in the third place, consider the nature and quality of the things whereupon judgment is given, how apt they are to deceive us. Truth is many times so like an error, and error comes so near to truth, that he had need be careful and circumspect that shall distinguish them in some cases. And in others again, truth lies hid under many folds, especially ambiguity of words, the common cheat of all students, who are more often deceived into opinions than convinced. It is not strange to see so many go astray from the Church, to whom the things of it are represented under the covert of false names, when they hear the government of it called tyranny; obedience, slavery; contempt, courage; license, liberty; frenzy, zeal; order, superstition. How easily thus may simple people mistake their way, and fall into the pit that's covered over with shadows and false names of things? When he hath studied this point well,

4. Let him, in the fourth place, be well advised in what manner he proceeds in judgment, and upon what evidence: For, allowing the conscience to be a judge, it must not trespass upon the rules of good judicature, as, both sides must be heard impartially, which is seldom done; the *conscience* must not be misled no more than other judges, by prejudice, passion, or favour; for what can that judgment be worth which is perverted by any of these. Now if we examine how most men come to pass sentence against the Church, we shall find it to be upon very slight evidence: It may be their education, they have been always brought up that way; for sects commonly run in a blood, in a family: Or they have been so taught, they say, by good men; that indeed is the sum and upshot of the faith of most that dissent, the credit given to some weak, private, ignorant instructor, whose person they have in admiration, without any great cause, God knows; whereas their private judgments, because they are parties, ought always to be suspected, if we be wise;

and because against their governors, to be condemned, if we be obedient.

All these well studied, may make for peace, when possibly arguments, and disputes, and punishments too will not do it. And yet if still none of these will make our student quiet,

Let him, in the last place, make trial of a common remedy that prevails in all cases of difficulty: Let him but study his own security, the safest course, and he shall find that better provided for in the Church's judgment, than in his own; for, if he should err in following the Church, or his governors, for that is possible, the greatest part of that guilt, some say all, I say only the greatest part, must lie at their door that command that which is unlawful: But if they should err in following their own judgment, or a judge of their own choosing, for that makes it their own too, and that is more than possible, all the blame and guilt then must of necessity and inexcusably fall upon themselves. Upon these principles, setting aside all those that may convince our judgments in particulars, from these alone, I say, we see how safe, how prudent, how religious a thing it is to submit our private judgments to the public, for the peace of the Church.

It remains only now, that we employ our best endeavour and study for it, which is the second part of the text, and the last thing to be considered,

That ye study.

Study is an earnest intention of the mind, by diligent search and enquiry. Wishing well to quiet, or speaking well of it, will not serve; the greatest disturbers of peace will do that many times, give it a good word, when they will not part with a fancy for it. And yet quiet is a thing that requires care and pains somewhat more than ordinary: For when St. Peter likewise speaks of peace, it is in words of the same import, *Seek peace, and ensue it* [I Peter 3:11]. If it be hidden, seek it out; if it flies from you, pursue after it. It is a busy thing to be quiet. The

word here translated, *study*, is in the original φιλοτιμέομαι [philotimeomai], *be ambitious of it;* that is, pursue and study it as you would do honour and preferment: And that, I think, is as much as can be desired; and yet not more than quiet both deserves and needs.

First, it deserves it. For though quiet be rather *Status vitæ* [a state of life], than *virtus* [a virtue]; it is no virtue itself, yet the best soil to plant virtue in. *The fruits of righteousness are sown in peace,* Jam. 3:18. So are all the fruits of industry; learning, arts, sciences, traffic, commerce, flourish most in the calm temperate clime; but in troubles and dissensions every good thing goes backward, only mischief thrives. It fares with troubled times, as in troubled waters; all the filth, dirt and mire in the bottom gets then up to the top. We saw as much when our waters were lately troubled; what a deal of filth, dirt and mire, what sordid stuff was then got up to the top and highest place of rule and command? So much are we the more obliged to study that peace and quiet, which hath sunk them to their proper place again, the bottom: And there let them lie, if you would be quiet.

2. As it deserves therefore our study, so it needs it too; for it is a difficult thing to be quiet, the way to it lies through so many parts and duties of religion, and not the easiest of them neither: To deny ourselves, by humility and lowliness of mind to acknowledge our own weakness and frailty, to submit our judgments to others, as better and wiser than ourselves; to subdue our passions and lusts, from whence the Apostle observes wars and contentions to come, *from our lusts* [James 4:1]; and to all these the flesh hath naturally a reluctance. Our student therefore hath need to contend with himself to be at peace with others.

St. Paul was at Athens when he wrote this epistle, a famous University for the study of all liberal arts and sciences. I cannot say he had these in his thought, when he commended this study to the

Thessalonians, as an art of more use than any he found at Athens: Yet when I see him so passionately earnest for it, to beseech them to study, we have reason to value it as an art well worthy of schools, and professors, and students. And they would make a Royal Society, whereof the King himself is Master, who is our peacemaker by office, and by a care equal to that, hath by law provided, that *under Him we may live a peaceable and quiet life in all godliness and honesty* [I Timothy 2:2]. He hath little sense of honour, that will not enter himself a student under that conduct. The very word for *study*, φιλοτιμέομαι, carries honour in it.

And yet I can tell them of a higher school for it than this, and wherein Kings themselves are content to be students. Our Lord Christ, the great Mediator of our eternal peace with Heaven, would not be brought into the world without a song of peace on Earth, by Angels: And when he left the world, bequeathed it as a legacy after him, *My peace I leave with you* [John 14:27]. And when he comes again to judge the world, we have reason to look that he will call us to a reckoning how we use his legacy. And so he will too; for he is that Lord, Matth. 24, that when he came and found some smiting their fellow-servants, commanded them to be cut asunder, and have their portion with hypocrites: A punishment well fitted to the offence; there was a schism in the fault, and there shall be another schism in the punishment; they who sundered and divided from their brethren, should themselves be cut asunder, and have their portion with hypocrites. But for the peace-makers, when he comes, he will provide better company, for *they shall be called the children of God* [Matthew 5:9]. Blessed are they then whom the Lord when he comes shall find at their studies of that quiet which gives them so fair a title to eternal rest and peace in Heaven with Christ, and all the children of God.

—1665

A Sermon Preached before the King At Whitehall, March 18, 1666

I THESSALONIANS 4:11
—And to do your own business.

The whole verse, whereof these words are a part, is an exhortation to the study of two lessons; one for *quiet*, the other for *business: That ye study to be quiet*, and to *do your own business.*

Of the former, the last time I had the honor to be called to this service, we treated particularly; and it was a point well worthy our care and study. But the lesson we are now to learn, seems not much to deserve or need it.

I have not (I confess) sought far for a text, but took that which came next to hand. Nor doth the text put you to seek far what you are to do; It is but your own business. In both respects it may be thought unfit for this audience, which is not of that quality to be entertained with no better provision than what comes next to hand; and especially, if that should prove plain and homely, as that is, *To do our own business*; and as it follows, *To work with our own hands*: This is but a kind of *mechanical* doctrine; and what should that do here in Court?

Not to leave myself and the text under this prejudice; That I sought no farther for it, was not of easiness or neglect, but choice; Because I found it not only in conjunction and company with the excellent study of *quiet*, to which any kind of retainer at large might deserve respect; but also, because I saw it set by the Apostle, in a place of near and intimate relation, a principle and foundation to it. The next way to be *quiet* abroad, is to be *busy* at home....This doing *our own business*,...is a practical principle, whereupon depends much of the business of our whole lives, and so hath the fate of other foundations, to be little seen and regarded; It lies low under ground, and we overlook it, as a thing not worthy any man's thought or care. But to give it the due, we must not look upon what it is in *sight*, but what it is in *virtue*; a principle and foundation whereupon is built that which is the desire of all good men, the public peace and quiet of the Church and Kingdom. And then we may allow it to be good doctrine which hath so good a use. It is a good tree that brings forth good fruit.

But then you will say, It must be in *season* too. Now the wise man tells us, *There is a time for war,* as well as *a time for peace* [Ecclesiastes 3:8]. And can it then be seasonable again and again thus to importune the study of such things as make for peace, at a time when we are all, and have cause to be in preparation for war? Indeed if it were such a peace, as would weaken the hands of any in the pursuit of that just, necessary and royal expedition, it were a most unseasonable solecism. But we must know, as there is a war that makes for peace, so there is a peace that makes for war. Unity among ourselves, binds us close together; we are the stronger for it…. Domestic peace then, though it comes not out of the artillery, is good ammunition for war: And it falls in well too, with the express letter and doctrine of the text, it is our own business. As it is the proper business of a King to protect his subjects from the insolencies and injuries of proud insulting neighbours; so it is the business of every good subject too, to assist him in it with their lives and fortunes. Whether therefore we seek for peace at home, or have cause of war abroad, the duty of the text is for us. We are doing our own business. But though it be a good foundation to build on every way; yet, *except the Lord build the house, their labour is but lost that build.* Let us therefore before we go farther in the work, go to him for a blessing upon it.

. . . .

[I]n this lesson there will fall to be learned these particulars:

1. That, there is and ought to be a propriety in business;[1] that to everyone there belongs something that he may properly call his own.

2. The obligation of duty and religion, to confine himself to that which is his own.

3. The operation it hath had in the world upon our quiet or disquiet.

4. From these is inferred a necessity to study it; *That ye study to do your own business.*

I. First, That there is a propriety in business. This must be laid for a ground; all the rest else will fall to nothing. It will be no religion to keep it; no sin to break it; no need to study it….

There is a busy humour in the world, to *lay all common*; and it is grown to be a sect of religion; yea, more than one; as many as there are kinds of propriety, so many sects endeavour to fling down the enclosures.

1. As first, there is a propriety in goods and possessions; and against this, there rises a sect of *Levellers*, who tell us from the Psalmist, *The Heavens are the Lord's; but the Earth hath he given to the Children of men* [Psalms 115:16].[2] That to which every man hath a right by the gift of God, the pride and covetousness of a few have engrossed, and made their own.

2. There is a right and propriety of respect and honour due to some above others. Against this arises another sect of Levellers they call *Quakers*, who refuse to give honour to whom honour belongs.[3] Though this looks like a religion against good manners only, or were but some quarrel with the grammarians against proper names; the mischief of it lies deeper, and is of the spirit of *Anabaptism*, who oppose the very powers and dignities them-

---

[1] *propriety* property or ownership.

[2] For this kind of communitarian argument, see the selection by Gerrard Winstanley.

[3] Founded by George Fox in the late 1640s, the Quaker movement became notorious in the period for its members' refusal to acknowledge social superiority (by doffing hats, etc.).

selves, which they despise in their titles; for they cannot be so foolish, though simple enough, as to make a religion of names only. These are dangerous sects of Levellers both; but they lie not in our way. The text toucheth only *Levellers of business*, who think they are not to be barred the liberty of doing anything that is good....But that there is a title and propriety in some to business, wherein it is not permitted to everyone to interpose, a necessity in Nature requires. The world is replenished with infinite variety of things, and a great deal of work is to be done to make them useful and serviceable to us. Now it is not possible for everyone to do all, and hardly all, in any one thing, to gain the full use and benefit of it. But when the works are distributed severally to some, the benefit may redound to all.

All the business of the world refers either to a *spiritual* end, the good of the soul; or to a *temporal* and civil, our well-being while we live here upon earth: And to both these ends God hath appointed and assigned particular persons; he did not leave them in common. In the temporal there is private business and public. For private use, as in families, there is the business of the husband and wife, the parent and children, the master and servants. And out of families, for private use likewise, there is the business of physicians and advocates, husbandmen, merchants and mariners, mechanics and labourers; and all these are of private nature, though of common benefit. Then is there the public business, by which all these are ordered and governed, and they are by St. Peter distinguished to our hands, as that of the *King as supreme*, and of *Governors sent by him* [I Peter 2:13–14]; and they are magistrates and judges for peace, captains and commanders for war. And besides these, there is the business of ministers and assistants to the supreme power, counsellors, lawyers, officers and servants; and all these are for that temporal end.

And for the spiritual, whose business refers to the soul, there is likewise a propriety; as in bishops to ordain, institute and order the rest of the clergy specially, and of the whole diocese occasionally, as the necessity of it shall require. Then is there the business of the Presbyters, in the several parts of the diocese, in a more particular and immediate cure and charge, to be directed by, and accountable to the bishop. There be others diaconal and ministerial to both. And all together, temporal and spiritual, as several members, make one body; *and every Member*, saith the Apostle, *hath not the same office*, Rom. 12:4. God divided his gifts to everyone severally as he will, I Cor. 12:11, he did not scatter them in common, but divide them, and all hold in severalty.

And as that severance and propriety stands upon good authority; so authority was, no doubt, induced upon reason of profit and interest. It conduceth more to the common good, than community itself could.

1. First, it brings order into the common business of the world, and that takes away confusion, which never did anything well....

2. In reason all business will be best done too, by those to whom they are peculiar and proper.... Men are most trusted in their own trades. We trust the lawyer with our estates, the physician with our bodies. I say nothing of our souls; we are so wise at that work, as to trust none but ourselves.

3. Yet thirdly, the nature and condition of the business itself, may require it. Some are so difficult, that everyone cannot do, though he would; and some are so mean, that every one would not do, though he could: and all are such, as through the mercy of God we need not do if we will, unless it be our own business.

We are now fallen upon the second part, that as everyone hath some business that is his own, so duty and religion obligeth him to take upon him no business but his own.

II. This lesson will not be so easily learned as the former: all confinement of itself seems uneasy.

He that hath no mind to go abroad, would not be tied to stay at home. And he that cares for no business, will take it ill to be barred any. But this confinement besides, nips the growth and increase of good, whereof they think, more would be done if everyone have free liberty to do it; and therefore it is just and reasonable to allow any one a concurrent jurisdiction with others in any thing that is otherwise good, though that be to govern with the King, to pray & preach, or what they please, with the Priest. And they have as much of propriety as any can have to business; yet even to these, they think any man may make a sufficient title, that hath *understanding* to know what is to be done, as well as any other, and *affection* to do it, perhaps more than others. And all have *right* and interest in the public, especially that wherein religion and the soul is concerned; how God may be best served, and wherein his glory may be most promoted. Will not all these make a title good enough to any business?

…In that everyone hath liberty to improve his understanding and knowledge for the best, as well for his own soul as the public good: In that let the glory of God be the star to guide him. But all these do not make the business ours; they are a good qualification in any for business, yet give no right or title to it. Great knowledge and skill in the laws will not set a man upon the bench; nor of divinity, in the bishop's chair; nor will the dexterous glib-gifted tongue put a man into the pulpit. There must be besides a title and commission to make them ours.

But must all the obligations we have to the public good, and to God's honour, stoop to commissions, titles and proprieties, which are but the creatures and constitutions of men?

To this question, I answer in the words of Job 13:7: *Will you speak wickedly for God, and talk deceitfully for him?* It is deceitful talking, to plead for God against himself; for though it should be granted, that the sorting of several employments and functions have something of *man* in them; yet the confirmation and approbation of God makes it his, and so divine: for as God hath founded a divine moral law, upon the propriety of goods and possessions, *Thou shalt not steal*; yea, thou shalt not covet that which is another's; and yet it comes not to be another's, but by human laws. So though different states of life and employment have somewhat in them by disposition of law, or our own choice; yet upon them also is founded this moral duty, to keep within those bounds: For though men laid the *landmarks*, yet God commanded *They should not be removed*, Deut. 19:14.

It is a kind of burglary to break into another man's business, as well as into another man's house: or if you will not allow it to be theft to have another's business found with you, as it is to have another's goods; it is as ill as theft in St. Peter's opinion. *The murtherer, the thief, the evil-doer, the busy-body*; there's a mess of them, he puts them all alike together, Pet. 4:15.

To shut up this point, If the *glory of God,* and the *public good*, and such like fair pretences, might let us loose upon one another's business, it would quickly bring us round, where we were, to that confusion and disorder, for remedy whereof, the Apostle added this lesson to the former. We shall never learn to be quiet well, unless we learn also to keep within our own business.

Yet I deny not, but that discord and dissention have other causes besides, for, of *Pride cometh contention*, saith Solomon, Prov. 13:10. And *from covetousness*, saith St. James, *they desire, and have not*, James 4:2. It is true of other lusts, wrath, revenge, envy, slander, and curiosity too, break the peace too often, and had need be bound to their good behaviour all. Yet we may observe it, That none of all these do actually any great mischief that way, till they first bring it to this, till it draws us from our own station, and fling us upon something that is none of our own business.

III. The truth of this will more fully be seen in the third part, which comes next to be considered, The operation it hath had in the world, by disturbing the peace and quiet of it. *Meum* and *Tuum* [mine and thine] hath not filled it with more suits and contentions in our goods and possessions, than it hath in the actions and business of our lives, What is our own, and what is not our own.

To arraign all that are guilty of breaking this rule in several kinds, would ask a long process. We will therefore take notice only here of the attempts upon *Government* and *Religion*, by those whose business it was not; because the most and greatest tempests and storms in the Christian World, have blown from that coast.

.   .   .   .

2. We were in a sad case not long since in this Kingdom by a civil war. I meddle not with the fault, let that sleep under the *Act of Oblivion*.[1] We may, I trust, without offence, enquire into the cause of it. What were they doing that gave us that disquiet? Look upon the Standard set up for the war; I mean, the most execrable COVENANT,[2] *Quomodo legis?* how read you there? was it not meddling with business was none of their own? They Covenanted first to extirpate the Government of the Church established by law. That law, with hands lifted up to Heaven, they swore they would abolish. The legislative power we know in whom it is, to make or mend laws; it was none of their business. In this they were certainly too bold with the King's *scepter*. At the next turn they take hold of his *sword* too, and engage themselves to a mutual defence against all opposition. This also was none of their business. For though a self-defence may be allowed as natural

to all; it is against private, not public opposition.... The sword is the King's, and *he that takes it* from any hand but his, where God hath placed it, *shall perish with the sword.* In this the Covenanters, as ill as they like bishops, would be, in the Apostle's phrase,...the worst sort of Bishops, that is, meddlers in business was none of their own [I Peter 4:15]. The worshippers of the Covenant have therefore been well dealt with, as the worshippers of the Golden Calf were by Moses, Exod. 32:20.... But the Covenant is past, and let it go. I wish for quiet sake, we may never hear of the like again.

3. This was transient: But there still remains a permanent and habitual disturbance of our peace, in the multitude and swarms of SECTS and factions in religions, to which it is naturally and inseparably inherent: An incurable mischief; like the leprosy on the walls, that could not be cleansed, but by pulling down the house. From these we have felt already but too much, and have cause yet to fear more.

But can we charge them with doing a business is none of their own? Can any thing be more properly our own business, than the *care of our souls*, and to *serve God in the best manner that our understandings and consciences shall direct us?*

They are mistaken that think the charge lies upon this issue, what every man may do for himself and his own salvation. He may without question do very much, for he may keep all God's commandments, if he can....And again, he may serve and worship God with as much fervency and devotion as he can and will; he may abound in charity, meekness, humility, patience and temperance, and all other Christian virtues. And *so long as ye thus follow that which is good*, saith St. Peter, *who will harm you?* [I Peter 3:13] And I may say too, who can hinder you in all this? but if he makes himself a party in a sect, if there be assembling together in companies, gather congregations, incorporate in a body, module Churches, give laws of doctrine and worship, set up teachers and leaders of their own; to

---

[1] The Act of Indemnity and Oblivion (1660) provided a general amnesty (excluding some named individuals), and prohibited public laying of blame for the wars.

[2] the Solemn League and Covenant (1643), in which the Long Parliament agreed to institute Presbyterianism in England in exchange for Scottish military support.

all this they have as little right, as they have need. A man may go far, ye see, in Religion, without troubling any; and if then they fall into some error or misbelief in religion, they ought not to be severely handled; but when they betake themselves to a sect, that alters the case, it will then be compassion mistaken. A locust alone is no such perilous beast to be feared or regarded by any; but when they come in shoals and swarms, and cover the face of the earth, they are a plague to the country where they light. So to look upon a sectary single, who out of simplicity and good meaning follows his conscience, our hearts should be every whit as tender for them, as their consciences are. But if we look upon them in company, they are as ill and dangerous as the company they are found in; and the danger of all popular meetings, and associations to a state, makes it the proper business of a King and his ministers to look to it, and to provide against it; wherein the care hath been taken, deserves a just commendation.

And yet when I assert and refer this business to the KING, I look to be called to an account for that; For they take the boldness by way of recrimination, to turn the text upon the King himself, *That His Power is Civil, and Matters of the Church and Religion are Ecclesiastical*, and so none of his business.

This is, I confess, too weighty a matter to be here thrust into the corner of a sermon; yet it will be necessary to say so much as may somewhat lay that loud clamour against it: For the *Papists* and *Presbyterians* both, how ill soever they may agree in other matters, hunt in couples against the King's power and *SUPREMACY*. But as we deny not all to others in their places; so we claim not all for the King. If I shall but only now set out *his* part in matters of the Church, it will appear sufficiently, that he…takes not upon him business which is not his own.

. . . .

They say, he claims by his title of *supremacy*, To govern *all persons in all causes, as well ecclesiastical as civil.*

We acknowledge this to be his just title; but deny, that he doth any thing by it, which is not properly his own business, and in right of his crown. That he is the fountain also of all ecclesiastical jurisdiction, though it be not expressly in his title, we acknowledge to be in his power.

. . . .

6. But lastly, is not this the same wrong and illusion we charge the *Pope* with, who in order to his spiritual end, usurps the temporal power; so the King in order to his temporal government, invades the ecclesiastical?

No, the case is far different. If the Pope did order temporals by spiritual means only,…we had the less to say against him; he is not out of the way of a bishop's power, though he should abuse it. But he for his spiritual end, usurps temporal means, and takes upon him to dispose of temporal estates, that is none of his business…. To return to our sectaries, who put us upon this digression, they still remain as we left them, guilty of doing much that is none of their own business.

What then is to be done with them? According to a late statute, a *mittimus* (I think) might be made to send them to prison;[1] but the Apostle here deals more kindly with them, and sends them only to school to study better, which is my fourth and last point.

IV. That ye *study to do your own business*. I will take no more out of the word *study*, than what any one understands to be in it: a serious weighing and considering of the matter; and there is need of it.

---

[1] The Five-Mile Act (1665) prohibited nonconformist ministers from preaching, teaching, or coming within five miles of the parish where they had officiated; *mittimus* a warrant to commit to prison.

1. The first thing the student is to do before he takes in hand any matter of importance, is to set down and consider whether it be his own business, or no; what *title* he can make to it. It is utterly a fault amongst us, to think that no part of our business, to consider whether it be our business or no. If a qualm comes over the stomach, that we begin to grow government-sick, or that the ceremonies and superstitions of the Church offend us, presently without further dispute, what ever comes of it, it is resolved we will have a better government, and a more pure and reformed Church. That is commonly concluded, before this be disputed. No good student will do so, conclude without premises. We must see whether it be our own business first, how we can derive a title to it.

We know, that *government* and *religion* come both originally from God; to which none can have right, but they to whom God hath set over, and entrusted the care and charge of either: Our part is to see by what mean conveyance it comes from them to us. If we have nothing to show that either of them have been particularly committed to us, we may safely and certainly conclude, it is none of our business.

2. Every student must observe a good method in his study; whereof one rule is, to proceed *à manifestis ad obscuriora* [from the obvious to the obscure]: Let him begin at that which is without question his own business. Hath he done all that belongs to his proper place and function, which is certainly his own? Or hath he a family at home to govern, that no doubt is his too? Are his wife, and children, and servants well ordered, all as they should be? St. Paul gives a charge to Timothy, not to set a bishop over the Church, who hath *not governed his own family well*. Though some have not a family without, yet everyone hath a family within, and a large one too: To rule his passions and inordinate desires only, asks a world of work, and they will find it so, whenever they set themselves upon it.

What a preposterous method and course is it to hunt eagerly after liberty from some imaginary pressure in government, or some poor ceremony in the Church, while in the mean time we are true slaves to some base, vile lust within us. Here we should begin to set our selves at liberty from our selves. And this the method of charity requires, as well as the method of art. Charity begins always at home, at our own business....

3. Study will be therefore needful in this case, because otherwise unconsidering men are apt to be carried away with the fair show of zeal and religion in reforming others; they take it for a wrong from any that think not so of it: But by considering well, they will find they are disappointed of that hope; for whatsoever sets them on work, it cannot be true religion, that is not contrary to itself. All students know, that one truth is not repugnant to another; nor one virtue to another.

1. Religion doth not make men tools, to employ themselves in that whereof there comes no good. All we do in other men's business, runs waste....

2. And yet, secondly, there is a worse matter in it than idleness. It charges our account more than needs; and there is no wisdom in that; for when the conscience brings us in more work than either God or man particularly requires, though it be not our own of duty here, it will be our own in account hereafter: For the conscience of doing it, makes it ours howsoever; and so guilty both of it, and all the mischief that comes by it.

3. 'Tis against justice....Justice lets every man enjoy his own. He that takes upon him another man's business, because he can do it better (for that's the great pretence, to do that which is *best*), may as well take another man's purse, because he will spend the money better. I think we will hardly allow of that justice.

4. 'Tis against hope, that Christian hope which supports us in all our sufferings and afflictions....

Lastly, as it disappoints them of the hope of that mercy from God; so it casts them *into the snare of the Devil*....There is no better fence against the Devil, than this...if he finds us diligently employed at home in our own business.

If for all this, the meddling reformers of others would be thought the men of religion, and of the *first rate* too; Let them know, That it is of such a religion as hath neither *prudence* in it, nor *charity*, nor *justice*, nor *hope*, nor *safety*. And when he hath weighed all these mischiefs that follow the breaking this rule:

Let him in the next place, consider the benefit that comes by keeping it. At that I began, and with that I will conclude. This lesson was set us of purpose by the Apostle to second and enforce the other of peace and quiet. The best way to be *quiet* with others, is to be busy with ourselves. It is the natural and genuine effect of it. All discord and dissension must be between two, either persons or parties; and that which commonly kindles the fire, is envy, or some supposed injury; now he that intends his own business only, can give no occasion to others, of either envy or complaint; and so in recompence of keeping to his own business, he shall quietly sit under his own vine, and under his own fig tree; he shall have own for own.

Lastly, besides this outward quiet with others, it will produce another within us, the *quiet* and *tranquillity of the conscience*, without which, outward peace may prove to some but a quiet passage here, to eternal misery hereafter. But this makes it a thorough quiet, both sides alike, within and without; for it lays those busy, unsatisfied thoughts within us, which otherwise gives trouble both to our selves and others: That when we see not, or think we see not all things so well carried in the Church and government, as we could wish; yet having gone as far to mend it, as the *line* of our own business will reach, and the farthest end of that is, having peaceably moved for it, and heartily prayed for it, we may with a safe and quiet conscience, leave the rest to God, and those to whom he hath committed that care and charge, whose proper business it is. And as many as walk according to this rule, peace be on them, and mercy from the God of peace and mercy; to whom be all honour, glory and praise, for ever. *Amen.*

—1666

William Cavendish, Duke of Newcastle
1592 – 1676

Born at Welbeck Abbey, the family estate, and educated at St. John's College, Cambridge, Cavendish inherited a great fortune. He was created Earl of Newcastle in 1628, and in the early 1630s spent about £20,000 (a huge sum at that time) on two elaborate entertainments for Charles I. These included masques commissioned from Ben Jonson. In 1638 he was made a member of the Privy Council and was appointed governor of the Prince of Wales, the future Charles II. In the early years of the civil war he gave a great deal of money to the royal cause, and raised and commanded a troop of gentlemen for the King. With the defeat of the Royalist armies he moved to the continent, living in Paris (1645–48), where he appointed Thomas Hobbes as tutor to Prince Charles, and Antwerp (1648–60). It was also while in Paris that he met and married his second wife, Margaret Lucas, whose works would include a *Life* (1667) of her husband (for more on the Duchess of Newcastle, see the introduction to the selections from her works). After the Restoration Cavendish regained most of his estates and received a dukedom, though the Duchess of Newcastle in her *Life* calculated that the wars had cost him over £900,000 in unpaid rents and other losses. He was patron to James Shirley, Dryden, and Thomas Shadwell, and was himself the author of several poems and plays, though his best known publications were two books on horsemanship (famous among book collectors for their engraved illustrations).

Newcastle's lengthy letter of advice to Charles II (one extant manuscript is eighty-eight pages long) was a private document, and was not printed until this century. Presented to Charles in the spring of 1659, it was the last in a series of letters of instruction he had written since the late 1630s, when he had been appointed governor to the Prince. There is no evidence that the King read the letter, but it has been suggested that the pleasure-loving Cavendish, an accomplished horseman, fencer, and dancer, was an important influence on Charles (for the King's personality, see the character written by the Marquis of Halifax). As political advice, the letter has been described as both Machiavellian and Hobbesian. Cavendish's invocation of Elizabethan *exempla* also reflects a pervasive post-civil war nostalgia for the confidence, security, and apparent tranquility of Elizabethan England.

❧❧❧

Advice to Charles II

May it please your most sacred Majesty,

I am bold humbly to present this book to your Majesty which is written particularly for your Majesty when you are enthroned. Why I present it now is because I think your Majesty will have more time and leisure to read it now than when you are enthroned. Besides, it is intended wholly for your Majesty's service and if it prove that which I am confident it will, I shall have reached my full intention, which service I would not have frustrated by my death. There is no oratory in it, or anything stolen out of books, for I seldom or ever read any. These discourses are out of my long experience, to present your Majesty with truths which great monarchs seldom hear. These truths are not only the most honest, but also the wisest, that a dutiful servant can offer to so gracious a master, and so wise a king as to be able to judge between truth and falsehood, though that falsehood be ever so subtly disguised. I ask pardon for the method, having no notes by me at all. If your Majesty like it, I have achieved my purpose with unspeakable joy and contentment; if you like it not, Sire, I humbly beg that favor of your Majesty to throw it into the fire so it may become a flaming sacrifice of my duty to your Majesty. May the great God ever preserve your Majesty.

* * * * *

FOR TRADE

Your Majesty will be pleased to consider that trade is a different business from the Church or the Law; these last two rob the hive of the commonwealth of its honey, and bring none to the hive. No, Sire, it is the merchant alone that brings honey to the hive. It is he alone who enriches kingdoms through trade, especially your Majesty's kingdom of England that is ordained for it. It is not a bad winter that the country man complains about that makes scarcity of money, but the decay of trade. A certain rule that never fails is that when everything is cheap, there is a scarcity of money; when everything is dear, then the kingdom is full of money. For example, imagine all the commonwealth in four or five persons, and they having five pounds apiece; a sixth person is to sell them a horse and that sixth person needs to sell it. Then he must sell it for no more than five pounds, for nobody has more to give, and he can get no more than there is. But put the case that these five persons had one hundred pounds apiece, then this sixth man that is to sell his horse may get one hundred pounds for him because those five persons have one hundred pounds apiece to give for it. Thus, your Majesty sees that plenty of money makes everything dear, and scarcity of money must of necessity make everything cheap. Therefore, your Majesty will be pleased to keep up the merchants; they alone can fill your kingdom with riches, and consequently enrich your Majesty, for if your kingdom is poor, where can your Majesty get wealth? Nowhere....

FOR CEREMONY AND ORDER

Although ceremony is nothing in itself, yet it does everything. For what is a king more than a subject, but for ceremony and order? When that fails him, he is ruined. What is the Church without ceremony and order? When that fails, the Church is ruined. What is the law without ceremony and order? When that fails, the law goes down. What are the universities, and all schools, without ceremony and order? Nothing. What are all corporations without ceremony and order? Nothing. What is a Lord more than a footman without ceremony and order? A despised title. What are parents and children, masters and servants, officers of all kinds in the commonwealth, without ceremony and order? Nothing at all. Aye, what is an army without ceremony and order? And there the strictest ceremony and order, for he that continues longest in order, which is in bodies [of men], wins the battle. What are all councils and states without ceremony and order? Nothing but confusion and ruin. So that ceremony and order, together with force, govern over all, in peace and in war, and keep every man and every thing within the circle of their own conditions. Aye, even bear-baiting, without ceremony and order, would be in more confusion than it is, and many other such things.

Therefore, your Majesty will be pleased to keep it up strictly, in your own person and at Court, to be a precedent to the rest of your nobles, and not make yourself too cheap by too much familiarity which, as the proverb says, breeds contempt. But when you appear, show yourself gloriously to your people, like a God, for the Holy Writ says: we have called you Gods.[1] When the people see you thus, they will get down on their knees, worship and pray for you with trembling fear and love as they did to Queen Elizabeth whose government is absolutely

---

[1] See Psalm 82:6. James VI/I discusses this biblical passage in his 1610 *Speech* to Parliament.

the best precedent for England's government. It is only that these horrid times must make a few amendments to set things straight and to keep them so. The Queen would say: "God bless you, my good people." Although this saying was no great matter in itself, yet, I assure your Majesty, it had a deep impact on the people. Aye, of a Sunday when she opened the window, the people would cry: "Oh Lord, I saw her hand, I saw her hand"; and some woman would cry out: "Oh Lord, the Queen is a woman!" There is certainly nothing that keeps up a king more than ceremony and order which creates distance, and this brings respect and duty, [hence] obedience, which is everything....

So if your Majesty pleases, speak to your heralds, set down the ceremony and order for all degrees of your nobility, as for barons, viscounts, earls, marquises, and dukes, and to have it printed, and so for all the great officers, their ceremony and order, not any to intrench one upon the other, but to keep only what is right, and due, for their places and dignities. As one thing, none under the degree of a baroness can have carpets by her bed, and she but one or two at the most. And now every Turkey merchant's wife will have all her floor over with carpets, so now every citizen's wife will have six horses in her coach, which is most unfitting ... this your Majesty will rectify very easily. So to make no difference between great ladies and citizen's wives in apparel is abominable. No, they should go to their little black velvet caps, small gold chains, and little ruffs, as they were in my time, and their apprentices in their round black caps.[1]

But this must take a little time, for fear of offending too fast, until your Majesty is well settled in your saddle. When any of these orders are violated, [the offender] must be brought into the Marshall's Court and punished there.[2] That court, though it was spoken against in Parliament, is a most excellent court, for it keeps up ceremony and order, provided the court be kept within its bounds. Certainly, degrees of apparel [appropriate] to the several conditions and callings is of great consequence to the peace of the kingdom, for when lower degrees strive to outbrave higher degrees, it breeds envy in the better sort, pride in the meaner sort, and contempt of the nobility by the vulgar, all of which breeds faction and disorder, which are the causes of a civil war. Therefore, Sire, keep up your nobility and gentry to all their just rights and dignities. For was it not a part of the nobility and gentry that kept up your Royal Father so long when he had no money—that which is the sinews of war—maintaining themselves and the war almost at their own charge, and holding out beyond all expectation? It was neither the Church nor the Law that kept the King up so long, but part of the nobility and gentry; therefore your Majesty's wisdom will cherish them....

THE ERRORS OF STATE AND THEIR REMEDIES

The greatest error in these last two reigns was that the kings were always in want of money, which is the greatest error a king can make, whether it was out of profuseness in gifts or in unnecessary things, such as pictures, jewels, or the like, or for being cozened. It is certain that want, in a king, will, in the end, bring ruin, for being in necessity makes him put up many illegal taxes which much offend the people. Then the next Parliament becomes inflamed and the king is forced to remedy them in order to give contentments to his people, and so he falls in the opinion of his subjects, and makes even the clowns see that Parliament can order him

---

[1] Most early modern countries had sumptuary legislation that regulated what clothing could be worn by people of different social ranks and occupations; Cavendish suggests a return to such regulations as one way to reassert traditional social hierarchies.

[2] *Marshall's Court* Marshalsea, a court originally held before the steward and marshall of the royal household to settle disputes between members of the household; in the seventeenth century it dealt with debts and with cases committed within twelve miles of the court.

[about],[1] and so many will think that a Parliament has the transcendent power which it has not; on the contrary, far from it. Aye, even should none of those taxes be presented, but it was your necessity that urged you to call a Parliament, that Parliament would think they had your Majesty on the hip and would play upon you accordingly. They would give you no money until they had what they desired; this cannot be a free Parliament, for they would bargain with you and play upon your necessity, getting ten times the worth of what they buy, very much to your prejudice. Therefore, as the old saying goes, put your money in your purse and keep it. Henry the seventh, your royal ancestor, was a wise king and he did this; he would often say that England was a good farm if it were well husbanded, and his Majesty was the best husband of it that ever I heard of, and so he was not put to such plunges as princes in necessity are. A sparing prince is good for himself and for his people, but not for the courtiers, who are but a few in comparison with the rest. When you are rich, even your important neighbours will fear you; if you are poor, they will not care about you. When you are rich, and call a Parliament, your Majesty is then master of the field and you may do what you please, and they will have no ground to work off against you. In a king, oh Sire, riches, both at home and abroad, are more advantageous than I can express. Therefore, Sire, put money in your purse and be rich....

THE RECREATIONS FOR YOUR MAJESTY'S PEOPLE BOTH IN THE CITY AND THE COUNTRY

First for London: Paris Gardens will hold good for the meaner people.[2] Then for the several playhouses. There were at least five in my time: Black-Friars, The Cockpit, Salisbury Court, The Fortune

and The Red Bull.[3] There were the boys that played at Black-Friars and at Paul's, while the King's Players acted at The Globe, now called The Phoenix.[4] Some played at The Boar's Head and at The Curtain-in-the-Fields and some at The Hope, which is The Bear Garden, and others at The White Friars.[5] But five or six playhouses are enough for all sorts of diversion and pleasure of that kind. Then there will be puppet plays to please them besides, as also dancers of the ropes with jugglers and tumblers, besides strange sights of beasts, birds, monsters and many other things, with several sorts of music and dancing. And all the old holidays,[6] with their mirth and rites set up again. There will be daily feasting in merry England, for England is so plentiful of all provisions, that if we do not eat them they will eat us, so we feast in our defence.

For the Country Recreations

May games, Morris dances, the Lord of the May, and the Lady of the May, the fool, and the hobby horse must not be forgotten, as also the Whitsun Lord and Lady, the thrashing of hens at Shrovetide, carols and wassails at Christmas, with good plum

---

[1] *clowns* rustic, ignorant, or ill-bred people (*OED* clown 1, 2).

[2] *Paris Gardens* a tract of about one hundred wooded acres in Southwark, open to the public.

[3] *in my time* that is, before the theatres were closed in 1642. Blackfriars was demolished in 1655; the Cockpit (also known as the Phoenix) was reopened at the Restoration but closed within a few years due to competition from the Theatre Royal; Salisbury Court had its interior destroyed by soldiers in 1649, but was restored and reopened at the Restoration, only to be destroyed in the Great Fire; the Fortune was also dismantled by soldiers in 1649, and pulled down completely in 1661; the Red Bull reopened in 1660 but was demolished within a few years.

[4] The Globe, rebuilt after a fire in 1613, was demolished in the mid-1640s; Newcastle is confusing its name change with the Cockpit, which was renamed the Phoenix when rebuilt after a fire in 1617.

[5] The Boar's Head was one of the largest and most famous taverns in Eastcheap; the Curtain was a playhouse that had fallen into disuse by the mid-1620s; the Hope was a theatre converted from a bear-baiting arena that had probably reverted to baiting by about 1617; Whitefriars had been abandoned by about 1614.

[6] *the old holidays* treated in more detail in the following section on "country recreations."

porridge and pies which are now forbidden as profane, ungodly things at wakes.[1] Fairs and markets maintain commerce and trade. And after evening prayer every Sunday and holiday, the country people with their fresher lasses will trip on the town green about the May Pole, to the loudest bagpipes, there to be refreshed with ale and cakes. King James, of blessed memory, wrote a little book,[2] not only in defence of dancing, but also commanded that his good people should rejoice themselves with dancing after evening prayer.

Then there should be players to go up and down the countryside. In my time, most noble men had country players, rope-dancers, jugglers, tumblers, and indeed most of all those things I formerly spoke of goes down into the country. And these things will much divert and please the people. Mr. Thomas Killigrew, your Majesty's Master of the Revels,[3] I know, will manage all these things most discreetly for your Majesty's honour and the good of the commonwealth, looking least after his own interests, or else I am much mistaken. These divertissements will amuse the people's thoughts, and keep them in harmless action which will free your Majesty from faction and rebellion.

—(1659)

---

[1] Parliamentary legislation in the 1640s had banned the celebration of traditional holiday rites and pastimes; support of these traditions subsequently became a mark of Royalist loyalty (in e.g. the poetry of Robert Herrick). Cockthrashing involved tethering a cock by a leg and throwing objects at it in the attempt to knock it over.

[2] The *Declaration of Sports* (1618, reissued 1633), popularly known as the Book of Sports, responded to Puritan sabbatarianism by decreeing that traditional holiday pastimes be allowed on Sundays.

[3] The Revels Office was the regulatory body that licensed plays and theatre companies. Killigrew (1612–1683), playwright and theatre manager, did not officially become Master of the Revels until 1673, when his predecessor Sir Henry Herbert died.

Edward Winslow
1595 – 1655

One of the founders of the Plymouth colony in Massachusetts, Winslow was born in Droitwich, Worcester, and moved to Leiden in 1617 to join John Robinson's Separatist church. One document from this period describes him as a printer by trade; he may be the same Edward Winslow who was made a freeman of the Stationers' Company in 1634. Winslow sailed to North America in the Mayflower, arriving with the other pilgrim settlers in November 1620. His first wife died during that winter, and his marriage to the widow Mrs. Susanna White was the colony's first. Winslow sat on the ruling council of the colony for more than twenty years, and served as Governor for three one-year periods in the 1630s and 1640s. During a visit to England in the 1630s he was imprisoned briefly by Archbishop William Laud for his role in the Plymouth church. In 1646 he returned to England to defend the colony against accusations made against it by the religious radical Samuel Gorton, and spent the following nine years holding minor posts under Oliver Cromwell. In 1655 he was sent as a commissioner to the West Indies, but died on board ship near Jamaica.

One of Winslow's responsibilities in the colony was to negotiate with the local native tribe, the Wampanoag, on whose friendliness the colony depended; he succeeded in winning the friendship of their chief, Massasoit. Winslow appended the following discussion of native religion and manners to his *Good News from New England* (1624), a narrative of the colony's activities in its first few years. In addition to works of religious controversy, Winslow edited *The Glorious Progress of the Gospel amongst the Indians in New England* (1649). For another European account of native North American life and manners, see the selections from Pierre-Esprit Radisson.

❧❧❧

Good News from New England
(excerpt)

THE RELIGION AND CUSTOMS OF THE INDIANS NEAR NEW PLYMOUTH

A few things I thought meet to add hereunto, which I have observed amongst the Indians, both touching their religion, and sundry other customs amongst them.

And first, whereas myself and others, in former Letters (which came to the press against my will and knowledge) wrote,[1] that the Indians about us, are a people without any religion, or knowledge of any God; therein I erred, though we could then gather no better. For as they conceive of many divine powers: so of one, whom they call *Kiehtan*,[2] to be the principal and maker of all the rest; and to be made by none. He (they say) created the heavens, earth, sea, and all creatures contained therein. Also that he made one man and one woman; of whom they, and we, and all mankind came: but how they became so far dispersed, that know they not.

At first, they say, there was no *Sachem*, or King, but *Kiehtan*; who dwelleth above in the heavens: whither all good men go when they die, to see their friends, and have their fill of all things. This his

---

[1] referring to *A Relation, or Journal, of the Beginning and Proceedings of the English Plantation Settled at Plymouth, in New England*, commonly known as *Mourt's Relation* from the name of the editor, printed in London in 1622 while Winslow was still in New England. The *Relation* is based on letters and journals by Winslow, William Bradford, and others.

[2] The meaning of the word *Kiehtan*, I think hath reference to antiquity: for *Chise* is an old man; *Kiehchise*, a man that exceedeth in age [note by Winslow].

habitation lieth far westward in the heavens, they say. Thither the bad men go also, and knock at his door: but he bids them, *Quatchet,* that is to say, Walk abroad, for there is no place for such; so that they wander in restless want and penury. Never man saw this *Kiehtan.* Only old men tell them of him: and bid them tell their children, yea, to charge them, to teach their posterities the same, and lay the like charge on them. This power they acknowledge to be good; and when they would obtain any great matter, meet together, and cry unto him: and so likewise, for plenty, victory, &c., sing, dance, feast, give thanks; and hang up garlands and other things, in memory of the same.

Another power they worship, whom they call *Hobbamock*; and to the northward of us, *Hobbamoqui.* This, as far as we can conceive, is the Devil; him they call upon to cure their wounds and diseases. When they are curable, he persuades them he sends the same for some conceived anger against them; but upon their calling on him, can and doth help them. But when they are mortal, and not curable in nature, then he persuades them, *Kiehtan* is angry, and sends them, which none can cure. Insomuch as, in that respect only, they somewhat doubt whether he be simply good, and therefore in sickness never call upon him.

This *Hobbamock* appears in sundry forms unto them, as in the shape of a man, a deer, a fawn, an eagle, &c., but most ordinarily a snake. He appears not to all, but the chiefest and most judicious amongst them, though all of them strive to attain to that hellish height of honour.

He appeareth most ordinary and is most conversant with three sorts of people.[1] One I confess I neither know by name nor office directly: of these they have few but esteem highly of them; and think that no weapon can kill them. Another they call by the name of *Powah*; and the third *Pinese.*

The office and duty of the *Powah* is to be exercised principally in calling upon the Devil, and curing diseases of the sick or wounded. The common people join with him in the exercise of invocation, but do but only assent, or as we term it, say *Amen* to what he saith; yet sometime break out into a short musical note with him. The *Powah* is eager and free in speech, fierce in countenance, and joineth many antic and laborious gestures with the same over the party diseased. If the party be wounded, he will also seem to suck the wound, but if they be curable (as they say) he toucheth it not; but a *Skooke,* that is the snake, or *Wobsacuck,* that is the eagle, sitteth on his shoulder and licks the same. This none sees but the *Powah*; who tells them he doth it himself. If the party be otherwise diseased, it is accounted sufficient if in any shape he but come into the house, taking it for an undoubted sign of recovery.

And as in former ages Apollo had his temple at Delphos, and Diana at Ephesus; so have I heard them call upon some as if they had their residence in some certain places, or because they appeared in those forms, in the same. In the *Powah's* speech he promiseth to sacrifice many skins of beasts, kettles, hatchets, beads, knives, and other the best things they have to the fiend, if he will come to help the party diseased: But whether they perform it I know not. The other practices I have seen, being necessarily called at some times to be with their sick, and have used the best arguments I could make them understand against the same. They have told me I should see the Devil at those times come to the party, but I assured myself and them of the contrary, which so proved: yea, themselves have confessed they never saw him when any of us were present. In desperate and extraordinary travail in childbirth, when the party cannot be delivered by the ordinary means, they send for this *Powah,* though ordinarily their travail is not so extreme as in our parts of the world, they being of a more

---

[1] *appeareth most ordinary* appears ordinarily to.

hardy nature. For on the third day after childbirth I have seen the mother with the infant upon a small occasion in cold weather in a boat upon the sea.

Many sacrifices the Indians use, and in some cases kill children. It seemeth they are various in their religious worship in a little distance, and grow more and more cold in their worship to *Kiehtan*; saying in their memory he was much more called upon. The *Nanohiggansets* [Narragansetts] exceed in their blind devotion, and have a great spacious house wherein only some few (that are, as we may term them, priests) come. Thither at certain known times resort all their people, and offer almost all the riches they have to their gods, as kettles, skins, hatchets, beads, knives, &c., all which are cast by the priests into a great fire that they make in the midst of the house, and there consumed to ashes. To this offering every man bringeth freely, and the more he is known to bring, hath the better esteem of all men. This the other Indians about us approve of as good, and wish their *Sachems* would appoint the like: and because the plague hath not reigned in *Nanohigganset* as at other places about them,[1] they attribute to this custom there used.

The *Pineses* are men of great courage and wisdom, and to these also the Devil appeareth more familiarly than to others, and as we conceive maketh covenant with them to preserve them from death, by wounds with arrows, knives, hatchets, &c. or at least both themselves and especially the people think themselves to be freed from the same. And although against their battles all of them by painting disfigure themselves, yet they are known by their courage and boldness, by reason whereof one of them will chase almost a hundred men, for they account it death for whomsoever stand in their way. These are highly esteemed of all sorts of people, and are of the *Sachem's* council, without whom they will not war or undertake any weighty business. In war

their *Sachems* for their more safety go in the midst of them. They are commonly men of the greatest stature and strength, and such as will endure most hardness, and yet are more discreet, courteous, and humane in their carriages than any amongst them, scorning theft, lying, and the like base dealings, and stand as much upon their reputation as any men.

And to the end they may have store of these,[2] they train up the most forward and likeliest boys from their childhood in great hardness, and make them abstain from dainty meat, observing divers orders prescribed, to the end that when they are of age the Devil may appear to them; causing to drink the juice of sentry and other bitter herbs, till they cast,[3] which they must disgorge into the platter, and drink again, and again, till at length through extraordinary oppressing of nature it will seem to be all blood, and this the boys will do with eagerness at the first, and so continue till by reason of faintness they can scarce stand on their legs, and then must go forth into the cold. Also they beat their shins with sticks, and cause them to run through bushes, stumps, and brambles, to make them hardy and acceptable to the Devil, that in time he may appear unto them.

Their *Sachems* cannot be all called Kings, but only some few of them, to whom the rest resort for protection, and pay homage unto them. Neither may they war without their knowledge and approbation, yet to be commanded by the greater as occasion serveth. Of this [greater] sort is *Massassowat* our friend, and *Conanacus* of *Nanohigganset* our supposed enemy.

Every *Sachem* taketh care for the widow and fatherless, also for such as are aged, and any way maimed, if their friends be dead or not able to provide for them.

---

[1] *Nanohigganset* now Rhode Island.

[2] *store* supply (of *Pineses*).

[3] *sentry* centaury, a plant of the gentian family with medicinal properties; *cast* vomit.

A *Sachem* will not take any to wife but such a one as is equal to him in birth; otherwise they say their seed would in time become ignoble. And though they have many other wives, yet are they no other than concubines or servants, and yield a kind of obedience to the principal, who ordereth the family, and them in it. The like their men observe also, and will adhere to the first during their lives; but put away the others at their pleasure.

This government is successive and not by choice. If the father die before the son or daughter be of age, then the child is committed to the protection and tuition of some one amongst them, who ruleth in his stead till he be of age, but when that is I know not.

Every *Sachem* knoweth how far the bounds and limits of his own country extendeth, and that is his own proper inheritance. Out of that if any of his men desire land to set their corn, he giveth them as much as they can use, and sets them their bounds. In this circuit whosoever hunteth, if they kill any venison, bringeth him his fee, which is the fore parts of the same, if it be killed on the land, but if in the water, then the skin thereof. The great *Sachems* or Kings, know their own bounds or limits of land, as well as the rest.

All travellers or strangers for the most part, lodge at the *Sachem's*; when they come they tell them how long they will stay, and to what place they go, during which time they receive entertainment according to their persons, but want not.

Once a year the *Pineses* use to provoke the people to bestow much corn on the *Sachem*. To that end they appoint a certain time and place near the *Sachem's* dwelling, where the people bring many baskets of corn, and make a great stack thereof. There, the *Pineses* stand ready to give thanks to the people on the *Sachem's* behalf, and after acquainteth the *Sachem* therewith, who fetcheth the same, and is no less thankful, bestowing many gifts on them.

When any are visited with sickness, their friends resort unto them for their comfort, and continue with them oft times till their death or recovery. If they die they stay a certain time to mourn for them. Night and morning they perform this duty many days after the burial in a most doleful manner, insomuch as though it be ordinary and the note musical, which they take one from another, and all together, yet it will draw tears from their eyes, and almost from ours also. But if they recover then because their sickness was chargeable, they send corn and other gifts unto them at a certain appointed time, whereat they feast and dance, which they call *Commoco*.

When they bury the dead, they sew up the corpse in a mat and so put it in the earth. If the party be a *Sachem* they cover him with many curious mats, and bury all his riches with him, and inclose the grave with a pale.[1] If it be a child the father will also put his own most special jewels and ornaments in the earth with it, also will cut his hair and disfigure himself very much in token of sorrow. If it be the man or woman of the house, they will pull down the mats and leave the frame standing, and bury them in or near the same, and either remove their dwelling, or give over house-keeping.

The men employ themselves wholly in hunting, and other exercises of the bow, except at some times they take some pains in fishing.

The women live a most slavish life. They carry all their burdens, set and dress their corn, gather it in, seek out for much of their food, beat and make ready the corn to eat, and have all household care lying upon them.

The younger sort reverence the elder; and do all mean offices whilst they are together, although they be strangers. Boys and girls may not wear their hair like men and women, but are distinguished thereby.

---

[1] *pale* palisade, fence (*OED* pale *sb* 1, 2).

A man is not accounted a man till he do some notable act, or show forth such courage and resolution as becometh his place. The men take much tobacco, but for boys so to do they account it odious.

All their names are significant and variable; for when they come to the state of men and women, they alter them according to their deeds and dispositions.

When a maid is taken in marriage she first cutteth her hair, and after weareth a covering on her head till her hair be grown out. The women are diversely disposed, some as modest as they will scarce talk one with another in the company of men, being very chaste also: yet other some light, lascivious and wanton.

If a woman have a bad husband, or cannot affect him,[1] and there be war or opposition between that and any other people, she will run away from him to the contrary party and there live, where they never come unwelcome: for where are most women, there is greatest plenty.

When a woman hath her monthly terms she separateth her self from all other company, and liveth certain days in a house alone: after which she washeth her self and all that she hath touched or used, and is again received to her husband's bed or family.

For adultery the husband will beat his wife and put her away, if he please. Some common strumpets there are as well as in other places, but they are such as either never married, or widows, or put away for adultery: for no man will keep such a one to wife.

In matters of unjust and dishonest dealing, the *Sachem* examineth and punisheth the same. In cases of thefts, for the first offence he is disgracefully rebuked, for the second beaten by the *Sachem* with a cudgel on the naked back, for the third he is beaten with many strokes, and hath his nose slit upward, that thereby all men may both know and shun him. If any man kill another, he must likewise for the same. The *Sachem* not only passeth the sentence upon malefactors, but executeth the same with his own hands, if the party be then present; if not, sendeth his own knife, in case of death, in the hands of others to perform the same. But if the offender be to receive other punishment, he will not receive the same but from the *Sachem* himself, before whom being naked he kneeleth, and will not offer to run away though he beat him never so much, it being a greater disparagement for a man to cry during the time of his correction, than is his offence and punishment.

As for their apparel they wear breeches and stockings in one like some Irish, which is made of deer skins, and have shoes of the same leather. They wear also a deer skin loose about them like a cloak, which they will turn to the weather side. In this habit they travel, but when they are at home or come to their journey's end, presently they pull off their breeches, stockings, and shoes, wring out the water if they be wet, and dry them, and rub or chafe the same. Though these be off, yet have they another small garment that covereth their secrets. The men wear also when they go abroad in cold weather an otter or fox skin on their right arm, but only their bracer on the left.[2] Women and all of that sex wear strings about their legs, which the men never do.

The people are very ingenious and observative. They keep account of time by the moon, and winters or summers; they know divers of the stars by name, in particular, they know the North Star and call it *maske*, which is to say "the bear." Also they have many names for the winds. They will guess very well at the wind and weather beforehand, by observations in the heavens. They report also, that some of them can cause the wind to blow in

---

[1] *cannot affect him* has no affection for him.

[2] *bracer* a wristguard used in archery (*OED* bracer[2]).

what part they list, can raise storms and tempests which they usually do when they intend the death or destruction of other people, that by reason of the unseasonable weather they may take advantage of their enemies in their houses. At such times they perform their greatest exploits, and in such seasons when they are at enmity with any, they keep more careful watch than at other times.

As for the language it is very copious, large, and difficult. As yet, we cannot attain to any great measure thereof; but can understand them, and explain ourselves to their understanding, by the help of those that daily converse with us. And though there be difference in a hundred miles distance of place, both in language and manners, yet not so much but that they very well understand each other. And thus much of their lives and manners.

Instead of records and chronicles, they take this course. Where any remarkable act is done, in memory of it, either in the place, or by some pathway near adjoining, they make a round hole in the ground about a foot deep, and as much over, which when others passing by behold, they enquire the cause and occasion of the same, which being once known, they are careful to acquaint all men, as occasion serveth therewith. And lest such holes should be filled, or grown up by an accident, as men pass by they will oft renew the same. By which means many things of great antiquity are fresh in memory. So that as a man travelleth, if he can understand his guide, his journey will be the less tedious, by reason of the many historical discourses will be related to him.

—1624

Rachel Speght
ca. 1597 – post 1621

Rachel Speght, the poet and polemical pamphle-teer, was the daughter of James Speght, a Calvinist minister and rector of the London churches of St. Mary Magdalene, Milk Street (1592–1637) and St. Clement, Eastcheap (1611–1637). Her mother's identity is unknown. James Speght wrote *A brief demonstration, who have, and of the certainty of their salvation, that have the Spirit of Christ* (1613), and an epiphany sermon, *The Day-spring of Comfort* (1615). Speght's writings reveal that she had received some instruction in rhetoric and logic, a thorough knowledge of Scripture, a facility in Latin, and a familiarity with a wide range of authoritative classical and Christian texts.

In her first publication, *A Muzzle for Melastomus, the Cynical Baiter of, and foul mouthed Barker against Eve's Sex* (1617), Speght defends the nature and worth of women in response to Joseph Swetnam's notorious anti-feminist pamphlet, the *Arraignment of Lewd, Idle, Froward and Unconstant Women* (1615).[1] Of the three direct refutations of Swetnam's treatise, Speght's was the first and the only one published under the author's own name.[2] In 1621, the year of her marriage to William Procter, Speght published *Mortality's Memorandum with a Dream Prefixed*. The title poem of *Mortality's Memorandum* is an extended meditation on death, while the prefixed dream is an allegorical dream vision. In "The Dream" Speght allegorizes the female struggle to acquire knowledge, progressing from ignorance to enlightenment. "The Dream" may be read as a counter-myth to the Edenic tragedy in which female knowledge is inextricably bound up with sin and death. Nothing is known of Speght's life after her marriage.

❧❧❧

A Muzzle for Melastomus

Not unto the veriest Idiot that ever set Pen to Paper, but to the Cynical Baiter of Women, or metamorphosed Misogunes, Joseph Swetnam. [3]

From standing water, which soon putrifies, can no good fish be expected; for it produceth no other creatures but those that are venomous or noisome, as snakes, adders, and such like.[4] Semblably, no better stream can we look, should issue from your idle corrupt brain, than that whereto the rough of your fury (to use your own words) hath moved you to open the sluice.[5] In which excrement of your roving cogitations you have used such irregularities touching concordance, and observed so disordered a method, as I doubt not to tell you, that a very accidence scholar would have quite put you down in both.[6] You appear herein not unlike that painter, who seriously endeavouring to portray Cupid's bow, forgot the string: for you being greedy to botch up your mingle mangle invective against women, have not therein observed, in many places,

---

[1] *Melastomus* "black mouth"; *Swetnam* Swetnam published under the pseudonym of Thomas Tel-troth.

[2] The two other responses to Swetnam's defamation of women were Ester Sowernam's *Esther Hath Hang'd Haman* (1617) and Constantia Munda's *The Worming of a Mad Dog: or, A Sop For Cerberus the Jailer of Hell* (1617). Later, an anonymous play was published, *Swetnam the Woman-hater Arraigned by Women* (1620).

[3] *Misogunes* a woman-hater (i.e. misogynist) (*OED* misogyne).

[4] *noisome* injurious (*OED* noisome *a* 1).

[5] *Semblably* similarly (*OED* semblably *adv* 1); *rough of…own words* Swetnam wrote, "I being in a great choler against some women, I mean more than one; And so in the rough of my fury, taking my pen in hand…." (sig. A2); *sluice* dam (*OED* sluice *sb.* 1b).

[6] *excrement* superfluous outgrowth (excretions) (*OED* excrement[2] 2); *concordance* grammatical agreement between words as parts of speech (*OED* concord *sb*[1] 6); *accidence scholar* schoolboy learning the rudiments of grammar (*OED* accidence[1] 1).

so much as a grammar sense.[1] But the emptiest barrel makes the loudest sound; and so we will account of you.

Many propositions have you framed, which (as you think) make much against women, but if one would make a logical assumption, the conclusion would be flat against your own sex.[2] Your dealing wants so much discretion, that I doubt whether to bestow so good a name as the dunce upon you: but minority bids me keep within my bounds;[3] and therefore I only say unto you, that your corrupt heart and railing tongue, hath made you a fit scribe for the devil.

In that you have termed your virulent foam, *the Bear-baiting of women*, you have plainly displayed your own disposition to be cynical, in that there appears no other dog or bull, to bait them, but yourself.[4] Good had it been for you to have put on that muzzle, which Saint James would have all Christians to wear; *Speak not evil one of another*: and then had you not seemed so like the serpent Porphyrus, as now you do; which, though full of deadly poison, yet being toothless, hurteth none so much as himself.[5] For you having gone beyond the limits not of humanity alone, but of Christianity, have done greater harm unto your own soul, than unto women, as may plainly appear. First, in dishonouring of God by palpable blasphemy, wresting and perverting every place of Scripture, that you have alleged; which by the testimony of Saint Peter, is to the destruction of them that so do.[6] Secondly, it appears by your disparaging of, and opprobrious speeches against, that excellent work of God's hands, which in his great love he perfected for the comfort of man. Thirdly, and lastly, by this your hodge-podge of heathenish sentences, similes, and examples, you have set forth yourself in your right colours, unto the view of the world: and I doubt not but the judicious will account of you according to your demerit: As for the vulgar sort, which have no more learning than you have showed in your book, it is likely they will applaud you for your pains.[7]

· · · · · · ·

*Of Woman's Excellency,
with the causes of her creation, and of the
sympathy which ought to be in man and wife
each toward other.*

The work of creation being finished, this approbation thereof was given by God himself, that *All was very good*:[8] If all, then woman, who, excepting man, is the most excellent creature under the canopy of heaven. But if it be objected by any:

First, that woman, though created good, yet by giving ear to Satan's temptations, brought death and misery upon all her posterity.

Secondly, that *Adam was not deceived, but that the woman was deceived, and was in the transgression*.[9]

Thirdly, that Saint Paul saith, *It were good for a man not to touch a woman*.[10]

Fourthly, and lastly, that of Solomon, who seems to speak against all of our sex; *I have found*

---

[1] *to botch up* to compose in a bungling manner (*OED* botch *v*[1] 3).

[2] *one* one proposition.

[3] *wants* lacks (*OED* want *v* 2a); *minority* youth (*OED* minority 2b).

[4] *the Bear-baiting of women* an allusion to the fourth chapter of Swetnam's treatise: "The Bear-baiting, or the Vanity of Widows."

[5] "James 4:1" (original marginalia); *Porphyrus* a serpent in India that lacks fangs, but whose vomit is venomous.

[6] "I Pet. 3:16" (original marginalia); Speght actually alludes to II Peter 3:16.

[7] *vulgar* persons belonging to the ordinary or common class, esp. the uneducated or ignorant (*OED* vulgar *sb* 2a).

[8] "Gen. 1:31" (original marginalia).

[9] "I Tim. 2:14" (original marginalia).

[10] "I Cor. 7:1" (original marginalia).

one man of a thousand, but a woman among them all have I not found, whereof in its due place.[1]

To the first of these objections I answer; that Satan first assailed the woman, because where the hedge is lowest, most easy it is to get over, and she being the weaker vessel was with more facility to be seduced: like as a crystal glass sooner receives a crack than a strong stone pot.[2] Yet we shall find the offence of Adam and Eve almost to parallel: For as an ambitious desire of being made like unto God, was the motive which caused her to eat, so likewise was it his; as may plainly appear by that *Ironia, Behold, man is become as one of us:*[3] Not that he was so indeed; but hereby his desire to attain a greater perfection than God had given him, was reproved. Woman sinned, it is true, by her infidelity in not believing the Word of God, but giving credit to Satan's fair promises, that *she should not die*; but so did the man too:[4] And if Adam had not approved of that deed which Eve had done, and been willing to tread the steps which she had gone, he being her head would have reproved her, and have made the commandment a bit to restrain him from breaking his Maker's injunction: For if a man burn his hand in the fire, the bellows that blowed the fire are not to be blamed, but himself rather, for not being careful to avoid the danger: Yet if the bellows had not blowed, the fire had not burnt; no more is woman simply to be condemned for man's transgression: for by the free will, which before his fall he enjoyed, he might have avoided, and been free from being burnt, or singed with that fire which was kindled by Satan, and blown by Eve. It therefore served not his turn a whit, afterwards to say, *The woman which thou gavest me, gave me of the tree, and I did eat:*[5] For a penalty was inflicted upon him, as well as on the woman, the punishment of her transgression being particular to her own sex, and to none but the female kind:[6] but for the sin of man the whole earth was cursed.[7] And he being better able, than the woman, to have resisted temptation, because the stronger vessel, was first called to account,[8] to show, that to whom much is given, of them much is required; and that he who was the sovereign of all creatures visible, should have yielded greatest obedience to God.

.   .   .   .

To the second objection I answer, that the Apostle doth not hereby exempt man from sin, but only giveth to understand, that the woman was the primary transgressor; and not the man, but that man was not at all deceived, was far from his meaning: for he afterward expressly saith, that as *in Adam all die, so in Christ shall all be made alive.*[9]

For the third objection, *It is good for a man not to touch a woman*: the Apostle makes it not a positive prohibition, but speaks it only because of the Corinthians' present necessity, who were then persecuted by the enemies of the Church, for which cause, and no other, he saith, *Art thou loosed from a wife? Seek not a wife*:[10] meaning whilst the time of these perturbations should continue in their heat; *but if thou art bound, seek not to be loosed: if thou marriest,*

---

[1] "Eccles. 7:30" (original marginalia); the reference is to the Geneva Bible; in the AV, see Ecclesiastes 7:28.

[2] *weaker vessel* a phrase from I Peter 3:7, used in the *Homily on Matrimony*.

[3] *Ironia...us* The statement is ironic because it is spoken by God; "Gen. 3:22" (original marginalia).

[4] "Gen. 3:4" (original marginalia).

[5] "Genesis 3:12" (original marginalia).

[6] *the punishment...female kind* "Unto the woman he [God] said, I will greatly multiply thy sorrow and thy conception; in sorrow thou shalt bring forth children; and thy desire shall be to thy husband, and he shall rule over thee" (Genesis 3:16).

[7] *but for...was cursed* "And unto Adam he said, Because thou hast hearkened unto the voice of thy wife, and hast eaten of the tree... cursed is the ground for thy sake; in sorrow shalt thou eat of it all the days of thy life" (Genesis 3:17).

[8] "Genesis 3:17" (original marginalia).

[9] "I Cor. 15:22" (original marginalia).

[10] "I Cor. 7" (original marginalia); *loosed* freed (*OED* loose *v* 1a).

thou sinnest not, only increasest thy care: *for the married careth for the things of this world, and I wish that you were without care, that ye might cleave fast unto the Lord without separation:*

. . . .

The fourth and last objection, is that of Solomon, *I have found one man among a thousand, but a woman among them all have I not found*: for answer of which, if we look into the story of his life, we shall find therein a commentary upon this enigmatical sentence included: for it is there said, that Solomon had seven hundred wives, and three hundred concubines, which number connexed make one thousand.[1] These women turning his heart away from being perfect with the Lord his God, sufficient cause had he to say, that among the said thousand women found he not one upright. He saith not, that among a thousand women never any man found one worthy of commendation, but speaks in the first person singularly, *I have not found*, meaning in his own experience: for this assertion is to be holden a part of the confession of his former follies, and no otherwise, his repentance being the intended drift of Ecclesiastes.

. . . .

The other end for which woman was made, was to be a companion and helper for man; and if she must be an helper, and but an helper, then are those husbands to be blamed, which lay the whole burden of domestical affairs and maintenance on the shoulders of their wives. For, as yoke-fellows they are to sustain part of each other's cares, griefs, and calamities: But as if two oxen be put in one yoke, the one being bigger than the other, the greater bears most weight; so the husband being the stronger vessel is to bear a greater burden than his wife; and therefore, the Lord said to Adam, *In the sweat of thy face shalt thou eat thy bread, till thou return to the dust.* And Saint Paul saith, *That he that provideth not for his household is worse than an infidel.* Nature hath taught senseless creatures to help one another; as the male pigeon, when his hen is weary with sitting on her eggs, and comes off from them, supplies her place, that in her absence they may receive no harm, until such time as she is fully refreshed....Seeing then that these unreasonable creatures, by the instinct of nature, bear such affection each to other, that without any grudge, they willingly, according to their kind, help one another, I may reason *à minore ad maius*, that much more should man and woman, which are reasonable creatures, be helpers each to other in all things lawful, they having the Law of God to guide them, his Word to be a lantern unto their feet, and a light unto their paths, by which they are excited to a far more mutual participation of each other's burden, than other creatures.[2] So that neither the wife may say to her husband, nor the husband unto his wife, I have no need of thee, no more than the members of the body may so say each to other, between whom there is such a sympathy, that if one member suffer, all suffer with it....[3] Marriage is a merry-age, and this world's Paradise, where there is mutual love.

—1617

---

[1] *connexed* joined together (*OED* connex *v Obs* 1).

[2] *à minore ad maius* from the lesser to the greater; *his Word... their paths* Psalm 119:105.

[3] "I Cor. 12:21" (original marginalia).

Thomas Edwards
1599 – 1647

As a preacher at Cambridge, Edwards earned the nickname "young Luther," and his Presbyterianism kept him in trouble with church authorities throughout the 1630s. But the civil war enabled him to switch from persecuted to persecutor. With the rise to power of the Presbyterian party in the early 1640s, Edwards emerged as one of their most tireless supporters. The threat posed by the growing popularity of Independency in mid-decade prompted Edwards to publish virulent attacks on the rapidly evolving beliefs of religious radicals. The most notorious of his books was *Gangraena: or a Catalogue and Discovery of Many of the Errours, Heresies, Blasphemies, and Pernicious Practices of the Sectaries of this Time*, which appeared in three substantial parts in 1646 and attracted numerous responses, including a remarkable series of pamphlets by William Walwyn which defended the ideal of religious toleration. Milton refers to "shallow Edwards" in his sonnet "On the New Forcers of Conscience under the Long Parliament." By 1647, the Independents were in the ascendant, and the resentment caused by Edwards' abuse led him to retire to Holland, where he soon died of the ague.

Edwards began the first part of *Gangraena* with the following catalogue of errors and heresies. While he goes on to name names and provide particulars, he here summarizes the arguments and practices that he believed were leading the country to ruin: toleration, pacifism, women preachers, the priesthood of all believers, denial of predestination, denial of the need for a state church, denial of the need for set forms of worship, and denial of the authority of the magistrate in matters of religion. For works by some of the writers Edwards was arguing against, see the selections by Richard Overton, John Milton, William Walwyn, and Lawrence Clarkson.

೧ംഌ

Gangraena
(excerpt)

The Catalogue of the Errors, Heresies, Blasphemies, is as follows

OF THE SCRIPTURES

1. That the Scriptures cannot be said to be the word of God; there is no word but Christ, the Scriptures are a dead letter, and no more to be credited than the writings of men, not divine, but human invention.

2. That the Scripture, whether a true manuscript or no, whether Hebrew, Greek or English, is but human, and so not able to discover a divine God. Then where is your command to make that your rule or discipline, that cannot reveal you God, nor give you power to walk with God? so that Christ letting out himself as he is in himself, ought to be a Christian's rule in obedience to himself.[1]

3. That the Scriptures are insufficient and uncertain, there is no certainty to build any doctrine upon them, they are not an infallible foundation of faith.

4. As the condition of Adam, Noah, Abraham, Moses, &c. was, that they did walk with God by the teaching of God, so is ours: that is not to limit Christ to Adam, Noah, Abraham, Moses, David, John and the Disciples. As they were not to tie God to any things before them recorded, but each of them had a new record; so are not we to limit God in the general records of those paths, but wait upon

---

[1] Here and in number 4 below, the second sentence appears to be Edwards' rebuttal of the opinion in question.

him in the enlargement of the Gospel what he will record you; and far be it from me to conclude either in doctrine or practice, that half of his glory is revealed as yet: As that I should enclose Christ in such a small compass as we have recorded: though I rejoice to understand it in the searching thereof, yet pressing toward the mark for the price of the high calling of God, waiting what he will record in my heart, and in that measure worship him in spirit and truth from the teaching of the spirit.

5. That the holy writings and sayings of Moses and the Prophets, of Christ and his Apostles, and the proper names, persons and things contained therein are allegories, and these allegories are the mystery and spiritual meaning of them.

6. That the penmen of Scripture, every one of them, writ as themselves conceived, they were the actions of their own spirit; and for what is said they were moved by the holy Ghost, that was no other spirit than that which moved them to write and speak other things, for in him we live and move and have our being.

7. That the Scriptures of the Old Testament do not concern nor bind Christians now under the New Testament: so that when places of Scripture are brought out of the Old Testament to prove points, many sectaries make slight of them, and say, Give us a text out of the New, we are ignorant of the Old; and hereupon some of them do not bind the Old Testament with the New, nor read it.

8. That right reason is the rule of faith, and that we are to believe the Scriptures, and the doctrine of the Trinity, Incarnation, Resurrection, so far as we see them agreeable to reason, and no farther.

9. That the New Testament, nor no place of Scripture in it, binds any further than the spirit for present reveals to us that such a place is the Word of God.

10. To read Scripture in English to a mixed congregation without present expounding it, is dangerous, and worse than to read it in Latin; for in Latin, as it doth no good, so it doth no harm.

OF GOD

11. That God hath a hand in, and is the author of, the sinfulness of his people; that he is the author not of those actions alone, in and with which sin is, but of the very pravity, ataxy, anomie, irregularity and sinfulness itself which is in them.[1]

12. That all lies come forth from out of the mouth of God.

13. 'Tis the will and command of God, that since the coming of his Son the Lord Jesus, a permission of the most Paganish, Jewish, Turkish, or Antichristian consciences and worships be granted to all men in all nations and countries: and they are only to be fought against with the sword of God's spirit, the word of God; and for the Parliament to use any civil coercive means to compel men of different judgment, is one of the greatest sins that can be named, 'tis committing a greater rape, than if they had forced or ravished the bodies of all the women in the world. Yea, if it be men's consciences, the Magistrate may not punish for blasphemies, nor for denying the Scriptures, nor for denying there is a God.

14. That no man was cast into Hell for any sin, but only because God would have it so.

15. That man had life before God breathed into him, and that which God breathed into him was part of the divine essence, and shall return into God again.

16. That we should think of ourselves no better than was meet, for God loves the creatures that creep upon the ground as well as the best Saints;[2] and there's no distance between the flesh of a man, and the flesh of a toad.

---

[1] *pravity* depravity, moral corruption (*OED*); *ataxy* want of order or discipline (*OED*); *anomie* disregard of divine law (*OED* anomy).

[2] *Saints* not traditional saints, but the living Saints: another term for the Godly, the religious Independents.

17. That the prince of the air that rules in the children of disobedience is God;[1] and that there is no other spirit but one, which spirit is God.

18. That God hath not decreed all the actions of men, because men doing what God decreed, do not sin.

19. That God was never angry nor displeased with man; for if he were ever displeased and pleased again, then there is a changeableness in God.

20. That God loved not one man more than another before the world, neither is there an absolute particular election, but only general and conditional upon perseverance; and the Scripture nowhere speaks of reprobates or reprobation.

21. That the soul dies with the body, and all things shall have an end, but God only shall remain forever.

22. Every creature in the first estate of creation was God, and every creature is God, every creature that hath life and breath being an efflux from God,[2] and shall return into God again, be swallowed up in him as a drop is in the ocean.

23. That to a saving knowledge of God, it sufficeth not to know him in the book of nature; nor secondly as revealed in the holy Scriptures, but that we must know him as abstract from his mercies and all his attributes.

24. That in the unity of the God-head there is not a trinity of persons, but the Doctrine of the Trinity believed and professed in the Church of God, is a popish tradition and a doctrine of Rome.

25. There are not three distinct persons in the divine essence, but only three offices; the Father, Son and holy Ghost are not three persons, but offices.

26. That there is but one person in the divine nature.

OF CHRIST

27. That Jesus Christ is not very God, not God essentially, but nominally, not the eternal Son of God by eternal generation, no otherwise may he be called the Son of God but as he was man.

28. That Christ's human nature is defiled with original sin as well as ours, Christ had from the birth to his death the same original corruption as ours, he took our sin into his nature as well as our flesh upon him: Christ is not of a holier nature than we; but in this appears God's love to us, that he will take one of us in the same condition, to convince us of what he is to us, and hath made us to be in him: methinks the beholding of Christ to be holy in the flesh is a dishonour to God, in that we should conceive holiness out of God, and again a discomfort to the Saints, that he should be of a more holy nature than they, as being no ground for them to come near with boldness to God.

29. That we did look for great matters from one crucified at Jerusalem 16 hundred years ago, but that does us no good, it must be a Christ formed in us, the deity united to our humanity, Christ came into the world to live thirty two years, and to do nothing else that he knew, and blessed God he never trusted in a crucified Christ.

30. Christ was true man when he created us: yea from eternity, and though he had not flesh, yet was he very man without flesh.

31. That Christ died for all men alike, for the reprobate as well as for the elect, and that not only sufficiently, but effectually, for Judas as well as Peter, for the damned in Hell as well as the saints in Heaven.

32. That by Christ's death, all the sins of all the men in the world, Turks, pagans, as well as Christians committed against the moral law and first Covenant, are actually pardoned and forgiven, and this is the everlasting Gospel.

---

[1] See Ephesians 2:2.

[2] *efflux* a flowing outward (*OED*).

33. That Christ did only satisfy for the sins against the first Covenant, but not for the sins against the second Covenant, as unbelief, he died not for the unbelief of any.

34. Christ died only for sins past, i.e. before the Gospel is revealed to the sinner, and the sins of men committed after conversion Christ died not for, but they are pardoned by his being a continual sacrifice.

35. Every man satisfies for himself for the sins against the second Covenant, namely unbelief: because he that believes not, the wrath of God abides upon him; so that for a year's unbelief a man bears a year's wrath, and this is all the satisfaction God requires.

36. That no man shall perish or go to Hell for any sin but unbelief only.

37. That the heathen who never heard of Christ by the word, have the Gospel, for every creature, as the sun, moon and stars preach the Gospel to men, and in them is revealed the knowledge of Christ crucified, and sin pardoned, if they had eyes to see it.

38. Those heathen that perish, do perish only for not believing according to the Gospel they enjoy.

39. Christ did not by his death purchase life and salvation for all, no nor for the elect: For it was not the end of God in the coming of Christ to purchase love and life; but Christ himself was purchased by love, that he might make out love and purchase us to love. For Christ came not to reconcile God to man, but man to God, for though Christ doth hold forth love and life, yet he did not purchase it, but was purchased by it.

40. Christ Jesus came into the world to witness and declare the love of God to us, not to procure it for us, or to satisfy God (as some say,) Christ was a most glorious publisher of the Gospel, he was sent to preach the Gospel, to heal the broken hearted, to preach deliverance to the captives: in all that Christ saith to be the end of his coming, is not a word mentioned of anything done by him in way of satisfying God. Christ's coming was more like a conqueror to destroy the enmity in our nature, and so to convince us of the love of God to us, by destroying in our nature that which we thought stood between God and us.

41. That the unction which the saints are said to receive from the holy One, 1 John 2:20, is one with the Christ-hood of Christ.

42. That Christ was a legal preacher, for till after his ascension the Gospel was not preached; Christ lived in a dark time, and so he preached the Law, but afterward then the Gospel came to be preached.

43. That Christ shall come and live again upon the earth, and for a thousand years reign visibly as an earthly monarch over all the world, in outward glory and pomp, putting down all monarchy and empires.

44. That when Christ in his own person hath subdued the disobedient nations, then the Church of the Jews and Gentiles shall live without any disturbance, from within or without it: all Christians shall live without sin, without the Word, sacraments or any ordinance, they shall pass those thousand years in worldly delights, begetting many children, eating and drinking, and enjoying all lawful pleasures which all the creatures then redeemed from their ancient slavery can afford.

45. That men may be saved without Christ, and the very heathens are saved, if they serve God according to the knowledge God hath given them, though they never heard of Christ.

46. That the least truth is of more worth than Jesus Christ himself.

47. Christ by his death hath freed all men from a temporal death which Adam's sin only deserved, by purchasing them a resurrection, and hath opened them a way to come to the Father if they will: thus far he died for all, no farther for any.

Of the Spirit of God, and of Sanctification

48. The Spirit of God dwells not, nor works in any: it is but our conceits and mistakes to think so, 'tis no spirit that works but our own.

49. That the same spirit which works in the children of disobedience is that spirit which sanctifies the hearts of the elect.

50. That there is a perfect way in this life, not by Word, sacraments, prayer and other ordinances, but by the experience of the spirit in a man's self.

51. That a man baptized with the holy Ghost, knows all things even as God knows all things, which point is a deep mystery and great ocean, where there is no casting anchor, nor sounding the bottom.

52. That if a man by the spirit knew himself to be in the state of grace, though he did commit murder or drunkenness, God did see no sin in him.

53. That sanctification is not an evidence of justification, and all notes and signs of a Christian's estate are legal and unlawful.[1]

54. Believers have no inherent sanctification, nor spiritual habits of grace infused into their hearts, but all their sanctification is that which is inherent in Christ, and they for this and no other cause, are said in Scripture phrase to be sanctified, but because of Christ's sanctification and inherent holiness.

Of Adam and Mankind

55. Though Adam had continued in his estate of innocency, and not fallen, yet he had died a natural death, for death now is not a fruit of sin to believers.

56. God's image on man, is only our face and countenance; and every wicked man hath therefore God's image as well as good men.

57. That Adam, and so mankind in him, lost not the image of God by his fall, only incurred a tempo-ral or corporal death, which was suspended for a time upon the promise of a Saviour.

58. There is no original sin in us, only Adam's first sin was original sin.

59. That the guilt of Adam's sin is imputed to no man, no man is punished for Adam's sin.

60. That one man is no more spiritual than another, nor is there any such inward difference between man and man; but all the spiritualness and difference lies without us in the word, which guides some men, and not others.

61. That all men who have the Gospel preached to them, and so manifested to their understandings, are immediately without any more ado able of themselves to believe and receive Christ.

62. There is no free-will in man either to good or evil, either in his natural estate or glorified estate.

63. That there is a power in man to resist grace, and that the grace which would convert one man, would not convert another.

64. Natural men may do such things as whereunto God hath by way of promise annexed grace and acceptation, and that if men improve their natural abilities to the utmost in seeking grace, they shall find it.

65. That regenerate men who have true grace, may fall totally and finally away from the state of grace.

Of the Moral Law, Justification, Faith, Repentance, Good Works

66. That the moral law is of no use at all to believers, that 'tis no rule for believers to walk by, nor to examine their lives by, and that Christians are freed from the mandatory power of the law.

67. Persons justified, are not justified by faith, but are justified from all eternity.

68. Neither faith, nor repentance, nor humiliation, nor self-denial, nor use of ordinances, nor doing as one would be done to, are duties required

---

[1] *legal* probably legalistic, a term applied to the doctrine of justification by works (*OED* legalism, legalist).

of Christians, or such things as they must exercise themselves in, or they can have no part in Christ.

69. True faith is without all doubts of salvation, and if any man have doubts of his salvation, his faith is to be noted with a black mark.

70. That to *credere* [believe], faith in a proper sense is imputed to justification, and not Christ's righteousness imputed to justification.

71. That the doctrine of repentance is a soul-destroying doctrine.

72. In the old Covenant (that is before Christ came in the flesh) in the Prophets' days, repentance is declared as a means to obtain remission, and neither remission nor the knowledge of remission to go before, but to follow contrition; but this is not the Gospel which is established upon better promises.

73. That 'tis as possible for Christ himself to sin, as for a child of God to sin.

74. That there ought to be no fasting days under the Gospel and that men ought not to afflict their souls, no not in a day of humiliation.

75. That God doth not chastise any of his children for sin, and let believers sin as fast as they can, there is a fountain open for them to wash in, and that not for the sins of God's people, but for swearers and drunkards the land is punished.

76. That believers have nothing to do to take care, or to look to themselves to keep from sin, God must look to them, if he will.

77. God loves his children as well sinning, as praying, hearing and doing the holiest duties, he accounts of them never the better for their good works, nor never the worse for their ill works.

78. That God's children are not at all to be humbled, troubled or grieved for sin after conversion, and what Peter did in this kind after his foul fact of denying his Master, issued from the weakness of his faith.

79. That God's children are not to ask the pardon and forgiveness of their sins, they need not,

they ought not, and 'tis no less than blasphemy for a child of God to ask pardon of sins, 'tis infidelity to ask pardon of sins, and David's asking forgiveness of sin was his weakness.

80. That when Abraham denied his wife, and in outward appearance seemed to lie in his distrust, lying, dissembling and equivocating that his wife was his sister, even then truly all his thoughts, words and deeds were perfectly holy and righteous from all spot of sin in the sight of God freely.

81. The called of God have sin in the flesh, they have sin in the conversation, but they have no sin, neither can they have any in the conscience, for the true faith of God's elect, and sin in the conscience, can no more stand together than light and darkness, and this reconciles those two Scriptures, *if we say we have no sin, we deceive ourselves* [1 John 1:8], and *he that is born of God doth not commit sin, neither can he, because he is born of God* [1 John 3:9].

82. The great Antichrist is that mystical body of iniquity which opposeth Jesus Christ, and not the Pope of Rome, or any particular succession of men, only he is a part of Antichrist. Denn makes the opposition of Antinomian errors to be the man of sin and the great Antichrist, as is to be seen in several pages of his *Man of Sin Discovered*.[1] And sectaries make them who deny Christ's dying for all, to be Antichrist: others make Antichristianism to consist in the coercive power of the Magistrate in matters of religion.

Of Man after this Life; of the Soul; Resurrection from the Dead; Heaven and Hell

83. That the soul of man is mortal as the soul of a beast, and dies with the body.

84. That the souls of the faithful after death, do sleep till the day of judgment, and are not in a

---

[1] Henry Denne, *The Man of Sin Discovered* (1645). Antinomianism was the belief that divine grace freed true believers from the need to observe any moral law.

capacity of acting anything for God, but 'tis with them as 'tis with a man that is in some pleasing dream.[1]

85. That the bodies of the faithful shall not rise again at the Resurrection (namely the same that died) but their souls shall have other bodies made fit for them, either by creation or faction from some pre-existing matter, and though the bodies be new, yet the men are the same, because the same souls remain still.

86. Infants rise not again, because they are not capable of knowing God, and therefore not of enjoying him.

87. That the perfection and resurrection spoken of by Paul, 1 Cor. 15:51, 52, 53, 54, 55, 56, 57, the hope set before us, the eternal inheritance, a city having foundations, whose builder and maker is God, are to be attained in the fullness and perfection of them now in this present time before the common death of the body.

88. That none of the souls of the Saints go to Heaven where Christ is, but Heaven is empty of the Saints till the resurrection of the dead.

89. There is no resurrection at all of the bodies of men after this life, nor no Heaven nor Hell after this life, nor no devils.

90. There shall be in the last day a resurrection from the dead of all the brute creatures, all beasts and birds that ever lived upon the earth, every individual of every kind of them that died shall rise again, as well as of men, and all these creatures shall live for ever upon the earth.

91. There is no Hell, but in this life, and that's the legal terrors and fears which men have in their consciences.

---

[1] The entries on the mortality of the soul probably refer to Richard Overton, *Mans Mortallitie* (1643, 1644). This pamphlet was named, along with Milton's *Doctrine and Discipline of Divorce* (1643), as the subject of a Parliamentary inquiry. Sir Thomas Browne discusses "mortalism" in *Religio Medici* as one of the ancient heresies with which he sympathized.

OF THE CHURCH, GOSPEL, MINISTRY AND SACRAMENTS

92. That there is no Church of Christ upon the earth, no true ministry, no sacraments, no Gospel, no faith, because there are no visible nor infallible gifts.

93. No man is damned but for rejecting the Gospel, and none can reject the Gospel, but those who have it tendered unto them, as they had it in the Apostles' days being confirmed by miracles.

94. That the pure preaching of the Word, and right administration of the sacraments, are no notes nor signs of a true visible Church.

95. 'Tis the will of God that miracles should attend the ministry, the Apostles make a marriage of doctrine and miracles, so that they who preach the Gospel, must be so gifted as to confirm it by signs and wonders.

96. That many Christians in these days have more knowledge than the Apostles, and when the time is come that there shall be true churches and ministry erected, they shall have greater gifts, and do greater miracles than the Apostles ever did, because the Christian Church was but then in its infancy.

97. That there ought to be in these times no making or building of churches, nor use of church ordinances, as ministering of the Word, sacraments, but waiting for a church, being in readiness upon all occasions to take knowledge of any passenger, of any opinion or tenet whatsoever, the Saints as pilgrims do wander as in a temple of smoke, not able to find religion, and therefore should not plant it by gathering or building a pretended supposed house, but should wait for the coming of the Spirit, as the Apostles did.

98. There is a salvation that shall be revealed in the last times, which was not known to the Apostles themselves.

99. That within a while God will raise up Apostles, men extraordinarily endowed with visible and infallible gifts to preach the Gospel, and that shall precede the fall of Rome.

100. That in points of religion, even in the articles of faith, and principles of religion, there's nothing certainly to be believed and built on, only that all men ought to have liberty of conscience, and liberty of prophesying.

101. That the Scriptures nowhere speak of sacraments, name or thing.

102. That the covenant whereof circumcision was the seal, was only of temporal promises, as e.g. of the land of Canaan; that the covenant God made with Abraham, had nothing spiritual in it; and that circumcision was a seal of the righteousness of faith to no other but to Abraham alone *quatenus* [in so far as] a father, and not to his children.

103. That baptism is not a seal nor sign of the covenant of grace.

104. That paedobaptism is unlawful and antichristian, and that 'tis as lawful to baptize a cat, or a dog or a chicken, as to baptize the infants of believers.

105. 'Tis as lawful to break any of the Ten Commandments, as to baptize an infant: yea, 'tis as lawful to commit adultery and murder, as to baptize a child.

106. That baptizing belongs not to ministers only, all gifted brethren and preaching disciples (though no ministers) may baptize.

107. Baptizedness is not essential to the baptizer, nor essential to preaching; so that persons, not only not in office, but not so much as baptized, may both baptize and preach.

108. Miracles are essential to the administration holden forth in the commission of baptism, Matthew 28:19.

109. That none are to be admitted to the Lord's Supper, though believers and Saints, nor their children to be baptized, but only they who are members in a church-way.

110. There is no Scripture against a man's being often baptized; neither is it more unlawful to be baptized often, than to receive the Lord's Supper often.

111. That Christ's words in the institution of his Supper, *This is my body*, and *This is my blood*, are to be understood literally.[1]

112. That Christians in receiving the Lord's Supper should receive with their hats on, with their heads covered, but the ministers should administer it with their hats off, uncovered.

113. That 'tis as necessary to be joined in church fellowship, as with Christ the head; and there's such a necessity of entering into a church-way, as there is no expectation of salvation without it.

114. That the Church of England and the ministry thereof is antichristian, yea of the devil, and that 'tis absolutely sinful and unlawful to hear any of their ministers preach in their assemblies.

115. That the Church of Rome was once a true church, but so was the Church of England never, therefore 'tis likelier the Church of Rome should be in the right in the doctrines of free-will, universal redemption, original sin, &c. than the Church of England.

116. That the calling and making of ministers of the Word and sacraments are not *jure Divino* [by divine right], but a minister comes to be so, as a merchant, bookseller, tailor, and such like.

117. That all settled certain maintenance for ministers of the Gospel, especially that which is called tithes, is unlawful, Jewish and antichristian.

118. That ministers of the Gospel in these days ought to work with their hands, and to follow some calling, that they may not be chargeable to the Church.

---

[1] Matthew 26:26–28; Mark 14:22–24; Luke 22:19–20.

119. That there ought to be no distinct order of ministers, nor such calling of some persons distinct and separated from the people, but that all men who have gifts are in their turns and courses, by the appointment of the rest of the company, to preach, pray, baptize, and they are for that turn instead of ministers, and as ministers.

Of Preaching and Hearing, of Praying, Singing of Psalms, of the Christian Sabbath or Lord's-day

120. That all days are alike to Christians under the New Testament, and they are bound no more to the observation of the Lord's day, or first day of the week than to any other.

121. That the Jewish Sabbath or Saturday is still to be kept by Christians for their Sabbath.

122. That Christians are not bound to meet one day in seven constantly, according to the manner of the nations, nor to pray and preach thus long, and in this manner two or three hours, according to the custom of the nations.

123. No man hath more to do to preach the Gospel than another, but every man may preach the Gospel, as well as any.

124. That 'tis lawful for women to preach, and why should they not, having gifts as well as men? and some of them do actually preach, having great resort to them.[1]

125. 'Tis a part of the Christian liberty of Christians, not to hear their own ministers, but to go and hear where they will, and whom they think they may profit most by.

126. That 'tis unlawful to worship God in places consecrated, and in places where superstition and idolatry have been practised, as in our churches.

127. That men ought to preach and exercise their gifts without study and premeditation, and not to think of what they are to say till they speak, because it shall be given them in that hour, and the Spirit shall teach them.

128. That there is no need of human learning, nor of reading authors for preachers, but all books and learning must go down, it comes from the want of the Spirit, that men write such great volumes, and make such ado of learning.

129. There are some women, ten or eleven in one town or vicinity, who hold it unlawful to hear any man preach, either publicly or privately, because they must not be like those women in [1] Timothy [2:11], ever learning, and never coming to the knowledge of the truth.

130. That 'tis unlawful to preach at all, sent or not sent out (as in a Church-state) but only thus, a man may preach as a waiting disciple, that is, Christians may not preach in a way of positive asserting and declaring things, but all they may do, is to confer, reason together, and dispute out things.

131. That 'tis unlawful for the Saints to join in receiving the Lord's Supper, where any wicked men are present, and that such mixed Communion doth pollute and defile them.

132. 'Tis unlawful for the Saints to join in prayer where wicked men are, or to pray with any of the wicked.

133. That 'tis unlawful for Christians to pray so much as privately with those (though godly) that are not members of a true church, but are members of the Church of England, and the assemblies thereof.

134. That how ever conference and discourse may be had with all, yet 'tis not lawful to join in prayer or giving of thanks, no not before meat, with those (though otherwise acknowledged Saints and godly, and are members of churches in the church-way) that are not of the same judgment and way.

135. That 'tis unlawful for Christians to pray at all with any others (either as being the mouth in prayer, or as joining in prayer), though never so

---

[1] Again, the second sentence is Edwards' outraged comment on the practical consequences of this opinion.

godly, and of their own judgments, either in the public assemblies, or in their families, unless such persons who prayed had an infallible spirit, as the Apostles.

136. That Christians are not bound to pray constantly every day at set times, as morning and evening, but only at such times as the Spirit moves them to it, and if they find not themselves so moved in many days and weeks together, they ought not to pray.

137. That wicked and unregenerate men ought not to pray to God at all.

138. That all singing of psalms, as David's, or any other holy songs of Scripture, is unlawful, and not to be joined with.

139. That the singing which Christians should use, is that of hymns and spiritual songs, framed by themselves, composed by their own gifts, and that upon special occasions, as deliverances, &c. sung in the congregation by one of the assembly, all the rest being silent.

140. That love-feasts, or feasts of love (with which the Lord's Supper is to be administered also) is a perpetual ordinance of Christ, at which only church-members are to be present, and to partake.

Of Church Government

141. That there is no distinction concerning government of ecclesiastical and civil, for all that government which concerns the church, ought to be civil, but the maintaining of that distinction is for maintaining the interests of church-men.

142. That a few private Christians, as six or seven gathering themselves into a covenant and church-fellowship, have an absolute entire power of the keys,[1] and all government within themselves, and are not under any authoritative power of any clas-ses, synods, or general councils, whatsoever they do, or what ways soever they take.

143. That the Presbytery and Presbyterial government, are the false prophet, and the beast spoken of in the Revelations: Presbytery is a third part of the city of Rome, yea that beast, in Revelation 11[:7] that ascends, and shall kill the two witnesses, namely the Independents.

Of Revelations and Miracles

144. That there are revelations and visions in these times, yea to some they are more ordinary, and shall be to the people of God generally within a while.

145. That the gift of miracles is not ceased in these times, but that some of the sectaries have wrought miracles, and miracles have accompanied them in their baptism, &c. and the people of God shall have power of miracles shortly.

146. That anointing the sick with oil by the elders praying over them, with laying on of hands, is a church-ordinance for church members that are sick, for their recovery.

147. 'Tis ordinary for Christians now in these days, with Paul to be rapt up to the third Heavens [11 Corinthians 12:2], and to hear words unutterable, and they cannot well have assurance of being Christians, that have not found and had experience of this.

Of the Civil Magistrate

148. That Christian magistrates have no power at all to meddle in matters of religion, or things ecclesiastical, but in civil only concerning the bodies and goods of men.

149. That for a people to wait upon man for a form to worship God by, was idolatry: Nay, for a people to wait upon Parliament or assembly for a

---

[1] *the keys*   perhaps the keys of the kingdom of Heaven (Matthew 16:19), but more likely Edwards is referring to the practical issue of his opponents' claim to be independent of any higher church authority.

form to worship God by, was worse than corporal idolatry.[1]

150. Whatsoever errors or miscarriages in religion the church should bear withal in men, continuing them still in communion with them, as brethren, these the magistrates should bear with in men, continuing them in the Kingdom or Commonwealth in the enjoyment of the liberty of subjects.

151. That the Parliament having their power from, and being entrusted by the people, the people may call them to an account for their actions, and let them right and straight: and seeing this present Parliament doth engross law-making and also law-executing into their own hands, contrary both to reason, and the true meaning of the law, the freemen of England ought not only to choose new members where they are wanting once every year, but also to renew and enquire once a year after the behaviour and carriage of those they have chosen. And if they find they never did any good, or are groundedly suspected to be unserviceable, that then those that choose and sent them may have liberty to choose more faithful, able, and better men in their places.

152. If God command such a thing to be done in his word, and the magistrate now come and command the same to be done, though a Christian ought to have, and would have done it, because of God's command, yet now he ought not to do it, because the magistrate commands it.

153. All the earth is the Saints', and there ought to be a community of goods, and the Saints should share in the lands and estates of gentlemen, and rich men.

Of Marriage and of Parents and Children

154. That 'tis lawful for a man to put away his wife upon indisposition, unfitness, or contrariety of mind arising from a cause in nature unchangeable;[2] and for disproportion and deadness of spirit, or something distasteful and averse in the immutable bent of nature; and man in regard of the freedom and eminency of his creation, is a law to himself in this matter, being head of the other sex, which was made for him, neither need he hear any judge therein above himself.

155. 'Tis lawful for one man to have two wives at once.

156. That children are not bound to obey their parents at all, if they be ungodly.

157. That parents are not to catechise their little children, nor to set them to read the Scripture, or to teach them to pray, but must let them alone for God to teach them.

Of War, and of Fighting and Killing

158. 'Tis unlawful for Christians to defend religion with the sword, or to fight for it when men come with the sword to take it away, religion will defend itself.

159. 'Tis unlawful for Christians to fight, and take up arms for their laws and civil liberties.

160. 'Tis unlawful to fight at all, or to kill any man, yea to kill any of the creatures for our use, as a chicken, or on any other occasion.

[Additional Subjects]

161. That using of set forms of prayer prescribed is idolatry.

162. David's saying, *I am a worm, and no man* [Psalm 22:6] must be understood literally: yea, he was both a man, and no man in the same literal sense.

163. That the Scripture speaks but of one kind of faith.

---

[1] referring to the Presbyterian *Directory of Public Worship* (1645) published by the Westminster Assembly of Divines.

[2] A marginal note indicates that Edwards is referring to arguments made by Milton in his *Doctrine and Discipline of Divorce* (1643).

164. Some of the sectaries in London do hold, that in Suffolk there is a prophet raised up to come and preach the everlasting Gospel to them, and he stays but for a vocal call from Heaven to send him, which is expected daily, and that this man is that prophet spoken of in the Scripture, 1 John 25; that prophet in that Scripture, distinguished from Christ and Elias, is this man raised up in Suffolk.

165. That it could not stand with the goodness of God, to damn his own creatures eternally.

166. That God the Father did reign under the law, God the Son under the Gospel, and now God the Father and God the Son are making over the Kingdom to God the holy Ghost, and he shall reign and be poured out upon all flesh.

167. That there shall be a general restoration, wherein all men shall be reconciled to God and saved, only those who now believe and are Saints before this restoration shall be in a higher condition than those that do not believe.

168. That 'tis not lawful for a Christian to be a magistrate, but upon turning Christian he should lay down his magistracy; neither do we read after Cornelius was baptized (though he were a Centurion before, and a man in command and authority) that ever he meddled any more with his band *called the Italian band* [Acts 10:1].

169. Man lost no more by the fall, than all the rest of the whole creation fell into with Adam, all the world being condemned to death and desolation, yea the heavens and the earth also: so that you may as safely conclude that all the whole creation lost life and salvation to glorification by Adam's transgression, as to conclude that man lost salvation by Adam's transgression.

170. Man hath not by Christ brought unto him eternal life and salvation, but only such a life as all the whole creation hath together with him, for the second Adam hath not purchased eternal life to glorification for man.

171. All the creatures shall assuredly partake of the Gospel of peace, and that our Lord the great Prophet spake something to this purpose, when he saith, Go preach the gospel to every creature, though they cannot hear to life and glorification; and Christ is the great prophet of his Father, to declare his Father's counsel to the whole creation, and he is the great High Priest, which offereth up himself a sacrifice of full satisfaction, not for all men only, but for all that by man was lost, even the whole creation of God.

172. That a Directory,[1] or order to help in the way of worship, is a breach of the second Commandment, and there is no word of God to warrant the making of that Directory book, more than Jeroboam had for the making of calves of gold, which he set upon two high places, one at Dan, the other at Bethel, to the confusion of himself and his posterity [1 Kings 12:28-30].

173. No man is yet in Hell, neither shall any be there until the judgment; for God doth not hang first, and judge after.

174. Men say that faith is supernatural, but how can it be above nature to believe that which we see sufficient ground to believe; and to believe anything of which we have no plain ground and reason, is so far from being above nature, that it is below it, and proper to fools and not to reasonable men.

175. The Law doth not pronounce eternal death in hell-fire on those that obey it not, nor were men to have perished in hell-fire in relation to the law or Adam's sin, but the Gospel pronounceth eternal death in hell-fire on those that obey it not; and if we had been to suffer Hell in relation to Adam or the Law, then Christ also should have suffered in Hell for us, to have redeemed us from thence, which he did not.

176. It is not suitable to God, to pick and choose amongst men in showing mercy; if the love of God

---

[1] another reference to the *Directory of Public Worship* (1645).

be manifested to a few, it is far from being infinite; if God show not mercy to all, to ascribe it to his will or pleasure, is to blaspheme his excellent name and nature.

Now unto these many more might be added that I know of, and are commonly known to others, which have been preached and printed within these four last years in England (as the necessity of dipping and burying underwater all persons to be baptized, and the necessity of a church covenant, as that ministers may not lawfully baptize, or administer the Lord's Supper out of their own particular congregations, neither preach ministerially, but as gifted brethren, out of their own church, with many such errors of the church way) but because they are but light in comparison, I will not name them.

I could relate also to you other errors, that have been reported to me and others by honest understanding men, to have been vented (and 'tis likely enough they may be true) as that 'tis lawful for wives to give without their husbands' consents something out of their husbands' estates, for the maintenance of the Church and ministers whereunto they belong: as that the Lord's Prayer, called and cried up by many to be so, it could not be the Lord's Prayer in regard there was a petition for pardon of sins, which Christ would not have taught, or words to that purpose; as also that if a man were strongly moved by the spirit to kill, to commit adultery, &c. and upon praying against it again and again it continued, and yet was still strongly pressed, he should then do it; but because I have not these upon so good grounds, nor such a concurrence of circumstances, or further confirmation upon enquiry, I therefore forbear to put them down particularly in the catalogue of errors, or to assert them with that authority.

—1646

King Charles I
1600 – 1649

In the summer of 1637, King Charles I and William Laud, the Archbishop of Canterbury, attempted to introduce a revised Prayer Book for use in the Church of Scotland. Many Scots, however, failed to see why an English desire for uniformity of worship meant that they were the ones who needed to change. The new liturgy subsequently became a focus for discontent, a symbol of a royal policy that had imposed numerous administrative, legal, and religious changes on Scotland over the previous decades. Well-planned riots greeted readings of the new service, followed over the next two years by the chain of events that comprise what is often called the Scottish Revolution. In February 1638, the Scots drafted the National Covenant, vowing to withstand innovations and maintain the Presbyterian cause. Charles tried to subdue the Covenanters by force, but a series of compromises and English humiliations culminated in the Scottish occupation of Newcastle upon Tyne in the summer of 1640. These two "Bishops' Wars" (1639–40) played a significant role in the buildup to the civil wars that would soon engulf all three nations Charles ruled.

The following royal proclamation was written in response to a widely circulated Scottish pamphlet, *An Information to All Good Christians within the Kingdom of England* (Edinburgh, 1639), in which the Covenanter leaders blamed the troubles on the "popishly affected" English bishops and appealed to an English Parliament to judge their case. Realizing that the Scots had gone over his head by using the press to present their side of events to an English audience, Charles responded in kind by printing ten thousand copies of this proclamation and ordering it to be read in every church in the kingdom. The ensuing paper skirmishes between King and Covenanter set the pattern for the subsequent pamphlet warfare between King and Parliament: while both sides continued the formality of addressing their texts to one another, their primary audience was the public, an entity increasingly recognized as one that could be addressed in print.

৩৩৩

A Proclamation and Declaration to Inform Our Loving Subjects of Our Kingdom of England of the Seditious Practices of Some in Scotland, Seeking to Overthrow Our Regal Power under False Pretences of Religion

Whereas we have endeavoured now for a long time together by all calm and fair ways to appease the disorders and tumultuous carriages caused by some evil affected persons in our realm of Scotland, but hitherto all in vain, we have now thought it not only fit, but necessary in general to inform all our loving subjects in this our realm of England, what the truth is of our proceedings, what our leniency and gentleness hath been towards them, and what froward and perverse returns they have made to us, notwithstanding all their specious pretences, the better to insinuate themselves and their odious cause into the minds of our loyal subjects here. These disorders and tumults have been thus raised in Scotland, and fomented by factious spirits, and those traitorously affected, begun upon pretences of religion, the common cloak for all disobedience; but now it clearly appears, the aim of these men is not religion (as they falsely pretend and publish) but it is to shake off all monarchical government, and to vilify our regal power justly descended upon us over them: Nay their malice reaches so far, both against our power and person, as that in a most cunning and subtle way they have endeavoured to poison the hearts of our good and loyal subjects of this our kingdom, and to seduce them (were it in their power) to the like rebellious courses with themselves: Now though we are most confident of our people's affections towards us (of which they have given us clear testimony by their ready and cheerful assistance in this cause) and have not the least thought that those turbulent spirits shall any way prevail with them; yet we cannot but hold it requisite to give them timely notice of their traitorous intentions, which very many ways appears unto us.

As first, by the multitude of their printed pamphlets, or rather indeed infamous libels, stuffed full of calumnies against our regal authority, and our most just proceedings, and spreading of them in divers parts of this our kingdom.

Secondly, by their sending of letters to private persons, to incite them against us, and sending of some of their fellow-Covenanters to be at private meetings in London, and elsewhere, to pervert our good people from their duty; and some of these meetings we know, and some of those letters (lewd enough) we have seen.

Thirdly, by their public contemning of all our just commands, and their mutinous protesting against them, a course not fit to be endured in any well ordered kingdom.

Fourthly, by their rejecting of the Covenant commanded by our authority, because it was commanded by us, whereas no Covenant or band of that nature in that kingdom hath ever been or can be legal and warrantable, which hath not been commanded, or at least assented unto by royal authority... : By which Covenant of theirs, they have treacherously induced many of our people to swear to a band against us; which band and Covenant (or rather conspiracy) of theirs, could not be with God, being against us the Lord's anointed over them: But it was and is a band and Covenant pretended to be with God, that they may with the better countenance do the works of the devil; such as all treasons and rebellions are.

And lastly, by their most hostile preparations in all kinds, as if we were not their King, but their sworn enemy: For what can their intentions be, being thus prepared, but to invade this Kingdom, should they not find us ready, both to resist their force and to curb their insolences: For many, and some of the chiefest among them, are men, not only of unquiet spirits, but of broken fortunes, and would be very glad of any occasion (especially under the colour of religion) to make them whole upon the lands and goods of our subjects in England, who we presume (besides their allegiance to us) will look better to themselves and their estates, than to share them with such desperate hypocrites, who seek to be better, and cannot well be worse. We demand again, what intentions else they can have; for we have already often assured them by our published proclamations, that we are so far from thinking of any innovation or alteration of religion, that we are resolved to maintain the same constantly, and as it is established by law in that our Kingdom; nay, so desirous have we been to give content unto them, as that we have in a manner condescended to all which they petitioned for; nay, our princely clemency in these produced no better effect, than increasing and daring insolences, to our dishonour both at home and abroad: Yet we passed by all till they struck at the very root of kingly government; for they have now assumed to themselves regal power; for whereas the print is the king's in all kingdoms, these seditious men have taken upon them to print what they please, though we forbid it, and to prohibit what they dislike, though we command it; and with the greater affront have forbid and dismissed the printer whom we established: Besides, they have taken upon them to convene our subjects, raise armies, block up and besiege our castles, to lay impositions and taxes upon our people, threatening such as continue in loyalty to us, with force and violence. To this we shall add that they have slighted the directions and power of our council table in that kingdom, and have set up tables of their own, at which, some of their leaders sit under the name of committees from the late pretended General Assembly or their deputies. And thus they meet when and where they please, treat and conclude what they please, and send their edicts through all parts of the kingdom without any consent, nay without all knowledge of us, our commissioner, or council, and directly contrary to many standing laws at this day in force in that kingdom, and yet pretend violation of their laws, as one of the main causes of their brain-sick distempers.

Here therefore, we take God and the world to witness, we hold our self forced and constrained to arm, not only to reclaim them, and to set our kingly authority right again in that our ancient and native Kingdom, but also for the safety of this Kingdom, our loyal subjects in it, with their wives, children, and goods, as well as our own, against the rage and fury of these men and their Covenant. And this we think fit to let you further know, that we hope in time to make the best of them see that we will endure no such Covenant and band in our Kingdom, to which we shall not consent: So the question is not now, whether a service book to be received or not; nor whether episcopal government shall be continued, or presbyterial admitted, but whether we are their king or not....

We further give you to understand, that there is a large Declaration coming forth, containing all the particular passages which have occurred in this business from the very beginning,[1] attested with their own foul acts, to disannul and shame their fair, but false words. But because this cannot so soon be made ready, we hold it most expedient to let this short Declaration forerun it, that our loyal subjects here and elsewhere, may not be infected with their false, wicked, specious, but most seditious informations. For example sake in their last pamphlet (beside divers other false, base, and fawning passages) there are these scandalous and most notorious untruths: As first, they say, that we have committed the arms we now take, and the armies we now raise, into the hands of professed papists, which is not more dishonourable to our self, and the noble persons entrusted by us, than odiously and notoriously false. Again they say, that some of power in the hierarchy of England have been the cause of our taking arms to invade our native Kingdom, and of meddling with their religion, whereas it is most certain, that no one of them have done any thing therein, but by our own princely direction and command. And for arms, it is notoriously known to all our council then present, that their counsels were for peace, and have been the persuaders (as much as in them lay) of the undeserved moderation wherewith we have hitherto proceeded towards so great offenders.

And further they say, that they intend no act of hostility against England, unless they shall be necessitated in their own defence. We would fain know, defence of what? Is it of disobedience? Defence against whom? Is it now against us their true and lawful sovereign? If they will defend against us, it ought to be by law, and not by arms: That defence we shall never deny them: This by arms we shall never permit them. Now our laws which they seem so much to value, are in a manner oppressed by them, in so much that our judges are so awed, as that they dare hardly proceed according to law.

With these, and the like mutinous libels, we desire our good subjects should not be infected, but that all of them might know the present necessity we have to arm our self, which is for no other end, save only for the safety and security of this our

---

[1] The folio *A Large Declaration Concerning the Late Tumults in Scotland* (1639) was published under the King's name, but was largely compiled by Walter Balcanquhall.

Kingdom, the reestablishment of our authorities in that, and the suppressing of such as have misled and abused our subjects there, and would (if not prevented) do the like here; but is no way to enforce any innovation of religion established in that Kingdom, or any ways to infringe the laws thereof, or any of their liberties whatsoever, which are according to law.

These are therefore to will and command all our loving subjects of this our Kingdom, that they receive no more of their seditious pamphlets sent from Scotland, or any other place, concerning those affairs, which can have no other use or influence than to draw the hearts of our loyal people to the like rebellious courses. And that such of our subjects here, as have already received any of these rebellious pamphlets, do presently deliver them to the next Justice of Peace, that he may send them to one of our secretaries, as both they and the Justices of Peace will answer it at their uttermost perils.

And our further will and pleasure is, that this our Proclamation and Declaration be read in time of divine service in every church within the Kingdom, that all our people to the meanest, may see the notorious carriages of these men, and likewise the justice and mercy of all our proceedings.

Given at our court at Whitehall the seven and twentieth day of February, in the fourteenth year of our reign of England, Scotland, France, and Ireland.[1]

God save the King.

—1639

---

[1] *France* English monarchs laid claim to the French crown in the fourteenth century, and England held land in France until the loss of Calais in 1558; it was not until the Treaty of Amiens (1802), however, that the English monarchy formally withdrew its long-absurd claim to the French title.

Bathsua Makin

ca. 1600 – ca. 1675

Bathsua Makin was the daughter of the linguist and schoolmaster Henry Reginald. The eminent mathematician John Pell was her brother-in-law.[1] She attended her father's school in the street of St. Mary Axe, not far from London, where she was instructed in classical and modern languages. Makin began her writing career as early as sixteen with the publication of *Musa Virginea* (1616), a collection of Greek, Latin, Hebrew, Spanish, German, French and Italian verse dedicated to James I. The King may have been unimpressed with this display of female erudition, for Makin is probably the "learned maid" referred to in the anecdote noted in John Collet's commonplace book: "When a learned maid was presented to King James for an English rarity, because she could speak and write pure Latin, Greek, and Hebrew, the King asked, 'But can she spin?'"

Bathsua married Richard Makin in the parish of St. Andrew Undershaft on March 5, 1621. She obtained a position at court as the tutor of Princess Elizabeth (1636–1650), the daughter of Charles I. She instructed Elizabeth in Greek, Latin, Hebrew, French, Italian and mathematics. At this time, she corresponded with the renowned Continental scholar Anna Maria van Schurman. When Parliament took Princess Elizabeth into custody in 1642, Makin may have remained her attendant for several years. During the Interregnum, she suffered financial difficulties. Her petition to the Council of State, for the "payment of the arrears of £40 a year granted her for life, for her attendance on the late King's children," was dismissed in 1655. Makin eventually found employment as a tutor in the household of Lucy Hastings, Dowager Countess of Huntingdon. The account books of the Hastings household indicate that she was there employed until October, 1662. Makin wrote three poems for Lucy Hastings, two of which are elegies for the Countess's children.

It has been thought that Makin wrote *An Essay to Revive the Ancient Education of Gentlewomen* (1673) to advertise the school she ran at Tottenham High Cross, a few miles from London. In this treatise the author, as Christine de Pizan had done, produces a catalogue of learned women from biblical and classical sources to demonstrate that the education of women is neither a new nor a dangerous social practice. The standard arguments of those who would "breed women low" are then brought forth in order to be controverted and corrected. The pedagogy of the treatise was greatly influenced by the writings of the philosopher and educationalist Johan Amos Komensky (Comenius). The question of attribution cannot be regarded as satisfactorily settled.[2]

---

[1] It was long thought that she was the daughter of John Pell, rector of Southwick, Sussex, and the sister of John Pell. See Frances Teague, *Bathsua Makin, Woman of Learning* (Lewisburg: Bucknell UP, 1998); Jean R. Brink, "Bathsua Reginald Makin: 'Most Learned Matron'," *Huntington Library Quarterly* 54 (1991), 313–326.

[2] The work is anonymous, and it has recently been argued that at least its second half was either copied from or written by Makin's colleague Mark Lewis, a follower of Comenius, whose *Apologie for Grammar* had been published in 1671. See Noel Malcolm's review of Francis Teague's book, headed "The lady vanishes," in the *Times Literary Supplement*, No. 5040, November 5, 1999, p. 28.

✑✑✑

An Essay to Revive the Ancient Education of Gentlewomen, in Religion, Manners, Arts & Tongues

To all Ingenious and Virtuous Ladies,
more especially to her Highness the Lady Mary,
Eldest Daughter to his Royal Highness
the Duke of York [1]

Custom, when it is inveterate, hath a mighty influence: it hath the force of nature itself. The barbarous custom to breed women low, is grown general amongst us, and hath prevailed so far, that it is verily believed (especially amongst a sort of debauched sots) that women are not endued with such reason, as men; nor capable of improvement by education, as they are. It is looked upon as a monstrous thing, to pretend the contrary.[2] A learned woman is thought to be a comet, that bodes mischief, whenever it appears.[3] To offer to the world the liberal education of women is to deface the image of God in man, it will make women so high, and men so low, like fire in the housetop, it will set the whole world in a flame.

These things and worse than these, are commonly talked of, and verily believed by many, who think themselves wise men: to contradict these is a bold attempt; where the attempter must expect to meet with much opposition. Therefore, ladies, I beg the candid opinion of your sex, whose interest I assert. More especially I implore the favour of your Royal Highness, a person most eminent amongst them, whose patronage alone will be a sufficient protection. What I have written is not out of humour to show how much may be said of a trivial thing to little purpose. I verily think, women were formerly educated in the knowledge of arts and tongues, and by their education, many did rise to a great height in learning. Were women thus educated now, I am confident the advantage would be very great: the women would have honour and pleasure, their relations profit, and the whole nation advantage. I am very sensible it is an ill time to set on foot this design: wherein not only learning but virtue itself is scorned and neglected, as pedantic things, fit only for the vulgar.[4] I know no better way to reform these exorbitancies, than to persuade women to scorn those toys and trifles, they now spend their time about, and to attempt higher things, here offered: This will either reclaim the men; or make them ashamed to claim the sovereignty over such as are more wise and virtuous than themselves.

Were a competent number of schools erected to educate ladies ingenuously,[5] methinks I see how ashamed men would be of their ignorance, and how industrious the next generation would be to wipe off their reproach.

I expect to meet with many scoffs and taunts from inconsiderate and illiterate men, that prize their own lusts and pleasure more than your profit and content. I shall be the less concerned at these, so long as I am in your favour; and this discourse may be a weapon in your hands to defend yourselves, whilst you endeavour to polish your souls, that you may glorify God, and answer the end of

---

[1] *Lady Mary* Mary Stuart (1662–1694), the daughter of James Stuart, the Duke of York (1663–1701), and Anne Hyde.

[2] *debauched sots* depraved fools.

[3] *comet* Comets were superstitiously regarded as heralds of strange or disastrous events (*OED* comet 1a).

[4] *vulgar* persons belonging to the ordinary or common class, especially the uneducated or ignorant (*OED* vulgar *sb* 2a).

[5] *ingenuously* in the liberal arts (*OED* ingenuously *adv* 2a).

your creation, to be meet helps to your husbands.[1] Let not your ladyships be offended, that I do not (as some have wittily done) plead for female preeminence.[2] To ask too much is the way to be denied all. God has made the man the head: if you be educated and instructed, as I propose, I am sure you will acknowledge it, and be satisfied that you are helps, that your husbands do consult and advise with you (which if you be wise they will be glad of) and that your husbands have the casting voice, in whose determinations you will acquiesce.[3] That this may be the effect of this education in all ladies that shall attempt it, is the desire of

YOUR SERVANT.

.   .   .   .

CARE OUGHT TO BE TAKEN BY US TO EDUCATE WOMEN IN LEARNING

That I may be more distinct in what I intend, I shall distinguish of women,

Women are of two sorts,
$$\left. \begin{array}{c} \text{RICH} \\ \text{POOR} \end{array} \right\} \quad \left\{ \begin{array}{l} \textit{Of good natural parts.}^{5} \\ \textit{Of low parts.} \end{array} \right.$$

I do not mean, that it is necessary to the *esse*, to the subsistence, or to the salvation of women, to be thus educated.[6] Those that are mean in the world, have not an opportunity for this education: Those that are of low parts, though they have opportunity, cannot reach this; *Ex quovis ligno non fit Minerva*:[7] My meaning is, persons that God has blessed with the things of this world, that have competent natural parts, ought to be educated in knowledge; that is, it is much better they should spend the time of their youth, to be competently instructed in those things usually taught to gentlewoman at schools, and the overplus of their time to be spent in gaining arts, and tongues,[8] and useful knowledge, rather than to trifle away so many precious minutes merely to polish their hands and feet, to curl their locks, to dress and trim their bodies; and in the meantime to neglect their souls, and not at all, or very little to endeavour to know God, Jesus Christ, themselves, and the things of nature, arts and tongues, subservient to these. I do not deny but women ought to be brought up to a comely and decent carriage, to their needle, to neatness, to understand all those things that do particularly belong to their sex. But when these things are competently cared for, and where there are endowments of nature and leisure, then higher things ought to be endeavoured after. Merely to teach gentlewomen to frisk and dance, to paint their faces, to curl their hair, to put on a whisk, to wear gay clothes, is not truly to adorn, but to adulterate their bodies;[9] yea (what is worse) to defile their souls. This (like Circe's cup) turns them to beasts;[10] whilst their belly is their God, they become swine;

---

[1] *meet helps to your husbands* "And the Lord God said, It is not good that man should be alone; I will make him an help meet for him" (Genesis 2:18).

[2] *Let not...female preeminence* an allusion to Cornelius Agrippa's *Of the Nobility and Preeminence of the Female Sex* (1532), translated by Edward Fleetwood in 1652.

[3] *God has...man the head* "But I would have you know, that the head of every man is Christ; and the head of the woman is the man; and the head of Christ is God" (I Corinthians 12:3); *casting voice* the deciding voice (*OED* casting *ppl.a* 2).

[5] *parts* abilities, especially of an intellectual kind (*OED* part *sb* A.II.12).

[6] *esse* essence, essential nature (*OED* esse 2).

[7] *Ex quovis ligno non fit Minerva* "Minerva is not made from any piece of wood." Minerva is traditionally identified with Pallas Athena, the goddess of wisdom, war, and the liberal arts. The sense is given by Burton in his passage on the miseries of scholars in the *Anatomy of Melancholy*: "a Mercury is not to be made out of every log: we can make mayors and officers every year, but not scholars."

[8] *overplus* surplus (*OED* overplus *a* C).

[9] *frisk* a brisk and lively movement in dancing (*OED* frisk *sb* 1); *whisk* a neckerchief (*OED* whisk *sb*[1] II.2).

[10] *Circe's cup* When Odysseus and his crew landed on Aeaea, the goddess Circe turned the crew to swine by giving them wine containing a mixture of malignant drugs (*The Odyssey*, Book X).

whilst lust, they become goats; and whilst pride is their God, they become very devils. Doubtless this under-breeding of women began amongst heathens and barbarous people; it continues with the Indians, where they make their women mere slaves, and wear them out in drudgery. It is practised amongst degenerate and apostate Christians, upon the same score, and now is a part of their religion;[1] it would therefore be a piece of reformation to correct it; and it would notably countermine them who fight against us, as Satan against Adam, by seducing our women, who then easily seduce their husbands.

Had God intended woman only as a finer sort of cattle, he would not have made them reasonable. Brutes, a few degrees higher than drills or monkeys (which the Indians use to do many offices),[2] might have better fitted some men's lust, pride, and pleasure; especially those that desire to keep them ignorant to be tyrannized over.

God intended women as a help-meet to man, in his constant conversation, and in his concerns of his family and estate, when he should most need, in sickness, weakness, absence, death, etc. Whilst we neglect to fit them for these things, we renounce God's blessing, he hath appointed women for, are ungrateful to him, cruel to them, and injurious to ourselves.

.   .   .   .

If any desire distinctly to know what they should be instructed in? I answer, I cannot tell where to begin to admit women, nor from what part of learning to exclude them, in regard of their capacities. The whole encyclopaedia of learning may be useful some way or other to them. Respect indeed is to be had to the nature and dignity of each art and science, as they are more or less subservient to religion, and may be useful to them in their station. I would not deny them the knowledge of grammar

and rhetoric, because they dispose to speak handsomely. Logic must be allowed, because it is the key to all sciences. Physic, especially visibles, as herbs, plants, shrubs, drugs, etc., must be studied, because this will exceedingly please themselves, and fit them to be helpful to others. The tongues ought to be studied, especially the Greek and Hebrew; these will enable to the better understanding of the Scriptures.

The mathematics, more especially geography, will be useful; this puts life into history. Music, painting, poetry, etc., are a great ornament and pleasure. Some things that are more practical are not so material, because public employments in the field and courts, are usually denied to women: yet some have not been inferior to many men even in these things also.

.   .   .   .

This kind of education will be very useful to women:

1. The profit will be to themselves. In the general they will be able to understand, read, write, and speak their mother tongue, which they cannot well do without this. They will have something to exercise their thoughts about, which are busy and active. Their quality ties them at home;[3] if learning be their companion, delight and pleasure will be their attendants: for there is no pleasure greater, nor more suitable to an ingenious mind, than what is founded in knowledge; it is the first fruits of heaven, and a glimpse of that glory we afterwards expect. There is in all an innate desire of knowing, and the satisfying [of] this is the greatest pleasure. Men are very cruel that give them leave to look at a distance, only to know they do not know; to make any thus to tantalize, is a great torment.

This will be a hedge against heresies. Men are furnished with arts and tongues for this purpose, that they may stop the mouths of their adversaries. And women ought to be learned, that they may stop

---

[1] *apostate*   one who forsakes his religious faith (*OED* apostate *sb* A1).

[2] *drills*   baboons of a west African species (*OED* drill *sb*³).

[3] *quality*   rank or position in society (*OED* quality *sb* 3a).

their ears against seducers. It cannot be imagined so many persons of quality would be so easily carried aside with every wind of doctrine, had they been furnished with these defensive arms;[1] I mean, had they been instructed in the plain rules of artificial reasoning, so as to distinguish a true and forcible argument, from a vain and captious fallacy.[2] Had they been furnished with examples of the most frequent illusions of erroneous seducers. Heresiarchs creep into houses, and lead silly women captive, then they lead their husbands, both their children;[3] as the devil did Eve, she her husband, they their posterity.

It is none of the least considerations, that a woman thus educated, who modestly uses her learning, is, in despite of envy, honoured by most, especially wise and good men; such a one is admired and even adored by the vulgar and illiterate.

.   .   .   .

2. Women thus educated, will be beneficial to their relations. It is a great blessing of God to a family, to provide a good wife for the head, if it be eminent; and a presage of ruin, when he sends a ranting Jezebel to a soft Ahab.[4]

One Athaliah, married to Joram, plucks ruin upon the house of Jehoshaphat.[5] How many families have been ruined by this one thing, the bad

education of women? Because the men find no satisfactory converse or entertainment at home,[6] out of mere weariness they seek abroad; hence they neglect their business, spend their estates, destroy their bodies, and oftentimes damn their souls.

The Italians slight their wives, because all necessary knowledge, that may make them serviceable (attainable by institution) is denied them: but they court, adore, and glory in their courtesans, though common whores; because they are polished with more generous breeding.

Many learned men, having married wives of excellent parts, have themselves instructed them in all kinds of learning, the more to fit them for their converse, and to endear them and their society to them, and to make them admired by others. The woman is the glory of the man;[7] we joy in our children when eminent, and in our wives when excellent, either in body or mind.

.   .   .   .

Before I mention the objections, I shall state the propositions I have endeavoured to prove. That which I intend is this, that persons of competent natural parts, indifferently inclined and disposed to learning, whom God hath blessed with estates, that they are not cumbered in the world, but have liberty and opportunity in their childhood; and afterwards, being competently instructed in all things now useful that concern them as women, may and ought to be improved in more polite learning, in religion, arts, and the knowledge of things, in tongues also as subservient to these, rather than to spend the overplus time of their youth, in making points for bravery, in dressing and trimming themselves like Bartholomew-babies, in painting and dancing, in

---

[1] *every wind of doctrine* Ephesians 4:14.

[2] *artificial* scholarly (*OED* artificial *a* A.II.7); *captious fallacy* a deceptive argument designed to entrap.

[3] *Heresiarchs* leaders or founders of a heresy (*OED* heresiarch); *silly* unlearned (*OED* silly *a* A.3).

[4] *Jezebel to a soft Ahab* Jezebel, the wife of Israel's "wicked" King Ahab, worshiped Baal, persecuted the Hebrew prophets, and arranged for the murder of Naboth to secure his land, a crime for which she was cursed by Elijah. The curse was realized when she was thrown from a window, and her corpse eaten by dogs (I Kings 16–21; II Kings 9).

[5] *Athaliah...Jehoshaphat* Athaliah, the wife of Jehoram (not Joram), counseled her son Ahaziah (the grandson of Jehoshaphat, King of Judah) "to do wickedly" during his reign. When her son was killed, she murdered almost "all the seed royal" of Judah and ruled for six years before she was put to death (II Kings 8,11; II Chronicles 22–23).

[6] *converse* conversation (*OED* converse *sb*[1]1).

[7] *The woman...glory of man* "For a man indeed ought not to cover his head, forasmuch as he is the image and glory of God: but the woman is the glory of the man" (I Corinthians 11:7).

making flowers of coloured straw, and building houses of stained paper, and such like vanities.[1]

Objection. *Nobody means gentlewomen should be thus educated in matters of mere vanity; but in practising their needle, in knowing and doing those things that concern good housewifery, which is women's particular qualification.*

Answer. I know not what may be meant, but I see what is generally done. In most schools for educating this sex, little more is proposed by the undertakers, or expected by the parents. As far as I can observe, the less anything of solidity is taught, the more such places are frequented. I do acknowledge, in the state of the question, that women should be accomplished in all those things that concern them as women. My meaning is, the overplus time may be employed in polishing their minds with the knowledge of such things as may be honourable, pleasant and profitable to them, and their relations afterwards.

Before I proceed further to answer the remaining objections, I desire this may be taken notice of, that whatever is said against this manner of educating women, may commonly be urged against the education of men.

Objection. *If we bring up our daughters to learning, no persons will adventure to marry them.*

Answer. 1. Many men, silly enough, (God knows) think themselves wise, and will not dare to marry a wise woman, lest they should be overtopped.[2]

2. As some husbands, debauched themselves, desire their wives should be chaste, and their children virtuous: So some men, sensible of their own want (caused by their parents' neglect), will choose a learned woman, in whom they may glory, and by whose prudence their defect may be supplied.[3]

3. Learned men, to be sure, will choose such the rather, because they are suitable. Some men marrying wives of good natural parts, have improved themselves in arts and tongues, the more to fit them for their converse.

4. Many women formerly have been preferred for this very thing.

Athenais, daughter to Leontius the philosopher, left destitute by him, was entertained by his sister Placida for her learning, and was after married to the Emperor Theodosius, charmed by her worth, being fitted by her education for that high place; she is recorded for an excellent Empress. Upon her being baptized, she was called Eudocea.[4]

Constantine married Helena the daughter of Lois, more for her learning, than any other accomplishments.[5]

We may probably imagine Hortensia, Terentia, Tullia, and diverse others, had never been married to such brave men, had not their education preferred them.[6]

If this way of educating gentlewomen should now be set on foot, there will not be so great a number bred; but (as degenerate as times are) there would be found learned men enough, to whom they may be preferred for their very education.

---

[3] *want* deficiency (*OED* want *sb*[2] 2a).

[4] *Athenais...Eudocea* Theodosius II (b. 401 C.E.) married Eudocia (d. 460) in 421 C.E. He was greatly influenced by his wife until they fell from favour (early 440s).

[5] *Constantine married Helena* presumably in reference to Helena, the wife or concubine of Constantius Chlorus and mother of Constantine the Great (285–337 C.E.).

[6] *Hortensia, Terentia, Tullia* Hortensia (first century B.C.E.), the daughter of Roman politician and orator Quintus Hortensius Hortalus, was herself an orator. Terentia (first century B.C.E.), the first wife of Cicero, was frequently addressed in his *Letters*. When Cicero divorced her, she married Sallust. Tullia (ca. 79–45 B.C.E.), the daughter of Cicero and Terentia, was first married to C. Piso, then to Furius Crassipes, and finally to Dolabella, military commander and politician.

---

[1] *making points for bravery* making lace for display (*OED* point *sb*[1] A.VI.32a; *OED* bravery 3); *Bartholomew-babies* dolls sold at Bartholomew's Fair, held annually at West Smithfield (*OED* Bartholomew d).

[2] *overtopped* surpassed (*OED* overtop *v* 2b).

Objection. *It is against custom to educate gentlewomen thus.*

Answer. Bad customs ought to be broken, or else many good things would never come into use. I have showed this is a heathenish custom, or a worse, continued amongst us upon very bad grounds.

Objection. *Solomon's good housewife is commended for rising early, employing her servants, making garments, by which her husband was known in the gate.*[1] *It seems she was of quality, she had so many servants, and her husband a magistrate; their courts of judicature were at the gate: no mention is made of arts or tongues.*

Answer. It seems persons of quality were more industrious in those times than they are now. I do not intend to hinder good housewifery, neither have I called any from their necessary labour to their book. My design is upon such persons whose leisure is a burden.

Further, if Solomon's good housewife was accomplished with arts and tongues, she would have more reverence from her servants, and by her knowledge in economics, know better how to manage so great a family.

Solomon describes an industrious woman. I am suggesting what persons ought to do that are about these things. Those that deny this, deserve no answer, but are to be thought on with scorn, as that duke that thought women wise enough that knew their husband's doublet and breeches asunder.[2]

If there be any persons so vain, and are yet pleased with this apish kind of breeding now in use, that desire their daughters should be outwardly dressed like puppets, rather than inwardly adorned with knowledge, let them enjoy their humour; but never wonder if such marmosets married to buffoons, bring forth and breed up a generation of baboons, that have little more wit than apes and hobby-horses.[3] I cannot say enough against this barbarous rudeness—to suffer one part, I had almost said the better part, of ourselves to degenerate (as far as possible) into brutality.

Objection. *Women are of ill natures, and will abuse their education. They will be proud, and not obey their husbands; they will be pragmatic, and boast of their parts and improvements.*[4] *The ill nature that is in them, will become more wicked, the more wit you furnish them with.*

Answer. This is the killing objection, and every thick-skulled fellow that babbles this out, thinks no Billingsgate woman can answer it.[5] I shall take the objection in pieces:

1. *They will abuse learning.]* So do men; he is egregiously simple, that argues against the use of a necessary or very convenient thing from the abuse of it.[6] By this argument no men should be liberally brought up; strong drinks should never be used any more in the world, and a hundred such like things.

2. *They are of ill natures.]* This is an impudent calumny;[7] as if the whole sex of women, or the greatest part of them, had that malice infused into their very natures and constitutions, that they are ordinarily made worse by that education that makes men generally better.

---

[1] *Solomon's good housewife* For Solomon's description of the virtuous woman whose "price is far above rubies," see Proverbs 31:10–31.

[2] *doublet* a close-fitting body garment, with or without sleeves (*OED* doublet 1); *breeches* a garment covering the loins and thighs, ending only just below the knee (*OED* breech *sb* 1c). Compare the Athenian Society's "Some indeed think they [women] have learned enough, if they can distinguish between their husband's breeches and another man's" (*Athenian Mercury* Vol. 1, No. 18).

[3] *marmosets* literally, in early use, any small monkeys; *fig.* applied to a person as a term of playful reproach (*OED* marmoset 2a,3a).

[4] *pragmatic* conceited in their opinion, opinionated (*OED* pragmatic *a* A.3).

[5] *Billingsgate* the name of one of the gates of London, and hence of the fish market there established. References to the abusive language of this market are frequent (*OED* Billingsate 1).

[6] *egregiously* remarkably (*OED* egregiously *adv*).

[7] *calumny* slander (*OED* calumny *sb* 2).

——— *Ingenuas didicisse fideliter artes*
Emollit mores, nec sinit esse feros.[1]

The heathen found that arts wrought upon men, the rougher sex.[2] Surely it is want of fidelity in the instructor, if it have not the like effect upon softer and finer materials.

3. *They will be proud, and not obey their husbands.]* To this I answer: what is said of philosophy, is true of knowledge; a little philosophy carries a man from God, but a great deal brings him back again;[3] a little knowledge, like windy bladders, puffs up, but a good measure of true knowledge, like ballast in a ship, settles down, and makes a person move more even in his station; 'tis not knowing too much, but too little that causes the irregularity. This same argument may be turned upon men; whatever they answer for themselves, will defend women.

Those that desire a farther answer, let them peruse Erasmus, his dialogue of the Ignorant Abbot and the Learned Woman.[4] An ignorant magistrate, or minister, may as well plead against improvement of knowledge in all below them, lest they should be wiser than themselves, and so deride them. Do not deny women their due, which is to be as well instructed as they can; but let men do their duty, to be wiser than they are. If this doth not please, let silly men let wise women alone; the rule is, all should be (as near as they can) equally yoked.

Objection. *The end of learning is public business, which women are not capable of. They must not speak in the church; and it is more proper for men to act in the commonwealth than they.*[5]

Answer. They may not speak in the church, but they may inquire of their husbands at home; it is private instruction I plead for; not public employment. Yet there is no such contradiction in the terms: Miriam and Deborah were extraordinarily called forth by God, as well as Aaron and Barak.[6] Sometimes women may have occasions for public business, as widows, and wives when their husbands are absent; but especially persons born to government. The Salic law hath not prevailed all the world over, and good reason too; for women upon thrones have been as glorious in their governing, as many men, as I have showed before.[7] But lay all this aside; there are other ends of learning, besides pleading in the hall, and appearing in the pulpit. Private persons (as I have before showed) may many ways please themselves, and benefit others. This objection also will turn the point upon all men that are in a private capacity.

Objection. *They will not mind their household affairs.*

Answer. Men are judged to be more capable of country business by liberal education. Most ingenious contrivances, even in husbandry and trades,

---

1. *Ingenuas...feros* "Faithful study of the liberal arts softens character and permits it not to be cruel" (Ovid, *Ex Ponto* II.ix.47).

2. *wrought upon men* performed on men (the desired effect) (*OED* work *v* B.I.1).

3. *What is said...back again* "It is true that a little philosophy inclineth man's mind to atheism, but depth in philosophy bringeth men's minds about to religion" (Bacon, *Of Atheism*).

4. *Erasmus...Learned Woman* Though the learned woman provides many reasons why women should be educated, the ignorant abbot only gives one response: "That women would never be kept in subjection if they were learned" and therefore would "never be such tame fools and very slaves" (*An Essay*, 23).

5. *They must not...the church* "And if they will learn any thing, let them ask their husbands at home: for it is a shame for women to speak in the church" (I Corinthians 14:35). See Margaret Fell's defence of women speaking in church: *Women's Speaking Justified* (1666).

6. *Miriam...Barak* Miriam, the prophetess, and Aaron, the high priest of Israel, were called by God to help their brother Moses free the Israelites from Egyptian bondage (Exodus 15:20–21). Deborah, the prophetess and judge, and Barak were likewise called to lead a coalition of Israelite tribal militias to victory over a Canaanite army commanded by Sisera (Judges 4–5). Both Miriam and Deborah composed victory odes.

7. *Salic law* the alleged fundamental law of the French monarchy by which females were excluded from succession to the crown; hence, generally a law excluding females from dynastic succession (*OED* salic *a* 1).

have been invented by scholars. You may as well say, a gentleman that hath country affairs to manage, ought not to be a scholar, because he will be poring upon his book, when he should be looking after his plowmen.

Objection. *They have other things to do.*

Answer. Those which have, may mind those things for ought I have said: The question is of persons at leisure, whether these had not better be employed in some good literature, than in pilling straws, or doing nothing, which is the certain seed of doing mischief?[1]

Objection. *Women do not desire learning.*

Answer. Neither do many boys (as schools are now ordered), yet I suppose you do not intend to lay fallow all children that will not bring forth fruit of themselves, to forbear to instruct those which at present do not thank you for it.

But I have said, there is in all an innate desire of knowing, in women as well as men: if the ways to the Temple of Pallas be so tedious and intricate, that they confound or tire her servants;[2] or, if you dress up learning in such an ugly and monstrous shape, that you affright children; I have nothing to say to such, but that they should reform their schools, or else all will think they have no desire any, either male or female, should be instructed.

Objection. *Women are of low parts.*

Answer. So are many men; we plead only for those which have competent parts. To be sure, some women are as capable of learning, and have attained to as great height in it as most men; witness those examples before produced.[3]

If this be true, their parts generally are lower than men's, there is the more need they should by all convenient means be improved. Crutches are for infirm persons.

Objection. *Women are of softer natures, more delicate and tender constitutions, not so fixed and solid as men.*

Answer. If their natures are soft, they are more capable of good impressions; if they are weak, more shame for us to neglect them, and defraud them of the benefit of education, by which they may be strengthened.

Objection. *It is against custom to educate gentlewomen thus; those that do attempt it, will make themselves ridiculous.*

Answer. This argument might have been used to the Irish, not to use traces at plow and cart, but to draw their horses by their tails, which was a general custom amongst them.[4] Bad customs (when it is evident they are so) ought to be broken, or else good customs can never come into use. That this is a bad custom, is evident, continued upon a bad ground. Let women be fools, and then you may easily make them slaves.

.   .   .   .

If all I have said may conveniently be done, I expect many will deride this design. I am contented, let them abound in their own sense, and have wives as silly as themselves desire, over whom they may tyrannize.

I hope I shall by this discourse persuade some parents to be more careful for the future of the breeding of their daughters. You cark and care to get great portions for them, which sometimes occasions their ruin.[5] Here is a sure portion, an easy way to make them excellent. How many born to good fortunes, when their wealth hath been wasted,

---

[1] *pilling straws* to pick [pill] straws was an expression for sleepiness, here in the sense of idleness (*OED* straw *sb*[1] II.9d).

[2] *Pallas* Pallas Athena.

[3] *witness...produced* Earlier in *An Essay*, a history of women eminent in linguistics, oratory, philosophy, mathematics and poetry is set forth.

[4] *traces* the ropes, by means of which horses draw a carriage, plough, or harrow (*OED* theat *sb*).

[5] *cark* labour anxiously (*OED* cark *v* 3); *portions* marriage portions (*OED* portion *sb* I.3).

have supported themselves and families too by their wisdom?

I hope some of these considerations will at least move some of this abused sex to set a right value upon themselves, according to the dignity of their creation, that they might, with an honest pride and magnanimity, scorn to be bowed down and made to stoop to such follies and vanities, trifles and nothings, so far below them, and unproportionable to their noble souls, nothing inferior to those of men, and equally precious to God in Christ, in whom there is neither male nor female.

Let a generous resolution possess your minds, seeing men in this age have invaded women's vices, in a noble revenge, reassume those virtues, which men sometimes unjustly usurped to themselves, but ought to have left them in common to both sexes.

POSTSCRIPT

If any enquire where this education may be performed, such may be informed, that a school is lately erected for gentlewomen at Tottenham High Cross, within four miles of London, in the road to Ware, where Mrs. Makin is governess, who was sometimes tutoress to the Princess Elizabeth, Daughter to King Charles the First; where, by the blessing of God, gentlewomen may be instructed in the principles of religion; and in all manner of sober and virtuous education.

.　　.　　.　　.　　.　　.

—1673

William Walwyn
1600 – 1681

William Walwyn was a leader of the Leveller movement and the author of some of the civil war period's most remarkable arguments for religious toleration, freedom of conscience, and the ability of individuals to form their own judgements on important issues without deferring to political or religious authorities. The younger son of a Worcester gentleman, Walwyn was apprenticed to the silk trade and by the late 1630s was a moderately prosperous merchant with a love for reading. He published the first of his approximately thirty pamphlets in 1641. Many of these works display Walwyn's general opposition to political and religious authoritarianism. While he remained associated with the Presbyterian church throughout the civil wars, for example, Walwyn challenged not only royal absolutism but also Presbyterian intolerance, particularly in a series of pamphlets written against the heretic-hunting Thomas Edwards (see the selection from Edwards' *Gangraena*). Less flamboyant than the other Leveller leaders John Lilburne and Richard Overton, Walwyn complemented their work by focussing on the principles of justice, reason, and equity that underlay the Leveller platform. Some hostile contemporaries thought Walwyn's reasoned, persuasive arguments and his intellectual coherence made him the most dangerous Leveller polemicist. Some time in the 1650s, after the defeat of the Leveller movement, Walwyn appears to have become a lay physician, publishing pamphlets that advocated commonsense treatment of the sick and dispensing herbal medicines that, while they might not have cured patients, almost certainly did not harm them in the ways common to the period's more conventional remedies.

The Bloody Project displays Walwyn's central concern for the liberty of the individual conscience. Published in August 1648 at the height of the Second Civil War, Walwyn asks soldiers on both sides if they truly know why they are being asked to kill their fellow Englishmen. He urges his readers to examine the political and religious rhetoric used to justify the war, and points out how neither side has lived up to the promises implied in their rhetoric. The pamphlet concludes by asking what causes are truly worth fighting for, and answers the question with a sketch of key elements in the Leveller platform, including the supremacy of the Commons, religious toleration, and social and legal reform. For more on the Levellers, see the selections from the Putney Debates and Richard Overton.

❧❧❧

The Bloody Project

In all undertakings which may occasion war or bloodshed, men have great need to be sure that their cause be right, both in respect of themselves and others: for if they kill men themselves, or cause others to kill, without a just cause, and upon the extremest necessity, they not only disturb the peace of men, and families, and bring misery and poverty upon a nation, but are indeed absolute murderers.

Nor will it in any measure satisfy the conscience, or God's justice, to go on in uncertainties, for in doubtful cases men ought to stand still, and consider, until certainty do appear, especially when killing and slaying of men (the most horrid work to nature and scripture) is in question.

Far be it from any man hastily to engage in any undertaking which may occasion a war, before the cause he is to fight for be rightly and plainly stated, well considered, and thoroughly understood to be just, and of absolute necessity to be maintained; nothing being more abominable in the sight of God or good men, than such persons who run but to shed blood for money, or to support this or the other interest, but neither consider the cause for which they engage, nor ought else, but pay, interest, honour, &c. Such are they who so eagerly endeavour to support the interest of a King, by the destruction of the people's interest; the interest of the Scots against the interest of the English; the interest of the Independents, by the ruin of the Presbyterians: and because it best consists with their present honour, profit, or humours, make it their business to pick quarrels, and increase divisions and jealousies, that so they may fish in the waters which they themselves have troubled.

But let such know, who ever they be, that though they may and do for a while brave it out, and flourish, yet a time is coming, and draweth on apace, when for all the murders they have caused, and mischiefs they have committed, they shall come to judgement, and then their consciences will be as a thousand witnesses against them.

But especially let men pretending conscience take heed how they either engage themselves, or persuade others to engage to fight and kill men, for a cause not rightly stated, or not thoroughly understood to be just, and of necessity to be maintained; for it is one of the most unreasonable, unchristian, and unnatural things that can enter into the mind of man, though it be to be feared that more than a few that have of late, both in the city and country, been (and at present are) active to engage in killing and slaying of men, cannot acquit themselves of this abomination.

I beseech you (you that are so forward and active to engage in the defence of the King's, Presbyterian, or Independent interest, and yet know no just cause for either) consider, was it sufficient that the King at first invited you in general terms to join with him, for the defence of the true Protestant religion, his own just prerogatives, the privileges of Parliament, and the liberty of the subject; but never declared in particular what that Protestant religion was he would have defended, or what prerogative would please him, what privileges he would allow the Parliament, or what freedoms the people?

Or was it sufficient think you now, that the Parliament invited you at first upon general terms to fight for the maintenance of the true Protestant religion, the liberties of the people, and privileges of Parliament; when neither themselves knew, for ought is yet seen, nor you, nor anybody else, what they meant by the true Protestant religion, or what the liberties of the people were, or what those privileges of Parliament were, for which yet nevertheless thousands of men have been slain, and thousands of families destroyed?

It is very like that some of you that joined with the King upon his invitation thought that, though the King had formerly countenanced popery and superstition, [and] had stretched his prerogative to the oppression and destruction of his people, by patents, projects,[1] &c., yet for the future he would have been more zealous for the truth, and more tender of his people, and not have persisted (notwithstanding his new protestations) to maintain his old principles.

And so likewise many of you that joined with the Parliament, who had formerly seen, felt, or considered the persecution of godly conscientious people by the Bishops and their clergy, with the reproaches cast upon them, and their grievous and destructive imprisonment, did believe the Parliament, under the notion of religion, intended to free the nation from all compulsion in matters of religion, and from molestation or persecution for

---

[1] *patents, projects* trade monopolies and business schemes. Despite Parliamentary and popular opposition, Charles had continued the traditional practice of awarding aristocratic favourites with highly profitable monopolies on the manufacture of or trade in commodities (e.g., salt, pots, sweet wine, oil, lead, bottles); holders of these patents frequently raised the price of the commodity to increase their profits.

opinions, or non-conformity; and that all laws or statutes tending thereunto should have been repealed: But since you find (by killing and destroying their opposers) you have enabled them to perform all things that might concern your freedom, or be conducible to the peace of the Kingdom. But do you now find that they do mean that, or the contrary? And will your consciences give you leave any longer to fight or engage in the cause of religion, when already you see what fruits you and your friends reap thereby?

And no doubt many of you understood by the liberties of the people, that they intended to free the Commons in Parliament, the people's representative, from a negative voice in King or Lords,[1] and would have declared themselves the highest authority, and so would have proceeded to have removed the grievances of the Commonwealth: And when you had seen patents, projects, and ship money taken away,[2] the High Commission and Star Chamber abolished,[3] did you ever imagine to have seen men and women examined upon interrogatories, and questions against themselves,[4] and imprisoned for refusing to answer? Or to have seen Commoners frequently sentenced and imprisoned by the Lords? Did you ever dream that the oppressions of Committees would have exceeded those of the Council table;[5] or that in the place of patents and projects, you should have seen an excise established, ten-fold surpassing all those and ship money together? You thought rather that tithes would have been esteemed an oppression, and that trade would have been made perfectly free, and that customs if continued would have been abated, and not raised for the support of domineering factions, and enrichment of four or five great men, as they have been of late times, to the sorrow and astonishment of all honest men, and the great prejudice of the trade of the nation.

Doubtless you hoped that both laws and lawyers, and the proceeding in all courts, should have been abbreviated, and corrected, and that you should never more have seen a beggar in England.

You have seen the Commonwealth enslaved for want of Parliaments, and also by their sudden dissolution, and you rejoiced that this Parliament was not to be dissolved by the King; but did you conceive it would have sat seven years to so little purpose, or that it should ever have come to pass, to be esteemed a crime to move for the ending thereof? Was the perpetuating of this Parliament, and the oppressions they have brought upon you and yours, a part of that liberty of the people you fought for? Or was it for such a privilege of Parliament, that they only might have liberty to oppress at their pleasure, without any hope of remedy? If all these put together make not up the cause for which you fought, what was the cause? What have ye obtained to the people but these liberties, for they must not be called oppressions? These are the fruits of all those vast disbursements, and those thousands of lives that have been spent and destroyed in the late War.

And though the army seemed to be sensible of these gross jugglings, and declared and engaged

---

[1] *negative voice* power of veto.

[2] *ship money* a controversial and unpopular tax levied by Charles I from 1635 to 1640.

[3] *High Commission and Star Chamber* respectively, the most unpopular ecclesiastical and secular courts. Both were associated with the maintenance of royal authority, and both were abolished by the Long Parliament.

[4] referring to the notorious oath *ex officio*, which required prisoners to answer questions against themselves even in the absence of the traditional two witnesses. The right against self-incrimination was a central plank in the Leveller platform of legal reform: Walwyn himself was jailed in 1649 for refusing on principle to answer questions.

[5] *Committees…Council table* that is, did you ever dream that committees of the House of Commons would prove as oppressive as the King's Privy Council?

against them, and professed that they took not pains as a mercenary army, hired to fight for the arbitrary ends of a state, but in judgement and conscience, for the preservation of their own and the people's just rights and liberties: Yet when they had prevailed against those their particular opposers, and accomplished the ends by them aimed at, all these things were forgotten, and those persons that appeared for the people's freedoms, by them esteemed and proceeded against as mutineers, or incendiaries.

In like manner, the present ruling party of Presbyterians make a great show of their apprehensions of the great slavery and servitude brought upon the people by the exercise of an arbitrary power in the Parliament, and by the jurisdiction of the sword in the hands of the army: They tell us that by this means the trade of the nation is destroyed, and that without the removal of these things, the peace of the nation cannot be secured. And it is exceeding true. But I beseech you consider, whether they do not revive the same play, and drive the same design, which was acted by the Parliament at first, and by the army the last summer.

First, they cry out against the exercise of an arbitrary power in the Parliament, and yet labour to invest it in the King, nay challenge the exercise of it by themselves: for what greater arbitrary power can there be in the world, than that a priest or two, and a few lay elders, under the name of a Presbytery, should have power to bind or loose, bring in, or cast out, save or destroy at their pleasure, and enforce all persons within the limits of their jurisdiction to believe as they believe and submit to whatever they command, or else to be by them delivered over to Satan.

Nay, if you look into those of that party of the magistracy of this city that are the great promoters of the present work: do there any men in the world exercise a more arbitrary power? Do not many of them act only by the rule of will and pleasure, and have they not openly professed themselves to be obliged to observe no other rule than discretion?

And though they decry against the power of the sword in the hands of the Independents, yet do they not with all their might labour to get it into the hands of the Presbyterians? and being there, will they not do that themselves, which they complain of in others? will they not say that there are gainsayers whose mouths must be stopped and with the sword rather than fail, and though Royalists or Independents may not use the sword to enforce their principles, yet Presbyterians may, as if all knowledge of the truth were centred in a Presbytery, consisting of half Scotch, half English, part Puritan, part Cavalier, lukewarm Christianity, neither hot nor cold, zealous for the truth which they know not, only by hearsay, and only because they love not Independency, that being too pure, nor Episcopacy, that being too profane, they will be between both (but not in a golden mean, for that were well), but more zealous than either in outward performances, but for the power of godliness. – I cease to judge, but we say we may know the tree by the fruit, and certain I am that thistles never bore figs.

But if you shall examine what grounds of freedom they propose in all their papers; what equal rules of justice they offer to be insisted on as a sure foundation for a lasting peace? Surely if you look but seriously into the bottom of their design, you will find that the peace they aim at is only their own, not the nation's; and that their own ease, honour and dominion, is the only thing they pursue, and so they could enjoy ease and plenty, and stretch themselves upon beds of down, they would never care what the poor country should suffer.

To be short, all the quarrel we have at this day in the kingdom, is no other than a quarrel of interests and parties, a pulling down of one tyrant to set up another, and instead of liberty, heaping upon ourselves a greater slavery than that we fought against: certainly this is the liberty that is so much strove for, and for which there are such fresh endeavours to engage men; but if you have not killed and destroyed men enough for this, go on and destroy, kill and slay, till your consciences are swollen so full with the blood of the people that they burst again, and upon your deathbeds may you see yourselves the most horrid murderers that ever lived, since the time that Cain killed his brother without a just cause; for where, or what is your cause? Believe it ye have a heavy reckoning to make, and must undergo a sad repentance, or it will go ill with you at the great day, when all the sophistry of your great reformers will serve you to little purpose, every man for himself being to give an account for the things which he hath done in the body, whether they be good or evil. Then it will serve you to little purpose to say, the King, Parliament, Army, Independents, Presbyterians, such an officer, magistrate, or minister deluded me; no more than it did Adam, to say the woman whom thou gavest, &c. It being thus decreed in heaven, the soul which sinneth shall surely die.

And though what is past cannot be recalled, yet it must be repented of, and special care taken for the future, that you sin no more in this kind, and either stand still or go right for the future, to which end, let these following directions be your guide.

1. You are to know, that a people living under a government, as this nation hath done, and doth, cannot lawfully put themselves into arms, or engage in war, to kill and slay men, but upon a lawful call and invitation from the supreme authority, or law-making power.

Now if the supreme authority of this nation were never yet so plainly declared, as that you understand certainly where it is, and who are invested therewith, you have then had no warrant for what you have done, nor have any plea in law

for your indemnity, as some of all parties have lately found to their costs.

And that this point of supreme authority was ever certainly stated, is absolutely denied; for according to the common supposition, it is three estates, which till within these few years were ever taken to be 1) Lords Spiritual, 2) Lords Temporal, 3) the Commons in Parliament assembled.

Now if these three were essential and equal, as all former times seem to allow, how could the Lords Temporal and the Commons cast out the Lords Spiritual? For by the same rule, the Lords Spiritual and Lords Temporal might have cast out the Commons, but the casting out the bishops hath both answered the question, and ended the controversy.

Since when the supreme authority is pretended to rest in the King, Lords, and Commons; and if so, when did the King assent to your proceedings in this war, which all the art in the world will not persuade him to be for him, but against him, and to ruin him and his? Or when did the Parliament assent to the proceedings of you that joined with the King in the late war pretendedly raised for the defence of religion, the privileges of Parliament, and liberty of the subject; and if the supreme power reside in all three, King, Lords, and Commons, how can the King justly do anything without the consent of the Lords and Commons, or the Lords and Commons without the King? May not the King and Lords as justly proceed to make laws, war, or peace without the Commons as they without the King? If they are not equal, which of them are supreme, and declared and proved by convincing reason so to be? If any, that you are to observe? If none, what have you done? what can you lawfully do?

That there should be either three or two distinct estates equally supreme is an absurd nullity in government, for admit two of them agree, and not the third, then there can be no proceedings or determination, and if there be but two, as is now pretended, in Lords and Commons, whose ordinances have served (how justly judge you) to make war and confiscate men's estates: admit they agree not, then also nothing can be done, which in government is ridiculous to imagine; besides it is now a known case that their ordinances are not pleadable against the laws, and give no indemnity, which were they the known supreme authority, could not but be effectual. That the King single and alone is the supreme authority himself never pretended to it, claiming only a negative voice in the law-making power, by which rule nothing can be done without him, than which nothing is more unreasonable. The Lords also never pretended to more than an equal share with the Commons, which in effect is a negative voice and as unreasonable as in the King. And when the Commons have been by petitioners styled the supreme authority, they have punished the petitioners, and disclaimed the supreme authority: and as two years since, so very lately they have voted that the Kingdom shall be governed by King, Lords, and Commons; which is a riddle that no man understands; for who knoweth what appertains to the King, what to the Lords, or what to the House of Commons? It is all out as uncertain as at first; and if the trumpet give an uncertain sound, who shall prepare himself for the battle? If by all your endeavours you cannot prevail to have the supreme authority declared and proved, how can you lawfully fight, or upon what grounds with a good conscience can you engage yourselves, or persuade others to engage in killing and slaying of men?

And if you should have the supreme authority rationally proved and declared to be in the Commons distinct from any other, as being the sole representative of the people; you must note that you are a free people, and are not to be pressed or enforced to serve in wars like horses and brute beasts, but are to use the understanding God hath given you, in judging of the cause, for defence whereof they desire you to fight, for it is not sufficient to fight by lawful authority, but you must be sure to fight for what is just: Lawful authority being sometimes mistaken, and many times so perverted and corrupted, as to command the killing and imprisoning men for doing that which is just and commendable, and for opposing what is unjust and destructive. Therefore as you are to forbear till you see the supreme authority distinctly and rationally stated; so also you are not to engage till the cause be expressly declared, lest after your next engagement you are as far to seek of a just cause as now you are; and after you have prevailed, instead of finding yourselves and your associates freemen, you find yourselves more enslaved than you were formerly. For by experience you now find you may be made slaves as effectually by a Parliament, as by any other kind of government; why then persist you to divide and fall into factions? to kill and slay men for you know not what, to advance the honor and interest of you know not whom; the King, Parliament, great men in the city and army can do nothing without you, to disturb the peace of the nation; upon you therefore both soldiers and people, who fight, pay and disburse your estates, is to be charged all the evil that hath been done; if you on all hands had not been and were not so hasty to engage for the advancement of interests to the prejudice of the nation, it is very likely we had not only escaped those late bloody turmoils that have happened among us, but also might prevent greater threatened dangers, which like an inundation begin to break in upon us. And if you now stop not, your consciences will be loaded with all that is to come, which threateneth far worse than what is past. Therefore, if ye are either men or Christians, hold your hands till you know what you fight for, and be sure that you have the truth of freedom in it, or never meddle, but desist, and let who will both fight and pay.

Certainly there is none so vile, considering what hath been said, that will again incur the guilt of murderers and fight before the cause be plainly stated and published, and if that were done as it ought to be, possibly it may be attained without fighting, and might have been all this while, the difference not being so great as was imagined. Besides, where is the man that would fight against the supreme authority, and a just cause? and certainly there is none of you (whether Royalists, Presbyterians, or Independents) so wicked as to desire to kill men without exceeding just grounds and upon the greatest necessity, it being the saddest work in the world.

For the preventing whereof, let us, I beseech you, examine what good things there are wanting, that are essential to the peace, freedom, and happiness of the nation, that may not be obtained without fighting.

1. Is there wanting the certain knowledge where the supreme authority is, and of right ought to be? It is confessed no one thing is more wanting, nor can the nation ever be quiet or happy without it.

But can it be anywhere justly and safely but in the House of Commons, who are chosen and trusted by the people? Certainly did men consider that in opposing thereof, they renounce and destroy their own freedoms, they would not do it for any thing in the world.

If the consideration of the manifold evils brought upon us by this House of Commons deter them, the next thing that is wanting is, That a set time be appointed for the ending of this Parliament, and a certainty for future Parliaments, both for their due elections, meeting, and dissolving: And who will be so unreasonable as to oppose any of these? certainly the number cannot be considerable.

Is it also necessary that Parliaments be abridged the power of impressing men, to serve as brute beasts in the wars, who will be against their being bounded therein? a good cause never wanted men, nor an authority that had money to pay them.

Hath it proved destructive in Parliaments to meddle in religion, and to compel and restrain in matters of God's worship? Are they evidently such things as cannot be submitted to judgment? Doth every man find it so that hath a living conscience? Who then will be against their binding herein, though they be entrusted to establish an uncompulsive public way of worship for the nation?

Is it unreasonable that any person should be exempt from those proceedings of law, unto which the generality of the people are to be subject? Who is there then that will not willingly have all from the highest to the lowest bound alike?

That Parliaments should have no power to punish any person for doing that which is not against a known declared law, or to take away general property, or to force men to answer to questions against themselves, or to order trials or proceed by any other ways than by twelve sworn men, who would not rejoice to have such boundaries?

Then, that the proceedings in law might be rectified, and all laws and the duty of magistrates written and published in English.[1] That the excise might have a speedy end, and no taxes but by way of subsidies. That trade might be free, and a less burdensome way for the maintenance of ministers be established, than that of tithes; and that work and necessaries be provided for all kind of poor people. Certainly for the obtaining of these things a man may justly adventure his life; all these being for a common good, and tend not to the setting up of any one party or faction of men.

These then are the causes to be insisted on, or nothing: And if the supreme authority adhere to this cause, they need neither fear Scotch, French,

---

1 *written and published in English* As part of their platform for reform of the legal system, the Levellers called for the translation of England's laws from Anglo-Norman ("Law French") into English so they could be understood by everyone, without the need for legal training. The legal profession successfully withstood this particular reform until well after the period covered by this anthology.

nor English enemies; but if they decline this cause, they are to be declined; the just freedom and happiness of a nation being above all constitutions, whether of Kings, Parliaments, or any other.

For shame therefore (Royalists, Presbyterians, Independents), before you murder another man hold forth your cause plainly and expressly; and if any adversaries appear either within or without the land, reason it out with them if it be possible, deal as becometh Christians, argue, persuade, and use all possible means to prevent another war, and greater bloodshed; your great ones, whether the King, Lords, Parliament men, rich citizens, &c. feel not the miserable effects thereof, and so cannot be sensible; but you and your poor friends that depend on farms, trades, and small pay, have many an aching heart when these live in all pleasure and deliciousness. The accursed thing is accepted by them, wealth and honor, and both come by the bleeding miserable distractions of the Commonwealth, and they fear an end of trouble would put an end to their glory and greatness.

Oh therefore all you soldiers and people that have your consciences alive about you, put to your strength of judgment, and all the might you have to prevent a further effusion of blood; let not the covetous, the proud, the bloodthirsty man bear sway amongst you; fear not their high looks, give no ear to their charms, their promises, or tears; they have no strength without you, forsake them and ye will be strong for good, adhere to them, and they will be strong to evil; for which you must answer, and give an account at the last day.

The King, Parliament, great men in the city and army, have made you but the stairs by which they have mounted to honour, wealth, and power. The only quarrel that hath been, and at present is but this, namely, whose slaves the people shall be. All the power that any hath, was but a trust conveyed from you to them, to be employed by them for your good; they have mis-employed their power, and instead of preserving you, have destroyed you: all power and authority is perverted from the King to the constable, and it is no other but the policy of statesmen to keep you divided by creating jealousies and fears among you, to the end that their tyranny and injustice may pass undiscovered and unpunished; but the people's safety is the supreme law; and if a people must not be left without a means to preserve itself against the King, by the same rule they may preserve themselves against the Parliament and army too, if they pervert the end for which they received their power, to wit the nation's safety; therefore speedily unite yourselves together, and as one man stand up for the defence of your freedom, and for the establishment of such equal rules of government for the future, as shall lay a firm foundation of peace and happiness to all the people without partiality. Let justice be your breastplate, and you shall need to fear no enemies, for you shall strike a terror to your now insulting oppressors, and force all the nation's peace to fly before you. Prosecute and prosper.

POSTSCRIPT

Can there be a more bloody project than to engage men to kill one another, and yet no just cause declared? Therefore I advise all men that would be esteemed religious or rational, really to consider what may be done for the future that is conducible to the peace of the nation. If the peace of the nation cannot be secured without the restoration of the King, let it be done speedily and honorably, and provide against his mis-government for the future; let his power be declared and limited by law.

If the peace of the nation cannot be secured by the continuance of this Parliament, let a period be set for the dissolution thereof, but first make certain provision for the successive calling, electing and sitting of Parliaments for the future; let their privileges be declared and power limited, as to what they are empowered and what not; for doubtless in Parliaments rightly constituted consists the freedom of a nation. And in all things do as you would be done unto, seek peace with all men.

But above all things, abandon your former actings for a King against a Parliament, or an army against both; for the Presbyterians against the Independents, &c., for in so doing you do but put a sword into your enemies' hands to destroy you, for hitherto, which of them soever were in power, they played the tyrants and oppressed, and so it will ever be when parties are supported. Therefore if you engage at all, do it by lawful authority, let your cause be declared, and just also, and let it be for the good of the whole nation, without which you will not only hazard being slaves, but also contract upon yourselves and posterities the guilt of murderers.
—1648

John Earle

?1601 – 1665

Educated at Christ Church and Merton College, Oxford, Earle received his MA in 1624 and was successively appointed Proctor of the University (1631), chaplain to the Earl of Pembroke, chaplain and tutor to the future Charles II (1641), and Chancellor of Salisbury Cathedral. Earle was a member of the famous literary and theological circle that surrounded Lucius Cary, second Viscount Falkland, at Great Tew, a group that included among others Jonson, Suckling, Waller, and Clarendon. Like most Royalist divines, Earle was deprived of his offices during the civil wars, and he travelled with the exiled court to France, where he served as Charles II's chaplain and made a Latin translation of *Eikon Basilike,* ascribed by Royalists to Charles I. At the Restoration he was appointed Dean of Westminster, and ended his career as Bishop of Salisbury, a position from which he opposed the persecution of Nonconformists. His friends in later life included Pepys and Evelyn, and he was admired by people across the political and religious spectrum: Clarendon wrote that Earle "was amongst the few excellent men who never had, nor never could have, an enemy."

The following literary "characters" are from Earle's collection *Microcosmography,* published in 1628 but written while he was a student at Oxford. The book was very successful, going through numerous editions in his lifetime. Like all character-writers (see the selections by Breton, Felltham, Butler and the Overburian character), Earle followed the model provided by the Greek writer Theophrastus. Earle's characters, however, tend to reflect his moderation of temper, and some respond to the Overburian writers' harsher and more satiric portraits.

❧❧❧

To the Reader, Genteel or Gentle

I have for once adventured to play the midwife's part, helping to bring forth these infants into the world which the father would have smothered, who, having left them lapped up in loose sheets, as soon as his fancy was delivered of them, written especially for his private recreation to pass away the time in the country, and by the forcible request of friends drawn from him, yet passing severally from hand to hand in written copies grew at length to be a pretty number in a little volume; and among so many sundry dispersed transcripts some very imperfect and surreptitious had like to have passed the press if the author had not used speedy means to prevention, when, perceiving the hazard he ran to be wronged, was unwillingly willing to let them pass as now they appear to the world. If any faults have escaped the press—as few books can be printed without—impose them not on the author, I intreat thee, but rather impute them to mine and the printer's oversight, who seriously promise on the re-impression hereof by greater care and diligence for this our former default to make thee ample satisfaction. In the meantime I remain

Thine
Edward Blount[1]

A Child

Is a man in a small letter, yet the best copy of Adam before he tasted of Eve or the apple; and he is happy whose small practice in the world can

[1] *Edward Blount* well known bookseller in London from 1594–1632, best known for his extensive publishing of drama, including works by his friend Christopher Marlowe and, in conjunction with others, Shakespeare's first folio (1623).

only write his character. He is nature's fresh picture newly drawn in oil, which time, and much handling, dims and defaces. His soul is yet a white paper unscribbled with observations of the world, wherewith, at length, it becomes a blurred notebook. He is purely happy, because he knows no evil, nor hath made means by sin to be acquainted with misery. He arrives not at the mischief of being wise, nor endures evils to come, by foreseeing them. He kisses and loves all, and, when the smart of the rod is past, smiles on his beater. Nature and his parents alike dandle him and entice him on with a bait of sugar to a draught of wormwood. He plays yet, like a young 'prentice the first day, and is not come to his task of melancholy. All the language he speaks yet is tears, and they serve him well enough to express his necessity. His hardest labor is his tongue, as if he were loath to use so deceitful an organ; and he is best company with it when he can but prattle. We laugh at his foolish sports, but his game is our earnest; and his drums, rattles, and hobby-horses, but the emblems and mocking of man's business. His father hath writ him as his own little story, wherein he reads those days of his life that he cannot remember, and sighs to see what innocence he has out-lived. The older he grows, he is a stair lower than God; and, like his first father, much worse in his breeches.[1] He is the Christian's example, and the old man's relapse; the one imitates his pureness, and the other falls into his simplicity. Could he put off his body with his little coat, he had got eternity without a burden, and exchanged but one heaven for another.

—1628

---

[1] *first father* Adam; a pun on Genesis 3:7 which, in the Geneva Bible, says that after their first disobedience Adam and Eve "made themselves breeches."

A Surgeon

Is one that has some business about this building or little house of man, whereof nature is as it were the tiler, and he the plasterer. It is ofter out of reparations than an old parsonage,[2] and then he is set on work to patch it again. He deals most with broken commodities, as a broken head or a mangled face, and his gains are very ill got, for he lives by the hurts of the commonwealth.[3] He differs from a physician as a sore does from a disease, or the sick from those that are not whole; the one distempers you within, the other blisters you without.[4] He complains of the decay of valour in these days, and sighs for that slashing age of sword and buckler; and thinks the law against duels was made merely to wound his vocation.[5] He had been long since undone if the charity of the stews had not relieved him,[6] from whom he has his tribute as duly as the pope; or a wind-fall sometimes from a tavern, if a quart pot hit right. The rareness of his custom makes him pitiless when it comes, and he holds a patient longer than our courts a cause. He tells you what danger you had been in if he had stayed but a minute longer, and though it be but a pricked finger, he makes of it much matter. He is a reasonable cleanly man, considering the scabs he has to deal with, and your finest ladies are now and then beholden to him for their best dressings. He curses old gentlewomen and their charity that makes his trade their alms; but his envy is never stirred so much as when gentlemen go over to fight upon Cal-

---

[2] *ofter out of reparations* more often in need of repair.

[3] *commonwealth* a pun on the traditional metaphoric identification of the human body with the body politic.

[4] Surgeons were confined to treating the body's exterior; university-trained physicians were allowed to treat internal complaints.

[5] James I issued a *Proclamation against Private Challenges* in 1613.

[6] *stews* brothels.

ais sands,[1] whom he wishes drowned ere they come there, rather than the French shall get his custom.

—1628

Paul's Walk [2]

Is the land's epitome, or you may call it the lesser Isle of Great Britain. It is more than this, the whole world's map, which you may here discern in its perfectest motion, justling and turning. It is a heap of stones and men, with a vast confusion of languages; and were the steeple not sanctified, nothing liker Babel. The noise in it is like that of bees, a strange humming or buzz mixed of walking tongues and feet: it is a kind of still roar or loud whisper. It is the great exchange of all discourse, and no business whatsoever but is here stirring and a-foot. It is the synod of all pates politic, jointed and laid together in most serious posture, and they are not half so busy at the Parliament. It is the antic of tails to tails, and backs to backs, and for vizards you need go no further than faces. It is the market of young lecturers, whom you may cheapen here at all rates and sizes. It is the general mint of all famous lies, which are here like the legends of popery, first coined and stamped in the church. All inventions are emptied here, and not few pockets. The best sign of a temple in it is, that it is the thieves' sanctuary, which rob more safely in the crowd than a wilderness, whilst every searcher is a bush to hide them. It is the other expense of the day, after plays, tavern, and a bawdy-house; and men have still some oaths left to swear here. The visitants are all men without exceptions, but the principal inhabitants and possessors are stale knights and captains out of service; men of long rapiers and breeches, which after all turn merchants here and traffic for news. Some make it a preface to their dinner, and travel for a stomach; but thriftier men make it their ordinary, and board here very cheap. Of all such places it is least haunted with hobgoblins, for if a ghost would walk more, he could not.

—1628

---

[1] *Calais sands* off the coast of France; often used by English duellists since outside the jurisdiction of the law.

[2] *Paul's Walk* St. Paul's Cathedral, a general gathering place and the centre of the trade in books and information.

Owen Felltham
?1604 – 1668

Felltham was a popular writer in his lifetime, and his *Resolves* played an important role in the development of the English essay, but relatively little is known of their author. Born into the prosperous Suffolk gentry, Felltham was probably educated by private tutors. From the early 1630s to the end of his life he served as steward to the Earls of Thomond in Northamptonshire. He was, however, well known in London literary circles: in addition to publishing the *Resolves*, he wrote poems that appear to have circulated widely in manuscript, and he contributed to a collection of lyrics in honour of Ben Jonson and to other printed miscellanies. He added 41 of his poems to the 1661 edition of the *Resolves*. His other works include *A Brief Character of the Low Countries*, which circulated in manuscript and in pirated editions until an authorized version appeared in 1652. Felltham's "Epitaph to the Eternal Memory of Charles the First," which includes the line "Here Charles the First, and Christ the second lies," indicates that he was an ardent Royalist, though he seems not to have played any active role in the civil wars.

The first edition of the *Resolves*, comprising 100 short, untitled prose works, appeared in 1623, before Felltham was twenty years old. He added 100 longer, titled essays in 1628, and this "duple century" reached seven editions by 1647. In 1661, Felltham revised or replaced the original century with 85 lengthier, more personal essays; this folio edition was reissued three more times before the end of the century. In this selection, "A Rule for Reading Authors" is one of the original century; the remainder were added in 1628. The translations are all Felltham's own. He often does not identify the source of his quotations: the essay, he explains, "of all writing is the nearest to a running discourse," a kind of conversation in which notes would be pedantic and ungentlemanly. For other examples of the essay form, see the selections from Francis Bacon; for the literary "character," see the selections from Nicholas Breton, John Earle, Samuel Butler, and the Overburan Character.

☙☙☙

Resolves
(selections)

OF PURITANS

I find many that are called *Puritans*; yet few, or none that will own the name.[1] Whereof the reason sure is this; that 'tis for the most part held a name of infamy; and is so new, that it hath scarcely yet obtained a definition: nor is it an appellation derived from one man's name, whose tenets we may find, digested into a volume: whereby we do much err in the application. It imports a kind of excellency above another; which man (being conscious of his own frail bendings) is ashamed to assume to himself. So that I believe there are men which *would be* Puritans: but indeed not any that *are*. One will have him one that lives religiously, and will not revel it in a shoreless excess. Another, him that separates from our divine assemblies.[2] Another, him that in some tenets only is peculiar. Another, him that will not swear. Absolutely to define him, is a work, I think, of difficulty; some I know that

---

[1] *Puritans* Almost always used pejoratively, the term "Puritan" first appeared in the late 1560s to describe the more extreme English Protestants who sought to "purify" the Elizabethan Church of the remnants of Catholicism. As Felltham points out, the term was flexible, a polemical signifier rather than a strict party label.

[2] *him that separates* Separatists (later called Independents or Congregationalists) believed in the autonomy of each local congregation, thereby challenging the legal, financial, and disciplinary authority of the state church.

rejoice in the name; but sure they be such, as least understand it. As he is more generally in these times taken, I suppose we may call him a Church-rebel, or one that would exclude order,[1] that his brain might rule. To decline offences; to be careful and consciable in our several actions, is a purity that every man ought to labour for, which we may well do, without a sullen segregation from all society. If there be any privileges, they are surely granted to the children of the King;[2] which are those that are the children of Heaven. If mirth and recreations be lawful, sure such a one may lawfully use it. If wine were given to cheer the heart, why should I fear to use it for that end? Surely, the merry soul is freer from intended mischief, than the thoughtful man. A bounded mirth, is a patent adding time and happiness to the crazed life of man. Yet if Laertius reports him rightly, Plato deserves a censure for allowing drunkenness at festivals; because, says he, as then, the Gods themselves reach wines to present men.[3] God delights in nothing more than in a cheerful heart, careful to perform him service. What parent is it, that rejoiceth not to see his child pleasant, in the limits of a filial duty? I know, we read of Christ's weeping, not of his laughter: yet we see, he graceth a feast with his first miracle; and that a feast of joy: And can we think that such a meeting could pass without the noise of laughter? What a lump of quickened care is the melancholic man! Change anger into mirth, and the precept will hold good still: Be merry, but sin not. As there be many, that in their life assume too great a liberty; so I believe there are some, that abridge themselves of what they might lawfully use. Ignorance is an ill steward, to provide for either soul, or body. A man that submits to reverent order, that sometimes unbends

himself in a moderate relaxation; and in all, labours to approve himself, in the sereneness of a healthful conscience: such a Puritan I will love immutably. But when a man, in things but ceremonial,[4] shall spurn at the grave authority of the Church, and out of a needless nicety, be a thief to himself of those benefits which God hath allowed him: or out of a blind and uncharitable pride, censure and scorn others as reprobates: or out of obstinacy, fill the world with brawls about undeterminable tenets: I shall think him one of those, whose opinion hath fevered his zeal to madness and distraction. I have more faith in one Solomon, than in a thousand Dutch parlours of such opinionists.[5] Behold then, what I have seen good! That it is comely to eat, and to drink, and to take pleasure in all his labour wherein he travaileth under the sun, the whole number of the days of his life, which God giveth him. For, this is his portion. Nay, "there is no profit to man, but that he eat, and drink, and delight his soul with the profit of his labour."[6] For, he that saw other things but vanity, saw this also, that it was the hand of God. Me thinks the reading of Ecclesiastes, should make a Puritan undress his brain, and lay off all those fanatic toys that jingle about his understanding. For my own part, I think the world hath not better men, than some that suffer under that name: nor withal, more scelestic villainies.[7] For, when they are once elated with that pride, they so

---

[1] *order* Anglican liturgy and ritual.

[2] *King* God.

[3] That is, they pass wine to the mortals present. Diogenes Laertius in fact says only that Plato approved of drinking at the "feasts of the god who was the giver of wine" (*Lives of Eminent Philosophers*, III.39).

[4] *in things but ceremonial* The status of church ceremonies was hotly debated: many reformers believed them "adiaphora" ("things indifferent" or unnecessary to salvation) and argued that participation in ceremonies not explicitly commanded by the Scriptures should not be compulsory.

[5] *Dutch parlours* Many English reformers moved to Holland in the early seventeenth century. Felltham contrasts the presumably endless arguments of these "opinionists" with the decisiveness of the famously wise biblical king.

[6] a paraphrase of Ecclesiastes 2:24. The "he" of the next sentence is the speaker in Ecclesiastes, who concluded that "all was vanity" (in 1:2, 2:11).

[7] *scelestic* wicked (*OED*).

contemn others, that they infringe the laws of all humane society.

OF POVERTY

The poverty of the poor man is the least part of his misery. In all the storms of fortune, he is the first that must stand the shock of extremity. Poor men are perpetual sentinels, watching in the depth of night against the incessant assaults of want; while the rich lie stoved in secure reposes:[1] and compassed with a large abundance. If the land be russeted with a bloodless famine,[2] are not the poor the first that sacrifice their lives to hunger? If war thunders in the trembling country's lap, are not the poor those that are exposed to the enemy's sword and outrage? If the plague, like a loaded sponge, flies, sprinkling poison through a populous kingdom, the poor are the fruit that are shaken from the burdened tree: while the rich, furnished with the helps of fortune, have means to wind out themselves, and turn these sad indurances on the poor,[3] that cannot avoid them. Like salt marshes, that lie low, they are sure, whensoever the sea of this world rages, to be first under, and imbarrenn'd with a fretting care.[4] Who like the poor are harrowed with oppression, ever subject to the imperious taxes, and the gripes of mightiness? Continual care checks the spirit: continual labour checks the body: and continual insultation both. He is like one rolled in a vessel full of pikes; which way soever he turns, he something finds that pricks him. Yet besides all these, there is another transcendent misery: and this is, that it maketh men contemptible.

Nil habet infoelix, &c.[5]

---

[1] *stoved*   kept in a heated room (*OED*).

[2] *russeted*   made red (*OED*).

[3] *indurances*   endurances, hardships (*OED* endurance 3).

[4] *imbarrenn'd*   made barren, unproductive (*OED* embarren).

[5] Juvenal, *Satires*, III.152.

Unhappy *want* hath nothing harder in it,
Than that it makes men scorned.——

As if the poor man were but fortune's dwarf; made lower than the rest of men, to be laughed at. The philosopher (though he were the same mind, and the same man) in his squalid rags, could not find admission, when better robes procured both an open door, and reverence. Though outward things can add nothing to our essential worth: yet, when we are judged on, by the help of others' outward senses, they much conduce to our value or disesteem. A diamond set in brass would be taken for a crystal, though it be not so, whereas a crystal set in gold will by many be thought a diamond. A poor man wise, shall be thought a fool; though he have nothing to condemn him but his being poor. The complaint is as old as Solomon: "The wisdom of the poor is despised; and his words not heard" [Ecclesiastes 9:16]. Poverty is a gulf, wherein all good parts are swallowed. Poor men, though wise, are but like satins without a gloss; which every man will refuse to look upon. Poverty is a reproach, which clouds the lustre of the purest virtue. It turns the wise man fool, to humour him that is a fool. Good parts in poverty show like beauty after sickness; pallid and pulingly deadish. And if all these calamities be but attendants, what may we judge that she is in herself? Undoubtedly, whatsoever we preach of contentedness in want, no precepts can so gain upon Nature, as to make her a non-sensitive. 'Tis impossible to find content in gnawing penury. Lack of things necessary, like a heavy load, and an ill saddle, is perpetually wringing of the back that bears it. Extreme poverty one calls a lantern, that lights us to all miseries. And without doubt, when 'tis urgent and importunate, it is ever chafing, upon the very heart of nature. What pleasure can he have in life, whose whole life is gripped by some or other misfortune? Living no time free, but that, wherein he does not live, his sleep. His mind is ever at jar, either with desire, fear, care, or sorrow: his appetite unappeasedly craving supply of food, for his body; which is either numbed with cold, in idleness; or stewed in sweat, with labour: nor can it be, but it will imbase even the purest metal in man:[1] it will alchemy the gold of virtue, and mix it with more dull alloy. It will make a man submit to those coarse ways, which another estate would scorn: nay, it will not suffer the soul to exercise that generous freedom, which equal nature has given it; but hales it to such low indecencies, as pull disdain upon it. Counsel and discretion, either quite leave a man; or else are so limited, by irresistible necessity, as they lose the brightness that they use to shine withal.

Crede mihi, miseros, prudentia prima reliquit,
Et sensus cum re, consiliumque fugit.[2]

Believe it, wisdom leaves the man distressed:
With wealth, both wit and counsel quits the breast.

Certainly, extreme poverty is worse than abundance. We may be good in plenty, if we will: in biting penury we cannot, though we would. In one, the danger is casual: in the other, 'tis necessitating. The best is that which partakes of both, and consists of neither. He that hath too little, wants feathers to fly withal: He that hath too much, is but cumbered with too large a tail. If a flood of wealth could profit us, it would be good to swim in such a sea: but it can neither lengthen our lives, nor enrich us after the end. I am pleased with that epigram, which is so like Diogenes,[3] that it makes him bite in his grave:

Effigiem, Rex Croese, tuam ditissime regum,
Vidit apud manes, Diogenes Cynicus:

Constitit; utque procul, solito maiore cachinno
Concussus, dixit: Quid tibi divitiae
Nunc prosunt, Regum Rex ô ditissime, cùm sis
Sicut ego solus, me quoque pauperior?
Nam quaecunque habui, mecum fero, cùm nihil ipse
Ex tantis tecum, Croese, fer as opibus:

When the Tubbed Cynic went to Hell, and there
Found the pale ghost of golden Croesus bare,
He stops, and jeering till he shuggs again,[4]
Says: O thou richest King of Kings, what gain
Have all thy large heaps brought thee, since I spy
Thee here alone, and poorer now than I?
For, all I had, I with me bring: but thou,
Of all thy wealth, hast not one farthing now.

Of what little use does he make the mines of this same opulent man? Surely, estates be then best, when they are likest minds that be worst: I mean, neither hot, nor cold: neither distended with too much, nor narrowly pent with too little: yet nearer to a plenty than want. We may be at ease in a room larger than ourselves: in a room that is less, we cannot. We need not use more than will serve: but we cannot use less. We see all things grow violent, and struggle, when we would imprison them in anything less than themselves. Fire, shut up, is furious. Exhalations inclouded, break out with thunder. Water, compressed, spurteth through the stretched strainer. 'Tis harder to contract many grains into one, than to cause many spring out of one. Where the channel is too little for the flood, who can wonder at the overflowing.

Quisquis inops peccat, minor est reus.

He is less guilty, that offends for want;

was the charity of Petronius Arbiter.[5] There is not in the world such another object of pity, as the

---

[1] *imbase* debase (*OED* embase 4).

[2] Ovid, *Ex Ponto*, IV.xii.47.

[3] Diogenes (ca. 412–323 B.C.E.), celebrated ancient Greek Cynic philosopher; he took up residence in a tub (hence "Tubbed Cynic" of Felltham's translation). The epigram is unidentified.

[4] *shuggs* variant of shog, to shake (here, with laughter) (*OED* shog 2).

[5] Petronius, *Satyricon*, ch. 133, sec. 3.

pinched state; which no man being secured from, I wonder at the tyrant's braves, and contempt. Questionless, I will rather with charity help him that is miserable, as I may be; than despise him that is poor, as I would not be. They have flinty and steeled hearts, that can add calamities to him, that is already but one entire mass.

OF WOMAN

Some are so uncharitable, as to think all women bad: and others are so credulous, as they believe they all are good. Sure: though every man speaks as he finds, there is reason to direct our opinion, without experience of the whole sex; which in a strict examination, makes more for their honour, than most men have acknowledged. At first, she was created his equal; only the difference was in the sex: otherwise, they both were Man. If we argue from the text, that male and female made man: so the man being put first, was worthier. I answer, "So the evening and the morning was the first day": yet few will think the night the better.[1] That man is made her governor, and so above her, I believe rather the punishment of her sin, than the prerogative of his worth: Had they both stood, it may be thought, she had never been in that subjection: for then had it been no curse, but a continuance of her former estate: which had nothing but blessedness in it. Peter Martyr indeed is of opinion, that man before the fall, had priority: But Chrysostome, he says does doubt it.[2] All will grant her body more admirable, more beautiful than man's: fuller of curiosities, and noble nature's wonders: both for conception, and fostering the producted birth. And can we think God would put a worser soul into a better body? When man was created, 'tis said, "God made man":

but when woman, 'tis said, "God builded her": as if he had then been about a frame of rarer rooms, and more exact composition.[3] And, without doubt, in her body, she is much more wonderful: and by this, we may think her so in her mind. Philosophy tells us, though the soul be not caused by the body, yet in the general it follows the temperament of it: so the comeliest outsides are naturally (for the most part) more virtuous within. If place can be any privilege, we shall find her built in Paradise, when man was made without it. 'Tis certain, they are by constitution colder than the boiling man:[4] so by this, more temperate: 'tis heat that transports man to immoderation and fury: 'tis that, which hurries him to a savage and libidinous violence. Women are naturally the more modest: and modesty is the seat and dwelling place of virtue. Whence proceed the most abhorred villainies, but from a masculine unblushing impudence? What a deal of sweetness do we find in a mild disposition? When a woman grows bold and daring, we dislike her, and say, "she is too like a man": yet in our selves, we magnify what we condemn in her. Is not this injustice? Every man is so much the better, by how much he comes nearer to God. Man in nothing is more like him, than in being merciful. Yet woman is far more merciful than man: It being a sex, wherein pity and compassion have dispersed far brighter rays. God is said to be love; and I am sure, everywhere woman is spoken of, for transcending in that quality. It was never found, but in two men only, that their love exceeded that of the feminine sex: and if you observe them, you shall find they were both of melting dispositions.[5] I know, when they prove bad, they are a sort of the vilest creatures: yet still the same reason

---

[1] See Genesis 1:27 and 1:5.

[2] Peter Martyr Vermigli (1500–1562), Italian theologian and reformer; Saint John Chrysostom (347?–407), patriarch of Constantinople.

[3] Genesis 2:22; the Geneva translation glossed "made he a woman" as "built."

[4] In classical and Renaissance physiology, women were associated with cold and moist qualities, men with hot and dry.

[5] *two men only* the biblical David and Jonathan; see esp. II Samuel 1:26.

gives it: for, *Optima corrupta, pessima*: the best things corrupted, become the worst. They are things, whose souls are of a more ductible temper,[1] than the harder metal of man: so may be made both better and worse. The representations of Sophocles and Euripides may be both true:[2] and for the tongue-vice, talkativeness, I see not but at meetings men may very well vie words with them. 'Tis true, they are not of so tumultuous a spirit, so not so fit for great actions. Natural heat does more actuate the stirring genius of man. Their easy natures make them somewhat more unresolute; whereby men have argued them of fear and inconstancy. But men have always held the Parliament, and have enacted their own wills, without ever hearing them speak: and then, how easy is it to conclude them guilty? Besides, education makes more difference between men and them, than nature: and all their aspersions are less noble, for that they are only from their enemies, men. Diogenes snarled bitterly when, walking with another, he spied two women talking, and said, "See, the viper and the asp are changing poison." The poet was conceited that said, after they were made ill, that God made them fearful, that man might rule them; otherwise they had been past dealing with. Catullus his conclusion was too general, to collect a deceit in all women, because he was not confident of his own:

> *Nulli se dicit mulier mea nubere malle*
> *Quàm mihi: non si se Jupiter ipse petat.*
> *Dicit: sed mulier Cupido quod dicit amanti,*
> *In vento, & rapida scribere oportet aqua.*[3]

My mistress swears, she'd leave all men for me:
Yea, though that Jove himself should suitor be.

She says it: but, what women swear to kind
Loves, may be writ in rapid streams, and wind.

I am resolved to honour virtue, in what sex soever I find it. And I think, in the general, I shall find it more in women, than men; though weaker, and more infirmly guarded. I believe, they are better, and may be wrought to be worse. Neither shall the faults of many, make me uncharitable to all: nor the goodness of some, make me credulous of the rest. Though hitherto, I confess, I have not found more sweet and constant goodness in man, than I have found in woman: and yet of these, I have not found a number.

Of Poets and Poetry

Surely he was a little wanton with his leisure, that first invented poetry. 'Tis but a play, which makes words dance, in the evenness of a cadency: yet without doubt, being a harmony, it is nearer to the mind than prose: for that itself is a harmony in height. But the words being rather the drossy part, conceit I take to be the principal. And here though it digresseth from truth, it flies above her, making her more rare, by giving curious raiment to her nakedness. The name the Grecians gave the men that wrote thus, showed how much they honoured it: they called them makers.[4] And had some of them had power to put their conceits in art, how near would they have come to deity? And for the virtues of men; they rest not on the bare demeanour, but slide into imagination: so proposing things above us, they kindle the reader to wonder and imitation. And certainly, poets that write thus, Plato never meant to banish.[5] His own practice shows he excluded not all. He was content to hear Antimachus recite his poem, when all the herd had left

---

[1] *ductible* malleable, pliable (*OED*).

[2] This probably refers to their differing characterizations of Electra, a more sympathetic figure in Sophocles' tragedy of that name than in Euripedes'.

[3] Catullus, *Poems*, lxx.

[4] *they called them makers* Ben Jonson discusses this point in *Discoveries*.

[5] Plato banished poets from his ideal Republic (*Republic* III.397).

him: and he himself wrote both tragedies and other pieces. Perhaps he found them a little too busy with his gods: and he being the first that made philosophy divine, and rational, was modest in his own beginnings. Another name they had of honour too, and that was Vates.[1] Nor know I how to distinguish between the prophets and poets of Israel. What is Jeremiah's Lamentation, but a kind of Sapphic elegy?[2] David's Psalms are not only poems; but songs, snatches and raptures of a flaming spirit. And this indeed I observe, to the honour of poets; I never found them covetous, or scrapingly-base. The Jews had not two such Kings in all their catalogue, as Solomon, and his father; poets both.[3] There is a largeness in their souls, beyond the narrowness of other men: and why may we not then think, this may embrace more, both of Heaven, and God? I cannot but conjecture this to be the reason, that they, most of them, are poor: They find their minds so solaced with their own flights, that they neglect the study of growing rich: and this, I confess again, I think, turns them to vice, and unmanly courses. Besides, they are for the most part mighty lovers of their palates; and this is known an impoverisher. Antigonus, in the tented field, found Antagoras cooking of a conger himself.[4] And they all are friends to the grape and liquor: though I think, many, more out of a ductible nature, and their love to pleasant company, than their affection to the juice alone. They are all of free natures; and are the truest definition of that philosopher's man, which gives him, animal risible.[5] Their grossest fault is, that you may conclude them sensual: yet this does

not touch them all. Ingenious for the most part they are. I know there be some rhyming fools; but what have they to do with poetry? When Sallust would tell us that Sempronia's wit was not ill, says he,— *Potuit versus facere, & jocum movere*: She could make a verse, and break a jest.[6] Something there is in it more than ordinary: in that it is all in such measured language, as may be marred by reading. I laugh heartily at Philoxenus his jest, who passing by, and hearing some masons mis-sensing his lines (with their ignorant sawing of them), falls to breaking their bricks amain: They ask the cause, and he replies, They spoil his work, and he theirs. Certainly, a worthy poet is so far from being a fool, that there is some wit required in him that shall be able to read him well: and without the true accent, numbered poetry does lose of the gloss. It was a speech becoming an able poet of our own, when a Lord read his verses crookedly, and he beseeched his Lordship, not to murder him in his own lines. He that speaks false Latin, breaks Priscian's head:[7] but he that repeats a verse ill, puts Homer out of joint. One thing commends it beyond oratory: it ever complieth to the sharpest judgements. He is the best orator that pleaseth all; even the crowd and clowns. But poetry would be poor, that they should all approve of. If the learned and judicious like it, let the throng bray. These, when 'tis best, will like it the least. So, they contemn what they understand not: and the neglected poet falls by want. Calpurnius makes one complain the misfortune.

Frange puer calamos, & inanes defere Musas:
Et potiùs glandes, rubicundaq; collige corna
Duc ad mulctra greges, & lac venale per urbem
Non tacitus porta: Quid enim tibi Fistula reddet,
Quo tutere famem? certè, mea carmina nemo
Praeter ab his Scopulis vent osa remurmurat Eccho.[8]

---

[1] *Vates* divinely inspired poet or bard; prophet-poet.

[2] the biblical book of Lamentations; *Sapphic* a metrical form named for the Greek lyric poet Sappho (seventh century B.C.E.).

[3] *his father* King David.

[4] *tented field* military encampment; *conger* eel.

[5] *animal risible* the laughing animal, a traditional philosophical definition of humans.

[6] Sallust, *Bellum Catilinae*, ch. 25.

[7] Priscian (fl. 500 C.E.), the best known Latin grammarian.

[8] Calpurnius Siculus, Eclogue IV, 23.

Boy, break thy pipes, leave, leave thy fruitless Muse:
Rather the mast, and blood-red cornill choose.[1]
Go lead thy flocks to milking; sell and cry
Milk through the city: What can learning buy,
To keep back hunger? None my verses mind,
But Echo babbling from these rocks and wind.

Two things are commonly blamed in poetry: nay, you take away that, if them: and these are lies, and flattery. But I have told them in the worst words: For, 'tis only to the shallow insight that they appear thus. Truth may dwell more clearly in an allegory, or a moraled fable, than in a bare narration. And for flattery, no man will take poetry literal: since in commendations, it rather shows what men should be, than what they are. If this were not, it would appear uncomely. But we all know, hyperboles in poetry, do bear a decency, nay, a grace along with them. The greatest danger that I find in it, is, that it wantons the blood, and imagination; as carrying a man in too high a delight. To prevent these, let the wise poet strive to be modest in his lines. First, that he dash not the Gods: next, that he injure not chastity, nor corrupt the ear with lasciviousness. When these are declined, I think a grave poem the deepest kind of writing. It wings the soul up higher, than the slacked pace of prose. Flashes that do follow the cup, I fear me, are too spritely to be solid: they run smartly upon the loose, for a distance or two; but then being foul, they give in, and tire. I confess, I love the sober muse, and fasting: From the other, matter cannot come so clear, but that it will be misted with the fumes of wine. Long poetry some cannot be friends withal: and indeed, it palls upon the reading. The wittiest poets have been all short, and changing soon their subject; as Horace, Martial, Juvenal, Seneca, and the two comedians.[2] Poetry should be rather like a coranto,[3] short, and nimbly-lofty; than a dull lesson, of a day long. Nor can it but be deadish, if distended: For, when 'tis right, it centers conceit, and takes but the spirit of things: and therefore foolish poesy, is of all writing the most ridiculous. When a goose dances, and a fool versifies, there is sport alike. He is twice an ass, that is a rhyming one. He is something the less unwise, that is unwise but in prose. If the subject be history, or contexted fable, then I hold it better put in prose, or blanks:[4] for ordinary discourse never shows so well in metre, as in the strain that it may seem to be spoken in: the commendation is, to do it to the life: Nor is this any other, than poetry in prose. Surely, though the world think not so, he is happy to himself, that can play the poet. He shall vent his passions by his pen, and ease his heart of their weight: and he shall often raise himself a joy in his raptures, which no man can perceive, but he. Sure, Ovid found a pleasure in't, even when he writ his *Tristia*.[5] It gently delivers the mind of distempers; and works the thoughts to a sweetness, in their searching conceit. I would not love it for a profession: and I would not want it for a recreation. I can make myself harmless, nay, amending mirth with it; while I should perhaps be trying of a worser pastime. And this I believe in it further, unless conversation corrupts his easiness, it lifts a man to nobleness; and is never in any rightly, but it makes him of a royal and capacious soul.
—1628

---

[1] *mast* a collective name for the fruit of the beech, oak, chestnut, and other forest trees, especially as food for swine (*OED* mast *sb* [2] 1); *cornill* the fruit of the Cornelian cherry tree, a fruit the size and shape of an olive (*OED* cornel [3] 1b).

[2] *the two comedians* the Roman dramatists Plautus and Terence.

[3] *coranto* a predecessor of the newspaper; a short pamphlet of public news (OED coranto[2]).

[4] *blanks* blank verse.

[5] *Tristia* "Sorrows," a collection of elegiac poems written while Ovid was in exile on the shores of the Black Sea.

A Rule in Reading Authors

Some men read authors as our gentlemen use flowers, only for delight and smell, to please their fancy, and refine their tongue. Others like the bee, extract only the honey, the wholesome precepts, and this alone they bear away, leaving the rest as little worth, of small value. In reading I will care for both, though for the last, most: the one serves to instruct the mind; the other fits her to tell what she hath learned: pity it is, they should be divided: he that hath worth in him, and cannot express it, is a chest keeping a rich jewel, and the key lost. Concealing goodness, is vice; virtue is better by being communicated. A good style, with wholesome matter, is a fair woman with a virtuous soul, which attracts the eyes of all; the good man thinks chastely, and loves her beauty for her virtue; which he still thinks more fair, for dwelling in so fair an outside. The vicious man hath lustful thoughts; and he would for her beauty fain destroy her virtue: but coming to solicit his purpose, finds such divine lectures from her angel's tongue, and those delivered with so sweet a pleasing modesty, that he thinks virtue is dissecting her soul to him, to ravish man with a beauty which he dreamed not of. So he could now curse himself for desiring that lewdly, which he hath learned since only to admire and reverence: Thus he goes away better, that came with an intent to be worse. Quaint phrases on a good subject, are baits to make an ill man virtuous: how many vile men seeking these, have found themselves converts? I may refine my speech without harm: but I will endeavour more to reform my life. 'Tis a good grace both of oratory, or the pen, to speak or write proper: but that is the best work, where the Graces and the Muses meet.

—1623

Sir Thomas Browne
1605 – 1682

Born in London, the son of a prosperous cloth merchant, Browne was educated at Winchester and Broadgates Hall (Pembroke College), Oxford, then after a period of travel proceeded to study at the three great medical schools of his age, the universities of Montpellier, Padua, and Leiden. In 1637 he settled as a practising physician in Norwich, where he remained until his death. Browne married in 1641 (despite a passage in *Religio Medici* expressing reservations about matrimony); only four of his twelve children survived into adulthood. He was a devoted Royalist throughout the civil wars and Commonwealth, though he was not active militarily and did not contribute any explicitly polemical works to the debates of the period. In addition to pursuing his profession as a provincial doctor, Browne retained a life-long interest in antiquities and natural history: among others, he corresponded with John Evelyn and Anthony à Wood, and his house was described as resembling one large cabinet of curiosities. In 1671 he was knighted by Charles II.

Browne probably composed *Religio Medici* in about 1635, when he was thirty years old. Two unauthorized editions appeared in 1642, leading Browne to publish an authorized version in 1643. The book was an immediate success, establishing Browne's reputation for wit (in the seventeenth-century sense of the word) in England and, with the appearance of a Latin translation in 1644, on the continent; other translations into Dutch, French, and German followed. In 1658, Brown published two of the most remarkable prose works of the period, *Hydriotaphia* (excerpted here) and *The Garden of Cyrus*. His other major work was *Pseudodoxia Epidemica: or Enquiries into very many Received Tenets and Commonly Presumed Truths* (1646, revised and augmented editions in 1650, 1658, 1672), popularly known as *Vulgar Errors*. An encyclopedic study of contemporary beliefs and the sources of error in a wide variety of fields, *Pseudodoxia* established Browne's reputation as a man of learning throughout Europe.

⸏⸎⸏

Religio Medici
(excerpts)

To the Reader

Certainly that man were greedy of life, who should desire to live when all the world were at an end; and he must needs be very impatient who would repine at death in the society of all things that suffer under it. Had not almost every man suffered by the press; or were not the tyranny thereof become universal; I had not wanted reason for complaint: but in times wherein I have lived to behold the highest perversion of that excellent invention; the name of his Majesty defamed, the honour of Parliament depraved, the writings of both depravedly, anticipatively, counterfeitly im-printed; complaints may seem ridiculous in private persons, and men of my condition may be as incapable of affronts,[1] as hopeless of their reparations. And truly had not the duty I owe unto the importunity of friends, and the allegiance I must ever acknowledge unto truth prevailed with me; the inactivity of my disposition might have made these sufferings continual, and time that brings other things to light, should have satisfied me in the remedy of its oblivion. But because things evidently false are not only printed, but many things of truth most falsely set forth; in this latter I could not but think my self engaged: for though we have no

---

[1] That is, when the King is being insulted, private individuals might be thought too unimportant to be affronted by the freedom of the press.

power to redress the former, yet in the other the reparation being within ourselves, I have at present represented unto the world a full and intended copy of that piece which was most imperfectly and surreptitiously published before.

This I confess about seven years past, with some others of affinity thereto, for my private exercise and satisfaction I had at leisurable hours composed; which being communicated unto one, it became common unto many, and was by transcription successively corrupted until it arrived in a most depraved copy at the press. He that shall peruse that work and shall take notice of sundry particularities and personal expressions therein, will easily discern the intention was not public: and being a private exercise directed to myself, what is delivered therein was rather a memorial unto me than an example or rule unto any other: and therefore if there be any singularity therein correspondent unto the private conceptions of any man, it doth not advantage them; or if dissentaneous thereunto, it no way overthrows them. It was penned in such a place and with such disadvantage, that (I protest) from the first setting of pen unto paper, I had not the assistance of any good book, whereby to promote my invention or relieve my memory; and therefore there might be many real lapses therein, which others might take notice of, and more that I suspected my self. It was set down many years past, and was the sense of my conceptions at that time, not an immutable law unto my advancing judgement at all times, and therefore there might be many things therein plausible unto my past apprehension, which are not agreeable unto my present self. There are many things delivered rhetorically, many expressions therein merely tropical,[1] and as they best illustrate my intention; and therefore also there are many things to be taken in a soft and flexible sense, and not to be called unto the rigid

test of reason. Lastly all that is contained therein is in submission unto maturer discernments, and as I have declared shall no further father them than the best and learned judgements shall authorize them; under favour of which considerations I have made its secrecy public and committed the truth thereof to every ingenuous reader.

Thomas Browne

THE FIRST PART

SECT. 1 For my religion, though there be several circumstances that might persuade the world I have none at all, as the general scandal of my profession,[2] the natural course of my studies, the indifferency of my behaviour, and discourse in matters of religion, neither violently defending one, nor with that common ardour and contention opposing another; yet in despite hereof I dare, without usurpation, assume the honorable style of a Christian:[3] not that I merely owe this title to the font,[3] my education, or clime wherein I was born, as being bred up either to confirm those principles my parents instilled into my unwary understanding; or by a general consent proceed in the religion of my country: But having, in my riper years, and confirmed judgment, seen and examined all, I find myself obliged by the principles of grace, and the law of mine own reason, to embrace no other name but this; neither doth herein my zeal so far make me forget the general charity I owe unto humanity, as rather to hate than pity Turks, infidels, and (what is worse) Jews, rather contenting myself to enjoy that happy style, than maligning those who refuse so glorious a title.

SECT. 2 But because the name of a Christian is become too general to express our faith, there being a geography of religions as well as lands, and every

---

[1] *tropical* figurative (of or pertaining to tropes).

[2] *the general scandal of my profession* Physicians were traditionally reputed to be irreligious.

[3] *to the font* to baptism.

clime distinguished not only by their laws and limits, but circumscribed by their doctrines and rules of faith; to be particular, I am of that reformed new-cast religion, wherein I dislike nothing but the name,[1] of the same belief our Saviour taught, the Apostles disseminated, the Fathers authorised, and the martyrs confirmed; but by the sinister ends of princes, the ambition and avarice of prelates, and the fatal corruption of times, so decayed, impaired, and fallen from its native beauty, that it required the careful and charitable hand of these times to restore it to its primitive integrity: Now the accidental occasion whereon, the slender means whereby, the low and abject condition of the person by whom so good a work was set on foot,[2] which in our adversaries begets contempt and scorn, fills me with wonder, and is the very same objection the insolent pagans first cast at Christ and his disciples.

SECT. 3 Yet have I not so shaken hands with those desperate resolutions, who had rather venture at large their decayed bottom, than bring her in to be new trimmed in the dock; who had rather promiscuously retain all, than abridge any, and obstinately be what they are, than what they have been, as to stand in diameter and swords point with them: we have reformed from them, not against them; for omitting those improperations and terms of scurrility betwixt us,[3] which only difference our affections, and not our cause, there is between us one common name and appellation, one faith, and necessary body of principles common to us both; and therefore I am not scrupulous to converse and live with them, to enter their churches in defect of ours, and either pray with them, or for them: I could never perceive any rational consequence from those many texts which prohibit the children of Israel to pollute themselves with the temples of the heathens; we being all Christians, and not divided by such detested impieties as might profane our prayers, or the place wherein we make them; or that a resolved conscience may not adore her Creator any where, especially in places devoted to his service; where if their devotions offend him, mine may please him, if theirs profane it, mine may hallow it; holy water and crucifix (dangerous to the common people) deceive not my judgment, nor abuse my devotion at all: I am, I confess, naturally inclined to that, which misguided zeal terms superstition; my common conversation I do acknowledge austere, my behaviour full of rigour, sometimes not without morosity; yet at my devotion I love to use the civility of my knee, my hat, and hand, with all those outward and sensible motions, which may express, or promote my invisible devotion. I should violate my own arm rather than a church, nor willingly deface the memory of saint or martyr. At the sight of a cross or crucifix I can dispense with my hat, but scarce with the thought or memory of my Saviour; I cannot laugh at but rather pity the fruitless journeys of pilgrims, or contemn the miserable condition of friars; for though misplaced in circumstance, there is something in it of devotion: I could never hear the *Ave Marie* bell without an elevation,[4] or think it a sufficient warrant, because they erred in one circumstance, for me to err in all, that is in silence and dumb contempt; whilst therefore they directed their devotions to her, I offered mine to God, and rectified the errors of their prayers by rightly ordering mine own; at a solemn procession I have wept abundantly, while my consorts, blind with opposition and prejudice, have fallen into an access of scorn and laughter: There are questionless both in Greek, Roman, and African churches,

---

[1] *the name* Protestant.

[2] *the person* Martin Luther, whose father was a miner.

[3] *improperations* taunts, reproaches (*OED*); Browne is referring to disputes between Protestants and Catholics, the "them" of the sentence.

---

[4] *Ave Marie bell* a Church bell that tolls every day at 6 and 12 of the clock, at the hearing whereof every one in that place soever either of house or street betakes him to his prayer, which is commonly directed to the Virgin [Browne's note].

solemnities, and ceremonies, whereof the wiser zeals do make a Christian use, and stand condemned by us; not as evil in themselves, but as allurements and baits of superstition to those vulgar heads that look asquint on the face of truth, and those unstable judgments that cannot consist in the narrow point and centre of virtue without a reel or stagger to the circumference.

SECT. 4 As there were many reformers, so likewise many reformations; every country proceeding in a particular way and method, according as their national interest together with their constitution and clime inclined them, some angrily and with extremity, others calmly, and with mediocrity,[1] not rending, but easily dividing the community, and leaving an honest possibility of a reconciliation, which though peaceable spirits do desire, and may conceive that revolution of time, and the mercies of God may effect; yet that judgment that shall consider the present antipathies between the two extremes, their contrarieties in condition, affection and opinion, may with the same hopes expect an union in the poles of Heaven.

SECT. 5 But to difference myself nearer, and draw into a lesser circle: There is no church whose every part so squares unto my conscience, whose articles, constitutions, and customs seem so consonant unto reason, and as it were framed to my particular devotion, as this whereof I hold my belief, the Church of England, to whose faith I am a sworn subject, and therefore in a double obligation, subscribe unto her articles, and endeavour to observe her constitutions: whatsoever is beyond, as points indifferent, I observe according to the rules of my private reason, or the humor and fashion of my devotion, neither believing this, because Luther affirmed it, or disproving that, because Calvin hath disavouched it. I condemn not all things in the Council of Trent, nor approve all in the Synod of Dort.[2] In brief, where the Scripture is silent, the church is my text; where that speaks, 'tis but my comment: where there is a joint silence of both, I borrow not the rules of my religion from Rome or Geneva, but the dictates of my own reason. It is an unjust scandal of our adversaries, and a gross error in ourselves, to compute the nativity of our religion from Henry the Eight, who though he rejected the Pope, refused not the faith of Rome, and effected no more than what his own predecessors desired and assayed in ages past, and was conceived the State of Venice would have attempted in our days.[3] It is as uncharitable a point in us to fall upon those popular scurrilities and opprobrious scoffs of the Bishop of Rome, whom as a temporal Prince, we owe the duty of good language: I confess there is cause of passion between us; by his sentence I stand excommunicated, heretic is the best language he affords me; yet can no ear witness I ever returned to him the name of Antichrist, man of sin, or whore of Babylon; it is the method of charity to suffer without reaction: those usual satires, and invectives of the pulpit may perchance produce a good effect on the vulgar, whose ears are opener to rhetoric than logic, yet do they in no wise confirm the faith of wiser believers, who know that a good cause needs not to be patroned by a passion, but can sustain itself upon a temperate dispute.

SECT. 6 I could never divide myself from any man upon the difference of an opinion, or be angry with his judgment for not agreeing with me in that, from which perhaps within a few days I should dissent myself: I have no genius to disputes in religion, and have often thought it wisdom to decline them, especially upon a disadvantage, or

---

[1] *mediocrity* moderation, temperance (*OED* mediocrity 2).

[2] The Council of Trent (1545–1563) defined the doctrines of the Catholic Counter-Reformation; the Synod of Dort (1618–1619) defined Calvinist doctrines (the "Rome or Geneva" respectively of the following sentence).

[3] In 1606 Pope Paul V excommunicated the entire Venetian Republic for repudiating papal authority.

when the cause of truth might suffer in the weakness of my patronage: where we desire to be informed, 'tis good to contest with men above ourselves; but to confirm and establish our opinions, 'tis best to argue with judgments below our own, that the frequent spoils and victories over their reasons may settle in ourselves an esteem, and confirmed opinion of our own. Every man is not a proper champion for truth, nor fit to take up the gauntlet in the cause of verity: Many from the ignorance of these maxims, and an inconsiderate zeal unto truth, have too rashly charged the troops of error, and remain as trophies unto the enemies of truth: A man may be in as just possession of truth as of a city, and yet be forced to surrender; 'tis therefore far better to enjoy her with peace, than to hazard her on a battle. If therefore there rise any doubts in my way, I do forget them, or at least defer them, till my better settled judgment, and more manly reason be able to resolve them; for I perceive every man's own reason is his best Oedipus,[1] and will upon a reasonable truce, find a way to loose those bonds wherewith the subtleties of error have enchained our more flexible and tender judgments. In philosophy where truth seems double-faced, there is no man more paradoxical than myself; but in divinity I love to keep the road, and though not in an implicit, yet an humble faith, follow the great wheel of the church, by which I move, not reserving any proper poles or motion from the epicycle of my own brain; by this means I leave no gap for heresies, schisms, or errors, of which at present, I hope I shall not injure truth, to say, I have no taint or tincture; I must confess my greener studies have been polluted with two or three, not any begotten in the latter centuries, but old and obsolete, such as could never have been revived, but by such extravagant and irregular heads as mine; for indeed heresies perish not with their authors, but like the river

Arethusa, though they lose their currents in one place, they rise up again in another:[2] one general council is not able to extirpate one single heresy, it may be cancelled for the present, but revolution of time and the like aspects from Heaven, will restore it, when it will flourish till it be condemned again; for as though there were a metempsychosis, and the soul of one man passed into another, opinions do find after certain revolutions, men and minds like those that first begat them. To see ourselves again we need not look for Plato's year;[3] every man is not only himself; there have been many Diogenes, and as many Timons,[4] though but few of that name; men are lived over again, the world is now as it was in ages past, there was none then, but there hath been someone since that parallels him, and is as it were his revived self.

SECT. 7 Now the first of mine was that of the Arabians, that the souls of men perished with their bodies, but should yet be raised again at the last day; not that I did absolutely conceive a mortality of the soul, but if that were, which faith, not philosophy hath yet thoroughly disproved, and that both entered the grave together, yet I held the same conceit thereof that we all do of the body, that it should rise again.[5] Surely it is but the merits of our unworthy natures, if we sleep in darkness, until the last alarum: A serious reflex upon my own unworthiness did make me backward from challenging this prerogative of my soul; so I might enjoy my

---

[1] *his best Oedipus* his best solver of problems; Oedipus saved Thebes by solving the Sphinx's riddle.

[2] *Arethusa* a mythical river from Ovid's *Metamorphoses* that crossed under the Adriatic and reappeared on the other side.

[3] *Plato's year* a revolution of certain thousand years when all things should return unto their former estate and he [Plato] be teaching again in his school as when he delivered this opinion [Browne's note].

[4] Diogenes and Timon were, respectively, the archetypal cynic and misanthropist.

[5] *it should rise again* Mortalism or soul-sleeping became a controversial heresy only a few years after Browne wrote *Religio Medici*; it is one of the beliefs attacked by Thomas Edwards in *Gangraena*. The doctrine was defended in pamphlets by the Leveller Richard Overton, and apparently sanctioned by Milton in *Paradise Lost* (10.792).

Saviour at the last, I could with patience be nothing almost unto eternity. The second was that of Origen, that God would not persist in his vengeance forever, but after a definite time of his wrath he would release the damned souls from torture;[1] which error I fell into upon a serious contemplation of the great attribute of God his mercy, and did a little cherish it in myself, because I found therein no malice, and a ready weight to sway me from the other extreme of despair, whereunto melancholy and contemplative natures are too easily disposed. A third there is which I did never positively maintain or practice, but have often wished it had been consonant to truth, and not offensive to my religion, and that is the prayer for the dead; whereunto I was inclined from some charitable inducements, whereby I could scarce contain my prayers for a friend at the ringing of a bell, or behold his corpse without an orison for his soul:[2] 'Twas a good way me thought to be remembered by posterity, and far more noble than an history. These opinions I never maintained with pertinacity, or endeavoured to inveigle any man's belief unto mine, nor so much as ever revealed or disputed them with my dearest friends; by which means I neither propagated them in others, nor confirmed them in myself, but suffering them to flame upon their own substance, without addition of new fuel, they went out insensibly of themselves; therefore these opinions, though condemned by lawful councils, were not heresies in me, but bare errors, and single lapses of my understanding, without a joint depravity of my will: Those have not only depraved understandings but diseased affections, which cannot enjoy a singularity without a heresy, or be the author of an opinion, without they be of a sect also; this was the villainy of the first schism of Lucifer, who was not content to err alone, but drew into his faction many legions of spirits; and upon this experience he tempted only Eve, as well understanding the communicable nature of sin, and that to deceive but one, was tacitly and upon consequence to delude them both.

SECT. 8 That heresies should arise we have the prophecy of Christ,[3] but that old ones should be abolished we hold no prediction. That there must be heresies, is true, not only in our church, but also in any other: even in doctrines heretical there will be super-heresies, and Arians not only divided from their church, but also among themselves:[4] for heads that are disposed unto schism and complexionally propense to innovation, are naturally indisposed for a community, nor will ever be confined unto the order or economy of one body; and therefore when they separate from others they knit but loosely among themselves; nor contented with a general breach or dichotomy with their church, do subdivide and mince themselves almost into atoms. 'Tis true, that men of singular parts and humors have not been free from singular opinions and conceits in all ages; retaining something not only beside the opinion of his own church or any other, but also any particular author: which notwithstanding a sober judgment may do without offence or heresy; for there is yet after all the decrees of councils and the niceties of the schools, many things untouched, unimagined, wherein the liberty of an honest reason may play and expatiate with security and far without the circle of an heresy.

SECT. 9 As for those wingy mysteries in divinity, and airy subtleties in religion, which have unhinged the brains of better heads, they never stretched the pia mater of mine; methinks there be not impossibilities enough in religion for an active faith; the deepest mysteries ours contains, have not only been illustrated, but maintained by syllogism, and the rule of reason: I love to lose myself in a

[1] Origen (ca. 185–ca. 254 C.E.), Alexandrian Biblical critic, theologian, and spiritual writer.

[2] *orison* prayer.

[3] See Matthew 24:11.

[4] St. Augustine described several competing factions of Arians, who denied the divinity of Christ.

mystery, to pursue my reason to an *O altitudo*.[1] 'Tis my solitary recreation to pose my apprehension with those involved enigmas and riddles of the Trinity, with incarnation and resurrection. I can answer all the objections of Satan, and my rebellious reason, with that odd resolution I learned of Tertullian, *Certum est quia impossibile est*.[2] I desire to exercise my faith in the difficultest points, for to credit ordinary and visible objects is not faith, but persuasion. Some believe the better for seeing Christ his sepulchre, and when they have seen the Red Sea, doubt not of the miracle. Now contrarily I bless myself, and am thankful that I lived not in the days of miracles, that I never saw Christ nor his disciples; I would not have been one of those Israelites that passed the Red Sea, nor one of Christ's patients, on whom he wrought his wonders; then had my faith been thrust upon me, nor should I enjoy that greater blessing pronounced to all that believe and saw not. 'Tis an easy and necessary belief to credit what our eye and sense hath examined: I believe he was dead, and buried, and rose again; and desire to see him in his glory, rather than to contemplate him in his cenotaph, or sepulchre. Nor is this much to believe, as we have reason, we owe this faith unto history: they only had the advantage of a bold and noble faith, who lived before his coming, who upon obscure prophesies and mystical types could raise a belief, and expect apparent impossibilities.

SECT. 10 'Tis true, there is an edge in all firm belief, and with an easy metaphor we may say the sword of faith; but in these obscurities I rather use it, in the adjunct the Apostle gives it, a buckler;[3] under which I perceive a wary combatant may lie invulnerable. Since I was of understanding to know we knew nothing, my reason hath been more

pliable to the will of faith; I am now content to understand a mystery without a rigid definition in an easy and platonic description.[4] That allegorical description of Hermes, pleaseth me beyond all the metaphysical definitions of divines;[5] where I cannot satisfy my reason, I love to humour my fancy; I had as leave you tell me that *anima est angelus hominis, est Corpus Dei,* as *Entelechia; Lux est umbra Dei,* as *actus perspicui:*[6] where there is an obscurity too deep for our reason, 'tis good to set down with a description, periphrasis, or adumbration; for by acquainting our reason how unable it is to display the visible and obvious effect of nature, it becomes more humble and submissive unto the subtleties of faith: and thus I teach my haggard and unreclaimed reason to stoop unto the lure of faith. I believe there was already a tree whose fruit our unhappy parents tasted, though in the same chapter, when God forbids it, 'tis positively said, the plants of the field were not yet grown; for God had not caused it to rain upon the earth.[7] I believe that the serpent (if we shall literally understand it) from his proper form and figure, made his motion on his belly before the curse. I find the trial of the Pucellage and virginity of women, which God ordained the Jews,[8] is very fallible. Experience, and history informs me, that not only many particular women, but likewise

[1] *O altitudo* referring to Romans 11:33: "O the depth of the riches both of the wisdom and the knowledge of God!"

[2] Tertullian, *De carne Christi,* 5: "It is certain, because it is impossible."

[3] *buckler* the shield of faith from Ephesians 6:16.

[4] *platonic description* meaning here a generalized or abstract description.

[5] Hermes Trismegistus was a mythical Egyptian writer credited with writing a body of ancient mystical texts, the *Corpus Hermeticum;* one of these texts defined the divine as "A sphere whose centre is everywhere, circumference nowhere."

[6] That is, he prefers the idea that "the soul is the angel of man, is the body of God" to thinking about the concept "essence"; or that "Light is the shadow of God" to the concept "actual transparency." Each pair contrasts metaphorical definitions from Renaissance philosophy (Paracelsus and Marsilio Ficino respectively) with the traditional Aristotelian terms; Browne's point is that he prefers the imaginative, metaphorical approach when the issues involved are beyond reason.

[7] See Genesis 2:5, 17.

[8] See Deuteronomy 22:13–21; *Pucellage* virginity (*OED*).

whole nations have escaped the curse of childbirth, which God seems to pronounce upon the whole sex;[1] yet do I believe that all this is true, which indeed my reason would persuade me to be false; and this I think is no vulgar part of faith to believe a thing not only above, but contrary to reason, and against the arguments of our proper senses.

SECT. 11 In my solitary and retired imagination (*Neque enim cum porticus aut me lectulus accepit, desum mihi*),[2] I remember I am not alone, and therefore forget not to contemplate him and his attributes who is ever with me, especially those two mighty ones, his wisdom and eternity; with the one I recreate, with the other I confound my understanding: for who can speak of eternity without a solecism, or think thereof without an ecstasy? Time we may comprehend, 'tis but five days elder than ourselves, and hath the same horoscope with the world; but to retire so far back as to apprehend a beginning, to give such an infinite start forward, as to conceive an end in an essence that we affirm hath neither the one nor the other; it puts my reason to Saint Paul's sanctuary;[3] my philosophy dares not say the angels can do it; God hath not made a creature that can comprehend him, 'tis the privilege of his own nature; "I am that I am," was his own definition unto Moses [Exodus 3:14]; and 'twas a short one, to confound mortality, that durst question God, or ask him what he was; indeed he only is, all others have and shall be, but in eternity there is no distinction of tenses; and therefore that terrible term "predestination," which hath troubled so many weak heads to conceive, and the wisest to explain, is in respect to God no prescious determination of our estates to come,[4] but a definitive blast of his will already fulfilled, and at the instant that he first decreed it; for to his eternity which is indivisible, and altogether, the last triumph is already sounded, the reprobates in the flame, and the blessed in Abraham's bosom. Saint Peter speaks modestly, when he saith, a thousand years to God are but as one day [II Peter 3:8]: for to speak like a philosopher, those continued instances of time which flow into thousand years, make not to him one moment; what to us is to come, to his eternity is present, his whole duration being but one permanent point without succession, parts, flux, or division.

SECT. 12 There is no attribute that adds more difficulty to the mystery of the Trinity, where though in a relative way of father and son, we must deny a priority. I wonder how Aristotle could conceive the world eternal, or how he could make good two eternities:[5] his similitude of a triangle, comprehended in a square,[6] doth somewhat illustrate the trinity of our souls, and that the triple unity of God; for there is in us not three, but a trinity of souls, because there is in us, if not three distinct souls, yet differing faculties, that can, and do subsist apart in different subjects, and yet in us are so united as to make but one soul and substance; if one soul were so perfect as to inform three distinct bodies, that were a petty trinity: conceive the distinct number of three, not divided nor separated by the intellect, but actually comprehended in its unity, and that is a perfect trinity. I have often admired the mystical way of Pythagoras, and the secret magic of numbers;[7] Beware of philosophy [Colossians 2:8], is a precept not to be received in

[1] in Genesis 3:16.

[2] Horace, *Satires*, 1.4.133–34: "For when the colonnade or my couch entertains me, I do not fail myself."

[3] the "O altitudo" of Romans 11:13 cited earlier.

[4] *prescious* prescient, foreknowing (*OED*).

[5] *De coelo*, 1.10–12.

[6] *De anima*, 2.3.

[7] Pythagoras (sixth century B.C.E.) discovered the mathematical basis of musical intervals; his disciples argued that everything in the universe was governed by numerical relations. Numerology remained popular throughout the seventeenth century. Browne explores "the secret magic of numbers" at length in his *Garden of Cyrus* (1658).

too large a sense; for in this mass of nature there is a set of things that carry in their front, though not in capital letters, yet in stenography, and short characters, something of divinity, which to wiser reasons serve as luminaries in the abyss of knowledge, and to judicious beliefs, as scales and roundels to mount the pinnacles and highest pieces of divinity.[1] The severe schools shall never laugh me out of the philosophy of Hermes, that this visible world is but a picture of the invisible, wherein as in a portrait, things are not truly, but in equivocal shapes; and as they counterfeit some more real substance in that invisible fabric.

SECT. 13 That other attribute wherewith I recreate my devotion, is his wisdom, in which I am happy; and for the contemplation of this only, do not repent me that I was bred in the way of study: The advantage I have of the vulgar, with the content and happiness I conceive therein, is an ample recompense for all my endeavours, in what part of knowledge soever. Wisdom is his most beauteous attribute, no man can attain unto it, yet Solomon pleased God when he desired it. He is wise because he knows all things, and he knoweth all things because he made them all, but his greatest knowledge is in comprehending that he made not, that is himself. And this is also the greatest knowledge in man. For this do I honour my own profession and embrace the council even of the Devil himself: had he read such a lecture in Paradise as he did at Delphos,[2] we had better known ourselves, nor had we stood in fear to know him. I know he is wise in all, wonderful in what we conceive, but far more in what we comprehend not, for we behold him but asquint upon reflex or shadow; our understanding is dimmer than Moses' eye,[3] we are ignorant of the

backparts, or lower side of his divinity; therefore to pry into the maze of his counsels, is not only folly in man, but presumption even in Angels; like us, they are his servants, not his senators; he holds no council, but that mystical one of the Trinity, wherein though there be three persons, there is but one mind that decrees, without contradiction; nor needs he any, his actions are not begot with deliberation, his wisdom naturally knows what's best; his intellect stands ready fraught with the superlative and purest ideas of goodness; consultation and election, which are two motions in us, make but one in him; his actions springing from his power, at the first touch of his will. These are contemplations metaphysical, my humble speculations have another method, and are content to trace and discover those expressions he hath left in his creatures, and the obvious effects of nature; there is no danger to profound these mysteries, no *Sanctum sanctorum* in philosophy:[4] The world was made to be inhabited by beasts, but studied and contemplated by man: 'tis the debt of our reason we owe unto God, and the homage we pay for not being beasts; without this the world is still as though it had not been, or as it was before the sixth day when as yet there was not a creature that could conceive, or say there was a world. The wisdom of God receives small honour from those vulgar heads, that rudely stare about, and with a gross rusticity admire his works; those highly magnify him whose judicious enquiry into his acts, and deliberate research into his creatures, return the duty of a devout and learned admiration.

.   .   .   .

SECT. 15 *Natura nihil agit frustra* [Nature does nothing in vain] is the only indisputed axiom in philosophy. There are no grotesques in nature; not anything framed to fill up empty cantons, and unnecessary spaces.[5] In the most imperfect crea-

---

[1] *roundels* ladder rungs (*OED* roundel 7).

[2] The motto *nosce teipsum* ("Know thyself") was inscribed on the temple of the Delphic oracle.

[3] See Exodus 33:23.

[4] *Sanctum sanctorum* holy of holies (from Exodus 26:33–34).

[5] *cantons* corners or nooks (*OED* canton *sb*[1] 1).

tures, and such as were not preserved in the ark, but, having their seeds and principles in the womb of nature, are everywhere where the power of the sun is, in these is the wisdom of his hand discovered. Out of this rank Solomon chose the object of his admiration.[1] Indeed, what reason may not go to school to the wisdom of bees, ants, and spiders? what wise hand teacheth them to do what reason cannot teach us? Ruder heads stand amazed at these prodigious pieces of nature, whales, elephants, dromedaries and camels; these, I confess, are the colossus and majestic pieces of her hand: but in these narrow engines there is more curious mathematics; and the civility of these little citizens more neatly sets forth the wisdom of their Maker. Who admires not Regiomontanus his fly beyond the eagle,[2] or wonders not more at the operation of two souls in those little bodies, than but one in the trunk of a cedar? I could never content my contemplation with those general pieces of wonder, the flux and reflux of the sea, the increase of the Nile, the conversion of the needle to the north; and have studied to match and parallel those in the more obvious and neglected pieces of nature, which without further travel I can do in the cosmography of myself. We carry with us the wonders we seek without us: there is all Africa and her prodigies in us; we are that bold and adventurous piece of nature, which he that studies wisely learns in a compendium what others labor at in a divided piece and endless volume.

SECT. 16 Thus there are two books from whence I collect my divinity; besides that written one of God, another of his servant nature, that universal and public manuscript, that lies expansed unto the eyes of all; those that never saw him in the one, have discovered him in the other: This was the scripture and theology of the heathens; the natural motion of the sun made them more admire him, than its supernatural station did the children of Israel;[3] the ordinary effect of nature wrought more admiration in them, than in the other all his miracles; surely the heathens knew better how to join and read these mystical letters, than we Christians, who cast a more careless eye on these common hieroglyphics, and disdain to suck divinity from the flowers of nature. Nor do I so forget God, as to adore the name of nature; which I define not with the schools, the principle of motion and rest, but, that straight and regular line, that settled and constant course the wisdom of God hath ordained the actions of his creatures, according to their several kinds. To make a revolution every day is the nature of the sun, because that necessary course which God hath ordained it, from which it cannot swerve, but by a faculty from that voice which first did give it motion. Now this course of nature God seldom alters or perverts, but like an excellent artist hath so contrived his work, that with the self same instrument, without a new creation he may effect his obscurest designs. Thus he sweeteneth the water with a wood, preserveth the creatures in the Ark, which the blast of his mouth might have as easily created: for God is like a skilful geometrician, who when more easily, and with one stroke of his compass, he might describe, or divide a right line, had yet rather do this in a circle or longer way, according to the constituted and forelaid principles of his art: yet this rule of his he doth sometimes pervert, to acquaint the world with his prerogative, lest the arrogancy of our reason should question his power, and conclude he could not; and thus I call the effects of nature the works of God, whose hand and instrument she only is; and therefore to ascribe his actions unto her, is to devolve the honor of the

---

[1] Proverbs 6:6: "Go to the ant, thou sluggard; consider her ways, and be wise."

[2] *Regiomontanus* Johann Muller (1436–1475), reputed to have built an iron fly and a wooden eagle, both capable of flying; Browne argues that the fly is the more wondrous because smaller.

[3] *station* standing still; see Joshua 19:12–13.

principal agent, upon the instrument; which if with reason we may do, then let our hammers rise up and boast they have built our houses, and our pens receive the honour of our writings. I hold there is a general beauty in the works of God, and therefore no deformity in any kind or species of creature whatsoever: I cannot tell by what logic we call a toad, a bear, or an elephant, ugly, they being created in those outward shapes and figures which best express the actions of their inward forms. And having past that general visitation of God, who saw that all that he had made was good, that is, conformable to his will, which abhors deformity, and is the rule of order and beauty; there is no deformity but in monstrosity, wherein notwithstanding there is a kind of beauty, Nature so ingeniously contriving the irregular parts, as they become sometimes more remarkable than the principal fabric. To speak yet more narrowly, there was never anything ugly, or misshapen, but the chaos; wherein notwithstanding to speak strictly, there was no deformity, because no form, nor was it yet impregnate by the voice of God: Now nature is not at variance with art, nor art with nature; they being both the servants of his providence: Art is the perfection of nature: Were the world now as it was the sixth day, there were yet a chaos: Nature hath made one world, and Art another. In brief, all things are artificial, for nature is the art of God.

SECT. 17 This is the ordinary and open way of his providence, which art and industry have in a good part discovered, whose effects we may foretell without an oracle; to foreshow these is not prophesy, but prognostication. There is another way full of meanders and labyrinths, whereof the Devil and spirits have no exact ephemerides;[1] and that is a more particular and obscure method of his providence, directing the operations of individuals and single essences: this we call Fortune, that serpentine and crooked line, whereby he draws those actions his wisdom intends in a more unknown and secret way. This cryptic and involved method of his providence have I ever admired, nor can I relate the history of my life, the occurrences of my days, the escapes of dangers, and hits of chance, with a *bezo las manos* [kiss of the hands] to Fortune, or a bare gramercy to my good stars. Abraham might have thought the ram in the thicket came thither by accident; humane reason would have said that mere chance conveyed Moses in the ark to the sight of Pharaoh's daughter [Exodus 2:3–10]; what a labyrinth is there in the story of Joseph [Genesis 37–48], able to convert a Stoic? Surely there are in every man's life certain rubs, doublings, and wrenches which pass awhile under the effects of chance, but at the last, well examined, prove the mere hand of God. 'Twas not dumb chance that, to discover the fougade or powder-plot, contrived a miscarriage in the letter.[2] I like the victory of '88 the better for that one occurrence which our enemies imputed to our dishonour, and the partiality of Fortune, to wit, the tempests and contrariety of winds.[3] King Philip did not detract from the nation when he said he sent his Armada to fight with men, and not to combat with the winds. Where there is a manifest disproportion between the powers and forces of two several agents, upon a maxim of reason we may promise the victory to the superior; but when unexpected accidents slip in, and unthought of occurrences intervene, these must proceed from a power that owes no obedience to those axioms: where, as in the writing upon the wall, we behold the hand, but see not the spring that moves it.

---

[1] *ephemerides* almanacs.

[2] The Gunpowder Plot (1605), a plan to blow up Parliament, was revealed when one of the conspirators wrote to warn a friend not to take his seat in Parliament that day; *fougade* French for mine.

[3] The English victory over the Spanish Armada in 1588 owed a great deal to favourable winds.

The success of that petty province of Holland (of which the Grand Seigneur proudly said, That if they should trouble him as they did the Spaniard, he would send his men with shovels and pick-axes, and throw it into the sea) I cannot altogether ascribe to the ingenuity and industry of the people, but to the mercy of God, that hath disposed them to such a thriving genius; and to the will of providence, that dispenseth her favour to each country in their preordinate season. All cannot be happy at once, for because the glory of one State depends upon the ruin of another, there is a revolution and vicissitude of their greatness, which must obey the swing of that wheel, not moved by intelligences, but by the hand of God, whereby all estates arise to their zenith and vertical points, according to their predestinated periods. For the lives not only of men, but of commonweales, and the whole world, run not upon an helix that still enlargeth, but on a circle where arriving to their meridian, they decline in obscurity, and fall under the horizon again.

SECT. 18 These must not therefore be named the effects of fortune, but in a relative way, and as we term the works of nature. It was the ignorance of man's reason that begat this very name, and by a careless term miscalled the providence of God; for there is no liberty for causes to operate in a loose and straggling way, nor any effect whatsoever, but hath its warrant from some universal or superior cause. 'Tis not a ridiculous devotion, to say a prayer before a game at tables; for even in sortileges and matters of greatest uncertainty, there is a settled and preordered course of effects; 'tis we that are blind, not Fortune: because our eye is too dim to discover the mystery of her effects, we foolishly paint her blind, and hoodwink the providence of the Almighty. I cannot justify that contemptible proverb, That fools only are fortunate, or that insolent paradox, That a wise man is out of the reach of Fortune; much less those opprobrious epithets of poets, whore, baud, and strumpet: 'Tis I confess the common fate of men of singular gifts of mind to be destitute of those of fortune; which doth not any way deject the spirit of wiser judgements, who thoroughly understand the justice of this proceeding; and being enriched with higher donatives, cast a more careless eye on these vulgar parts of felicity. 'Tis a most unjust ambition, to desire to engross the mercies of the Almighty, nor to be content with the goods of mind, without a possession of those of body or fortune: and 'tis an error worse than heresy, to adore these complemental and circumstantial pieces of felicity, and undervalue those perfections and essential points of happiness, wherein we resemble our Maker. To wiser desires 'tis satisfaction enough to deserve, though not to enjoy the favours of Fortune; let providence provide for fools: 'tis not partiality, but equity in God, who deals with us but as our natural parents; those that are able of body and mind, he leaves to their deserts; to those of weaker merits he imparts a larger portion, and pieces out the defect of one by the excess of the other.

Thus have we no just quarrel with Nature, for leaving us naked, or to envy the horns, hoofs, skins, and furs of other creatures, being provided with reason, that can supply them all. We need not labour with so many arguments to confute judicial astrology; for if there be a truth therein, it doth not injure Divinity; if to be born under Mercury disposeth us to be witty, under Jupiter to be wealthy, I do not owe a knee unto these, but unto that merciful hand that hath ordered my indifferent and uncertain nativity unto such benevolous aspects. Those that held that all things were governed by Fortune had not erred, had they not persisted there: the Romans, that erected a temple to Fortune, acknowledged therein, though in a blinder way, somewhat of Divinity; for in a wise supputation all things begin and end in the Almighty. There is a nearer way to heaven than Homer's chain; an easy logic may conjoin heaven and earth in one argument, and with less than a sorites resolve all things into God.[1] For though we christen effects by their most sensible and nearest causes, yet is God the true and infallible cause of all, whose concourse though it be general, yet doth it subdivide itself into the particular actions of every thing, and is that spirit, by which each singular essence not only subsists, but performs its operations.

Sect. 19. The bad construction and perverse comment on these pair of second causes, or visible hands of God, have perverted the devotion of many into atheism; who forgetting the honest advisoes of Faith, have listened unto the conspiracy of Passion and Reason. I have therefore always endeavoured to compose those feuds and angry dissentions between affection, faith, and reason: For there is in our soul a kind of triumvirate, or triple government of three competitors, which distract the peace of this our commonwealth, not less than did that other the state of Rome.

As Reason is a rebel unto Faith, so Passion unto Reason. As the propositions of Faith seem absurd unto Reason, so the theorems of Reason unto Passion, and both unto Faith; yet a moderate and peaceable discretion may so state and order the matter, that they may be all kings, and yet make but one monarchy, every one exercising his sovereignty and prerogative in a due time and place, according to the restraint and limit of circumstance. There are, as in philosophy, so in Divinity, sturdy doubts and boisterous objections, wherewith the unhappiness of our knowledge too nearly acquainteth us. More of these no man hath known than my self, which I confess I conquered, not in a martial posture, but on my knees. For our endeavours are not only to combat with doubts, but always to dispute with the Devil; the villainy of that spirit takes a hint of infidelity from our studies, and by

demonstrating a naturality in one way, makes us mistrust a miracle in another.

Thus having perused the Archidoxis and read the secret sympathies of things, he would dissuade my belief from the miracle of the brazen serpent, make me conceit that image worked by sympathy, and was but an Egyptian trick to cure their diseases without a miracle.[2] Again, having seen some experiments of bitumen, and having read far more of naptha, he whispered to my curiosity the fire of the altar might be natural, and bid me mistrust a miracle in Elias, when be entrenched the altar round with water;[3] for that inflammable substance yields not easily unto water, but flames in the arms of its antagonist: and thus would he inveigle my belief to think the combustion of Sodom might be natural, and that there was an asphaltic and bituminous nature in that lake before the fire of Gomorrah. I know that manna is now plentifully gathered in Calabria, and Josephus tells me in his days 'twas as plentiful in Arabia; the Devil therefore made the quaere, Where was then the miracle in the days of Moses? The Israelites saw but that in his time, the natives of those countries behold in ours. Thus the Devil played at chess with me, and yielding a pawn, thought to gain a Queen of me, taking advantage of my honest endeavours; and whilst I laboured to raise the structure of my reason, he strived to undermine the edifice of my faith.

.   .   .   .

SECT. 27 That miracles are ceased I can neither prove nor absolutely deny, much less define the time and period of their cessation; that they survived Christ is manifest upon record of Scripture; that they out-lived the Apostles also, and were

---

[1] *Homer's chain* See *Iliad* 8.18–26; *sorites* a term from logic for a series of linked propositions (*OED*).

[2] *Archidoxis* the *Archidoxis Magica*, a compilation of occult lore by the Renaissance mage Paracelsus; for the miracle of the brazen serpent, see Numbers 21:9.

[3] *fire of the altar* See Leviticus 6:13 and II Macabees 1:19–36; *miracle in Elias* I Kings 18.

revived at the conversion of nations many years after, we cannot deny, if we shall not question those writers whose testimonies we do not controvert in points that make for our own opinions; therefore that may have some truth in it that is reported by the Jesuits of their miracles in the Indies. I could wish it were true, or had any other testimony than their own pens: they may easily believe those miracles abroad, who daily conceive a greater at home, the transmutation of those visible elements into the body and blood of our Saviour: for the conversion of water into wine, which he wrought in Cana, or what the Devil would have had him done in the wilderness, of stones into bread, compared to this will scarce deserve the name of a miracle.[1] Though indeed, to speak properly, there is not one miracle greater than another, they being the extraordinary effects of the hand of God, to which all things are of an equal facility; and to create the world as easy as one single creature. For this is also a miracle, not only to produce effects against or above nature, but before nature; and to create nature as great a miracle, as to contradict or transcend her. We do too narrowly define the power of God, restraining it to our capacities. I hold that God can do all things; how he should work contradictions, I do not understand, yet dare not therefore deny. I cannot see why the Angel of God should question Esdras to recall the time past,[2] if it were beyond his own power; or that God should pose mortality in that, which he was not able to perform himself. I will not say God cannot, but he will not perform many things, which we plainly affirm he cannot: this I am sure is the mannerliest proposition, wherein notwithstanding I hold no paradox. For strictly his power is the same with his will, and they both with all the rest do make but one God.

---

[1] *water into wine* John 2:1–10; *stones into bread* Matthew 4:3, Luke 4:3.

[2] *Esdras* in the apocryphal II Esdras 4:5.

SECT. 28 Therefore that miracles have been I do believe, that they may yet be wrought by the living I do not deny: but have no confidence in those which are fathered on the dead; and this hath ever made me suspect the efficacy of relics, to examine the bones, question the habits and appurtenances of Saints, and even of Christ himself. I cannot conceive why the cross that Helena found and whereon Christ himself died should have power to restore others unto life;[3] I excuse not Constantine from a fall off his horse, or a mischief from his enemies, upon the wearing those nails on his bridle which our Saviour bore upon the cross in his hands. I compute among your *piae fraudes* [pious frauds], nor many degrees before consecrated swords and roses, that which Baldwin King of Jerusalem returned the Genovese for their cost and pains in his war, to wit the ashes of John the Baptist. Those that hold the sanctity of their souls doth leave behind a tincture and sacred faculty on their bodies, speak naturally of miracles, and do not salve the doubt. Now one reason I tender so little devotion unto relics, is, I think, the slender and doubtful respect I have always held unto antiquities: for that indeed which I admire is far before antiquity, that is, eternity, and that is God himself; who though he be styled the Ancient of Days [Daniel 7:9], cannot receive the adjunct of antiquity, who was before the world, and shall be after it, yet is not older then it; for in his years there is no climacteric; his duration is eternity, and far more venerable then antiquity.

SECT. 29 But above all things, I wonder how the curiosity of wiser heads could pass that great and indisputable miracle, the cessation of oracles: and in what swoon their reasons lay, to content themselves and sit down with such far-fetched and ridiculous reasons as Plutarch allegeth for it. The Jews that can believe that supernatural solstice of the sun in the days of Joshua have yet the impu-

---

[3] *Helena* mother of the Emperor Constantine, who allegedly found the true cross in 326.

dence to deny the eclipse, which even pagans confessed at his death:[1] but for this, it is evident beyond contradiction the Devil himself confessed it.[2] Certainly it is not a warrantable curiosity to examine the verity of Scripture by the concordance of human history, or seek to confirm the chronicle of Hester or Daniel by the authority of Megasthenes or Herodotus. I confess I have had an unhappy curiosity this way, till I laughed myself out of it with a piece of Justine, where he delivers that the children of Israel for being scabbed were banished out of Egypt. And truly since I have understood the occurrences of the world, and know in what counterfeit shapes and deceitful vizards times present represent on the stage things past; I do believe them little more than things to come. Some have been of my opinion, and endeavoured to write the history of their own lives; wherein Moses hath outgone them all, and left not only the story of his life, but as some will have it of his death also.

SECT. 30 It is a riddle to me how this story of oracles hath not wormed out of the world that doubtful conceit of spirits and witches; how so many learned heads should so far forget their metaphysics, and destroy the ladder and scale of creatures, as to question the existence of spirits: for my part, I have ever believed, and do now know, that there are witches; they that doubt of these do not only deny them, but spirits; and are obliquely and upon consequence a sort, not of infidels, but atheists. Those that to confute their incredulity desire to see apparitions shall questionless never behold any, nor have the power to be so much as witches; the Devil hath them already in a heresy as capital as witchcraft, and to appear to them, were but to convert them. Of all the delusions wherewith he deceives mortality, there is not any that puzzleth me more than the legerdemain of changelings. I do not credit those transformations of reasonable creatures into beasts, or that the Devil hath a power to transpeciate a man into a horse, who tempted Christ (as a trial of his divinity) to convert but stones into bread. I could believe that spirits use with man the act of carnality, and that in both sexes; I conceive they may assume, steal, or contrive a body, wherein there may be action enough to content decrepit lust, or passion to satisfy more active veneries; yet in both, without a possibility of generation: and therefore that opinion, that Antichrist should be born of the tribe of Dan by conjunction with the Devil, is ridiculous, and a conceit fitter for a Rabbi than a Christian. I hold that the Devil doth really possess some men, the spirit of melancholy others, the spirit of delusion others; that as the Devil is concealed and denied by some, so God and good angels are pretended by others, whereof the late detection of the Maid of Germany hath left a pregnant example.[3]

SECT. 31 Again, I believe that all that use sorceries, incantations, and spells are not witches, or, as we term them, magicians. I conceive there is a traditional magic, not learned immediately from the Devil, but at second hand from his scholars, who having once the secret betrayed, are able and do empirically practice without his advice, they both proceeding upon the principles of nature: where actives, aptly conjoined to disposed passives, will under any master produce their effects. Thus I think at first a great part of philosophy was witchcraft, which being afterward derived from one to another, proved but philosophy, and was indeed no more than the honest effects of nature. What invented by us is philosophy, learned from him is magic. We do surely owe the honour of many secrets to the discovery of good and bad angels. I could never pass that sentence of Paracelsus without

---

[1] *his death* Christ's; see Luke 23:44–45.

[2] In his oracles to Augustus [Browne's note].

[3] That lived without meat upon the smell of a rose [Browne's note]. Probably referring to Eva Flegan, who allegedly stopped eating in 1597 and was exposed as a fraud in 1628.

an asterisk or annotation: *Ascendens constellatum multa revelat, quaerentibus magnalia naturae,* i.e. *opera Dei.*[1] I do think that many mysteries ascribed to our own inventions have been the courteous revelations of spirits; for those noble essences in heaven bear a friendly regard unto their fellow natures on earth; and therefore [I] believe that those many prodigies and ominous prognostics, which fore-run the ruins of states, princes, and private persons, are the charitable premonitions of good angels, which more careless enquiries term but the effects of chance and nature....

SECT. 33   Therefore for spirits I am so far from denying their existence, that I could easily believe, that not only whole countries, but particular persons have their tutelary, and guardian angels: it is not a new opinion of the Church of Rome, but an old one of Pythagoras and Plato; there is no heresy in it, and if not manifestly defined in Scripture, yet is it an opinion of a good and wholesome use in the course and actions of a man's life, and would serve as an hypothesis to salve many doubts, whereof common philosophy affordeth no solution. Now if you demand my opinion and metaphysics of their natures, I confess them very shallow, most of them in a negative way, like that of God; or in a comparative, between ourselves and fellow creatures; for there is in this universe a stair, or manifest scale of creatures, rising not disorderly, or in confusion, but with a comely method and proportion. Between creatures of mere existence and things of life, there is a large disproportion of nature; between plants and animals or creatures of sense, a wider difference; between them and man, a far greater: and if the proportion hold on, between man and angels there should be yet a greater. We do not comprehend their natures, who retain the first definition of Porphyry and distinguish them from ourselves by immortality; for before his fall, man also was im-

mortal; yet must we needs affirm that he had a different essence from the angels: having therefore no certain knowledge of their natures, 'tis no bad method of the schools, whatsoever perfection we find obscurely in ourselves, in a more complete and absolute way to ascribe unto them....

SECT. 34   These are certainly the magisterial and masterpieces of the Creator, the flower (or as we may say) the best part of nothing; actually existing, what we are but in hopes, and probability; we are only that amphibious piece between a corporal and spiritual essence, that middle form that links those two together, and makes good the method of God and nature, that jumps not from extremes, but unites the incompatible distances by some middle and participating natures. That we are the breath and similitude of God, it is indisputable, and upon record of holy Scripture, but to call ourselves a microcosm, or little world, I thought it only a pleasant trope of rhetoric, till my near judgement and second thoughts told me there was a real truth therein: for first we are a rude mass, and in the rank of creatures which only are, and have a dull kind of being not yet privileged with life, or preferred to sense or reason; next we live the life of plants, the life of animals, the life of men, and at last the life of spirits, running on in one mysterious nature those five kinds of existences, which comprehend the creatures not only of the world, but of the universe. Thus is man that great and true amphibium, whose nature is disposed to live not only like other creatures in diverse elements, but in divided and distinguished worlds; for though there be but one world to sense, there are two to reason; the one visible, the other invisible, whereof Moses seems to have left no description, and of the other so obscurely, that some parts thereof are yet in controversy; and truly for the first chapters of Genesis, I must confess a great deal of obscurity; though divines have to the power of human reason endeavoured to make all go in a literal meaning, yet those allegorical interpreta-

---

[1]   Thereby is meant our good Angel appointed us from our nativity [Browne's note].

tions are also probable, and perhaps the mystical method of Moses bred up in the hieroglyphical schools of the Egyptians....

SECT. 36 The whole creation is a mystery, and particularly that of man; at the blast of his mouth were the rest of the creatures made, and at his bare word they started out of nothing: but in the frame of man (as the text describes it) he played the sensible operator, and seemed not so much to create, as make him; when he had separated the materials of other creatures, there consequently resulted a form and soul, but having raised the walls of man, he was driven to a second and harder creation of a substance like himself, an incorruptible and immortal soul.... In our study of anatomy there is a mass of mysterious philosophy, and such as reduced the very heathens to divinity; yet amongst all those rare discoveries and curious pieces I find in the fabric of man, I do not so much content myself as in that I find not, that is, no organ or proper instrument for the rational soul; for in the brain, which we term the seat of reason, there is not anything of moment more than I can discover in the crany of a beast: and this is a sensible and no inconsiderable argument of the inorganity of the soul, at least in that sense we usually so receive it. Thus we are men, and we know not how; there is something in us, that can be without us, and will be after us; though it is strange that it hath no history, what it was before us, nor cannot tell how it entered in us.

SECT. 37 Now for these walls of flesh, wherein the soul doth seem to be immured before the Resurrection, it is nothing but an elemental composition, and a fabric that must fall to ashes. "All flesh is grass," is not only metaphorically, but literally true, for all those creatures we behold are but the herbs of the field, digested into flesh in them, or more remotely carnified in ourselves. Nay further, we are what we all abhor, anthropophagi and cannibals, devourers not only of men, but of our-

selves; and that not in an allegory, but a positive truth; for all this mass of flesh which we behold came in at our mouths: this frame we look upon hath been upon our trenchers. In brief, we have devoured ourselves, I cannot believe the wisdom of Pythagoras did ever positively, and in a literal sense, affirm his metempsychosis, or impossible transmigration of the souls of men into beasts: of all metamorphoses or transmigrations, I believe only one, that is of Lot's wife, for that of Nebuchadnezzar proceeded not so far.[1] In all others I conceive no further verity than is contained in their implicit sense and morality: I believe that the whole frame of a beast doth perish, and is left in the same estate after death as before it was materialed into life; that the souls of men know neither contrary nor corruption; that they subsist beyond the body, and outlive death by the privilege of their proper natures, and without a miracle; that the souls of the faithful, as they leave earth, take possession of Heaven: that those apparitions and ghosts of departed persons are not the wandering souls of men, but the unquiet walks of Devils, prompting and suggesting us unto mischief, blood and villainy, instilling and stealing into our hearts that the blessed spirits are not at rest in their graves but wander solicitous of the affairs of the world. That those phantasms appear often, and do frequent cemeteries, charnel houses and churches, it is because those are the dormitories of the dead, where the Devil like an insolent champion beholds with pride the spoils and trophies of his victory in Adam.

.   .   .   .

SECT. 48 How shall the dead arise, is no question of my faith; to believe only possibilities, is not faith, but mere philosophy; many things are true in divinity, which are neither inducible by reason, nor confirmable by sense, and many things in philosophy confirmable by sense, yet not inducible by

---

[1] *Lot's wife* who turned into a pillar of salt (Genesis 19:26); for Nebuchadnezzar, see Daniel 4:33.

reason. Thus it is impossible by any solid or demonstrative reasons to persuade a man to believe the conversion of the needle to the north; though this be possible, and true, and easily credible, upon a single experiment unto the sense. I believe that our estranged and divided ashes shall unite again, that our separated dust after so many pilgrimages and transformations into the parts of minerals, plants, animals, elements, shall at the voice of God return into their primitive shapes; and join again to make up their primary and predestinate forms. As at the Creation, there was a separation of that confused mass into its species, so at the destruction thereof there shall be a separation into its distinct individuals. As at the creation of the world, all the distinct species that we behold, lay involved in one mass, till the fruitful voice of God separated this united multitude into its several species: so at the last day, when these corrupted relics shall be scattered in the wilderness of forms, and seem to have forgot their proper habits, God by a powerful voice shall command them back into their proper shapes, and call them out by their single individuals: Then shall appear the fertility of Adam, and the magic of that sperm that hath dilated into so many millions. I have often beheld as a miracle, that artificial resurrection and revivification of mercury, how being mortified into thousand shapes, it assumes again its own, and returns into its numerical self. Let us speak naturally, and like philosophers, the forms of alterable bodies in these sensible corruptions perish not; nor, as we imagine, wholly quit their mansions, but retire and contract themselves into their secret and unaccessible parts, where they may best protect themselves from the action of their antagonist. A plant or vegetable consumed to ashes, to a contemplative and school philosopher seems utterly destroyed, and the form to have taken his leave forever: But to a sensible artist the forms are not perished, but withdrawn into their incombustible part, where they lie secure from the action of that devouring element. This is made good by experience, which can from the ashes of a plant revive the plant, and from its cinders recall it into its stalk and leaves again. What the art of man can do in these inferior pieces, what blasphemy is it to affirm the finger of God cannot do in these more perfect and sensible structures? This is that mystical philosophy, from whence no true scholar becomes an atheist, but from the visible effects of nature, grows up a real divine, and beholds not in a dream, as Ezekiel [37:1–14], but in an ocular and visible object the types of his resurrection.

.   .   .   .

SECT. 57   I believe many are saved who to man seem reprobated, and many are reprobated, who in the opinion and sentence of man, stand elected; there will appear at the last day strange and unexpected examples both of his justice and his mercy, and therefore to define either is folly in man, and insolency even in the devils; those acute and subtle spirits, in all their sagacity, can hardly divine who shall be saved; which if they could prognosticate, their labour were at an end; nor need they compass the earth, seeking whom they may devour. Those who upon a rigid application of the Law, sentence Solomon unto damnation, condemn not only him, but themselves, and the whole world; for by the letter and written word of God, we are without exception in the state of death, but there is a prerogative of God, and an arbitrary pleasure above the letter of his own Law, by which alone we can pretend unto salvation, and through which Solomon might be as easily saved as those who condemn him.

SECT. 58   The number of those who pretend unto salvation, and those infinite swarms who think to pass through the eye of this needle, hath much amazed me. That name and compellation of "little flock" [Luke 12:32], doth not comfort but deject my devotion, especially when I reflect upon mine own unworthiness, wherein, according to my humble apprehensions, I am below them all. I believe there shall never be an anarchy in Heaven, but as there are hierarchies amongst the angels, so shall there be degrees of priority amongst the Saints. Yet is it (I protest) beyond my ambition to aspire unto the first ranks; my desires only are, and I shall be happy therein, to be but the last man, and bring up the rear in Heaven.

SECT. 59 Again, I am confident, and fully persuaded, yet dare not take my oath of my salvation; I am as it were sure, and do believe, without all doubt, that there is such a city as Constantinople, yet for me to take my oath thereon were a kind of perjury, because I hold no infallible warrant from my own sense to confirm me in the certainty thereof. And truly, though many pretend an absolute certainty of their salvation, yet when an humble soul shall contemplate her own unworthiness, she shall meet with many doubts and suddenly find how little we stand in need of the precept of Saint Paul, *Work out your salvation with fear and trembling*. That which is the cause of my election, I hold to be the cause of my salvation, which was the mercy and *beneplacit* of God, before I was, or the foundation of the world. Before Abraham was, I am, is the saying of Christ, yet is it true in some sense if I say it of myself, for I was not only before my self, but Adam, that is, in the idea of God, and the decree of that synod held from all eternity. And in this sense, I say, the world was before the creation, and at an end before it had a beginning; and thus was I dead before I was alive; though my grave be England, my dying place was Paradise, and Eve miscarried of me before she conceived of Cain.

SECT. 60 Insolent zeals that do decry good works and rely only upon faith, take not away merit: for depending upon the efficacy of their faith, they enforce the condition of God, and in a more sophistical way do seem to challenge Heaven. It was decreed by God, that only those that lapped in the waters like dogs, should have the honour to destroy the Midianites [Judges 7:5–7], yet could none of those justly challenge, or imagine he deserved that honour thereupon. I do not deny, but that true faith, and such as God requires, is not only a mark or token, but also a means of our salvation, but where to find this is as obscure to me, as my last end. And if our Saviour could object unto his own disciples and favourites, a faith that to the quantity of a grain of mustard seed is able to remove mountains; surely, that which we boast of is not anything, or at the most but a remove from nothing. This is the tenor of my belief, wherein, though there be many things singular, and to the humour of my irregular self, yet, if they square not with maturer judgements, I disclaim them, and do no further father them, than the learned and best judgements shall authorize them.

THE SECOND PART

SECT. 1 Now for that other virtue of charity, without which faith is a mere notion, and of no existence, I have ever endeavoured to nourish the merciful disposition and humane inclination I borrowed from my parents, and regulate it to the written and prescribed laws of charity; and if I hold the true anatomy of myself, I am delineated and naturally framed to such a piece of virtue: for I am of a constitution so general, that it consorts and sympathizeth with all things; I have no antipathy, or rather idiosyncracy, in diet, humour, air, anything; I wonder not at the French for their dishes of frogs, snails, and toadstools, nor at the Jews for locusts and grasshoppers, but being amongst them, make them my common viands; and I find they agree with my stomach as well as theirs; I could digest a salad gathered in a church-yard, as well as in a garden. I cannot start at the presence of a serpent, scorpion, lizard, or salamander; at the sight of a toad or viper I find in me no desire to take up a stone to destroy them. I feel not in myself those common antipathies that I can discover in others. Those national repugnances do not touch me, nor do I behold with prejudice the French, Italian, Spaniard, or Dutch; but where I find their actions in balance with my countrymen's, I honour, love, and embrace them in the same degree. I was born in the eighth climate,[1] but seem to be framed and constellated unto all; I am no plant that will not prosper out of a garden. All places, all airs make unto me one country; I am in England everywhere, and under any meridian: I have been shipwrecked, yet am not enemy with the sea or winds; I can study, play, or sleep in a tempest. In brief, I am averse from nothing, neither plant, animal, nor spirit; my conscience would give me the lie if I should say I absolutely detest or hate any essence but the Devil, or so at least abhor anything but that we might come to composition. If there be any among those common objects of hatred I do condemn and laugh at, it is that great enemy of reason, virtue, and religion, the multitude: that numerous piece of monstrosity, which taken asunder seem men, and the reasonable creatures of God; but confused together, make but one great beast, and a monstrosity more prodigious than Hydra; it is no breach of charity to call these fools, it is the style all holy writers have afforded them, set down by Solomon in canonical Scripture, and a point of our faith to believe so. Neither in the name of multitude do I only include the base and minor sort of people; there is a rabble even amongst the gentry, a sort of plebeian heads, whose fancy moves with the same wheel as these; men in the same level with mechanics, though their fortunes do somewhat gild their infirmities, and their purses compound for their follies. But as in casting account, three or four men together come short in account of one man placed by himself below them: so neither are a troop of these ignorant Dorados of that true esteem and value,[2] as many a forlorn person, whose condition doth place him below their feet. Let us speak like politicians; there is a nobility without heraldry, a natural dignity whereby one man is ranked with another, another filed before him, according to the quality of his desert, and preeminence of his good parts. Though the corruption of these times and the bias of present practise wheel another way, thus it was in the first and primitive commonwealths, and is yet in the integrity and cradle of well-ordered polities, till corruption getteth ground, ruder desires labouring after that which wiser considerations condemn, everyone having a liberty to amass and heap up riches, and they a license or faculty to do or purchase anything.

. . . .

SECT. 5 There is I think no man that apprehends his own miseries less than myself, and no man that so nearly apprehends another's. I could lose an arm without a tear, and with a few groans, methinks, be quartered into pieces; yet can I weep most seriously at a play, and receive with a true passion the counterfeit griefs of those known and professed impostors. It is a barbarous part of inhumanity to add unto any afflicted party's misery, or endeavour to multiply in any man a passion, whose single nature is already above his patience; this was the greatest affliction of Job, and those oblique expostulations of his friends a deeper injury than the downright blows of the Devil. It is not the tears of our own eyes only, but of our friends also, that do exhaust the current of our sorrows, which, falling into many streams, runs more peaceably, and is contented with a narrower channel. It is an act within the power of charity, to translate a passion out of one breast into another, and to divide a sorrow almost out of itself; for an affliction, like a

---

[1] *eighth climate*   the eighth of the twenty-four climatic belts between the equator and the North Pole.

[2] *Dorados*   wealthy persons.

dimension, may be so divided, as if not indivisible, at least to become insensible. Now with my friend I desire not to share or participate, but to engross his sorrows, that by making them mine own, I may more easily discuss them; for in mine own reason, and within my self I can command that which I cannot entreat without myself, and within the circle of another. I have often thought those noble pairs and examples of friendship not so truly histories of what had been, as fictions of what should be, but I now perceive nothing in them but possibilities, nor anything in the heroic examples of Damon and Pythias, Achilles and Patroclus, which methinks upon some grounds I could not perform within the narrow compass of myself. That a man should lay down his life for his friend, seems strange to vulgar affections, and such as confine themselves within that worldly principle, charity begins at home. For mine own part I could never remember the relations that I hold unto myself, nor the respect I owe unto mine own nature, in the cause of God, my country, and my friends. Next to these three, I do embrace myself; I confess I do not observe that order that the schools ordain our affections, to love our parents, wives, children, and then our friends; for excepting the injunctions of religion, I do not find in myself such a necessary and indissoluble sympathy to all those of my blood. I hope I do not break the fifth commandment, if I conceive I may love my friend before the nearest of my blood, even those to whom I owe the principles of life. I never yet cast a true affection on a woman, but I have loved my friend as I do virtue, my soul, my God. From hence me-thinks I do conceive how God loves man, what happiness there is in the love of God. Omitting all other, there are three most mystical unions: two natures in one person; three persons in one nature; one soul in two bodies. For though indeed they be really divided, yet are they so united, as they seem but one, and make rather a duality then two distinct souls.

SECT. 6 There are wonders in true affection, it is a body of enigmas, mysteries, and riddles, wherein two so become one, as they both become two; I love my friend before myself, and yet methinks I do not love him enough; some few months hence my multiplied affection will make me believe I have not loved him at all; when I am from him, I am dead till I be with him, when I am with him, I am not satisfied, but would still be nearer him; united souls are not satisfied with embraces, but desire to be truly each other, which being impossible, their desires are infinite, and must proceed without a possibility of satisfaction. Another misery there is in affection, that whom we truly love like our own selves, we forget their looks, nor can our memory retain the idea of their faces; and it is no wonder, for they are ourselves, and our affection makes their looks our own. This noble affection falls not on vulgar and common constitutions, but on such as are marked for virtue; he that can love his friend with this noble ardour, will in a competent degree affect all. Now, if we can bring our affections to look beyond the body, and cast an eye upon the soul, we have found out the true object, not only of friendship but charity; and the greatest happiness that we can bequeath the soul, is that wherein we all do place our last felicity, salvation, which though it be not in our power to bestow, it is in our charity and pious invocations to desire, if not to procure. And further, I cannot contentedly frame a prayer for myself in particular, without a catalogue of my friends, nor request a happiness wherein my sociable disposition doth not desire the fellowship of my neighbour. I never hear the toll of a passing bell, though in my mirth and at a tavern, without my prayers and best wishes for the departing spirit; I cannot go to cure the body of my patient, but I forget my profession, and call unto God for his soul; I cannot see one say his prayers, but instead of imitating him, I fall into a supplication for him, who perhaps is no more to me than a common nature: and if God hath vouchsafed an ear to my supplications, there are surely many happy that never saw me, and enjoy the blessing of mine unknown devotions. To pray for enemies, that is, for their salvation, is no harsh precept, but the practise of our daily and ordinary devotions.

.   .   .   .

SECT. 8 I thank God, amongst those millions of vices I do inherit and hold from Adam, I have escaped one, and that a mortal enemy to charity, the first and father sin, not only of man but of the devil, pride, a vice whose name is comprehended in a monosyllable, but in its nature not circumscribed with a world. I have escaped it in a condition that can hardly avoid it: those petty acquisitions and reputed perfections that advance and elevate the conceits of other men add no feathers unto mine; I have seen a grammarian tower and plume himself over a single line in Horace, and show more pride in the construction of one ode, than the author in the composure of the whole book. For my own part, besides the jargon and *patois* of several provinces, I understand no less then six languages, yet I protest I have no higher conceit of myself, than had our fathers before the confusion of Babel, when there was but one language in the world, and none to boast himself either linguist or critic. I have not only seen several countries, beheld the nature of their climes, the chorography of their provinces, topography of their cities, but understood their several laws, customs and policies; yet cannot all this persuade the dullness of my spirit unto such an opinion of myself, as I behold in nimbler and conceited heads, that never looked a degree beyond their nests. I know the names, and somewhat more, of all the constellations in my horizon, yet I have seen a prating mariner, that could only name the pointers and the North Star, out-talk me, and conceit himself a whole sphere above me. I know most of the plants of my country, and of those about me; yet methinks I do not know so many as when I did but know an hundred, and had scarcely ever simpled further than Cheapside:[1] for indeed heads of capacity, and such as are not full with a handful, or easy measure of knowledge, think they know nothing, till they know all; which being impossible, they fall upon the opinion of Socrates, and only know they know not anything...: we do but learn today what our better advanced judgements will unteach us tomorrow: and Aristotle doth but instruct us, as Plato did him; that is, to confute himself. I have run through all sects, yet find no rest in any; though our first studies and junior endeavours may style us peripatetics, stoics, or academics, yet I perceive the wisest heads prove at last almost all sceptics, and stand like Janus in the field of knowledge. I have therefore one common and authentic philosophy I learned in the schools, whereby I discourse and satisfy the reason of other men; another more reserved and drawn from experience, whereby I content mine own. Solomon that complained of ignorance in the height of knowledge, hath not only humbled my conceits, but discouraged my endeavours. There is yet another conceit that hath sometimes made me shut my books; which tells me it is a vanity to waste our days in the blind pursuit of knowledge; it is but attending a little longer, and we shall enjoy that by instinct and infusion which we endeavour at here by labour and inquisition: it is better to sit down in a modest ignorance, and rest contented with the natural blessing of our own reasons, than buy the uncertain knowledge of this life with sweat and vexation, which death gives every fool gratis, and is an accessory of our glorification.

SECT. 9 I was never yet once,[2] and commend their resolutions who never marry twice; not that I disallow of second marriage, as neither in all cases of

---

[1] *simpled*   gathered simples (medicinal herbs) (*OED* simple v^2).

[2] Browne married in 1641.

polygamy, which, considering some times and the unequal number of both sexes, may be also necessary. The whole woman was made for man, but the twelfth part of man for woman: man is the whole world and the breath of God, woman the rib and crooked piece of man. I could be content that we might procreate like trees, without conjunction, or that there were any way to perpetuate the world without this trivial and vulgar way of coition. It is the foolishest act a wise man commits in all his life, nor is there any thing that will more deject his cold imagination, when he shall consider what an odd and unworthy piece of folly he hath committed. I speak not in prejudice, nor am averse from that sweet sex, but naturally amorous of all that is beautiful; I can look a whole day with delight upon a handsome picture, though it be but of an horse. It is my temper, and I like it the better, to affect all harmony, and sure there is music even in the beauty, and the silent note which Cupid strikes, far sweeter than the sound of an instrument. For there is a music wherever there is a harmony, order, or proportion; and thus far we may maintain the music of the spheres; for those well ordered motions and regular paces, though they give no sound unto the ear, yet to the understanding they strike a note most full of harmony. Whosoever is harmonically composed delights in harmony; which makes me much mistrust the symmetry of those heads which declaim against all Church music. For myself, not only from my obedience, but my particular genius, I do embrace it; for even that vulgar and tavern music, which makes one man merry, another mad, strikes me into a deep fit of devotion, and a profound contemplation of the first composer; there is something in it of divinity more than the ear discovers. It is an hieroglyphical and shadowed lesson of the whole world, and the creatures of God; such a melody to the ear, as the whole world well understood, would afford the understanding. In brief, it is a sensible fit of that harmony, which intellectually

sounds in the ears of God. It unties the ligaments of my frame, takes me to pieces, dilates me out of myself, and by degrees, methinks, resolves me into Heaven. I will not say with Plato, the soul is an harmony, but harmonical, and hath its nearest sympathy unto music: thus, some whose temper of body agrees and humours the constitution of their souls are born poets, though indeed all are naturally inclined unto rhythm…

I feel not in me those sordid and unchristian desires of my profession; I do not secretly implore and wish for plagues, rejoice at famines, revolve ephemerides, and almanacks in expectation of malignant aspects, fatal conjunctions, and eclipses: I rejoice not at unwholesome springs, nor unseasonable winters; my prayer goes with the husbandman's; I desire every thing in its proper season, that neither men nor the times be out of temper. Let me be sick myself, if sometimes the malady of my patient be not a disease unto me; I desire rather to cure his infirmities than my own necessities; where I do him no good methinks it is scarce honest gain, though I confess 'tis but the worthy salary of our well-intended endeavours. I am not only ashamed, but heartily sorry, that besides death, there are diseases incurable, yet not for my own sake, or that they be beyond my art, but for the general cause and sake of humanity, whose common cause I apprehend as mine own. And to speak more generally, those three noble professions which all civil commonwealths do honour, are raised upon the fall of Adam, and are not anyway exempt from their infirmities; there are not only diseases incurable in physic, but cases indissoluble in laws, vices incorrigible in divinity. If general councils may err, I do not see why particular courts should be infallible; their perfectest rules are raised upon the erroneous reason of man, and the laws of one do but condemn the rules of another; as Aristotle ofttimes the opinions of his predecessors, because, though agreeable to reason, yet were not consonant to his own rules, and the logic of his proper principles. Again, to speak nothing of the sin against the Holy Ghost, whose cure not only, but whose nature is unknown, I can cure the gout or stone in some, sooner than divinity, pride or avarice in others. I can cure vices by physic, when they remain incurable by divinity, and shall obey my pills, when they condemn their precepts. I boast nothing, but plainly say, we all labour against our own cure, for death is the cure of all diseases. There is no catholicon or universal remedy I know but this, which though nauseous to queasy stomachs, yet to prepared appetites is nectar, and a pleasant potion of immortality....

SECT. 11 Now for my life, it is a miracle of thirty years, which to relate were not an history, but a piece of poetry, and would sound to common ears like a fable; for the world, I count it not an inn, but an hospital, and a place not to live, but to die in. The world that I regard is myself; it is the microcosm of mine own frame that I cast mine eye on; for the other, I use it but like my globe, and turn it round sometimes for my recreation. Men that look upon my outside, perusing only my condition and fortunes, do err in my altitude; for I am above Atlas his shoulders. The earth is a point not only in respect of the heavens above us, but of that heavenly and celestial part within us: that mass of flesh that circumscribes me, limits not my mind: that surface that tells the heavens it hath an end, cannot persuade me I have any; I take my circle to be above three hundred and sixty; though the number of the ark do measure my body, it comprehendeth not my mind: whilst I study to find how I am a microcosm or little world, I find myself something more than the great. There is surely a piece of divinity in us, something that was before the elements and owes no homage unto the sun. Nature tells me I am the image of God, as well as scripture; he that understands not thus much hath not his introduction or first lesson, and is yet to begin the alphabet of man.

Let me not injure the felicity of others, if I say I am as happy as any, I have that in me can convert poverty into riches, adversity into prosperity: I am more invulnerable than Achilles, fortune hath not one place to hit me; *Ruat coelum, Fiat voluntas tua* [may your will be done though the heavens fall] salveth all; so that whatsoever happens, it is but what our daily prayers desire. In brief, I am content, and what should providence add more? Surely this is it we call happiness, and this do I enjoy; with this I am happy in a dream, and as content to enjoy a happiness in a fancy as others in a more apparent truth and reality.

. . . .

SECT. 15 I conclude therefore and say, there is no happiness under (or as Copernicus will have it, above) the sun, nor any crambe in that repeated verity and burden of all the wisdom of Solomon, *All is vanity and vexation of spirit*; there is no felicity in that the world adores.[1] Aristotle whilst he labours to refute the ideas of Plato, falls upon one himself: for his *summum bonum* [greatest good] is a chimæra, and there is no such thing as his felicity. That wherein God himself is happy, the holy angels are happy, in whose defect the Devils are unhappy; that dare I call happiness: whatsoever conduceth unto this, may with an easy metaphor deserve that name; whatsoever else the world terms happiness, is to me a story out of Pliny, an apparition, or neat delusion, wherein there is no more of happiness than the name. Bless me in this life with but the peace of my conscience, command of my affections, the love of thyself and my dearest friends, and I shall be happy enough to pity Caesar. These are O Lord the humble desires of my most reasonable ambition and all I dare call happiness on earth: wherein I set no rule or limit to thy hand or providence. Dispose of me according to the wisdom of thy pleasure. Thy will be done, though in my own undoing.

—1643

---

[1] *crambe* a tiresome repetition; for Solomon, see Ecclesiastes 2:11.

Hydriotaphia, Urne-Burial,
or A Discourse of the Sepulchral Urnes
Lately found in Norfolk
(excerpts)

TO MY WORTHY AND HONOURED FRIEND,
THOMAS LE GROS, OF CROSTWICK, ESQUIRE

When the funeral pyre was out, and the last valediction over, men took a lasting adieu of their interred friends, little expecting the curiosity of future ages should comment upon their ashes, and, having no old experience of the duration of the relics, held no opinion of such after-considerations.

But who knows the fate of his bones, or how often he is to be buried? who hath the oracle of his ashes, or whither they are to be scattered? The relics of many lie like the ruins of Pompey's, in all parts of the earth; and when they arrive at your hands, these may seem to have wandered far, who in a direct and meridian travel, have but few miles of known Earth between yourself and the pole.

That the bones of Theseus should be seen again in Athens was not beyond conjecture, and hopeful expectation; but that these should arise so opportunely to serve yourself, was an hit of fate and honour beyond prediction.

We cannot but wish these urns might have the effect of theatrical vessels, and great Hippodrome urns in Rome,[1] to resound the acclamations and honour due unto you. But these are sad and sepulchral pitchers, which have no joyful voices; silently expressing old mortality, the ruins of forgotten times, and can only speak with life, how long in this corruptible frame, some parts may be uncorrupted; yet able to outlast bones long unborn, and noblest pile among us.

We present not these as any strange sight or spectacle unknown to your eyes, who have beheld the best of urns and noblest variety of ashes; who are yourself no slender master of antiquities, and can daily command the view of so many imperial faces,[2] which raiseth your thoughts unto old things, and consideration of times before you, when even living men were antiquities; when the living might exceed the dead, and to depart this world, could not be properly said to go unto the greater number. And so run up your thoughts upon the ancient of days, the antiquary's truest object, unto whom the eldest parcels are young, and earth itself an infant; and without Egyptian account makes but small noise in thousands.

We were hinted by the occasion, not catched the opportunity to write of old things, or intrude upon the antiquary. We are coldly drawn unto discourses of antiquities, who have scarce time before us to comprehend new things, or make out learned novelties. But seeing they arose as they lay, almost in silence among us, at least in short account suddenly passed over; we were very unwilling they should die again, and be buried twice among us.

Beside, to preserve the living, and make the dead to live, to keep men out of their urns, and discourse of human fragments in them, is not impertinent unto our profession; whose study is life and death, who daily behold examples of mortality, and of all men least need artificial mementos, or coffins by our bedside, to mind us of our graves.

'Tis time to observe occurrences, and let nothing remarkable escape us. The supinity of elder days hath left so much in silence, or time hath so martyred the records, that the most industrious heads do find no easy work to erect a new *Britannia*.[3]

'Tis opportune to look back upon old times, and contemplate our forefathers. Great examples grow thin, and to be fetched from the passed world. Simplicity flies away, and inequity comes at long

---

[1] Conceived to resound the voices of people at their shows [Browne's note]; the Hippodrome was the site of horse races.

[2] *imperial faces* on coins.

[3] *Britannia* a famous antiquarian work (1586) by William Camden.

strides upon us. We have enough to do to make up ourselves from present and passed times, and the whole stage of things scarce serveth for our instruction. A complete piece of virtue must be made from the centos of all ages,[1] as all the beauties of Greece could make but one handsome Venus.

When the bones of King Arthur were digged up, the old race might think they beheld therein some originals of themselves; unto these of our urns none here can pretend relation, and can only behold the relics of those persons who in their life giving the laws unto their predecessors, after long obscurity, now lie at their mercies. But, remembering the early civility they brought upon these countries, and forgetting long passed mischiefs, we mercifully preserve their bones, and piss not upon their ashes.

In the offer of these antiquities we drive not at ancient families, so long outlasted by them. We are far from erecting your worth upon the pillars of your forefathers, whose merits you illustrate. We honour your old virtues, conformable unto times before you, which are the noblest armoury. And, having long experience of your friendly conversation, void of empty formality, full of freedoms, constant and generous honesty. I look upon you as a gem of the old rock, and must profess myself even to urn and ashes,

Your every faithful friend and servant,

Thomas Browne

CHAPTER 1

In the deep discovery of the subterranean world, a shallow part would satisfy some enquirers; who, if two or three yards were open about the surface, would not care to rake the bowels of Potosi,[2] and regions towards the centre. Nature hath furnished one part of the Earth, and man another. The trea-

sures of time lie high, in urns, coins, and monuments, scarce below the roots of some vegetables. Time hath endless rarities, and shows of all varieties; which reveals old things in heaven, makes new discoveries in earth, and even earth itself a discovery. That great antiquity America lay buried for a thousand years; and a large part of the earth is still in the urn unto us.

Though if Adam were made out of an extract of the earth, all parts might challenge a restitution, yet few have returned their bones far lower than they might receive them; not affecting the graves of giants, under hilly and heavy coverings, but content with less than their own depth, have wished their bones might lie soft, and the earth be light upon them. Even such as hope to rise again would not be content with central interment, or so desperately to place their relics as to lie beyond discovery, and in no way to be seen again; which happy contrivance hath made communication with our forefathers, and left unto our view some parts, which they never beheld themselves.

.   .   .   .

CHAPTER 2

The solemnities, ceremonies, rites of their cremation or interment, so solemnly delivered by authors, we shall not disparage our reader to repeat. Only the last and lasting part in their urns, collected bones and ashes, we cannot wholly omit or decline that subject, which occasion lately presented, in some discovered among us.

In a field of old Walsingham, not many months past, were digged up between forty and fifty urns, deposited in a dry and sandy soil, not a yard deep, nor far from one another. Not all strictly of one figure, but most answering these described: some containing two pounds of bones, distinguishable in skulls, ribs, jaws, thighbones, and teeth, with fresh impressions of their combustion. Besides the extra-

---

[1] *centos* scraps.

[2] *Potosi* the rich mountain of Peru [Browne's note].

neous substances, like pieces of small boxes, or combs handsomely wrought, handles of small brass instruments, brazen nippers, and in one some kind of opal.

Near the same plot of ground, for about six yards compass, were digged up coals and incinerated substances, which begat conjecture that this was the *ustrina* or place of burning their bodies, or some sacrificing place unto the *manes* [spirit], which was properly below the surface of the ground, as the *aræ* and altars unto the gods and heroes above it.

That these were the urns of Romans from the common custom and place where they were found, is no obscure conjecture,[1] not far from a Roman garrison, and but five miles from Brancaster, set down by ancient record under the name of Brannodunum. And where the adjoining town, containing seven parishes, in no very different sound, but Saxon termination, still retains the name of Burnham, which being an early station, it is not improbable the neighbour parts were filled with habitations, either of Romans themselves, or Brittains romanised, which observed the Roman customs....

Than the time of these urns deposited, or precise antiquity of these relics, nothing of more uncertainty. For since the lieutenant of Claudius seems to have made the first progress into these parts, since Boadicea was overthrown by the forces of Nero, and Agricola put a full end to these conquests; it is not probable the country was fully garrisoned or planted before; and therefore however these urns might be of later date, not likely of higher antiquity.[2]

And the succeeding Emperors desisted not from their conquests in these and other parts; as testified by history and medal inscriptions yet extant. The province of Britain, in so divided a distance from Rome, beholding the faces of many imperial persons, and in large account no fewer than Cæsar, Claudius, Britannicus, Vespasian, Titus, Adrian, Severus, Commodus, Geta, and Caracalla.

A great obscurity herein, because no medal or Emperor's coin enclosed, which might denote the date of their interments, observable in many urns, and found in those of Spitalfields by London, which contained the coins of Claudius, Vespasian, Commodus, Antoninus, attended with lachrymatories,[3] lamps, bottles of liquor, and other appurtenances of affectionate superstition, which in these rural interments were wanting.

Some uncertainty there is from the period or term of burning, or the cessation of that practise. Macrobius affirmeth it was disused in his days. But most agree, though without authentic record, that it ceased with the Antonini. Most safely to be understood after the reign of those Emperors, which assumed the name of Antoninus, extending unto Heliogabalus. Not strictly after Marcus: for about fifty years later we find the magnificent burning and consecration of Severus; and if we so fix this period or cessation, these urns will challenge above thirteen hundred years.[4]

But whether this practise was only then left by Emperors and great persons, or generally about Rome, and not in other provinces, we hold no authentic account. For after Tertullian, in the days of Minucius it was obviously objected upon Christians that they condemned the practise of burning. And we find a passage in Sidonius, which asserteth that practise in France unto a lower account. And perhaps not fully disused till Christianity fully

---

1 Browne suggests that the urns date from the Roman occupation of Britain (43–410 C.E.). On the basis of an engraved illustration of the urns in the original edition, they have been identified instead as pre-Christian Saxon.

2 *For since...antiquity* Browne argues that the urns could not be earlier than 78 C.E., after the first Roman excursions into Norfolk by Publius Ostorius Scapula ("the lieutenant of Claudius"), the suppression of native uprisings led by Queen Boadicea (d. 62), and the beginning of systematic pacification by Gnaeus Julius Agrippa.

3 *lachrymatories* glass phials found in Roman tombs, presumably designed to hold tears.

4 *this period* the beginning of the third century C.E.

established, which gave the final extinction to these sepulchral bonfires.

Whether they were the bones of men or women or children, no authentic decision from ancient custom in distinct places of burial. Although not improbably conjectured, that the double sepulchre or burying place of Abraham had in it such intention. But from exility of bones, thinness of skulls, smallness of teeth, ribs, and thighbones; not improbable that many thereof were persons of minor age, or women. Confirmable also from things contained in them: in most were found substances resembling combs, plates like boxes, fastened with iron pins, and handsomely overwrought like the necks or bridges of musical instruments, long brass plates overwrought like the handles of neat implements, brazen nippers to pull away hair, and in one a kind of opal, yet maintaining a bluish colour.

Now that they accustomed to burn or bury with them things wherein they excelled, delighted, or which were dear unto them, either as farewells unto all pleasure, or vain apprehension that they might use them in the other world, is testified by all antiquity. Observable from the gem or beryl ring upon the finger of Cynthia, the mistress of Propertius, when after her funeral pyre her ghost appeared unto him. And notably illustrated from the contents of that Roman urn preserved by Cardinal Farnese, wherein besides great number of gems with heads of gods and goddesses were found an ape of agate, a grasshopper, an elephant of amber, a crystal ball, three glasses, two spoons, and six nuts of crystal, and beyond the content of urns, in the monument of Childerick the first, and fourth king from Pharamond, casually discovered three years past at Tournay, restoring unto the world much gold richly adorning his sword, two hundred rubies, many hundred Imperial coins, three hundred golden bees, the bones and horseshoe of his horse interred with him, according to the barbarous magnificence of those days in their sepulchral obsequies. Although

if we steer by the conjecture of many and Septuagint expression, some trace thereof may be found even with the ancient Hebrews, not only from the sepulchral treasure of David, but the circumcision knives which Joshua also buried.

Some men considering the contents of these urns, lasting pieces and toys included in them, and the custom of burning with many other nations, might somewhat doubt whether all urns found among us were properly Roman relics, or some not belonging unto our British, Saxon, or Danish forefathers.

In the form of burial among the ancient Brittains, the large discourses of Cæsar, Tacitus, and Strabo are silent. For the discovery whereof, with other particulars, we much deplore the loss of that letter which Cicero expected or received from his brother Quintus, as a resolution of British customs; or the account which might have been made by Scribonius Largus, the physician accompanying the Emperor Claudius, who might have also discovered that frugal bit of the old Britains, which in the bigness of a bean could satisfy their thirst and hunger.[1]

But that the Druids and ruling priests used to burn and bury, is expressed by Pomponius. That Bellinus, the brother of Brennus and King of the Brittains, was burnt is acknowledged by Polydorus. That they held that practise in Gallia, Cæsar expressly delivereth. Whether the Brittains (probably descended from them, of like religion, language and manners) did not sometimes make use of burning; or whether at least such as were after civilized unto the Roman life and manners, conformed not unto this practise, we have no historical assertion or denial. But since, from the account of Tacitus the Romans early wrought so much civility upon the British stock, that they brought them to build temples, to wear the gown, and study the Roman

---

[1] *frugal bit* mentioned in Dio Cassius, *Roman History*, 72.12.

laws and language, that they conformed also unto their religious rites and customs in burials, seems no improbable conjecture.

.   .   .   .

CHAPTER 5

Now since these dead bones have already out-lasted the living ones of Methuselah,[1] and in a yard under-ground, and thin walls of clay, out-worn all the strong and specious buildings above it; and quietly rested under the drums and tramplings of three conquests;[2] What Prince can promise such diuturnity unto his relics,[3] or might not gladly say,

Sic ego componi versus in ossa velim.[4]

Time which antiquates antiquities, and hath an art to make dust of all things, hath yet spared these minor monuments. In vain we hope to be known by open and visible conservatories, when to be unknown was the means of their continuation and obscurity into protection: If they died by violent hands, and were thrust into their urns, these bones become considerable, and some old philosophers would honour them, whose souls they conceived most pure, which were thus snatched from their bodies; and to retain a stronger propension unto them: whereas they weariedly left a languishing corps, and with faint desires of reunion. If they fell by long and aged decay, yet wrapt up in the bundle of time, they fall into indistinction, and make but one blot with infants. If we begin to die when we live, and long life be but a prolongation of death; our life is a sad composition; we live with death, and die not in a moment. How many pulses made

up the life of Methuselah, were work for Archimedes: Common counters sum up the life of Moses his man [Psalm 90:10]. Our days become considerable like petty sums by minute accumulations; where numerous fractions make up but small round numbers; and our days of a span long make not one little finger.[5]

If the nearness of our last necessity, brought a nearer conformity unto it, there were a happiness in hoary hairs, and no calamity in half senses. But the long habit of living indisposeth us for dying; when avarice makes us the sport of death; when even David grew politickly cruel; and Solomon could hardly be said to be the wisest of men. But many are too early old, and before the date of age. Adversity stretcheth our days, misery makes Alcmenas nights,[6] and time hath no wings unto it. But the most tedious being is that which can unwish itself, content to be nothing, or never to have been, which was beyond the malcontent of Job, who cursed not the day of his life, but his nativity: Content to have so far been, as to have a title to future being; although he had lived here but in an hidden state of life, and as it were an abortion.

What song the Sirens sang, or what name Achilles assumed when he hid himself among women, though puzzling questions are not beyond all conjecture.[7] What time the persons of these ossuaries entered the famous nations of the dead, and slept with princes and counsellors, might admit a wide solution. But who were the proprietaries of these bones, or what bodies these ashes made up, were a question above antiquarianism. Not to be resolved by man, nor easily perhaps by spirits,

---

[1] *Methuselah* traditionally, the oldest human; he lived 969 years (Genesis 5:27).

[2] *three conquests* Saxon, Danish, and Norman.

[3] *diuturnity* long-lastingness (*OED*).

[4] Tibullus, iii.2.26: "Thus let me be placed when I am turned to bones."

[5] according to the ancient arithmetic of the hand wherein the little finger of the right hand contracted, signified an hundred [Browne's note].

[6] *Alcmenas nights* Zeus extended one night to the length of three when he seduced Alcmene, the mother of Hercules.

[7] the puzzling questions of Tiberius unto Grammarians [Browne's note]. Suetonius, *Life of Tiberius*, 70.

except we consult the provincial guardians, or tutelary observators. Had they made as good provision for their names, as they have done for the reliques, they had not so grossly erred in the art of perpetuation. But to subsist in bones, and be but pyramidally extant, is a fallacy in duration. Vain ashes, which in the oblivion of names, persons, times, and sexes, have found unto themselves, a fruitless continuation, and only arise unto late posterity, as emblems of mortal vanities; antidotes against pride, vain-glory, and madding vices. Pagan vain-glories which thought the world might last forever, had encouragement for ambition, and finding no Atropos unto the immortality of their names, were never damped with the necessity of oblivion.[1] Even old ambitions had the advantage of ours, in the attempts of their vain-glories, who acting early, and before the probable meridian of time, have by this time found great accomplishment of their designs, whereby the ancient heroes have already outlasted their monuments, and mechanical preservations. But in this latter scene of time we cannot expect such mummies unto our memories, when ambition may fear the prophecy of Elias,[2] and Charles the Fifth can never hope to live within two Methuselahs of Hector.[3]

And therefore restless inquietude for the diuturnity of our memories unto present considerations, seems a vanity almost out of date, and superannuated piece of folly. We cannot hope to live so long in our names, as some have done in their persons, one face of Janus holds no proportion unto the other. 'Tis too late to be ambitious. The great mutations of the world are acted, or time may be too short for our designs. To extend our memories by monuments, whose death we daily pray for, and whose duration we cannot hope, without injury to our expectations, in the advent of the last day, were a contradiction to our beliefs. We whose generations are ordained in this setting part of time, are providentially taken off from such imaginations. And being necessitated to eye the remaining particle of futurity, are naturally constituted unto thoughts of the next world, and cannot excusably decline the consideration of that duration, which maketh pyramids pillars of snow, and all that's past a moment.

Circles and right lines limit and close all bodies, and the mortal right-lined circle,[4] must conclude and shut up all. There is no antidote against the opium of time, which temporally considereth all things; our Fathers find their graves in our short memories, and sadly tell us how we may be buried in our survivors. Gravestones tell truth scarce forty years:[5] Generations pass while some trees stand, and old families last not three oaks. To be read by bare inscriptions like many in Gruter,[6] to hope for eternity by enigmatical epithets, or first letters of our names, to be studied by antiquaries, who we were, and have new names given us like many of the mummies,[7] are cold consolations unto the students of perpetuity, even by everlasting languages.

To be content that times to come should only know there was such a man, not caring whether they knew more of him, was a frigid ambition in

---

[1] *Atropos* in mythology, one of the three Fates, responsible for cutting the thread of life.

[2] that the world may last but six thousand years [Browne's note].

[3] Hector's fame lasting above two lives of Methuselah, before that famous prince was extant [Browne's note]. The world was commonly thought to have been created about 4000 years B.C.E.; if it were to last for 6000 years, the Holy Roman Emperor Charles V (born in 1500) had only 500 years in which to be famous before the world ended.

[4] *the mortal right-lined circle* Θ (theta), the first letter of the Greek word for death.

[5] old ones being taken up, and other bodies laid under them [Browne's note].

[6] *Gruter* Janus Gruterus, *Inscriptiones antiquae totius orbis Romani* (1603), a collection of Roman inscriptions.

[7] which men show in several Countries, giving them what names they please; and unto some the names of the old Egyptian Kings out of Herodotus [Browne's note].

Cardan:[1] disparaging his horoscopal inclination and judgment of himself. Who cares to subsist like Hippocrates' patients, or Achilles' horses in Homer, under naked nominations, without deserts and noble acts, which are the balsam of our memories, the *entelechia* and soul of our subsistences.[2] To be nameless in worthy deeds exceeds an infamous history. The Canaanitish woman lives more happily without a name, than Herodias with one.[3] And who had not rather have been the good thief, than Pilate?

But the iniquity of oblivion blindly scattereth her poppy, and deals with the memory of men without distinction to merit of perpetuity. Who can but pity the founder of the Pyramids? Herostratus lives that burnt the Temple of Diana, he is almost lost that built it; time hath spared the epitaph of Adrian's horse, confounded that of himself. In vain we compute our felicities by the advantage of our good names, since bad have equal durations; and Thersites is like to live as long as Agamemnon.[4] Who knows whether the best of men be known? or whether there be not more remarkable persons forgot, than any that stand remembered in the known account of time? without the favour of the everlasting register the first man had been as unknown as the last,[5] and Methuselah's long life had been his only chronicle.

Oblivion is not to be hired: The greater part must be content to be as though they had not been, to be found in the register of God, not in the record of man. Twenty-seven names make up the first story,[6] and the recorded names ever since contain not one living century. The number of the dead long exceedeth all that shall live. The night of time far surpasseth the day, and who knows when was the equinox? Every hour adds unto that current arithmetic, which scarce stands one moment. And since death must be the Lucina of life,[7] and even pagans could doubt whether thus to live, were to die. Since our longest sun sets at right descensions, and makes but winter arches, and therefore it cannot be long before we lie down in darkness, and have our light in ashes.[8] Since the brother of death daily haunts us with dying mementos,[9] and time that grows old itself, bids us hope no long duration: Diuturnity is a dream and folly of expectation.

Darkness and light divide the course of time, and oblivion snares with memory, a great part even of our living beings; we slightly remember our felicities, and the smartest strokes of affliction leave but short smart upon us. Sense endureth no extremities, and sorrows destroy us or themselves. To weep into stones are fables.[10] Afflictions induce callosities, miseries are slippery, or fall like snow upon us, which notwithstanding is no unhappy stupidity. To be ignorant of evils to come, and forgetful of evils past, is a merciful provision in nature, whereby we digest the mixture of our few and evil days, and our delivered senses not relapsing into cutting remembrances, our sorrows are not kept raw by the edge of repetitions. A great part of antiquity contented their hopes of subsistency with a transmigration of their souls. A good way to continue their memories, while having the advantage of plural successions, they could not but act something remarkable in

---

[1] *Cardan* Girolamo Cardano, *De propria vita* (1614), p. 42.

[2] *entelechia* informing spirit, soul (transliterated Greek; see *OED* entelechy 2).

[3] *The Canaanitish woman* Matthew 15:22–28; *Herodias* Matthew 14:3–11 and Mark 6:17–28.

[4] In the *Iliad*, Thersites was a rancorous reviler of his Greek leaders, while Agamemnon was the heroic head of the Greek army.

[5] *everlasting register* the Bible.

[6] before the flood [Browne's note].

[7] *Lucina* Roman goddess of childbirth.

[8] according to the custom of the Jews, who place a lighted wax-candle in a pot of ashes by the corpse [Browne's note].

[9] *the brother of death* sleep.

[10] In mythology, Niobe turned into a stone from weeping.

such variety of beings, and enjoying the fame of their passed selves, make accumulation of glory unto their last durations. Others rather than be lost in the uncomfortable night of nothing, were content to recede into the common being, and make one particle of the public soul of all things, which was no more than to return into their unknown and divine original again. Egyptian ingenuity was more unsatisfied, contriving their bodies in sweet consistences, to attend the return of their souls. But all was vanity, feeding the wind, and folly. The Egyptian mummies, which Cambyses or time hath spared,[1] avarice now consumeth. Mummy is become merchandise, Mizraim cures wounds, and Pharaoh is sold for balsams.[2]

In vain do individuals hope for immortality, or any patent from oblivion, in preservations below the moon: Men have been deceived even in their flatteries above the sun, and studied conceits to perpetuate their names in heaven. The various cosmography of that part hath already varied the names of contrived constellations; Nimrod is lost in Orion, and Osiris in the Dog-star. While we look for incorruption in the heavens, we find they are but like the Earth; durable in their main bodies, alterable in their parts: whereof beside comets and new stars, perspectives begin to tell tales.[3] And the spots that wander about the sun, with Phaeton's favour,[4] would make clear conviction.

There is nothing strictly immortal, but immortality; whatever hath no beginning may be confident of no end. All others have a dependent being, and within the reach of destruction, which is the peculiar of that necessary essence that cannot destroy itself; and the highest strain of omnipotency to be so powerfully constituted, as not to suffer even from the power of itself. But the sufficiency of Christian immortality frustrates all earthly glory, and the quality of either state after death, makes a folly of posthumous memory. God who can only destroy our souls, and hath assured our resurrection, either of our bodies or names hath directly promised no duration. Wherein there is so much of chance that the boldest expectants have found unhappy frustration; and to hold long subsistence, seems but a scape in oblivion. But man is a noble animal, splendid in ashes, and pompous in the grave, solemnizing nativities and deaths with equal lustre, not omitting ceremonies of bravery, in the infamy of his nature.

Life is a pure flame, and we live by an invisible sun within us. A small fire sufficeth for life, great flames seemed too little after death, while men vainly affected precious pyres, and to burn like Sardanapalus,[5] but the wisdom of funeral laws, found the folly of prodigal blazes, and reduced undoing fires, unto the rule of sober obsequies, wherein few could be so mean as not to provide wood, pitch, a mourner, and an urn.

Five languages secured not the epitaph of Gordianus;[6] the man of God lives longer without a tomb than any by one, invisibly interred by angels, and adjudged to obscurity, though not without some marks directing humane discovery. Enoch and Elias without either tomb or burial,[7] in an anomalous state of being, are the great examples of perpetuity, in their long and living memory, in strict

---

[1] *Cambyses* conqueror of Egypt in the sixth century B.C.E.

[2] *Mummy* a medicinal drug made from mummies (*OED* mummy *sb*[1] 1); *Mizraim* an ancient Egyptian (Genesis 10:6), hence a potential ingredient in mummy, like any Pharaoh.

[3] *perspectives* telescopes.

[4] In mythology, Phaeton rashly insisted on driving the sun chariot for a day, could not control the immortal horses, and had to be killed before he set fire to the Earth; the sunspots follow a similarly erratic path.

[5] *Sardanapalus* ancient Assyrian king who burned himself, his wives, and all he owned when his estate was under siege.

[6] in Greek, Latin, Hebrew, Egyptian, Arabic, defaced by Licinius the Emperor [Browne's note].

[7] Enoch and Elias were both taken directly to Heaven (Genesis 5:24, II Kings 2:11).

account being still on this side death, and having a late part yet to act upon this stage of earth. If in the decretory term of the world we shall not all die but be changed, according to received translation; the last day will make but few graves; at least quick resurrections will anticipate lasting sepultures; some graves will be opened before they be quite closed, and Lazarus be no wonder. When many that feared to die shall groan that they can die but once, the dismal state is the second and living death, when life puts despair on the damned; when men shall wish the coverings of mountains, not of monuments, and annihilation shall be courted.

While some have studied monuments, others have studiously declined them: and some have been so vainly boisterous, that they durst not acknowledge their graves; wherein Alaricus seems most subtle, who had a river turned to hide his bones at the bottom.[1] Even Sylla that thought himself safe in his urn, could not prevent revenging tongues, and stones thrown at his monument.[2] Happy are they whom privacy makes innocent, who deal so with men in this world, that they are not afraid to meet them in the next, who when they die, make no commotion among the dead, and are not touched with that poetical taunt of Isaiah.[3]

Pyramids, arches, obelisks, were but the irregularities of vain-glory, and wild enormities of ancient magnanimity. But the most magnanimous resolution rests in the Christian religion, which trampleth upon pride, and sets on the neck of ambition, humbly pursuing that infallible perpetuity, unto which all others must diminish their diameters, and be poorly seen in angles of contingency.[4]

Pious spirits who passed their days in raptures of futurity, made little more of this world, than the world that was before it, while they lay obscure in the chaos of pre-ordination, and night of their forebeings. And if any have been so happy as truly to understand Christian annihilation, extasis, exolution, liquefaction, transformation, the kiss of the spouse, gustation of God, and ingression in the divine shadow,[5] they have already had an handsome anticipation of heaven; the glory of the world is surely over, and the earth in ashes unto them.

To subsist in lasting monuments, to live in their productions, to exist in their names, and predicament of chimeras, was large satisfaction unto old expectations, and made one part of their Elysiums.[6] But all this is nothing in the metaphysics of true belief. To live indeed is to be again ourselves, which being not only an hope but an evidence in noble believers; 'Tis all one to lie in St. Innocent's churchyard,[7] as in the sand of Egypt: ready to be anything, in the ecstasy of being ever, and as content with six foot as the moles of Adrianus.[8]

Lucan:
—*Tabesne cadavera solvat*
An rogus haud refert.[9]

—1658

---

[1] *Alaricus* King of the Goths (d. 410 C.E.).

[2] *Sylla* Lucius Cornelius Sulla Felix (ca. 138–78 B.C.E.), elected Dictator of Rome.

[3] See Isaiah 14:4–17.

[4] *Angulus contingentiae*, the least of angles [Browne's note].

[5] all terms from the Christian mystical tradition: *exstasis* ecstasy (*OED* ecstasis); *exolution* release, setting free (*OED* exolution 1c); *kiss of the spouse* the divine kiss; *gustation* tasting (*OED*); *ingression* entrance (*OED*).

[6] *predicament of chimeras* category of wild or fanciful conceptions. In classical mythology, a chimera was a monster with a lion's head, goat's body, and serpent's tail.

[7] in Paris where bodies soon consume [Browne's note].

[8] a stately mausoleum or sepulchral pyle built by Adrianus in Rome, where now standeth the Castle of St. Angelo [Browne's note].

[9] Lucan, *Pharsalia*, 7.809–10: "It matters not whether the corpses are burnt on the pyre or decompose with time."

John Milton
1608 – 1674

Had Milton not published a line of verse, he would still hold a place in the canon of seventeenth-century writing by virtue of his prose. Milton was a major prose writer and a formidable polemicist, in Latin as well as English. He was also prolific (the modern scholarly edition of his complete prose occupies ten thick volumes), and wide-ranging in the subjects he addressed. Milton published numerous works of religious and political controversy (including defences of the regicide and of republicanism); he also tackled theology, reform of the divorce laws, educational theory, press censorship, grammar, logic, and the histories of Britain and Muscovia; in several pamphlets he wrote about himself. Written across thirty years of complex history, Milton's polemical works negotiate a shifting ideological landscape: his ideas are not static, nor even is his style (inimitable as it is). But at heart what unites all of Milton's polemic is his defence of liberties—religious, political, intellectual, personal, and civic.

The first of the three examples of Milton's prose below is the autobiographical preface to the second book of *The Reason of Church Government Urged against Prelaty* (dated 1641, but probably published in early 1642), one of the five anti-prelatical tracts Milton published in the early 1640s. Here Milton sets aside for a moment his arguments against church government by bishops and writes instead of his poetic ambitions, the intellectual training to which he has committed himself, and his reasons for entering the public sphere before completing "the full circle of my private studies."

The second selection is the complete text of *Areopagitica* (1644), Milton's response to a Parliamentary Order (June 1643) that banned the publication of any book that had not been licensed before publication: what Milton attacks is *pre*-publication censorship, not censorship in general. His main strategy is to link pre-publication licensing to its Laudian and ultimately Catholic antecedents, in effect accusing Parliament and the then-politically dominant Presbyterians with instituting a tyranny as egregious as the one they had fought to overthrow. (William Walwyn, Richard Overton, and Mary Howgill make the same charge in their attacks on the powers that in turn succeeded the Presbyterians, the New Model Army and Oliver Cromwell. For a text that sought to renew censorship after the Restoration, see Roger L'Estrange.) *Areopagitica* takes the form of an oration to Parliament: Milton's title invokes the *Areopagite Discourse* (ca. 355 B.C.E.) by Isocrates, who exhorted a return to the days when the Athenian court of the Areopagus (a kind of Supreme Court) was a model of virtue, wisdom, and responsibility. Milton might also expect his readers to remember that Paul delivered an oration on the Areopagus, the hill outside Athens that gave its name to the court that met there (Acts 17:19–34).

The final text is *Of True Religion* (1673), the last work Milton published in his lifetime and one of the many responses generated by Charles II's Declaration of Indulgence in 1672. The King had promised a measure of religious toleration in the Declaration of Breda (1660), but in the early years of his reign Parliament passed a series of statutes, collectively known as the Clarendon code, that made life very difficult for the large Nonconformist community. The Declaration of Indulgence offered to suspend penal laws on religious matters, and invited Nonconformists to apply for licenses permitting public worship; it also allowed Catholics freedom of worship in their homes. The King's principal aim was to initiate a softening of penalties on Catholicism: in the secret Treaty of Dover (1670) with Louis XIV of France, Charles promised the eventual announcement of his own conversion and the reestablishment of Catholicism in England. The Declaration however sparked a wave of "no popery" agitation, Parliament asserted its power in matters ecclesiastical, and the King was forced to withdraw it in 1673, though a bill was passed that eased restrictions on "his Majesty's subjects that are Dissenters in matters of Religion."

Milton likely wrote *Of True Religion* upon hearing that Parliament was considering some measure of toleration for dissenting Protestants. The pamphlet encourages support for the bill by opposing the Declaration and by making other conciliatory gestures to the Church of England; he takes care that his arguments for toleration, unlike the more general arguments from Christian liberty he had made in *A Treatise of Civil Power* (1659), do not apply to Catholics.

ഇൗ

The Reason of Church Government
Preface to the Second Book

How happy were it for this frail, and as it may be truly called, mortal life of man, since all earthly things which have the name of good and convenient in our daily use are withal so cumbersome and full of trouble, if knowledge, yet which is the best and lightsomest possession of the mind were, as the common saying is, no burden, and that what it wanted of being a load to any part of the body, it did not with a heavy advantage overlay upon the spirit. For not to speak of that knowledge that rests in the contemplation of natural causes and dimensions, which must needs be a lower wisdom, as the object is low, certain it is that he who hath obtained in more than the scantiest measure to know anything distinctly of God, and of his true worship; and what is infallibly good and happy in the state of man's life, what in itself evil and miserable, though vulgarly not so esteemed; he that hath obtained to know this, the only high valuable wisdom indeed, remembering also that God, even to a strictness, requires the improvement of these his entrusted gifts, cannot but sustain a sorer burden of mind, and more pressing, than any supportable toil or weight which the body can labour under, how and in what manner he shall dispose and employ those sums of knowledge and illumination, which God hath sent him into this world to trade with.

And that which aggravates the burden more is, that having received amongst his allotted parcels certain precious truths, of such an orient lustre as no diamond can equal, which nevertheless he has in charge to put off at any cheap rate, yea, for nothing to them that will, the great merchants of this world, fearing that this course would soon discover and disgrace the false glitter of their deceitful wares wherewith they abuse the people, like poor Indians with beads and glasses, practise by all means how they may suppress the vending of such rarities, and at such a cheapness as would undo them, and turn their trash upon their hands. Therefore, by gratifying the corrupt desires of men in fleshly doctrines, they stir them up to persecute with hatred and contempt all those that seek to bear themselves uprightly in this their spiritual factory:[1] which they foreseeing, though they cannot but testify of truth, and the excellency of that heavenly traffic which they bring, against what opposition or danger soever, yet needs must it sit heavily upon their spirits, that being in God's prime intention and their own, selected heralds of peace and dispensers of treasure inestimable without price to them that have no pence, they find in the discharge of their commission that they are made the greatest variance and offence, a very sword and fire both in house and city over the whole earth.

This is that which the sad prophet Jeremiah laments: "Woe is me, my mother, that thou hast borne me, a man of strife and contention" [Jeremiah 15:10]. And although divine inspiration must certainly have been sweet to those ancient prophets, yet the irksomeness of that truth which they

---

[1] *factory* trading post.

brought was so unpleasant unto them, that everywhere they call it a burden. Yea, that mysterious book of Revelation, which the great evangelist was bid to eat, as it had been some eye-brightening electuary of knowledge and foresight, thought it were sweet in his mouth and in the learning, it was bitter in his belly, bitter in the denouncing.[1] Nor was this hid from the wise poet Sophocles, who in that place of his tragedy where Tiresias is called to resolve King Oedipus in a matter which he knew would be grievous, brings him in bemoaning his lot, that he knew more than other men.[2] For surely to every good and peaceable man, it must in nature needs be a hateful thing to be the displeaser and molester of thousands; much better would it like him doubtless to be the messenger of gladness and contentment, which is his chief intended business to all mankind, but that they resist and oppose their own true happiness. But when God commands to take the trumpet, and blow a dolorous or a jarring blast, it lies not in man's will what he shall say, or what he shall conceal. If he shall think to be silent as Jeremiah did, because of the reproach and derision he met with daily, "And all his familiar friends watched for his halting," to be revenged on him for speaking the truth, he would be forced to confess as he confessed: "His word was in my heart as a burning fire shut up in my bones; I was weary with forbearing, and could not stay" [Jeremiah 20:8–10]. Which might teach these times not suddenly to condemn all things that are sharply spoken or vehemently written as proceeding out of stomach, virulence, and ill-nature; but to consider rather that, if the prelates have leave to say the worst that can be said, or do the worst that can be done, while they strive to keep to themselves, to their great pleasure and commodity, those things which they ought to render up, no man can be justly offended with him

that shall endeavour to impart and bestow, without any gain to himself, those sharp but saving words which would be a terror and a torment in him to keep back.

For me, I have determined to lay as the best treasure and solace of a good old age, if God vouchsafe it me, the honest liberty of free speech from my youth, where I shall think it available in so dear a concernment as the Church's good. For if I be, either by disposition or what other cause, too inquisitive, or suspicious of myself and mine own doings, who can help it? But this I foresee, that should the Church be brought under heavy oppression, and God have given me ability the while to reason against that man that should be the author of so foul a deed; or should she, by blessing from above on the industry and courage of faithful men, change this her distracted estate into better days, without the least furtherance or contribution of those few talents which God at that present had lent me;[3] I foresee what stories I should hear within myself, all my life after, of discourage and reproach: "Timorous and ungrateful, the Church of God is now again at the foot of her insulting enemies, and thou bewailest. What matters it for thee, or thy bewailing? When time was, thou couldst not find a syllable of all that thou hast read, or studied, to utter in her behalf. Yet ease and leisure was given thee for thy retired thoughts, out of the sweat of other men. Thou hast the diligence, the parts, the language of a man, if a vain subject were to be adorned or beautified; but when the cause of God and his Church was to be pleaded, for which purpose that tongue was given thee which thou hast, God listened if he could hear thy voice among his zealous servants, but thou wert dumb as a beast; from henceforward be that which thine own brutish silence hath made thee."

---

[1] *mysterious book* See Revelation 10:9–10; *electuary* a medicine made palatable by being mixed with honey or syrup.

[2] Sophocles, *Oedipus the King*, ll. 316–17.

[3] *those few talents* See the parable of the talents in Matthew 25:14–31; Milton also invokes the parable in his Sonnet 19.

Or else I should have heard on the other ear: "Slothful, and ever to be set light by, the Church hath now overcome her late distresses after the unwearied labours of many her true servants that stood up in her defence; thou also wouldst take upon thee to share amongst them of their joy: but wherefore thou? Where canst thou show any word or deed of thine which might have hastened her peace? Whatever thou dost now talk, or write, or look, is the alms of other men's active prudence and zeal. Dare not now to say or do anything better than thy former sloth and infancy; or if thou darest, thou dost impudently to make a thrifty purchase of boldness to thyself out of the painful merits of other men; what before was thy sin is now thy duty, to be abject and worthless."

These, and such like lessons as these, I know would have been my matins duly, and my evensong.[1] But now by this little diligence, mark what a privilege, I have gained with good men and saints, to claim my right of lamenting the tribulations of the Church, if she should suffer, when others that have ventured nothing for her sake have not the honour to be admitted mourners. But if she lift up her drooping head and prosper, among those that have something more than wished her welfare, I have my charter and freehold of rejoicing to me and my heirs. Concerning therefore this wayward subject against prelaty, the touching whereof is so distasteful and disquietous to a number of men, as by what hath been said I may deserve of charitable readers to be credited, that neither envy nor gall hath entered me upon this controversy, but the enforcement of conscience only, and a preventive fear lest the omitting of this duty should be against me, when I would store up to myself the good provision of peaceful hours: so, lest it be still imputed to me, as I have found it hath been, that some

self-pleasing humour of vain-glory hath incited me to contest with men of high estimation, now while green years are upon my head; from this needless surmisal I shall hope to dissuade the intelligent and equal auditor, if I can but say successfully that which in this exigent behooves me; although I would be heard only, if it might be, by the elegant and learned reader, to whom principally for a while I shall beg leave I may address myself.

To him it will be no new thing, though I tell him that if I hunted after praise by the ostentation of wit and learning, I should not write thus out of mine own season when I have neither yet completed to my mind the full circle of my private studies, although I complain not of any insufficiency to the matter in hand; or were I ready to my wishes, it were a folly to commit anything elaborately composed to the careless and interrupted listening of these tumultuous times. Next, if I were wise only to my own ends, I would certainly take such a subject as of itself might catch applause, whereas this hath all the disadvantages on the contrary; and such a subject as the publishing whereof might be delayed at pleasure, and time enough to pencil it over with all the curious touches of art, even to the perfection of a faultless picture; whenas in this argument the not deferring is of great moment to the good speeding, that, if solidity have leisure to do her office, art cannot have much. Lastly, I should not choose this manner of writing, wherein knowing myself inferior to myself, led by the genial power of nature to another task, I have the use, as I may account, but of my left hand.

And though I shall be foolish in saying more to this purpose, yet, since it will be such a folly wisest men go about to commit, having only confessed and so committed, I may trust with more reason, because with more folly, to have courteous pardon. For although a poet, soaring in the high region of his fancies, with his garland and singing robes about him, might, without apology, speak more of himself

---

[1] *matins…evensong* morning and evening prayers (in both the Church of England and the Roman Catholic Church, though Milton's meaning is probably generic).

than I mean to do; yet for me sitting here below in the cool element of prose, a mortal thing among many readers of no empyreal conceit, to venture and divulge unusual things of myself, I shall petition to the gentler sort, it may not be envy to me.

I must say, therefore, that after I had for my first years, by the ceaseless diligence and care of my father (whom God recompense!), been exercised to the tongues and some sciences, as my age would suffer, by sundry masters and teachers, both at home and at the schools, it was found that whether aught was imposed me by them that had the overlooking, or betaken to of mine own choice in English, or other tongue, prosing or versing, but chiefly by this latter, the style, by certain vital signs it had, was likely to live. But much latelier in the private academies of Italy, whither I was favoured to resort, perceiving that some trifles which I had in memory, composed at under twenty or thereabout (for the manner is, that everyone must give some proof of his wit and reading there), met with acceptance above what was looked for; and other things which I had shifted in scarcity of books and conveniences to patch up amongst them were received with written encomiums,[1] which the Italian is not forward to bestow on men of this side the Alps; I began thus far to assent both to them and divers of my friends here at home, and not less to an inward prompting which now grew daily upon me, that by labour and intense study (which I take to be my portion in this life), joined with the strong propensity of nature, I might perhaps leave something so written to aftertimes, as they should not willingly let it die.

These thoughts at once possessed me, and these other; that if I were certain to write as men buy leases, for three lives and downward, there ought no regard be sooner had than to God's glory, by the honour and instruction of my country. For which

cause, and not only for that I knew it would be hard to arrive at the second rank among the Latins, I applied myself to that resolution, which Ariosto followed against the persuasions of Bembo,[2] to fix all the industry and art I could unite to the adorning of my native tongue; not to make verbal curiosities the end (that were a toilsome vanity), but to be an interpreter and relater of the best and sagest things among mine own citizens throughout this island in the mother dialect. That, what the greatest and choicest wits of Athens, Rome, or modern Italy, and those Hebrews of old did for their country, I, in my proportion, with this over and above, of being a Christian, might do for mine; not caring to be once named abroad, though perhaps I could attain to that, but content with these British islands as my world; whose fortune hath hitherto been that, if the Athenians, as some say, made their small deeds great and renowned by their eloquent writers, England hath had her noble achievements made small by the unskillful handling of monks and mechanics.

Time serves not now, and perhaps I might seem too profuse, to give any certain account of what the mind at home in the spacious circuits of her musing hath liberty to propose to herself, though of highest hope and hardest attempting; whether that epic form whereof the two poems of Homer, and those other two of Virgil and Tasso,[3] are a diffuse, and the book of Job a brief model: or whether the rules of Aristotle herein are strictly to be kept, or nature to be followed, which in them that know art, and use judgment, is no transgression, but an enriching of art; and lastly, what king or knight, before the

---

[1] *encomiums* poems of praise; five from Milton's Italian friends were published with his *Poems* in 1645.

[2] *Ariosto…Bembo* Pietro Bembo (1470–1547) reputedly advised Ludovico Ariosto (1474–1533) to write his epic *Orlando Furioso* in Latin rather than Italian; Ariosto declined, claiming that he preferred to be first-rate in his native tongue rather than second-rate among the Latin poets.

[3] *Tasso* Torquato Tasso (1544–1595), Italian poet whose work greatly influenced English writers, author of the epic *Gerusalemme Liberata* (1580–1581), translated by Edward Fairfax as *Jerusalem Delivered* (1600).

conquest, might be chosen in whom to lay the pattern of a Christian hero. And as Tasso gave to a prince of Italy his choice whether he would command him to write of Godfrey's expedition against the Infidels, or Belisarius against the Goths, or Charlemain against the Lombards; if to the instinct of nature and the emboldening of art aught may be trusted, and that there be nothing adverse in our climate,[1] or the fate of this age, it haply would be no rashness, from an equal diligence and inclination, to present the like offer in our own ancient stories. Or whether those dramatic constitutions, wherein Sophocles and Euripides reign, shall be found more doctrinal and exemplary to a nation.

The scripture also affords us a divine pastoral drama in the Song of Solomon, consisting of two persons and a double chorus, as Origen rightly judges.[2] And the Apocalypse of St John is the majestic image of a high and stately tragedy, shutting up and intermingling her solemn scenes and acts with a sevenfold chorus of hallelujahs and harping symphonies: and this my opinion the grave authority of Paraeus, commenting that book, is sufficient to confirm.[3] Or if occasion shall lead, to imitate those magnific odes and hymns, wherein Pindarus and Callimachus are in most things worthy, some others in their frame judicious, in their matter most and end faulty. But those frequent songs throughout the law and prophets beyond all these, not in their divine argument alone, but in the very critical art of composition, may be easily made appear over all the kinds of lyric poesy to be incomparable.

These abilities, wheresoever they be found, are the inspired gift of God, rarely bestowed, but yet to some (though most abuse) in every nation; and are of power, beside the office of a pulpit, to imbreed and cherish in a great people the seeds of virtue and public civility, to allay the perturbations of the mind, and set the affections in right tune; to celebrate in glorious and lofty hymns the throne and equipage of God's almightiness, and what he works, and what he suffers to be wrought with high providence in his Church; to sing victorious agonies of martyrs and saints, the deeds and triumphs of just and pious nations, doing valiantly through faith against the enemies of Christ; to deplore the general relapses of kingdoms and states from justice and God's true worship.

Lastly, whatsoever in religion is holy and sublime, in virtue amiable or grave, whatsoever hath passion or admiration in all the changes of that which is called fortune from without, or the wily subtleties and refluxes of man's thoughts from within; all these things with a solid and treatable smoothness to paint out and describe. Teaching over the whole book of sanctity and virtue, through all the instances of example, with such delight to those especially of soft and delicious temper, who will not so much as look upon truth herself, unless they see her elegantly dressed; that whereas the paths of honesty and good life appear now rugged and difficult, though they be indeed easy and pleasant, they will then appear to all men both easy and pleasant, though they were rugged and difficult indeed. And what a benefit this would be to our youth and gentry, may be soon guessed by what we know of the corruption and bane which they suck in daily from the writings and interludes of libidinous and ignorant poetasters; who, having scarce ever heard of that which is the main consistence of a true poem, the choice of such persons as they ought to introduce, and what is moral and decent to each one, do for the most part lay up vicious principles in sweet pills to be swallowed down, and make the taste of virtuous documents harsh and sour.

---

[1] *climate* Milton expresses his fear that the English climate was inimical to the artistic intellect in *Paradise Lost* 9.44–45.

[2] *Origen* one of the most influential early Christian theologians (d. 254).

[3] *Paraeus* the biblical commentator David Paraeus (1548–1622).

But because the spirit of man cannot demean itself lively in this body, without some recreating intermission of labour and serious things, it were happy for the commonwealth if our magistrates, as in those famous governments of old, would take into their care not only the deciding of our contentious law-cases and brawls but the managing of our public sports and festival pastimes; that they might be, not such as were authorized a while since,[1] the provocations of drunkenness and lust, but such as may inure and harden our bodies by martial exercises to all warlike skill and performance; and may civilize, adorn, and make discreet our minds by the learned and affable meeting of frequent academies, and the procurement of wise and artful recitations, sweetened with eloquent and graceful enticements to the love and practice of justice, temperance, and fortitude, instructing and bettering the nation at all opportunities, that the call of wisdom and virtue may be heard everywhere, as Solomon saith: "She crieth without, she uttereth her voice in the streets, in the top of high places, in the chief concourse, and in the openings of the gates" [Proverbs 1:20–21; 8:2–3]. Whether this may not be not only in pulpits but after another persuasive method, at set and solemn paneguries, in theatres, porches,[2] or what other place or way may win most upon the people to receive at once both recreation and instruction, let them in authority consult.

The thing which I had to say, and those intentions which have lived within me ever since I could conceive myself anything worth to my country, I return to crave excuse that urgent reason hath plucked from me, by an abortive and foredated discovery. And the accomplishment of them lies not but in a power above man's to promise; but that none hath by more studious ways endeavoured, and with more unwearied spirit that none shall, that I dare almost aver of myself, as far as life and free leisure will extend; and that the land had once enfranchised herself from this impertinent yoke of prelaty, under whose inquisitorious and tyrannical duncery no free and splendid wit can flourish.

Neither do I think it shame to covenant with any knowing reader, that for some few years yet I may go on trust with him toward the payment of what I am now indebted, as being a work not to be raised from the heat of youth, or the vapours of wine; like that which flows at waste from the pen of some vulgar amorist, or the trencher fury of a rhyming parasite; nor to be obtained by the invocation of Dame Memory and her siren daughters; but by devout prayer to that eternal Spirit who can enrich with all utterance and knowledge, and sends out his seraphim with the hallowed fire of his altar to touch and purify the lips of whom he pleases:[3] to this must be added industrious and select reading, steady observation, insight into all seemly and generous arts and affairs; till which in some measure be compassed, at mine own peril and cost, I refuse not to sustain this expectation from as many as are not loath to hazard so much credulity upon the best pledges that I can give them.

Although it nothing content me to have disclosed thus much beforehand, but that I trust hereby to make it manifest with what small willingness I endure to interrupt the pursuit of no less hopes than these, and leave a calm and pleasing solitariness, fed with cheerful and confident thoughts, to embark in a troubled sea of noises and hoarse disputes, put from beholding the bright countenance of truth in the quiet and still air of delightful studies, to come into the dim reflection

---

[1] *such as were authorized* referring to the *Book of Sports*, issued by James I in 1618 and re-issued by Charles I in 1633, which sought to combat Puritan sabbatarianism by authorizing the performance on Sundays and other holidays of such traditional pastimes as dancing around May poles, archery, and morris dancing.

[2] *paneguries* public assemblies during religious festivals; *porches* probably church porches or side-chapels.

[3] *hallowed fire* See Isaiah 6:1–7.

of hollow antiquities sold by the seeming bulk, and there be fain to club quotations with men whose learning and belief lies in marginal stuffings; who, when they have, like good sumpters,[1] laid ye down their horse-loads of citations and fathers at your door with a rhapsody of who and who were bishops here or there, ye may take off their pack-saddles, their day's work is done, and episcopacy, as they think, stoutly vindicated. Let any gentle apprehension that can distinguish learned pains from unlearned drudgery, imagine what pleasure or profoundness can be in this, or what honour to deal against such adversaries.

But were it the meanest under-service, if God by his secretary conscience enjoin it, it were sad for me if I should draw back; for me especially, now when all men offer their aid to help, ease, and lighten the difficult labours of the Church, to whose service, by the intentions of my parents and friends, I was destined of a child, and in mine own resolutions: till coming to some maturity of years, and perceiving what tyranny had invaded the Church, that he who would take orders must subscribe slave, and take an oath withal,[2] which unless he took with a conscience that would retch, he must either straight perjure, or split his faith; I thought it better to prefer a blameless silence before the sacred office of speaking, bought and begun with servitude and forswearing. Howsoever thus Church-outed by the prelates, hence may appear the right I have to meddle in these matters, as before the necessity and constraint appeared.

—1642

---

[1] *sumpters* drivers of pack-horses (*OED*).

[2] *take an oath* A candidate for ordination had to swear allegiance to the King and subscribe to the Book of Common Prayer, its thirty-nine articles of belief, and the hierarchical government of the Church of England.

Areopagitica:
A Speech of Mr. John Milton for the Liberty of Unlicensed Printing, to the Parliament of England

This is true Liberty, when free born men
Having to advise the public may speak free,
Which he who can, and will, deserves high praise,
Who neither can nor will, may hold his peace;
What can be juster in a State than this?
Euripedes, *The Suppliants*

They who to states and governors of the Commonwealth direct their speech, High Court of Parliament, or, wanting such access in a private condition, write that which they foresee may advance the public good; I suppose them, as at the beginning of no mean endeavour, not a little altered and moved inwardly in their minds: some with doubt of what will be the success, others with fear of what will be the censure; some with hope, others with confidence of what they have to speak. And me perhaps each of these dispositions, as the subject was whereon I entered, may have at other times variously affected;[3] and likely might in these foremost expressions now also disclose which of them swayed most, but that the very attempt of this address thus made, and the thought of whom it hath recourse to, hath got the power within me to a passion, far more welcome than incidental to a preface.

Which though I stay not to confess ere any ask, I shall be blameless, if it be no other than the joy and gratulation which it brings to all who wish and promote their country's liberty; whereof this whole discourse proposed will be a certain testimony, if not a trophy. For this is not the liberty which we can hope, that no grievance ever should arise in the Commonwealth—that let no man in this world

---

[3] *other times* Milton had published seven prose works before *Areopagitica*.

expect; but when complaints are freely heard, deeply considered and speedily reformed, then is the utmost bound of civil liberty attained that wise men look for. To which if I now manifest by the very sound of this which I shall utter, that we are already in good part arrived, and yet from such a steep disadvantage of tyranny and superstition grounded into our principles as was beyond the manhood of a Roman recovery, it will be attributed first, as is most due, to the strong assistance of God our deliverer, next to your faithful guidance and undaunted wisdom, Lords and Commons of England. Neither is it in God's esteem the diminution of his glory, when honourable things are spoken of good men and worthy magistrates; which if I now first should begin to do, after so fair a progress of your laudable deeds, and such a long obligement upon the whole realm to your indefatigable virtues, I might be justly reckoned among the tardiest, and the unwillingest of them that praise ye.

Nevertheless there being three principal things, without which all praising is but courtship and flattery: First, when that only is praised which is solidly worth praise: next, when greatest likelihoods are brought that such things are truly and really in those persons to whom they are ascribed: the other, when he who praises, by showing that such his actual persuasion is of whom he writes, can demonstrate that he flatters not; the former two of these I have heretofore endeavoured, rescuing the employment from him who went about to impair your merits with a trivial and malignant encomium;[1] the latter as belonging chiefly to mine own acquittal, that whom I so extolled I did not flatter, hath been reserved opportunely to this occasion.

For he who freely magnifies what hath been nobly done, and fears not to declare as freely what might be done better, gives ye the best covenant of his fidelity; and that his loyalist affection and his hope waits on your proceedings. His highest praising is not flattery, and his plainest advice is a kind of praising. For though I should affirm and hold by argument, that it would fare better with truth, with learning and the Commonwealth, if one of your published Orders, which I should name, were called in; yet at the same time it could not but much redound to the lustre of your mild and equal government, whenas private persons are hereby animated to think ye better pleased with public advice, than other statists have been delighted heretofore with public flattery. And men will then see what difference there is between the magnanimity of a triennial Parliament, and that jealous haughtiness of prelates and Cabin Counsellors that usurped of late, whenas they shall observe ye in the midst of your victories and successes more gently brooking written exceptions against a voted Order than other Courts, which had produced nothing worth memory but the weak ostentation of wealth, would have endured the least signified dislike at any sudden Proclamation.

If I should thus far presume upon the meek demeanour of your civil and gentle greatness, Lords and Commons, as what your published Order hath directly said, that to gainsay, I might defend myself with ease, if any should accuse me of being new or insolent, did they but know how much better I find ye esteem it to imitate the old and elegant humanity of Greece, than the barbaric pride of a Hunnish and Norwegian stateliness. And out of those ages, to whose polite wisdom and letters we owe that we are not yet Goths and Jutlanders, I could name him who from his private house wrote that discourse to the Parliament of Athens, that persuades them to change the form of democracy which was then established.[2] Such honour was done in those days to men who professed the study of wisdom and elo-

---

[1] *from him* Bishop Joseph Hall, whose *Humble Remonstrance* (1641) sparked the Smectymnuan controversy, to which Milton contributed *Animadversions* (1641) and *Apology against a Pamphlet* (1642).

[2] *him* Isocrates (436–338 B.C.E.), whose *Areopagitic Discourse* provided a formal model for *Areopagitica.*

quence, not only in their own country, but in other lands, that cities and signiories heard them gladly, and with great respect, if they had aught in public to admonish the state. Thus did Dion Prusaeus, a stranger and a private orator, counsel the Rhodians against a former edict;[1] and I abound with other like examples, which to set here would be superfluous.

But if from the industry of a life wholly dedicated to studious labours, and those natural endowments haply not the worse for two and fifty degrees of northern latitude, so much must be derogated, as to count me not equal to any of those who had this privilege, I would obtain to be thought not so inferior, as yourselves are superior to the most of them who received their counsel: and how far you excel them, be assured, Lords and Commons, there can no greater testimony appear, than when your prudent spirit acknowledges and obeys the voice of reason from what quarter soever it be heard speaking; and renders ye as willing to repeal any Act of your own setting forth, as any set forth by your predecessors.

If ye be thus resolved, as it were injury to think ye were not, I know not what should withhold me from presenting ye with a fit instance wherein to show both that love of truth which ye eminently profess, and that uprightness of your judgment which is not wont to be partial to yourselves; by judging over again that Order which ye have ordained to regulate Printing: *that no book, pamphlet, or paper shall be henceforth printed, unless the same be first approved and licensed by such*, or at least one of such, as shall thereto be appointed. For that part which preserves justly every man's copy to himself, or provides for the poor, I touch not, only wish they be not made pretences to abuse and persecute honest and painful men, who offend not in either of these particulars. But that other clause of Licensing

Books, which we thought had died with his brother quadragesimal and matrimonial when the prelates expired,[2] I shall now attend with such a homily, as shall lay before ye, first the inventors of it to be those whom ye will be loath to own; next what is to be thought in general of reading, whatever sort the books be; and that this Order avails nothing to the suppressing of scandalous, seditious, and libellous books, which were mainly intended to be suppressed. Last, that it will be primely to the discouragement of all learning, and the stop of Truth, not only by disexercising and blunting our abilities in what we know already, but by hindering and cropping the discovery that might be yet further made both in religious and civil Wisdom.

I deny not, but that it is of greatest concernment in the Church and Commonwealth to have a vigilant eye how books demean themselves as well as men; and thereafter to confine, imprison, and do sharpest justice on them as malefactors. For books are not absolutely dead things, but do contain a potency of life in them to be as active as that soul was whose progeny they are; nay, they do preserve as in a vial the purest efficacy and extraction of that living intellect that bred them. I know they are as lively, and as vigorously productive, as those fabulous dragon's teeth; and being sown up and down, may chance to spring up armed men.[3] And yet, on the other hand, unless wariness be used, as good almost kill a man as kill a good book. Who kills a man kills a reasonable creature, God's image; but he who destroys a good book, kills reason itself, kills the image of God, as it were in the eye. Many a man lives a burden to the earth; but a good book is the precious life-blood of a master spirit, embalmed and treasured up on purpose to a life beyond life. 'Tis

---

[1] *Dion Prusaeus* Greek rhetorician (d. ca. 117 C.E.) famous as a spokesman for republican ideals in Rome.

[2] *quadragesimal* pertaining to Lent and referring to dispensations from dietary restrictions given by bishops, who also had the power to dispense with certain restrictions governing marriage licenses.

[3] *dragon's teeth* In Greek mythology, the teeth of a dragon slain by Cadmus bred armed men when sown.

true, no age can restore a life, whereof perhaps there is no great loss; and revolutions of ages do not oft recover the loss of a rejected truth, for the want of which whole nations fare the worse.

We should be wary therefore what persecutions we raise against the living labours of public men, how we spill that seasoned life of man, preserved and stored up in books; since we see a kind of homicide may be thus committed, sometimes a martyrdom, and if it extend to the whole impression, a kind of massacre; whereof the execution ends not in the slaying of an elemental life, but strikes at that ethereal and fifth essence, the breath of reason itself, slays an immortality rather than a life. But lest I should be condemned of introducing licence, while I oppose licensing, I refuse not the pains to be so much historical, as will serve to show what hath been done by ancient and famous commonwealths against this disorder, till the very time that this project of licensing crept out of the inquisition, was catched up by our prelates, and hath caught some of our presbyters.

In Athens, where books and wits were ever busier than in any other part of Greece, I find but only two sorts of writings which the magistrate cared to take notice of; those either blasphemous and atheistical, or libellous. Thus the books of Protagoras were by the judges of Areopagus commanded to be burnt, and himself banished the territory for a discourse begun with his confessing not to know 'whether there were gods, or whether not.' And against defaming, it was agreed that none should be traduced by name, as was the manner of *Vetus Comoedia*,[1] whereby we may guess how they censured libelling. And this course was quick enough, as Cicero writes, to quell both the desperate wits of other atheists, and the open way of defaming, as the event showed. Of other sects and opinions, though tending to voluptuousness, and the denying of Divine Providence, they took no heed.

Therefore we do not read that either Epicurus, or that libertine school of Cyrene, or what the Cynic impudence uttered, was ever questioned by the laws. Neither is it recorded that the writings of those old comedians were suppressed, though the acting of them were forbid; and that Plato commended the reading of Aristophanes, the loosest of them all, to his royal scholar Dionysius, is commonly known, and may be excused, if holy Chrysostom,[2] as is reported, nightly studied so much the same author and had the art to cleanse a scurrilous vehemence into the style of a rousing sermon.

That other leading city of Greece, Lacedaemon, considering that Lycurgus their lawgiver was so addicted to elegant learning, as to have been the first that brought out of Ionia the scattered works of Homer, and sent the poet Thales from Crete to prepare and mollify the Spartan surliness with his smooth songs and odes, the better to plant among them law and civility, it is to be wondered how museless and unbookish they were, minding nought but the feats of war. There needed no licensing of books among them, for they disliked all but their own laconic apothegms, and took a slight occasion to chase Archilochus out of their city, perhaps for composing in a higher strain than their own soldierly ballads and roundels could reach to. Or if it were for his broad verses, they were not therein so cautious but they were as dissolute in their promiscuous conversing; whence Euripides affirms in *Andromache*, that their women were all unchaste. Thus much may give us light after what sort of books were prohibited among the Greeks.

The Romans also, for many ages trained up only to a military roughness resembling most the Lacedaemonian guise, knew of learning little but what their twelve Tables, and the Pontific College

---

[1] *Vetus Comoedia* the "Old Comedy" of ancient Greece, characterized by virulent personal satire.

[2] *Chrysostom* St. John Chrysostom (ca. 347–407), one of the most influential of the Greek Church Fathers.

with their augurs and flamens taught them in religion and law,[1] so unacquainted with other learning, that when Carneades and Critolaus, with the Stoic Diogenes coming ambassadors to Rome, took thereby occasion to give the city a taste of their philosophy, they were suspected for seducers by no less a man than Cato the Censor, who moved it in the Senate to dismiss them speedily, and to banish all such Attic babblers out of Italy. But Scipio and others of the noblest senators withstood him and his old Sabine austerity; honoured and admired the men; and the censor himself at last, in his old age, fell to the study of what whereof before he was so scrupulous. And yet at the same time, Naevius and Plautus, the first Latin comedians, had filled the city with all the borrowed scenes of Menander and Philemon. Then began to be considered there also what was to be done to libellous books and authors; for Naevius was quickly cast into prison for his unbridled pen, and released by the tribunes upon his recantation; we read also that libels were burnt, and the makers punished by Augustus. The like severity, no doubt, was used, if aught were impiously written against their esteemed gods. Except in these two points, how the world went in books, the magistrate kept no reckoning.

And therefore Lucretius without impeachment versifies his Epicurism to Memmius, and had the honour to be set forth the second time by Cicero, so great a father of the commonwealth; although himself disputes against that opinion in his own writings. Nor was the satirical sharpness or naked plainness of Lucilius, or Catullus, or Flaccus, by any order prohibited. And for matters of state, the story of Titus Livius, though it extolled that part which Pompey held, was not therefore suppressed by Octavius Caesar of the other faction. But that Naso

was by him banished in his old age,[2] for the wanton poems of his youth, was but a mere covert of state over some secret cause: and besides, the books were neither banished nor called in. From hence we shall meet with little else but tyranny in the Roman empire, that we may not marvel, if not so often bad as good books were silenced. I shall therefore deem to have been large enough, in producing what among the ancients was punishable to write; save only which, all other arguments were free to treat on.

By this time the emperors were become Christians, whose discipline in this point I do not find to have been more severe than what was formerly in practice. The books of those whom they took to be grand heretics were examined, refuted, and condemned in the general Councils; and not till then were prohibited, or burnt, by authority of the emperor. As for the writings of heathen authors, unless they were plain invectives against Christianity, as those of Porphyrius and Proclus, they met with no interdict that can be cited, till about the year 400, in a Carthaginian Council, wherein bishops themselves were forbid to read the books of Gentiles, but heresies they might read: while others long before them, on the contrary, scrupled more the books of heretics than of Gentiles. And that the primitive Councils and bishops were wont only to declare what books were not commendable, passing no further, but leaving it to each one's conscience to read or to lay by, till after the year 800, is observed already by Padre Paolo, the great unmasker of the Trentine Council.[3]

After which time the Popes of Rome, engrossing what they pleased of political rule into their own

---

[1] *twelve Tables* the basic texts of the Roman legal code; *Pontific College* supreme ecclesiastical authority of ancient Rome; *augurs* Roman priests responsible for reading omens; *flamens* Roman priests responsible for maintaining the sacrificial fires.

[2] *Naso* Ovid, banished from Rome to a town on the Black Sea at the age of 43; the true cause of his exile remains unknown.

[3] *Padre Paolo* Paolo Servita (Pietro Sarpi); his influential *History of the Council of Trent* (1619) cast a sceptical eye on the Council of Trent (1545-1563), which affirmed Roman Catholic doctrine against the challenge posed by the Reformation.

hands, extended their dominion over men's eyes, as they had before over their judgments, burning and prohibiting to be read what they fancied not; yet sparing in their censures, and the books not many which they so dealt with: till Martin V, by his bull, not only prohibited, but was the first that excommunicated the reading of heretical books; for about that time Wycliffe and Huss, growing terrible, were they who first drove the Papal Court to a stricter policy of prohibiting.[1] Which course Leo X and his successors followed, until the Council of Trent and the Spanish Inquisition engendering together brought forth, or perfected, those Catalogues and expurging Indexes, that rake through the entrails of many an old good author, with a violation worse than any could be offered to his tomb. Nor did they stay in matters heretical, but any subject that was not to their palate, they either condemned in a Prohibition, or had it straight into the new Purgatory of an Index.

To fill up the measure of encroachment, their last invention was to ordain that no book, pamphlet, or paper should be printed (as if St. Peter had bequeathed them the keys of the press also out of Paradise) unless it were approved and licensed under the hands of two or three glutton friars. For example:[2]

Let the Chancellor Cini be pleased to see if in this present work be contained ought that may withstand the printing
Vincent Rabbatta, Vicar of Florence

I have seen this present work, and find nothing athwart the catholic faith and good manners: In witnesse whereof I have given, &c.
Nicolò Cini, Chancellor of Florence

Attending the precedent relation, it is allowed that this present work of Davanzati may be printed,
Vincent Rabbatta, &c.

It may be printed, July 15.
Friar Simon Mompei d'Amelia, Chancellor of the holy office in Florence

Sure they have a conceit, if he of the bottomless pit had not long since broke prison, that this quadruple exorcism would bar him down. I fear their next design will be to get into their custody the licensing of that which they say Claudius intended,[3] but went not through with. Vouchsafe to see another of their forms the Roman stamp:

Imprimatur, if it seem good to the reverend master of the holy Palace,
Belcastro, Vicegerent

Imprimatur
Friar Nicolò Rodolphi, master of the holy Palace

Sometimes five *Imprimatur*s are seen together dialogue-wise in the piazza of one title-page, complimenting and ducking each to other with their shaven reverences, whether the author, who stands by in perplexity at the foot of his epistle, shall to the press or to the sponge. These are the pretty responsories, these are the dear antiphonies, that so bewitched of late our Prelates and their chaplains with the goodly echo they made; and besotted us to

---

[1] *Martin V...prohibiting* In 1418 Pope Martin V published a bull that condemned the works of John Wycliffe (ca. 1324–1384) and John Huss (ca. 1373–1415), founders of influential movements for religious reform in England and Bohemia respectively.

[2] What follows are Milton's translations of the permissions printed with Bernardo Davanzati's *Scisma d'Inghilterra* (1638).

[3] "Quo veniam daret flatum crepitumque ventris in convivio emittendi" [Milton's marginal note]: Claudius "thought of an edict allowing the privilege of breaking wind quietly or noisily at table" (Suetonius, *Life of Claudius*, 32).

the gay imitation of a lordly *Imprimatur*, one from Lambeth House, another from the west end of Pauls; so apishly romanizing, that the word of command still was set down in Latin; as if the learned grammatical pen that wrote it would cast no ink without Latin; or perhaps, as they thought, because no vulgar tongue was worthy to express the pure conceit of an *Imprimatur*; but rather, as I hope, for that our English, the language of men, ever famous and foremost in the achievements of liberty, will not easily find servile letters enow to spell such a dictatory presumption English.

And thus ye have the inventors and the original of booklicensing ripped up and drawn as lineally as any pedigree. We have it not, that can be heard of, from any ancient state, or polity or church; nor by any statute left us by our ancestors elder or later; nor from the modem custom of any reformed city or church abroad; but from the most antichristian council and the most tyrannous inquisition that ever inquired. Till then books were ever as freely admitted into the world as any other birth; the issue of the brain was no more stifled than the issue of the womb: no envious Juno sat cross-legged over the nativity of any man's intellectual offspring; but if it proved a monster, who denies, but that it was justly burnt, or sunk into the sea? But that a book, in worse condition than a peccant soul, should be to stand before a jury ere it be born to the world, and undergo yet in darkness the judgment of Radamanth and his colleagues, ere it can pass the ferry backward into light, was never heard before, till that mysterious iniquity, provoked and troubled at the first entrance of Reformation, sought out new limbos and new hells wherein they might include our books also within the number of their damned. And this was the rare morsel so officiously snatched up, and so ill-favouredly imitated by our inquisiturient bishops, and the attendant minorities their chaplains. That ye like not now these most certain authors of this licensing order, and that all sinister

intention was far distant from your thoughts, when ye were importuned the passing it, all men who know the integrity of your actions, and how ye honour Truth, will clear ye readily.

But some will say, What though the inventors were bad, the thing for all that may be good? It may be so; yet if that thing be no such deep invention, but obvious, and easy for any man to light on, and yet best and wisest commonwealths through all ages and occasions have forborne to use it, and falsest seducers and oppressors of men were the first who took it up, and to no other purpose but to obstruct and hinder the first approach of Reformation; I am of those who believe it will be a harder alchemy than Lullius ever knew, to sublimate any good use out of such an invention.[1] Yet this only is what I request to gain from this reason, that it may be held a dangerous and suspicious fruit, as certainly it deserves, for the tree that bore it, until I can dissect one by one the properties it has. But I have first to finish, as was propounded, what is to be thought in general of reading books, whatever sort they be, and whether be more the benefit or the harm that thence proceeds?

Not to insist upon the examples of Moses, Daniel, and Paul, who were skilful in all the learning of the Egyptians, Chaldeans, and Greeks, which could not probably be without reading their books of all sorts; in Paul especially, who thought it no defilement to insert into Holy Scripture the sentences of three Greek poets, and one of them a tragedian;[2] the question was notwithstanding sometimes controverted among the primitive doctors, but with great odds on that side which affirmed it both lawful and profitable; as was then evidently perceived, when Julian the Apostate and subtlest enemy to our faith made a decree forbidding Christians the study of heathen learning: for, said he, they wound us with

---

[1] *Lullius* Ramón Lull (d. 1315), the best-known medieval alchemist.

[2] Acts 17:28 (quoting Aratus); I Corinthians 15:33 (Euripedes, probably via Menander); Titus 1:12 (Epimenides).

our own weapons, and with our own arts and sciences they overcome us. And indeed the Christians were put so to their shifts by this crafty means, and so much in danger to decline into all ignorance, that the two Apollinarii were fain, as a man may say, to coin all the seven liberal sciences out of the Bible, reducing it into divers forms of orations, poems, dialogues, even to the calculating of a new Christian grammar. But, saith the historian Socrates, the providence of God provided better than the industry of Apollinarius and his son, by taking away that illiterate law with the life of him who devised it.[1] So great an injury they then held it to be deprived of Hellenic learning; and thought it a persecution more undermining, and secretly decaying the Church, than the open cruelty of Decius or Diocletian.

And perhaps it was the same politic drift that the devil whipped St. Jerome in a Lenten dream, for reading Cicero; or else it was a phantasm bred by the fever which had then seized him. For had an angel been his discipliner, unless it were for dwelling too much upon Ciceronianisms, and had chastised the reading, not the vanity, it had been plainly partial; first to correct him for grave Cicero, and not for scurril Plautus, whom he confesses to have been reading not long before; next to correct him only, and let so many more ancient fathers wax old in those pleasant and florid studies without the lash of such a tutoring apparition; insomuch that Basil teaches how some good use may be made of Margites, a sportful poem, not now extant, writ by Homer; and why not then of Morgante, an Italian romance much to the same purpose?[2]

But if it be agreed we shall be tried by visions, there is a vision recorded by Eusebius, far ancienter than this tale of Jerome to the nun Eustochium, and, besides, has nothing of a fever in it. Dionysius Alexandrinus was about the year 240 a person of great name in the Church for piety and learning, who had wont to avail himself much against heretics by being conversant in their books; until a certain presbyter laid it scrupulously to his conscience, how he durst venture himself among those defiling volumes. The worthy man, loath to give offence, fell into a new debate with himself what was to be thought, when suddenly a vision sent from God (it is his own epistle that so avers it) confirmed him in these words: Read any books whatever come to thy hands, for thou art sufficient both to judge aright, and to examine each matter. To this revelation he assented the sooner, as he confesses, because it was answerable to that of the Apostle to the Thessalonians, "Prove all things, hold fast that which is good" [I Thessalonians 5:21]. And he might have added another remarkable saying of the same author: "To the pure, all things are pure" [Titus 1:15], not only meats and drinks, but all kind of knowledge whether of good or evil; the knowledge cannot defile, nor consequently the books, if the will and conscience be not defiled.

For books are as meats and viands are; some of good, some of evil substance; and yet God, in that unapocryphal vision, said without exception, "Rise, Peter; kill and eat" [Acts 10:13], leaving the choice to each man's discretion. Wholesome meats to a vitiated stomach differ little or nothing from unwholesome; and best books to a naughty mind are not unappliable to occasions of evil. Bad meats will scarce breed good nourishment in the healthiest concoction; but herein the difference is of bad books, that they to a discreet and judicious reader serve in many respects to discover, to confute, to forewarn, and to illustrate. Whereof what better witness can ye expect I should produce, than one of your own now sitting in Parliament, the chief of learned men reputed in this land, Mr. Selden;

---

[1] *the two Apollinarii* a fourth-century father and son who, when the Emperor Julian forbade Christians from studying secular literature, translated Scripture into verse, drama, and dialogues; Milton's source is Socrates Scholasticus, *Ecclesiastical History*, 3.14.

[2] *Morgante* a mock-heroic romance (1481) by Luigi Pulci.

whose volume of natural and national laws proves, not only by great authorities brought together, but by exquisite reasons and theorems almost mathematically demonstrative, that all opinions, yea errors, known, read, and collated, are of main service and assistance toward the speedy attainment of what is truest.[1] I conceive, therefore, that when God did enlarge the universal diet of man's body, saving ever the rules of temperance, he then also, as before, left arbitrary the dieting and repasting of our minds; as wherein every mature man might have to exercise his own leading capacity.

How great a virtue is temperance, how much of moment through the whole life of man! Yet God commits the managing so great a trust, without particular law or prescription, wholly to the demeanour of every grown man. And therefore when he himself tabled the Jews from heaven, that omer which was every man's daily portion of manna [Exodus 16:33] is computed to have been more than might have well sufficed the heartiest feeder thrice as many meals. For those actions which enter into a man, rather than issue out of him, and therefore defile not, God uses not to captivate under a perpetual childhood of prescription, but trusts him with the gift of reason to be his own chooser; there were but little work left for preaching, if law and compulsion should grow so fast upon those things which heretofore were governed only by exhortation. Solomon informs us, that much reading is a weariness to the flesh [Ecclesiastes 12:12]; but neither he nor other inspired author tells us that such or such reading is unlawful: yet certainly had God thought good to limit us herein, it had been much more expedient to have told us what was unlawful than what was wearisome. As for the burning of those Ephesian books by St. Paul's converts; 'tis replied the books were magic, the Syriac so renders them [Acts 19:19]. It was a private act, a voluntary act, and leaves us to a voluntary imitation: the men in remorse burnt those books which were their own; the magistrate by this example is not appointed; these men practised the books, another might perhaps have read them in some sort usefully.

Good and evil we know in the field of this world grow up together almost inseparably; and the knowledge of good is so involved and interwoven with the knowledge of evil, and in so many cunning resemblances hardly to be discerned, that those confused seeds which were imposed upon Psyche as an incessant labour to cull out, and sort asunder, were not more intermixed.[2] It was from out the rind of one apple tasted, that the knowledge of good and evil, as two twins cleaving together, leaped forth into the world. And perhaps this is that doom which Adam fell into of knowing good and evil, that is to say of knowing good by evil. As therefore the state of man now is; what wisdom can there be to choose, what continence to forbear without the knowledge of evil? He that can apprehend and consider vice with all her baits and seeming pleasures, and yet abstain, and yet distinguish, and yet prefer that which is truly better, he is the true wayfaring Christian.

I cannot praise a fugitive and cloistered virtue, unexercised and unbreathed, that never sallies out and sees her adversary, but slinks out of the race, where that immortal garland is to be run for, not without dust and heat. Assuredly we bring not innocence into the world, we bring impurity much rather; that which purifies us is trial, and trial is by what is contrary. That virtue therefore which is but a youngling in the contemplation of evil, and knows not the utmost that vice promises to her followers, and rejects it, is but a blank virtue, not a pure; her whiteness is but an excremental whiteness.[3] Which

---

[1] John Selden (1584–1654), one of the period's best known legal historians; Milton refers to the preface of *De jure naturali* (1640).

[2] *Psyche* Apuleius tells the story of Cupid and Psyche in *The Golden Ass*; Psyche's impossible task was set by her mother-in-law, Venus.

[3] *excremental* superficial (*OED* a[2]).

was the reason why our sage and serious poet Spenser, whom I dare be known to think a better teacher than Scotus or Aquinas, describing true temperance under the person of Guyon, brings him in with his Palmer through the cave of Mammon, and the bower of earthly bliss, that he might see and know, and yet abstain.[1] Since therefore the knowledge and survey of vice is in this world so necessary to the constituting of human virtue, and the scanning of error to the confirmation of truth, how can we more safely, and with less danger, scout into the regions of sin and falsity than by reading all manner of tractates and hearing all manner of reason? And this is the benefit which may be had of books promiscuously read.

But of the harm that may result hence three kinds are usually reckoned. First, is feared the infection that may spread; but then all human learning and controversy in religious points must remove out of the world, yea the Bible itself; for that ofttimes relates blasphemy not nicely, it describes the carnal sense of wicked men not unelegantly, it brings in holiest men passionately murmuring against Providence through all the arguments of Epicurus: in other great disputes it answers dubiously and darkly to the common reader. And ask a Talmudist what ails the modesty of his marginal Keri, that Moses and all the prophets cannot persuade him to pronounce the textual Chetiv.[2] For these causes we all know the Bible itself put by the Papist into the first rank of prohibited books. The ancientest fathers must be next removed, as Clement of Alexandria, and that Eusebian book of Evangelic preparation,

transmitting our ears through a hoard of heathenish obscenities to receive the Gospel.[3] Who finds not that Irenaeus, Epiphanius, Jerome, and others discover more heresies than they well confute, and that oft for heresy which is the truer opinion?

Nor boots it to say for these, and all the heathen writers of greatest infection, if it must be thought so, with whom is bound up the life of human learning, that they writ in an unknown tongue, so long as we are sure those languages are known as well to the worst of men, who are both most able, and most diligent to instil the poison they suck, first into the courts of princes, acquainting them with the choicest delights and criticisms of sin. As perhaps did that Petronius whom Nero called his Arbiter, the master of his revels; and the notorious ribald of Arezzo, dreaded and yet dear to the Italian courtiers.[4] I name not him for posterity's sake, whom Henry VIII named in merriment his Vicar of hell.[5] By which compendious way all the contagion that foreign books can infuse will find a passage to the people far easier and shorter than an Indian voyage, though it could be sailed either by the north of Cataio eastward,[6] or of Canada westward, while our Spanish licensing gags the English press never so severely.

But on the other side that infection which is from books of controversy in religion is more doubtful and dangerous to the learned than to the ignorant; and yet those books must be permitted untouched by the licenser.[7] It will be hard to instance where any ignorant man hath been ever seduced by

---

[1] Milton famously misremembers *The Faerie Queene*: while Guyon, the Knight of Temperance, does resist the Bower of Bliss (II.xii.42ff.) with the aid of his Palmer (a pilgrim who has been to the Holy Land, and a figure for the reason that restrains passion), his settled habits of temperance allow Guyon to withstand the temptations of Mammon's cave on his own (II.vii.2; viii.3).

[2] *Keri...Chetiv* terms from Hebraic textual criticism: if a given reading (*Chetiv*) was thought corrupt or unseemly, a marginal note (*Ketiv*) provided an emendation or euphemism.

[3] The Church Fathers Clement of Alexandria (second century) and Eusebius (third century) both wrote texts that described pagan rites in great if disapproving detail.

[4] *the notorious ribald* Pietro Aretino (1492–1557), a writer of famously explicit sonnets, published in illustrated editions.

[5] *Vicar of hell* Sir Francis Brian, a minor poet and cousin to Anne Boleyn.

[6] *Cataio* Cathay, or China.

[7] The Licensing Order in fact specifically provided for such books.

papistical book in English, unless it were commended and expounded to him by some of that clergy: and indeed all such tractates, whether false or true, are as the prophecy of Isaiah was to the eunuch, not to be understood without a guide [Acts 8:27–35]. But of our priests and doctors how many have been corrupted by studying the comments of Jesuits and Sorbonists,[1] and how fast they could transfuse that corruption into the people, our experience is both late and sad. It is not forgot, since the acute and distinct Arminius was perverted merely by the perusing of a nameless discourse written at Delft, which at first he took in hand to confute.[2]

Seeing, therefore, that those books, and those in great abundance, which are likeliest to taint both life and doctrine, cannot be suppressed without the fall of learning and of all ability in disputation, and that these books of either sort are most and soonest catching to the learned, from whom to the common people whatever is heretical or dissolute may quickly be conveyed, and that evil manners are as perfectly learnt without books a thousand other ways which cannot be stopped, and evil doctrine not with books can propagate, except a teacher guide, which he might also do without writing, and so beyond prohibiting, I am not able to unfold, how this cautelous enterprise of licensing can be exempted from the number of vain and impossible attempts.[3] And he who were pleasantly disposed could not well avoid to liken it to the exploit of that gallant man who thought to pound up the crows by shutting his park gate.

Besides another inconvenience, if learned men be the first receivers out of books and dispreaders both of vice and error, how shall the licensers themselves be confided in, unless we can confer upon them, or they assume to themselves above all others in the land, the grace of infallibility and uncorruptedness? And again, if it be true that a wise man, like a good refiner, can gather gold out of the drossiest volume, and that a fool will be a fool with the best book, yea or without book; there is no reason that we should deprive a wise man of any advantage to his wisdom, while we seek to restrain from a fool, that which being restrained will be no hindrance to his folly. For if there should be so much exactness always used to keep that from him which is unfit for his reading, we should in the judgment of Aristotle not only, but of Solomon and of our Saviour, not vouchsafe him good precepts, and by consequence not willingly admit him to good books; as being certain that a wise man will make better use of an idle pamphlet, than a fool will do of sacred Scripture.

'Tis next alleged we must not expose ourselves to temptations without necessity, and next to that, not employ our time in vain things. To both these objections one answer will serve, out of the grounds already laid, that to all men such books are not temptations, nor vanities, but useful drugs and materials wherewith to temper and compare effective and strong medicines, which man's life cannot want. The rest, as children and childish men, who have not the art to qualify and prepare these working minerals, well may be exhorted to forbear, but hindered forcibly they cannot be by all the licensing that sainted Inquisition could ever yet contrive. Which is what I promised to deliver next, That this order of licensing conduces nothing to the end for which it was framed; and hath almost prevented me by being clear already while thus much hath been explaining. See the ingenuity of Truth, who, when she

---

[1] *Sorbonists* the theology faculty at the University of Paris.

[2] *Arminius* Jacobus Arminius (1560–1609); his "corruption" was not a conversion to Catholicism but a move to what became known as Arminianism, a form of Protestantism that challenged the strict predestinarian theology of Calvinism. Milton held Arminian views, as is clear from his major poems.

[3] *cautelous* deceitful, crafty (*OED*).

gets a free and willing hand, opens herself faster than the pace of method and discourse can overtake her.

It was the task which I began with, to show that no nation, or well-instituted state, if they valued books at all, did ever use this way of licensing; and it might be answered, that this is a piece of prudence lately discovered. To which I return, that as it was a thing slight and obvious to think on, so if it had been difficult to find out, there wanted not among them long since who suggested such a course; which they not following, leave us a pattern of their judgment that it was not the not knowing, but the not approving, which was the cause of their not using it.

Plato, a man of high authority, indeed, but least of all for his commonwealth, in the book of his Laws, which no city ever yet received, fed his fancy by making many edicts to his airy burgomasters, which they who otherwise admire him wish had been rather buried and excused in the genial cups of an Academic night sitting. By which laws he seems to tolerate no kind of learning but by unalterable decree, consisting most of practical traditions, to the attainment whereof a library of smaller bulk than his own Dialogues would be abundant. And there also enacts, that no poet should so much as read to any private man what he had written, until the judges and law-keepers had seen it, and allowed it.[1] But that Plato meant this law peculiarly to that commonwealth which he had imagined, and to no other, is evident. Why was he not else a lawgiver to himself, but a transgressor, and to be expelled by his own magistrates; both for the wanton epigrams and dialogues which he made, and his perpetual reading of Sophron Mimus and Aristophanes, books of grossest infamy, and also for commending the latter of them, though he were the malicious libeller of his chief friends, to be read by the tyrant Dionysius, who had little need of such trash to spend his time

on? But that he knew this licensing of poems had reference and dependence to many other provisos there set down in his fancied republic, which in this world could have no place: and so neither he himself, nor any magistrate, or city ever imitated that course, which, taken apart from those other collateral injunctions, must needs be vain and fruitless. For if they fell upon one kind of strictness, unless their care were equal to regulate all other things of like aptness to corrupt the mind, that single endeavour they knew would be but a fond labour; to shut and fortify one gate against corruption, and be necessitated to leave others round about wide open.

If we think to regulate printing, thereby to rectify manners, we must regulate all recreations and pastimes, all that is delightful to man. No music must be heard, no song be set or sung, but what is grave and Doric.[2] There must be licensing dancers, that no gesture, motion, or deportment be taught our youth but what by their allowance shall be thought honest; for such Plato was provided of; it will ask more than the work of twenty licensers to examine all the lutes, the violins, and the guitars in every house; they must not be suffered to prattle as they do, but must be licensed what they may say. And who shall silence all the airs and madrigals that whisper softness in chambers? The windows also, and the balconies must be thought on; there are shrewd books, with dangerous frontispieces, set to sale; who shall prohibit them, shall twenty licensers? The villages also must have their visitors to inquire what lectures the bagpipe and the rebeck reads,[3] even to the ballatry and the gamut of every municipal fiddler, for these are the countryman's Arcadias, and his Montemayors.[4]

---

[2] *Doric*   used by Plato (*Republic* III.398–99) to describe music that was manly and dignified (see *Paradise Lost* 1.550).

[3] *rebeck*   a three-stringed violin.

[4] That is, music is the rural equivalent to sophisticated prose romances, such as Sir Philip Sidney's *Arcadia* (1590) and Jorge de Montemayor's *Diana* (ca. 1559).

---

[1] a paraphrase of Plato, *Laws*, VII.801.

Next, what more national corruption, for which England hears ill abroad, than household gluttony: who shall be the rectors of our daily rioting? And what shall be done to inhibit the multitudes that frequent those houses where drunkenness is sold and harboured? Our garments also should be referred to the licensing of some more sober work-masters to see them cut into a less wanton garb. Who shall regulate all the mixed conversation of our youth, male and female together, as is the fashion of this country? Who shall still appoint what shall be discoursed, what presumed, and no further? Lastly, who shall forbid and separate all idle resort, all evil company? These things will be, and must be; but how they shall be least hurtful, how least enticing, herein consists the grave and governing wisdom of a state.

To sequester out of the world into Atlantic and Utopian polities which never can be drawn into use will not mend our condition; but to ordain wisely as in this world of evil, in the midst whereof God hath placed us unavoidably. Nor is it Plato's licensing of books will do this, which necessarily pulls along with it so many other kinds of licensing, as will make us all both ridiculous and weary, and yet frustrate; but those unwritten, or at least unconstraining, laws of virtuous education, religious and civil nurture, which Plato there mentions as the bonds and ligaments of the commonwealth, the pillars and the sustainers of every written statute; these they be which will bear chief sway in such matters as these, when all licensing will be easily eluded. Impunity and remissness, for certain, are the bane of a commonwealth; but here the great art lies, to discern in what the law is to bid restraint and punishment, and in what things persuasion only is to work.

If every action which is good or evil in man at ripe years were to be under pittance and prescription and compulsion, what were virtue but a name, what praise could be then due to well-doing, what

gramercy to be sober, just, or continent? Many there be that complain of Divine Providence for suffering Adam to transgress; foolish tongues! When God gave him reason, he gave him freedom to choose, for reason is but choosing; he had been else a mere artificial Adam, such an Adam as he is in the motions. We ourselves esteem not of that obedience, or love, or gift, which is of force: God therefore left him free, set before him a provoking object, ever almost in his eyes; herein consisted his merit, herein the right of his reward, the praise of his abstinence. Wherefore did he create passions within us, pleasures round about us, but that these rightly tempered are the very ingredients of virtue?

They are not skillful considerers of human things, who imagine to remove sin by removing the matter of sin; for, besides that it is a huge heap increasing under the very act of diminishing, though some part of it may for a time be withdrawn from some persons, it cannot from all, in such a universal thing as books are; and when this is done, yet the sin remains entire. Though ye take from a covetous man all his treasure, he has yet one jewel left, ye cannot bereave him of his covetousness. Banish all objects of lust, shut up all youth into the severest discipline that can be exercised in any hermitage, ye cannot make them chaste, that came not thither so: such great care and wisdom is required to the right managing of this point. Suppose we could expel sin by this means; look how much we thus expel of sin, so much we expel of virtue: for the matter of them both is the same; remove that, and ye remove them both alike.

This justifies the high providence of God, who, though he commands us temperance, justice, continence, yet pours out before us, even to a profuseness, all desirable things, and gives us minds that can wander beyond all limit and satiety. Why should we then affect a rigour contrary to the manner of God and of nature, by abridging or scanting those means, which books freely permitted are, both to the trial of virtue and the exercise of truth? It would be better done, to learn that the law must needs be frivolous, which goes to restrain things, uncertainly and yet equally working to good and to evil. And were I the chooser, a dram of well-doing should be preferred before many times as much the forcible hindrance of evil-doing. For God sure esteems the growth and completing of one virtuous person more than the restraint of ten vicious.

And albeit whatever thing we hear or see, sitting, walking, travelling, or conversing, may be fitly called our book, and is of the same effect that writings are, yet grant the thing to be prohibited were only books, it appears that this order hitherto is far insufficient to the end which it intends. Do we not see, not once or oftener, but weekly, that continued court-libel against the Parliament and City, printed, as the wet sheets can witness, and dispersed among us, for all that licensing can do?[1] yet this is the prime service a man would think, wherein this Order should give proof of itself. If it were executed, you'll say. But certain, if execution be remiss or blindfold now, and in this particular, what will it be hereafter and in other books? If then the Order shall not be vain and frustrate, behold a new labour, Lords and Commons, ye must repeal and proscribe all scandalous and unlicensed books already printed and divulged; after ye have drawn them up into a list, that all may know which are condemned, and which not; and ordain that no foreign books be delivered out of custody, till they have been read over. This office will require the whole time of not a few overseers, and those no vulgar men. There be also books which are partly useful and excellent, partly culpable and pernicious; this work will ask as many more officials, to make expurgations and expunctions, that the Common-wealth of Learning be not damnified. In fine, when

the multitude of books increase upon their hands, ye must be fain to catalogue all those printers who are found frequently offending, and forbid the importation of their whole suspected typography. In a word, that this your order may be exact and not deficient, ye must reform it perfectly according to the model of Trent and Seville, which I know ye abhor to do.

Yet though ye should condescend to this, which God forbid, the Order still would be but fruitless and defective to that end whereto ye meant it. If to prevent sects and schisms, who is so unread or so uncatechized in story, that hath not heard of many sects refusing books as a hindrance, and preserving their doctrine unmixed for many ages, only by unwritten traditions? The Christian faith, for that was once a schism, is not unknown to have spread all over Asia, ere any Gospel or Epistle was seen in writing. If the amendment of manners be aimed at, look into Italy and Spain, whether those places be one scruple the better, the honester, the wiser, the chaster, since all the inquisitional rigour that hath been executed upon books.

Another reason, whereby to make it plain that this Order will miss the end it seeks, consider by the quality which ought to be in every licenser. It cannot be denied but that he who is made judge to sit upon the birth or death of books, whether they may be wafted into this world or not, had need to be a man above the common measure, both studi-ous, learned, and judicious; there may be else no mean mistakes in the censure of what is passable or not; which is also no mean injury. If he be of such worth as behoves him, there cannot be a more tedious and unpleasing journey-work, a greater loss of time levied upon his head, than to be made the perpetual reader of unchosen books and pamphlets, ofttimes huge volumes. There is no book that is acceptable unless at certain seasons; but to be enjoined the reading of that at all times, and in a hand scarce legible, whereof three pages would not

---

[1] *court libel* The Royalist newspaper *Mercurius aulicus*, published weekly from 1642 to 1645 and sporadically afterward.

down at any time in the fairest print, is an imposition which I cannot believe how he that values time and his own studies, or is but of a sensible nostril, should be able to endure. In this one thing I crave leave of the present licensers to be pardoned for so thinking; who doubtless took this office up, looking on it through their obedience to the Parliament, whose command perhaps made all things seem easy and unlaborious to them; but that this short trial hath wearied them out already, their own expressions and excuses to them who make so many journeys to solicit their licence are testimony enough. Seeing therefore those who now possess the employment by all evident signs wish themselves well rid of it; and that no man of worth, none that is not a plain unthrift of his own hours, is ever likely to succeed them, except he mean to put himself to the salary of a press corrector; we may easily foresee what kind of licensers we are to expect hereafter, either ignorant, imperious, and remiss, or basely pecuniary. This is what I had to show, wherein this Order cannot conduce to that end whereof it bears the intention.

I lastly proceed from the no good it can do, to the manifest hurt it causes, in being first the greatest discouragement and affront that can be offered to learning, and to learned men.

It was the complaint and lamentation of prelates, upon every least breath of a motion to remove pluralities,[1] and distribute more equally Church revenues, that then all learning would be for ever dashed and discouraged. But as for that opinion, I never found cause to think that the tenth part of learning stood or fell with the clergy: nor could I ever but hold it for a sordid and unworthy speech of any churchman who had a competency left him. If therefore ye be loath to dishearten heartily and discontent, not the mercenary crew of false pretenders to learning, but the free and ingenuous sort of

such as evidently were born to study, and love learning for itself, not for lucre or any other end but the service of God and of truth, and perhaps that lasting fame and perpetuity of praise which God and good men have consented shall be the reward of those whose published labours advance the good of mankind, then know that, so far to distrust the judgment and the honesty of one who hath but a common repute in learning, and never yet offended, as not to count him fit to print his mind without a tutor and examiner, lest he should drop a schism, or something of corruption, is the greatest displeasure and indignity to a free and knowing spirit that can be put upon him.

What advantage is it to be a man over it is to be a boy at school, if we have only escaped the ferula to come under the fescue of an *Imprimatur*,[2] if serious and elaborate writings, as if they were no more than the theme of a grammar-lad under his pedagogue, must not be uttered without the cursory eyes of a temporizing and extemporizing licenser? He who is not trusted with his own actions, his drift not being known to be evil, and standing to the hazard of law and penalty, has no great argument to think himself reputed in the Commonwealth wherein he was born for other than a fool or a foreigner. When a man writes to the world, he summons up all his reason and deliberation to assist him; he searches, meditates, is industrious, and likely consults and confers with his judicious friends; after all which done he takes himself to be informed in what he writes, as well as any that writ before him. If, in this the most consummate act of his fidelity and ripeness, no years, no industry, no former proof of his abilities can bring him to that state of maturity, as not to be still mistrusted and suspected, unless he carry all his considerate diligence, all his midnight watchings

---

[1] *pluralities* multiple church livings held by one person.

[2] *ferula...fescue* respectively, a cane used for disciplining school children and a straw or twig used as a pointer in instruction.

and expense of Palladian oil,[1] to the hasty view of an unleisured licenser, perhaps much his younger, perhaps far his inferior in judgment, perhaps one who never knew the labour of bookwriting, and if he be not repulsed or slighted, must appear in print like a punie with his guardian,[2] and his censor's hand on the back of his title to be his bail and surety that he is no idiot or seducer, it cannot be but a dishonour and derogation to the author, to the book, to the privilege and dignity of Learning.

And what if the author shall be one so copious of fancy, as to have many things well worth the adding come into his mind after licensing, while the book is yet under the press, which not seldom happens to the best and diligentest writers; and that perhaps a dozen times in one book? The printer dares not go beyond his licensed copy; so often then must the author trudge to his leave-giver, that those his new insertions may be viewed; and many a jaunt will be made, ere that licenser, for it must be the same man, can either be found, or found at leisure; meanwhile either the press must stand still, which is no small damage, or the author lose his accuratest thoughts, and send the book forth worse than he had made it, which to a diligent writer is the greatest melancholy and vexation that can befall.

And how can a man teach with authority, which is the life of teaching, how can he be a doctor in his book as he ought to be, or else had better be silent, whenas all he teaches, all he delivers, is but under the tuition, under the correction of his patriarchal licenser to blot or alter what precisely accords not with the hidebound humour which he calls his judgment? When every acute reader, upon the first sight of a pedantic licence, will be ready with these like words to ding the book a quoit's distance from him: I hate a pupil teacher, I endure not an instructor that comes to me under the wardship of an overseeing fist. I know nothing of the licenser, but that I have his own hand here for his arrogance; who shall warrant me his judgment? The State, sir, replies the stationer, but has a quick return: The State shall be my governors, but not my critics; they may be mistaken in the choice of a licenser, as easily as this licenser may be mistaken in an author; this is some common stuff; and he might add from Sir Francis Bacon, "That such authorized books are but the language of the times."[3] For though a licenser should happen to be judicious more than ordinary, which will be a great jeopardy of the next succession, yet his very office and his commission enjoins him to let pass nothing but what is vulgarly received already.

Nay, which is more lamentable, if the work of any deceased author, though never so famous in his lifetime and even to this day, come to their hands for licence to be printed, or reprinted, if there be found in his book one sentence of a venturous edge, uttered in the height of zeal and who knows whether it might not be the dictate of a divine spirit, yet not suiting with every low decrepit humour of their own, though it were Knox himself, the Reformer of a Kingdom,[4] that spake it, they will not pardon him their dash: the sense of that great man shall to all posterity be lost, for the fearfulness or the presumptuous rashness of a perfunctory licenser. And to what an author this violence hath been lately done, and in what book of greatest consequence to be faithfully published, I could now instance, but shall forbear till a more convenient season.[5]

---

[3] from a government brief Bacon wrote in 1589 about the government's response to the Martin Marprelate controversy, first printed in 1641 as *A Wise and Moderate Discourse*.

[4] John Knox (ca. 1505–1572), leader of the Reformation in Scotland.

[5] Among the texts suggested as the one Milton has in mind are Edward Coke's *Institutes* (1641) and John Knox's *History of the Reformation* (1644), both cut by censors.

---

[1] *Palladian* pertaining to Pallas Athena, goddess of wisdom.

[2] *punie* from the French *puis-ne*, a minor.

Yet if these things be not resented seriously and timely by them who have the remedy in their power, but that such iron moulds as these shall have authority to gnaw out the choicest periods of exquisitest books, and to commit such a treacherous fraud against the orphan remainders of worthiest men after death, the more sorrow will belong to that hapless race of men, whose misfortune it is to have understanding. Henceforth let no man care to learn, or care to be more than worldly-wise; for certainly in higher matters to be ignorant and slothful, to be a common steadfast dunce, will be the only pleasant life, and only in request.

And as it is a particular disesteem of every knowing person alive, and most injurious to the written labours and monuments of the dead, so to me it seems an undervaluing and vilifying of the whole Nation. I cannot set so light by all the invention, the art, the wit, the grave and solid judgment which is in England, as that it can be comprehended in any twenty capacities how good soever, much less that it should not pass except their superintendence be over it, except it be sifted and strained with their strainers, that it should be uncurrent without their manual stamp. Truth and understanding are not such wares as to be monopolized and traded in by tickets and statutes and standards. We must not think to make a staple commodity of all the knowledge in the land, to mark and licence it like our broadcloth and our woolpacks. What is it but a servitude like that imposed by the Philistines, not to be allowed the sharpening of our own axes and coulters,[1] but we must repair from all quarters to twenty licensing forges? Had anyone written and divulged erroneous things and scandalous to honest life, misusing and forfeiting the esteem had of his reason among men, if after conviction this only censure were adjudged him that he should never henceforth write but what were first examined by an appointed officer, whose hand should be annexed to pass his credit for him that now he might be safely read; it could not be apprehended less than a disgraceful punishment. Whence to include the whole Nation, and those that never yet thus offended, under such a diffident and suspectful prohibition, may plainly be understood what a disparagement it is. So much the more, whenas debtors and delinquents may walk abroad without a keeper, but unoffensive books must not stir forth without a visible jailer in their title.

Nor is it to the common people less than a reproach; for if we be so jealous over them, as that we dare not trust them with an English pamphlet, what do we but censure them for a giddy, vicious, and ungrounded people; in such a sick and weak state of faith and discretion, as to be able to take nothing down but through the pipe of a licenser? That this is care or love of them, we cannot pretend, whenas, in those popish places where the laity are most hated and despised, the same strictness is used over them. Wisdom we cannot call it, because it stops but one breach of licence, nor that neither: whenas those corruptions, which it seeks to prevent, break in faster at other doors which cannot be shut.

And in conclusion it reflects to the disrepute of our Ministers also, of whose labours we should hope better, and of the proficiency which their flock reaps by them, than that after all this light of the Gospel which is, and is to be, and all this continual preaching, they should still be frequented with such an unprincipled, unedified and laic rabble, as that the whiff of every new pamphlet should stagger them out of their catechism, and Christian walking. This may have much reason to discourage the Ministers when such a low conceit is had of all their exhortations, and the benefiting of their hearers, as that they are not thought fit to be turned loose to three sheets of paper without a licenser; that all the sermons, all the lectures preached, printed, vented in such numbers, and such volumes, as have now

---

[1] *coulters* A coulter is the sharpened edge of a plough.

well nigh made all other books unsaleable, should not be armour enough against one single enchiridion,[1] without the castle of St Angelo of an *Imprimatur*.[2]

And lest some should persuade ye, Lords and Commons, that these arguments of learned men's discouragement at this your Order are mere flourishes, and not real, I could recount what I have seen and heard in other countries, where this kind of inquisition tyrannizes; when I have sat among their learned men, for that honour I had, and been counted happy to be born in such a place of philosophic freedom, as they supposed England was, while themselves did nothing but bemoan the servile condition into which learning amongst them was brought; that this was it which had damped the glory of Italian wits; that nothing had been there written now these many years but flattery and fustian. There it was that I found and visited the famous Galileo, grown old a prisoner to the Inquisition, for thinking in astronomy otherwise than the Franciscan and Dominican licensers thought.

And though I knew that England then was groaning loudest under the prelatical yoke, nevertheless I took it as a pledge of future happiness, that other nations were so persuaded of her liberty. Yet was it beyond my hope that those Worthies were then breathing in her air, who should be her leaders to such a deliverance, as shall never be forgotten by any revolution of time that this world hath to finish. When that was once begun, it was as little in my fear that, what words of complaint I heard among learned men of other parts uttered against the Inquisition, the same I should hear by as learned men at home uttered in time of Parliament against an order of licensing; and that so generally that, when I had disclosed myself a companion of their

discontent, I might say, if without envy, that he whom an honest quaestorship had endeared to the Sicilians was not more by them importuned against Verres,[3] than the favourable opinion which I had among many who honour ye, and are known and respected by ye, loaded me with entreaties and persuasions, that I would not despair to lay together that which just reason should bring into my mind, toward the removal of an undeserved thraldom upon learning. That this is not therefore the disburdening of a particular fancy, but the common grievance of all those who had prepared their minds and studies above the vulgar pitch to advance truth in others, and from others to entertain it, thus much may satisfy.

And in their name I shall for neither friend nor foe conceal what the general murmur is; that if it come to inquisitioning again and licensing, and that we are so timorous of ourselves, and so suspicious of all men, as to fear each book and the shaking of every leaf, before we know what the contents are; if some who but of late were little better than silenced from preaching shall come now to silence us from reading, except what they please, it cannot be guessed what is intended by some but a second tyranny over learning: and will soon put it out of controversy, that Bishops and Presbyters are the same to us, both name and thing. That those evils of Prelaty, which before from five to six and twenty sees were distributively charged upon the whole people, will now light wholly upon learning, is not obscure to us: whenas now the pastor of a small unlearned parish on the sudden shall be exalted Archbishop over a large diocese of books, and yet not remove, but keep his other cure too, a mystical pluralist. He who but of late cried down the sole ordination of every novice Bachelor of Art, and denied sole jurisdiction over the simplest parishioner, shall now at home in his private chair assume

---

[1] *enchiridion*   a hand-book, but probably also punning on another meaning of the word in Greek, a hand-knife.

[2] *St Angelo*   the papal fortress across from the Vatican.

[3] *he...Verres*   Cicero, whose oratory drove Gaius Verres from office.

both these over worthiest and excellentest books and ablest authors that write them.

This is not, ye Covenants and Protestations that we have made,[1] this is not to put down Prelaty; this is but to chop an Episcopacy; this is but to translate the Palace Metropolitan from one kind of dominion into another; this is but an old canonical sleight of commuting our penance. To startle thus betimes at a mere unlicensed pamphlet will after a while be afraid of every conventicle, and a while after will make a conventicle of every Christian meeting. But I am certain that a State governed by the rules of justice and fortitude, or a Church built and founded upon the rock of faith and true knowledge, cannot be so pusillanimous. While things are yet not constituted in Religion, that freedom of writing should be restrained by a discipline imitated from the Prelates and learnt by them from the Inquisition, to shut us all up again into the breast of a licenser, must needs give cause of doubt and discouragement to all learned and religious men.

Who cannot but discern the fineness of this politic drift, and who are the contrivers? That while Bishops were to be baited down, then all Presses might be open; it was the people's birthright and privilege in time of Parliament, it was the breaking forth of light? But now, the Bishops abrogated and voided out the Church, as if our Reformation sought no more but to make room for others into their seats under another name, the episcopal arts begin to bud again, the cruse of truth must run no more oil, liberty of printing must be enthralled again under a prelatical commission of twenty, the privilege of the people nullified, and, which is worse, the freedom of learning must groan again, and to her old fetters: all this the Parliament yet sitting. Although their own late arguments and defences against the Prelates might remember them,

that this obstructing violence meets for the most part with an event utterly opposite to the end which it drives at: instead of suppressing sects and schisms, it raises them and invests them with a reputation. "The punishing of wits enhances their authority," said the Viscount St. Albans; "and a forbidden writing is thought to be a certain spark of truth that flies up in the faces of them who seek to tread it out."[2] This Order therefore may prove a nursing-mother to sects, but I shall show how it will be a step-dame to Truth: and first by disenabling us to the maintenance of what is known already.

Well knows he who uses to consider, that our faith and knowledge thrives by exercise, as well as our limbs and complexion. Truth is compared in Scripture to a streaming fountain;[3] if her waters flow not in a perpetual progression, they sicken into a muddy pool of conformity and tradition. A man may be a heretic in the truth; and if he believe things only because his Pastor says so, or the Assembly so determines, without knowing other reason, though his belief be true, yet the very truth he holds becomes his heresy.

There is not any burden that some would gladlier post off to another than the charge and care of their Religion. There be—who knows not that there be?—of Protestants and professors who live and die in as arrant an implicit faith as any lay Papist of Loretto. A wealthy man, addicted to his pleasure and to his profits, finds Religion to be a traffic so entangled and of so many piddling accounts, that of all mysteries he cannot skill to keep a stock going upon that trade. What should he do? fain he would have the name to be religious, fain he would bear up with his neighbours in that. What does he therefore, but resolve to give over toiling, and to find himself out some factor, to whose care and credit he may commit the whole managing of his

---

[1] Milton deploys the rhetorical strategy of addressing the texts that led to the abolishment of episcopacy, including the Scottish National Covenant (1638) and the Solemn League and Covenant (1643).

[2] from Bacon's *A Wise and Moderate Discourse* (1641).

[3] Psalm 85:11.

religious affairs? some Divine of note and estimation that must be. To him he adheres, resigns the whole warehouse of his religion, with all the locks and keys, into his custody; and indeed makes the very person of that man his religion; esteems his associating with him a sufficient evidence and commendatory of his own piety. So that a man may say his religion is now no more within himself, but is become a dividual movable, and goes and comes near him, according as that good man frequents the house. He entertains him, gives him gifts, feasts him, lodges him; his religion comes home at night, prays, is liberally supped, and sumptuously laid to sleep, rises, is saluted, and after the malmsey or some well-spiced brewage, and better breakfasted than he whose morning appetite would have gladly fed on green figs between Bethany and Jerusalem, his Religion walks abroad at eight, and leaves his kind entertainer in the shop trading all day without his Religion.

Another sort there be who, when they hear that all things shall be ordered, all things regulated and settled, nothing written but what passes through the custom-house of certain publicans that have the tonnaging and poundaging of all free-spoken truth,[1] will straight give themselves up into your hands, make 'em and cut 'em out what religion ye please: there be delights, there be recreations and jolly pastimes that will fetch the day about from sun to sun, and rock the tedious year as in a delightful dream. What need they torture their heads with that which others have taken so strictly and so unalterably into their own purveying? These are the fruits which a dull ease and cessation of our knowledge will bring forth among the people. How goodly and how to be wished were such an obedient unanimity as this, what a fine conformity would it starch us all

into! Doubtless a staunch and solid piece of framework, as any January could freeze together.

Nor much better will be the consequence even among the clergy themselves. It is no new thing never heard of before, for a parochial minister, who has his reward and is at his Hercules' pillars in a warm benefice,[2] to be easily inclinable, if he have nothing else that may rouse up his studies, to finish his circuit in an English concordance and a topic folio, the gatherings and savings of a sober graduateship, a Harmony and a Catena;[3] treading the constant round of certain common doctrinal heads, attended with the uses, motives, marks, and means, out of which, as out of an alphabet, or sol-fa,[4] by forming and transforming, joining and disjoining variously, a little bookcraft, and two hours' meditation, might furnish him unspeakably to the performance of more than a weekly charge of sermoning: not to reckon up the infinite helps of interlinearies, breviaries, synopses, and other loitering gear. But as for the multitude of sermons ready printed and piled up, on every text that is not difficult, our London trading St. Thomas in his vestry, and add to boot St. Martin and St. Hugh, have not within their hallowed limits more vendible ware of all sorts ready made: so that penury he never need fear of pulpit provision, having where so plenteously to refresh his magazine. But if his rear and flanks be not impaled, if his back door be not secured by the rigid licenser, but that a bold book may now and then issue forth and give the assault to some of his old collections in their trenches, it will concern him then to keep waking, to stand in watch, to set good guards and sentinels about his received opinions, to walk the round and counter-round with his fellow

---

1 *publicans* here, tax collectors; Milton links the Licensing Order with tunnage and poundage, a tariff that Charles I had attempted to collect on his own authority (that is, without Parliament).

2 *Hercules' pillars* Gibraltar and Abyla, which mark the limit of the Mediterranean; hence, a symbol for any ultimate achievement.

3 *topic folio... Catena* reference books that could provide shortcuts to sermon making, respectively a commonplace book, a parallel edition of the gospels, and extracts from the Church Fathers.

4 *sol-fa* musical scale.

inspectors, fearing lest any of his flock be seduced, who also then would be better instructed, better exercised and disciplined. And God send that the fear of this diligence, which must then be used, do not make us affect the laziness of a licensing Church.

For if we be sure we are in the right, and do not hold the truth guiltily, which becomes not, if we ourselves condemn not our own weak and frivolous teaching, and the people for an untaught and irreligious gadding rout, what can be more fair than when a man judicious, learned, and of a conscience, for aught we know, as good as theirs that taught us what we know, shall not privily from house to house, which is more dangerous, but openly by writing publish to the world what his opinion is, what his reasons, and wherefore that which is now thought cannot be sound? Christ urged it as wherewith to justify himself, that he preached in public; yet writing is more public than preaching; and more easy to refutation, if need be, there being so many whose business and profession merely it is to be the champions of Truth; which if they neglect, what can be imputed but their sloth, or unability?

Thus much we are hindered and disinured by this course of licensing toward the true knowledge of what we seem to know. For how much it hurts and hinders the licensers themselves in the calling of their ministry, more than any secular employment, if they will discharge that office as they ought, so that of necessity they must neglect either the one duty or the other, I insist not, because it is a particular, but leave it to their own conscience, how they will decide it there.

There is yet behind of what I proposed to lay open, the incredible loss and detriment that this plot of licensing puts us to; more than if some enemy at sea should stop up all our havens and ports and creeks, it hinders and retards the importation of our richest merchandise, Truth; nay, it was first established and put in practise by Antichristian malice and mystery on set purpose to extinguish, if it were possible, the light of Reformation, and to settle falsehood; little differing from that policy wherewith the Turk upholds his Alcoran, by the prohibiting of printing. 'Tis not denied, but gladly confessed, we are to send our thanks and vows to Heaven louder than most of nations, for that great measure of truth which we enjoy, especially in those main points between us and the Pope, with his appurtenances the Prelates: but he who thinks we are to pitch our tent here, and have attained the utmost prospect of reformation that the mortal glass wherein we contemplate can show us, till we come to beatific vision, that man by this very opinion declares that he is yet far short of Truth.

Trust indeed came once into the world with her Divine Master, and was a perfect shape most glorious to look on: but when he ascended, and his Apostles after him were laid asleep, then straight arose a wicked race of deceivers, who, as that story goes of the Egyptian Typhon with his conspirators, how they dealt with the good Osiris,[1] took the virgin Truth, hewed her lovely form into a thousand pieces, and scattered them to the four winds. From that time ever since, the sad friends of Truth, such as durst appear, imitating the careful search that Isis made for the mangled body of Osiris, went up and down gathering up limb by limb, still as they could find them. We have not yet found them all, Lords and Commons, nor ever shall do, till her Master's second coming; he shall bring together every joint and member, and shall mold them into an immortal feature of loveliness and perfection. Suffer not these licensing prohibitions to stand at every place of opportunity, forbidding and disturbing them that continue seeking, that continue to do

---

[1] *Typhon...Osiris* Milton's source for this allegory about the search for truth is likely Plutarch's "On Isis and Osiris." Typhon (the Egyptian Set) tears up and scatters the body of Osiris (sacred text), which Isis, the sister of Osiris, then collects and pieces together.

our obsequies to the torn body of our martyred saint.

We boast our light; but if we look not wisely on the Sun itself, it smites us into darkness. Who can discern those planets that are oft combust, and those stars of brightest magnitude that rise and set with the Sun, until the opposite motion of their orbs bring them to such a place in the firmament, where they may be seen evening or morning? The light which we have gained was given us, not to be ever staring on, but by it to discover onward things more remote from our knowledge. It is not the unfrocking of a priest, the unmitring of a bishop, and the removing him from off the Presbyterian shoulders, that will make us a happy nation. No, if other things as great in the Church, and in the rule of life both economical and political, be not looked into and reformed, we have looked so long upon the blaze that Zwinglius and Calvin hath beaconed up to us, that we are stark blind.[1] There be who perpetually complain of schisms and sects, and make it such a calamity that any man dissents from their maxims. 'Tis their own pride and ignorance which causes the disturbing, who neither will hear with meekness, nor can convince; yet all must be suppressed which is not found in their syntagma.[2] They are the troublers, they are the dividers of unity, who neglect and permit not others to unite those dissevered pieces which are yet wanting to the body of Truth. To be still searching what we know not by what we know, still closing up truth to truth as we find it (for all her body is homogeneal and proportional), this is the golden rule in theology as well as in arithmetic, and makes up the best harmony in a Church; not the forced and outward union of cold and neutral, and inwardly divided minds.

Lords and Commons of England, consider what nation it is whereof ye are, and whereof ye are the governors: a nation not slow and dull, but of a quick, ingenious and piercing spirit, acute to invent, subtle and sinewy to discourse, not beneath the reach of any point, the highest that human capacity can soar to. Therefore the studies of Learning in her deepest sciences have been so ancient and so eminent among us, that writers of good antiquity and ablest judgment have been persuaded that even the school of Pythagoras and the Persian wisdom took beginning from the old philosophy of this island. And that wise and civil Roman, Julius Agricola, who governed once here for Caesar, preferred the natural wits of Britain before the laboured studies of the French.[3] Nor is it for nothing that the grave and frugal Transylvanian sends out yearly from as far as the mountainous borders of Russia, and beyond the Hercynian wilderness, not their youth, but their staid men, to learn our language and our theologic arts.[4]

Yet that which is above all this, the favour and the love of Heaven, we have great argument to think in a peculiar manner propitious and propending towards us. Why else was this nation chosen before any other, that out of her, as out of Sion, should be proclaimed and sounded forth the first tidings and trumpet of Reformation to all Europe? And had it not been the obstinate perverseness of our prelates against the divine and admirable spirit of Wycliffe, to suppress him as a schismatic and innovator, perhaps neither the Bohemian Huss and Jerome, no nor the name of Luther or of Calvin, had been ever known: the glory of reforming all our neighbours had been completely ours. But now, as our obdurate clergy have with violence demeaned the matter, we are become hitherto the latest and backwardest scholars, of whom God offered to have

---

[1] Ulrich Zwingli (1484–1531) and John Calvin (1509–1564), leading figures of the Reformation.

[2] *syntagma* systematic treatise or body of doctrine.

[3] Tacitus, *Agricola*, 21.

[4] Many theologians from strongly Protestant Transylvania came to study in western European universities in the period.

made us the teachers. Now once again by all concurrence of signs, and by the general instinct of holy and devout men, as they daily and solemnly express their thoughts, God is decreeing to begin some new and great period in his Church, even to the reforming of Reformation itself: what does he then but reveal himself to his servants, and as his manner is, first to his Englishmen? I say, as his manner is, first to us, though we mark not the method of his counsels, and are unworthy.

Behold now this vast city: a city of refuge, the mansion house of liberty, encompassed and surrounded with his protection; the shop of war hath not there more anvils and hammers waking, to fashion out the plates and instruments of armed Justice in defence of beleaguered Truth, than there be pens and heads there, sitting by their studious lamps, musing, searching, revolving new notions and ideas wherewith to present, as with their homage and their fealty, the approaching Reformation: others as fast reading, trying all things, assenting to the force of reason and convincement. What could a man require more from a nation so pliant and so prone to seek after knowledge? What wants there to such a towardly and pregnant soil but wise and faithful labourers, to make a knowing people, a nation of prophets, of sages, and of worthies? We reckon more than five months yet to harvest; there need not be five weeks; had we but eyes to lift up, the fields are white already.[1]

Where there is much desire to learn, there of necessity will be much arguing, much writing, many opinions; for opinion in good men is but knowledge in the making. Under these fantastic terrors of sect and schism, we wrong the earnest and zealous thirst after knowledge and understanding which God hath stirred up in this city. What some lament of, we rather should rejoice at, should rather praise this pious forwardness among men, to reas-

sume the ill-reputed care of their Religion into their own hands again. A little generous prudence, a little forbearance of one another, and some grain of charity might win all these diligences to join, and unite in one general and brotherly search after Truth; could we but forgo this prelatical tradition of crowding free consciences and Christian liberties into canons and precepts of men. I doubt not, if some great and worthy stranger should come among us, wise to discern the mold and temper of a people, and how to govern it, observing the high hopes and aims, the diligent alacrity of our extended thoughts and reasonings, in the pursuance of truth and freedom, but that he would cry out as Pyrrhus did, admiring the Roman docility and courage: If such were my Epirots,[2] I would not despair the greatest design that could be attempted, to make a Church or Kingdom happy.

Yet these are the men cried out against for schismatics and sectaries; as if, while the temple of the Lord was building, some cutting, some squaring the marble, others hewing the cedars, there should be a sort of irrational men who could not consider there must be many schisms and many dissections made in the quarry and in the timber, ere the house of God can be built. And when every stone is laid artfully together, it cannot be united into a continuity, it can but be contiguous in this world; neither can every piece of the building be of one form; nay rather the perfection consists in this, that, out of many moderate varieties and brotherly dissimilitudes that are not vastly disproportional, arises the goodly and the graceful symmetry that commends the whole pile and structure.

Let us therefore be more considerate builders, more wise in spiritual architecture, when great reformation is expected. For now the time seems come, wherein Moses the great prophet may sit in heaven rejoicing to see that memorable and glorious

---

[1] an adaptation of John 4:35.

[2] Pyrrhus, King of Epirus, defeated a Roman army in 280 B.C.E.

wish of his fulfilled, when not only our seventy Elders, but all the Lord's people, are become prophets. No marvel then though some men, and some good men too perhaps, but young in goodness, as Joshua then was, envy them. They fret, and out of their own weakness are in agony, lest these divisions and subdivisions will undo us. The adversary again applauds, and waits the hour: When they have branched themselves out, saith he, small enough into parties and partitions, then will be our time. Fool! he sees not the firm root, out of which we all grow, though into branches: nor will beware until he see our small divided maniples cutting through at every angle of his ill-united and unwieldy brigade.[1] And that we are to hope better of all these supposed sects and schisms, and that we shall not need that solicitude, honest perhaps though overtimorous of them that vex in this behalf, but shall laugh in the end at those malicious applauders of our differences, I have these reasons to persuade me.

First, when a city shall be as it were besieged and blocked about, her navigable river infested, inroads and incursions round, defiance and battle oft rumoured to be marching up even to her walls and suburb trenches, that then the people, or the greater part, more than at other times, wholly taken up with the study of highest and most important matters to be reformed, should be disputing, reasoning, reading, inventing, discoursing, even to a rarity and admiration, things not before discoursed or written of, argues first a singular goodwill, contentedness and confidence in your prudent foresight and safe government, Lords and Commons; and from thence derives itself to a gallant bravery and well-grounded contempt of their enemies, as if there were no small number of as great spirits among us, as his was, who when Rome was nigh besieged by Hannibal, being in the city, bought that piece of ground at no cheap rate, whereon Hannibal himself encamped his own regiment.

Next, it is a lively and cheerful presage of our happy success and victory. For as in a body, when the blood is fresh, the spirits pure and vigorous, not only to vital but to rational faculties, and those in the acutest and the pertest operations of wit and subtlety, it argues in what good plight and constitution the body is so when the cheerfulness of the people is so sprightly up, as that it has not only wherewith to guard well its own freedom and safety, but to spare, and to bestow upon the solidest and sublimest points of controversy and new invention, it betokens us not degenerated, nor drooping to a fatal decay, but casting off the old and wrinkled skin of corruption to outlive these pangs and wax young again, entering the glorious ways of truth and prosperous virtue, destined to become great and honourable in these latter ages. Methinks I see in my mind a noble and puissant nation rousing herself like a strong man after sleep, and shaking her invincible locks. Methinks I see her as an eagle mewing her mighty youth,[2] and kindling her undazzled eyes at the full midday beam; purging and unscaling her long-abused sight at the fountain itself of heavenly radiance; while the whole noise of timorous and flocking birds, with those also that love the twilight, flutter about, amazed at what she means, and in their envious gabble would prognosticate a year of sects and schisms.

What would ye do then? should ye suppress all this flowery crop of knowledge and new light sprung up and yet springing daily in this city? should ye set an oligarchy of twenty engrossers over it, to bring a famine upon our minds again, when we shall know nothing but what is measured to us by their bushel? Believe it, Lords and Commons, they who counsel ye to such a suppressing do as good as bid ye suppress yourselves; and I will soon

---

[1] *maniples* infantry companies in the Roman army.

[2] *mewing* "muing" in the original; "mew" is a term from falconry meaning to moult, leading to a connection with ideas of renewal.

show how. If it be desired to know the immediate cause of all this free writing and free speaking, there cannot be assigned a truer than your own mild and free and humane government. It is the liberty, Lords and Commons, which your own valorous and happy counsels have purchased us, liberty which is the nurse of all great wits; this is that which hath rarefied and enlightened our spirits like the influence of heaven; this is that which hath enfranchised, enlarged and lifted up our apprehensions degrees above themselves.

Ye cannot make us now less capable, less knowing, less eagerly pursuing of the truth, unless ye first make yourselves, that made us so, less the lovers, less the founders of our true liberty. We can grow ignorant again, brutish, formal and slavish, as ye found us; but you then must first become that which ye cannot be, oppressive, arbitrary and tyrannous, as they were from whom ye have freed us. That our hearts are now more capacious, our thoughts more erected to the search and expectation of greatest and exactest things, is the issue of your own virtue propagated in us; ye cannot suppress that, unless ye reinforce an abrogated and merciless law, that fathers may dispatch at will their own children. And who shall then stick closest to ye, and excite others? not he who takes up arms for coat and conduct and his four nobles of Danegelt.[1] Although I dispraise not the defence of just immunities, yet love my peace better, if that were all. Give me the liberty to know, to utter, and to argue freely according to conscience, above all liberties.

What would be best advised, then, if it be found hurtful and so unequal to suppress opinions for the newness or the unsuitableness to a customary acceptance, will not be my task to say. I only shall repeat what I have learned from one of your own honourable number, a right noble and pious lord, who, had he not sacrificed his life and fortunes to the Church and Commonwealth, we had not now missed and bewailed a worthy and undoubted patron of this argument. Ye know him, I am sure; yet I for honour's sake, and may it be eternal to him, shall name him, the Lord Brook.[2] He writing of Episcopacy and by the way treating of sects and schisms, left ye his vote, or rather now the last words of his dying charge, which I know will ever be of dear and honoured regard with ye, so full of meekness and breathing charity, that next to his last testament, who bequeathed love and peace to his disciples, I cannot call to mind where I have read or heard words more mild and peaceful. He there exhorts us to hear with patience and humility those, however they be miscalled, that desire to live purely, in such a use of God's ordinances, as the best guidance of their conscience gives them, and to tolerate them, though in some disconformity to ourselves. The book itself will tell us more at large, being published to the world, and dedicated to the Parliament by him who, both for his life and for his death, deserves that what advice he left be not laid by without perusal.

And now the time in special is, by privilege to write and speak what may help to the further discussing of matters in agitation. The temple of Janus with his two controversal faces might now not unsignificantly be set open. And though all the winds of doctrine were let loose to play upon the earth, so Truth be in the field, we do injuriously, by licensing and prohibiting, to misdoubt her strength. Let her and Falsehood grapple; who ever knew Truth put to the worse, in a free and open encounter? Her confuting is the best and surest suppressing. He who hears what praying there is for light and clearer knowledge to be sent down among us,

---

[1] *coat and conduct* a tax that provided clothing and transportation of new troops; *noble* a coin worth 6s 8d; *Danegelt* ship money, a tax originally levied to support the building of ships with which to oppose invading Danes but controversially resurrected by Charles I.

[2] Robert Greville, second Lord Brooke (1608–1643), a leading Parliamentarian and general, killed in battle; Milton cites his *Discourse of Episcopacie* (1641).

would think of other matters to be constituted beyond the discipline of Geneva, framed and fabricked already to our hands. Yet when the new light which we beg for shines in upon us, there be who envy and oppose, if it come not first in at their casements. What a collusion is this, whenas we are exhorted by the wise man to use diligence, to seek for wisdom as for hidden treasures early and late, that another order shall enjoin us to know nothing but by statute? When a man hath been labouring the hardest labour in the deep mines of knowledge; hath furnished out his findings in all their equipage; drawn forth his reasons as it were a battle ranged; scattered and defeated all objections in his way; calls out his adversary into the plain, offers him the advantage of wind and sun, if he please, only that he may try the matter by dint of argument: for his opponents then to skulk, to lay ambushments, to keep a narrow bridge of licensing where the challenger should pass, though it be valour enough in soldiership, is but weakness and cowardice in the wars of Truth.

For who knows not that Truth is strong, next to the Almighty? She needs no policies, nor stratagems, nor licensings to make her victorious; those are the shifts and the defences that error uses against her power. Give her but room, and do not bind her when she sleeps, for then she speaks not true, as the old Proteus did, who spake oracles only when he was caught and bound,[1] but then rather she turns herself into all shapes, except her own, and perhaps tunes her voice according to the time, as Micaiah did before Ahab, until she be adjured into her own likeness [I Kings 22:9–28]. Yet is it not impossible that she may have more shapes than one. What else is all that rank of things indifferent, wherein Truth may be on this side or on the other, without being unlike herself? What but a vain shadow else is the abolition of those ordinances, that handwriting

nailed to the cross? What great purchase is this Christian liberty which Paul so often boasts of? His doctrine is, that he who eats or eats not, regards a day or regards it not, may do either to the Lord. How many other things might be tolerated in peace, and left to conscience, had we but charity, and were it not the chief stronghold of our hypocrisy to be ever judging one another?

I fear yet this iron yoke of outward conformity hath left a slavish print upon our necks; the ghost of a linen decency yet haunts us.[2] We stumble and are impatient at the least dividing of one visible congregation from another, though it be not in fundamentals; and through our forwardness to suppress, and our backwardness to recover any enthralled piece of truth out of the grip of custom, we care not to keep truth separated from truth, which is the fiercest rent and disunion of all. We do not see that, while we still affect by all means a rigid external formality, we may as soon fall again into a gross conforming stupidity, a stark and dead congealment of wood and hay and stubble, forced and frozen together, which is more to the sudden degenerating of a Church than many subdichotomies of petty schisms.

Not that I can think well of every light separation, or that all in a Church is to be expected gold and silver and precious stones: it is not possible for man to sever the wheat from the tares, the good fish from the other fry; that must be the angels' ministry at the end of mortal things. Yet if all cannot be of one mind—as who looks they should be?—this doubtless is more wholesome, more prudent, and more Christian that many be tolerated, rather than all compelled. I mean not tolerated popery, and open superstition, which, as it extirpates all religions and civil supremacies, so itself should be extirpate, provided first that all charitable and compassionate means be used to win and regain the weak and the

---

[1] *Proteus* a shape-shifting sea deity; see *Odyssey* 4.383–459.

[2] *linen decency* referring to the vestments that Archbishop Laud insisted ministers wear in the interests of uniformity.

misled: that also which is impious or evil absolutely either against faith or manners no law can possibly permit, that intends not to unlaw itself: but those neighbouring differences, or rather indifferences, are what I speak of, whether in some point of doctrine or of discipline, which, though they may be many, yet need not interrupt the unity of Spirit, if we could but find among us the bond of peace.

In the meanwhile if any one would write, and bring his helpful hand to the slow-moving Reformation which we labour under, if Truth have spoken to him before others, or but seemed at least to speak, who hath so bejesuited us that we should trouble that man with asking licence to do so worthy a deed? and not consider this, that if it come to prohibiting, there is not aught more likely to be prohibited than truth itself; whose first appearance to our eyes, bleared and dimmed with prejudice and custom, is more unsightly and unplausible than many errors, even as the person is of many a great man slight and contemptible to see to. And what do they tell us vainly of new opinions, when this very opinion of theirs, that none must be heard, but whom they like, is the worst and newest opinion of all others; and is the chief cause why sects and schisms do so much abound, and true knowledge is kept at distance from us; besides yet a greater danger which is in it?

For when God shakes a Kingdom with strong and healthful commotions to a general reforming, 'tis not untrue that many sectaries and false teachers are then busiest in seducing; but yet more true it is, that God then raises to his own work men of rare abilities, and more than common industry, not only to look back and revise what hath been taught heretofore, but to gain further and go on some new enlightened steps in the discovery of truth. For such is the order of God's enlightening his Church, to dispense and deal out by degrees his beam, so as our earthly eyes may best sustain it.

Neither is God appointed and confined, where and out of what place these his chosen shall be first heard to speak; for he sees not as man sees, chooses not as man chooses, lest we should devote ourselves again to set places, and assemblies, and outward callings of men; planting our faith one while in the old Convocation house, and another while in the Chapel at Westminster; when all the faith and religion that shall be there canonized is not sufficient without plain convincement, and the charity of patient instruction to supple the least bruise of conscience, to edify the meanest Christian, who desires to walk in the Spirit, and not in the letter of human trust, for all the number of voices that can be there made; no, though Harry VII himself there, with all his liege tombs about him, should lend them voices from the dead, to swell their number.

And if the men be erroneous who appear to be the leading schismatics, what withholds us but our sloth, our self-will, and distrust in the right cause, that we do not give them gentle meeting and gentle dismissions, that we debate not and examine the matter thoroughly with liberal and frequent audience; if not for their sakes, yet for our own? seeing no man who hath tasted learning, but will confess the many ways of profiting by those who, not contented with stale receipts, are able to manage and set forth new positions to the world. And were they but as the dust and cinders of our feet, so long as in that notion they may yet serve to polish and brighten the armoury of Truth, even for that respect they were not utterly to be cast away. But if they be of those whom God hath fitted for the special use of these times with eminent and ample gifts, and those perhaps neither among the Priests nor among the Pharisees, and we in the haste of a precipitant zeal shall make no distinction, but resolve to stop their mouths, because we fear they come with new and dangerous opinions, as we commonly forejudge them ere we understand them, no less than woe to us, while, thinking thus to defend the Gospel, we are found the persecutors.

There have been not a few since the beginning of this Parliament, both of the Presbytery and others, who by their unlicensed books, to the contempt of an *Imprimatur*, first broke that triple ice clung about our hearts, and taught the people to see day: I hope that none of those were the persuaders to renew upon us this bondage which they themselves have wrought so much good by contemning. But if neither the check that Moses gave to young Joshua [Numbers 11:27-29], nor the countermand which our Saviour gave to young John, who was so ready to prohibit those whom he thought unlicensed [Luke 9:49-50], be not enough to admonish our Elders how unacceptable to God their testy mood of prohibiting is, if neither their own remembrance what evil hath abounded in the Church by this let of licensing, and what good they themselves have begun by transgressing it, be not enough, but that they will persuade and execute the most Dominican part of the Inquisition over us, and are already with one foot in the stirrup so active at suppressing, it would be no unequal distribution in the first place to suppress the suppressors themselves: whom the change of their condition hath puffed up, more than their late experience of harder times hath made wise.

And as for regulating the Press, let no man think to have the honour of advising ye better than yourselves have done in that Order published next before this, "that no book be Printed, unless the Printer's and the Author's name, or at least the Printer's, be registered."[1] Those which otherwise come forth, if they be found mischievous and libellous, the fire and the executioner will be the timeliest and the most effectual remedy that man's prevention can use. For this authentic Spanish policy of licensing books, if I have said aught, will prove the most unlicensed book itself within a short while; and was the immediate image of a Star Chamber decree to that purpose made in those very times when that Court did the rest of those her pious works, for which she is now fallen from the stars with Lucifer. Whereby ye may guess what kind of state prudence, what love of the people, what care of Religion or good manners there was at the contriving, although with singular hypocrisy it pretended to bind books to their good behaviour. And how it got the upper hand of your precedent Order so well constituted before, if we may believe those men whose profession gives them cause to inquire most, it may be doubted there was in it the fraud of some old patentees and monopolizers in the trade of bookselling; who under pretence of the poor in their Company not to be defrauded, and the just retaining of each man his several copy, which God forbid should be gainsaid, brought divers glosing colours to the House, which were indeed but colours, and serving to no end except it be to exercise a superiority over their neighbours; men who do not therefore labour in an honest profession to which learning is indebted, that they should be made other men's vassals. Another end is thought was aimed at by some of them in procuring by petition this Order, that, having power in their hands, malignant books might the easier scape abroad, as the event shows.

But of these sophisms and elenchs of merchandise I skill not.[2] This I know, that errors in a good government and in a bad are equally almost incident; for what Magistrate may not be misinformed, and much the sooner, if liberty of Printing be reduced into the power of a few? But to redress willingly and speedily what hath been erred, and in highest authority to esteem a plain advertisement more than others have done a sumptuous bribe, is a virtue (honoured Lords and Commons) answer-

---

[1] Milton cites an Order of January 29, 1642.

[2] *sophisms and elenchs* differing forms of logical deceit, the first a positive expression, the second a refutation.

able to your highest actions, and whereof none can participate but greatest and wisest men.

—1644

Of True Religion, Heresy, Schism, and Toleration

It is unknown to no man, who knows ought of concernment among us, that the increase of Popery is at this day no small trouble and offence to greatest part of the Nation; and the rejoicing of all good men that it is so; the more their rejoicing, that God hath given a heart to the people to remember still their great and happy deliverance from Popish thraldom, and to esteem so highly the precious benefit of his Gospel, so freely and so peaceably enjoyed among them. Since therefore some have already in public with many considerable arguments exhorted the people to beware the growth of this Romish weed; I thought it no less than a common duty to lend my hand, how unable soever, to so good a purpose. I will not now enter into the labyrinth of Councils and fathers, an entangled wood which the Papist loves to fight in, not with hope of victory, but to obscure the shame of an open overthrow: which yet in that kind of combat, many heretofore, and one of late,[1] hath eminently given them. And such manner of dispute with them, to learned men, is useful and very commendable. But I shall insist now on what is plainer to common apprehension, and what I have to say, without longer introduction.

True religion is the true worship and service of God, learnt and believed from the word of God only. No man or Angel can know how God would be worshipped and served unless God reveal it: He hath revealed and taught it us in the holy Scriptures by inspired Ministers, and in the Gospel by his own Son and his Apostles, with strictest command to reject all other traditions or additions whatsoever. According to that of St. Paul, "Though we or an Angel from Heaven preach any other Gospel unto you, than that which we have preached unto you, let him be anathema, or accursed" [Galatians 1:8]. And Deut. 4:2: "Ye shall not add to the word which I command you, neither shall you diminish ought from it." Rev. 22:18, 19: "If any man shall add, &c. If any man shall take away from the words," &c. With good and religious reason therefore all Protestant churches with one consent, and particularly the Church of England in her thirty-nine articles, Artic. 6th, 19th, 20th, 21st, and elsewhere, maintain these two points, as the main principles of true religion: that the rule of true religion is the word of God only: and that their faith ought not to be an implicit faith, that is, to believe, though as the Church believes, against or without express authority of Scripture. And if all Protestants as universally as they hold these two principles, so attentively and religiously would observe them, they would avoid and cut off many debates and contentions, schisms and persecutions, which too oft have been among them, and more firmly unite against the common adversary.[2] For hence it directly follows, that no true Protestant can persecute, or not tolerate his fellow Protestant, though dissenting from him in some opinions, but he must flatly deny and renounce these two his own main principles, whereon true religion is founded; while he compels his brother from that which he believes as the manifest word of God, to an implicit faith (which he himself condemns) to the endangering of his brother's soul, whether by rash belief, or outward conformity: "for whatsoever is not of faith, is sin" [Romans 14:23].

I will now as briefly show what is false religion or heresy, which will be done as easily: for of contraries the definitions must needs be contrary. Heresy

---

1 *one of late* probably Edward Stillingfleet, *A Discourse Concerning the Idolatry Practised in the Church of Rome* (1671), which had gone through three editions by the year Milton was writing.

2 *the common adversary* Catholicism.

therefore is a religion taken up and believed from the traditions of men and additions to the word of God. Whence also it follows clearly, that of all known sects or pretended religions at this day in Christendom, Popery is the only or the greatest heresy: and he who is so forward to brand all others for heretics, the obstinate Papist, the only heretic. Hence one of their own famous writers found just cause to style the Romish church "Mother of Error, School of Heresy."[1] And whereas the Papist boasts himself to be a Roman Catholic, it is a mere contradiction, one of the Pope's bulls, as if he should say, universal particular a Catholic schismatic. For Catholic in Greek signifies universal: and the Christian church was so called, as consisting of all nations to whom the Gospel was to be preached, in contradistinction to the Jewish church, which consisted for the most part of Jews only.

Sects may be in a true church as well as in a false, when men follow the doctrine too much for the teacher's sake, whom they think almost infallible; and this becomes, through infirmity, implicit faith; and the name sectary, pertains to such a disciple.

Schism is a rent or division in the church, when it comes to the separating of congregations; and may also happen to a true church, as well as to a false; yet in the true needs not tend to the breaking of communion; if they can agree in the right administration of that wherein they communicate, keeping their other opinions to themselves, not being destructive to faith. The Pharisees and Sadducees were two sects, yet both met together in their common worship of God at Jerusalem. But here the Papist will angrily demand, what! Are Lutherans, Calvinists, Anabaptists, Socinians, Arminians,[2] no heretics? I answer, all these may have some errors, but are no heretics. Heresy is in the will and choice professedly against Scripture; error is against the will, in misunderstanding the Scripture after all sincere endeavours to understand it rightly: Hence it was said well by one of the ancients, "Err I may, but a heretic I will not be."[3] It is a human frailty to err, and no man is infallible here on earth. But so long as all these profess to set the word of God only before them as the rule of faith and obedience; and use all diligence and sincerity of heart, by reading, by learning, by study, by prayer for illumination of the holy Spirit, to understand the rule and obey it, they have done what man can do: God will assuredly pardon them, as he did the friends of Job,[4] good and pious men, though much mistaken, as there it appears, in some points of doctrine. But some will say, with Christians it is otherwise, whom God hath promised by his Spirit to teach all things. True, all things absolutely necessary to salvation: But the hottest disputes among Protestants calmly and charitably enquired into, will be found less than such. The Lutheran holds consubstantiation;[5] an error indeed, but not mortal. The Calvinist is taxed with predestination,[6] and to make God the author of sin; not with any dishonourable thought of God, but it may be over zealously asserting his absolute power, not without plea of Scripture. The Anabaptist is accused of denying infants their right to

---

[1] Petrarch (1304–1374) had described the Church as "scola d'errori e templo d'eresia" (sonnet 107) on account of papal corruption.

[2] respectively, mainstream Protestant movements founded on the theology of Martin Luther (1483–1546) and John Calvin (1509–1564); the name of several groups associated with the radical fringe of the German Reformation and linked by their repudiation of infant

baptism; followers of the unitarian theology of Fausto Paolo Sozzini (1539–1604), who denied the essential divinity of Christ; and followers of the Dutch theologian Jacobus Arminius (1560–1609), who challenged the strict predestination of the Calvinists.

[3] a dictum attributed in the period to Augustine.

[4] Job 42:7–10.

[5] *consubstantiation* the Lutheran doctrine of the Eucharist, which holds that the substances of both the blood and body of Christ and of the bread and wine co-exist in union with one another.

[6] *predestination* the belief that certain persons, the elect, are by divine decree guided to salvation, while others, the reprobate, are excluded, all without reference to their individual merits.

baptism; again they say, they deny nothing but what the Scripture denies them.[1] The Arian and Socinian are charged to dispute against the Trinity:[2] they affirm to believe the Father, Son, and Holy Ghost, according to Scripture, and the Apostolic Creed; as for terms of trinity, triniunity, coessentiality, tripersonality, and the like, they reject them as scholastic notions, not to be found in Scripture, which by a general Protestant maxim is plain and perspicuous abundantly to explain its own meaning in the properest words, belonging to so high a matter and so necessary to be known; a mystery indeed in their sophistic subtleties, but in Scripture a plain doctrine. Their other opinions are of less moment. They dispute the satisfaction of Christ,[3] or rather the word *Satisfaction*, as not scriptural: but they acknowledge him both God and their saviour. The Arminian lastly is condemned for setting up free will against free grace;[4] but that imputation he disclaims in all his writings, and grounds himself largely upon Scripture only. It cannot be denied that the authors or later revivers of all these sects or opinions, were learned, worthy, zealous, and religious men, as appears by their lives written, and the same of their many eminent and learned followers, perfect and powerful in the Scriptures, holy and unblameable in their lives: and it cannot be imagined that God would desert such painful and zealous labourers in his Church,[5] and oft times great

sufferers for their conscience, to damnable errors and a reprobate sense, who had so often implored the assistance of his Spirit; but rather, having made no man infallible, that he hath pardoned their errors, and accepts their pious endeavours, sincerely searching all things according to the rule of Scripture, with such guidance and direction as they can obtain of God by prayer. What Protestant then who himself maintains the same principles, and disavows all implicit faith, would persecute, and not rather charitably tolerate such men as these, unless he mean to abjure the principles of his own religion? If it be asked, how far they should be tolerated? I answer doubtless equally, as being all Protestants; that is on all occasions to give account of their faith, either by arguing, preaching in their several assemblies, public writing, and the freedom of printing. For if the French and Polonian Protestants enjoy all this liberty among Papists,[6] much more may a Protestant justly expect it among Protestants; and yet some times here among us, the one persecutes the other upon every slight pretence.

But he is wont to say he enjoins only things indifferent.[7] Let them be so still; who gave him authority to change their nature by enjoining them? If by his own principles, as is proved, he ought to tolerate controverted points of doctrine not slightly grounded on Scripture, much more ought he not impose things indifferent without Scripture. In religion nothing is indifferent, but, if it come once to be imposed, is either a command or a prohibition, and so consequently an addition to the word

---

[1] Milton agreed with "the Anabaptist" on the issue of infant baptism.

[2] Arianism and Socinianism are both doctrines which denied the divinity of Christ. The Arian position is argued in *De doctrina Christiana*, a manuscript certainly connected with and generally thought to be by Milton.

[3] *satisfaction* a theological term for payment of a penalty due God on account of sin; often applied to the atonement, with Christ's death a satisfaction for the sins of the world.

[4] *free will against free grace* As a result of their more liberal attitude to predestination, Arminians were accused by Calvinists of linking salvation to the exercise of the human will, thus diminishing God's majesty.

[5] *painful* painstaking.

[6] The models offered by France and Poland were often cited in tolerationist pamphlets, though the freedom of Protestants in both countries was seriously undermined in the last few decades of the seventeenth century.

[7] *things indifferent* referring to the doctrine of adiaphora, or "things indifferent" to salvation. The Church of England valued uniformity of practice on matters such as church ceremonies and vestments, arguing that conformity on these "indifferent" issues should not trouble a dissenting conscience. Milton proceeds to summarize a primary Nonconformist counter-argument.

of God, which he professes to disallow. Besides, how unequal, how uncharitable must it needs be, to impose that which his conscience cannot urge him to impose, upon him whose conscience forbids him to obey? What can it be but love of contention for things not necessary to be done, to molest the conscience of his brother, who holds them necessary to be not done? To conclude, let such a one but call to mind his own principles above mentioned, and he must necessarily grant, that neither he can impose, nor the other believe or obey ought in religion, but from the word of God only. More amply to understand this, may be read the 14th and 15th chapters to the Romans, and the contents of the 14th, set forth no doubt but with full authority of the Church of England; the gloss is this: "Men may not contemn, or condemn one the other for things indifferent." [1] And in the 6th Article above mentioned, "whatsoever is not read in Holy Scripture, nor may be proved thereby, is not to be required of any man as an article of faith, or necessary to salvation." And certainly what is not so, is not to be required at all; as being an addition to the word of God expressly forbidden.

Thus this long and hot contest, whether Protestants ought to tolerate one another, if men will be but rational and not partial, may be ended without need of more words to compose it.

Let us now enquire whether Popery be tolerable or no. Popery is a double thing to deal with, and claims a twofold power, ecclesiastical, and political, both usurped, and the one supporting the other.

But ecclesiastical is ever pretended to political. The Pope by this mixed faculty, pretends right to kingdoms and states, and especially to this of England, thrones and unthrones Kings, and ab-solves the people from their obedience to them; [2] sometimes interdicts to whole nations the public worship of God, shutting up their churches: [3] and was wont to drain away greatest part of the wealth of this then miserable land, as part of his patrimony, to maintain the pride and luxury of his court and prelates: [4] and now since, through the infinite mercy and favour of God, we have shaken off his Babylonish yoke, hath not ceased by his spies and agents, bulls and emissaries, once to destroy both King and Parliament; [5] perpetually to seduce, corrupt, and pervert as many as they can of the people. Whether therefore it be fit or reasonable, to tolerate men thus principled in religion towards the State, I submit it to the consideration of all magistrates, who are best able to provide for their own and the public safety. As for tolerating the exercise of their religion, supposing their state activities not to be dangerous, I answer, that toleration is either public or private; and the exercise of their religion, as far as it is idolatrous, can be tolerated neither way: not publicly, without grievous and unsufferable scandal given to all conscientious beholders; not privately, without great offence to God, declared against all kind of idolatry, though secret. Ezekiel 8:7, 8: "And he brought me to the door of the court, and when I looked, behold a hole in the wall. Then said he unto me, Son of Man, dig now in the wall; and when I had digged, behold a door, and he said unto me, go in, and behold the wicked abominations that they do here." And verse 12: "Then said he unto me, Son of Man, hast thou seen what the ancients

---

[1] Milton omits what follows in the gloss: "But take heed that they give no offence in them."

[2] Pope Innocent III excommunicated King John in 1209, and Pope Pius V excommunicated Queen Elizabeth in 1569, absolving her subjects from the oath of allegiance.

[3] referring again to Pope Innocent III's struggles with John, when England was placed under interdiction from 1208 to 1214.

[4] Papal taxation was much resented in the thirteenth and fourteenth centuries.

[5] referring to the Gunpowder Plot, a Catholic conspiracy to blow up the Houses of Parliament and James I on November 5, 1605.

of the house of Israel do in the dark?" &c. And it appears by the whole chapter, that God was no less offended with these secret idolatries, than with those in public; and no less provoked, than to bring on and hasten his judgments on the whole land for these also.

Having shown thus, that Popery, as being idolatrous, is not to be tolerated either in public or in private; it must be now thought how to remove it and hinder the growth thereof, I mean in our natives, and not foreigners, privileged by the Law of Nations. Are we to punish them by corporal punishment, or fines in their estates, upon account of their religion? I suppose it stands not with the clemency of the Gospel, more than what appertains to the security of the State: But first we must remove their idolatry, and all the furniture thereof, whether idols, or the mass wherein they adore their God under bread and wine:[1] for the commandment forbids to adore, not only "any graven image, but the likeness of anything in Heaven above, or in the earth beneath, or in the water under the earth, thou shalt not bow down to them nor worship them, for I the Lord thy God am a jealous God" [Exodus 20:5]. If they say that by removing their idols we violate their consciences, we have no warrant to regard conscience which is not grounded on Scripture: and they themselves confess in their late defences, that they hold not their images necessary to salvation, but only as they are enjoined them by tradition.

Shall we condescend to dispute with them? The Scripture is our only principle in religion; and by that only they will not be judged, but will add other principles of their own, which, forbidden by the word of God, we cannot assent to. And the common maxim also in logic is, "against them who deny principles, we are not to dispute."[2] Let them bound their disputations on the Scripture only, and an ordinary Protestant, well read in the Bible, may turn and wind their doctors. They will not go about to prove their idolatries by the word of God, but run to shifts and evasions, and frivolous distinctions: Idols they say are laymen's books, and a great means to stir up pious thoughts and devotion in the learnedest. I say they are no means of God's appointing, but plainly the contrary: Let them hear the Prophets; Jerem. 10:8: "The stock is a doctrine of vanities." Habakkuk 2:18: "What profiteth the graven image that the maker thereof hath graven it: The molten image and a teacher of lies?" But they allege in their late answers, that the laws of Moses given only to the Jews, concern not us under the Gospel: and remember not that idolatry is forbidden as expressly (in several places of the Gospel). But with these wiles and fallacies "compassing sea and land, like the Pharisees of old, to make one Proselyte," they lead away privily many simple and ignorant souls, men or women, "and make them twofold more the children of Hell than themselves," Matt. 23:15. But the Apostle hath well warned us, I may say, from such deceivers as these, for their mystery was then working. "I beseech you brethren," saith he, "mark them which cause divisions and offences, contrary to the doctrine which ye have learned, and avoid them; for they that are such serve not our Lord Jesus Christ, but their own belly, and by good words and fair speeches deceive the heart of the simple," Rom. 16:17, 18.

The next means to hinder the growth of Popery will be to read duly and diligently the Holy Scriptures, which as St. Paul saith to Timothy, who had known them from a child, "are able to make wise unto salvation" [II Timothy 3:15]. And to the whole Church of Colossi; "Let the word of Christ dwell in you plentifully, with all wisdom," Coloss. 3:16. The Papal Antichristian Church permits not her laity to read the Bible in their own tongue: Our Church on the contrary hath proposed it to all men,

---

[1] The equation of transubstantiation with idolatry was common in Protestant polemic.

[2] Aristotle, *Physics*, I.ii.

and to this end translated it into English, with profitable notes on what is met with obscure, though what is most necessary to be known be still plainest: that all sorts and degrees of men, not understanding the original, may read it in their mother tongue. Neither let the countryman, the tradesman, the lawyer, the physician, the statesman, excuse himself by his much business from the studious reading thereof. Our Saviour saith, Luke 10:41, 42: "Thou art careful and troubled about many things, but one thing is needful." If they were asked, they would be loath to set earthly things, wealth, or honour before the wisdom of salvation. Yet most men in the course and practice of their lives are found to do so; and through unwillingness to take the pains of understanding their religion by their own diligent study, would fain be saved by a deputy. Hence comes implicit faith, ever learning and never taught, much hearing and small proficiency, till want of fundamental knowledge easily turns to superstition or Popery: Therefore the Apostle admonished [Ephesians] 4:14: "That we henceforth be no more children tossed to and fro and carried about with every wind of doctrine, by the sleight of men, and cunning craftiness whereby they lie in wait to deceive." Every member of the Church, at least of any breeding or capacity, so well ought to be grounded in spiritual knowledge, as, if need be, to examine their teachers themselves, Act. 17:11: "They searched the Scriptures daily, whether those things were so." Rev. 2:2: "Thou hast tried them which say they are Apostles, and are not." How should any private Christian try his teachers unless he be well grounded himself in the rule of Scripture, by which he is taught. As therefore among Papists, their ignorance in Scripture chiefly upholds Popery; so among Protestant people, the frequent and serious reading thereof will soonest pull Popery down.

Another means to abate Popery arises from the constant reading of Scripture, wherein believers who agree in the main, are everywhere exhorted to mutual forbearance and charity one towards the other, though dissenting in some opinions. It is written that the coat of our Saviour was without seam [John 19:23]: whence some would infer that there should be no division in the Church of Christ. It should be so indeed; yet seams in the same cloth, neither hurt the garment, nor misbecome it; and not only seams, but schisms will be while men are fallible: But if they who dissent in matters not essential to belief, while the common adversary is in the field, shall stand jarring and pelting at one another, they will be soon routed and subdued. The Papist with open mouth makes much advantage of our several opinions; not that he is able to confute the worst of them, but that we by our continual jangle among ourselves make them worse than they are indeed. To save ourselves therefore, and resist the common enemy, it concerns us mainly to agree within ourselves, that with joint forces we may not only hold our own, but get ground; and why should we not? The Gospel commands us to tolerate one another, though of various opinions, and hath promised a good and happy event thereof, Phil. 3:15: "Let us therefore as many as be perfect be thus minded; and if in any thing ye be otherwise minded, God shall reveal even this unto you." And we are bid, I Thess. 5:21: "Prove all things, hold fast that which is good." St. Paul judged that not only to tolerate, but to examine and prove all things, was no danger to our holding fast of that which is good. How shall we prove all things, which includes all opinions at least founded on Scripture, unless we not only tolerate them, but patiently hear them, and seriously read them? If he who thinks himself in the truth professes to have learnt it, not by implicit faith, but by attentive study of the Scriptures and full persuasion of heart, with what equity can he refuse to hear or read him, who demonstrates to have gained his knowledge by the same way? is it a fair course to assert truth by arrogating to himself the only freedom of speech, and stopping the mouths of others equally gifted? This is the direct way to bring in that Papistical implicit faith which we all disclaim. They pretend it would unsettle the weaker sort: the same groundless fear is pretended by the Romish clergy in prohibiting the Scripture. At least then let them have leave to write in Latin while the common people understand not; that what they hold may be discussed among the learned only. We suffer the idolatrous books of Papists, without this fear, to be sold and read as common as our own. Why not much rather of Anabaptists, Arians, Arminians, and Socinians? There is no learned man but will confess he hath much profited by reading controversies, his senses awaked, his judgment sharpened, and the truth which he holds more firmly established. If then it be profitable for him to read; why should it not at least be tolerable and free for his adversary to write? In Logic they teach, that contraries laid together more evidently appear: it follows then that all controversies being permitted, falsehood will appear more false, and truth the more true: which must needs conduce much, not only to the confounding of Popery, but to the general confirmation of unimplicit truth.

The last means to avoid Popery, is to amend our lives: it is a general complaint that this nation of late years, is grown more numerously and excessively vicious than heretofore; pride, luxury, drunkenness, whoredom, cursing, swearing, bold and open atheism everywhere abounding: Where these grow, no wonder if Popery also grow apace. There is no man so wicked, but at sometimes his conscience will wring him with thoughts of another world, and the peril of his soul: the trouble and melancholy which he conceives of true repentance and amendment he endures not; but inclines rather to some carnal superstition, which may pacify and lull his conscience with some more pleasing doctrine. None more ready and officious to offer herself than the Romish, and opens wide her office, with all her faculties to receive him; easy confession, easy absolution, pardons, indulgences, masses for him both quick and dead, *Agnus Dei*'s,[1] relics, and the like: and he, instead of "working out his salvation with fear and trembling" [Philippians 2:12], straight thinks in his heart (like another kind of fool than he in the Psalms)[2] to bribe God as a corrupt judge; and by his proctor, some priest or friar, to buy out his peace with money, which he cannot with his repentance. For God, when men sin outrageously, and will not be admonished, gives over chastizing them, perhaps by pestilence, fire, sword, or famine,[3] which may all turn to their good, and takes up his severest punishments, hardness, besottedness of heart, and idolatry, to their final perdition. Idolatry brought the heathen to heinous transgressions, Romans [1:21–32]. And heinous transgressions oft times bring the slight professors of true religion, to gross idolatry: [II] Thess. 2:11, 12: "For this cause, God shall send them strong delusion that they should believe a lie, that they all might be damned who believe not the truth, but had pleasure in unrighteousness." And Isaiah 44:18: Speaking of idolaters, "They have not known nor understood, for he hath shut their eyes that they cannot see, and their hearts that they cannot understand." Let us therefore using this last means, last here spoken of, but first to be done, amend our lives with all speed; least through impenitency we run into that stupidly, which we now seek all means so warily to avoid, the worst of superstitions, and the heaviest of all God's judgments, Popery.

—1673

---

[1] An *Agnus Dei* ("Lamb of God") was a devotional medallion made of wax depicting the lamb, a figure of Christ.

[2] Psalm 14:1: "The fool hath said in his heart, There is no God."

[3] The London plague of 1665, the Great Fire of 1666, and English defeats in the Dutch Wars were often cited as divine judgments against England.

Queen Henrietta Maria
1609 –1669

Henrietta Maria, born at the Louvre in November, 1609, was the youngest daughter of Henry IV of France and his second wife Marie de Medici. Her marriage to Charles I in 1625 created an alliance between France and England. The marriage took place on the agreement that Charles would suspend the recusancy laws in England, that the English would serve as allies to the French against the Huguenot rebels at La Rochelle, and that Henrietta Maria would be permitted to have Catholic attendants in her service. Henrietta Maria had use of a chapel at Somerset House, which was open to members of the court, and Capuchin priests were sent from France to officiate. In 1629, Henrietta Maria bore her first child, a son who lived only a few hours. The following year, Charles (II) was born, and Henrietta attended mass with the child until her husband forbade it in February 1636. Between 1630 and 1644, Henrietta Maria bore five other children: Mary, James (II), Elizabeth, Henry and Henrietta. Henrietta Maria's political role included her raising £20,000 from English Catholics to assist Charles in the impending war against the Scottish forces. This action was followed by a series of foreign-aid and military plots which she devised to support Charles against Parliament. In 1641, Henrietta Maria arranged a marriage between her eldest daughter Mary and William of Orange in an attempt to secure funds from William which would enable Charles to resist Parliament. Mary and William were married in 1642, and in the same year, Henrietta Maria left for the Continent with some of the crown jewels which she pawned in Amsterdam to raise funds for munitions of war. Despite threats to her safety, Henrietta Maria returned to England with a large sum of money and arms in 1643, joining Newcastle's army at York. Meeting her husband at Edgehill, she rode with him to Oxford on July 14, 1643. The following year, Henrietta Maria gave birth to her youngest child Henrietta, and returned to St. Germains, France on July 14, 1644. In her letters to Charles I during the first civil war, we read of her personal attachments and political stratagems as Queen consort. However, her political negotiations failed to save the life of her husband. By 1646, Charles had placed himself in Scottish hands, an act which served as the prelude to his death. Her application for a passport to plead for her husband's life in 1648 was unsuccessful; she heard of his execution in February, 1649. After arranging a marriage between Henrietta and the Duke of Orleans, brother to Louis XIV, Henrietta Maria returned to England in 1660 to secure a portion for Henrietta. She did so, and lived in Somerset House on £60,000 per annum. Roman Catholic services continued to be performed in her chapel. Henrietta Maria left London in 1665 and never returned to England, retiring in Colombes near Paris. She was buried in the church of St. Denis.

ↄ⫝⫝ↄↄↄ

The Queen's Letter [1]

Royal Sir, though I have been a long time absent from you in person, yet am I still and ever will ✔

be present with you in affection. No distance of place can divide our hearts, nor any length of time can lessen the real and unfeigned love that is equal between us. My heart's desire is to see you, and once more to behold a happy union between your Majesty and your Parliament.

—1642

---

[1] *The Queen's Letter* was printed at the conclusion of the pamphlet *The Best News from York, That ever came to London and Westminster Containing, His Majesty's most gracious Resolution to return to his Parliament* (London, 1642).

The Queen's Letter Sent to the King's most excellent Majesty from Holland [1]

Most royal and illustrious monarch of great Britain, my great, my good and worthy liege, the most regal object of my loving heart, best affections and utmost endeavours; be pleased to let this paper in all humility to salute your princely hands, and to give your princely cogitations some account of my endeavours (as I am bound in duty, and as I am your spouse and loyal wife), for your Majesty in my absence, my love having now no other ways left of expression, but by being your humble and faithful agent in accommodating and promoting your high affairs, wherein if my words, the pledges, and earnest solicitors for the improvement of your present fame and glory, may carry in them any strength of persuasion, I would earnestly incite your princely thoughts to a remembrance of your Majesty's resolution to carry forward your designs until they grow to a famous maturity and ripeness. Maintain and continue your cause in the hardy prosecution of your affairs, without any mitigation, unless an honourable satisfaction may make you disbandon and raise your former intentions. Now you have a large field given you, wherein the illustrious virtues inherent in your royal person may be actually expressed, and give the whole Christian world which are now spectators, and the eye of all Christendom upon your person, a clear approbation and testimony that your Majesty merits that noble attribute annexed to your royal title, *Defender of the Faith*. For by such like actions as these, princes live when they have paid their debt to nature, and will be their own monument, which shall be everlasting, and more durable than that of marble. Be therefore constant in your princely resolutions, full of your own cause, and your Majesty shall never want external accommodations and foreign compliances, which by my earnest endeavours and solicitations have of late been somewhat advanced, having obtained a list from our brother the Prince of Orange, from whence as the special merit did distinguish them in worth, I have selected out of that number some choice, well-experienced and serviceable soldiers, such as shall be forward with courageous affections to maintain your princely affairs, and to amplify your renown and glory in the engagement of present actions. [2] And out of these deserving men, I have chosen stout commanders, who will be always ready to do your Majesty service in your army, and that I might further supply and serve your present occasions, I have caused 400 barrels of powder, and 10 pieces of ordnance, to be conveyed to your Majesty, besides good store of all other ammunition, necessary upon all warlike occasions. The compliance of our noble brother the Prince of Orange is so settled in a firm complexion, sympathising, and affectionately agreeing with the present condition of affairs, that he hath by many demonstrations given testimony thereof, and by raising diverse sums of money for my use hath endeavoured the inclination of his particular affections, amongst other accommodations lest your Majesty should be any way necessitated. I am to certify your Majesty, that the jewels of your crown are for present receipts engaged to some certain Jews of Amsterdam. [3] Moreover I am to give your Highness cause to esteem the cheerful undertakings and forward alacrity of our brother

---

[1] from *The Queen's Letter from Holland: Directed to the King's Most Excellent Majesty* (London, 1642/3).

[2] *Prince of Orange* Though Henrietta Maria had originally opposed a marriage between her eldest daughter Mary and William, Prince of Orange, she now encouraged the alliance in the hopes that William would supply money or troops to resist Parliament. On April 19, 1641 William arrived in England with a substantial amount of money. Parliament learned from an intercepted letter of November 26, 1642 that William had advanced her additional funds.

[3] *that the jewels...of Amsterdam* By June of 1642, news reached England that Henrietta Maria had been selling or pawning a great part of the crown jewels at Amsterdam and had purchased stores of munitions of war for the King's service.

the Prince of Orange, who will with all careful vigilancy be ready to take all opportunities for your Majesty's advantage, and will with clear intentions wherein you may repose trust, be ready to express himself in all Christian offices. My acknowledgment of Prince Robert's valiant courage and love expressed in personal actions, and those adhering to your Majesty, being arrived to my knowledge by a letter lately sent to Mr. Jermyn, must needs deserve my approbation and highest commendation, since his worth and noble actions are of such transcendent expression of princely merit.[1] Amongst the other endeavours of my affectionate desires, the States have been earnestly solicited for their aid and assistance, which as yet cannot be induced upon them to grant, nor can I by any persuasion obtain the effect of my urgent motion, though I hope my letters sent unto my brother the French king, shall infuse a royal flame into his breast, and make him through accompable fullness of your Highness's cause, give such aid unto your Majesty, as may express him royal in his thoughts, and tender of his regal relation unto your Highness;[2] but if my letter should be so unhappy as not fully to inflame and instigate his mind to awake his power in your aid and defence, I cannot nor will not see your actions brought on with so much expectation any way disanimated, but since the age's hopes must be the production and business of your weighty affairs, my personal solicitation shall at my going into France induce and incline my most Christian brother to appear in promoting and assisting your Majesty's cause and actions, which are so full of honourable justice.[3] Though absent till we be resident in your princely heart, and believe my affections and endeavours are ever ready to serve your Majesty.

Sir, I am and always shall be your most dutiful wife and liege woman.

HENRIETTA MARIA

—1642/3

---

[1] *Prince Robert* Prince Rupert; the name was often so Anglicized by English writers; *Mr. Jermyn* Henry Jermyn was Henrietta Maria's "man of business." He and the cavalier poet Sir John Suckling devised a plot by which Henrietta Maria could bring up the English army in the north to support the King.

[2] *accompable* probably meaning "sufficient for the occasion."

[3] *disanimated* discouraged (*OED* disanimate *v* 2).

Edward Hyde, Earl of Clarendon
1609 –1674

One of the most prominent statesmen of the century, Clarendon (as he is usually called, though he was not created Earl until 1661) was the son of a Wiltshire country gentleman. He was educated at Magdalen Hall, Oxford, and trained as a lawyer at the Middle Temple. His friends included many of the most distinguished intellectual and literary figures of the day, among them Ben Jonson, Thomas Carew, Edmund Waller, and John Earle; he also enjoyed connections with the Duke of Buckingham, Lucius Cary, and William Laud. Clarendon began his political career when he was elected to both the Short and Long Parliaments in 1640. While playing an active role in Parliament's early attempts at political reform, he opposed any alteration in ecclesiastical matters and eventually led Royalist opposition to the Grand Remonstrance. Clarendon became one of the King's leading advisors throughout the wars, responsible for administrative and financial rather than military issues; in addition, he wrote most of the King's numerous declarations and pamphlets until 1645. He accompanied Prince

Charles to Jersey in 1646, where he began to write his *History*. With the renewal of war in 1648, he joined the Prince in France and from 1651 on was chief advisor to Charles II, as Secretary of State and (from 1658) Lord Chancellor. Clarendon was one of the architects of the Restoration settlement, and for a few years after 1660 was virtually head of government. In 1667, popular opposition and court intrigues led to his downfall, and he fled into France, where he lived the remainder of his life.

During this final period of exile Clarendon wrote an autobiography, and then combined this *Life* with the draft of the *History* he had begun 25 years earlier in Jersey and some new material to produce the final *History of the Rebellion*. The excerpts below combine passages from the final *History* and the *Life*, both of which were first published, separately, in the eighteenth century. For more on William Laud, the subject of one of Clarendon's famous character sketches, see the selection from Laud's *Diary*; for other accounts of the Great Fire, see the accounts by John Evelyn and Samuel Pepys.

🙠🙡

From *The Life of Edward Earl of Clarendon*
and *The History of the Rebellion and
Civil Wars in England*
(excerpts)

THE CHARACTER OF WILLIAM LAUD

It was within one week after the king's return from Scotland [in August 1633], that [Archbishop of Canterbury George] Abbot died at his house at Lambeth. And the king took very little time to consider who should be his successor, but the very next time the bishop of London (who was longer upon his way home than the king had been) came to him, his majesty entertained him very cheerfully

with this compellation,[1] "My lord's grace of Canterbury, you are very welcome"; and gave order the same day for the dispatch of all the necessary forms for the translation:[2] so that within a month or thereabouts after the death of the other archbishop, he [Laud] was completely invested in that high dignity, and settled in his palace at Lambeth. This great prelate had been before in great favour with the duke of Buckingham,[3] whose great confidant he

---

[1] *compellation* appellation, the name or title by which a person is addressed (*OED* compellation 2b,c).

[2] *translation* the move of a bishop to another bishopric.

[3] *the duke of Buckingham* George Villiers (1592–1628); for more information, see the selection of anti-Buckingham poems.

was, and by him recommended to the king, as fittest to be trusted in the conferring all ecclesiastical preferments, when he was but bishop of St. David's, or newly preferred to Bath and Wells; and from that time he entirely governed that province without a rival: so that his promotion to Canterbury was long foreseen and expected; nor was it attended with any increase of envy or dislike.

He was a man of great parts, and very exemplary virtues, allayed and discredited by some unpopular natural infirmities; the greatest of which was (besides a hasty, sharp way of expressing himself) that he believed innocence of heart, and integrity of manners, was a guard strong enough to secure any man in his voyage through this world, in what company soever he travelled, and through what ways soever he was to pass: and sure never any man was better supplied with that provision. He was born of honest parents, who were well able to provide for his education in the schools of learning, from whence they sent him to St. John's college in Oxford, the worst endowed at that time of any in that famous university. From a scholar he became a fellow, and then the president of that college, after he had received all the graces and degrees (the proctorship and the doctorship) could be obtained there. He was always maligned and persecuted by those who were of the Calvinian faction, which was then very powerful, and who, according to their useful maxim and practice, call every man they do not love, papist; and under this senseless appellation they created him many troubles and vexations; and so far suppressed him, that though he was the king's chaplain, and taken notice of for an excellent preacher, and a scholar of the most sublime parts, he had not any preferment to invite him to leave his poor college, which only gave him bread, till the vigour of his age was past: and when he was promoted by king James, it was but to a poor bishopric in Wales, which was not so good a support for a

bishop, as his college was for a private scholar, though a doctor.

Parliaments in that time were frequent,[1] and grew very busy; and the party under which he had suffered a continual persecution, appeared very powerful, and full of design, and they who had the courage to oppose them, began to be taken notice of with approbation and countenance: and under this style he came to be first cherished by the duke of Buckingham, after he had made some experiments of the temper and spirit of the other people, nothing to his satisfaction. From this time he prospered at the rate of his own wishes, and being transplanted out of his cold barren diocese of St. David's, into a warmer climate, he was left, as was said before, by that omnipotent favourite in that great trust with the king, who was sufficiently indisposed towards the persons or the principles of Mr. Calvin's disciples.

When he came into great authority, it may be, he retained too keen a memory of those who had so unjustly and uncharitably persecuted him before; and, I doubt, was so far transported with the same passions he had reason to complain of in his adversaries, that, as they accused him of popery, because he had some doctrinal opinions which they liked not, though they were nothing allied to popery; so he entertained too much prejudice to some persons, as if they were enemies to the discipline of the church, because they concurred with Calvin in some doctrinal points; when they abhorred his discipline, and reverenced the government of the church, and prayed for the peace of it with as much zeal and fervency as any in the kingdom; as they made manifest in their lives, and in their sufferings with it, and for it. He had, from his first entrance into the world, without any disguise or dissimulation, declared his own opinion of that classis of

---

[1] *in that time* the 1620s. Laud was made Bishop of St. David's in 1621, at the age of 48.

men;[1] and, as soon as it was in his power, he did all he could to hinder the growth and increase of that faction, and to restrain those who were inclined to it, from doing the mischief they desired to do. But his power at court could not enough qualify him to go through with that difficult reformation, whilst he had a superior in the church, who, having the reins in his hand, could slacken them according to his own humour and indiscretion; and was thought to be the more remiss, to irritate his choleric disposition. But when he had now the primacy in his own hand, the king being inspired with the same zeal, he thought he should be to blame, and have much to answer, if he did not make haste to apply remedies to those diseases, which he saw would grow apace.

In the end of September of the year 1633, he was invested in the title, power, and jurisdiction of archbishop of Canterbury, and entirely in possession of the revenue thereof, without a rival in church or state; that is, no man professed to oppose his greatness; and he had never interposed or appeared in matter of state to this time. His first care was, that the place he was removed from might be supplied with a man who would be vigilant to pull up those weeds, which the London soil was too apt to nourish, and so drew his old friend and companion Dr. Juxon as near to him as he could.[2] They had been fellows together in one college in Oxford, and, when he was first made bishop of St. David's, he made him president of that college: when he could no longer keep the deanery of the chapel royal, he made him his successor in that near attendance upon the king: and now he was raised to archbishop, he easily prevailed with the king to make the other, bishop of London, before, or very soon

after, he had been consecrated bishop of Hereford, if he were more than elect of that church.

It was now a time of great ease and tranquillity; the king (as hath been said before) had made himself superior to all those difficulties and straits he had to contend with the four first years he came to the crown at home; and was now reverenced by all his neighbours, who all needed his friendship, and desired to have it; the wealth of the kingdom notorious to all the world, and the general temper and humour of it little inclined to the papists, and less to the puritan. There were some late taxes and impositions introduced, which rather angered than grieved the people, who were more than repaired by the quiet, peace, and prosperity they enjoyed; and the murmur and discontent that was, appeared to be against the excess of power exercised by the crown, and supported by the judges in Westminster-hall. The church was not repined at, nor the least inclination to alter the government and discipline thereof, or to change the doctrine. Nor was there at that time any considerable number of persons of any valuable condition throughout the kingdom, who did wish either; and the cause of so prodigious a change in so few years after was too visible from the effects. The archbishop's heart was set upon the advancement of the church, in which he well knew he had the king's full concurrence, which he thought would be too powerful for any opposition; and that he should need no other assistance.

Though the nation generally, as was said before, was without any ill talent to the church,[3] either in the point of the doctrine, or the discipline, yet they were not without a jealousy that popery was not enough discountenanced, and were very averse from admitting any thing they had not been used to, which they called innovation, and were easily persuaded, that any thing of that kind was but to

---

[1] *classis* one of the governing hierarchies in the Presbyterian church. Clarendon here uses the term more generally, as in "class" or "type" of men (he uses the same word below to describe Royalists).

[2] *Dr. Juxon* William Juxon (1582–1663); he became Archbishop of Canterbury at the Restoration.

[3] *talent* inclination, will, disposition (*OED* talent *sb* 2,3).

please the papists. Some doctrinal points in controversy had been, in the late years, agitated in the pulpits with more warmth and reflections, than had used to be; and thence the heat and animosity increased in books pro and con upon the same arguments: most of the popular preachers, who had not looked into the ancient learning, took Calvin's word for it, and did all they could to propagate his opinions in those points: they who had studied more, and were better versed in the antiquities of the church, the fathers, the councils, and the ecclesiastical histories, with the same heat and passion in preaching and writing defended the contrary.

The archbishop had, all his life, eminently opposed Calvin's doctrine in those controversies, before the name of Arminius was taken notice of, or his opinions heard of;[1] and thereupon, for want of another name, they had called him a papist, which nobody believed him to be, and he had more manifested the contrary in his disputations and writings, than most men had done; and it may be the other found the more severe and rigorous usage from him, for their propagating that calumny against him. He was a man of great courage and resolution, and being most assured within himself, that he proposed no end in all his actions or designs, than what was pious and just (as sure no man had ever a heart more entire to the king, the church, or his country), he never studied the best ways to those ends; he thought, it may be, that any art or industry that way would discredit, at least make the integrity of the end suspected, let the cause be what it will. He did court persons too little; nor cared to make his designs and purposes appear as candid as they were, by showing them in any other dress than their own natural beauty and roughness; and did not consider enough what men said, or were like to say of him. If the faults and vices were fit to be looked into, and discovered, let the persons be who they would that were guilty of them, they were sure to find no connivance or favour from him. He intended the discipline of the church should be felt, as well as spoken of, and that it should be applied to the greatest and most splendid transgressors, as well as to the punishment of smaller offences, and meaner offenders; and thereupon called for or cherished the discovery of those who were not careful to cover their own iniquities, thinking they were above the reach of other men's, or their power or will to chastise. Persons of honour and great quality, of the court, and of the country, were every day cited, into the high-commission court,[2] upon the fame of their incontinence, or other scandal in their lives, and were there prosecuted to their shame and punishment: and as the shame (which they called an insolent triumph upon their degree and quality, and levelling them with the common people) was never forgotten, but watched for revenge; so the fines imposed there were the most questioned, and repined against, because they were assigned to the rebuilding and repairing St. Paul's church; and thought therefore to be the more severely imposed, and the less compassionately reduced and excused; which likewise made the jurisdiction and rigour of the star-chamber more felt,[3] and murmured against, which sharpened many men's humours against the bishops, before they had any ill intention towards the church.

The archbishop had not been long at Canterbury, when there was another great alteration in the

---

[1] *Arminius* Jacobus Arminius (1560–1609), a celebrated Dutch Reformed theologian who challenged the Calvinist doctrine of predestination. In England, Laud's movement toward an anti-Calvinistic, more ceremonial church polity was widely termed "Arminian."

[2] *high-commission court* an ecclesiastical court that investigated heresy and other irregularities. Widely unpopular for its arbitrary procedures and its use by the monarchy to enforce the royal prerogative, it was abolished by Parliament in 1641.

[3] *star-chamber* a court of law used extensively by Charles I to maintain royal authority, subsequently abolished by the Long Parliament.

court by the death of the earl of Portland,[1] high treasurer of England; a man so jealous of the archbishop's credit with the king, that he always endeavoured to lessen it by all the arts and ways he could; which he was so far from effecting, that, as it usually falls out, when passion and malice make accusation, by suggesting many particulars which the king knew to be untrue, or believed to be no faults, he rather confirmed his majesty's judgment of him, and prejudiced his own reputation. His death caused no grief to the archbishop; who was upon it made one of the commissioners of the treasury and revenue, which he had reason to be sorry for, because it engaged him in civil business and matters of state, in which he had little experience, and which he had hitherto avoided. But being obliged to it now by his trust, he entered upon it with his natural earnestness and warmth, making it his principal care to advance and improve the king's revenue by all the ways which were offered, and so hearkened to all informations and propositions of that kind; and having not had experience of that tribe of people who deal in that traffic (a confident, senseless, and for the most part a naughty people), he was sometimes misled by them to think better of some projects than they deserved: but when he was so entirely devoted to what would be beneficial to the king, that all propositions and designs, which were for the profit (only or principally) of particular persons how great soever, were opposed and crossed, and very often totally suppressed and stifled in their birth, by his power and authority; which created him enemies enough in the court, and many of ability to do mischief, who knew well how to recompense discourtesies, which they always called injuries.

And the revenue of too many of the court consisted principally in enclosures,[2] and improvement of that nature, which he still opposed passionately, except they were founded upon law; and then, if it would bring profit to the king, how old and obsolete soever the law was, he thought he might justly advise the prosecution. And so he did a little too much countenance the commission for depopulation,[3] which brought much charge and trouble upon the people, which was likewise cast upon his account.

He had observed, and knew it must be so, that the principal officers of the revenue, who governed the affairs of money, had always access to the king, and spent more time with him in private than any of his servants or counsellors, and had thereby frequent opportunities to do good or ill offices to many men; of which he had had experience, when the earl of Portland was treasurer, and the lord Cottington chancellor of the exchequer;[4] neither of them being his friends; and the latter still enjoying that place, and having his former access, and so continuing a joint commissioner of the treasury with him, and understanding that province much better, he still opposed, and commonly carried everything against him: so that he was weary of the toil and vexation of that business; as all other men were, and still are of the delays which are in dispatches, whilst that office is executed by commission.

The treasurer's is the greatest office of benefit in the kingdom, and the chief in precedence next the archbishop's, and the great seal:[5] so that the eyes of all men were at gaze who should have this great office; and the greatest of the nobility, who were in

---

[1] *earl of Portland* Sir Richard Weston (1577–1635).

[2] *enclosures* privately owned enclosed fields, which had begun in the sixteenth century to replace the open-field system of farming.

[3] *commission for depopulation* one of the crown's unpopular money-raising strategies, in this case a commission that enforced fines on landowners who allowed fields to go uncultivated and thereby encouraged workers to leave the countryside.

[4] *Lord Cottington* Francis Cottington, Baron Cottington (1578?–1652), a convert to Catholicism.

[5] *the great seal* a metonymy for the Lord Chancellor, in whose custody was kept the Great Seal, used to authenticate royal documents.

the chiefest employments, looked upon it as the prize of one of them; such offices commonly making way for more removes and preferments: when on a sudden the staff was put into the hands of the bishop of London [Juxon], a man so unknown, that his name was scarce heard of in the kingdom, who had been within two years before but a private chaplain to the king, and the president of a poor college in Oxford. This inflamed more men than were angry before, and no doubt did not only sharpen the edge of envy and malice against the archbishop (who was the known architect of this new fabric), but most unjustly indisposed many towards the church itself; which they looked upon as the gulf ready to swallow all the great offices, there being others in view, of that robe who were ambitious enough to expect the rest.

In the meantime the archbishop himself was infinitely pleased with what was done, and unhappily believed he had provided a stronger support for the church; and never abated any thing of his severity and rigour towards men of all conditions, or in the sharpness of his language and expressions, which was so natural to him, that he could not debate any thing without some commotion, when the argument was not of moment, nor bear contradiction in debate, even in the council, where all men are equally free, with that patience and temper that was necessary; of which they who wished him not well took many advantages, and would therefore contradict him, that he might be transported with some indecent passion; which, upon a short recollection, he was always sorry for, and most readily and heartily would make acknowledgment. No man so willingly made unkind use of all those occasions, as the lord Cottington, who being a master of temper, and of the most profound dissimulation, knew too well how to lead him into a mistake, and then drive him into choler, and then expose him upon the matter, and the manner, to the judgment of the company; and he chose to do

this most when the king was present; and then he would dine with him the next day.

. . . . .

The person [Clarendon] whose life this discourse is to recollect (and who had so great an affection and reverence for the memory of that prelate, [archbishop Laud,] that he never spake of him without extraordinary esteem, and believed him to be a man of the most exemplar virtue and piety of any of that age)[1] was wont to say, the greatest want the archbishop had was of a true friend, who would seasonably have told him of his infirmities, and what people spake of him; and he said, he knew well that such a friend would have been very acceptable to him; and upon that occasion he used to mention a story of himself: that when he was a young practiser of the law, being in some favour with him (as is mentioned before), he went to visit him in the beginning of a Michaelmas term,[2] shortly after his return from the country, where he had spent a month or two of the summer.

He found the archbishop early walking in the garden; who received him according to his custom, very graciously; and continuing his walk, asked him, "What good news in the country?" to which he answered, "there was none good; the people were universally discontented; and (which troubled him most) that every [one] spoke extreme ill of his grace, as the cause of all that was amiss." He replied, "that he was sorry for it; he knew he did not deserve it; and that he must not give over serving the king and the church, to please the people, who otherwise would not speak well of him." Mr. Hyde told him, "he thought he need not lessen his zeal for either; and that it grieved him to find persons of the best condition, and who loved both king and church, exceedingly indevoted to him; complaining of his

---

[1] *exemplar* exemplary (*OED* exemplar *a* 4).

[2] *Michaelmas term* the university or court term beginning on the Feast of St. Michael and All Angels (September 29).

manner of treating them, when they had occasion to resort to him, it may be, for his direction." And then named him two persons of the most interest and credit in Wiltshire, who had that summer attended the council board in some affairs which concerned the king and the county: that all the lords present used them with great courtesy, knowing well their quality and reputation; but that he alone spake very sharply to them, and without any thing of grace, at which they were much troubled; and one of them, supposing that somebody had done him ill offices, went the next morning to Lambeth, to present his service to him, and to discover, if he could, what misrepresentation had been made of him: that after he had attended very long, he was admitted to speak with his grace, who scarce hearing him, sharply answered him, that "he had no leisure for compliments"; and so turned away; which put the other gentleman much out of countenance: and that this kind of behaviour of his was the discourse of all companies of persons of quality; every man continuing any such story with another like it, very much to his disadvantage, and to the trouble of those who were very just to him.

He heard the relation very patiently and attentively, and discoursed over every particular with all imaginable condescension; and said, with evident show of trouble, that "he was very unfortunate to be so ill understood; that he meant very well; that he remembered the time when those two persons were with the council; that upon any deliberations, when any thing was resolved, or to be said to any body, the council enjoined him to deliver their resolutions; which he did always according to the best of his understanding: but by the imperfection he had by nature, which he said often troubled him, he might deliver it in such a tune, and with a sharpness of voice, that made men believe he was angry, when there was no such thing; that when those gentlemen were there, and he had delivered what he was to say, they made some stay, and spake with some of the lords, which not being according to order, he thought he gave them some reprehension; they having at that time very much other business to do: that he did well remember that one of them (who was a person of honour) came afterwards to him at a time he was shut up about an affair of importance, which required his full thoughts; but that as soon as he heard of the other's being without, he sent for him, himself going into the next room, and receiving him very kindly, as he thought; and supposing that he came about business, asked him what his business was; and the other answering, that he had no business, but continuing his address with some ceremony, he had indeed said, that he had not time for compliments: but he did not think that he went out of the room in that manner: and concluded, that it was not possible for him, in the many occupations he had, to spend any time in unnecessary compliments; and that if his integrity and uprightness, which never should be liable to reproach, could not be strong enough to preserve him, he must submit to God's good pleasure."

He was well contented to hear Mr. Hyde reply very freely upon the subject, who said, "he observed by what his grace himself had related, that the gentlemen had too much reason for the report they made; and he did not wonder that they had been much troubled at his carriage towards them; that he did exceedingly wish that he would more reserve his passion towards all persons, how faulty soever; and that he would treat persons of honour, and quality, and interest in their country, with more courtesy and condescension; especially when they came to visit him, and make offer of their service." He said, smiling, that "he could only undertake for his heart; that he had very good meaning; for his tongue, he could not undertake, that he would not sometimes speak more hastily and sharply than he should do (which oftentimes he was sorry for and reprehended himself for), and in a tune which might be liable to misinterpretation with them who were not very well acquainted with him, and so knew that it was an infirmity, which his nature and education had so rooted in him, that it was in vain to contend with it." For the state and distance he kept with men, he said, "he thought it was not more than was suitable to the place and degree he held in the church and state; or so much as others had assumed to themselves who had sat in his place; and thereupon he told him some behaviour and carriage of his predecessor, Abbot (who he said was not better born than himself), towards the greatest nobility of the kingdom, which he thought was very insolent and inexcusable"; and was indeed very ridiculous.

After this bold enterprise, [Mr. Hyde] ever found himself more graciously received by him, and treated with more familiarity; upon which he always concluded, that if the archbishop had had any true friend, who would, in proper seasons, have dealt frankly with him in the most important matters, and wherein the errors were like to be most penal, he would not only have received it very well, but have profited himself by it. But it is the misfortune of most persons of that education (how worthy soever), that they have rarely friendships with men above their own condition; and that their ascent being commonly sudden, from low to high, they have afterwards rather dependants than friends, and are still deceived by keeping somewhat in reserve to themselves, even from those with whom they seem most openly to communicate; and which is worse, receive for the most part their informations and advertisements from clergymen who understand the least, and take the worst measure of human affairs, of all mankind that can write and read.

The archbishop of Canterbury had lain prisoner in the Tower, from the beginning of the parliament, full four years, without any prosecution till this time, when they brought him to the bars of both houses;[1] charging him with several articles of high treason; which, if all that was alleged against him had been true, could not have made him guilty of treason. They accused him of a design to bring in popery, and of having correspondence with the pope, and such like particulars, as the consciences of his greatest enemies absolved him from. No man was a greater or abler enemy to popery; no man a more resolute and devout son of the church of England. He was prosecuted by lawyers, assigned to that purpose, out of those, who from their own antipathy to the church and bishops, or from some disobligations received from him, were sure to bring passion, animosity, and malice enough of their own; what evidence soever they had from others. And they did treat him with all the rudeness, reproach, and barbarity imaginable; with which his judges were not displeased.

He defended himself with great and undaunted courage, and less passion than was expected from his constitution; answered all their objections with clearness and irresistible reason; and convinced all men of his integrity, and his detestation of all treasonable intentions. So that though few excellent men have ever had fewer friends to their persons, yet all reasonable men absolved him from any foul crime that the law could take notice of, and punish. However, when they had said all they could against him, and he all for himself that need to be said, and no such crime appearing, as the lords, as the supreme court of judicatory, would take upon them to judge him to be worthy of death, they resorted to their legislative power, and by ordinance of parliament, as they called it, that is, by a determination of those members who sat in the houses (whereof in the house of peers there were not above twelve), they appointed him to be put to death, as guilty of high treason. The first time that two houses of parliament had ever assumed that jurisdiction, or that ever ordinance had been made to such a purpose; nor could any rebellion be more against the law, than that murderous act.

---

[1] Laud was committed to the Tower in 1641, and tried in 1644.

When the first mention was made of their monstrous purpose, of bringing the archbishop to a trial for his life, the chancellor of the exchequer,[1] who had always a great reverence and affection for him, had spoken to the king of it, and proposed to him, that in all events, there might be a pardon prepared, and sent to him, under the great seal of England; to the end, if they proceeded against him in any form of law, he might plead the king's pardon; which must be allowed by all who pretended to be governed by the law; but if they proceeded in a martial, or any other extraordinary way, without any form of law, his majesty should declare his justice and affection to an old faithful servant, whom he much esteemed, in having done all towards his preservation that was in his power to do. The king was wonderfully pleased with the proposition; and took from thence occasion to commend the piety and virtue of the archbishop with extraordinary affection; and commanded the chancellor of the exchequer to cause the pardon to be drawn, and his majesty would sign and seal it with all possible secrecy; which at that time was necessary. Whereupon the chancellor sent for sir Thomas Gardiner, the king's solicitor, and told him the king's pleasure; upon which he presently prepared the pardon, and it was signed and sealed with the great seal of England, and carefully sent, and delivered into the archbishop's own hand, before he was brought to his trial; who received it with great joy, as it was a testimony of the king's gracious affection to him, and care of him, without any opinion that they who endeavoured to take away the king's life would preserve his by his majesty's authority.

When the archbishop's council had perused the pardon, and considered that all possible exceptions would be taken to it, though they should not reject it, they found, that the impeachment was not so distinctly set down in the pardon as it ought to be; which could not be helped at Oxford,[2] because they had no copy of it; and therefore had supplied it with all those general expressions, as, in any court of law, would make the pardon valid against any exceptions the king's own council could make against it. Hereupon, the archbishop had, by the same messenger, returned the pardon again to the chancellor, with such directions and copies as were necessary; upon which it was perfected accordingly, and delivered safely again to him, and was in his hands during the whole time of his trial. So when his trial was over, and the ordinance passed for the cutting off his head, and he called and asked, according to custom in criminal proceedings, what he could say more, why he should not suffer death? he told them, that he had the king's gracious pardon, which he pleaded, and tendered to them, and desired that it might be allowed.

Whereupon he was sent to the Tower, and the pardon read in both Houses; where, without any long debate, it was declared to be of no effect, and that the king could not pardon a judgment of parliament. And so, without troubling themselves farther, they gave orders for his execution; which he underwent with all Christian courage and magnanimity, to the admiration of the beholders, and confusion of his enemies. Much hath been said of the person of this great prelate before, of his great endowments, and natural infirmities; to which shall be added no more in this place (his memory deserving a particular celebration), than that his learning, piety, and virtue, have been attained by very few, and the greatest of his infirmities are common to all, even to the best men.

---

[1] Hyde himself; he succeeded Cottington as Chancellor of the Exchequer in 1643.

[2] *Oxford* the location of the King and his court at the time.

THE TEMPER AND SPIRIT OF THE NATION
AFTER 1660

It will be convenient here, before we descend to those particulars which had an influence upon the minds of men, to take a clear view of the temper and spirit of that time; of the nature and inclination of the army; of the disposition and interest of the several factions in religion; all which appeared in their several colours, without dissembling their principles, and with equal confidence demanded the liberty of conscience they had enjoyed in and since the time of Cromwell; and the humour and the present purpose and design of the parliament itself, to whose judgment and determination the whole settlement of the kingdom, both in church and state, stood referred by the king's own declaration from Breda,[1] which by God's inspiration had been the sole visible motive to that wonderful change that had ensued.[2] And whosoever takes a prospect of all those several passions and appetites and interests, together with the divided affections, jealousies, and animosities of those who had been always looked upon as the king's party, which, if united, would in that conjuncture have been powerful enough to have balanced all the other; I say, whoever truly and ingenuously considers and reflects upon all this composition of contradictory wishes and expectations, must confess that the king was not yet the master of the kingdom, nor his authority and security such as the general noise and acclamation, the bells and the bonfires, proclaimed it to be; and that there was in no conjuncture more need, that the virtue and wisdom and industry of a prince should be evident, and made manifest in the preservation of his dignity, and in the application of his mind to the government of his affairs; and that all

who were eminently trusted by him should be men of unquestionable sincerity, who with industry and dexterity should first endeavour to compose the public disorders, and to provide for the peace and settlement of the kingdom, before they applied themselves to make or improve their own particular fortunes. And there is little question, but if this good method had been pursued, and the resolutions of that kind, which the king had seriously taken beyond the seas, when he first discerned his good fortune coming towards him, had been executed and improved; the hearts and affections of all degrees of men were so prepared by their own natural inclinations and integrity, by what they had seen and what they had suffered, by their observations and experience, by their fears, or by their hopes; that they might have been all kneaded into as firm and constant an obedience and resignation to the king's authority, and to a lasting establishment of monarchic power, in all the just extents which the king could expect, or men of any public or honest affections could wish or submit to.

There was yet added to this slippery and uneasy posture of affairs, another mortification, which made a deeper impression upon the king's spirit than all the rest, and without which the worst of the other would have been in some degree remediable; that was, the constitution and disunion of those who were called and looked upon as his own party, which without doubt in the whole kingdom was numerous enough, and capable of being powerful enough to give the law to all the rest; which had been the ground of many unhappy attempts in the late time; that if any present force could be drawn together, and possessed of any such place in which they might make a stand without being overrun in a moment, the general concurrence of the kingdom would in a short time reduce the army,[3] and make the king superior to all his enemies; which imagina-

---

[1] *declaration from Breda* the declaration (April 4, 1660) in which the King promised the political and religious concessions that ushered in the Restoration; it is included in this anthology.

[2] *that wonderful change* the Restoration of the monarchy in 1660.

[3] *the army* Parliament's New Model Army.

tion was enough confuted, though not enough extinguished, by the dearbought experience in the woeful enterprise at Worcester.[1] However, it had been now a very justifiable presumption in the king, to believe as well as hope, that he could not be long in England without such an apparency of his own party, that wished all that he himself desired, and such a manifestation of their authority, interest and power, that would prevent, or be sufficient to subdue, any froward disposition that might grow up in the parliament, or more extravagant demands in the army itself. An appearance there was of that people, great enough, who had all the wishes for the king which he entertained for himself. But they were so divided and disunited by private quarrels, factions, and animosities; or so unacquainted with each other; or, which was worse, so jealous of each other; the understandings and faculties of many honest men were so weak and shallow, that they could not be applied to any great trust; and others, who wished and meant well, had a peevishness, frowardness, and opiniatrety, that they would be engaged only in what pleased themselves, nor would join in any thing with such and such men whom they disliked. The severe and tyrannical government of Cromwell and the parliament had so often banished and imprisoned them upon mere jealousies, that they were grown strangers to one another, without any communication between them: and there had been so frequent betrayings and treacheries used, so many discoveries of meetings privately contrived, and of discourses accidentally entered into, and words and expressions rashly and unadvisedly uttered without any design, upon which multitudes were still imprisoned and many put to death; so that the jealousy was so universal, that few men who had never so good affections for the king, durst confer with any freedom together.

But these unhappy and fatal miscarriages, and the sad spectacles which ensued, made not those impressions upon the affections and spirits of the king's friends as they ought to have done; nor rendered the wariness and discretion of those who had dissuaded the enterprise, and who were always imprisoned upon suspicion, how innocent soever, the more valued and esteemed: on the contrary, it increased the reproaches against the knot, as if their *lâcheté* and want of appearance and engaging had been the sole cause of the misfortune.[2] And after some short fits of dejection and acquiescence, upon the shedding so much blood of their friends and confederates, and the notorious discovery of being betrayed by those, who had been trusted by them, of the army; they began again to resume courage, to meet and enter upon new counsels and designs, imputing the former want of success to the want of skill and conduct in the undertakers, not to the all-seeing vigilance of Cromwell and his instruments, or to the formed strength of his government, not to be shaken by weak or ill-seconded conspiracies. Young men were grown up, who inherited their fathers' malignity, and were too impatient to revenge their death, or to be even with their oppressors, and so entered into new combinations as unskilful, and therefore as unfortunate as the former; and being discovered even before they were formed, Cromwell had occasion given him to make himself more terrible in new executions, and to exercise greater tyranny upon the whole party, in imprisonments, penalties, and sequestrations;[3] making those who heartily desired to be quiet, and who as much abhorred any rash and desperate insurrection, to pay their full shares of the folly of

---

[1] *the woeful enterprise at Worcester* Cromwell decisively defeated an invading Scottish Royalist army under Charles II at the battle of Worcester (September 3, 1651).

[2] *the knot* the "Sealed Knot," the official (though ineffective) body for Royalist conspiracy in England; *lâcheté* feebleness, weakness, or cowardice.

[3] *sequestrations* Sequestration was the seizure of income from an estate, a money-raising tactic used extensively by Parliament against Royalists during the civil wars.

the other, as if all were animated by the same spirit. And this unjust and unreasonable rigour increased the reproaches and animosities in the king's friends against each other: the wiser and more sober part, who had most experience, and knew how impossible it was to succeed in such enterprises, and had yet preserved or redeemed enough of their fortunes to sit still and expect some hopeful revolution, were inexpressibly offended, and bitterly inveighed against those, who without reason disturbed their peace and quiet, by provoking the state to fresh persecutions of them who had given them no offence: and the other stirring and enraged party, with more fierceness and public disdain, protested against and reviled those who refused to join with them, as men who had spent all their stock of allegiance, and meant to acquiesce with what they had left under the tyranny and in the subjection of Cromwell. And thus they who did really wish the same things, and equally the overthrow of that government, which hindered the restoration of the king, grew into more implacable jealousies and virulencies against each other, than against that power that oppressed them both, and "poured out their blood like water" [Psalm 79:3]. And either party conveyed their apologies and accusations to the king: one insisting upon the impertinency of all such attempts; and the other insisting that they were ready for a very solid and well-grounded enterprise, were sure to be possessed of good towns, if, by his majesty's positive command, the rest, who professed such obedience to him, would join with them.

I have thought myself obliged to renew the memory of all these particulars, that the several vicissitudes and stages may be known, by which the jealousies, murmurs, and disaffections in the royal party amongst themselves, and against each other, had mounted to that height which the king found them at when he returned; when in truth very few men of active minds, and upon whom he could depend in any sudden occasion that might probably press him, can be named, who had any confidence in each other. All men were full of bitter reflections upon the actions and behaviour of others, or of excuses and apologies for themselves for what they thought might be charged upon them. The woeful vice of drinking, from the uneasiness of their fortune, or the necessity of frequent meetings together, for which taverns were the most secure places, had spread itself very far in that classis of men, as well as upon other parts of the nation, in all counties; and had exceedingly weakened the parts, and broken the understandings of many, who had formerly competent judgments, and had been in all respects fit for any trust; and had prevented the growth of parts in many young men, who had good affections, but had been from their entering into the world so corrupted with that excess, and other license of the time, that they only made much noise, and by their extravagant and scandalous debauches, brought many calumnies and disestimation upon that cause which they pretended to advance. They who had suffered much in their fortunes, and by frequent imprisonments and sequestrations and compositions,[1] expected large recompenses and reparations in honours which they could not support, or offices which they could not discharge, or lands and money which the king had not to give; as all dispassioned men knew the conditions which the king was obliged to perform, and that the act of indemnity discharged all those forfeitures which could have been applied to their benefit: and therefore they who had been without comparison the greatest sufferers in their fortunes, and in all respects had merited most, never made any inconvenient suits to the king, but modestly left the memory and consideration of all they had done or undergone, to his majesty's own gracious reflections. They were observed to be most importunate, who had deserved least, and were least capable to perform any notable

---

[1] *compositions* fines paid by Royalists to avoid prosecution or confiscation of their estates.

service; and none had more esteem of themselves, and believed preferment to be more due to them, than a sort of men, who had most loudly begun the king's health in taverns, especially if for any disorders which had accompanied it they had suffered imprisonment, without any other pretence of merit, or running any other hazard.

This unhappy temper and constitution of the royal party, with whom he had always intended to have made a firm conjunction against all accidents and occurrences which might happen at home or from abroad, did wonderfully displease and trouble the king; and, with the other perplexities, which are mentioned before, did so break his mind, and had that operation upon his spirits, that finding he could not propose any such method to himself, by which he might extricate himself out of those many difficulties and labyrinths in which he was involved, nor expedite those important matters which depended upon the goodwill and despatch of the parliament, which would proceed by its own rules, and with its accustomed formalities, he grew more disposed to leave all things to their natural course, and God's providence; and by degrees unbent his mind from the knotty and ungrateful part of his business, grew more remiss in his application to it, and indulged to his youth and appetite that license and satisfaction that it desired, and for which he had opportunity enough, and could not be without ministers abundant for any such negotiations; the time itself, and the young people thereof of either sex having been educated in all the liberty of vice, without reprehension or restraint. All relations were confounded by the several sects in religion, which discountenanced all forms of reverence and respect, as relics and marks of superstition. Children asked not blessing of their parents; nor did they concern themselves in the education of their children; but were well content that they should take any course to maintain themselves, that they might be free from that expense. The young women conversed without any circumspection or modesty, and frequently met at taverns and common eating houses; and they who were stricter and more severe in their comportment, became the wives of the seditious preachers, or of officers of the army. The daughters of noble and illustrious families bestowed themselves upon the divines of the time, or other low and unequal matches. Parents had no manner of authority over their children, nor children any obedience or submission to their parents; but "everyone did that which was good in his own eyes" [Judges 17:6, 21:25]. This unnatural antipathy had its first rise from the beginning of the rebellion, when the fathers and sons engaged themselves in the contrary parties, the one choosing to serve the king, and the other the parliament; which division and contradiction of affections was afterwards improved to mutual animosities and direct malice, by the help of the preachers, and the several factions in religion, or by the absence of all religion: so that there were never such examples of impiety between such relations in any age of the world, Christian or heathen, as that wicked time, from the beginning of the rebellion to the king's return; of which the families of Hotham and Vane are sufficient instances;[1] though other more illustrious houses may be named, where the same accursed fruit was too plentifully gathered, and too notorious to the world. The relation between masters and servants had been long since dissolved by the parliament, that their army might be increased by the prentices against their masters' consent, and that they might

---

[1] *Hotham and Vane* Sir John Hotham (d. 1645) was appointed Governor of Hull by the King in 1639, but turned the city over to Parliament in 1642; he and his son of the same name fought against the King during the First Civil War, but were both executed by Parliament in 1645 for negotiating their return to the Royalist party. Sir Henry Vane the elder (1589–1655) had been Secretary of State but joined Parliament in 1641; his son, Sir Henry Vane the younger (1613–1662), had also held offices under the King, but became a leading official in the Commonwealth and was executed after the Restoration.

have intelligence of the secret meetings and transactions in those houses and families which were not devoted to them; from whence issued the foulest treacheries and perfidiousness that were ever practised: and the blood of the master was frequently the price of the servant's villainy.

Cromwell had been most strict and severe in the forming the manners of his army, and in chastising all irregularities; insomuch that sure there was never any such body of men so without rapine, swearing, drinking, or any other debauchery, but the wickedness of their hearts: and all persons cherished by him, were of the same leaven, and to common appearance without the practice of any of those vices which were most infamous to the people, and which drew the public hatred upon those who were notoriously guilty of them. But then he was well pleased with the most scandalous lives of those who pretended to be for the king, and wished that all his were such, and took all the pains he could that they might be generally thought to be such; whereas in truth the greatest part of those who were guilty of those disorders were young men, who had never seen the king, and had been born and bred in those corrupt times, "when there was no king in Israel" [Judges 17:6, 18:1, 19:1, 21:25]. He was equally delighted with the luxury and voluptuousness of the Presbyterians, who, in contempt of the thrift, sordidness, and affected ill-breeding of the Independents, thought it became them to live more generously, and were not strict in restraining or mortifying the unruly and inordinate appetite of flesh and blood, but indulged it with too much and too open scandal, from which he reaped no small advantage; and wished all those, who were not his friends, should not only be infected, but given over to the practice of the most odious vices and wickedness.

In a word, the nation was corrupted from that integrity, good nature, and generosity, that had been peculiar to it, and for which it had been signal and celebrated throughout the world; in the room whereof the vilest craft and dissembling had succeeded. The tenderness of the bowels, which is the quintessence of justice and compassion, the very mention of good nature was laughed at and looked upon as the mark and character of a fool; and a roughness of manners, or hard-heartedness and cruelty was affected. In the place of generosity, a vile and sordid love of money was entertained as the truest wisdom, and any thing lawful that would contribute towards being rich. There was a total decay, or rather a final expiration of all friendship; and to dissuade a man from any thing he affected, or to reprove him for any thing he had done amiss, or to advise him to do any thing he had no mind to do, was thought an impertinence unworthy a wise man, and received with reproach and contempt. These dilapidations and ruins of the ancient candour and discipline were not taken enough to heart, and repaired with that early care and severity that they might have been; for they were not then incorrigible; but by the remissness of applying remedies to some, and the unwariness in giving a kind of countenance to others, too much of that poison insinuated itself into minds not well fortified against such infection: so that much of the malignity was transplanted, instead of being extinguished, to the corruption of many wholesome bodies, which, being corrupted, spread the diseases more powerfully and more mischievously.

THE PLAGUE AND THE FIRE OF LONDON, 1665–6

There begun now [Spring 1665] to appear another enemy, much more formidable than the Dutch,[1] and more difficult to be struggled with; which was the plague, that brake out in the winter, and made such an early progress in the spring, that

---

[1] *the Dutch* with whom England was then at war, caused primarily by commercial rivalry (the second Anglo-Dutch war, 1665–1667).

though the weekly numbers did not rise high, and it appeared to be only in the outskirts of the town, and in the most obscure alleys, amongst the poorest people; yet the ancient men, who well remembered in what manner the last great plague (which had been near forty years before) first brake out, and the progress it afterwards made, foretold a terrible summer. And many of them removed their families out of the city to country habitations; when their neighbours laughed at their providence, and thought they might have stayed without danger: but they found shortly that they had done wisely.

In March it spread so much, that the parliament was very willing to part: which was likewise the more necessary, in regard that so many of the members of the house of commons were assigned to so many offices and employments which related to the war, and which required their immediate attendance.

After Christmas the rage and fury of the pestilence began in some degree to be mitigated, but so little, that nobody who had left the town had yet the courage to return thither: nor had they reason; for though it was a considerable abatement from the height it had been at, yet there died still between three and four thousand in the week, and of those, some men of better condition than had fallen before. The general [Albemarle][1] writ from thence, "that there still arose new difficulties in providing for the setting out the fleet, and some of such a nature, that he could not easily remove them without communication with his majesty, and receiving his more positive directions; and how to bring that to pass he knew not, for as he could by no means advise his majesty to leave Oxford, so he found many objections against his own being absent from London." Windsor was thought upon as a place where the king might safely reside, there being then no infection there: but the king had adjourned the

term thither, which had possessed the whole town; and he was not without some apprehension, that the plague had got into one house.

In the end, towards the end of February, the king resolved that the queen and duchess and all their families should remain in Oxford; and that his majesty and his brother, with prince Rupert, and such of his council and other servants as were thought necessary or fit, would make a quick journey to Hampton-Court, where the general might be every day, and return again to London at night, and his majesty gave such orders as were requisite for the carrying on his service, and so after two or three days' stay there return again to Oxford; for no man did believe it counsellable, that his majesty should reside longer there, than the despatch of the most important business required: and with this resolution his majesty made his journey to Hampton-Court.

It pleased God, that the next week after his majesty came thither, the number of those who died of the plague in the city decreased one thousand; and there was a strange universal joy there for the king's being so near. The weather was as it could be wished, deep snow and terrible frost, which very probably stopped the spreading of the infection, though it might put an end to those who were already infected, as it did, for in a week or two the number of the dead was very little diminished. The general came and went as was intended: but the business every day increased; and his majesty's remove to a further distance was thought inconvenient, since there appeared no danger in remaining where he was.

And after a fortnight's or three weeks' stay, he resolved, for the quicker despatch of all that was to be done, to go to Whitehall, when there died above fifteen hundred in the week, and when there was not in a day seen a coach in the streets, but those which came in his majesty's train; so much all men were terrified from returning to a place of so much

---

[1] *The general* George Monck, first Duke of Albemarle (1608–1670), largely responsible for the conduct of the Dutch war.

mortality. Yet it can hardly be imagined what numbers flocked thither from all parts upon the fame of the king's being at Whitehall, all men being ashamed of their fears for their own safety, when the king ventured his person. The judges at Windsor adjourned the last return of the term to Westminster-hall, and the town every day filled marvellously; and which was more wonderful, the plague every day decreased. Upon which the king changed his purpose, and, instead of returning to Oxford, sent for the queen and all the family to come to Whitehall: so that before the end of March the streets were as full, the exchange as much crowded, and the people in all places as numerous, as they had ever been seen, few persons missing any of their acquaintance, though by the weekly bills there appeared to have died above one hundred and threescore thousand persons: and many, who could compute very well, concluded that there were in truth double that number who died; and that in one week, when the bill mentioned only six thousand, there had in truth fourteen thousand died. The frequent deaths of the clerks and sextons of parishes hindered the exact account every week; but that which left it without any certainty was the vast number that was buried in the fields, of which no account was kept. Then of the Anabaptists and other sectaries, who abounded in the city, very few left their habitations; and multitudes of them died, whereof no churchwarden or other officer had notice; but they found burials, according to their own fancies, in small gardens or the next fields. The greatest number of those who died consisted of women and children, and the lowest and poorest sort of the people; so that, as I said before, few men missed any of their acquaintance when they returned, not many of wealth or quality or of much conversation being dead; yet some of either sort there were.

THE FIRE

It was upon the first day of that September, in the dismal year of 1666 (in which many prodigies were expected, and so many really fell out),[1] that that memorable and terrible fire brake out in London, which begun about midnight, or nearer the morning of Sunday, in a baker's house at the end of Thames Street next the Tower, there being many little narrow alleys and very poor houses about the place where it first appeared; and then finding such store of combustible materials, as that street is always furnished with in timber-houses, the fire prevailed so powerfully, that that whole street and the neighbourhood was in so short a time turned to ashes, that few persons had time to save and preserve any of their goods; but were a heap of people almost as dead with the sudden distraction, as the ruins were which they sustained. The magistrates of the city assembled quickly together, and with the usual remedies of buckets, which they were provided with: but the fire was too ravenous to be extinguished with such quantities of water as those instruments could apply to it, and fastened still upon new materials before it had destroyed the old. And though it raged furiously all that day, to that degree that all men stood amazed as spectators only, no man knowing what remedy to apply, nor the magistrates what orders to give; yet it kept within some compass, burned what was next, and laid hold only on both sides; and the greatest apprehension was of the Tower, and all considerations entered upon how to secure that place.

But in the night the wind changed, and carried the danger from thence, but with so great and irresistible violence, that as it kept the English and

---

[1] *the dismal year of 1666 (in which many prodigies were expected)* When Bibles became readily available in the vernacular, many were fascinated by the prophetic parts of such books as Revelation. The end of the world was thought to be imminent, and was expected to be heralded by remarkable events. 1666 was an especially popular date among those who forecast the millennium, because 666 was the number of the Beast who had first to be overthrown (Revelation 13:18).

Dutch fleets from grappling when they were so near each other, so it scattered the fire from pursuing the line it was in with all its force, and spread it over the city: so that they, who went late to bed at a great distance from any place where the fire prevailed, were awakened before morning with their own houses being in a flame; and whilst endeavour was used to quench that, other houses were discovered to be burning, which were near no place from whence they could imagine the fire could come; all which kindled another fire in the breasts of men, almost as dangerous as that within their houses.[1]

Monday morning produced first a jealousy, and then an universal conclusion, that this fire came not by chance, nor did they care where it began; but the breaking out in several places at so great distance from each other made it evident, that it was by conspiracy and combination. And this determination could not hold long without discovery of the wicked authors, who were concluded to be all the Dutch and all the French in the town, though they had inhabited the same places above twenty years. All of that kind, or, if they were strangers, of what nation soever, were laid hold of; and after all the ill usage that can consist in words, and some blows and kicks, they were thrown into prison. And shortly after, the same conclusion comprehended all the Roman Catholics, the papists, who were in the same predicament of guilt and danger, and quickly found that their only safety consisted in keeping within doors; and yet some of them, and of quality, were taken by force out of their houses, and carried to prison.

When this rage spread as far as the fire, and every hour brought reports of some bloody effects of it, worse than in truth they were, the king distributed many of the privy-council into several quarters of the city, to prevent, by their authorities, those inhumanities which he heard were commit-

ted. In the mean time, even they or any other person thought it not safe to declare, that they believed that the fire came by accident, or that it was not a plot of the Dutch and the French and papists to burn the city; which was so generally believed, and in the best company, that he who said the contrary was suspected for a conspirator, or at best a favourer of them. It could not be conceived how a house that was distant a mile from any part of the fire could suddenly be in a flame, without some particular malice; and this case fell out every hour. When a man at the furthest end of Bread Street, had made a shift to get out of his house his best and most portable goods, because the fire had approached near them; he no sooner had secured them, as he thought, in some friend's house in Holborn, which was believed a safe distance, but he saw that very house, and none else near it, in a sudden flame. Nor did there want, in this woeful distemper, the testimony of witnesses who saw this villainy committed, and apprehended men who they were ready to swear threw fireballs into houses, which were presently burning.

The lord Hollis and lord Ashley, who had their quarters assigned about Newgate Market and the streets adjacent, had many brought to them in custody for crimes of this nature; and saw, within a very little distance from the place where they were, the people gathered together in great disorder; and as they came nearer saw a man in the middle of them without a hat or cloak, pulled and hauled and very ill used, whom they knew to be a servant to the Portugal ambassador, who was presently brought to them. And a substantial citizen was ready to take his oath, "that he saw that man put his hand in his pocket, and throw into a shop a fireball; upon which he saw the house immediately on fire: whereupon, being on the other side of the way, and seeing this, he cried out to the people to stop that gentleman, and made all the haste he could himself"; but the people had first seized upon him, and taken

---

[1] *another fire* that is, fear that the fires were being deliberately set.

away his sword, which he was ready to draw; and he not speaking nor understanding English, they had used him in the manner set down before. The lord Hollis told him what he was accused of, and "that he was seen to have thrown somewhat out of his pocket, which they thought to be a fireball, into a house which was now on fire": and the people had diligently searched his pockets to find more of the same commodities, but found nothing that they meant to accuse him of. The man standing in great amazement to hear he was so charged, the lord Hollis asked him, "what it was that he pulled out of his pocket, and what it was he threw into the house": to which he answered, "that he did not think that he had put his hand into his pocket; but he remembered very well, that as he walked in the street, he saw a piece of bread upon the ground, which he took up, and laid upon a shelf in the next house"; which is a custom or superstition so natural to the Portuguese, that if the king of Portugal were walking, and saw a piece of bread upon the ground, he would take it up with his own hand, and keep it till he saw a fit place to lay it down.

The house being in view, the lords with many of the people walked to it, and found the piece of bread just within the door upon a board, where he said he laid it; and the house on fire was two doors beyond it, which the man who was on the other side of the way, and saw this man put his hand into the house without staying, and presently after the fire break out, concluded to be the same house; which was very natural in the fright that all men were in: nor did the lords, though they were satisfied, set the poor man at liberty; but, as if there remained ground enough of suspicion, committed him to the constable, to be kept by him in his own house for some hours, when they pretended they would examine him again. Nor were any persons who were seized upon in the same manner, as multitudes were in all the parts of the town, especially if they were strangers or papists, presently dis-

charged, when there was no reasonable ground to suspect; but all sent to prison, where they were in much more security than they could have been in full liberty, after they were once known to have been suspected; and most of them understood their commitment to be upon that ground, and were glad of it.

The fire and the wind continued in the same excess all Monday, Tuesday, and Wednesday, till afternoon, and flung and scattered brands burning into all quarters; the nights more terrible than the days, and the light the same, the light of the fire supplying that of the sun. And indeed whoever was an eyewitness of that terrible prospect, can never have so lively an image of the last conflagration till he beholds it; the faces of all people in a wonderful dejection and discomposure, not knowing where they could repose themselves for one hour's sleep, and no distance thought secure from the fire, which suddenly started up before it was suspected; so that people left their houses and carried away their goods from many places which received no hurt, and whither they afterwards returned again; all the fields full of women and children, who had made a shift to bring thither some goods and conveniences to rest upon, as safer than any houses, where yet they felt such intolerable heat and drought, as if they had been in the middle of the fire. The king and the duke, who rode from one place to another, and put themselves into great dangers amongst the burning and falling houses, to give advice and direction what was to be done, underwent as much fatigue as the meanest, and had as little sleep or rest; and the faces of all men appeared ghastly and in the highest confusion. The country sent in carts to help those miserable people who had saved any goods: and by this means, and the help of coaches, all the neighbour villages were filled with more people than they could contain, and more goods than they could find room for; so that those fields became likewise as full as the other about London and Westminster.

It was observed that where the fire prevailed most, when it met with brick buildings, if it was not repulsed, it was so well resisted that it made a much slower progress; and when it had done its worst, that the timber and all the combustible matter fell, it fell down to the bottom within the house, and the walls stood and enclosed the fire, and it was burned out without making a further progress in many of those places; and then the vacancy so interrupted the fury of it, that many times the two or three next houses stood without much damage. Besides the spreading, insomuch as all London seemed but one fire in the breadth of it, it seemed to continue in its full fury a direct line to the Thames side, all Cheapside from beyond the Exchange, through Fleet Street; insomuch as for that breadth, taking in both sides as far as the Thames, there was scarce a house or church standing from the bridge to Dorset-house, which was burned on Tuesday night after Baynard's Castle.

On Wednesday morning, when the king saw that neither the fire decreased nor the wind lessened, he even despaired of preserving Whitehall, but was more afraid of Westminster Abbey. But having observed by his having visited all places, that where there were any vacant places between the houses, by which the progress of the fire was interrupted, it changed its course and went to the other side; he gave order for pulling down many houses about Whitehall, some whereof were newly built and hardly finished, and sent many of his choice goods by water to Hampton Court; as most of the persons of quality in the Strand, who had the benefit of the river, got barges and other vessels, and sent their furniture for their houses to some houses some miles out of the town. And very many on both sides the Strand, who knew not whither to go, and scarce what they did, fled with their families out of their houses into the streets, that they might not be within when the fire fell upon their houses.

But it pleased God, contrary to all expectation, that on Wednesday, about four or five of the clock in the afternoon, the wind fell: and as in an instant the fire decreased, having burned all on the Thames side to the new buildings of the Inner Temple next to Whitefriars, and having consumed them, was stopped by that vacancy from proceeding further into that house; but laid hold on some old buildings which joined to Ram Alley, and swept all those into Fleet Street. And the other side being likewise destroyed to Fetter Lane, it advanced no further; but left the other part of Fleet Street to the Temple Bar, and all the Strand, unhurt, but what damage the owners of the houses had done to themselves by endeavouring to remove; and it ceased in all other parts of the town near the same time: so that the greatest care then was, to keep good guards to watch the fire that was upon the ground, that it might not break out again. And this was the better performed, because they who had yet their houses standing had not the courage to sleep, but watched with much less distraction; though the same distemper still remained in the utmost extent, that all this had fallen out by the conspiracy of the French and Dutch with the papists; and all jails were filled with those who were every hour apprehended upon that jealousy; or rather upon some evidence that they were guilty of the crime. And the people were so sottish, that they believed that all the French in the town (which no doubt were a very great number) were drawn into a body, to prosecute those by the sword who were preserved from the fire: and the inhabitants of a whole street have run in a great tumult one way, upon the rumour that the French were marching at the other end of it; so terrified men were with their own apprehensions.

When the night, though far from being a quiet one, had somewhat lessened the consternation, the first care the king took was, that the country might speedily supply markets in all places, that they who had saved themselves from burning might not be in danger of starving; and if there had not been extraordinary care and diligence used, many would have perished that way. The vast destruction of corn, and all other sorts of provisions, in those parts where the fire had prevailed, had not only left all that people destitute of all that was to be eat or drank; but the bakers and brewers, which inhabited the other parts which were unhurt, had forsaken their houses, and carried away all that was portable: insomuch as many days passed, before they were enough in their wits and in their houses to fall to their occupations; and those parts of the town which God had spared and preserved were many hours without anything to eat, as well as they who were in the fields. And yet it can hardly be conceived, how great a supply of all kinds was brought from all places within four and twenty hours. And which was more miraculous, in four days, in all the fields about the town, which had seemed covered with those whose habitations were burned, and with the goods which they had saved, there was scarce a man to be seen: all found shelter in so short a time, either in those parts which remained of the city and in the suburbs, or in the neighbour villages; all kind of people expressing a marvellous charity towards those who appeared to be undone. And very many, with more expedition than can be conceived, set up little sheds of brick and timber upon the ruins of their own houses, where they chose rather to inhabit than in more convenient places, though they knew they could not long reside in those new buildings.

The king was not more troubled at any particular, than at the imagination which possessed the hearts of so many, that all this mischief had fallen out by a real and formed conspiracy; which, albeit he saw no colour to believe, he found very many intelligent men, and even some of his own council, who did really believe it. Whereupon he appointed the privy-council to sit both morning and evening, to examine all evidence of that kind that should be brought before them, and to send for any persons

who had been committed to prison upon some evidence that made the greatest noise; and sent for the lord chief justice, who was in the country, to come to the town for the better examination of all suggestions and allegations of that kind, there having been some malicious report scattered about the town, that the court had so great a prejudice against any kind of testimony of such a conspiracy, that they discountenanced all witnesses who came before them to testify what they knew; which was without any colour of truth. Yet many who were produced as if their testimony would remove all doubts, made such senseless relations of what they had been told, without knowing the condition of the persons who told them, or where to find them, that it was a hard matter to forbear smiling at their evidence. Some Frenchmen's houses had been searched, in which had been found many of those shells for squibs and other fireworks, frequently used in nights of joy and triumph; and the men were well known, and had lived many years there by that trade, and had no other: and one of these was the king's servant, and employed by the office of ordnance for making grenades of all kinds, as well for the hand as for mortar pieces. Yet these men were looked upon as in the number of the conspirators, and remained still in prison till their neighbours solicited for their liberty. And it cannot be enough wondered at, that in this general rage of the people no mischief was done to the strangers, that no one of them was assassinated outright, though many were sorely beaten and bruised.

Let the cause be what it would, the effect was very terrible; for above two parts of three of that great city were burned to ashes, and those the most rich and wealthy parts of the city, where the greatest warehouses and the best shops stood. The Royal Exchange, with all the streets about it, Lombard Street, Cheapside, Paternoster Row, St. Paul's church, and almost all the other churches in the city, with the Old Bailey, Ludgate, all Paul's churchyard even to the Thames, and the greatest part of Fleet Street, all which were places the best inhabited, were all burned without one house remaining.

The value or estimate of what that devouring fire consumed, over and above the houses, could never be computed in any degree: for besides that the first night (which in a moment swept away the vast wealth of Thames Street) there was [not] any thing that could be preserved in respect of the suddenness and amazement (all people being in their beds till the fire was in their houses, and so could save nothing but themselves), the next day with the violence of the wind increased the distraction; nor did many believe that the fire was near them, or that they had reason to remove their goods, till it was upon them, and rendered it impossible. Then it fell out at a season in the year, the beginning of September, when very many of the substantial citizens and other wealthy men were in the country, whereof many had not left a servant in their houses, thinking themselves upon all ordinary accidents more secure in the goodness and kindness of their neighbours, than they could be in the fidelity of a servant; and whatsoever was in such houses was entirely consumed by the fire, or lost as to the owners. And of this *classis* of absent men, when the fire came where the lawyers had houses, as they had in many places, especially Sergeants Inn in Fleet Street, with that part of the Inner Temple that was next it and Whitefriars, there was scarce a man to whom those lodgings appertained who was in town: so that whatsoever was there, their money, books, and papers, besides the evidences of many men's estates deposited in their hands, were all burned or lost, to a very great value. But of particular men's losses could never be made any computation.

It was an incredible damage that was and might rationally be computed to be sustained by one small company, the company of stationers, in books,

paper, and the other lesser commodities which are vendible in that corporation, which amounted to no less than two hundred thousand pounds: in which prodigious loss there was one circumstance very lamentable. All those who dwelt near Paul's carried their goods, books, paper, and the like, as others of greater trades did their commodities, into the large vaults which were under St. Paul's church, before the fire came thither: which vaults, though all the church above the ground was afterwards burned, with all the houses round about, still stood firm and supported the foundation, and preserved all that was within them; until the impatience of those who had lost their houses, and whatsoever they had else, in the fire, made them very desirous to see what they had [saved], upon which all their hopes were founded to repair the rest.

It was the fourth day after the fire ceased to flame, though it still burned in the ruins, from whence there was still an intolerable heat, when the booksellers especially, and some other tradesmen, who had deposited all they had preserved in the greatest and most spacious vault, came to behold all their wealth, which to that moment was safe: But the doors were no sooner opened, and the air from without fanned the strong heat within, but first the driest and most combustible matters, broke into a flame, which consumed all, of what kind soever, that till then had been unhurt there. Yet they who had committed their goods to some lesser vaults, at a distance from that greater, had better fortune; and having learned from the second ruin of their friends to have more patience, attended till the rain fell, and extinguished the fire in all places, and cooled the air: and then they securely opened the doors, and received all from thence that they had there.

If so vast a damage as two hundred thousand pounds befell that little company of stationers in books and paper and the like, what shall we conceive was lost in cloth (of which the country clothiers lost all that they had brought up to Blackwell

Hall against Michaelmas, which was all burned with that fair structure), in silks of all kinds, in linen, and those richer manufactures? Not to speak of money, plate, and jewels, whereof some were recovered out of the ruins of those houses which the owners took care to watch, as containing somewhat that was worth the looking for, and in which deluge there were men ready enough to fish.

The lord mayor, though a very honest man, was much blamed for want of sagacity in the first night of the fire, before the wind gave it much advancement: for though he came with great diligence as soon as he had notice of it, and was present with the first, yet having never been used to such spectacles, his consternation was equal to that of other men, nor did he know how to apply his authority to the remedying the present distress; and when men who were less terrified with the object pressed him very earnestly, that he would give order for the present pulling down those houses which were nearest, and by which the fire climbed to go further (the doing whereof at that time might probably have prevented much of the mischief that succeeded), he thought it not safe counsel, and made no other answer, than that he durst not do it without the consent of the owners. His want of skill was the less wondered at, when it was known afterwards, that some gentlemen of the Inner Temple would not endeavour to preserve the goods which were in the lodgings of absent persons, nor suffer others to do it, "because," they said, "it was against the law to break up any man's chamber."

The so sudden repair of those formidable ruins, and the giving so great beauty to all deformity (a beauty and a lustre that city had never before been acquainted with), is little less wonderful than the fire that consumed it.

It was hoped and expected that this prodigious and universal calamity, for the effects of it covered the whole kingdom, would have made impression, and produced some reformation in the license of the court: for as the pains the king had taken night and day during the fire, and the dangers he had exposed himself to, even for the saving the citizens' goods, had been very notorious,[1] and in the mouths of all men, with good wishes and prayers for him; so his majesty had been heard during that time to speak with great piety and devotion of the displeasure that God was provoked to. And no doubt the deep sense of it did raise many good thoughts and purposes in his royal breast. But he was narrowly watched and looked to, that such melancholic [thoughts] might not long possess him, the consequence and effect whereof was like to be more grievous than that of the fire itself; of which that loose company that was too much cherished, even before it was extinguished, discoursed as of an argument for mirth and wit to describe the wildness of the confusion all people were in; in which the scripture itself was used with equal liberty, when they could apply it to their profane purposes. And Mr. May presumed to assure the king, "that this was the greatest blessing that God had ever conferred upon him, his restoration only excepted: for the walls and gates being now burned and thrown down of that rebellious city, which was always an enemy to the crown, his majesty would never suffer them to repair and build them up again, to be a bit in his mouth and a bridle upon his neck; but would keep all open, that his troops might enter upon them whenever he thought necessary for his service, there being no other way to govern that rude multitude but by force."[2]

This kind of discourse did not please the king, but was highly approved by the company; and for the wit and pleasantness of it was repeated in all companies, infinitely to the king's disservice, and corrupted the affections of the citizens and of the country, who used and assumed the same liberty to

---

[1] *notorious* well known, famous.

[2] probably Baptist May, *bon viveur* and holder of a minor court office.

publish the profaneness and atheism of the court. And as nothing was done there in private, so it was made more public in pasquils and libels,[1] which were as bold with reflections of the broadest nature

upon the king himself, and upon those in whose company he was most delighted, as upon the meanest person.

—1702–04, 1759

---

[1] *pasquils* satires, lampoons, particularly those posted in public.

Gerrard Winstanley
1609 – ?1676

Born in Lancashire, the son of a mercer (a dealer in fabrics) with puritan sympathies, Winstanley worked in the London cloth trade until his business failed in 1643, when he moved to Cobham in Surrey to earn a living as a farm labourer. Most of the activities and writings (about twenty pamphlets and broadsheets) for which he is known date from the period 1648–1652. Like many other radicals of the revolutionary period, Winstanley disappears from the records after 1660, though he may be the Gerrard Winstanley who died a Quaker and corn chandler in 1676.

Winstanley's early pamphlets participate in the tradition of radical religious mysticism represented by Lawrence Clarkson (in his Seeker and Antinomian phases) and Abiezer Coppe. Like Coppe, Winstanley's search for Scripture's spiritual meaning led to a concern for social justice: Hell, he believed, was a mechanism of control used by clerics and the rich to oppress the poor. But Winstanley is best known for the political revelation that led to the Digger movement, a vision of agrarian communism first proclaimed in *The New Law of Righteousness* (1649) and set out in its most elaborate form in his last publication, *The Law of Freedom in a Platform* (1652). Winstanley argued that men could be free only when private property was abolished, all had access to the land and worked it in common, and no one worked for wages: social and economic inequities, he wrote, were a function of inequities in the distribution of property. While several Digger

communes were founded to put these ideas into practice, the most famous was on St. George's Hill, near Winstanley's home in Cobham. Winstanley and others began to till the commons land there in April 1649; alarmed local landowners complained to Thomas Fairfax and the Council of State, who proved not to share their anxieties. But the owners persisted, pursued the Diggers in court, and led a mob to trample their crops. The Diggers resettled nearby, but were finally driven out in 1650. The experiment and the attempts to suppress it were widely reported at the time. The following *Declaration* was the second of two manifestos published to explain the project.

While the Digger movement is best known for Winstanley's political writings, Digger communities around the country produced a variety of texts, including songs written to popularize their cause. In 1650, the Digger community on St. George's Hill published *The Diggers Mirth*, a short pamphlet containing "verses composed and fitted to tunes, for the delight and recreation of all those who Dig, or own that work, in the Commonwealth of England." "The Digger's Song" included here was not among the songs published at the time, but was discovered in the manuscript papers of William Clarke, secretary to Cromwell's Council of War. Like the other Digger songs, its authorship is uncertain, though its similarity to verses scattered in Winstanley's pamphlets has led some to credit him with writing it.

❦

A Declaration from the Poor Oppressed People of England

We whose names are subscribed, do in the name of all the poor oppressed people in England, declare unto you, that call yourselves lords of manors, and lords of the land, that in regard the King of Righteousness, our Maker, hath enlightened our hearts so far, as to see that the earth was not made purposely for you to be lords of it, and we to be your slaves, servants, and beggars; but it was made to be a common livelihood to all, without respect of persons: And that your buying and selling of land, and the fruits of it, one to another, is *the cursed thing*, and was brought in by war; which hath, and still does establish murder, and theft, in the hands of some branches of mankind over others, which is the greatest outward burden, and unrighteous power, that the creation groans under: For the power of enclosing land, and owning propriety,[1] was brought into the creation by your ancestors by the sword; which first did murder their fellow creatures, men, and after plunder or steal away their land, and left this land successively to you, their children. And therefore, though you did not kill or thieve, yet you hold that cursed thing in your hand, by the power of the sword; and so you justify the wicked deeds of your fathers; and that sin of your fathers shall be visited upon the head of you, and your children, to the third and fourth generation, and longer too, till your bloody and thieving power be rooted out of the land.

And further, in regard the King of Righteousness hath made us sensible of our burdens, and the cries and groanings of our hearts are come before him: We take it as a testimony of love from him, that our hearts begin to be freed from slavish fear of men, such as you are; and that we find resolutions in us, grounded upon the inward law of love, one towards another, to dig and plough up the commons and waste lands through England; and that our conversation shall be so unblameable, that your laws shall not reach to oppress us any longer, unless you by your laws will shed the innocent blood that runs in our veins.

For though you and your ancestors got your propriety by murder and theft, and you keep it by the same power from us, that have an equal right to the land with you, by the righteous law of creation,

yet we shall have no occasion of quarrelling (as you do) about that disturbing devil, called *particular propriety*:[2] For the earth, with all her fruits of corn, cattle, and such like, was made to be a common storehouse of livelihood to all mankind, friend and foe, without exception.

And to prevent your scrupulous objections, know this, that we must neither buy nor sell; money must not any longer (after our work of the earth's community is advanced) be the great god, that hedges in some, and hedges out others; for money is but part of the earth: And surely, the Righteous Creator, who is King, did never ordain, that unless some of mankind do bring that mineral (silver and gold) in their hands to others of their own kind, that they should neither be fed, nor be clothed; no surely, for this was the project of tyrant-flesh (which landlords are branches of) to set his image upon money. And they make this unrighteous law, that none should buy or sell, eat, or be clothed, or have any comfortable livelihood among men, unless they did bring his image stamped upon gold or silver in their hands.

And whereas the Scriptures speak that the mark of the Beast is 666, the number of a man; and that those that do not bring that mark in their hands, or in their foreheads, they should neither buy nor sell, Revel. 13:16[–18]. And seeing the numbering letters round about the English money make 666,[3] which is the number of that kingly power and glory (called a Man), and seeing the age of the Creation is now come to the image of the Beast, or half day, and seeing 666 is his mark, we expect this to be the last tyrannical power that shall reign;[4] and that people shall live freely in the enjoyment of the Earth, without bringing the mark of the Beast in

---

[1] *propriety* property, but also possessions or ownership in general. See the brief discussion by Thomas Hobbes in *Leviathan*, chapter 18, where he lists protecting propriety as the seventh power of the sovereign; and the Putney Debates.

[2] *particular propriety* private property or ownership.

[3] that is, when the letters in the Latin abbreviations on some coinage were translated (selectively) into their equivalents in Roman numerals.

[4] referring to the British monarchy, overthrown with the execution of Charles I in January 1649.

their hands, or in their promise;[1] and that they shall buy wine and milk, without money, or without price, as Isaiah speaks.[2]

For after our work of the earthly community is advanced, we must make use of gold and silver, as we do of other metals, but not to buy and sell withal; for buying and selling is the great cheat that robs and steals the earth one from another: It is that which makes some lords, other beggars, some rulers, others to be ruled; and makes great murderers and thieves to be imprisoners and hangers of little ones, or of sincere-hearted men.

And while we are made to labor the earth together, with one consent and willing mind; and while we are made free, that every one, friend and foe, shall enjoy the benefit of their creation, that is, to have food and raiment from the earth, their mother; and every one subject to give account of his thoughts, words, and actions to none, but to the one only righteous judge, and prince of peace; the spirit of righteousness that dwells, and that is now rising up to rule in every creature, and in the whole globe. We say, while we are made to hinder no man of his privileges given him in his creation, equal to one, as to another; what law then can you make, to take hold upon us, but laws of oppression and tyranny, that shall enslave or spill the blood of the innocent? And so yourselves, your judges, lawyers, and justices, shall be found to be the greatest transgressors, in, and over mankind.

But to draw nearer to declare our meaning, what we would have, and what we shall endeavour to the uttermost to obtain, as moderate and righteous reason directs us; seeing we are made to see our privileges, given us in our creation, which have hitherto been denied to us and our fathers since the power of the sword began to rule, and the secrets of the creation have been locked up under the tradi-

tional, parrot-like speaking, from the universities and colleges for scholars, and since the power of the murdering and thieving sword, formerly, as well as now of late years, hath set up a government, and maintains that government; for what are prisons, and putting others to death, but the power of the sword to enforce people to that government which was got by conquest and sword, and cannot stand of itself, but by the same murdering power? That government that is got over people by the sword and kept by the sword, is not set up by the King of Righteousness to be his law, but by covetousness, the great god of the world; who hath been permitted to reign for a time, times, and dividing of time, and his government draws to the period of the last term of his allotted time; and then the nations shall see the glory of that government that shall rule in righteousness, without either sword or spear,

And seeing, further, the power of righteousness in our hearts, seeking the livelihood of others as well as ourselves, hath drawn forth our bodies to begin to dig, and plough, in the commons and waste land, for the reasons already declared,

And seeing and finding ourselves poor, wanting food to feed upon, while we labor the earth to cast in seed, and to wait till the first crop comes up; and wanting ploughs, carts, corn, and such materials to plant the commons withal, we are willing to declare our condition to you, and to all, that have the treasury of the earth, locked up in your bags, chests, and barns, and will offer up nothing to this public treasury; but will rather see your fellow creatures starve for want of bread, that have an equal right to it with yourselves, by the law of creation: But this by the way we only declare to you, and to all that follow the subtle art of buying and selling the earth, with her fruits, merely to get the treasury thereof into their hands, to lock it up from them, to whom

---

[1] without using coins or notes, that is, without buying or selling.

[2] Isaiah 55:1.

it belongs; that so, such covetous, proud, unrighteous, selfish flesh, may be left without excuse in the day of judgment.

And therefore, the main thing we aim at, and for which we declare our resolutions to go forth, and act, is this, to lay hold upon, and as we stand in need, to cut and fell, and make the best advantage we can of the woods and trees that grow upon the commons. To be a stock for ourselves, and our poor brethren, through the land of England, to plant the commons withal; and to provide us bread to eat, till the fruit of our labors in the earth bring forth increase; and we shall meddle with none of your proprieties (but what is called commonage) till the spirit in you, make you cast up your lands and goods, which were got, and still is kept in your hands by murder, and theft; and then we shall take it from the spirit that hath conquered you, and not from our swords, which is an abominable and unrighteous power, and a destroyer of the creation: But the son of man comes not to destroy, but to save.

And we are moved to send forth this Declaration abroad, to give notice to everyone whom it concerns, in regard we hear and see, that some of you, that have been lords of manors, do cause the trees and woods that grow upon the commons, which you pretend a royalty unto, to be cut down and sold for your own private use, whereby the common land, which your own mouths do say belongs to the poor, is impoverished, and the poor oppressed people robbed of their rights, while you give them cheating words, by telling some of our poor oppressed brethren that those of us that have begun to dig and plough up the commons, will hinder the poor; and so blind their eyes, that they see not their privilege, while you, and the rich free-holders make the most profit of the commons, by your overstocking of them with sheep and cattle; and the poor that have the name to own the commons, have the least share therein; nay, they are checked by you,

if they cut wood, heath, turf, or furseys,[1] in places about the common, where you disallow.

Therefore we are resolved to be cheated no longer, nor be held under the slavish fear of you no longer, seeing the earth was made for us, as well as for you: And if the common land belongs to us who are the poor oppressed, surely the woods that grow upon the commons belong to us likewise: therefore we are resolved to try the uttermost in the light of reason, to know whether we shall be free men, or slaves. If we lie still, and let you steal away our birthrights, we perish; and if we petition we perish also, though we have paid taxes, given free quarter, and ventured our lives to preserve the nation's freedom as much as you, and therefore by the law of contract with you, freedom in the land is our portion as well as yours, equal with you: And if we strive for freedom, and your murdering, governing laws destroy us, we can but perish.

Therefore we require, and we resolve to take both common land and common woods to be a livelihood for us, and look upon you as equal with us, not above us, knowing very well that England the land of our nativity is to be a common treasury of livelihood to all, without respect of persons....

And we hope we may not doubt (at least we expect) that they that are called the great Council and powers of England, who so often have declared themselves, by promises and covenants, and confirmed them by multitude of fasting days, and devout protestations, to make England a free people, upon condition they would pay moneys, and adventure their lives against the successor of the Norman conqueror;[2] under whose oppressing power England was enslaved; and we look upon that freedom promised to be the inheritance of all, without respect of persons; and this cannot be, unless the land of England be freely set at liberty

---

[1] *furseys* furze or gorse, a kind of shrub (*OED* furzy).

[2] *the successor of the Norman conqueror* meaning King Charles I.

from proprietors, and become a common treasury to all her children, as every portion of the land of Canaan was the common livelihood of such and such a tribe, and of every member in that tribe, without exception, neither hedging in any, nor hedging out.[1]

We say we hope we need not doubt of their sincerity to us herein, and that they will not gainsay our determinate course; howsoever, their actions will prove to the view of all, either their sincerity, or hypocrisy: We know what we speak is our privilege, and our cause is righteous, and if they doubt of it, let them but send a child for us to come before them, and we shall make it manifest four ways.

First, by the National Covenant,[2] which yet stands in force to bind Parliament and people to be faithful and sincere, before the Lord God Almighty, wherein every one in his several place hath covenanted to preserve and seek the liberty each of other, without respect of persons.

Secondly, by the late victory over King Charles, we do claim this our privilege, to be quietly given us, out of the hands of tyrant-government, as our bargain and contract with them; for the Parliament promised, if we would pay taxes, and give free quarter, and adventure our lives against Charles and his party, whom they called the common enemy, they would make us a free people; these three being all done by us, as well as by themselves, we claim this our bargain, by the law of contract from them, to be a free people with them, and to have an equal privilege of common livelihood with them, they being chosen by us, but for a peculiar work, and for an appointed time, from among us, not to be our oppressing lords, but servants to succour us. But these two are our weakest proofs. And yet by them

(in the light of reason and equity that dwells in men's hearts) we shall with ease cast down, all those former enslaving Norman reiterated laws, in every King's reign since the conquest, which are as thorns in our eyes, and pricks in our sides, and which are called the ancient government of England.

Thirdly, we shall prove, that we have a free right to the land of England, being born therein as well as elder brothers, and that it is our right equal with them, and they with us, to have a comfortable livelihood in the earth, without owning any of our own kind, to be either lords or landlords over us: And this we shall prove by plain text of Scripture, without exposition upon them, which the scholars and great ones generally say, is their rule to walk by.

Fourthly, we shall prove it by the righteous law of our creation, that mankind in all his branches is the lord of the earth and ought not to be in subjection to any of his own kind without him, but to live in the light of the law of righteousness, and peace established in his heart.

And thus in love we have declared the purpose of our hearts plainly, without flattery, expecting love, and the same sincerity from you, without grumbling or quarrelling, being creatures of your own image and mould, intending no other matter herein, but to observe the law of righteous action, endeavouring to shut out of the creation the cursed thing, called *particular propriety*, which is the cause of all wars, bloodshed, theft, and enslaving laws, that hold the people under misery.

Signed for and in behalf of all the poor oppressed people of England, and the whole world.

Gerrard Winstanley [and forty-four others]
—1649

---

[1] See Numbers 34; Joshua 13–19.

[2] The Solemn League and Covenant, sworn by members of the House of Commons in September 1643, was a pledge to protect constitutional and Parliamentary liberties as well as to reform the church on Presbyterian lines.

The Diggers' Song

You noble Diggers all, stand up now, stand up
 now,
 You noble Diggers all, stand up now,
The waste land to maintain, seeing Cavaliers by
 name
Your digging does disdain, and persons all defame
5   Stand up now, stand up now.

Your houses they pull down, stand up now, stand
 up now,
 Your houses they pull down, stand up now.
Your houses they pull down to fright poor men in
 town,
But the gentry must come down, and the poor
 shall wear the crown.
10   Stand up now, Diggers all.

With spades and hoes and plows, stand up now,
 stand up now,
 With spades and hoes and plows stand up now,
Your freedom to uphold, seeing Cavaliers are bold
To kill you if they could, and rights from you to
 hold.
15   Stand up now, Diggers all.

Their self-will is their law, stand up now, stand
 up now,
 Their self-will is their law, stand up now.
Since tyranny came in they count it now no sin
To make a gaol a gin,[1] to starve poor men therein.
20   Stand up now, stand up now.

The gentry are all round, stand up now, stand up
 now,
 The gentry are all round, stand up now.
The gentry are all round, on each side they are
 found,

Their wisdom's so profound, to cheat us of our
 ground.
25   Stand up now, stand up now.

The lawyers they conjoin, stand up now, stand up
 now,
 The lawyers they conjoin, stand up now,
To arrest you they advise, such fury they devise,
The devil in them lies and hath blinded both their
 eyes.
30   Stand up now, stand up now.

The clergy they come in, stand up now, stand up
 now,
 The clergy they come in, stand up now.
The clergy they come in, and say it is a sin
That we should now begin, our freedom for to win.
35   Stand up now, Diggers all.

The tithe they yet will have, stand up now, stand
 up now,
 The tithes they yet will have, stand up now.
The tithes they yet will have, and lawyers their
 fees crave,
And this they say is brave, to make the poor their
 slave.
40   Stand up now, Diggers all.

'Gainst lawyers and gainst Priests, stand up now,
 stand up now,
 Gainst lawyers and gainst Priests stand up now.
For tyrants they are both even flat against their
 oath,
To grant us they are loath, free meat, and drink,
 and cloth.
45   Stand up now, Diggers all.

The club is all their law, stand up now, stand up
 now,
 The club is all their law, stand up now.
The club is all their law to keep men in awe,

---

[1] *gin* a snare or trap, or even an engine of torture (*OED* gin *sb*[1] 4, 5).

But they no vision saw to maintain such a law.
50   Stand up now, Diggers all.

The Cavaliers are foes, stand up now, stand up
    now,
    The Cavaliers are foes, stand up now;
The Cavaliers are foes, themselves they do disclose
By verses not in prose to please the singing boys
55   Stand up now, Diggers all.

To conquer them by love, come in now, come in
    now,
    To conquer them by love, come in now;
To conquer them by love, as it does you behove,
For he is King above, no power is like to love.
60   Glory here Diggers all.
  —CA. 1649–50

Anne Bradstreet
ca. 1612 — 1672

Born in 1612, Anne was the second of six children of Thomas and Dorothy Yorke. When she was six years old, her father became page to Lord Compton who was then steward to the fourth Earl of Lincoln, a prominent Puritan. The family moved, as a result, to Sempringham Manor in Lincolnshire, where Anne was educated by tutors and able to access the libraries of both her father and the Earl. She contracted smallpox in 1628, and was married later that year to Simon Bradstreet, son of a nonconformist minister in Lincolnshire, a fortunate union by her own account. In 1630, the Bradstreets and Dudleys set sail for New England, landing at Salem, Massachusetts. They moved immediately to Charlestown, then to Newtown, and finally settled in Ipswich for several years before moving to Andover, where Anne spent the remainder of her life. Thomas Dudley became the governor of Massachusetts colony in 1634, the same year that Anne bore the first of eight children. In 1642, she distributed her first collection of poems in manuscript form. These poems were well received, inspiring the Puritan divine Cotton Mather to describe her as "a crown to her father." Without her knowledge, Bradstreet's brother-in-law John Woodbridge published her work in England under the title *The Tenth Muse Lately Sprung up in America* (1650). In 1661, Anne had a long and serious illness, but her husband, now secretary of the colony, was required to travel to England on state business. It was during his absence that she wrote her "poetical epistles" to her husband. Her later writing consisted mainly of elegies, occasional meditations and poems of supplication in the face of illness, affliction, and the absence of her family. Bradstreet died of consumption at Andover, September 16, 1672. A second edition of her poems was published posthumously in 1678 (*Several Poems*), but her prose contemplations, meditations and additional poems, preserved by her son Simon (the Andover Manuscript) remained unpublished until 1867. Bradstreet's corpus exhibits a facility in historical, political and religious verse as well as intensity and candour in the expression of personal grief, domestic pleasure and religious faith.

❧❧❧

To My Dear Children [1]

This book by any yet unread,
I leave for you when I am dead,
That being gone, here you may find
What was your living mother's mind.
Make use of what I leave in love
And God shall bless you from above.

A.B.

My dear children,

I knowing by experience that the exhortations of parents take most effect when the speakers leave to speak, and those especially sink deepest which are spoke latest, and being ignorant whether on my death bed I shall have opportunity to speak to any of you much less to all, thought it the best whilst I was able to compose some short matters, (for what else to call them I know not) and bequeath to you, that when I am no more with you, yet I may be daily in your remembrance, (although it is the least in my aim in what I now do) but that you may gain some spiritual advantage by my experience. I have not studied in this you read to show my skill, but to declare the truth, not to set forth myself, but the glory of God. If I had minded the former it had

---

[1] This spiritual autobiography addressed to her children was found in the Andover Manuscript and remained unpublished until 1867.

been perhaps better pleasing to you, but seeing the last is the best, let it be best pleasing to you.

The method I will observe shall be this—I will begin with God's dealing with me from my childhood to this day.

In my young years about 6 or 7 as I take it I began to make conscience of my ways, and what I knew was sinful as lying, disobedience to parents, etc. I avoided it. If at any time I was overtaken with the like evils, it was a great trouble, and I could not be at rest 'till by prayer I had confessed it unto God.[1] I was also troubled at the neglect of private duties though too often tardy that way. I also found much comfort in reading the Scriptures, especially those places I thought most concerned my condition, and as I grew to have more understanding, so the more solace I took in them.

In a long fit of sickness which I had on my bed I often communed with my heart, and made my supplication to the Most High who set me free from that affliction.

But as I grew up to be about 14 or 15 I found my heart more carnal, and sitting loose from God, vanity and the follies of youth take hold of me.

About 16 the Lord laid his hand sore upon me and smote me with the smallpox. When I was in my affliction I besought the Lord, and confessed my pride and vanity and he was entreated of me, and again restored me. But I rendered not to him according to the benefit received.

After a short time I changed my condition and was married, and came into this country, where I found a new world and new manners at which my heart rose. But after I was convinced it was the way of God, I submitted to it and joined to the church at Boston.

After some time I fell into a lingering sickness like a consumption together with a lameness which correction I saw the Lord sent to humble and try

me and do me good: and it was not altogether ineffectual.

It pleased God to keep me a long time without a child which was a great grief to me, and cost me many prayers and tears before I obtained one, and after him gave me many more, of whom I now take the care, that as I have brought you into the world, and with great pains, weakness, cares and fears brought you to this, I now travail in birth again of you till Christ be formed in you.

Among all my experiences of God's gracious dealings with me I have constantly observed this that he hath never suffered me long to sit loose from him, but by one affliction or other hath made me look home, and search what was amiss. So usually thus it hath been with me that I have no sooner felt my heart out of order, but I have expected correction for it, which most commonly hath been upon my own person, in sickness, weakness, pains, sometimes on my soul in doubts and fears of God's displeasure, and my sincerity towards him. Sometimes he hath smote a child with sickness, sometimes chastened by losses in estate, and these times (through his great mercy) have been the times of my greatest getting and advantage; yea I have found them the times when the Lord hath manifested the most love to me. Then have I gone to searching, and have said with David, "Lord search me and try me, see what ways of wickedness are in me, and lead me in the way everlasting":[2] and seldom or never but I have found either some sin I lay under which God would have reformed, or some duty neglected which he would have performed, and by his help I have laid vows and bonds upon my soul to perform his righteous commands.

If at any time you are chastened of God take it as thankfully and joyfully as in greatest mercies, for if ye be his ye shall reap the greatest benefit by it: It hath been no small support to me in times of

---

[1] *with the like evils* Harvard edition; the Twayne edition reads "with the evils."

[2] *Lord search me...way everlasting* Psalm 139:23-24.

darkness when the Almighty hath hid his face from me, that yet I have had abundance of sweetness and refreshment after affliction and more circumspection in my walking after I have been afflicted.[1] I have been with God like an untoward child, that no longer than the rod has been on my back (or at least in sight) but I have been apt to forget him and myself too. Before I was afflicted I went astray, but now I keep thy statutes.

I have had great experience of God's hearing my prayers, and returning comfortable answers to me, either in granting the thing I prayed for, or else in satisfying my mind without it, and I have been confident it hath been from him, because I have found my heart through his goodness enlarged in thankfulness to him.

I have often been perplexed that I have not found that constant joy in my pilgrimage and refreshing which I supposed most of the servants of God have, although he hath not left me altogether without the witness of his Holy Spirit who hath oft given me his word and set to his seal that it shall be well with me. I have sometimes tasted of that hidden manna that the world knows not, and have set up my Ebenezer and have resolved with myself that against such a promise, such tastes of sweetness the gates of hell shall never prevail:[2] yet have I many times sinkings and droopings, and not enjoyed that felicity that sometimes I have done. But when I have been in darkness and seen no light, yet have I

desired to stay myself upon the Lord, and when I have been in sickness and pain, I have thought if the Lord would but lift up the light of his countenance upon me, although he ground me to powder it would be but light to me; yea oft have I thought were I in hell itself and could there find the love of God toward me, it would be a heaven and could I have been in heaven without the love of God, it would have been a hell to me for in truth it is the absence and presence of God that makes heaven or hell.[3]

Many times hath Satan troubled me concerning the verity of the Scriptures, many times by atheism how I could know whether there was a God; I never saw any miracles to confirm me, and those which I read of how did [I] know but they were feigned. That there is a God my reason would soon tell me by the wondrous works that I see, the vast frame of the heaven and the earth, the order of all things night and day, summer and winter, spring and autumn, the daily providing for this great household upon the earth, the preserving and directing of all to its proper end. The consideration of these things would with amazement certainly resolve me that there is an Eternal Being. But how should I know he is such a God as I worship in Trinity, and such a Saviour as I rely upon. Though this hath thousands of times been suggested to me, yet God hath helped me over. I have argued thus with myself, that there is a God I see. If ever this God hath revealed himself it must be in his word, and this must be it or none. Have I not found that operation by it that no human invention can work upon the soul, hath no judgments befallen diverse who have scorned and contemned it, hath it not been preserved through all ages maugre all the heathen tyrants and all of the enemies who have opposed it? Is there any story but that which shows the beginnings of times, and how the world came to

---

[1] *hid his face* "But your iniquities have separated between you and your God, and your sins have hid his face from you, that he will not hear" (Isaiah 59:2). "For he hath not despised nor abhorred the affliction of the afflicted; neither hath he hid his face from him; but when he cried unto him, he heard" (Psalm 22:21).

[2] *hidden manna* "He that has an ear, let him hear what the Spirit saith unto the churches; To him that overcometh will I give to eat of the hidden manna...." (Revelation 2:17); *set up my Ebenezer* "Then Samuel took a stone, and set it between Mizpeh and Shen, and called the name of it Ebenezer, saying, Hitherto hath the Lord helped us" (I Samuel 7:12); *gates of hell* "And I say unto thee, that thou art Peter, and upon this rock I shall build my church: and the gates of hell shall not prevail against it" (Matthew 16:18).

[3] *were I in hell itself* Harvard edition; the Twayne edition reads: "were it hell itself."

be as we see? Do we not know the prophecies in it fulfilled which could not have been so long foretold by any but God himself?

When I have got over this block then have I another put in my way, that admit this be the true God whom we worship, and that be his word, yet why may not the Popish religion be the right. They have the same God, the same Christ, the same word. They only interpret it one way we another.

This hath sometimes stuck with me, and more it would, but the vain fooleries that are in their religion together with their lying miracles, and cruel persecutions of the saints, which admit were they as they term them yet not so to be dealt withal.

The consideration of these things and many the like would soon turn me to my own religion again.

But some new troubles I have had since the world has been filled with blasphemy, and sectaries, and some who havest been accounted sincere Christians have been carried away with them, that sometimes I have said, "Is there faith upon the earth?" and I have not known what to think. But then I have remembered the words of Christ that so it must be, and that if it were possible the very elect should be deceived.[1] "Behold," saith our Saviour, "I have told you before." That hath stayed my heart, and I can now say, "Return O my soul to thy rest, upon this rock Christ Jesus will I build my faith, and if I perish, I perish." But I know all the powers of hell shall never prevail against it. I know whom I have trusted, and whom I have believed and that he is able to keep that I have committed to his charge.[2]

Now to the King immortal, eternal invisible, the only wise God, be honour and glory for ever and ever,[3]

Amen.

This was written in much sickness and weakness, and is very weakly and imperfectly done, but if you can pick any benefit out of it, it is the mark which I aimed at.

—1867

---

[1] *words of Christ…be deceived* "For there shall arise false Christs, and false prophets, and shall shew great signs and wonders; insomuch that, if it were possible, they shall deceive the very elect" (Matthew 24:24; see also Mark 13:22).

[2] *I know whom…committed to his charge* II Timothy 1:12.

[3] *Now to the King…for ever and ever* I Timothy 1:17.

Jeremy Taylor
1613 — 1667

The son of a Cambridge barber, Taylor was educated at Perse School and Gonville and Caius College, Cambridge, taking holy orders in 1633 and his M.A. the year following. His eloquence as a substitute preacher at St. Paul's attracted the attention of Archbishop William Laud, who sent Taylor to Oxford, where he was made a fellow of All Souls College. He was chaplain to Laud and Charles I in the late 1630s, and served as chaplain to the King's household in Oxford during the first half of the 1640s (shortly before he was executed, Charles I sent Taylor a watch and some jewels). During a visit to Wales in 1645, he was captured and imprisoned by Parliamentary forces; upon his release he remained in Wales, living with the Earl of Carbery at his estate of Golden Grove in Carmarthenshire. It was during his years at Golden Grove that Taylor produced much of his most important work, including *Holy Living* (1650) and *Holy Dying* (1651), as well as many sermons. In 1655 Taylor was arrested once more and briefly imprisoned, for reasons that remain unclear. Two years later he was presented, at the suggestion of John Evelyn, with a lectureship in Lisburn in Ireland, where he would spend much of the remainder of his life; after the Restoration he was made Bishop of Down and Connor, and subsequently of Dromore, though his pleas for an English bishopric went unheeded. His other works include an argument for toleration, *A Discourse of the Liberty of Prophesying* (1647); a life of Christ, *The Great Exemplar* (1649); *XXVIII Sermons Preached at Golden Grove* (1651); and *XXV Sermons* (1653).

For other meditations on death (a subject of both the funeral sermon for Lady Carbery and *Holy Dying*), see the selections from John Donne's *Devotions*; for the social role of women and issues connected with childbirth (both touched on in the funeral sermon), see the selections from *The Gentlewoman's Companion* and Elizabeth Clinton.

❧❧❧

A Funeral Sermon, Preached at the Obsequies of the Right Honourable and Most Virtuous Lady The Lady Frances, Countess of Carbery[1]

For we must needs die, and are as water spilt on the ground, which cannot be gathered up again; neither doth God respect any person; yet doth he devise means that his banished be not expelled from him.
II Sam. 14:14.

When our blessed Saviour and his disciples viewed the temple, some one amongst them cried out, *Magister aspice, quales lapides,* "Master, behold what fair, what great stones are here!" Christ made no other reply but foretold their dissolution, and a world of sadness and sorrow which should bury that whole nation, when the teeming cloud of God's displeasure should produce a storm which was the daughter of the biggest anger, and the mother of the greatest calamity which ever crushed any of the sons of Adam, "The time shall come that there shall not be left one stone upon another."[2] The whole temple and the religion, the ceremonies ordained by God, and the nation beloved by God, and the fabric erected for the service of God, shall run to their own period, and lie down in their

---

[1] Frances, Countess Carbery (d. 1650) and her husband, Richard Vaughan, second Earl of Carbery (ca. 1600–1686), were Taylor's patrons during the decade he spent in Wales.

[2] Mark 13:1–2. The Latin is from the Vulgate; the English translations are likely Taylor's own.

several graves. Whatsoever had a beginning can also have an ending, and it shall die, unless it be daily watered with the purls flowing from the fountain of life,[1] and refreshed with the dew of heaven, and the wells of God. And therefore God had provided a tree in paradise to have supported Adam in his artificial immortality: immortality was not in his nature, but in the hands and arts, in the favour and superadditions of God. Man was always the same mixture of heat and cold, of dryness and moisture; ever the same weak thing, apt to feel rebellion in the humours, and to suffer the evils of a civil war in his body natural: and therefore health and life was to descend upon him from heaven, and he was to suck life from a tree on earth; himself being but ingraffed into a tree of life, and adopted into the condition of an immortal nature: but he that in the best of his days was but a scion of this tree of life,[2] by his sin was cut off from thence quickly, and planted upon thorns, and his portion was for ever after among the flowers, which today spring and look like health and beauty, and in the evening they are sick, and at night are dead, and the oven is their grave. And as before, even from our first spring from the dust on earth, we might have died if we had not been preserved by the continual flux of a rare providence; so now that we are reduced to the laws of our own nature, "we must needs die." It is natural, and therefore necessary: it is become a punishment to us, and therefore it is unavoidable; and God hath bound the evil upon us by bands of natural and inseparable propriety, and by a supervening unalterable decree of heaven; and we are fallen from our privilege, and are returned to the condition of beasts, and buildings, and common things. And we see temples defiled unto the ground, and they die by sacrilege; and great empires die by their own

plenty and ease, full humours, and factious subjects; and huge buildings fall by their own weight, and the violence of many winters eating and consuming the cement, which is the marrow of their bones; and princes die like the meanest of their servants; and every thing finds a grave and a tomb; and the very tomb itself dies by the bigness of its pompousness and luxury,

> ——— *Phario nutantia pondera saxo*
> *Quæ cineri vanus dat ruitura labor* [3]

and becomes as friable and uncombined dust as the ashes of the sinner or the saint that lay under it, and is now forgotten in his bed of darkness. And to this catalogue of mortality man is enrolled with a *statutum est*, "it is appointed for all men once to die, and after death comes judgment." And if a man can be stronger than nature, or can wrestle with a decree of heaven, or can escape from a divine punishment by his own arts, so that neither the power nor the providence of God, nor the laws of nature, nor the bands of eternal predestination can hold him, then he may live beyond the fate and period of flesh, and last longer than a flower: but if all these can hold us and tie us to conditions, then we must lay our heads down upon a turf, and entertain creeping things in the cells and little chambers of our eyes, and dwell with worms till time and death shall be no more. "We must needs die," that's our sentence: but that's not all;—

"We are as water spilt on the ground, which cannot be gathered up again." Stay,

1. We are as water, weak, and of no consistence, always descending, abiding in no certain place, unless where we are detained with violence; and every little breath of wind makes us rough and tempestuous, and troubles our faces; every trifling accident discomposes us; and as the face of the

---

[1] *purls* small streams (*OED* purl *sb*[2] 1).

[2] *scion* a shoot of a plant cut for grafting or planting; by extension, a young descendant, usually of a noble family (*OED* scion 1, 2). The literal and metaphoric meanings both apply here.

[3] Martial, *Epigrams*, 1.88: "masses of Parian stone, gifts of vain labor doomed to fall."

waters wafting in a storm so wrinkles itself that it makes upon its forehead furrows deep and hollow like a grave; so do our great and little cares and trifles first make the wrinkles of old age, and then they dig a grave for us: and there is in nature nothing so contemptible, but it may meet with us in such circumstances, that it may be too hard for us in our weaknesses; and the sting of a bee is a weapon sharp enough to pierce the finger of a child or the lip of a man; and those creatures which nature hath left without weapons, yet they are armed sufficiently to vex those parts of men which are left defenceless and obnoxious to a sunbeam, to the roughness of a sour grape, to the unevenness of a gravelstone, to the dust of a wheel, or the unwholesome breath of a star looking awry upon a sinner.

2. But besides the weaknesses and natural decayings of our bodies, if chances and contingencies be innumerable, then no man can reckon our dangers, and the preternatural causes of our death; so that he is a vain person whose hopes of life are too confidently increased by reason of his health: and he is too unreasonably timorous, who thinks his hopes at an end when he dwells in sickness. For men die without rule, and with and without occasions; and no man suspecting or foreseeing any of death's addresses, and no man in his whole condition is weaker than another. A man in a long consumption is fallen under one of the solemnities and preparations to death: but at the same instant the most healthful person is as near death, upon a more fatal and a more sudden, but a less discerned cause. There are but few persons upon whose foreheads every man can read the sentence of death written in the lines of a lingering sickness, but they (sometimes) hear the passing-bell ring for stronger men, even long before their own knell calls at the house of their mother to open her womb, and make a bed for them....There are sicknesses that walk in darkness, and there are exterminating angels that fly wrapt up in the curtains of immateriality and an uncommunicating nature; whom we cannot see, but we feel their force and sink under their sword, and from heaven the veil descends that wraps our heads in the fatal sentence. There is no age of man but it hath proper to itself some posterns and outlets for death, besides those infinite and open ports out of which myriads of men and women every day pass into the dark, and the land of forgetfulness. Infancy hath life but *in effigie*,[1] or like a spark dwelling in a pile of wood: the candle is so newly lighted, that every little shaking of the taper, and every ruder breath of air puts it out, and it dies. Childhood is so tender, and yet so unwary; so soft to all the impressions of chance, and yet so forward to run into them, that God knew there could be no security without the care and vigilance of an angel-keeper: and the eyes of parents and the arms of nurses, the provisions of art, and all the effects of human love and providence, are not sufficient to keep one child from horrid mischiefs, from strange and early calamities and deaths, unless a messenger be sent from heaven to stand sentinel, and watch the very playings and sleepings, the eatings and drinkings of the children; and it is a long time before nature makes them capable of help: for there are many deaths, and very many diseases to which poor babes are exposed; but they have but very few capacities of physic: to show that infancy is as liable to death as old age, and equally exposed to danger, and equally incapable of a remedy: with this only difference, that old age hath diseases incurable by nature, and the diseases of childhood are incurable by art: and both the states are the next heirs of death.

3. But all the middle way the case is altered: nature is strong, and art is apt to give ease and remedy, but still there is no security; and there the case is not altered. 1) For there are so many diseases in men that are not understood. 2) So many new ones every year. 3) The old ones are so changed in

---

[1] That is, infancy has but the form or likeness of life.

circumstance, and intermingled with so many collateral complications. 4) The symptoms are oftentimes so alike. 5) Sometimes so hidden and fallacious. 6) Sometimes none at all; as in the most sudden and most dangerous imposthumations.[1] 7) And then, the diseases in the inward parts of the body are oftentimes such to which no application can be made. 8) They are so far off, that the effects of all medicines can no otherwise come to them, than the effect and juices of all meats; that is, not till after two or three alterations and decoctions, which change the very species of the medicament. 9) And after all this, very many principles in the art of physic are so uncertain, that after they have been believed seven or eight ages, and that upon them much of the practice hath been established, they come to be considered by a witty man, and others established in their stead; by which men must practise, and by which three or four generations of men more (as happens) must live or die. 10) And all this while the men are sick, and they take things that certainly make them sicker for the present, and very uncertainly restore health for the future: that it may appear of what a large extent is human calamity, when God's providence hath not only made it weak and miserable upon the certain stock of a various nature, and upon the accidents of an infinite contingency; but even from the remedies which are appointed, our dangers and our troubles are certainly increased: so that we may well be likened to water; our nature is no stronger, our abode no more certain; if the sluices be opened, "it falls away and runneth apace" [Psalm 58:7]; if its current be stopped, it swells and grows troublesome, and spills over with a great diffusion; if it be made to stand still it putrefies: and all this we do. For,

4. In all the process of our health we are running to our grave: we open our own sluices by viciousness and unworthy actions; we pour in drink, and let out life; we increase diseases, and know not how to bear them; we strangle ourselves with our own intemperance; we suffer the fevers and the inflammations of lust, and we quench our souls with drunkenness; we bury our understandings in loads of meat and surfeits: and then we lie down upon our beds, and roar with pain and disquietness of our souls: nay, we kill one another's souls and bodies with violence and folly, with the effects of pride and uncharitableness; we live and die like fools, and bring a new mortality upon ourselves; wars and vexatious cares, and private duels and public disorders, and every thing that is unreasonable, and every thing that is violent: so that now we may add this fourth gate to the grave: besides nature—and chance—and the mistakes of art—men die with their own sins, and then enter into the grave in haste and passion, and pull the heavy stone of the monument upon their own heads. And thus we make ourselves like water spilt on the ground; we throw away our lives as if they were unprofitable (and indeed most men make them so), we let our years slip through our fingers like water; and nothing is to be seen, but like a shower of tears upon a spot of ground; there is a grave digged, and a solemn mourning, and a great talk in the neighbourhood, and when the days are finished, they shall be, and they shall be remembered no more: and that's like water too, when it is spilt, "it cannot be gathered up again."

There is no redemption from the grave.

> ———inter se mortales mutua vivunt,
> Et quasi cursores vitai lampada tradunt.[2]

Men live in their course and by turns; their light burns a while, and then it burns blue and faint, and men go to converse with spirits, and then they reach the taper to another; and as the hours of yesterday

---

[1] *imposthumations* swellings or abscesses on the body (*OED*).

[2] Lucretius, *De rerum natura*, II.76, 79: "mortal creatures live dependent one upon another, and like runners pass on the torch of life."

can never return again, so neither can the man whose hours they were, and who lived them over once, he shall never come to live them again, and live them better....

This consideration I intend to you as a severe monitor and an advice of carefulness, that you order your affairs so that you may be partakers of the first resurrection; that is, from sin to grace, from the death of vicious habits to the vigour, life, and efficacy of an habitual righteousness. For..."Blessed are they that have part in the first resurrection, upon them the second death shall have no power" [Revelation 20:6]: meaning that they who by the power of Christ and his holy spirit were raised to life again, were holy and blessed souls, and such who were written in the book of God; and that this grace happened to no wicked and vicious person: so it is most true in the spiritual and intended sense: you only that serve God in a holy life; you who are not dead in trespasses and sins; you who serve God with an early diligence and an unwearied industry, and a holy religion, you and you only shall come to life eternal, you only shall be called from death to life; the rest of mankind shall never live again, but pass from death to death; from one death to another, to a worse; from the death of the body to the eternal death of body and soul. And therefore in the apostles' creed there is no mention made of the resurrection of wicked persons, but of "the resurrection of the body to everlasting life."[1] The wicked indeed shall be haled forth from their graves, from their everlasting prisons, where in chains of darkness they are kept unto the judgment of the great day: but this therefore cannot be called *in sensu favoris* [in the best or true sense] "a resurrection," but the solemnities of the eternal death; it is nothing but a new capacity of dying again; such a dying as cannot signify rest; but where death means nothing but an intolerable and never-ceasing calam-

ity: and therefore these words of my text are otherwise to be understood of the wicked, otherwise of the godly: the wicked are spilt like water and shall never be gathered up again; no, not in the gatherings of eternity; they shall be put into vessels of wrath and set upon the flames of hell; but that is not a gathering but a scattering from the face and presence of God. But the godly also come under the sense of these words: they descend into their graves, and shall no more be reckoned among the living; they have no concernment in all that is done under the sun. Agamemnon hath no more to do with the Turks' armies invading and possessing that part of Greece where he reigned,[2] than had the hippocentaur who never had a being:[3] and Cicero hath no more interest in the present evils of Christendom, than we have to do with his boasted discovery of Catiline's conspiracy.[4] What is it to me that Rome was taken by the Gauls? and what is it now to Camillus if different religions be tolerated amongst us?[5] These things that now happen concern the living, and they are made the scenes of our duty or danger respectively: and when our wives are dead and sleep in charnel-houses, they are not troubled when we laugh loudly at the songs sung at the next marriage-feast; nor do they envy when another snatches away the gleanings of their husbands' passion.

It is true, they envy not, and they lie in a bosom where there can be no murmur; and they that are consigned to kingdoms, and to the feast of the marriage-supper of the Lamb, the glorious and eternal Bridegroom of holy souls, they cannot think our marriages here, our lighter laughings and vain

---

[1] *apostles' creed* a fourth-century statement of faith included in the Anglican liturgy.

[2] *Agamemnon* in Homer, the King of Mycenae and commander of the Greek army against Troy.

[3] *hippocentaur* centaur; a creature part man, part horse.

[4] Cicero made his "boasted discovery" in his oration *On Catiline*.

[5] *Camillus* the saviour of Rome after the Gallic invasion (387/6 B.C.E.).

rejoicings, considerable as to them. And yet there is a relation continued still: Aristotle said that to affirm the dead take no thought for the good of the living, is a disparagement to the laws of that friendship which in their state of separation they cannot be tempted to rescind.[1] And the church hath taught in general that they pray for us, they recommend to God the state of all their relatives, in the union of the intercession that our blessed Lord makes for them and us; and S. Ambrose gave some things in charge to his dying brother Satyrus, that he should do for him in the other world: he gave it him, I say, when he was dying, not when he was dead. And certain it is that though our dead friends' affection to us is not to be estimated according to our low conceptions, yet it is not less, but much more than ever it was; it is greater in degree, and of another kind.

But then we should do well also to remember that in this world we are something besides flesh and blood; that we may not without violent necessities run into new relations, but preserve the affections we bore to our dead when they were alive. We must not so live as if they were perished, but so as pressing forward to the most intimate participation of the communion of saints. And we also have some ways to express this relation, and to bear a part in this communion, by actions of intercourse with them, and yet proper to our state: such as are, strictly performing the will of the dead, providing for, and tenderly and wisely educating their children, paying their debts, imitating their good example, preserving their memories privately, and publicly keeping their memorials, and desiring of God with hearty and constant prayer that God would give them a joyful resurrection, and a merciful judgment (for so S. Paul prayed in behalf of Onesiphorus), that "God would show them mercy in that day" [II Timothy 1:18], that fearful, and yet much to be desired day, in which the most righteous person hath need of much mercy and pity, and shall find it. Now these instances of duty show that the relation remains still; and though the relict of a man or woman hath liberty to contract new relations,[2] yet I do not find they have liberty to cast off the old, as if there were no such thing as immortality of souls. Remember that we shall converse together again; let us therefore never do any thing of reference to them which we shall be ashamed of in the day when all secrets shall be discovered, and that we shall meet again in the presence of God: in the mean time, God watcheth concerning all their interest, and he will in his time both discover and recompense. For though, as to us, they are like water spilt; yet to God they are as water fallen into the sea, safe and united in his comprehension and inclosures.

But we are not yet past the consideration of the sentence. This descending to the grave is the lot of all men, "neither doth God respect the person of any man"; the rich is not protected for favour, nor the poor for pity, the old man is not reverenced for his age, nor the infant regarded for his tenderness; youth and beauty, learning and prudence, wit and strength, lie down equally in the dishonours of the grave. All men, and all natures, and all persons resist the addresses and solemnities of death, and strive to preserve a miserable and unpleasant life; and yet they all sink down and die. For so have I seen the pillars of a building assisted with artificial props bending under the pressure of a roof, and pertinaciously resisting the infallible and prepared ruin,

Donec longa dies omni compage soluta
Ipsum cum rebus subruat auxilium,[3]

---

[2] *relict* widow or widower (*OED* relict *sb* 2).

[3] Maximianus, *Elegies*, I.173–74: "right then long time destroys our careful efforts, brings down the building with the props we fashioned."

---

[1] *Nicomachean Ethics*, 1.11.

till the determined day comes, and then the burden sunk upon the pillars, and disordered the aids and auxiliary rafters into a common ruin and a ruder grave: so are the desires and weak arts of man; with little aids and assistances of care and physic we strive to support our decaying bodies, and to put off the evil day; but quickly that day will come, and then neither angels nor men can rescue us from our grave; but the roof sinks down upon the walls, and the walls descend to the foundation; and the beauty of the face, and the dishonours of the belly, the discerning head and the servile feet, the thinking heart and the working hand, the eyes and the guts together shall be crushed into the confusion of a heap, and dwell with creatures of an equivocal production, with worms and serpents, the sons and daughters of our own bones, in a house of dirt and darkness.

.   .   .   .

I have now done with my text, but yet am to make you another sermon. I have told you the necessity and the state of death, it may be, too largely for such a sad story; I shall therefore now with a better *compendium* teach you how to live,[1] by telling you a plain narrative of a life, which if you imitate, and write after the copy, it will make that death shall not be an evil, but a thing to be desired, and to be reckoned amongst the purchases and advantages of your fortune. When Martha and Mary went to weep over the grave of their brother, Christ met them there, and preached a funeral sermon, discoursing of the resurrection, and applying to the purposes of faith, and confession of Christ, and glorification of God [John 11:17–27]. We have no other, we can have no better precedent to follow: and now that we are come to weep over the grave of our dear sister, this rare personage, we

cannot choose but have many virtues to learn, many to imitate, and some to exercise.

1. I chose, not to declare her extraction and genealogy; it was indeed fair and honourable; but having the blessing to be descended from worthy and honoured ancestors, and herself to be adopted and ingraffed into a more noble family; yet she felt such outward appendages to be none of hers, because not of her choice, but the purchase of the virtues of others, which although they did engage her to do noble things, yet they would upbraid all degenerate and less honourable lives than were those which began and increased the honour of the families. She did not love her fortune for making her noble; but thought it would be a dishonour to her if she did not continue a nobleness and excellency of virtue fit to be owned by persons relating to such ancestors. It is fit for us all to honour the nobleness of a family: but it is also fit for them that are noble to despise it, and to establish their honour upon the foundation of doing excellent things, and suffering in good causes, and despising dishonourable actions, and in communicating good things to others. For this is the rule in nature; those creatures are most honourable which have the greatest power, and do the greatest good: and accordingly myself have been a witness of it, how this excellent lady would by an act of humility and Christian abstraction strip herself of all that fair appendage and exterior honour which decked her person and her fortune, and desired to be owned by nothing but what was her own, that she might only be esteemed honourable according to that which is the honour of a Christian and a wise person.

2. She had a strict and severe education, and it was one of God's graces and favours to her: for being the heiress of a great fortune, and living amongst the throng of persons in the sight of vanities and empty temptations, that is, in that part of the kingdom where greatness is too often expressed in great follies and great vices, God had

---

[1] *compendium*   an abbreviation, perhaps also with the Latin implication of a saving or profit (*OED*).

provided a severe and angry education to chastise the forwardness of a young spirit and a fair fortune, that she might for ever be so far distant from a vice, that she might only see it and loathe it, but never taste of it, so much as to be put to her choice whether she be virtuous or no. God, intending to secure this soul to himself, would not suffer the follies of the world to seize upon her by way of too near a trial or busy temptation.

3. She was married young; and besides her business of religion, seemed to be ordained in the providence of God to bring to this honourable family a part of a fair fortune, and to leave behind her a fairer issue, worth ten thousand times her portion: and as if this had been all the public business of her life, when she had so far served God's ends, God in mercy would also serve hers, and take her to an early blessedness.

4. In passing through which line of providence, she had the art to secure her eternal interest, by turning her condition into duty, and expressing her duty in the greatest eminency of a virtuous, prudent, and rare affection, that hath been known in any example. I will not give her so low a testimony, as to say only that she was chaste; she was a person of that severity, modesty, and close religion, as to that particular, that she was not capable of uncivil temptation; and you might as well have suspected the sun to smell of the poppy that he looks on, as that she could have been a person apt to be sullied by the breath of a foul question.

5. But that which I shall note in her, is that which I would have exemplar to all ladies, and to all women: she had a love so great for her lord, so entirely given up to a dear affection, that she thought the same things, and loved the same loves, and hated according to the same enmities, and breathed in his soul, and lived in his presence, and languished in his absence; and all that she was or did, was only for and to her dearest lord:

Si gaudet, si flet, si tacet, hunc loquitur;
Cœnat, propinat, poscit, negat, innuit; unus
Nævius est;—— [1]

And although this was a great enamel to the beauty of her soul, yet it might in some degrees be also a reward to the virtue of her lord: for she would often discourse it to them that conversed with her, that he would improve that interest which he had in her affection to the advantages of God and of religion; and she would delight to say, that he called her to her devotions, he encouraged her good inclinations, he directed her piety, he invited her with good books; and then she loved religion, which she saw was not only pleasing to God, and an act or state of duty, but pleasing to her lord, and an act also of affection and conjugal obedience; and what at first she loved the more forwardly for his sake, in the using of religion, left such relishes upon her spirit, that she found in it amiability enough to make her love it for its own. So God usually brings us to him by instruments of nature and affections, and then incorporates us into his inheritance by the more immediate relishes of heaven, and the secret things of the Spirit. He only was (under God) the light of her eyes, and the cordial of her spirits, and the guide of her actions, and the measure of her affections, till her affections swelled up into a religion, and then it could go no higher, but was confederate with those other duties which made her dear to God: which rare combination of duty and religion I choose to express in the words of Solomon, "She forsook not the guide of her youth, nor brake the covenant of her God" [Proverbs 2:17].

6. As she was a rare wife, so she was an excellent mother: for in so tender a constitution of spirit as hers was, and in so great a kindness towards her

---

[1] Martial, *Epigrams*, 1.6: "if glad, if fearful, if mute, of her he speaks. He dines, drinks healths, asks, denies, or nods: Naevia is everything."

children, there hath seldom been seen a stricter and more curious care of their persons, their deportment, their nature, their disposition, their learning, and their customs: and if ever kindness and care did contest, and make parties in her, yet her care and her severity was ever victorious; and she knew not how to do an ill turn to their severer part, by her more tender and forward kindness. And as her custom was, she turned this also into love to her lord: for she was not only diligent to have them bred nobly and religiously, but also was careful and solicitous that they should be taught to observe all the circumstances and inclinations, the desires and wishes of their father; as thinking that virtue to have no good circumstances, which was not dressed by his copy, and ruled by his lines, and his affections. And her prudence in the managing her children was so singular and rare, that whenever you mean to bless this family, and pray a hearty and a profitable prayer for it, beg of God that the children may have those excellent things which she designed to them, and provided for them in her heart and wishes, that they may live by her purposes, and may grow thither whither she would fain have brought them. All these were great parts of an excellent religion, as they concerned her greatest temporal relations.

7. But if we examine how she demeaned herself towards God, there also you will find her not of a common, but of an exemplar piety. She was a great reader of Scripture, confining herself to great portions every day; which she read not to the purposes of vanity and impertinent curiosities, not to seem knowing or to become talking, not to expound and rule; but to teach her all her duty, to instruct her in the knowledge and love of God and of her neighbours; to make her more humble, and to teach her to despise the world and all its gilded vanities; and that she might entertain passions wholly in design and order to heaven. I have seen a female religion that wholly dwelt upon the face and tongue; that like a wanton and an undressed tree spends all its juice in suckers and irregular branches, in leaves and gum, and after all such goodly outsides you should never eat an apple, or be delighted with the beauties or the perfumes of a hopeful blossom. But the religion of this excellent lady was of another constitution; it took root downward in humility, and brought forth fruit upward in the substantial graces of a Christian, in charity and justice, in chastity and modesty, in fair friendships and sweetness of society. She had not very much of the forms and outsides of godliness, but she was hugely careful for the power of it, for the moral, essential, and useful parts; such which would make her be, not seem to be, religious.

8. She was a very constant person at her prayers, and spent all her time which nature did permit to her choice, in her devotions, and reading and meditating, and the necessary offices of household government; every one of which is an action of religion, some by nature, some by adoption. To these also God gave her a very great love to hear the word of God preached; in which because I had sometimes the honour to minister to her, I can give this certain testimony, that she was a diligent, watchful, and attentive hearer: and to this had so excellent a judgment, that if ever I saw a woman whose judgment was to be revered, it was hers alone: and I have sometimes thought that the eminency of her discerning faculties did reward a pious discourse, and placed it in the regions of honour and usefulness, and gathered it up from the ground, where commonly such homilies are spilt, or scattered in neglect and inconsideration. But her appetite was not soon satisfied with what was useful to her soul: she was also a constant reader of sermons, and seldom missed to read one every day; and that she might be full of instruction and holy principles, she had lately designed to have a large book, in which she purposed to have a stock of religion transcribed in such assistances as she would choose, that she might be "readily furnished and

instructed to every good work."[1] But God prevented that, and hath filled her desires, not out of cisterns and little aqueducts, but hath carried her to the fountain, where she "drinks of the pleasure of the river" [Psalm 36:8] and is full of God.

9. She always lived a life of much innocence, free from the violences of great sins: her person, her breeding, her modesty, her honour, her religion, her early marriage, the guide of her soul, and the guide of her youth, were as so many fountains of restraining grace to her, to keep her from the dishonours of a crime. *Bonum est portare jugum ab adolescentia*, "it is good to bear the yoke of the Lord from our youth" [Lamentations 3:27]; and though she did so, being guarded by a mighty providence, and a great favour and grace of God from staining her fair soul with the spots of hell, yet she had strange fears and early cares upon her, but these were not only for herself, but in order to others, to her nearest relatives. For she was so great a lover of this honourable family of which now she was a mother, that she desired to become a channel of great blessings to it unto future ages, and was extremely jealous lest any thing should be done, or lest any thing had been done, though an age or two since, which should entail a curse upon the innocent posterity; and therefore (although I do not know that ever she was tempted with an offer of the crime) yet she did infinitely remove all sacrilege from her thoughts, and delighted to see her estate of a clear and disentangled interest: she would have no mingled rights with it; she would not receive any thing from the church, but religion and a blessing: and she never thought a curse and a sin far enough off, but would desire it to be infinitely distant; and that as to this family God had given much honour and a wise head to govern it, so he would also for ever give many more blessings: and because she knew the sins of parents descend upon children, she endeavoured

by justice and religion, by charity and honour to secure that her channel should convey nothing but health, and a fair example and a blessing.

10. And though her accounts to God was made up of nothing but small parcels, little passions, and angry words, and trifling discontents, which are the allays of the piety of the most holy persons; yet she was early at her repentance; and toward the latter end of her days, grew so fast in religion, as if she had had a revelation of her approaching end, and therefore that she must go a great way in a little time: her discourses more full of religion, her prayers more frequent, her charity increasing, her forgiveness more forward, her friendships more communicative, her passion more under discipline; and so she trimmed her lamp, not thinking her night was so near, but that it might shine also in the daytime, in the temple, and before the altar of incense.

But in this course of hers, there were some circumstances, and some appendages of substance, which were highly remarkable.

1. In all her religion, and in all her actions of relation towards God, she had a strange evenness and untroubled passage, sliding toward her ocean of God and of infinity with a certain and silent motion. So have I seen a river deep and smooth passing with a still foot and a sober face, and paying to the *fiscus*,[2] the great exchequer of the sea, the prince of all the watery bodies, a tribute large and full: and hard by it a little brook skipping and making a noise upon its unequal and neighbour bottom: and after all its talking and bragged motion, it paid to its common audit no more than the revenues of a little cloud, or a contemptible vessel. So have I sometimes compared the issues of her religion to the solemnities and famed outsides of another's piety; it dwelt upon her spirit, and was incorporated with

---

[1] II Timothy 3:17. The "large book" would have had blank pages for manuscript transcription of passages from other texts.

[2] *fiscus* state treasury (Latin).

the periodical work of every day; she did not believe that religion was intended to minister to fame and reputation, but to pardon of sins, to the pleasures of God, and the salvation of souls. For religion is like the breath of heaven; if it goes abroad into the open air, it scatters and dissolves like camphor: but if it enters into a secret hollowness, into a close conveyance, it is strong and mighty, and comes forth with vigour and great effect at the other end, at the other side of this life, in the days of death and judgment.

2. The other appendage of her religion, which also was a great ornament to all the parts of her life, was a rare modesty and humility of spirit, a confident despising and undervaluing of herself. For though she had the greatest judgment, and the greatest experience of things and persons that I ever yet knew in a person of her youth, and sex, and circumstances; yet as if she knew nothing of it, she had the meanest opinion of herself; and like a fair taper, when she shined to all the room, yet round about her own station she had cast a shadow and a cloud, and she shined to everybody but herself. But the perfectness of her prudence and excellent parts could not be hid; and all her humility and arts of concealment, made the virtues more amiable and illustrious. For as pride sullies the beauty of the fairest virtues, and makes our understanding but like the craft and learning of a devil: so humility is the greatest eminency and art of publication in the whole world; and she in all her arts of secrecy and hiding her worthy things, was but "like one that hideth the wind, and covers the ointment of her right hand" [Proverbs 27:16].

I know not by what instrument it happened; but when death drew near, before it made any show upon her body or revealed itself by a natural signification, it was conveyed to her spirit: she had a strange secret persuasion that the bringing this child should be her last scene of life: and we have known, that the soul when she is about to disrobe herself of her upper garment, sometimes speaks rarely,

Magnifica verba mors prope admota excutit;[1]

sometimes it is prophetical; sometimes God by a superinduced persuasion wrought by instruments or accidents of his own, serves the ends of his own providence and the salvation of the soul. But so it was, that the thought of death dwelt long with her, and grew from the first steps of fancy and fear, to a consent, from thence to a strange credulity and expectation of it; and without the violence of sickness she died, as if she had done it voluntarily, and by design, and for fear her expectation should have been deceived, or that she should seem to have had an unreasonable fear, or apprehension; or rather (as one said of Cato) *sic abiit e vita ut causam moriendi nactam se esse gauderet,* "she died, as if she had been glad of the opportunity."[2]

And in this I cannot but adore the providence, and admire the wisdom and infinite mercies of God. For having a tender and soft, a delicate and fine constitution and breeding, she was tender to pain, and apprehensive of it, as a child's shoulder is of a load and burden. *Grave est teneræ cervici jugum:*[3] and in her often discourses of death, which she would renew willingly and frequently, she would tell, that she feared not death, but she feared the sharp pains of death. *Emori nolo, me esse mortuam non curo;*[4] the being dead, and being freed from the troubles and dangers of this world, she hoped would be for her advantage, and therefore that was no part of her fear: but she believing the pangs of death were great, and the use and aids of reason little, had reason to fear lest they should do violence to her spirit and the decency of her resolution. But God, that knew her fears and her jealousy

[1] Seneca, *Troades,* 1.575: "when death draws near it drives out boastful words."

[2] Cicero, *Tusculan Disputations,* 1.30.74.

[3] Seneca, *On Providence,* IV.7: "to the tender neck the yoke is heavy."

[4] Cicero, *Tusculan Disputations,* 1.8.15 (quoting Epicharmus): "Dying I shun; of being dead I nothing reck."

concerning herself, fitted her with a death so easy, so harmless, so painless, that it did not put her patience to a severe trial. It was not (in all appearance) of so much trouble as two fits of a common ague; so careful was God to remonstrate to all that stood in that sad attendance that this soul was dear to him: and that since she had done so much of her duty towards it, he that began would also finish her redemption, by an act of a rare providence, and a singular mercy. Blessed be that goodness of God, who does so careful actions of mercy for the ease and security of his servants. But this one instance was a great demonstration that the apprehension of death is worse than the pains of death; and that God loves to reprove the unreasonableness of our fears, by the mightiness, and by the arts of his mercy.

She had in her sickness (if I may so call it, or rather in the solemnities and graver preparations towards death) some curious and well-becoming fears, concerning the final state of her soul: but from thence she passed into a *deliquium*, or a kind of trance, and as soon as she came forth of it, as if it had been a vision, or that she had conversed with an angel, and from his hand had received a label or scroll of the book of life, and there seen her name enrolled, she cried out aloud, "Glory be to God on high; now I am sure I shall be saved." Concerning which manner of discoursing we are wholly ignorant what judgment can be made: but certainly there are strange things in the other world; and so there are in all the immediate preparations to it; and a little glimpse of heaven, a minute's conversing with an angel, any ray of God, any communication extraordinary from the Spirit of comfort, which God gives to his servants in strange and unknown manners, are infinitely far from illusions; and they shall then be understood by us, when we feel them, and when our new and strange needs shall be refreshed by such unusual visitations.

But I must be forced to use summaries and arts of abbreviature in the enumerating those things in which this rare personage was dear to God and to all her relatives.

If we consider her person, she was in the flower of her age,

Jucundum quum ætas florida ver ageret; [1]

of a temperate, plain and natural diet, without curiosity or an intemperate palate; she spent less time in dressing than many servants; her recreations were little and seldom, her prayers often, her reading much: she was of a most noble and charitable soul; a great lover of honourable actions, and as great a despiser of base things; hugely loving to oblige others, and very unwilling to be in arrear to any upon the stock of courtesies and liberality; so free in all acts of favour, that she would not stay to hear herself thanked, as being unwilling that what good went from her to a needful or an obliged person should ever return to her again; she was an excellent friend, and hugely dear to very many, especially to the best and most discerning persons; to all that conversed with her, and could understand her great worth and sweetness: she was of an honourable, a nice, and tender reputation; and of the pleasures of this world, which were laid before her in heaps, she took a very small and inconsiderable share, as not loving to glut herself with vanity, or take her portion of good things here below.

If we look on her as a wife, she was chaste and loving, fruitful and discreet, humble and pleasant, witty and compliant, rich and fair; and wanted nothing to the making her a principal and precedent to the best wives of the world, but a long life, and a full age.

If we remember her as a mother, she was kind and severe, careful and prudent, very tender, and

---

[1] Catullus 68, 1. 16: "when my youth in its flower was keeping jocund spring-time."

not at all fond, a greater lover of her children's souls than of their bodies, and one that would value them more by the strict rules of honour and proper worth, than by their relation to herself.

Her servants found her prudent, and fit to govern, and yet open-handed, and apt to reward; a just exactor of their duty, and a great rewarder of their diligence.

She was in her house a comfort to her dearest lord, a guide to her children, a rule to her servants, an example to all.

But as she related to God in the offices of religion, she was even and constant, silent and devout, prudent and material; she loved what she now enjoys, and she feared what she never felt, and God did for her what she never did expect: her fears went beyond all her evil; and yet the good which she hath received was, and is, and ever shall be beyond all her hopes.

She lived as we all should live and she died as I fain would die;

> *Et cum supremos Lachesis perneverit annos,*
> *Non aliter cineres mando jacere meos.*[1]

I pray God I may feel those mercies on my death-bed that she felt, and that I may feel the same effect of my repentance which she feels of the many degrees of her innocence. Such was her death, that she did not die too soon; and her life was so useful and so excellent, that she could not have lived too long. *Nemo parum diu vixit qui virtutis perfectæ perfecto functus et munere.*[2] And as now in the grave it shall not be enquired concerning her, how long she lived, but how well; so to us who live after her, to suffer a longer calamity, it may be some ease to our sorrows, and some guide to our lives, and some security to our conditions, to consider that God

hath brought the piety of a young lady to the early rewards of a never ceasing and never dying eternity of glory. And we also, if we live as she did, shall partake of the same glories; not only having the honour of a good name, and a dear and honoured memory, but the glories of these glories, the end of all excellent labours, and all prudent counsels, and all holy religion, even the salvation of our souls in that day when all the saints, and amongst them this excellent woman, shall be shown to all the world to have done more, and more excellent things than we know of or can describe. *Mors illos consecrat, quorum exitum et qui timent, laudant,* "death consecrates and makes sacred that person whose excellency was such, that they that are not displeased at the death, and cannot dispraise the life; but they that mourn sadly, think they can never commend sufficiently."[3]

—1650

Holy Living and *Holy Dying*
(excerpts)

The Rule and Exercises of Holy Living

CHAP. I.
Consideration of the general instruments, and means serving to a holy life: by way of introduction

It is necessary that every man should consider, that since God hath given him an excellent nature, wisdom and choice, an understanding soul, and an immortal spirit, having made him Lord over the beasts, and but a little lower than the angels; he hath also appointed for him a work and a service great enough to employ those abilities, and hath also designed him to a state of life after this, to which he can only arrive by that service and obedi-

---

[1] Martial, *Epigrams*, 1.88: "when Lachesis shall spin my last years out, I charge that my ashes lie thus and not otherwise."

[2] Cicero, *Tusculan Disputations*, 1.45.109: "No one has lived too short a life who has discharged the perfect work of perfect virtue."

[3] Seneca, *On Providence*, 2; more literally, "death consecrates those whose end even those who fear must praise."

ence. And therefore as every man is wholly God's own portion by the title of creation: so all our labours and care, all our powers and faculties must be wholly employed in the service of God, even all the days of our life, that this life being ended, we may live with him for ever.

Neither is it sufficient that we think of the service of God as a work of the least necessity, or of small employment; but that it be done by us as God intended it; that it be done with great earnestness and passion, with much zeal and desire: that we refuse no labour, that we bestow upon it much time, that we use the best guides, and arrive at the end of glory by all the ways of grace, of prudence and religion.

And indeed if we consider how much of our lives is taken up by the needs of nature, how many years are wholly spent before we come to any use of reason, how many years more before that reason is useful to us to any great purposes, how imperfect our discourse is made by our evil education, false principles, ill company, bad examples, and want of experience; how many parts of our wisest and best years are spent in eating and sleeping, in necessary businesses, and unnecessary vanities, in worldly civilities, and less useful circumstances, in the learning arts and sciences, languages or trades; that little portion of hours that is left for the practises of piety and religious walking with God, is so short and trifling, that were not the goodness of God infinitely great, it might seen unreasonable or impossible for us to expect of him eternal joys in heaven, even after the well spending those few minutes which are left for God, and God's service, after we have served ourselves, and our own occasions.

And yet it is considerable, that the fruit which comes from the many days of recreation and vanity is very little, and although we scatter much, yet we gather but little profit: but from the few hours we spend in prayer and the exercises of a pious life, the return is great and profitable; and what we sow in the minutes and spare portions of a few years, grows up to crowns and sceptres in a happy and a glorious eternity.

1. Therefore, although it cannot be enjoined, that the greatest part of our time be spent in the direct actions of devotion and religion, yet it will become, not only a duty, but also a great providence to lay aside for the services of God, and the businesses of the Spirit as much as we can: because God rewards our minutes with long and eternal happinesses; and the greater portion of our time we give to God, the more we treasure up for ourselves; and *No man is a better merchant than he that lays out his time upon God, and his money upon the poor.*

2. Only it becomes us to remember and to adore God's goodness for it, that God hath not only permitted us to serve the necessities of our nature, but hath made them to become parts of our duty; that if we by directing these actions to the glory of God intend them as instruments to continue our persons in his service, he by adopting them into religion may turn our nature into grace, and accept our natural actions, as actions of religion. God is pleased to esteem it for a part of his service, if we eat or drink; so it be done temperately, and as may best preserve our health, that our health may enable our services towards him: And there is no one minute of our lives (after we are come to the use of reason) but we are, or may be doing the work of God, even then when we most of all serve ourselves.

3. To which if we add, that in these and all other actions of our lives we always stand before God, acting, and speaking and thinking in his presence, and that it matters not that our conscience is sealed with secrecy, since it lies open to God, it will concern us to behave ourselves carefully, as in the presence of our judge.

These three considerations rightly managed, and applied to the several parts and instances of our lives, will be like Elisha stretched upon the child [1

Kings 17:17–22], apt to put life and quickness into every part of it, and to make us live the life of grace, and do the work of God.

. . . .

—1650

The Rule and Exercises of Holy Dying

CHAP. 2
*A general preparation towards a holy and blessed death,
by way of exercise*

SECT. 1
*Three precepts preparatory to a holy death
to be practised in our whole life*

1. *He that would die well must always look for death, every day knocking at the gates of the grave,*[1] and then the gates of the grave shall never prevail upon him to do him mischief. This was the advice of all the wise and good men of the world; who especially in the days and periods of their joy and festival egressions chose to throw some ashes into their chalices,[2] some sober remembrances of their fatal period. Such was the black shirt of Saladine, the tombstone presented to the Emperor of Constantinople on his Coronation day; the Bishop of Rome's two reeds with flax and wax taper, the Egyptian skeleton served up at feasts,[3] and Trimalchio's banquet in Petronius,[4] in which was brought in the image of a dead man's bones of silver with spondiles exactly turning to every of the guests,[5] and saying to everyone, that you, and you must die, and look not one upon another, for everyone is equally concerned in this sad representment. These in phantastic semblances declare a severe counsel and useful meditation; and it is not easy for a man to be gay in his imagination, or to be drunk with joy or wine, pride or revenge, who considers sadly that he must ere long dwell in a house of darkness and dishonour, and his body must be the inheritance of worms, and his soul must be what he pleases, even as a man makes it here by his living good or bad. I have read of a young hermit who being passionately in love with a young lady could not by all the arts of religion and mortification suppress the trouble of that fancy, till at last being told that she was dead and had been buried about fourteen days, he went secretly to her vault, and with the skirt of his mantle wiped the moisture from the carcase, and still at the return of his temptation laid it before him, saying, Behold this is the beauty of the woman thou didst so much desire; and so the man found his cure.[6] And if we make death as present to us, our own death, dwelling and dressed in all its pomp of fancy and proper circumstances, if anything will quench the heats of lust, or the desires of money, or the greedy passionate affections of this world, this must do it. But withall, the frequent use of this meditation, by curing our present inordinations will make death safe and friendly, and by its very custom will make that the King of terrors shall come to us without his affrighting dresses; and that we shall sit down in the grave as we compose ourselves to sleep, and do the duties of nature and choice. The old people that lived near the Riphæan mountains, were taught to converse with death, and to handle it on all sides and to discourse of it, as of a thing that will

---

[1] Taylor cites Seneca, Epistle CI.8, 10: "Begin at once to live, and count each separate day as a separate life" and "a day differs not a whit from eternity"; and Martial, *Epigrams*, IV.liv.3–4: "If thou art wise, use to the full, Collinus, all thy days, and ever deem that each day is thy last."

[2] *egressions* processions.

[3] *Saladine…Egyptian skeleton* Taylor's source for these four allusions to the use of objects as reminders of death (the *memento mori* tradition) was Philipp Camerarius, *The Walking Library*, trans. (from Latin) by John Molle (1621 and later eds.), I.xii.35–36.

[4] Trimalchio's banquet is in Petronius, *Satyricon*, 34.

[5] *spondiles* vertebrae (*OED* spondyle).

[6] Taylor's source for this story remains unidentified.

certainly come, and ought so to do.[1] Thence their minds and resolutions became capable of death, and they thought it a dishonourable thing, with greediness to keep a life that must go from us, to lay aside its thorns, and to return again circled with a glory and a diadem.

2. *He that would die well must all the days of his life lay up against the day of death*,[2] not only by the general provisions of holiness and a pious life indefinitely, but, provisions proper to the necessities of that great day of expense, in which a man is to throw his last cast for an eternity of joys or sorrows; ever remembering, that this alone well performed is not enough to pass us into Paradise, but that alone done foolishly is enough to send us to hell; and the want of either a holy life, or death, makes a man to fall short of the mighty price of our high calling. In order to this rule we are to consider what special graces we shall then need to exercise, and by the proper arts of the Spirit, by a heap of proportioned arguments, by prayers, and a great treasure of devotion laid up in Heaven, provide before hand a reserve of strength and mercy. Men in the course of their lives walk lazily and incuriously as if they had both their feet in one shoe, and when they are passively revolved to the time of their dissolution they have no mercies in store, no patience, no faith, no charity to God, or despite of the world, being without gust or appetite for the land of their inheritance, which Christ with so much pain and blood had purchased for them. When we come to die indeed, we shall be very much put to it to stand firm upon the two feet of a Christian, *faith* and *patience*. When we ourselves are to use the articles, to turn our former discourses into present practise, and to feel what we never felt before, we shall find

it to be quite another thing to be willing presently to quit this life, and all our present possessions for the hopes of a thing which we were never suffered to see, and such a thing of which we may fail so many ways, and of which if we fail anyway we are miserable forever. Then we shall find how much we have need to have secured the Spirit of God, and the grace of faith by an habitual, perfect unmovable resolution. The same also is the case of patience, which will be assaulted with sharp pains, disturbed fancies, great fears, want of a present mind, natural weaknesses, frauds of the Devil, and a thousand accidents and imperfections. It concerns us therefore highly in the whole course of our lives, not only to accustom ourselves to a patient suffering of injuries and affronts, of persecutions and losses, of cross accidents and unnecessary circumstances; but also by representing death as present to us, to consider with what arguments then to fortify our patience; and by assiduous and fervent prayer to God, all our life long call upon God to give us patience, and great assistances, a strong faith and a confirmed hope, the Spirit of God, and his Holy angels' assistants at that time, to resist and to subdue the devil's temptations and assaults; and so to fortify our hearts that it break not into intolerable sorrows and impatience, and end in wretchlessness and infidelity.[3] But this is to be the work of our life, and not to be done at once; but as God gives us time by succession, by parts and little periods. For it is very remarkable that God who giveth plenteously to all creatures, he hath scattered the firmament with stars as a man sows corn in his fields, in a multitude bigger than the capacities of humane order; he hath made so much variety of creatures, and gives us great choice of meats and drinks, although any one of both kinds would have served our needs; and so in all instances of nature; yet in the distribution of our time, God seems to be strait-

---

[1] Taylor cites Lucan, *Pharsalia*, I.458–62. In classical writing, the Riphæan mountains were a mythical range north of the known parts of Europe.

[2] Taylor cites Seneca, Epistle CI.8: "one who daily puts the finishing touches to his life is never in want of time."

[3] *wretchlessness* recklessness (*OED*).

handed, and gives it to us, not as nature gives us rivers, enough to drown us, but drop by drop, minute after minute, so that we never can have two minutes together, but he takes away one when he gives us another. This should teach us to value our time, since God so values it, and by his so small distribution of it, tells us, it is the most precious thing we have. Since therefore in the day of our death, we can have but still the same little portion of this precious time, let us in every minute of our life, I mean, in every discernable portion lay up such a stock of reason and good works, that they may convey a value to the imperfect and shorter actions of our death-bed; while God rewards the piety of our lives by his gracious acceptation and benediction, upon the actions preparatory to our death-bed.

3. *He that desires to die well and happily, above all things must be careful, that he do not live a soft, a delicate and voluptuous life*; but a life severe, holy, and under the discipline of the cross; under the conduct of prudence and observation, a life of warfare and sober counsels, labour and watchfulness. No man wants cause of tears and a daily sorrow. Let every man consider what he feels and acknowledge his misery; let him confess his sin and chastise it; let him bear his cross patiently, and his persecutions nobly, and his repentances willingly and constantly; let him pity the evils of all the world, and bear his share of the calamities of his brother; let him long and sigh for the joys of Heaven; let him tremble and fear because he hath deserved the pains of hell; let him commute his eternal fear with a temporal suffering, preventing God's judgement by passing one of his own; let him groan for the labours of his pilgrimage, and the dangers of his warfare; and by that time he hath summed up all these labours; and duties, and contingencies, all the proper causes, instruments and acts of sorrow, he will find, that for a secular joy and wantonness of spirit, there are not left many

void spaces of his life. It was Saint James's advice; "Be afflicted, and mourn, and weep; let your laughter be turned into mourning, and your joy into weeping" [James 4:9]: And Bonaventure in the life of Christ, reports that the H. Virgin Mother said to S. Elizabeth, "That Grace does not descend into the soul of a man but by prayer and by affliction."[1] Certain it is, that a mourning spirit, and an afflicted body are great instruments of reconciling God to a sinner, and they always dwell at the gates of atonement and restitution. But besides this; a delicate and prosperous life is hugely contrary to the hopes of a blessed eternity. "Woe be to them that are at ease in Sion" [Amos 6:1]; so it was said of old; and our B. Lord said, "Woe be to you that laugh, for you shall weep" [Luke 6:25]: but "Blessed are they that mourn, for they shall be comforted" [Matthew 5:4]. Here or hereafter we must have our portion of sorrows. *He that now goeth on his way weeping and beareth forth good seed with him, shall doubtless come again with joy, and bring his sheaves with him* [Psalm 126:6]. And certainly , he that sadly considers the portion of Dives [Luke 16:19–31], and remembers that the account which Abraham gave him for the unavoidableness of his torment, was because he had *his good things in this life*, must in all reason, with trembling run from a course of banquets, and *faring deliciously every day*, as being a dangerous estate, and a consignation to an evil greater than all danger, the pains and torment of unhappy souls. If either by patience or repentance, by compassion or persecution, by choice or by conformity, by severity or discipline, we allay the festival follies of a soft life, and profess under the cross of Christ, we shall more willingly and more safely enter into our grave: But the death-bed of a voluptuous man upbraids his little and cozening prosperities, and exacts pains made sharper by the passing from soft beds, and a softer mind. *He that would die holily and happily,*

---

[1] St. Bonaventure, *Meditationes vitae Christi*, sect. 3.

must in this world love tears, humility, solitude and repentance.[1]

SECT. 2
Of daily examination of our actions, in the whole course of our health, preparatory to our death-bed

He that will die well and happily, must dress his soul by a diligent and frequent scrutiny: He must perfectly understand, and watch the state of his soul; he must set his house in order before he be fit to die. And for this there is great reason, and great necessity.

Reasons for a daily examination

1. For if we consider the disorders of every day, the multitude of impertinent words, the great portions of time spent in vanity, the daily omissions of duty, the coldness of our prayers, the indifference of our spirit in holy things, the uncertainty of our secret purposes, our infinite deceptions and hypocrisies, sometimes not known, very often not observed by ourselves; our want of charity, our not knowing in how many degrees of action and purpose every virtue is to be exercised, the secret adherencies of pride, and too forward complacency in our best actions, our failings in all our relations, the niceties of difference between some virtues and some vices, the secret indiscernible passages from lawful to unlawful in the first instances of change, the perpetual mistakings of permissions for duty, and licentious practises for permissions, our daily abusing the liberty that God gives us, our unsuspected sins in the managing a course of life certainly lawful, our little greedinesses in eating, our surprises in the proportions of our drinkings, our too great freedoms and fondnesses in lawful loves, our aptness for things sensual, and our deadness and tediousness of spirit in spiritual employments, besides infinite

variety of cases of conscience that do occur in the life of every man, and in all intercourses of every life, and that the productions of sin are numerous and increasing, like the families of the Northern people, or the genealogies of the first patriarchs of the world; from all this we shall find that the computations of a man's life are busy as the table of sines and tangents, and intricate as the accounts of eastern merchants: and therefore it were but reason we should sum up our accounts at the foot of every page, I mean, that we call ourselves to scrutiny every night when we compose ourselves to the little images of death.

2. For if we make but one general account, and never reckon till we die, either we shall only reckon by great sums, and remember nothing but clamorous and crying sins, and never consider concerning particulars, or forget very many; or if we could consider all that we ought, we must needs be confounded with the multitude and variety. But if we observe all the little passages of our life, and reduce them into the order of accounts and accusations, we shall find them multiply so fast, that it will not only appear to be an ease to the accounts of our death-bed, but by the instrument of shame will restrain the inundation of evils; it being a thing intolerable to humane modesty to see sins increase so fast, and virtues grow up so slow; to see every day stained with the spots of leprosy, or sprinkled with the marks of a lesser evil.

3. It is not intended, we should take accounts of our lives only to be thought religious, but that we may see our evil and amend it, that we dash our sins against the stones, that we may go to God, and to a spiritual guide, and search for remedies and apply them. And indeed no man can well observe his own growth in grace, but by accounting seldomer returns of sin, and a more frequent victory over temptations; concerning which every man makes his observations according as he makes his inquiries and search after himself: In order to this it was that

---

[1] Taylor cites Lucan, *Pharsalia*, VIII.21–23.

Saint Paul wrote; before receiving the Holy Sacrament "Let a man examine himself, and so let him eat" [I Corinthians 11:28]. This precept was given in those days when they communicated every day,[1] and therefore *a daily examination* also was intended.

4. And it will appear highly fitting, if we remember that at the day of judgement, not only the greatest lines of life, but every branch and circumstance of every action, every word, and thought shall be called to scrutiny and severe judgement; insomuch that it was a great truth which one said; "Woe be to the most innocent life if God should search into it, without mixtures of mercy."[2] And therefore we are here to follow S. Paul's advice; "Judge yourselves and you shall not be judged of the Lord" [I Corinthians 11:31]. The way to prevent God's anger is to be angry with ourselves, and by examining our actions and condemning the criminal, by being assessors in God's tribunal, at least we shall obtain the favour of the court. *As therefore,*

every night we must make our bed the memorial of our grave, so let our evening thoughts be an image of the days of judgement.

5. This advice was so reasonable and proper an instrument of virtue, that it was taught even to the scholars of Pythagoras by their master. "Let not sleep seize upon the regions of your senses, before you have three times recalled the conversation and accidents of the day":[3] Examine what you have committed against the Divine Law, what you have omitted of your duty, and in what you have made use of the Divine Grace to the purposes of virtue and religion, *joining the Judge reason to the legislative mind or conscience*, that God may reign there as a law-giver and a judge. Then Christ's kingdom is set up in our hearts; then we always live in the eye of our judge, and live by the measures of reason, religion, and sober counsels.

—1651

---

[1] *communicated* received communion.

[2] St. Augustine, *Confessions*, IX.xiii.34.

[3] Taylor cites Hierocles, *Commentarius in aurea carmina.*

Samuel Butler
1613 – 1680

Little is known of Samuel Butler's life. The son of a Worcestershire farmer and clerk, he was educated at King's School, Worcester, and according to one source proceeded to Cambridge, although no records of his matriculation have been found. Butler worked as a clerk in various households including that of one of Cromwell's generals, Sir Samuel Luke, on whom the figure of Hudibras may be based. His first publication, when he was forty-seven, was an anonymous tract supporting the Stuart cause. In 1661 Butler held a stewardship to Richard Vaughan, Earl of Carbery, at Ludlow Castle, but he held this position only briefly. In December 1661 the first part of *Hudibras* was published and Butler achieved instant fame. The poem delighted the court, but apparently little was done to help Butler financially. The second part of *Hudibras* was printed a year later, and the third section was introduced at the end of 1677. Butler's financial position appears to have deteriorated after he resigned his post at Ludlow, and Charles did little to alleviate his situation until 1677 when Butler was finally awarded a pension, three years before he died of consumption.

❧❧❧

A Romance-Writer [1]

Pulls down old histories to build them up finer again, after a new model of his own designing. He takes away all the lights of truth in history to make it the fitter tutoress of life; for Truth herself has little or nothing to do in the affairs of the world, although all matters of the greatest weight and moment are pretended and done in her name, like a weak princess that has only the title, and falsehood all the power. He observes one very fit decorum in dating his histories in the days of old and putting all his own inventions upon ancient times; for when the world was younger, it might perhaps love and fight, and do generous things at the rate he describes them; but since it is grown old, all these heroic feats are laid by and utterly given over, nor ever like to come in fashion again; and therefore all his images of those virtues signify no more than the statues upon dead men's tombs, that will never make them live again. He is like one of Homer's gods, that sets men together by the ears and fetches them off again how he pleases; brings armies into the field like Janello's leaden soldiers; [2] leads up both sides himself, and gives the victory to which he pleases, according as he finds it fit the design of his story; makes love and lovers too, brings them acquainted, and appoints meetings when and where he pleases, and at the same time betrays them in the height of all their felicity to miserable captivity, or some other horrid calamity; for which he makes them rail at the gods and curse their own innocent stars when he only has done them all the injury; makes men villains, compels them to act all barbarous inhumanities by his own directions, and after inflicts the cruellest punishments upon them for it. He makes all his knights fight in fortifications, and storm one another's armor before they can come to encounter body for body, and always matches them so equally one with

---

[1] The following two works of prose are extracts from Butler's *Characters*, a work in which he represents numerous human types. For other examples, see the selections from the Overburian Character, Felltham, Earle, and Breton.

[2] *Janello* Butler's first editor, Robert Thyer, writes "this alludes to some Kind of Puppet-Performance in those Times, as I find the name Janello, in another imperfect piece of Butler's introduced as belonging to a famous Operator in that Art." Thyer's edition was first published in 1759.

another that it is a whole page before they can guess which is likely to have the better; and he that has it is so mangled that it had been better for them both to have parted fair at first; but when they encounter with those that are no knights, though ever so well armed and mounted, ten to one goes for nothing. As for the ladies, they are every one the most beautiful in the whole world, and that's the reason why no one of them, nor all together with all their charms, have power to tempt away any knight from another. He differs from a just historian as a joiner does from a carpenter; the one does things plainly and substantially for use, and the other carves and polishes merely for show and ornament.[1]

—1759 (CA. 1667-69)

A Rabble

Is a congregation or assembly of the States-general[2] sent from their several and respective shops, stalls, and garrets. They are full of controversy, and every one of a several judgment concerning the business under present consideration, whether it be mountebank, show, hanging, or ballad-singer. They meet, like Democritus's[3] atoms, *in vacuo*,[4] and by a fortuitous jostling together produce the greatest and most savage beast in the whole world; for though the members of it may have something of human nature while they are asunder, when they are put together they have none at all, as a multitude of several sounds make one great noise unlike all the rest, in which no one particular is distinguished. They are a great dunghill where all sorts of dirty and nasty humours meet, stink, and ferment, for all the parts are in a perpetual tumult. 'Tis no wonder they make strange Churches, for they take naturally to any imposture, and have a great antipathy to truth and order as being contrary to their original confusion. They are a herd of swine possessed with a dry devil that run after hanging instead of drowning. Once a month they go on pilgrimage to the gallows, to visit the sepulchres of their ancestors, as the Turks do once a week. When they come there they sing psalms, quarrel, and return full of satisfaction and narrative. When they break loose they are like a public ruin, in which the highest parts lie undermost, and make the noblest fabrics heaps of rubbish. They are like the sea, that's stirred into a tumult with every blast of wind that blows upon it, till it become a watery Apennine, and heap mountain billows upon one another, as once the giants did in the war with heaven. A crowd is their proper element, in which they make their way with their shoulders as pigs creep through hedges. Nothing in the world delights them so much as the ruin of great persons or any calamity in which they have no share, though they get nothing by it. They love nothing but themselves in the likeness of one another, and, like sheep, run all that way the first goes, especially if it be against their governors, whom they have a natural disaffection to.

—1759 (CA. 1667-69)

---

[1] *joiner* a worker in wood who does lighter and more ornamental work than that of a carpenter, as the construction of the furniture and fittings of a house or ship (*OED* joiner *sb* 2).

[2] *States-general* a legislative assembly representing the three estates, viz. clergy, nobles and commons or burghers of a whole realm, principality, or commonwealth (*OED*).

[3] *Democritus* (ca. 460–ca. 370 B.C.E.) Greek philosopher who taught of the atom and its relation to the world.

[4] *in vacuo* in a vacuum.

Margaret Fell
1614 – 1702

Born in Marsh Grange, Lancashire, to John Askew and Margaret Pyper, Margaret Fell was to become the most prominent female Quaker of the seventeenth century. In 1632, she married the barrister Thomas Fell of Swarthmore Hall, near Ulverston, by whom she had nine children. Thomas Fell later served as a Member of Parliament for Lancashire. While her husband was in London in 1652, Fell received George Fox into her home, not an uncommon event, for she often opened her house to religious persons. However, in this instance, Fox converted Fell, her children and many of her servants to Quakerism during his stay. On his return, Thomas Fell accommodated his wife's beliefs, though he never converted to Quakerism. Swarthmore Hall was to become the centre of Quakerism for the next thirty-eight years, and Margaret Fell one of its staunchest defenders.

After her conversion, Fell vigorously advocated liberty of conscience in matters of religion in a series of pamphlets published over a forty-year period. She wrote to both Oliver Cromwell and Charles II to protest the persecution of the Quakers. In response to her pleas, Charles II agreed to let the Quakers have their liberty, but despite his promise, they were "hardly used, and taken up at their meetings generally, even until many prisons throughout the nation was filled with them." (Fell's brief autobiography, from which this quotation is taken, is published in *A Brief Collection of Remarkable Passages* [London, 1710].) In 1663, five years after her husband's death, Fell was called before the magistrates at Ulverston for permitting illegal meetings at Swarthmore Hall. Upon refusing the oath of allegiance, she was committed to prison at Lancaster Castle. She remained imprisoned until 1668 because she refused to agree to any stipulation preventing Quaker meetings at Swarthmore Hall. During her imprisonment at Lancaster Castle, Fell wrote *Women's Speaking Justified* (1666), a judicious and thorough defence of a woman's right to speak in church. Her treatise should be read in light of the Quaker call for women's public ministry which, as Trevett reminds us, "encompassed not just preaching, prophecy and other overtly 'religious' activity, but also any witnessing to the faith, be it in the home, the marketplace or workplace, in the steeple-house, the law-courts and the prison" (Christine Trevett, *Women and Quakerism in the 17th Century* [York: The Ebor P, 1995], 58).

In 1669, Fell married George Fox. The happiness of their union was short-lived as Fell was imprisoned in Lancaster Castle early in 1670 and not released until the following year. When not visiting the imprisoned, sharing brief interludes with George Fox, or arranging interviews with royalty, Fell resided at Swarthmore for the remainder of her life and continued to be fined for permitting Quaker meetings to be held in her home. She outlived her second husband by eleven years, dying at Swarthmore in 1702.

☙☙

Women's Speaking Justified, Proved, and Allowed of by the Scriptures [1]

Whereas it has been an objection in the minds of many, and several times hath been objected by the clergy, or ministers, and others, against women's speaking in the church; and so consequently may be taken, that they are condemned for meddling in the things of God; the ground of which objection, is taken from the Apostle's words, which he writ in his First Epistle to the Corinthians, chap. 14. vers. 34, 35.[2] And also what he writ to Timothy in the First Epistle, chap. 2 vers. 11, 12. But how far they wrong the Apostle's intentions in these Scriptures, we shall show clearly when we come to them in their course and order. But first let me lay down how God himself hath manifested his will and mind concerning women, and unto women.

And first, when *God created man in his own image: in the image of God created he them, male and female: And God blessed them, and God said unto them, Be fruitful, and multiply: And God said, Behold I have given you of every herb*, etc. Gen. 1.[3] Here God joins them together in his own image, and makes no such distinctions and differences as men do; for though they be weak, he is strong; and as he said to the Apostle, His *grace is sufficient*, and his *strength is made manifest in weakness*, II Cor. 12:9. And such has the Lord chosen, even *the weak things of the world, to confound the things which are mighty;*

and *things which are despised, hath God chosen, to bring to nought things that are*, I Cor. 1.[4] And God hath put no such difference between the male and female as men would make.

It is true, *The serpent that was more subtle than any other beast of the field*, came unto the woman, with his temptations, and with a lie: his subtlety discerning her to be more inclinable to hearken to him, when he said, *If ye eat, your eyes shall be opened*: and the woman saw that *the fruit was good to make one wise*: there the temptation got into her, and *she did eat, and gave to her husband, and he did eat* also, and so they were both tempted into the transgression and disobedience; and therefore God said unto Adam, when that he hid himself when he heard his voice, *Hast thou eaten of the tree which I commanded thee that thou shouldest not eat?* And Adam said, *The woman which thou gavest me, she gave me of the tree, and I did eat. And the Lord said unto the woman, What is this that thou hast done?* And the woman said, *The serpent beguiled me, and I did eat*. Here the woman spoke the truth unto the Lord. See what the Lord saith, vers. 15. after he had pronounced sentence on the serpent: *I will put enmity between thee and the woman, and between thy seed and her seed; it shall bruise thy head, and thou shalt bruise his heel*, Gen. 3.[5]

Let this word of the Lord, which was from the beginning, stop the mouths of all that oppose women's speaking in the power of the Lord; for he hath put enmity between the woman and the serpent; and if the seed of the woman speak not, the seed of the serpent speaks; for God hath put enmity between the two seeds, and it is manifest, that those that speak against the woman and her seed's speaking, speak out of the enmity of the old serpent's

---

[1] This treatise was first published in 1666. The present text is taken from the 1667 edition.

[2] *the Apostle's words* The Apostle Paul writes, "Let your women keep silence in the churches: for it is not permitted unto them to speak; but they are commanded to be under obedience, as also saith the law. And if they will learn any thing, let them ask their husbands at home: for it is a shame for women to speak in the church" (I Corinthians 14:34–35). "Let the woman learn in silence with all subjection. But I suffer not a woman to teach, nor to usurp authority over the man, but to be in silence" (I Timothy 2:11–12).

[3] Genesis 1:27–29.

[4] I Corinthians 1:27–28.

[5] Genesis 3:1, 5, 6, 11–13, 15.

seed;[1] and God hath fulfilled his word and his promise, *When the fullness of time was come, he hath sent forth his Son, made of a woman, made under the law, that we might receive the adoption of sons,* Gal. 4:4, 5.

Moreover, the Lord is pleased, when he mentions his church, to call her by the name of woman, by his prophets, saying, I *have called thee as a woman forsaken, and grieved in spirit, and as a wife of youth,* Isa. 54.[2] Again, *How long wilt thou go about, thou backsliding daughter? For the Lord hath created a new thing in the earth, a woman shall compass a man,* Jer. 31:22. And David, when he was speaking of Christ and his church, he saith, *The king's daughter is all glorious within, her clothing is of wrought gold; she shall be brought unto the king: with gladness and rejoicing shall they be brought; they shall enter into the king's palace,* Psal. 45.[3] And also King Solomon in his Song, where he speaks of Christ and his church, where she is complaining and calling for Christ, he saith, *If thou knowest not, O thou fairest among women, go thy way by the footsteps of the flock,* Cant.1:8.c. 5.9. And John, when he saw the wonder that was in heaven, he saw *a woman clothed with the sun, and the moon under her feet, and upon her head a crown of twelve stars; and there appeared another wonder in heaven, a great red dragon stood ready to devour her child*: here the enmity appears that God put between the woman and the dragon, Revelations 12.[4]

Thus much may prove that the church of Christ is a woman, and those that speak against the woman's speaking, speak against the church of Christ, and the seed of the woman, which seed is Christ;

that is to say, those that speak against the power of the Lord, and the Spirit of the Lord speaking in a woman, simply, by reason of her sex, or because she is a woman, not regarding the seed, and Spirit, and power that speaks in her; such speak against Christ, and his church, and are of the seed of the serpent, wherein lodgeth the enmity. And as God the Father made no such difference in the first creation, nor never since between the male and the female, but always out of his mercy and loving kindness, had regard unto the weak, so also, his Son, Christ Jesus, confirms the same thing. When the Pharisees came to him, and asked him, if it were lawful for a man to put away his wife, he answered and said unto them, *Have you not read, that he that made them in the beginning, made them male and female, And said, For this cause shall a man leave father and mother, and shall cleave unto his wife, and they twain shall be one flesh, wherefore they are no more twain but one flesh; what therefore God hath joined together, let no man put asunder,* Mat. 19.[5]

Again, Christ Jesus, when he came to the city of Samaria, where Jacob's well was, where the woman of Samaria was; you may read, in John 4, how he was pleased to preach the everlasting gospel to her; and when the woman said unto him, *I know that when the Messiah cometh (which is called Christ), when he cometh, he will tell us all things; Jesus saith unto her, I that speak unto thee am he;*[6] this is more than ever he said in plain words to man or woman (that we read of) before he suffered. Also he said unto Martha, when she said, she knew that her brother should rise again in the last day, Jesus said unto her, *I am the resurrection and the life: he that believeth on me, though he were dead, yet shall he live; and whosoever liveth and believeth shall never die. Believest thou this?* She answered, *Yea Lord, I believe thou art the Christ, the Son of God.* Here she mani-

---

[1] *old serpent* "And the great dragon was cast out, that old serpent, called the Devil, and Satan, which deceiveth the whole world" (Revelation 12:9).

[2] Isaiah 54:6.

[3] Psalm 45:13–15.

[4] Revelation 12:1,3–4.

---

[5] Matthew 19:4–6.

[6] John 4:25–26.

fested her true and saving faith, which few at that day believed so on him, John 11:25, 26.

Also that woman that came unto Jesus with an alabaster box of very precious ointment, and poured it on his head as he sat at meat; it's manifested that this woman knew more of the secret power and wisdom of God, than his disciples did, that were filled with indignation against her; and therefore Jesus saith, *Why do ye trouble the woman, for she hath wrought a good work upon me? Verily, I say unto you, wheresoever this gospel shall be preached in the whole world, there shall also this that this woman hath done, be told for a memorial of her,* Matt. 26, Mark 14:3.[1] Luke saith further, *She was a sinner,* and that *she stood at his feet behind him weeping, and began to wash his feet with her tears and did wipe them with the hair of her head, and kissed his feet, and anointed them with ointment.* And when Jesus saw the heart of the Pharisee that hath bidden him to his house, he took occasion to speak unto Simon, as you may read in Luke 7 and he turned to the woman, and said, *Simon, Seest thou this woman? Thou gavest me no water to my feet but she hath washed my feet with tears, and wiped them with the hair of her head: Thou gavest me no kiss, but this woman, since I came in, hath not ceased to kiss my feet: My head with oil thou didst not anoint, but this woman hath anointed my feet with ointment: Wherefore I say unto thee, her sins, which are many, are forgiven her, for she hath loved much,* Luke 7:37, to the end.[2]

Also there was many women which followed Jesus from Galilee ministering unto him, and stood afar off when he was crucified, Mat. 28:55,[3] Mark 15. Yea even the women of Jerusalem wept for him insomuch that he said unto them, *Weep not for me, ye daughters of Jerusalem, but weep for yourselves, and for your children,* Luke 23:28.

And certain women which had been healed of evil spirits and infirmities, Mary Magdalen, and Joanna the wife of Chuza, Herod's steward's wife, *and many others which ministered unto him of their substance,* Luke 8:2, 3.

Thus we see that Jesus owned the love and grace that appeared in women, and did not despise it, and by what is recorded in the Scriptures, he received as much love, kindness, compassion, and tender dealing towards him from women, as he did from any others, both in his lifetime, and also after they had exercised their cruelty upon him, for Mary Magdalene, and Mary the mother of Jesus, beheld where he was laid: *And when the sabbath was past, Mary Magdalen, and Mary the mother of James, and Salome, had brought sweet spices that they might anoint him: And very early in the morning, the first day of the week, they came unto the sepulchre at the rising of the sun; and they said among themselves, who shall roll us away the stone from the door of the sepulchre? And when they looked, the stone was rolled away, for it was very great*: Mark 16:1, 2, 3, 4, Luke 24:1, 2, *and they went down into the sepulchre,* and as Matthew saith, *The angel rolled away the stone, and he said unto the women, Fear not, I know whom ye seek, Jesus which was crucified: He is not here, he is risen,* Mat. 28.[4] Now Luke saith thus, That *there stood two men by them in shining apparel, and as they were perplexed and afraid, the men said unto them, He is not here; remember how he said unto you when he was in Galilee, that the Son of Man must be delivered into the hands of sinful men, and be crucified, and the third day rise again, and they remembered his words, and returned from the sepulchre, and told all these things to the eleven, and to all the rest.*[5]

It was Mary Magdalene and Joanna, and Mary the mother of James, and the other women that were with them, which told these things to the Apostles. And

---

[1] Matthew 26:10,13; Mark 14:3–9.

[2] Luke 7:37,38,44–47.

[3] The biblical verse actually cited is Matthew 27:55.

[4] Matthew 28:2,5–6.

[5] Luke 24:4–9.

their words seemed unto them as idle tales, and they believed them not.[1] Mark this, ye despisers of the weakness of women, and look upon yourselves to be so wise: But Christ Jesus doth not so, for he makes use of the weak: For when he met the women after he was risen, he said unto them, *All Hail*, and they came and held him by the feet, and worshipped him; then said Jesus unto them, *Be not afraid, go tell my brethren that they go into Galilee, and there they shall see me*, Mat. 28:10, Mark 16:9. And John saith, when Mary was weeping at the sepulchre, that Jesus said unto her, *Woman, why weepest thou? what seekest thou?* And when she supposed him to be the gardener, *Jesus saith unto her, Mary; she turned herself, and saith unto him, Rabboni, which is to say, Master. Jesus saith unto her, Touch me not, for I am not yet ascended to my Father, but go to my brethren, and say unto them I ascend unto my Father, and your Father, and to my God, and your God*, John 20:16, 17.

Mark this, you that despise and oppose the message of the Lord God that he sends by women. What had become of the redemption of the whole body of mankind, if they had not believed the message that the Lord Jesus sent by these women, of and concerning his resurrection? And if these women had not thus, out of their tenderness and bowels of love, who had received mercy, and grace, and forgiveness of sins, and virtue, and healing from him, which many men also had received the like, if their hearts had not been so united and knit unto him in love, that they could not depart as the men did, but sat watching, and waiting, and weeping about the sepulchre until the time of his resurrection, and so were ready to carry his message, as is manifested, else how should his disciples have known, who were not there?

Oh blessed and glorified be the glorious Lord, for this may all the whole body of mankind say,

though the wisdom of man, that never knew God, is always ready to except against the weak; but the weakness of God is stronger than men, and the foolishness of God is wiser than men.[2]

And in Acts 18, you may read how Aquila and Priscilla took unto them Apollos, and expounded unto him the way of God more perfectly; who was an eloquent man, and mighty in the Scriptures: yet we do not read that he despised what Priscilla said, because she was a woman, as many now do.

And now to the Apostle's words, which is the ground of the great objection against women's speaking: And first, I Cor. 14. let the reader seriously read that chapter, and see the end and drift of the Apostle in speaking these words: For the Apostle is there exhorting the Corinthians unto charity, and to desire spiritual gifts, and not to speak in an unknown tongue, and not to be children in understanding, but to be children in malice, but in understanding to be men; and that the spirits of the prophets should be subject to the prophets, for God is not the author of confusion, but of peace: And then he saith, *Let your women keep silence in the church*, etc.[3]

Where it doth plainly appear that the women, as well as others, that were among them, were in confusion, for he saith, *How is it brethren? when ye come together, every one of you hath a psalm, hath a doctrine, hath a tongue, hath a revelation, hath an interpretation. Let all things be done to edifying.*[4] Here was no edifying, but all was in confusion speaking together: Therefore he saith, *If any man speak in an unknown tongue, let it be by two, or at most by three, and that by course, and let one interpret; but if there by no interpreter, let him keep silence in the church.*[5] Here the man is commanded to keep

---

[1] Luke 24:10–11.

[2] I Corinthians 1:25.

[3] I Corinthians 14:34.

[4] I Corinthians 14:26.

[5] I Corinthians 14:27–28.

silence as well as the woman, when they are in confusion and out of order.

But the Apostle saith further, *They are commanded to be in obedience, as also saith the law; and if they will learn any thing, let them ask their husbands at home, for it is a shame for a woman to speak in the church.*[1]

Here the Apostle clearly manifests his intent; for he speaks of women that were under the law, and in that transgression as Eve was, and such as were to learn, and not to speak publicly, but they must first ask their husbands at home, and it was a shame for such to speak in the church: And it appears clearly, that such women were speaking among the Corinthians, by the Apostle's exhorting them from malice and strife, and confusion, and he preacheth the law unto them, and he saith, in the law it is written, *With men of other tongues, and other lips, will I speak unto this people*, vers. 2.[2]

And what is all this to women's speaking that have the everlasting Gospel to preach, and upon whom the promise of the Lord is fulfilled, and his Spirit poured upon them according to his word, Acts 2:16, 17, 18?[3] And if the Apostle would have stopped such as had the Spirit of the Lord poured upon them, why did he say just before, *If any thing be revealed to another that sitteth by, let the first hold his peace* and *you may all prophesy one by one?*[4] Here he did not say that such women should not prophesy as had the revelation and Spirit of God poured upon them, but their women that were under the law, and in the transgression, and were in strife,

confusion and malice in their speaking, for if he had stopped women's praying or prophesying, why doth he say: *Every man praying or prophesying having his head covered, dishonoureth his head; but every woman that prayeth or prophesieth with her head uncovered dishonoureth her head? Judge in yourselves, Is it comely that a woman pray or prophesy uncovered? For the woman is not without the man, neither is the man without the woman, in the Lord*, I Cor. 11:3, 4, 13.[5]

Also that other Scripture, in I Tim. 2, where he is exhorting that prayer and supplication be made everywhere, lifting up holy hands without wrath and doubting; he saith in the like manner also, That *women must adorn themselves in modest apparel, with shamefastness and sobriety, not with broidered hair, or gold, or pearl[s], or costly array*; He saith, *Let women learn in silence with all subjection, but I suffer not a woman to teach, nor to usurp authority over the man, but to be in silence; for Adam was first formed, then Eve; and Adam was not deceived, but the woman being deceived was in the transgression.*[6]

Here the Apostle speaks particularly to a woman in relation to her husband, to be in subjection to him, and not to teach, nor usurp authority over him, and therefore he mentions Adam and Eve: But let it be strained to the utmost, as the opposers of women's speaking would have it, that is, that they should not preach nor speak in the church, of which there is nothing here: Yet the Apostle is speaking to such as he is teaching to wear their apparel, what to wear, and what not to wear; such as were not come to wear modest apparel, and such as were not come to shamefastness and sobriety, but he was exhorting them from broidered hair, gold, and pearls, and costly array; and such are not to usurp authority over the man, but to learn in silence with all subjection, as it becometh women professing godliness, with good works.

---

[1] I Corinthians 14:34–35.

[2] The biblical verse actually cited is I Corinthians 14:21.

[3] "But this is that which was spoken by the prophet Joel; And it shall come to pass in the last days, saith God, I will pour out of my Spirit upon all flesh: and your sons and your daughters shall prophesy, and your young men shall see visions, and your old men shall dream dreams: And on my servants and on my handmaidens I will pour out in those days of my Spirit; and they shall prophesy" (Acts 2:16–18).

[4] I Corinthians 14:30–31.

[5] The biblical verses actually cited are I Corinthians 11:4,5,13 and 11.

[6] I Timothy 2:9, 11–14.

And what is all this to such as have the power and Spirit of the Lord Jesus poured upon them, and have the message of the Lord Jesus given unto them? Must not they speak the word of the Lord because of these undecent and unreverent women that the Apostle speaks of, and to, in these two Scriptures? And how are the men of this generation blinded, that bring these Scriptures, and pervert the Apostle's words, and corrupt his intent in speaking of them, and by these Scriptures endeavour to stop the message and word of the Lord God in women, by contemning and despising of them? If the Apostle would have had women's speaking stopped, and did not allow of them, why did he entreat his true yoke-fellow to help those women who laboured with him in the Gospel? Phil. 4:3. And why did the Apostles join together in prayer and supplication with the women, and Mary the mother of Jesus, and with his brethren, Acts 1:14, if they had not allowed, and had union and fellowship with the Spirit of God, wherever it was revealed in women as well as others? But all this opposing and gainsaying of women's speaking hath risen out of the bottomless pit, and spirit of darkness that hath spoken for these many hundred years together in this night of apostasy, since the revelations have ceased and been hid, and so that spirit hath limited and bound all up within its bond and compass, and so would suffer none to speak, but such as that spirit of darkness, approved of, man or woman.[1]

And so here hath been the misery of these last ages past, in the time of the reign of the beast, that John saw when he stood upon the sand of the sea, rising out of the sea, and out of the earth, having seven heads and ten horns, Rev. 13. In this great city of Babylon, which is the woman that hath sitten so long upon the scarlet-coloured beast, full of names, of blasphemy, having seven heads and ten horns; and this woman hath been arrayed and decked with gold, and pearls, and precious stones, and she hath had a golden cup in her hand, full of abominations, and hath made all nations drunk with the cup of her fornication; and all the world hath wondered after the beast, and hath worshipped the dragon that gave power to the beast; and this woman hath been drunk with the blood of the saints, and with the blood of the martyrs of Jesus;[2] and this hath been the woman that hath been speaking and usurping authority for many hundred years together: And let the times and ages past testify how many have been murdered and slain, in ages and generations past; every religion and profession (as it hath been called) killing and murdering one another, that would not join one with another. And thus the Spirit of Truth, and the power of the Lord Jesus Christ hath been quite lost among them that have done this; and this mother of harlots hath sitten as a queen, and said, *She should see no sorrow,* but though her days have been long, even many hundred of years, for there was power given unto the beast, to continue forty and two months, and to make war with the saints, and to overcome them;[3] and all that have dwelt upon the earth have worshipped him, whose names are not written in the book of the life of the Lamb, slain from the foundation of the world.[4]

But blessed be the Lord, his time is over, which was above twelve hundred years, and the darkness is past, and the night of apostasy draws to an end, and the true light now shines, the morning-light, the bright morning star, the root and offspring of David, he is risen, he is risen, glory to the highest for evermore; and the joy of the morning is come, and the bride, the Lamb's wife, is making herself ready, as a bride that is adorning for her husband,

---

[1] *apostasy* abandonment or renunciation of one's religious faith or moral allegiance (*OED* apostasy 1).

[2] *In this great...martyrs of Jesus* Here Fell paraphrases Revelation 17:2–6.

[3] *She should see no sorrow* Revelation 18:7; *power given unto...two months* Revelation 13:5.

[4] *and all that...of the world* Revelation 13:8.

and to her is granted that she shall be arrayed in fine linen, clean and white, and the fine linen is the righteousness of the saints: The holy Jerusalem is descending out of heaven from God, having the glory of God, and her light is like a jasper stone, clear as crystal.[1]

And this is that free woman that all the children of the promise are born of; not the children of the bondwoman, which is Hagar, which genders to strife and to bondage, and which answers to Jerusalem which is in bondage with her children; but this is *the Jerusalem which is free, which is the mother of us all.*[2] And so this bondwoman and her children, that are born after the flesh, have persecuted them that are born after the Spirit, even until now; but now the bondwoman and her seed is to be cast out, that hath kept so long in bondage and in slavery, and under limits; this bondwoman and her brood is to be cast out, and our holy city, the new Jerusalem, is coming down from heaven, and her light will shine throughout the whole earth, even as a jasper stone, clear as crystal, which brings freedom and liberty, and perfect redemption to her whole seed; and this is that woman and image of the eternal God, that God hath owned, and doth own, and will own for evermore.

More might be added to this purpose, both out of the Old Testament and New, where it is evident that God made no difference, but gave his good Spirit, as it pleased him, both to man and woman, as Deborah, Huldah and Sarah.[3] The Lord calls by his prophet Isaiah, *Hearken unto me, ye that follow after righteousness, ye that seek the Lord, look unto the rock from whence ye were hewn, and to the hole of the pit from whence ye were digged; look unto Abraham your father and to Sarah that bare you, for the Lord will comfort Sion,* etc. Isa. 5.[4] And Anna the prophetess, *who was a widow of fourscore and four years of age, which departed not from the temple, but served God with fastings and prayers night and day, she coming in at that instant,* (when old Simeon took the child Jesus in his arms, and) *she gave thanks unto the Lord, and spake of him to all them who looked for redemption in Jerusalem,* Luke 2:36, 37, 38. And Philip the evangelist, into whose house the Apostle Paul entered, who was one of the seven, Acts 6:3. He had four daughters which were virgins, that did prophesy, Acts 21.

And so let this serve to stop that opposing spirit that would limit the power and Spirit of the Lord Jesus, whose Spirit is poured upon all flesh, both sons and daughters, now in his resurrection; and since that the Lord God in the creation, when he made man in his own image, he made them male and female; and since that Christ Jesus, as the Apostle saith, was made of a woman, and the power of the highest overshadowed her, and the Holy Ghost came upon her, and the holy thing that was born of her, was called the *Son of God,* and when he was upon the earth, he manifested his love, and his will, and his mind, both to the woman of Samaria, and Martha, and Mary her sister, and several others, as hath been showed;[5] and after his resurrection also manifested himself unto them first of all, even

---

[1] This passage is a collation and paraphrase of Revelation 22:16,17, Revelation 19:7–8, and Revelation 21:2,11.

[2] *not the children...of us all* Hagar was the Egyptian bondwoman of Abraham's wife Sarah. When Sarah was infertile, Abraham fathered a child (Ishmael) upon Hagar. After the birth of her son Isaac, Sarah asked Abraham to "cast out this bondwoman and her son" (Genesis 21). Fell cites Paul's typological exposition of Genesis 21: "For it is written that Abraham had two sons, the one by a bondmaid, the other by a freewoman. But he who was of the bondwoman was born after the flesh; but he of the freewoman was by promise. Which things are an allegory: for these are the two covenants; the one from the mount Sinai, which gendereth to bondage, which is Agar. For this Agar is mount Sinai in Arabia, and answereth to Jerusalem which now is, and is in bondage with her children. But Jerusalem which is above is free, which is the mother of us all" (Galatians 4:22–26).

[3] For biblical accounts of these three women, see Judges 4–5, II Kings 22:14, and Genesis 12–23 respectively.

[4] The biblical verses actually cited are Isaiah 51:1–3.

[5] *and since...of a woman* Galatians 4:4; *and the power...of God* Luke 1:35.

before he ascended unto his Father. *Now when Jesus was risen, the first day of the week, he appeared first unto Mary Magdalene*, Mark 16:9. And thus the Lord Jesus hath manifested himself and his power, without respect of persons, and so let all mouths be stopped that would limit him, whose power and Spirit is infinite, that is pouring it upon all flesh.

And thus much in answer to these two Scriptures, which have been such a stumbling block; that the ministers of darkness have made such a mountain of: But the Lord is removing all this, and taking it out of the way.

—1667

Lawrence Clarkson (or Claxton)
1615 – 1667

The confusion about this author's name derives from the fact that it is written Clarkson in the earlier tracts and Claxton in the later ones. The correct form is likely to be Clarkson, a common name around Preston, in Lancashire, where he was born, but there pronounced "Clackson." Clarkson was brought up in the Church of England, but developed a puritan intolerance of May poles and dancing on the Sabbath, and set off on a religious journey that took him through virtually all of the many forms of Christianity available in the England of his time. He was successively a Presbyterian, Independent, Antinomian, Anabaptist or "Dipper," Seeker, Ranter and, finally, Muggletonian. In one of these phases he turned against conventional sexual morality, and preached sexual liberation for women. He was imprisoned as an Anabaptist, and only freed when he renounced "dipping." He was also imprisoned by the House of Commons for a tract considered blasphemous, after which he was to be banished, "and not to return upon pain of death." In fact he did not leave the country, but travelled around earning his living through preaching, astrology, a magic act, and quack medicine.

Clarkson's spiritual journey demonstrates in one person's experience the increasingly radical religious options available in the 1640s and 1650s, and incidentally records a great deal of social history. His travels reflect the new mobility of the 1640s, with marching soldiers and the politically or religiously restless mingling with local populations to an un-precedented degree; they also reveal how radicalized individuals or communities made and maintained contact with one another, and the important role played in these communities by printers and booksellers.

The Lost Sheep Found has an agenda: it represents a bid for the leadership of the Muggletonian sect after the death of co-founder John Reeve (born 1608) in 1658. Clarkson signals his ambition on the title page of the book, where he describes himself as "the only true converted Messenger of Christ Jesus," an implicit snub to the claims of Reeve's cousin, and co-founder of the sect, Lodowick Muggleton (1609–1698). Clarkson lost this battle, however, and went on to accept a subordinate role in the sect, with which he remained affiliated for the rest of his life. (For Clarkson's relations with the Muggletonians, see A.L. Morton, *The World of the Ranters* [London: Lawrence and Wishart, 1970], pp. 138–42.)

Clarkson's death was probably an indirect result of the Fire of London. He borrowed money to lend to those who needed capital to rebuild, and was imprisoned for debt after someone defaulted on a loan. Given the mortality rate in seventeenth-century prisons, it is not surprising that he should die after a year's incarceration. *The Lost Sheep Found* (1660) is one of the liveliest and most interesting "spiritual autobiographies" of the time. For other examples of the genre, see the selections from John Bunyan's *Grace Abounding* and Anne Bradstreet.

၎ၜၜ

The Lost Sheep Found:
or, The Prodigal returned to his Father's house, after many a sad and weary Journey through many Religious Countries

Having published several writings in confirmation of this spiritual last commission that ever shall appear in this unbelieving world,[1] a well-wisher to this commission, yea a man of no mean

---

[1] Muggleton and Reeve claimed to be the "two witnesses" promised in Revelation 11:3–6, whose arrival marked the end of this world and the beginning of the new age of the spirit; the revelation of their role was to be God's last intervention in the world.

parts nor parentage in this, reason's kingdom,[1] much importuned me to publish to this perishing world, the various leadings forth of my spirit through each dispensation,[2] from the year 1630, to this year 1660, and that for no other end, than that reason, or the devil's mouth might be stopped, with the hypocrisy of his heart laid naked, and the tongues of faith with praises opened, to consider what variety of by-paths, and multiplicity of seeming realities, yet absolute notions, the souls of the elect may wander or travel through, seeking rest, and yet find none till the day unexpected, that soul as a brand be plucked out of the fire of his own righteousness, or professed wickedness, unto the true belief of a real commission which quencheth all the fiery darts of sin that dispensations have left cankering in his soul, (mind this) as have but patience, and thou shalt hear the more I labored for perfect cure and peace in my soul, the further I was from it, insomuch that I was resolved to seek forth no more, supposing my self in as perfect health and liberty in my spirit, as any then professing an unknown God whatsoever.

As do but seriously mind this ensuing epistle, and thou mayest in me read thy own hypocrisy and dissimulation in point of worship all along; as in that year 1630, being of the age of fifteen years, and living with my parents in the town of Preston in Amounderness,[3] where I was born, and educated in the form and worship of the Church of England, then established in the title of the Episcopal, or Bishops' Government; then, and in that year, my heart began to enquire after the purest ministry held forth under that form, not being altogether void of some small discerning, who preached Christ more truly and powerfully, as I thought, than another,

and unto them was I only resolved to follow their doctrine above any other, and to that end my brethren being more gifted in the knowledge of the Scriptures than myself, and very zealous in what they knew, that they did often prevail with Mr. Hudson our town-lecturer,[4] to admit of such ministers as we judged were true laborious ministers of Christ, who when they came, would thunder against superstition, and sharply reprove sin, and profaning the Lord's-day; which to hear, tears would run down my cheeks for joy: so having a pitiful superstitious fellow the minister of our town,[5] I spared no pains to travel to Standish and other places, where we could hear of a Godly minister, as several times I have gone ten miles, more or less, fasting all the day, when my parents never knew of it, and though I have been weary and hungry, yet I came home rejoicing. Then the ministers had an order, that none should receive the sacrament, but such as would take it at the railed altar kneeling,[6] which I could not do, and therefore went to such ministers in the country that gave it fitting. Now a while after Mr. Starby the minister of our town, taking notice of leaving our parish, informed our father the danger of his children going into heresy, and the trouble that would ensue upon our father and his children, besides the disgrace of all good church-men, which did much incense our father, but all to no purpose, for I thought it conscience to obey God before man; however I being under my father's tuition, he cast a strict eye over me, and would force me to read over the prayers in the *Book of Common Prayer* and

---

[1] Muggleton and Reeve taught that reason was the creation of the devil.

[2] *dispensation* religious system.

[3] in Lancashire.

[4] Lecturers were ordained stipendiary ministers (often deacons) appointed by town corporations or parishes for regular preaching; the position was often associated with Puritanism.

[5] an orthodox Church of England minister; "superstitious" was a pejorative term used to link the Church of England with Catholicism.

[6] one of many directives made by the Archbishop of Canterbury, William Laud. "The Godly" regarded Laud's efforts to promote ceremony in worship as innovatory and Catholicizing.

Practice of Piety,[1] which I have done, till they have fallen asleep and my self, this was our devotion in those days; but increasing in knowledge, I judged to pray another man's form, was vain babbling, and not acceptable to God:[2] and then the next thing I scrupled, was asking my parents' blessing, that often times in the winter mornings, after I have been out of my bed, I have stood freezing above, and durst not come down till my father was gone abroad, and the reason I was satisfied, the blessing or prayers of a wicked man God would not hear, and so should offend God to ask him blessing; for either of these two ways I must, down on my knees, and say, father pray to God to bless me, or give me your blessing for God's sake, either of which I durst not use with my lips, but was in me refrained; and I improved my knowledge in the doctrine of those men I judged was the true Ministers of God, so that with tears many times I have privately sought the Lord as I thought, whether those things that the puritanical priests preached, was my own, and the more I was troubled, that I could not pray without a book as my brethren did, fain would I have been judged a professor with them, but wanted parts,[3] yet often times have had motions to tender my self to prayer amongst them, but durst not, and to that end I might be admitted to pray with them, I have prayed alone to try how I could pray, but could not utter my self as I knew they did: so I remember there was a day of humiliation to be set apart by the Puritans so called, to seek God by prayer and expounding of Scriptures, against which day I took my pen, and writ a pretty form of words, so got them by heart, and when the day came I was called to improve my gifts, at which I was glad, yet in a trembling condi-

tion lest I should be foiled; however, to prayer I went, with a devotion as though I had known the true God, but alas, when I was in the midst of that prayer, I left my form of words, and so was all in a sweat as though I had been sick, and so came off like a hypocrite as I was, which so seized on my soul, that I thought for my hypocrisy damnation would be my portion; however it humbled me, that I was glad to become one of the meanest of the number, still full of fears that when I died, I should go to hell; in which time I writ all the hypocrisy of my heart in a letter to send to Mr. Hudson our lecturer, to know his judgement whether such a soul as there related might be saved? in the interim comes a motion within me, saying, *Ah fool, why dost thou send to man that knows not what will become of his own soul? burn it, and wait upon me*; which letter I did burn, and not many weeks after I had a gift of prayer that was not inferior to my brethren, for which I was glad for the goodness of God to my soul; and as I increased in knowledge, so was my zeal, that I have many times privately prayed with rough hard cinders under my bare knees, that so God might hear me; and when I could not end my prayers with tears running down my cheeks, I was afraid some sin shut the attention of God from me: and thus did I do for a few years, in which time the bishops began to totter and shake, yea, for their cruelty and superstition, was totally routed.

Now if then you had asked me what I thought God was, the devil was, what the angels' nature was, what Heaven and Hell was, and what would become of my soul after death?

My answer had plainly been this: That my God was a grave, ancient, holy, old man, as I supposed sat in Heaven in a chair of gold, but as for his nature I knew no more than a child: and as for the devil, I really believed was some deformed person out of man, and that he could where, when, and how, in what shape appear he pleased; and therefore the devil was a great scarecrow, in so much that

---

[1] *Practice of Piety* a popular devotional treatise by Lewis Bayley (second edition published 1612), and one of the books John Bunyan mentions in *Grace Abounding* as an influence.

[2] A belief in the authenticity of extempory over set forms of prayer was one of the broad defining elements of Puritanism.

[3] *parts* abilities, talents, skills (*OED* part 12).

every black thing I saw in the night, I thought was the devil. But as for the angels, I knew nothing at all; and for Heaven I thought was a glorious place, with variety of rooms suitable for Himself, and his son Christ, and the Holy Ghost: and Hell, where it was I knew not, but judged it a local place, all dark, fire and brimstone, which the devils did torment the wicked in, and that forever; but for the soul at the hour of death, I believed was either by an angel or a devil fetched immediately to Heaven or Hell. This was the height of my knowledge under the Bishops' Government, and I am persuaded was the height of all Episcopal ministers then living; so that surely if they shall be established for a national ministry, they will not impose such ceremonies as then they did, but are grown wiser about God and devil; for they will find the major part of England is grown wiser, so cannot stoop to an inferior light; therefore if ye now begin to stand, take heed lest ye fall.

Secondly, after this I travelled into the church of the Presbyterians,[1] where still I made brick of straw and clay, nay there I found my soul the more oppressed, and further ensnared in the land of Egypt, burning brick all the day; but I knowing no further light, I was willing to bear their yoke, and sometimes found it pleasant; for herein consisted the difference of the Presbyterian and Episcopal, only in a few superstitious rites and ceremonies,[2] as also their doctrine was more lively than the Episcopal, for they would thunder the pulpit with an unknown God, which then I thought was true, and sharply reprove sin, though since I saw we were the greatest sinners; but however their doctrine I liked, it being the highest I then heard of. So war being

begun betwixt the Episcopal and the Presbyterian,[3] I came for London, where I found them more precise than in our popish country of Lancashire; for with us the Lord's-day was highly profaned by the toleration of maypoles, dancing and rioting, which the Presbyterians hated, and in their doctrine cried out against, which thing my soul also hated, though yet I was not clear but the steeple was the house of God, from that saying of David, Psalm 84:10, saying, "For a day in thy courts is better than a thousand: I had rather be a door-keeper in the house of my God, than to dwell in the tents of wickedness"; so that I finding out the ablest teachers in London; as then I judged was Mr. Calamy, Case, Brooks,[4] and such like, unto whom I daily resorted, if possible, to get assurance of salvation, not neglecting to receive the ordinance of breaking of bread from them, judging in so doing, I "showed forth the Lord's death till he came."[5] Now the persecution of the bishops fell so heavy upon the Presbyterian ministers, that some fled for New England; and Hooker had left several books in print,[6] which so tormented my soul, that I thought it impossible to be saved; however, I labored what in me lay, to find those signs and marks in my own soul, and to that end neglected all things that might hinder it; and thus for a certain time I remained a hearer of them till such time that wars began to be hot, and they pressed the people to send out their husbands and servants to help the Lord against the mighty, by which many a poor soul knowing no better, was murdered, and murdered others, taking the Bible in

---

[1] *Presbyterians* the logical next step, from being a "puritan" within the established Church to being a "puritan" outside it, within an alternative system of church government.

[2] an argument Milton summarizes in his sonnet "On the New Forcers of Conscience" as "*New Presbyter* is but *Old Priest* writ Large."

[3] The Bishops' Wars (1639–1640); see Charles I, *A Proclamation* (1639) and *Information from the Scottish Nation* (1640).

[4] Presbyterian divines Edmund Calamy (1600–1666) and Thomas Case (1598–1682), and the Independent minister Thomas Brooks (1608–1680).

[5] I Corinthians 11:26.

[6] Thomas Hooker (?1586–1647), New England divine.

their pockets, and the Covenant in their hats,[1] by me was esteemed the work and command of the Lord, not at all minding the command of the second commission to the contrary, as in II Cor. 10:4 saying, "We do not war after the flesh, for the weapons of our warfare are not carnal, but mighty through God to the pulling down of strong holds, &c." This was not by me understood, but as they did in the old time in Moses his commission, so I thought we might do then; in which time the Presbyterians began to be a great people, and in high esteem, and at that time there was a great slaughter of the Protestants in Ireland,[2] that London was thronged with their ministers and people, and several collections was gathered for them: but this I observed, that as the Presbyterians got power, so their pride and cruelty increased against such as was contrary to them, so that:

Thirdly I left them, and travelled to the Church of the Independents;[3] for this I observed as wars increased, so variety of judgements increased: and coming to them, of which was Mr. Goodwin,[4] and some others, I discerned their doctrine clearer, and of a more moderate spirit. Now the greatest difference betwixt them, was about baptizing of infants, pleading by Scripture, that none but the infants or children of believers ought to be baptized; and that none of them must receive the Sacrament, as then it was called, but such as was church-members, judging all that was not congregated into fellowship, were not of God, but the world: so that about these things I was searching the truth thereof, and

labored in the letter of the Scripture to satisfy my judgement; in the interim hearing of one Doctor Crisp,[5] to him I went, and he held forth against all the aforesaid churches, that let his people be in society or no, though walked all alone, yet if he believed that Christ Jesus died for him, God beheld no iniquity in him: and to that end I seriously perused his books, and found it proved by Scripture, as it is written Number 23:21: "He hath not beheld iniquity in Jacob, neither hath he seen perverseness in Israel." This was confirmed by other Scriptures, that I conceived whose sins Christ died for, their sin was to be required no more; for thus thinking when the debt was paid, the creditor would not look upon him as indebted to him, yet this I ever thought Christ never died for all, though the Scripture was fluent to that purpose, yet I found Scriptures to the contrary, and was ever as touching that satisfied, that as Christ prayed for none but such as was given him out of the world, "I pray for them, I pray not for the world,"[6] so that I thought he did not die for them he would not pray for, which thought now I know is true, and have by pen, and can by tongue make good the same. But I must return to the time then under Doctor Crisp's doctrine, in which I did endeavor to become one of those that God saw no sin, and in some measure I began to be comforted therewith, but how, or which way to continue in the same I could not tell; having as yet but little understanding in the Scripture I was silent, only still enquiring after the highest perch of light then held forth in London, in which time Mr. Randel appeared, with Mr. Simpson, with such a doctrine as Doctor Crisp, only higher and clearer, which then was called antino-

---

[1] *Covenant* the Scottish National Covenant (1638), the signers of which vowed to maintain the Presbyterian cause against royal and Laudian innovations.

[2] *a great slaughter* during the Irish rebellion of 1641.

[3] *Independents* also known as Congregationalists; believers in the independence or autonomy of each local congregation (and therefore deniers of the legitimacy of a state church).

[4] Thomas Goodwin (1600–1680), the Independent divine who would attend Cromwell on his deathbed.

[5] Tobias Crisp (1600–1643), Puritan minister linked with the rise of Antinomianism (see below). The three volumes of his *Christ Alone Exalted* were published in 1643 (vols. 1–2) and 1648 (vol. 3).

[6] John 17:9.

mians, or against the law,[1] so that I left all church-fellowship, and burning of brick in Egypt, and travelled with them up and down the borders, part Egypt, and part wilderness.

Fourthly, take notice in this sect [the Antinomians] I continued a certain time, for church it was none, in that it was but part form, and part none; in which progress I had a great sort of professors acquainted with me, so began to be somebody amongst them, and having a notable gift in prayer, we often assembled in private, improving my gifts, judging then the best things of this world was only prepared for the Saints, of which then I judged my self one, not knowing any other but that God was a spirit, and did motion in and out into his Saints, and that this was God's kingdom, and we his people; and therefore I judged God did fight for us against our enemies, that so we might enjoy him in liberty. At which time Paul Hobson brake forth with such expressions of the in-comes and out-goes of God,[2] that my soul much desired such a gift of preaching, which after a while Hobson and I being acquainted, he had a captain's place under Colonel Fleetwood for Yarmouth,[3] so that thither with him I went, and there tarried a soldier with them, at which time I had a small gift of preaching, and so by degrees increased into a method, that I attempted the pulpit at Mr. Wardel's parish in Suffolk, and so acquainted my gifts more and more in public, that having got acquaintance at Norwich, I left the company at Yarmouth; so after a few days I was admitted into a pulpit two or three times: so

coming a man from Pulom [Pulham] side in Norfolk and hearing of me, was greatly affected with my doctrine, but especially my prayer, and was very urgent with me to go to their parish of Russel, which within two weeks after I assented to be there such a day, which was against the Fast-day; for at that time the Parliament had established a monthly fast, which was the last Wednesday of the month: at the set time I came to the place appointed, where this man had given notice to the best affected people in those parts, what a rare man was to preach that day, which thing I was ambitious of, as also to get some silver. Well, to the master I went, and as was my doctrine, so was their understanding, though I say't, as young as I was, yet was not I inferior to any priest in those days. So in conclusion of my day's work there came several in the church-yard to me, and gave me thanks for my pains, yea, hoped the Lord would settle me among them, which news I was glad to hear; so for the next Lord's-day by goodman Mays and Burton was I invited to preach at Pulom, which was a great parish; so upon liking I went, and was well approved of by all the godly, so there for a time I was settled for twenty shillings a week, and very gallantly was provided for, so that I thought I was in Heaven upon earth judging the priests had a brave time in this world, to have a house built for them, and means provided for them, to tell the people stories of other men's works. Now after I had continued half a year, more or less, the ministers began to envy me for my doctrine, it being free grace,[4] so contrary to theirs, and that the more, their people came from their own parish to hear me, so that they called me "sheep-stealer" for robbing them of their flock, and to that end came to catch and trap me at several lectures where I was called, that at last they prevailed with the heads of the parish to turn me out, so I slighting them as they

---

[1] Giles Randall (born ca. 1608), charged in the Star Chamber in 1643 with Anabaptism, Antinomianism, and Familism; and John Simpson (d. 1662). Antinomianism is the general name for the belief that the "new dispensation" of divine grace won by Christ's sacrifice freed Christians from the need to observe any moral law.

[2] Paul Hobson (d. 1666); a Particular Baptist and a captain in the New Model Army whose frequent preaching around the country attracted the ire of heretic hunters such as Thomas Edwards.

[3] George Fleetwood (1623–1672), Colonel of Horse in the New Model Army, later one of the regicides (pardoned).

[4] *free grace* the doctrine of the unmerited favour of God.

could me, we parted, and then having many friends, I was importuned to come and live with them, so above all I chose Robert Marchant's house my lodging place, because his daughter I loved; and for a certain time preached up and down several churches, both of Suffolk and Norfolk, and many times in private, that I had a great company. Now in the interim there was one John Tyler a Colchester man frequented those parts where then I inhabited, who was a teacher of the Baptists,[1] and had a few scattered up and down the country, which several times we had meetings and converse about a lawful minister. Now I knowing no other but that those sayings, "Go ye teach all nations, baptizing them, and lo I am with you to the end of the world";[2] that continuance to the end of the world, was the loadstone that brought me to believe that the baptism of the Apostles was as much in force now, as in their days, and that command did as really belong to me as to them; so being convinced, for London I went to be further satisfied, so that after a little discourse with Patience, I was by him baptized in the water that runneth about the Tower,[3] after which I stayed at London about a week.

Fifthly, then for Suffolk again I travelled through the Church of the Baptists, and was of Robert Marchant's family received with joy, for I had the love of all the family; and though he had four daughters marriageable, yet there was one I loved above any in that country; though I was beloved of other friends' daughters far beyond her in estate, yet for her knowledge and moderation in spirit, I loved her; so there up and down a certain

time I continued preaching the gospel, and very zealous I was for obedience to the commands of Christ Jesus; which doctrine of mine converted many of my former friends and others to be baptized, and so into a church fellowship was gathered to officiate the order of the Apostles, so that really I thought if ever I was in a true happy condition, then I was, knowing no other but as aforesaid, that this command of Christ did as really belong to me as to them; and we having the very same rule, as elders and deacons, with dipping, and breaking of bread in the same manner as they, I was satisfied we only were the Church of Christ in this world.

Thus having a great company, and baptizing of many into that faith, there was no small stir among the priests what to do with me, which afterwards they got a warrant from the Parliament, to apprehend Mr. Knowles and my self,[4] for then Knowles was about Ipswich preaching that doctrine, and baptizing certain people into that faith; now they apprehended Mr. Knowles in Ipswich gaol, and from thence with their warrant came to secure me, so in the week day after privately assembled in a friend's house, within three miles of Ay, there came in an officer from the Parliament with certain soldiers, and two constables, with some of the parish, having clubs and staves surrounded the house, I being earnest in my doctrine, and at that time was very much pressing the people, that without submitting to baptism all their profession was nothing, proving by Scripture that as Christ was our pattern, so we must follow him as example, which could not be unless we kept his commandments, as it is written, "If ye love me, keep my commandments":[5] Now dipping being a command of Christ; I judged them rebels that did profess the name of Christ, and not submit their bodies to the ordinance of Christ, and that Christ requires obedi-

---

[1] *Baptists* proponents of the conscious baptism of believers as the basis of a gathered church. After the Restoration, Baptists moved closer in temper to Presbyterians and Independents; in the decades before 1660, however, they were associated with the period's more radical religious and political movements.

[2] Matthew 28:19–20.

[3] the Tower of London. Clarkson was baptised on November 6, 1644.

[4] Hanserd Knollys (ca. 1599–1691), Particular Baptist; later associated with the Fifth Monarchists.

[5] John 14:15.

ence from none but such as was capable of being taught, and therefore no children, but men and women, ought to receive the ordinance of baptism, in which time some of the officers hearing me, interrupted me in my doctrine, and told me I must leave off, and go along with them, showing me the authority they had from the Parliament; however, some of our friends would have opposed them, but I saw it was in vain, and so desired our friends to be quiet, and said, we must not only profess Christ, but also suffer for him; so it being in the winter-time, and almost night, they hasted me for Ay, though I, with our friends, desired but so much liberty as to go to my wife's father's house for linen and other necessaries, and they would engage for my appearance before the committee at Bury; but all in vain, then my wife told them they should provide a horse for her, for whither ever I went, she would go: at which they were very much incensed, but all to no purpose, so at last a trooper would have her to ride behind him, but she with scorn refused, then they got her furniture to ride behind me, so taking leave with our friends, to Ay that night we were carried; now one of them went before to provide lodging, so the town having intelligence they had taken a great Anabaptist,[1] there was no small waiting for my coming, that when I came into the entering of the town, the inhabitants had beset both sides of the streets to see my person, supposing an Anabaptist had been a strange creature, but when they beheld me, with my wife, they said one to another, he is like one of us, yea, they are a very pretty couple, it is pity I should suffer: so to the inn I came, where a great company was in the yard to behold me; so being unhorsed, they guarded me to our lodging, and great provision was made for

supper, where many a pot was spent that night to see my face;[2] so to bed we went, and in the next room by soldiers guarded, so in the morning we were hasted for St. Edmonds Bury, which that morning Captain Harvey gave out many sad and grievous words what the committee would do with me, but the devil was deceived; however I said little: so they came to me with a bill what I had to pay for beer, wine, and meat; unto which I said, I had none, but if I had, I would pay none, it was sufficient I was wrongfully deprived of my freedom, and not to pay for their rioting; however they told me, I must before I go; then keep me here still: surely, said I, your masters that set you on work, are able to pay you your wages. Well, they said before I came out of prison, if I were not hanged, I should pay it; then said I, rest your selves contented till that day: so towards Bury we took our journey, and one was gone before to inform the committee I was taken; against my appearance they were assembled in a full committee, of which as I take it, Captain Bloyes of Woodbridge was then chairman. So to the hall I was guarded, the room being full, I was conveyed up to the chairman, who asked, my name? To which I replied, this was strange that you had a warrant to take me, and know not my name. Well, that was no matter, do you tell us your name; so I told them. What countryman are you? I said Lanca-shire. What made you travel so far off into these parts? The like motions that moved others, moved me. How long have you professed this way of dipping? Not so long as I ought to have done, had my understanding been enlightened. What then, you approve of what you do? Otherways I should not do it. How many have you dipped in these parts? I being a free born subject of this nation ought not to accuse my self; but you are to prove your charge, by sufficient witness against me, but however I being brought before you for my obedi-

---

[1] *Anabaptist*   a name used of various radical religious groups on the continent with roots in the German Reformation, groups whose beliefs were the subject of a great deal of fear-mongering. Used in England as a term of abuse, with implications of polygamy, the denial of private property, and the erasure of all hierarchy.

[2] that is, many drinks (sold in pots) were bought at the inn as an excuse to see the prisoner.

ence to the commands of Christ, I am neither afraid nor ashamed to tell you what I have done: but to give you an account how many I have dipped, that I cannot tell. Then you have dipped some? Yea, that I have. After what manner do you dip them? After a decent order. We are informed you dip both men and women naked? As unto that you are not rightly informed. Where is your Jordan you dip them in? Though it is not Jordan, yet there are several places convenient. Do you not dip them in the night? Yea. And why do you not dip them in the day, it being an ordinance of Christ as you say? Because such as you are not able to bear the truth. Then said Sir William Spring, but Mr. Claxton, have not you forced some in the water against their wills? That is contrary to Scripture. Did you not one time, being on horseback, with a switch force some into the water? Let them that so informed you, affirm it before you to my face. But Mr. Claxton, who were those that you dipped about Framingham? At this time I cannot remember, but several I have dipped there aways. Did not you dip six sisters there about at one time? I never dipped six at one time. Then said Sir John Rowse, we are informed you dipped six sisters one night naked. That is nothing to me what you are informed, for I never did such a thing; nay further, it is reported, that which of them you liked best, you lay with her in the water? Surely your experience teacheth you the contrary, that nature hath small desire to copulation in water, at which they laughed; But, said I, you have more cause to weep for the unclean thoughts of your heart. Mr. Claxton have not you a wife? One that brought me, said she is in town. Where is she? Fetch her hither. She being without the door, came in quickly, and took me by the hand. Well, said the chairman, you are a loving woman, is this your husband? Yes, he is my husband. How long have you been married? About two months. Where were you married? At Waybread in my father's house. Who married you? My husband, with the consent of my parents, and the church. At that there was a great laughter, and said, your husband marry you to himself, that is against the law; I being vexed at their folly, answered, marriage is no other, but a free consent in love each to the other before God, and who was sufficient to publish the contract as my self? Nay but Mr. Claxton, you are not rightly informed as touching a true marriage. I say I was married according to truth: then if your marriage be lawful, we are not lawfully married. I question not yours, look ye to that; but this I know, and can prove, I am married according to the word of God; neither can your law repeal the contract of that couple, that hath their parents' consent, and the church confirming the same. Well, well, we shall give you the hearing, but how many was present when you took her to your wife? About twelve. What did you say to her and the church? First, I sought the Lord by prayer for a blessing upon that ordinance, and then I declared unto her parents and the church what had passed betwixt she and I, and that before them all I took her by the hand, and asked her if she was not willing to take me for her husband during life? To which she assented, as also her parents approved of it, and gave her to me with the confirmation of the church. Then said the chairman, what think you gentlemen, of this marriage? They said it was a strange marriage. What then Mrs. Claxton, you look upon this man your lawful husband? Yea, I deny all other men in the world. Then you have lain with him? I ought to lie with no other. But Mrs. Claxton, did your husband dip you before, or after he became your husband? Before I was contracted in public? How or after what manner did your husband dip you? in your clothes or naked? Sir, we defy any indecent carriage, if you were dipped in your clothes you would spoil them, and besides it might endanger your life with cold: we have clothes for both men and women provided for that purpose. What, were you plunged over head and ears? So saith the Scripture. What

Mr. Claxton, did you go with her into the water?
No, I stood on the bank side. Mrs. Claxton, were
not you amazed, or almost drowned? No sir, the
obedience to the command of God did shut out all
fear and cold. What, did not you go to bed after
dipped? I had a warm bed with dry linen provided.
Did not your husband lodge with you that night?
There is no such wickedness among us. Why what
matter, you were married before God. Till we were
publicly before witness, we had no such custom,
and let me tell you, if it be the practice of your
church, it is not so in ours. Nay woman, be not
angry, I do not say you did so, for truly I am as
much against sin as you are. But Mrs. Claxton, we
have an order to secure your husband, and there to
endure the pleasure of the Parliament, what will you
do? we have no order to stay you. If you stay my
husband, you must stay me also. Why, are you
willing to go to gaol with your husband? For the
cause of Christ I am willing to suffer imprisonment.
Then you are resolved yours is the way of truth.
Then said I, for the present I know no truth but
this. Well Mr. Claxton, after a while you will be
otherwise informed. Never to turn back again. We
are to commit you to custody, that so you may
seduce no more people. Sir, I must obey your
pleasure, but I shall not deny to be obedient to the
command of Christ. Well, we shall talk with you
another time: so they ordered to make my mittimus,[1] and in my presence gave it Captain Poe my
keeper, and said, Mr. Claxton, you may take notice
that the Parliament is favorable to you, that they
will not send you to the common gaol, but to a
house where none but men of quality are kept in
custody. Then said Poe, who was my gaoler, what
shall his wife do? Then said my wife, where ever my
husband is, there will I be, then the committee
ordered her with me: so coming thither, there was
none but two papist knights, and a sea captain, so

after we had supped, we were directed to our
chamber, which was a large chamber, and pretty
good furniture. Now under a week I told Captain
Poe that I was not able to board at half a crown a
meal. Then, saith he, you must go to the common
gaol. Thither would I go, for I am not ashamed to
sit in the stocks in the marketplace, for the name of
Christ. So he informed the committee, but they
would not remove me, and said, he must agree for
the chamber, and I find my self diet. At this Poe
was vexed, and sent up his handmaid mistress Tuck,
to agree with me for the chamber at four shillings a
week, which for the space of half a year I gave her,
in which time our people increased, there being
William Muly and some others of this way in Bury,
I had oftentimes money from the army, and the
churches at London and Colchester, so that I
wanted for nothing; and some came to my chamber, and there I preached unto them, in so much
that the keeper informed the committee, who that
Sunday at night assembled, to consider what to do
with me: in conclusion they shut me close prisoner,
and kept my wife from me, which was more grief to
me than the rest. Well, against the next Lord's-day
I appointed our friends to stand before my window
on the Angel-hill, that being the way for all the
great ones of the town to go to their worship, so at
the very instant time putting my head forth of the
window, I did boldly exhort the people to beware of
the priests, and while it is the time of your health,
submit your souls and bodies in obedience to the
true baptism, and be no longer deluded to think
that your infants are commanded to obey, or capable of an ordinance imposed upon them. Oh for
shame, if not for fear, stand still and hear the truth
related by his true and lawful minister, otherwise
turn back again; at which a great sort of people gave
attention, which did enrage the priest and magistrate, yet they knew not what to do with me, but
charged me to do so no more. Then said I, take
heed how you keep my wife from me: is this to do

---

[1] *mittimus*   warrant committing a person to prison.

445

as you would be done unto? so they forthwith took off the padlock, and let my friends come to me. After this I had the liberty of the whole house, nay, to sit at the street-door; for he had no prisoners but such as gave in great security for their safe imprisonment; and as for me, and Westrop my fellow-prisoner, they feared not our going away, only they were afraid I should dip some. So a little after, spring coming on, I got liberty, not being well, to go abroad with a keeper, and Captain Gray, who was called Captain Drink-water, was to go with me. Now above all the rest, I desired Captain Gray to go with me to a wood a mile distant from me; it having rained over night, the brook was up, so a man coming with a pole, I desired him to lay it over, which he did, so I went over first, and the Captain followed me, and shaking the pole, he fell in to the middle in water, and in a trembling condition he was, lest the committee should hear of it;[1] so to the wood we went, and there he dried his hose and stockings, so after we came to prison again, the committee hearing of it, questioned Captain Gray, but he told them the truth, at which they laughed. After I had lain there a long time, Mr. Sedgewick and Mr. Erbery came to visit me,[2] with whom I had great discourse, and after they were gone, I had a great contest in my mind, as touching the succession of baptism, which I could not see but in the death of the Apostles, there was never since no true administrator; for I could not read there was ever any that had power by imposition of hands, to give the Holy Ghost, and work miracles as they did; so that in the death of them I concluded baptism to either young or old, was ceased. Now observe, I could discern this, but could not by the same rule see that preaching and prayer was to

cease: for this now I know, as in the death of the Apostles, and them commissionated by them, the commission ceased, as unto all their form and worship. So finding I was but still in Egypt burning brick, I was minded to travel into the wilderness; so seeing the vanity of the Baptists, I renounced them and had my freedom. Then:

Sixthly, I took my journey into the society of those people called Seekers,[3] who worshipped God only by prayer and preaching, therefore to Ely I went, to look for Sedgewick and Erbery but found them not, only their people were assembled: with whom I had discourse, but found little satisfaction; so after that for London I went to find Seekers there, which when I came, there was divers fallen from the Baptists as I had done, so coming to Horn in Fleet-lane and Fleten in Seacoal-lane, they informed me that several had left the church of patience, in seeing the vanity of Kiffen and others,[4] how highly they took it upon them, and yet could not prove their call successively; so glad was I there was a people to have society withal; then was I moved to put forth a book which was the first that ever I writ, bearing this title, *The Pilgrimage of Saints, by church cast out, in Christ found, seeking truth*,[5] this being a suitable piece of work in those days, that it wounded the churches; which book Randel owned, and sold many for me.[6] Now as I was going over London-bridge, I met with Thomas Gun a teacher of the Baptists, who was a man of a very humble, moderate spirit, who asked me if I owned the *Pilgrimage of Saints*? I told him yea: then

[1] in case they might think he had been baptised.

[2] William Sedgwick (ca. 1610–1663), Independent minister with connections to the Seekers, and William Erbery or Erbury (1604–1654), New Model Army chaplain, political radical, and Seeker (see below).

[3] Seekers rejected all forms of the visible church (e.g., baptism), in anticipation of a new dispensation that would supersede those offered by the Old and New Testaments.

[4] William Kiffin or Kiffen (1616–1701), merchant and Baptist minister. In the early 1640s he had been apprenticed to John Lilburne.

[5] No copies are extant of this book, published in 1646; it appears from the title to adopt a Seeker stance.

[6] Giles Randall, a London bookseller responsible for the publication of several books expounding the doctrine of the spirit within.

said he, you have writ against the church of Christ, and have discovered your self an enemy to Christ. Then I said, it is better be a hypocrite to man than to God, for I find as much dissimulation, covetousness, back-biting and envy, yea as filthy wickedness among some of them, as any people I know: and notwithstanding your heaven-like carriage, if all your faults were written in your forehead, for ought I know, you are a hypocrite as well as I; which afterwards it was found out he had lain with his landlady many times; and that he might satisfy his lust, upon slighty [slight] errands he sent her husband into the country, that so he might lodge with his wife all night; which being found out, so smote his conscience, that he privately took a pistol and shot himself to death in Georges-fields. As all along in this my travel I was subject to that sin, and yet as saint-like, as though sin were a burden to me, so that the fall of this Gun did so seize on my soul, that I concluded there was none could live without sin in this world; for notwithstanding I had great knowledge in the things of God, yet I found my heart was not right to what I pretended, but full of lust and vain-glory of this world, finding no truth in sincerity that I had gone through, but merely the vain pride and conceit of reason's imagination, finding my heart with the rest, seeking nothing but the praise of men in the height of my prayer and preaching, yet in my doctrine through all these opinions, pleading the contrary, yea abasing myself, and exalting a Christ that then I knew not. Now after this I returned to my wife in Suffolk, and wholly bent my mind to travel up and down the country, preaching for monies, which then I intended for London, so coming to Colchester where I had John Aplewhit, Purkis, and some other friends, I preached in public; so going for London, a mile from Colchester, I set my cane upright upon the ground, and which way it fell, that way would I go; so falling towards Kent, I was at a stand what I should do there, having no acquaintance, and but little money, yet whatever hardship I met withal, I was resolved for Gravesend, so with much ado I got that night to a town called Bilrekey, it being in the height of summer, and in that town then having no friends, and I think but six pence, I lodged in the Church porch all night, so when day appeared, I took my journey for Gravesend, and in the way I spent a groat of my six pence, and the other two pence carried me over the water; so being in the town, I enquired for some strange opinionated people in the town, not in the least owning of them, but seemingly to ensnare them, which they directed me to one Rugg a victualler, so coming in, though having no monies, yet I called for a pot of ale, so after a few words uttered by me, the man was greatly taken with my sayings, in so much that he brought me some bread and cheese, with which I was refreshed, and bid me take no care, for I should want for nothing, you being the man that writ *The Pilgrimage of Saints*, I have had a great desire to see you, with some soldiers and others, so for the present he left me, and informed Cornet Lokier[1] and the rest, that I was in town, who forthwith came to me, and kindly received me, and made way for me to preach in the Blockhouse; so affecting my doctrine, they quartered me in the officers' lodging, and two days after they carried me to Dartford, where there I preached; so against the next Lord's-day came for Gravesend; and there preached in the marketplace, which was such a wonder to the town and country, that some for love, and others for envy, came to hear, that the priest of the town had almost none to hear him, that if the magistrate durst, he would have apprehended me; for I boldly told them God dwelled not in the temple made with hands; neither was any place more holy than another, proving by Scripture, that where two or three were gathered in his name, God was in the midst of them, and that every believer was the

---

[1] Nicholas Lockyer, later a Leveller agitator and participant in the Putney Debates.

temple of God, as it is written, "God dwelleth with a humble and contrite spirit";[1] So after this we went to Maidston and Town-maulin, and there I preached up and down, so at last having given me about five pounds, I went to my wife and promised in two weeks to return again, which I did, but I found not Lokier nor the rest so affectionate as before, for he had a gift of preaching, & therein did seek honor, so suspicious of my blasting his reputation, slighted and persecuted me, so that I left them, and towards Maidston travelled, so one Bulfinch of Town-maulin having friends towards Canterbury, persuaded me to go with them, and so against the next Lord's-day, having no steeple free, we had a gentleman's barn free, where a great company was assembled: then for Sandwich I went, and up and down found friends, so coming to Canterbury there was some six of this way, amongst whom was a maid of pretty knowledge, who with my doctrine was affected, and I affected to lie with her, so that night prevailed, and satisfied my lust, afterwards the maid was highly in love with me, and as gladly would I have been shut of her, lest some danger had ensued, so not knowing I had a wife she was in hopes to marry me, and so would have me lodge with her again, which fain I would, but durst not, then she was afraid I would deceive her, and would travel with me, but by subtlety of reason I persuaded her to have patience, while I went into Suffolk, and settled my occasions, then I would come and marry her, so for the present we parted, and full glad was I that I was from her delivered, so to Maidston I came, and having got some six pounds, returned to my wife, which a while after I went for Kent again, but found none of the people so zealous as formerly, so that my journey was but a small advantage to me, and then I heard the maid had been in those parts to seek me, but not hearing of me, returned home again, and not long after was

married to one of that sect, and so there was an end of any further progress into Kent. Then not long after I went for London, and some while remained preaching at Bowe in Mr. Sterry's place,[2] and London-stone, but got nothing; so to Suffolk I went, and having but one child, put it to nurse, intending to go to my parents in Lancashire. So leaving my wife at my cousin Anderton's, I hearing of Seekers in Hartfordshire, went thither, and at last was hired by Mr. Hickman to preach at Peters in St. Albans, so being liked, I was hired for a month longer, so fetched my wife, and there continued till such time the town of Sanderidge took me for their minister, and settled me in the vicarage, where Sir John Garret, Colonel Cox, and Justice Robotom came constantly to hear me, and gave me several gifts, so that in Heaven I was again; for I had a high pitch of free grace, and mightily flown in the sweet discoveries of God, and yet not at all knowing what God was, only an infinite Spirit, which when he pleased did glance into his people the sweet breathings of his Spirit; and therefore preached, it was not sufficient to be a professor, but a possessor of Christ, the possession of which would cause a profession of him, with many such high-flown notions, which at that time I knew no better, nay, and in truth I speak it, there was few of the clergy able to reach me in doctrine or prayer; yet notwithstanding, not being an university man, I was very often turned out of employment, that truly I speak it, I think there was not any poor soul so tossed in judgement, and for a poor livelihood, as then I was. Now in this my prosperity I continued not a year, but the patron being a superstitious cavalier, got an order from the Assembly of Divines to call me in question for my doctrine,[3] and so put in a drunken

---

[1] Isaiah 57:15.

[2] *Mr. Sterry's place* possibly Peter Sterry (1613–1672), Independent minister and later Cromwell's chaplain.

[3] *Assembly of Divines* also known as the Westminster Assembly. A body of 151 nominated members representing a wide spectrum of religious views (though dominated by Presbyterians), appointed by the

fellow in my room: and thus was I displaced from my Heaven upon earth, for I was dearly beloved of Smiths and Thrales, the chief of the parish. Well, there was no other way but for London again, and after a while sent my goods for Suffolk by water: now at this I concluded all was a cheat, yea preaching itself, and so with this apprehension went up and down Hartfordshire, Bedford, and Buckinghamshire, and by my subtlety of reason got monies more or less; as of one at Barton, I had twelve pounds for the printing of a book against the commonalty of England,[1] impeaching them for traitors, for suffering the Parliament their servants, to usurp over them, judging the commonwealth was to cut out the form, and shape of their grievances, and send it up to their servants the Parliament to finish, showing, as the commonwealth gave the Parliament power, so they were greater than the Parliament, with matter to the effect. And then being presented to a small parish in Lincolnshire, thither I went, but finding no society to hear, I grew weary thereof, and stayed with some friends at Oford, so with a little monies went home again, and not long after going into Lincolnshire, I preached in several places, that at last Captain Cambridge hearing of me, and was much affected with me, and made me teacher to their company, and said I should have all necessaries provided me and a man allowed me; then I was well recruited and horsed, so that I judged it was the mercy of God to me, my distress being great, and my care for my family. Now after a while our regiment went for London, so though I had preached in Lincoln, Horncastle, Spilsby, and many other places, yet they would excuse me for two months, having no need of preaching at London, so with what monies I had I went to my wife, and stayed there a while, and so

came for London. Now our regiment being Twistons [George Twisleton's], quartered in Smith-field, but I quartered in a private house, who was a former friend of mine, asked me if I heard not of a people called *My one flesh*?[2] I said no, what was their opinion, and how should I speak with any of them? Then she directed me to Giles Calvert.[3] So that now friends, I am travelling further into the wilderness, having now done burning of brick, I must still wander in the mountains and deserts; so coming to Calvert, and making enquiry after such a people, he was afraid I came to betray them, but exchanging a few words in the height of my language, he was much affected, and satisfied I was a friend of theirs, so he writ me a note to Mr. Brush, and the effect thereof was, the bearer hereof is a man of the greatest light I ever yet heard speak, and for ought I know indeed of receiving of him you may receive an angel, so to Mr. Brush I went, and presented this note, which he perused, so bid me come in, and told me if I had come a little sooner, I might have seen Mr. Coppe,[4] who then had lately appeared in a most dreadful manner; so there being Mary Lake, we had some discourse, but nothing to what was in me, however they told me, if next Sunday I would come to Mr. Melis in Trinity-lane, there would that day some friends meet. Now observe at this time my judgment was this, that there was no man could be freed from sin, till he had acted that so called sin, as no sin, this a certain time had been burning within me, yet durst not reveal it to any, in that I

Long Parliament to reform the English church.

[1] *A Generall Charge or, Impeachment of High Treason, in the Name of Justice Equity, against the Communality of England* (1647), an uncharacteristically political pamphlet with ideas close to those of the Levellers.

[2] *My one flesh* Nothing is known of this group other than what Clarkson writes here; he clearly intends readers to associate it with the Ranters (see below).

[3] *Giles Calvert* a bookseller active in London from 1639 to his death in 1663. In the late 1640s, Calvert published Ranter, Leveller, and Digger works (including about half of Gerrard Winstanley's writings); in the 1650s he published early Quaker literature and was appointed one of the official printers to the Council of State.

[4] *Coppe* Abiezer Coppe (1619–1672), Ranter. See the introduction to the selections from his *A Fiery Flying Roll*.

thought none was able to receive it, and a great desire I had to make trial, whether I should be troubled or satisfied therein: so that:

Seventhly, I took my progress into the wilderness, and according to the day appointed, I found Mr. Brush, Mr. Rawlinson, Mr. Goldsmith, with Mary Lake, and some four more: now Mary Lake was the chief speaker, which in her discourse was something agreeable, but not so high as was in me experienced, and what I then knew with boldness declared, in so much that Mary Lake being blind, asked who that was that spake? Brush said the man that Giles Calvert sent to us, so with many more words I affirmed that there was no sin, but as man esteemed it sin, and therefore none can be free from sin, till in purity it be acted as no sin, for I judged that pure to me, which to a dark understanding was impure, for to the pure all things, yea all acts were pure: thus making the Scripture a writing of wax, I pleaded the words of Paul, "That I know, and am persuaded by the Lord Jesus, that there was nothing unclean, but as man esteemed it,"[1] unfolding that was intended all acts, as well as meats and drinks, and therefore till you can lie with all women as one woman, and not judge it sin, you can do nothing but sin: now in Scripture I found a perfection spoken of, so that I understood no man could attain perfection but this way, at which Mr. Rawlinson was much taken, and Sarah Kullin being then present, did invite me to make trial of what I had expressed, so as I take it, after we parted, she invited me to Mr. Wats in Rood-lane, where was one or two more like her self, and as I take it, lay with me that night: now against next Sunday it was noised abroad what a rare man of knowledge was to speak at Mr. Brush's; at which day there was a great company of men and women, both young and old; and so from day to day increased, that now I had choice of what before I aspired after, insomuch that

it came to our officer's ears; but having got my pay I left them, and lodged in Rood-lane; where I had clients many, that I was not able to answer all desires, yet none knew our actions but our selves; however I was careful with whom I had to do. This lustful principle increased so much, that the Lord Mayor with his officers came at midnight to take me, but knowing thereof, he was prevented. Now Coppe was by himself with a company ranting and swearing, which I was seldom addicted to, only proving by Scripture the truth of what I acted; and indeed Solomon's writings was the original of my filthy lust, supposing I might take the same liberty as he did, not then understanding his writings was no Scripture, that I was moved to write to the world what my principle was, so brought to public view a book called *The Single Eye*,[2] so that men and women came from many parts to see my face, and hear my knowledge in these things, being restless till they were made free, as then we called it. Now I being as they said, *Captain of the Rant*,[3] I had most of the principal women came to my lodging for knowledge, which then was called the Headquarters. Now in the height of this ranting, I was made still careful for moneys for my wife, only my body was given to other women: so our company increasing, I wanted for nothing that heart could desire, but at last it became a trade so common, that all the froth and scum broke forth into the height of this wickedness, yea began to be a public reproach, that I broke up my quarters, and went into the country

---

[1] Romans 14:14.

[2] *A Single Eye All Light, No Darkness; or Light and Darkness One* (London: Giles Calvert, 1650), a sustained argument that no act is intrinsically sinful, that "swearing, drunkenness, adultery, and theft" are sins only if the person committing them believes them to be so. Parliament ordered this "impious and blasphemous" book burned in September 1650.

[3] Clarkson is the only source for this claim to leadership. The term "Ranter" was applied pejoratively to a loose assortment of religious and social radicals of the period; it is unclear how organized a group the Ranters were, or even if they could be called a group at all except in the imagination of those seeking to define unacceptable behaviour in a time of rapid religious, political, and social change.

to my wife, where I had by the way disciples plenty, which then Major Rainsborough,[1] and Doctor Barker was minded for Mr. Walis of Elford, to there I met them, where was no small pleasure and delight in praising of a God that was an infinite nothing, what great and glorious things the Lord had done, in bringing us out of bondage, to the perfect liberty of the sons of God, and yet then the very notion of my heart was to all manner of theft, cheat, wrong, or injury that privately could be acted, though in tongue I professed the contrary, not considering I brake the law in all points (murder excepted:) and the ground of this my judgement was, God had made all things good, so nothing evil but as man judged it; for I apprehended there was no such thing as theft, cheat, or a lie, but as man made it so: for if the creature had brought this world into no propriety, as mine and thine, there had been no such title as theft, cheat, or a lie; for the prevention hereof Everard and Gerrard Winstanley did dig up the Commons,[2] that so all might have to live of themselves, then there had been no need of defrauding, but unity one with another, not then knowing this was the devil's kingdom, and reason lord thereof, and that reason was naturally inclined to love itself above any other, and to gather to itself what riches and honor it could, that so it might bear sway over its fellow creature; for I made it appear to Gerrard Winstanley there was a self-love and vain-glory nursed in his heart, that if possible, by digging to have gained people to him, by which his name might become great among the poor commonalty of the nation, as

afterwards in him appeared a most shameful retreat from Georges-hill,[3] with a spirit of pretended universality, to become a real tithe-gatherer of propriety; so what by these things in others, and the experience of my own heart, I saw all that men spake or acted, was a lie, and therefore my thought was, I had as good cheat for something among them, and that so I might live in prosperity with them, and not come under the lash of the law; for here was the thought of my heart from that saying of Solomon, Eccles. 3:19: "For that which befalleth the sons of men, befalleth beasts, even one thing befalleth them; as the one dieth, so dieth the other, yea, they have all one breath, so that a man hath no preeminence above a beast; for all is vanity, all go into one place, all art of the dust, and all turn to dust again." So that the 18th and 19th verses of Ecclesiastes was the rule and direction of my spirit, to eat and to drink, and to delight my soul in the labor of my mind all the days of my life, which I thought God gave me as my portion, yea to rejoice in it as the gift of God, as said that wise head-piece Solomon; for this then, and ever after, till I came to hear of a commission,[4] was the thought of my heart, that in the grave there was no more remembrance of either joy or sorrow after. For this I conceived, as I knew not what I was before I came in being, so for ever after I should know nothing after this my being was dissolved; but even as a stream from the ocean was distinct in itself while it was a stream, but when returned to the ocean, was therein swallowed and become one with the ocean; so the spirit of man while in the body, was distinct from God, but when death came it returned to God, and so became one

---

[1] William Rainsborough, a New Model Army officer with Leveller sympathies, and a participant in the Putney debates. In 1650 he was cited in the Commons for countenancing Clarkson's (prohibited) *A Single Eye*.

[2] William Everard (fl. 1643–49) and Winstanley (ca. 1609–?1676), the major figures of the Digger movement, a form of agrarian communism. They believed that true freedom was possible only when private property was abolished, and that the common lands should be worked to the benefit of all. See the selections from Winstanley.

[3] St. George's Hill, near Cobham in Surrey, the site of the best known Digger experiment in tilling commons and waste lands (summer 1649). The settlement was dispersed as a result of pressure from local landowners. Clarkson implies that Winstanley's "retreat" was from his principles.

[4] *a commission* the Muggletonian commission.

with God, yea God itself; yet notwithstanding this, I had sometimes a relenting light in my soul, fearing this should not be so, as indeed it was contrary; but however, then a cup of wine would wash away this doubt.

But now to return to my progress, I came for London again, to visit my old society; which then Mary Midleton of Chelsford and Mrs. Star was deeply in love with me, so having parted with Mrs. Midleton, Mrs. Star and I went up and down the country as man and wife, spending our time in feasting and drinking, so that taverns I called the house of God; and the drawers,[1] messengers; and sack, divinity; reading in Solomon's writings it must be so, in that it made glad the heart of God; which before, and at that time, we had several meetings of great company, and that some, no mean ones neither, where then, and at that time, they improved their liberty, where Doctor Paget's maid stripped herself naked, and skipped among them, but being in a cook's shop, there was no hunger, so that I kept myself to Mrs. Star, pleading the lawfulness of our doings as aforesaid, concluding with Solomon all was vanity. In the interim the Parliament had issued forth several warrants into the hands of church-members, which knew me not by person, but by name, so could not take me, though several times met with me, that at last the Parliament to him that could bring me before them, would give a hundred pounds, so that one Jones for lucre of money, knowing me, got a warrant to apprehend me, who meeting me in the four swans within Bishopsgate, told me he had a warrant from the High Court of Parliament to take me. Let me see it, said I, you have no power to serve it without an officer, and so would have escaped, but could not the people so thronged about me, and a great tumult there was, some fighting with him for an informer, but being a city trooper, and some more

of his company with him, they carried me, as I take it, to Alderman Andrews, where they searched my pockets; but having dropped an almanac that had the names of such as sold my books for me, they found it, and carried it to the Parliament, so informed the House I was taken, and likewise desired to know what they should do with me, who gave order to bring me by water to Whitehall-stairs, and deliver me to Barkstead's [Colonel John Barkstead's] soldiers, where after a while a messenger was sent to take me into custody, where I was lodged in Whitehall over against the Dial, and two soldiers guarded me night and day, for which I was to pay; but some being of my principle, they would guard me for nothing, and a captain of theirs would give me moneys; so after two days I was sent for before the committee of Parliament to be examined: so being called in, they asked me my name, my country, with many such frivolous things; so coming to the business in hand, Mr. Weaver being the chairman, asked me if I lodged in Rood-lane? To which I answered, once I did. Wherefore did you lodge there? Because I had a friend there of whom I hired a chamber. What company of men and women were those that came to you? To instance their names I cannot, but some came as they had business with me. Who were those women in black bags that came to you? As now I know not. But Mr. Claxton, we are informed, you have both wives and maids that lodgeth with you there? Those that informed you, let them appear face to face, for I never lay with any but my own wife. No: for you call every woman your wife? I say I lie with none but my wife, according to law, though in the unity of the spirit, I lie with all the creation. That is your sophistication, but deal plainly before God and man, did not you lie with none in Rood-lane, and others' places, besides your wife? I do deal plainly as you, but I being a free-born subject ought not to accuse myself, in that you are to prove your charge. Mr. Claxton confess the truth, it will be better for you:

---

[1] *drawers* tapsters.

for we assure you shall suffer no wrong. What I know is truth, I have, and shall speak. What did you at Mrs. Croes' in Rederiff? I had conference with the people. As you were preaching, you took a pipe of tobacco, and women came and saluted you, and others above was committing adultery. This is more than I remember? No, you will not remember any thing against you: but surely you cannot but remember this almanac is yours, and these men's names your own handwriting. Yea I did write them. Was not these men your disciples? They were not mine, but their own. Did not Major Rainsborough, and the rest lie with other women? Not as I know. But Mr. Claxton do you remember this book is yours? I never saw that before, but may be some of the like nature I have. Why, did not you write this book? That you are to prove. Here is the two first letters of your name. What is that to me? it may serve for other names as well as mine. Did not Major Rainsborough and these men give you monies to print this book? How should they give me monies to print that which neither I nor they knew of. This book must be yours, for it speaks your language, suitable to your practise. I being but a stranger to you, how should you know my language or practise? Though you will confess nothing, yet we have witness to prove it. Let them be examined in my presence: so calling Jones that betrayed me, did you never see Mr. Claxton lie with no woman? I have heard him talk of such things, but saw no act. Though you cannot, there is some will, therefore Mr. Claxton deal plainly, that though you lay with none, yet did not you allow it none others? I saw no evil in them to disallow; and gentlemen let me speak freely to you, suppose I were your servant, entrusted with your secrets, and knew that you were traitors against this present power, would you take it well for me to impeach you, and bear witness against you? At which, either the Earl of Denby, or the Earl of Salisbury said, no: such a servant deserved to be hanged; at which they laughed and said, this was a case of another nature. I say as it is in the one, so it is in the other. Well then, Mr. Claxton, you will not confess the truth. You say you have witness to prove it. However the truth I have confessed, and no more can be expected. Do not you know one Coppe? Yea I know him, and that is all, for I have not seen him above two or three times. Then they said, this is a sad principle, which if not routed, all honest men will have their wives deluded. One of them said, he feared not his wife she was too old, so they dismissed me to the place from whence I came, and said we shall report it to the House, that so with speed you may have your trial, but I think it was about fourteen weeks before I received the sentence of the House, which took up the House a day and half work, as John Lilborn said,[1] stood the nation in a thousand pounds. And thus they sat spending the commonwealth's monies, about frivolous things. Now having passed some votes, at last they carried the day for my banishment, which vote that day was printed, and pasted upon many posts about the city of London, that Lawrence Claxton "should remain in New-Bridewel a month and a day, and then the High Sheriff of London conduct him to the High Sheriff in Kent, and so to be banished England, Scotland and Ireland, and the Territories thereof during life, and Major Rainsborough to be no longer Justice during his life."[2] Now when my month was expired, their vote was not executed, so after a while I came forth of prison, and then took my journey with my wife to my house in Stainfield, and from thence I took my progress into Cambridgeshire, to the towns of Foxen and Orwel where still I continued my ranting principle, with a high hand.

Now in the interim I attempted the art of astrology and physic, which in a short time I gained, and therewith travelled up and down

---

[1] John Lilburne (1615–1657), Leveller leader and pamphleteer; Lilburne often refers to financial issues in his writings.

[2] The banishment was ordered on September 17, 1650.

Cambridgeshire and Essex, as Linton and Saffron-walden, and other country towns, improving my skill to the utmost, that I had clients many, yet could not be therewith contented, but aspired to the art of magic, so finding some of Doctor Ward's and Woolerd's manuscripts,[1] I improved my genius to fetch goods back that were stolen, yea to raise spirits, and fetch treasure out of the earth, with many such diabolical actions, as a woman of Sudbury in Suffolk assisted me, pretending she could do by her witch-craft whatever she pleased; now something was done, but nothing to what I pretended, however monies I gained, and was up and down looked upon as a dangerous man, that the ignorant and religious people was afraid to come near me, yet this I may say, and speak the truth, that I have cured many desperate diseases, and one time brought from Glenford to a village town wide of Laxham to Doctor Clark,[2] two women and one man that had bewitched his daughter, who came in a frosty cold night, tormented in what then Clark was a doing, and so after that his daughter was in perfect health, with many such like things, that it puffed up my spirit, and made many fools believe in me, for at that time I looked upon all was good, and God the author of all, and therefore have several times attempted to raise the devil, that so I might see what he was, but all in vain, so that I judged all was a lie, and that there was no devil at all, nor indeed no God but only nature, for when I have perused the Scriptures I have found so much contradiction as then I conceived, that I had no faith in it at all, no more than a history, though I would talk of it, and speak from it for my own advantage, but if I had really then related my thoughts, I neither believed that Adam was the first creature, but that there was a creation before him, which world I thought was eternal, judging that land of Nod where Cain took his wife, was inhabited a long time before Cain, not considering that Moses was the first writer of Scripture, and that we were to look no further than what there was written; but I really believed no Moses, Prophets, Christ, or Apostles, nor no resurrection at all: for I understood that which was life in man, went into that infinite bulk and bigness, so called God, as a drop into the ocean, and the body rotted in the grave, and forever so to remain.

In the interim came forth a people called Quakers,[3] with whom I had some discourse, from whence I discerned that they were no further than burning brick in Egypt, though in a more purer way than their fathers before them; also their God, their devil, and their resurrection and mine, was all one, only they had a righteousness of the law which I had not; which righteousness I then judged was to be destroyed, as well as my unrighteousness, and so kept on my trade of preaching, not minding anything after death, but as aforesaid, as also that great cheat of astrology and physic I practised, which not long after I was beneficed in Mersland, at Terington and St. Johns, and from thence went to Snetsham in Norfolk, where I was by all the town received, and had most of their hands for the presentation, then for London I went, and going to visit Chetwood my former acquaintance, she, with the wife of Middleton, related to me the two witnesses;[4] so having some conference with Reeve the prophet, and reading his writings, I was in a trembling condition; the nature thereof you may read in the introduction of that book (*Look about you, for the*

---

[1] possibly Samuel Ward (d. 1643) of Cambridge. Woolerd remains unidentified.

[2] possibly Gilbert Clark, a student of Samuel Ward's.

[3] *Quakers* founded by George Fox (1624–1691) in the late 1640s. Their reliance on the inner light led Quakers to dispense with consecrated buildings, ordained ministers, or set liturgy of any kind; their refusal to take oaths, pay tithes, or acknowledge social hierarchy led to widespread persecution. Clarkson wrote against the Quakers in *The Quakers Downfal* (1659).

[4] Muggleton and Reeve, who claimed to be the "two witnesses" promised in Revelation 11:3–6.

devil that you fear is in you)[1] considering how sadly I had these many years spent my time, and that in none of these seven churches could I find the true God, or right devil;[2] for indeed that is not in the least desired, only to prate of him, and pray to him we knew not, though it is written, "It is life eternal to know the true God,"[3] yet that none of them minds, but from education believeth him to be an eternal, infinite spirit, here, there, and everywhere; which after I was fully persuaded, that there was to be three commissions upon this earth,[4] to bear record to the three titles above, and that this was the last of those three: upon the belief of this I came to the knowledge of the two seeds, by which I knew the nature and form of the true God, and the right devil, which in all my travels through the seven churches I could never find, in that now I see, it was only from the revelation of this commission to make it known.

Now being at my journey's end, as in point of notional worship, I came to see the vast difference of faith from reason, which before I conclude, you shall hear, and how that from faith's royal prerogative all its seed in Adam was saved, and all reason in the fallen angel was damned, from whence I came to know my election and pardon of all my former transgressions; after which my revelation growing, moved me to publish to the world, what my Father was, where he liveth, and the glory of his house, as is confirmed by my writings now in public; so that now I can say, of all my formal righteousness, and professed wickedness, I am stripped naked, and in room thereof clothed with innocency of life, perfect assurance, and seed of discerning with the spirit of revelation.

[The autobiographical narrative over, the text continues with a theological question-and-answer section about Muggletonian doctrine.]
—1660

---

[1] by Clarkson, published in 1659.

[2] *seven churches* the seven churches he passed through from the Church of England to Ranting; Clarkson probably chose the number (and consequently organized his narrative) to coincide with the "seven churches" of Revelation 1:4.

[3] John 17:3.

[4] *three commissions* a doctrine based ultimately on the writings of the mystic Joachim of Fiore (ca. 1132–1202), in which all of history is divided into three great periods: the age of the Father, lived under Law until the end of the Old Testament dispensation; the age of the Son, lived under grace until the end of the New Testament dispensation; and the forthcoming age of the Spirit. Joachimite ideas, with their promise of the dawning of a new religious order, were very popular among the radical religious sects of the 1640s.

Richard Overton
fl. 1640 – 1664

Little is known of Overton's life before 1640, though he might be the Richard Overton who matriculated at Queen's College, Cambridge, in 1631 and acted in the college company. Some scholars think he spent the 1630s as a professional actor and/or playwright; this speculation is based primarily on the "theatricality" of his polemical writing. Overton began his rise to prominence in 1640–42, when he published numerous pamphlets attacking the foundations of English religious, political, legal, and economic life. Using an imaginative variety of satiric and fictive strategies, Overton targeted episcopacy, economic monopolies, the civil law, and royal councillors, often singling out individuals, particularly archbishop William Laud, for special attention. In late 1642 or 1643, he apparently spent some time in the radical religious communities in Amsterdam. He also wrote *Mans Mortalitie* (1644), a theological work in which he denied the immortality of the soul between death and the Resurrection; along with Milton's *Doctrine and Discipline of Divorce* (1644), this tract provoked the Parliamentary investigation of unlicensed printing that would lead Milton to write *Areopagitica* (1644). In 1645–46, Overton attacked the growing intolerance of the victorious Presbyterians in a series of pamphlets that employed the persona of Martin Marpriest (adopted from the late sixteenth-century Martin Marprelate tracts). The best known is *The Araignement of Mr. Persecution* (1645), an allegorical trial that might have inspired John Bunyan's Vanity Fair trial scene in *The Pilgrim's Progress*. In the second half of the 1640s, Overton worked closely with other Leveller leaders, writing or co-writing dozens of pamphlets and newspaper editorials calling for the political, social, and economic reforms that constituted the basis of the Leveller programme. Little again is known of Overton after the waning of the Levellers in 1649. In the 1650s he was involved in various shadowy plots aimed against Oliver Cromwell, and a warrant for his arrest in 1663 implies he survived into the Restoration. But the place and date of his death are unknown.

The following narrative is excerpted from *The Picture of the Councel of State* (1649), which contains narratives by Overton, John Lilburne, and Thomas Prince describing their arrest in March 1649 for their role in the publication of *The Second Part of England's New Chains Discovered* (1649), an attack on Cromwell's Council of State. Along with William Walwyn, all were imprisoned for their refusal to answer questions and thereby incriminate themselves. Overton spends much of his narrative refuting the politically resonant charge that he was caught sleeping with another man's wife. Political and religious radicals of the period were frequently accused of advocating free love (the "community of women," as the officer who arrests Overton puts it). The charge stemmed largely from anxiety that these radical platforms threatened all property—which included wives—and concomitant gender hierarchies: what might wives do if given this freedom? Characteristic of Overton's writing is his use of dialogue to dramatize his confrontation with authorities, and his legalistic reproduction of the actual documents involved. For more on the Levellers, see the selections from the Putney Debates and William Walwyn.

❧❧❧

The Proceedings of the Council of State Against Richard Overton, now Prisoner in the Tower of London, 1649

Upon the twenty eighth of March 1649, a party of horse and foot commanded by Lieut. Colonel [Daniel] Axtel (a man highly pretending to religion,) came betwixt five and six of the morning to the house where I then lodged, in that hostile manner to apprehend me, as by the sequel appeared.

But now, to give an account of the particular circumstances attending that action, may seem frivolous, as to the public; but in regard the Lieutenant Colonel was pleased so far to out-strip the capacity of a saint, as to betake himself to the venomed arrows of lying calumnies and reproaches, to wound (through my sides) the too much forsaken cause of the poor oppressed people of this long wasted Commonwealth: like as it hath been the practice of all perfidious tyrants in all ages. I shall therefore trouble the reader with the rehearsal of all the occurrent circumstances which attended his apprehension of me, that the world may clearly judge betwixt us. And what I here deliver from my pen as touching this matter, I do deliver it to be set upon the record of my account, as I will answer it at the dreadful day of judgment, when the secrets of all hearts shall be opened, and every one receive according to his deeds done in the flesh: and God so deal with me at that day, as in this thing I speak the truth: And if the rancorous spirits of men will not be satisfied therewith, I have no more to say but this, to commit myself to God in the joyful rest of a good conscience, and not value what insatiable envy can suggest against me. Thus then to the business itself.

In the house where I then lodged that night there lived three families, one of the gentlemen being my very good friend, with whom all that night he and I only lay in bed together, and his wife and child lay in another bed by themselves: and when they knocked at the door, the gentleman was up and ready, and his wife also, for she rose before him, and was suckling her child: and I was also up, but was not completely dressed; and of this the gentleman (her husband) hath taken his oath before one of the Masters of the Chancery.[1] And we three were together in a chamber discoursing, he and I intending about our business immediately to go abroad, and hearing them knock, I said, Yonder they are come for me. Whereupon, some books that lay upon the table in the room, were thrown into the beds betwixt the sheets (and the books were all the persons he found there in the beds, except he took us for printed papers, and then there were many;) and the gentleman went down to go to the door; and as soon as the books were cast aside, I went to put on my boots; and before the gentleman could get down the stairs, a girl of the house had opened the door, and let them in, and so meeting the gentleman upon the stairs, Axtel commanded some of the soldiers to seize upon him, and take him into custody, and not suffer him to come up: And I hearing a voice from below, that one would speak with me, I went to the chamber door (it being open) and immediately appeared a musketeer (Corporal Neaves, as I take it) and he asked me if my name were not Mr. Overton: I answered, it was Overton; and so I sat me down upon the bed side to pull on my other boot, as if I had but new risen, the better to shelter the books; and that Corporal was the first man that entered into the chamber, and after him one or two more, and then followed the Lieutenant Colonel; and the Corporal told me, I was the man they were come for, and bade me make me ready: and the Lieutenant Colonel when he came in, asked me how I did, and told me, they

---

[1] *hath taken his oath* Overton reproduces the affidavit at the end of the narrative. The Chancery was the court of the Lord Chancellor, a Master one of the Chancellor's twelve assistants.

would use me civilly, and bid me put on my boots, and I should have time enough to make me ready: And immediately upon this the Lieutenant Colonel began to abuse me with scandalous language, and asked me, if the gentlewoman who then sat suckling her child, were not one of my wives, and averred that she and I lay together that night. Then the gentleman hearing his wife called whore, and abused so shamefully, got from the soldiers, and ran up stairs; and coming into the room where we were, he taxed the Lieutenant Colonel for abusing of his wife and me, and told him, that he and I lay together that night: But the Lieutenant Colonel, out of that little discretion he had about him, took the gentleman by the hand, saying, How dost thou, brother cuckold? using other shameful ignorant and abusive language, not worthy repeating. Well, upon this his attempt thus to make me his prisoner, I demanded his warrant; and he showed me a warrant from the Council of State, with Mr. Bradshaw's hand to it,[1] and with the broad seal of England to it, (as he called it) to apprehend Lieutenant Colonel Lilburne, Mr. Walwyn, Mr. Prince,[2] and myself, wherever they could find us. And as soon as I was dressed, he commanded the musketeers to take me away; and as soon as I was down stairs, he remanded me back again into the chamber where he took me, and then told me, he must search the house, and commanded the trunks to be opened, or they should be broken open: and commanded one of the soldiers to search my pockets. I demanded his warrant for that: He told me, he had a warrant, I had seen it. I answered, That was for the apprehen-

sion of my person; and bid him show his warrant for searching my pockets, and the house: and according to my best remembrance, he replied, He should have a warrant. So little respect had he to law, justice, and reason; and *vi & armis* [by force of arms], right or wrong, they fell to work, (inconsiderately devolving all law, right, and freedom betwixt man and man into their sword; for the consequence of it extends from one to all) and his party of armed horse and foot (joined to his over-hasty exorbitant will) was his irresistible warrant: And so they searched my pockets, and took all they found in them, my money excepted, and searched the trunks, chests, beds, &c. And the Lieutenant Colonel went into the next chamber, where lived an honest soldier (one of the Lieutenant General's [Cromwell's] regiment) and his wife, and took away his sword, and vilified the gentleman and his wife, as if she had been his whore, and took him prisoner for lying with a woman, as he said. He also went up to the gentleman who lets out the rooms, and cast the like imputations upon his wife, as also upon a maid that lives in the house, and gave it out in the court and street, amongst the soldiers and neighbours that it was a bawdy-house, and that all the women that lived in it were whores, and that he had taken me in bed with another man's wife. Well, he having ransacked the house, found many books in the beds, and taken away all such writings, papers, and books, of what sort or kind soever, that he could find, and given them to the soldiers, (amongst which he took away certain papers which were my former meditations upon the works of the creation, entitled *God's Word confirmed by his Works*;[3] wherein I endeavoured the probation of a God,[4] a creation, a state of innocence, a fall, a resurrection, a restorer, a day of judgment, &c. barely from the consideration of

---

[1] John Bradshaw (1602–1659), president from 1649–1652 of the Council of State, the country's executive body throughout the Interregnum; Bradshaw presided at the trial of Charles I.

[2] The three Leveller leaders arrested at the same time as Overton: John Lilburne (1615–1657), a Lieutenant-Colonel of dragoons when he left the Parliamentary army in 1645; William Walwyn (1600–1680); and Thomas Prince (fl. 1640–1653). Lilburne and Walwyn both published numerous pamphlets on liberty and toleration in addition to their work on behalf of the Leveller cause.

---

[3] This book, apparently a theological treatise, does not appear to have been subsequently published.

[4] *probation* proof, demonstration.

things visible and created: and these papers I reserved to perfect and publish as soon as I could have any rest from the turmoils of this troubled Commonwealth: and for the loss of those papers I am only troubled: all that I desire of my enemies' hands, is but the restitution of those papers, that whatever becomes of me, they may not be buried in oblivion, for they may prove useful to many). Well, when the Lieutenant Colonel had thus far mistaken himself, his religion and reason thus unworthily to abuse me and the household in that scandalous nature, unbeseeming the part of a gentleman, a soldier, or a Christian (all which titles he claimeth) and had transgressed the limits of his authority, by searching, ransacking, plundering, and taking away what he pleased, he marched me in the head of his party to Paul's Church-yard, and by the way commanded the soldiers to lead me by the arm; and from thence, with a guard of three companies of foot, and a party of horse, they forced me to Whitehall; and the soldiers carried the books some upon their muskets, some under their arms: but by the way (upon our march) the Corporal that first entered the room (whose word in that respect is more valuable than Axtel's) confessed unto me (in the audience of the soldier they took also with them from the place of my lodging) that the Lieutenant Colonel had dealt uncivilly and unworthily with me, and that there was no such matter of taking me in bed with an other woman, &c. And this the said soldier will depose upon his oath.

When I came to Whitehall, I was delivered into the hands of Adjutant General Stubber, where I found my worthy friends Lieutenant Colonel John Lilburne, Mr. Walwyn, and Mr. Prince in the same captivity under the martial usurpation: and after I had been there a while, upon the motion of Lieutenant Colonel Lilburne, that Lieutenant Colonel Axtel, and I might be brought face to face about the matter of scandal that was raised, he coming there unto us, and questioned about the report he had

given out, there averred, that he took me abed with another man's wife; and being asked if he saw us actually in bed together, he answered, we were both in the chamber together, and the woman had scarce got on her coats, (which was a notorious untruth) and she sat suckling of her child, and from these circumstances he did believe we did lie together, and that he spake according to his conscience what he believed: These were his words, or to the like effect, to which I replied, as aforementioned. But how short this was of a man pretending so much conscience and sanctity as he doth I leave to all unprejudiced people to judge: it is no point of Christian faith (to which [he] is so great a pretender) to foment a lie for a wicked end, and then to plead it his belief and conscience, for the easier credence of his malicious aspersion: but though the words "belief" and "conscience" be too specious evangelical terms, no truly conscientious person will say they are to be used, or rather abused to such evil ends. Well in that company I having taxed him for searching my pockets, and without warrant, he answered; that because I was so base a fellow, he did what he could to destroy me. And then the better to make up the measure of the reproach he had raised, he told us, it was now an opinion amongst us to have community of women;[1] I desired him to name one of that opinion, he answered me, It may be that I was of that opinion, and I told him, it may be that he was of that opinion, and that my may be was as good as his may be: whereupon he replied, that I was a saucy fellow. Surely the Lieutenant Colonel at that instance had forgot the bugget from whence he dropped,[2] I presume when he was a peddler in Harfordshire he had not so lofty an esteem of himself, but now the case is altered, the gentleman is become one of the grandees of the Royal palace:

---

[1] *community of women*   free love; see headnote. An accusation also made against the Ranters and other religious radicals.

[2] *bugget*   a budget; a pouch, bag, or wallet, usually made of leather (*OED* budget 1); referring to the officer's "peddler" pedigree.

one of the (mock-) Saints in season, now judging the earth, inspired with providence and opportunities at pleasure of their own invention as quick and nimble as an hocas spocas, or a fiend in a juggler's box, they are not flesh and blood, as are the wicked, they are all spiritual, all heavenly, the pure chameleons of the time, they are this or that or what you please, in a trice, in a twinkling of an eye; there is no form, no shape that you can fancy among men, into which their spiritualities are not changeable at pleasure; but for the most part, these holy men present themselves in the perfect figure of angels of light, of so artificial resemblance, enough to deceive the very elect if possible, that when they are entered into their sanctum sanctorum [holy of holies], their holy convocation at Whitehall, they then seem no other than a choir of archangels, of cherubims and seraphims, chanting their false holy Hallelujahs of victory over the people, having put all principalities and powers under their feet, and the Kingdom and dominion and the greatness of the Kingdom is theirs, and all dominions, even all the people shall serve and obey them, (excuse me, it is but their own counterfeit dialect, under which their pernicious hypocrisy is veiled that I retort into their bosoms, that you may know them within and without, not that I have any intention of reflection upon holy writ) and now these men of Jerusalem (as I may term them) those painted sepulchres of Sion after their long conjuring together of providences, opportunities and seasons one after another, dressed out to the people in the sacred shade of God's time, (as after the language of their new fangled saintships I may speak it) they have brought their seasons to perfection, even to the season of seasons, now to rest themselves in the large and full enjoyment of the creature for a time, two times and half a time, resolving now to wear out the true asserters of the people's freedom,[1] and to change the time

and laws to their exorbitant ambition and will; while all their promises, declarations and engagements to the people must be nulled and made cyphers, and cast aside as waste paper, as unworthy the fulfilment, or once the remembrance of those gentlemen, those magnificent stems of our new upstart nobility, for now it is not with them as in the days of their engagement at Newmarket and Triploe heath,[2] but as it was in the days of old with corrupt persons, so is it in ours, *Tempora mutantur*—.[3]

But to proceed to the story: the Lieutenant Colonel did not only show his weakness, (or rather his iniquity) in his dealing with me, but he convents the aforesaid soldier of Lieutenant General's regiment before divers of the officers at Whitehall, and there he renders the reason wherefore he made him a prisoner, because said he, he takes Overton's part, for he came and asked him how he did, and bid him be of good comfort, and he lay last night with a woman: To which he answered, It is true, but the woman was my wife. Then they proceeded to ask, when they were married, and how they should know she was his wife, and he told them where and when, but that was not enough, they told him, he must get a certificate from his Captain that he was married to her and then he should have his liberty.

Friends and country-men, where are you now? what shall you do that have no captains to give you certificates? sure you must have the banns of matrimony re-asked at the Conventicle of Gallants at Whitehall, or at least you must thence have a congregational licence, (without offence be it

---

[1] *true asserters of the people's freedom*   the Levellers.

[2] *their engagement at Newmarket and Triploe heath*   high points of army radicalism and unity: a general rendezvous of the New Model Army was held in Newmarket on June 4–5, 1647 during which officers and soldiers engaged not to disband until various grievances had been redressed; a second rendezvous was held on Triploe Heath, not far from Cambridge, a few days later on June 10.

[3] *Tempora mutantur nos et metamur in illis*   "times change and we change with them," an epigram attributed to John Owen (1560?–1622).

spoken to true churches) to lie with your wives, else how shall your wives be chaste or the children legitimate? they have now taken cognizance over your wives and beds, whither will they next? Judgement is now come into the hand of the armed-fury saints. My masters have a care what you do, or how you look upon your wives, for the new Saints militant are paramount all laws, King, Parliament, husbands, wives, beds, &c. But to let that pass.

Towards the evening we were sent for, to go before the Council of State at Darby-house, and after Lieutenant Colonel John Lilburne, and Mr. Walwyn had been before them, then I was called in, and Mr. Bradshaw spake to me, to this effect.

Master Overton, the Parliament hath seen a book, entitled *The Second Part of England's New Chains Discovered*, and hath passed several votes thereupon, and hath given order to this Council to make inquiry after the authors and publishers thereof, and proceed upon them as they see cause, and to make a return thereof unto the House: And thereupon he commanded Mr. Frost their secretary to read over the said votes unto me, which were to this purpose, as hath since been publicly proclaimed:

Die Martis 27 Martii, 1649. [Tuesday 27 March]
The House being informed of a scandalous and seditious book printed, entitled, *The Second Part of England's New Chains Discovered*.

The said book was this day read.
Resolved upon the question by the Commons assembled in Parliament, That this printed paper, entitled, *The Second Part of England's New Chains Discovered* etc. doth contain most false, scandalous, and reproachful matter, and is highly seditious and destructive to the present government, as it is now declared and settled by Parliament, tends to division and mutiny in the army, and the raising of a new war in the Commonwealth, and to hinder the present relief of Ireland, and to the continuing of

free-quarter:[1] And this House doth further declare, that the authors, contrivers, and framers of the said papers, are guilty of high treason, and shall be proceeded against as traitors; and that all persons whatsoever, that shall join with, or adhere unto, and hereafter voluntarily aid or assist the authors, framers, and contrivers of the aforesaid paper, in the prosecution thereof, shall be esteemed as traitors to the Commonwealth, and be proceeded against accordingly.

Then Mr. Bradshaw spake to me much after this effect:

Master Overton, this Council having received information, that you had a hand in the contriving and publishing of the book, sent for you by their warrant to come before them; besides, they are informed of other circumstances at your apprehension against you, that there were divers of the books found about you. Now Mr. Overton, if you will make any answer thereunto, you have your liberty.

To which I answered in these words, or to the like effect:

Sir, what title to give you, or distinguish you by, I know not; indeed, I confess I have heard by common report, that you go under the name of a Council of State; but for my part, what you are I cannot well tell; but this I know, that had you (as you pretend) a just authority from the Parliament, yet were not your authority valuable or binding, till solemnly proclaimed to the people: so that for my part, in regard you were pleased thus violently to bring me before you, I shall humble crave at your hands, the production of your authority, that I may know what it is, for my better information how to demean my self.[2]

PRESIDENT: Mr. Overton, we are satisfied in our authority.

---

[1] *free-quarter* the obligatory provision of room and board to soldiers.

[2] *your authority* A few months earlier, King Charles had at his trial challenged the authority of a judicial body headed by John Bradshaw in similar terms, though for different reasons.

R. OVERTON Sir, if I may not know it, however I humbly desire, that I may be delivered from under the force of the military power; for having a natural and legal title to the rights of an Englishman, I shall desire that I may have the benefit of the law of England, (which law taketh no cognizance of the sword). And in case you or any man pretend matter of crime against me, in order to a trial, I desire I may be resigned up to the civil magistrate, and receive a free and legal trial in some ordinary court of justice, according to the known law of the land; that if I be found a transgressor of any established declared law of England, on God's name let me suffer the penalty of that law.

Further, Sir, in case I must still be detained a prisoner, it is my earnest desire, that I may be disposed to some prison under the jurisdiction and custody of the civil authority: For, as for my own part, I cannot in conscience (to the common right of the people) submit myself in any wise to the trial or custody of the sword; for I am no soldier, neither hath the army any authority over me, I owe them neither duty nor obedience, they are no sheriffs, justices, bailiffs, constables, or other civil magistrates: So that I cannot, neither will I submit unto their power, but must take the boldness to protest against it.

PRESIDENT: Mr. Overton, if this be your answer, you may withdraw.

R. OVERTON: Sir, I humbly desire a word or two more.

LIEUT. GEN. [CROMWELL]: Let him have liberty.

PRESIDENT: Mr. Overton, you may speak on.

R. OVERTON: Gentlemen, for future peace and security sake, I shall humbly desire to offer this unto your consideration; namely, that if you think it meet: That you would choose any four men in England, pick and choose where you please; and we (for my part, I speak it freely in my own behalf, and I think I may say as much in theirs) shall endeavour to the utmost of our power by a fair and moderate discourse, to give the best account and satisfaction concerning the matter of difference betwixt us, that we can, that if possible, peace and agreement may be made: And this, after the weakness of my small understanding, I judge to be a fair and reasonable way: if you shall be pleased to accept of it, you may; if not, you may use your pleasure; I am in your hand, do with me as you think good, I am not able to hinder you.

PRESIDENT: Mr. Overton, if this be all you have to say, withdraw.

R. OVERTON: Sir, I have said.

So I was commanded into a little withdrawing room close by the Council; and I supposed they would have taken my motion into consideration: But after I had been there a while, I was ordered to the room again, where Lieutenant Colonel Lilburne, Mr. Walwyn, &c. were.

And now that it may be clear unto the whole world, that we heartily desire the prevention and cessation of all differences and divisions that may be bred and break forth in the land, to the hazard, if not actual embroilment thereof in a new exundation of blood in the prosecution of this controversy,[1] we do freely from the heart (that heaven and earth may bear witness betwixt our integrity to the peace of the Commonwealth, and their dealings with us) make this proffer as to be known to the whole world; that we (in the first place I may best speak for myself; and I so far know the minds of Lieutenant Colonel John Lilburne, Mr. Walwyn, and Mr. Prince, that I may as freely speak it in their behalfs) will, by the assistance of God, give any four men in England that they shall choose (although the Lieutenant General, and the Commissary General be two of them)[2] a free and moderate debate (if they

---

[1] *exundation* overflow, inundation (*OED*).

[2] *Commissary General* Henry Ireton (1611–1651), Commissary-General of Horse, Oliver Cromwell's son-in-law, and a leader in the negotiations among the army, the King, and the Parliament in the later 1640s.

shall think it no scorn) touching all matters of difference betwixt us, as to the business of the Commonwealth (for therein doth consist the controversy betwixt us) that if possibly, new flames and combustions may be quenched, and a thorough and an hearty composure be made betwixt us, upon the grounds of an equal and just government. And that the business may be brought to a certain issue betwixt us, let them, if they please, choose two umpires out of the House, or elsewhere, and we will choose two; and for our parts, we shall stand to the free determination or sentence, that these four, or any three of them shall pass betwixt us. Or else, if they please but to center upon the *Agreement of the People* with amendments according to our late sad apprehensions,[1] presented to the House upon the 26 of February 1648 [that is, 1649], for our parts, we shall seal a contract of oblivion for all bypast matters, relating either to good name, life, liberty or estate; saving, of making accompt for the public monies of the Commonwealth: And in such an agreement we will center, to live and die with them in the prosecution thereof. And if this be not a fair and peaceable motion, let all well-minded people judge.

But if nothing will satisfy them but our blood, we shall not (through the might of God) be sparing of that, to give witness to the right and freedom of this Commonwealth against their usurpation and tyranny; but let them know this, that building hath a bad foundation that is laid in the blood of honest men, such as their own knowledge and consciences bear them record, are faithful to the common interest and safety of the people: out of our ashes may possibly arise their destruction. This I know, God is just, and he will repay the blood of the innocent upon the head of the tyrant. But to return to the narrative.

After some small space that we had all been before them, we were called in again; first, Lieutenant Colonel John Lilburne, then Mr. Walwyn, and then myself: And coming before them the second time, Mr. Bradshaw, spake to this effect:

PRESIDENT: Mr. Overton, the Council hath taken your answer into consideration, and they are to discharge their duty to the Parliament, who hath ordered them to make enquiry after the book, entitled, *The Second Part of England's New Chains, &c.* And thereof they are to give an account to the House: And the Council hath ordered me to put this question unto you. Whether you had an hand in the contriving or publishing this book, or no?

R. OVERTON: Sir, I well remember, that since you cut off the King's head, you declared (or at least the Parliament, from whence you pretend the derivation of your authority) that you would maintain the known fundamental laws of the land, and preserve them inviolable, that the meanest member of this Commonwealth, with the greatest, might freely and fully enjoy the absolute benefit thereof. Now gentlemen, it is well known, and that unto yourselves, that in cases criminal, as now you pretend against me, it is against the fundamental laws of this Commonwealth to proceed against any man by way of interrogatories against himself, as you do against me: and I believe (gentlemen) were you in our cases, you would not be willing to be so served yourselves; (what you would have other men do unto you, that do you unto them.) So that for my part, gentlemen, I do utterly refuse to make answer unto any thing in relation to my own person, or any man or men under heaven; but do humbly desire, that if you intend by way of charge to proceed to any trial of me, that it may be (as before I desired at your hands) by the known established law of England, in some ordinary court of justice appointed for such cases (extraordinary ways being never to be used,

---

[1] *Agreement of the People* a revised version of the Leveller manifesto, first published in October 1647 (see the selection from the Putney Debates), republished by Lilburne, Walwyn, Prince, and Overton in May 1649 while they were prisoners in the Tower.

but abominated, where ordinary ways may be had) and I shall freely submit to what can be legally made good against me.

But I desire that in the mean time you would be pleased to take notice, that though in your eye I seem so highly criminal, as by those votes you pretend; yet am I guilty of nothing, not of this paper, entitled, *The Second Part of England's New Chains*, in case I had never so much an hand in it, till it be legally proved: for the law looketh upon no man to be guilty of any crime, till by law he be convicted; so that, I cannot esteem myself guilty of any thing, till by the law you have made the same good against me.

And further sir, I desire you to take notice, that I cannot be guilty of the transgression of any law, before that law be in being: it is impossible to offend that which is not; where there is no law there is no transgression: Now, those votes on which you proceed against me are but of yesterday's being; so that, had I an hand in that book whereof you accuse me, provided it were before those votes, you cannot render me guilty by those votes: If I had done any thing in it, since the votes (provided you had solemnly proclaimed the same) then you might have had some colour to have proceeded against me: but I have but newly heard the votes, and since that you know I could do nothing.

PRESIDENT: Mr. Overton, I would correct your judgment in one thing: We are not upon any trial of you; we are only upon the discharge of our duty, and that trust committed unto us by the Parliament, to make enquiry after the authors, contrivers and framers of the book; and having information against yourself and your comrades, we sent for you, and are to return your answer to the House, howsoever you dispute their authority.

R. OVERTON: Dispute their authority, Sir! That's but your supposition, and supposition is no proof. And Sir, as you say you are to discharge your duty, so must I discharge mine. And as for matter of trial,

I am sure you tax me in a criminal way, and proceed to question me thereupon. But Sir, I conceive it my duty to answer to none of your questions in that nature, and therefore shall utterly refuse.

Now gentlemen, I desire you to take notice, that I do not oppose you as you are members of the Commonwealth; for it is well known, and I think to some here, that I have ever been an opposer of oppression and tyranny, even from the days of the bishops to this present time; and the books that I have writ and published do in some measure bear witness thereof, and it is well known, that my practice hath ever been answerable thereunto. I suppose no man can accuse me, but that I have opposed tyranny where-ever I found it: It is all one to me under what name or title soever oppression be exercised, whether under the name of King, Parliament, Council of State, under the name of this, or that, or any thing else; for tyranny and oppression is tyranny and oppression to me where-ever I find it, and where-ever I find it I shall oppose it, without respect of persons.

I know I am mortal and finite, and by the course of nature my days must have a period, how soon I know not; and the most you can do, it is but to proceed to life; and for my part, I had rather die in the just vindication of the cause of the poor oppressed people of this Commonwealth, than to die in my bed; and the sooner it is, the welcomer, I care not if it were at this instant, for I value not what you can do unto me.

But gentlemen, I humbly desire yet a word or two. I confess, I did not expect so much civility at your hands as I have found, and for the same I return you hearty thanks.

Now whereas you commonly say, That we will have no bottom, center no where, and do tax us by the votes you read unto me, of destruction to the present government, division and mutiny in the army, &c. But here I do profess unto you, as in the presence of the all-seeing God, before whom one day I must give an account of all my actions, that in case you will but conclude upon an equal and just government by way of an Agreement of the People, as was honourably begun by the general officers of the army; and but free that article in it which concerns the liberty of God's worship from the vexatious entanglements and contradictions that are in it, that so conscientious people might freely (without any fear of an insulting clergy) live quietly and peaceably in the enjoyment of their consciences; as also to add unto it a bar against regality, and the House of Lords; as also to make provision in it against the most weighty oppressions of the land; that thereby they may be utterly removed, and for the future prevented, and the people settled in freedom and safety: And then, for my part, neither hand, foot, pen, tongue, mouth or breath of mine shall move against you; but I shall with my utmost power, with hand, heart, life and blood, assist you in the prosecution thereof, and therein center. Try me, and if I fail of my word, then let me suffer.

PRESIDENT: Mr. Overton, if you have no more to say, you may withdraw.

R. OVERTON: Sir, I humbly crave the further addition of a word or two. Gentlemen, I desire (as I did before) that I may (according to the common right of the people of England) be forthwith freed from under the power of the sword, and be delivered into the hands of the Civil Magistrate, in case I shall be still detained a prisoner; for I am so much against the intrusion of the military power into the seat of the Magistrate, that I had rather you would fetter me legs and hands, and tie me neck and heels together, and throw me into a dungeon, and not allow me so much as the benefit of bread and water till I be starved to death, than I would accept of the best down-bed in England, with suitable accommodation, under the custody of the sword.

PRESIDENT: Mr. Overton, I would correct your judgment a little, you are not under the military power, but under the civil authority; for by the

authority of Parliament this Council by their warrant hath sent for you.

R. OVERTON: Sir, it is confessed, that *pro forma tantum*, for matter of form, ink or paper, I am under the civil authority, but essentially and really, I am under the martial power; for that warrant by which I was taken, was executed upon me by the military power, by a party of horse, and divers companies of foot in arms, and in that hostile manner (like a prisoner of war) I was led captive to Whitehall, and there ever since, till commanded hither, I was kept amongst the soldiers, and I am still under the same force: Besides, Sir, these men are mere soldiers, no officers of the magistracy of England, they brought no warrant to me from any Justice of Peace, neither did carry me before any Justice of Peace, but seized on me, and kept me by their own force: Therefore it is evident and clear to me, that I am not under the civil, but the martial power.

PRESIDENT: Master Overton, if this be your answer, you may withdraw.

R. OVERTON: Sir, I have said.

And so I was conducted to the room where they had disposed Lieutenant Colonel Lilburne and Mr. Walwyn: And the next news we heard from them, was, of our commitment to the Tower, and Master Prince and I were joined as yoke-fellows in one warrant; a copy whereof is as followeth;

These are to will and require you, to receive herewith into your custody the persons of Master Richard Overton, and Master Thomas Prince, and them safely to keep in your prison of the Tower of London, until you receive further order: They being committed to you upon suspicion of High Treason; of which you are not to fail; and for which this shall be your warrant: Given at the Council of State at Darby-House this twenty-eighth day of March, 1649.

Signed in the name, and by the order of the Council of State, appointed by authority of Parliament.

To the Lieutenant of the Tower,

Jo. Bradshaw, President.

Thus all uninterested, unprejudiced persons, (who measure things as they are in themselves, having nothing in admiration with respect of persons, who simply and sincerely mind the freedom and prosperity of the Commonwealth) may clearly see, as in a glass, by this taste of aristocratical tyranny towards us, a perfect and lively resemblance of the Council of State; *Ex pede Leonem*, you may know a lion by his foot, or a bear by his paw: by this you may see their nature and kind, what and from whence they are, and whether they tend, by this line you may measure the height depth and breadth of their new architecture of state, and by making our case but yours, you will find yourselves new fettered in chains, such as never England knew or tasted before; that you may (truly if you will but measure it in the consequence thereof,) break forth and cry out, their little finger is thicker than our father's loins; our fathers made our yoke heavy, but these add unto our yoke; our fathers chastised us with whips, but these chastise us with scorpions.[1] Who would have thought in the days of their glorious pretences for freedom, in the days of their engagements, declarations and remonstrances, while they were the hope of the oppressed, the joy of the righteous, and had the mighty confluence of all the afflicted and well-minded people of the land about them, (I principally reflect upon the victors of the times) I say, who would have thought to have heard, seen, or felt such things from their hands as we have done? Who would have thought such glorious and hopeful beginnings should have vanished into tyranny? Who would have thought to

have seen those men end in the persecution and imprisonment of persons whom their own consciences tell them, to be men of known integrity to the Commonwealth; and which is so evident and demonstrative, that thousands in this nation can bear record thereof; and that those men should be so devilish, so tyrannical and arbitrary, as after their imprisonment, to rake hell, and skim the devil, to conjure out matter of charge or accusation against them, that they might have their blood, as in our case they have done, sending abroad their bloodhounds to search and pry out in every corner, what could be made out against us, going up and down like roaring lions seeking how they might devour us; one offering Mistress Prince her husband's liberty, and the £1000 they owe him, if he will but discover what he knoweth (as they are pleased to imagine) against us; and not only so, but some members of the House (as Mr. Kiffin confessed in respect of himself)[2] negotiate with the principal leaders of several congregations of religious people about the town, to promote a petition, which was no other but in order to their bloody design against us; that those conscientious people (surprised by their fraudulent suggestions and craft) might (not truly understanding the business) appear in the disownment and discountenance of us; and in the approbation and furtherance of the prosecutors of their bloody votes of High Treason, intentionally breathed out against us: for could they by their delusions overwhelm us once in the odium of religious people; with the venomous contagion of their malicious clamours, bug-bears, reproaches and lies, beget us under the anathema of the churches, then they think they may with ease and applause cut us off; for that's the venom lieth under the leaf, how finely soever they zeal it over; that so our friends and brethren (thus surprised and overtaken) may become our butchers, and think they do God and

---

[1] a reference to II Chronicles 10:10–11.

[2] *Mr. Kiffin* William Kiffin (1616–1701), a prominent Baptist minister.

their country good service while they slay us; but let them beware how they contract the guilt of our blood upon their heads; for assuredly the blood of the innocent will be upon them, and God will repay it; I speak not this to beg their mercy, I abhor it, I bid defiance to what all the men and devils in earth or hell can do against me in the discharge of my understanding and conscience for the good of this Commonwealth; for I know my redeemer liveth, and that after this life I shall be restored to life and immortality, and receive according to the innocency and uprightness of my heart: Otherwise, I tell you plainly, I would not thus put my life and well-being in jeopardy, and expose myself to those extremities and necessities that I do; I would creaturize, be this or that or any thing else, as were the times, eat, drink, and take my pleasure; turn Judas or any thing to flatter great men for promotion: but blessed be the God of heaven and earth, he hath given me a better heart, and better understanding. But to proceed;

That which is most to our astonishment, we understand of a truth, that Master Kiffin (to whose congregation my back-friend Axtel is a retainer) Master Spilsbury, Master Patience (who vilified the book entitled *The Second Part of England's New Chains*, and yet confessed he never saw it or heard it read, as by evidence can be made good) Mr. Fountain, Mr. Drapes, Mr. Richardson, Mr. Couset, Mr. Tomlins, and Mr. Wade the schoolmaster became their pursuivants or bloodhounds, to hunt us to the Bar of the House of Commons with a petition (most evidently and clearly in pursuance of our blood) entitled *The Humble Petition and Representation of the several Churches of God in London commonly (though falsely) called Anabaptists*, April 12, 1649, tacitly and curiously in a most religious veil pointing at, and reflecting upon us, as interrupters of the settlement of the liberty and freedom of this Commonwealth;[1] heady, high-minded, unruly, disobedient, presumptuous, self-willed, condemners of rulers, dignities and civil government, whoremasters, drunkards, cheaters, &c. as if it were not with those men, as with the publican and sinner, disowning the book entitled *The Second Part*, &c. which at that juncture of time, all circumstances duly weighed, was an absolute justification of those votes of High Treason, and of prosecution against us as traitors, for the tendency of those votes were vented at us, and that their own knowledge and consciences tells them to be true, so that they could have done no more in order to our blood, than what they did in that matter, so as to hand it off fairly and covertly preserving to themselves the reputation of the churches of God: and to add unto their impiety against us, they juggle with the churches, present it in the name of the churches of God in London called Anabaptists, and in their names remonstrate that they (meaning the churches, as by the title they speak) neither had nor have heart nor hand in the framing, contriving, abetting, or promotion of the said paper, which though read in several of our public meetings, we do solemnly profess, it was without our consent, being there openly opposed by us. Notwithstanding it is notoriously evident, that the generality of the people dissented from their petition against us; and as upon good intelligence I am informed, they had scarce ten in some congregations to sign it, in some not above 2 or 3, in some none; and in the main they had not the tithe of the people:[2] and yet those men like a consistory of bishops, a synod of presbyters, or a New England classis, presume upon the

---

[1] This pamphlet, signed by a number of Independent ministers, reflected the split between the Independents (politically ascendent after the execution of the King), and the Levellers, who pushed for further reforms on religious and political issues. In it, the ministers disavow support for the Leveller text, *England's New Chains Discovered* (1649), that appears to have been submitted to them for signature.

[2] *tithe* ten percent.

assumption of the name of several churches of God,[1] as if to themselves they had purchased the monopoly or patent thereof, or as if the persons of Mr. Kiffin, Mr. Patience, &c. were so many several churches, (hence sprang the papal, prelatical, and presbyterial supremacy over the consciences of people) and therefore it behoveth the people to have a care of their leaders.

We have had the name of King, the name of Parliament, the name of the army, &c. surprised, abused, and usurped against us by the hand of our exorbitant enemies, but never before, the name of several churches of God, and those styled Anabaptists; hear O heavens, and judge O earth! Was there ever the like fact attempted or perpetrated amongst the churches of God? such wickedness is not once to be named amongst them: And I do not doubt but the well-minded Christian people of those several churches presented by that petition, will vindicate themselves from the aspersion thereby laid upon them; for I cannot believe till I see it, that those people would do any thing, or own any thing that might but so much as seemingly tend to our blood, or our imprisonment; I am confident they abhor it: And they cannot in conscience do less than to disavow that bloody petition (as to its tendency against us) and till they do it, they will be sharers in the public guilty of our imprisonment, yea, and of our blood, for (however God may divert the wicked purposes of men), that petition is guilty of our blood.

I confess, for my part, I am a man full of sin, and personal infirmities, and in that relation I will not take upon me to clear or justify myself; but as for my integrity and uprightness to the Commonwealth, to whatsoever my understanding tells me is for the good of mankind, for the safety, freedom,

and tranquillity of my country, happiness and prosperity of my neighbours, to do to my neighbour as I would be done by, and for the freedom and protection of religious people: I say as to those things, (according to the weak measure of my understanding and judgment) I know my integrity to be such, that I shall freely (in the might of God) sacrifice my life to give witness thereunto; and upon that accompt I am now in bonds, a protestor against the aristocratical tyranny of the Council of State, scorning their mercy, and bidding defiance to their cruelty, had they ten millions more of armies, & Cromwells to perpetrate their inhumanities upon me; for I know they can pass but to this life; when they have done that, they can do no more; and in this case of mine, he that will save his life shall lose it; I know my life is hid in Christ, and if upon this accompt I must yield it, welcome, welcome, welcome by the grace of God.

And as for those reproaches and scandals like the smoke of the bottomless pit, that are fomented against me; whereby too many zealous tender spirited people are prejudiced against my person, ready to abhor the thing I do, though never so good, for my person sake; I desire such to remove their eyes from persons to things: if the thing I do be good, it is of God; and so look upon it, and not upon me, and so they shall be sure not to mistake themselves, nor to wrong me: And I further desire such to consider, that tales, rumours, slanderings, backbitings, lies, scandals &c. tossed up and down like clouds with the wind, are not the fruits of the spirit, neither are they weapons of God's warfare, they are of the devil and corruption, and betray in the users of them an evil mind: It is a certain badge of a deceiver to take up whisperings and tales of men's personal failings to inflect them to the cause those persons maintain, by such means to gain advantages upon them.

Consider whether the things I hold forth and profess as in relation to the Commonwealth, be not

---

[1] *consistory...synod...classis* judicial bodies for ecclesiastical causes in the established, Presbyterian, and Independent churches respectively; Overton objects to the presumption of representation made by these and similar bodies.

for the good of mankind, and the preservation of God's people: and if they be, my personal failings are not to be reckoned as a counter-balance against them. As I am in myself in respect to my own personal sins and transgressions; so I am to myself and to God, and so I must give an account; the just must stand by his own faith: But as I am in relation to the Commonwealth, that all men have cognizance of, because it concerns their own particular lives, livelihoods and beings, as well as my own; and my failings and evils in that respect I yield up to the cognizance of all men, to be righteously used against me. So that the business is, not how great a sinner I am, but how faithful and real to the Commonwealth; that's the matter concerneth my neighbour, and whereof my neighbour is only in this public controversy to take notice; and for my personal sins that are not of civil cognizance or wrong unto him, to leave them to God, whose judgment is righteous and just. And till persons professing religion be brought to this sound temper, they fall far short of Christianity; the spirit of love, brotherly charity, doing to all men as they would be done by, is not in them; without which they are but as a sounding brass, and a tinkling cymbal, a whited wall, rottenness and corruption, let their ceremonial formal practice of religion be never so angel-like or specious.

There is a great noise of my sins and iniquities: but which of my asperser's ox or ass have I stolen? which of them have I wronged the value of a farthing? They tax me with filthiness, and strange impieties; but which amongst them is innocent? he that is innocent, let him throw the first stone; otherwise let him lay his hand on his mouth: I have heard of as odious failings, even of the same nature whereof they tax me (and it may be, upon better evidence) amongst them, laid open to me, even of the highest in present power, as well as amongst eminent persons in churches; which I ever have counted unworthy to be used as an engine against

them in the controversy of the Commonwealth: But if they will not be quiet, I shall be forced, in honour to my own reputation, to open the cabinet of my asperser's infirmities, that the world may see what sort of men they are that they say unto others, thou shalt not steal, and steal themselves: I shall be sorry to be forced to it; but if they will not be content, necessity hath no law, I shall (as Mr. John Goodwin said to Mr. Edwards, if he would not be quiet)[1] make all their reputations as a stinking carcass.

And although they think they have such firm matters against me, let them not be too hasty to pursue me with reproach any further, lest it recoil with a vengeance upon themselves: for it is an old and a true saying, One tale is good till another be told. Therefore let no man judge before the time, lest he be judged; for I am able to vindicate myself to all rational men, as clear as the sun at noon day, in what I have done.

Much I might have said as in relation to the illegality of our apprehension, commitment, &c. But for the present I shall omit it to further opportunity, or the engagement of some more abler pen: And so I shall commit myself and my ways to God alone, with cheerfulness and alacrity of spirit, rejoicing that he hath counted me worthy to bear witness once more against the oppressors of the people, and to suffer for the sake of the poor, against the insulting tyrants of the times.

RICHARD OVERTON

From my aristocratical captivity in the Tower of London; April 4, 1649.

Dulce est pro Patria mori.[2]

---

[1] John Goodwin (1594?–1665), prominent Independent minister and controversialist; Thomas Edwards (1599–1647), a zealous Presbyterian who attacked the Independents among others in repeatedly updated editions of *Gangraena* (1646); for more on Edwards, see the selection from *Gangraena*.

[2] From Horace, *Odes*, III.ii.13: "it is sweet to die for one's country."

POSTSCRIPT

Courteous Reader, for thy better satisfaction concerning the infamous scandal raised by Lieutenant Colonel Axtel upon me, I thought meet to subjoin hereunto a copy of an affidavit concerning the matter: But I have forborne the publishing of the deponent's name in print, upon his own desire; yet those of my friends who are desirous, I shall be ready to show unto them the original copy: A transcript whereof is as followeth.

A.B. of the parish of St. Anne Aldersgate, citizen and pewterer of London, aged thirty six years or thereabouts, maketh oath, that whereas Lieutenant Colonel Axtel, upon his apprehending of Mr. Richard Overton, upon Wednesday, between five and six of the clock in the morning, being the twenty ninth of March last past, 1649, by an order from the Council of State, did raise and make a report, that he took the said Mr. Overton in bed with this deponent's wife, that that report was and is altogether false and scandalous; for that this deponent and the said Mr. Overton, the Tuesday night next preceding the said Wednesday, did lie both together all that night in one and the self same bed; and this deponent's wife and his little child in another bed of this deponent's house or lodgings. And that the next morning, before the said Lieutenant Colonel Axtel knocked at the door, this deponent, with his wife, with the said Mr. Overton, were all up and ready (saving that Mr. Overton had not put on his boots, band and cuffs) and were altogether in a chamber of this deponent's house, where this deponent's wife was then suckling of her child: and this deponent hearing some body knock at the door, went down to open it; which was readily done by a girl of the same house. Whereupon the said Lieutenant Colonel Axtel (meeting this deponent upon the stairs, and asking him if he were Mr. Overton; to which this deponent replying, No;) commanded the musketeers (who attended him) to take this deponent into custody, and he himself went directly up into the chamber with some musketeers attending him. All which this deponent affirmeth upon his oath to be true.

A.B.

Jurat. 4 Aprilis, 1649
Rob. Aylet[1]
—1649

---

[1] *Jurat...Aylet* the *jurator* or sworn assessor, an assistant to a judge; the person in front of whom this affidavit was signed.

Sir Roger L'Estrange
1616 – 1704

Born into a well-to-do Norfolk family and studying probably at Cambridge, L'Estrange served in the King's army under Prince Rupert and spent three years in a Parliamentary prison for his part in a Royalist plot. Upon his release in 1648 he promoted an unsuccessful Royalist uprising in Kent, then fled to Holland; Edward Hyde (later Earl of Clarendon) put him to work in the service of the exiled Charles II. L'Estrange returned to England in 1653, and in the late 1650s was writing pamphlets in favour of the monarchy. At the Restoration he worked as pamphleteer, government spy, and journalist, serving as editor of the semi-official papers *The News* and *The Intelligencer* (1663–66) and later *The Observator* (1681–87). The primary targets of his early work were Republicans (a 1660 pamphlet entitled *No Blind Guides* answered Milton) and Presbyterians (whom he blamed for the wars and the execution of Charles I); his later work attacked Whigs and dissenters. He was knighted by James II.

L'Estrange's denunciation of liberty of the press in this 1663 text won him an appointment as Surveyor of the Press, a position he would hold almost continuously up to the 1688 Revolution. In addition to providing a great deal of information about seventeenth-century printing and the book trade, L'Estrange's *Considerations* reveals how seriously the power of the press was taken by those who blamed the civil wars on pamphleteering: "persons are pardoned," L'Estrange writes, "but not books." Drawing on an extensive web of informers, he sought to curb a trade that had greatly expanded since the early 1640s. L'Estrange bragged in 1670 of having suppressed 600 pamphlets, and one printer, John Twyn, was hanged, drawn, and quartered on L'Estrange's evidence. But on the whole his efforts were not very successful, and his was one of the last attempts in England to enforce a rigid control of printing. L'Estrange lost his position after the Revolution, and supported himself by writing translations, including the fables of Aesop (1692) and the works of Josephus (1702).

❧❧❧

Considerations and Proposals in Order to the Regulation of the Press

I think no man denies the necessity of suppressing licentious and unlawful pamphlets, and of regulating the press; but in what manner, and by what means this may be effected, that's the question. The two main points are printing, and publishing.[1]

The instruments of setting the work afoot are these. The adviser, author, compiler, writer, corrector, and the persons for whom, and by whom; that is say, the stationer (commonly), and the printer. To which may be added, the letter-founders, and the smiths, and joiners, that work upon presses.

The usual agents for publishing are the printers themselves, stitchers,[2] binders, stationers, hawkers, mercury-women,[3] peddlers, ballad-singers, posts, carriers, hackney-coachmen, boatmen, and mariners. Other instruments may be likewise employed, against whom a general provision will be sufficient. Hiding, and concealing of unlawful books, is but in order to publishing, and may be brought under the same rule.

Touching the adviser, author, compiler, writer, and corrector, their practices are hard to be retrieved, unless the one discover the other.

---

[1] *publishing* distributing.

[2] *stitchers* in bookbinding, those who sewed the gatherings together.

[3] *mercury-women* the (usually female) sellers of pamphlets or newsbooks, which were often called "mercuries" (*OED* mercury *sb* 2e).

This discovery may be procured partly by a penalty upon refusing to discover, and partly by a reward to the discoverer; but let both the penalty and the reward be considerable, and certain: and let the obligation of discovery run quite through, from the first mover of the mischief to the last disperser of it.…

Concerning the confederacy of stationers and printers, we shall speak anon: but the thing we are now upon, is singly printing, and what necessarily relates to it.

One great evil is the multiplicity of private presses, and consequently of printers, who for want of public and warrantable employment are forced either to play the knaves in corners, or to want bread.

The remedy is, to reduce all printers and presses that are now in employment to a limited number; and then to provide against private printing for the time to come, which may be done by the means following.

First: the number of printers and presses being resolved upon, let the number of their journeymen[1] and apprentices be likewise limited: and in like manner, the number of master-founders,[2] and of their journeymen and their apprentices; all which to be allowed of and approved by such person or persons, as shall be authorised for that purpose; neither let any joiner, carpenter, or smith presume to work for or upon any printing press, without such allowance as aforesaid, according to the direction of the late act for printing.[3]

Secondly, let all such printers, letter-founders, joiners, carpenters, and smiths, as shall hereafter be allowed, as aforesaid, be respectively and severely interrogated before their admittance, in order to the discovery of supernumerary printers and presses. That is:

1. Let the printers be questioned about private presses they have at any time wrought upon for so many years last past, and the time when, and for, and with whom: and what other printers and presses they know of at present, beside those of the present establishment.

2. Let the founders be also examined, what letter they have furnished since such a time;[4] when and for whom, and what other printers &c.

3. Let the joiners, carpenters, and smiths be questioned likewise what presses they have erected, or amended, &c. when, and for whom? and what other presses, printers, &c.—as before.

And if after such examination it shall appear at any time within so many months, that any man has wilfully concealed or denied the truth, let him forfeit his employment as a person not fit to be trusted, and let the informer be taken into his place if he be capable of it, and desire it; or else, let him be rewarded some other way. The same course may be taken also concerning English printers and presses beyond the seas.

This may serve as to the discovery of private printers and presses already in employment: Now to prevent underhand-dealing for the future, and to provide against certain other abuses in such as are allowed.

First: Let a special care be taken of card-makers, leather-gilders, flock-workers, and quoif-drawers;[5] either by expressly inhibiting their use of such presses as may be applied to printing of books, or by tying them up to the same terms and conditions

---

[1] *journeymen* craftsmen who have served their apprenticeship and are qualified to work for wages.

[2] *master-founders* makers of type for printing.

[3] *An Act for Preventing the Frequent Abuses in Printing Seditious… Books…and for Regulating of Printing and Printing Presses* (1662), called "The Licensing Act" for its restitution of the licensing system instituted by Archbishop Laud in 1637.

[4] *letter* type.

[5] all trades that could use a press of some sort in their work: respectively, makers of playing cards or maps and charts; leather decorators; workers of flock, a material made from wool or cloth refuse; and makers of head-coverings (coifs).

with printers; and let no other tradesman whatso-ever presume to make use of a printing-press, but upon the same conditions, and under the same penalties with printers.

Secondly. Let no press or printing house be erected or let, and let no joiner, carpenter, smith, or letter-founder work for a printing-house, without notice (according to the late Act).

Thirdly. Let no materials belonging to printing, no letters ready founded, or cast, be imported or bought without the like notice, and for whom (according to the late Act).

Fourthly. Let every master printer be bound at least, if not sworn, not to print, cause or suffer to be printed in his house, or press, any book or books without lawful licence (according to the late Act).

Fifthly. Let no master printer be allowed to keep a press but in his own dwelling house, and let no printing house be permitted with a back door to it.

Sixthly. Let every master printer certify what warehouses he keeps, and not change them without giving notice.

Seventhly. Let every master printer set his name to whatsoever he prints, or causes to be printed (according to the late Act).

Eighthly. Let no printer presume to put upon any book, the title, marque, or vignette, of any other person who has the privilege of sole printing the same, without the consent of the person so privileged (according to the late Act) and let no man presume to print another man's copy.

Ninthly. Let no printer presume either to re-print, or change the title of any book formerly printed, without licence; or to counterfeit a licence, or knowingly to put any man's name to a book as the author of it, that was not so.

Tenthly. Let it be penal to antedate any book; for by so doing, new books will be shuffled among old ones to the increase of the stock.

Eleventhly. Let the price of books be regulated.

Twelfthly. Let no journeyman be employed without a certificate from the master where he wrought last.

Thirteenthly. Let no master discharge a journey-man, nor he leave his master, under 14 days notice, unless by consent.

Fourteenthly. Let the persons employed be of known integrity, so near as may be; free of the said mysteries, and able in their trades (according to the late Act)....

Next to printing follows publishing or dispers-ing, which, in and about the town, is commonly the work of printers, stitchers, binders, stationers, mercury-women, hawkers, peddlers, and ballad singers.

Concerning printers, stitchers, and binders; the penalty may be double, where the fault is so: That is, where the same person (for example) is found to be both printer and disperser of the same unlawful books, he may be punished in both capacities: of the rest (the stationer excepted) little need be said but that they may be punishable, and the penalty suited to the quality of the offender.

The most dangerous people of all are the confed-erate stationers, and the breaking of that knot would do the work alone. For the closer carriage of their business they have here in the town, their private warehouses, and receivers.

Let every stationer certify, what warehouses he keeps, and not change them without giving notice.

Let the receivers and concealers of unlawful or unlicensed books be punished as the dispersers of them, unless within 12 hours after such receipt they give notice to [a person to be named] that they have such quantities of books in their custody, and to whom they belong.

They hold intelligence abroad by the means of posts, carriers, hackney-coachmen, boatmen, and mariners: and for fear of interceptions they correspond by false names, and private tokens; so that if a letter or packet miscarry, people may not know what to make on't. As for the purpose: so many dozen of gloves stands for so many dozen of books. Such a marque for such a price, &c.

They enter in their day books, only in general terms, such and such parcels of books, without naming particulars.

1. Let every stationer living in or about London be obliged to keep a day book of the particulars of all the unlicensed books and papers which he sends, causes or allows to be sent, by any of the messengers above-mentioned, into any parts of his Majesty's Dominions; and let him enter the names likewise of the persons to whom he sends them, under a penalty; if either he be proved to have kept a false book, or to have corresponded under a false name, and let every stationer elsewhere (i.e. within the Kingdom of England, and Dominion of Wales) be obliged to keep a day book likewise, of what unlicensed books and papers he receives, and from whom, upon the like penalty.

2. Let no stationer presume to send, cause or allow to be sent, either by land, or water, any dry-fats, bales, packs, maunds, or other fardells,[1] or packets of printed books, or papers, without superscribing them in such sort, that they may be known to be books, together with the names of the persons from whom they are sent, and to whom they are directed: under pain of forfeiting all parcels of books that are not so superscribed, or otherwise that are advertised under false names.

3. Let every hackney-coachman, carrier, boatman, or mariner, that knowingly transgresses in the private conveyance of such letters or packets as aforesaid, be subjected to a particular penalty.

Concerning books imported. They must be first prepared beyond the seas; secondly, conveyed hither; and thirdly, received and distributed here.

Let the English printer, vender, or utterer of any books written in the English tongue, or by an English man, in any other tongue and printed beyond the seas, to the dishonour of his Majesty or of the established government, be required to appear from beyond the seas, by a certain day, and under such a penalty; which if he refuse, or wilfully fail to do, let it be made penal for any person living within his Majesty's Dominions (after sufficient notice of his such contempt), to hold any further correspondence with him, either by message, letter, or otherwise, till he hath given satisfaction for his offence.

Let a general penalty be laid upon the importers of any English books, whatsoever, printed beyond the seas. And so likewise upon the contractors: for the receivers, concealers, and dispersers of any books whatsoever, imported into this realm, and disposed of without due authority. It rests now to be considered. First what books are to be suppressed, and secondly, into what hands the care of the press is to be committed.

The books to be suppressed are as follows

First, all printed papers pressing the murder of the late King.

Secondly, all printed justifications of that execrable act.

Thirdly, all treatises denying his Majesty's title to the Crown of England.

Fourthly, all libels against the person of his sacred Majesty, his blessed father, or the Royal Family.

Fifthly, all discourses manifestly tending to stir up the people against the established government.

Sixthly, all positions terminating in this treasonous conclusion, that his Majesty may be arraigned,

---

[1] all containers for transporting goods: *dry-fat* any large vessel (cask, barrel, tub) used to hold dry goods (*OED*); *maunds* wicker or woven baskets (*OED*); *fardells* bundles or parcels (*OED*).

judged, and executed, by his people: such as are these following:

Coordination;[1] the sovereignty of the two houses, or of the House of Commons; or of the diffusive body of the people, in case of necessity. The justification of the war raised in 1642 in the name of King and Parliament. The defence of the legality and obligation of the covenant.[2] The separation of the King's person from his authority. The denial of his Majesty's power in ecclesiastical affairs. The maintaining that the Long Parliament is not yet dissolved.

If it be objected that this looks too far back; it may be answered that persons are pardoned, but not books. But to more particular reasons for the suppressing of old pamphlets.

First, it is (with reverence) a duty both from his sacred Majesty and his Parliament, to the honour, and memory of the late King, to deliver the reputation of that blessed martyr from the diabolical calumnies and forgeries which are yet extant against his person, and government.

Secondly, it is as much a duty toward our present sovereign, of whose Royal Family, and person, as much ill is said, and published, as is possible for the wit of man to utter, or for the malice of Hell to invent.

Thirdly, in relation to political ends, and to the security of the public, they ought to be suppressed: for they do not only revile, and slander his Majesty's royal person, but many of them disclaim his very title to the crown; and others subject his prerogative, and consequently his sacred life to the sovereign power of the people; and this is done too, with all the advantages of a pestilent and artificial imposture. Now why a pamphlet should be allowed to proclaim this treason to the world, which but whispered in a corner would certainly bring a man to the gallows, is not easily comprehended.

Fourthly, it makes the English nation cheap in the eyes of the world, to find the blood and virtues of the late King, appear so little to be considered, beside the hazardous consequence of blasting the Royal cause, and of discouraging loyalty to future generations, by transmitting the whole party of the Royalists, in so many millions of virulent libels, to posterity, for a prostitute rabble of villains and traitors.

Fifthly, these desperate libels and discourses do not only defame the government, encourage and enrich the faction, and poison the people; but, while they are permitted, those stationers and printers that would otherwise be honest are forced either to play the knaves for company, or to break: for there's scarce any other trading for them, but in that trash. Their customers will be supplied, and if they ask for any of these treasonous books, they must either furnish them, or lose their custom.

Sixthly, the same reason that prohibits new pamphlets, requires also the suppressing of old ones (of the same quality), for 'tis not the date that does the mischief, but the matter, and the number. If they be plausible, and cunning enough to deceive, and then numerous enough to spread, Buchanan and Knox will do the business as sure as Baxter and Calamy.[3] Besides that in some respects, the old ones have a great advantage of the new: for being written in times of freedom, and managed by great masters of the popular style, they speak plainer and strike

---

[1] *Coordination* in this context, the idea that the three estates (King, Lords, and Commons) shared or co-ordinated executive power, the King being just one of three.

[2] *the covenant* the *Solemn League and Covenant* (1643), an agreement between the Scottish Covenanters and Parliament to impose Presbyterianism in England and Ireland and to safeguard constitutional liberties won by Parliament.

[3] George Buchanan (1506–1582), Scottish historian and political theorist who opposed royal absolutism; John Knox (1515?–1572), the dominant figure of the Scottish reformation; Richard Baxter (1615–1691), prolific puritan divine; Edmund Calamy (1600–1666), English Presbyterian divine.

homer to the capacity and humour of the multitude; whereas they that write in the fear of a law, are forced to cover their meaning under ambiguities, and hints, to the greater hazard of the libeller, than of the public.

Seventhly, they must be suppressed, in order to a future regulation: for otherwise 'tis but antedating new books, and making them pass for old ones (which may be done with very little hazard of detection) or else, as any saleable book grows scarce 'tis but reprinting it with a false date, and by these additions, and recruits, a stock of seditious pamphlets shall be kept in motion to the end of the world. In fine, if they are not fit to be sold, they are not fit to be kept; for a verbal prohibition without an actual seizure will be rather an advantage to the private trade, than a hindrance; and bring profit to the factious book-sellers and printers, that have copies lie upon their hands, by enhancing the prices.

. . . .

[L'Estrange prints excerpts from a variety of texts expressing opinions he thinks unacceptable.] I could add more, and worse to the instances already given, but these shall suffice for a taste. The question is now, by whom the government and oversight of the press is to be undertaken, and the contest lies at present betwixt the booksellers and printers, which although concorporate by an ancient grant, are in this point become competitors; and since they have divided themselves, they shall be here likewise distinctly considered.

The Stationers are not to be entrusted with the care of the press, for these following reasons

First, they are both parties and judges: for diverse of them have brought up servants to the mystery of printing which they still retain in dependence: Others again are both printers and stationers, themselves; so that they are entrusted (effectually) to search for their own copies; to destroy their own interests; to prosecute their own agents, and to punish themselves: for they are the principal authors of those mischiefs which they pretend now to redress, and the very persons against whom the penalties of this intended regulation are chiefly levelled.

Secondly, it is not advisable to rely upon the honesty of people (if it may be avoided) where that honesty is to their loss: especially if they be such as have already given proof that they prefer their private gain before the well-fare of the public: which has been the stationer's case throughout our late troubles, some few excepted, whose integrity deserves encouragement.

Thirdly, in this trust, they have not only the temptation of profit to divert them from their duty (a fair part of their stock lying in seditious ware) but the means of transgressing with great privacy and safety: for, make them overseers of the press, and the printers become totally at their devotion; so that the whole trade passes through the fingers of their own creatures, which, upon the matter, concludes rather in a combination, than a remedy.

Fourthly, it seems a little too much to reward the abusers of the press with the credit of superintending it: upon a confidence that they that destroyed the last king for their benefit, will now make it their business to preserve this to their loss.

Fifthly, it will cause a great disappointment of searches, when the persons most concerned shall have it in their power to spoil all, by notices, partiality, or delay....

The Printers are not to be trusted with the government of the press

First, all the arguments already objected against the stationers hold good also against the printers, but not fully so strong. That is, they are both parties, and judges. Self-ended, (upon experiment) under the temptation of profit. Offenders as well as the stationers; and in all abuses of the press, confederate with them. Besides, they will have the same influence upon searches; and they have probably as little stomach to a regulation, as the other…

Secondly, it were a hard matter to pick out twenty master-printers, who are both free of the trade, of ability to manage it, and of integrity to be entrusted with it: most of the honester sort being impoverished by the late times, & the great business of the press being engrossed by Oliver [Cromwell's] creatures.…

To conclude: both printers and stationers, under colour of offering a service to the public, do effectually design one upon another. The printers would beat down the book-selling trade, by managing the press as themselves please, and by working upon their own copies. The stationers, on the other side, they would subject the printers to be absolutely their slaves; which they effected in a large measure already, by so increasing the number, that the one half must either play the knaves, or starve.

The expedient for this must be some way to disengage the printers from that servile and mercenary dependence upon the stationers, upon which they are at present subjected. The true state of the business being as follows.

First, the number of master-printers is computed to be about 60, whereas 20 or 24 would dispatch all the honest work of the nation.

Secondly, these master-printers have above 100 apprentices (that is, at least 20 more than they ought to have by the law).

Thirdly, there are, beside aliens,[1] and those that are free of other trades,[2] at least 150 journey-men, of which number, at least 30 are superfluous; to which 30 there will be added about 36 more, beside

above 50 supernumerary apprentices, upon the reduction of the master-printers to 24.…

These supernumerary printers were at first introduced by the book-sellers, as a sure way to bring them both to their prices and purposes; for the number being greater than could honestly live upon the trade, the printers were enforced either to print treason, or sedition, if the stationer offered it, or to want lawful work, by which necessity on the one side, and power on the other, the combination became exceeding dangerous, and so it still continues; but how to dissolve it, whether by dis-incorporating the Company of Stationers, and subjecting the printers to rules apart, and by themselves; or by making them two distinct companies, I do not meddle.

This only may be offered, that in case those privileges and benefits should be granted to both stationers and printers, which they themselves desire in point of trade; yet in regard that several interests are concerned, that of the kingdom on the one side, and only that of the companies on the other; it is but reason that there should be several super-intending powers, and that the smaller interest should give place, and be subordinate to the greater: That is, the master and wardens to manage the business of their respective trade, but withal, to be subjected to some superior officer, that should over-look them both on behalf of the public. [L'Estrange proposes six surveyors of the press, independent of the Company of Stationers, each of whom would examine and license books before publication.]

Now concerning penalties and rewards

1. The gain of printing some books is ten times greater, if they escape, than the loss, if they be taken: so that the damage bearing such a disproportion to the profit, is rather an allurement to offend, than a discouragement.

---

[1] *aliens* resident foreigners.

[2] *free of other trades* Completion of apprenticeship within any guild could allow a "freeman" to work in another trade.

2. As the punishment is too small, for the offender; so is the reward also, for the informer: for reckon the time, trouble, and money, which it shall cost the prosecutor to recover his allotment, he shall sit down at last a loser by the bargain: and more than that, he loses his credit, and employment, over and above, as a betrayer of his fellows; so great is the power and confidence of the delinquent party.

The way to help this, is, to augment both the punishment and the reward; and to provide that the inflicting of the one, and the obeying of the other, may be both easy and certain: for to impose a penalty and to leave the way of raising it, so tedious and difficult as in this case hitherto it is, amounts to no more than this: if the informer will spend ten pound 'tis possible he may recover five: and so the prosecutor must impose a greater penalty upon himself, than the law does upon the offender; or else all comes to nothing.

An expedient for this inconvenience is highly necessary; and why may not the oath of one credible witness or more, before a Master of the Chancery, or a Justice of the Peace, serve for a conviction. Especially the person accused being left at liberty before such oath taken, either to appear to the Privy-Council, or to abide the decision.

Now to the several sorts of penalties, and to the application of them.

The ordinary penalties I find to be these: death, mutilation, imprisonment, banishment, corporal pains, disgrace, pecuniary mulcts:[1] which penalties are to applied with regard to the quality of the offence, and to the condition of the delinquent.

The offence is either blasphemy, heresy, schism, treason, sedition, scandal, or contempt of authority.

The delinquents are the advisers, authors, compilers, writers, printers, correctors, stitchers, and binders of unlawful books and pamphlets: together with all publishers, dispersers and concealers of them in general: and all stationers, posts, hackney-coachmen, carriers, boatmen, mariners, hawkers, mercury-women, peddlers, and balladsingers so offending, in particular.

Penalties of disgrace ordinarily in practice are many, and more may be added.

Pillory, stocks, whipping, carting, stigmatizing, disablement to bear office, or testimony. Public recantation, standing under the gallows with a rope about the neck, at a public execution. Disfranchisement (if free-men), cashiering (if soldiers),[2] degrading (if persons of condition),[3] wearing some badge of infamy: condemnation to work either in mines, plantations, or houses of correction.

Under the head of pecuniary mulcts, are comprehended forfeitures, confiscations, loss of any beneficial office, or employment, incapacity to hold or enjoy any: and finally, all damages accruing, and imposed, as a punishment for some offence.

Touching the other penalties before-mentioned, it suffices only to have named them, and so to proceed to the application of them, with respect to the crime, and to the offender.

The penalty ought to bear proportion to the malice, and influence of the offence, but with respect to the offender too: for the same punishment (unless it be death itself) is not the same thing to several persons; and it may be proper enough to punish one man in his purse, another in his credit, a third in his body, and all for the same offence.

The grand delinquents are the authors or compilers (which I reckon as all one), the printers, and stationers.

For the authors, nothing can be too severe, that stands with humanity, and conscience. First, 'tis the way to cut off the fountain of our troubles. Sec-

---

[1] *pecuniary mulcts* fines (*OED*).

[2] *cashiering* dismissal from military service (*OED* cashier *v* 2).

[3] *degrading* reducing from a higher to a lower social or other kind of rank (*OED* degrade *v* 2).

ondly, there are not many of them in an age, and so the less work to do.

The printer and stationer come next, who beside the common penalties of money, loss of copies, or printing materials, may be subjected to these further punishments.

Let them forfeit the best copy they have,[1] at the choice of that surveyor of the press, under whose cognisance the offence lies; the profit whereof the said officer shall see thus distributed one third to the King, a second to the informer, reserving the remainder to himself.

In some cases, they may be condemned to wear some visible badge, or marque of ignominy, as a halter instead of a hat-band,[2] one stocking blue, and another red; a blue bonnet with a red *T* or *S* upon it, to denote the crime to be either treason, or sedition; and if at any time the person so condemned shall be found without the said badge or marque, during the time of his obligation to wear it, let him incur some further penalty, provided only, that if within the said time, he shall discover and seize, or cause to be seized any author, printer, or stationer, liable at the time of that discovery and seizure to be proceeded against, for the matter of treasonous, or seditious pamphlets, the offender aforesaid shall from the time of that discovery be discharged from wearing it any longer.

This proposal may seem fantastic at first sight; but certainly there are many men who had rather suffer any other punishment than be made publicly ridiculous.

It is not needful here to run through every particular, and to direct, in what manner, and to what degree, these and other offenders in the like kind shall be punished, so as to limit, and appropriate, the punishment: but it shall suffice, having specified the several sorts of offenders, and offences; to have laid down likewise the several species of penalties, sortable to every man's condition, and crime.

Concerning rewards, something is said already, and I shall only add for a conclusion, that they are every jot as necessary as punishments; and ought to be various, according to the several needs, tempers, and qualities of the persons upon whom they are to be conferred. Money is a reward for one; honour for another: and either of these misplaced, would appear rather a mockery, than a benefit.

—1663

---

[1] *best copy* the best-selling or most profitable book they own the right to publish.

[2] *halter* noose.

Abraham Cowley
1618 – 1667

Abraham Cowley was the seventh child of Thomas Cowley, a London stationer. He was born after his father's death, and probably named after his godfather. When he was about ten he opened Spenser's *Faerie Queene* by chance, was "infinitely delighted" and resolved to be a poet himself. One of the most precocious of English poets, he was fifteen when *Poetical Blossoms* was published in 1633, but much of it may have been ready for the press two years earlier. Rumour of its impending publication may have been the occasion of the sonnet "How soon hath Time," by Milton, who was ten years older. 1633 was also notable as the year when the poems of John Donne and George Herbert first achieved print publication. Cowley has been thought of as the last of "the school of Donne." Cowley was educated at Westminster School and in 1636 went up to Trinity College, Cambridge, where he became a close friend of Richard Crashaw and of William Hervey, the first cousin of Henry Jermyn, who was to become Henrietta Maria's secretary and eventually Earl of St. Albans. This connection was later to become important to Cowley. As a young man, Cowley was ambitious for fame as a poet, imagining himself crossing the Alps of success as "the Muse's Hannibal." This ambition may explain his unwise attempt to write a religious epic, the *Davideis*, which was never completed. In 1642 he wrote a comedy, *The Guardian*, for a visit to Cambridge of the Prince of Wales; any hopes of becoming a professional dramatist were dashed by Parliament's banning of all stage performances shortly afterwards. In 1644 he was deprived of his position at Cambridge by the Earl of Manchester's commission, which required subscription to the Solemn League and Covenant. By then Cowley had already departed for Oxford, at that point in the hands of the Royalists; he became a member of the Great Tew circle which congregated around Lord Falkland, and was regarded as a leading Royalist poet. In the early summer of 1643 he began work on a long poem, *The Civil War*, which he abandoned after the first battle of Newbury (September 20, 1643) when it became apparent that history was providing the wrong plot.

Henrietta Maria left England in April 1644, never to see Charles I again. Some time before June 1646 Cowley was in Paris, in Jermyn's household. For several years he managed Henrietta Maria's correspondence (in cipher) with Charles, and, after Charles's death, with the Duke of York. Cowley may have been responsible for drawing Crashaw to the attention of Henrietta Maria. In Paris he is likely to have met Thomas Hobbes, whose philosophy, it has been argued, was important for the development of Cowley's poetic; he also met the diarist John Evelyn, who was to become a great friend, and Edmund Waller, his chief rival as a love poet. Having earlier declared his ambition to be "the Muse's Hannibal," he now decided that he would be "Love's Columbus." His poems in *The Mistress* (1647) provoked Dr. Johnson to say that they "might have been written for penance by a hermit, or for hire by a philosophical rhymer who had only heard of another sex."

In 1651 Cowley went to Scotland with letters for Charles II, and then to Jersey, still a Royalist stronghold, with a mission to sell Crown lands there to raise funds for the royal exiles. Hyde, later to be Lord Chancellor and the most powerful subject in the first years of the Restoration, suspected that Cowley had skimmed off a disproportionate commission. By the summer of 1654 he was back in England, with Cromwell's permission, studying medicine, perhaps as a cover, and now suspected by both sides. In April 1655 he was seized on suspicion of a plot against Cromwell, and only released when his friend, the doctor Charles Scarborough, put up a thousand pounds as warranty for his good behaviour. Like Lovelace, Cowley seems to have been profoundly affected by imprisonment, and the publication he prepared while incarcerated was to ensure that his years of work as a Royalist agent were not rewarded as he had hoped after the Restoration. The *Poems* of 1656, with its famous preface and the often enigmatic Pindaric Odes, have received a good deal of critical attention, in the hope that they might yield a sense of what Cowley's true political opinions were, and whether they were revealed or masked in the preface. His biographer, Bishop Sprat, wrote that he believed "that it would be a meritorious service to the King if any man who was known to have followed his interest could insinuate into the usurpers' minds that men of his principles were now willing to be quiet, and could persuade the poor oppressed Royalists to conceal their affections for better occasions." Unfortunately for Cowley, neither Hyde nor Charles saw it that way, Hyde being angered at the apparent desertion of the Royalist cause expressed in the preface and Charles perhaps concerned by the apparent endorsement of the assassination of a ruler in the "Brutus" ode. It is worth noting, though, that the *Poems* of 1656, like *The Mistress* of 1647, were published by Humphrey Moseley, the leading Royalist publisher of the period.

After his release from prison, Cowley lived in London under surveillance from both sides. He was admitted to the degree of "doctor of physick" at Oxford in December 1657, but there is no evidence that he ever practised. A more notable defector from the Royalist cause at that time was the Duke of Buckingham, who was an admirer of Cowley's work and became a consistent supporter. Another important friend made at this time was Thomas Sprat, still an undergraduate at Wadham College, Oxford, as was the future Earl of Rochester. When it finally became clear that Charles II would be restored to the throne, Cowley tried to rid himself of the suspicion caused by the *Poems* of 1656, writing a long letter to Ormonde at the royal headquarters in Brussels on December 26, 1659. He received no direct help from Charles, but the King did order Trinity College to reinstate him in his fellowship and Cowley was allowed to resume his service to Jermyn. His suit for the mastership of the Savoy, a lucrative sinecure which had been promised him by Charles I, was unsuccessful; his poem in response to this disappointment, "The Complaint," cannot be regarded as a model of stoic fortitude. However, Cowley was far from impoverished during the seven years that remained to him after the Restoration. He had the income from his Cambridge fellowship, a profitable association with Davenant in the newly revived London theatre, with two of his own plays quite popular, and, from 1662, a substantial grant of lands from Henrietta Maria. Moreover, he continued to lead an active intellectual life, with friends among those who founded the Royal Society. He was among those who floated a plan to regularize the English language, and he turned his retirement from affairs of state to good account by becoming a keen amateur gardener, with the help of his friend John Evelyn. His essays, among the most attractive of his writings, are the product of these retired years. He was regarded, by the time of his death, as the greatest poet of his age, and according to Evelyn "near one hundred coaches of noblemen and persons of quality" attended his funeral. He was buried in Westminster Abbey next to Chaucer and Spenser.

༄༅༅

Extracts from the Preface to the Poems of 1656.

And if in quiet and flourishing times [poets] meet with so small encouragement, what are they to expect in rough and troubled ones? If *Wit* be such a *Plant*, that it scarce receives heat enough to preserve it alive even in the *Summer* of our cold Cli-mate, how can it choose but wither in a long and sharp *winter*? A warlike, various and a tragical age is best to *write of*, but worst to *write in*.

. . . .

Neither is the present constitution of my *Mind* more proper than that of the *Times* for this exercise, or rather divertisement. There is nothing that requires so much serenity and cheerfulness of *Spirit*;

it must not be either overwhelmed with the cares of *Life*, or overcast with the *Clouds of Melancholy* and *Sorrow*, or shaken and disturbed with the storms of injurious *Fortune*; it must like the *Halcyon*, have *fair weather* to breed in. The *Soul* must be filled with bright and delightful *Ideas*, when it undertakes to communicate delight to others; which is the main end of *Poesie*.

.   .   .   .

I have cast away all such pieces as I wrote during the time of the late troubles, with any relation to the differences that caused them; as among others, *three Books of the Civil War itself*, reaching as far as the first *Battle of Newbury*, where the succeeding *misfortunes* of the *party* stopped the *work*, for it is so uncustomary, as to become almost *ridiculous*, to make *Laurels* for the *Conquered*. Now though in all *Civil Dissentions*, when they break into open hostilities, the *War* of the *Pen* is allowed to accompany that of the *Sword*, and everyone is in a manner obliged with his *Tongue*, as well as *Hand*, to serve and assist the side which he engages in; yet when the event of battle, and the unaccountable *Will* of *God* has determined the controversy, and that we have submitted to the conditions of the *Conqueror*, we must lay down our *Pens* as well as *Arms*, we must *march* out of our *Cause* itself, and *dismantle* that, as well as our *Towns* and *Castles*, of all the *Works* and *Fortifications* of *Wit* and *Reason* by which we defended it. We ought not sure, to begin ourselves to revive the remembrance of those times and actions for which we have received a *General Amnesty*, as a *favor* from the *Victor*. The truth is, neither *We*, nor *They*, ought by the *Representation* of *Places* and *Images* to make a kind of *Artificial Memory* of those things wherein we are all bound to desire like *Themistocles*, the *Art of Oblivion*.[1] The *enmities* of

Fellow-Citizens should be, like that of *Lovers*, the *Redintegration* of their *Amity*.[2] The names of *Party*, and *Titles* of *Division*, which are sometimes in effect the whole quarrel, should be extinguished and forbidden in peace under the notion of *Acts* of *Hostility*. And I would have it accounted no less unlawful to *rip up old wounds*, than to *give new ones*; which has made me not only abstain from printing any things of this kind, but to burn the very copies, and inflict a severer punishment on them myself, than perhaps the most rigid Officer of *State* would have thought that they deserved.

—1656

Of Solitude

Nunquam minus solus, quam cum solus, is now become a very vulgar saying.[3] Every man and almost every boy for these seventeen hundred years, has had it in his mouth. But it was at first spoken by the excellent Scipio, who was without question a most eloquent and witty person, as well as the most wise, most worthy, most happy, and the greatest of all mankind.[4] His meaning no doubt was this, that he found more satisfaction to his mind, and more improvement of it by solitude than by company, and to show that he spoke not this loosely or out of vanity, after he had made Rome, mistress of almost the whole world, he retired himself from it by a voluntary exile, and at a private house in the middle of a wood near Liternum, passed the remainder of his glorious life no less gloriously. This house Seneca went to see so long after with great veneration, and among other things describes his baths to have been of so mean a struc-

---

[1] *Themistocles* a celebrated Athenian statesman. Lives were written by Plutarch and Cornelius Nepos, and there is a famous sketch of his character in the first book of Thucydides (*Oxford Companion to Classical Literature*); *Oblivion* was a politically loaded word.

[2] *Redintegration* restoration, renewal (*OED*).

[3] "Never less alone, than when alone."

[4] *the excellent Scipio* Scipio Africanus Major, ca. 236–ca. 183 B.C.E. After a successful military career, he retired to his private estate at Liternum in Campania.

ture, that now, says he, the basest of the people would despise them, and cry out, poor Scipio understood not how to live. What an authority is here for the credit of retreat? and happy had it been for Hannibal, if adversity could have taught him as much wisdom as was learnt by Scipio from the highest prosperities.[1] This would be no wonder if it were as truly as it is colourably and wittily said by Monsieur de Montagne. That ambition itself might teach us to love solitude; there's nothing does so much hate to have companions. 'Tis true, it loves to have its elbows free, it detests to have company on either side, but it delights above all things in a train behind, aye, and ushers too before it. But the greatest part of men are so far from the opinion of that noble Roman, that if they chance at any time to be without company, they're like a becalmed ship, they never move but by the wind of other men's breath, and have no oars of their own to steer withal. It is very fantastical and contradictory in human nature, that men should love themselves above all the rest of the world, and yet never endure to be with themselves. When they are in love with a mistress, all other persons are importunate and burdensome to them. *Tecum vivere amem, tecum obeam Lubens*, They would live and die with her alone.

> Sic ego secretis possum bené vivere silvis
> Quà nulla humano sit via trita pedé,
> Tu mihi curarum requies, tu nocte vel atrâ
> Lumen, & in solis tu mihi turba locis.

With thee forever I in woods could rest,
Where never human foot the ground has pressed,

Thou from all shades the darkness canst exclude,
And from a desert banish solitude.

And yet our dear self is so wearisome to us, that we can scarcely support its conversation for an hour together. This is such an odd temper of mind as Catullus expresses towards one of his mistresses, whom we may suppose to have been of a very unsociable humour.

> Odi & Amo, quanám id faciam ratione requiris?
> Nescio, sed fieri sentio, & excrucior.[2]

I hate, and yet I love thee too;
How can that be? I know not how;
Only that so it is I know,
And feel with torment that 'tis so.

It is a deplorable condition, this, and drives a man sometimes to pitiful shifts in seeking how to avoid himself.

The truth of the matter is, that neither he who is a fop in the world, is a fit man to be alone; nor he who has set his heart much upon the world, though he have never so much understanding; so that solitude can be well fitted and set right, but upon a very few persons. They must have enough knowledge of the world to see the vanity of it, and enough virtue to despise all vanity; if the mind be possessed with any lust or passions, a man had better be in a fair, than in a wood alone. They may like petty thieves cheat us perhaps, and pick our pockets in the midst of company, but like robbers they use to strip and bind, or murder us when they catch us alone. This is but to retreat from men, and fall into the hands of devils. 'Tis like the punishment of parricides among the Romans, to be sewed into a

---

[1] *Hannibal* the Carthaginian leader who was defeated by Scipio at the battle of Zama in Africa, 202 B.C.E. His father had pledged him, when he was still a boy, to undying hatred of Rome, and Hannibal continued to stir up trouble after his defeat, with the result that the Romans hunted him down until he took his own life (*OCCL*).

[2] A modern text reads: *Odi et amo, quare id faciam, fortasse requiris?/ nescio, sed fieri sentio et excrucior.* For this reading, accompanied by a lively translation, see *The Poems of Catullus*, translated by James Michie, Bristol Classical P, 1989, pages 198–9.

bag with an ape, a dog, and a serpent. The first work therefore that a man must do to make himself capable of the good of solitude, is, the very eradication of all lusts, for how is it possible for a man to enjoy himself while his affections are tied to things without himself? In the second place, he must learn the art and get the habit of thinking; for this too, no less than well speaking, depends upon much practice, and cogitation is the thing which distinguishes the solitude of a god from a wild beast. Now because the soul of man is not by its own nature or observation furnished with sufficient materials to work upon; it is necessary for it to have continual recourse to learning and books for fresh supplies, so that the solitary life will grow indigent, and be ready to starve without them; but if once we be thoroughly engaged in the love of letters, instead of being wearied with the length of any day, we shall only complain of the shortness of our whole life.

> *O vita, stulto longa, sapienti brevis!*
> O life, long to the fool, short to the wise!

The first Minister of State has not so much business in public, as a wise man has in private; if the one have little leisure to be alone, the other has less leisure to be in company; the one has but part of the affairs of one nation, the other all the works of God and Nature under his consideration. There is no saying shocks me so much as that which I hear very often, that a man does not know how to pass his time. 'Twould have been but ill spoken by Methusalem in the nine hundred sixty-ninth year of his life,[1] so far it is from us, who have not time enough to attain to the utmost perfection of any part of any science, to have cause to complain that we are forced to be idle for want of work. But this you'll say is work only for the learned, others are not capable either of the employments or divertisse-

ments that arrive from letters. I know they are not; and therefore cannot much recommend solitude to a man totally illiterate. But if any man be so unlearned as to want entertainment of the little intervals of accidental solitude, which frequently occur in almost all conditions (except the very meanest of the people, who have business enough in the necessary provisions for life) it is truly a great shame both to his parents and himself, for a very small portion of any ingenious art will stop up all those gaps of our time, either music, or painting, or designing, or chemistry, or history, or gardening, or twenty other things will do it usefully and pleasantly; and if he happen to set his affections upon poetry (which I do not advise him too immoderately) that will over do it; no wood will be thick enough to hide him from the importunities of company or business, which would abstract him from his beloved.

> —*O quis me gelidis sub montibus Æmi*
> *Sistat, & ingenti ramorum protegat umbra!*—[2]
> Virg. Georg.

1

Hail, old patrician trees, so great and good!
　　Hail ye plebeian under wood!
　　　Where the poetic birds rejoice,
And for their quiet nests and plenteous food,
5　　Pay with their grateful voice.

2

Hail, the poor Muses' richest manor seat!
　　Ye country houses and retreat,
　　　Which all the happy gods so love,
That for you oft they quit their bright and great
10　　Metropolis above.

---

[1] *Methusalem in the nine hundred sixty-ninth year of his life* Genesis 6:27.

[2] "O for one to set me under the cool mountains of Haemus, and shield me under the branches' mighty shade" (Virgil, *Georgics,* Book 2, lines 488–9). Modern texts differ slightly from the one quoted by Cowley.

3

Here Nature does a house for me erect,
   Nature the wisest architect,
   Who those fond artists does despise
That can the fair and living trees neglect;
15   Yet the dead timber prize.

4

Here let me careless and unthoughtful lying, .
   Hear the soft winds above me flying,
   With all their wanton boughs dispute,
And the more tuneful birds to both replying,
20   Nor be myself too mute.

5

A silver stream shall rule his waters near,
   Gilt with the sun-beams here and there
   On whose enamelled bank I'll walk,
And see how prettily they smile, and hear
25   How prettily they talk.

6

Ah wretched, and too solitary he
   Who loves not his own company!
   He'll feel the weight of't many a day
Unless he call in sin or vanity
30   To help to bear't away.

7

Oh Solitude, first state of human-kind!
   Which blest remained till man did find
   Even his own helper's company.
As soon as two (alas!) together joined,
35   The serpent made up three.

8

Though God himself, through countless ages thee
   His sole companion chose to be,

Thee, sacred Solitude alone,
Before the branchy head of number's tree
40   Sprang from the trunk of one. [1]

9

Thou (though men think thine an unactive part)
   Dost break and tame th'unruly heart,
   Which else would know no settled pace,
Making it move, well managed by thy art,
45   With swiftness and with grace.

10

Thou the faint beams of reason's scattered light,
   Dost like a burning-glass unite,
   Dost multiply the feeble heat,
And fortify the strength, till thou dost bright
50   And noble fires beget.

11

Whilst this hard truth I teach, methinks, I see
   The monster London laugh at me,
   I should at thee too, foolish city,
If it were fit to laugh at misery,
55   But thy estate I pity.

12

Let but thy wicked men from out thee go,
   And all the fools that crowd the so,
   Even thou who dost thy millions boast,
A village less then Islington wilt grow,
60   A solitude almost.
—1668

---

[1] *Before the branchy head of number's tree / Sprang from the trunk of one* before the unity of God brought forth the multiplicity of the phenomenal world.

Of Obscurity

Nam neque divitibus contingunt gaudia solis,
Nec vixit male, qui natus moriensque fefellit.
—Hor. Epist. *l.* 1.17.

God made not pleasures only for the rich,
Nor have those men without their share too liv'd,
Who both in life and death the world deceiv'd.

This seems a strange sentence thus literally translated, and looks as if it were in vindication of the men of business (for who else can deceive the world?) whereas it is in commendation of those who live and die so obscurely, that the world takes no notice of them. This Horace calls deceiving the world, and in another place uses the same phrase.

> *Secretum iter & fallentis semita vitæ.*— Ep. 18. [1]
> The secret tracks of the deceiving life.

It is very elegant in Latin, but our English word will hardly bear up to that sense, and therefore Mr. Broom translates it very well,[2]

> Or from a life, led as it were by stealth.

Yet we say in our language, a thing deceives our sight, when it passes before us unperceived, and we may say well enough out of the same author,

> Sometimes with sleep, sometimes with wine we
>   strive,
> The cares of life and troubles to deceive.

But that is not to deceive the world, but to deceive ourselves, as Quintilian says, *Vitam fallere*, To draw on still, and amuse, and deceive our life, till it be advanced insensibly to the fatal period, and fall into that pit which nature hath prepared for it.[3] The meaning of all this is no more than that most vulgar saying, *Bene qui latuit, bene vixit*, He has lived well, who has lain well hidden. Which if it be a truth, the world (I'll swear) is sufficiently deceived: For my part, I think it is, and that the pleasantest condition of life, is *in Incognito*. What a brave privilege is it to be free from all contentions, from all envying or being envied, from receiving and from paying all kind of ceremonies? It is in my mind, a very delightful pastime, for two good and agreeable friends to travel up and down together, in places where they are by nobody known, nor know anybody. It was the case of Æneas and his Achates, when they walked invisibly about the fields and streets of Carthage, Venus herself

> A veil of thickened air around them cast,
> That none might know, or see them as they passed.

The common story of Demosthenes's confession that he had taken great pleasure in hearing of a tanker-woman say as he passed;[4] This is that Demosthenes, is wonderful ridiculous from so solid an orator.[5] I myself have often met with that temptation to vanity (if it were any) but am so far from finding it any pleasure, that it only makes me run faster from the place, till I get, as it were out of sight-shot. Democritus relates, and in such a manner, as if he gloried in the good fortune and com-

---

[1] This is also from Book I of Horace's *Epistles*.

[2] *Mr. Broom* unidentified. Alexander Brome is perhaps the likeliest candidate; another possibility is the playwright Richard Brome.

[3] *Quintilian* Marcus Fabius Quintilianus (ca. 36–ca. 95 C.E.) was the first person to receive an official salary as a teacher of oratory at Rome. He became wealthy and famous, and after twenty years retired to write his great work, *Institutio Oratoria* (*The Education of an Orator*). This work was influential in the Renaissance, as Quintilian's conception of the purpose of education, to produce a man of high character and general culture, was in harmony with that of the humanists (*OCCL*).

[4] *tanker-woman* a female tankard-bearer; see *OED* tanker and tankard 4.

[5] *Demosthenes* (383–322 B.C.E.), a great Athenian orator and statesman, generally considered to be the greatest of Greek orators.

modity of it, that when he came to Athens nobody there did so much as take notice of him;[1] and Epicurus lived there very well, that is, lay hid many years in his gardens, so famous since that time, with his friend Metrodorus:[2] after whose death, making in one of his letters a kind commemoration of the happiness which they two had enjoyed together, he adds at last, that he thought it no disparagement to those great felicities of their life, that in the midst of the most talked-of and talking country in the world, they had lived so long, not only without fame, but almost without being heard of. And yet within a very few years afterward, there were no two names of men more known or more generally celebrated. If we engage into a large acquaintance and various familiarities, we set open our gates to the invaders of most of our time: we expose our life to a *quotidian ague* of frigid impertinencies, which would make a wise man tremble to think of. Now, as for being known much by sight, and pointed at, I cannot comprehend the honour that lies in that: Whatsoever it be, every mountebank has it more than the best doctor, and the hangman more than the Lord Chief Justice of a city. Every creature has it both of nature and art if it be any ways extraordinary. It was as often said, This is that Bucephalus, or, This is that Incitatus,[3] when they were led prancing through the streets, as, this is that Alexander, or this is that Domitian; and truly for the

latter, I take Incitatus to have been a much more honourable beast then his master, and more deserving the consulship, then he the Empire. I love and commend a true good fame, because it is the shadow of virtue, not that it doth any good to the body which it accompanies, but 'tis an efficacious shadow, and like that of St. Peter cures the diseases of others.[4] The best kind of glory, no doubt, is that which is reflected from honesty, such as was the glory of Cato and Aristides,[5] but it was harmful to them both, and is seldom beneficial to any man whilst he lives, what it is to him after his death, I cannot say, because, I love not philosophy merely notional and conjectural, and no man who has made the experiment has been so kind as to come back to inform us. Upon the whole matter, I account a person who has a moderate mind and fortune, and lives in the conversation of two or three agreeable friends, with little commerce in the world besides, who is esteemed well enough by his few neighbours that know him, and is truly irreproachable by anybody, and so after a healthful quiet life, before the great inconveniences of old age, goes more silently out of it than he came in (for I would not have him so much as cry in the exit), this innocent deceiver of the world, as Horace calls him, this *Muta persona*, I take to have been more happy in his part, than the greatest actors that fill the stage with show and noise, nay, even than Augustus himself, who asked with his last breath, Whether he had not played his farce very well.

[1] *Democritus* Democritus of Abdera, born ca. 460 B.C.E., sometimes known as "the laughing philosopher."

[2] *Epicurus* Epicurus (341-270 B.C.E.), founder of the Epicurean school of philosophy. His school was known as the "Gardens," from the gardens in which he taught (*OCCL*).

[3] *Bucephalus* the horse of Alexander the Great (*OCCL*); *Incitatus* Cowley's memory is perhaps at fault here; it was Caligula, not Domitian, who proposed to make his favourite horse, Incitatus, a consul.

[4] *an efficacious shadow, and like that of St. Peter cures the diseases of others* Acts 5:15.

[5] *Cato* Cato of Utica (95–46 B.C.E.). He was the chief political antagonist of Caesar and the triumvirate and was described by the Roman historian Livy as "the conscience of Rome." When he saw that his cause was lost, he took his own life; *Aristides* (born 520 B.C.E.), an Athenian statesman and soldier. "His reputation for honesty went back to his contemporaries, and later became proverbial" (*OCD*).

Seneca, ex Thyeste,
Act. 2. Chor.

*Stet quicunque volet, potens
Aulæ culmine lubrico, &c.*

Upon the slippery tops of human state,
The gilded pinnacles of fate,
Let others proudly stand, and for a while
　　The giddy danger to beguile,
With joy, and with disdain look down on all,
Till their heads turn, and down they fall.
Me, O ye Gods, on Earth, or else so near
　　That I no fall to Earth may fear,
And, O ye gods, at a good distance seat
　　From the long ruins of the great.
Here wrapped in th' arms of quiet let me lie;
Quiet, companion of obscurity.
Here let my life, with as much silence slide,
　　As time that measures it does glide.
Nor let the breath of infamy or fame,
From town to town echo about my name.
Nor let my homely death embroidered be
　　With scutcheon or with elegy.
　　An old plebeian let me die,
Alas, all then are such as well as I.
　　To him, alas, to him, I fear,
The face of death will terrible appear:
Who in his life flattering his senseless pride
By being known to all the world beside,
Does not himself, when he is dying, know
Nor what he is, nor whither he's to go.
—1668

Of My Self

It is a hard and nice subject for a man to write of himself, it grates his own heart to say anything of disparagement, and the reader's ears to hear anything of praise from him. There is no danger from me of offending him in this kind; neither my mind, nor my body, nor my fortune, allow me any materi-

als for that vanity. It is sufficient, for my own contentment, that they have preserved me from being scandalous, or remarkable on the defective side. But besides that, I shall here speak of myself, only in relation to the subject of these precedent discourses, and shall be likelier thereby to fall into the contempt, than rise up to the estimation of most people. As far as my memory can return back into my past life, before I knew, or was capable of guessing what the world, or glories, or business of it were, the natural affections of my soul gave me a secret bent of aversion from them, as some plants are said to turn away from others, by an antipathy imperceptible to themselves, and inscrutable to man's understanding. Even when I was a very young boy at school, instead of running about on holy days and playing with my fellows; I was wont to steal from them, and walk into the fields, either alone with a book, or with some one companion, if I could find any of the same temper. I was then too, so much an enemy to all constraint, that my masters could never prevail on me, by any persuasions or encouragements, to learn without book the common rules of grammar, in which they dispensed with me alone, because they found I made a shift to do the usual exercise out of my own reading and observation. That I was then of the same mind as I am now (which I confess, I wonder at myself) may appear by the latter end of an ode, which I made when I was but thirteen years old, and which was then printed with many other verses. The beginning of it is boyish, but of this part which I here set down (if a very little were corrected) I should hardly now be much ashamed.

9

This only grant me, that my means may lie
Too low for envy, for contempt too high.
　　Some honor I would have
Not from great deeds, but good alone.
The unknown are better than ill known.

Rumour can ope' the grave,
Acquaintance I would have, but when 't depends
Not on the number, but the choice of friends.

10

Books should, not business entertain the light,
And sleep, as undisturbed as death, the night.
　　My house a cottage, more
Than palace, and should fitting be
For all my use, no luxury.
　　My garden painted o'er
With Nature's hand, not art's; and pleasures yield,
Horace might envy in his Sabine field.

11

Thus would I double my life's fading space,
For he that runs it well, twice runs his race.
　　And in this true delight,
These unbought sports, this happy state,
I would not fear nor wish my fate,
　　But boldly say each night,
Tomorrow let my sun his beams display,
Or in clouds hide them; I have lived today.

You may see by it, I was even then acquainted
with the poets (for the conclusion is taken out of
Horace); and perhaps it was the immature and
immoderate love of them which stamped first, or
rather engraved these characters in me: They were
like letters cut into the bark of a young tree, which
with the tree still grow proportionably. But, how
this love came to be produced in me so early, is a
hard question: I believe I can tell the particular little
chance that filled my head first with such chimes of
verse, as have never since left ringing there: For I
remember when I began to read, and to take some
pleasure in it, there was wont to lie in my Mother's
parlour (I know not by what accident, for she
herself never in her life read any book but of devotion) but there was wont to lie Spenser's *Works*; this
I happened to fall upon, and was infinitely de-

lighted with the stories of the knights, and giants,
and monsters, and brave houses, which I found
everywhere there (though my understanding had
little to do with all this): and by degrees with the
tinkling of the rhyme and dance of the numbers, so
that I think I had read him all over before I was
twelve years old, and was thus made a poet as
irremediably as a child is made an eunuch. With
these affections of mind, and my heart wholly set
upon letters, I went to the university; but was soon
torn from thence by that violent public storm
which would suffer nothing to stand where it did,
but rooted up every plant, even from the princely
cedars to me, the hyssop. Yet I had as good fortune
as could have befallen me in such a tempest; for I
was cast by it into the family of one of the best
persons, and into the court of one of the best
princesses of the world. Now though I was here
engaged in ways most contrary to the original
design of my life, that is, into much company, and
no small business, and into a daily sight of greatness, both militant and triumphant (for that was the
state then of the English and French courts) yet all
this was so far from altering my opinion, that it
only added the confirmation of reason to that
which was before but natural inclination. I saw
plainly all the paint of that kind of life, the nearer I
came to it; and that beauty which I did not fall in
love with, when, for ought I knew, it was real, was
not like to bewitch, or entice me, when I saw that it
was adulterate. I met with several great persons,
whom I liked very well, but could not perceive that
any part of their greatness was to be liked or desired, no more then I would be glad, or content to
be in a storm, though I saw many ships which rid
safely and bravely in it: A storm would not agree
with my stomach, if it did with my courage.
Though I was in a crowd of as good company as
could be found anywhere, though I was in business
of great and honourable trust, though I eat at the
best table, and enjoyed the best conveniences for

present subsistence that ought to be desired by a man of my condition in banishment and public distresses; yet I could not abstain from renewing my old schoolboy's wish in a copy of verses to the same effect.

> Well then; I now do plainly see
> This busy world and I shall ne'er agree, &c.

And I never then proposed to myself any other advantage from his Majesty's happy restoration, but the getting into some moderately convenient retreat in the country, which I thought in that case I might easily have compassed, as well as some others, with no greater probabilities or pretences have arrived to extraordinary fortunes: But I had before written a shrewd prophesy against my self, and I think Apollo inspired me in the truth, though not in the elegance of it.

> Thou, neither great at court nor in the war,
> Nor at th' exchange shal't be, nor at the
>   wrangling bar;
> Content thyself with the small barren praise
> Which neglected verse does raise, &c.

However by the failing of the forces which I had expected, I did not quit the design which I had resolved on, I cast myself into it *A Corps Perdu*, without making capitulations, or taking counsel of fortune. But God laughs at a man, who says to his soul, "Take thy ease": I met presently not only with many little encumbrances and impediments, but with so much sickness (a new misfortune to me) as would have spoiled the happiness of an emperor as well as mine: Yet I do neither repent nor alter my course. *Non ego perfidum Dixi Sacramentum*; Nothing shall separate me from a mistress, which I have loved so long, and have now at last married; though she neither has brought me a rich portion, nor lived yet so quietly with me as I hoped from her.

> _____ *Nec vos, dulcissima mundi*
> *Nomina, vos Musæ, Libertas, Otia, Libri,*
> *Hortique Sylvæq; anima remanente relinquam.*

> Nor by me ere shall you,
> You of all names the sweetest, and the best,
> You Muses, books, and liberty and rest;
> You gardens, fields, and woods forsaken be,
> As long as life itself forsakes not me.

But this is a very petty ejaculation; because I have concluded all the other chapters with a copy of verses, I will maintain the humour to the last.
—1668

Abiezer Coppe
1619 – 1672

Born in Warwick, and educated at the grammar school there, Coppe entered All Souls College, Oxford in 1636, transferring later to Merton College. He left without taking a degree, and his subsequent spiritual journey resembles Lawrence Clarkson's progression through increasingly radical religious beliefs. Coppe became a Presbyterian, then a Baptist, and claimed to have preached throughout Warwickshire during the 1640s. His earliest writings, dating from 1649, are pointedly antinomian, arguing that true belief freed Christians from the need to observe any moral law. In the same year Coppe was imprisoned in Warwick, where he had a vision ordering him to go to London and proclaim the judgement of God against the "great ones of the earth." The message he delivered in sermons on the streets of London and in the two parts of *A Fiery Flying Roll* combined radical religious and political ideas. Coppe adopts a prophetic voice and a mystical, millennial antinomianism, but at the same time denounces economic and social privilege in terms that align him with writers such as John Lilburne and Gerrard Winstanley (Coppe describes God as "the mighty Leveller" throughout *A Fiery Flying Roll*). Coppe's distinctive style of writing reflects his effort to render mystical experience into words—an attempt he admits is impossible. His lack of faith in language's ability to name and describe inner experience was shared by several writers usually grouped together as Ranters; their belief that language was a code, that words as well as actions were only shadows or signs of an ineffable spiritual reality, represents the culmination of one tradition of seventeenth-century religious writing.

A Fiery Flying Roll (the two parts were issued together) was immediately controversial, and in February 1650 it was ordered burned as blasphemous. Coppe was imprisoned and in 1651 recanted, but appears to have continued to preach. After the Restoration he changed his name to Higham and combined preaching with a medical practice in Surrey, where he died in 1672. For more on the Ranters, see the notes to Clarkson's *The Lost Sheep Found*, which mentions Coppe at several points. Coppe is sometimes described as a Ranter leader, but it is important to remember that most of what is known of the Ranters comes from hostile opponents. Seeking to define what was most threatening in a period of rapid social and political change, their accounts possibly overstated the extent to which the Ranters were an organized group.

❦❧❦❧

A Fiery Flying Roll
and *A Second Fiery Flying Roll*
(excerpts)

THE PREFACE

An inlet into the Land of Promise, the New Jerusalem, and a gate into the ensuing discourse, worthy of serious consideration.

My dear one.
All or none.
Everyone under the sun.
Mine own.

My most Excellent Majesty (in me) hath strangely and variously transformed this form.

And behold, by mine own almightiness (in me) I have been changed in a moment, in the twinkling of an eye, at the sound of the trump.[1]

---

[1] See I Corinthians 15:52. Coppe's text is densely interwoven with biblical language; only a few specific references have been annotated.

And now the Lord is descended from Heaven, with a shout, with the voice of the archangel, and with the trump of God.

And the sea, the earth, yea all things are now giving up their dead. And all things that ever were, are, or shall be visible—are the grave wherein the King of Glory (the eternal, invisible almightiness, hath lain as it were) dead and buried.

But behold, behold, he is now risen with a witness, to save Zion with vengeance, or to confound and plague all things into himself; who by his mighty angel is proclaiming (with a loud voice) that sin and transgression is finished and ended; and everlasting righteousness brought in; and the everlasting Gospel preaching; which everlasting Gospel is brought in with most terrible earthquakes, and heaven-quakes, and with signs and wonders following.

Amen

And it hath pleased my most Excellent Majesty (who is universal love, and whose service is perfect freedom), to set this form (the writer of this roll) as no small sign and wonder in fleshly Israel; as you may partly see in the ensuing discourse.

And now (my dear ones!) everyone under the sun, I will only point at the gate; through which I was led into that new city, new Jerusalem, and to the spirits of just men, made perfect, and to God the judge of all.

First, all my strength, my forces were utterly routed, my house I dwelt in fired; my father and mother forsook me, the wife of my bosom loathed me, mine old name was rotted, perished; and I was utterly plagued, consumed, damned, rammed, and sunk into nothing, into the bowels of the still eternity (my mother's womb) out of which I came naked, and whetherto I returned again naked. And lying a while there, rapt up in silence, at length (the body or outward form being awake all this while) I heard with my outward ear (to my apprehension) a most terrible thunder-clap, and after that a second.

And upon the second thunder-clap, which was exceeding terrible, I saw a great body of light, like the light of the sun, and red as fire, in the form of a drum (as it were) whereupon with exceeding trembling and amazement on the flesh, and with joy unspeakable in the spirit, I clapped my hands, and cried out, *Amen, Hallelujah, Hallelujah, Amen*. And so lay trembling, sweating and smoking (for the space of half an hour) at length with a loud voice (I inwardly) cried out, Lord, what wilt thou do with me; my most excellent majesty and eternal glory (in me) answered and said, Fear not, I will take thee up into mine everlasting Kingdom. But thou shalt (first) drink a bitter cup, a bitter cup, a bitter cup; whereupon (being filled with exceeding amazement) I was thrown into the belly of hell (and take what you can of it in these expressions, though the matter is beyond expression) I was among all the Devils in hell, even in their most hideous hue.

And under all this terror, and amazement, there was a little spark of transcendent, transplendent, unspeakable glory, which survived, and sustained itself, triumphing, exulting, and exalting itself above all the fiends. And confounding the very blackness of darkness (you must take it in these terms, for it is infinitely beyond expression). Upon this the life was taken out of the body (for a season) and it was thus resembled, as if a man with a great brush dipped in whiting, should with one stroke wipe out, or sweep off a picture upon a wall, &c. after a while, breath and life was returned into the form again; whereupon I saw various streams of light (in the night) which appeared to the outward eye; and immediately I saw three hearts (or three appearances in the form of hearts), of exceeding brightness; and immediately an innumerable company of hearts, filling each corner of the room where I was. And methoughts there was variety and distinction, as if there had been several hearts, and yet most strangely and inexpressibly complicated or folded up in unity. I clearly saw distinction, diversity, variety, and as clearly saw all swallowed up into unity. And it hath been my song many times since, within and without, unity, universality, universality, unity, Eternal Majesty, &c. And at this vision, a most strong, glorious voice uttered these words, *The spirits of just men made perfect.*[1] The spirits &c, with whom I had as absolute, clear, full communion, and in a two-fold more familiar way, than ever I had outwardly with my dearest friends, and nearest relations. The visions and revelations of God, and the strong hand of eternal invisible almightiness, was stretched out upon me, within me, for the space of four days and nights, without intermission.

The time would fail if I would tell you all, but it is not the good will and pleasure of my most excellent Majesty in me, to declare any more (as yet) than thus such further: That amongst those various voices that were then uttered within, these were some, *Blood, blood, where, where? upon the hypocritical holy heart,* &c. Another thus, *Vengeance, vengeance, vengeance, plagues, plagues, upon the inhabitants of the earth; fire, fire, fire, sword, sword, &c. upon all that bow now down to eternal Majesty, universal love; I'll recover, recover, my wool, my flax, my money. Declare, declare, fear thou not the faces of any; I am (in thee) a munition of rocks,* &c.[2]

Go up to London, to London,[3] that great city, write, write, write. And behold I writ, and lo a hand was sent to me, and a roll of a book was therein, which this fleshly hand would have put wings to, before the time. Whereupon it was snatched out of my hand, and the roll thrust into my mouth; and I eat it up, and filled my bowels with it (Eze. 2:8 &c. cha. 3:1, 2, 3), where it was as bitter as worm-wood; and it lay broiling, and burning in my stomach, till I brought it forth in this form.

And now I send it flying to thee, with my heart, And all

Per AUXILIUM PATRIS בן [4]

A Second Fiery Flying Roll

CHAPTER III

A strange, yet most true story: under which is couched that lion, whose roaring shall make all the beasts of the field tremble, and all the kingdoms of the earth quake. Wherein also (in part) the subtlety of the well-favoured harlot is discovered, and her flesh burning with that fire, which shall burn down all churches, except that of the first born, &c.

Follow me, who, last Lord's day September 30, 1649, met him in open field, a most strange deformed man, clad with patched clouts: who looking wishly on me, mine eye pitied him; and my heart, or the day of the Lord, which burned as an oven in me, set my tongue on flame to speak to him, as followeth.

How now friend, art thou poor?

He answered, yea Master very poor.

Whereupon my bowels trembled within me, and quivering fell upon the worm-eaten chest (my corpse I mean), that I could not hold a joint still.

And my great love within me (who is the great God within that chest, or corpse), was burning hot toward him; and made the lock-hole of the chest, to wit, the mouth of the corpse, again to open: Thus.

Art poor?

Yea, very poor, said he.

---

[1] Hebrews 12:23.

[2] Hosea 2:9.

[3] It not being shown to me, what I should do, more than preach and print something, &c. very little expecting I should be so strangely acted, as to (my exceeding joy and delight) I have been, though to the utter cracking of my credit, and to the rotting of my old name which is damned, and cast out (as a toad to the dunghill) that I might have a new name, with me, upon me, within me, which is, I am— [marginal note by Coppe].

---

[4] by the help of the father, A C [his initials in Hebrew].

Whereupon the strange woman who flattereth with her lips,[1] and is subtle of heart, said within me.

It's a poor wretch, give him two-pence.

But my excellency and majesty (in me) scorned her words, confounded her language; and kicked her out of his presence.

But immediately the well-favoured harlot (whom I carried not upon my horse behind me) but who rose up in me, said:

It's a poor wretch give him *6d* and that's enough for a squire or knight, to give to one poor body.

Besides (saith the holy scripturian whore) he's worse than an infidel that provides not for his own family.

True love begins at home, &c.

Thou, and thy family, are fed as the young ravens, strangely, though thou hast been a constant preacher, yet thou hast abhorred both tithes and hire; and thou knowest not aforehand, who will give thee the worth of a penny.

Have a care of the main chance.

And thus she flattereth with her lips, and her words being smoother than oil; and her lips dropping as the honey comb, I was fired to hasten my hand into my pocket; and pulling out a shilling, said to the poor wretch, give me six pence, here's a shilling for thee.[2]

He answered, I cannot, I have never a penny.

Whereupon I said, I would fain have given thee something if thou couldst have changed my money.

Then saith he, God bless you.

Whereupon with much reluctancy, with much love, and with amazement (of the right stamp) I turned my horse head from him, riding away. But a while after I was turned back (being advised by my Demilance)[3] to wish him call for six pence, which I would leave at the next town at one's house, which I thought he might know, (Sapphira like) keeping back part.[4]

But (as God judged me) I, as she, was struck down dead.

And behold the plague of God fell into my pocket; and the rust of my silver rose up in judgment against me, and consumed my flesh as with fire: so that I, and my money perished with me.

I being cast into that lake of fire and brimstone.

And all the money I had about me to a penny (though I thought through the instigation of my quondam mistress to have reserved some, having rode about 8 miles, not eating one mouth-full of bread that day, and had drunk but one small draught of drink; and had between 8 or 9 miles more to ride, ere I came to my journey's end: my horse being lame, the ways dirty, it raining all the way, and I not knowing what extraordinary occasion I might have for money). Yet (I say) the rust of my silver did so rise up in judgment against me, and burnt my flesh like fire: and the 5th of James thundered such an alarm in mine ears,[5] that I was fain to call all I had into the hands of him, whose visage was more marred than any man's that ever I saw.

This is a true story, most true in the history.

It's true also in the mystery.

And there are deep ones couched under it, for it's a shadow of various, glorious (though strange), good things to come.

---

[3] *Demilance* here, a horseman armed with a short lance (*OED* demilance 2), another personification of the speaker's self-interested instincts. The term was becoming obsolete in the seventeenth century, and was often used in humorous or satiric contexts, like "cavalier."

[4] Acts 5; Sapphira and her husband Ananias kept back some money when they gave the Apostles a donation; both died when confronted with their unwillingness to give everything they had.

[5] a chapter condemning the wealthy; it begins "Go to now, ye rich men, weep and howl for your miseries that shall come upon you. Your riches are corrupted, and your garments are moth-eaten."

---

[1] here and subsequently, a gendered personification of the adulterous heart, of the instincts that justify self-interest over doing what is right.

[2] A shilling was worth twelve pence; he is asking for six pence change.

Well! to return—after I had thrown my rusty cankered money into the poor wretch's hands, I rode away from him, being filled with trembling, joy, and amazement, feeling the sparkles of a great glory arising up from under these ashes.

After this, I was made (by that divine power which dwelleth in this ark, or chest) to turn my horse's head—whereupon I beheld this poor deformed wretch, looking earnestly after me: and upon that, was made to put off my hat, and bow to him seven times, and was (at that strange posture) filled with trembling and amazement, some sparkles of glory arising up also from under this; as also from under these ashes, yet I rode back once more to the poor wretch, saying, because I am a King, I have done this, but you need not tell anyone.

The day's our own.

This was done on the last Lord's day, September 30 in the year 1649, which is the year of the Lord's recompenses for Zion, and the day of his vengeance, the dreadful day of Judgment. But I have done (for the present) with this story, for it is the latter end of the year 1649.

—1649

John Evelyn
1620 – 1706

Evelyn was born into a wealthy commercial family and educated at Balliol College, Oxford. After inheriting a large fortune on his father's death in 1640, he travelled extensively in Europe for most of the 1640s. Though absent from England during the civil wars, he was a steadfast Royalist, acting several times as a messenger in France for the royal family. He returned to England in 1652, and after the Restoration held a number of public offices. A founding member and secretary of The Royal Society, Evelyn was a Restoration virtuoso, interested in all branches of the arts and sciences and a recognised authority on numismatics, antiquities, painting, architecture, engraving, landscape gardening, and arboriculture. His publications ranged from works on education to urban planning, from horticulture to the arrangement of libraries; his translations from French brought into England the latest continental ideas in his many areas of interest.

Evelyn's diary, first published in the nineteenth century, covers his life from the early 1640s to his death, making it along with Pepys's diary one of the most substantial personal records of the period. Evelyn is less spontaneous and confessional than Pepys. But he knew and described many of the most distinguished men and women of the era, and his diary provides an invaluable record of Restoration intellectual, artistic, and scientific life. For other accounts of the Restoration, see the selections from Burnet, Clarendon, Wood, and the *Declaration of Breda*; for other accounts of the Great Fire, see the selections from Clarendon and Pepys.

☙❧

The Diary of John Evelyn
(selections)

THE RESTORATION

1660

Feb. 3   General Monck came now to London out of Scotland, but no man knew what he would do, or declare, yet was he met on all his way by the Gentlemen of all the counties which he passed, with petitions that he would recall the old long interrupted Parliament, and settle the Nation in some order, being at this time in a most prodigious confusion, and under no government, every body expecting what would be next, and what he would do.[1]

Feb. 10   Now were the gates of the city broken down by General Monck, which exceedingly exasperated the city; the soldiers marching up and down as triumphing over it, and all the old army of the fanatics put out of their posts, and sent out of town.

Feb. 11   A signal day: Monck perceiving how infamous and wretched a pack of knaves would have still usurped the supreme power, and having intelligence that they intended to take away his commission, repenting of what he had done to the city, and where he and his forces quartered; marches to Whitehall, dissipates that nest of robbers, and convenes the old Parliament, the "rump-parliament" (so called as retaining some few rotten members of the other) being dissolved; and for joy whereof, were many thousands of rumps roasted publicly in the streets at the bonfires this night, with ringing of bells, and universal jubilee: this was the first good omen.

---

[1] *Monck*   George Monck, Duke of Albemarle (1608–1670). Monck fought for Charles I during the first two years of the Civil War, but afterward for Cromwell and the Commonwealth; in 1659–60 he used the army under his command in Scotland to force the recall of the "Rump" Parliament and then to have the restored Parliament make the political changes that led to the Restoration.

May 3 Came the most happy tidings of his Majesty's gracious Declaration,[1] and applications to the Parliament, General, and people &c and their dutiful acceptance and acknowledgment, after a most bloody and unreasonable rebellion of near 20 years. Praised be forever the Lord of heaven, who only dost wondrous things, because thy mercies endure forever.

May 8…This day was his Majesty proclaimed in London: &c.

May 9 I was desired and designed to accompany my Lord Berkeley with the public address of the Parliament,[2] General &c: and invite him to come over, and assume his kingly government, he being now at Breda; but being yet so weak and convalescent, I could not make that journey by sea, which was not a little to my detriment &c: so I went to London to excuse my self, returning the 10th, having yet received a gracious message from his Majesty, by Major Scot & Colonel Tuke.

May 24 Came to me Colonel Morley about procuring his pardon, and now too late saw his horrible error and neglect of the counsel I gave him, by which he had certainly done the great work, with the same ease that Monck did it.[3] Who was then in Scotland, and Morley in a post to have done what he pleased, by which he made himself the greatest person in England next the King: but his jealousy and fear kept him from that blessing, and honor. I addressed him to my Lord Mordaunt, then in great favour, for his pardon, which he obtained at the cost of 1000 pounds, as I heard: O the sottish omission of this gentleman: What did I not undergo of danger in this negotiation, to have brought him over to his Majesty's interest when it was entirely in his hands.

May 29 This day came in his Majesty Charles the 2d to London after a sad, and long exile, and calamitous suffering both of the King and Church: being 17 years: This was also his birthday, and with a triumph of above 20,000 horse and foot, brandishing their swords and shouting with unexpressible joy: The ways strewed with flowers, the bells ringing, the streets hung with tapestry, fountains running with wine: The Mayor, Aldermen, all the Companies in their liveries, chains of gold, banners; Lords and nobles, cloth of silver, gold and velvet everybody clad in, the windows and balconies all set with Ladies, trumpets, music, and myriads of people flocking the streets and was as far as Rochester, so as they were seven hours in passing the city, even from two in the afternoon 'til nine at night: I stood in the strand, and beheld it, and blessed God: And all this without one drop of blood, and by that very army, which rebelled against him: but it was the Lord's doing, *et mirabile in oculis nostri*:[4] for such a Restoration was never seen in the mention of any history, ancient or modern, since the return of the Babylonian captivity, nor so joyful a day, and so bright, ever seen in this nation: this happening when to expect or effect it, was past all humane policy.

THE FIRE OF LONDON

1666

Sept. 2 This fatal night about ten, began that deplorable fire, near Fish Street in London: I had

---

[1] The *Declaration of Breda* (April 4, 1660), in which Charles promised the concessions that paved the way to the Restoration.

[2] *Berkeley* John Berkeley, first Baron Berkeley of Stratton (d. 1678), soldier and ambassador.

[3] Herbert Morley (1616–1667); a colonel in the Parliamentary army, Morley refused to act as a judge in the King's trial, opposed Cromwell as long as possible, and withdrew into private life during the Commonwealth. In 1659 he raised troops and helped restore Parliament. Evelyn's estimate of the options available to Morley at the time is inaccurate.

[4] "It is marvellous in our eyes" (Psalm 118:23; Matthew 21:42; Mark 12:11).

public prayers at home:[1] after dinner the fire continuing, with my wife and son took coach and went to the bank side in Southwark, where we beheld that dismal spectacle, the whole city in dreadful flames near the water side, and had now consumed all the houses from the bridge all Thames Street and upwards towards Cheapside, down to the Three Cranes, and so returned exceedingly astonished, what would become of the rest.

Sept. 3   The fire having continued all this night (if I may call that night, which was as light as day for 10 miles round about after a dreadful manner) when conspiring with a fierce eastern wind, in a very dry season, I went on foot to the same place, when I saw the whole south part of the city burning from Cheapside to the Thames, and all along Cornhill (for it likewise kindled back against the wind, as well as forward), Tower Street, Fenchurch Street, Gracious Street, and so along to Baynard's Castle, and was now taking hold of St. Paul's Church, to which the scaffolds contributed exceedingly;[2] the conflagration was so universal, and the people so astonished, that from the beginning (I know not by what desponding or fate), they hardly stirred to quench it, so as there was nothing heard or seen but crying out and lamentation, and running about like distracted creatures, without at all attempting to save even their goods; such a strange consternation there was upon them, so as it burned both in breadth and length, the churches, public halls, Exchange, hospitals, monuments, and ornaments, leaping after a prodigious manner from house to house and street to street, at great distance one from the other, for the heat (with a long set of fair and warm weather) had even ignited the air, and prepared the materials to conceive the fire,

which devoured after an incredible manner, houses, furniture and everything: Here we saw the Thames covered with goods floating, all the barges and boats laden with what some had time and courage to save, as on the other, the carts &c carrying out to the fields, which for many miles were strewed with movables of all sorts, and tents erecting to shelter both people and what goods they could get away: O the miserable and calamitous spectacle, such as haply the whole world had not seen the like since the foundation of it, nor to be out done, 'til the universal conflagration of it, all the sky were of a fiery aspect, like the top of a burning oven, and the light seen above 40 miles round about for many nights: God grant mine eyes may never behold the like, who now saw above ten thousand houses all in one flame, the noise and crackling and thunder of the impetuous flames, the shrieking of women and children, the hurry of people, the fall of towers, houses and churches was like an hideous storm, and the air all about so hot and inflamed that at the last one was not able to approach it, so as they were forced to stand still, and let the flames consume on which they did for near two whole miles in length and one in breadth: The clouds also of smoke were dismal, and reached upon computation near 50 miles in length: Thus I left it this afternoon burning, a resemblance of Sodom, or the last day: It called to mind that of 4 Heb: *non enim hic habemus stabilem Civitatem*:[3] the ruins resembling the picture of Troy: London was, but is no more: Thus I returned.

Sept. 4   The burning still rages; I went now on horseback, and it was now gotten as far as the Inner Temple; all Fleet Street, Old Bailey, Ludgate hill, Warwick Lane, Newgate, Paul's Chain, Wattling Street now flaming and most of it reduced to ashes, the stones of Paul's flew like grenades, the lead

[1] *public prayers at home*   that is, prayers attended by all members of the household (family and servants) and led by Evelyn.

[2] *scaffolds*   wooden construction scaffolds erected before the fire for repairs to the church.

[3] Actually Hebrews 13:14, "For here we have no continuing city." Evelyn is citing from the Latin translation by Theodore Beza.

melting down the streets in a stream, and the very pavements of them glowing with fiery redness, so as nor horse nor man was able to tread on them, and the demolitions had stopped all the passages, so as no help could be applied; the eastern wind still more impetuously driving the flames forwards: Nothing but the almighty power of God was able to stop them, for vain was the help of man: on the fifth it crossed towards Whitehall, but O the confusion was then at that Court: It pleased his Majesty to command me among the rest to look after the quenching of Fetter-lane end, to preserve (if possible) that part of Holborn, whilst the rest of the Gentlemen took their several posts, some at one part, some at another, for now they began to bestir themselves, and not 'til now, who 'til now had stood as men interdict, with their hands a cross, and began to consider that nothing was like to put a stop, but the blowing up of so many houses, as might make a (wider) gap, than any had yet been made by the ordinary method of pulling them down with engines; This some stout seamen proposed early enough to have saved the whole city; but some tenacious and avaricious men, aldermen &c. would not permit, because their houses must have been of the first: It was therefore now commanded to be practised, and my concern being particularly for the Hospital of St. Bartholomew's near Smithfield, where I had many wounded and sick men, made me the more diligent to promote it; nor was my care for the Savoy less: So as it pleased Almighty God by abating of the wind, and the industry of people, now when all was lost, infusing a new spirit into them (and such as had if exerted in time undoubtedly preserved the whole) that the fury of it began sensibly to abate, about noon, so as it came no farther than the Temple westward, nor than the entrance of Smithfield north; but continued all this day and night so impetuous toward Cripplegate, and the Tower, as made us even all despair; It also brake out again in the Temple: but

the courage of the multitude persisting, and innumerable houses blown up with gunpowder, such gaps and desolations were soon made, as also by the former three day's consumption, as the back fire did not so vehemently urge upon the rest, as formerly: There was yet no standing near the burning and glowing ruins near a furlong's space; The coal and wood wharfs and magazines of oil, rosin, chandler &c:[1] did infinite mischief; so as the invective I but a little before dedicated to his Majesty and published, giving warning what might probably be the issue of suffering those shops to be in the city,[2] was looked on as prophetic: but there I left this smoking and sultry heap, which mounted up in dismal clouds night and day, the poor inhabitants dispersed all about St. George's, Moorfields, as far as Highgate, and several miles in circle, some under tents, others under miserable huts and hovels, without a rag, or any necessary utensils, bed or board, who from delicateness, riches and easy accommodations in stately and well furnished houses, were now reduced to extremest misery and poverty: In this calamitous condition I returned with a sad heart to my house, blessing and adoring the distinguishing mercy of God, to me and mine, who in the midst of all this ruin, was like Lot, in my little Zoar, safe and sound.[3]

Sept. 6   It is not indeed imaginable how extraordinary the vigilance and activity of the King and Duke was, even labouring in person, and being present, to command, order, reward, and encourage

---

[1] *chandler* This word is an interlinear addition to Evelyn's text, and does not make sense syntactically. The reference is probably to the highly combustible stores of the ship's chandlers on the river bank, stocked with cordage, canvas and tar.

[2] *the invective I...published* referring to *Fumifugium: or The Inconveniencie of the Aer and Smoak of London Dissipated* (1661), in which Evelyn had warned of the danger of fires from factories and warehouses (hence "invective," here meaning a polemical work).

[3] See Genesis 19:20–22.

workmen; by which he showed his affection to his people, and gained theirs.[1]

Sept. 7   I went this morning on foot from White-hall as far as London Bridge, through the late Fleet Street, Ludgate hill, by St. Paul's, Cheapside, Exchange, Bishopsgate, Aldersgate, and out to Moorfields, thence through Cornhill, &c with extraordinary difficulty, clambering over mountains of yet smoking rubbish, and frequently mistaking where I was, the ground under my feet so hot, as made me not only sweat, but even burnt the soles of my shoes, and put me all over in sweat: In the mean time his Majesty got to the Tower by water, to demolish the houses about the Graft, which being built entirely about it, had they taken fire, and attacked the white Tower, where the magazines of powder lay, would undoubtedly have not only beaten down and destroyed all the bridge, but sunk and torn all the vessels in the river, and rendered the demolition beyond all expression for several miles even about the country at many miles distance: At my return I was infinitely concerned to find that goodly church St. Paul's now a sad ruin, and that beautiful portico (for structure comparable to any in Europe, as not long before repaired by the late King) now rent in pieces, flakes of vast stone split in sunder, and nothing remaining entire but the inscription in the architrave which showing by whom it was built, had not one letter of it defaced: which I could not but take notice of: It was aston-ishing to see what immense stones the heat had in a manner calcined, so as all the ornaments, col-umns, friezes, capitals and projectures of massy Portland stone flew off, even to the very roof, where a sheet of lead covering no less than six acres by measure, being totally melted, the ruins of the vaulted roof falling, broke into St. Faith's, which being filled with the magazines of books, belonging

to the Stationers, and carried thither for safety, they were all consumed burning for a week following:[2] It is also observable, that the lead over the altar at the east end was untouched; and among the divers monuments, the body of one bishop remained entire. Thus lay in ashes that most venerable church, one of the ancientest pieces of early piety in the Christian world, beside near 100 more; the lead, ironwork, bells, plate &c melted; the exquisitely wrought Mercer's Chapel, the sumptuous Ex-change, the august fabric of Christ Church, all the rest of the companies' halls, sumptuous buildings, arches, entries, all in dust. The fountains dried up and ruined, whilst the very waters remained boiling; the voragos of subterranean cellars, wells and dun-geons,[3] formerly warehouses, still burning in stench and dark clouds of smoke like hell, so as in five or six miles traversing about, I did not see one load of timber unconsumed, nor many stones but what were calcined white as snow, so as the people who now walked about the ruins, appeared like men in some dismal desert, or rather in some great city, laid waste by an impetuous and cruel enemy, to which was added the stench that came from some poor creatures' bodies, beds, and other combustible goods: Sir Thomas Gresham's statue,[4] though fallen to the ground from its niche in the Royal Exchange, remained entire, when all those of the kings since the conquest were broken to pieces: also the Stan-dard in Cornhill, and Queen Elizabeth's effigies, with some arms on Ludgate continued with but little detriment, whilst the vast iron chains of the city streets, vast hinges, bars and gates of prisons were many of them melted, and reduced to cinders

---

[1] *Duke* James, Duke of York, the King's brother and later James II.

[2] *Stationers* Stationers included booksellers and printers; many had shops in the yard around St. Paul's, and had put their stock in the crypt beneath the church for safekeeping. The loss to the book trade was considerable.

[3] *voragos* A vorago is an abyss or chasm (*OED*).

[4] Gresham (1519?–1579) founded the Royal Exchange as a meeting place for merchants and bankers.

by the vehement heats: nor was I yet able to pass through any of the narrower streets, but kept the widest, the ground and air, smoke and fiery vapour, continued so intense, my hair being almost singed, and my feet insufferably surbated:[1] The by-lanes and narrower streets were quite filled up with rubbish, nor could one have possibly known where he was, but by the ruins of some church, or hall, that had some remarkable tower or pinnacle remaining: I then went towards Islington, and Highgate, where one might have seen two hundred thousand people of all ranks and degrees dispersed, and laying along by their heaps of what they could save from the *Incendium*, deploring their loss, and though ready to perish for hunger and destitution, yet not asking one penny for relief, which to me appeared a stranger sight, than any I had yet beheld: His Majesty and Council indeed took all imaginable care for their relief, by Proclamation, for the country to come in and refresh them with provisions: when in the midst of all this calamity and confusion, there was (I know not how) an alarm begun, that the French and Dutch (with whom we were now in hostility) were not only landed, but even entering the city; there being in truth, great suspicion some days before, of those two nations joining, and even now, that they had been the occasion of firing the town: This report did so terrify, that on a sudden there was such an uproar and tumult, that they ran from their goods, and taking what weapons they could come at, they could not be stopped from falling on some of those nations whom they casually met, without sense or reason, the clamor and peril growing so excessive, as made the whole Court amazed at it, and they did with infinite pains, and great difficulty reduce and appease the people,[2] sending guards and troops of soldiers, to cause them to retire into the fields again,

where they were watched all this night when I left them pretty quiet, and came home to my house, sufficiently weary and broken: Their spirits thus a little sedated, and the affright abated, they now began to repair into the suburbs about the city, where such as had friends or opportunity got shelter and harbour for the present: to which his Majesty's Proclamation also invited them. Still the plague, continuing in our parish, I could not without danger adventure to our church.

Sept. 10   I went again to the ruins, for it was now no longer a city.

Sept. 13   …on the 13, I presented his Majesty with a survey of the ruins, and a plot for a new city, with a discourse on it, whereupon, after dinner his Majesty sent for me into the Queen's bed chamber, her Majesty and the Duke only present, where they examined each particular, and discoursed upon them for near a full hour, seeming to be extremely pleased with what I had so early thought on.

Oct. 10   This day was indicted a general fast through the nation, to humble us, upon the late dreadful conflagration, added to the plague and war, the most dismal judgments could be inflicted, and indeed but what we highly deserved for our prodigious ingratitude, burning lusts, dissolute court, profane and abominable lives, under such dispensations of God's continued favour, in restoring Church, Prince, and people from our late intestine calamities,[3] of which we were altogether unmindful even to astonishment.

Oct. 18   To London: Star-Chamber: thence to court, it being the first time of his Majesty's putting himself solemnly into the eastern fashion of vest, changing doublet, stiff collar, bands and cloak &c:

---

[1] *surbated* bruised or sore with much walking (*OED*).

[2] *reduce* subdue, calm.

---

[3] *intestine calamities* internal calamities, that is, the Civil War.

into a comely vest, after the Persian mode with girdle or sash, and shoe strings and garters, into buckles, of which some were set with precious stones, resolving never to alter it, and to leave the French mode, which had hitherto obtained to our great expense and reproach: upon which divers courtiers and gentlemen gave his Majesty gold, by way of wager, that he would not persist in this resolution: I had some time before indeed presented an Invectique against that inconstancy, and our so much affecting the French fashion, to his Majesty in which I took occasion to describe the comeliness and usefulness of the Persian clothing in the very same manner his Majesty clad himself; this pamphlet I entitled *Tyrannus* or the mode,[1] and give it his Majesty to read; I do not impute the change which soon happened to this discourse, but it was an identity, that I could not but take notice of: This night was acted my Lord Brahal's tragedy called *Mustapha* before their Majesties &c: at Court:[2] at which I was present, very seldom at any time, going to the public theaters, for many reasons, now as they were abused, to an atheistical liberty, foul and indecent; women now (and never 'till now) permitted to appear and act, which inflaming several young noblemen and gallants, became their whores, and to some their wives, witness the Earl of Oxford, Sir R. Howard, Prince Rupert, the Earl of Dorset, and another greater person than any of these,[3] who fell into their snares, to the reproach of their noble families, and ruin both of body and soul: I was invited to see this tragedy, exceedingly well writ, by my Lord Chamberlain, though in my mind, I did not approve of any such pastime, in a season of such judgements and calamity.

—(1660, 1666)

---

[1] *Tyrannus or the Mode: in a Discourse of Sumptuary Lawes* (1661); *Invectique* a form of "invective," meaning a polemical work.

[2] *Lord Brahal's tragedy* a play by Roger Boyle, Baron Broghill and first Earl of Orrery (1621–1679), statesman, soldier, and dramatist.

[3] *another greater person than any of these* King Charles II.

Lucy Hutchinson
1620 – ca. 1675

Lucy Apsley Hutchinson was born in the Tower of London, the daughter of Lucy St. John and Sir Allen Apsley, Lieutenant of the Tower. While pregnant with Lucy, her mother dreamt of a star settling in her hand as she walked in the garden. Lucy's father interpreted this to mean that she would bear "a daughter of some extraordinary eminency." In an autobiographical fragment, Lucy paints herself as a particularly bright child, eagerly reading and listening to sermons by the age of four. At seven, she was instructed by eight tutors in language, music, dancing, writing and needlework, yet was continually drawn into the world of texts, eventually displaying competence in French, Latin, Greek and Hebrew. It was her pleasure in writing "witty songs and amorous sonnets" that drew the attentions of her future husband, John Hutchinson, who was compelled to make her acquaintance after detecting a "rationality in the sonnet, beyond the customary reach of a she-wit." Though struck down with smallpox in 1638, later that year she wed Hutchinson, by whom she had eight children. In 1640, Lucy moved to Owthorpe, the Hutchinson family home, where she soon turned her attention to the translation of the six books of Lucretius. Although this translation, written in the schoolroom of her children, was not published, it enjoyed circulation amongst friends. Such tranquillity was soon interrupted by the turbulence of the civil wars. Hutchinson, a Parliamentarian, was governor of the castle in Nottingham, and in 1646 assumed a seat in the Long Parliament. Appointed one of the judges at the trial of the King, he was to sign Charles I's death sentence, an act which led to his imprisonment in the Tower after the Restoration. When he was removed to Sandown Castle in Kent in 1663, the unhealthy conditions weakened his health and, despite Lucy's daily visits and medical efforts, he died the following year. To console herself, Lucy became her husband's biographer. In the *Memoirs of Colonel Hutchinson*, Hutchinson emerges as virtuous and valorous, suffering saint and noble warrior. The *Memoirs* do not, however, merely eulogize but offer a compelling and detailed, if partisan, account of the Civil War. Prefaced to the *Memoirs* is a fragment of "The Life of Mrs. Hutchinson," strangely more forthcoming on the history of Britain than it is on the childhood of Lucy or the workings of her mind. In later life, Lucy Hutchinson wrote two religious treatises, *On the Principles of Christian Religion* and *On Theology*, for the benefit of her children, yet never ventured to publish any of her work. She had once declared that silence was the most becoming virtue in women, which may well explain her distaste for publication. The date of Lucy Hutchinson's death is unknown.

 భసాద

The Life of Mrs. Lucy Hutchinson Written by Herself, A Fragment

The almighty author of all beings, in his various providences, whereby he conducts the lives of men from the cradle to the tomb, exercises no less wisdom and goodness than he manifests power and greatness, in their creation; but such is the stupidity of blind mortals, that instead of employing their studies in these admirable books of providence, wherein God daily exhibits to us glorious characters of his love, kindness, wisdom, and justice, they ungratefully regard them not, and call the most wonderful operations of the great God the common accidents of human life, especially if they be such as are usual, and exercised towards them in ages wherein they are not very capable of observation, and whereon they seldom employ any reflection; for in things great and extraordinary, some, perhaps, will take notice of God's working, who either forget or believe not that he takes as well a care and account of their smallest concernments, even the hairs of their heads.

Finding myself in some kind guilty of this general neglect, I thought it might be a means to stir up my thankfulness for things past, and to encourage my faith for the future, if I recollected as much as I have heard or can remember of the passages of my youth, and the general and particular providences exercised to me, both in the entrance and progress of my life. Herein I meet with so many special indulgences as require a distinct consideration, they being all of them to be regarded as talents intrusted to my improvement for God's glory. The parents by whom I received my life, the places where I began and continued it, the time when I was brought forth to be a witness of God's wonderful workings in the earth, the rank that was given me in my generation, and the advantages I received in my person, each of them carries along with it many mercies which are above my utterance, and as they give me infinite cause of glorifying God's goodness, so I cannot reflect on them without deep humiliation for the small improvement I have made of so rich a stock; which, that I may yet by God's grace better employ, I shall recall and seriously ponder: and, first, as far as I have since learnt, set down the condition of things in the place of my nativity, at that time when I was sent into the world. It was on the 29th day of January, in the year of our Lord 1619–20, that in the Tower of London, the principal city of the English isle, I was, about four of the clock in the morning, brought forth to behold the ensuing light. My father was Sir Allen Apsley, lieutenant of the Tower of London; my mother, his third wife, was Lucy, the youngest daughter of Sir John St. John, of Lidiard Tregooze, in Wiltshire, by his second wife. My father had then living a son and a daughter by his former wives, and

by my mother three sons, I being her eldest daughter. The land was then at peace (it being towards the latter end of the reign of King James),[1] if that quietness may be called a peace, which was rather like the calm and smooth surface of the sea, whose dark womb is already impregnated with a horrid tempest.

Whoever considers England will find it no small favour of God to have been made one of its natives, both upon spiritual and outward accounts. The happiness of the soil and air contribute all things that are necessary to the use or delight of man's life. The celebrated glory of this isle's inhabitants, ever since they received a mention in history, confers some honour upon every one of her children, and with it an obligation to continue in that magnanimity and virtue, which hath famed this island, and raised her head in glory higher than the great kingdoms of the neighbouring continent. Britain hath been as a garden enclosed, wherein all things that man can wish, to make a pleasant life, are planted and grow in her own soil, and whatsoever foreign countries yield, to increase admiration and delight, are brought in by her fleets.[2] The people, by the plenty of their country, not being forced to toil for bread, have ever addicted themselves to more generous employments, and been reckoned, almost in all ages, as valiant warriors as any part of the world sent forth: insomuch, that the greatest Roman captains thought it not unworthy of their expeditions, and took great glory in triumphs for imperfect conquests. Lucan upbraids Julius Caesar for returning hence with a repulse, and it was two hundred years before the land could be reduced into a Roman province, which at length was done, and such of the nation, then called Picts, as scorned servitude, were driven into the barren country of

---

[1] *latter end of the reign* James I reigned until 1625.

[2] *Britain has been as a garden enclosed* Wilderness, garden and hedge metaphors are commonplace in works published during the civil wars and interregnum.

Scotland, where they have ever since remained a perpetual trouble to the successive inhabitants of this place.[1] The Britons, that thought it better to work for their conquerors in a good land, than to have the freedom to starve in a cold or barren quarter, were by degrees fetched away, and wasted in the civil broils of these Roman lords, till the land, almost depopulated, lay open to the incursions of every borderer, and were forced to call a stout warlike people, the Saxons, out of Germany, to their assistance.[2] These willingly came at their call, but were not so easily sent out again, nor persuaded to let their hosts inhabit with them, for they drove the Britons into the mountains of Wales, and seated themselves in those pleasant countries which from the new masters received a new name, and ever since retained it, being called England; and on which the warlike Dane made many attempts, with various success, but after about two or three hundred years' vain contest, they were for ever driven out, with shame and loss, and the Saxon Heptarchy melted into a monarchy, which continued till the superstitious prince, who was sainted for his ungodly chastity, left an empty throne to him that could seize it. He who first set up his standard in it, could not hold it, but with his life left it again for the Norman usurper, who partly by violence, partly by falsehood, laid here the foundation of his monarchy, in the people's blood, in which it hath swam about five hundred years, till the flood that bore it was ploughed into such deep furrows as had almost sunk the proud vessel.[3] Of those Saxons that remained subjects to the Norman conqueror, my father's family descended; of those Normans that came in with him, my mother's was derived; both of them, as all the rest in England, contracting such affinity, by mutual marriages, that the distinction remained but a short space; Normans and Saxons becoming one people, who by their valour grew terrible to all the neighbouring princes, and have not only bravely acquitted themselves in their own defence, but have showed abroad how easily they could subdue the world, if they did not prefer the quiet enjoyment of their own part above the conquest of the whole.

Better laws and a happier constitution of government no nation ever enjoyed, it being a mixture of monarchy, aristocracy, and democracy, with sufficient fences against the pest of every one of those forms—tyranny, faction, and confusion; yet is it not possible for man to devise such just and excellent bounds, as will keep in wild ambition, when princes' flatterers encourage that beast to break his fence, which it hath often done, with miserable consequences both to the prince and people; but could never in any age so tread down popular liberty, but that it arose again with renewed vigour, till at length it trod on those that trampled it before. And in the just bounds, wherein our kings were so well hedged in, the surrounding princes have with terror seen the reproof of their usurpa-

---

[1] *Lucan upbraids…with a repulse* Marcus Annaeus Lucanus (39–65 C.E.), the poet and historian, notes Caesar's failure in his epic poem *Bellum Civile* ("The Civil War"), also known as *Pharsalia*. Lucan's text became an important cultural touchstone in the period because he wrote from a Republican point of view.

[2] *and were forced…to their assistance* The Anglo-Saxons, led by Hengist, came to Britain in 449 C.E. at the invitation of King Vortigern and were granted lands in the eastern part of the island in exchange for military service.

[3] *warlike Dane…Norman usurper* Under attack by the Danes, the Wessex forces joined under the leadership of King Alfred the Great (849–899 C.E.), who ruled England from 871 until his death. Battles between the Dane Canute (ca. 994–1035) and the Wessex kings in the eleventh century resulted in a pact in which Edmund Ironside held Wessex and Canute Mercia. On Edmund's death (1017), Canute succeeded to the whole realm of England. Hutchinson follows the line of King Alfred the Great to Edward the Confessor, whose monastic chastity left him childless. When he died without an heir, there were two claimants to the throne: the Anglo-Saxon Harold, son of Godwin, and William of Normandy. Harold ruled for forty weeks and a day before William invaded England and killed Harold at the Battle of Hastings (1066).

tions over their free brethren, whom they rule rather as slaves than subjects, and are only served for fear, but not for love; whereas this people have ever been as affectionate to good, as unpliable to bad sovereigns.

Nor is it only valour and generosity that renown this nation; in arts we have advanced equal to our neighbours, and in those that are most excellent, exceeded them. The world hath not yielded men more famous in navigation, nor ships better built or furnished. Agriculture is as ingeniously practised; the English archers were the terror of Christendom, and their clothes the ornament; but these low things bounded not their great spirits, in all ages it hath yielded men as famous in all kinds of learning, as Greece or Italy can boast of.

And to complete the crown of all their glory, reflected from the lustre of their ingenuity, valour, wit, learning, justice, wealth, and bounty, their piety and devotion to God, and his worship, hath made them one of the most truly noble nations in the Christian world, God having as it were enclosed a people here, out of the waste common of the world, to serve him with a pure and undefiled worship. Lucius the British king was one of the first monarchs of the earth that received the faith of Christ into his heart and kingdom;[1] Henry the Eighth, the first prince that broke the antichristian yoke off from his own and his subjects' necks.[2] Here it was that the first Christian emperor received his crown; here began the early dawn of gospel light, by Wycliffe and other faithful witnesses, whom God raised up after the black and horrid midnight of antichristianism; and a more plentiful harvest of

devout confessors, constant martyrs, and holy worshippers of God, hath not grown in any field of the church, throughout all ages, than those whom God hath here glorified his name and gospel by.[3] Yet hath not this wheat been without its tares;[4] God in comparison with other countries hath made this as a paradise, so, to complete the parallel, the serpent hath in all times been busy to seduce, and not unsuccessful; ever stirring up opposers to the infant truths of Christ.[5]

No sooner was the faith of Christ embraced in this nation, but the neighbouring heathens invaded the innocent Christians, and slaughtered multitudes of them; and when, by the mercy of God, the conquering pagans were afterwards converted, and there were none left to oppose the name of Christ with open hostility, then the subtle serpent put off his own horrid appearance, and comes out in a Christian dress, to persecute Christ in his poor prophets, that bore witness against the corruption of the times.[6] This intestine quarrel hath been more successful to the devil, and more afflictive to the church, than all open wars; and, I fear, will never happily be decided, till the Prince of Peace come to conclude the controversy, which at the time of my birth was working up into that tempest, wherein I have shared many perils, many fears, and many sorrows; and many more mercies, consolations, and

---

[1] *Lucius* Lucius wrote to Pope Eleutherius some time between 177 and 180 C.E. asking to be made a Christian by his direction. This request was granted and the Britons converted (Bede, I.4)

[2] *Henry the Eighth…subjects' necks* When Pope Clement VII refused to consent to Henry VIII's divorce from Catherine of Aragon, Henry broke from papal allegiance, arranged for Parliament to make him Supreme Head of the Church of England, and married Anne Boleyn in 1533.

[3] *Wycliffe* John Wycliffe (ca. 1330–1384), founder of the Lollards, a movement for religious reform often seen by English Protestants as anticipating the Protestant Reformation.

[4] *Yet hath not…its tares* A reference to the parable of the wheat and tares (Matthew 13:24–30).

[5] *the serpent* "that old serpent, which is the Devil, and Satan" (Revelation 20:2).

[6] *the neighbouring heathens…afterwards converted* The pagan Angles, Saxons and Jutes infiltrated England and achieved power in the fifth and sixth centuries. Sent by Pope Gregory to England in 596 C.E., Augustine converted the peoples to Christianity and was consecrated Archbishop of the English nation (Bede, I.23–27).

preservations, which I shall have occasion to mention in other places.[1]

From the place of my birth I shall only desire to remember the goodness of the Lord, who hath caused my lot to fall in a good ground; who hath fed me in a pleasant pasture, where the well-springs of life flow to all that desire to drink of them. And this is no small favour, if I consider how many poor people perish among the heathen, where they never hear the name of Christ; how many poor Christians spring up in countries enslaved by Turkish and antichristian tyrants, whose souls and bodies languish under miserable slavery. None know what mercy it is to live under a good and wholesome law, that have not considered the sad condition of being subject to the will of an unlimited man; and surely it is too universal a sin in this nation, that the common mercies of God to the whole land are so slightly regarded, and so inconsiderately passed over; certainly these are circumstances which much magnify God's loving-kindness and his special favour to all that are of English birth, and call for a greater return of duty from us than from all other people of the world.

Nor is the place only, but the time of my coming into the world, a considerable mercy to me. It was not in the midnight of popery, nor in the dawn of the gospel's restored day, when light and shades were blended and almost undistinguished, but when the Sun of truth was exalted in his progress, and hastening towards a meridian glory. It was, indeed, early in the morning, God being pleased to allow me the privilege of beholding the admirable growth of gospel light in my days: and oh! that my soul may never forget to bless and praise his name for the wonders of power and goodness, wisdom and truth, which have been manifested in this my time.

The next blessing I have to consider in my nativity is my parents, both of them pious and virtuous in their own conversation, and careful instructors of my youth, not only by precept but example; which, if I had leisure and ability, I should have transmitted to my posterity, both to give them the honour due from me in such a grateful memorial, and to increase my children's improvement of the patterns they set them; but since I shall detract from those I would celebrate, by my imperfect commemorations, I shall content myself to sum up some few things for my own use, and let the rest alone, which I either knew not, or have forgotten, or cannot worthily express.

My grandfather by the father's side was a gentleman of a competent estate, about £700 or £800 a year, in Sussex. He being descended of a younger house, had his residence at a place called Pulborough; the family out of which he came was an Apsley of Apsley, a town where they had been seated before the Conquest, and ever since continued, till of late the last heir male of that eldest house, being the son of Sir Edward Apsley, died without issue, and his estate went with his sister's daughters into other families. Particularities concerning my father's kindred or country I never knew much of, by reason of my youth at the time of his death, and my education in far distant places; only in general I have heard, that my grandfather was a man well reputed and beloved in his country, and that it had been such a continued custom for my ancestors to take wives at home, that there was scarce a family of any note in Sussex to which they were not by intermarriages nearly related; but I was myself a stranger to them all, except my Lord Goring, who living at court, I have seen with my father, and heard of him, because he was appointed one of my father's executors, though he declined the

---

[1] *that tempest* Hutchinson presents the civil wars largely as a battle between religious opponents, proponents of Papistry and Arminianism ("children of darkness") and proponents of Calvinism ("children of light"). She describes the latter faction, of which she is a member, as those who "zealous for God's glory or worship, could not endure blasphemous oaths, ribald conversation, profane scoffs, sabbath breaking, derision of the word of God."

trouble.[1] My grandfather had seven sons, of which my father was the youngest; to the eldest he gave his whole estate, and to the rest, according to the custom of those times, slight annuities.[2] The eldest brother married to a gentlewoman of a good family, and by her had only one son, whose mother dying, my uncle married himself again to one of his own maids, and by her had three more sons, whom, with their mother, my cousin William Apsley, the son of the first wife, held in such contempt, that a great while after, dying without children, he gave his estate of inheritance to my father, and two of my brothers, except about £100 a year to the eldest of his half brothers, and annuities of £30 a piece to the three for their lives. He died before I was born, but I have heard very honourable mention of him in our family. The rest of my father's brothers went into the wars in Ireland and the Low Countries, and there remained none of them, nor their issues, when I was born, but only three daughters who bestowed themselves meanly, and their generations are worn out, except two or three unregarded children.[3] My father, at the death of my grandfather, being but a youth at school, had not patience to stay the perfecting of his studies, but put himself into present action, sold his annuity, bought himself good clothes, put some money in his purse, and came to London; and by means of a relation at court, got a place in the household of Queen Elizabeth, where

he behaved himself so that he won the love of many of the court; but being young, took an affection to gaming, and spent most of the money he had in his purse. About that time, the Earl of Essex was setting forth on a voyage to Cadiz, and my father, that had a mind to quit his idle court life, procured an employment from the victualler of the navy, to go along with that fleet.[4] In which voyage he demeaned himself with so much courage and prudence, that after his return he was honoured with a very noble and profitable employment in Ireland. There a rich widow, that had many children, cast her affections upon him, and he married her; but she not living many years with him, and having no children by him, after her death he distributed all her estate among her children, for whom he ever preserved a fatherly kindness, and some of her grandchildren were brought up in his house after I was born. He, by God's blessing, and his fidelity and industry, growing in estate and honour, received a knighthood from King James soon after his coming to the crown,[5] for some eminent service done to him in Ireland, which, having only heard in my childhood, I cannot perfectly set down. After that, growing into a familiarity with Sir George Carew, made now by the king Earl of Totness, a niece of this earl's, the daughter of Sir Peter Carew, who lived a young widow in her uncle's house, fell in love with him, which her uncle perceiving, procured a marriage between them.[6] She had diverse children by my

---

[1] *Lord Goring* perhaps George Goring, Receiver-General of the Court of Wards from 1584 to 1594. He owned several Sussex manors. He died owing the Crown £19,777 and court gossip had it that he had engaged in fraudulent financial practices.

[2] *the custom of those times* The right of primogeniture was the feudal rule of inheritance by which the property and title of an intestate, excluding only the widow's dower or jointure, passed to the eldest son. The remaining children were granted an annual sum of money for a term of years, for life, or in perpetuity.

[3] *wars in Ireland* During the reign of Elizabeth I, English troops were intermittently deployed to quell uprisings against England's colonial rule; *Low Countries* Beginning in the 1580s, English soldiers assisted the Dutch in their revolt against Spanish rule.

[4] *Earl of Essex...to Cadiz* During England's war with Spain, Robert Devereux (1576–1601), second Earl of Essex, led an expedition against Cadiz in June 1596; *victualler* one who supplies an army or armed force with necessary provisions (*OED* victualler 2a).

[5] *received a knighthood...to the crown* In her *Diary* (Knole Diary), Anne Clifford described King James's propensity to bestow knighthoods immediately after he ascended the throne in 1603: "Likewise he created many barons among which my Uncle Russell was made Lord Russell of Thorney, and for knights, they were innumerable."

[6] *Sir George Carew...Earl of Totness* George, first and only Lord Carew of Clopton. He was appointed President of Munster in February 1600.

father, but only two of them, a son and daughter, survived her, who died whilst my father was absent from her in Ireland. He led, all the time of his widowhood, a very disconsolate life, careful for nothing in the world but to educate and advance the son and daughter, the dear pledges she had left him, for whose sake he quitted himself of his employments abroad, and procured himself the office of Victualler of the Navy, a place then both of credit and great revenue. His friends, considering his solitude, had procured him a match of a very rich widow, who was a lady of as much discretion as wealth; but while he was upon this design he chanced to see my mother, at the house of Sir William St. John, who had married her eldest sister; and though he went on his journey, yet something in her person and behaviour, which he carried along with him, would not let him accomplish it, but brought him back to my mother. She was of a noble family, being the youngest daughter of Sir John St. John, of Liddiard Tregooze in the county of Wilts; her father and mother died when she was not above five years of age, and yet at her nurse's, from whence she was carried to be brought up in the house of the Lord Grandison, her father's younger brother; an honourable and excellent person, but married to a lady so jealous of him, and so ill-natured in her jealous fits, to anything that was related to him, that her cruelties to my mother exceeded the stories of stepmothers. The rest of my aunts, my mother's sisters, were dispersed to several places, where they grew up till my uncle, Sir John St. John, being married to the daughter of Sir Thomas Laten, they were all again brought home to their brother's house. There were not in those days so many beautiful women found in any family as these, but my mother was by the most judgments preferred before all her elder sisters, who, something envious at it, used her unkindly. Yet all the suitors that came to them still turned their addresses to her, which she in her youthful innocency neglected, till

one of greater name, estate, and reputation than the rest, happened to fall deeply in love with her, and to manage it so discreetly, that my mother could not but entertain him. My uncle's wife, who had a mother's kindness for her, persuaded her to remove herself from her sisters' envy, by going along with her to the Isle of Jersey, where her father was governor; which she did, and there went into the town, and boarded in a French minister's house, to learn the language, that minister having been, by the persecution in France, driven to seek his shelter there. Contracting a dear friendship with this holy man and his wife, she was instructed in their Geneva discipline, which she liked so much better than our more superstitious service, that she could have been contented to have lived there, had not a powerful passion in her heart drawn her back.[1] But at her return she met with many afflictions; the gentleman who had professed so much love to her, in her absence had been, by most vile practices and treacheries, drawn out of his senses, and into the marriage of a person, whom, when he recovered his reason, he hated. But that served only to augment his misfortune, and the circumstances of that story not being necessary to be here inserted, I shall only add that my mother lived in my uncle's house, secretly discontented at this accident, but was comforted by the kindness of my uncle's wife, who had contracted such an intimate friendship with her, that they seemed to have but one soul. And in this kindness she had some time a great solace, till some malicious persons had wrought some jealousies, which were very groundless, in my uncle concerning his wife; but his nature being inclinable to that passion, which was fomented in him by subtle wicked persons, and my mother endeavouring to vindicate injured innocence, she was herself not well treated by my uncle, whereupon she left his house, with a resolution to withdraw herself

---

[1] *Geneva discipline* Presbyterianism, contrasted with the "superstitious" (that is, Catholicizing) Church of England.

into the island, where the good minister was, and there to wear out her life in the service of God. While she was deliberating, and had fixed upon it in her own thoughts, resolving to impart it to none, she was with Sir William St. John, who had married my aunt, when my father accidentally came in there, and fell so heartily in love with her, that he persuaded her to marry him, which she did, and her melancholy made her conform cheerfully to that gravity of habit and conversation, which was becoming the wife of such a person, who was then forty-eight years of age, and she not above sixteen. The first year of their marriage was crowned with a son, called after my father's name, and born at East Smithfield, in that house of the king's which belonged to my father's employment in the navy. The next year they removed to the Tower of London, whereof my father was made lieutenant, and there had two sons more before me, and four daughters, and two sons after; of all which only three sons and two daughters survived him at the time of his death, which was in the sixty-third year of his age, after he had three years before languished of a consumption, that succeeded a fever which he got in the unfortunate voyage to the Isle of Rhee.[1]

He died in the month of May, 1630, sadly bewailed by not only all his dependants and relations, but by all that were acquainted with him; for he never conversed with any to whom he was not at some time or in some way beneficial; and his nature was so delighted in doing good, that it won him the love of all men, even his enemies, whose envy and malice it was his custom to overcome with obligations. He had great natural parts, but was too active

in his youth to stay the heightening of them by study of dead writings; but in the living books of men's conversations he soon became so skilful that he was never mistaken, but where his own good would not let him give credit to the evil he discerned in others. He was a most indulgent husband, and no less kind to his children; a most noble master, who thought it not enough to maintain his servants honourably while they were with him, but, for all that deserved it, provided offices or settlements, as for children. He was a father to all his prisoners, sweetening with such compassionate kindness their restraint, that the affliction of a prison was not felt in his days. He had a singular kindness for all persons that were eminent either in learning or arms, and when, through the ingratitude and vice of that age, many of the wives and children of Queen Elizabeth's glorious captains were reduced to poverty, his purse was their common treasury, and they knew not the inconvenience of decayed fortunes till he was dead: many of those valiant seamen he maintained in prison, many he redeemed out of prison, and cherished with an extraordinary bounty. If among his excellencies one outshined the rest, it was the generous liberality of his mind, wherein goodness and greatness were so equally distributed that they mutually embellished each other. Pride and covetousness had not the least place in his breast. As he was in love with true honour, so he contemned vain titles; and though in his youth he accepted an addition to his birth, in his riper years he refused a baronetcy, which the king offered him. He was severe in the regulating of his family, especially would not endure the least immodest behaviour or dress in any woman under his roof. There was nothing he hated more than an insignificant gallant, that could only make his legs and prune himself, and court a lady, but had not brains to employ himself in things more suitable to

[1] *Isle of Rhee* In the *Memoirs*, Hutchinson writes of the ill-fated expedition to the Isle of Rhé to assist the Huguenots: "The protestants abroad were all looked upon as puritans, and their interests, instead of being protected sadly betrayed; ships were let out to the French king to serve against them; and all the flower of the English gentry were lost in an ill-managed expedition to the Isle of Rhee, under pretence of helping them, but so ordered that it proved the loss of Rochelle, the strong fort and best defence of all the protestants in France."

man's nobler sex.[1] Fidelity in his trust, love and loyalty to his prince, were not the least of his virtues, but those wherein he was not excelled by any of his own or succeeding times. The large estate he reaped by his happy industry, he did many times over as freely resign again to the king's service, till he left the greatest part of it at his death in the king's hands. All his virtues wanted not the crown of all virtue, piety and true devotion to God. As his life was a continued exercise of faith and charity, it concluded with prayers and blessings, which were the only consolations his desolate family could receive in his death. Never did any two better agree in magnanimity and bounty than he and my mother, who seemed to be actuated by the same soul, so little did she grudge any of his liberalities to strangers, or he contradict any of her kindness to all her relations;[2] her house being a common home to all of them, and a nursery to their children. He gave her a noble allowance of £300 a year for her own private expense, and had given her all her own portion to dispose of how she pleased, as soon as she was married; which she suffered to increase in her friend's hands; and what my father allowed her she spent not in vanities, although she had what was rich and requisite upon occasions, but she laid most of it out in pious and charitable uses. Sir Walter Raleigh and Mr. Ruthin being prisoners in the Tower, and addicting themselves to chemistry, she suffered them to make their rare experiments at her cost, partly to comfort and divert the poor prisoners, and partly to gain the knowledge of their experiments, and the medicines to help such poor people as were not able to seek physicians.[3] By these

means she acquired a great deal of skill, which was very profitable to many all her life. She was not only to these, but to all the other prisoners that came into the Tower, as a mother. All the time she dwelt in the Tower, if any were sick she made them broths and restoratives with her own hands, visited and took care of them, and provided them all necessaries; if any were afflicted she comforted them, so that they felt not the inconvenience of a prison who were in that place. She was not less bountiful to many poor widows and orphans, whom officers of higher and lower rank had left behind them as objects of charity. Her own house was filled with distressed families of her relations, whom she supplied and maintained in a noble way. The worship and service of God, both in her soul and her house, and the education of her children, were her principal care. She was a constant frequenter of week-day lectures, and a great lover and encourager of good ministers, and most diligent in her private reading and devotions.[4]

When my father was sick she was not satisfied with the attendance of all that were about him, but made herself his nurse, and cook, and physician, and, through the blessing of God, and her indefatigable labours and watching, preserved him a great while longer than the physicians thought it possible for his nature to hold out. At length, when the Lord took him to rest, she showed as much humility and patience, under that great change, as moderation and bounty in her more plentiful and prosperous condition, and died in my house at Owthorpe, in the county of Nottingham, in the year 1659. The privilege of being born of, and educated by, such

---

[1] *make his legs* bow: "an obeisance made by drawing back one leg and bending the other" (*OED* leg *v* 2; leg *sb* 4); *prune himself* to trim, dress up with minute nicety (*OED* prune *v*[1] B.2)

[2] *actuated* rendered actual or active (*OED* actuated *ppl.a*).

[3] *Sir Walter Raleigh* After his secret marriage to Elizabeth Throckmorton, Sir Walter Raleigh (ca. 1552–1618) was imprisoned in the Tower in 1592, condemned to death and then reprieved. He was

imprisoned in 1603 for allegedly conspiring to assassinate James I and crown Arabella Stuart. He was freed in 1616 to undertake an expedition to Guiana in search of gold, during the course of which a Spanish settlement was burnt. On the failure of the expedition and at the insistence of the Spanish ambassador, Raleigh was arrested, and executed on October 29, 1618.

[4] *lectures* sermons.

excellent parents, I have often revolved with great thankfulness for the mercy, and humiliation that I did no more improve it.[1] After my mother had had three sons, she was very desirous of a daughter, and when the women at my birth told her I was one, she received me with a great deal of joy; and the nurses fancying, because I had more complexion and favour than is usual in so young children, that I should not live, my mother became fonder of me, and more endeavoured to nurse me. As soon as I was weaned a French woman was taken to be my dry-nurse, and I was taught to speak French and English together.[2] My mother, while she was with child of me, dreamed that she was walking in the garden with my father, and that a star came down into her hand, with other circumstances, which, though I have often heard, I minded not enough to remember perfectly; only my father told her, her dream signified she should have a daughter of some extraordinary eminency; which thing, like such vain prophecies, wrought as far as it could its own accomplishment: for my father and mother fancying me then beautiful, and more than ordinarily apprehensive, applied all their cares, and spared no cost to improve me in my education, which procured me the admiration of those that flattered my parents.[3] By the time I was four years old I read English perfectly, and having a great memory, I was carried to sermons; and while I was very young could remember and repeat them exactly, and being caressed, the love of praise tickled me, and made me attend more heedfully. When I was about seven years of age, I remember I had at one time eight tutors in several qualities, languages, music, dancing, writing, and needlework; but my genius was quite averse from all but my book, and that I was so eager of, that my mother thinking it prejudiced my health, would moderate me in it; yet this rather animated me than kept me back, and every moment I could steal from my play I would employ in any book I could find, when my own were locked up from me. After dinner and supper I still had an hour allowed me to play, and then I would steal into some hole or other to read. My father would have me learn Latin, and I was so apt that I outstripped my brothers who were at school, although my father's chaplain, that was my tutor, was a pitiful dull fellow. My brothers, who had a great deal of wit, had some emulation at the progress I made in my learning, which very well pleased my father; though my mother would have been contented if I had not so wholly addicted myself to that as to neglect my other qualities. As for music and dancing, I profited very little in them, and would never practise my lute or harpsichords but when my masters were with me; and for my needle I absolutely hated it. Play among other children I despised, and when I was forced to entertain such as came to visit me, I tired them with more grave instructions than their mothers, and plucked all their babies to pieces, and kept the children in such awe, that they were glad when I entertained myself with elder company; to whom I was very acceptable, and living in the house with many persons that had a great deal of wit, and very profitable serious discourses being frequent at my father's table and in my mother's drawing-room, I was very attentive to all, and gathered up things that I would utter again, to great admiration of many that took my memory and imitation for wit. It pleased God that, through the good instructions of my mother, and the sermons she carried me to, I was convinced that the knowledge of God was the most excellent study, and accordingly applied myself to it, and to practise as I was taught. I used to exhort my mother's maids much, and to turn their idle discourses to good

---

[1] *revolved* meditated upon (*OED* revolve *v* II.10).

[2] *dry-nurse* a woman who takes care and attends a child but does not suckle it (*OED* dry-nurse *sb* 1).

[3] *my education* Compare the education of Lucy Hutchinson described here to that prescribed in *An Essay to Revive the Ancient Education of Gentlewomen* (1673).

subjects; but I thought, when I had done this on the Lord's day, and every day performed my due tasks of reading and praying, that then I was free to anything that was not sin; for I was not at that time convinced of the vanity of conversation which was not scandalously wicked. I thought it no sin to learn or hear witty songs and amorous sonnets or poems, and twenty things of that kind, wherein I was so apt that I became the confidant in all the loves that were managed among my mother's young women; and there was none of them but had many lovers, and some particular friends beloved above the rest. Among these I have....[1] Five years after me my mother had a daughter that she nursed at her own breast, and was infinitely fond of above all the rest; and I being of too serious a temper was not so pleasing to my...[2]

—1806

Memoirs of the Life of Colonel Hutchinson
(excerpts)

The court of this king was a nursery of lust and intemperance;[3] he had brought in with him a company of poor Scots, who, coming into this plentiful kingdom, were surfeited with riot and debaucheries, and got all the riches of the land only to cast away. The honour, wealth, and glory of the nation, wherein Queen Elizabeth left it, were soon prodigally wasted by this thriftless heir; and the nobility of the land was utterly debased by setting honours to public sale, and conferring them on persons that had neither blood nor merit fit to wear, nor estates to bear up their titles, but were fain to invent projects to pill the people, and pick their purses for the maintenance of vice and lewdness.[4]

The generality of the gentry of the land soon learned the court fashion, and every great house in the country became a sty of uncleanness. To keep the people in their deplorable security, till vengeance overtook them, they were entertained with masks, stage plays, and various sorts of ruder sports. Then began murder, incest, adultery, drunkenness, swearing, fornication, and all sort of ribaldry, to be no concealed but countenanced vices, because they held such conformity with the court example. Next to this, a great cause of these abominations was the mixed marriages of papist and protestant families, which, no question, was a design of the popish party to compass and procure; and so successful, that I have observed that there was not one house in ten, where such a marriage was made, but the better party was corrupted, the children's souls were sacrificed to devils, the worship of God was laid aside in that family, for fear of distasting the idolater; the kindred, tenants, and neighbours, either quite turned from it, or cooled in their zeal for religion. As the fire is most fervent in a frosty season, so the general apostacy from holiness, if I may so call it, and defection to lewdness, stirred up sorrow, indignation, and fear, in all that retained any love of God in the land, whether ministers or people; the ministers warned the people of the approaching judgments of God, which could not be expected but to follow such high provocations; God in his mercy sent his prophets into all corners of the land, to preach repentance, and cry out against the ingratitude of England, who thus requited so many rich mercies that no nation could ever boast of more;[5] and by these a few were everywhere converted and established in faith and holiness; but at court they were hated, disgraced, and reviled, and in scorn had the name of Puritan fixed upon them.

---

[1] Many pages have been torn out, apparently by Hutchinson herself.

[2] Hutchinson's narrative ends here rather abruptly.

[3] *this king* James I (1566–1625), who reigned from 1603–1625.

[4] *pill* plunder, pillage (*OED* pill *v*[1] I.1a).

[5] *God in his mercy...of the land* Hutchinson echoes the apocalyptic rhetoric of Ezekiel: "Also, thou son of man, thus saith the Lord GOD unto the land of Israel; An end, the end is come upon the four corners of the land" (7:2).

And now the ready way to preferment there was to declare an opposition to the power of godliness, under that name; so that their pulpits might justly be called the scorner's chair, those sermons only pleasing that flattered them in their vices, and told the poor king that he was Solomon, and that his sloth and cowardice, by which he betrayed the cause of God and honour of the nation, was gospel meekness and peaceableness; for which they raised him up above the heavens, while he lay wallowing like a swine in the mire of his lust.[1] He had a little learning, and this they called the spirit of wisdom, and so magnified him, so falsely flattered him, that he could not endure the words of truth and soundness, but rewarded these base, wicked, unfaithful fawners with rich preferments, attended with pomps and titles, which heaped them up above a human height. With their pride, their envy swelled against the people of God, whom they began to project how they might root out of the land; and when they had once given them a name, whatever was odious or dreadful to the king, they fixed upon the puritan, who, according to their character, was nothing but a factious hypocrite.

The king had upon his heart the dealings both of England and Scotland with his mother, and harboured a secret desire of revenge upon the godly in both nations, yet had not courage enough to assert his resentment like a prince, but employed a wicked cunning he was master of, and called king-craft, to undermine what he durst not openly oppose,—the true religion;[2] this was fenced with the liberty of the people, and so linked together, that it was impossible to make them slaves, till they were brought to be idolaters of royalty and glorious lust;[3] and as impossible to make them adore these gods, while they continued loyal to the government of Jesus Christ. The payment of civil obedience to the king and the laws of the land satisfied not; if any durst dispute his impositions in the worship of God, he was presently reckoned among the seditious and disturbers of the public peace, and accordingly persecuted; if any were grieved at the dishonour of the kingdom, or the griping of the poor, or the unjust oppressions of the subject, by a thousand ways, invented to maintain the riots of the courtiers, and the swarms of needy Scots the king had brought in to devour like locusts the plenty of this land, he was a puritan; if any, out of mere morality and civil honesty, discountenanced the abominations of those days, he was a puritan, however he conformed to their superstitious worship; if any showed favour to any godly honest persons, kept them company, relieved them in want, or protected them against violent or unjust oppression, he was a puritan; if any gentleman in his country maintained the good laws of the land, or stood up for any public interest, for good order or government, he was a puritan: in short, all that crossed the views of the needy courtiers, the proud encroaching priests, the thievish projectors, the lewd nobility and gentry—whoever was zealous for God's glory or worship, could not endure blasphemous oaths, ribald conversation, profane scoffs, sabbath breaking, derision of the word of God, and the like— whoever could endure a sermon, modest habit or conversation, or anything good,—all these were puritans;[4] and if puritans, then enemies to the king

---

[1] *while he lay...his lust* "For when they speak great swelling words of vanity, they allure through the lusts of the flesh, through much wantonness.... But it is happened unto them according to the true proverb, The dog is turned to his own vomit again; and the sow that was washed to her wallowing in the mire" (II Peter 2:18,22); there is much in II Peter 2 that is relevant to Hutchinson's description of James I.

[2] *his mother* Mary Queen of Scots (1542–1587), who was imprisoned by the Scots for complicity in the murder of her husband, Henry Stuart, Lord Darnley. She was later imprisoned for more than twenty years by the English, who eventually convicted her of treason and executed her.

[3] *fenced...people* fortified by association with the idea of popular liberty (*OED* fence *v* 6).

[4] *projectors* schemers (*OED* projector 1b).

and his government, seditious, factious, hypocrites, ambitious disturbers of the public peace, and finally, the pest of the kingdom. Such false logic did the children of darkness use to argue with against the hated children of light, whom they branded besides as an illiterate, morose, melancholy, discontented, crazed sort of men, not fit for human conversation; as such they made them not only the sport of the pulpit, which was become but a more solemn sort of stage, but every stage, and every table, and every puppet-play, belched forth profane scoffs upon them, the drunkards made them their songs, and all fiddlers and mimics learned to abuse them, as finding it the most gameful way of fooling.[1] Thus the two factions in those days grew up to great heights and enmities one against the other; while the papist wanted not industry and subtlety to blow the coals between them, and was so successful that, unless the mercy of God confound them by their own imaginations, we may justly fear they will at last obtain their full wish.

.   .   .   .

The face of the court was much changed in the change of the king, for King Charles was temperate, chaste, and serious; so that the fools and bawds, mimics and catamites,[2] of the former court, grew out of fashion; and the nobility and courtiers, who did not quite abandon their debaucheries, yet so reverenced the king as to retire into corners to practise them. Men of learning and ingenuity in all arts were in esteem, and received encouragement from the king, who was a most excellent judge and great lover of paintings, carvings, gravings, and many other ingenuities, less offensive than the bawdry and profane abusive wit which was the only exercise of the other court.[3] But, as in the primitive

times, it is observed that the best emperors were some of them stirred up by Satan to be the bitterest persecutors of the church, so this king was a worse encroacher upon the civil and spiritual liberties of his people by far than his father. He married a papist, a French lady, of a haughty spirit, and a great wit and beauty, to whom he became a most uxorious husband.[4] By this means the court was replenished with papists, and many who hoped to advance themselves by the change, turned to that religion. All the papists in the kingdom were favoured, and, by the king's example, matched into the best families; the puritans were more than ever discountenanced and persecuted, insomuch that many of them chose to abandon their native country, and leave their dearest relations, to retire into any foreign soil or plantation, where they might, amidst all outward inconveniences, enjoy the free exercise of God's worship. Such as could not flee were tormented in the bishops' court, fined, whipped, pilloried, imprisoned, and suffered to enjoy no rest, so that death was better than life to them; and notwithstanding their patient sufferance of all these things, yet was not the king satisfied till the whole land was reduced to perfect slavery. The example of the French king was propounded to him, and he thought himself no monarch so long as his will was confined to the bounds of any law; but knowing that the people of England were not pliable to an arbitrary rule, he plotted to subdue them to his yoke by a foreign force, and till he could effect it, made no conscience of granting anything to the people, which he resolved should not oblige him longer than it served his turn; for he was a prince that had nothing of faith or truth, justice or generosity, in him. He was the most obstinate person in his self-will that ever was, and so bent upon being an absolute, uncontrollable sovereign, that he was resolved either to be such a king or

---

[1] *every stage* See, for example, Ben Jonson's characters Zeal-of-the-Land Busy and Tribulation Wholesome in *Bartholomew Fair* and *The Alchemist* respectively.

[2] *catamites* boys "kept for unnatural purposes" (*OED* catamite).

[3] *bawdry* lewd, obscene (*OED* bawdry 3).

---

[4] *uxorious* dotingly or submissively fond (*OED* uxorious *a* 1a).

none. His firm adherence to prelacy was not for conscience of one religion more than another, for it was his principle that an honest man might be saved in any profession;[1] but he had a mistaken principle that kingly government in the state could not stand without episcopal government in the church; and, therefore, as the bishops flattered him with preaching up his sovereign prerogative, and inveighing against the puritans as factious and disloyal, so he protected them in their pomp and pride, and insolent practices against all the godly and sober people of the land.

.   .   .   .

But there were two above all the rest, who led the van of the king's evil counsellors, and these were Laud, archbishop of Canterbury, a fellow of mean extraction and arrogant pride, and the Earl of Strafford, who as much outstripped all the rest in favour as he did in abilities, being a man of deep policy, stern resolution, and ambitious zeal to keep up the glory of his own greatness.[2] In the beginning of this king's reign, this man had been a strong asserter of the liberties of the people, among whom he had gained himself an honourable reputation, and was dreadful to the court party; who thereupon strewed snares in his way, and when they found a breach at his ambition, his soul was that way entered and captivated. He was advanced first to be lord president of the council in the north, to be a baron, afterwards an earl, and then deputy of Ireland; he was the nearest to a favourite of any man since the death of the Duke of Buckingham, who was raised by his first master, and kept up by the second, upon no account of personal worth or any deserving abilities in him, but only from the violent and private inclinations of the princes.[3] But the Earl of Strafford wanted not any accomplishment that could be desired in the most serviceable minister of state: besides, he having made himself odious to the people by his revolt from their interest to that of the oppressive court, he was now obliged to keep up his own interest with his new party, by all the malicious practices that pride and revenge could inspire him with. But above all these the king had another instigator of his own violent purpose, more powerful than all the rest, and that was the queen, who, grown out of her childhood, began to turn her mind from those vain extravagancies she lived in at first, to that which did less become her, and was more fatal to the kingdom; which is never in any place happy where the hands which were made only for distaffs affect the management of sceptres.[4]—If any one object the fresh example of Queen Elizabeth, let them remember that the felicity of her reign was the effect of her submission to her masculine and wise counsellors; but wherever male princes are so effeminate as to suffer women of foreign birth and different religions to intermeddle with the affairs of state, it is always found to produce sad desolations; and it hath been observed that a French queen never brought any happiness to England. Some kind of fatality, too, the English imagined to be in her name of Marie, which, it is said, the king rather chose to have her called by than her other, Henrietta, because the land should find a blessing in

---

[1] *prelacy* the system of church government by prelates or bishops of lordly rank (*OED* prelacy 4).

[2] *there were two…own greatness* William Laud, Archbishop of Canterbury (1572–1645), and Sir Thomas Wentworth, first Earl of Strafford (1593–1641). Puritans adamantly opposed the Arminian theology and "Anglican" ecclesiology of Laud, the son of a Reading clothier. He was imprisoned in 1641 and executed in 1645. Strafford, Lord President of the Council of the North and Deputy of Ireland, was the chief advisor of Charles I from 1639 onwards. In 1640, he was impeached by the Commons and imprisoned in the Tower of London, and in 1641 was executed for treason; *deep* grave (*OED* deep *a* II.7a).

[3] *Duke of Buckingham* George Villiers, first Duke of Buckingham (1592–1628), was a favorite of both James I and Charles I. See the selection of poems on the Duke of Buckingham.

[4] *distaffs* the staff of a hand spinning-wheel; used symbolically for female authority (*OED* distaff 2,3b).

that name, which had been more unfortunate;[1] but it was not in his power, though a great prince, to control destiny. This lady being by her priests affected with the meritoriousness of advancing her own religion, whose principle it is to subvert all other, applied that way her great wit and parts, and the power her haughty spirit kept over her husband, who was enslaved in his affection only to her, though she had no more passion for him than what served to promote her designs. Those brought her into a very good correspondence with the archbishop and his prelatical crew, both joining in the cruel design of rooting the godly out of the land. The foolish protestants were meditating reconciliations with the church of Rome, who embraced them as far as they would go, carrying them in hand, as if there had been a possibility of bringing such a thing to pass; meanwhile they carried on their design by them, and had so ripened it, that nothing but the mercy of God prevented the utter subversion of protestantism in the three kingdoms.—But how much soever their designs were framed in the dark, God revealed them to his servants, and most miraculously ordered providences for their preservation.

.   .   .   .

[Jan. 1644]

...The enemy being entered, possessed themselves of St. Peter's church and certain houses near the castle, from whence they shot into the castle-yard and wounded one man and killed another, which was all the hurt that was done our men that day.[2]

The governor was very angry with the horse for coming up so suddenly, and stirred them up to such a generous shame, that they dismounted, and all took muskets to serve as foot, with which they did such very good service, that they exceedingly well regained their reputations.[3] Having taken foot arms, the governor sent one of his own companies with part of them, and they beat the cavaliers out of the nearest lanes and houses, which they had possessed, and so made a safe way for the rest to sally out and retreat, as there should be occasion.

When this was done, which was about noon, the governor sent out all the rest of the horse and foot, to beat the enemy out of the town. Sir Charles Lucas, who was the chief commander of all the forces there, had prepared a letter to send up to the governor to demand of him the castle; or if he would not deliver it, that then he should send down the mayor and aldermen, threatening, that if they came not immediately, he would sack and burn the town.[4] There were, at that time, above a thousand cavaliers in the town, and as many in a body without the town, to have beaten off the Derby and Leicester forces, if they should have made any attempt to come in, to the assistance of their friends in Nottingham. On the other side of the Trent were all the forces Mr. Hastings could bring out from his own garrison and Belvoir and Wiverton to force the bridges. All the cavalier forces that were about the town, were about three thousand. When Sir Charles Lucas had written his letter, he could find none that would undertake to carry it to the castle, whereupon they took the mayor's wife, and with threats, compelled her to undertake it; but just as she went out of the house from them, she heard an outcry, that "the roundheads were sallying forth," whereupon she flung down their letter and ran away; and they

---

[1] *her name of Marie...unfortunate* probably a reference to the execution of Mary Queen of Scots, though possibly an allusion to Mary Tudor (1516–1558), the Catholic queen dubbed "Bloody Mary" by Protestants.

[2] *The enemy* Royalist forces (Cavaliers); *the castle* Nottingham Castle.

[3] *governor* Colonel Hutchinson was appointed governor of Nottingham Castle and the town by order of Parliament November 20, 1643.

[4] *Charles Lucas* the brother of Margaret Lucas, afterwards Margaret Cavendish, Duchess of Newcastle. William Cavendish, then Marquis of Newcastle, had secured the north of England for the King at the inception of the first civil war (1642–46).

ran as fast, from four hundred soldiers, who came furiously upon them out of the castle, and surprised them;[1] while they were secure the castle would not have made so bold an attempt. But the governor's men chased them from street to street, till they had cleared the town of them, who ran away confusedly: the first that went out shot their pistols into the thatched houses to have fired them, but by the mercy of God neither that, nor other endeavours they showed to have fired the town, as they were commanded, took effect. Between thirty and forty of them were killed in the streets, fourscore were taken prisoners, and abundance of arms were gathered up, which the men flung away in haste, as they ran; but they put some fire into a hay barn and hay mows, and all other combustible things they could discern in their haste, but by God's mercy, the town, notwithstanding, was preserved from burning. While their foot marched away, their horse faced the town in a valley where their reserve stood, till towards evening, and then they all drew off. Many of them died on their return, and were found dead in the woods and in the towns they passed through. Many of them, discouraged by this service, ran away, and many of their horses were quite spoiled: for two miles they left a great track of blood, which froze as it fell upon the snow, for it was such bitter weather that the foot had waded almost to the middle in snow as they came, and

were so numbed with cold when they came into the town, that they were fain to be rubbed to get life into them, and in that condition were more eager for fires and warm meat than for plunder; which, together with their feeling of security, saved many men's goods; as they did not believe that an enemy, who had unhandsomely, to speak truth, suffered them to enter the town without any dispute, would have dared, at such great odds, to have set upon driving them out. Indeed, no one can believe, but those that saw that day, what a strange ebb and flow of courage and cowardice there was in both parties on that day. The cavaliers marched in with such terror to the garrison, and such gallantry, that they startled not when one of their leading files fell before them all at once, but marched boldly over the dead bodies of their friends, under their enemies' cannon, and carried such valiant dreadfulness about them, as made very courageous stout men recoil. Our horse, who ran away frighted at the sight of their foes, when they had breastworks before them, and the advantage of freshness to beat back assailants already vanquished with the sharpness of the cold and a killing march, within three or four hours, as men that thought nothing too great for them, returned fiercely upon the same men, after their refreshment, when they were entered into defensible houses. If it were a romance, one should say, after the success, that the heroes did it out of excess of gallantry, that they might the better signalise their valour upon a foe who was not vanquished to their hands by the inclemency of the season: but we are relating wonders of Providence, and must record this as one not to be conceived of, but by those who saw and shared in it. It was indeed a great instruction, that the best and highest courages are but the beams of the Almighty; and when He withholds His influence, the brave turn cowards, fear unnerves the most mighty, makes the most generous base, and great men to do those things they blush to think on; when God again

---

[1] *roundheads* Elsewhere in the *Memoirs* Hutchinson explains the genesis of the label "roundheads": "This name of roundhead coming so importunely in, I shall make a little digression to tell you how it came up. When puritanism grew into a faction, the zealots distinguished themselves, both men and women, by several affectations of habit, look and words....Among other affected habits, few of the puritans, what degree soever they were of, wore their hair long enough to cover their ears, and the ministers and many others cut it close round their heads, with so many little peaks, as was something ridiculous to behold....From this custom of wearing their hair, that name of roundhead became the scornful term given to the whole parliament party, whose army indeed marched out as if they had been only sent out till their hair was grown....It was very ill applied to Mr. Hutchinson, who, having naturally a very fine thickset head of hair, kept it clean and handsome, so that it was a great ornament to him."

inspires, the fearful and the feeble see no dangers, believe no difficulties, and carry on attempts whose very thoughts would, at another time, shiver their joints like agues. The events of this day humbled the pride of many of our stout men, and made them afterwards more carefully seek God, as well to inspire as prosper their valour; and the governor's handsome reproaches of their faults, with showing them the way to repair them, retrieved their straggling spirits, and animated them to very wonderful and commendable actions.

.   .   .   .

[January, 1649]

In January 1649, the court sat, the king was brought to his trial, and a charge drawn up against him for levying war against the parliament and people of England, for betraying the public trust reposed in him, and for being an implacable enemy to the commonwealth. But the king refused to plead, disowning the authority of the court, and after three several days persisting in contempt thereof, he was sentenced to suffer death. One thing was remarked in him by many of the court, that when the blood spilt in many of the battles where he was in his own person, and had caused it to be shed by his own command, was laid to his charge, he heard it with disdainful smiles, and looks and gestures which rather expressed sorrow that all the opposite party to him were not cut off, than that any were: and he stuck not to declare in words, that no man's blood spilt in this quarrel troubled him except one, meaning the Earl of Strafford. The gentlemen that were appointed his judges, and divers others, saw in him a disposition so bent on the ruin of all that opposed him, and of all the righteous and just things they had contended for, that it was upon the consciences of many of them, that if they did not execute justice upon him, God would require at their hands all of the blood and desolation which should ensue by their suffering him to escape, when God had brought him into

their hands. Although the malice of the malignant party and their apostate brethren seemed to threaten them, yet they thought they ought to cast themselves upon God, while they acted with a good conscience for him and for their country. Some of them afterwards, for excuse, belied themselves, and said they were under the awe of the army, and overpersuaded by Cromwell, and the like;[1] but it is certain that all men herein were left to their free liberty of acting, neither persuaded nor compelled; and as there were some nominated in the commission who never sat, and others who sat at first, but durst not hold on, so all the rest might have declined it if they would, when it is apparent they would have suffered nothing by so doing. For those who then declined were afterwards, when they offered themselves, received in again, and had places of more trust and benefit than those who ran the utmost hazard; which they deserved not, for I know upon certain knowledge that many, yea the most of them, retreated, not for conscience, but from fear and worldly prudence, foreseeing that the insolency of the army might grow to that height as to ruin the cause, and reduce the kingdom into the hands of the enemy; and then those who had been most courageous in their country's cause would be given up as victims. These poor men did privately animate those who appeared most publicly, and I know several of them in whom I lived to see that saying of Christ fulfilled, "He that will save his life shall lose it, and he that for my sake will lose his life shall save it";[2] when afterwards it fell out that all their prudent declensions saved not the lives of some nor the estates of others. As for Mr. Hutchinson, although he was very much confirmed in his judgment concerning the cause, yet herein being called to an extraordinary action, whereof many were of several minds, he addressed himself to

---

[1] *Cromwell*   Oliver Cromwell, Lord Protector (1599–1658).

[2] *He that…save it*   Matthew 16:25.

God by prayer; desiring the Lord that, if through any human frailty he were led into any error or false opinion in these great transactions, he would open his eyes, and not suffer him to proceed, but that he would confirm his spirit in the truth, and lead him by a right enlightened conscience; and finding no check, but a confirmation in his conscience that it was his duty to act as he did, he, upon serious debate, both privately and in his addresses to God, and in conferences with conscientious, upright, unbiased persons, proceeded to sign the sentence against the king. Although he did not then believe but that it might one day come to be again disputed among men, yet both he and others thought they could not refuse it without giving up the people of God, whom they had led forth and engaged themselves unto by the oath of God, into the hands of God's and their own enemies; and therefore he cast himself upon God's protection, acting according to the dictates of a conscience which he had sought the Lord to guide, and accordingly the Lord did signalize his favour afterwards to him.

After the death of the king it was debated and resolved to change the form of government from a monarchy into a commonwealth, and the house of lords was voted dangerous and useless thereunto, and dissolved. A council of state was to be annually chosen for the management of affairs, accountable to the parliament, out of which, consisting of forty councillors and a president, twenty were every year to go off by lot, and twenty new ones to be supplied. It is true, that at that time almost every man was fancying a form of government, and angry, when this came forth, that his invention took not place; and among these John Lilburne, a turbulent-spirited man, who ever was quiet in anything, published libels;[1] and the Levellers made a disturbance with a kind of insurrection, which Cromwell

soon appeased, they indeed being betrayed by their own leaders.

But how the public business went on...I shall leave to the stories that were then written; and only in general say that the hand of God was mightily seen in prospering and preserving the parliament till Cromwell's ambition unhappily interrupted them.

.   .   .   .

[April, 1660]

The colonel and Mr. Stanhope went up to the parliament, which began on the 25th day of April, 1660; to whom the king sending a declaration from Breda, which promised, or at least intimated, liberty of conscience, remission of all offences, enjoyment of liberties and estates;[2] they voted to send commissioners to invite him. And almost all the gentry of all parties went, some to fetch him over, some to meet him at the sea side, some to fetch him into London, into which he entered on the 29th day of May, with a universal joy and triumph, even to his own amazement; who, when he saw all the nobility and gentry of the land flowing in to him, asked where were his enemies. For he saw nothing but prostrates, expressing all the love that could make a prince happy. Indeed it was a wonder in that day to see the mutability of some, and the hypocrisy of others, and the servile flattery of all. Monk, like his better genius, conducted him, and was adored like one that had brought all the glory and felicity of mankind home with this prince.[3]

The officers of the army had made themselves as fine as the courtiers, and all hoped in this change to change their condition, and disowned all things they before had advised. Every ballad singer sang up

---

[1] *John Lilburne* Lilburne (1615–1657), political radical and leader of the Leveller movement; their *Agreement of the People* offered a kind of constitutional blueprint.

[2] *the king* Charles II; *declaration from Breda* a conciliatory Declaration issued by Charles II at Breda in April 1660, which ushered in the Restoration; it is included in this anthology.

[3] *Monk* George Monck, first Duke of Albemarle (1608–1670). Before he was captured by Fairfax in 1644, Monck fought for Charles I. He later became a trusted friend of Cromwell. In 1659, Monck resolved to restore Charles II to the throne and was created Baron Monck, Earl of Torrington, and Duke of Albemarle.

and down the streets ribald rhymes, made in reproach of the late commonwealth, and of all those worthies that therein endeavoured the people's freedom and happiness.

The presbyterians were now the white boys,[1] and according to their nature fell a thirsting, and then hunting after blood, urging that God's blessing could not be upon the land, till justice had cleansed it from the late king's blood. First that fact was disowned, then all the acts made after it rendered void, then an inquisition made after those that were guilty thereof, but only seven were nominated of those that sat in judgement on that prince, for exemplary justice, and a proclamation sent for the rest to come in, upon penalty of losing their estates.

While these things were debating in the house, at the first, divers persons concerned in that business sat there, and when the business came into question, every one of them spoke of it according to their present sense. But Mr. Lenthall, son to the late Speaker of that parliament, when the presbyterians first called that business into question, though not at all concerned in it himself, stood up and made such a handsome and honourable speech in defence of them all, as deserves eternal honour.[2] But the presbyterians called him to the bar for it, where, though he mitigated some expressions, which might be ill taken of the house, yet he spoke so generously, that it will never be forgotten of him. Herein he behaved himself with so much courage and honour as was not matched at that time in England, for which he was looked on with an evil eye, and, upon a pretence of treason, put in prison; from whence his father's money, and the lieutenant of the tower's jealousy, delivered him. When it came to Ingoldsby's turn, he, with many tears, professed his repentance for that murder, and told a false tale, how Cromwell held his hand, and forced him to subscribe the sentence, and made a most whining recantation, after which he retired;[3] and another had almost ended, when Colonel Hutchinson, who was not there at the beginning, came in, and was told what they were about, and that it would be expected he should say something. He was surprised with a thing he expected not, yet neither then, nor in any like occasion, did he ever fail himself, but told them, "That for his actings in those days, if he had erred, it was the inexperience of his age, and the defect of his judgement, and not the malice of his heart, which had ever prompted him to pursue the general advantage of his country more than his own; and if the sacrifice of him might conduce to the public peace and settlement, he should freely submit his life and fortunes to their disposal; that the vain expense of his age, and the great debts his public employments had run him into, as they were testimonies that neither avarice nor any other interest had carried him on, so they yielded him just cause to repent that he ever forsook his own blessed quiet, to embark in such a troubled sea, where he had made shipwreck of all things but a good conscience; and as to that particular action of the king, he desired them to believe he had that sense of it that befitted an Englishman, a Christian, and a gentleman." What he expressed was to this effect, but so very handsomely delivered, that it took generally the whole house; only one gentleman stood up and said, he had expressed himself as one that was much more sorry for the events and consequences than the actions; but another replied, that when a man's words might admit of two interpreta-

---

2 *Mr. Lenthall* Sir John Lenthall (1625–1681), son of William Lenthall, was knighted by Cromwell in 1658, and served as a colonel in the Parliamentary army in 1659. Expelled from the House May 12, 1660, he was eventually knighted by Charles II (1677).

---

3 *Ingoldsby* Sir Richard Ingoldsby (d. 1685) was appointed colonel of a regiment of foot in the New Model Army in 1645. He was one of the King's judges and signed his death warrant. With the fall of Richard Cromwell in 1659, he met with the agents of Charles II, whom he helped to restore to the throne. He was therefore spared the punishment of the other regicides and was created a Knight of the Bath at Charles II's coronation.

tions, it befitted gentlemen always to receive that which might be most favourable. As soon as the colonel had spoken, he retired into a room where Ingoldsby was with his eyes yet red, who had called up a little spite to succeed his whinings, and embracing Colonel Hutchinson, "O colonel," said he, "did I ever imagine we could be brought to this? Could I have suspected it, when I brought them Lambert in the other day, this sword should have redeemed us from being dealt with as criminals, by that people for whom we had so gloriously exposed ourselves."[1] The colonel told him he had foreseen, ever since those usurpers thrust out the lawful authority of the land to enthrone themselves, it could end in nothing else; but the integrity of his heart, in all he had done, made him as cheerfully ready to suffer as to triumph in a good cause. The result of the house that day was to suspend Colonel Hutchinson and the rest from sitting in the house. Monk, after all his great professions, now sat still, and had not one word to interpose for any person, but was as forward to set vengeance on foot as any man.

Mrs. Hutchinson, whom to keep quiet, her husband had hitherto persuaded that no man would lose or suffer by this change, at this beginning was awakened, and saw that he was ambitious of being a public sacrifice, and therefore, herein only in her whole life, resolved to disobey him, and to improve all the affection he had to her for his safety, and prevailed with him to retire; for she said, she would not live to see him a prisoner. With her unquietness, she drove him out of her own lodgings into a custody of a friend, in order to his further retreat, if occasion should be, and then made it her business to solicit all her friends for his safety. Meanwhile, it

was first resolved in the house, that mercy should be shown to some, and exemplary justice to others; then the number was defined, and voted it should not exceed seven; then upon the king's own solicitation, that his subjects should be put out of their fears, those seven were named, and after that a proclamation was sent for the rest to come in. Colonel Hutchinson not being of the number of those seven, was advised by all his friends to surrender himself, in order to secure his estate, and he was very earnest to do it, when Mrs. Hutchinson would by no means hear of it: but being exceedingly urged by his friends, that she would hereby obstinately lose all their estate, she would not yet consent that the colonel should give himself into custody, and she had wrought him to a strong engagement, that he would not dispose of himself without her. At length, being accused of obstinacy, in not giving him up, she devised a way to try the house, and wrote a letter in his name to the Speaker, to urge what might be in his favour, and to let him know, that by reason of some inconveniency it might be to him, he desired not to come under custody, and yet should be ready to appear at their call; and if they intended any mercy to him, he begged they would begin it in permitting him his liberty upon his parole, till they should finally determine of him. This letter she conceived would try the temper of the house; if they granted this, she had her end, for he was still free; if they denied it, she might be satisfied in keeping him from surrendering himself.

Having contrived and written this letter, before she carried it to the colonel, a friend came to her out of the house, near which her lodgings then were, and told her that if they had but any ground to begin, the house was that day in a most excellent temper towards her husband; whereupon she wrote her husband's name to the letter, and ventured to send it in, being used sometimes to write the letters he dictated, and her character not much differing from his. These gentlemen who were moved to try

---

[1] *Lambert* Major-General John Lambert (1619–1683) took up arms for the Parliament when the civil war began. In a dispute between the army and Parliament in 1647, he presented the army's grievances. As he did not take part in the trial of Charles I, he was imprisoned rather than executed when the monarchy was restored.

this opportunity, were not the friends she relied on; but God, to show that it was he, not they, sent two common friends, who had such good success that the letter was very well received; and upon that occasion all of all parties spoke so kindly and effectually for him, that he had not only what he desired, but was voted to be free without any engagement; and his punishment was only that he should be discharged from the present parliament, and from all offices, military or civil, in the state for ever; and upon his petition of thanks for this, his estate also was voted to be free from all mulcts and confiscations. Many providential circumstances concurred in this thing. That which put the house into so good a humour towards the colonel that day, was, that having taken the business of the king's trial into consideration, certain committees were found to be appointed to order the prepara-

tion of the court, the chairs and cushions, and other formalities, wherein Colonel Hutchinson had nothing to do; but when they had passed their votes for his absolute discharge and came to the sitting of the court, he was found not to have been one day away.[1] A rogue that had been one of their clerks had brought in all these informations; and above all, poor Mrs. Hacker, thinking to save her husband, had brought up the warrant for execution, with all their hands and seals.

—1806

---

[1] *but when they passed…one day away* According to Nelson's *Trial of Charles I,* Colonel Hutchinson was absent on Friday, January 12, when a committee was appointed for ordering and managing the King's trial. However, he attended most days and signed the sentence and the warrant for execution. Colonel Hutchinson was ultimately imprisoned in Sandown Castle in Kent, where he died on September 11, 1664.

Margaret Cavendish, Duchess of Newcastle
1623 – 1673

Margaret Cavendish was born in Colchester, Essex, the youngest of eight children of Sir Thomas Lucas, a wealthy landowner, and Elizabeth Leighton. In "A True Relation of my Birth, Breeding, and Life" Margaret recalls that she was raised by her mother after her father's death in accordance with "her birth and the nature of her sex" *(Nature's Pictures*, 1656). Her education, however, was limited to the traditional "feminine arts," a condition which Cavendish laments throughout her writings. When Queen Henrietta Maria appeared in Oxford in 1643, Margaret had a "great desire to be one of her maids of honour," and having obtained permission from her mother, she travelled to Oxford to become her attendant. Soon after her departure, Margaret's mother and brothers were sequestered from their estate and plundered of their goods. Elizabeth Lucas, however, managed to maintain Margaret in good condition to avoid her shameful exit from court. When the court went into exile in France (1644), Margaret met the exiled widower William Cavendish, Marquis (later Duke) of Newcastle, thirty years her senior (a selection from his writing is included in this anthology). Despite the difference in age, William successfully wooed Margaret, drawn, as she claims, to her "bashful fears which many condemned," for he would "choose such a wife as he might bring to his own humours; and not such a one as was wedded to self-conceit, or one that had been tempered to the humours of another." They were married in Paris in 1645. From Paris, they travelled to Rotterdam where they resided for six months until settling in Antwerp, where they remained until the Restoration. There were no children of the marriage.

In 1651, Margaret returned to England in an attempt to save William's estates. However, her application for funds from the sequestration committee was unsuccessful, and but for the assistance of Charles Cavendish, William's brother, they would have had little means of support. The same year, Margaret returned to Antwerp where she lived lavishly on credit. She published her first book of poetry, *Poems and Fancies*, in 1653. She followed this publication with collections of philosophical epistles and treatises, and short prose fictional works before returning to England in 1660. After her return, Margaret spent much of her time at the Newcastle estate writing closet drama, social and philosophical essays, poetry, prose fiction, and her husband's biography.

Viewed as an eccentric because of her unusual dress, her novel scientific notions, and her desire to write for publication, Margaret was criticized by many of her contemporaries including Samuel Pepys and Dorothy Osborne. However, her work was celebrated in some quarters. She was praised by such contemporary female authors as Katherine Philips and Bathsua Makin. Margaret's strengths as a writer lie in her refusal to operate within social and literary convention. She self-consciously engaged in generic innovation, adopted positions in the "masculine" discourses of natural philosophy and history, and challenged the philosophical conceptions of Descartes, Hobbes, More, and Van Helmont. Cavendish was a member of the political rearguard and the philosophical vanguard, and her writing exhibits a struggle between conservative and radical impulses, most notably in her treatment of women and of the non-human world. Margaret Cavendish died in London and was buried in Westminster Abbey.

❧❧❧

The Philosophical and Physical Opinions [1]

To the Two Universities

Most famously learned,

I here present the sum of my works, not that I think wise schoolmen, and industrious, laborious students should value my book for any worth, but to receive it without a scorn, for the good encouragement of our sex, lest in time we should grow irrational as idiots, by the dejectedness of our spirits, through the careless neglects, and despisements of the masculine sex to the effeminate, thinking it impossible we should have either learning or understanding, wit or judgement, as if we had not rational souls as well as men, and we out of a custom of dejectedness think so too, which makes us quit all industry towards profitable knowledge being employed only in low, and petty employments, which takes away not only our abilities towards arts, but higher capacities in speculations, so as we are become like worms that only live in the dull earth of ignorance, winding ourselves sometimes out, by the help of some refreshing rain of good educations which seldom is given us; for we are kept like birds in cages to hop up and down in our houses, not suffered to fly abroad to see the several changes of fortune, and the various humors, ordained and created by nature; thus wanting the experiences of nature, we must needs want the understanding and knowledge and so consequently prudence, and invention of men: thus by an opinion, which I hope is but an erroneous one in men, we are shut out of all power, and authority by reason we are never employed either in civil nor martial affairs, our counsels are despised and laughed at, the best of our actions are trodden down with scorn, by the over-weaning conceit men have

of themselves and through a despisement of us.

But I considering with myself, that if a right judgement, and a true understanding, and a respectful civility live anywhere, it must be in learned universities, where nature is best known, where truth is oftenest found, where civility is most practised, and if I find not a resentment here, I am very confident I shall find it nowhere,[2] neither shall I think I deserve it, if you approve not of me, but if I deserve not praise, I am sure to receive so much courtship from this sage society, as to bury me in silence; thus I may have a quiet grave, since not worthy a famous memory; but to lie entombed under the dust of an university will be honour enough for me, and more than if I were worshipped by the vulgar as a deity. Wherefore if your wisdoms cannot give me the bays, let your charity strew me with cypress;[3] and who knows but after my honourable burial, I may have a glorious resurrection in following ages, since time brings strange and unusual things to pass, I mean unusual to men, though not in nature: and I hope this action of mine, is not unnatural, though unusual for a woman to present a book to the university, nor impudence, for the action is honest, although it seem vainglorious, but if it be, I am to be pardoned, since there is little difference between man and beast, but what ambition and glory makes.

—1655

---

[1] *The Philosophical and Physical Opinions* which this letter prefaced was published in London in 1655.

[2] *resentment* appreciation or understanding (*OED* resentment 6).

[3] *bays* The leaves or sprigs of the bay laurel were woven into a wreath or garland to reward a conqueror or poet; hence, figuratively, the fame and repute attained by these (*OED* bay *sb*¹ 3); cypress used for habiliments of mourning (*OED* cypress³ *Obs* 1c). Compare Bradstreet's "If e'er you deign these lowly lines, your eyes / Give wholesome parsley wreath, I ask no bays" ("The Prologue" ll.44–45).

Nature's Pictures Drawn by Fancy's Pencil to the Life [1]

The Loving Cuckold

There was a gentleman that had married a wife, beautiful, modest, chaste, and of a mild and sweet disposition; and after he had been married some time, he began to neglect her, and make courtship to other women; which she perceiving, grew very melancholy; and sitting one day very pensive alone, in comes one of her husband's acquaintance to see him; but this lady told him, her husband was abroad.

Said he, "I have been to visit him many times, and still he is gone abroad."

Said she, "my husband finds better company abroad than he hath at home, or at least thinks so, which makes him go so often forth."

So he, discoursing with the lady, told her, he thought she was of a very melancholy disposition.

She said, she was not naturally so, but what her misfortunes caused.

Said he, "can fortune be cruel to a beautiful lady?"

"'Tis a sign," said she, "I am not beautiful, to match me to an unkind husband."

Said he, "to my thinking it is as impossible for your husband to be unkind, as fortune to be cruel."

Said she, "you shall be judge whether he be not so;" "for first," said she, "I have been an obedient wife, observed his humours, and obeyed his will in everything; next, I have been a thrifty, cleanly, patient and chaste wife; thirdly, I brought him a great portion; and lastly, my neighbours say I am handsome, and yet my husband doth neglect me, and despise me, making courtships to other women,

and sometimes, to vex me the more, before my face."

Said he, "your husband is not worthy of you; therefore if I may advise you, I would cast aside the affection I had placed upon him, and bestow it upon a person that will worship you with an idolatrous zeal; and if you please to bestow it on me, I will offer my heart on the altar of your favours, and sacrifice my services thereon; and my love shall be as the vestal fire that never goeth out, but perpetually burn with a religious flame."[2]

Thus speaking and pleading, made courtship to her, but she at first did not receive it; but he having opportunity by reason her husband was much from home, and using importunity, at last corrupted her, and she making a friendship with this gentleman, began to neglect her husband as much as he had done her;[3] which he perceiving, began to pull in the bridle of his loose carriage: but when he perceived his acquaintance was her courtly admirer, he began to woo her anew to gain her from him; but it would not be; for she became from a meek, modest, obedient, and thrifty wife, to be a ranting, flaunting, bold, imperious wife.

But her husband grew so fond of her, that he sought all the ways he could to please her, and was the observants creature to her that might be, striving to please her in all things or ways he could devise;[4] insomuch as observing she was never pleased but when she had gallants to court her, he would invite gentlemen to his house, and make entertainments for them; and those she seemed most to favour, he would make dear friendships with; and would often be absent, to give them opportunities to be with his wife alone, hoping to

---

[1] In *Nature's Pictures* (London, 1656), Cavendish includes a collection of prose and verse fiction from a wide range of genres and a brief autobiography.

[2] *vestal fire* sacred fire; originally the sacred fire in the temple of Vesta at Rome, over which the priestesses (the vestal virgins) had charge (*OED* vestal *a* A.2).

[3] *importunity* constancy of action or troublesome pertinacity in solicitation (*OED* importunity 3,4).

[4] *observants* presumably in the sense of "most observant."

get a favourable look, or a kiss for his good services, which she would craftily give him to encourage him.

But the other gentleman that made the first addresses to her, being a married man, his wife hearing her husband was so great a lover of that lady, and that that lady's husband was reformed from his incontinent life, and was become a doting fond wittal, loving and admiring her for being courted and made love to, esteeming that most that others seemed to like well of;[1] she began to imitate her; which her husband perceiving, gave her warning not to do so, but she would take no warning, but entertained those that would address themselves; whereupon her husband threatened her: but at last she was so delighted with variety that she regarded not his threats; whereupon he used her cruelly, but nothing would reclaim her, only she would make more secret meetings, wherewith she was better pleased; for secret meetings, as I have heard, give an edge to adultery; for it is the nature of mankind to be most delighted with that which is most unlawful. But her husband finding no reformation could be made, he parted with her, for he thought it a greater dishonour to be a wittal than a cuckold, although he was very much troubled to be either; for though he was willing to make a cuckold, yet he was not willing to be one himself. Thus you may see the different natures of men.

—1656

---

[1] *incontinent* wanting in self-restraint, chiefly with reference to sexual appetites (*OED* incontinent *a* A.1); *wittal* a man who is aware of and complaisant about the infidelity of his wife (*OED* wittol *sb* 1a).

Orations of Diverse Sorts, Accommodated to Diverse Places [2]

An Oration for Liberty of Conscience

Fellow Citizens,

It is very probable, we shall fall into a civil war, through the diverse opinions in one and the same religion; for what hath been the cause of this hash in religion, but the suffering of theological disputations in schools, colleges, churches, and chambers, as also books of controversies? All which ought not to have been suffered, but prohibited, by making laws of restraint; but since that freedom hath been given, the inconveniency cannot be avoided, unless the magistrates will give, or at least not oppose a free liberty to all; for if the people of this nation is so foolish, or wilful, or factious, or irreligious, as not to agree in one opinion, and to unite in one religion, but will be of diverse opinions, if not of diverse religions, the governors must yield, or they will consume the civil government with the fire of their zeal; indeed they will consume themselves at last in their own confusion. Wherefore, the best remedy to prevent their own ruin, with the ruin of the commonwealth, is, to let them have liberty of conscience, conditionally, that they do not meddle with civil governments or governors; and for security that they shall not, there must be a law made and enacted, that, whosoever doth preach, dispute, or talk against the government or governors, not only in this, but of any other nation, shall be punished either with death, banishment, or fine; also for the quiet and peace of this kingdom, there ought to be a strict law, that no governor or magistrate

---

[2] In her address "To the Readers" prefacing *Orations of Diverse Sorts* (London, 1662), Cavendish explains the purpose of her text: "I have endeavoured in this book to express perfect orators, that speak perfect orations, as to cause their auditors to act, or believe, according to the orator's opinion, judgment, design, or desire."

shall in any kind infringe our just rights, our civil or common laws, nor our ancient customs; for if the one law should be made, and not the other, the people would be slaves, and the governors their tyrants.

An Oration against Liberty of Conscience

Fellow Citizens,

I am not of the former orator's opinion; for if you give liberty in the church, you must give liberty in the state, and so let everyone do what they will, which will be a strange government, or rather I may say, no government: for if there be no rules, there can be no laws, and if there be no laws, there can be no justice, and if no justice, no safety, and if no safety, no propriety, neither of goods, wives, children, nor lives, and if there be no propriety, there will be no husbandry, and the lands will lie unmanured, also there will be neither trade nor traffic, all which will cause famine, war, and ruin, and such a confusion, as the kingdom will be like a chaos, which the gods keep us from.

An Oration proposing a Mean betwixt the two former Opinions

Fellow Citizens,

I am not of the two former orators' opinions, neither for an absolute liberty, nor a forced unity, but between both, as neither to give them such liberty, as for several opinions, to gather into several congregations, nor to force them to such ceremonies, as agree not with their consciences; and if those sects or separatists disturb not the canon, common, or civil laws, not to disturb their bodies, minds, or estates: for if they disturb not the public weal, why should you disturb their private devotions? Wherefore, give them leave to follow their several opinions, in their particular families, other-

wise if you force them, you will make them furious, and if you give them an absolute liberty, you will make them factious.

—1662

CCXI Sociable Letters [1]

IX

MADAM,

In your last letter I perceive that the Lady N.P. is an actor in some state-design, or at least would be thought so, for our sex in this age, is ambitious to be state-ladies, that they may be thought to be wise women; but let us do what we can, we shall prove ourselves fools, for wisdom is an enemy to our sex, or rather our sex is an enemy to wisdom. 'Tis true, we are full of designs and plots, and ready to side into factions; but plotting, designing, factions, belong nothing to wisdom, for wisdom never intermeddles therein or therewith, but renounces them; it is only cheating craft and subtlety that are the managers thereof: and for deceiving craft, women are well practised therein, and most of them may be accounted politicians; for no question but women may, can, and oftentimes do make wars, especially civil wars; witness our late civil war, wherein women were great, although not good actors; for though women cannot fight with warring arms themselves, yet they can easily inflame men's minds against the governors and governments, unto

---

[1] Cavendish delineates the purpose of *CCXI Sociable Letters* (1664) in the Preface: "But, noble readers, I do not intend to present you here with long compliments in short letters, but with short descriptions in long letters; the truth is, they are rather scenes than letters, for I have endeavoured under the cover of letters to express the humors of mankind, and the actions of man's life by the correspondence of two ladies, living at some short distance from each other, which make it not only their chief delight and pastime, but their tie in friendship, to discourse by letters, as they would do if they were personally together, so that these letters are an imitation of a personal visitation and conversation, which I think is better (I am sure more profitable) than those conversations that are an imitation of romantical letters, which are but empty words, and vain compliments."

which men are too apt even without the persuasion of women, as to make innovation through envy and emulation, in hopes of advancement in title, fortune, and power, of which women are as ambitious as men; but I wish for the honour of our sex, that women could as easily make peace as war, though it is easier to do evil than good, for every fool can make an uproar, and a tumultuous disorder, such as the wisest can hardly settle into order again. But women in state-affairs can do as they do with themselves, they can, and do often make themselves sick, but when they are sick, not well again: so they can disorder a state, as they do their bodies, but neither can give peace to th'one, nor health to th'other; but their restless minds, and unsatiable appetites, do many times bring ruin to the one, and death to the other; for temperance and quietness are strangers to our sex. But leaving the Lady N.P. to her petty designs, and weak plots, I rest,

Madam,

Your very faithful Fr. and S.

XVII

MADAM,

The pure lady, or Lady Puritan, is so godly, as to follow all those ministers she thinks are called and chosen by the Holy Spirit, to preach the Word of God, whereas those ministers preach more their own words, than God's, for they interpret the Scripture to their own sense, or rather to their factious humours and designs, and after their sermons, their female flocks gossip Scripture, visiting each other to confer notes, and make repetitions of the sermons, as also to explain and expound them; for first the minister expounds the Scripture, and then the women-hearers expound the sermon; so that there are expoundings upon expoundings, and preaching upon preaching, insomuch as they make such a medley or hash of the Scripture, as certainly the right and truth is so hidden and obscured, that none can find it; and surely the Holy Spirit, whom they talk so much of, knows not what they mean or preach, being so much and such nonsense in their sermons, as God himself cannot turn to sense; but howsoever, it works on some to a good effect and causes as much devotion amongst many, as if they preached learnedly, eloquently, and interpreted rightly, and to the true sense and meaning; for many sorrowful and penitent tears are shed, but whether they be bottled up in heaven, I know not:[1] certainly Mary Magdalene could not weep faster for the time, or fetch deeper sighs, or stronger groans for her sins, than they do, which shows that they have been grievous sinners; but whether their sins were of the same kind as hers were, I cannot tell, and I think they would not confess, for confession they account popish. But truly, and verily, the Lady Puritan who hath been to visit me this afternoon, hath so tired me with her preaching discourse, as I think I shall not recover my weary spirits and deafened ears, this two days, unless a quiet sleep cure me; nay, she hath so filled my head with words, as I doubt it will hinder my silent repose; howsoever I'll try: and so taking my leave as going to bed, I rest,

Madam,

Your faithful Fr. and S.

XXVI

MADAM,

We have no news here, unless to hear that the Lady C.R. did beat her husband, and because she would have witness enough, she beat him in a public assembly, nay, being a woman of none of the least sizes, but one of the largest, and having anger added to her strength, she did beat him soundly, and it is said, that he did not resist her, but endured

---

[1] *bottled up in heaven* "Thou tellest my wanderings: put thou my tears into thy bottle: are they not in thy book?" (Psalm 56:8).

patiently; whether he did it out of fear to show his own weakness, being not able to encounter her, or out of a noble nature, not to strike a woman, I know not; yet I believe the best: and surely, if he doth not, or cannot tame her spirits, or bind her hands, or for love will not leave her, if she beat him often, he will have but a sore life. Indeed I was sorry when I heard of it, not only for the sake of our sex, but because she and he are persons of dignity, it belonging rather to mean-born and bred women to do such unnatural actions, for certainly, for a wife to strike her husband, is as much, if not more, as for a child to strike his father; besides, it is a breach of matrimonial government, not to obey all their husbands' commands; but those women that strike or cuckold their husbands, are matrimonial traitors, for which they ought to be highly punished; as for blows, they ought to be banished from their husband's bed, house, family, and for adultery, they ought to suffer death, and their executioner ought to be their husband. 'Tis true, passion will cause great indiscretion, and women are subject to violent passions, which makes or causes them so often to err in words and actions, which, when their passion is over, they are sorry for; but unruly passions are only a cause of uncivil words and rude actions, whereas adultery is caused by unruly appetites; wherefore women should be instructed and taught more industriously, carefully, and prudently, to temper their passions, and govern their appetites, than men, because there comes more dishonour from their unruly passions and appetites, than from men's; but for the most part women are not educated as they should be, I mean those of quality, for their education is only to dance, sing, and fiddle, to write complimental letters, to read romances, to speak some language that is not their native, which education, is an education of the body, and not of the mind, and shows that their parents take more care of their feet than their head, more of their words than their reason, more of their music than

their virtue, more of their beauty than their honesty,[1] which methinks is strange, as that their friends and parents should take more care, and be at greater charge to adorn their bodies, than to endue their minds, to teach their bodies arts, and not to instruct their minds with understanding; for this education is more for outward show, than inward worth, it makes the body a courtier, and the mind a clown, and oftentimes it makes their body a bawd, and their mind a courtesan, for though the body procures lovers, yet it is the mind that is the adulteress, for if the mind were honest and pure, they would never be guilty of that crime; wherefore those women are best bred, whose minds are civilest, as being well taught and governed, for the mind will be wild and barbarous, unless it be enclosed with study, instructed by learning, and governed by knowledge and understanding, for then the inhabitants of the mind will live peaceably, happily, honestly and honourably, by which they will rule and govern their associate appetites with ease and regularity, and their words, as their household servants, will be employed profitably. But leaving the Lady C.R. and her husband to passion and patience, I rest,

Madam,

Your faithful Friend and Servant.

LV

MADAM,

You were pleased in your last letter to tell me, that you had been in the country, and that you did almost envy the peasants for living so merrily; it is a sign, Madam, they live happily, for mirth seldom dwells with troubles and discontents, neither doth riches nor grandeur live so easily, as that unconcerned freedom that is in low and mean fortunes and persons, for the ceremony of grandeur

---

[1] *honesty* chastity.

530

is constrained and bound with forms and rules, and a great estate and high fortune is not so easily managed as a less, a little is easily ordered, where much doth require time, care, wisdom and study as considerations; but poor, mean peasants that live by their labour, are for the most part happier and pleasanter than great rich persons, that live in luxury and idleness, for idle time is tedious, and luxury is unwholesome, whereas labour is healthful and recreative, and surely country housewives take more pleasure in milking their cows, making their butter and cheese, and feeding their poultry, than great ladies do in painting, curling, and adorning themselves, also they have more quiet and peaceable minds and thoughts, for they never, or seldom, look in a glass to view their faces, they regard not their complexions, nor observe their decays, they defy time's ruins of their beauties, they are not peevish and froward if they look not as well one day as another, a pimple or spot in their skin tortures not their minds, they fear not the sun's heat, but out-face the sun's power, they break not their sleeps to think of fashions, but work hard to sleep soundly, they lie not in sweats to clear their complexions, but rise to sweat to get them food, their appetites are not queasy with surfeits,[1] but sharpened with fasting, they relish with more savour their ordinary coarse fare, than those who are pampered do their delicious rarities; and for their mirth and pastimes, they take more delight and true pleasure, and are more inwardly pleased and outwardly merry at their wakes, than the great ladies at their balls, and though they dance not with such art and measure, yet they dance with more pleasure and delight, they cast not envious, spiteful eyes at each other, but meet friendly and lovingly. But great ladies at public meetings take not such true pleasures, for their envy at each other's beauty and bravery disturbs their pastimes, and obstructs their mirth, they

rather grow peevish and froward through envy, than loving and kind through society, so that whereas the country peasants meet with such kind hearts and unconcerned freedom as they unite in friendly jollity, and depart with neighbourly love, the greater sort of persons meet with constrained ceremony, converse with formality, and for the most part depart with enmity; and this is not only amongst women, but amongst men, for there is amongst the better sort a greater strife for bravery than for courtesy, for place than friendship, and in their societies there is more vainglory than pleasure, more pride than mirth, and more vanity than true content; yet in one thing the better sort of men, as the nobles and gentry, are to be commended, which is, that though they are oftener drunken and more debauched than peasants, having more means to maintain their debaucheries, yet at such times as at great assemblies, they keep themselves more sober and temperate than peasants do, which are for the most part drunk at their departing;[2] but to judge between the peasantry and nobles for happiness, I believe where there's one noble that is truly happy, there are a hundred peasants; not that there be more peasants than nobles, but that they are more happy, number for number, as having not the envy, ambition, pride, vainglory, to cross, trouble, [and] vex them, as nobles have; when I say nobles, I mean those that have been ennobled by time as well as title, as the gentry. But, Madam, I am not a fit judge for the several sorts or degrees, or courses of lives, or actions of mankind, as to judge which is happiest, for happiness lives not in outward show or concourse, but inwardly in the mind, and the minds of men are too obscure to be known, and too various and inconstant to fix a belief in them, and since we cannot know ourselves, how should we know others? Besides, pleasure and true delight lives

---

[1] *surfeits* excesses (*OED* surfeit *sb* 1).

[2] *debauched* seduced from duty or virtue; depraved in morals; given up to sensual pleasures or loose living (*OED* debauched *ppl.a*).

in everyone's own delectation;[1] but let me tell you, my delectation is, to prove my self,

Madam,

Your Faithful Fr. and S.
I, M.N.

CXXIII

MADAM,

I wonder how that person you mention in your letter, could either have the conscience, or confidence to dispraise Shakespeare's plays, as to say they were made up only with clowns, fools, watchmen, and the like; but to answer that person, though Shakespeare's wit will answer for himself, I say, that it seems by his judging, or censuring, he understands not plays, or wit; for to express properly, rightly, usually, and naturally, a clown's, or fool's humour, expressions, phrases, garbs, manners, actions, words, and course of life, is as witty, wise, judicious, ingenious, and observing, as to write and express the expressions, phrases, garbs, manners, actions, words, and course of life, of kings and princes; and to express naturally, to the life, a mean country wench, as a great lady, a courtesan, as a chaste woman, a mad man, as a man in his right reason and senses, a drunkard, as a sober man, a knave, as an honest man, and so a clown, as a well-bred man, and a fool, as a wise man; nay, it expresses and declares a greater wit, to express, and deliver to posterity, the extravagancies of madness, the subtlety of knaves, the ignorance of clowns, and the simplicity of naturals, or the craft of feigned fools, than to express regularities, plain honesty, courtly garbs, or sensible discourses, for 'tis harder to express nonsense than sense, and ordinary conversations, than that which is unusual; and 'tis harder, and requires more wit to express a jester, than a grave statesman; yet Shakespeare did not

want wit, to express to the life all sorts of persons, of what quality, profession, degree, breeding, or birth soever; nor did he want wit to express the diverse, and different humours, or natures, or several passions in mankind; and so well he hath expressed in his plays all sorts of persons, as one would think he had been transformed into every one of those persons he hath described; and as sometimes one would think he was really himself the clown or jester he feigns, so one would think, he was also the king, and privy counsellor; also as one would think he were really the coward he feigns, so one would think he were the most valiant, and experienced soldier; who would not think he had been such a man as his Sir John Falstaff? and who would not think he had been Harry the Fifth? and certainly Julius Cæsar, Augustus Cæsar, and Antonius, did never really act their parts better, if so well, as he hath described them, and I believe that Antonius and Brutus did not speak better to the people, than he hath feigned them; nay, one would think that he had been metamorphosed from a man to a woman, for who could describe Cleopatra better than he hath done, and many other females of his own creating, as Nan Page, Mrs. Page, Mrs. Ford, the doctor's maid, Beatrice, Mrs. Quickly, Doll Tearsheet, and others, too many to relate?[2] and in his tragic vein, he presents passions so naturally, and misfortunes so probably, as he pierces the souls of his readers with such a true sense and feeling thereof, that it forces tears through their eyes, and almost persuades them, they are really actors, or at least present at those tragedies. Who would not swear he had been a noble lover, that could woo so well? and there is not any person he hath described

---

[1] *delectation* the action of delighting (*OED* delectation).

[2] ll. 34–43 Cavendish refers to characters in *Henry IV* (Falstaff, Henry V, Mistress Quickly, Doll Tearsheet), *Henry V* (Falstaff, Henry V, Hostess Quickly), *Anthony and Cleopatra* (Cleopatra), *Much Ado About Nothing* (Beatrice), *Julius Cæsar* (Julius Cæsar, Octavius Cæsar, Marcus Antonius, Marcus Brutus), *The Merry Wives of Windsor* (Mistress Ford, Mistress Page, Anne Page, Mistress Quickly-servant to Doctor Caius).

in his book, but his readers might think they were well acquainted with them; indeed Shakespeare had a clear judgment, a quick wit, a spreading fancy, a subtle observation, a deep apprehension, and a most eloquent elocution; truly, he was a natural orator, as well as a natural poet, and he was not an orator to speak well only on some subjects, as lawyers, who can make eloquent orations at the bar, and plead subtly and wittily in law-cases, or divines, that can preach eloquent sermons, or dispute subtly and wittily in theology, but take them from that, and put them to other subjects, and they will be to seek; but Shakespeare's wit and eloquence was general, for, and upon all subjects, he rather wanted subjects for his wit and eloquence to work on, for which he was forced to take some of his plots out of history, where he only took the bare designs, the wit and language being all his own; and so much he had above others, that those, who writ after him, were forced to borrow of him, or rather to steal from him; I could mention diverse places, that others of our famous poets have borrowed, or stolen, but lest I should discover the persons, I will not mention the places, or parts, but leave it to those that read his plays, and others, to find them out. I should not have needed to write this to you, for his works would have declared the same truth: but I believe, those that dispraised his plays, dispraised them more out of envy, than simplicity or ignorance, for those that could read his plays, could not be so foolish to condemn them, only the excellency of them caused an envy to them. By this we may perceive, envy doth not leave a man in the grave, it follows him after death, unless a man be buried in oblivion, but if he leave any thing to be remembered, envy and malice will be still throwing aspersion upon it, or striving to pull it down by detraction. But leaving Shakespeare's works to their own

defence, and his detractors to their envy, and you to your better employments, than reading my letter, I rest,

Madam,

Your faithful Friend
and humble Servant

—1664

Philosophical Letters: or, Modest Reflections [1]

XXXVI (sect. 1)

MADAM,

That all other animals, besides man, want reason, your author endeavours to prove in his *Discourse of Method*,[2] where his chief argument is, that other animals cannot express their mind, thoughts or conceptions, either by speech or any other signs, as man can do: For, says he, "it is not for want of the organs belonging to the framing of words, as we may observe in parrots and pies,[3] which are apt enough to express words they are taught, but understand nothing of them." My answer is, that one man expressing his mind by speech or words to another, doth not declare by it his excellency and supremacy above all other creatures, but for the most part more folly, for a talking man is not so wise as a contemplating man. But by reason other creatures cannot speak or discourse with each other as men, or make certain signs, whereby to express

---

[1] In the Preface to *Philosophical Letters* (1664), Cavendish describes the nature of her work, "I took the liberty to declare my own opinions as other philosophers do, and to that purpose I have here set down several famous and learned authors' opinions, and my answers to them in the form of letters, which was the easiest way for me to write." In particular, Cavendish formulates her theory of natural philosophy by addressing and judging the validity of the works by Descartes, Hobbes, More and Van Helmont.

[2] *Discourse of Method* published in 1637. In particular, Cavendish addresses Descartes's account of the irrational animal in Discourse 5.

[3] *pies* magpies.

themselves as dumb and deaf men do, should we conclude they have neither knowledge, sense, reason, or intelligence? Certainly, this is a very weak argument; for one part of a man's body, as one hand, is not less sensible than the other, nor the heel less sensible than the heart, nor the leg less sensible than the head, but each part hath its sense and reason, and so consequently its sensitive and rational knowledge; and although they cannot talk or give intelligence to each other by speech, nevertheless each hath its own peculiar and particular knowledge, just as each particular man has his own particular knowledge, for one man's knowledge is not another man's knowledge; and if there be such a peculiar and particular knowledge in every several part of one animal creature, as man, well may there be such in creatures of different kinds and sorts: But this particular knowledge belonging to each creature, doth not prove that there is no intelligence at all betwixt them, no more than the want of human knowledge doth prove the want of reason; for reason is the rational part of matter, and makes perception, observation, and intelligence different in every creature, and every sort of creatures, according to their proper natures, but perception, observation and intelligence do not make reason, reason being the cause, and they the effects. Wherefore though other creatures have not the speech, nor mathematical rules and demonstrations, with other arts and sciences, as men; yet may their perceptions and observations be as wise as men's, and they may have as much intelligence and commerce betwixt each other, after their own manner and way, as men have after theirs: To which I leave them, and man to his conceited prerogative and excellence, resting,

Madam,

Your faithful Friend,
and Servant.

—1664

Mary Howgill
1623 – before 1681

Mary Howgill, a prophetic writer, is best known for her public defense of the non-conformist Society of Friends, commonly referred to as the Quakers. It is presumed that Howgill was the sister of the eminent Quaker preacher Francis Howgill of Grayrigg, Westmorland, as he was known to have a sister who engaged in "publishing truth." Both Mary and Francis Howgill addressed letters to Oliver Cromwell, amongst others, complaining of persecutions, and both suffered imprisonment as a result. It is believed she converted to Quakerism shortly after her brother's conversion in 1652, as she was imprisoned in Kendal in 1653 for her public assertion of Quaker doctrine, later enduring imprisonment in Exeter during 1656. Recent research has raised some questions about the identity of Howgill, as there were two Mary Howgills who prophesied. Contemporary records document that the Mary Howgill indicted at Lancaster Assizes in March 1654/5 for abusing Thomas Shaw, Rector of Aldingham, was of Overkellet, Lancashire, not Grayrigg, Westmorland. Only two pamphlets written by Howgill were published. Written within the context of religious persecution, *A Remarkable Letter* challenged political and religious authorities which responded to freedom of religious conscience with the confiscation of property, imprisonment and physical violence.

❧❦❧

A Remarkable Letter of Mary Howgill to Oliver Cromwell, Called Protector

TO THEE
OLIVER CROMWELL

When thou wast a soldier for the Lord, thou wast low, and little in thine own eyes; then thou remembredst the Lord, and stood in his fear, and he was thy strength; but now thou art in thy own strength, and hast forgot that time: I say, thou hast denied the Lord God, and thy own law with the pride of thy own heart; and the pride of thy heart is now acting all manner of cruelty against them who are in the fear of the Lord.

When thou wast low, the Lord was thy strength, but now thou hast departed from him, and thy strength is in man; thou hast trusted in the arm of flesh and not in God;[1] thou hast chosen the glory of this world, and art as a stinking dunghill in the sight of God; thou hast shut thyself out of the kingdom, and them who are in the kingdom, all manner of evil is done and acted to them in thy name; and so thou hast strengthened all the wicked, and instead of serving the Lord, thou has served thy own glory, and thy own pleasures, and thou art going on in all thy power; but verily him whom thou once served, which thou now art turned from, he will overtake thee, for thou hast almost filled up thy measure;[2] many fair things hast thou promised to them whom the Lord is their strength, but they see thee and all thy subtlety: For verily, hast not thou suffered in thy name (whose name is Oliver Lord Protector) many bloody actions to be done in thy name? And he that protects thee now is unrighteous Mammon, and so him that is our Protector will rule thee, to him must thou bow, for verily the

---

[1] *arm of flesh* "With him is an arm of flesh; but with us is the Lord our God to help us, and to fight our battles" (II Chronicles 32:8).

[2] *filled up thy measure* Jesus said to the scribes and Pharisees: "Wherefore ye be witnesses unto yourselves, that ye are the children of them which killed the prophets. Fill ye up then the measure of your Fathers. Ye serpents, ye generation of vipers, how can you escape the damnation of hell" (Matthew 23:32–33).

law of God shall overturn thee:[1] And when thou hast filled up thy measure in thy cruel bloody actions, who hast suffered the innocent to be persecuted, yea unto death, and some hath suffered stoning and sore bruising.

Therefore in the name of the Lord God, whom we serve, and whom once thou trusted in, verily, I say unto thee, thy condition above all men is most lamentable; for them who are born again,[2] and witness a new birth in him, whom we receive tribute from; we are all soldiers against all sin and deceit, and have overcome death, hell, and the grave; and being of them who partake of the resurrection of Christ, the second death hath no power over. And so in the power of God we all stand to follow the Lamb wherever he goes, and so we follow the Lord in the new generation.[3] But I say unto thee, thou hast forgot thy promise, and what the Lord did for thee when he gave thee victory over unreasonable men.

Woe is me for thee, that ever thou shouldest depart from that of God that was once in thee, and hast trusted in the arm of flesh, and so thou art one with them whom once thou foughtest against! For there is that in thy conscience will let thee see thou art one with a proud man, one with a drunken man, one with a covetous man, and one with all them that are in the evil, the light in thy conscience will let thee see all these things; for verily, that in thee which should have brought forth fruit unto God, hath brought forth nothing but wild grapes, bram-

bles, briers, and thorns;[4] and thy crown which thou hast now is nothing but thorns.[5]

Oh! thou hadst better had the angels to have guarded thee, and the Lord to have protected thee, than to have trusted in the arm of flesh.

For verily his Son is brought forth in them who have believed in his name, and all the angels shall worship him: But thou hast crucified the Son of God, and hast chosen thy own way, and thy own strength, and thou art one with all them who are set against Christ; for verily I say unto thee, he will overtake thee when thou hast filled up thy measure; for he who is Lord of heaven and earth, is ready to deliver thee into the hands of thy enemies within and without; for I say unto thee, thy way is now darkness, and thou hast turned thy back on him who is all our strength and light, in whose strength, I tell thee, thou hast even owned him who is the god of this world, and the glory of the world is thy portion and delight, and that which is of another world is crucified by thee.[6]

Oh! my heart is sad for thee, that ever thou shouldest be found where thou art; many true messengers the Lord hath sent to thee for the good of thy soul; but thou wouldest not lend thy ears to them, and so thou must have no peace with them; for them who would have loved thy soul, thou wouldst not hear, and the soul is more worth than the glory of this world. But verily thou must have thy portion amongst them who are in their own glory; for we who know the Lord, and have found him whom our souls loved, our glory is not of this world, nor in our own glory, nor in our own strength, but in the Lord our God, who is our glory, and hath crowned us with his everlasting glory, and we stand in his glory, and in his power,

---

[1] *Mammon* the Aramaic word for "riches," occurring in the Greek text of Matthew 6:24 and Luke 16:9–13, and retained in the Vulgate. From the sixteenth century onwards it has been current in English usage as a term for opprobrium of wealth regarded as an idol or as an evil influence (*OED*).

[2] *born again* spiritual birth as distinct from physical birth: "Being born again, not of corruptible seed, but of incorruptible, by the word of God, which liveth and abideth for ever" (I Peter 1:23). See also John 3:5–8.

[3] *we all stand to follow the Lamb* those redeemed from among men (Revelation 14:4).

[4] *hath brought forth…briers, and thorns* an allusion to the parable of the sower (Matthew 13:3–23; Mark 4:3–13).

[5] *and thy Crown* emended from "and Crown thy."

[6] *thy way is now of darkness* "The way of the wicked is as darkness: they know not at what they stumble" (Proverbs 4:19).

and so we stand in the righteousness of God, who hath brought us into the innocency, and in that we know our being and our habitation with the Lord, and with him to reign for evermore; for *them who suffer with him shall reign with him.*[1] But thou, where thou standest, thy reign shall be but for a time, for misery and great condemnation shall be thy portion, and all them who have forgotten the Lord our God; for we have the Lord to be our strength, and thou who acts against him, the time is come that we are justified, and with him that justifies us shalt thou be condemned, and thou shalt know that thou hadst better that thy tongue had been cloven to the roof of thy mouth, ere these things had been acted in thy name (we are kept in perfect peace).[2] And them who have suffered to death in prison, their blood, yea the blood of the innocent shall be required of thee, whom the Lord set in the place, but thou hast departed from that place; and so thou dost not, nor canst not bear rule for God, but against him; but he is coming upon thee, whom thou hast acted against, which thou shalt know, and all thy gallant glory will he bring down; for no flesh shall glory in his presence, for dreadful will he be to thy glory, even him whom thou hast crucified, the Lamb slain from the foundation of the world:[3] I say unto thee in the name of the Lord, whom we all know, and for whom we are a witness against thee, this shall witness for us; for thou must have condemnation with the light which thou hast turned from, which witness is in thy conscience, which thou once wast in, and heard speak, and breathed after the Lord, and many dear servants of God have warned thee of thy earthly glory; the Lord did send me once before now to thee, for the good of thy soul, and I could have done anything once for thee, for the seed's sake, that thou mightst have known the way of truth; but thou hast counted us all of small worth.

Woe is me for thee, that thou canst not see him whom thou hast pierced, nor canst lay it to heart what thou hast done.

Hold thee once before, that thou hadst crucified the Lamb of God, and trodden the blood of the new covenant under thy feet, and counted it a vain thing:[4] Thou askedst me once what it was; and I told thee the blood of Christ cleansed from all sin, and his water washed, and his Spirit made alive;[5] but thou couldest not receive these things, for all the cry that thou couldest hear which was in thee; for verily I say, thou couldest not hear, but hast hardened thy heart; for the righteous hath cried to thee for righteousness's sake but it could not be heard, neither in thyself, nor in others; and all that ever thou didst do for God is now in vain, for thou hast now chosen thy own way, and so the cry could never be heard, how the righteous hath cried for righteousness's sake, that they might have had justice in the land, that many a one might have worshipped God without any disturbance.

Thou hast suffered thy soldiers, which are in the abomination with thyself, to disturb peaceable meetings, and to hale men to prison: Thou hast many colours for thy deceit, but thou hast none for

---

[1] *for them who suffer...reign with him* "If we suffer, we shall also reign with him: if we deny him, he also will deny us" (II Timothy 2:12).

[2] *we are kept in perfect peace* "Thou wilt keep him in perfect peace, whose mind is stayed on thee: because he trusteth in thee" (Isaiah 26:3).

[3] *the Lamb slain from...the world* "And all that dwell upon the earth shall worship him, whose names are not written in the book of life of the Lamb slain from the foundation of the world" (Revelation 13:8).

[4] *new covenant* The "old covenant," the contractual agreement between God and the Israelites established through the Mosaic covenant at Sinai, is one of obligations, subject to sanctions of blessings and curses. The "new covenant" promises peace for both Jew and Gentile through the sacrifice of Christ, the high priest (mediator) in covenant renewal. Paul describes the "old covenant" as the letter of the law which "killeth" and the new covenant as the "spirit" which gives "life" (II Corinthians 3).

[5] *the blood of Christ...made alive* "But if we walk in the light, as he is in the light, we have fellowship one with another, and the blood of Jesus Christ his Son cleanseth us from all sin" (I John 1:7).

these men which were met peaceably together;[1] for violently they came amongst them with their horses, and acted violently, by treading amongst simple and harmless people.

Oh! what shameless things are done in thy name, and by thy authority! yea verily the righteous spirit of God is grieved with thee: And all these things shalt thou know; for all the cunning and subtleties of thy heart is seen and known by them who are come into the everlasting spirit: And when thou givest account for all those actions which have been acted by thee and in thy name and by thy power, oh what a day will it be with thee![2] For as my soul lives, these things shall be laid all to thy charge: And for us, whom the Lord hath redeemed from the vain-glory of the world, and hath graffed

us into himself, he will plead our cause, yea the righteous cause of himself, and he will make thee an example to all great ones in the world;[3] and when that day comes upon thee, thou shalt me remember, that thou wast warned of all thy evil

By a lover of thy soul, whose
name in the flesh is

MARY HOWGILL

This in one of its first copies was delivered to Oliver Cromwell's own hands by the author herself, at or about the eighth day of the fourth month 1656 about ten o'clock at night, with whom thereupon she had much discourse.

—1656

---

[1] *colours* fair pretenses to conceal or to cloak the truth (*OED* colour *sb*[1] III.11a,12a).

[2] *givest account* "So then every one of us shall give account of himself to God" (Romans 14:12).

---

[3] *graffed* grafted.

Lady Anne Halkett
1623 – 1699

The autobiographer Lady Anne Halkett was born in London. Her parents were Thomas Murray, Provost of Eton College and former tutor of Charles I, and Jane Drummond, later governess of the Duke of Gloucester and the Princess Elizabeth. Her father died three months after her birth. Her mother employed tutors to teach her to write, speak French, play the lute and virginals, and dance. Halkett also studied medical science, which later proved useful when she tended soldiers wounded in the Battle of Dunbar. In 1644, she fell in love with Thomas Howard, the eldest son of Edward, first Lord Howard of Escrick, but her mother opposed the match because of Howard's small fortune. Halkett's autobiographical narrative of thwarted love and unexpected treachery in this and other liaisons has been compared to Richardson's *Clarissa* and Austen's *Pride and Prejudice*. Soon after her disappointment with Howard, Halkett helped Colonel Joseph Bampfield to effect the escape of James Stuart, the Duke of York, in April, 1648. Shortly afterwards, Bampfield,

posing as a widower, successfully proposed marriage to Halkett. The relationship continued for several years before Bampfield's wife was proven to be alive. In 1656, Anne married Sir James Halkett, a widower with two sons and two daughters, and took up residence at his estate at Pitfirrane in Scotland. She bore four children, three of whom died in infancy, before her husband's death in 1670. Between 1677 and 1678, Halkett wrote her memoirs, a vivid and candid account of historical events, political intrigue and personal relationships. After 1683, Halkett supplemented her income by caring for and tutoring children. On his accession in 1685, James II granted her a pension of £100 a year for her service to him when he was Duke of York. Halkett died leaving more than twenty manuscript volumes of devotional prose, dating from 1649 onward. Though selections from several of her religious writings were published shortly after her death, her memoirs remained unpublished until 1875.

❧❧❧

The Memoirs of Anne, Lady Halkett

In the year 1644 I confess I was guilty of an act of disobedience, for I gave way to the address of a person whom my mother, at the first time that ever he had occasion to be conversant with me, had absolutely discharged me ever to allow of:[1] and though before ever I saw him several did tell me that there would be something more than ordinary betwixt him and me (which I believe they fudged from the great friendship betwixt his sister and me, for we were seldom asunder at London, and she and

I were bedfellows when she came to my sister's house at Charleton, where for the most part she stayed while we continued in the country), yet he was half a year in my company before I discovered anything of a particular inclination for me more than another, and as I was civil to him both for his own merit and his sister's sake, so any particular civility I received from him I looked upon it as flowing from the affection he had to his sister and her kindness to me.[2]

After that time it seems he was not so much master of himself as to conceal it any longer. And

---

[1] *address* courtship (*OED* address *sb* II.9); *person* Thomas Howard (1625–1678), son of Edward, first Lord Howard of Escrick.

[2] *fudged* to fudge is to fit in with what is anticipated (*OED* fudge *v* 2); *his sister* Anne Howard, daughter of Lord Howard of Escrick; *my sister's house at Charleton* Elizabeth Murray was married to Sir Henry Newton, who had an estate at Charlton in Kent.

having never any opportunity of being alone with me to speak himself, he employed a young gentleman (whose confidante he was in an amour betwixt him and my Lady Anne, his cousin-german) to tell me how much he had endeavoured all this time to smother his passion which he said began the first time that ever he saw me, and now was come to that height that if I did not give him some hopes of favour he was resolved to go back again into France (from whence he had come when I first saw him) and turn Capuchin.[1]

Though this discourse disturbed me, yet I was a week or ten days before I would be persuaded so much as to hear him speak of this subject, and desired his friend to represent several disadvantages that it would be to him to pursue such a design. And knowing that his father had sent for him out of France with an intention to marry him to some rich match that might improve his fortune, it would be high ingratitude in me to do anything to hinder such a design, since his father had been so obliging to my mother and sister as to use his Lordship's interest with the Parliament to prevent the ruin of my brother's house and k[in].[2] But when all I could say to him by his friend could not prevail, but that he grew so ill and discontented that all the house took notice, I did yield so far to comply with his desire as to give him liberty one day when I was walking in the gallery to come there and speak to me. What he said was handsome and short, but much disordered, for he looked pale as death, and his hand trembled when he took mine to lead me, and with a great sigh said, "If I loved you less I could say more."

I told him I could not but think myself much obliged to him for his good opinion of me, but it would be a higher obligation to confirm his esteem of me by following my advice, which I should now give him myself, since he would not receive it by his friend. I used many arguments to dissuade him from pursuing what he proposed, and in conclusion told him I was 2 or 3 year[s] older than he, and were there no other objection, yet that was of such weight with me as would never let me allow his further address.

"Madam," said he, "what I love in you may well increase, but I am sure it can never decay."

I left arguing and told him I would advise him to consult with his own reason and that would let him see I had more respect to him in denying than in granting what with so much passion he desired.

After that, he sought, and I shunned, all opportunities of private discourse with him; but one day in the garden his friend took his sister by the hand and led her into another walk and left him and I together. And he with very much seriousness began to tell me that he had observed ever since he had discovered his affection to me that I was more reserved and avoided all converse with him, and therefore, since he had no hopes of my favour, he was resolved to leave England, since he could not be happy in it. And that whatever became of him that might make him displease either his father or his friends, I was the occasion of it, for if I would not give him hopes of marrying him, he was resolved to put himself out of a capacity of marrying any other and go immediately into a convent, and that he had taken order to have post horses ready against the next day.[3]

I confess this discourse disturbed me, for though I had had no respect for him, his sister, or his family, yet religion was a tie upon me to endeavour

---

[1] *Lady Anne* Lady Ann Howard, daughter of the second Earl of Suffolk; *cousin-german* first cousin; *Capuchin* a friar of the order of St. Francis, of the new rule of 1528.

[2] *since his father…and k[in]* Edward Howard, first Lord Escrick, had interceded with Parliamentarians to reduce the fines levied on Sir Henry Newton, who had fought in King Charles's army.

[3] *convent* an institution which houses a body of monks or friars (*OED* convent *sb* 4).

the prevention of the hazard of his soul.[1] I looked on this as a violent passion which would not last long and perhaps might grow the more by being resisted, when as a seeming complaisance might lesson it. I told him I was sorry to have him entertain such thoughts as could not but be a ruin to him and a great affliction to all his relations, which I would willingly prevent if it were in my power.

He said it was absolutely in my power, for if I would promise to marry him he should esteem himself the most happy man living, and he would wait whatever time I thought most convenient for it. I replied I thought it was unreasonable to urge me to promise that which ere long he might repent the asking, but this I would promise to satisfy him, that I would not marry till I saw him first married. He kissed my hand upon that with as much joy as if I had confirmed to him his greatest happiness and said he could desire no more, for he was secure I should never see nor hear of that till it was to myself. Upon this we parted, both well pleased, for he thought he had gained much in what I promised, and I looked upon my promise as a cure to him, but no inconvenience to myself, since I had no inclination to marry any. And though I had, a delay in it was the least return I could make to so deserving a person.

But I deceived myself by thinking this was the way to moderate his passion, for now he gave way to it without any restraint and thought himself so secure of me as if there had been nothing to oppose it, though he managed it with that discretion that it was scarce visible to any within the house; not so much as either his sister or mine had the least suspicion of it, for I had enjoined him not to let them or any other know what his designs were because I would not have them accessory, whatever fault might be in the prosecution of it.

Thus it continued till towards winter that his sister was to go home to her father again, and then, knowing he would want much of the opportunity he had to converse with me, he was then very importunate to have me consent to marry him privately, which it seems he pleased himself so with the hopes of prevailing with me that he had provided a wedding ring and a minister to marry us.[2] I was much unsatisfied with his going that length, and in short, told him he need never expect I would marry him without his father's and my mother's consent.[3] If that could be obtained, I should willingly give him the satisfaction he desired, but without that I could not expect God's blessing neither upon him nor me, and I would do nothing that was so certain a way to bring ruin upon us both. He used many arguments from the examples of others who had practised the same and were happy both in their parents' favour and in one another, but finding me fixed beyond any persuasion, he resolved to acquaint my sister with it and to employ her to speak of it to his father and my mother.

She very unwillingly undertook it, because she knew it would be a surprise to them and very unwelcome. But his importunity prevailed, and she first acquainted my mother with it, who was so passionately offended with the proposal that, whereas his father might have been brought to have given his consent (having ever had a good opinion of me and very civil), she did so exasperate him against it that nothing could satisfy her, but presently to put it to Mr. H.'s choice either presently to marry a rich citizen's daughter that his father had designed for him, or else to leave England. The reason I believe that made my mother the more incensed was, first, that it was what in the begin-

---

[2] *want*   lack (*OED* want *v* 2).

[3] *going that length*   going to such an extent or extremity (*OED* length *sb* I.5b).

---

[1] *though*   even if (*OED* though *conj* B.II.2a).

ning of our acquaintance she had absolutely discharged my having a thought of allowing such an address; and though in some respect his quality was above mine and therefore better than any she could expect for me, yet my Lord H.'s fortune was such as had need of a more considerable portion than my mother could give me, or else it must ruin his younger children.[1] And therefore my mother would not consent to it, though my Lord H. did offer to do the utmost his condition would allow him if she would let me take my hazard with his son. But my mother would not be persuaded to it upon no consideration, lest any should have thought it was began with her allowance; and to take away the suspicion of that, did, I believe, make her the more violent in opposing it and the more severe to me.

My sister made choice of Sunday to speak of it; first, because she thought that day might put them both in a calmer frame to hear her, and confine their passion, since it would be the next day before they would determine anything. But finding both by my mother and my Lord H. that they intended nothing but to part us so as never to meet again, except it was as strangers, Mr. H. was very importunate to have an opportunity to speak with me that night, which I gave. My sister being only with me, we came down together to the room appointed to meet with him. I confess I never saw those two passions of love and regret more truly represented, nor could any person express greater affection and resolution of constancy, which with many solemn oaths he sealed of never loving or marrying any but myself. I was not satisfied with his swearing to future performances, since I said both he and I might find it most convenient to retract, but this I did assure him, as long as he was constant he should

never find a change in me, for though duty did oblige me not to marry any without my mother's consent, yet it would not tie me to marry without my own.

My sister at this rises and said, "I did not think you would have engaged me to be a witness of both your resolutions to continue what I expected you would rather have laid aside, and therefore I will leave you."

"Oh, Madam," said he, "can you imagine I love at that rate as to have it shaken with any storm? No, were I secure your sister would not suffer in my absence by her mother's severity, I would not care what misery I were exposed to, but to think I should be the occasion of trouble to the person in the earth that I love most is unsupportable."

And with that he fell down in a chair that was behind him, but as one without all sense, which I must confess did so much move me that, laying aside all former distance I had kept him at, I sat down upon his knee, and laying my head near his I suffered him to kiss me, which was a liberty I never gave before; nor had not then had I not seen him so overcome with grief, which I endeavoured to suppress with all the encouragement I could, but still pressing him to be obedient to his father, either in going abroad or staying at home as he thought most convenient.

"No," says he, "since they will not allow me to converse with you, France will be more agreeable to me than England, nor will I go there except I have liberty to come here again and take my leave of you." To that I could not disagree if they thought fit to allow it, and so my sister and I left him, but she durst not own to my mother where she had been.

The next morning early my Lord H. went away, and took with him his son and daughter, and left me to the severities of my offended mother, who nothing could pacify. After she had called for me and said as many bitter things as passion could

---

[1] *quality* rank or position in society (*OED* quality *sb* 3a); *Lord H.'s...younger children* Lord Howard had five children; Thomas was his eldest son and heir. Halkett's mother believed that if Lord H.'s eldest son failed to marry an heiress with a substantial portion (dowry), his four younger children would not be provided for.

dictate upon such a subject, she discharged me to see him and did solemnly vow that if she should hear I did see Mr. H. she would turn me out of her doors and never own me again. All I said to that part was that it should be against my will if ever she heard of it.

.   .   .   .

At this time my Lord H. had a sister in France who gloried much of her wit and contrivance and used to say she never designed anything but she accomplished it.[1] My Lord H. thought she was the fittest person to divert his son from his amour, and to her he writes and recommends it to her management, who was not negligent of what she was entrusted with, as appeared in the conclusion; though her carriage was a great disappointment to Mr. H., for he expected by her mediation to have obtained what he desired, and that made him the more willing to comply with her, who designed her own advantage by this to oblige her brother, who might be the more useful to her in a projected marriage she had for her own son.

Upon Thursday the 13th of February, 1645/6, word was brought to my mother that the Countess of B. was come out of France and Mr. H. with her, which was a great surprise to her and all his relations. My mother examined me if I had sent for him or knew anything of his coming, which I assured her I had not, and she said not much more. But I was as much disturbed as any, sometimes thinking he was come with an assurance from his aunt that she would accomplish what he had so passionately desired, or else that he had laid all thoughts of me aside and was come with a resolution to comply with his father's desires. The last opinion I was a little confirmed in, having never received any word or letter from him in ten days after his return; and meeting him accidently where I was walking, he crossed the way, and another time was in the room where I came in to visit some young ladies, and neither of these times took any notice of me more than of one I had never seen. I confess I was a little disordered at it, but made no conclusions till I saw what time would produce.

Upon Tuesday the 4th of March, my Lady Anne W. his cousin came to my mother's, and having stayed a convenient time for a visit with my mother (for then it was not usual for mothers and daughters to be visited apart), I waited on her down, and taking me aside she told me she was desired by her cousin T.H. to present his most faithful service to me and to desire me not to take it ill that he did not speak to me when he met me.[2] For finding his aunt not his friend as he expected, he seemed to comply with her desire only to have the opportunity of coming home with her, and had resolved for a time to forbear all converse with me and to make love to all that came in his way; but assured me it was only to make his friends think he had forgot me, and then he might with the less suspicion prosecute his design, which was never to love or marry any but me. And this, she said, he confirmed with all the solemn oaths imaginable.

In pursuance of this he visited all the young ladies about the town. But an earl's daughter gave him the most particular welcome, whose mother not allowing him to come as a pretender, she made appointment with him and met him at her cousin's house frequently, which I knew and he made sport of. The summer being now advancing, my mother and her family went with my sister to her house in the country, which being not far from London we heard often how affairs went there, and amongst other discourse that it was reported Mr. H. was in love with my Lady E.M. and she with him; at which some smiled and said it might be her wit had taken

---

[1] *my Lord H. had a sister* Lord Howard's sister was Elizabeth Knollys Vaux, Countess of Banbury.

[2] *Lady Anne W.* Lady Ann Walsingham.

him, but certainly not her beauty (for she had as little of that as myself).[1]

Though these reports put me upon my guard, yet I confess I did not believe he was real in his address there; neither did his sister, who was sometimes a witness of their converse and gave me account of it. But I approved not of his way, for I thought it could not but reflect upon himself and injure either that lady or me. But she took a way to secure herself; for upon the last Tuesday in July, 1646, a little before supper, I received a letter from Mrs. H., a particular friend of mine, who writ me word that upon the Tuesday before Mr. H. was privately married to my Lady E.M., and the relations of both sides was unsatisfied.[2]

I was alone in my sister's chamber when I read the letter, and flinging myself down upon her bed, I said, "Is this the man for whom I have suffered so much? Since he hath made himself unworthy my love, he is unworthy my anger or concern." And rising, immediately I went out into the next room to my supper as unconcernedly as if I had never had an interest in him, nor had never lost it.

.   .   .   .

This gentleman came to see me sometimes in the company of ladies who had been my mother's neighbours in St. Martin's Lane, and sometimes alone.[3] But whenever he came, his discourse was serious, handsome, and tending to impress the advantages of piety, loyalty, and virtue;[4] and these subjects were so agreeable to my own inclination

that I could not but give them a good reception, especially from one that seemed to be so much an owner of them himself. After I had been used to freedom of discourse with him, I told him I approved of his advice to others, but I thought his own practice contradicted much of his profession, for one of his acquaintance had told me he had not seen his wife in a twelvemonth; and it was impossible, in my opinion, for a good man to be an ill husband, and therefore he must defend himself from one before I could believe the other of him. He said it was not necessary to give everyone that might condemn him the reason of his being so long from her, yet to satisfy me he would tell me the truth, which was that, he being engaged in the king's service, he was obliged to be at London, where it was not convenient for her to be with him, his stay in any place being uncertain.[5] Besides, she lived amongst her friends, who though they were kind to her yet were not so to him, for most of that country had declared for the Parliament and were enemies to all that had, or did, serve the king; and therefore his wife, he was sure, would not condemn him for what he did by her own consent. This seeming reasonable, I did insist no more upon that subject.

At this time he had frequent letters from the king, who employed him in several affairs, but that of the greatest concern which he was employed in was to contrive the Duke of York's escape out of St. James' (where His Highness and the Duke of Gloucester and the Princess Elizabeth lived under the care of the Earl of Northumberland and his Lady).[6] The difficulties of it were represented by

---

[1] *Lady E.M.* Lady Elizabeth Mordaunt, daughter of John, first Earl of Peterborough (1599–1643).

[2] *upon the Tuesday…my Lady E.M.* Thomas Howard married Lady Elizabeth Mordaunt on July 21, 1646.

[3] *This gentleman* Colonel Joseph Bampfield, a soldier and secret agent for Charles I. Though Bampfield helped to effect the escape of the Duke of York from St. James's Palace in April 1648, he later served Oliver Cromwell's government.

[4] *handsome* appropriate; also clever (*OED* handsome *a* A.2a); *impress* imprint on the mind; urge (*OED* impress *v*[1]I.3).

[5] *engaged in the king's service* Charles I was currently imprisoned at Carisbrooke Castle on the Isle of Wight.

[6] *Duke of York* James Stuart, the Duke of York (1633–1701), the second son of Charles I; *St. James'* St. James's Palace, in which the Duke of York had been born; *Duke of Gloucester* Henry Stuart (1639–1660), the third son of Charles I; *Princess Elizabeth* Elizabeth Stuart (1635–1650), the second daughter of Charles I; *Earl of Northumberland* Algernon Percy, tenth Earl of Northumberland

Colonel B., but His Majesty still pressed it, and I remember this expression was in one of the letters: *I believe it will be difficult, and if he miscarry in the attempt it will be the greatest affliction that can arrive to me, but I look upon James' escape as Charles's preservation, and nothing can content me more.*[1] *Therefore be careful what you do.*

This letter amongst others he showed me, and where the king approved of his choice of me to entrust with it, for to get the Duke's clothes made and to dress him in his disguise.[2] So now all C.B.'s business and care was how to manage this business of so important concern which could not be performed without several persons' concurrence in it. For he being generally known as one whose stay at London was in order to serve the king, few of those who were entrusted by the Parliament in public concerns durst own converse or hardly civility to him, lest they should have been suspect by their party, which made it difficult for him to get access to the Duke.[3] But (to be short) having communicated the design to a gentleman attending His Highness, who was full of honour and fidelity, by his means he had private access to the Duke, to whom he presented the king's letter and order to His Highness for consenting to act what C.B.

should contrive for his escape;[4] which was so cheerfully entertained and so readily obeyed, that being once designed there was nothing more to do than to prepare all things for the execution.

I had desired him to take a ribbon with him and bring me the bigness of the Duke's waist and his length to have clothes made fit for him. In the meantime C.B. was to provide money for all necessary expense, which was furnished by an honest citizen. When I gave the measure to my tailor to enquire how much mohair would serve to make a petticoat and waistcoat to a young gentlewoman of that bigness and stature, he considered it a long time and said he had made many gowns and suits, but he had never made any to such a person in his life. I thought he was in the right; but his meaning was, he had never seen any women of so low a stature have so big a waist. However, he made it as exactly fit as if he had taken the measure himself. It was a mixed mohair of a light hair colour and black, and the under-petticoat was scarlet.

All things being now ready, upon the 20th of April, 1648, in the evening was the time resolved on for the Duke's escape. And in order to that, it was designed for a week before every night as soon as the Duke had supped, he and those servants that attended His Highness (till the Earl of Northumberland and the rest of the house had supped) went to a play called hide and seek, and sometimes he would hide himself so well that in half an hour's time they could not find him.[5] His Highness had so used them to this that when he went really away they thought he was but at the usual sport. A little before the Duke went to supper that night, he called for the gardener (who only had

---

(1602–1668), initially held military posts under Charles I before aligning himself with the Parliamentarians.

[1] *I look upon... me more* Charles I appears aware of the plan proposed by Cromwell and others to depose him, disinherit the Prince of Wales, and crown the Duke of York. With the Duke of York's escape, the royal succession would not be threatened and the motivation for disinheriting, even assassinating, the Prince of Wales would be removed.

[2] *approved of his choice of me* Though Charles I may not have known Halkett personally, her father had served as his tutor and secretary, her mother had been under-governess and later governess of the Duke of Gloucester and the Princess Elizabeth, and her brothers Henry and Charles had been Grooms of the King's Bedchamber.

[3] *own converse* admit conversation (*OED* own *sb* 1).

[4] *a gentleman attending His Highness* In his memoirs, James II mentions "the assistance of Mr. George Howard brother to the Earl of Suffolk who at that time was his Master of Horse."

[5] *hide and seek* As the Duke of York was a boy of fourteen at the time of his escape, his interest in playing hide and seek would not have caused suspicion.

a treble key, besides that which the Duke had) and bid him give him that key till his own was mended, which he did.[1] And after His Highness had supped, he immediately called to go to the play, and went down the privy stairs into the garden and opened the gate that goes into the park, treble locking all the doors behind him.[2] And at the garden gate C.B. waited for His Highness, and putting on a cloak and periwig, hurried him away to the park gate where a coach waited that carried them to the water side.[3] And taking the boat that was appointed for that service, they rode to the stairs next the bridge, where I and Miriam waited in a private house hard by that C.B. had prepared for dressing His Highness, where all things were in a readiness.[4]

But I had many fears, for C.B. had desired me, if they came not there precisely by ten o'clock, to shift for myself, for then I might conclude they were discovered, and so my stay there could do no good, but prejudice myself.[5] Yet this did not make me leave the house though ten o'clock did strike, and he that was entrusted, [who] often went to the landing-place and saw no boat coming, was much discouraged, and asked me what I would do. I told him I came there with a resolution to serve His Highness and I was fully determined not to leave that place till I was out of hopes of doing what I came there for, and would take my hazard.[6] He left me to go again to the water side, and while I was fortifying myself against what might arrive to me, I heard a great noise of many as I thought coming up

stairs, which I expected to be soldiers to take me; but it was a pleasing disappointment, for the first that came in was the Duke, who with much joy I took in my arms and gave God thanks for his safe arrival. His Highness called, "Quickly, quickly, dress me," and putting off his clothes I dressed him in the women's habit that was prepared, which fitted His Highness very well and was very pretty in it. After he had eaten something I made ready while I was idle, lest His Highness should be hungry, and having sent for a Woodstreet cake (which I knew he loved) to take in the barge,[7] with as much haste as could be His Highness went cross the bridge to the stairs where the barge lay, C.B. leading him, and immediately the boatmen plied the oar so well that they were soon out of sight, having both wind and tide with them. But I afterwards heard the wind changed and was so contrary that C.B. told me he was terribly afraid they should have been blown back again. And the Duke said, "Do anything with me rather than let me go back again," which put C.B. to seek help where it was only to be had, and after he had most fervently supplicated assistance from God, presently the wind blew fair and they came safely to their intended landing place. But I heard there was some difficulty before they got to the ship at Graves-End, which had like to have discovered them had not Colonel Washington's lady assisted them.[8]

After the Duke's barge was out of sight of the bridge, I and Miriam went where I appointed the coach to stay for me and made drive as fast as the coachman could to my brother's house, where I stayed.[9] I met none in the way that gave me any

[1] *treble key* a key used to open a treble lock, which operates by three turns of the key (*OED* treble *a* A.3).

[2] *privy* private; possibly concealed (*OED* privy *a* A.II.5).

[3] *periwig* an artificial imitation of a head of hair worn by women (*OED* periwig *sb* 1).

[4] *next the bridge...private house* on the north bank of the Thames; *Miriam* Halkett's personal maid; *hard by* close by (*OED* hard by *prep* A).

[5] *to shift for* to make provision for (*OED* shift *v* I.4a).

[6] *hazard* chances (*OED* hazard *sb* 2).

[7] *Woodstreet cake* probably so named after Wood Street in the Cheapside market.

[8] *Graves-End* a port twenty-four miles south-east of London, on the south bank of the Thames; *discovered* revealed (*OED* discover *v* 4); *Colonel Washington's lady* probably Elizabeth, the wife of Colonel Henry Washington (1615–1664).

[9] *my brother's house* the house of Henry Murray, her oldest brother.

apprehension that the design was discovered, nor was it noised abroad till the next day. For (as I related before) the Duke having used to play at hide and seek, and to conceal himself a long time when they missed him at the same play, thought he would have discovered himself as formerly when they had given over seeking him.[1] But a much longer time being passed than usually was spent in that divertisement,[2] some began to apprehend that His Highness was gone in earnest past their finding, which made the Earl of Northumberland (to whose care he was committed), after strict search made in the house of St. James and all thereabouts to no purpose, to send and acquaint the Speaker of the House of Commons that the Duke was gone, but how or by what means he knew not; but desired that there might be orders sent to the Cinque Ports for stopping all ships going out till the passengers were examined and search made in all suspected places where His Highness might be concealed.[3]

Though this was gone about with all the vigilancy imaginable, yet it pleased God to disappoint them of their intention by so infatuating those several persons who were employed for writing orders that none of them were able to write one right, but ten or twelve of them were cast by before one was according to their mind.[4] This account I had from Mr. N., who was mace-bearer to the Speaker at that time and a witness of it.[5] This disorder of the clerks contributed much to the Duke's safety, for he was at sea before any of the orders came to the ports and so was free from what was designed if they had taken His Highness.

Though several were suspected for being accessory to the escape, yet they could not charge any with it but the person who went away, and he being out of their reach, they took no notice as either to examine or imprison others.

. . . .

To allay the joy that all the Loyal Party had for the king's return, there was two great occasions for disturbance, the one being strengthened by the other:[6] Cromwell coming in with an army when there was so great divisions both in Church and State, and such unsuitable things proposed for accommodation as I wish were buried in perpetual silence. After the king had been invited to several places and entertained suitably to what could be expected, His Majesty returned again to Dunfermline, having ordered the forces to march; and one morning came letters from the army lying at Dunbar that they had so surrounded the enemy that there was no possibility for them to escape, which news gave great joy and much security. But the sad effects made us see how little confidence should be placed in anything but God, who in his justice thought fit to punish this kingdom and bring it under subjection to an usurper because they paid not that subjection that was due to their lawful king.

The unexpected defeat which the king's army had at Dunbar put everyone to new thoughts how to dispose of themselves, and none was more perplexed than I where to go or what to do…. Upon Saturday, the 7th of September, we left Dunfermline and came that night to Kinrose, where we stayed till Monday. I cannot omit to insert here the

---

[1] *given over* ceased from, given up (*OED* give *v.* B.XVI.63a).

[2] *divertisement* recreation (*OED* divertisement 1).

[3] *the Speaker…of Commons* William Lenthall (1591–1662), Member of Parliament for Woodstock, Oxfordshire (1640–1653); *Cinque Ports* a group of sea-ports (originally five, whence the name) on the south coast of England.

[4] *infatuating* rendering them utterly foolish (*OED* infatuating *v* 2).

[5] *Mr. N.* Sergeant Norfolk.

[6] *king's return* The Prince of Wales (considered King Charles II by Royalists after his father's execution in 1649) landed in the Firth of Cromarty, June 16, 1650. Cromwell, commander of the New Model Army, invaded Scotland on July 22, 1650 and defeated the army of the Scottish Covenanters who fought for Charles II at Dunbar on September 3, 1650. Halkett traveled to Scotland to visit the King and to recover her interest in a property in Scotland.

opportunity I had of serving many poor wounded soldiers; for as we were riding to Kinrose I saw two that looked desperately ill, who were so weak they were hardly able to go along the high way; and inquiring what ailed them, they told me they had been soldiers at Dunbar and were going towards Kinrose, if their wounds would suffer them.[1] I bid them when they came there enquire for the Countess of D.'s lodging and there would be one there would dress them. It was late, it seems, before they came, and so till the next morning I saw them not, but then they came, attended with twenty more. And betwixt that time and Monday that we left that place, I believe threescore was the least that was dressed by me and my woman and Ar. Ro., who I employed to such as was unfit for me to dress; and besides the plasters or balsam I applied, I gave every one of them as much with them as might dress them 3 or 4 times, for I had provided myself very well of things necessary for that employment, expecting they might be useful.[2]

Amongst the many variety of wounds amongst them, two was extraordinary. One was a man whose head was cut so that the [   ] was very visibly seen and the water came bubbling up, which when Ar. R. saw he cried out, "Lord have mercy upon thee, for thou art but a dead man." I seeing the man who had courage enough before begin to be much disheartened, I told him he need not be discouraged with what he that had no skill said, for if it pleased God to bless what I should give him he might do well enough; and this I said more to hearten him up than otherwise, for I saw it a very dangerous wound. And yet it pleased God he recovered, as I heard afterwards.... The other was a youth about 16 that had been run through the body with a tuke.[3] It went in under his right shoulder and came out under his left breast, and yet [he] had little inconvenience by it, but his greatest prejudice was from so infinite a swarm of creatures that it is incredible for any that were not eye witnesses of it.[4] I made a contribution and bought him other clothes to put on him and made the fire consume what else had been impossible to destroy.

—1875 (CA. 1677–78)

---

[1] *suffer* allow (*OED* suffer *v* II.12).

[2] *plasters* an external curative application consisting of a medicinal substance spread on a piece of muslin (*OED* plaster *sb* I.1a).

[3] *tuke* rapier (*OED* tuck *sb³*).

[4] *prejudice* injury (*OED* prejudice *sb* I.1b).

Katharine Evans and Sarah Chevers
? – d. 1692; ? – d. 1664

Little is known of the early lives of Katharine Evans and Sarah Chevers. In documents from the Inquisition in Malta, it is recorded that Katharine Evans advised Inquisitors that she was the daughter of Anne and Roger "Canual," while Sarah Chevers said that she was the daughter of Margaret and William "Shenel."[1] Katharine Evans was married to the Quaker John Evans and resided in Englishbatch, Somersetshire. Chevers, her traveling companion, was married to Henry Chevers from Slaughterford, Wiltshire. Both women left their husbands and children to serve as Quaker missionaries and frequently experienced indignities during their travels. Evans was banished from the Isle of Wight some time between the years 1655 and 1657 and during the same time period, a soldier came to her bedside on the Isle of Man and carried her on shipboard. Her insistence on public preaching resulted in an imprisonment in Cornwall, and both Evans and Chevers suffered the humiliation of being "stripped and tied to a whipping-post in the market of Salisbury and there whipped" (1657).[2] In 1658, Evans and Chevers undertook a sea-voyage to Alexandria to extend their missionary work. These plans were thwarted when they were apprehended by the Inquisition on the Island of Malta, and imprisoned for more than three years. During their confinement, Evans and Chevers wrote *This is a Short Relation of Some of the Cruel Sufferings (For the Truth's Sake) of Katharine Evans and Sarah Chevers* (1662), a spiritual autobiography which details their endurance in the face of physical and psychological affliction. After their release in July, 1662, Evans and Chevers embarked on a series of missionary trips to Scotland, Wales and Ireland. Chevers died in 1664, but Evans continued her ministry and was imprisoned at Welchpool in Montgomeryshire (1666) and Newgate prison in Bristol (1682) before her death in 1692.

෴

This is a Short Relation of Some of the Cruel Sufferings (For the Truth's Sake) of Katharine Evans and Sarah Chevers, in the Inquisition in the Isle of Malta

A true declaration concerning the Lord's love to us in all our voyage: We were at sea, between London and Plymouth, many weeks, and one day we had some trials; and between Plymouth and Legorn we were 31 days, and we had many trials and storms within and without;[3] but the Lord did deliver us out of all: And when we came to Legorn, with the rest of our friends, we went into the town after we had product,[4] and stayed there many days, where we had service every day; for all sorts of people came unto us, but no man did offer to hurt us, yet we gave them books and having got passage in a Dutch ship we sailed towards Cyprus, intending to go to Alexandria, but the Lord had appointed

---

[1] The historian Stefano Villani, who has inspected the Inquisition Archive in Malta, believes (based on the fact that Inquisitors wrote English names in the same way they pronounced them) that "Canual" is likely "Canwal" and "Shenel" is likely "Channel." For more information on the events relating to the missionary service of Evans and Chevers in Malta, see Villani, *Tremolantie Papisti: Missioni Quacchere Nell'Italia Del Seicento* (Roma: Edizioni de Storia e Letterature, 1996), 115–135.

[2] Friends House in London provided us with a typescript of their forthcoming *Dictionary of Quaker Biography* to supply information not available until recently on early female Quakers.

[3] *Legorn* Legorno (now Livorno), Italy, a major port.

[4] *had product* obtained provisions (*OED* product *sb*[1] 2c).

something for us to do by the way, as he did make it manifest to us, as I did speak, for the master of the ship had no business in the place; but being in company with another ship which had some business at the city of Malta (in the Island of Malta where Paul suffered shipwreck)[1] and being in the harbour, on the first day of the week, we being moved of the Lord, went into the town, and the English consul met us on the shore, and asked us concerning our coming, and we told him truth, and gave him some books, and a paper, and he told us there was an Inquisition, and he kindly entreated us to go to his house, and said all that he had was at our service while we were there. And in the fear and dread of the Lord we went, and there came many to see us, and we called them to repentance, and many of them were tender; but the whole city is given to idolatry. And we went a ship-board that night; and the next day we being moved to go into the city again, dared not to fly the cross, but in obedience went, desiring the will of God to be done. And when we came to the governor, he told us that he had a sister in the nunnery did desire to see us if we were free; and in the fear of God we went, and talked with them, and gave them a book, and one of their priests was with us (at the nunnery) and had us into their place of worship, and some would have us bow to the high altar, which we did deny; and having a great burden, we went to the consul again, and were waiting upon the Lord what to do, that we might know.

And the Inquisitors sent for us, and when we came before them, they asked our names, and the names of our husbands, and the names of our fathers and mothers, and how many children we had; and they asked us, wherefore we came into that country? And we told them, we were the servants of the living God, and were moved to come and call them to repentance; and many other questions, and they went away, but commanded that we should be stayed there. And the next day they came again, and called for us, and we came; but they would examine us apart, and called Sarah, and they asked, whether she was a true Catholic? She said, that she was a true Christian that worshippeth God in spirit and in truth; and they proffered her the crucifix, and would have had her swear that she would speak the truth; and she said, she should speak the truth, but she would not swear, for Christ commanded her not to swear, saying, *Swear not at all*:[2] And the English consul persuaded her with much entreating to swear, saying, none should do her any harm: But she denied; and they took some books from her, and would have had her swear by them, but she would not: And they asked, wherefore she brought the books? And she said, because we could not speak their language, and they might know wherefore we came; and they asked of her, what George Fox was;[3] and she said, he was a minister. And they asked, wherefore she came thither? She said, to do the will of God, as she was moved of the Lord. And they asked, how the Lord did appear unto her? And she said, by his spirit. And they asked, where she was when the Lord appeared unto her? And she said, upon the way. And they asked, whether she

---

[1] *where Paul suffered shipwreck*   After Paul was arrested in Jerusalem, he appealed to Caesar and was taken by ship to Rome. When the ship was wrecked, Paul escaped, landing on an island called "Melita," which has commonly been interpreted as "Malta" (Acts 28:1).

[2] *Christ commanded...Swear not at all*   "But I say unto you, Swear not at all; neither by heaven; for it is God's throne" (Matthew 5:34). Judicial swearing was considered profane by Quakers. After 1662, an Act was passed to prevent "mischiefs and dangers that may arise by certain persons called Quakers, and others refusing to take oaths," making it illegal to refuse to take an oath. In a short treatise, George Fox made the following response: "The world saith, 'Kiss the book,' but the book saith, 'Kiss the Son, lest He be angry.' And the Son saith, 'Swear not at all, but keep to Yea and Nay in all your communications, for whatsoever is more than this cometh of evil.'"

[3] *George Fox*   George Fox (1624–1691) was the founder of the Children of Light, later known as the Society of Friends. In 1650, Fox reports in his *Journal* that Justice Bennet of Derby was the first to name Fox and his followers Quakers because Fox "bade them tremble at the word of the Lord."

did see his presence, and hear his voice? And she said, she did hear his voice, and saw his presence; and they asked, what he said to her? And she said, the Lord told her, she must go over the seas to do his will; and then they asked, how she knew it was the Lord? And she said, he bid her go, and his living presence should go with her, and he was faithful that had promised, for she did feel his living presence; and so they went away.

．　．　．　．　．　．　．　．　．

The next second day came a magistrate, two friars, and the man with the black rod, and a scribe, and the keeper, to the Inquisition, to sit upon judgment, and examined us apart concerning our faith in Christ. The magistrate would have had us to swear, and we answered, No; Christ said, *Swear not at all*; and so said James the apostle.[1] He asked, if we would speak truth? We said, yea. He asked, whether we did believe the creed?[2] We said, we did believe in God, and in Jesus Christ, which was born of the Virgin Mary, and suffered at Jerusalem under Pilate, and arose again from the dead the third day, and ascended to his Father, and shall come to judgment, to judge both quick and dead. He asked, how we did believe the resurrection? We answered, we did believe that the just and the unjust should arise, according to the Scriptures. He said, *Do you believe in the saints, and pray to them*? We said, we

did believe the communion of saints;[3] but we did not pray to them, but to God only, in the name of Jesus Christ. He asked, whether we did believe in the Catholic Church? We said, we did believe the true Church of Christ; but the word Catholic we have not read in Scripture. He asked, if we believed a purgatory?[4] We said, no; but a heaven and a hell. The friar said, we were commanded to pray for the dead;[5] for those that were in heaven had no need; and they that were in hell there is no redemption; therefore there must be a purgatory. He asked, if we believed their holy sacrament? We said, we never read (the word) sacrament in Scripture.[6] The friar replied, where we did read in our Bibles sanctification, it was sacrament in theirs. He said, their holy sacrament was bread and wine, which they converted into the flesh and blood of Christ by the virtue of Christ.[7] We said, they did work miracles

---

[3] *communion of saints* The phrase "communion of the saints" is taken from the Apostles' Creed and is generally interpreted to refer to the union of all believers, living or dead, in Christ. Roman Catholics frequently referred to this phrase as a justification for the practice of prayers for the dead.

[4] *purgatory* According to Roman Catholic and Greek Orthodox teachings, purgatory is a place of temporal punishment in the intermediate realm. Those who die at peace with the church but who are not yet perfect must endure purgative suffering, during which time, Aquinas claims, "the stain of sinful habit is removed from the soul."

[5] *commanded to pray for the dead* The custom of praying for the dead appears to have arisen in the church at the end of the second century. II Maccabees 12:44 (Apocrypha) is often cited to support such a practice.

[6] *sacrament* According to Catholicism, the following sacraments were channels of divine grace: Eucharist, Baptism, Marriage, Holy Orders, Confirmation, Penance, and Extreme Unction. Protestants recognized only two sacraments, Eucharist (Holy Communion) and Baptism, which were seen as reminders rather than vehicles of divine grace. The Quakers argued that they experienced mystical union with God independent of the sacraments, rendering them unnecessary.

[7] *Holy Sacrament...virtue of Christ* Evans and Chevers are asked whether they accept the Roman Catholic doctrine of transubstantiation: that the bread and wine in Eucharist are literally transformed into Christ's body and blood. Luther had rejected transubstantiation, coining the term consubstantiation to express his belief that the bread and wine remain along with the body and blood of Christ. However,

---

[1] *and so said James the apostle* "But above all things, my brethren, swear not, neither by heaven, neither by the earth, neither by any other oath: but let your yea be yea; and your nay, nay; lest ye fall into condemnation" (James 5:12).

[2] *creed* The word "creed" derives from the Latin *credo*, "I believe" denoting a body of beliefs and a confession of faith. In Christian history three creeds are noteworthy: the Nicene Creed (381 C.E.), the Apostles' Creed (390) and the Athanasian Creed (fourth or fifth century). The response made by Evans and Chevers suggests that the Inquisitors were referring to the Apostles' Creed whose predecessor was the Old Roman Creed.

then, for Christ's virtue is the same as it was when he turned water into wine at the marriage in Cana.[1] He said, if we did not eat the flesh, and drink the blood of the Son of God, we had no life in us. We said, the flesh and blood of Christ is spiritual, and we do feed upon it daily; for that which is begotten of God in us, can no more live without spiritual food, than our temporal bodies can without temporal food. He said, that we did never hear Mass. We said, we did hear the voice of Christ, he only had the words of eternal life, and that was sufficient for us.[2] He said, we were heretics and heathens. We said, they were heretics that lived in sin and wickedness, and such were heathens that knew not God. He asked about our meetings in England? And we told them the truth to their amazement. And they asked, who was the head of our Church? We said, *Christ*. And they asked, what George Fox is. And we said, *He is a minister of Christ*. They asked, whether he sent us? We said, *No, the Lord did move us to come*. The friar said, we were deceived, and had not the faith; but we had all virtues. We said, that faith was the ground from whence virtues do proceed. They said, if we would take their holy sacrament, we might have our liberty; or else the Pope would not leave us for millions of gold, but we should lose our souls and our bodies too. We said, the Lord had provided for our souls, and our bodies were freely given up to serve the Lord. They asked us, if we did not believe marriage was a sacrament? We said, it was an ordinance of God. They asked us, if we did believe men could forgive sins? We said none could

forgive sin, but God only. They brought us that Scripture, *Whose sins ye remit in earth, shall be remitted in heaven*.[3] We said, all power was God's, and he could give it to whom he would (that were born of the eternal spirit, and guided by the same; such have power to do the Father's will, as I answered a friar also in the city of Naples) and they were silent, the power greatly working. We asked them wherein we had wronged them, that we should be kept prisoners all [the] days of our lives, and said, our innocent blood would be required at their hands.

   ·   ·   ·   ·   ·   ·   ·

The tenth day of my fast there came two friars, the chancellor, the man with the black rod, and a physician, and the keeper; and the friar commanded my dear friend to go out of the room, and he came and pulled my hand out of the bed, and said, *Is the Devil so great in you, that you cannot speak?* I said, *Depart from me thou worker of iniquity, I know thee not; the power of the Lord is upon me, and thou callest him Devil*. He took his crucifix to strike me in the mouth; and I said, *Look here!* and I asked him, whether it were that cross which crucified Paul to the world, and the world unto him?[4] And he said, it was. I denied him, and said, the Lord had made me a witness for himself against all workers of iniquity. He bid me be obedient, and went to strike me: I said, *Wilt thou strike me?* He said, he would. I said, *Thou art out of the apostles' doctrine, they were no strikers; I deny thee to be any of them who went in the name of the Lord*. He said, he had brought me a physician in charity. I said, the Lord was my physician, and my saving-health. He said I should be whipped, and quartered, and burnt that night in

---

many Protestant groups regarded Holy Communion as no more than a symbol of Christ's presence, a reminder of the crucifixion and resurrection.

[1] *water into wine...in Cana* The first miracle performed by Jesus was his transformation of water into wine (John 2:2–10).

[2] *we did never...sufficient for us* Quaker worship is based on the indwelling of the Holy Spirit, not limited by place, time or persons. The emphasis on the inward nature of one's relation to the divine, of Christ's presence in the "hearts of His people" as George Fox describes it, renders Mass a "vain tradition."

[3] *Whose sins ye...remitted in heaven* The friar appears to be referring to John 20:23, "Whose soever sins ye remit, they are remitted unto them; and whose soever sins ye remit, they are retained."

[4] *cross which crucified...world unto him* "But God forbid that I should glory, save in the cross of our Lord Jesus Christ, by whom the world is crucified unto me, and I unto the world" (Galatians 6:14).

Malta, and my mate too: wherefore did we come to teach them? I told him I did not fear, the Lord was on our side, and he had no power but what he had received; and if he did not use it to the same end the Lord gave it him, the Lord would judge him. And they were all smitten as dead men, and went away.

And as soon as they were gone, the Lord said unto me, *The last enemy that shall be destroyed, is death*; and the life arose over death, and I glorified God. The friar went to my friend, and told her, I called him worker of iniquity. *Did she*, said Sarah? *Art thou without sin?* He said he was; *Then she hath wronged thee.* (But I say, the wise reader may judge:) For between the eighth and ninth hour in the evening, he sent a drum to proclaim at the prison gate; we know not what it was, but the fire of the Lord consumed it. And about the fourth hour in the morning they were coming with a drum and guns; and the Lord said unto me, *Arise out of thy grave clothes.* And we arose, and they came up to the gate to devour us in a moment. But the Lord lifted up his standard with his own Spirit (of might) and made them to retreat, and they fled as dust before the wind; praises and honour be given to our God forever. I went to bed again, and the Lord said unto me, *Herod will seek the young child's life to destroy it yet again*;[1] and great was my affliction; so that my dear fellow and labourer in the work of God, did look every hour when I should depart the body for many days together, and we did look every hour when we should be brought to the stake day and night, for several weeks, and Isaac was freely offered up. But the Lord said, he had provided a ram in the bush.[2] Afterwards the friar came again

with his physician; I told him, that I could not take anything, unless I was moved of the Lord. He said, we must never come forth of that room while we lived, and we might thank God and him it was no worse, for it was like to be worse. We said, if we had died, we had died as innocent as ever did servants of the Lord. He said, it was well we were innocent. They did (also) look still when I would die.

The friar bid my friend take notice what torment I would be in at the hour of death, thousands of devils (he said) would fetch my soul to hell. She said, she did not fear any such thing.

And he asked if I did not think it expedient for the elders of the Church to pray over the sick? I said, yea, such as were eternally moved of the spirit of the Lord. He fell down on[3] his knees and did howl, and wish bitter wishes upon himself if he had not the true faith; but we denied him. The physician was in a great rage at Sarah, because she could not bow to him, but to God only.[4]

The last day of my fast I began to be a hungry, but was afraid to eat, the enemy was so strong; but the Lord said unto me, *If thine enemy hunger, feed him; if he thirst, give him drink. In so doing thou shalt heap coals of fire upon his head; be not overcome of evil, but overcome evil with good.*[5] I did eat, and was refreshed, and glorified God; and in the midst of our extremity the Lord sent his holy angels to comfort us, so that we rejoiced and magnified God;

---

[1] *Herod will seek…yet again* an allusion to Herod's attempt to kill the Christ child by slaying all children two years and younger resident in Bethlehem, and in all the coasts thereof (Matthew 2:13–16).

[2] *Isaac was freely…the bush* God tested Abraham's faith by requiring him to offer up his long-awaited son Isaac as a sacrifice. When Abraham demonstrated his faith by binding Isaac to an altar and preparing the knife, God withdrew his request, providing a ram as a substitute sacrifice. In the New Testament, Paul interprets Abraham's

act as an *exemplum* of faith and as a type of Christ's universal sacrifice (Hebrews 11:17; see also James 2:21).

[3] *on* emended from 'of' in the 1662 text.

[4] *could not bow…but God only* In his journal, George Fox writes that God: "forbade me to put off my hat to any, high or low; and I was required to say Thee and Thou to all men and women, without any respect to rich or poor, great or small. And as I travelled up and down, I was not to bid people Good-morrow, or Good-evening, neither might I bow or scrape my leg to any one, and this made the sects and professions to rage." In accordance with Fox's principles, Evans and Chevers refuse to acknowledge social or religious hierarchy by bowing to ecclesiastical officials.

[5] *If thine enemy…evil with good* Romans 12:20–21.

and in the time of our great trial, the sun and earth did mourn visibly three days, and the horror of death and pains of hell was upon me: the sun was darkened, the moon was turned into blood, and the stars did fall from heaven, and there was great tribulation ten days, such as never was from the beginning of the world: and then did I see the Son of Man coming in the clouds, with power and great glory, triumphing over his enemies; the heavens were on fire, and the elements did melt with fervent heat, and the trumpet sounded out of Sion, and an alarm was struck up in Jerusalem, and all the enemies of God were called to the great day of battle of the Lord. And I saw a great wonder in heaven, the woman clothed with the sun, and had the moon under her feet and a crown of twelve stars upon her head, and she travailed in pain ready to be delivered of a man-child, and there was a great dragon stood ready to devour the man-child as soon as it was born; and there was given to the woman two wings of a great eagle to carry her into the desert, where she should be nourished for a time, times, and half a time; and the dragon cast a flood out of his mouth, etc. And I saw war in heaven, Michael and his angels against the dragon and his angels, and the Lamb and his army did overcome them; and there was a trumpet sounded in heaven, and I heard a voice saying to me, *The city is divided into three parts*, and I heard another trumpet sounding, and I looked and saw an angel go down into a great pool of water, and I heard a voice saying unto me, *Whosoever goeth down next after the troubling of the waters, shall be healed of whatsoever disease he hath.* And I heard another trumpet sounding, and I heard a voice, saying, *Babylon is fallen, is fallen, Babylon the great is fallen.* And I looked, and saw the smoke of her torment, how it did ascend; and I heard another trumpet sounding, and I heard a voice saying, *Rejoice and be exceeding glad, for great is your reward in heaven; for he that is mighty hath magnified you, and holy is his name; and from henceforth all*

generations shall call you blessed: And I heard another trumpet sounding in heaven, and I heard a voice saying unto me, *Behold!* and I looked, and I saw Pharaoh and his host pursuing the children of Israel, and he and his host were drowned in the sea.[1]

Dear friends and people, whatsoever I have written is not because it is recorded in the Scripture, or that I have heard of such things; but in obedience to the Lord I have written the things which I did hear, see, tasted and handled of the good word of God, to the praise of his name forever.

And all this time my dear sister in Christ Jesus was in as great affliction as I (in a manner) to see my strong travail night and day; yet she was kept in the patience, and would willingly have given me up to death, that I might have been at rest; yet she would have been left in as great danger, woe and misery, as ever was any poor captive for the Lord's truth; for they did work night and day with their divinations, enchantments and temptations, thinking thereby to bring us under their power; but the Lord prevented them every way, so that great was their rage, and they came often with their physician, and said it was in charity; I asked them whether they did keep us in that hot room to kill us, and bring us a physician to make us alive.

The friar said, the Inquisitor would lose his head if he should take us thence; and it was better to keep us there, than to kill us.

The room was so hot and so close, that we were fain to rise often out of our bed, and lie down at a chink of their door for air to fetch breath; and with the fire within, and the heat without, our skin was like sheep's leather, and the hair did fall off our heads, and we did fail often; our afflictions and

---

[1] *and in that time…in the sea*   Despite the claim that this apocalyptic vision was experiential rather than textually-based, this passage is a collage of biblical allusions: Psalm 116:3; Joel 2:31; Acts 2:20; Revelation 6:12; Matthew 24:29; Mark 13:25; Revelation 2:10; Matthew 24:30; II Peter 3:12; Revelation 12:1–4, 7,14,16; Revelation 16:9; Isaiah 41:18; John 5:4; Revelation 16:9; Revelation 18:12; Matthew 5:12; Luke 1:48-49; Exodus 14:23.

burdens were so great, that when it was day we wished for night; and when it was night we wished for day; we sought death, but could not find it; we desired to die, but death fled from us. We did eat our bread weeping, and mingled our drink with our tears. We did write to the Inquisitor, and laid before him our innocency, and our faithfulness, in giving our testimony for the Lord amongst them; and I told him, if it were our blood they did thirst after, they might take it any other way, as well as to smother us up in that hot room. So he sent the friar, and he took away our inkhorns (they had our Bibles before). We asked why they took away our goods? They said, it was all theirs, and our lives too, if they would. We asked how we had forfeited our lives unto them; they said, for bringing books and papers. We said, if there were any thing in them that was not true, they might write against it. They said, they did scorn to write to fools and asses that did not know true Latin. And they told us, the Inquisitor would have us separated, because I was weak, and I should go into a cooler room; but Sarah should abide there. I took her by the arm, and said, *The Lord hath joined us together and woe be to them that should part us.*[1] I said, I rather choose to die there with my friend, than to part from her. He was smitten, and went away, and came no more in five weeks, and the door was not opened in that time. Then they came again to part us; but I was sick, and broken out from head to foot. They sent for a doctor, and he said, we must have air, or else we must die. So the Lord compelled them to go to the Inquisitor, and he gave order for the door to be set open six hours in a day; they did not part us till ten weeks after: But oh the dark clouds and the sharp showers the Lord did carry us through! Death itself had been better than to have parted in that place. They said, we corrupted each other, and that they thought when we were parted, we would have bowed to them. But they found we were more stronger afterwards than we were before; the Lord our God did fit us for every condition. They came and brought a scourge of small hemp and asked us, if we would have any of it. They said, they did whip themselves till the blood did come. We said, that could not reach the Devil, he sat upon the heart. They said, all the men and women of Malta were for us, if we would be Catholics, for there would be none like unto us. We said, the Lord had changed us into that which changed not. They said, all their holy women did pray for us, and we should be honored of all the world if we would turn. We said, we were of God, and the whole world did lie in wickedness; and we denied the honor of the world, and the glory too. They said, we should be honored of God too, but now we were hated of all. We said, it is an evident token whose servants we are; the servant is not greater than the Lord, and that Scripture was fulfilled which saith, *All this will I give thee, if thou wilt fall down and worship me.*[2]

.   .   .   .

And there were two or three English ships there, came into harbour, and Sarah saw the coming of them in a vision of the night, and there was great pleading for us, that we saw; but she heard a voice, saying, we could not go now. So we were made willing to wait the Lord's time.

Then they sent for us forth when the ships were gone, and asked us if we would be Catholics: And we said, we were true Christians, and had received the spirit of Christ, and he that had not the spirit of

---

[1] *The Lord has...part us* Evans alludes to the passage traditionally used to support the sanctity of marriage: "And [Jesus] said, For this cause shall a man leave father and mother, and shall cleave to his wife: and they twain shall be one flesh? Wherefore they are no more twain, but one flesh. What therefore God hath joined together, let no man put asunder" (Matthew 19:5–6).

[2] *All this will...and worship me* This passage is taken from the temptation of Christ during his forty-day fast in the desert: "Again, the devil taketh him [Jesus] up into an exceeding high mountain, and sheweth him all the kingdoms of the world, and the glory of them; And saith unto him, All these things will I give thee, if thou wilt fall down and worship me" (Matthew 4:8–9).

Christ, was none of his. The English consul told us of the ships, and said, they would not let us go unless we would be Catholics; and that we must suffer more imprisonment yet; and said, he did what he could for us. One of the magistrates showed us the cross; we told them, and said, we did take up the cross of Christ daily, which is the great power of God to crucify sin and iniquity.[1] So we told them that one of their Fathers did promise us our liberty. We did think that friar was too tender hearted to stay among them; he did take a great deal of pains for us (the captain said);[2] we told him, he

would never have cause to repent it; the blessing of God would be upon him for any thing he should do for us; for we were the servants of the living God, and he promised us our freedoms in a little time.[3]
—1662

---

[1] *take up the cross of Christ daily* "And he [Jesus] said to them all, If any man will come after me, let him deny himself, and take up his cross daily, and follow me" (Luke 9:23).

[2] *that friar...(the captain said)* In an earlier passage, Evans and Chevers describe attempts to free them from imprisonment: "They did not tell us of any English that were there; but there was one Francis Steward of London, a captain of a ship, and a friar of Ireland, which came to the city together (for what we know) and they did take great pains for us, and went to their ruler, and the Inquisitor, and to several magistrates and friars, and the new English consul with them, and wrought much amongst them that all were willing to let us go, save the Inquisitor."

---

[3] *he promised...in a little time* Evans and Chevers were both released in 1662 on condition that they immediately return to England.

John Aubrey
1626 – 1697

John Aubrey was one of the leading antiquaries of the second half of the seventeenth century, a period increasingly interested in documenting Britain's architectural, archeological, cultural, and folkloric past before it disappeared in the face of social change and political upheaval. He attended Trinity College, Oxford, though his education there was interrupted by the Civil War. In 1649 he uncovered the megalithic ruins at Avebury, ignored until that time; in 1662 he was nominated one of the original fellows of The Royal Society; and in the 1670s he made thorough antiquarian surveys of Surrey and his native Wiltshire. The only book Aubrey published in his lifetime was *Miscellanies* (1696), a collection of folklore and ghost stories. But he left a great deal of antiquarian and historical material in manuscript, much of which was used by later researchers or published after his death.

Aubrey is best known for his *Brief Lives*, a collection of biographical notes on more than four hundred British men and some women, almost all of whom lived in the sixteenth and seventeenth centuries. The *Lives* range in length from single sentences to detailed biographical sketches, and their subjects include writers (the largest group), mathematicians and scientists (the second largest), statesmen, clergymen, lawyers, physicians, educators, artists, merchants, well-known members of society, and Aubrey's own friends. Compiled over many years, Aubrey's material was originally intended as a contribution to Anthony à Wood's *Athenae Oxoniensis*. But after quarrelling with the difficult Wood over the use he was making of these notes, Aubrey withdrew them, and the *Lives* remained in manuscript until they were first published in the nineteenth century. Though he has been criticized for inaccuracy and credulity, Aubrey took his research seriously, interviewing friends, descendants, and relatives of his subjects, as well as checking local records and legal documents. But his *Lives* are famous less for their biographical facts than for Aubrey's shrewd eye for the character-revealing detail, and for his willingness to record the anecdotes, rumours, and scandals that vividly reveal the personalities of the men and women whose lives he recorded. For more biographical information on Andrewes, Bacon, Hobbes (a life-long friend of Aubrey's), Marvell, and Milton, see the headnotes to the selections from their works.

❦❦❦

Brief Lives
(excerpts)

LANCELOT ANDREWES (1555–1626)

Lancelot Andrewes, Lord Bishop of Winton, was born in London; went to school at Merchant Taylor's school. Mr. Mulcaster was his schoolmaster, whose picture he hung in his study.

Old Mr. Sutton…was his school fellow, and said that Lancelot Andrewes was a great long boy of 18 years old at least before he went to the university.

The Puritan faction did begin to increase in those days, and especially at Emmanuel College. This party had a great mind to draw in this learned young man, whom (if they could make theirs) they knew would be a great honour to them. They carried themselves outwardly with great sanctity and strictness. They preached up very strict keeping and observing the Lord's day: made, upon the matter, damnation to break it, and that 'twas less sin to kill a man. Yet these hypocrites did bowl in a private green at their college every Sunday after sermon; and one of the college (a loving friend to Mr. L. Andrewes) to satisfy him, one time lent him the key of a private back door to the bowling green, on a Sunday evening, which he opening, discovered these zealous preachers with their gowns off, earnest at play. But they were strangely surprised to see the entry of one that was not of *the brotherhood*.

There was then at Cambridge a good fat Alderman that was wont to sleep at church, which the Alderman endeavoured to prevent but could not. Well! this was preached against as a sign of *reprobation*. The good man was exceedingly troubled at it, and went to Andrewes his chamber to be satisfied in point of conscience. Mr. Andrewes told him, that it was an ill habit of body, not of mind, and that it was against his will; advised him on Sundays to make a more sparing meal, and to mend it at supper. The Alderman did so, but sleep comes on again for all that, and was preached at; comes again to be resolved with tears in his eyes. Andrewes then told him he would have him make a good hearty meal as he was wont to do, and presently take out his full sleep. He did so, came to St. Mary's where the Preacher was prepared with a sermon to damn all who slept at sermon, a certain sign of reprobation. The good Alderman, having taken his full nap before, looks on the preacher all sermon time, and spoiled the design. But I should have said that Andrewes was most extremely spoken against and preached against for offering to assoil or excuse a sleeper in sermon time.[1] But he had learning and wit enough to defend himself.

His good learning quickly made him known in the University, and also to King James, who much valued him for it, and advanced him, and at last made him Bishop of Winchester: which bishopric he ordered with great prudence as to government of the parsons, preferring of ingenious persons that were staked to poor livings and did *delitescere* [lie hidden]. He made it his enquiry to find out such men. Amongst several others (whose names have

escaped my memory) Nicholas Fuller (he wrote *Critica Sacra*), Minister of Allington, near Amesbury in Wilts, was one. The Bishop sent for him, and the poor man was afraid and knew not what hurt he had done. Makes him sit down to dinner and, after the dessert, was brought in, in a dish, his Institution and Induction, or the donation of a Prebend; which was his way...

He had not that smooth way of oratory, as now. It was a shrewd and severe animadversion of a Scottish Lord, who, when King James asked him how he liked Bishop Andrewes' sermon, said that he was learned, but he did play with his text, as a Jack-an-apes does, who takes up a thing and tosses and plays with it, and then he takes up another, and plays a little with it. Here's a pretty thing, and there's a pretty thing!

SIR FRANCIS BACON (1561–1626)

In his Lordship's prosperity, Sir Fulke Greville, Lord Brooke was his great friend and acquaintance; but when he was in disgrace and want, he was so unworthy as to forbid his butler to let him have any more small beer, which he had often sent for, his stomach being nice, and the small beer of Gray's Inn not liking his palate. This has done his memory more dishonour than Sir Philip Sidney's friendship engraven on his monument hath done him honour....[2]

Mr. Ben Jonson was one of his friends and acquaintance, as doth appear by his excellent verses on his Lordship's birthday, and in his *Underwoods*, where he gives him a character, and concludes that about his time and within his view were born all the wits that could honour a nation or help study.

The learned and great Cardinal Richelieu was a great admirer of the Lord Bacon....

---

[1] *assoil* absolve, pardon, forgive (*OED*).

[2] *his monument* Fulke Greville (1554–1628) described himself on his monument as "Servant to Queen Elizabeth, Counsellor to King James, Friend to Sir Philip Sidney."

Mr. Thomas Hobbes was beloved by his Lordship, who was wont to have him walk with him in his delicate groves where he did meditate: and when a notion darted into his mind, Mr. Hobbes was presently to write it down, and his Lordship was wont to say that he did it better than anyone else about him; for that many times, when he read their notes he scarce understood what they writ, because they understood it not clearly themselves.

In short, all that were great and good loved and honoured him....

At every meal, according to the season of the year, he had his table strewed with sweet herbs and flowers, which he said did refresh his spirits and memory.

When his Lordship was at his country house at Gorhambery, St. Albans, [it] seemed as if the court were there, so nobly did he live. His servants had liveries with his crest (a boar); his watermen were more employed by gentlemen than any other, even the King's....

He was wont to say to his servant Hunt (who was a notable thrifty man, and loved the world...), "The world was made for man, Hunt; and not man for the world."

None of his servants durst appear before him without Spanish leather boots; for he would smell the neat's leather, which offended him....

He was a παιδεραστής [paiderastes].[1] His Ganymedes and favourites took bribes; but his Lordship always gave judgement *secundum aequum et bonum* [according as was just and good]. His decrees in Chancery stand firm, i.e. there are fewer of his decrees reversed than of any other Chancellor.

His dowager married her gentleman-usher Sir Thomas (I think) Underhill, whom she made deaf

and blind with too much of Venus. She was living since the beheading of the late King.

He had a uterine brother, Anthony Bacon, who was a very great statesman, and much beyond his brother Francis for the politics, a lame man; he was a pensioner to and lived with the Earl of Essex. And to him he dedicates the first edition of his *Essayes*, a little book no bigger than a primer, which I have seen in the Bodleian Library....

He had a delicate, lively, hazel eye; Dr. Harvey told me it was like the eye of a viper....

The Bishop of London did cut down a noble cloud of trees at Fulham. The Lord Chancellor told him that he was a good expounder of dark places.

Upon his being in disfavour his servants suddenly went away; he compared them to the flying of the vermin when the house was falling....

Within the bounds of the walls of this old city of Verulam (his Lordship's Baronry) was Verulam House; which his Lordship built, the most ingeniously contrived little pile that ever I saw. No question but his Lordship was the chiefest architect; but he had for his assistant a favourite of his, a St. Albans' man, Mr. Dobson, who was his Lordship's right hand....

This house did cost nine or ten thousand [pounds] the building, and was sold about 1665 or 1666 by Sir Harbottle Grimston, Baronet, to two carpenters for four hundred pounds; of which they made eight hundred pounds. I am sorry I measured not the front and breadth; but I little suspected it would be pulled down for the sale of the materials....

The garden is large, which was (no doubt) rarely planted and kept in his Lordship's time. Here is a handsome door, which opens into oak wood; over this door in golden letters on blue are six verses.

The oaks of this wood are very great and shady. His Lordship much delighted himself here: under every tree, he planted some fine flower, or flowers,

---

[1] Latin *paederastes*; the older/active partner in a sexual relationship between men of unequal ages. But not the English "pederast": Aubrey claims that Bacon's partners were not boys but young men (his "Ganymedes," from the name of the young man beloved by Zeus in Greek mythology, were old enough to take bribes).

some whereof are there still (1656) viz. peonies, tulips.

From this wood a door opens into a place as big as an ordinary park, the west part whereof is coppice wood,[1] where are walks cut out as straight as a line, and broad enough for a coach, a quarter of a mile long or better. Here his Lordship much meditated, his servant Mr. Bushell attending him with his pen and ink horn to set down his present notions.

The east of this parquet was heretofore, in his Lordship's prosperity, a paradise; now is a large ploughed field. The walks, both in the coppices and other boscages,[2] were most ingeniously designed: at several good views were erected elegant summer houses well built of Roman architecture, well wainscotted and ceiled; yet standing, but defaced, so that one would have thought the Barbarians had made a conquest here.

The figures of the ponds were thus: they were pitched at the bottoms with pebbles of several colours, which were worked in to several figures, as of fishes, etc., which in his Lordship's time were plainly to be seen through the clear water, now over-grown with flags and rushes. If a poor body had brought his Lordship half a dozen pebbles of a curious colour, he would give them a shilling, so curious was he in perfecting his fishponds, which I guess do contain four acres. In the middle of the middlemost pond, in the island, is a curious banqueting house of Roman architecture, paved with black and white marble; covered with Cornish slate, and neatly wainscotted....

In April, and the springtime, his Lordship would, when it rained, take his coach (open) to receive the benefit of irrigation, which he was wont to say was very wholesome because of the nitre in the air and the Universal Spirit of the world.

Mr. Hobbes told me that the cause of his Lordship's death was trying an experiment; viz. as he was taking the air in a coach with Dr. Witherborne (a Scotchman, physician to the King) towards Highgate, snow lay on the ground, and it came into my Lord's thoughts, why flesh might not be preserved in snow, as in salt. They were resolved they would try the experiment presently. They alighted out of the coach and went into a poor woman's house at the bottom of Highgate hill, and bought a hen, and made the woman exenterate it,[3] and then stuffed the body with snow, and my Lord did help to do it himself. The snow so chilled him that he immediately fell so extremely ill, that he could not return to his lodging (I suppose then at Gray's Inn) but went to the Earl of Arundel's house at Highgate, where they put him into a good bed warmed with a pan, but it was a damp bed that had not been lain in about a year before, which gave him such a cold that in two or three days as I remember Mr. Hobbes told me, he died of suffocation.

This October, 1681, it rang over all St. Albans that Sir Harbottle Grimston, Master of the Rolls, had removed the coffin of this most renowned Lord Chancellor to make room for his own to lie-in in the vault there at St. Michael's church.

VENETIA DIGBY (1600-33) [4]

Venetia Stanley was the daughter of Sir Edward Stanley. She was a most beautiful desirable creature, and being *matura viro* [ready for a man] was left by her father to live with a tenant and servants at Enston Abbey in Oxfordshire: but as private as that

---

[1] *coppice*   a small wood or thicket grown for the purpose of periodic cutting (*OED*).

[2] *boscages*   thickets or groves (*OED*).

[3] *extenterate*   a latinism not in the *OED*; from context, eviscerate.

[4] One of the famous beauties of the age, Venetia Stanley secretly married Sir Kenelm Digby in 1625; her death prompted commemorative verse by many prominent poets of the period, including Ben Jonson.

place was, it seems her beauty could not lie hid. The young eagles had espied her, and she was sanguine and tractable, and of much suavity (which to abuse was great pity).[1]

In those days, Richard, Earl of Dorset (eldest son and heir to the Lord Treasurer) lived in the greatest splendor of any nobleman in England. Among other pleasures that he enjoyed, Venus was not the least. This pretty creature's fame quickly came to his Lordship's ears, who made no delay to catch at such an opportunity.

I have now forgot who first brought her to town, but I have heard my uncle Danvers say (who was her contemporary) that she was so commonly courted, and that by Grandees, that 'twas written over her lodging one night in *literis uncialibus* [capital letters]:

PRAY COME NOT NEAR,
FOR DAME VENETIA STANLEY LODGETH HERE.

The Earl of Dorset aforesaid was her greatest gallant, who was extremely enamoured of her, and had one, if not more children by her. He settled on her an annuity of 500 pounds per annum.

Among other young sparks of that time, Sir Kenelm Digby grew acquainted with her, and fell so much in love with her that he married her, much against the good will of his mother, but he would say that a wise man, and lusty, could make an honest woman out of a brothel house.

Sir Edmund Wild had her picture (and you may imagine was very familiar with her) which picture is now at Droitwich, in Worcestershire, at an Inn in an entertaining room, where now the town keep their meetings. Also at Mr. Rose's, a jeweller in Henrietta Street in Convent Garden, is an excellent piece of hers, drawn after she was newly dead.

She had a most lovely and sweet turned face, delicate dark brown hair. She had a perfect healthy constitution; strong; good skin; well proportioned; much inclining to a *Bona Roba* (near altogether).[2] Her face, a short oval; dark brown eyebrow, about which much sweetness, as also in the opening of her eyelids. The colour of her cheeks was just that of the damask rose, which is neither too hot nor too pale. She was of a just stature, not very tall.

Sir Kenelm had several pictures of her by Vandyke, &c. He had her hands cast in plaster, and her feet and face. See Ben Jonson's second volume, where he hath made her live in poetry, in his drawing of her both body and mind:

> Sitting, and ready to be drawn,
> What makes these tiffany, silks, and lawn,
> Embroideries, feathers, fringes, lace,
> When every limb takes like a face! etc.[3]

When these verses were made she had three children by Sir Kenelm, who are there mentioned, viz. Kenelm, George and John.

She died in her bed, suddenly. Some suspected that she was poisoned. When her head was opened there was found but little brain, which her husband imputed to her drinking of viper-wine;[4] but spiteful women would say 'twas a viper husband who was jealous of her that she would steal a leap. I have heard some say, e.g. my cousin Elizabeth Falkner, that after her marriage she redeemed her honour by her strict living. Once a year the Earl of Dorset invited her and Sir Kenelm to dinner, where the Earl would behold her with much passion, and only kiss her hand.

About 1676 or 5, as I was walking through Newgate Street, I saw Dame Venetia's bust from off

---

[2] *Bona Roba* defined by John Florio in the sixteenth century as "a good wholesome plum-cheeked wench" (*OED* bona-roba).

[3] The first four lines from the third song (of ten) of Jonson's "Eupheme; or the Fair Fame Left to Posterity of that Truly-Noble Lady, the Lady Venetia Digby."

[4] *viper-wine* wine medicated by an extract obtained from vipers, supposedly lending it restorative powers (*OED* viper 5).

---

[1] *suavity* sweetness and agreeableness (*OED*).

her tomb standing at a stall at the Golden Cross, a brazier's shop. I perfectly remembered it, but the fire had got off the gilding; but taking notice of it to one that was with me, I could never see it afterwards exposed to the street. They melted it down. How these curiosities would be quite forgot, did not such idle fellows as I am put them down.

THOMAS FAIRFAX (1612–71) [1]

Thomas, Lord Fairfax of Cameron, Lord General of the Parliament army. When Oxford was surrendered, the first thing General Fairfax did was to set a good guard of soldiers to preserve the Bodleian Library. 'Tis said there was more hurt done by the Cavaliers (during their garrison) by way of embezzling and cutting off chains of books, than there was since. He was a lover of learning, and had he not taken this special care, that noble library had been utterly destroyed, for there were ignorant Senators enough who would have been contented to have had it so.

THOMAS HOBBES (1588–1679)

The day of his birth was April the fifth, Anno Domini 1588, on a Friday morning, which that year was Good Friday. His mother fell in labour with him upon the fright of the invasion of the Spaniards....

At fourteen years of age, he went away a good school scholar to Magdalen Hall, in Oxford. It is not to be forgotten that before he went to the University, he had turned Euripides' *Medea* out of Greek into Latin iambics, which he presented to his Master. Mr. H. told me that he would fain have had them, to see how he did grow. Twenty odd years ago I searched all old Mr. Latimer's papers,

but could not find them; the oven had devoured them.

At Oxford Mr. T. H. used, in the summer time especially, to rise very early in the morning, and would tie the leaden counters with packthreads, which he did besmear with birdlime, and bait then with parings of cheese, and the jackdaws would spy them a vast distance up in the air, and as far as Osney Abbey, and strike at the bait, and so he harled in the string, which the weight of the counter would make cling about their wings. (This story he happened to tell me, discoursing of the optics, to instance such sharpness of sight in so little an eye.) He did not much care for logic, yet he learned it, and thought himself a good disputant. He took great delight there to go to the bookbinders' shops, and lie gaping on maps.

After he had taken his Bachelor of Arts degree, the then principal of Magdalen Hall (Sir James Hussee: a great encourager of towardly youths) recommended him to his young Lord (the Earl of Devonshire) when he left Oxon, who had a conceit that he should profit more in his learning if he had a scholar of his own age to wait on him than if he had the information of a grave Doctor. He was his Lordship's page, and rode a hunting and hawking with him, and kept his privy purse.

By this way of life he had almost forgot his Latin. He therefore bought him books of an Amsterdam print that he might carry in his pocket (particularly Caesar's *Commentaries*) which he did read in the lobby, or ante-chamber, whilst his Lord was making his visits.

He spent two years in reading romances and plays, which he has often repented and said that these two years were lost of him—wherein perhaps he was mistaken too. For it might furnish him with copy of words.

The Lord Chancellor Bacon loved to converse with him. He assisted his Lordship in translating several of his essays into Latin, one, I well remem-

---

[1] Lord Fairfax, Commander-in-Chief of the Parliamentary army from 1645.

ber, is that "Of the Greatness of Cities": the rest I have forgot....

When the Parliament sat that began in April 1640 and was dissolved in May following, and in which many points of the regal power, which were necessary for the peace of the Kingdom and safety of his Majesty's person, were disputed and denied, Mr. Hobbes wrote a little treatise in English, wherein he did set forth and demonstrate, that the said powers and rights were inseparably annexed to the sovereignty, which sovereignty they did not then deny to be in the King; but it seems understood not, or would not understand, that inseparability. Of this treatise, though not printed, many gentlemen had copies, which occasioned much talk of the author; and had not his Majesty dissolved the Parliament, it had brought him in danger of his life.

Bishop Manwaring (of St. David's) preached his [Hobbes'] doctrine; for which, among others, he was sent prisoner to the Tower. Then thought Mr. Hobbes, 'tis time now for me to shift for myself, and so withdrew into France, and resided at Paris. This little manuscript treatise grew to be his book *De Cive*, and at last grew there to be the so formidable *Leviathan*; the manner of writing of which book (he told me) was thus. He said that he sometimes would set his thoughts upon researching and contemplating, always with this rule that he very much and deeply considered one thing at a time (*scilicet* [namely], a week or sometimes a fortnight). He walked much and contemplated, and he had in the head of his staff a pen and ink horn, carried always a notebook in his pocket, and as soon as a notion darted, he presently entered it into his book, or else he should perhaps have lost it. He had drawn the design of the book into chapters, etc. so he knew whereabout it would come in. Thus that book was made.

He wrote and published the *Leviathan* far from the intention either of disadvantage to his Majesty, or to flatter Oliver [Cromwell] (who was not made Protector till three or four years after) on purpose to facilitate his return; for there is scarce a page in it that he does not upbraid him.

His Majesty was displeased with him (at Paris) for a while, but not very long, by means of some's complaining of and misconstruing his writing. But his Majesty had a good opinion of him, and said openly, that he thought Mr. Hobbes never meant him hurt....

It happened, about two or three days after his Majesty's happy return, that, as he was passing in his coach through the Strand, Mr. Hobbes was standing at Little Salisbury House gate (where his Lord then lived). The King espied him, put off his hat very kindly to him, and asked him how he did. About a week after, he had oral conference with his Majesty at Mr. S. Cowper's, where, as he sat for his picture, he was diverted by Mr. Hobbes' pleasant discourse. Here his Majesty's favours were redintegrated to him,[1] and order was given that he should have free access to his Majesty, who was always much delighted in his wit and smart repartees.

The wits at court were wont to bait him. But he feared none of them, and would make his part good. The King would call him the bear: here comes the bear to be baited (this is too low wit to be published)....

He had very few books. I never saw (nor Sir William Petty) above half a dozen about him in his chamber. Homer and Virgil were commonly on his Table; sometimes Xenophon, or some probable history, and Greek Testament, or so.

He had read much, if one considers his long life; but his contemplation was much more than his reading. He was wont to say that if he had read as much as other men, he should have known no more than other men.

He was wont to say that he had rather have the advice, or take physic from an experienced old

---

[1] *redintegrated* restored (OED).

woman, that had been at many sick people's bed-sides, than from the learnedst but unexperienced physician.

'Tis not consistent with an harmonical soul to be a woman-hater, neither had he an abhorrence to good wine, but he was, even in his youth (generally) temperate, both as to wine and women....

For his last 30+ years, his diet, etc., was very moderate and regular. He rose about seven, had his breakfast of bread and butter; and took his walk, meditating till ten; then he did put down the minutes of his thoughts, which he penned in the afternoon. He thought much and with excellent method and steadiness, which made him seldom make a false step....

When Mr. T. Hobbes was sick in France, the divines came to him, and tormented him (both Roman Catholic, Church of England, and Geneva). Said he to them, let me alone, or else I will detect all your cheats from Aaron to yourselves....

There was a report (and surely true) that in Parliament, not long after the King was settled, some of the Bishops made a motion to have the good old gentleman burnt for a heretic. Which, he hearing, feared that his papers might be searched by their order, and he told me he had burnt part of them; among other things, a poem, in Latin hexameter and pentameter, of the encroachment of the clergy (both Roman and Reformed) on the civil power.

That he was a Christian 'tis clear, for he received the sacrament of Dr. Pierson, and in his confession to Dr. John Cosins, on his (as he thought) death-bed, declared that he liked the religion of the Church of England best of all other....

Mr. Benjamin Jonson, Poet Laureate, was his loving and familiar friend and acquaintance....

When he was at Florence, he contracted a friendship with the famous Galileo Galilei, whom he extremely venerated and magnified; and not only as he was a prodigious wit, but for his sweetness of nature and manners. They pretty well resembled one another as to their countenances, as by their pictures doth appear; were both cheerful and melancholic sanguine; and had both a consimility of Fate, to be hated and persecuted by the ecclesiastics....

Mr. John Dryden, Poet Laureate, is his great admirer, and oftentimes makes use of his doctrine in his plays (from Mr. Dryden himself)....

He fell sick about the middle of October 1679. His disease was the stranguary,[1] and the physicians judged it incurable by reason of his great age and natural decay. About the 20th of November, my Lord being to remove from Chatsworth to Hard-wick, Mr. Hobbes would not be left behind; and therefore with a featherbed laid into the coach, upon which he lay warm clad, he was conveyed safely, and was in appearance as well after that little journey as before it. But seven or eight days after, his whole right side was taken with the dead palsy, and at the same time he was made speechless. He lived after this seven days, taking very little nourishment, slept well, and by intervals endeavoured to speak, but could not. In the whole time of his sickness he was free from fever. He seemed therefore to die rather for want of the fuel of life (which was spent in him) and mere weakness and decay, than by the power of his disease, which was thought to be only an effect of his age and weakness. He was put into a woollen shroud and coffin, which was covered with a white sheet, and upon that a black hearse cloth, and so carried upon men's shoulders, a little mile to church. The company, consisting of the family and neighbours that came to his funeral, and attended him to his grave, were very hand-somely entertained with wine, burned and raw, cake, biscuit, etc.

---

[1] *stranguary* a disease of the urinary tract.

ROBERT HOOKE (1635–1703) [1]

Mr Robert Hooke, curator of The Royal Society at London, was borne at Freshwater in the Isle of Wight; his father was minister there....

John Hoskyns, the painter, being at Freshwater to draw pictures, Mr. Hooke observed what he did, and, thought he, why cannot I do so too? So he gets him chalk, and ruddle,[2] and coal, and grinds them, and puts them on a trencher, got a pencil, and to work he went, and made a picture: then he copied (as they hung up in the parlour) the pictures there, which he made like. Also, being a boy there, at Freshwater, he made a dial on a round trencher; never having had any instruction. His father was not mathematical at all.

When his father died, his son Robert was but thirteen years old, to whom he left one hundred pounds, which was sent up to London with him, with an intention to have bound him apprentice to Mr. [Peter] Lilly the painter, with whom he was a little while upon trial; who liked him very well, but Mr. Hooke quickly perceived what was to be done, so, thought he, why cannot I do this by myself and keep my hundred pounds?

He went to Mr. Busby's the schoolmaster of Westminster, at whose house he was; and he made very much of him. With him he lodged his hundred pounds. There he learned to play twenty lessons on the organ. He there in one week's time made himself master of the first six books of Euclid, to the admiration of Mr. Busby. At school here he was very mechanical, and (amongst other things) he invented thirty several ways of flying....

Anno Domini 1658 he was sent to Christ Church in Oxford, where he had a chorister's place (in those days when the church music was put down) which was a pretty good maintenance. He

lay in the chamber in Christ Church that was Mr. [Robert] Burton's, of whom 'tis whispered that, *non obstante* [notwithstanding] all his astrology and his book of *Melancholy*, he ended his days in that chamber by hanging himself.

He was there assistant to Dr. Thomas Willis in his chemistry; who afterwards recommended him to the Honourable Robert Boyle, Esquire, to be useful to him in his chemical operations. Anno Domini 1662 Mr. Robert Boyle recommended Mr. Robert Hooke to be Curator of the Experiments of The Royal Society, wherein he did an admirable good work to the Commonwealth of Learning, in recommending the fittest person in the world to them.

Anno Domini 1666 the great conflagration of London happened, and then he was chosen one of the two Surveyors of the city of London; by which he hath got a great estate. He built Bedlam, the Physicians' College, Montague House, the pillar on Fish Street Hill, and Theatre there; and he is much made use of in designing buildings....

As he is of prodigious inventive head, so is a person of great virtue and goodness. Now when I have said his inventive faculty is so great, you cannot imagine his memory to be excellent, for they are like two buckets, as one goes up, the other goes down. He is certainly the greatest mechanic this day in the world.

'Twas Mr. Robert Hooke that invented the pendulum watches, so much more useful than the other watches. He hath invented an engine for the speedy working of division, etc., or for the speedy and immediate finding out the divisor.

Before I leave this town, I will get of him a catalogue of what he hath wrote; and as much of his inventions as I can. But they are many hundreds; he believes not fewer than a thousand. 'Tis such a hard matter to get people to do themselves right.

Mr. Robert Hooke did in Anno 1670 write a discourse called *An Attempt to Prove the Motion of the Earth*, which he then read to The Royal Society;

---

[1] scientist, architect, astronomer, and inventor; Secretary of The Royal Society, 1677–82.

[2] *ruddle* a red ochre, used for marking sheep (*OED*).

wherein he has delivered the theory of explaining the celestial motions mechanically: his words are these: "I shall explain a system of the world, differing in many particulars from any yet known, answering in all things to the common rules of mechanical motions. This depends upon three suppositions; first, that all celestial bodies whatsoever have an attractive or gravitating power towards their own centers, whereby they attract not only their own parts, and keep them from flying from them, as we may observe the Earth to do, but that they do also attract all the other celestial bodies that are within the sphere of their activity, and consequently that not only the Sun and the Moon have an influence upon the body and motion of the Earth, and the Earth upon them, but that Mercury also, Venus, Mars, Saturn, and Jupiter, by their attractive powers have a considerable influence upon its motion, as, in the same manner, the corresponding attractive power of the Earth hath a considerable influence upon every one of their motions also. The second supposition is this, that all bodies whatsoever that are put into direct and simple motion will so continue to move forwards in a straight line, till they are by some other effectual powers deflected and bent into a motion describing a circle, ellipsis, or some other uncompounded curve line. The third supposition is, that these attractive powers are so much the more powerful in operating, by how much nearer the body wrought upon is to their own centers."

About nine or ten years ago, Mr. Hooke wrote to Mr. Isaac Newton, of Trinity College, Cambridge, to make a demonstration of this theory, not telling him, at first, the proportion of the gravity to the distance, nor what was the curved line that was thereby made. Mr. Newton, in his answer to the letter, did express that he had not thought of it; and in his first attempt about it, he calculated the curve by supposing the attraction to be the same at all distances: upon which Mr. Hooke sent, in his next letter, the whole of his hypothesis, *scil.* that the gravitation was reciprocal to the square of the distance: which is the whole celestial theory, concerning which Mr. Newton has made a demonstration, not at all owning he received the first intimation of it from Mr. Hooke. Likewise Mr. Newton has in the same book printed some other theories and experiments of Mr. Hooke's, without acknowledging from whom he had them. This is the greatest discovery in nature that ever was since the world's creation. It never was so much as hinted by any man before. I wish he had writ plainer, and afforded a little more paper.

Andrew Marvell (1621–78)

He was of middling stature, pretty strong set, roundish faced, cherry cheeked, hazel eye, brown hair. He was in his conversation very modest, and of very few words: and though he loved wine he would never drink hard in company, and was wont to say that, he would not play the goodfellow in any man's company in whose hands he would not trust his life. He had not a general acquaintance.

In the time of Oliver the Protector he was Latin Secretary. He was a great master of the Latin tongue; an excellent poet in Latin or English: for Latin verses there was no man could come into competition with him.

I remember I have heard him say that the Earl of Rochester was the only man in England that had the true vein of satire.

His native town of Hull loved him so well that they elected him for their representative in Parliament, and gave him an honourable pension to maintain him.

He kept bottles of wine at his lodging, and many times he would drink liberally by himself to refresh his spirits, and exalt his muse....

Obiit Londini [died London], Aug. 18, 1678; and is buried in St. Giles Church in-the-fields about the middle of the south aisle. Some suspect that he was poisoned by the Jesuits, but I cannot be positive.

SIR ROBERT MORAY (d. 1673)

Sir Robert Moray, Knight, was of the ancient family of the Morays in Scotland. He was born (as I take it) in the Highlands. The Highlanders (like the Swedes) can make their own clothes; and I have heard Sir Robert say that he could do it. I have heard some of Oliver Cromwell's army say, that the Highlanders ate only oatmeal and water and milk: that their rivers did abound with trouts but they had not the wit to take them till the English taught 'em.

He spent most of his time in France. After his juvenile education at school and the University he betook himself to military employment in the service of Louis the 13th. He was at last a Lieutenant Colonel. He was a great master of the Latin tongue and was very well read. They say he was an excellent soldier.

He was far from the rough humour of the camp-breeding, for he was a person the most obliging about the Court and the only man that would do a kindness gratis upon an account of friendship. A lackey could not have been more obsequious and diligent. What I do now aver I know to be true upon my own score as well as others. He was a most humble and good man, and as free from covetousness as a Carthusian. He was abstemious and abhorred women. His Majesty was wont to tease at him. 'Twas pity he was a Presbyterian.

He was the chief appuy of his countrymen and their good angel.[1] There had been formerly a great friendship between him and the Duke of Lauderdale, till, about a year or two before his death, he went to the Duke on his return from Scotland and told him plainly that he had betrayed his country.

He was one of the first contrivers and institutors of The Royal Society and was our first President, and performed his charge in the Chair very well.

He was my most honoured and obliging friend, and I was more obliged to him than to all the courtiers besides. I had a great loss in his death, for, had he lived, he would have got some employment or other for me before this time. He had the King's ear as much as anyone, and was indefatigable in his undertakings. I was often with him. I was with him three hours the morning he died; he seemed to be well enough. I remember he drank at least 1/2 pint of fair water, according to his usual custom.

His lodging where he died was the leaded pavilion in the garden at Whitehall. He died suddenly July 4th about 8 hours p.m. A.D. 1673. Had but one shilling in his pocket, i.e. in all. The King buried him. He lies by Sir William Davenant in Westminster Abbey.

He was a good chemist and assisted his Majesty in his chemical operations.

JOHN MILTON (1608–74)

Mr. John Milton was of an Oxfordshire family. His grandfather was a Roman Catholic of Holton, in Oxfordshire, near Shotover.

His father was brought up in the University of Oxon, at Christ Church, and his grandfather disinherited him because he kept not to the Catholic religion (he found a Bible in English, in his chamber). So thereupon he came to London, and became a scrivener (brought up by a friend of his; was not an apprentice) and got a plentiful estate by it, and left it off many years before he died. He was an ingenious man; delighted in music; composed many songs now in print, especially that of "Oriana." I have been told that the father composed a song of fourscore parts for the Lantgrave of Hess, for which his Highness sent a medal of gold, or a

---

[1] *appuy* support, prop (*OED* appui).

noble present. He died about 1647; buried in Cripplegate church from his house in the Barbican.

His son John was born the 9th of December, 1608, *die Veneris* [Friday], half an hour after six in the morning, in Bread Street, in London, at the Spread Eagle, which was his house (he had also in that street another house, the Rose; and other houses in other places). Anno Domini 1619, he was ten years old; and was then a poet. His schoolmaster then was a Puritan, in Essex, who cut his hair short.

He went to school to old Mr. Gill, at Paul's school. Went, at his own charge only, to Christ's College in Cambridge at fifteen, where he stayed eight years at least. Then he traveled into France and Italy (had Sir Henry Wotton's commendatory letters). At Geneva he contracted a great friendship with the learned Dr. Deodati of Geneva. He was acquainted with Sir Henry Wotton, Ambassador at Venice, who delighted in his company. He was several years beyond sea, and returned to England just upon the breaking out of the Civil Wars.

From his brother, Christopher Milton: when he went to school, when he was very young, he studied very hard, and sat up very late, commonly till twelve or one o'clock at night, and his father ordered the maid to sit up for him, and in those years (10) composed many copies of verses which might well become a riper age. And was a very hard student in the University, and performed all his exercises there with very good applause. His first tutor there was Mr. Chapell; from whom receiving some unkindness (whipped him) he was afterwards (though it seemed contrary to the rules of the College) transferred to the tuition of one Mr. Tovell, who died Parson of Lutterworth. He went to travel about the year 1638 and was abroad about a year's space, chiefly in Italy.

Immediately after his return he took a lodging at Mr Russell's, a tailor, in St. Bride's Churchyard,

and took into his tuition his sister's two sons, Edward and John Philips, the first ten, the other nine years of age; and in a year's time made them capable of interpreting a Latin author at sight. And within three years they went through the best of Latin and Greek poets—Lucretius and Manilius, of the Latins (and with him the use of the globes, and some rudiments of arithmetic and geometry) Hesiod, Aratus, Dionysius Afer, Oppian, Apollonii *Argonautica*, and Quintus Calaber. Cato, Varro and Columella *De re rustica* were the very first authors they learned. As he was severe on the one hand, so he was most familiar and free in his conversation to those to whom most sour in his way of education. N.B. he made his nephews songsters, and sing, from the time they were with him.

His first wife (Mrs. Powell, a Royalist) was brought up and lived where there was a great deal of company and merriment, dancing, etc. And when she came to live with her husband, at Mr. Russell's, in St. Bride's Churchyard, she found it very solitary; no company came to her; oftimes heard his nephews beaten and cry. This life was irksome to her, and so she went to her parents at Fost-hill. He sent for her, after some time; and I think his servant was evilly entreated: but as for matter of wronging his bed, I never heard the least suspicions; nor had he, of that, any jealousy.

Two opinions do not well on the same bolster; she was a Royalist, and went to her mother to the King's quarters, near Oxford. I have perhaps so much charity to her that she might not wrong his bed: but what man, especially contemplative, would like to have a young wife environed and stormed by the sons of Mars, and those of the enemy party? He parted from her, and wrote the Triplechord about divorce.[1]

He had a middle wife, whose name was Katharine Woodcock. No child living by her.

---

[1] *Triplechord* referring to *Tetrachordon* (1645), one of Milton's four pamphlets about divorce.

He married his third wife, Elizabeth Minshull, the year before the sickness: a gentle person, a peaceful and agreeable humour.

Hath two daughters living: Deborah was his amanuensis (he taught her Latin, and to read Greek to him when he had lost his eyesight).

His sight began to fail him at first upon his writing against Salmasius, and before 'twas full completed one eye absolutely failed. Upon the writing of other books, after that, his other eye decayed. His eyesight was decaying about twenty years before his death. His father read without spectacles at 84. His mother had very weak eyes, and used spectacles presently after she was thirty years old.

His harmonical and ingenious soul did lodge in a beautiful and well proportioned body. He was a spare man. He was scarce so tall as I am (of middle stature).

He had brown hair. His complexion exceeding fair—he was so fair that they called him "the Lady of Christ's College." Oval face. His eye a dark gray.

He was very healthy and free from all diseases: seldom took any physic (only sometimes he took manna):[1] only towards his latter end he was visited with the gout, spring and fall.

He had a delicate tuneable voice, and had good skill. His father instructed him. He had an organ in his house; he played on that most. Of a very cheerful humour. He would be cheerful even in his gout fits, and sing.

He had a very good memory; but I believe that his excellent method of thinking and disposing did much to help his memory.

His widow has his picture, drawn very well and like, when a Cambridge scholar, which ought to be engraven; for the Pictures before his books are not at all like him.

His exercise was chiefly walking. He was an early riser (*scil.* at four o'clock *manè* [in the morning]), yea, after he lost his sight. He had a man to read to him. The first thing he read was the Hebrew bible, and that was at four *manè*, 1/2 hour plus. Then he contemplated.

At seven his man came to him again, and then read to him again, and wrote till dinner; the writing was as much as the reading. His daughter, Deborah, could read to him in Latin, Italian and French, and Greek. Married in Dublin to one Mr. Clark (sells silk, etc.) very like her father. The other sister is Mary, more like her mother.

After dinner he used to walk three or four hours at a time (he always had a garden where he lived) went to bed about nine.

Temperate man, rarely drank between meals. Extreme pleasant in his conversation, and at dinner, supper, etc.; but satirical. (He pronounced the letter "R" very hard—a certain sign of a satirical wit—from John Dryden.)

All the time of writing his *Paradise Lost*, his vein began at the autumnal equinoctial, and ceased at the vernal or thereabouts (I believe about May) and this was four or five years of his doing it. He began about two years before the King came in, and finished about three years after the King's Restoration.

In the fourth book of *Paradise Lost* there are about six verses of Satan's exclamation to the Sun, which Mr. E. Philips remembers about 15 or 16 years before ever his poem was thought of, which verses were intended for the beginning of a tragedy which he had designed, but was diverted from it by other business.

He was visited much by the learned; more than he did desire. He was mightily importuned to go into France and Italy. Foreigners came much to see him, and much admired him, and offered to him great preferments to come over to them; and the only inducement of several foreigners that came

---

[1] *manna* a medicinal juice obtained from the bark of the Manna-ash or other plants (*OED* manna 4).

over into England, was chiefly to see Oliver Protector, and Mr. John Milton; and would see the house and chamber where he was born. He was much more admired abroad than at home.

His familiar learned acquaintance were Mr. Andrew Marvell, Mr. Skinner, Dr. Pagett, M.D.

John Dryden, esq., Poet Laureate, who very much admires him, went to him to have leave to put his *Paradise Lost* into a drama in rhyme. Mr. Milton received him civilly, and told him *he would give him leave to tag his verses*.

His widow assures me that Mr. T. Hobbes was not one of his acquaintance, that her husband did not like him at all, but he would acknowledge him to be a man of great parts, and a learned man. Their interests and tenets did run counter to each other.

Whatever he wrote against monarchy was out of no animosity to the King's person, or out of any faction or interest, but out of a pure zeal to the liberty of mankind, which he thought would be greater under a free state than under a monarchical government. His being so conversant in Livy and the Roman authors, and the greatness he saw done by the Roman Commonwealth, and the virtue of their great commanders, induced him to [this belief].

—(WRITTEN CA. 1667–1692)

Dorothy Osborne
1627 – 1695

Dorothy Osborne was born in Bedfordshire, the daughter of Sir Peter Osborne and Lady Dorothy Danvers. At the age of twenty-one, she travelled with her brother to St. Malo, where her father, the Lieutenant-Governor of Guernsey, defended a garrison for the King. They stopped at an inn on the Isle of Wight, where Osborne met and fell in love with Sir William Temple (1628–1699), who was en route to France. Though Temple had been brought up by his uncle, the renowned theologian and Royalist Dr. Henry Hammond, his father sat in the Long Parliament and held an office in Ireland under Cromwell. When Sir John Temple heard that his son had accompanied Osborne to St. Malo, he instructed him to continue to Paris posthaste. In 1649, Osborne returned with her father to England, retiring to the family ancestral home, Chicksands, in Bedfordshire.

Though they rarely saw one another, Osborne and Temple continued their courtship, at times through secret correspondence, for seven years. Both families hoped for wealthier partners for their children, and opposed the match. During her extended courtship, Osborne rejected numerous suitors including Henry Cromwell, son of the Lord Protector. Shortly after the death of her father in March 1654,

Osborne insisted that her engagement to Temple be made public, and by June negotiations for the marriage settlement had begun. Though Osborne contracted smallpox during these negotiations, she and Temple were married soon after her recovery. Over the course of her forty-year marriage, she served as ambassador's wife in Brussels, The Hague, Ireland and London, enjoyed intimate friendships with royalty, and was known as a patron of the arts. She outlived all of her children. Osborne died at Moor Park, the Temple estate in Surrey.

The love letters from Osborne to Temple written during their courtship remained unpublished until 1836, when extracts from forty-two of her letters were issued as a supplement to Thomas Courtenay's *Memoirs of the Life, Works, and Correspondence of Sir William Temple*. Temple had informed Osborne that she wrote "better than the most extraordinary person in the kingdom." Her letters have been appreciated for their expression of personal desire in the face of frustrated love, for their witty treatment of the morals and social life of the aristocracy and landed gentry during the Interregnum, and for their insight into political events of local and national significance.

ↄ৩ↄ৩

The Letters of Dorothy Osborne to Sir William Temple, 1652–54

[Saturday, January 8, 1653]

SIR, There is nothing moves my charity like gratitude; and when a beggar's thankful for a small relief, I always repent it was not more. But seriously, this place will not afford much towards the enlarging of a letter, and I am grown so dull with living in't (for I am not willing to confess that I was always so) as to need all helps. Yet you shall see I will endeavour to satisfy you, upon condition you will tell me why you quarrelled so at your last letter. I cannot guess at it, unless it were that you repented you told me so much of your story, which I am not apt to believe neither, because it would not become our friendship, a great part of it consisting (as I have been taught) in a mutual confidence. And to let you see that I believe it so, I will give you an account of myself, and begin my story, as you did yours, from our parting at Goring House.[1]

I came down hither not half so well pleased as I went up, with an engagement upon me that I had little hope of ever shaking off, for I had made use of all the liberty my friends would allow me to preserve my own, and 'twould not do; he was so weary of his, that he would part with't upon my terms. As my last refuge I got my brother to go down with him to see his house, who, when he came back, made the relation I wished. He said the seat was as ill as so good a country would permit, and the house so ruined for want of living in't, as it would ask a good proportion of time and money to make it fit for a woman to confine herself to. This (though it were not much) I was willing to take hold of, and made it considerable enough to break the engagement. I had no quarrel to his person or his fortune, but was in love with neither, and much out of love with a thing called marriage; and have since thanked God I was so, for 'tis not long since one of my brothers writ me word of him that he was killed in a duel, though since I hear that 'twas the other that was killed, and he is fled upon 't, which does not mend the matter much. Both made me glad I had 'scaped him, and sorry for his misfortune, which in earnest was the least return his many civilities to me could deserve.

Presently, after this was at an end, my mother died, and I was left at liberty to mourn her loss awhile. At length my aunt (with whom I was when you last saw me) commanded me to wait on her at London;[2] and when I came she told me how much I was in her care, how well she loved me for my mother's sake, and something for my own, and drew out a long set speech which ended in a good motion (as she called it);[3] and truly I saw no harm in 't, for by what I had heard of the gentleman I guessed he expected a better fortune than mine. And it proved so. Yet he protested he liked me so well, that he was very angry my father would not be persuaded to give a £1,000 more with me; and I him so ill, that I vowed if I had £1,000 less I should have thought it too much for him. And so we parted. Since, he has made a story with a new mistress that is worth your knowing, but too long for a letter. I'll keep it for you.

After this, some friends that had observed a gravity in my face which might become an elderly man's wife (as they termed it) and a mother-in-law, proposed a widower to me, that had four daughters, all old enough to be my sisters;[4] but he had a great estate, was as fine a gentleman as ever England bred, and the very pattern of wisdom. I that knew how much I wanted it, thought this the safest place for me to engage in, and was mightily pleased to think I had met with one at last that had wit enough for himself and me too. But shall I tell you what I thought when I knew him (you will say nothing on't): 'twas the vainest, impertinent, self-conceited learned coxcomb that ever yet I saw; to say more were to spoil his marriage, which I hear he is towards with a daughter of my Lord of Coleraine's;[5] but for his sake I shall take heed of a fine gentleman as long as I live.

Before I had quite ended with him, coming to town about that and some other occasions of my own, I fell in Sir Thomas's way;[6] and what humour took him I cannot imagine, but he made very formal addresses to me, and engaged his mother and my brother to appear in't. This bred a story pleasanter than any I have told you yet, but so long a one that I must reserve it till we meet, or make it

---

[1] *Goring House* the London residence of the Earl of Norwich.

[2] *my aunt* Osborne's maternal aunt, Lady Gargrave.

[3] *motion* proposal (*OED* motion *sb* 7a).

[4] *a widower* Sir Justinian Isham (1610–1674).

[5] *daughter of …Coleraine's* daughter of Hugh Hare, first Baron Coleraine (1606?–1667).

[6] *Sir Thomas's* Sir Thomas Osborne's; Sir Thomas was Osborne's cousin on her mother's side.

a letter of itself. Only by this you may see 'twas not for nothing he commended me, though to speak seriously, it was because it was to you. Otherwise I might have missed of his praises for we have hardly been cousins since the breaking up of that business.[1]

The next thing I desired to be rid on was a scurvy spleen that I had ever been subject to, and to that purpose was advised to drink the waters.[2] There I spent the latter end of the summer, and at my coming home found that a gentleman (who has some estate in this country) had been treating with my brother, and it yet goes on fair and softly.[3] I do not know him so well as to give you much of his character: 'tis a modest, melancholy, reserved man, whose head is so taken up with little philosophical studies, that I admire how I found a room there. 'Twas sure by chance; and unless he is pleased with that part of my humour which other people think worst, 'tis very possible the next new experiment may crowd me out again. Thus you have all my late adventures, and almost as much as this paper will hold. The rest shall be employed in telling you how sorry I am you have got such a cold. I am the more sensible of your trouble by my own, for I have newly got one myself. But I will send you that which used to cure me. 'Tis like the rest of my medicines: if it do no good, 'twill be sure to do no harm, and 'twill be no great trouble to you to eat a little on't now and then; for the taste, as it is not excellent, so 'tis not very ill. One thing more I must tell you, which is that you are not to take it ill that I mistook your age by my computation of your journey through this country; for I was persuaded t'other day that I could not be less than thirty years

old by one that believed it himself, because he was sure it was a great while since he had heard of such a one in the world

As your humble servant.

[THURSDAY-SATURDAY, JUNE 2–4, 1653]

SIR, I have been reckoning up how many faults you lay to my charge in your last letter, and I find I am severe, unjust, unmerciful, and unkind. Oh me, how should one do to mend all these! 'Tis work for an age, and 'tis to be feared I shall be so old before I am good, that 'twill not be considerable to anybody but myself whether I am so or not. I say nothing of the pretty humour you fancied me in, in your dream, because 'twas but a dream. Sure, if it had been anything else, I should have remembered that my Lord L. loves to have his chamber and his bed to himself.[4] But seriously, now, I wonder at your patience. How could you hear me talk so senselessly, though 'twere but in your sleep, and not to be ready to beat me? What nice mistaken points of honour I pretend to, and yet could allow him a room in the same bed with me! Well, dreams are pleasant things to people whose humours are so; but to have the spleen and to dream upon't, is a punishment I would not wish my greatest enemy. I seldom dream, or never remember them, unless they have been so sad as to put me into such disorder as I can hardly recover when I am awake, and some of those I am confident I shall never forget.

You ask me how I pass my time here. I can give you a perfect account not only of what I do for the present, but of what I am likely to do this seven years if I stay here so long. I rise in the morning reasonably early, and before I am ready I go round the house till I am weary of that, and then into the garden till it grows too hot for me. About ten

---

[1] *for we have...that business* Attempts had been made to arrange a marriage between Osborne and Sir Thomas.

[2] *scurvy spleen* The spleen was regarded as the seat of melancholy or ill humour; *scurvy fig.* worthless, irritating; *drink the waters* The waters at Epsom Wells in Surrey were alleged to improve fits of ill temper caused by an ailing spleen.

[3] *treating with* negotiating terms with (*OED* treating *vbl sb* 1).

[4] *Lord L.* presumably Philip, Lord Lisle (1619–1698), third Earl of Leicester, under whom Temple served.

o'clock I think of making me ready, and when that's done I go into my father's chamber, from thence to dinner, where my cousin Molle and I sit in great state in a room and at a table that would hold a great many more.[1] After dinner we sit and talk till Mr. B. comes in question, and then I am gone.[2] The heat of the day is spent in reading or working, and about six or seven o'clock I walk out into a common that lies hard by the house, where a great many young wenches keep sheep and cows, and sit in the shade singing of ballads. I go to them and compare their voices and beauties to some ancient shepherdesses that I have read of, and find a vast difference there; but, trust me, I think these are as innocent as those could be. I talk to them, and find they want nothing to make them the happiest people in the world but the knowledge that they are so. Most commonly, when we are in the midst of our discourse, one looks about her, and spies her cows going into the corn, and then away they all run as if they had wings at their heels. I, that am not so nimble, stay behind; and when I see them driving home their cattle, I think 'tis time for me to retire too. When I have supped, I go into the garden, and so to the side of a small river that runs by it, where I sit down and wish you with me (you had best say this is not kind neither). In earnest, 'tis a pleasant place, and would be much more so to me if I had your company. I sit there sometimes till I am lost with thinking; and were it not for some cruel thoughts of the crossness of our fortunes that will not let me sleep there, I should forget that there were such a thing to be done as going to bed.[3]

Since I writ this my company is increased by two, my brother Harry and a fair niece, the eldest of my brother Peyton's daughters.[4] She is so much a woman that I am almost ashamed to say I am her aunt; and so pretty, that, if I had any design to gain a servant, I should not like her company;[5] but I have none, and therefore shall endeavour to keep her here as long as I can persuade her father to spare her, for she will easily consent to it, having so much of my humour (though it be the worst in her) as to like a melancholy place and little company. My brother John is not come down again, nor am I certain when he will be here. He went from London into Gloucestershire to my sister who was very ill, and his youngest girl, of which he was very fond, is since dead.[6] But I believe by that time his wife has a little recovered her sickness and the loss of her child, he will be coming this way. My father is reasonably well, but keeps his chamber still, and will hardly, I am afraid, ever be so perfectly recovered as to come abroad again.

I am sorry for poor Walker, but you need not doubt of what he has of yours in his hands, for it seems he does not use to do his work himself.[7] I speak seriously, he keeps a Frenchman that sets all his seals and rings. If what you say of my Lady Leppington be of your own knowledge, I shall believe you, but otherwise I can assure you I have heard from people that pretend to know her very well, that her kindness to Compton was very moderate, and that she never liked him so well as when he died and gave her his estate.[8] But they might be deceived, and 'tis not so strange as that you should

---

[1] *making me ready* dressing myself (*OED* ready *a* III.13b); *my cousin Molle* Henry Molle, a distant relative.

[2] *Mr. B.* Osborne's current suitor, Levinus Bennet, Sheriff of Cambridgeshire.

[3] *crossness* opposition (*OED* crossness 2).

[4] *a fair niece* Dorothy Peyton, the daughter of Osborne's eldest sister Elizabeth (d. 1642) and her brother-in-law Thomas Peyton of Knowlton, Kent.

[5] *servant* a professed lover (*OED* servant *sb* 4b).

[6] *sister* sister-in-law.

[7] *Walker* the goldsmith who had set Osborne's seals.

[8] *If what you…his estate* In May, 1652, Colonel Henry Crompton was killed by George Brydges, Lord Chandos, in a duel fought over Mary Carey, Lady Leppington, to whom Crompton bequeathed his estates. Chandos was convicted of manslaughter.

imagine a coldness and an indifference in my letters
where I so little meant it; but I am not displeased
you should desire my kindness enough to apprehend the loss of it when it is safest. Only I would
not have you apprehend it so far as to believe it
possible—that were an injury to all the assurances
I have given you, and if you love me you cannot
think me unworthy. I should think myself so, if I
found you grew indifferent to me, that I have had
so long and so particular a friendship for; but, sure,
this is more than I need to say. You are enough in
my heart to know all my thoughts, and if so, you
know better than I can tell you how much I am

Yours.

[OCTOBER 1653]

SIR, You would have me say something of my
coming.[1] Alas! how fain I would have something to
say, but I know no more than you saw in that letter
I sent you. How willingly would I tell you anything
that I thought would please you; but I confess I do
not love to give uncertain hopes, because I do not
care to receive them. And I thought there was no
need of saying I would be sure to take the first
occasion, and that I waited with impatience for it,
because I hoped you had believed all that already;
and so you do, I am sure. Say what you will, you
cannot but know my heart enough to be assured
that I wish myself with you, for my own sake as well
as yours. 'Tis rather that you love to hear me say it
often, than that you doubt it; for I am no dissembler. I could not cry for a husband that were indifferent to me (like your cousin); no, nor for a husband that I loved neither. I think 'twould break my
heart sooner than make me shed a tear. 'Tis ordinary griefs that only make me weep. In earnest, you
cannot imagine how often I have been told that I
had too much *franchise* in my humour, and that

'twas a point of good breeding to disguise handsomely;[2] but I answered still for myself, that 'twas
not to be expected I should be exactly bred, that
had never seen a Court since I was capable of
anything. Yet I know so much—that my Lady
Carlisle would take it very ill if you should not let
her get the point of honour;[3] 'tis all she aims at, to
go beyond everybody in compliment. But are not
you afraid of giving me a strange vanity with telling
me that I write better than the most extraordinary
person in the kingdom? If I had not the sense to
understand that the reason why you like my letters
better is only because they are kinder than hers,
such a word might have undone me.

But my Lady Isabella, that speaks, and looks,
and sings, and plays, and all so prettily, why cannot
I say that she is as free from faults as her sister
believes her?[4] No; I am afraid she is not, and sorry
that those she has are so generally known. My
brother did not bring them for an example, but I
did, and made him confess she had better have
married a beggar than that beast with all his estate.
She cannot be excused; but certainly they run a
strange hazard that have such husbands as makes
them think they cannot be more undone, whatever
course they take.[5] Oh, 'tis ten thousand pities! I
remember she was the first woman that ever I took
notice of for extremely handsome; and, in earnest,
she was then the loveliest thing that could be looked
on, I think. But what should she do with beauty
now? Were I as she, I would hide myself from all

---

[1] *my coming* Osborne had hoped to travel to London.

[2] *franchise* freedom or license (*OED* franchise *sb*. II.8).

[3] *Lady Carlisle* Lucy Hay, Countess of Carlisle (1599–1660), was
praised by the poets of her day. Her beauty and wit afforded her a
central position in Charles I's Court. After Strafford's execution in
1641, she allied herself with the Parliamentarians. Her political
intrigues led to an eighteen-month imprisonment in the Tower; *point
of honour* the obligation to demand satisfaction for a wrong or an
insult (*OED* point *sb*[1] D.9).

[4] *Lady Isabella* sister of Lady Diana Rich and wife of Sir James
Thynne.

[5] *undone* ruined (*OED* undone *ppl.a*[2]).

the world; I should think all people that looked on me read it in my face and despised me in their hearts; and at the same time they made me a leg, or spoke civilly to me, I should believe they did not think I deserved their respect.[1] I'll tell you who he urged for an example though, my Lord Pembroke and my Lady, who, they say, are upon parting after all his passion for her, and his marrying her against the consent of all his friends;[2] but to that I answered, that though he pretended great kindness he had for her, I never heard of much she had for him, and knew she married him merely for advantage. Nor is she a woman of that discretion as to do all that might become her, when she must do it rather as things fit to be done than as things she is inclined to. Besides that, what with a *spleenatick* side and a *chimickall* head, he is but an odd body himself.[3]

But is it possible what they say, that my Lord Leicester and my Lady are in great disorder, and that after forty years' patience he has now taken up the cudgels and resolves to venture for the mastery?[4] Methinks he wakes out of his long sleep like a froward child, that wrangles and fights with all that comes near it. They say he has turned away almost every servant in the house, and left her at Penshurst to digest it as she can.[5]

What an age do we live in, where 'tis a miracle if in ten couple that are married, two of them live so as not to publish to the world that they cannot agree. I begin to be of the opinion of him that (when the Roman Church first propounded whether it were not convenient for priests not to marry) said that it might be convenient enough, but sure it was not our Saviour's intention, for He commanded that all should take up their cross and follow Him;[6] and for his part, he was confident there was no such cross as a wife. This is an ill doctrine for me to preach; but to my friends I cannot but confess that I am afraid much of the fault lies in us; for I have observed that generally in great families, the men seldom disagree, but the women are always scolding; and 'tis most certain, that let the husband be what he will, if the wife have but patience (which, sure, becomes her best), the disorder cannot be great enough to make a noise;[7] his anger alone, when it meets with nothing that resists it, cannot be loud enough to disturb the neighbours. And such a wife may be said to do as a kinswoman of ours that had a husband who was not always himself; and when he was otherwise, his humour was to rise in the night, and with two bedstaves tabour upon the table an hour together.[8] She took care every night to lay a great cushion upon the table for him to strike on, that nobody might hear him, and so discover his madness. But 'tis a sad thing when all one's happiness is only that the world does not know you are miserable.

For my part, I think it were very convenient that all such as intend to marry should live together in the same house some years of probation; and if, in all that time, they never disagreed, they should then be permitted to marry if they pleased; but how few would do it then! I do not remember that I ever saw

---

[1] *made me a leg*   bowed (*OED* leg *sb* 4).

[2] *my Lord Pembroke and my Lady*   probably Philip Herbert, fifth Earl of Pembroke (1619–1669), and his second wife Catherine, the daughter of Sir William Villiers.

[3] *spleenatick*   ill-tempered, peevish; *chimickall* engaged in the practice or study of chemistry (*OED* chemical *a* 5).

[4] *Lord Leicester and my Lady*   Robert Sidney, second Earl of Leicester (1595–1677), and his wife Dorothy Percy (d. 1659), daughter of Henry, ninth Earl of Northumberland. Lady Leicester was the sister of Lady Carlisle; *taken up the cudgels*   engaged in a vigorous contest; cudgels are literally clubs (*OED* cudgel *sb* 2).

[5] *digest*   endure, put up with (*OED* digest *v* 6).

[6] *take up their cross and follow him*   a comical allusion to Matthew 16:24, "Then said Jesus unto his disciples, If any man will come after me, let him deny himself, and take up his cross, and follow me."

[7] *noise*   disturbance (*OED* noise *sb* 1a).

[8] *bedstaves*   staffs or sticks used in some way about a bed; formerly well-known as a ready weapon (*OED* bedstaff *Obs*); *tabour* beat (*OED* tabour *v* 3).

or heard of any couple that were bred up so together (as many you know are, that are designed for one another from children), but they always disliked one another extremely; and parted, if it were left in their choice. If people proceeded with this caution, the world would end sooner than is expected, I believe; and because, with all my wariness, 'tis not impossible but I may be caught, nor likely that I should be wiser than everybody else, 'twere best, I think, that I said no more in this point.

What would I give to know that sister of yours that is so good at discovery;[1] sure she is excellent company; she had reason to laugh at you when you would have persuaded her the "moss was sweet." I remember Jane brought some of it to me, to ask me if I thought it had no ill smell, and whether she might venture to put it in the box or not.[2] I told her as I thought, she could not put a more innocent thing there, for I did not find that it had any smell at all; besides that I was willing it should do me some service in requital of the pains I had taken for it. My niece and I wandered through some six hundred acres of wood in search of it, to make rocks and strange things that her head is full of, and she admires it more than you did. If she had known I had consented it should have been used to fill up a box, she would have condemned me extremely. I told Jane that you liked her present, and she, I find, is resolved to spoil your compliment, and make you confess at last that they are not worth the eating; she threatens to send you more, but you would forgive her if you saw how she baits me every day to go to London; all that I can say will not satisfy her. When I urge (as 'tis true) that there is a necessity of my stay here, she grows furious, cries you will die with melancholy, and confounds me so with stories of your ill-humour, that I'll swear I think I should go merely to be at quiet, if it were possible, though

there were no other reason for it. But I hope 'tis not so ill as she would have me believe it, though I know your humour is strangely altered from what it was, and am sorry to see it. Melancholy must needs do you more hurt than to another to whom it may be natural, as I think it is to me; therefore if you loved me you would take heed on't. Can you believe that you are dearer to me than the whole world besides, and yet neglect yourself? If you do not, you wrong a perfect friendship; and if you do, you must consider my interest in you, and preserve yourself to make me happy. Promise me this, or I shall haunt you worse than she does me. Scribble how you please, so you make your letter long enough; you see I give you good example; besides, I can assure you we do perfectly agree if you receive no satisfaction but from my letters, I have none but what yours give me.

[OCTOBER 1653]

SIR, Why are you so sullen, and why am I the cause? Can you believe that I do willingly defer my journey? I know you do not. Why, then, should my absence now be less supportable to you than heretofore? It cannot, nay it shall not be long (if I can help it), and I shall break through all inconveniences rather than deny you anything that lies in my power to grant. But by your own rules, then, may not I expect the same from you? Is it possible that all I have said cannot oblige you to a care of yourself? What a pleasant distinction you make when you say 'tis not melancholy makes you do these things, but a careless forgetfulness. Did ever anybody forget themselves to that degree that was not melancholy in extremity. Good God! how are you altered; and what is it that has done it? I have known you when of all the things in the world you would not have been taken for a discontent;[3] you were, as I thought,

---

[1] *that sister of yours* Martha Temple (d. 1722), who lived with Temple and their father, Sir John Temple, in London.

[2] *Jane* Jane Wright, Osborne's companion and chaperone.

[3] *a discontent* a malcontent.

perfectly pleased with your condition; what has made it so much worse since? I know nothing you have lost, and am sure you have gained a friend. A friend that is capable of the highest degree of friendship you can propound, that has already given an entire heart for that which she received, and 'tis no more in her will than in her power ever to recall it or divide it; if this be not enough to satisfy you, tell me what I can do more? I shall find less difficulty in the doing it than in imagining what it may be; and will not you then do so much for my sake as to be careful of a health I am so infinitely concerned in and which those courses must needs destroy? If you loved me you would, I am sure you would, and let me tell you, you can never be that perfect friend you describe if you can deny me this. But will not your wife believe there is such a friendship?[1] I am not of her opinion at all, but I do not wonder neither that she is of it. Alas! how few there are that ever heard of such a thing, and fewer that understand it. Besides it is not to be taught or learned. It must come naturally to those that have it, and those must believe it before they can know it. But I admire, since she has it not, how she can be satisfied of her condition; nothing else, sure, can recompense the alterations you say it made in her fortune. What was it took her? Her husband's good face? What could invite her where there was neither fortune, wit, nor good usage, and a husband to whom she was but indifferent; which is all one to me, if not worse than an aversion, and I should sooner hope to gain upon one that hated me than upon one that did not consider me enough either to love or hate me. I'll swear she is a great deal easier to please than I should be.

There are a great many ingredients must go to the making me happy in a husband. First, as my cousin Franklin says, our humours must agree;[2] and to do that he must have that kind of breeding that I have had, and used that kind of company. That is, he must not be so much a country gentleman as to understand nothing but hawks and dogs, and be fonder of either than of his wife; nor of the next sort of them whose aim reaches no further than to be Justice of Peace, and once in his life High Sheriff, who reads no books but statutes, and studies nothing but how to make a speech interlarded with Latin that may amaze his disagreeing poor neighbours, and fright them rather than persuade them into quietness. He must not be a thing that began the world in a free school,[3] was sent from thence to the university, and is at his furthest when he reaches the Inns of Court, has no acquaintance but those of his form in these places, speaks the French he has picked out of old laws, and admires nothing but the stories he has heard of the revels that were kept there before his time. He must not be a town gallant neither, that lives in a tavern and an ordinary,[4] that cannot imagine how an hour should be spent without company unless it be in sleeping, that makes court to all the women he sees, thinks they believe him, and laughs and is laughed at equally. Nor a travelled Monsieur whose head is all feather inside and outside, that can talk of nothing but dances and duels, and has courage enough to wear slashes when everybody else dies with cold to see him.[5] He must not be a fool of no sort, nor peevish, nor ill-natured, nor proud, nor covetous; and to all this must be added, that he must love me and I him as much as we are capable of loving. Without all

---

[1] *your wife* the person who assumes the role of your "wife" by giving such advice.

[2] *humours* temperaments (*OED* humour *sb* II.4).

[3] *free school* a school in which learning is given without pay (though this definition has been disputed) (*OED* free *a* A.IV.32b).

[4] *an ordinary* an eating house where public meals are provided at a fixed price. In the expensive ordinaries, dinner was followed by gambling, and the term was often used as synonymous with "gambling-house" (*OED* ordinary *sb* III.14b).

[5] *slashes* vertical slits made in garments in order to expose to view a lining or under garment of a different or contrasting colour (*OED* slash *sb*[1] 3a).

this, his fortune, though never so great, would not satisfy me; and with it, a very moderate one would keep me from ever repenting my disposal.

I have been as large and as particular in my descriptions as my cousin Molle in his of Moor Park—but that you know the place so well I would send it you—nothing can come near his patience in writing it, but my reading on't. But would you had sent me your father's letter, it would not have been less welcome to me than to you; and you may safely believe that I am equally concerned with you in anything. I should be pleased, too, to see something of my Lady Carlisle's writing, because she is so extraordinary a person.[1] I have been thinking of sending you my picture till I could come myself; but a picture is but dull company, and that you need not; besides, I cannot tell whether it be very like me or not, though 'tis the best I ever had drawn for me, and Mr. Lely will have it that he never took more pains to make a good one in his life, and that was it I think that spoiled it.[2] He was condemned for making the first he drew for me a little worse than I, and in making this better he has made it as unlike as t'other. He is now, I think, at my Lord Paget's at Marlow, where I am promised he shall draw a picture of my Lady for me—she gives it me, she says, as the greatest testimony of her friendship to me, for by her own rule she is past the time of having pictures taken of her.[3] After eighteen, she says, there is no face but decays apparently; I would

fain have had her excepted such as had never been beauties, for my comfort, but she would not.

When you see your friend Mr. Heningham, you may tell him in his ear there is a willow garland coming towards him.[4] He might have sped better in his suit if he had made court to me, as well as to my Lady Ruthin.[5] She has been my wife this seven year, and whosoever pretends there must ask my leave.[6] I have now given my consent that she shall marry a very pretty little gentleman, Sir Christopher Yelverton's son, and I think we shall have a wedding ere it be long.[7] My Lady her mother, in great kindness, would have recommended Heningham to me, and told me in a compliment that I was fitter for him than her daughter, who was younger, and therefore did not understand the world so well; that she was certain if he knew me he would be extremely taken for I would make just that kind of wife he looked for. I humbly thanked her, but said that without knowing him more than by relation, I was certain he would not make that kind of husband I looked for—and so it went no further.

I expect my elder brother here shortly, whose fortune is well mended by my other brother's death, so as if he were satisfied himself with what he has done, I know no reason why he might not be very happy; but I am afraid he is not. I have not seen my sister since I knew she was so;[8] but, sure, she can have lost no beauty, for I never saw any that she had, but good black eyes, which cannot alter. He loves her, I think, at the ordinary rate of husbands,

[1] *I should be...a person* Temple later sends Osborne one of Lady Carlisle's letters, of which she writes: "Methinks the hand and the style both show her a great person, and 'tis writ in the way that's now affected by all that pretend to wit and breeding; only, I am a little scandalised I confess that she uses the word faithful—she that never knew how to be so in her life" (Sunday October 23, 1653).

[2] *Mr. Lely* Peter Lely, the Dutch portrait painter, lived in England from 1641 until his death in 1679. See Lovelace's poem addressed to him, p. 767.

[3] *Lord Paget's* Sir William Paget, fifth Baron Paget (1609–1678), was married to Lady Frances Rich. Frances was the sister of Osborne's close friend Lady Diana Rich, referred to throughout these letters as "my Lady."

[4] *Mr. Heningham* apparently an unsuccessful suitor of Osborne's; he is mentioned in a letter of May 25, 1654 as having also been jilted by Mrs. Gerard; *willow garland* a symbol of grief for unrequited love (*OED* willow *sb* I.1d).

[5] *Lady Ruthin* Susan, Lady Grey de Ruthin, daughter of Charles Longueville, Lord Grey de Ruthin.

[6] *my wife* an expression used between close women friends.

[7] *Sir Christopher Yelverton's son* Sir Harry Yelverton, who did marry Lady Ruthin as Osborne hoped.

[8] *sister* sister-in-law; John Osborne's new wife Eleanor Danvers.

but not enough, I believe, to marry her so much to his disadvantage if it were to do again; and that would kill me were I as she, for I could be infinitely better satisfied with a husband that had never loved me in hope he might, than with one that began to love me less than he had done.

I am yours.

[SATURDAY, FEBRUARY 4, 1654]

SIR, 'Tis well you have given over your reproaches; I can allow you to tell me of my faults kindly and like a friend. Possibly it is a weakness in me to aim at the world's esteem, as if I could not be happy without it; but there are certain things that custom has made almost of absolute necessity, and reputation I take to be one of those. If one could be invisible I should choose that; but since all people are seen and known, and shall be talked of in spite of their teeth,[1] who is it that does not desire, at least, that nothing of ill may be said of them, whether justly or otherwise? I never knew any so satisfied with their own innocence as to be content the world should think them guilty. Some out of pride have seemed to contemn ill reports when they have found they could not avoid them, but none out of strength of reason, though many have pretended to it. No, not my Lady Newcastle with all her philosophy, therefore you must not expect it from me.[2] I shall never be ashamed to own that I have a particular value for you above any other, but 'tis not the greatest merit of person will excuse a want of fortune; in some degree I think it will, at least with the most rational part of the world, and, as far as that will reach, I desire it should. I would

not have the world believe I married out of interest and to please my friends;[3] I had much rather they should know I chose the person, and took his fortune, because 'twas necessary, and that I prefer a competency with one I esteem infinitely before a vast estate in other hands. 'Tis much easier, sure, to get a good fortune than a good husband; but whosoever marries without any consideration of fortune shall never be allowed to do it out of so reasonable an apprehension,[4] the whole world (without any reserve) shall pronounce they did it merely to satisfy their giddy humour.

Besides, though you imagine 'twere a great argument of my kindness to consider nothing but you, in earnest I believe 'twould be an injury to you. I do not see that it puts any value upon men when women marry them for love (as they term it); 'tis not their merit, but our folly that is always presumed to cause it; and would it be any advantage to you to have your wife thought an indiscreet person? All this I can say to you; but when my brother disputes it with me I have other arguments for him, and I drove him up so close t'other night that for want of a better gap to get out at he was fain to say that he feared as much your having a fortune as your having none, for he saw you held my Lord Lisle's principles.[5] That religion or honour were things you did not consider at all, and that he was confident you would take any engagement, serve in any employment, or do anything to advance yourself. I had no patience for this. To say you were a beggar, your father not worth £4000 in the whole world, was nothing in comparison of having no religion nor no honour. I forgot all my disguise,

---

[1] *in spite of their teeth*   notwithstanding their opposition (*OED* tooth *sb* III.5).

[2] *Lady Newcastle*   Margaret Cavendish, Duchess of Newcastle (1623–1673), published *Philosophical Fancies* in 1653. She was viewed by many as an eccentric because of her unusual apparel, her novel philosophic ideas, and her desire to write for publication.

[3] *interest*   financial interest.

[4] *apprehension*   notion (*OED* apprehension II.9).

[5] *Lord Lisle's principles*   Lord Lisle held republican opinions. He was favoured by Cromwell, sat in the "Little Parliament" and was a member of both the councils of state elected by it. He was also a member of the two councils of state of the protectorate and sat in Cromwell's House of Lords.

and we talked ourselves weary;[1] he renounced me again, and I defied him, but both in as civil language as it would permit, and parted in great anger with the usual ceremony of a leg and a courtesy, that you would have died with laughing to have seen us.

The next day I, not being at dinner, saw him not till night; then he came into my chamber, where I supped but he did not. Afterwards Mr. Gibson and he and I talked of indifferent things till all but we two went to bed. Then he sat half-an-hour and said not one word, nor I to him. At last, in a pitiful tone, "Sister," says he, "I have heard you say that when anything troubles you, of all things you apprehend going to bed, because there it increases upon you, and you lie at the mercy of all your sad thoughts, which the silence and darkness of the night adds a horror to; I am at that pass now. I vow to God I would not endure another night like the last to gain a crown." I, who resolved to take no notice what ailed him, said 'twas a knowledge I had raised from my spleen only, and so fell into a discourse of melancholy and the causes, and from that (I know not how) into religion; and we talked so long of it, and so devoutly, that it laid all our anger.[2] We grew to a calm and peace with all the world. Two hermits conversing in a cell they equally inhabit, never expressed more humble, charitable kindness, one towards another, than we. He asked my pardon and I his, and he has promised me never to speak of it to me whilst he lives, but leave the event to God Almighty; and till he sees it done, he will be always the same to me that he is;[3] then he shall leave me, he says, not out of want of kindness to me, but because he cannot see the ruin of a person that he loves so passionately, and in whose happiness he had laid up all his. These are the terms we are at, and I am confident he will keep his word with me, so that you have no reason to fear him in any respect; for though he should break his promise, he should never make me break mine. No, let me assure you this rival, nor any other, shall ever alter me, therefore spare your jealousy, or turn it all into kindness.

I will write every week, and no miss of letters shall give us any doubts of one another. Time nor accidents shall not prevail upon our hearts, and, if God Almighty please to bless us, we will meet the same we are, or happier. I will do all you bid me. I will pray, and wish, and hope, but you must do so too, then, and be so careful of yourself that I may have nothing to reproach you with when you come back.

That vile wench lets you see all my scribbles, I believe;[4] how do you know I took care your hair should not be spoiled? 'Tis more than ere you did, I think, you are so negligent on't, and keep it so ill, 'tis pity you should have it. May you have better luck in the cutting it than I had with mine. I cut it two or three years agone, and it never grew since. Look to it; if I keep the lock you give me better than you do all the rest, I shall not spare you; expect to be soundly chidden. What do you mean to do with all my letters? Leave them behind you? If you do, it must be in safe hands, some of them concern you, and me, and other people besides us very much, and they will almost load a horse to carry.

Do not my cousins at Moor Park mistrust us a little? I have a great belief they do. I'm sure Robin Cheke told my brother of it since I was last in town.[5] Of all things, I admire my cousin Molle has not got it by the end, he that frequents that family so much, and is at this instant at Kimbolton. If he

---

[1] *disguise* counterfeit semblance or show (*OED* disguise *sb* 4).

[2] *laid* appeased (*OED* lay *v*[1] I.3a).

[3] *sees it done* witnesses our marriage.

[4] *vile wench* Nan Stacy, who may at one time have been Osborne's servant. She apparently lived in London, and Temple may have lodged with her and her mother.

[5] *Robin Cheke* a distant relative; presumably the son of Sir Thomas Cheke, Osborne's great-uncle.

has, and conceals it, he is very discreet; I could never discern by anything that he knew it. I shall endeavour to accustom myself to the noise on't, and make it as easy to me as I can, though I had much rather it were not talked of till there were an absolute necessity of discovering it, and you can oblige me in nothing more than in concealing it.[1] I take it very kindly that you promise to use all your interest in your father to persuade him to endeavour our happiness, and he appears so confident of his power that it gives me great hopes.

Dear! shall we ever be so happy, think you? Ah! I dare not hope it. Yet 'tis not want of love gives me these fears. No, in earnest, I think; (nay, I am sure) I love you more than ever, and 'tis that only gives me these despairing thoughts; when I consider how small a proportion of happiness is allowed in this world, and how great mine would be in a person for whom I have a passionate kindness, and who has the same for me. As it is infinitely above what I can deserve, and more than God Almighty usually allots to the best people, I can find nothing in reason but seems to be against me; and, methinks, 'tis as vain in me to expect it as 'twould be to hope I might be a queen (if that were really as desirable a thing as 'tis thought to be); and it is just it should be so.

We complain of this world, and the variety of crosses and afflictions it abounds in, and yet for all this who is weary on't (more than in discourse), who thinks with pleasure of leaving it, or preparing for the next? We see old folks, that have outlived all the comforts of life, desire to continue it, and nothing can wean us from the folly of preferring a mortal being, subject to great infirmity and unavoidable decays, before an immortal one, and all the glories that are promised with it. Is this not very like preaching? Well, 'tis too good for you; you shall have no more on't. I am afraid you are not mortified enough for such discourses to work upon

(though I am not of my brother's opinion, neither, that you have no religion in you). In earnest, I never took anything he ever said half so ill, as nothing, sure, is so great an injury. It must suppose one to be a devil in human shape. Oh, me! now I am speaking of religion, let me ask you is not his name Bagshawe that you say rails on love and women?[2] Because I heard one t'other day speaking of him, and commending his wit, but withal, said he was a perfect atheist. If so, I can allow him to hate us, and love, which, sure, has something of divine in it, since God requires it of us. I am coming into my preaching vein again. What think you, were it not a good way of preferment as the times are? If you advise me to it I'll venture. The woman at Somerset House was cried up mightily. Think on't.

Dear, I am yours.

[SATURDAY, FEBRUARY 11, 1654]

SIR, The lady was in the right. You are a very pretty gentleman and a modest; were there ever such stories as these you tell? The best on't is, I believe none of them, unless it be that of my Lady Newport, which I must confess is so like her that if it be not true 'twas at least excellently fancied.[3] But my Lord Rich is not caught, though he was near it.[4] My Lady Devonshire, whose daughter his first wife was, has engaged my Lord Warwick to put a stop to the business.[5] Otherwise, I think his present want of

---

[1] *noise* rumour (*OED* noise *sb* 2a); *discovering* disclosing (*OED* discover *v* 3a).

[2] *Bagshawe* Edward Bagshawe the Elder (d. 1662), a lawyer. Originally a staunch Puritan, he later joined the King's party.

[3] *Lady Newport* wife of the Earl of Newport and mother of Lady Anne Blunt, of whose scandal Osborne writes in a previous letter.

[4] *Lord Rich* Robert, Baron Rich (d. 1659), eldest son of Robert Rich, second Earl of Warwick. His first wife was Anne Cavendish, daughter of William Cavendish, Earl of Devonshire. His second wife was Anne, daughter of Sir Thomas Cheke.

[5] *My Lord Warwick* Robert Rich, second Earl of Warwick (1587–1658). The nature of the business that he must "put a stop to" is not known, though it appears Lady Devonshire wants to prevent a

fortune, and the little sense of honour he has, might have been prevailed on to marry her.

'Tis strange to see the folly that possesses the young people of this age, and the liberties they take to themselves. I have the charity to believe they appear very much worse than they are, and that the want of a Court to govern themselves by is in great part the cause of their ruin; though that was no perfect school of virtue, yet Vice there wore her mask, and appeared so unlike herself that she gave no scandal. Such as were really as discreet as they seemed to be gave good example, and the eminency of their condition made others strive to imitate them, or at least they durst not own a contrary course. All who had good principles and inclinations were encouraged in them, and such as had neither were forced to put on a handsome disguise that they might not be out of countenance at themselves. 'Tis certain (what you say) that where divine or human laws are not positive we may be our own judges; nobody can hinder us, nor is it in itself to be blamed. But, sure, it is not safe to take all the liberty that is allowed us—there are not many that are sober enough to be trusted with the government of themselves; and because others judge us with more severity than our indulgence to ourselves will permit, it must necessarily follow that 'tis safer being ruled by their opinion than by our own. I am disputing again, though you told me my fault so plainly.

I'll give it over, and tell you that *Parthenissa* is now my company. My brother sent it down, and I have almost read it.[1] 'Tis handsome language; you would know it to be writ by a person of good quality though you were not told it; but, in the whole, I am not very much taken with it. All the stories have too near a resemblance with those of other romances, there is nothing of new or *surprenant* in them;[2] the ladies are all so kind they make no sport, and I meet only with one that took me by doing a handsome thing of the kind. She was in a besieged town, and persuaded all those of her sex to go out with her to the enemy (which were a barbarous people) and die by their swords, that the provision of the town might last the longer for such as were able to do service in defending it. But how angry was I to see him spoil this again by bringing out a letter this woman left behind her for the governor of the town, where she discovers a passion for him, and makes *that* the reason why she did it. I confess I have no patience for our *faiseurs de Romance* when they make women court.[3] It will never enter into my head that 'tis possible any woman can love where she is not first loved, and much less that if they should do that, they could have the face to own it. Methinks he that writes *L'illustre Bassa* says well in his epistle that we are not to imagine his hero to be less taking than those of other romances because the ladies do not fall in love with him whether he will or not.[4] 'Twould be an injury to the ladies to suppose they could do so, and a greater to his hero's civility if he should put him upon being cruel to them, since he was to love but one. Another fault I find, too, in the style—'tis affected. *Ambitioned* is a great word with him, and *ignore*; *my concern*, or of *great concern*, is, it seems, properer than *concernment*: and though he makes his people say fine handsome things to one another,

---

proposed second marriage.

[1] *Parthenissa* a romance written by Roger Boyle, Baron Broghill, later Earl of Orrery (1621–1679). Its first instalment was published in 1651, the last in 1669, though it was chiefly published during the years 1654–1656.

[2] *surprenant* surprising.

[3] *faiseurs de Romance* makers of Romance.

[4] *L'illustre Bassa* a romance written by Madelein de Scudery, and translated by Henry Cogan in 1652. The passage to which Osborne refers reads: "And if you see not my hero persecuted with love by women, it is not because he was not amiable, and that he could not be loved, but because it would clash with civility in the persons of ladies, and with true resemblance in that of men, who rarely show themselves cruel unto them, nor in doing it could have any good grace."

yet they are not easy and *naïve* like the French, and there is a little harshness in most of the discourses that one would take to be the fault of a translator rather than of an author. But perhaps I like it the worse for having a piece of *Cyrus* by me that I am hugely pleased with, and that I would fain have you read:[1] I'll send it [to] you. At least read one story that I'll mark you down, if you have time for no more. I am glad you stay to wait on your sister.[2] I would have my gallant civil to all, much more when it is so due, and kindness too.

I have the cabinet, and 'tis in earnest a pretty one;[3] though you will not own it for a present. I'll keep it as one, and 'tis like to be yours no more but as 'tis mine. I'll warrant you would ne'er have thought of making me a present of charcoal as my servant James would have done, to warm my heart I think he meant it.[4] But the truth is, I had been inquiring for some (as 'tis a commodity scarce enough in this country), and he hearing of it, told the bailiff he would give him some if 'twere for me. But this is not all. I cannot forbear telling you the other day he made me a visit, and I, to prevent his making discourses to me, made Mrs. Goldsmith and Jane sit by all the while.[5] But he came better provided that I could have imagined. He brought a letter with him, and gave it me as one that he had met with directed to me, he thought it came out of Northamptonshire. I was upon my guard, and suspecting all he said, examined him so strictly where he had it before I would open it, that he was hugely confounded, and I confirmed that 'twas his.

I laid it by and wished then they would have left us, that I might have taken notice on't to him. But I had forbid it them so strictly before, that they offered not to stir farther than to look out at [the] window, as not thinking there was any necessity of giving us their eyes as well as their ears; but he that saw himself discovered took that time to confess to me (in a whispering voice that I could hardly hear myself) that the letter (as my Lord Broghill says) was of *great concern* to him, and begged I would read it, and give him my answer. I took it up presently, as if I had meant it, but threw it, sealed as it was, into the fire, and told him (as softly as he had spoke to me) I thought that the quickest and best way of answering it.[6] He sat awhile in great disorder, without speaking a word, and so rose and took his leave. Now what think you, shall I ever hear of him more?

You do not thank me for using your rival so scurvily nor are not jealous of him, though your father thinks my intentions were not handsome towards you, which methinks is another argument that one is not to be one's own judge; for I am very confident they were, and with his favour shall never believe otherwise. I am sure I have no ends to serve of my own in what I did—it could be no advantage to me that had firmly resolved never to marry; but I thought it might be an injury to you to keep you in expectation of what was never likely to be, as I apprehended. Why do I enter into this wrangling discourse? Let your father think me what he pleases, if he ever comes to know me, the rest of my actions shall justify me in this; if he does not, I'll begin to practise upon him (what you have so often preached to me) to neglect the report of the world, and satisfy myself in my own innocency.

'Twill be pleasinger to you, I am sure, to tell you how fond I am of your lock. Well, in earnest now, and setting aside all compliment, I never saw finer

---

[1] *Cyrus* Madelein de Scudery's *Artamenes, or The Grand Cyrus,* translated by F.G. in 1653.

[2] *I am glad…your sister* Temple delayed his departure to Ireland, in order to accompany his sister Martha.

[3] *cabinet* a case for the safe custody of jewels, or other valuables, letters, documents, etc. (*OED* cabinet *sb* I.5).

[4] *servant James* Osborne's suitor James Beverley of Bedfordshire.

[5] *Mrs. Goldsmith* the wife of Daniel Goldsmith, the rector of Campton, in which parish Chicksands was situated.

[6] *presently* without delay (*OED* presently *adv* 3).

hair, nor of a better colour; but cut no more on't, I would not have it spoiled for the world. If you love me, be careful on't. I am combing, and curling, and kissing this lock all day, and dreaming on't all night. The ring, too, is very well, only a little of the biggest. Send me a tortoise-shell one to keep it on, that is a little less than that I sent for a pattern. I would not have the rule absolutely true without exception that hard hairs are ill natured, for then I should be so. But I can allow that all soft hairs are good, and so are you, or I am deceived as much as you are if you think I do not love you enough. Tell me, my dearest, am I? You will not be if you think I am

Yours.

[MARCH 18, 1654]

How true it is that a misfortune never comes single; we live in expectation of some one happiness that we propose to ourselves, an age almost, and perhaps miss it at the last; but sad accidents have wings to overtake us, and come in flocks like ill-boding ravens. You were no sooner gone but (as if that had not been enough) I lost the best father in the world; and though, as to himself, it was an infinite mercy in God Almighty to take him out of a world that can be pleasing to none, and was made more uneasy to him by many infirmities that were upon him, yet to me it is an affliction much greater than people judge it. Besides all that is due to nature and the memory of many (more than ordinary) kindnesses received from him, besides what he was to all that knew him, and what he was to me in particular, I am left by his death in the condition (which of all others) is the most insupportable to my nature, to depend upon kindred that are not friends, and that, though I pay as much as I should do to a stranger,

yet think they do me a courtesy.[1] I expect my eldest brother to-day; if he comes, I shall be able to tell you before I seal up this where you are likely to find me. If he offers me to stay here, this hole will be more agreeable to my humour than any place that is more in the world. I take it kindly that you used arts to conceal our story and satisfy my nice apprehensions, but I'll not impose that constraint upon you any longer, for I find my kind brother publishes it with more earnestness than ever I strove to conceal it;[2] and with more disadvantage than anybody else would. Now he has tried all ways to what he desires, and finds it is vain, he resolves to revenge himself upon me, by representing this action in such colours as will amaze all people that know me, and do not know him enough to discern his malice to me; he is not able to forbear showing it now, when my condition deserves pity from all the world, I think, and that he himself has newly lost a father, as well as I; but takes this time to torment me, which appears (at least to me) so barbarous a cruelty, that though I thank God I have charity enough perfectly to forgive all the injuries he can do me, yet I am afraid I shall never look upon him as a brother more. And now do you judge whether I am not very unhappy, and whether that sadness in my face you used to complain of was not suited to my fortune. You must confess it; and that my kindness for you is beyond example. All these troubles and persecutions that make me weary of the world before my time, cannot lessen the concernment I have for you, and instead of being persuaded, as they would have me, by their malicious stories, methinks I am obliged to love you more in recompense of all the injuries they have done you upon my score. I shall need nothing but my own heart to fortify me in this resolution, and desire nothing in return of it but that your care of

---

[1] *though I pay...a courtesy* Osborne probably paid for her board and lodging at Chicksands out of her private income.

[2] *nice* tender, delicate (*OED* nice *a* 4c).

yourself may answer that which I shall always have for your interests.

    I received your letter of the 10th of this month; and I hope this will find you at your journey's end. In earnest, I have pitied your sister extremely, and can easily apprehend how troublesome this voyage must needs be to her, by knowing what others have been to me; yet, pray assure her I would not scruple at undertaking it myself to gain such an acquaintance, and would go much farther than where (I hope) she now is to serve her. I am afraid she will not think me a fit person to choose for a friend, that cannot agree with my own brother; but I must trust you to tell my story for me, and will hope for a better character from you than he gives me; who, lest I should complain, resolves to prevent me, and possess my friends first that he is the injured party.[1] I never magnified my patience to you, but I begin to have a good opinion on't since this trial; yet, perhaps, I have no reason, and it may be as well a want of sense in me as of passion; however, you will not be displeased to know that I can endure all that he or anybody else can say, and that setting aside my father's death and your absence, I make nothing an affliction to me, though I am sorry, I confess, to

see myself forced to keep such distances with one of his relations, because religion and nature and the custom of the world teaches otherwise. I see I shall not be able to satisfy you in this how I shall dispose of myself, for my brother is not come;[2] the next will certainly tell you. In the meantime, I expect with great impatience to hear of your safe arrival. 'Twas a disappointment that you missed those fair winds. I pleased myself extremely with a belief that they had made your voyage rather a diversion than a trouble, either to you or your company, but I hope your passage was as happy, if not as sudden as you expected it; let me hear often from you, and long letters. I do not count this so. Have no apprehensions for me, but all the care of yourself that you please. My melancholy has no danger in't; and I believe the accidents of my life would work more upon any other than they do upon me, whose humour is always more prepared for them than that of gayer persons. I hear nothing that is worth your knowing; when I do, you shall have it. Tell me if there be anything I can do for you, and assure yourself I am perfectly

                                    Yours.

—1888 (1652–54)

---

[1] *possess* persuade, convince (*OED* possess *v* II.9b).

[2] *in this* in this letter.

John Bunyan
1628 – 1688

Born in the village of Elstow, near Bedford, the son of a brazier (tinker), Bunyan learned to read and write at the village school and was trained in his father's trade. During the civil wars he was drafted into the Parliamentary army and stationed at Newport Pagnell from 1644 to 1646–47, though it is doubtful if he saw much if any military action. In 1649 he married his first wife, the daughter of one of "the godly," who introduced Bunyan to the popular devotional manuals that would become his primary reading matter along with the Bible and John Foxe's *Acts and Monuments* (the *Book of Martyrs*). After the lengthy spiritual struggles depicted in *Grace Abounding* (1666), Bunyan joined the Separatist congregation in Bedford in 1655, and began to preach the following year. He soon began to publish on religious subjects, basing his early books on sermons and his public disputations with local Quakers, Anglicans, and Presbyterians; by the late 1650s, the congregation in Bedford was being described as "Bunyan's people." The Restoration saw the resurrection of laws against dissent, and in November 1660 Bunyan was arrested for preaching without a license and holding a "conventicle," a religious gathering outside the established Church. The penalty was three months' imprisonment; Bunyan, however, refused to give up preaching, and consequently remained in prison for the following twelve years, though he was allowed out occasionally to visit friends and family. Many of his subsequent books, including *Grace Abounding* and the first part of *The Pilgrim's Progress* (probably completed during a second period of imprisonment in 1676), were written while Bunyan was in jail. Released under the Declaration of Indulgence in 1672, Bunyan returned to the congregation at Bedford and continued to preach for the remainder of his days.

Bunyan published dozens of books, many of which went through numerous editions before the end of the seventeenth century. Early copies of his books tend to be rare, since they were read to pieces—many are extant in only a few copies. The publication of the first part of *The Pilgrim's Progress* in 1678 brought Bunyan a measure of fame: it was reprinted over twenty times before 1700 (including an American edition printed in Boston), and translated into several languages before Bunyan's death. A second part, relating the spiritual journey of Christian's wife Christiana and her children, was first published in 1684. Bunyan's other principal works are *The Life and Death of Mr. Badman* (1680) and *The Holy War* (1682); a collected *Works* was first published in 1692.

❦

Grace Abounding to the Chief of Sinners
(excerpt)

In this my relation of the merciful working of God upon my soul, it will not be amiss, if in the first place, I do, in a few words, give you a hint of my pedigree, and manner of bringing up; that thereby the goodness and bounty of God towards me, may be the more advanced and magnified before the sons of men.

For my descent then, it was, as is well known by many, of a low and inconsiderable generation; my father's house being of that rank that is meanest, and most despised of all the families in the land.[1] Wherefore I have not here, as others, to boast of noble blood, or of a high-born state according to

---

[1] Bunyan exaggerates the lowliness of his family's social position to display the Christian humility expected by readers of personal religious testaments. While his father was a tradesman, he was not itinerant, and the family owned a small freehold.

the flesh; though all things considered, I magnify the Heavenly Majesty, for that by this door he brought me into this world, to partake of the grace and life that is in Christ by the Gospel.

But yet notwithstanding the meanness and inconsiderableness of my parents, it pleased God to put it into their heart, to put me to school, to learn both to read and write; the which I also attained, according to the rate of other poor men's children, though to my shame I confess, I did soon lose that little I learned, even almost utterly, and that long before the Lord did work his gracious work of conversion upon my soul.

As for my own natural life, for the time that I was without God in the world, it was indeed according to the course of this world, and the spirit that now worketh in the children of disobedience: Eph. 2:2, 3 it was my delight to be taken captive by the Devil "at his will," II Tim. 2:6 being filled with all unrighteousness; the which did also so strongly work, and put forth itself, both in my heart and life, and that from a child, that I had but few equals (especially considering my years, which were tender, being few), both for cursing, swearing, lying and blaspheming the holy name of God.

Yea, so settled and rooted was I in these things, that they became as a second nature to me; the which, as I also have with soberness considered since, did so offend the Lord, that even in my childhood he did scare and affright me with fearful dreams, and did terrify me with dreadful visions. For often, after I had spent this and the other day in sin, I have in my bed been greatly afflicted, while asleep, with the apprehensions of Devils, and wicked spirits, who still, as I then thought, laboured to draw me away with them; of which I could never be rid.

Also I should at these years be greatly afflicted and troubled with the thoughts of the day of Judgment, and that both night and day, and should tremble at the thoughts of the fearful torments of Hell-fire; still fearing that it would be my lot to be found at last amongst those Devils and hellish fiends, who are there bound down with the chains and bonds of eternal darkness.

These things I say, when I was but a child, about nine or ten years old, did so distress my soul, that then in the midst of my many sports and childish vanities, amidst my vain companions, I was often much cast down and afflicted in my mind therewith, yet could I not let go my sins; yea, I was so overcome with despair of life and Heaven, that then I should often wish, either that there had been no Hell, or that I had been a Devil; supposing they were only tormentors; that if it must needs be, that I indeed went thither, I might be rather a tormentor, than tormented my self.

A while after, these terrible dreams did leave me, which also I soon forgot; for my pleasures did quickly cut off the remembrance of them, as if they had never been: wherefore, with more greediness, according to the strength of nature, I did still let loose the reins to my lusts, and delighted in all transgression against the law of God: so that until I came to the state of marriage, I was the very ringleader of all the youth that kept me company, into all manner of vice and ungodliness.

Yea, such prevalency had the lusts and fruits of the flesh, in this poor soul of mine, that had not a miracle of precious grace prevented, I had not only perished by the stroke of eternal justice, but had also laid my self open, even to the stroke of those laws, which bring some to disgrace and open shame before the face of the world.

In these days, the thoughts of religion was very grievous to me; I could neither endure it myself, nor that any other should; so that when I have but seen some read in those books that concerned Christian piety, it would be as it were a prison to me. Then I said unto God, "depart from me, for I desire not the knowledge of thy ways," Job 21:14, 15. I was now void of all good consideration; Heaven and

Hell were both out of sight and mind; and as for saving and damning, they were least in my thoughts. O Lord, thou knowest my life, and my ways were not hid from thee.

Yet this I well remember, that though I could myself sin with the greatest delight and ease, and also take pleasure in the vileness of my companions; yet even then, if I have at any time seen wicked things by those who professed goodness, it would make my spirit tremble. As once above all the rest, when I was in my height of vanity, yet hearing one to swear that was reckoned for a religious man, it had so great a stroke upon my spirit, as it made my heart to ache.

But God did not utterly leave me, but followed me still, not now with convictions, but judgements, yet such as were mixed with mercy. For once I fell into a crick of the sea, and hardly escaped drowning: another time I fell out of a boat into Bedford River, but mercy yet preserved me alive: Besides, another time being in the field, with one of my companions, it chanced that an adder passed over the highway, so I having a stick in mine hand, struck her over the back; and having astounded her, I forced open her mouth with my stick, and plucked her sting out with my fingers, by which act had not God been merciful to me, I might by my desperateness have brought myself to mine end.

This also have I taken notice of with thanksgiving; when I was a soldier,[1] I with others were drawn out to go to such a place to besiege it; but when I was just ready to go, one of the company desired to go in my room, to which, when I had consented he took my place; and coming to the siege, as he stood sentinel, he was shot into the head with a musket bullet and died.

Here, as I said, were judgements and mercy, but neither of them did awaken my soul to righteousness, wherefore I sinned still, and grew more and more rebellious against God, and careless of mine own salvation.

Presently after this, I changed my condition into a married state, and my mercy was, to light upon a wife whose father was counted godly: this woman and I, though we came together as poor as poor might be (not having so much household stuff as a dish or spoon betwixt us both), yet this she had for her part, *The Plain Man's Path-way to Heaven*, and *The Practice of Piety*,[2] which her father had left her when he died. In these two books I should sometimes read with her, wherein I also found some things that were somewhat pleasing to me (but all this while I met with no conviction). She also would be often telling of me what a godly man her father was, and how he would reprove and correct vice, both in his house, and amongst his neighbours; what a strict and holy life he lived in his day, both in word and deed.

Wherefore these books, with this relation, though they did not reach my heart to awaken it about my sad and sinful state, yet they did beget within me some desires to religion: so that, because I knew no better, I fell in very eagerly with the religion of the times,[3] to wit, to go to church twice a day, and that too with the foremost, and there should very devoutly both say and sing as others did; yet retaining my wicked life: but withal, I was so overrun with the spirit of superstition, that I adored, and that with great devotion, even all things (both the high place, priest, clerk, vestments, service, and what else), belonging to the church; counting all things holy that were therein contained; and especially the priest and clerk most happy, and without doubt greatly blessed, because

[1] Bunyan served in the Parliamentary army, though it is doubtful if he saw much, if any, military action.

[2] frequently reprinted works of popular devotion by Arthur Dent (first published 1601) and Lewis Bayley (first published before 1612) respectively.

[3] Though Bunyan's emphasis on ritual appears to refer to Anglican services, he is writing of a time (the late 1640s and early 1650s) when the Presbyterians controlled the national church.

they were the servants, as I then thought, of God, and were principal in the holy temple, to do his work therein.

This conceit grew so strong in little time upon my spirit, that had I but seen a priest (though never so sordid and debauched in his life), I should find my spirit fall under him, reverence him, and knit unto him; yea, I thought for the love I did bear unto them (supposing they were the Ministers of God), I could have lain down at their feet, and have been trampled upon by them; their name, their garb, and work, did so intoxicate and bewitch me.

After I had been thus for some considerable time, another thought came into my mind, and that was, Whether we were of the Israelites, or no: for finding in the Scriptures that they were once the peculiar People of God, thought I, if I were one of this race, my soul must needs be happy. Now again I found within me a great longing to be resolved about this question, but could not tell how I should: at last, I asked my father of it, who told me, "No, we were not": wherefore then I fell in my spirit, as to the hopes of that, and so remained.

But all this while, I was not sensible of the danger and evil of sin; I was kept from considering that sin would damn me, what religion soever I followed, unless I was found in Christ: nay, I never thought of him, nor whether there was one or no. Thus man, while blind, doth wander, but wearieth himself with vanity: for he knoweth not the way to the City of God, Eccles. 10:15.

But one day (amongst all the sermons our parson made), his subject was, to treat of the Sabbath day, and of the evil of breaking that, either with labour, sports, or otherwise (now I was, notwithstanding my religion, one that took much delight in all manner of vice, and especially that was the day that I did solace my self therewith). Wherefore I fell in my conscience under his sermon, thinking and believing that he made that sermon on purpose to show me my evil doing; and at that time

I felt what guilt was, though never before, that I can remember; but then I was for the present greatly loaded therewith, and so went home when the sermon was ended, with a great burden upon my spirit.

This, for that instant, did benumb the sinews of my best delights, and did embitter my former pleasures to me: but behold, it lasted not; for before I had well dined, the trouble began to go off my mind, and my heart returned to its old course: but oh how glad was I, that this trouble was gone from me, and that the fire was put out, that I might sin again without control! Wherefore, when I had satisfied nature with my food, I shook the sermon out of my mind, and to my old custom of sports and gaming I returned with great delight.

But the same day, as I was in the midst of a game at cat,[1] and having struck it one blow from the hole; just as I was about to strike it the second time, a voice did suddenly dart from Heaven into my soul, which said, "Wilt thou leave thy sins, and go to Heaven? or have thy sins, and go to Hell?" At that I was put to an exceeding maze; wherefore, leaving my cat upon the ground, I looked up to Heaven, and was as if I had with the eyes of my understanding, seen the Lord Jesus looking down upon me, as being very hotly displeased with me, and as if he did severely threaten me with some grievous punishment for these, and other my ungodly practices.

I had no sooner thus conceived in my mind, but suddenly this conclusion was fastened on my spirit (for the former hint did set my sins again before my face), *That I had been a great and grievous sinner, and that it was now too late for me to look after Heaven; for Christ would not forgive me, nor pardon*

---

[1] *game at cat* also called tip-cat. Played with a cudgel and a wooden cylinder (the cat) tapering to a point at both ends; the cat was tipped into the air and then hit, with points scored for correctly estimating the distance it would go. The hole is the place on the ground where the cat was laid (*OED* tip-cat 2).

my transgressions. Then I fell to musing upon this also; and while I was thinking on it, and fearing lest it should be so, I felt my heart sink in despair, concluding it was too late; and therefore I resolved in my mind I would go on in sin: for thought I, if the case be thus, my state is surely miserable; miserable if I leave my sins; and but miserable if I follow them: I can but be damned; and if I must be so, I had as good be damned for many sins, as be damned for few.

Thus I stood in the midst of my play, before all that then were present; but yet I told them nothing: but, I say, I having made this conclusion, I returned desperately to my sport again; and I well remember, that presently this kind of despair did so possess my soul, that I was persuaded I could never attain to other comfort than what I should get in sin; for Heaven was gone already, so that on that I must not think: wherefore I found within me a great desire to take my fill of sin, still studying what sin was set to be committed, that I might taste the sweetness of it; and I made as much haste as I could to fill my belly with its delicates, lest I should die before I had my desire; for that I feared greatly. In these things, I protest before God, I lie not, neither do I feign this sort of speech: these were really, strongly, and with all my heart, my desires; *the good Lord, whose mercy is unsearchable, forgive me my transgressions.*

(And I am very confident, that this temptation of the Devil is more than usual amongst poor creatures than many are aware of, even to over-run their spirits with a scurvy and seared frame of heart, and benumbing of conscience: which frame, he stilly and slyly supplieth with such despair, that though not much guilt attendeth the soul, yet they continually have a secret conclusion within them, that there is no hopes for them; "for they have loved sins, therefore after them they will go," Jer. 2:25 & 18:12).

Now therefore I went on in sin with great greediness of mind, still grudging that I could not be so satisfied with it as I would: this did continue with me about a month, or more. But one day, as I was standing at a neighbour's shop window, and there cursing and swearing, and playing the madman, after my wonted manner, there sat within the woman of the house, and heard me; who, though she was a very loose and ungodly wretch, yet protested that I swore and cursed at that most fearful rate, that she was made to tremble to hear me; and told me further, "That I was the ungodliest fellow for swearing that ever she heard in all her life; and that I, by thus doing, was able to spoil all the youth in a whole town, if they came but in my company."

At this reproof I was silenced, and put to secret shame; and that too, as I thought, before the God of Heaven: wherefore, while I stood there, and hanging down my head, I wished with all my heart that I might be a little child again, that my father might learn me to speak without this wicked way of swearing: for, thought I, I am so accustomed to it, that it is but in vain for me to think of a reformation, for I thought it could never be.

But how it came to pass I know not, I did from this time forward so leave my swearing, that it was a great wonder to myself to observe it; and whereas before I knew not how to speak unless I put an oath before, and another behind, to make my words have authority, now, I could, without it, speak better, and with more pleasantness then ever I could before: all this while I knew not Jesus Christ, neither did I leave my sports and play.

But quickly after this, I fell in company with one poor man that made profession of religion; who, as I then thought, did talk pleasantly of the Scriptures, and of the matters of religion: wherefore falling into some love and liking to what he said, I betook me to my Bible, and began to take great pleasure in reading, but especially with the historical part thereof: for, as for Paul's Epistles, and Scriptures of that nature, I could not away with them, being as yet but ignorant either of the corruptions of my nature, or of the want and worth of Jesus Christ to save me.

Wherefore I fell to some outward reformation, both in my words and life, and did set the Commandments before me for my way to Heaven: which Commandments I also did strive to keep; and, as I thought, did keep them pretty well sometimes, and then I should have comfort; yet now and then should break one, and so afflict my conscience; but then I should repent, and say I was sorry for it, and promise God to do better next time, and there get help again, for then I thought I pleased God as well as any man in England.

Thus I continued about a year, all which time our neighbours did take me to be a very godly man, a new and religious man, and did marvel much to see such a great and famous alteration in my life and manners; and indeed so it was, though yet I knew not Christ, nor grace, nor faith, nor hope; and truly as I have well seen since, had I then died, my state had been most fearful: well, this I say, continued about a twelve-month, or more.

But, I say, my neighbours were amazed at this my great conversion, from prodigious profaneness, to something like a moral life; and, truly, so they well might; for this my conversion was as great, as for Tom of Bethlem to become a sober man.[1] Now, therefore, they began to praise, to commend, and to speak well of me, both to my face, and behind my back. Now, I was, as they said, become godly; now, I was become a right honest man. But Oh! when I understood that these were their words and opinions of me, it pleased me mighty well: For though, as yet, I was nothing but a poor painted hypocrite, yet I loved to be talked of as one that was truly godly. I was proud of my godliness; and, I did all I did, either to be seen of, or to be well spoken of, by

men: well, this I say, continued for about a twelve-month or more.

Now you must know, that before this I had taken much delight in ringing,[2] but my conscience beginning to be tender, I thought that such a practice was but vain, and therefore forced myself to leave it, yet my mind hankered, wherefore I should go to the steeple house, and look on: though I durst not ring. But I thought this did not become religion neither, yet I forced myself and would look on still; but quickly after, I began to think, how, if one of the bells should fall: then I chose to stand under a main beam that lay over thwart the steeple from side to side, thinking there I might stand sure: But then I should think again, should the bell fall with a swing, it might first hit the wall, and then rebounding upon me, might kill me for all this beam; this made me stand in the steeple door, and now thought I, I am safe enough, for if a bell should then fall, I can slip out behind these thick walls, and so be preserved notwithstanding.

So after this, I would yet go to see them ring, but would not go further than the steeple door; but then it came into my head, how if the steeple itself should fall, and this thought (it may fall for ought I know), would when I stood and looked on, continually so shake my mind, that I durst not stand at the steeple door any longer, but was forced to fly, for fear it should fall upon my head.

Another thing was my dancing, I was a full year before I could quite leave it; but all this while, when I thought I kept this or that Commandment, or did by word or deed anything that I thought were good, I had great peace in my conscience, and should think with myself, God cannot choose but be now pleased with me, yea, to relate it in mine own way, I thought no man in England could please God better than I.

---

[1] *Tom of Bethlem* a generic name for a madman, derived from Bethlehem (often corrupted to Bedlam) Hospital outside London, where the insane were kept.

[2] *ringing* bell-ringing, a popular pastime requiring a team of ringers; Bunyan's church in Elstow had five tuned bells.

But poor wretch as I was, I was all this while ignorant of Jesus Christ, and going about to establish my own righteousness, had perished therein, had not God in mercy showed me more of my state by nature.

But upon a day, the good providence of God did cast me to Bedford,[1] to work on my calling; and in one of the streets of that town, I came where there was three or four poor women sitting at a door in the sun, and talking about the things of God; and being now willing to hear them discourse, I drew near to hear what they said; for I was now a brisk talker also myself in the matters of religion; but now I may say, "I heard, but I understood not"; for they were far above out of my reach, for their talk was about a new birth, the work of God on their hearts, also how they were convinced of their miserable state by nature: they talked how God had visited their souls with his love in the Lord Jesus, and with what words and promises they had been refreshed, comforted, and supported against the temptations of the Devil; moreover, they reasoned of the suggestions and temptations of Satan in particular, and told to each other by which they had been afflicted, and how they were borne up under his assaults: they also discoursed of their own wretchedness of heart, of their unbelief, and did contemn, slight, and abhor their own righteousness, as filthy, and insufficient to do them any good.

And me thought they spake as if joy did make them speak: they spake with such pleasantness of Scripture language, and with such appearance of grace in all they said, that they were to me as if they had found a new world, as if they were people that dwelt alone, and were not to be reckoned among their neighbours, Num. 23:9.

At this I felt my own heart began to shake, as mistrusting my condition to be naught; for I saw that in all my thoughts about religion and salvation,

the new birth did never enter into my mind, neither knew I the comfort of the word and promise, nor the deceitfulness and treachery of my own wicked heart. As for secret thoughts, I took no notice of them; neither did I understand what Satan's temptations were, nor how they were to be withstood and resisted, &c.

Thus therefore when I had heard and considered what they said, I left them, and went about my employment again: but their talk and discourse went with me, also my heart would tarry with them, for I was greatly affected with their words, both because by them I was convinced that I wanted the true tokens of a truly godly man, and also because by them I was convinced of the happy and blessed condition of him that was such a one.

—1666

The Pilgrim's Progress
(excerpt)

CHRISTIAN AND FAITHFUL VISIT VANITY FAIR

Then I saw in my dream, that when they were got out of the wilderness, they presently saw a town before them, and the name of that town is Vanity; and at the town there is a fair kept called Vanity Fair:[2] It is kept all the year long, it beareth the name of Vanity Fair, because the town where 'tis kept, is lighter than vanity; and also, because all that is there sold, or that cometh thither, is vanity. As is the saying of the wise, "All that cometh is vanity."[3]

This fair is no new erected business, but a thing of ancient standing; I will show you the original of it.

Almost five thousand years agone, there were pilgrims walking to the celestial city, as these two

---

[1] Bunyan moved to Bedford in 1655 and joined the Separatist congregation there; he began to preach in 1656.

[2] Bunyan's Vanity Fair is probably modeled in some details on the great annual fair held at Stourbridge, near Cambridge, which had its own court to try offences committed in the fair.

[3] Bunyan cites Isaiah 40:17 and Ecclesiastes 1:2, 11, 17.

honest persons are; and Beelzebub, Apollyon, and Legion, with their companions, perceiving by the path that the pilgrims made, that their way to the city lay through this town of Vanity, they contrived here to set up a fair; a fair wherein should be sold of all sorts of vanity, and that it should last all the year long. Therefore at this fair are all such merchandise sold, as houses, lands, trades, places, honours, preferments, titles, countries, kingdoms, lusts, pleasures, and delights of all sorts, as whores, bawds, wives, husbands, children, masters, servants, lives, blood, bodies, souls, silver, gold, pearls, precious stones, and what not.

And moreover, at this fair there is at all times to be seen jugglings, cheats, games, plays, fools, apes, knaves, and rogues, and that of all sorts.

Here are to be seen too, and that for nothing, thefts, murders, adulteries, false swearers, and that of a blood-red colour.

And as in other fairs of less moment, there are the several rows and streets under their proper names, where such and such wares are vended, so here likewise, you have the proper places, rows, streets (*viz.* countries, and kingdoms), where the wares of this fair are soonest to be found: Here is the Britain row, the French row, the Italian row, the Spanish row, the German row, where several sorts of vanities are to be sold. But as in other fairs, some one commodity is as the chief of all the fair, so the ware of Rome and her merchandise is greatly promoted in this fair.[1] Only our English nation, with some others, have taken a dislike thereat.

Now, as I said, the way to the celestial city lies just through this town, where this lusty fair is kept; and he that will go to the city, and yet not go through this town, must needs go out of the world. The prince of princes himself, when here, went through this town to his own country, and that upon a Fair-day too: Yea, and as I think it was Beelzebub, the chief Lord of this fair, that invited him to buy of his vanities; yea, would have made him Lord of the fair, would he but have done him reverence as he went through the town. Yea, because he was such a person of honour, Beelzebub had him from street to street, and showed him all the kingdoms of the world in a little time, that he might if possible allure that blessed one, to cheapen and buy some of his vanities. But he had no mind to the merchandise, and therefore left the town; without laying out so much as one farthing upon these vanities. This fair therefore is an ancient thing, of long standing, and a very great fair.

Now these pilgrims, as I said, must needs go through this fair: Well, so they did; but behold, even as they entered into the fair, all the people in the fair were moved, and the town itself as it were in a hubbub about them; and that for several reasons: For,

First, the pilgrims were clothed with such kind of raiment, as was diverse from the raiment of any that traded in that fair. The people therefore of the fair made a great gazing upon them: Some said they were fools, some they were bedlams, and some they were outlandish men.[2]

Secondly, and as they wondered at their apparel, so they did likewise at their speech; for few could understand what they said; they naturally spoke the language of Canaan; but they that kept the fair, were the men of this world: so that from one end of the fair to the other, they seemed barbarians each to the other.

Thirdly, but that which did not a little amuse the merchandisers,[3] was, that these pilgrims set very light by all their wares, they cared not so much as to look upon them: and if they called upon them to buy, they would put their fingers in their ears, and

---

[1] *ware of Rome* Roman Catholic doctrines and rites.

[2] *outlandish men* foreigners.

[3] *amuse* amaze, bewilder (*OED* amuse *v* 2).

cry, "Turn away mine eyes from beholding vanity";[1] and look upwards, signifying that their trade and traffic was in Heaven.

One chanced mockingly, beholding the carriages of the men, to say unto them, What will ye buy? but they, looking gravely upon him, said, "We buy the truth."[2] At that, there was an occasion taken to despise the men the more; some mocking, some taunting, some speaking reproachfully, and some calling upon others to smite them. At last things came to an hubbub, and great stir in the fair; insomuch that all order was confounded. Now was word presently brought to the great one of the fair, who quickly came down, and deputed some of his most trusty friends to take these men into examination, about whom the fair was almost overturned. So the men were brought to examination; and they that sat upon them, asked them whence they came, whither they went, and what they did there in such an unusual garb? The men told them, that they were pilgrims and strangers in the world, and that they were going to their own country, which was the heavenly Jerusalem; and that they had given none occasion to the men of the town, nor yet to the merchandisers, thus to abuse them, and to let them in their journey,[3] except it was, for that, when one asked them what they would buy, they said, they would buy the truth. But they that were appointed to examine them, did not believe them to be any other then bedlams and mad, or else such as came to put all things into a confusion in the fair. Therefore they took them, and beat them, and besmeared them with dirt, and then put them into the cage, that they might be made a spectacle to all the men of the fair. There therefore they lay for some time, and were made the objects of any man's sport, or malice, or revenge, the great one of the fair

laughing still at all that befell them. But the men being patient, and not rendering railing for railing, but contrariwise blessing, and giving good words for bad, and kindness for injuries done: Some men in the fair that were more observing, and less prejudiced than the rest, began to check and blame the baser sort for their continual abuses done by them to the men: They therefore in angry manner let fly at them again, counting them as bad as the men in the cage, and telling them that they seemed confederates, and should be made partakers of their misfortunes. The other replied, that for ought they could see, the men were quiet, and sober, and intended nobody any harm; and that there were many that traded in their fair, that were more worthy to be put into the cage, yea, and pillory too, than were the men that they had abused. Thus, after divers words had passed on both sides (the men behaving themselves all the while very wisely, and soberly before them), they fell to some blows, among themselves, and did harm one to another. Then were these two poor men brought before their examiners again, and there charged as being guilty of the late hubbub that had been in the fair. So they beat them pitifully, and hanged irons upon them, and led them in chains up and down the fair, for an example and a terror to others, lest any should further speak in their behalf, or join themselves unto them. But Christian and Faithful behaved themselves yet more wisely, and received the ignominy and shame that was cast upon them, with so much meekness and patience, that it won to their side (though but few in comparison of the rest) several of the men in the fair. This put the other party yet into a greater rage, insomuch that they concluded the death of these two men. Wherefore they threatened that neither the cage, nor irons, should serve their turn, but that they should die, for the abuse they had done, and for deluding the men of the fair.

---

[1] Psalm 119:37.

[2] Proverbs 23:23.

[3] *let* hinder.

Then were they remanded to the cage again, until further order should be taken with them. So they put them in, and made their feet fast in the stocks.

Here also they called again to mind what they had heard from their faithful friend Evangelist, and were the more confirmed in their way and sufferings, by what he told them would happen to them.[1] They also now comforted each other, that whose lot it was to suffer, even he should have the best on't; therefore each man secretly wished that he might have that preferment: but committing themselves to the all-wise dispose of him that ruleth all things, with much content they abode in the condition in which they were, until they should be otherwise disposed of.

Then a convenient time being appointed, they brought them forth to their trial in order to their condemnation. When the time was come, they were brought before their enemies and arraigned; the Judge's name was Lord Hategood.[2] Their indictment was one and the same in substance, though somewhat varying in form; the contents whereof was this:

"That they were enemies to, and disturbers of their trade; that they had made commotions and divisions in the town, and had won a party to their own most dangerous opinions, in contempt of the law of their Prince."[3]

Then Faithful began to answer, That he had only set himself against that which had set itself against him that is higher than the highest. And, said he, As for disturbance, I make none, being myself a man of peace; the party that were won to us, were won, by beholding our truth and innocence, and they are only turned from the worse to the better. And as to the King you talk of; since he is Beelzebub, the enemy of our Lord, I defy him and all his angels.

Then proclamation was made, that they that had ought to say for the Lord the King against the prisoner at the bar, should forthwith appear, and give in their evidence. So there came in three witnesses, to wit, Envy, Superstition, and Pickthank.[4] They were then asked, If they knew the prisoner at the bar? and what they had to say for their Lord the King against him?

Then stood forth Envy, and said to this effect; My Lord, I have known this man a long time, and will attest upon my oath before this honourable bench, that he is—

Judge. Hold, give him his oath: So they sware him. Then he said, My Lord, this man, notwithstanding his plausible name, is one of the vilest men in our country; he neither regardeth Prince nor people, law nor custom; but doth all that he can to possess all men with certain of his disloyal notions, which he in the general calls principles of faith and holiness. And in particular, I heard him once myself affirm, "That Christianity, and the customs of our town of Vanity, were diametrically opposite, and could not be reconciled." By which saying, my Lord, he doth at once, not only condemn all our laudable doings, but us in the doing of them.

Judge. Then did the Judge say to him, Hast thou any more to say?

Envy. My Lord, I could say much more, only I would not be tedious to the court. Yet if need be,

---

[1] Evangelist had told Faithful and Christian that in Vanity Fair they would "be hardly beset with enemies who will strain hard but they will kill you; and be sure that one or both of you must seal the testimony which you hold, with blood: but be faithful unto death, and the King will give you a crown of life. He that shall die there, although his death will be unnatural, and his pain perhaps great, he will yet have the better of his fellow; not only because he will be arrived at the Celestial City soonest, but because he will escape many miseries that the other will meet with in the rest of his journey."

[2] a character probably based on the Lord Chief Justice George Jeffreys (1648–89), who was notoriously harsh in his treatment of Dissenters.

[3] Throughout the trial, Bunyan observes the formulas and procedures of contemporary English legal practice.

---

[4] *Pickthank* flatterer.

when the other gentlemen have given in their evidence, rather than anything shall be wanting that will dispatch him, I will enlarge my testimony against him. So he was bid stand by. Then they called Superstition, and bid him look upon the prisoner; they also asked, What he could say for their Lord the King against him? Then they sware him, so he began.

Superstition. My Lord, I have no great acquaintance with this man, nor do I desire to have further knowledge of him; however this I know, that he is a very pestilent fellow, from some discourse that the other day I had with him in this town; for then talking with him, I heard him say, "That our religion was naught, and such by which a man could by no means please God": which sayings of his, my Lord, your Lordship very well knows, what necessarily thence will follow, to wit, That we still do worship in vain, are yet in our sins, and finally shall be damned; and this is that which I have to say.

Then was Pickthank sworn, and bid say what he knew, in behalf of their Lord the King against the prisoner at the bar.

Pickthank. My Lord, and you gentlemen all, This fellow I have known of a long time, and have heard him speak things that ought not to be spoke. For he hath railed on our noble Prince Beelzebub, and hath spoke contemptibly of his honourable friends, whose names are the Lord Old Man, the Lord Carnal Delight, the Lord Luxurious, the Lord Desire of Vain-glory, my old Lord Lechery, Sir Having Greedy, with all the rest of our nobility; and he hath said moreover, that if all men were of his mind, if possible, there is not one of these noblemen should have any longer a being in this town. Besides, he hath not been afraid to rail on you, my Lord, who are now appointed to be his Judge, calling you an ungodly villain, with many other such like vilifying terms, with which he hath bespattered most of the gentry of our town. When this Pickthank had told his tale, the Judge directed

his speech to the prisoner at the bar, saying, Thou runagate, heretic, and traitor, hast thou heard what these honest gentlemen have witnessed against thee.

Faithful. May I speak a few words in my own defence?

Judge. Sirrah, sirrah, thou deservest to live no longer, but to be slain immediately upon the place; yet that all men may see our gentleness towards thee, let us hear what thou hast to say.

Faithful. 1. I say then in answer to what Mr. Envy hath spoken, I never said ought but this, "That what rule, or laws, or custom, or people, were flat against the word of God, are diametrically opposite to Christianity." If I have said amiss in this, convince me of my error, and I am ready here before you to make my recantation.

2. As to the second, to wit, Mr. Superstition, and his charge against me, I said only this, "That in the worship of God there is required a divine faith; but there can be no divine faith, without a divine revelation of the will of God: therefore whatever is thrust into the worship of God, that is not agreeable to divine revelation, cannot be done but by an humane faith, which faith will not profit to eternal life."

3. As to what Mr. Pickthank hath said, I say (avoiding terms, as that I am said to rail, and the like), "That the Prince of this town, with all the rabblement his attendants, by this gentleman named, are more fit for a being in Hell, than in this town and country"; And so the Lord have mercy upon me.

Then the Judge called to the jury (who all this while stood by, to hear and observe), "Gentlemen of the jury, you see this man about whom so great an uproar hath been made in this town: you have also heard what these worthy gentlemen have witnessed against him; also you have heard his reply and confession: It lieth now in your breasts to hang him, or save his life. But yet I think meet to instruct you into our law.

"There was an act made in the days of Pharaoh the Great, servant to our Prince, That lest those of a contrary religion should multiply and grow too strong for him, their males should be thrown into the river. There was also an act made in the days of Nebuchadnezzar the Great, another of his servants, That whoever would not fall down and worship his golden image, should be thrown into a fiery furnace. There was also an act made in the days of Darius, That who so, for some time, called upon any God but his, should be cast into the lion's den. Now the substance of these laws this rebel has broken, not only in thought (which is not to be borne), but also in word and deed; which must therefore needs be intolerable.

"For that of Pharaoh, his law was made upon a supposition, to prevent mischief, no crime being yet apparent; but here is a crime apparent. For the second and third, you see he disputeth against our religion; and for the treason he hath confessed, he deserveth to die the death."

Then went the jury out, whose names were Mr. Blind-man, Mr. No-good, Mr. Malice, Mr. Love-lust, Mr. Live-loose, Mr. Heady, Mr. High-mind, Mr. Enmity, Mr. Liar, Mr. Cruelty, Mr. Hate-light, and Mr. Implacable, who everyone gave in his private verdict against him among themselves, and afterwards unanimously concluded to bring him in guilty before the Judge. And first Mr. Blind-man, the foreman, said, "I see clearly that this man is an heretic." Then said Mr. No-good, "Away with such a fellow from the earth." "Ay," said Mr. Malice, "for I hate the very looks of him." Then said Mr. Love-lust, "I could never endure him." "Nor I," said Mr. Live-loose, "for he would always be condemning my way." "Hang him, hang him," said Mr. Heady. "A sorry scrub," said Mr. High-mind. "My heart riseth against him," said Mr. Enmity. "He is a rogue," said Mr. Liar. "Hanging is too good for him," said Mr. Cruelty. "Let's dispatch him out of the way," said Mr. Hate-light. Then said Mr.

Implacable, "Might I have all the world given me, I could not be reconciled to him, therefore let us forthwith bring him in guilty of death": And so they did, therefore he was presently condemned, To be had from the place where he was, to the place from whence he came, and there to be put to the most cruel death that could be invented.

They therefore brought him out, to do with him according to their law; and first they scourged him, then they buffeted him, then they lanced his flesh with knives; after that they stoned him with stones, then pricked him with their swords, and last of all they burned him to ashes at the stake.[1] Thus came Faithful to his end. Now, I saw that there stood behind the multitude, a chariot and a couple of horses, waiting for Faithful, who (so soon as his adversaries had dispatched him) was taken up into it,[2] and straightway was carried up through the clouds, with sound of trumpet, the nearest way to the celestial gate. But as for Christian, he had some respite, and was remanded back to prison; so he there remained for a space: But he that over-rules all things, having the power of their rage in his own hand, so wrought it about, that Christian for that time escaped them, and went his way.

And as he went he sang:

> Well Faithful, thou hast faithfully profest
> Unto thy Lord: with him thou shalt be blest;
> When Faithless ones, with all their vain
>   delights,
> Are crying out under their hellish plights.
> Sing, Faithful, sing; and let thy name survive;
> For though they kill'd thee, thou art yet alive.

—1678

---

[1] Bunyan draws on the descriptions of Protestant martyrdoms in John Foxe's *Acts and Monuments* (often known as the *Book of Martyrs*), first published in 1563 and frequently reprinted in increasingly expanded editions.

[2] like Elijah, in II Kings 2:11.

King Charles II
1630 – 1685

In February 1660, General George Monck marched his army from Scotland to London and forced the recall of the members of Parliament expelled in Pride's Purge (1648). The augmented House voted to dissolve the Long Parliament, and in March a Convention Parliament was elected in which the republicans were routed. The final obstacle to the restoration of the monarchy was removed in April, when Charles issued a declaration from Breda, his residence in southwestern Netherlands, in which he promised a general pardon to those who had acted against the crown in the previous twenty years (with exceptions to be named), liberty of conscience in religion (where it "did not disturb the peace of the kingdom"), and the determination of all disputed matters (such as the sale of Royalist lands) in Parliament. The Earl of Clarendon, who had helped write the text, believed that the Declaration of Breda "by God's inspiration had been the sole visible motive to that wonderful change that had ensued." All clauses were subject to ratification by Parliament. The sale of Royalist lands was eventually confirmed, and the Act of Indemnity and Oblivion (1660) gave legislative effect to the promised general amnesty, with the exception of fifty named individuals (thirteen regicides were eventually executed). The promise of religious toleration, however, was to prove unacceptable to the "Cavalier" Parliament, which passed instead an Act of Uniformity (1662) that led to the resignation of a large number of dissenting clergy.

പ്രപ്ര

The Declaration of Breda

Charles R.

Charles, by the grace of God, King of England, Scotland, France and Ireland, Defender of the Faith, &c. To all our loving subjects, of what degree or quality soever, greeting.

If the general distraction and confusion which is spread over the whole kingdom doth not awaken all men to a desire and longing that those wounds which have so many years together been kept bleeding, may be bound up, all we can say will be to no purpose; however, after this long silence, we have thought it our duty to declare how much we desire to contribute thereunto; and that as we can never give over the hope, in good time, to obtain the possession of that right which God and nature hath made our due, so we do make it our daily suit to the Divine Providence, that He will, in compassion to us and our subjects, after so long misery and sufferings, remit and put us into a quiet and peaceable possession of that our right, with as little blood and damage to our people as is possible; nor do we desire more to enjoy what is ours, than that all our subjects may enjoy what by law is theirs, by a full and entire administration of justice throughout the land, and by extending our mercy where it is wanted and deserved.

And to the end that the fear of punishment may not engage any, conscious to themselves of what is past, to a perseverance in guilt for the future, by opposing the quiet and happiness of their country, in the restoration of King, Peers and people to their just, ancient and fundamental rights, we do, by these presents, declare, that we do grant a free and general pardon, which we are ready, upon demand, to pass under our Great Seal of England, to all our subjects, of what degree or quality soever, who, within forty days after the publishing hereof, shall lay hold upon this our grace and favour, and shall, by any public act, declare their doing so, and that they return to the loyalty and obedience of good subjects; excepting only such persons as shall hereafter be excepted by Parliament, those only to be excepted. Let all our subjects, how faulty soever, rely upon the word of a King, solemnly given by this present declaration, that no crime whatsoever, committed against us or our royal father before the publication of this, shall ever rise in judgment, or be brought in question, against any of them, to the least endamagement of them, either in their lives, liberties or estates, or (as far forth as lies in our power) so much as to the prejudice of their reputations, by any reproach or term of distinction from the rest of our best subjects; we desiring and ordaining that henceforth all notes of discord, separation and difference of parties be utterly abolished among all our subjects, whom we invite and conjure to a perfect union among themselves, under our protection, for the re-settlement of our just rights and theirs in a free Parliament, by which, upon the word of a King, we will be advised.

And because the passion and uncharitableness of the times have produced several opinions in religion, by which men are engaged in parties and animosities against each other (which, when they shall hereafter unite in a freedom of conversation, will be composed or better understood), we do declare a liberty to tender consciences, and that no man shall be disquieted or called in question for differences of opinion in matter of religion, which do not disturb the peace of the kingdom; and that we shall be ready to consent to such an Act of Parliament, as, upon mature deliberation, shall be offered to us, for the full granting that indulgence.

And because, in the continued distractions of so many years, and so many and great revolutions, many grants and purchases of estates have been made to and by many officers, soldiers and others, who are now possessed of the same, and who may be liable to actions at law upon several titles, we are likewise willing that all such differences, and all things relating to such grants, sales and purchases, shall be determined in Parliament, which can best provide for the just satisfaction of all men who are concerned.

And we do further declare, that we will be ready to consent to any Act or Acts of Parliament to the purposes aforesaid, and for the full satisfaction of all arrears due to the officers and soldiers of the army under the command of General Monck; and that they shall be received into our service upon as good pay and conditions as they now enjoy.

Given under our Sign Manual and Privy Signet, at our Court at Breda, this 14 day of April, 1660, in the twelfth year of our reign.[1]

—1660

---

[1] The reign is dated from the execution of Charles I in January 1649.

Anthony à Wood
1632 – 1695

The antiquary Anthony à Wood (the "à" was his characteristically idiosyncratic addition) was born in Oxford in a house across from Merton College, which he entered as an undergraduate in 1647; he would live in the same house for the rest of his life, surviving on a modest inherited income and compiling materials for the history of the university and its members. In his lifetime Wood published *Historia et Antiquitates Universitatis Oxoniensis* (Oxford, 1674) and a biographical dictionary, *Athenae Oxoniensis: An Exact History of all the Writers and Bishops who have had their Education in the University of Oxford* (1691–92). In addition, he left at his death a mass of manuscript papers, including substantial autobiographical material, much of which has been subsequently edited. Wood's quarrelsome personality and frank opinions made him unpopular at Oxford: contemporaries resented his "slanderous and saucy reflections" on the characters of the men he wrote about, and in 1693 *Athenae Oxoniensis* was accused of libelling the Earl of Clarendon and publicly burned. But the collections Wood compiled are an invaluable resource for historians and literary scholars, and are in many ways most interesting for Wood's gossipy and often abusive accounts of people and events in Oxford during the second half of the seventeenth century.

The nineteenth-century editor of Wood's *Life and Times* produced his five-volume text by combining an autobiographical narrative with journals and other manuscript sources Wood left at his death. In the autobiography, Wood refers to himself in the third person. The short passages omitted between the selected entries presented here include such information as lists of books loaned, death notices, transcriptions of Latin inscriptions, College election results, genealogical charts, and money spent on food, drink, and pamphlets. The biographies of Jeremy Taylor and Robert Burton are selected from *Athenae Oxoniensis*; for more on these writers, see the introductions to the selections from their works.

૭൦ഽൗ

The Life and Times of Anthony à Wood
(extracts)

Notes on Oxford during the Interregnum

Now for a conclusion I shall make bold to show you in what esteem the University stood in the late broken times, viz. from the year 1648 to 1660, and then a character of the members thereof in general of that time....

'Tis well known that the Universities of this land have had their beginnings and continuances to no other end but to propagate religion and good manners and supply the nation with persons chiefly professing the three famous faculties of Divinity, Law, and Physick. But in these late times when the dregs of people grew wiser than their teachers, and pretended to have received revelations, visions, inspirations, and I know not what, and therefore above all religion ordinarily professed, nothing could satisfy their insatiable desires but aiming at an utter subversion of them [the Universities], church, and schools, or those places that they thought might put a curb to their proceedings. Intelligent men knew and saw very well that it was their intent to rout up all and to ruin those things that smelt of an Academy, never rejoicing more than when they could trample on the gown and bring humane learning and arts into disgrace. This I may very boldly say and none can deny it that these domestic confusions among ourselves about matters of religion, and insurrections of seditious subjects that have and do pretend to reformation, hath been the only reason why these nurseries must first feel the smart of their implacasy,[1] supposing thereby that unless they were subverted nothing of their designs as to the settlement of their opinions can take place.

Some there were also that made it their common practice to preach against them, styling them "the nurseries of wickedness, the nests of mutton tuggers, the dens of formal drones"; ever and anon styling the Colleges and Halls "cages of unclean birds"; and such like....

And as it was a common matter to declaim against Universities in public, so was it also in the private meetings and conventicles of Anabaptists, Quakers, and such like unstable people, challenging also sometimes the gown itself to oppose what they did and said, and this ever in the Universities themselves, they being backed by force of arms or else some authority....

Furthermore also some there were that endeavoured in their writings to make a reformation of the Universities not as to manners, but discipline; not as to a settlement and well-ordering of their lands, but to the taking them away "to the end that drones might not be nursed up"; not to the increasing or augmenting of several nurseries in the Universities, but to the decreasing, by joining several into one....

Manners: factious, saucy, and some impudent and conceited, morose (incident to most that are sedentary and studious),[2] false, factious in College, and delighting in petty plots and raising in basin of water,[3] reserved (being always jealous that what they said or did should be told to others to disadvantage). Scorning at anything that seemed formal;

laughing at a man in a cassock or canonical coat or long cloak to the heels, at those praying with hats before their eyes when they come into the church or kneeling down against a pillar or form. Scorning and laughing at those that used the Lord's prayer. Never styled any church by the name of "St." as "St. Mary's," "St. Peter's" etc.; but "he preached at Mary's," "Peter's" etc.

Discipline: by constant preaching and praying they worked very much upon the affections of people, and some in so great manner that they proved no better than crazed people, or such that are dreamers of dreams, that pretend to revelations, to be instructed by visions.... Disputing constantly, and many good disputants they bred up, especially in philosophy; for divinity, I think none, for few or none had respect for the fathers and schoolmen, and scholars made use of them in disputing. Philosophical disputations often in the Greek tongue in those times (but since this Restoration seldom or never); but fighting in the schools and other times in the streets (to the great scandal of the gown), frequent. The sale of books very much, practical divinity and quaint discourses, and money plenty;[4] not so after the Restoration. Quaint discourses extant; since, nothing but plays and sermons, and foolish drollery.

[They used to] love and encourage instrumental music; but did not care for vocal, because that was used in church by the prelatical party. They would not go to ale-houses or taverns, but send for their liquors to their respective chambers and tipple it there. Some would go in public; but then, if overtaken [with drink] they were so cunning as to dissemble it in their way home by a lame leg or that some sudden pain there had taken them. [They would] countenance none but such that "had the grace of God in them." No public spirits, but

[1] *implacasy* apparently coined by Wood from "implacable."

[2] *incident to most that are...studious* Robert Burton discusses this belief at some length in the selection from *The Anatomy of Melancholy* (in "Love of Learning, or Overmuch Study. With a Digression of the Misery of Scholars").

[3] *raising in basin of water* making storms in a teacup.

[4] In another version of this note, Wood expands: "Money then stirring, and coming in from the new gentlemen."

minded only their endearments and comfortable importances....

They were great enemies to May-games and would never suffer anything thereof to be done in the University or city, as May-poles, morrises, Whitsun ales; nay, scarce wakes.

They would not suffer any common players to come into the University, nor scholars to act in private but what they did by stealth; yet at Act times they would permit dancing the rope, drolls, or monstrous sights to be seen.

They would not suffer any swearing or cursing; and if a scholar was found guilty of either, expulsion for the most part was his punishment: if any town-man, a forfeiture of money, the stocks, or prison.

[They did] avoid the company of royalists and the prelatical party, as the protestants did the papists and popishly affected after the plot was discovered in the latter end of September 1678.[1]

They suffered not public drunkenness but punished it very severely, and did make the boon party that were guilty of it so scandalous in their discourse, nay, in sermons, that it frighted the young fry from it and their company.

Being taken off from these pleasing matters, they became factious among themselves, and ever and anon carrying tales to the great persons and endeavouring to lift one another out; so that every man carrying himself wary and being jealous, seldom free discourse or company was made. We had no coffee houses then.

Many also of them that were the sons of upstart gentlemen, such that had got the good places into their hands belonging to the law-courts and had bought the lands of the clergy and gentry, were generally very proud, saucy, impudent, and seldom gave respect to any but the leading person. As for any of the old stock, they laughed and flouted at them, scarce gave them the wall, much less the common civility of a hat:[2] and so it was that the ancient gentry of the nation were despised.

The inferior sort or juniors went very lavishly in their apparel; they always wore hats with ribbon, powdered hair, laced bands and tassel or snake-bow band-strings, half shirts, and long cuffs: and no wonder, seeing Dr. [John] Owen when vice-chancellor had always his hair powdered, cambric band with large costly band-strings, velvet jacket, his breeches set round at knee with ribbons pointed, Spanish leather boots with cambric tops, etc. And all this was in opposition to a prelatical cut.

Gowns with wide sleeves (as wide as surplices), brought by the Cambridge bachelors; imitated by undergraduates. Masters' gowns long, draggling on the ground, sleeves also not used by ancient scholars, faced with velvet.

The University flourished in number, but few nobility; few gentry also, unless to Colleges where an old Head and some Fellows remained. After the Restoration it did in some manner decay in number: Presbyterians and Independents and other fanatical people did forbear to send them for fear of orthodox principles. Another party thought an University too low a breeding; entertained one [a tutor] at home, who infused principles of atheism. Others sent them beyond the seas and they return home factious and propagate faction. Another party (the papists), they send also beyond sea.

THE RESTORATION

Feb. 13, Monday, at night, was great rejoicing here in Oxon [Oxford] for the news that then was

---

[1] *the plot* the Popish Plot (1678), a fictitious Jesuit plot to assassinate Charles II and place the Catholic James, Duke of York, on the throne; reports of the plot caused widespread panic.

[2] *old stock* the pre-war Masters of Arts and Fellows of Colleges who still remained in Oxford; *give the wall* a mark of courtesy: when two people approached one another on a street, the junior of the two was expected to let the senior pass closest to the building, where the ground was likely less messy; *civility of the hat* undergraduates were expected to raise their cap to any M.A. or Fellow.

brought, that there should suddenly be a free parliament. The bells rang, and bonfires were made, and some rumps or tails of sheep were flung into a bonfire at Queen's College gate. Dr. John Palmer, a great rumper, warden of All Souls College in the place of Dr. [Gilbert] Sheldon, being then very ill and weak, had a rump thrown up from the street at his windows. He had been one of the rump parliament, and a favourite of Oliver [Cromwell]....

At this time [February 1660] A. W. [Anthony Wood] being resolved to set himself to the study of antiquities and do something in them in the house where he was born, he set up a chimney in the upper room looking eastward; and in the next room joining he put out a window next to the street, and made it a study, in which he composed for the most part those things which he afterwards published....

The pictures of prophets, apostles, saints, &c. that had been painted on the back-side of the stalls in Merton College choir, in various and antique shapes, about the beginning of the reign of King Henry 7, were daubed over with paint by the command of the usurpers, about 1651, to the sorrow of curious men that were admirers of ancient painting. But that daubing wearing away in two or three years, they were all painted over in oil colours this year [1660] and the ancient pictures quite obliterated. While the workmen were performing this work, several of the brass plates, with inscriptions, on gravestones were most sacrilegiously torn up, and taken away, either by some of the painters, or other workmen then working in the chapel. A.W. complained of these things to the Fellows and desired them to look after the offenders; but, with shame be it spoken, not one of them did resent the matter, or enquire after the sacrilegists, such were their degenerated and poor spirits. However A.W. had before this time transcribed them, which were afterwards printed....[1]

Some cavaliers that were restored [to positions at Oxford] were good scholars, but the generality dunces. And of those good scholars but few preferred....

In this month (April) all tokens of monarchy restored. Arms that had been plastered over in the broken times, especially those in the Public Schools were all plastered over. The sign of the King's Head that had been dashed out or daubed over in paint tempore Olivari [in Oliver's time] (and in its place was written "This was the King's Head"), was new painted....

May.— Upon the votes in the Parliament House, May 1, Tuesday, the King's arms are everywhere renewed, etc.

May 1, Tuesday, May poles, May games. A May pole against the Bear [Inn] in Allhallows parish, set up on purpose to vex the Presbyterians and Independents. Dr. John Conant, then vice-chancellor, came with his beadles and servants to have it sawed down, but before he had entered an inch into it, he and his party were forced to leave that place....

May 24, Thursday, there was a most excellent music lecture of the practick part in the public school of that faculty, where A.W. performed a part on the violin. There were also voices; and by the direction of Edward Low, organist of Christ Church, who was then the Deputy Professor for Dr. John Wilson, all things were carried very well and gave great content to the most numerous auditory. This meeting was to congratulate his majesty's safe arrival to his kingdoms. The school was exceeding full, and the gallery at the end of the school was full of the female sex. After all was concluded, Mr. Low and some of the performers, besides others that did not perform, retired to the Crowne Tavern where

---

[1] in Wood's *Historia et Antiquitates*, lib. 2, p. 91.

they drank a health to the king, the two dukes,[1] George Monck,[2] &c....

May 29, Tuesday, the day of restoration of King Charles 2 observed in all or most places in England, particularly at Oxon which did exceed any place of its bigness. Many from all parts flocked to London to see his entry; but A.W. was not there, but at Oxon, where the jollity of the day continued till next morning. The world of England was perfectly mad. They were freed from the chains of darkness and confusion which the Presbyterians and fanatics had brought upon them; yet some of them seeing then what mischief they had done, tacked about to participate of the universal joy, and at length closed with the royal party.

This Holy Thursday [May 31] the people of Oxon were so violent for May poles in opposition to the Puritans that there was numbered 12 May poles besides 3 or 4 morrisses, etc. But no opposition appearing afterwards, the rabble flagged in their zeal; and seldom after above 1 or 2 in a year....

June 16, Saturday, John Milton's and John Goodwin's books called in and burned.[3] Taken out of those libraries where they were, especially out of the Public Library. About the same time, William Prynne's book against the bishops and books against archbishop Laud were taken out of the Public Library and put in the study in the gallery.[4]

—(CA. 1660)

---

[1] *the two dukes* the King's brothers, James, Duke of York, and Henry, Duke of Gloucester (who died in September 1660).

[2] George Monck (1608–1670), first Duke of Albemarle; he commanded the army whose entrance into London in 1660 initiated the events that would lead to the restoration of the monarchy.

[3] Parliament ordered the burning of Milton's *Eikonoklastes* (1649) and *Defensio pro populo Anglicano* (1651), and Goodwin's *Hybristodikai. The Obstructours of Justice* (1649); all three books defended the trial and execution of the King. John Goodwin (1594?–1665) was a prominent Independent minister and polemicist.

[4] For Prynne, a militant Presbyterian who published numerous anti-episcopal works, see the preface to William Laud's *Diary*.

Athenae Oxoniensis
(excerpts)

ROBERT BURTON, known otherwise to scholars by the name of Democritus Junior, younger brother to William Burton, whom I shall mention under the year 1645, was born of an ancient and genteel family at Lindley in Leicestershire, 8 Feb. 1576, and therefore in the titles of several of his choice books which he gave to the public library, he added to his surname *Lindliacus Leycestrensis*. He was educated in grammar learning in the free school of Sutton-Colfield in Warwickshire, whence he was sent to Brasen-nose College in the long vacation, *an.* 1593, where he made a considerable progress in Logic and Philosophy in the condition of a commoner. In 1599, he was elected student of Christ Church and for form sake, though he wanted not a tutor, he was put under the tuition of Dr. John Bancroft, afterwards Bishop of Oxon. In 1614, he was admitted to the reading of the sentences,[5] and on the 29 Nov. 1616, he had the vicarage of St. Thomas's parish in the west suburb of Oxon conferred on him by the Dean and Canons of Christ Church (to the parishioners whereof, he always gave the sacrament in wafers), which, with the rectory of Segrave in Leicestershire, given to him some years after by George Lord Berkeley, he kept with much ado to his dying day. He was an exact mathematician, a curious calculator of nativities, a general read scholar, a thorough-paced philologist, and one that understood the surveying of lands well. As he was by many accounted a severe student, a devourer of authors, a melancholy and humorous person;[6] so by others, who knew him well, a person of great honesty, plain dealing and charity. I have heard

---

[5] *admitted to the reading of the sentences* that is, he was awarded his Bachelor of Divinity. In the medieval university, being admitted to B.D. meant that a scholar could lecture on the *Sentences* of Peter Lombard (ca. 1100–1160), the standard textbook of Catholic theology.

[6] *humorous* subject to his humour of melancholy.

some of the ancients of Christ Church often say that his company was very merry, facete and juvenile,[1] and no man in his time did surpass him for his ready and dextrous interlarding his common discourses among them with verses from the poets or sentences from classical authors. Which being then all the fashion in the University, made his company more acceptable. He hath written,

The Anatomy of Melancholy.—First printed in quarto [1621] and afterwards several times in folio *an.* 1624, [1628,] 1632, 1638, and 1652, &c. to the great profit of the bookseller, who got an estate by it. 'Tis a book so full of variety of reading, that gentlemen who have lost their time and are put to a push for invention, may furnish themselves with matter for common or scholastical discourse and writing. Several authors have unmercifully stolen matter from the said book without any acknowledgment, particularly one William Greenwood, in his book entitled *A Description of the Passion of Love,* &c. (London, 1657, octavo). Who, as others of the like humour do, sometimes takes his quotations without the least mention of Democritus Junior. He the said Robert Burton paid his last debt to nature, in his chamber in Christ Church at, or very near that time, which he had some years before foretold from the calculation of his own nativity. Which being exact, several of the students did not forbear to whisper among themselves, that rather than there should be a mistake in the calculation, he sent up his soul to Heaven through a slip about his neck. His body was afterwards with due solemnity buried near that of Dr. Robert Weston, in the North Aisle which joins next to the Choir of the Cathedral of Christ Church, on the 27 of January in sixteen hundred thirty and nine. Over his grave was soon after erected a comely monument on the upper pillar of the said aisle, with his bust painted to the life: On the right hand of which, is the calculation of his nativity, and under the bust this inscription made by himself; all put up by the care of William Burton his brother. *Paucis notus, paucioribus ignotus, hic jacet Democritus junior, cui vitam dedit, & mortem Melancholia. Obiit viii. Id. Jan. A.C. MDCXXXIX.*[2] He left behind him a very choice library of books, many of which he bequeathed to that of Bodley, and a hundred pounds to buy five pounds yearly for the supplying of Christ Church library with books.

JEREMY TAYLOR tumbled out of his mother's womb into the lap of the muses at Cambridge, was educated in Gonville and Caius College there till he was M. of A. Afterwards entering into holy orders, he supplied for a time the Divinity Lecturer's place in the Cathedral of St. Paul in London, where behaving himself with great credit and applause far above his years, came to the cognisance of that great encourager of learning, ingenuity, and virtue, Dr. Laud Archbishop of Canterbury, who thinking it for the advantage of the world that such mighty parts should be afforded better opportunity of study and improvement, than a course of constant preaching would allow of, he caused him to be elected Fellow of All Souls College *an.* 1636: where being settled, love and admiration still waited upon him; while he improved himself much in books. But this the reader is to know that tho' he came in merely by the paramount interest of the said Archbishop, yet it was done against the statutes of the College in these two respects. First because he had exceeded the age, within which the said statutes make candidates capable of being elected, and secondly that he had not been of three years standing in the University of Oxon, only a week or two before he was put in. However he being a person of most wonderful parts and like to be an ornament thereunto, he was

---

[1] *facete* graceful, polished, elegant (*OED* facete 2); *juvenile* youthful (without the pejorative implication).

[2] "Known by few, unknown by fewer, here lies Democritus Junior, to whom Melancholy gave both life and death. Died eight days after the ides of January [actually January 25] 1639 [i.e. 1640]."

dispensed with, and thereby obtained in that house much of that learning, wherewith he was enabled to write casuistically. About the same time he was in a ready way to be confirmed a member of the Church of Rome, as many of that persuasion have said, but upon a sermon delivered in St. Mary's Church in Oxon on the 5 of Nov. (Gun-powder-treason day) *an.* 1638, wherein several things were put in against the Papists by the then Vice-chancellor he was afterwards rejected with scorn by those of that party, particularly by Fr. à S. Clara his intimate acquaintance;[1] to whom afterwards he expressed some sorrow for those things he had said against them, as the said S. Clara hath several times told me.[2] About that time, he became one of the chaplains to the said Archbishop of Canterbury who bestowed upon him the rectory of Uppingham in Rutlandshire, and other matters he would have done for him in order to his advance in the Church, had not the rebellion unluckily broke out. In the year 1642 he was with others, by virtue of his Majesty's letters sent to this University, actually created D. of D. [Doctor of Divinity] in that noted convocation held on the first day of Nov. the same year, he being then Chaplain in Ordinary to his said Majesty, and a frequent preacher before him and the court in Oxon. Afterwards he attended in his Majesty's army in the condition of a Chaplain, where tho' he had not a command of his time and books, yet he laid the foundation of several treatises in defence of Episcopacy, the Liturgy, Ministry, and Church of England. Upon the declining of the King's cause, he retired into Wales, where he was suffered under the loyal Earl of Carbury of the Golden Grove in Caermarthenshire to officiate, and keep school, to maintain him and his children. From which, tho' it continued but a few years were several youths most loyally educated, and afterwards sent to the universities. In this solitude he began to write his excellent discourses which are enough of themselves to furnish a library, and will be famous to all succeeding generations for the exactness of wit, profoundness of judgment, richness of fancy, clearness of expression, copiousness of invention, and general usefulness to all purposes of a Christian. By which he soon after got a great reputation among all persons of judgment and indifference and his name grew greater still,[3] as the world grew better and wiser. When he had spent some years in this retirement, in a private corner, as 'twere, of the world, his family was visited with sickness, and thereby lost the dear pledges of God's favour, three sons of great hopes, within the space of two or three months. And tho' he had learned a quiet submission to the divine will, yet this affliction touched him so sensibly, that it made him desirous to leave the country: And going to London, he there for a time officiated in a private congregation of Loyalists to his great hazard and danger. At length meeting with Edward Lord Conway, a person of great honour and generosity, that Lord, after he had understood his condition, made him a kind proffer, which our author Taylor embracing, it carried him over into Ireland, and settled him at Portmore, a place made for study and contemplation; which he therefore dearly loved. And there he wrote his *Cases of Conscience*,[4] a book that is able alone to give its author

---

[1] Christopher Davenport (1598–1680) assumed the name Franciscus à Sancta Clara upon becoming a Franciscan friar. He was chaplain to Queen Henrietta Maria and Catherine of Braganza, and a friend of William Laud's.

[2] Wood's account is somewhat unclear. His story is that Taylor was compelled to preach a sermon which contained anti-Catholic passages added by the Vice-Chancellor, that these passages offended Taylor's Catholic friends, and that he apologized to them for the incident. Taylor denied that he had considered conversion, and there is no evidence that this sermon contains the work of anybody other than Taylor. Wood's source is a Catholic friar with an interest in encouraging the belief that a prominent member of the Church of England considered converting to Catholicism.

[3] *indifference* impartiality.

[4] *Ductor Dubitantium, or the Rule of Conscience* (1660), which Taylor entitled *Cases of Conscience* in later editions.

immortality. By this time the wheel of providence brought about the King's happy restoration, and out of a confused chaos beauty and order began to appear: Whereupon our loyal author went over to congratulate the Prince and people's happiness, and bear a part in the universal triumph. It was not long after his sacred Majesty began the settlement of the Church, and Dr. Taylor being resolved upon for the Bishopric of Downe and Connor, was consecrated thereinto at Dublin on the 27th of January 1660, and on the 21st of June 1661 he had the administration of the See of Dromore granted to him by his Majesty, in consideration, that he had been the Church's champion, and that he had suffered much in defence of its cause. With what care and faithfulness he discharged his office, all upon the place knew well, and what good rules and directions he gave to his clergy, and how he taught them the practice of them by his own example. Upon his being made Bishop he was constituted a Privy Counsellor, and the University of Dublin gave him their testimony, by recommending him for their Vice-chancellor, which honourable office he kept to his dying day. He was esteemed by the generality of persons a complete artist, accurate logician, exquisite, quick and acute in his reasonings, a person of great fluency in his language and prodigious readiness in his learning.... But he had not only the accomplishments of a gentleman, but so universal were his parts, that they were proportioned to everything. And tho' his spirit and humour were made up of smoothness and gentleness, yet he could bear with the harshness and roughness of the schools, and was not unseen in their subtleties and spinosities.[1] His skill was great both in the civil and canon law and casuistical divinity: And he was a rare conductor of souls, and knew how to counsel, and to advise; to solve difficulties, and determine cases, and quiet consciences. To these may be added his great acquaintance with the fathers and ecclesiastical writers, and the doctors of the first and purest age both of the Greek and Latin Church; which he hath made use of against the Roman Catholics, to vindicate the Church of England from the challenge of innovation, and to prove her ancient, Catholic, and apostolical. Add to all these, he was a person of great humility, had nothing in him of pride and humour, but was courteous and affable and of easy access. He was withal a person of great charity and hospitality: and whosoever compares his plentiful incomes with the inconsiderable estate he left at his death, will be easily convinced that charity was steward for a great proportion of his revenue. To sum up all in a few words of another author, "This great Prelate had the good humour of a gentleman, the eloquence of an orator, the fancy of a poet, the acuteness of a schoolman, the profoundness of a philosopher, the wisdom of a chancellor, the sagacity of a prophet, the reason of an angel, and the piety of a saint. He had devotion enough for a cloister, learning enough for an university, and wit enough for a College of Virtuosi. And had his parts and endowments been parcelled out among his poor clergy that he left behind him, it would perhaps have made one of the best dioceses in the world."...[2]

[He] being overtaken with a violent fever, surrendered up his pious soul to the omnipotent at Lisburne alias Lisnegarvy on the thirteenth day of August in sixteen hundred sixty and seven, and was buried in a chapel of his own erection on the ruins of the old Cathedral of Dromore.

—1691–92

---

[1] *spinosities*   to be spinous is to be thorny; figuratively, difficult or unprofitable arguments or theories (*OED* spinosity 2).

[2] from George Rust, *A Funeral Sermon Preached at the Obsequies of … Jeremy Lord Bishop of Down* (1668).

John Locke

1632 – 1704

Born at Wrington in Somerset, the son of an attorney, Locke attended Westminster School and Christ Church, Oxford, where he was made an M.A. and Fellow in 1658. At Oxford he met Robert Boyle, who would become a life-long friend, and other scientists who would later be involved in the establishment of The Royal Society (which Locke joined in 1668). In the early 1660s Locke was appointed to university positions in Greek, rhetoric, and moral philosophy; in addition he devoted himself to scientific and medical studies. Locke left Oxford in 1667 to become confidential advisor to Anthony Ashley Cooper (later the Earl of Shaftesbury), who employed Locke as secretary to various government councils and commissions. In 1675 Locke travelled to France in hopes of improving his health, where he worked on the *Essay Concerning Human Understanding* and studied science, civil engineering, gardening, and politics. The fall of Shaftesbury and his Whig adherents in 1682 forced Locke to live in Holland from 1683 to 1689. He returned after the Revolution and was appointed Commissioner of Appeals (1689–1704) and made a member of the new Council of Trade (1696–1700). In 1691 Locke moved to Essex to live in the home of Sir Francis and Lady Masham, where he continued to write and publish.

An Essay Concerning Human Understanding was first published in 1690, though Locke had begun writing it twenty years earlier. He continued to revise the text for the three later editions published in his lifetime, and left further revisions that were included in a posthumously published fifth edition. The text was also translated into French and Latin, and an abridgement by an Oxford scholar was published in 1696. The classic statement of empiricist philosophy, *An Essay* would wield considerable influence throughout the following century. Locke's other works include the two *Treatises of Government* (1690), in which he denied the divine right of kings and argued that rulers were obligated to protect the liberties of citizens, three *Letters* on toleration (1689–1692), and *The Reasonableness of Christianity* (1695). The following excerpt, the chapter "Of Enthusiasm" (added to the fourth edition, in 1700), follows chapters "Of Reason" and "Of Faith and Reason, and Their Distinct Provinces." For Locke, faith involved assenting to truth revealed from God. It was up to reason, however, to decide if a given idea was genuinely revealed. Enthusiasm to Locke is the refusal to apply reason to ideas that the believer thinks are revealed truth, and the question he seeks to answer in this chapter is: how to distinguish between true revelation and mere enthusiasm?

❧❧❧

An Essay Concerning Human Understanding

OF ENTHUSIASM
BOOK IV, CHAPTER XIX

He that would seriously set upon the search of truth, ought in the first place to prepare his mind with a love of it. For he that loves it not, will not take much pains to get it; nor be much con- cerned when he misses it. There is nobody in the Commonwealth of Learning who does not profess himself a lover of truth: and there is not a rational creature that would not take it amiss to be thought otherwise of. And yet for all this one may truly say, there are very few lovers of truth for truth's sake, even amongst those who persuade themselves that they are so. How a man may know whether he be so in earnest is worth enquiry: And I think there is this one unerring mark of it, *viz.* The not entertaining any proposition with greater assurance than the proofs it is built upon will warrant. Whoever goes beyond this measure of assent, 'tis plain receives not truth in the love of it; loves not truth for truth's sake, but for some other bye end. For the evidence that any proposition is true (except such as are self-evident) lying only in the proofs a man has of it, whatsoever degrees of assent he affords it beyond the degrees of that evidence, 'tis plain all that surplusage of assurance is owing to some other affection, and not to the love of truth: It being as impossible, that the love of truth should carry my assent above the evidence that there is to me that it is true, as that the love of truth should make me assent to any proposition, for the sake of that evidence, which it has not, that it is true: which is in effect to love it as a truth, because it is possible or probably that it may not be true. In any truth that gets not possession of our minds by the irresistible light of self-evidence, or by the force of demonstration, the arguments that gain it assent are the vouchers and gage of its probability to us; and we can receive it for no other than such as they deliver it to our understandings. Whatsoever credit or authority we give to any proposition more than it receives from the principles and proofs it supports itself upon, is owing to our inclinations that way, and is so far a derogation from the love of truth as such: which as it can receive no evidence from our passions or interests, so it should receive no tincture from them.

The assuming an authority of dictating to others, and a forwardness to prescribe to their opinions, is a constant concomitant of this bias and corruption of our judgments. For how almost can it be otherwise, but that he should be ready to impose on others' belief, who has already imposed on his own? Who can reasonably expect arguments and conviction from him, in dealing with others, whose understanding is not accustomed to them in his dealing with himself? Who does violence to his own faculties, tyrannizes over his own mind, and usurps the prerogative that belongs to truth alone, which is to command assent by only its own authority, *i.e.* by and in proportion to that evidence which it carries with it.

Upon this occasion I shall take the liberty to consider a third ground of assent, which with some men has the same authority, and is as confidently relied on as either faith or reason, I mean enthusiasm. Which laying by reason would set up revelation without it. Whereby in effect it takes away both reason and revelation, and substitutes in the room of it, the ungrounded fancies of a man's own brain, and assumes them for a foundation both of opinion and conduct.

Reason is natural revelation, whereby the eternal Father of Light, and Fountain of all Knowledge, communicates to mankind that portion of truth which he has laid within the reach of their natural faculties: Revelation is natural reason enlarged by a new set of discoveries communicated by God immediately, which reason vouches the truth of, by the testimony and proofs it gives that they come from God. So that he that takes away reason, to make way for revelation, puts out the Light of both, and does much what the same, as if he would persuade a man to put out his eyes the better to receive the remote light of an invisible star by a telescope.

Immediate revelation being a much easier way for men to establish their opinions, and regulate their conduct, than the tedious and not always successful labour of strict reasoning, it is no wonder, that some have been very apt to pretend to revelation, and to persuade themselves that they are under the peculiar guidance of Heaven in their actions and opinions, especially in those of them, which they cannot account for by the ordinary methods of knowledge, and principles of reason. Hence we see, that in all ages, men in whom melancholy has mixed with devotion, or whose conceit of themselves has raised them into an opinion of a greater familiarity with God, and a nearer admittance to his favour than is afforded to others, have often flattered themselves with a persuasion of an immediate intercourse with the deity, and frequent communications from the divine spirit. God I own cannot be denied to be able to enlighten the understanding by a ray darted into the mind immediately from the Fountain of Light: This they understand he has promised to do, and who then has so good a title to expect it, as those who are his peculiar people, chosen by him and depending on him?

Their minds being thus prepared, whatever groundless opinion comes to settle itself strongly upon their fancies, is an illumination from the spirit of God, and presently of divine authority: And whatsoever odd action they find in themselves a strong inclination to do, that impulse is concluded to be a call or direction from Heaven, and must be obeyed; 'tis a commission from above, and they cannot err in executing it.

This I take to be properly enthusiasm, which though founded neither on reason, nor divine revelation, but rising from the conceits of a warmed or over-weening brain, works yet, where it once gets footing, more powerfully on the persuasions and actions of men, than either of those two, or both together: Men being most forwardly obedient to the impulses they receive from themselves; and the whole man is sure to act more vigorously, where the whole man is carried by a natural motion. For strong conceit like a new principle carries all easily with it, when got above common sense, and freed from all restraint of reason and check of reflection, it is heightened into a divine authority, in concurrence with our own temper and inclination.

Though the odd opinions and extravagant actions Enthusiasm has run men into, were enough to warn them against this wrong principle so apt to misguide them both in their belief and conduct: yet the love of something extraordinary, the ease and glory it is to be inspired and be above the common and natural ways of knowledge, so flatters many men's laziness, ignorance, and vanity, that when once they are got into this way of immediate revelation; of illumination without search; and of certainty without proof, and without examination, 'tis a hard matter to get them out of it. Reason is lost upon them, they are above it: they see the Light infused into their understandings, and cannot be mistaken; 'tis clear and visible there; like the light of bright sunshine, shows itself, and needs no other proof, but its own evidence: they feel the hand of God moving them within, and the impulses of the spirit, and cannot be mistaken in what they feel. Thus they support themselves, and are sure reason hath nothing to do with what they see and feel in themselves: what they have a sensible experience of admits no doubt, needs no probation. Would he not be ridiculous who should require to have it proved to him, that the Light shines, and that he sees it? It is its own proof, and can have no other. When the spirit brings Light into our minds, it dispels darkness. We see it, as we do that of the sun at noon, and need not the twilight of reason to show it us. This light from Heaven is strong, clear, and pure, carries its own demonstration with it, and we may as rationally take a glow-worm to assist us to discover the sun, as to examine the celestial ray by our dim candle, reason.

This is the way of talking of these men: they are sure, because they are sure: and their persuasions are right, only because they are strong in them. For, when what they say is stripped of the metaphor of seeing and feeling, this is all it amounts to: and yet these similes so impose on them, that they serve them for certainty in themselves, and demonstration to others.

But to examine a little soberly this internal Light, and this feeling on which they build so much. These men have, they say, clear Light, and they see; they have an awakened sense, and they feel:

this cannot, they are sure, be disputed them. For when a man says he sees or he feels, no body can deny it him, that he does so. But here let me ask: This seeing, is it the perception of the truth of the proposition, or of this, that it is a revelation from God? This feeling, is it a perception of an inclination or fancy to do something, or of the spirit of God moving that inclination? These are two very different perceptions, and must be carefully distinguished, if we would not impose upon ourselves. I may perceive the truth of a proposition, and yet not perceive that it is an immediate revelation from God. I may perceive the truth of a proposition in Euclid, without its being, or my perceiving it to be, a revelation: Nay I may perceive I came not by this knowledge in a natural way, and so may conclude it revealed, without perceiving that it is a revelation from God. Because there be Spirits,[1] which, without being divinely commissioned, may excite those Ideas in me, and lay them in such order before my mind, that I may perceive their connection. So that the knowledge of any proposition coming into my mind, I know not how, is not a perception that it is from God. Much less is a strong persuasion, that it is true, a perception that it is from God, or so much as true. But however it be called Light and seeing; I suppose, it is at most but belief, and assurance: and the proposition taken for a revelation is not such as they know to be true, but taken to be true. For where a proposition is known to be true, revelation is needless. And it is hard to conceive how there can be a revelation to any one of what he knows already. If therefore it be a proposition which they are persuaded, but do not know, to be true, whatever they may call it, it is not seeing, but believing. For these are two ways whereby truth comes into the

mind, wholly distinct, so that one is not the other. What I see I know to be so by the evidence of the thing itself: what I believe I take to be so upon the testimony of another: But this testimony I must know to be given, or else what ground have I of believing? I must see that it is God that reveals this to me, or else I see nothing. The question then here is, How do I know that God is the revealer of this to me; that this impression is made upon my mind by his holy spirit, and that therefore I ought to obey it? If I know not this, how great soever the assurance is that I am possessed with, it is groundless; whatever Light I pretend to, it is but Enthusiasm. For whether the proposition supposed to be revealed, be in itself evidently true, or visibly probable, or by the natural ways of knowledge uncertain, the proposition that must be well grounded and manifested to be true is this, that God is the revealer of it, and that what I take to be a revelation is certainly put into my mind by him, and is not an illusion dropped in by some other spirit, or raised by my own fancy. For if I mistake not, these men receive it for true, because they presume God revealed it. Does it not then stand them upon, to examine upon what grounds they presume it to be a revelation from God? or else all their confidence is mere presumption: and this Light they are so dazzled with, is nothing but an *ignis fatuus* that leads them continually round in this circle.[2] It is a revelation because they firmly believe it, and they believe it, because it is a revelation.

In all that is of divine revelation there is need of no other proof but that it is an inspiration from God: For he can neither deceive nor be deceived. But how shall it be known, that any proposition in our minds is a truth infused by God; a truth that is revealed to us by him, which he declares to us, and therefore we ought to believe? Here it is that Enthu-

---

[1] *Spirits* Locke argues earlier in the *Essay* for the existence of a wide range of spirits or angels, forming a continuous chain of being leading up to the perfection of God: "That there should be more species of intelligent creatures above us than there are of sensible and material below us is probable to me from hence: that in all the visible corporeal world we see no chasm or gaps" (bk. 3, ch. 6, sect. 12).

[2] *ignis fatuus* "false light"; the "will-o'-the-wisp" or phosphorescent gas (created by decaying organic matter) that could lead unwary travellers astray in marshy areas; metaphorically any delusive hope.

siasm fails of the evidence it pretends to. For men thus possessed boast of a Light whereby they say, they are enlightened, and brought into the knowledge of this or that truth. But if they know it to be a truth, they must know it to be so either by its own self-evidence to natural reason; or by the rational proofs that make it out to be so. If they see and know it to be a truth, either of these two ways, they in vain suppose it to be a revelation: For they know it to be true by the same way that any other man naturally may know that it is so without the help of revelation. For thus all the truths of what kind soever that men uninspired are enlightened with, came into their minds, and are established there. If they say they know it to be true, because it is a revelation from God, the reason is good: but then it will be demanded, how they know it to be a revelation from God. If they say by the Light it brings with it, which shines bright in their minds, and they cannot resist; I beseech them to consider, whether this be any more, than what we have taken notice of already, *viz.* that it is a revelation because they strongly believe it to be true. For all the Light they speak of is but a strong, though ungrounded persuasion of their own minds that it is a truth. For rational grounds from proofs that it is a truth they must acknowledge to have none, for then it is not received as a revelation, but upon the ordinary grounds that other truths are received: And if they believe it to be true, because it is a revelation, and have no other reason for its being a revelation, but because they are fully persuaded without any other reason that it is true, they believe it to be a revelation only because they strongly believe it to be a revelation, which is a very unsafe ground to proceed on, either in our tenets, or actions: And what readier way can there be to run ourselves into the most extravagant errors and miscarriages than thus to set up fancy for our supreme and sole guide, and to believe any proposition to be true, any action to be right, only because we believe it to be so? The strength of our persuasions are no evidence at all of their own rectitude: Crooked things may be as stiff and inflexible as straight: and men may be as positive and peremptory in error as in truth. How come else the intractable zealots in different and opposite parties? For if the Light, which everyone thinks he has in his mind, which in this case is nothing but the strength of his own persuasion, be an evidence that it is from God, contrary opinions may have the same title to be inspirations; and God will be not only the Father of Lights, but of opposite and contradictory Lights, leading men contrary ways; and contradictory propositions will be divine truths, if an ungrounded strength of assurance be an evidence that any proposition is a divine revelation.

This cannot be otherwise, whilst firmness of persuasion is made the cause of believing, and confidence of being in the right is made an argument of truth; St. Paul himself believed he did well, and that he had a call to it, when he persecuted the Christians, whom he confidently thought in the wrong: But yet it was he, and not they, who were mistaken.[1] Good men are men still, liable to mistakes, and are sometimes warmly engaged in errors, which they take for divine truths, shining in their minds with the clearest Light.

Light, true Light in the mind is, or can be nothing else but the evidence of the truth of any proposition; and if it be not a self-evident proposition, all the Light it has, or can have, is from the clearness and validity of those proofs, upon which it is received. To talk of any other Light in the understanding is to put ourselves in the dark, or in the power of the Prince of Darkness, and by our own consent, to give ourselves up to delusion to believe a lie. For if strength of persuasion be the Light, which must guide us; I ask how shall anyone distinguish between the delusions of Satan, and the inspirations of the Holy Ghost? He can transform

---

[1] Acts 8–9 (with Paul then known as Saul).

himself into an Angel of Light. And they who are led by this Son of the Morning are as fully satisfied of the illumination, *i.e.* are as strongly persuaded, that they are enlightened by the Spirit of God, as any one who is so: They acquiesce and rejoice in it, are acted by it: and nobody can be more sure, nor more in the right (if their own strong belief may be judge) than they.

He therefore that will not give himself up to all the extravagancies of delusion and error must bring this guide of his Light within to the trial. God when he makes the prophet does not unmake the man. He leaves all his faculties in their natural state, to enable him to judge of his inspirations, whether they be of divine original or no. When he illuminates the mind with supernatural Light, he does not extinguish that which is natural. If he would have us assent to the truth of any proposition, he either evidences that truth by the usual methods of natural reason, or else makes it known to be a truth, which he would have us assent to, by his authority, and convinces us that it is from him, by some marks which reason cannot be mistaken in. Reason must be our last judge and guide in every thing. I do not mean, that we must consult reason, and examine whether a proposition revealed from God can be made out by natural principles, and if it cannot, that then we may reject it: But consult it we must, and by it examine, whether it be a revelation from God or no: And if reason finds it to be revealed from God, reason then declares for it, as much as for any other truth, and makes it one of her dictates. Every conceit that thoroughly warms our fancies must pass for an inspiration, if there be nothing but the strength of our persuasions, whereby to judge of our persuasions: If reason must not examine their truth by something extrinsical to the persuasions themselves; inspirations and delusions, truth and falsehood will have the same measure, and will not be possible to be distinguished.

If this internal Light, or any proposition which under that title we take for inspired, be conformable to the principles of reason or to the word of God, which is attested revelation, reason warrants it, and we may safely receive it for true, and be guided by it in our belief and actions: If it receive no testimony nor evidence from either of these rules, we cannot take it for a revelation, or so much as for true, till we have some other mark that it is a revelation, besides our believing that it is so. Thus we see the holy men of old, who had revelations from God, had something else besides that internal Light of assurance in their own minds, to testify to them that it was from God. They were not left to their own persuasions alone, that those persuasions were from God; but had outward signs to convince them of the author of those revelations. And when they were to convince others, they had a power given them to justify the truth of their commission from Heaven; and by visible signs to assert the divine authority of the message they were sent with. Moses saw the bush burn without being consumed, and heard a voice out of it. This was something besides finding an impulse upon his mind to go to Pharaoh, that he might bring his brethren out of Egypt: and yet he thought not this enough to authorise him to go with that message, till God by another miracle, of his rod turned into a serpent, had assured him of a power to testify his mission by the same miracle repeated before them, whom he was sent to.[1] Gideon was sent by an angel to deliver Israel from the Mideanites, and yet he desired a sign to convince him, that this commission was from God.[2] These and several the like instances to be found among the prophets of old, are enough to show, that they thought not an inward seeing or persuasion of their own minds without any other proof a sufficient evidence that it was from God,

---

[1] Exodus 3:1–4; 4:1–5.

[2] Judges 6:11–21.

though the Scripture does not everywhere mention their demanding or having such proofs.

In what I have said I am far from denying, that God can, or doth sometimes enlighten men's minds in the apprehending of certain truths, or excite them to good actions by the immediate influence and assistance of the Holy Spirit, without any extraordinary signs accompanying it. But in such cases too we have reason and the Scripture, unerring rules to know whether it be from God or no. Where the truth embraced is consonant to the revelation in the written word of God; or the action conformable to the dictates of right reason or Holy Writ, we may be assured that we run no risk in entertaining it as such, because though perhaps it be not an immediate revelation from God, extraordinarily operating on our minds, yet we are sure it is warranted by that revelation which he has given us of truth. But it is not the strength of our private persuasion within ourselves, that can warrant it to be a Light or motion from Heaven: Nothing can do that but the written word of God without us, or that standard of reason which is common to us with all men. Where reason or Scripture is express for any opinion or action, we may receive it as of divine authority: But 'tis not the strength of our own persuasions which can by itself give it that stamp. The bent of our own minds may favour it as much as we please; that may show it to be a foundling of our own, but will by no means prove it to be an offspring of Heaven, and of divine original.

—1700

George Savile, Marquis of Halifax
1633 – 1695

The heir to one of Yorkshire's great county families, Halifax was educated at Shrewsbury and in France and Italy; he inherited his father's baronetcy in 1644. His background was Royalist—his father had been the Royalist governor of York—and he sat for Pontefract in the Convention Parliament of 1660. Halifax's involvement in public affairs began soon after the Restoration. Tolerant (he opposed the execution of both Catholic and Whig "plotters"), independent, urbane, witty, a fine orator, and a mediator by instinct, Halifax came to be known as the trimmer, a master of compromise and the middle way in politics. In an otherwise sympathetic sketch, Gilbert Burnet wrote that Halifax "changed sides so often, that in conclusion no side trusted him." He was ennobled in 1668 (eventually made Marquis in 1682), admitted to the Privy Council in 1672, dismissed from office in 1676, and reinstated three years later. He opposed the Exclusion Bill, though he did not like James II. He was initially neutral about the Revolution, though he served eventually as chief minister to William and Mary (1689–1690). Halifax appears in Dryden's *Absalom and Achitophel* as

"Jotham of piercing wit and pregnant thought, / Endued by nature and learning taught / To move assemblies" (lines 882–884).

As a writer and prose stylist, Halifax is best known for *The Character of a Trimmer*, a defence of political moderation first published in 1688 but circulated previously in manuscript; his other works include *A Letter to a Dissenter* (1687) and *Advice to a Daughter* (1688). *A Character of King Charles II* was first published in 1750, when it was edited from manuscript by Alexander Pope. Halifax wrote the sketch sometime between the death of the King in 1685 and his own death a decade later. The biographical character was a convention of history writing (for another Restoration example, see Clarendon's character of William Laud), though the genre did borrow from the psychology of the literary character as practised earlier in the century by writers such as Overbury, Earle, and Breton. For Halifax, this sketch was also in a sense a working political document, the product of years of careful observation necessitated by a life in court politics.

❧❧❧

A Character of King Charles II

OF HIS RELIGION

A character differeth from a picture only in this, every part of it must be like, but it is not necessary that every feature should be comprehended in it as in a picture, only some of the most remarkable.

This Prince at his first entrance into the world had adversity for his introducer, which is generally thought to be no ill one, but in his case it proved so, and laid the foundation of most of those misfortunes or errors that were the causes of the great objections made to him.

The first effect it had was in relation to his religion.

The ill-bred familiarity of the Scotch divines had given him a distaste of that part of the Protestant religion.[1] He was left then to the little remnant of the Church of England in the Fauxbourg St. Germain;[2] which made such a kind of figure, as might easily be turned in such a manner as to make him lose his veneration for it. In a refined country where

---

[1] After the execution of Charles I in 1649, the Scots proclaimed Charles II King of Scotland in 1649—but on the condition that he accept the Presbyterian *Solemn League and Covenant*.

[2] an Anglican chapel in Paris established by diplomat Sir Richard Browne.

religion appeared in pomp and splendor, the outward appearance of such unfashionable men was made an argument against their religion; and a young Prince not averse to raillery was the more susceptible of a contempt for it.

The company he kept, the men in his pleasures, and the arguments of State that he should not appear too much a Protestant whilst he expected assistance from a popish Prince;[1] all these, together with a habit encouraged by an application to his pleasures, did so loosen and untie him from his first impressions, that I take it for granted, after the first year or two, he was no more a Protestant. If you ask me what he was, my answer must be, that he was of the religion of a young Prince in his warm blood, whose enquiries were more applied to find arguments against believing, than to lay any settled foundations for acknowledging providence, mysteries, &c. A general creed, and no very long one, may be presumed to be the utmost religion of one, whose age and inclination could not well spare any thoughts that did not tend to his pleasures.

In this kind of indifference or unthinkingness, which is too natural in the beginnings of life to be heavily censured, I will suppose he might pass some considerable part of his youth. I must presume too that no occasions were lost, during that time, to insinuate everything to bend him towards popery. Great art without intermission, against youth and easiness, which are seldom upon their guard, must have its effect. A man is to be admired if he resisteth, and therefore cannot reasonably be blamed if he yieldeth to them. *When* the critical minute was, I'll not undertake to determine; but certainly the inward conviction doth generally precede the outward declarations: At what distances, dependeth upon men's several complexions and circumstances; no stated period can be fixed.

It will be said that he had not religion enough to have *conviction*; that is a vulgar error. Conviction indeed is not a proper word but where a man is convinced by reason; but in the common acceptation, it is applied to those who cannot tell why they are so: If men can be at least as positive in a mistake as when they are in the right; they may be as clearly convinced when they do not know why, as when they do.

I must presume that no man of the King's age, and his methods of life, could possibly give a good reason for changing his religion in which he was born, let it be what it will. But our passions are much oftener convinced than our reason. He had but little reading, and that tending to his pleasures more than to his instruction. In the library of a young Prince, the solemn folios are not much rumpled, books of a lighter digestion have the dog's ears.

Some pretend to be very precise in the time of his reconciling; the Cardinal de Retz, &c.[2] I will not enter into it minutely, but whenever it was, it is observable that the government of France did not think it advisable to discover it openly; upon which such obvious reflections may be made, that I will not mention them.

Such a secret can never be put into a place which is so closely stopped, that there shall be no chinks. Whispers went about, particularly men had intimations: Cromwell had his advertisements in other things,[3] and this was as well worth his paying for. There was enough said of it to startle a great many, though not universally diffused; so much, that if the government here, had not crumbled of itself, his right alone, with that and other clogs upon it, would hardly have thrown it down. I conclude that when he came into England he was as certainly a

---

[1] *a popish Prince* the King of France, Louis XIV.

[2] *Retz* Jean-François-Paul de Gondi, Cardinal de Retz (1613–1679), with whom Charles negotiated in 1658–1659 about Catholic support for an invasion of England.

[3] *advertisements* reports from his spies.

Roman Catholic, as that he was a man of pleasure; both very consistent by visible experience.

It is impertinent to give reasons for men's changing their religion. None can give them but themselves, as every man has quite a different way of arguing: A thing which may very well be accounted for. They are differing kinds of wit, to be quick to find a *fault*, and to be capable to find out a *truth*: There must be industry in the last; the first requires only a lively heat, that catcheth hold of the *weak* side of any thing, but to choose the *strong* one is another talent. The reason why men of wit are often the laziest in their enquiries is, that their heat carrieth their thoughts so fast that they are apt to be tired, and they faint in the drudgery of a continued application. Have not men of great wit in all times permitted their understandings to give way to their first impressions? It taketh off from the diminution when a man doth not *mind* a thing; and the King had then other business: The inferior part of the man was then in possession, and the faculties of the brain, as to serious and painful enquiries, were laid asleep at least, tho' not extinguished. Careless men are most subject to superstition. Those who do not study reason enough to make it their guide, have more unevenness: As they have neglects, so they have starts and frights; dreams will serve the turn; omens and sicknesses have violent and sudden effects upon them. Nor is the strength of an argument so effectual from its intrinsic force, as by its being well suited to the temper of the party.

The *genteel part* of the Catholic religion might tempt a Prince that had more of the fine gentleman than his governing capacity required: and the exercise of *indulgence* to *sinners* being more frequent in it, than of *inflicting penance*, might be some recommendation. Mistresses of that faith are stronger specifics in this case,[1] than any that are in physic.

The Roman Catholics complained of his breach of promise to them very early.[2] There were broad peepings out, glimpses so often repeated, that to discerning eyes it was flaring: In the very first year there were such suspicions as produced melancholy shakings of the head, which were very significant.[3] His unwillingness to *marry* a Protestant was remarkable, though both the Catholic and the Christian Crown would have adopted her. Very early in his youth, when any German Princess was proposed, he put off the discourse with raillery. A thousand little circumstances were a kind of accumulative evidence, which in these cases may be admitted.

Men that were earnest Protestants were under the sharpness of his displeasure, expressed by raillery, as well as by other ways. Men near him have made discoveries from sudden breakings out in discourse, &c. which showed there was a root. It was not the least skilful part of his concealing himself, to make the world think he leaned towards an indifference in religion.

He had sicknesses before his death, in which he did not trouble any Protestant divines; those who saw him upon his death-bed, saw a great deal.[4]

. . . .

His Amours, Mistresses, &c.

It may be said that his inclinations to love were the effects of health, and a good constitution, with as little mixture of the *seraphic* part as ever man had:[5]

---

[1] *Mistresses of that faith*   Louise de Kéroualle (later Duchess of Portsmouth) and Barbara Palmer (later Countess of Castlemaine and Duchess of Cleveland) were both Catholic (the latter a convert).

[2] Charles had promised toleration of Catholicism in the Declaration of Breda (1660).

[3] The first Act of Parliament passed after the Restoration contained a clause that sought to curb such speculations with a clause prohibiting anyone from saying that the King was Catholic.

[4] The Benedictine Father John Huddleston administered the Catholic rites to Charles on his deathbed.

[5] *seraphic*   devout, elevated (*OED* seraphic 2, 3b); Halifax is saying that the King's "inclinations to love" were spurred more by physical than emotional considerations.

And though from that foundation men often raise their passions; I am apt to think his stayed as much as any man's ever did in the *lower region*. This made him like easy mistresses: They were generally resigned to him while he was abroad, with an implied bargain. Heroic refined lovers place a good deal of their pleasure in the difficulty, both for the vanity of conquest, and as a better earnest of their kindness.

After he was restored, mistresses were recommended to him; which is no small matter in a *Court*, and not unworthy the thoughts even of a *Party*. A mistress either dexterous in herself, or well-instructed by those that are so, may be very useful to her friends, not only in the immediate hours of her ministry, but by her influences and insinuations at other times. It was resolved generally by others, whom he should have in his arms, as well as whom he should have in his councils. Of a man who was so capable of choosing, he chose as seldom as any man that ever lived.

He had more properly, at least in the beginning of his time, a good stomach to his mistresses, than any great passion for them. His taking them from others was never learnt in a romance; and indeed fitter for a philosopher than a knight-errant. His patience for their frailties showed him no exact lover. It is a heresy according to a true lover's creed, ever to forgive an infidelity, or the appearance of it. Love of ease will not do it, where the *heart* is much engaged; but where mere *nature* is the motive, it is possible for a man to think righter than the common opinion, and to argue, that a rival taketh away nothing but the heart, and leaveth all the rest.

In his latter times he had no *love*, but insensible engagements that made it harder than most might apprehend to untie them. The *politics* might have their part; a secret, a commission, a confidence in critical things, though it doth not give a lease for a precise term of years, yet there may be difficulties in

dismissing them; there may be no love all the while; perhaps the contrary.

He was said to be as little constant as they were thought to be. Though he had no love, he must have some appetite, or else he could not keep them for mere ease, or for the love of sauntering; mistresses are frequently apt to be uneasy; they are in all respects craving creatures; so that though the taste of those joys might be flattened, yet a man who loved pleasure so as to be very unwilling to part with it, might (with the assistance of his fancy, which doth not grow old so fast) reserve some supplemental entertainments, that might make their personal service be still of use to him. The definition of pleasure, is *what pleaseth*, and if that which grave men may call a corrupted fancy, shall administer any remedies for putting off mourning for the loss of youth, who shall blame it?

The *young* men seldom apply their censure to these matters; and the *elder* have an interest to be gentle towards a mistake, that seemeth to make some kind of amends for their decays.

He had wit enough to *suspect*, and he had wit enough too *not to care*: The ladies got a great deal more than would have been allowed to be an equal bargain in Chancery,[1] for what they did for it; but neither the manner, nor the measure of pleasure is to be judged by others.

Little inducements at first grew into strong reasons by degrees. Men who do not consider circumstances, but judge at a distance, by a general way of arguing, conclude if a mistress in some cases is not immediately turned off, it must needs be that the gallant is incurably subjected. This will by no means hold in private men, much less in Princes, who are under more entanglements, from which they cannot so easily loosen themselves.

His mistresses were as different in their humours, as they were in their looks. They gave matter

---

[1] *Chancery* the court concerned with remedying wrongs not covered under the common law.

of very different reflections. The last especially was quite out of the definition of an ordinary mistress; the causes and the manner of her being first introduced were very different.[1] A very peculiar distinction was spoken of, some extraordinary solemnities that might dignify, though not sanctify her function.[2] Her chamber was the true cabinet council. The King did always by his councils, as he did sometimes by his meals; he sat down out of form with the Queen, but he supped *below stairs*. To have the secrets of a King, who happens to have too many, is to have a King in chains: He must not only, not part with her, but he must in his own defence dissemble his dislike: The less kindness he hath, the more he must show: There is great difference between being *muffled*, and being *tied*: He was the first, not the last. If he had quarrelled at some times, besides other advantages, this mistress had a powerful *second* (one may suppose a kind of *guarantee*);[3] this to a man that loved his *ease*, though his *age* had not helped, was sufficient.

The thing called *sauntering*,[4] is a stronger temptation to Princes than it is to others. The being galled with importunities, pursued from one room to another with asking faces; the dismal sound of unreasonable complaints, and ill-grounded pretences; the deformity of fraud ill-disguised; all these would make any man run away from them; and I used to think it was the motive for making him walk so fast. So it was more properly taking sanctuary. To get into a room, where all business was to stay at the door, excepting such as he was disposed

to admit, might be very acceptable to a younger man than he was, and less given to his ease. He slumbered after dinner, had the noise of the company to divert him, without their solicitations to importune him. In these hours where he was more unguarded, no doubt the cunning men of the court took their times to make their observations, and there is as little doubt but he made his upon them too: Where man had chinks he would see through them as soon as any man about him. There was much more real business done there in his politic, than there was in his personal capacity, *Stans pede in uno*;[5] and there was the *French part* of *the Government*,[6] which was not the least.

In short, without endeavouring to find more arguments, he was *used* to it. Men do not care to put off a habit, nor do often succeed when they go about it. His was not an *unthinkingness*; he did not perhaps think so much of his subjects as they might wish; but he was far from being wanting to think of himself.

His Conduct to his Ministers

He lived with his ministers as he did with his mistresses; he used them, but he was not in love with them. He showed his judgment in this, that he cannot properly be said ever to have had a *favourite*, though some might look so at a distance. The present use he might have of them, made him throw favours upon them, which might lead the lookers on into that mistake; but he tied himself no more to them, than they did to him, which implied a sufficient liberty on either side.

---

[1] *The last* Louise de Kéroualle (1649–1734).

[2] In October 1671, John Evelyn noted in his diary that de Kéroualle "was bedded one of these nights, and the stocking flung, after the manner of a married bride."

[3] *second* a back-up (*OED* second v 2); in this case Louis XIV of France.

[4] *sauntering* as in its modern sense, to dawdle or trifle, to do anything in an aimless or leisurely way; this meaning of the word was new in the Restoration (*OED*).

[5] From Horace, *Satires*, I.iv.9–10: "Herein lay his fault: often in an hour, as though a great exploit, he would dictate two hundred lines while standing, as they say, on one foot"—a proverbial expression for doing something without effort.

[6] Louise de Kéroualle was assumed to represent the interests of Louis XIV.

Perhaps he made *dear purchases*: If he seldom gave profusely, but where he expected some unreasonable thing, great rewards were material evidences against those who received them.

He was free of access to them, which was a very gaining quality. He had at least as good a memory for the faults of his Ministers as for their services; and whenever they fell, the whole inventory came out; there was not a slip omitted.

That some of his Ministers seemed to have a superiority,[1] did not spring from his resignation to them, but to his ease. He chose rather to be *eclipsed* than to be *troubled*.

His brother was a Minister,[2] and he had his jealousies of him. At the same time that he raised him, he was not displeased to have him lessened. The cunning observers found this out, and at the same time that he reigned in the cabinet, he was very familiarly used at the private supper.

A Minister turned off is like a Lady's waiting-woman, that knoweth all her washes, and hath a shrewd guess at her strayings: So there is danger in turning them off, as well as in keeping them.

He had back stairs to convey informations to him, as well as for other uses; and though such informations are sometimes dangerous (especially to a Prince that will not take pains necessary to digest them), yet in the main, that humour of hearing every body against every body, kept those about him in much awe, than they would have been without it. I do not believe that ever he trusted any man, or any set of men so entirely, as not to have some secrets, in which they had *no share*: As this might make him less well served, so in some degree it might make him the less imposed upon.

You may reckon under this article his *Female Ministry*; for though he had Ministers of the Coun-cil, Ministers of the Cabinet, and Ministers of the Ruelle; the Ruelle was often the last appeal.[3] Those who were not well there, were used because they were *necessary* at the time, not because they were *liked*; so that their tenure was a little uncertain. His Ministers were to administer business to him as doctors do physic, wrap it up in something to make it less unpleasant; some skilful digressions were so far from being impertinent, that they could not many times fix him to a fair audience without them. His aversion to formality made him dislike a serious discourse, if very long, except it was mixed with something to entertain him. Some even of the graver sort too, used to carry this very far, and rather than fail, use the coarsest kind of youthful talk.

In general, he was upon pretty even terms with his Ministers, and could as easily bear *their* being *hanged* as some of them could *his* being *abused*.

OF HIS WIT AND CONVERSATION

His wit consisted chiefly in the quickness of his apprehension. His apprehension made him find faults, and that led him to short sayings upon them, not always equal, but often very good.

By his being abroad, he contracted a habit of conversing familiarly, which added to his natural genius, made him very apt to talk; perhaps more than a very nice judgment would approve.

He was apter to make *broad allusions* upon anything that gave the least occasion, than was altogether suitable with the very good breeding he showed in most other things. The company he kept whilst abroad, had so used him to that sort of dialect, that he was so far from thinking it a fault or an indecency, that he made it a matter of raillery upon those who could not prevail upon themselves to join in it. As a man who hath a good stomach

---

[1] probably referring to Edward Hyde, Earl of Clarendon; Thomas Osborne, Earl of Danby; and Charles Spencer, Earl of Sunderland.

[2] *His brother* James, Duke of York (later King James II), who was Lord High Admiral.

[3] *Ruelle* a reception room in which ladies of fashion would meet in the morning to entertain persons of distinction (*OED* ruelle 2).

loveth generally to talk of meat, so in the vigour of his age, he began that style, which by degrees grew so natural to him, that after he ceased to do it out of pleasure, he continued to do it out of custom. The hypocrisy of the former times inclined men to think they could not show too great an aversion to it, and that helped to encourage this unbounded liberty of talking, without the restraints of decency which were before observed. In his more familiar conversations with the ladies, even they must be passive, if they would not enter into it. How far sounds as well as objects may have their effects to raise inclination, might be an argument to him to use that style; or whether using liberty at its full stretch, was not the general inducement without any particular motives to it.

The manner of that time of *telling stories*, had drawn him into it; being commended at first for the faculty of telling a tale well, he might insensibly be betrayed to exercise it too often. Stories are dangerous in this, that the best expose a man most, by being oftenest repeated. It might pass for an evidence for the Moderns against the Ancients,[1] that it is now wholly left off by all that have any pretence to be distinguished by their good sense....

HIS TALENTS, TEMPER, HABITS, &C.

He had a mechanical head, which appeared in his inclination to shipping and fortification, &c. This would make one conclude, that his thoughts would naturally have been more fixed to business, if his pleasures had not drawn them away from it.

He had a very good memory, though he would not always make equal good use of it. So that if he had accustomed himself to direct his faculties to his business, I see no reason why he might not have been a good deal master of it. His chain of *memory* was longer than his chain of *thought*; the first could bear any burden, the other was tired by being carried on too long; it was fit to ride a heat, but it had not wind enough for a long course.

A very great memory often forgetteth how much time is lost by repeating things of no use. It was one reason of his talking so much; since a great memory will always have something to say, and will be discharging itself, whether in or out of season, if a good judgment doth not go along with it, to make it stop and turn. One might say of his memory, that it was a *Beauté Journaliere*:[2] Sometimes he would make shrewd applications, &c., at others he would bring things out of it, that never deserved to be laid in it.

He grew by age into a pretty exact distribution of his hours, both for his business, pleasures, and the exercise for his health, of which he took as much care as could possibly consist with some liberties he was resolved to indulge in himself. He walked by his watch, and when he pulled it out to look upon it, skilful men would make haste with what they had to say to him.

He was often retained in his *personal* against his *politic* capacity. He would speak upon those occasions most dexterously against himself; *Charles Stuart* would be bribed against the *King*; and in the distinction, he leaned more to his natural self, than his character would allow. He would not suffer himself to be so much fettered by his character as was convenient; he was still starting out of it, the power of nature was too strong for the dignity of his calling, which generally yielded as often as there was a contest.

It was not the best use he made of his back stairs to admit men to bribe him against himself, to

---

[1] *Moderns against the Ancients*   a long-running debate on the relative merits of ancient versus modern learning, most famously summarized in Jonathan Swift's *The Battle of the Books* (1704).

[2] *Beauté Journaliere*   beautiful but capricious or unpredictable.

procure a defalcation,[1] help a lame accountant to get off, or side with the farmers against the improvement of the revenue.[2] The King was made the instrument to defraud the Crown, which is somewhat extraordinary.

That which might tempt him to it probably was, his finding that those about him so often took money upon those occasions; so that he thought he might do well at least to be a partner. He did not take the money to hoard it; there were those at Court who watched those times, as the Spaniards do for the coming in of the Plate Fleet.[3] The beggars of both sexes helped to empty his Cabinet, and to leave room in them for a new lading upon the next occasion. These negotiators played double with him too, when it was for their purpose so to do. He knew it, and went on still; so he gained his present end, at the time, he was less solicitous to enquire into the consequences.

He could not properly be said to be either *covetous* or *liberal*; his desire to get was not with an intention to be rich; and his spending was rather an easiness in letting money go, than any premeditated thought for the distribution of it. He would do as much to throw off the burden of a present importunity, as he would to relieve a want.

When once the aversion to bear uneasiness taketh place in a man's mind, it doth so check all the passions, that they are damped into a kind of indifference; they grow faint and languishing, and come to be subordinate to that fundamental maxim, of not purchasing any thing at the price of a difficulty. This made that he had as little eagerness to oblige, as he had to hurt men; the motive of his giving bounties was rather to make men less uneasy

to him, than more easy to themselves; and yet no ill-nature all this while. He would slide from an asking face, and could guess very well. It was throwing a man off from his shoulders, that leaned upon them with his whole weight; so that the party was not gladder to receive, than he was to give. It was a kind of implied bargain; though men seldom kept it, being so apt to forget the advantage they had received, that they would presume the King would as little remember the good he had done them, so as to make it an argument against their next request.

This principle of making the love of ease exercise an entire sovereignty in his thoughts, would have been less censured in a private man, than might be in a Prince. The consequence of it to the public changeth the nature of that quality, or else a philosopher in his private capacity might say a great deal to justify it. The truth is, a King is to be such a distinct creature from a man, that their thoughts are to be put in quite a differing shape, and it is such a disquieting task to reconcile them, that Princes might rather expect to be lamented than to be envied, for being in a station that exposeth them, if they do not do more to answer men's expectations than human nature will allow.

That men have the less ease for their loving it so much, is so far from a wonder, that it is a natural consequence, especially in the case of a Prince. Ease is seldom got without some pains, but it is yet seldomer kept without them. He thought giving would make men more easy to him, whereas he might have known it would certainly make them more troublesome.

When men receive benefits from Princes, they attribute less to his generosity than to their own deserts; so that in their own opinion, their merit cannot be bounded; by that mistaken rule, it can as little be satisfied. They would take it for a diminution to have it circumscribed. Merit hath a thirst upon it that can never be quenched by golden showers. It is not only still ready, but greedy to

---

[1] *defalcation* a fraudulent shortcoming or misappropriation in financial matters (*OED* defalcation 5).

[2] referring to a political battle (1682–1683) over the "farming" of the excise tax: fee "farmers" are those who bought for a fixed sum the right to collect the profits of a tax or office.

[3] *Plate Fleet* the fleet carrying silver from mines in the New World.

receive more. This King Charles found in as many instances as any Prince that ever reigned, because the easiness of access introducing the good success of their first request, they were the more encouraged to repeat those importunities, which had been more effectually stopped in the beginning by a short and resolute denial. But his nature did not dispose him to that method, it directed him rather to put off the troublesome minute for the time, and that being his inclination, he did not care to struggle with it.

I am of an opinion, in which I am every day more confirmed by observation, that gratitude is one of those things that cannot be bought. It must be born with men, or else all the obligations in the world will not create it. An outward show may be made to satisfy decency, and to prevent reproach; but a real sense of a kind thing is a gift of nature, and never was, nor can be acquired.

The love of ease is an opiate, it is pleasing for the time, quieteth the spirits, but it hath its effects that seldom fail to be most fatal. The immoderate love of ease maketh a man's mind pay a passive obedience to any thing that happeneth: It reduceth the thoughts from having *desire* to be *content*.

It must be allowed he had a little over-balance on the well-natured side, not vigour enough to be earnest to do a kind thing, much less to do a harsh one; but if a hard thing was done to another man, he did not eat his supper the worse for it. It was rather a deadness than severity of nature, whether it proceeded from a dissipation of spirits, or by the habit of living in which he was engaged.

If a King should be born with more tenderness than might suit with his office, he would in time be hardened. The faults of his subjects make severity so necessary, that by the frequent occasions given to use it, it comes to be habitual, and by degrees the resistance that nature made at first groweth fainter, till at last it is in a manner quite extinguished.

In short, this Prince might more properly be said to have *gifts* than *virtues*, as affability, easiness of living, inclinations to give, and to forgive: Qualities that flowed from his nature rather than from his virtue.

He had not more application to any thing than the preservation of his *health*; it had an entire preference to any thing else in his thoughts, and he might be said without aggravation to study that, with as little intermission as any man in the world. He understood it very well, only in this he failed, that he thought it was more reconcilable with his *pleasures*, than it really was. It is natural to have such a mind to reconcile these, that 'tis the easier for any man that goeth about it, to be guilty of that mistake.

This made him overdo in point of nourishment, the better to furnish to those entertainments; and then he thought by great exercise to make amends, and to prevent ill effects of his blood being too much raised. The success he had in this method, whilst he had youth and vigour to support him in it, encouraged him to continue it longer than nature allowed. Age stealeth so insensibly upon us, that we do not think of suiting our way of reasoning to the several stages of life; so insensibly that not being able to pitch upon any *precise time*, when we cease to be young, we either flatter ourselves that we always continue to be so, or at least forget how much we are mistaken in it.

CONCLUSION

After all this, when some rough strokes of the pencil have made several parts of the picture look a little hard, it is a justice that would be due to every man, much more to a Prince, to make some amends, and to reconcile men as much as may be to it by the last finishing.

He had as good a claim to a kind interpretation as most men. First as a *Prince*: living and dead, generous and well-bred men will be gentle to them; next as an *unfortunate Prince* in the beginning of his time, and a *gentle* one in the rest.

A Prince neither sharpened by his misfortunes whilst abroad, nor by his power when restored, is such a shining character, that it is a reproach not to be so dazzled with it, as not to be able to see a fault in its full light. It would be a scandal in this case to have an exact memory. And if all who are akin to his vices, should mourn for him, never Prince would be better attended to his grave. He is under the protection of common frailty, that must engage men for their own sakes not to be too severe, where they themselves have so much to answer.

What therefore an angry philosopher would call *lewdness*, let frailer men call a warmth and sweetness of the blood, that would not be confined in the communicating itself; an over-flowing of good nature, of which he had such a stream, that it would not be restrained within the banks of a crabbed and unsociable virtue.

If he had sometimes less *firmness* than might have been wished; let the kindest reason be given, and if that should be wanting, the best excuse. I would assign the cause of it to be his loving at any rate to be easy, and his deserving the more to be indulged in it, by his desiring that everybody else should be so.

If he sometimes let a *servant fall*,[1] let it be examined whether he did not weigh so much upon his master, as to give him a fair excuse. That yielding-ness, whatever foundations it might lay to the disadvantage of posterity, was a specific to preserve us in peace for his own time. If he loved too much to lie upon his own down bed of ease, his subjects had the pleasure, during his reign, of lolling and stretching upon theirs. As a sword is sooner broken upon a feather bed than upon a table, so his pliant-ness broke the blow of a present mischief much better than a more immediate resistance would perhaps have done.

Ruin saw this, and therefore removed him first to make way for further overturnings.[2]

If he *dissembled*; let us remember, first, that he was a King, and that dissimulation is a Jewel of the Crown; next, that it is very hard for a man not to do sometimes too much of that, which he conclud-eth necessary for him to practice. Men should consider, that as there would be no false dice, if there were no true ones, so if dissembling is grown universal, it ceaseth to be foul play, having an implied allowance by the general practice. He that was so often forced to dissemble in his own defence, might the better have the privilege sometimes to be the aggressor, and to deal with men at their own weapon.

Subjects are apt to be as arbitrary in their cen-sure, as the most assuming Kings can be in their power. If there might be matter for objections, there is not less reason for excuses; the defects laid to his charge, are such as may claim indulgence from mankind.

Should nobody throw a stone at his faults but those who are free from them, there would be but a slender shower.

What private man will throw stones at him because he *loved*? Or what Prince, because he *dissembled*?

If he either *trusted*, or *forgave* his *enemies*, or in some cases *neglected* his *friends*, more than could in strictness be allowed; let not those errors be so arraigned as take away the privilege that seemeth to be due to Princely frailties. If Princes are under the misfortune of being accused to govern ill, their

---

[1] *let a servant fall* referring to the Earl of Clarendon, forced into exile in 1667, and the Earl of Danby, impeached in 1679.

[2] likely referring to the 1688 Revolution, contrasting Charles II's "pliantness" with James II's inflexibility; though possibly referring also to the Monmouth rebellion (1685) and/or James II's assault on the constitution and the Anglican privileges.

subjects have the less right to fall hard upon them, since they generally so little deserve to be governed well.

The truth is, the calling of a King, with all its glittering, hath such an unreasonable weight upon it, that they may rather expect to be lamented, than to be envied; for being set upon a pinnacle, where they are exposed to censure, if they do not do more to answer men's expectations, than corrupted nature will allow.

It is but justice therefore to this Prince, to give all due softening to the less shining parts of his life; to offer flowers and leaves to hide, instead of using aggravations to expose them.

Let his royal ashes then lie soft upon him, and cover him from harsh and unkind censures; which though they should not be unjust, can never clear themselves from being indecent.

—(CA. 1685–1695)

Samuel Pepys
1633 – 1703

Born in London, the son of a tailor who would rise to become a landowner, Pepys (pronounced "peeps") was educated at St. Paul's School and at Trinity Hall and Magdalene College, Cambridge; he received his B.A. in 1654 and his M.A. in 1660. In 1655 he married Elizabeth St. Michael, the daughter of a French Huguenot refugee. The following year Sir Edward Montagu, his father's first cousin, secured Pepys a clerical post in government, the beginning of a career in public affairs in which Pepys would serve as Clerk of the Privy Seal (1660), Surveyor-General of the navy victualling office (1665), and Secretary of the Admiralty (1672). A brilliant administrator, Pepys has been called "the saviour of the navy" for the economic and logistical reforms he introduced; his work also put him on good terms with the Lord High Admiral, the Duke of York (later James II). In 1679 he was implicated in the "Popish plot" and deprived of office, but was soon set free; he was reinstated to his admiralty position in 1684. In the same year he served as president of The Royal Society, which he had joined shortly after its foundation. He retired after the 1688 Revolution, when his long friendship with the deposed James II made him an object of suspicion.

Pepys kept his diary from 1660 to 1669, stopping only because he feared (unnecessarily, as it turned out) for his eyesight. Written in one of the seventeenth century's several shorthand systems mixed with codes of his own devising, the diary was not transcribed until the early nineteenth century; it has subsequently become not only the best known English diary but also an important source for information about Restoration social life. Always gregarious, an enthusiastic playgoer, amateur musician, and reader (his remarkable library, housed in the original bookcases he designed, remains intact at Magdalene College), Pepys knew and wrote about a wide range of people, from court personalities to local shopkeepers. In the following excerpt, the many names left unannotated are all various business, social, trade, and court acquaintances. For other accounts of the Great Fire, which destroyed much of the central city of London, see the selections from Pepys's friend and fellow diarist John Evelyn and from the Earl of Clarendon.

⊄⋊⊄⋊

The Diary of Samuel Pepys

THE FIRE OF LONDON

SEPTEMBER 2, 1666. LORD'S DAY.   Some of our maids sitting up late last night to get things ready against our feast today, Jane called us up, about 3 in the morning, to tell us of a great fire they saw in the city. So I rose, and slipped on my nightgown and went to her window, and thought it to be on the back side of Marke Lane at the furthest; but being unused to such fires as followed, I thought it far enough off, and so went to bed again and to sleep. About 7 rose again to dress myself, and there looked out at the window and saw the fire not so much as it was, and further off. So to my closet to set things to rights after yesterday's cleaning.[1] By and by Jane comes and tells me that she hears that above 300 houses have been burned down tonight by the fire we saw, and that it was now burning down all Fish Street by London Bridge. So I made myself ready presently, and walked to the Tower and there got up upon one of the high places, Sir J. Robinson's little son going up with me;[2] and there

---

[1] *closet* private (as opposed to public) room; in Pepys's case, a combination of home office and library. The "King's closet" below is a private apartment.

[2] Sir John Robinson was Lieutenant of the Tower of London.

I did see the houses at that end of the bridge all on fire, and an infinite great fire on this and the other side the end of the bridge—which, among other people, did trouble me for poor little Michell and our Sarah on the bridge.[1] So down, with my heart full of trouble, to the Lieutenant of the Tower, who tells me that it begun this morning in the King's baker's house in Pudding Lane, and that it hath burned down St. Magnes Church and most part of Fish Street already. So I down to the waterside and there got a boat and through bridge, and there saw a lamentable fire. Poor Michell's house, as far as the Old Swan, already burned that way and the fire running further, that in a very little time it got as far as the Steel-yard while I was there. Everybody endeavouring to remove their goods, and flinging into the river or bringing them into lighters that lay off.[2] Poor people staying in their houses as long as till the very fire touched them, and then running into boats or clambering from one pair of stair by the waterside to another. And among other things, the poor pigeons I perceive were loath to leave their houses, but hovered about the windows and balconies till they were some of them burned, their wings, and fell down.

Having stayed, and in an hour's time seen the fire rage every way, and nobody to my sight endeavouring to quench it, but to remove their goods and leave all to the fire; and having seen it get as far as the Steel-yard, and the wind mighty high and driving it into the city, and everything, after so long a drought, proving combustible, even the very stones of churches, and among other things, the poor steeple by which pretty Mrs. Horsley lives, and whereof my old school-fellow Elborough is parson, taken fire in the very top and there burned till it fall down—I to Whitehall with a gentleman with me

who desired to go off from the Tower to see the fire in my boat—to Whitehall, and there up to the King's closet in the chapel, where people came about me and I did give them an account dismayed them all; and word was carried in to the King, so I was called for and did tell the King and Duke of York what I saw, and that unless his Majesty did command houses to be pulled down, nothing could stop the fire. They seemed much troubled, and the King commanded me to go to my Lord Mayor from him and command him to spare no houses but to pull down before the fire every way. The Duke of York bid me tell him that if he would have any more soldiers, he shall; and so did my Lord Arlington afterward, as a great secret. Here meeting with Captain Cocke, I in his coach, which he lent me, and Creed with me,[3] to Paul's; and there walked along Watling Street as well as I could, every creature coming away loaded with goods to save—and here and there sick people carried away in beds. Extraordinary good goods carried in carts and on backs. At last met my Lord Mayor in Canning Street, like a man spent, with a handkerchief about his neck. To the King's message, he cried like a fainting woman, "Lord, what can I do? I am spent. People will not obey me. I have been pulling down houses. But the fire overtakes us faster than we can do it."[4] That he needed no more soldiers; and that for himself, he must go and refresh himself, having been up all night. So he left me, and I him, and walked home—seeing people all almost distracted and no manner of means used to quench the fire. The houses too, so very thick thereabouts, and full of matter for burning, as pitch and tar, in Thames Street—and warehouses of oil and wines and brandy and other things. Here I saw Mr. Isaccke Houblon, that handsome man—prettily

---

[1] Michael Mitchell kept a local tavern, though Pepys is probably referring to his wife, Betty, an old flame whom he elsewhere in the *Diary* describes as his "second wife." Sarah was a former servant.

[2] *lighters* flat-bottomed boats used for loading and unloading ships.

[3] George Cocke, merchant and navy contractor; John Creed, Pepys's principal rival for administrative advancement.

[4] *Lord Mayor* Sir Thomas Bludworth; he was subsequently much criticized for indecision (see entry for September 7 below).

dressed and dirty at his door at Dowgate, receiving some of his brothers' things whose houses were on fire; and as he says, have been removed twice already, and he doubts (as it soon proved) that they must be in a little time removed from his house also—which was a sad consideration. And to see the churches all filling with goods, by people who themselves should have been quietly there at this time.

By this time it was about 12 o'clock, and so home and there find my guests, which was Mr. Wood and his wife, Barbary Shelden, and also Mr. Moone—she mighty fine, and her husband, for aught I see a likely man. But Mr. Moone's design and mine, which was to look over my closet and please him with the sight thereof, which he hath long desired, was wholly disappointed, for we were in great trouble and disturbance at this fire not knowing what to think of it. However, we had an extraordinary good dinner, and as merry as at this time we could be.

While at dinner, Mrs. Batelier came to enquire after Mr. Woolfe and Stanes (who it seems are related to them), whose houses in Fish Street are all burned, and they in a sad condition. She would not stay in the fright.

As soon as dined, I and Moone away and walked through the city, the streets full of nothing but people and horses and carts loaded with goods, ready to run over one another, and removing goods from one burned house to another—they now removing out of Canning Street (which received goods in the morning) into Lumbard Street and further; and among others, I now saw my little goldsmith Stokes receiving some friend's goods, whose house itself was burned the day after. We parted at Paul's, he home and I to Paul's Wharf, where I had appointed a boat to attend me; and took in Mr. Carcasse and his brother, whom I met in the street, and carried them below and above bridge, to and again, to see the fire, which was now got further, both below and above, and no likelihood of stopping it. Met with the King and Duke of York in their barge, and with them to Queen-Hith and there called Sir Rd. Browne to them. Their order was only to pull down houses apace, and so below bridge at the waterside; but little was or could be done, the fire coming upon them so fast. Good hopes there was of stopping it at the Three Cranes above, and at Buttolph's Wharf below bridge, if care be used; but the wind carries it into the city, so as we know not by the waterside what it doth there. River full of lighters and boats taking in goods, and good goods swimming in the water; and only, I observed that hardly one lighter or boat in three that had the goods of a house in, but there was a pair of virginals in it.[1] Having seen as much as I could now, I away to Whitehall by appointment, and there walked to St. James's Park, and there met my wife and Creed and Wood and his wife and walked to my boat, and there upon the water again, and to the fire up and down, it still increasing and the wind great. So near the fire as we could for smoke; and all over the Thames, with one's face in the wind you were almost burned with a shower of firedrops—this is very true—so as houses were burned by these drops and flakes of fire, three or four, nay five or six houses, one from another. When we could endure no more upon the water, we to a little alehouse on the Bankside over against the Three Cranes, and there stayed till it was dark almost and saw the fire grow; and as it grow darker, appeared more and more, and in corners and upon steeples and between churches and houses, as far as we could see up the hill of the city, in a most horrid malicious bloody flame, not like the fine flame of an ordinary fire. Barbary and her husband away before us. We stayed till, it being darkish, we saw the fire as only one entire arch of fire from this to the other side the bridge, and in a bow up the hill, for an arch

[1] *pair of virginals* a single instrument, though referred to in the period in the plural; a type of keyboard (*OED* virginal *sb* 1b).

of above a mile long. It made me weep to see it. The churches, houses, and all on fire and flaming at once, and a horrid noise the flames made, and the cracking of houses at their ruin. So home with a sad heart, and there find everybody discoursing and lamenting the fire; and poor Tom Hater came with some few of his goods saved out of his house, which is burned upon Fish Street Hill. I invited him to lie at my house, and did receive his goods: but was deceived in his lying there,[1] the noise coming every moment of the growth of the fire, so as we were forced to begin to pack up our own goods and prepare for their removal. And did by moonshine (it being brave,[2] dry, and moonshine and warm weather) carry much of my goods into the garden, and Mr. Hater and I did remove my money and iron chests into my cellar—as thinking that the safest place. And got my bags of gold into my office ready to carry away, and my chief papers of accounts also there, and my tallies into a box by themselves. So great was our fear, as Sir W. Batten had carts come out of the country to fetch away his goods this night. We did put Mr. Hater, poor man, to bed a little; but he got but very little rest, so much noise being in my house, taking down of goods.

SEPTEMBER 3.   About 4 o'clock in the morning, my Lady Batten sent me a cart to carry away all my money and plate and best things to Sir W. Rider's at Bednall Green; which I did, riding myself in my nightgown in the cart; and Lord, to see how the streets and the highways are crowded with people, running and riding and getting of carts at any rate to fetch away things. I find Sir W. Rider tired with being called up all night and receiving things from several friends. His house full of goods—and much of Sir W. Batten and Sir W. Penn's. I am eased at

my heart to have my treasure so well secured. Then home with much ado to find a way. Nor any sleep all this night to me nor my poor wife. But then, and all this day, she and I and all my people labouring to get away the rest of our things, and did get Mr. Tooker to get me a lighter to take them in, and we did carry them (myself some) over Tower Hill, which was by this time full of people's goods, bringing their goods thither. And down to the lighter, which lay at the next quay above the Tower dock. And here was my neighbour's wife, Mrs. Buckworth, with her pretty child and some few of her things, which I did willingly give way to be saved with mine. But there was no passing with anything through the postern, the crowd was so great.

The Duke of York came this day by the office and spoke to us, and did ride with his guard up and down the city to keep all quiet (he being now General, and having the care of all).

This day, Mercer being not at home, but against her mistress' order gone to her mother's, and my wife going thither to speak with W. Hewer, met her there and was angry; and her mother saying that she was not a prentice girl, to ask leave every time she goes abroad, my wife with good reason was angry, and when she came home, bid her be gone again. And so she went away, which troubled me; but yet less than it would, because of the condition we are in fear of coming into in a little time, of being less able to keep one in her quality. At night, lay down a little upon a quilt of W. Hewer in the office (all my own things being packed up or gone); and after me, my poor wife did the like—we having fed upon the remains of yesterday's dinner, having no fire nor dishes, nor any opportunity of dressing anything.

SEPTEMBER 4.   Up by break of day to get away the remainder of my things, which I did by a lighter at the Iron Gate; and my hands so few, that it was the afternoon before we could get them all away.

---

[1] *was deceived*   was mistaken in making the offer.

[2] *brave*   fine (*OED* brave *a* 3b).

Sir W. Penn and I to Tower Street, and there met the fire burning three or four doors beyond Mr. Howell's; whose goods, poor man (his trays and dishes, shovels &c., were flung all along Tower Street in the kennels, and people working therewith from one end to the other), the fire coming on in that narrow street, on both sides, with infinite fury. Sir W. Batten, not knowing how to remove his wine, did dig a pit in the garden and laid it in there; and I took the opportunity of laying all the papers of my office that I could not otherwise dispose of. And in the evening Sir W. Penn and I did dig another and put our wine in it, and I my Parmesan cheese as well as my wine and some other things.

The Duke of York was at the office this day at Sir W. Penn's, but I happened not to be within. This afternoon, sitting melancholy with Sir W. Penn in our garden and thinking of the certain burning of this office without extraordinary means, I did propose for the sending up of all our workmen from Woolwich and Deptford yards (none whereof yet appeared), and to write to Sir W. Coventry to have the Duke of York's permission to pull down houses rather than lose this office, which would much hinder the King's business. So Sir W. Penn he went down this night, in order to the sending them up tomorrow morning; and I wrote to Sir W. Coventry about the business, but received no answer.

This night Mrs. Turner (who, poor woman, was removing her goods all this day—good goods, into the garden, and knew not how to dispose of them)—and her husband supped with my wife and I at night in the office, upon a shoulder of mutton from the cook's, without any napkin or anything, in a sad manner but were merry. Only, now and then walking into the garden and saw how horridly the sky looks, all on a fire in the night, was enough to put us out of our wits; and indeed it was extremely dreadful—for it looks just as if it was at us, and the whole heaven on fire. I after supper walked in the dark down to Tower Street, and there saw it all on fire at the Trinity house on that side and the Dolphin tavern on this side, which was very near us—and the fire with extraordinary vehemence. Now begins the practice of blowing up of houses in Tower Street, those next the Tower, which at first did frighten people more than anything; but it stopped the fire where it was done—it bringing down the houses to the ground in the same places they stood, and then it was easy to quench what little fire was in it, though it kindled nothing almost. W. Hewer this day went to see how his mother did, and comes late home, but telling us how he hath been forced to remove her to Islington, her house in Pye Corner being burned. So that it got so far that way and all the Old Bailey, and was running down to Fleet Street. And Paul's is burned, and all Cheapside. I wrote to my father this night; but the post-house being burned, the letter could not go.

SEPTEMBER 5. I lay down in the office again upon W. Hewer's quilt, being mighty weary and sore in my feet with going till I was hardly able to stand. About 2 in the morning my wife calls me up and tells of new cries of "Fire!"—it being come to Barking Church, which is the bottom of our lane. I up; and finding it so, resolved presently to take her away; and did, and took my gold (which was about £2350), W. Hewer, and Jane down by Poundy's boat to Woolwich. But Lord, what a sad sight it was by moonlight to see the whole city almost on fire—that you might see it plain at Woolwich, as if you were by it. There when I came, I find the gates shut, but no guard kept at all; which troubled me, because of discourses now begun that there is plot in it and that the French had done it.[1] I got the gates open, and to Mr. Shelden's, where I locked up

---

[1] *gates* the gates to the dockyard; if French agents were setting fires, the dockyard would provide a significant military target, hence Pepys's worries about the lack of a guard.

my gold and charged my wife and W. Hewer never to leave the room without one of them in it night nor day. So back again, by the way seeing my goods well in the lighters at Deptford and watched well by people. Home, and whereas I expected to have seen our house on fire, it being now about 7 o'clock, it was not. But to the fire, and there find greater hopes than I expected; for my confidence of finding our office on fire was such, that I durst not ask anybody how it was with us, till I came and saw it not burned. But going to the fire, I find, by the blowing up of houses and the great help given by the workmen out of the King's yards, sent up by Sir W. Penn, there is a good stop given to it, as well at Mark Lane end as ours—it having only burned the dial of Barking Church, and part of the porch, and was there quenched. I up to the top of Barking steeple, and there saw the saddest sight of desolation that I ever saw. Everywhere great fires. Oil cellars and brimstone and other things burning. I became afeared to stay there long; and therefore down again as fast as I could, the fire being spread as far as I could see it, and to Sir W. Penn's and there eat a piece of cold meat, having eaten nothing since Sunday but the remains of Sunday's dinner.

Here I met with Mr. Young and Whistler; and having removed all my things, and received good hopes that the fire at our end is stopped, they and I walked into the town and find Fanchurch Street, Gracious Street, and Lumbard Street all in dust. The Exchange a sad sight, nothing standing there of all the statues or pillars but Sir Tho. Gresham's picture in the corner.[1] Walked into Moorfields (our feet ready to burn, walking through the town among the hot coals) and find that full of people, and poor wretches carrying their goods there, and everybody keeping his goods together by themselves (and a great blessing it is to them that it is fair weather for them to keep abroad night and day);

drank there, and paid twopence for a plain penny loaf.

Thence homeward, having passed through Cheapside and Newgate Market, all burned—and seen Anthony Joyce's house in fire. And took up (which I keep by me) a piece of glass of Mercer's chapel in the street, where much more was, so melted and buckled with the heat of the fire, like parchment. I also did see a poor cat taken out of a hole in the chimney joining to the wall of the Exchange, with the hair all burned off the body and yet alive. So home at night, and find there good hopes of saving our office—but great endeavours of watching all night and having men ready; and so we lodged them in the office, and had drink and bread and cheese for them. And I lay down and slept a good night about midnight—though when I rose, I hear that there had been a great alarm of French and Dutch being risen—which proved nothing. But it is a strange thing to see how long this time did look since Sunday, having been always full of variety of actions, and little sleep, that it looked like a week or more. And I had forgot almost the day of the week.

SEPTEMBER 6.   Up about 5 o'clock, and there met Mr. Gawden at the gate of the office (I intending to go out, as I used every now and then to do, to see how the fire is) to call our men to Bishop's Gate, where no fire had yet been near, and there is now one broke out—which did give great grounds to people, and to me too, to think that there is some kind of plot in this (on which many by this time have been taken, and it hath been dangerous for any stranger to walk in the streets);[2] but I went with the men and we did put it out in a little time, so that that was well again. It was pretty to see how hard

---

[1] *picture* statue; Sir Thomas Gresham had founded the Royal Exchange, a meeting place for merchants and bankers.

[2] Many blamed the fire on foreign saboteurs, with suspicion falling on Catholics generally and the French in particular; the fire does, however, appear to have been accidental. Clarendon discusses these fears in more detail.

the women did work in the canals sweeping of water; but then they would scold for drink and be as drunk as devils. I saw good butts of sugar broke open in the street, and people go and take handfuls out and put into beer and drink it. And now all being pretty well, I took boat and over to Southwark, and took boat on the other side the bridge and so to Westminster, thinking to shift myself, being all in dirt from top to bottom. But could not there find any place to buy a shirt or pair of gloves, Westminster Hall being full of people's goods—those in Westminster having removed all their goods, and the Exchequer money put into vessels to carry to Nonsuch. But to the Swan, and there was trimmed. And then to Whitehall, but saw nobody, and so home. A sad sight to see how the river looks—no houses nor church near it to the Temple—where it stopped. At home did go with Sir W. Batten and our neighbour Knightly (who, with one more, was the only man of any fashion left in all the neighbourhood hereabouts, they all removing their goods and leaving their houses to the mercy of the fire) to Sir R. Ford's, and there dined, in an earthen platter a fried breast of mutton, a great many of us. But very merry; and indeed as good a meal, though as ugly a one, as ever I had in my life. Thence down to Deptford, and there with great satisfaction landed all my goods at Sir G. Carteret's, safe, and nothing missed I could see, or hurt. This being done to my great content, I home; and to Sir W. Batten's, and there with Sir R. Ford, Mr. Knightly, and one Withers, a professed lying rogue, supped well; and mighty merry and our fears over. From them to the office and there slept, with the office full of labourers, who talked and slept and walked all night long there. But strange it was to see Clothworker's Hall on fire these three days and nights in one body of flame—it being the cellar, full of oil.

September 7.   Up by 5 o'clock and, blessed by God, find all well, and by water to Paul's wharf.

Walked thence and saw all the town burned, and a miserable sight of Paul's Church, with all the roofs fallen and the body of the choir fallen into St. Faith's—Paul's school also—Ludgate—Fleet Street—my father's house, and the church, and a good part of the Temple the like. So to Creed's lodging near the New Exchange, and there find him laid down upon a bed—the house all unfurnished, there being fears of the fire's coming to them. There borrowed a shirt of him—and washed. To Sir W. Coventry at St. James's, who lay without curtains, having removed all his goods—as the King at Whitehall and everybody had done and was doing. He hopes we shall have no public distractions upon this fire, which is what everybody fears—because of the talk of the French having a hand in it. And it is a proper time for discontents—but all men's minds are full of care to protect themselves and save their goods. The militia is in arms everywhere. Our fleets, he tells me, have been in sight one of another, and most unhappily by foul weather were parted, to our great loss, as in reason they do conclude—the Dutch being come out only to make a show and please their people; but in very bad condition as to stores, victuals, and men. They are at Bullen, and our fleet come to St. Ellen's. We have got nothing, but have lost one ship, but he knows not what.[1]

Thence to the Swan and there drank; and so home and find all well. My Lord Brouncker at Sir W. Batten's, and tells us the General is sent for up to come to advise with the King about business at this juncture, and to keep all quiet—which is great honour to him, but I am sure is but a piece of dissimulation. So home and did give order for my house to be made clean; and then down to Woolwich and there find all well. Dined, and Mrs. Markeham came to see my wife. So I up again, and calling at Deptford for some things of W. Hewer, he being with me; and then home and spent the

---

[1] The English in fact lost several ships in this encounter.

evening with Sir R. Ford, Mr. Knightly, and Sir W. Penn at Sir W. Batten's. This day our merchants first met at Gresham College, which by proclamation is to be their Exchange. Strange to hear what is bid for houses all up and down here—a friend of Sir W. Rider's having £150 for what he used to let for £40 per annum. Much dispute where the Custom House shall be; thereby the growth of the city again to be foreseen. My Lord Treasurer, they say, and others, would have it at the other end of the town. I home late to Sir W. Penn, who did give me a bed—but without curtains or hangings, all being down. So here I went the first time into a naked bed, only my drawers on—and did sleep pretty well; but still, both sleeping and waking, had a fear of fire in my heart, that I took little rest. People do all the world over cry out of the simplicity of my Lord Mayor in general, and more particularly in this business of the fire, laying it all upon him. A proclamation is come out for markets to be kept at Leaden Hall and Mile-end Green and several other places about the town and Tower hill, and all churches to be set open to receive poor people.

SEPTEMBER 8.   Up, and with Sir W. Batten and Sir W. Penn by water to Whitehall, and they to St. James's. I stopped with Sir G. Carteret, to desire him to go with us and to enquire after money. But the first he cannot do, and the other as little, or says, "When can we get any, or what shall we do for it?" He, it seems, is employed in the correspondence between the city and the King every day, in settling of things. I find him full of trouble to think how things will go. I left him, and to St. James's, where we met first at Sir W. Coventry's chamber and there did what business we can without any books. Our discourse, as everything else, was confused. The fleet is at Portsmouth, there staying a wind to carry them to the Downes or toward Bullen, where they say the Dutch fleet is gone and stays. We concluded upon private meetings for a while, not having any

money to satisfy any people that may come to us. I bought two eels upon the Thames, cost me 6s.[1] Thence with Sir W. Batten to the Cockpit, whither the Duke of Albemarle is come. It seems the King holds him so necessary at this time, that he hath sent for him and will keep him here. Indeed, his interest in the city, being acquainted, and his care in keeping things quiet, is reckoned that wherein he will be very serviceable. We to him. He is courted in appearance by everybody. He very kind to us. I perceive he lays by all business of the fleet at present and minds the city, and is now hastening to Gresham College to discourse with the Aldermen. Sir W. Batten and I home (where met by my brother John, come to town to see how things are with us). And then presently he with me to Gresham College —where infinite of people; partly through novelty to see the new place, and partly to find out and hear what is become one man of another. I met with many people undone, and more that have extraordinary great losses. People speaking their thoughts variously about the beginning of the fire and the rebuilding of the city. Then to Sir W. Batten and took my brother with me, and there dined with a great company of neighbours, and much good discourse; among others, of the low spirits of some rich men in the city, in sparing any encouragement to the poor people that wrought for the saving their houses. Among others, Alderman Starling, a very rich man, without children, the fire at next door to him in our lane—after our men had saved his house, did give 2s 6d among 30 of them, and did quarrel with some that would remove the rubbish out of the way of the fire, saying that they came to steal. Sir W. Coventry told me of another this morning in Holborne, which he showed the King—that when it was offered to stop the fire near his house for such a reward, that came but to 2s 6d a man among the neighbours, he would give but

---

[1] three times the usual price of two shillings.

18*d*. Thence to Bednall Green by coach, my brother with me, and saw all well there and fetched away my journal book to enter for five days past; and then back to the office, where I find Bagwell's wife and her husband come home. Agreed to come [to] their house tomorrow, I sending him away back to his ship today. To the office, and late writing letters; and then to Sir W. Penn, my brother lying with me, and Sir W. Penn gone down to rest himself at Woolwich. But I was much frighted, and kept awake in my bed, by some noise I heard a great while below-stairs and the boys not coming up to me when I knocked. It was by their discovery of people stealing of some neighbour's wine that lay in vessels in the street. So to sleep. And all well all night.

SEPTEMBER 9.   Sunday. Up, and was trimmed, and sent my brother to Woolwich to my wife to dine with her. I to church, where our parson made a melancholy but good sermon—and many, and most, in the church cried, especially the women.

The church mighty full, but few of fashion, and most strangers. I walked to Bednall Green; and there dined well, but a bad venison pasty, at Sir W. Rider's. Good people they are, and good discourse. And his daughter Middleton, a fine woman and discreet. Thence home, and to church again, and there preached Dean Harding; but methinks a bad poor sermon, though proper for the time—nor eloquent, in saying at this time that the city is reduced from a large folio to a *decimo tertio*.[1] So to my office, there to write down my journal and take leave of my brother, whom I sent back this afternoon, though rainy—which it hath not done a good while before. But I had no room nor convenience for him here till my house is fitted; but I was very kind to him, and do take very well of him his journey. I did give him 40*s* for his pocket; and so he being gone, and it presently raining, I was troubled for him, though it is good for the fire. Anon to Sir W. Penn to bed, and made my boy Tom to read me asleep.
—(1666)

---

[1] *large folio…decimo tertio*   sizes of books, from the largest to the smallest.

Robert South

1634 – 1716

The son of a London merchant, South was educated at Westminster School and Christ Church, Oxford. After receiving his M.A. in 1657, he travelled on the continent where in 1658 he was privately ordained. After the Restoration, South held a succession of offices, becoming public orator of Oxford (1660–1667), domestic chaplain to the Earl of Clarendon (1660), chaplain to the Duke of York (1667), canon of Christ Church (1670), and rector of Islip in Oxfordshire (1668); later in life he turned down the offer of a bishopric.

South was a very popular preacher, known for a witty, pithy, sometimes sarcastic sermon style. Many of his sermons were published separately, and they were gathered in a six-volume collected edition (1679–1715). The following sermon, preached at about the time of the Restoration, draws a parallel between the biblical King Jeroboam and Oliver Cromwell in order to attack the Interregnum Independents and others who argued for the legitimacy of worship outside the established Church. His emphasis on the importance to the state of religious order and ceremony is similar to the pragmatic political advice William Cavendish was privately giving Charles II at the same time. In addition, South's picture of the thankless difficulties of the clerical life echoes Robert Burton's discussion of the melancholy of scholars. The sermon was first published in *Interest Deposed, and Truth Restored... Two Sermons* (1660).

❧❧❧

Ecclesiastical Policy the Best Policy:
or
Religion the Best Reason of State

Preached at Lincoln's Inn
[Before 25 May, 1660]

I Kings 13:33, 34. *After this thing Jeroboam returned not from his evil way, but made again of the lowest of the people priests of the high places: Whosoever would, he consecrated him, and he became one of the priests of the high places. And this thing became sin unto the house of Jeroboam, even to cut it off, and to destroy it from off the face of the earth.*

Jeroboam (from the name of a person become the character of impiety) is reported to posterity eminent, or rather infamous, for two things; usurpation of government, and innovation of religion. 'Tis confessed, the former is expressly said to have been from God; but since God may order, and dispose, what he does not approve; and use the wickedness of men, while he forbids it; the design of the first cause does not excuse the malignity of the second: And therefore, the advancement and sceptre of Jeroboam was in that sense only the work of God, in which it is said, Amos 3:6: "That there is no evil in the city which the Lord has not done." But from his attempts upon the civil power, he proceeds to innovate God's worship; and from the subjection of men's bodies and estates, to enslave their consciences, as knowing that true religion is no friend to an unjust title. Such was afterwards the way of Mahomet, to the tyrant to join the impostor, and what he had got by the sword to confirm by the Alcoran;[1] raising his empire upon two pillars, conquest, and inspiration. Jeroboam being thus advanced, and thinking policy the best piety, though indeed in nothing ever more befooled; the nature of sin being not only to defile, but to infatuate: In [I Kings] the 12th chapter, and the 27th verse, he thus argues: "If this people go up to do

---

[1] *Alcoran* the usual seventeenth-century spelling for the Qur'an (Koran).

sacrifice in the House of the Lord at Jerusalem, then shall the heart of this people turn again unto their Lord, even unto Rehoboam King of Judah, and they shall kill me, and go again unto Rehoboam King of Judah." As if he should have said, the true worship of God, and the converse of those that use it, dispose men to a considerate lawful subjection. And therefore I must take another course: My practice must not be better than my title; what was won by force, must be continued by delusion. Thus sin is usually seconded with sin: And a man seldom commits one sin to please, but he commits another to defend himself. As 'tis frequent for the adulterer to commit murder to conceal the shame of his adultery. But let us see Jeroboam's politic procedure in the next verse. "Whereupon the King took counsel, and made two calves of gold, and said unto them, It is too much for you to go up to Jerusalem, behold thy Gods, O Israel." As if he had made such an edict: "I Jeroboam, by the advice of my council, considering the great distance of the temple, and the great charges that poor people are put to in going thither; as also the intolerable burthen of paying the first-fruits and tithes to the priest, have considered of a way that may be more easy, and less burthensome to the people, as also more comfortable to the priests themselves; and therefore strictly enjoin, that none henceforth presume to repair to the temple at Jerusalem, especially since God is not tied to any place or form of worship; as also, because the devotion of men is apt to be clogged by such ceremonies; therefore both for the ease of the people, as well as for the advancement of religion, we require and command, that all henceforth forbear going up to Jerusalem." Questionless these, and such other reasons, the impostor used to insinuate his devout idolatry. And thus the calves were set up, to which oxen must be sacrificed; the God and the sacrifice out of the same herd. And because Israel was not to return to Egypt, Egypt was brought back to them: That is, the Egyptian way of worship, the Apis, or

Serapis, which was nothing but the image of a calf or ox, as is clear from most historians. Thus Jeroboam having procured his people Gods, the next thing was to provide priests. Hereupon, to the calves he adds a commission, for the approving, trying, and admitting the rascality and lowest of the people to minister in that service: Such as kept cattle, with a little change of their office, were admitted to make oblations to them. And doubtless, besides the approbation of these, there was a commission also to eject such of the priests and Levites of God, as being too ceremoniously addicted to the temple, would not serve Jeroboam before God, nor worship his calves for their gold, nor approve those two glittering sins for any reason of state whatsoever.

Having now perfected divine worship, and prepared both Gods and priests: In the next place, that he might the better teach his false priests the way of their new worship, he begins the service himself, and so countenances by his example, what he had enjoined by his command, in the 33 *v.* of this chapter, "And Jeroboam stood by the altar to burn incense." Burning of incense was then the ministerial office amongst them, as preaching is now amongst us. So that to represent to you the nature of Jeroboam's action: It was, as if in a Christian nation the chief governor should authorize and encourage all the scum and refuse of the people to preach,[1] and call them to the Ministry by using to preach, and invade the ministerial function himself. But Jeroboam rested not here, but while he was busy in his work, and a prophet immediately sent by God, declares against his idolatry, he endeavours to seize upon, and commit him; in the 4 *v.* "He held forth his hand from the altar, and said, Lay hold of him." Thus we have him completing his sin, and by a "strange imposition of hands" persecuting the true prophets, as well as ordaining false. But it

---

[1] Cromwell (a lively copy of Jeroboam) did so [note added when the sermon was published in a collected edition].

was a natural transition, and no ways wonderful to see him, who stood affronting God with false incense in the right hand, persecuting with the left, and abetting the idolatry of one arm with the violence of the other. Now, if we lay all these things together, and consider the parts, rise, and degrees of his sin, we shall find, that it was not for nothing, that the spirit of God so frequently and bitterly in Scripture stigmatizes this person; for it represents him, first encroaching upon the civil government, thence changing that of the church, debasing the office that God had made sacred; introducing a false way of worship, and destroying the true. And in this we have a full and fair description of a foul thing, that is, of an usurper and an impostor: or, to use one word more comprehensive than both, "of Jeroboam the Son of Nebat who made Israel to sin."

From the story and practice of Jeroboam, we might gather these observations.

1. That God sometimes punishes a notorious sin, by suffering the sinner to fall into a worse.

Thus God punishes the rebellion of the Israelites, by permitting them to fall into idolatry.

2. There is nothing so absurd, but may be obtruded upon the vulgar under pretence of religion.

Certainly, otherwise, a golden calf could never have been made, either the object, or the means of divine worship.

3. Sin, especially that of perverting God's worship, as it leaves a guilt upon the soul, so it perpetuates a blot upon the name.

Hence nothing so frequent, as for the spirit of God to express wicked, irreligious Kings, by comparing them to Ahab or Jeroboam. It being usual to make the first and most eminent in any kind, not only the standard for comparison, but also the rule of expression.

But I shall insist only upon the words of the text, and what shall be drawn from thence. Here are two things in the words that may seem to require explication.

1. What is meant by the High Places.

2. What by the consecration of the priests.

1. Concerning the High Places. The use of these in the divine worship was general and ancient. And as Dionysius Vossius observes in his notes upon Moses Maimonides, the first way that was used, long before temples were either built, or thought lawful. The reason of this seems to be, because those places could not be thought to shut up, or confine the immensity of God, as they supposed an house did; and withall gave his worshippers a nearer approach to Heaven by their height. Hence we read that the Samaritans worshipped upon Mount Gerizim, Joh. 4:20. And Samuel went up to the High Place to sacrifice, I Sam. 9:14. And Solomon sacrificed at the High Place in Gibeon, I King. 3:4. Yea, the temple itself was at length built upon a Mount or High Place, II Chron. 3:1. You will say then, Why are these places condemned? I answer, that the use of them was not condemned as absolutely and always unlawful in itself, but only after the temple was built, and that God had professed to put his name in that place and no other: Therefore, what was lawful in the practice of Samuel and Solomon before the Temple was in being was now detestable in Jeroboam, since that was constituted by God the only place for his worship. To bring this consideration to the times of Christianity. Because the Apostles and primitive Christians preached in houses, and had only private meetings, in regard they were under persecution, and had no churches; this cannot warrant the practice of those now-a-days, nor a toleration of them, that prefer houses before churches, and a conventicle before the congregation.[1]

---

[1] *conventicle* a private religious meeting or assembly, particularly of a Nonconformist congregation; John Bunyan was arrested for holding a conventicle.

2. For the second thing, which is the consecration of the priests; it seems to have been correspondent to ordination in the Christian church. Idolaters themselves were not so far gone, as to venture upon the priesthood without consecration and a call. To show all the solemnities of this, would be tedious, and here unnecessary: The Hebrew word which we render to consecrate, signifies "to fill the hand," which indeed imports the manner of consecration, which was done by filling the hand: for the priest cut a piece of the sacrifice, and put it into the hands of him that was to be consecrated; by which ceremony he received right to sacrifice, and so became a priest. As our ordination in the Christian church is said to have been heretofore transacted by the Bishop's delivering of the Bible into the hands of him that was to be ordained, whereby he received power ministerially to dispense the mysteries contained in it, and so was made a presbyter.[1] Thus much briefly concerning consecration.

There remains nothing else to be explained in the words: I shall therefore now draw forth the sense of them into these two propositions:

1. The surest means to strengthen, or the readiest to ruin the civil power, is either to establish, or destroy the worship of God in the right exercise of religion.

2. The next, and most effectual way to destroy religion is to embase the teachers and dispensers of it.

Of both these in their order.

For the prosecution of the former, we are to show,

1. The truth of the assertion, that it is so.

2. The reason of the assertion, why and whence it is so.

1. For the truth of it: It is abundantly evinced from all records both of divine and profane history, in which he that runs may read the ruin of the state in the destruction of the church; and that not only

portended by it, as its sign, but also inferred from it, as its cause.

2. For the reason of the point; it may be drawn,

1. From the judicial proceeding of God, the great King of Kings, and supreme ruler of the universe; who for his commands is indeed careful, but for his worship jealous: And therefore in states notoriously irreligious, by a secret and irresistible power, countermands their deepest project, splits their counsels, and smites their most refined policies with frustration and a curse; being resolved that the kingdoms of the world shall fall down before him, either in his adoration, or their own confusion.

2. The reason of the doctrine may be drawn from the necessary dependence of the very principles of government upon religion. And this I shall pursue more fully. The great business of government is to procure obedience, and keep off disobedience: the great springs upon which those two move, are rewards and punishments, answering the two ruling affections of man's mind, hope and fear. For since there is a natural opposition between the judgment and the appetite, the former respecting what is honest, the latter what is pleasing; which two qualifications seldom concur in the same thing, and since withall, man's design in every action is delight; therefore to render things honest also practicable, they must be first represented desirable, which cannot be, but by proposing honesty clothed with pleasure; and since it presents no pleasure to the sense, it must be fetched from the apprehension of a future reward. For questionless duty moves not so much upon command as promise. Now therefore, that which proposes the greatest and most suitable rewards to obedience, and the greatest terrors and punishments to disobedience, doubtless is the most likely to enforce one, and prevent the other. But it is religion that does this, which to happiness and misery joins eternity. And these,

---

[1] *a presbyter* in this case, a priest in the established Church, not an elder in the Presbyterian Church.

supposing the immortality of the soul, which philosophy indeed conjectures, but only religion proves, or (which is as good) persuades: I say these two things, eternal happiness and eternal misery, meeting with a persuasion that the soul is immortal, are, without controversy, of all others, the first the most desirable, and the latter the most horrible to humane apprehension. Were it not for these, civil government were not able to stand before the prevailing swing of corrupt nature, which would know no honesty but advantage, no duty but in pleasure, nor any law but its own will. Were not these frequently thundered into the understandings of men, the magistrate might enact, order, and proclaim; proclamations might be hung upon walls and posts, and there they might hang, seen and despised, more like malefactors, than laws: But when religion binds them upon the conscience, conscience will either persuade or terrify men into their practice. For, put the case, a man knew, and that upon the sure grounds, that he might do an advantageous murder or robbery, and not be discovered; what humane laws could hinder him, which, he knows, cannot inflict any penalty, where they can make no discovery? But religion assures him, that no sin, though concealed from humane eyes, can either escape God's sight in this world, or his vengeance in the other.... If there was not a Minister in every parish, you would quickly find cause to increase the number of constables: And if the churches were not employed to be places to hear God's law, there would be need of them to be prisons for the breakers of the laws of men....

Wherefore, having proved the dependence of government upon religion, I shall now demonstrate, that the safety of government depends upon the truth of religion. False religion is in its nature the greatest bane and destruction to government in the world. The reason is, because whatsoever is false, is also weak. *Ens* and *Verum* in philosophy are the same:[1] And so much as any religion has of falsity it loses of strength and existence. Falsity gains authority only from ignorance, and therefore is in danger to be known; for from being false, the next immediate step is to be known to be such. And what prejudice this would be to the civil government, is apparent, if men should be awed into obedience, and affrighted from sin by rewards and punishments, proposed to them in such a religion, which afterwards should be detected, and found a mere falsity and cheat; for if one part be but found to be false, it will make the whole suspicious. And men will then not only cast off obedience to the civil magistrate, but they will do it with disdain and rage, that they have been deceived so long, and brought to do that out of conscience, which was imposed upon them out of design: For though men are often willingly deceived, yet still it must be under an opinion of being instructed; though they love the deception, yet they mortally hate it under that appearance: Therefore it is no ways safe for a magistrate, who is to build his dominion upon the fears of men, to build those fears upon a false religion. 'Tis not to be doubted, but the absurdity of Jeroboam's calves, made many Israelites turn subjects to Rehoboam's government that they might be proselytes to his religion. Herein the weakness of the Turkish religion appears, that it urges obedience upon the promise of such absurd rewards, as, that after death they should have palaces, gardens, beautiful women, with all the luxury that could be: As if those things, that were the occasions and incentives of sin in this world, could be the rewards of holiness in the other. Besides many other inventions, false and absurd, that are like so many chinks and holes to discover the rottenness of the whole fabric, when God shall be pleased to give light to discover, and open their reasons to discern them. But you will say, What government more sure and

---

[1] *Ens and Verum* being or entity, and truth.

absolute than the Turkish, and yet what religion more false? Therefore, certainly government may stand sure and strong, be the religion professed never so absurd. I answer, that it may do so indeed by accident, through the strange peculiar temper, and gross ignorance of a people; as we see it happens in the Turks, the best part of whose policy, supposing the absurdity of their religion, is this, that they prohibit schools of learning; for this hinders knowledge and disputes, which such a religion would not bear. But suppose we, that the learning of these Western nations were as great there as here, and the Alcoran as common to them as the Bible to us, that they might have free recourse to search and examine the flaws and follies of it; and withall, that they were of as inquisitive a temper as we: And who knows, but as there are vicissitudes in the government, so there may happen the same also in the temper of a nation? If this should come to pass, where would be their religion? And then let every one judge, whether the *Arcana Imperii* and *Religionis* would not fall together.[1] They have begun to totter already; for Mahomet having promised to come and visit his followers, and translate them to Paradise after a thousand years, this being expired, many of the Persians began to doubt and smell the cheat, till the Mufti or Chief Priest told them, that it was a mistake in the figure, and assured them, that upon more diligent survey of the records, he found it two thousand instead of one. When this is expired, perhaps they will not be able to renew the fallacy. I say therefore, that though this government continues firm in the exercise of a false religion, yet this is by accident, through the present genius of the people, which may change; but this does not prove, but that the nature of such a religion (of which we only now speak), tends to subvert and betray the civil power. Hence Machiavel himself, in his ani-

madversions upon Livy,[2] makes it appear, that the weakness of Italy, which was once so strong, was caused by the corrupt practices of the papacy, in depraving and misusing religion to that purpose, which he, though himself a papist, says, could not have happened, had the Christian religion been kept in its first, and native simplicity. Thus much may suffice for the clearing of the first proposition.

The inferences from hence are two.

1. If government depends upon religion, then this shows the pestilential design of those, that attempt to disjoin the civil and ecclesiastical interest, setting the latter wholly out of the tuition of the former. But 'tis clear that the fanatics know no other step to the magistracy, but through the ruin of the Ministry. There is a great analogy between the body natural and politic; in which the ecclesiastical or spiritual part justly supplies the part of the soul; and the violent separation of this from the other, does as certainly infer death and dissolution, as the disjunction of the body and the soul in the natural; for when this once departs, it leaves the body of the commonwealth a carcass, noisome, and exposed to be devoured by birds of prey. The Ministry will be one day found, according to Christ's word, "the salt of the Earth" [Matthew 5:13], the only thing that keeps societies of men from stench and corruption....

2. If the safety of government is founded upon the truth of religion, then this shows the danger of any thing that may make even the true religion suspected to be false. To be false, and to be thought false is all one in respect of men, who act not according to truth, but apprehension. As on the contrary, a false religion, while apprehended true, has the force and efficacy of truth. Now there is nothing more apt to induce men to a suspicion of any religion, than frequent innovation and change:

---

[1] *Arcana Imperii and Religionis* mysteries of state and religion.

[2] Machiavelli's *Discorsi sopra la prima deca di Tito Livio* [Discourses on Livy] was written in 1513 and published in numerous editions and translations, including English.

for since the object of religion, God; the subject of it, the Soul of Man; and the business of it, Truth, is always one and the same: Variety and novelty is a just presumption of falsity. It argues sickness and distemper in the mind, as well as in the body, when a man is continually turning and tossing from one side to the other. The wise Romans ever dreaded the least innovation in religion: Hence we find the advice of Maecenas to Augustus Caesar, in Dion Cassius, in the 52 Book,[1] where he counsels him to detest and persecute all innovators of divine worship, not only as condemners of the Gods, but as the most pernicious disturbers of the state: For when men venture to make changes in things sacred, it argues great boldness with God, and this naturally imports little belief of him: which if the people once perceive, they will take their creed also, not from the magistrate's laws, but his example. Hence in England, where religion has been still purifying, and hereupon almost always in the fire and the furnace; atheists, and irreligious persons have took no small advantage from our changes. For in King Edward the Sixth's time, the divine worship was twice altered in two new liturgies. In the first of Queen Mary, the Protestant religion was persecuted with fire and faggot, by law and public council of the same persons, who had so lately established it. Upon the coming in of Queen Elizabeth, religion was changed again, and within a few days the public council of the nation made it death for a priest to convert any man to that religion, which before with so much eagerness of zeal had been restored. So that it is observed by an author, that in the space of twelve years there were four changes about religion made in England, and that by the public council and authority of the realm, which were more than were made by any Christian state throughout the world, so soon one after another, in the space of fifteen hundred years before. Hence it is, that the enemies of God take occasion to blaspheme, and call our religion Statism. And now adding to the former, those many changes that have happened since, I am afraid we shall not so easily claw off that name: Nor, though we may satisfy our own consciences in what we profess, be able to repel and clear off the objections of the rational world about us, which not being interested in our changes as we are, will not judge of them as we judge; but debate them by impartial reason, by the nature of the thing, the general practice of the church; against which *new lights, sudden impulses of the spirit, extraordinary calls,*[2] will be but weak arguments to prove anything but the madness of those that use them, and that the church must needs wither, being blasted with such inspirations. We see therefore how fatal and ridiculous innovations in the church are: And indeed when changes are so frequent, it is not properly religion, but fashion. This, I think, we may build upon as a sure ground, that where there is continual change, there is great show of uncertainty, and uncertainty in religion is a shrewd motive, if not to deny, yet to doubt of its truth.

Thus much for the first doctrine. I proceed now to the second, *viz. That the next, and most effectual way to destroy religion, is to embase the teachers and dispensers of it.* In the handling of this, I shall show,

1. How the dispensers of religion, the Ministers of the Word, are embased or rendered vile.

2. How the embasing or vilifying them is a means to destroy religion.

1. For the first of these, the Ministers and Dispensers of the Word are rendered base or vile two ways:

1. By divesting them of all temporal privileges and advantages, as inconsistent with their calling. It is strange, since the Priest's office heretofore was always splendid, and almost regal, that it is now looked upon as a piece of religion, to make it low

---

[1] in Dio Cassius, *Roman History*, LII.36.

[2] all terms or phrases associated with Puritan preaching and writing.

and sordid. So that the use of the word *Minister* is brought down to the literal signification of it, *a Servant*: for now to *serve* and to *minister, servile* and *ministerial*, are terms equivalent. But in the Old Testament the same word signifies a *Priest*, and a *Prince*, or chief ruler: hence, though we translate it *Priest* of On, Gen. 41:45, and *Priest* of Midiam, Exod. 3:1, and "as it is with the people so with the priest," Isa. 24:2, Junius and Tremellius render all these places, not by Sacerdos, priest; but by Præses, that is, a prince, or at least a chief counsellor, or Minister of State.[1] And it is strange, that the name should be the same, when the nature of the thing is so exceeding different. The like also may be observed in other languages, that the most illustrious titles are derived from things sacred, and belonging to the worship of God....

But why have I produced all these examples of the heathens? Is it to make these a ground of our imitation? No, but to show that the giving honor to the priesthood, was a custom universal amongst all civilized nations: And whatsoever is universal, is also natural, as not being founded upon compact, or the particular humours of men, but flowing from the native results of reason: and that which is natural, neither does nor can oppose religion. But you will say, this concerns not us, who have an express rule and word revealed. Christ was himself poor, and despised, and withall has instituted such a Ministry. To the first part of this plea I answer, that Christ came to suffer, yet the sufferings and miseries of Christ do not oblige all Christians to undertake the like. For the second, that the Ministry of Christ was low, and despised, by his institution, I utterly deny. It was so, indeed, by the malice and persecution of the heathen princes, but what does this argue or infer for a low, dejected Ministry in a flourishing state, which professes to encourage

Christianity? But to dash this cavil, read but the practice of Christian emperors and kings all along, down from the time of Constantine, in what respect, what honor and splendor they treated the Ministers; and then let our adversaries produce their puny, pitiful arguments for the contrary, against the general, clear, undoubted vogue and current of all antiquity. As for two or three little countries about us, the learned and impartial will not value their practice; in one of which places the Minister has been seen, for mere want, to mend shoes on the Saturday, and been heard to preach on the Sunday. In the other place, stating the several orders of the citizens, they place their Ministers after their apothecaries; that is, the physician of the soul after the drugster of the body: a fit practice for those, who if they were to rank things as well as persons, would place their religion after their trade.

And thus much concerning the first way of debasing the Ministers and Ministry.

2. The second way is by admitting ignorant, sordid, illiterate persons to this function. This is to give the royal stamp to a piece of lead. I confess, God has no need of any man's parts, or learning; but certainly then, he has much less need of his ignorance, and ill behaviour. It is a sad thing, when all other employments shall empty themselves into the Ministry: When men shall repair to it, nor for preferment, but refuge; like malefactors, flying to the altar, only to save their lives; or like those of Eli's race, I Sam. 2:36, that should come crouching, and seek to be put into the priest's office, that they might eat a piece of bread. Heretofore there was required splendor of parentage to recommend any one to the priesthood as Josephus witnesses in a treatise which he wrote of his own life; where he says, To have right to deal in things sacred, was, amongst them, accounted an argument of a noble and illustrious descent. God would not accept the offals of other professions. Doubtless many rejected Christ, upon this thought, that he was the carpen-

---

[1] *Junius and Tremellius* Franciscus Junius (1545–1602) and John Immanuel Tremellius (1510–1580) published (1569–1579) what would become the standard Protestant Latin version of the Bible.

ter's son, who would have embraced him, had they known him to have been the son of David. The preferring undeserving persons to this great service, was eminently Jeroboam's sin, and how Jeroboam's practice and offense has been continued amongst us in another guise, is not unknown: For has not learning unqualified men for approbation to the Ministry? Have not parts and abilities been reputed enemies to grace, and qualities no ways ministerial? While *friends, faction, well-meaning,* and *little understanding* have been accomplishments beyond study and the university; and to falsify a story of conversion, beyond pertinent answers and clear resolutions to the hardest and most concerning questions. So that matters have been brought to this pass, that if a man amongst his sons had any blind, or disfigured, he laid him aside for the Ministry; and such an one was presently approved, as having a *mortified countenance.* In short, it was a fiery furnace, which often approved dross, and rejected gold. But thanks be to God, those *spiritual wickednesses* are now discharged from *their High Places.*[1] Hence it was, that many rushed into the Ministry, as being the only calling that they could profess without serving an apprenticeship. Hence also we had those that could preach sermons, but not defend them. The reason of which is clear, because the works and writings of learned men might be borrowed, but not the abilities. Had indeed the old Levitical hierarchy still continued; in which it was part of the ministerial office to slay the sacrifices, to cleanse the vessels, to scour the flesh-forks, to sweep the temple, and carry the filth and rubbish to the brook Kidron,[2] no persons living had been fitter for the Ministry, and to serve in this nature at the altar. But since it is made a labour of the mind; as to inform men's judgments, and move their affections,

to resolve difficult places of scripture, to decide and clear off controversies; I cannot see how to be a butcher, scavenger, or any other such trade, does at all qualify, or prepare men for this work. But as unfit as they were, yet to clear a way for such into the Ministry, we have had almost all sermons full of gibes and scoffs at humane learning. Away with *vain philosophy, with the disputer of this world, and the enticing words of man's wisdom,* and set up *the foolishness of preaching, the simplicity of the Gospel.* Thus divinity has been brought in upon the ruins of humanity; by forcing the words of the scripture from the sense, and then haling them to the worst of drudgeries, to set a *Jus Divinum* [divine law] upon ignorance and imperfection, and recommend natural weakness for supernatural grace. Hereupon the ignorant have took heart to venture upon this great calling, and instead of cutting their way to it, according to the usual course, through the knowledge of the Tongues, the study of philosophy, school-divinity, the Fathers and Councils, they have taken another and a shorter cut, and having read perhaps a treatise or two *Upon the Heart, The Bruised Reed, The Crumbs of Comfort,* Wollebius in English, and some other little authors,[3] the usual furniture of old women's closets, they have set forth as accomplished divines, and forthwith they present themselves to the Service; and there have not been wanting Jeroboam's as willing to consecrate and receive them, as they to offer themselves. And this has been one of the most fatal, and almost irrecoverable blows that has been given to the Ministry.

And this may suffice concerning the second way of embasing God's Ministers; namely, by intrusting the Ministry with raw, unlearned, ill-bred persons; so that what Solomon speaks of a proverb in the

---

[1] referring back to the text that provides the sermon's subject.

[2] *brook Kidron* a valley outside Jerusalem, often mentioned in the Old Testament.

[3] popular devotional works by Puritan writers: Richard Sibbes, *The Bruised Reed* (earliest extant edition is the 6th, 1658); Michael Sparke, compiler, *Crums of Comfort* (earliest extant edition is the 30th, 1642); Johann Wolleb, *The Abridgement of Christian Divinity* (first pub. 1650). *Upon the Heart* could be a generic "Puritan" title.

mouth of a fool, the same may be said of the Ministry vested in them, that it is like a pearl in a swine's snout.

I proceed now to the second thing proposed in the discussion of this doctrine, which is to show, how the embasing of the Ministers tend to the destruction of religion.

This it does two ways.

1. Because it brings them under exceeding scorn and contempt; and then, let none think religion itself secure: For the vulgar have not such logical heads, as to be able to abstract such subtle conceptions, as to separate the man from the Minister, or to consider the same person under a double capacity, and so honour him as a divine, while they despise him as poor. But suppose they could, yet actions cannot distinguish, as conceptions do; and therefore every act of contempt strikes at both, and unavoidably wounds the Ministry through the sides of the Minister. And we must know, that the least degree of contempt weakens religion, because it is absolutely contrary to the nature of it; religion properly consisting in a reverential esteem of things sacred. Now, that which in any measure weakens religion, will at length destroy it: For the weakening of a thing is only a partial destruction of it. Poverty and meanness of condition expose the wisest to scorn, it being natural for men to place their esteem rather upon things great than good; and the poet observes, that this *infelix paupertas* [unhappy poverty] has nothing in it more intolerable than this, that it renders men ridiculous.[1] And then, how easy and natural it is for contempt to pass from the person to the office, from him that speaks, to the thing that he speaks of, experience proves: Counsel being seldom valued so much for the truth of the thing, as the credit of him that gives it.... [In] our judicatures, take away the trumpet, the scarlet, the attendance, and the Lordship, which would be to make Justice naked, as well as blind; and the Law would lose much of its terror, and consequently of its authority.[2] Let the Minister be abject and low, his interest inconsiderable, the Word will suffer for his sake: The message will still find reception according to the dignity of the messenger. Imagine an ambassador presenting himself in a poor frieze jerkin, and tattered clothes, certainly he would have but small audience, his embassy would speed rather according to the weakness of him that brought, than the majesty of him that sent it. It will fare alike with the ambassadors of Christ, the people will give them audience according to their presence. A notable example of which we have in the behaviour of some to Paul himself, I Cor. 10:10. Hence in the Jewish church it was cautiously provided in the law, that none that was blind or lame, or had any remarkable defect in his body, was capable of the priestly office; because these things naturally make a person contemned, and this presently reflects upon the function. This therefore is the first way by which the low, despised condition of the Ministers, tends to the destruction of the Ministry and religion: namely, because it subjects their persons to scorn, and consequently their calling: and it is not imaginable that men will be brought to obey what they cannot esteem.

2. The second way by which it tends to the ruin of the Ministry is, because it discourages men of fit parts and abilities from undertaking it.[3] And certain it is, that as the calling dignifies the man, so the man much more advances his calling. As a garment, though it warms the body, has a return with an advantage, being much more warmed by it. And how often a good cause may miscarry without a wise manager, and the faith for want of a defender, is, or at least may be known. 'Tis not the truth of an

---

[1] Juvenal, *Satires*, III. 152–53.

[2] William Cavendish makes the same point in his discussion of "order and ceremony" in his letter of advice to Charles II.

[3] Robert Burton addresses this issue in his discussion of the melancholy of scholars in the *Anatomy of Melancholy*.

assertion, but the skill of the disputant, that keeps off a baffle; not the justness of a cause, but the valour of the soldiers that must win the field: When a learned Paul was converted, and undertook the Ministry, it stopped the mouths of those that said, None but poor, weak fisher-men preached Christianity, and so his learning silenced the scandal, as well as strengthened the church: Religion, placed in a soul of exquisite knowledge and abilities, as in a castle, finds not only habitation, but defence… What is it that kept the Church of Rome strong, athletic, and flourishing for so many centuries, but the happy succession of the choicest wits engaged to her service by suitable preferments? And what strength, do we think, would that give to the true religion, that is able thus to establish a false? Religion in a great measure stands or falls according to the abilities of those that assert it. And if, as some observe, men's desires are usually as large as their abilities, what course have we took to allure the former, that we might engage the latter to our assistance? But we have took all ways to affright and discourage scholars from looking towards this sacred calling: For will men lay out their wit and judgment, upon that employment, for the undertaking of which, both will be questioned? Would men, not long since, have spent toilsome days, and watchful nights in the laborious quest of knowledge preparative to this work, at length to come and dance attendance for approbation upon a junta of petty tyrants, acted by party and prejudice, who denied fitness from learning, and grace from morality? Will a man exhaust his livelihood upon books, and his health, the best part of his life, upon study, to be at length thrust into a poor village, where he shall have his due precariously, and entreat for his own; and when he has it, live poorly and contemptibly upon it, while the same or less labour, bestowed upon any other calling, would bring not only comfort but splendor, not only maintenance but abundance? 'Tis, I confess, the duty of Ministers to endure this condition; but neither religion nor reason does oblige either them to approve, or others to choose it. Doubtless, parents will not throw away the towardness of a child, and the expense of education, upon a profession, the labour of which is increased, and the rewards of which are vanished: To condemn promising, lively parts to contempt and penury in a despised calling. What is it else but the casting of a Moses into the mud, or offering a son upon the altar, and instead of a Priest to make him a sacrifice? Neither let any here reply that it becomes not a ministerial spirit to undertake such a calling for reward; for they must know, that it is one thing to undertake it for a reward, and not to be willing to undertake it without one. It is one thing to perform good works only that we may receive the recompense of them in Heaven, and another thing not to be willing to follow Christ and forsake the world, if there were no such recompense. But besides, suppose it were the duty of scholars to choose this calling in the midst of all its discouragements: Yet a prudent Governor, who knows it to be his wisdom, as well as his duty, to take the best course to advance religion, will not consider men's duty, but their practice; not what they ought to do, but what they use to do: and therefore draw over the best qualified to his service, by such ways as are most apt to persuade and induce men. Solomon built his temple with the tallest cedars: and surely, when God refused the defective and the maimed for sacrifice, we cannot think that he requires them for the Priesthood. When learning, abilities, and what is excellent in the world, forsake the church, we may easily foretell its ruin, without the gift of prophecy. And when ignorance succeeds in the place of learning, weakness in the room of judgment, we may be sure, heresy and confusion will quickly come in the room of religion. For undoubtedly there is no way so effectual to betray the truth, as to procure it a weak defender.

Well now, instead of raising any particular uses from the point that has been delivered, let us make a brief recapitulation of the whole. Government, we see, depends upon religion, and religion upon the encouragement of those that are to dispense and assert it. For the further evidence of which truths, we need not travel beyond our own borders; but leave it to every one impartially to judge, whether from the very first day that our religion was unsettled, and church government flung out of doors, the civil government has ever been able to fix upon a sure foundation. We have been changing even to a proverb. The indignation of Heaven has been rolling and turning us from one form to another, till at length such a giddiness seized upon government, that it fell into the very dregs of sectaries, who threatened an equal ruin both to Minister and Magistrate; and how the State has sympathized with the Church, is apparent. For have not our princes as well as our priests been of the lowest of the people? Have not cobblers, draymen, mechanics, governed, as well as preached? Nay, have not they by preaching come to govern? Was ever that of Solomon more verified, *That servants have rid, while Princes and Nobles have gone on foot*? But God has been pleased by a miracle of mercy to dissipate this confusion and chaos, and to give us some openings, some dawnings of liberty and settlement. But now, let not those who are to rebuild our Jerusalem, think that the temple must be built last: For if there be such a thing as a God, and religion, as, whether men believe it or no, they will one day find and feel, assuredly he will stop our liberty, till we restore him his worship. Besides, it is a senseless thing in reason, to think that one of these interests can stand without the other, when in the very order of natural causes, government is preserved by religion. But to return to Jeroboam with whom we first began. He laid the foundation of his government in destroying, though doubtless he coloured it with the name of reforming God's worship: but see the issue. Consider him cursed by God, maintaining his usurped title by continual vexatious wars against the Kings of Judah; smote in his posterity, which was made like the dung upon the face of the earth, as low and vile as those priests whom he had employed. Consider him branded, and made odious to all after-ages. And now, when his kingdom and glory was at an end, and he and his posterity rotting under ground, and his name stinking above it; judge what a worthy prize he made in getting of a kingdom, by destroying the church. Wherefore the sum of all is this; to advise and desire those whom it may concern, to consider Jeroboam's punishment, and then they will have little heart to Jeroboam's sin.

—1660

Mary Rowlandson

ca. 1635 – ca. 1678/9

The autobiographer Mary Rowlandson was the daughter of John White and Joane West of South Petherton, Somersetshire. The White family migrated to Salem, Massachusetts in 1638, and eventually moved to the frontier town of Lancaster. John White was the wealthiest of the original proprietors of Lancaster, his estate being valued at almost £400. In 1656, Mary married Joseph Rowlandson, the first minister of Lancaster. She bore four children, one of whom died in infancy.

Rapid growth in New England over the next two decades resulted in a long series of jurisdictional and property disputes between Native tribes and the English colonizers. By 1675 hostility had peaked between the Wampanoag Chief Metacomet, named King Philip by the English, and the New England colonists. The Wampanoags joined other Algonquian tribes to forge a coalition against the Plymouth Colony. King Philip's War ensued, which commenced with a Wampanoag attack on outlying Plymouth Colony villages on June 20, 1675. Fearing invasion, Rowlandson's husband and her brother-in-law, Lieutenant Henry Kerley, traveled to Boston in search of military aid. During their absence, a contingent of Narragansetts attacked Lancaster on February 10, 1676. Rowlandson and her three children were captured, and forced to wander for eleven weeks through the forests of Massachusetts and New Hampshire. Her youngest child did not survive captivity, dying along the way from a gunshot wound and starvation. Rowlandson was ransomed for £20 on May 2, 1676, and the restoration of her surviving children soon followed.

The family lived in Boston until Joseph Rowlandson found a position as minister in Wethersfield, Connecticut in 1677. He died in November, 1678. The last historical document in which Rowlandson is named is dated 1679, and while she is likely to have lived until the publication of her captivity narrative, no record of her death exists. Rowlandson's account of her captivity was published in both Cambridge, New England, and London under the title *The Sovereignty and Goodness of God, Together, with the Faithfulness of His Promises Displayed; Being a Narrative of the Captivity and Restoration of Mrs. Mary Rowlandson* (1682). This spiritual autobiography chronicles Rowlandson's suffering, celebrates divine Providence in the face of affliction, and offers a colonial view of aboriginal life.

೮෨ೣ

The Sovereignty and Goodness of God Together, with the Faithfulness of His Promises Displayed; Being a Narrative of the Captivity and Restoration of Mrs. Mary Rowlandson

On the tenth of February 1676 came the Indians with great numbers upon Lancaster: Their first coming was about sunrising; hearing the noise of some guns, we looked out; several houses were burning, and the smoke ascending to heaven. There were five persons taken in one house, the father and the mother and a sucking child they knocked on the head; the other two they took and carried away alive. There were two others, who being out of their garrison upon some occasion were set upon; one was knocked on the head, the other escaped: Another there was who running along was shot and wounded and fell down; he begged of them his life, promising them money (as they told me) but they would not hearken to him but knocked him in [the] head, and stripped him naked, and split open his bowels. Another, seeing many of the Indians about his barn, ventured and went out but was quickly shot down. There were three others belonging to the same garrison who were killed; the Indians, getting up upon the roof of the barn, had advantage to shoot down upon them over their fortification. Thus these murderous wretches went on, burning, and destroying before them.

At length they came and beset our own house, and quickly it was the dolefullest day that ever mine eyes saw. The house stood upon the edge of a hill; some of the Indians got behind the hill, others into the barn, and others behind anything that could shelter them; from all which places they shot against the house, so that the bullets seemed to fly like hail; and quickly they wounded one man among us, then another, and then a third. About two hours (according to my observation, in that amazing time) they had been about the house before they prevailed to fire it (which they did with flax and hemp, which they brought out of the barn, and there being no defense about the house, only two flankers at two opposite corners and one of them not finished).[1] They fired it once, and one ventured out and quenched it, but they quickly fired it again, and that took. Now is that dreadful hour come, that I have often heard of (in time of war as it was the case of others) but now mine eyes see it. Some in our house were fighting for their lives, others wallowing in their blood, the house on fire over our heads, and the bloody heathen ready to knock us on the head, if we stirred out: Now might we hear mothers and children crying out for themselves, and one another, *Lord, what shall we do?* Then I took my children (and one of my sisters, hers) to go forth and leave the house, but as soon as we came to the door and appeared, the Indians shot so thick that the bullets rattled against the house, as if one had taken an handful of stones and threw them so that we were fain to give back.[2] We had six stout dogs belonging to our garrison, but none of them would stir, though another time, if any Indian had come to the door, they were ready to fly upon him and tear him down. The Lord hereby would make us the more to acknowledge his hand and to see that our help is always in him. But out we must go, the fire increasing and coming along behind us, roaring, and the Indians gaping before us with their guns, spears and hatchets to devour us. No sooner were we out of the house, but my brother-in-law (being before wounded in defending the house, in or near the throat) fell down dead, whereat the Indians scornfully shouted, halloed, and were presently upon him, stripping off his clothes.[3] The bullets flying thick, one went through my side, and the same (as would seem) through the bowels and hand of my dear child in my arms. One of my elder sister's children, named William, had then his leg broken, which the Indians perceiving, they knocked him on the head.[4] Thus were we butchered by those merciless heathen, standing amazed, with the blood running down to our heels. My eldest sister being yet in the house,[5] and seeing those woeful sights, the infidels hailing mothers one way, and children another, and some wallowing in their blood: and her elder son telling her that her son William was dead, and myself was wounded, she said, *And, Lord, let me die with them*; which was no sooner said, but she was struck with a bullet, and fell down dead over the threshold. I hope she is reaping the fruit of her good labours, being faithful to the service of God in her place. In her younger years she lay under much trouble upon spiritual accounts, till it pleased God to make that precious scripture take hold of

---

[1] *flankers* a fortification projecting so as to flank or defend another part (*OED* flanker *sb¹* 1).

[2] *fain to give back* inclined to retreat.

[3] *brother-in-law* John Divoll, the husband of Rowlandson's younger sister Hannah; *halloed* shouted in order to incite (*OED* halloo *v* 1b).

[4] *William* William Kerley, son of Elizabeth White Kerley.

[5] *eldest sister* Elizabeth White Kerley.

her heart, II Cor. 12:9, *And he said unto me, my grace is sufficient for thee*. More than twenty years after I have heard her tell how sweet and comfortable that place was to her. But to return: The Indians laid hold of us, pulling me one way and the children another, and said, *Come go along with us*; I told them they would kill me: they answered, if I were willing to go along with them they would not hurt me.

Oh, the doleful sight that now was to behold at this house! *Come, behold the works of the Lord, what desolation he has made in the earth*.[1] Of thirty-seven persons who were in this one house, none escaped either present death, or a bitter captivity, save only one, who might say as he, Job 1:15, *And I only am escaped alone to tell the news*.[2] There were twelve killed, some shot, some stabbed with their spears, some knocked down with their hatchets. When we are in prosperity, oh the little that we think of such dreadful sights, and to see our dear friends and relations lie bleeding out their heart-blood upon the ground. There was one who was chopped into the head with a hatchet, and stripped naked, and yet was crawling up and down. It is a solemn sight to see so many Christians lying in their blood, some here and some there, like a company of sheep torn by wolves, all of them stripped naked by a company of hell-hounds, roaring, singing, ranting and insulting, as if they would have torn our very hearts out; yet the Lord by his almighty power preserved a number of us from death, for there were twenty-four of us taken alive and carried captive.

I had often before this said, that if the Indians should come, I should choose rather to be killed by them than taken alive but when it came to the trial my mind changed; their glittering weapons so daunted my spirit that I chose rather to go along with those (as I may say) ravenous beasts, than that moment to end my days; and that I may the better declare what happened to me during that grievous captivity, I shall particularly speak of the several removes we had up and down the wilderness.

THE FIRST REMOVE

Now away we must go with those barbarous creatures, with our bodies wounded and bleeding, and our hearts no less than our bodies. About a mile we went that night, up upon a hill within sight of the town where they intended to lodge.[3] There was hard by a vacant house (deserted by the English before, for fear of the Indians).[4] I asked them whether I might not lodge in the house that night, to which they answered, *What, will you love English men still?* This was the dolefullest night that ever my eyes saw. Oh the roaring, and singing and dancing, and yelling of those black creatures in the night, which made the place a lively resemblance of hell. And as miserable was the waste that was there made of horses, cattle, sheep, swine, calves, lambs, roasting pigs, and fowl (which they had plundered in the town), some roasting, some lying and burning, and some boiling to feed our merciless enemies; who were joyful enough though we were disconsolate. To add to the dolefulness of the former day, and the dismalness of the present night, my thoughts ran upon my losses and sad bereaved condition. All was gone, my husband gone (at least separated from me, he being in the Bay;[5] and to add to my grief, the Indians told me they would kill him as he came homeward), my children gone, my relations and friends gone, our house and home and all our comforts within door, and without, all was gone

---

[1] *Come behold...in the earth* Psalm 46:8.

[2] *save only one* Ephraim Roper was believed to be the only inhabitant of Lancaster present during the attack to escape death or captivity.

[3] *a hill...the town* George Hill, the highest elevation in Lancaster.

[4] *hard by* close by (*OED* hard by *prep* A).

[5] *he being in the Bay* Reverend Joseph Rowlandson had traveled to Boston, the capital of the Massachusetts Bay Colony, in search of military assistance to defend Lancaster.

(except my life), and I knew not but the next moment that might go too. There remained nothing to me but one poor wounded babe, and it seemed at present worse than death that it was in such a pitiful condition, bespeaking compassion, and I had no refreshing for it, nor suitable things to revive it. Little do many think what is the savageness and brutishness of this barbarous enemy, ay, even those that seem to profess more than others among them, when the English have fallen into their hands.[1]

Those seven that were killed at Lancaster the summer before upon a Sabbath day, and the one that was afterward killed upon a week day, were slain and mangled in a barbarous manner, by one-eyed John, and Marlborough's praying Indians, which Capt. Mosely brought to Boston, as the Indians told me.[2]

THE SECOND REMOVE [3]

But now, the next morning, I must turn my back upon the town, and travel with them into the vast and desolate wilderness, I knew not whither. It is not my tongue, or pen can express the sorrows of my heart, and bitterness of my spirit, that I had at this departure: but God was with me, in a wonderful manner, carrying me along, and bearing up my spirit, that it did not quite fail. One of the Indians carried my poor wounded babe upon a horse; it went moaning all along, *I shall die, I shall die.* I went on foot after it, with sorrow that cannot be expressed. At length I took it off the horse, and carried it in my arms till my strength failed, and I fell down with it: Then they set me upon a horse with my wounded child in my lap, and there being no furniture upon the horse's back,[4] as we were going down a steep hill, we both fell over the horse's head, at which they like inhuman creatures laughed, and rejoiced to see it, though I thought we should there have ended our days, as overcome with so many difficulties. But the Lord renewed my strength still, and carried me along, that I might see more of his power; yea, so much that I could never have thought of had I not experienced it.

After this it quickly began to snow, and when night came on, they stopped:[5] and now down I must sit in the snow, by a little fire, and a few boughs behind me, with my sick child in my lap, and calling much for water, being now (through the wound) fallen into a violent fever. My own wound [was] also growing so stiff that I could scarce sit down or rise up; yet so it must be, that I must sit all this cold winter night upon the cold, snowy ground, with my sick child in my arms, looking that every hour would be the last of its life; and having no Christian friend near me, either to comfort or help me. Oh, I may see the wonderful power of God that my spirit did not utterly sink under my affliction: still the Lord upheld me with his gracious and merciful spirit, and we were both alive to see the light of the next morning.

THE THIRD REMOVE [6]

The morning being come, they prepared to go on their way. One of the Indians got up upon a

---

[1] *to profess* to affirm their faith in, or allegiance to, Christianity (*OED* profess *v* II.4a).

[2] *Those seven...Indians told me* These victims were killed during the attack of August 22, 1675 led by the Nashaway chieftain One-eyed John (whose Native names were Apequinsah and Monoco); *praying Indians* natives who converted to Christianity and adopted British customs; *Capt. Mosely* Captain Samuel Moseley of Boston was a key leader in the New England forces.

[3] Friday, February 11. The second remove took Rowlandson on a Native trail in the western part of Princeton, Massachusetts.

[4] *furniture* the harness, housings, trappings, etc. of a horse (*OED* furniture 4c).

[5] *they stopped* at Princeton, Massachusetts.

[6] From Saturday, February 12 to Sunday, February 27, Rowlandson traveled to the Native village Wenimesset (typically spelled Menameset).

horse, and they set me up behind him with my poor sick babe in my lap. A very wearisome and tedious day I had of it; what with my own wound, and my child's being so exceeding sick, in a lamentable condition with her wound. It may be easily judged what a poor feeble condition we were in, there being not the least crumb of refreshing that came within either of our mouths, from Wednesday night to Saturday night, except only a little cold water. This day in the afternoon, about an hour by sun, we came to the place where they intended, *viz.* an Indian town, called Wenimesset, norward of Quabaug. When we were come, oh the number of pagans (now merciless enemies) that there came about me, that I may say as David, Psal. 27:13, *I had fainted, unless I had believed, etc.* The next day was the Sabbath: I then remembered how careless I had been of God's holy time, how many Sabbaths I had lost and misspent, and how evilly I had walked in God's sight; which lay so close unto my spirit, that it was easy for me to see how righteous it was with God to cut the thread of my life, and cast me out of his presence forever. Yet the Lord still showed mercy to me, and upheld me; and as he wounded me with one hand, so he healed me with the other. This day there came to me one Robert Pepper (a man belonging to Roxbury) who was taken in Captain Beers his fight, and had been now a considerable time with the Indians; and up with them almost as far as Albany to see King Philip, as he told me, and was now very lately come into these parts.[1] Hearing, I say, that I was in this Indian town, he obtained leave to come and see me. He told me, he himself was wounded in the leg at Captain Beers his fight; and was not able some time to go, but as they carried him, and as he took oaken

leaves and laid to his wound, and through the blessing of God he was able to travel again. Then I took oaken leaves and laid to my side, and with the blessing of God it cured me also; yet before the cure was wrought, I may say, as it is in Psal. 38:5, 6 *My wounds stink and are corrupt, I am troubled, I am bowed down greatly, I go mourning all the day long.* I sat much alone with a poor wounded child in my lap, which moaned night and day, having nothing to revive the body, or cheer the spirits of her, but instead of that, sometimes one Indian would come and tell me one hour, that, *Your master will knock your child in the head.* And then a second, and then a third, *Your master will quickly knock your child in the head.*

This was the comfort I had from them, *Miserable comforters are ye all,* as he said.[2] Thus nine days I sat upon my knees, with my babe in my lap, till my flesh was raw again; my child being even ready to depart this sorrowful world, they bade me carry it out to another wigwam (I suppose because they would not be troubled with such spectacles) whither I went with a heavy heart, and down I sat with the picture of death in my lap. About two hours in the night, my sweet babe, like a lamb departed this life, on Feb. 18, 1676, it being about six years and five months old. It was nine days from the first wounding in this miserable condition, without any refreshing of one nature or other, except a little cold water. I cannot but take notice, how at another time I could not bear to be in the room where any dead person was, but now the case is changed; I must and could lie down by my dead babe, side by side all the night after. I have thought since of the wonderful goodness of God to me, in preserving me in the use of my reason and senses, in that distressed time, that I did not use wicked and violent means to end my own miserable life. In the morning, when they understood that my child was dead they sent for me

---

[1] *Robert Pepper...Captain Beers* In September, 1675, as Captain Richard Beers led a party of men to enforce the Northfield garrison, he was confronted by warriors led by Sagamore Sam. Robert Pepper was the only soldier captured. The others were slain alongside Beers or escaped; *King Philip* the Wampanoag Chief Metacomet, so named by the Plymouth colonists.

[2] *Miserable comforters are ye all* Job 16:2.

home to my master's wigwam: (by my master in this writing must be understood Quanopin, who was a sagamore and married [to] King Philip's wife's sister; not that he first took me, but I was sold to him by another Narragansett Indian, who took me when first I came out of the garrison).[1] I went to take up my dead child in my arms to carry it with me, but they bid me let it alone: there was no resisting, but go I must and leave it. When I had been at my master's wigwam, I took the first opportunity I could get, to go look after my dead child: when I came, I asked them what they had done with it. Then they told me it was upon the hill: then they went and showed me where it was, where I saw the ground was newly digged, and there they told me they had buried it: There I left that child in the wilderness, and must commit it, and myself also in this wilderness condition, to him who is above all. God having taken away this dear child, I went to see my daughter Mary, who was at this same Indian town, at a wigwam not very far off, though we had little liberty or opportunity to see one another: she was about ten years old, and taken from the door at first by a praying Indian and afterward sold for a gun. When I came in sight, she would fall a-weeping; at which they were provoked, and would not let me come near her, but bade me be gone; which was a heart-cutting word to me. I had one child dead, another in the wilderness, I knew not where, the third they would not let me come near to: *Me* (as he said) *have ye bereaved of my children, Joseph is not, and Simeon is not, and ye will take Benjamin also, all these things are against me.*[2] I could not sit still in this condition, but kept walking from one place to another. And as I was going along, my heart was even overwhelmed with the thoughts of my condition, and that I should have children, and a nation which I knew not ruled over them. Where-

upon I earnestly entreated the Lord, that he would consider my low estate, and show me a token for good, and if it were his blessed will, some sign and hope of some relief. And indeed quickly the Lord answered, in some measure, my poor prayers: for as I was going up and down mourning and lamenting my condition, my son came to me, and asked me how I did;[3] I had not seen him before, since the destruction of the town, and I knew not where he was, till I was informed by himself, that he was amongst a smaller parcel of Indians, whose place was about six miles off; with tears in his eyes he asked me whether his sister Sarah was dead; and told me he had seen his sister Mary; and prayed me, that I would not be troubled in reference to himself. The occasion of his coming to see me at this time, was this: There was, as I said, about six miles from us, a small plantation of Indians, where it seems he had been during his captivity: and at this time there were some forces of the Indians gathered out of our company, and some also from them (among whom was my son's master) to go to assault and burn Medfield: In this time of the absence of his master, his dame brought him to see me. I took this to be some gracious answer to my earnest and unfeigned desire. The next day, *viz.* to this, the Indians returned from Medfield, all the company, for those that belonged to the other small company, came through the town that now we were at. But before they came to us, oh! the outrageous roaring and whooping that there was: They began their din about a mile before they came to us. By their noise and whooping they signified how many they had destroyed (which was at that time twenty-three). Those that were with us at home, were gathered together as soon as they heard the whooping, and every time that the other went over their number, these at home gave [such] a shout that the very earth rung again: And thus they continued till those that

---

[1] *sagamore* the chief of an American aboriginal tribe (*OED* sachem 1).

[2] *Me...against me* Genesis 42:36.

[3] *my son* Joseph Rowlandson.

had been upon the expedition were come up to the sagamore's wigwam; and then, oh, the hideous insulting and triumphing that there was over some Englishmen's scalps that they had taken (as their manner is) and brought with them. I cannot but take notice of the wonderful mercy of God to me in those afflictions, in sending me a Bible. One of the Indians that came from Medfield fight, [who] had brought some plunder, came to me, and asked me, if I would have a Bible; he had got one in his basket. I was glad of it and asked him whether he thought the Indians would let me read. He answered, *Yes*; so I took the Bible, and in that melancholy time, it came into my mind to read first the 28. chapter of Deut. which I did, and when I had read it, my dark heart wrought on this manner, that there was no mercy for me, that the blessings were gone, and the curses come in their room, and that I had lost my opportunity. But the Lord helped me still to go on reading till I came to chapter 30, the seven first verses, where I found there was mercy promised again, if we would return to him by repentance; and though we were scattered from one end of the earth to the other, yet the Lord would gather us together, and turn all those curses upon our enemies. I do not desire to live to forget this scripture, and what comfort it was to me.

Now the Indians began to talk of removing from this place, some one way, and some another. There were now besides myself nine English captives in this place (all of them children, except one woman). I got an opportunity to go and take my leave of them; they being to go one way, and I another; I asked them whether they were earnest with God for deliverance. They told me they did as they were able, and it was some comfort to me, that the Lord stirred up children to look to him. The woman, *viz.* Goodwife Joslin, told me, she should never see me again, and that she could find in her heart to run away;[1] I wished her not to run away by any means, for we were near thirty miles from any English town and she very big with child, and had but one week to reckon; and another child in her arms, two years old, and bad rivers there were to go over, and we were feeble, with our poor and coarse entertainment.[2] I had my Bible with me; I pulled it out, and asked her whether she would read; we opened the Bible and lighted on Psal. 27, in which psalm we especially took notice of that *ver. ult., Wait on the Lord, be of good courage, and he shall strengthen thine heart, wait I say on the Lord.*

THE FOURTH REMOVE [3]

And now I must part with that little company I had. Here I parted from my daughter Mary (whom I never saw again till I saw her in Dorchester, returned from captivity) and from four little cousins and neighbours, some of which I never saw afterward: the Lord only knows the end of them. Amongst them also was that poor woman before mentioned, who came to a sad end, as some of the company told me in my travel: She, having much grief upon her spirit, about her miserable condition, being so near her time, she would be often asking the Indians to let her go home; they not being willing to that, and yet vexed with her importunity, gathered a great company together about her, and stripped her naked, and set her in the midst of them; and when they had sung and danced about her (in their hellish manner) as long as they pleased, they knocked her on [the] head, and the child in her arms with her: when they had done that, they made a fire and put them both into it, and told the other children that were with them, that if they attempted

---

[1] *Goodwife Joslin* Ann Joslin, the wife of Abraham Joslin of Lancaster.

[2] *entertainment* sustenance; treatment (*OED* entertainment 3,5).

[3] From Monday, February 28, to Friday, March 3, 1676, Rowlandson was at a camp near the Native village of Nichewaug.

to go home, they would serve them in like manner: The children said, she did not shed one tear, but prayed all the while. But to return to my own journey; we travelled about half a day or [a] little more, and came to a desolate place in the wilderness, where there were no wigwams or inhabitants before; we came about the middle of the afternoon to this place, cold and wet, and snowy, and hungry, and weary, and no refreshing, for man, but the cold ground to sit on, and our poor Indian cheer.

Heartaching thoughts here I had about my poor children, who were scattered up and down among the wild beasts of the forest: My head was light and dizzy (either through hunger or hard lodging, or trouble or all together), my knees feeble, my body raw by sitting double night and day, that I cannot express to man the affliction that lay upon my spirit, but the Lord helped me at that time to express it to himself. I opened my Bible to read, and the Lord brought that precious scripture to me, Jer. 31:16, *Thus saith the Lord, Refrain thy voice from weeping and thine eyes from tears, for thy work shall be rewarded, and they shall come again from the land of the enemy.* This was a sweet cordial to me, when I was ready to faint; many and many a time have I sat down, and wept sweetly over this scripture. At this place we continued about four days.

·   ·   ·   ·   ·   ·   ·

THE EIGHTH REMOVE [1]

.... But to return, we traveled on till night; and in the morning, we must go over the river to Philip's crew. When I was in the canoe, I could not but be amazed at the numerous crew of pagans that were on the bank on the other side. When I came ashore, they gathered all about me, I sitting alone in the midst: I observed they asked one another questions, and laughed, and rejoiced over their gains and victories. Then my heart began to fail: and I fell a-weeping, which was the first time to my remembrance, that I wept before them. Although I had met with so much affliction, and my heart was many times ready to break, yet could I not shed one tear in their sight: but rather had been all this while in a maze, and like one astonished: but now I may say, as Psal. 137:1, *By the rivers of Babylon, there we sat down: yea, we wept when we remembered Zion.* There one of them asked me, why I wept; I could hardly tell what to say: yet I answered, they would kill me: *No*, said he, *none will hurt you.* Then came one of them and gave me two spoonfulls of meal to comfort me, and another gave me half a pint of peas; which was more worth than many bushels at another time. Then I went to see King Philip. He bade me come in and sit down, and asked me whether I would smoke it (a usual compliment nowadays amongst saints and sinners) but this no way suited me.[2] For though I had formerly used tobacco, yet I had left it ever since I was first taken. It seems to be a bait the devil lays to make men lose their precious time: I remember with shame, how formerly, when I had taken two or three pipes, I was presently ready for another, such a bewitching thing it is: But I thank God, he has now given me power over it; surely there are many who may be better employed than to lie sucking a stinking tobacco pipe.

Now the Indians gather their forces to go against North-Hampton: overnight one went about yelling and hooting to give notice of the design. Whereupon they fell to boiling of groundnuts and parching of corn (as many as had it) for their provision: and in the morning away they went: During my abode in this place, Philip spoke to me to make a shirt for his boy, which I did, for which he gave me a shilling: I offered the money to my master, but he bade me keep it: and with it I bought a piece of

---

[1] On Wednesday, March 8, 1676, Rowlandson encamped on the west side of the Connecticut River at Coasset, South Vernon, Vermont.

[2] *compliment* act of courtesy; gift (*OED* compliment *sb* 1,3).

horseflesh. Afterwards he asked me to make a cap for his boy, for which he invited me to dinner. I went, and he gave me a pancake, about as big as two fingers; it was made of parched wheat, beaten and fried in bear's grease, but I thought I never tasted pleasanter meat in my life. There was a squaw who spoke to me to make a shirt for her *sannup*, for which she gave me a piece of bear.[1] Another asked me to knit a pair of stockings, for which she gave me a quart of peas: I boiled my peas and bear together, and invited my master and mistress to dinner, but the proud gossip, because I served them both in one dish, would eat nothing, except one bit that he gave her upon the point of his knife. Hearing that my son was come to this place, I went to see him and found him lying flat upon the ground: I asked him how he could sleep so. He answered me, that he was not asleep but at prayer; and lay so that they might not observe what he was doing. I pray God he may remember these things now he is returned in safety. At this place (the sun now getting higher) what with the beams and heat of the sun, and the smoke of the wigwams, I thought I should have been blind. I could scarce discern one wigwam from another. There was here one Mary Thurston of Medfield, who seeing how it was with me, lent me a hat to wear: but as soon as I was gone, the squaw who owned that Mary Thurston came running after me, and got it away again. Here was the squaw that gave me one spoonful of meal. I put it in my pocket to keep it safe: yet notwithstanding somebody stole it, but put five Indian corns in the room of it: which corns were the greatest provision I had in my travel for one day.

The Indians, returning from North-Hampton, brought with them some horses, and sheep, and other things which they had taken: I desired them, that they would carry me to Albany, upon one of those horses, and sell me for powder: for so they

had sometimes discoursed. I was utterly hopeless of getting home on foot, the way that I came. I could hardly bear to think of the many weary steps I had taken, to come to this place.

.   .   .   .

THE TWENTIETH REMOVE [2]

…. But to return again to my going home, where we may see a remarkable change of providence: At first they were all against it, except my husband would come for me; but afterwards they assented to it, and seemed much to rejoice in it; some asked me to send them some bread, others some tobacco, others shaking me by the hand, offering me a hood and scarf to ride in; not one moving hand or tongue against it. Thus hath the Lord answered my poor desire, and the many earnest requests of others put up unto God for me. In my travels an Indian came to me, and told me, if I were willing, he and his squaw would run away, and go home along with me: I told him *no*: I was not willing to run away, but desired to wait God's time, that I might go home quietly, and without fear. And now God has granted me my desire. O the wonderful power of God that I have seen, and the experience that I have had: I have been in the midst of those roaring lions, and savage bears, that feared neither God, nor man, nor the devil, by night and day, alone and in company: sleeping all sorts together, and yet not one of them ever offered me the least abuse of unchastity to me, in word or action. Though some are ready to say, I speak it for my own credit; but I speak it in the presence of God, and to his glory. God's power is as great now, and as sufficient to save as when he preserved Daniel in the lion's den; or the three children in the fiery furnace. I may well say as his Psal. 107:12, *Oh give thanks unto the Lord for he is good, for his mercy*

---

1 *sannup* the husband of a squaw (*OED* sannup).

2 Between Friday, April 28 and Tuesday, May 2, 1676, Rowlandson was encamped near the southern end of Wachusett Lake, Princeton, Massachusetts.

endureth for ever. Let the redeemed of the Lord say so, whom he hath redeemed from the hand of the enemy, especially that I should come away in the midst of so many hundreds of enemies quietly and peaceably, and not a dog moving his tongue. So I took my leave of them, and in coming along my heart melted into tears, more than all the while I was with them, and I was almost swallowed up with the thoughts that ever I should go home again. About the sun going down, Mr. Hoar, and myself, and the two Indians came to Lancaster, and a solemn sight it was to me.[1] There had I lived many comfortable years amongst my relations and neighbours, and now not one Christian to be seen, nor one house left standing. We went on to a farmhouse that was yet standing, where we lay all night: and a comfortable lodging we had, though nothing but straw to lie on. The Lord preserved us in safety that night, and raised us up again in the morning, and carried us along, that before noon, we came to Concord. Now was I full of joy, and yet not without sorrow: joy to see such a lovely sight, so many Christians together, and some of them my neighbours: There I met with my brother, and my brother-in-law, who asked me, if I knew where his wife was.[2] Poor heart! He had helped to bury her, and knew it not; she being shot down by the house [which] was partly burned: so that those who were at Boston at the desolation of the town, and came back afterward, and buried the dead, did not know her. Yet I was not without sorrow, to think how many were looking and longing, and my own children amongst the rest, to enjoy that deliverance that I had now received and I did not know whether ever I should see them again. Being re-

cruited with food and raiment,[3] we went to Boston that day, where I met with my dear husband, but the thoughts of our dear children, one being dead, and the other we could not tell where, abated our comfort each to other. I was not before so much hemmed in with the merciless and cruel heathen, but now as much with pitiful, tenderhearted, and compassionate Christians. In that poor, and distressed, and beggarly condition I was received in, I was kindly entertained in several houses: so much love I received from several (some of whom I knew, and others I knew not) that I am not capable to declare it. But the Lord knows them all by name: The Lord reward them sevenfold into their bosoms of his spirituals for their temporals. The twenty pounds, the price of my redemption, was raised by some Boston gentlemen, and Mrs. Usher, whose bounty and religious charity, I would not forget to make mention of.[4] Then Mr. Thomas Shepard of Charlestown received us into his house, where we continued eleven weeks; and a father and mother they were to us.[5] And many more tender-hearted friends we met with in that place. We were now in the midst of love, yet not without much and frequent heaviness of heart for our poor children, and other relations, who were still in affliction. The week following, after my coming in, the governor and council sent forth to the Indians again; and that not without success; for they brought in my sister,[6] and Goodwife Kettle:

.   .   .   .

Our family being now gathered together (those of us that were living), the South Church in Boston hired an house for us: Then we removed from Mr.

---

[1] *Mr. Hoar* John Hoar of Concord had assisted Rowlandson in the ransom negotiations.

[2] *my brother and my brother-in-law* Josiah White and Lieutenant Henry Kerley.

[3] *recruited* restored to a normal condition (*OED* recruit *sb* 6 and recruited *ppl.a*).

[4] *Mrs. Usher* the wife of Hezekiah Usher, a Boston bookseller.

[5] *Thomas Shepard* the son of the Reverend Thomas Shepard of Cambridge.

[6] *my sister* Hannah White Divoll.

Shepard's, those cordial friends, and went to Boston, where we continued about three-quarters of a year: Still the Lord went along with us, and provided graciously for us. I thought it somewhat strange to set up housekeeping with bare walls; but as Solomon says, *Money answers all things*;[1] and that we had through the benevolence of Christian friends, some in this town and some in that, and others, and some from England, that in a little time we might look, and see the house furnished with love. The Lord hath been exceeding good to us in our low estate, in that when we had neither house nor home, nor other necessaries; the Lord so moved the hearts of these and those towards us, that we wanted neither food, nor raiment for ourselves or ours, Prov. 18:24, *There is a friend which sticketh closer than a brother.* And how many such friends have we found, and now living amongst? And truly such a friend have we found him to be unto us, in whose house we lived, *viz.* Mr. James Whitcomb, a friend unto us near hand, and afar off.

I can remember the time, when I used to sleep quietly without workings in my thoughts, whole nights together, but now it is other ways with me. When all are fast about me, and no eye open, but his who ever waketh, my thoughts are upon things past, upon the awful dispensation of the Lord towards us; upon his wonderful power and might, in carrying of us through so many difficulties, in returning us in safety, and suffering none to hurt us. I remember in the night season, how the other day I was in the midst of thousands of enemies, and nothing but death before me: It [was] then hard work to persuade myself, that ever I should be satisfied with bread again. But now we are fed with the finest of the wheat, and, as I may say, *With honey out of the rock.*[2] Instead of the husk, we have the fatted calf: The thoughts of these things in the particulars of them, and of the love and goodness of God towards us, make it true of me, what David said of himself, Psal. 6:5, *I watered my couch with my tears.*[3] Oh! the wonderful power of God that mine eyes have seen, affording matter enough for my thoughts to run in, that when others are sleeping mine eyes are weeping.

I have seen the extreme vanity of this world: One hour I have been in health, and wealth, wanting nothing: but the next hour in sickness and wounds and death, having nothing but sorrow and affliction.

Before I knew what affliction meant, I was ready sometimes to wish for it. When I lived in prosperity, having the comforts of the world about me, my relations by me, my heart cheerful: and taking little care for anything; and yet seeing many, whom I preferred before myself, under many trials and afflictions, in sickness, weakness, poverty, losses, crosses, and cares of the world, I should be sometimes jealous lest I should have my portion in this life, and that scripture would come to mind, Heb. 12:6, *For whom the Lord loveth he chasteneth, and scourgeth every son whom he receiveth.* But now I see the Lord had his time to scourge and chasten me. The portion of some is to have their afflictions by drops, now one drop and then another; but the dregs of the cup, the wine of astonishment: like a sweeping rain that leaveth no food, did the Lord prepare to be my portion. Affliction I wanted, and affliction I had, full measure (I thought) pressed down and running over; yet I see, when God calls a person to anything, and through never so many difficulties, yet he is fully able to carry them

---

[1] *Money answers all things* "A feast is made for laughter, and wine maketh merry: but money answereth all things" (Ecclesiastes 10:19).

[2] *finest of...the rock* "He should have fed them also with the finest of the wheat: and with honey out of the rock should I have satisfied thee" (Psalm 81:16).

[3] *Psalm 6:5* actually Psalm 6:6.

through and make them see, and say they have been gainers thereby. And I hope I can say in some measure, as David did, *It is good for me that I have been afflicted.*[1] The Lord hath showed me the vanity of these outward things. That they are the *Vanity of vanities and vexation of spirit;*[2] that they are but a shadow, a blast, a bubble, and things of no continuance. That we must rely on God himself, and our whole dependence must be upon him. If trouble from smaller matters begin to arise in me, I have something at hand to check myself with, and say, why am I troubled? It was but the other day that if I had had the world, I would have given it for my freedom, or to have been a servant to a Christian. I have learned to look beyond present and smaller troubles, and to be quieted under them, as Moses said, Exod. 14:13, *Stand still and see the salvation of the Lord.*

—1682

---

[1] *It is good...afflicted* "It is good for me that I have been afflicted; that I might learn thy statutes" (Psalm 119:71).

[2] *That they...of spirit* "I have seen all the works that are done under the sun; and behold all is vanity and vexation of spirit" (Ecclesiastes 1:14; see also 2:11; 4:4, 6:9).

Thomas Sprat
1635 – 1713

In 1651 Sprat entered Wadham College, Oxford, at the time the centre of a scientific circle surrounding its Warden, John Wilkins. Wilkins would become the first Secretary of The Royal Society (founded in 1660, received royal charters in 1662 and 1663), and Sprat was nominated as one of the first members along with such scientific luminaries as Robert Boyle, Robert Hooke, William Petty, John Ray, and Christopher Wren. Sprat was a clergyman, not a scientist, and he appears to have been recruited to act as publicist and polemicist (other literary figures who would become members of the Society include John Aubrey, Abraham Cowley, John Dryden, John Evelyn, and Edmund Waller). In his clerical career, Sprat was a noted preacher who became Dean of Westminster (1680) and Bishop of Rochester (1683). In addition to the *History of the Royal Society*, first published in 1667, Sprat published poetry and a life of his friend Abraham Cowley.

Written only a few years after The Royal Society had been founded, Sprat's *History* sought to publicize the Society's goals and to defend its activities from critics, both at home (such as Samuel Butler) and on the continent. His concern for the language used in the Society's deliberations and publications derives ultimately from Sir Francis Bacon, who was the major philosophical inspiration behind the Society (see the selections from Bacon's *Aphorisms*). In addition, the reformation of language had political implications in the Restoration: many people blamed the civil wars on failures to communicate, or on the misuse of language for political and religious ends. For a philosophical text written in the empiricist mode the Society sought to promote, see the selections from John Locke. For a different kind of Restoration response to the problems of language, see the selection from Roger L'Estrange on censorship.

❧❧❧

The History of The Royal Society of London
(excerpts)

A Proposal for Erecting an English Academy
(extract from PT. I, SECT. 20)

But besides, if we observe well the English language; we shall find, that it seems at this time more than others, to require some such aid, to bring it to its last perfection. The truth is, it has been hitherto a little too carelessly handled; and I think, has had less labor spent about its polishing, than it deserves. Till the time of King Henry the Eighth, there was scarce any man regarded it, but Chaucer; and nothing was written in it, which one would be willing to read twice, but some of his poetry. But then it began to raise itself a little, and to sound tolerably well. From that age, down to the beginning of our late civil wars, it was still fashioning, and beautifying itself. In the wars themselves (which is a time, wherein all languages use, if ever, to increase by extraordinary degrees; for in such busy, and active times, there arise more new thoughts of men, which must be signified, and varied by new expressions) then I say, it received many fantastical terms, which were introduced by our religious sects; and many outlandish phrases, which several writers, and translators, in that great hurry, brought in, and made free as they pleased, and with all it was enlarged by many sound, and necessary forms, and idioms, which it before wanted. And now, when men's minds are somewhat settled, their passions allayed, and the peace of our country gives us the opportunity of such diversions: if some sober and judicious men, would take the whole mass of our

660

language into their hands, as they find it, and would set a mark on the ill words; correct those, which are to be retained; admit, and establish the good; and make some emendations in the accent, and grammar: I dare pronounce, that our speech would quickly arrive at as much plenty, as it is capable to receive; and at the greatest smoothness, which its derivation from the rough German will allow it.

THEIR MANNER OF DISCOURSE (PT. 2, SECT. 20)

Thus they [Society members] have directed, judged, conjectured upon, and improved experiments. But lastly, in these, and all other businesses, that have come under their care; there is one thing more, about which the Society has been most solicitous; and that is, the manner of their discourse: which, unless they had been very watchful to keep in due temper, the whole spirit and vigour of their design, had been soon eaten out, by the luxury and redundance of speech. The ill effects of this superfluity of talking, have already overwhelmed most other arts and professions; insomuch, that when I consider the means of happy living, and the causes of their corruption, I can hardly forbear recanting what I said before[1]; and concluding, that eloquence ought to be banished out of all civil societies, as a thing fatal to peace and good manners. To this opinion I should wholly incline; if I did not find, that it is a weapon, which may be as easily procured by bad men, as good: and that, if these should only cast it away, and those retain it; the naked innocence of virtue, would be upon all occasions exposed to the armed malice of the wicked. This is the chief reason, that should now keep up the ornaments of speaking, in any request: since they are so much degenerated from their original usefulness. They were at first, no doubt, an admirable instrument in the hands of wise men: when they were only employed to describe goodness, honesty, obedience; in

larger, fairer, and more moving images: to represent truth, clothed with bodies; and to bring knowledge back again to our very senses, from whence it was at first derived to our understandings. But now they are generally changed to worse uses: They make the fancy disgust the best things, if they come found, and unadorned: they are in open defiance against reason; professing, not to hold much correspondence with that; but with its slaves, the passions: they give the mind a motion too changeable, and bewitching, to consist with right practice. Who can behold, without indignation, how many mists and uncertainties, these specious tropes and figures have brought on our knowledge? How many rewards, which are due to more profitable, and difficult arts, have been still snatched away by the easy vanity of fine speaking? For now I am warmed with this just anger, I cannot withhold myself, from betraying the shallowness of all these seeming mysteries; upon which, we writers, and speakers, look so big. And, in few words, I dare say; that of all the studies of men, nothing may be sooner obtained, than this vicious abundance of phrase, this trick of metaphors, this volubility of tongue, which makes so great a noise in the world. But I spend words in vain; for the evil is now so inveterate, that it is hard to know whom to blame, or where to begin to reform. We all value one another so much, upon this beautiful deceit; and labour so long after it, in the years of our education: that we cannot but ever after think kinder of it, than it deserves. And indeed, in most other parts of learning, I look on it to be a thing almost utterly desperate in its cure: and I think, it may be placed amongst those general mischiefs; such, as the dissension of Christian Princes, the want of practice in religion, and the like; which have been so long spoken against, that men are become insensible about them; every one shifting off the fault from himself to others; and so they are only made bare common places of complaint. It will suffice my present purpose, to point

---

[1] *what I said before* in pt. 1, sect. 20, excerpted above.

out, what has been done by the Royal Society, towards the correcting of its excesses in natural philosophy; to which it is, of all others, a most professed enemy.

They have therefore been most rigorous in putting in execution the only remedy that can be found for this extravagance: and that has been, a constant resolution to reject all the amplifications, digressions, and swellings of style: to return back to the primitive purity, and shortness, when men delivered so many things, almost in an equal number of words. They have exacted from all their members, a close, naked, natural way of speaking; positive expressions; clear senses; a native easiness: bringing all things as near the mathematical plainness, as they can: and preferring the language of artisans, countrymen, and merchants, before that of wits, or scholars.

And here, there is one thing, not to be passed by; which will render this established custom of the Society, well nigh everlasting: and that is, the general constitution of the minds of the English. I have already often insisted on some of the prerogatives of England; whereby it may justly lay claim, to be the head of a philosophical league, above all other countries in Europe: I have urged its situation, its present genius, and the disposition of its merchants; and many more such arguments to encourage us, still remain to be used: But of all others, this, which I am now alleging, is of the most weighty, and important consideration. If there can be a true character given of the universal temper of any nation under Heaven: then certainly this must be ascribed to our countrymen: that they have commonly an unaffected sincerity; that they love to deliver their minds with a sound simplicity; that they have the middle qualities, between the reserved subtle southern, and the rough unhewn northern people: that they are not extremely prone to speak: that they are more concerned, what others will think of the strength, than of the fineness of what they say: and that an universal modesty possesses them. These qualities are so conspicuous, and proper to our soil; that we often hear them objected to us, by some of our neighbour satirists, in more disgraceful expressions. For they are wont to revile the English, with a want of familiarity; with a melancholy dumpishness; with slowness, silence, and with the unrefined sullenness of their behaviour. But these are only the reproaches of partiality, or ignorance: for they ought rather to be commended for an honourable integrity; for a neglect of circumstances, and flourishes; for regarding things of greater moment, more than less; for a scorn to deceive as well as to be deceived: which are all the best endowments, that can enter into a philosophical mind. So that even the position of our climate, the air, the influence of the heaven, the composition of the English blood; as well as the embraces of the ocean, seem to join with the labours of the Royal Society, to render our country, a land of experimental knowledge. And it is a good sign, that nature will reveal more of its secrets to the English, than to others; because it has already furnished them with a genius so well proportioned, for the receiving, and retaining its mysteries.

—1667

Thomas Traherne
1637 – 1674

Little is known about Traherne's life. He was the son of a Herefordshire shoemaker, of a Welsh family. He would have been five when the Civil War broke out, and Hereford was in the thick of the conflict, changing hands three times. It is possible that both of Traherne's parents died when he was young; nothing is heard of them, and Traherne and his brother Philip seem to have been adopted by an innkeeper, Philip Traherne senior. Traherne graduated from Brasenose College, one of the more Puritan of the Oxford colleges, in 1656, and was appointed rector of Credenhill near Hereford in 1657. He was ordained as an Anglican priest at the Restoration in 1660, and is known to have been a member of a religious circle centred upon a devout woman, Susanna Hopton. He kept in contact with Oxford, and his work *Roman Forgeries*, published in 1673, may represent work towards a Bachelor of Divinity degree. He became B.D. in 1669. While he retained his rectorship at Credenhill until his death, in 1669 he moved to London, as private chaplain to Sir Orlando Bridgeman, Lord Keeper of the Privy Seal. He was buried at Teddington in Middlesex.

The works by which Traherne is now best known, his poems and *Centuries of Meditation*, were not published in his lifetime. The manuscripts were found on two bookstalls, in different streets, in 1897, by a scholar who recognized that they were the work of the same writer. Many of the poems exist in two versions, one "improved" by Traherne's brother Philip. At first they were thought to be by Vaughan, because of some thematic similarities; but in fact Vaughan and Traherne are stylistically far apart, and Vaughan is by far the better poet, which is not to say that Traherne's work is without interest. The prose work, *Centuries of Meditation*, is generally considered to be superior to the verse.

There has been a good deal of excitement among scholars and devotees of Traherne in recent years, because manuscripts keep on turning up. In 1967, for example, his *Commentaries of Heaven* were discovered on a burning trash-heap by a man searching for car parts. He emigrated to Canada, and fifteen years after the discovery the manuscript was identified as Traherne's. Another manuscript of devotional prose was discovered in the late 1990s.

❧❧❧

The Third Century
(excerpt)

1

Will you see the infancy of this sublime and celestial greatness? Those pure and virgin apprehensions I had from the womb, and that divine light wherewith I was born, are the best unto this day, wherein I can see the universe. By the gift of God they attended me into the world, and by his special favor I remember them till now. Verily they seem the greatest gifts his wisdom could bestow, for without them all other gifts had been dead andx

vain. They are unattainable by book, and therefore I will teach them by experience. Pray for them earnestly: for they will make you angelical, and wholly celestial. Certainly Adam in Paradise had not more sweet and curious apprehensions of the world, than I when I was a child.

2

All appeared new, and strange at the first, inexpressibly rare, and delightful, and beautiful. I was a little stranger which at my entrance into the world was saluted and surrounded with innumerable joys. My knowledge was divine. I knew by intuition those things which since my apostasy,[1] I collected again, by the highest reason. My very ignorance was advantageous. I seemed as one brought into the estate of innocence. All things were spotless and pure and glorious: yea, and infinitely mine, and joyful and precious. I knew not that there were any sins, or complaints, or laws. I dreamed not of poverty's contentions or vices. All tears and quarrels, were hidden from mine eyes. Everything was at rest, free, and immortal. I knew nothing of sickness or death or exaction, in the absence of these I was entertained like an angel with the works of God in their splendor and glory; I saw all in the peace of Eden; Heaven and Earth did sing my creator's praises and could not make more melody to Adam, than to me. All time was eternity, and a perpetual Sabbath. Is it not strange, that an infant should be heir of the world, and see those mysteries which the books of the learned never unfold?

3

The corn was orient and immortal wheat,[2] which never should be reaped, nor was ever sown. I thought it had stood from everlasting to everlasting. The dust and stones of the street were as precious as gold. The gates were at first the end of the world, the green trees when I saw them first through one of the gates transported and ravished me; their sweetness and unusual beauty made my heart to leap, and almost mad with ecstacy, they were such strange and wonderful things: The men! O what venerable and reverend creatures did the aged seem! Immortal cherubims! And young men glittering and sparkling angels and maids strange seraphic pieces of life and beauty! Boys and girls tumbling in the street, and playing, were moving jewels. I knew not that they were born or should die. But all things abided eternally as they were in their proper places. Eter-

nity was manifest in the light of the day, and something infinite behind everything appeared: which talked with my expectation and moved my desire. The city seemed to stand in Eden, or to be built in Heaven. The streets were mine, the temple was mine, the people were mine, their clothes and gold and silver was mine, as much as their sparkling eyes, fair skins and ruddy faces. The skies were mine, and so were the sun and moon and stars, and all the world was mine, and I the only spectator and enjoyer of it. I knew no churlish proprieties,[3] nor bounds nor divisions: but all proprieties and divisions were mine: all treasures and the possessors of them. So that with much ado I was corrupted; and made to learn the dirty devices of this world. Which now I unlearn, and become as it were a little child again, that I may enter into the Kingdom of God.

4

Upon those pure and virgin apprehensions which I had in my infancy, I made this poem.[4]

1

That childish thoughts such joys inspire,
Doth make my wonder, and his glory higher;
His bounty, and my wealth more great:
It shows his Kingdom, and his work complete.
5   In which there is not any thing,
Not meet to be the joy of cherubim.

2

He in our childhood with us walks,
And with our thoughts mysteriously he talks;
He often visiteth our minds,
10   But cold acceptance in us ever finds.
We send him often grieved away,
Who else would show us all his kingdom's joy.

---

[1] *apostasy* his movement away from childhood innocence; see meditation 7 below.

[2] *orient* bright, glowing, shining (*OED* orient *adj* 2b).

[3] *proprieties* properties, possessions.

[4] *this poem* found also in manuscripts of Traherne's poems, where it is entitled "The Approach."

3

O Lord I wonder at thy love,
Which did my infancy so early move:
15   But more at that which did forbear
And move so long, though sleighted many a year:
        But most of all, at last that thou
Thy self shouldst me convert, I scarce know how.

4

        Thy gracious motions oft in vain
20 Assaulted me: My heart did hard remain
        Long time! I sent my God away
Grieved much, that he could not give me his joy.
        I careless was, nor did regard
The end for which he all those thoughts prepared.

5

25   But now, with new and open eyes,
I see beneath, as if I were above the skies:
        And as I backward look again
See all his thoughts and mine most clear and plain.
        He did approach, he me did woe.
30 I wonder that my God this thing would do.

6

        From nothing taken first I was;
What wondrous things his glory brought to pass!
        Now in the world I him behold,
And me, enveloped in precious gold;
35   In deep abysses of delights,
In present hidden glorious benefits.

7

        Those thoughts his goodness long before
Prepared as precious and celestial store:
        With curious art in me inlaid,
40 That childhood might itself alone be said
        My tutor teacher guide to be,
Instructed then even by the deity.

———————

5

Our Savior's meaning, when he said, he must be born again and become a little child that will enter into the Kingdom of Heaven:[1] is deeper far than is generally believed. It is not only in a careless reliance upon divine providence, that we are to become little children, or in the feebleness and shortness of our anger and simplicity of our passions: but in the peace and purity of all our soul. Which purity also is a deeper thing than is commonly apprehended. For we must disrobe ourselves of all false colors, and unclothe our souls of evil habits; all our thoughts must be infant-like and clear: the powers of our soul free from the leaven of this world, and disentangled from men's conceits and customs. Grit in the eye or the yellow jaundice will not let a man see those objects truly that are before it. And therefore it is requisite that we should be as very strangers to the thoughts, customs and opinions of men in this world as if we were but little children. So those things would appear to us only which do to children when they are first born. Ambitions, trades, luxuries, inordinate affections, casual and accidental riches invented since the fall would be gone, and only those things appear, which did to Adam in Paradise, in the same light, and in the same colors. God in his works, glory in the light, love in our parents, men, ourselves, and the face of Heaven. Every man naturally seeing those things, to the enjoyment of which he is naturally born.

6

Every one provideth objects, but few prepare senses whereby, and light wherein to see them. Since therefore we are born to be a burning and shining light, and whatever men learn of others, they see in the light of others' souls: I will in the light of my soul show you the universe. Perhaps it is celestial, and will teach you how beneficial we may be to each other. I am sure it is a sweet and curious light

———
[1] Mark 10:15, Luke 18:17.

665

to me: which had I wanted: I would have given all the gold and silver in all worlds to have purchased. But it was the gift of God and could not be bought with money. And by what steps and degrees I proceeded to that enjoyment of all eternity which now I possess I will likewise show you. A clear, and familiar light it may prove unto you.

7

The first light which shined in my infancy in its primitive and innocent clarity was totally eclipsed: insomuch that I was fain to learn all again. If you ask me how it was eclipsed? Truly by the customs and manners of men, which like contrary winds blew it out: by an innumerable company of other objects, rude, vulgar and worthless things that like so many loads of earth and dung did overwhelm and bury it: by the impetuous torrent of wrong desires in all others whom I saw or knew that carried me away and alienated me from it: by a whole sea of other matters and concernments that covered and drowned it: finally by the evil influence of a bad education that did not foster and cherish it. All men's thoughts and words were about other matters; they all prized new things which I did not dream of. I was a stranger and unacquainted with them; I was little and reverenced their authority; I was weak, and easily guided by their example: ambitious also, and desirous to approve myself unto them. And finding no one syllable in any man's mouth of those things, by degrees they vanished, my thoughts (as indeed what is more fleeting than a thought) were blotted out. And at last all the celestial great and stable treasures to which I was born, as wholly forgotten, as if they had never been.

8

Had any man spoken of it, it had been the most easy thing in the world, to have taught me, and to have made me believe, that Heaven and Earth was God's house, and that he gave it me. That the sun was mine and that men were mine, and that cities and kingdoms were mine also: that earth was better than gold, and that water was, every drop of it, a precious jewel. And that these were great and living treasures: and that all riches whatsoever else was dross in comparison. From whence I clearly find how docile our nature is in natural things, were it rightly entreated. And that our misery proceedeth ten thousand times more from the outward bondage of opinion and custom, than from any inward corruption or depravation of nature: And that it is not our parents' loins, so much as our parents' lives, that enthrals and blinds us, Yet is all our corruption derived from Adam: inasmuch as all the evil examples and inclinations of the world arise from his sin. But I speak it in the presence of God and of our Lord Jesus Christ, in my pure primitive virgin light, while my apprehensions were natural, and unmixed, I can not remember, but that I was ten thousand times more prone to good and excellent things, than evil. But I was quickly tainted and fell by others.
—(CA. 1669–74)

Aphra Behn
1640 – 1689

Little is certainly known about the early life of Aphra Behn. There are several biographical accounts, which present conflicting versions of her lineage, birthplace and youth. Within a decade of her death were published: *An Account of the Life of the Incomparable Mrs. Behn* (1696), *Memoirs of the Life of Mrs. Behn* (1696) and *The History of the Life and Memoirs of Mrs. Behn* (1698). These and other early references have led biographers to conclude that Aphra Behn was born in Harbledon near Canterbury on July 10, 1640, daughter to Bartholomew Johnson and Elizabeth Denham. It is believed that she spent several years in her early twenties (ca. 1663–64) in Surinam, where she met William Scot. Some time in 1664, she was married to a Mr. Behn, possibly a city merchant of Dutch extraction, who died of the plague in 1665. In August, 1666, during the Dutch war, she was dispatched as an official government spy to Antwerp, with a mission to persuade William Scot to act as a double agent. She returned to England in 1667 heavily in debt, and was briefly imprisoned in London. Despite repeated petitions, she received no compensation for her services, and undertook to live by the pen, writing at least eighteen plays. While her theatrical career dominated the first decade of her professional writing, Behn also produced translations from Latin and French, and wrote popular verse and prose fiction. As a writer of drama, novels, epistles, and poetry, she explored a variety of highly charged subjects not common in Restoration literature: female sexuality, lust, seduction, incest, rape. The themes upon which she wrote drew criticism from churchmen. Bishop Burnet wrote to Anne Wharton: "she is so abominably vile a woman, and rallies not only all Religion but all Virtue in so odious and obscene a manner, that I am heartily sorry that she has writ any thing in your commendation." Perhaps because of the subversive nature of her drama and prose fiction, Behn's role as Tory apologist most evident in her occasional verse has received less critical attention. Aphra Behn died in London and was buried in Westminster Abbey. Of her life and burial, Virginia Woolf was to write: "All women together ought to let flowers fall upon the tomb of Aphra Behn which is, most scandalously but rather appropriately, in Westminster Abbey, for it was she who earned them the right to speak their minds."

⌘

Love Letters by Mrs A. Behn [1]

LETTER I

You bid me write, and I wish it were only the effects of complaisance that makes me obey you;

I should be very angry with myself, and you, if I thought it were any other motive: I hope it is not, and will not have you believe otherwise. I cannot help however wishing you no mirth, nor any content in your dancing-design; and this unwonted malice in me I do not like, and would have concealed it if I could, lest you should take it for something which I am nor will believe myself guilty of. May your women be all ugly, ill-natured, ill-dressed, ill-fashioned, and unconversable; and, for your greater disappointment, may every moment of your time there be taken up with thoughts of me, (a sufficient curse); and yet you will be better enter-

---

[1] first published posthumously in *The Histories and Novels of the Late Ingenious Mrs. Behn: In One Volume* (London, 1696). The present text is taken from *Histories and Novels* (1700). Behn's biographers have suggested that these letters may have been addressed to John Hoyle, a (bi-sexual) lawyer. A contemporary, Roger Morris, wrote that Hoyle had "kept" Behn as his mistress. Others, however, consider these expressions of desire not to be autobiographical, reading them as eloquent fictional expressions of a tragic, frustrating passion.

tained than me, who possibly am, and shall be, uneasy with thoughts not so good. Perhaps you had eased me of some trouble, if you had let me seen, or known you had been well: but these are favours for better friends; and I'll endeavour not to resent the loss, or rather the miss of 'em. It may be, since I have so easily granted this desire of yours, in writing to you, you will fear you have pulled a trouble on—but do not: I do by this send for you.—You know what you gave your hand upon; the date of banishment is already out, and I could have wished you had been so good-natured as to have disobeyed me. Pray take notice therefore I am better natured than you: I am profoundly melancholy since I saw you; I know not why, and should be glad to see you when your occasions will permit you to visit.

Astrea

LETTER II

You may tell me a thousand years, my dear Lycidas, of your unbounded friendship; but after so unkind a departure as that last night, give me leave (when serious) to doubt it; nay, 'tis past doubt: I know you rather hate me; what else could hurry you from me, when you saw me surrounded with all the necessary impossibilities of speaking to you? I made as broad signs as one could do, who durst not speak, both for your sake and my own; I acted even imprudently to make my soul be understood, that was then (if I may say so) in real agonies for your departure. 'Tis a wonder a woman, so violent in all her passions as I, did not (forgetting all prudence, all considerations) fly out into absolute commands, or at least entreaties, that you would give me a moment's time longer. I burst to speak with you, to know a thousand things; but particularly how you came to be so barbarous, as to carry away all that could make my satisfaction: You carried away my letter, and you carried away Lycidas; I will not call him mine, because he has so

unkindly taken himself back. 'Twas with that design you came; for I saw all night with what reluctancy you spoke, how coldly you entertained me, and with what pain and uneasiness you gave me the only conversation I value in the world. I am ashamed to tell you this: I know your peevish virtue will misinterpret me: But take it how you will, think of it as you please; I am undone, and will be free; I will tell you, you did not use me well: I am ruined, and will rail at you—Come then, I conjure you, this evening, that after it I may shut those eyes that have been too long waking. I have committed a thousand madnesses in this; but you must pardon the faults you have created. Come and do so; for I must see you tonight, and that in a better humour than you were last night. No more; obey me as you have that friendship for me you profess; and assure yourself, to find a very welcome reception from,

Lycidas,

Your

Astrea

LETTER III

When shall we understand one another? for I thought, dear Lycidas, you had been a man of your parole:[1] I will as soon believe you will forget me, as that you have not remembered the promise you made me. Confess you are the teasingest creature in the world, rather than suffer me to think you neglect me, or would put a slight upon me, that have chosen you from all the whole creation, to give my entire esteem to. This I had assured you yesterday, but that I dreaded the effects of your censure today; and though I scorn to guard my tongue, as hoping 'twill never offend willingly, yet I can, with much ado, hold it, when I have a great mind to say a thousand things, I know will be taken in an ill sense. Possibly you will wonder what compels me to write, what moves me to send where I find so little

---

[1] *man of your parole* man of your word.

welcome; nay, where I meet with such returns, it may be I wonder too. You say I am changed: I had rather almost justify an ill, than repent, maintain false arguments, than yield I am in the wrong. In fine, charming friend Lycidas, whatever I was since you knew me, believe I am still the same in soul and thought; but that is, what shall never hurt you, what shall never be but to serve you; why then did you say, you would not sit near me? Was that, my friend, was that the esteem you profess? Who grows cold first? Who is changed? and who the aggressor? 'Tis I was first in friendship, and shall be last in constancy: You, by inclination, and not for want of friends, have I placed highest in my esteem; and for that reason your conversation is the most acceptable and agreeable of any in the world—and for this reason you shun mine. Take your course; be a friend like a foe, and continue to impose upon me, that you esteem me when you sly me: Renounce your false friendship, or let me see you give it entire to

Astrea

LETTER IV

I had rather, dear Lycidas, set myself to write to any man on earth than you, for I fear your severe prudence and discretion, so nice, may make an ill judgment of what I say: Yet you bid me not dissemble; and you need not have cautioned me, who so naturally hate those little arts of my sex, that I often run on freedoms, that may well enough bear a censure from people so scrupulous as Lycidas. Nor dare I follow all my inclinations neither, nor tell all the little secrets of my soul: Why I write them, I can give no account; 'tis but fooling myself, perhaps, into an undoing. I do not (by this soft entertainment) rook in my heart, like a young gamester, to make it venture its last stake:[1] This, I say may be the

danger; I may come off unhurt, but cannot be a winner: Why then should I throw an uncertain cast, where I hazard all, and you nothing?[2] Your staunch prudence is proof against love, and all the bank's on my side: You are so unreasonable, you would have me pay where I have contracted no debt; you would have me give, and you, like a miser, would distribute nothing. Greedy Lycidas! Unconscionable! and ungenerous! You would not be in love for all the world, yet wish I were so, Uncharitable!—Would my fever cure you? Or a curse on me make you blessed? Say Lycidas, will it? I have heard, when two souls kindly meet, 'tis a vast pleasure, as vast as the curse must be, when kindness is not equal; and why should you believe that necessary for me, that will be so very incommode for you?[3] Will you, dear Lycidas, allow then, that you have less good-nature than I? Pray be just, till you can give such proofs of the contrary, as I shall be judge of; or give me a reason for your ill-nature. So much for loving.

Now, as you are my friend, I conjure you to consider what resolution I took up, when I saw you last (which methinks is a long time), of seeing no man till I saw your face again; and when you remember that, you will possibly be so kind as to make what haste you can to see me again: Till then, have thoughts as much in favour of me as you can; for when you know me better, you will believe I merit all. May you be impatient and uneasy till you see me again; and bating that, may all the blessings of heaven and earth light on you, is the continued prayers of,

Dear Lycidas,

Your true   *Astrea*

---

[1] *rook in my heart, like a young gamester* cheat my heart, as if it were an inexperienced gambler (*OED* rook *v*[1]1).

[2] *an uncertain cast* a throw of dice.

[3] *incommode* inconvenient.

LETTER V

Though it be very late, I cannot go to bed; but I must tell thee, I have been very good ever since I saw thee, and have been a writing, and perhaps you had eased me of some trouble, if you had let me see, or know you had been well:[1] have seen no face of man, or other body, save my own people. I am mightily pleased with your kindness to me tonight; and 'twas, I hope, and believe, very innocent, and undisturbing on both sides. My Lycidas says, he can be soft and dear when he please to put off his haughty pride, which is only assumed to see how far I dare love him ununited. Since then my soul's delight you are, and may ever be assured I am, and ever will be yours, befall me what will and that all the devils of hell shall not prevail against thee: Show then, I say, my dearest love, thy native sweet temper: Show me all the love thou hast undissembled then, and never till then, shall I believe you love; and deserve my heart, for God's sake, to keep me well: and if thou hast love (as I shall never doubt, if thou art always as tonight) show that love, I beseech thee; there being nothing so grateful to God, and mankind, as plain-dealing. 'Tis too late to conjure thee farther:[2] I will be purchased with softness, and dear words, and kind expressions, sweet eyes, and a low voice.

Farewell; I love thee dearly, passionately, and tenderly, and am resolved to be eternally.

My only dear delight, and
Joy of my life, thy   *Astrea*

LETTER VI

Since you, my dearest Lycidas, have prescribed me laws and rules, how I shall behave myself to please and gain you; and that one of these is not

---

[1] *if you had let me see, or know you had been well* emended from "seen" and "known."

[2] *conjure* beseech, implore (*OED* conjure *v* II.4a).

lying or dissembling; and that I had tonight promised you should never have a tedious letter from me more, I will begin to keep my word, and stint my heart and hand. I promised though to write; and though I have no great matter to say more, than the assurance of my eternal love to you, yet to obey you, and not only so, but to oblige my own impatient heart, I must, late as 'tis say something to thee.

I stayed after thee tonight, till I had read a whole act of my new play too; and then he led me over all the way, saying, Gad you were the man: And beginning some rallying love-discourse after supper, which he fancied was not so well received as it ought, he said you were not handsome, and called Philly to own it; but he did not, but was of my side, and said you were handsome: So he went on a while, and all ended that concerned you. And this, upon my word, is all.

Your articles I have read over, and do not like 'em; you have broke one, even before you have sworn or sealed 'em; that is, they are writ with reserves. I must have a better account of your heart tomorrow, when you come. I grow desperate fond of you, and would fain be used well; if not, I will march off: But I will believe you mean to keep your word, as I will forever do mine. Pray make haste to see me tomorrow; and if I am not at home when you come, send for me over the way, where I have engaged to dine, there being an entertainment on purpose tomorrow for me.

For God's sake make no more niceties and scruples than need, in your way of living with me; that is, do not make me believe this distance is to ease you, when indeed 'tis meant to ease us both of love; and for God's sake, do not misinterpret my excess of fondness; and if I forget myself, let the check you give be sufficient to make me desist. Believe me, dear creature, 'tis more out of humour and jest, than any inclination on my side; for I could sit eternally with you, without part of disturbance: Fear me not, for you are (from that) as safe as in heaven itself. Believe me, dear Lycidas, this truth, and trust me. 'Tis late, farewell; and come, for God's sake, betimes tomorrow, and put off your foolish fear and niceties, and do not shame me with your perpetual ill opinion; my nature is proud and insolent, and cannot bear it: I will be used something better, in spite of all your apprehensions falsely grounded. Adieu, keep me as I am ever yours.   *Astrea*

By this letter, one would think I were the nicest thing on earth;[1] yet I know a dear friend goes far beyond me in that unnecessary fault.

LETTER VII

My charming unkind,
I would have gaged my life you could not have left me so coldly, so unconcerned as you did; but you are resolved to give me proofs of your no love: Your counsel, which was given you tonight, has wrought the effects which it usually does in hearts like yours. Tell me no more you love me; for 'twill be hard to make me think it, though it be the only blessing I ask on earth: But if love can merit a heart, I know who ought to claim yours. My soul is ready to burst with pride and indignation; and at the same time, love, with all his softness assails me, and will make me write: so that, between one and the other, I can express neither as I ought. What shall I do to make you know I do not use to condescend to so much submission, nor to tell my heart so freely? Though you think it use, methinks, I find my heart swell with disdain at this minute, for my being ready to make asseverations of the contrary, and to assure you I do not, nor never did, love, or talk at the rate I do to you, since I was born: I say, I would swear this, but something rolls up my bosom, and checks my very thoughts as it rises. You

ought, oh faithless, and infinitely adorable Lycidas! to know and guess my tenderness; you ought to see it grow, and daily increase upon your hands: If it be troublesome, 'tis because I fancy you lessen, whilst I increase, in passion; or rather, that by your ill judgment of mine, you never had any in your soul for me. Oh unlucky, oh vexatious thought! Either let me never see that charming face, or ease my soul of so tormenting an agony, as the cruel thought of not being beloved. Why, my lovely dear, should I flatter you? or, why make more words of my tenderness, than another woman, that loves as well, would do, as once you said? No, you ought rather to believe that I say more, because I love more than any woman can be capable of: My soul is formed of no other material than love; and all that soul of love was formed for my dear, faithless Lycidas—methinks I have a fancy, that something will prevent my going tomorrow morning: However, I conjure thee, if possible, to come tomorrow about seven or eight at night, that I may tell you in what a deplorable condition you left me tonight. I cannot describe it; but I feel it, and with you the same pain, for going so inhumanely: But, oh! you went to joys, and left me to torments! You went to love alone, and left me love and rage, fevers and calentures, even madness itself![2] Indeed, indeed, my soul! I know not to what degree I love you; let it suffice I do most passionately, and can have no thoughts of any other man, whilst I have life. No! Reproach me, defame me, lampoon me, curse me, and kill me, when I do, and let heaven do so too.

Farewell—I love you more and more every moment of my life—know it, and goodnight. Come tomorrow, being Wednesday, to, my adorable *Lycidas,* your   *Astrea*

---

[1] *the nicest thing on earth* probably in the sense of "delicate, needing tactful handling" (*OED* nice *a* 11b).

[2] *calentures* delirium, burning passion (*OED* calenture 1,2).

LETTER VIII

Why, my dearest charmer, do you disturb that repose I had resolved to pursue, by taking it unkindly that I did not write? I cannot disobey you, because indeed I would not, though 'twere better much for both I had been forever silent: I prophesy so, but at the same time cannot help my fate, and know not what force or credit there is in the virtue we both profess; but I am sure 'tis not good to tempt it: I think I am sure, and I think my Lycidas just; But, oh! to what purpose is all this fooling? You have often wisely considered it; but I never stayed to think till 'twas too late; whatever resolutions I make in the absence of my lovely friend, one single sight turns me all woman, and all his. Take notice then, my Lycidas, I will henceforth never be wise more; never make any vows against my inclinations, or the little-winged deity. I do not only see 'tis all in vain, but I really believe they serve only to augment my passion. I own I have neither the coldness of Lycidas, nor the prudence; I cannot either not love, or have a thousand arts of hiding it; I have nobody to fear, and therefore may have somebody to love: But if you are destined to be he, the Lord have mercy on me; for I am sure you'll have none. I expect a reprimand for this plain confession; but I must justify it, and I will, because I cannot help it: I was born to ill luck; and this loss of my heart is, possibly, not the least part on't.[1] Do not let me see you disapprove it, I may one day grow ashamed on't, and reclaim, but never, whilst you blow the flame, though perhaps against your will. I expect now a very wise answer; and, I believe, with abundance of discretion, you will caution me to avoid this danger that threatens. Do so, if you have a mind to make me launch farther into the main sea of love: Rather deal with me as with a right woman; make me believe myself infinitely

beloved. I may chance, from the natural inconstancy of my sex, to be as false as you would wish, and leave you in quiet: For as I am satisfied I love in vain, and without return, I am satisfied that nothing, but the thing that hates me, could treat me as Lycidas does; and 'tis only the vanity of being beloved by me can make you countenance a softness so displeasing to you. How could anything, but the man that hates me, entertain me so unkindly? Witness your excellent opinion of me, of loving others; witness your passing by the end of the street where I live, and squandering away your time at any coffee-house, rather than allow me what you know in your soul is the greatest blessing of my life, your dear dull melancholy company; I call it dull, because you can never be gay or merry where Astrea is. How could this indifference possess you, when your malicious soul knew I was languishing for you? I died, I fainted and pined for an hour of what you lavished out, unregardless of me, and without so much as thinking on me! What can you say, that judgment may not pass? that you may not be condemned for the worst-natured, incorrigible thing in the world? Yield, and at least say, my honest friend Astrea, I neither do love thee, nor can, nor ever will; at least let me say, you were generous, and told me plain blunt truth: I know it; nay worse, you impudently (but truly) told me your business would permit you to come every night, but your inclinations would not: At least this was honest, but very unkind, and not over civil. Do not you, my amiable Lycidas, know I would purchase your sight at any rate; why this neglect then? Why keeping distance? But as much as to say, "Astrea, truly you will make me love you, you will make me fond of you, you will please and delight me with your conversation, and I am a fellow that do not desire to be pleased, therefore be not so civil to me; for I do not desire civil company, nor company that diverts me." A pretty speech this; and yet if I do obey, desist being civil, and behave myself very rudely, as

---

[1] *possibly* emended from "possible"; the latter was used adverbially, but as an intensifer of "can" or "could."

I have done, you say, this two or three days—then, Oh, Astrea! where is your profession? Where your love so boasted? Your good-nature, etc? Why truly, my dear Lycidas, where it was, and ever will be, so long as you have invincible charms, and show your eyes, and look so dearly; though you may, by your prudent counsel, and your wise conduct of absence, and marching by my door without calling in, oblige me to stay my hand, and hold my tongue: I can conceal my kindness, though not dissemble one: I can make you think I am wise, if I list; but when I tell you I have friendship, love and esteem for you, you may pawn your soul upon't: Believe 'tis true, and satisfy yourself you have, my dear Lycidas, in your Astrea all she professes. I should be glad to see you as soon as possible (you say Thursday) you can: I beg you will, and shall, with impatience, expect you betimes. Fail me not, as you would have me think you have any value for   *Astrea*

I beg you will not fail to let me hear from you, today, being Wednesday, and see you at night if you can.

—1700

The Dumb Virgin:
Or, The Force of Imagination

Rinaldo, a senator of the great city, Venice, by a plentiful inheritance, and industrious acquisitions, was become master of a very plentiful estate; which, by the countenance of his family, sprung from the best houses in Italy, had rendered him extremely popular and honoured; he had risen to the greatest dignities of that state, all which offices he discharged with wisdom and conduct, befitting the importance of his charge, and character of the manager; but this great person had some accidents in his children, sufficient to damp all the pleasure of his more smiling fortunes; he married when young, a beautiful and virtuous lady, who had rendered

him the happy father of a son; but his joys were soon disturbed by the following occasion.

There stands an island in the Adriatic Sea, about twenty leagues from Venice, a place wonderfully pleasant in the summer, where art and nature seem to outrival each other, or seem rather to combine in rendering it the most pleasant of their products, being placed under the most benign climate in the world, and situated exactly between Italy and Greece, it appears an entire epitome of all the pleasures in them both; the proper glories of the island were not a little augmented by the confluence of gentlemen and ladies of the chiefest rank in the city, insomuch that this was a greater mart for beauty and gallantry, than Venice for trade. Among others, Rinaldo's lady begged her husband's permission to view this so much celebrated place.

He was unwilling to trust his treasure to the treachery of the watery element; but repeating her request, he yielded to her desires, his love not permitting him the least show of command, and so through its extent, conspiring its own destruction. His lady with her young son, (whom she would not trust from her sight) and a splendid attendance in a barge well fitted, sets out for the island. Rinaldo being detained at home himself about some important affairs relating to the public, committed the care of his dear wife and child to a faithful servant called Gaspar; and for their greater security against pirates, had obtained his brother, who commanded a Venetian galley, to attend them as convoy: in the evening they set out from Venice, with a prosperous gale, but a storm arising in the night, soon separated the barge from her convoy, and before morning drove her beyond the designed port, when instead of discovering the wished for island, they could see a Turkish pirate bearing towards them, with all her sail; their late apprehensions of shipwreck, were drowned in a greater danger of captivity and lasting slavery, their fears drove some into resolutions as extravagant as the terrors that caused them, but the confusion of all was so tumultuous, and the designs so various, that nothing could be put in execution for the public safety; the greatest share of the passengers being ladies, added strangely to the consternation; beauty always adds a pomp to woe, and by its splendid show, makes sorrow look greater and more moving. Some by their piteous plaints and wailings proclaimed their griefs aloud, whilst others bespoke their sorrows more emphatically by sitting mournfully silent; the fears of some animated them to extravagant actions, whilst the terrors of others were so mortifying, that they showed no sign of life, but by their trembling; some mourned the rigour of their proper fate, others conscious of the sorrows of their friends and relations should sustain through their loss, made the griefs of them their own; but the heaviest load of misfortunes lay on Rinaldo's lady, besides the loss of her liberty, the danger of her honour, the separation from her dear husband, the care for her tender infant wrought rueful distractions; she caught her child in her arms, and with tears extorted through fear and affection, she deplored the misfortune of her babe, the pretty innocent smiling in the embraces of its mother, showed that innocence could deride the persecution of fortune; at length she delivered the infant into the hands of Gaspar, begging him to use all endeavours in its preservation, by owning it for his, when they fell into the hands of the enemy.

But Gaspar, who amidst the universal consternation had a peculiar regard to his own safety, and master's interest, undertook a design desperately brave. Two long planks, which lay lengthwise in the barge, as seats, he had tied together with ropes, and taking the infant from the mother, whilst the whole vessel was in a distracted confusion, he fastened it to the planks, and shoving both overboard before him, plunged into the sea after, dragging the planks that bore the infant with one hand, and swimming with t'other, making the next land; he had swam about two hundred paces from the barge before his exploit

was discovered, but then the griefs of Rinaldo's lady were doubly augmented, seeing her infant exposed to the fury of the merciless winds and waves, which she then judged more rigorous than the Turks; for to a weak mind, that danger works still the strongest, that's most in view; but when the pirate, who by this time had fetched them within shot, began to fire, she seemed pleased that her infant was out of that hazard, though exposed to a greater. Upon their sign of yielding, the Turk launching out her boat, brought them all on board her; but she had no time to examine her booty, being saluted by a broadside vigorously discharged from a Venetian galley, which bore down upon them, whilst they were taking aboard their spoil; this galley was that commanded by Rinaldo's brother, which cruising that way in quest of the barge, happily engaged the Turk, before they had leisure to offer any violence to the ladies, and plying her warmly the space of two hours made her a prize, to the inexpressible joy of the poor ladies, who all this time under hatches, had sustained the horrors of ten thousand deaths by dreading one.

All the greater dangers over, Rinaldo's lady began to reflect on the strange riddle of her son's fortune, who by shunning one fate, had (in all probability) fallen into a worse, for they were above ten leagues from any land, and the sea still retained a roughness, unsettled since the preceding storm, she therefore begged her brother-in-law, to sail with all speed in search of her son and Gaspar; but all in vain, for cruising that day, and the succeeding night along the coasts, without making any discovery of what they sought, he sent a boat to be informed by the peasants, of any such landings upon their coast; but they soon had a dismal account, finding the body of Gaspar thrown dead on the sand, and near to him the planks, the unhappy occasion of his flight, and the faithless sustainers of the infant. So thinking these mournful objects testimonies enough of the infant's loss, they returned with the doleful relation to their captain and the lady; her grief at the recital of the tragic story, had almost transported her to madness; what account must she now make to the mournful father, who esteemed this child the chief treasure of his life; she feared that she might forfeit the affection of a husband by being the unfortunate cause of so great a loss; but her fears deceived her, for although her husband, received her with great grief, 'twas nevertheless moderated by the patience of a Christian, and the joy for recovering his beloved lady.

This misfortune was soon lessened by the growing hopes of another offspring, which made them divest their mourning, to make preparations for the joyful reception of this new guest into the world; but upon its appearance their sorrows were redoubled, 'twas a daughter, its limbs were distorted, its back bent, and though the face was the freest from deformity, yet had it no beauty to recompense the dis-symmetry of the other parts: Physicians being consulted in this affair, derived the cause from the frights and dismal apprehensions of the mother, at her being taken by the pirates; about which time they found by computation, the conception of the child to be; the mother grew very melancholy, rarely speaking, and not to be comforted by any diversion. She conceived again, but no hopes of better fortune could decrease her grief, which growing with her burden, eased her of both at once, for she died in childbirth, and left the most beautiful daughter to the world that ever adorned Venice, but naturally and unfortunately dumb; which defect the learned attributed to the silence and melancholy of the mother, as the deformity of the other was to the extravagance of her frights.

Rinaldo, waiving all intentions of a second marriage, directs his thoughts to the care of his children, their defects not lessening his inclination, but stirring up his endeavours in supplying the defaults of nature by the industry of art, he accordingly makes the greatest provision for their breeding and education, which proved so effectual in a little time, that their progress was a greater prodigy than themselves.

The eldest called Belvideera, was indefatigably addicted to study, which she had improved so far, that by the sixteenth year of her age, she understood all the European languages, and could speak most of 'em, but was particularly pleased with the English, which gave me the happiness of many hours conversation with her; and I may ingenuously declare, 'twas the most pleasant I ever enjoyed, for besides a piercing wit, and depth of understanding peculiar to herself, she delivered her sentiments with that easiness and grace of speech, that it charmed all her hearers.

The beauties of the second sister, named Maria, grew with her age, every twelve months saluting her with a new year's gift of some peculiar charm; her shapes were fine set off with a graceful and easy carriage, the majesty and softness of her face at once wrought love and veneration; the language of her eyes sufficiently paid the loss of her tongue, and there was something so commanding in her look, that it struck every beholder as dumb as herself; she was a great proficient in painting; which puts me in mind of a notable story I can't omit; her father had sent for the most famous painter in Italy to draw her picture, she accordingly sat for it; he had drawn some of the features of her face, and coming to the eye, desired to give him as brisk and piercing glance as she could; but the vivacity of her look so astonished the painter, that through concern he let his pencil drop and spoiled the picture; he made a second essay, but with no better success, for rising in great disorder, he swore it impossible to draw that which he could not look upon; the lady vexed at the weakness of the painter, took up his pencils and the picture, and sitting down to her glass finished it herself; she had improved her silent conversation with her sister so far, that she was understood by her, as if she had spoke, and I remember this lady was the first I saw use the significative way of discourse by the fingers; I dare not say 'twas she invented it (though it probably might have been an invention of these ingenious sisters) but I am positive none before her ever brought it to that perfection.

In the seventeenth of Belvideera's, and sixteenth year of Maria's age; Francisco, brother to Rinaldo, was made admiral of the Venetian fleet, and upon his first entrance upon his command, had obtained a signal victory over the Turks; he returning to Venice with triumph, applause and spoil, presented to the Great Duke a young English gentleman, who only as a volunteer in the action, had signalized himself very bravely in the engagement, but particularly by first boarding the Turkish admiral galley, and killing her commander hand to hand; the fame of this gentleman soon spread over all Venice, and the two sisters sent presently for me, to give an account of the exploits of my countryman, as their uncle had recounted it to them; I was pleased to find so great an example of English bravery, so far from home, and longed extremely to converse with him, vainly flattering myself, that he might have been of my acquaintance. That very night there was a grand ball and masquerade at the Great Duke's palace, for the more signal joy of the late success, thither Belvideera invited me to accompany her and Maria, adding withal as a motive, that we might there most probably meet and discourse with this young hero; and equipping me with a suit of masquerade, they carried me in their coach to the ball, where we had passed half an hour, when I saw enter a handsome gentleman in a rich English dress; I showed him to Belvideera, who moving towards him, with a gallant air, slaps him on the shoulder with her fan, he turning about, and viewing her person, the defaults of which were not altogether hidden by her disguise; "Sir," (said he) "if you are a man, know that I am one, and will not bear impertinence; but, if you are a lady, Madam, as I hope in

heavens you are not, I must inform you, that I am under a vow, not to converse with any female tonight"; "Know, then Sir," (answered Belvideera very smartly) "that I am a female, and you have broke your vow already; but methinks, Sir, the ladies are very little obliged to your vow, which would rob them of the conversation of so fine a gentleman."

"Madam," (said the gentleman) "the sweetness of your voice bespeaks you a lady, and I hope the breaking my vow will be so far from damning me, that I shall thereby merit heaven, if I may be blest in your divine conversation." Belvideera made such ingenious and smart repartees to the gentleman, who was himself a great courtier, that he was entirely captivated with her wit, insomuch, that he could not refrain making protestations of his passion; he talked about half an hour in such pure Italian, that I began to mistrust my Englishman, wherefore taking some occasion to jest upon his habit, I found 'twas only a masquerade to cloak a downright Venetian; in the meantime we perceived a gentleman gallantly attired with no disguise but a Turkish turban on, the richliest beset with jewels I ever saw; he addressed Maria with all the mien and air of the finest courtier; he had talked to her a good while before we heard him, but then Belvideera, knowing her poor sister incapable of any defence, "Sir," (said she) to the Venetian, "yonder is a lady of my acquaintance, who lies under a vow of silence as you were, I must therefore beg your pardon, and fly to her relief"; She can never be conquered, who has such a champion (replied the gentleman), upon which Belvideera turning from him, interposed between the gentleman and her sister, saying, "This lady, Sir, is under an obligation of silence, as a penance imposed by her Father Confessor"; "Madam," (replied the gentleman) "whoever imposed silence on these fair lips, is guilty of a greater offence than any, such a fair creature could commit"; "Why Sir," (said Belvideera) "have you seen the lady's beauty"; "Yes Madam;" (answered he) "for urging her to talk, which I found she declined, I promised to disengage her from any farther impertinence, upon a sight of her face; she agreed by paying the price of her liberty, which was ransom enough for anything under heavens, but her fair company;" he spoke in an accent that easily showed him a stranger; which Belvideera laying hold of, as an occasion of raillery, "Sir," (said she), "your tongue pronounces you a great stranger in this part of the world, I hope you are not what that turban represents; perhaps Sir, you think yourself in the seraglio";[1] "Madam," (replied he,) "this turban might have been in the Turkish seraglio, but never in so fair a one as this; and this turban (taking it off) is now to be laid at the foot of some Christian lady, for whose safety, and by whose protecting influence I had the happiness to win it from the captain of the Turkish admiral galley." We were all surprised, knowing him then the young English gentleman, we were so curious of seeing; Belvideera presently talked English to him, and made him some very pretty compliments upon his victory, which so charmed the young soldier, that her tongue claimed an equal share in his heart with Maria's eyes; "Madam," (said he to her) "if you have the beauty of that lady, or if she has your wit, I am the most happy, or the most unfortunate man alive." "Sir," said the Venetian coming up, "pray give me leave to share in your misfortunes." "Sir" (said Belvideera very smartly) "you must share in his good fortunes, and learn to conquer men, before you have the honour of being subdued by ladies, we scorn mean praises, Sir." "Madam," (said the Venetian in some choler) "perhaps I can subdue a rival." "Pray Sir," (said the stranger) "don't be angry with the lady, she's not your rival I hope, Sir." Said the Venetian, "I can't be angry at the lady, because I love her; but my anger must be levelled at him, who after this

declaration dare own a passion for her." "Madam," (said the English gentleman turning from the Venetian) "honour now must extort a confession from me, which the awfulness of my passion durst never have owned": "And I must declare," added he in a louder voice, "to all the world, that I love you, lest this gentleman should think his threats forced me to disown it": "O! then" (said Belvideera) "you're his rival in honour, not in love." "In honourable love I am Madam," answered the stranger. "I'll try," (said the Venetian, going off in choler), he whispered a little to a gentleman, that stood at some distance, and immediately went out; this was Gonzago, a gentleman of good reputation in Venice, his principles were honour and gallantry, but the former often swayed by passions raised by the latter. All this while Maria and I were admiring the stranger, whose person was indeed wonderfully amiable, his motions were exact, yet free and unconstrained; the tone of his voice carried a sweet air of modesty in it, yet were all his expressions manly; and to sum up all, he was as fine an English gentleman, as I ever saw step in the ball.

Poor Maria never before envied her sister the advantage of speech, or never deplored the loss of her own with more regret, she found something so sweet in the mien, person, and discourse of this stranger, that her eyes felt a dazzling pleasure in beholding him, and like flattering mirrors represented every action and feature, with some heightening advantage to her imagination: Belvideera also had some secret impulses of spirit, which drew her insensibly into a great esteem of the gentleman; she asked him, by what good genius, propitious to Venice, he was induced to live so remote from his country; he said, that he could not employ his sword better than against the common foe of Christianity; and besides, there was a peculiar reason, which prompted him to serve there, which time could only make known. I made bold to ask him some peculiar questions, about affairs at Court,

---

[1] *seraglio* a harem (*OED* seraglio I.1a).

to most of which he gave answers, that showed his education liberal, and himself no stranger to quality; he called himself Dangerfield, which was a name that so pleased me, that being since satisfied it was a counterfeit, I used it in a comedy of mine:[1] we had talked till the greater part of the company being dispersed, Dangerfield begged leave to attend us to our coach, and waiting us to the door, the gentleman whom Gonzago whispered, advanced and offered his service to hand Maria, she declined it, and upon his urging, she turned to the other side of Dangerfield, who by this action of the ladies finding himself entitled to her protection: "Sir," (said he) "favours from great beauties, as from great monarchs, must flow voluntarily, not by constraint, and whosoever would extort from either, are liable to the greatest severity of punishment"; "Oh, Sir," (replied the Venetian very arrogantly) "I understand not your monarchy, we live here under a free state; besides Sir, where there is no punishment to be dreaded, the law will prove of little force; and so, Sir, by your leave"; offering to push him aside, and lay hold on the lady. Dangerfield returned the jostle so vigorously, that the Venetian fell down the descent of some stairs at the door, and broke his sword: Dangerfield leaped down after him, to prosecute his chastisement, but seeing his sword broken, only whispered him, that if he would meet him next morning at six, at the back part of St Mark's Church, he would satisfy him for the loss of his sword; upon which the Venetian immediately went off, cursing his ill fate, that prevented his quarrelling with Dangerfield; to whom he had born a grudging envy ever since his success in the late engagement, and of whom, and his lodgings, he had

given Gonzago an account, when he whispered him at the ball. Dangerfield left us full of his praises, and went home to his lodgings, where he found a note directed to him to this effect:

Sir,
You declared publicly at the ball, you were my rival in love and honour, if you dare prove it by maintaining it; I shall be tomorrow morning at six, at the back part of St Mark's Church, where I shall be ready to fall a sacrifice to both.

Gonzago

Dangerfield on the perusal of this challenge began to reflect on the strangeness of that evening's adventure, which had engaged him in a passion for two mistresses, and involved him in two duels, and whether the extravagance of his passion, or the oddness of his fighting appointments were most remarkable, he found hard to determine; his love was divided between the beauty of one lady, and wit of another, either of which he loved passionately, yet nothing could satisfy him, but the possibility of enjoying both. He had appointed the gentleman at the ball to meet him at the same time and place, which Gonzago's challenge to him imported; this disturbance employed his thoughts till morning, when rising and dressing himself very richly, he walked to the appointed place. Erizo, who was the gentleman whose sword he had broke, was in the place before him, and Gonzago entered at the same time with him. Erizo was surprised to see Gonzago, as much as he was to find Erizo there. "I don't remember friend" (said Gonzago) "that I desired your company here this morning." "As much as I expected yours," answered Erizo. "Come gentlemen," (said Dangerfield interrupting them) "I must fight you both it seems, which shall I dispatch first." "Sir," (said Erizo) "you challenged me, and therefore I claim your promise." "Sir," (replied Gonzago) "he must require the same of me first, as I chal-

---

[1] *Dangerfield…comedy of mine* This name would have been familiar to Behn's readers; Thomas Dangerfield was one of the informants in the Meal-Tub Plot, designed to counter the Popish Plot by "exposing" a conspiracy amongst Protestants. Before this involvement, he had published a narrative of his international adventures (*Don Tomazo*, 1680). He was flogged to death in 1685. The name Dangerfield has not been discovered in any of Behn's extant plays.

lenged him." Said Erizo, "the affront I received was unpardonable, and therefore I must fight him first, lest if he fall by your hands, I be deprived of my satisfaction." "Nay," (replied Gonzago) "my love and honour being laid at stake, first claims his blood; and therefore Sir," (continued he to Dangerfield) "defend yourself." "Hold" (said Erizo) interposing, "if you thrust home, you injure me your friend." "You have forfeited that little," (said Gonzago all in choler) "and therefore if you stand not aside, I'll push at you." "Thrust home then," said Erizo, "and take what follows." They immediately assaulted each other vigorously. "Hold gentlemen" (said Dangerfield striking down their swords) "by righting yourselves you injure me, robbing me of that satisfaction, which you both owe me, and therefore gentlemen you shall fight me, before any private quarrel among yourselves defraud me of my revenge, and so one or both of you," thrusting first at Erizo. "I'm your man," said Gonzago, parrying the thrust made at Erizo.[1] The clashing of so many swords alarmed some gentlemen at their matins in the church among whom was Rinaldo, who since the death of his wife, had constantly attended morning service at that church, wherein she was buried.[2] He with two or three more, upon the noise ran out, and parting the three combatants, desired to know the occasion of their promiscuous quarrel. Gonzago and Erizo knowing Rinaldo, gave him an account of the matter, as also who the stranger was. Rinaldo was overjoyed to find the brave Briton, whom he had received so great a character of, from his brother the admiral, and accosting him very courteously, "Sir," (said he) "I'm sorry for our countrymen should be so ungrateful as to injure any person, who has been so serviceable to the state; and pray gentlemen," (added he, addressing the other two) "be entreated to suspend your animosities, and come dine with me at my house, where I hope to prevail with you to end your resentments." Gonzago and Erizo hearing him compliment the stranger at their expense, told him in a rage, they would choose some other place than his house, to end their resentments in, and walked off. Dangerfield, on Rinaldo's farther request, accompanied him to his house.

Maria had newly risen, and with her nightgown only thrown loose about her, had looked out of the window, just as her father and Dangerfield were approaching the gate, at the same instant she cast her eyes upon Dangerfield, and he accidentally looked up to the window where she stood, their surprise was mutual, but that of Dangerfield the greater; he saw such an amazing sight of beauty, as made him doubt the reality of the object, or distrust the perfection of his sight; he saw his dear lady, who had so captivated him the preceding day, he saw her in all the heightening circumstances of her charms, he saw her in all her native beauties, free from the encumbrance of dress, her hair as black as ebony, hung flowing in careless curls over her shoulders, it hung linked in amorous twinings, as if in love with its own beauties; her eyes not yet freed from the dullness of the late sleep, cast a languishing pleasure in their aspect, which heaviness of sight added the greatest beauties to those suns, because under the shade of such a cloud, their lustre could only be viewed; the lambent drowsiness that played upon her face, seemed like a thin veil not to hide, but to heighten the beauty which it covered; her nightgown hanging loose discovered her charming bosom, which could bear no name, but transport, wonder and ecstasy, all which struck his soul, as soon as the object hit his eye; her breasts with an easy heaving showed the smoothness of her soul and of her skin; their motions were so languishly soft, that they could not be said to rise and fall, but rather to swell up towards love, the heat of which

---

[1] *parrying* warding off or turning aside a weapon by opposing one's own weapon (*OED* parry *v*1).

[2] *matins* morning prayers.

seemed to melt them down again; some scattered jetty hairs, which hung confusedly over her breasts, made her bosom show like Venus caught in Vulcan's net, but 'twas the spectator, not she was captivated.[1] This Dangerfield saw, and all this at once, and with eyes that were adapted by a preparatory potion; what must then his condition be? He was stricken with such amazement, that he was forced to support himself, by leaning on Rinaldo's arm, who started at his sudden indisposition. "I'm afraid, Sir," (said he) "you have received some wound in the duel." "Oh! Sir," (said he) "I am mortally wounded"; but recollecting himself after a little pause, "Now I am better." Rinaldo would have sent for a surgeon to have it searched. "Your pardon Sir," (said Dangerfield) "my indisposition proceeds from an inward malady, not by a sword, but like those made by Achilles' spear, nothing can cure, but what gave the wound."[2] Rinaldo guessing at the distemper, but not the cause of it, out of good manners, declined any further enquiry, but conducting him in, entertained him with all the courtesy imaginable; but in half an hour a messenger came from the senate, requiring his immediate attendance; he lying under an indispensable necessity of making his personal appearance, begged Dangerfield's pardon, entreating him to stay, and command his house till his return, and conducting him to a fine library, said he might there find entertainment, if he were addicted to study; added withal, as a farther engagement of his patience, that he should meet the admiral at the senate, whom he would bring home as an addition to their company at dinner. Dangerfield needed none of these motives to stay, being detained by a secret inclination to the place; walking therefore into the library, Rinaldo went to the senate. Dangerfield when alone fell into deep ruminating on his strange condition, he knew himself in the house, with one of his dear charmers, but durst not hope to see her, which added to his torment, like Tantalus removed the farther from happiness, by being nearer to it, contemplated so far on the beauties that dear creature, that he concluded, if her wit were like that of his t'other mistress, he would endeavour to confine his passion wholly to that object.[3]

In the meantime Maria was no less confounded, she knew herself in love with a stranger, whose residence was uncertain, she knew her own modesty in concealing it; and alas! she knew her dumbness incapable of ever revealing it, at least, it must never expect any return; she had gathered from her sister's discourse, that she was her rival; a rival, who had the precedency in age, as the advantage of wit, and intrigue, which want of speech rendered her incapable of; these reflections, as they drew her farther from the dear object, brought her nearer despair; her sister was gone that morning with her uncle the admiral, about two miles from Venice, to drink some mineral waters, and Maria finding nothing to divert her, goes down to her father's library, to ease her melancholy by reading. She was in the same loose habit in which she appeared at the window, her distraction of thought not permitting her care in dressing herself; she entered whilst Dangerfield's thoughts were bent by a full contemplation of her idea, insomuch that his surprise represented her as a phantom only, created by the strength of his

---

[1] *Venus caught in Vulcan's net* Vulcan, god of fire and metallurgy, was the lame husband of Venus. Suspecting her infidelity, Vulcan trapped Venus, engaged in sexual intercourse with Mars, by covering the lovers with a net (*Odyssey*, ix.266–366).

[2] *Achilles' spear...gave the wound* On their way to Troy, the Greeks mistook Teuthrania for Troy and began an attack; Telephus resisted them and was wounded by Achilles. When the wound would not heal Telephus travelled to the Greek camp and asked Achilles to cure him as an oracle had told him that the wounder would be the healer. Achilles healed him by applying the rust of his spear to the wound.

[3] *Tantalus* As a punishment for killing and cooking his son Pelops, who was later restored to life, Tantalus was condemned to Hades and compelled for eternity to stand up in water to his chin, with fruit-laden trees over his head; when he attempted to drink, the water disappeared and when he reached for the fruit, the wind blew it out of reach.

fancy; her depth of thought had cast down her eyes, in a fixed posture so low, that she discovered not Dangerfield, till she stood close where he sat, but then so sudden an appearance of what she so loved, struck so violently on her spirits, that she fell in a swoon, and fell directly into Dangerfield's arms; this soon wakened him from his dream of happiness, to a reality of bliss, he found his phantom turned into the most charming piece of flesh and blood that ever was, he found her, whom just now he despaired of seeing; he found her with all her beauties flowing loose in his arms, the greatness of the pleasure raised by the two heightening circumstances of unexpectancy and surprise, was too large for the capacity of his soul, he found himself beyond expression happy, but could not digest the surfeit;[1] he had no sooner leisure to consider on his joy, but he must reflect on the danger of her that caused it, which forced him to suspend his happiness to administer some relief to her expiring senses: he had a bottle of excellent spirits in his pocket, which holding to her nose, soon recovered her; she finding herself in the arms of a man, and in so loose a dress, blushed now more red, than she looked lately pale; and disengaging herself in a confusion, would have flung from him; but he gently detaining her by a precarious hold, threw himself on his knees, and with the greatest fervency of passion cried out: "For heaven's sake, dearest creature, be not offended at the accidental blessing which fortune, not design hath cast upon me"; (she would have raised him up), "No Madam," (continued he) "never will I remove from this posture, till you have pronounced my pardon; I love you Madam to that degree, that if you leave me in a distrust of your anger, I cannot survive it; I beg, entreat, conjure you speak, your silence torments me worse than your reproaches could; am I so much disdained, that you will not afford me one word?" The lamen-

table plight of the wretched lady every one may guess, but nobody can comprehend; she saw the dearest of mankind prostrate at her feet, and imploring what she would as readily grant as he desire, yet herself under a necessity of denying his prayers, and her own easy inclinations; the motions of her soul, wanting the freedom of utterance, were like to tear her heart asunder by so narrow a confinement, like the force of fire pent up, working more impetuously; till at last he redoubled his importunity, her thoughts wanting conveyance by the lips, burst out at her eyes in a flood of tears, then moving towards a writing desk, he following her still on his knees, amidst her sighs and groans she took pen and paper, writ two lines, which she gave him folded up, then flinging from him ran up to her chamber; he strangely surprised at this odd manner of proceeding, opening the paper read the following words:

> *You can't my pardon, nor my anger move.*
> *For know, alas, I'm dumb, alas I love.*

He was wonderfully amazed reading these words. "Dumb," (cried he out) "naturally Dumb? O ye niggard powers, why was such a wondrous piece of art left imperfect?" He had many other wild reasonings upon the lamentable subject, but falling from these to more calm reflections, he examined her note again, and finding by the last words that she loved him, he might presently imagine, that if he found not some means of declaring the continuance of his love, the innocent lady might conjecture herself slighted, upon the discovery of her affection and infirmity: Prompted by which thought, and animated by the emotions of his passion, he ventured to knock at her door; she having by this time dressed herself, ventured to let him in; Dangerfield ran towards her, and catching her with an eager embrace, gave her a thousand kisses, "Madam," said he, "you find that pardoning offences only prepares more, by emboldening the offender; but I hope

---

[1] *surfeit* excess (*OED* surfeit *sb* I.1).

Madam," showing her the note, "this is a general pardon for all offences of this sort, by which I am so encouraged to transgress, that I shall never cease crimes of this nature"; kissing her again. His happiness was interrupted by Belvideera's coming home, who running up stairs, called "Sister, sister, I have news to tell you": Her voice alarms Maria, who fearing the jealousy of Belvideera, should she find Dangerfield in her bedchamber, made signs that he should run into the closet, which she had just locked as Belvideera came in; "Oh, sister," (said Belvideera) "in a lucky hour went I abroad this morning." In a more lucky hour stayed I at home this morning, thought Maria. "I have," continued she, "been instrumental in parting two gentlemen fighting this morning, and what is more, my father had parted them before, when engaged with the fine English gentleman we saw at the ball yesterday; but the greatest news of all is, that this fine English gentleman is now in the house, and must dine here today; but you must not appear sister, because 'twere a shame to let strangers know that you are dumb." Maria perceiving her jealousy, pointed to her limbs, intimating thereby, that it was as great a shame for her to be seen by strangers; but she made farther signs, that since it was her pleasure, she would keep her chamber all that day, and not appear abroad. Belvideera was extremely glad of her resolution, hoping that she should enjoy Dangerfield's conversation without any interruption. The consternation of the spark in the closet all this while was not little, he heard the voice of the charmer, that had so captivated him, he found that she was sister to that lady, whom he just now was making so many protestations to, but he could not imagine how she was instrumental in parting the two gentlemen, that should have fought with him: the occasion was this.

Gonzago and Erizo parting from Rinaldo and Dangerfield, had walked towards the Rialto, and both exasperated that they had missed their intended revenge against Dangerfield, turned their fury upon each other, first raising their anger by incensed expostulations, then drawing their swords engaged in a desperate combat, when a voice very loud calling ("Erizo hold") stopped their fury to see whence it proceeded; when a coach driving at full flight stopped close by them, and Francisco the Venetian admiral leaped out with his sword drawn, saying, "Gentlemen, pray let me be an instrument of pacification: as for your part, Erizo, this proceeding suits not well with the business I am to move in favour of you in the senate today; the post you sue for claims your blood to be spilt against the common foe, not in private resentment, to the destruction of a citizen; and therefore I entreat you as my friend, or I command you as your officer, to put up." Erizo, unwilling to disoblige his admiral, upon whose favour his advancement depended, told Gonzago, that he must find another time to talk with him. "No, no, gentlemen," (said the admiral) "you shall not part till I have reconciled you, and therefore let me know your cause of quarrel." Erizo therefore related to him the whole affair, and mentioning that Dangerfield was gone home to dine with Rinaldo, ("with Rinaldo? my father") said Belvideera from the coach, overjoyed with hopes of seeing Dangerfield at home. "Yes" (replied Gonzago surprised) "if Rinaldo the Senator be your father Madam." "Yes he is," replied Belvideera. Gonzago then knew her to be the lady he was enamoured of, and for whom he would have fought Dangerfield; and now cursed his ill fate, that he had denied Rinaldo's invitation, which lost him the conversation of his mistress, which his rival would be sure of. "Come, come, gentlemen," (said the admiral) "you shall accompany me to see this stranger at Rinaldo's house, I bear a great esteem for him, and so it behoves every loyal Venetian, for whose service he hath been so signal." Erizo, unwilling to deny the admiral, and Gonzago glad of an opportunity of his mistress's company, which he just now thought lost, consented to the proposal, and mounting all into the coach, the three gentlemen were set down at the senate, and the lady drove home as above mentioned.

Rinaldo in the meantime was not idle in the senate, there being a motion made for election of a captain to the Rialto galleon, made void by the death of its former commander in the late fight, and which was the post designed by the admiral for Erizo. Rinaldo catching an opportunity of obliging Dangerfield, for whom he entertained a great love and respect, proposed him as a candidate for the command, urging his late brave performance against the Turks, and how much it concerned the interest of the state to encourage foreigners. He being the admiral's brother, and being so fervent in the affair, had by an unanimous consent his commission signed just as his brother came into the senate, who fearing how things were carried, comforted Erizo by future preferment; but Erizo, however he stifled his resentment, was struck with envy, that a stranger, and his enemy should be preferred to him, and resolved revenge on the first opportunity. They all went home with Rinaldo, and arrived whilst Belvideera was talking above stairs with her sister. Rinaldo, impatient to communicate his success to Dangerfield, ran into the study, where he left him; but missing him there, went into the garden, and searching all about, returned to the company, telling them he believed Dangerfield had fallen asleep in some private arbor in the garden, where he could not find him, or else impatient of his long stay, had departed; but he was sure, if he had gone, he would soon return: However they went to dinner, and Belvideera came down, making an apology for her sister's absence, through an indisposition that had seized her. Gonzago had his wished for opportunity of entertaining his mistress, whilst she always expecting some news of Dangerfield, sat very uneasy in his company; whilst Dangerfield in the closet, was as impatient to see her. The short discourse she had with her sister, gave him assurance that his love would not be unacceptable. Maria durst not open the closet, afraid that her sister should come up every minute, besides, 'twas impossible to convey him out of the chamber undiscovered, until 'twas dark, which made him wonder what occasioned his long confinement; and being tired with sitting, got up to the window, and softly opening the casement, looked out to take the air; his footman walking accidentally in the court, and casting up his eye that way, spied him, which confirmed his patience in attending for him at the gate; at length it grew dark, and Maria knowing that her sister was engaged in a match at cards with her father, Gonzago and Erizo, the admiral being gone, she came softly to the closet, and innocently took Dangerfield by the hand, to lead him out, he clapped the dear soft hand to his mouth, and kissing it eagerly, it fired his blood, and the unhappy opportunity adding the temptation, raised him to the highest pitch of passion; he found himself with the most beautiful creature in the world, one who loved him, he knew they were alone in the dark, in a bed-chamber, he knew the lady young and melting, he knew besides she could not tell, and he was conscious of his power in moving; all these wicked thoughts concurring, established him in the opinion, that this was the critical minute of his happiness, resolving therefore not to lose it, he fell down on his knees, devouring her tender hand, sighing out in his passion, begging her to crown it with her love, making ten thousand vows and protestations of his secrecy and constancy, urging all the arguments that the subtlety of the devil or man could suggest. She held out against all his assaults above two hours, and often endeavoured to struggle from him, but durst make no great disturbance, through fear of alarming the company below, at last he redoubling his passion with sighs, tears, and all the rest of love's artillery, he at last gained the fort, and the poor conquered lady, all panting, soft, and trembling every joint, melted by his embraces, he there fatally enjoyed the greatest ecstasy of bliss, heightened by the circumstances of stealth, and difficulty in obtaining. The ruined lady now too late deplored the loss of her honour, but he endeavoured to comfort her by making vows of secrecy, and promising to salve her reputation by a speedy marriage, which he certainly intended, had not the unhappy crisis of his fate been so near;[1] the company by this time had gone off, and Belvideera had retired to her chamber, melancholy that she had missed her hopes of seeing Dangerfield. Gonzago and Erizo going out of the gate saw Dangerfield's footman, whom they knew, since they saw him with his master in the morning. Gonzago asked him why he waited there? "For my master, Sir," replied the footman. "Your master is not here sure," said Gonzago. "Yes, but he is Sir," said the servant, "for I attended him hither this morning with Rinaldo, and saw him in the afternoon look out of a window above stairs." "Ha!" said Gonzago, calling Erizo aside, "by heavens, he lies here tonight then, and perhaps with my mistress, I perceived she was not pressing our stay, but rather urging our departure: Erizo, Erizo, this block must be removed, he has stepped between you and a command today, and perhaps may lie between me and my mistress tonight." "By hell" (answered Erizo) "thou hast raised a fury in me, that will not be lulled asleep, but by a portion of his blood, let's dispatch this block-head first": and running at the footman with one thrust killed him. Dangerfield by this time had been let out, and hearing the noise ran to the place: they presently assaulted him; he defended himself very bravely the space of some minutes, having wounded Gonzago in the breast, when Rinaldo hearing the noise came out; but too late for Dangerfield's relief, and too soon for his own fate, for Gonzago exasperated by his wound, ran treacher-

ously behind Dangerfield, and thrust him quite through the body; he finding the mortal wound, and wild with rage, thrust desperately forward at Erizo, when at the instant Rinaldo striking in between to part them, received Dangerfield's sword to his body, which pierced him quite through; he no sooner fell than Dangerfield perceived his fatal error, and the other two fled. Dangerfield cursed his fate, and begged with all the prayers and earnestness of a dying man that Rinaldo would forgive him. "Oh!" said Rinaldo, "you have ill rewarded me for my care in your concerns in the senate today." The servants coming out took up Rinaldo, and Dangerfield leaning upon his sword they led in. Belvideera first heard the noise, and running down first met the horrid spectacle, her dear father breathing out his last, and her lover, whom she had all that day flattered herself with hopes of seeing, she now beheld in streams of his blood; but what must poor Maria's case be; besides the grief for her father's fate, she must view that dear man, lately happy in her embraces, now folded in the arms of death, she finds herself bereft of a parent, her love, her honour, and the defender of it, all at once; and the greatest torment is, that she must bear all this anguish, and cannot ease her soul by expressing it. Belvideera sat wiping the blood from her father's wound, whilst mournful Maria sat by Dangerfield, administering all the help she could to his fainting spirits; whilst he viewed her with greater excess of grief, than he had heretofore with pleasure; being sensible what was the force of her silent grief, and the wrong he had done her, which now could never redress: he had accidentally dropped his wig in the engagement, and inclining his head over the coach where he lay. Rinaldo casting his eye upon him, perceived the mark of a bloody dagger on his neck under his left ear: "Sir," (said Rinaldo, raising himself up) "I conjure you answer me directly, were you born with the mark of that dagger, or have you received it since by accident." "I was certainly born with it,"

---

[1] *salve* preserve (*OED* salve *v²Obs.* 4a).

answered he. "Just such a mark had my son Cosmo, who was lost in the Adriatic": "How" (replied Dangerfield, starting up with a wild confusion) "Lost! sayest thou in the Adriatic? your son lost in the Adriatic?" "Yes, yes," said Rinaldo, "too surely lost in the Adriatic." "O ye impartial powers" (said Dangerfield) "why did you not reveal this before? or why not always conceal it? how happy had been the discovery some few hours ago, and how tragical is it now? For know," continued he, addressing himself to Rinaldo, "know that my supposed father, who was a Turkey merchant,[1] upon his deathbed called me to him, and told me 'twas time to undeceive me, I was not his son, he found me in the Adriatic Sea tied to two planks in his voyage from Smyrna to London; having no children, he educated me as his own, and finding me worth his care, left me all his inheritance with this dying command, that I should seek my parents at Venice." Belvideera hearkening all this while to the lamentable story, then conjectured whence proceeded the natural affection the whole family bore him, and embracing him, cried out, "Oh my unhappy brother." Maria all this while had strong and wild convulsions of sorrow within her, till the working force of her anguish racking at once all the passages of her breast, by a violent impulse broke the ligament that doubled in her tongue, and she burst out with this exclamation; "Oh! incest, incest." Dangerfield echoed that outcry with this, "O! horror, horror, I have enjoyed my sister, and murdered my father." Maria running distracted about the chamber at last spied Dangerfield's sword by which he had supported himself into the house, and catching it up, reeking with the blood of her father, plunged it into her heart, and throwing herself into Dangerfield's arms, calls out, "O my brother, O my love," and expired. All the neighbourhood was soon alarmed by the outcries of the family. I lodged within three doors of Rinaldo's house, and running presently thither, saw a more bloody tragedy in reality, than what the most moving scene ever presented; the father and daughter were both dead, the unfortunate son was gasping out his last, and the surviving sister most miserable, because she must survive such misfortunes, cried to me! "O behold the fate of your wretched countryman." I could make no answer, being struck dumb by the horror of such woeful objects; but Dangerfield hearing her name his country, turning towards me, with a languishing and weak tone, "Madam," said he, "I was your countryman, and would to heavens I were so still; if you hear my story mentioned, on your return to England, pray give these strange turns of my fate not the name of crimes, but favour them with the epithet of misfortunes; my name is not Dangerfield; but Cla——" his voice there failed him, and he presently died; death seeming more favourable than himself, concealing the fatal author of so many misfortunes, for I could never since learn out his name; but have done him the justice, I hope, to make him be pitied for his misfortunes, not hated for his crimes. Francisco being sent for, had Gonzago and Erizo apprehended, condemned, and executed. Belvideera consigned all her father's estate over to her uncle, reserving only a competency to maintain her a recluse all the rest of her life.

—1700

---

[1] *a Turkey merchant* an English merchant who traveled to Turkey to engage in trade.

Pierre-Esprit Radisson
ca. 1640 – 1710

Born in France, possibly in the south near Avignon, Radisson emigrated to Trois Rivières in New France as a youth; he might have come to the New World with his half-sister, who married Médard Chouart Des Groseilliers, Radisson's partner in most of his explorations. The mid-seventeenth century was the period of the Huron-Iroquois wars, which scattered the Huron from their settlements in Southern Ontario to territory in Michigan and Wisconsin, ravaged French settlements along the St. Lawrence, and brought the fur trade to a halt. In 1651 Radisson was captured by the Iroquois (the "enemy" in the journal) and adopted into a native family, escaping in 1653 after many adventures. In 1657 his trip to the Jesuit mission at Onondaga (near Syracuse, NY) led to another miraculous escape. In 1659–60, he and his brother-in-law embarked on the year-long journey to Lake Superior described in the following journal. Despite the spectacular cargo of furs with which they returned,

the explorers received a cold welcome by the Governor of New France. In the 1660s the two consequently transferred their allegiance to England in search of the patronage with which they and others could begin to exploit the resources of this newly "discovered" land; the result was the founding of the Hudson's Bay Company in 1670. Ever discontented with his masters, Radisson served both English and French during his later travels and adventures, eventually dying in London.

Radisson wrote four journals of his early adventures, all extant in a seventeenth-century English scribal manuscript. While some scholars have speculated that these texts are translations from now lost French originals, their French characteristics (such as spelling and vocabulary) appear to indicate that Radisson wrote them for an English readership using the English he had learned during his three years on the fringes of the Stuart Court.

❧❧❧

Travel Journal: Lake Superior, 1659–60
(excerpts)

RADISSON AND DES GROSEILLIERS
ARE FORBIDDEN TO TRAVEL TO THE INTERIOR

The spring following we were in hopes to meet with some company, having been so fortunate the year before.[1] Now during the winter whether it was that my brother revealed to his wife what we had seen in our voyage and what we further intended,[2] or how it came to pass, it was known, so

much that the Father Jesuits were desirous to find out a way how they might get down the castors from the Bay of the North by the Sagnes,[3] and so make themselves masters of that trade. They resolved to make a trial as soon as the ice would permit them. So to discover our intentions they were very earnest with me to engage myself in that voyage, to the end that my brother would give over his: which I utterly denied them knowing that they could never bring it about; because I heard the wildmen say that although the way be easy, the wildmen that are feed at their doors would have

---

[1] *the year before* probably referring to a journey in 1657–58 to the Jesuit mission in Onondaga.

[2] *my brother* Médard Chouart Des Groseilliers (1618–1696?), who was married to Radisson's half-sister. His diaries were lost overboard in a canoe spill.

[3] *castors* beavers; one of the many French usages that suggest that the text is not a translation from a French original but one written in English by a Francophone; *Bay of the North by the Sagnes* Hudson Bay and the Saguenay river.

hindered them, because they make a livelihood of that trade.

In my last voyage I took notice of that that goes to three hands,[1] which is first from the people of the north to another nation, that the French call Squerells, and another nation that they call Porquepicque, and from them to the Montignes and Algonquins that live in or about Quebec; but the greatest hindrance is the scant of water and the horrid torrents and want of victuals, being no way to carry more than can serve fourteen days or three weeks navigation on that river. Nevertheless the Fathers are gone with the Governor's son of the three rivers and six other French and twelve wildmen.

During that time we made our proportion [propositions?] to the governor of Quebec that we were willing to venture our lives for the good of the country,[2] and go to travel to the remotest countries with two Hurons and that made their escape from the Iroquois. They wished nothing more than to be in those parts, where their wives and families were, about the Lake of the stairing haire;[3] to that intent would stay until August to see if anybody would come from thence. My brother and I were of one mind; and for more assurance my brother went to Montreal to bring those two men along. He came back, being in danger. The Governor gives him leave, conditionally that he must carry two of his servants along with him, and give them the *moitie* of the profit.[4] My brother was vexed at such an unreasonable demand, to take inexperted men to their ruin. All our knowledge and desire depended

only of this last voyage; besides that the Governor should compare two of his servants to us, that have ventured our lives so many years and maintained the country with our generosity in the presence of all; neither was there one that had the courage to undertake what we have done. We made the Governor a slight answer, and told him for our part we knew what we were; discoverers before governors. If the wildmen came down, the way [was the same?] for them as for us, and that we should be glad to have the honour of his company, but not of that of his servants, and that we were both masters and servants; the Governor was much displeased at this, and commanded us not to go without his leave.[5] We desired the Fathers to speak to him about it; our addresses were slight because of the shame was put upon them the year before of their return. Besides, they stayed for an opportunity to go there themselves; for their design is to further the Christian faith to the greatest glory of God, and indeed are charitable to all those that are in distress and needy, especially to those that are worthy or industrious in their way of honesty. This is the truth, let who he will speak otherwise, for this really I know myself by experience. I hope I offend none to tell the truth. We are forced to go back without doing anything.

The month of August that brings a company of the Sault,[6] who were come by the river of the three rivers with incredible pains, as they said. It was a company of seven boats, we wrote the news of their *arrivement* to Quebec. They send us word that they will stay until the two Fathers be turned from Sacquenes, that we should go with them. An answer without reason. Necessity obliged us to go. Those people are not to be enticed, for as soon as they have done their affair they go. The Governor of the

---

[1] trade that passes through the hands of three Native nations before reaching the French.

[2] *Governor* Pierre Voyer D'Argenson (1625–1709), governor of New France from 1659 to 1661.

[3] Lake Michigan, where the Ottawa (Odawa) lived; they wore their hair in a brush turned up, and the French called them "cheveux relevés" ("standing hairs").

[4] *moitie* half.

[5] French law forbade the French from travelling to the interior without permission. De Groseilliers was duly arrested when the two returned.

[6] *the Sault* the Saulteur, a branch of the Ojibwa.

place defends us to go.[1] We told him that the offense was pardonable because it was everyone's interest nevertheless we knew what we were to do, and that he should not be blamed for us, we made gifts to the wildmen, that wished with all their hearts that we might go along with them. We told them that the Governor minded to send servants with them, and forbids us to go along with them. The wildmen would not accept of their company, but told us that they would stay for us two days in the Lake of St Peter in the grass some six leagues from the three rivers; but we did not let them stay so long, for that very night my brother having the keys of the borough as being captain of the place, we embarked ourselves.

We made ready in the morning, so that we went, three of us about midnight. Being come opposite to the fort: they ask who is there, my brother tells his name, everyone knows what good services we had done to the country, and loved us, the inhabitants as well as the soldiers. The sentry answers him God give you a good voyage. We went on the rest of that night. At six in the morning we arrived to the appointed place, but found no body. We were well armed, and had a good boat. We resolved to go day and night to the river of the Meddows to overtake them.[2] The wildmen did fear that it was somewhat else, but three leagues beyond that of the fort of Richlieu, we saw them coming to us. We put ourselves upon our guards thinking they were enemy; but were friends, and received us with joy, and said that if we had not come in three days time, they would have sent their boats to know the reason of our delay. There we are in that river waiting for the night. Being come to the river of the Meddows, we did separate ourselves, three into three boats; the man that we have taken with us was put into a boat of three men and a woman, but not of the same

nation as the rest, but of one that we call sorcerers. They were going down to see some friends that lived with the Nation of the Fire, that now liveth with the Ponoestigonce or the Sault.[3] It is to be understood that this river is divided much into streams very swift and small, before you go to the river of Canada;[4] [because] of the great game that there is in it, the enemy is to be feared, which made us go through these torrents. This could make anyone afraid, who is inexpert in such voyages....

FRENCH AND HURONS BATTLE AGAINST THE IROQUOIS

The day following we were set upon by a company of Iroquois that fortified themselves in the passage where they waited of Octauack,[5] for they knew of their going down. Our wildmen seeing that there was no way to avoid them resolved to be together, being the best way for them to make a quick expedition, for the season of the year pressed us to make expedition, we resolved to give a combat. We prepared ourselves with targets [shields], now the business was to make a discovery.[6] I doubt not but the enemy was much surprised to see us so in number. The council was held, and resolution taken; I and a wildman were appointed to go and see their fort, I offered myself with a free will, to let them see how willing I was to defend them: that is the only way to gain the hearts of those wildmen. We saw that their fort was environed with great rocks, that there was no way to mine it, because there were no trees near it. The mine was nothing else but to cut the nearest tree, and so by his fall make a bracke, and so go and give an assault.[7] Their

---

[1] *defends* French *défendre*; forbids.

[2] *river of the Meddows* Rivière des Prairies, the channel running between Montreal Island and Isle Jésus.

[3] *sorcerers* Nipissings; *the Nation of the Fire* Algonquian-speaking Mascouten; *Ponoestigonce* Pawitikong, "of the rapids."

[4] *river of Canada* the St. Lawrence.

[5] *waited of Octauack* waited for the Ottawas (Odawa).

[6] *make a discovery* French *se découvrir*; to reveal ourselves.

[7] *mine* French *mine*, meaning a plot or plan; *bracke* an obstacle, as in "windbreak."

fort was nothing but trees one against another in a round, or square without sides.

The enemy seeing us come near, shot at us but in vain, for we have forewarned ourselves before we came there. It was a pleasure to see our wildmen with their guns and arrows, which agreed not together, nevertheless we told them when they received a bracke their guns would be to no purpose, therefore to put them by, and make use of their bows and arrows. The Iroquois saw themselves put to it, and the evident danger that they were in, but too late except they would run away, yet our wildmen were better footmen than they. These were Frenchmen that should give them good directions to overthrow them, resolved to speak for peace,[1] and throw necklaces of porcelaine over the stakes of their fort.[2] Our wildmen were dazzled at such gifts, because that the porcelaine is very rare and costly in their country, and then seeing themselves flattered with fair words, to which they gave ear, we trust them by force to put their first design in execution, but feared their lives and loved the porcelaine, seeing they had it without danger of any life. They were persuaded to stay till the next day, because now it was almost night. The Iroquois makes their escape. This occasion lost, our consolation was that we had that passage free, but vexed for having lost that opportunity, and contrary wise were contented of our side, for doubtless some of us had been killed in the battle.

The day following we embarked ourselves quietly, being upon our guards for fear of any surprise, for that enemy's danger scarcely began, who with his furore made himself so redoubted [dreaded], having been there up and down to make a new slaughter. This morning passes in assurance enough; in the afternoon the two boats that had

orders to land some two hundred paces from the landing place. One took only a small bundle very light [and] tends to the other side of the carriage [portage] imagining there to make the kettle boil, having killed two stags two hours ago, and was scarce half way when he meets the Iroquois, without doubt for that same business. I think both were much surprised. The Iroquois had a bundle of castor that he left behind without much ado, our wildmen did the same they both run away to their partners to give them notice. By chance my brothers meets them in the way. The wildmen seeing that they all were frightened and out of breath they asked the matter and was told Nadouuée,[3] and so soon said, he lets fall his bundle that he had upon his back into a bush, and comes back where he finds all the wildmen despaired. He desired me to encourage them, which I performed with all earnestness, we runned to the height of the carriage. As we were agoing they took their arms with all speed; in the way we found the bundle of castors that the enemy had left. By this means we found out that they were in a fright as we, and that they came from the wars of the upper country, which we told the wildmen, so encouraged them to gain the water side to discover their forces, where we no sooner came but two boats were landed and charged their guns, either to defend themselves or to set upon us. We prevented this affair by our diligence and shot at them with our bows and arrows, as with our guns.

They finding such an assault, immediately forsook the place; they would have gone into their boats, but we gave them not so much time. They threw themselves into the river to gain the other side. This river was very narrow, so that it was very violent. We had killed and taken them all, if two boats of theirs had not come to their succour, which made us gave over to follow them, and look to ourselves, for we knew not the number of their

---

[1] That is, the French, who should have shown their allies how to defeat the Iroquois, preferred a peaceful solution.

[2] *porcelaine* made of conch or cowrie shells; a highly valued commodity.

[3] *Nadouuée* Natowe, meaning "great serpents" (i.e. enemies).

men. Three of their men nevertheless were killed; the rest is on the other side of the river where there was a fort which was made long before. There they retired themselves with all speed. We pass our boats to augment our victory,[1] seeing that they were many in number, they did what they could to hinder our passage, but all in vain, for we made use of the bundle of castors that they left, which were to us instead of gabbions,[2] for we put them at the heads of our boats, and by that means got ground in spite of their noses. They killed one of our men as we landed. Their number was not to resist ours; they retired themselves into the fort and brought the rest of their [men?] in hopes to save it. In this they were far mistaken, for we furiously gave an assault, not sparing time to make us bucklers, and made use of nothing else but of castors tied together. So without any more ado we gathered together. The Iroquois spared not their powder, but made more noise than hurt. The darkness covered the earth, which was somewhat favorable for us, but to overcome them the sooner, we filled a barrel full of gun powder, and having stopped the hole of it well and tied it to the end of a long pole, being at the foot of the fort. Here we lost three of our mens; our machine did play with an execution. I may well say that the enemy never had seen the like. Moreover I took three or four pounds of powder, this I put into a rind of a tree, then a fuse to have the time to throw the rind, warning the wildmen as soon as the rind made his execution that they should enter in and break the fort upside down, with the hatchet and the sword in their hands.

In the meantime the Iroquois did sing, expecting death, or to their heels, at the noise of such a smoke and noise that our machines made with the slaughter of many of them; seeing themselves so betrayed,

they let us go free into their fort, that thereby they might save themselves; but having environed the fort, we are mingled pell mell, so that we could not know one another in that skirmish of blows. There was such an noise that should terrify the stoutest men. Now there falls a shower of rain and a terrible storm, that to my thinking there was something extraordinary that the Devil himself made that storm to give those men leave to escape from our hands, to destroy another time more of these innocents. In that darkness everyone looked about for shelter, not thinking of those braves that laid down half dead. To pursue them, it was a thing impossible, yet do believe that the enemy was not far. As the storm was over, we came together, making a noise, and I am persuaded that many thought themselves prisoners that were at liberty. Some sang their fatal song albeit without any wounds,[3] so that those that had the confidence to come near the others were comforted by assuring them the victory and that the enemy was routed. We presently made a great fire, and with all haste make up the fort again for fear of any surprise. We searched for those that were missing. Those that were dead and wounded were visited. We found eleven of our enemy slain and two only of ours, besides seven were wounded, who in a short time passed all danger of life. While some were busy in tying five of the enemy that could not escape, the others visited the wounds of their companions, who for to show their courage sung louder than those that were well. The sleep that we took that night did not make our heads giddy, although we had need of reposing. Many liked the occupation, for they filled their bellies with the flesh of their enemies, we broiled some of it and kettles full of the rest.[4] We burned our comrades, being their custom to reduce such

---

[1] *pass our boats* press on in our boats.

[2] *gabbions* wicker cylinders, filled with earth and used to build fortifications (*OED* gabion 1).

[3] *fatal song* death song.

[4] Radisson implies that he participated in the ritual cannibalism; his casualness in this passage may have been deliberate, to shock readers in Europe.

into ashes, being slain in battle. It is an honour to give them such a burial.

At the break of day we cooked what could accommodate us, and flung the rest away. The greatest mark of our victory was that we had ten heads and four prisoners, whom we embarked in hopes to bring them into our country, and there to burn them at our own leisures for the more satisfaction of our wives. We left that place of massacre with horrid cries. Forgetting the death of our parents, we plagued those unfortunates. We plucked out their nails one after another....

THE ARRIVAL AT LAKE SUPERIOR

Afterwards we entered into a strait which had ten leagues in length full of islands where we wanted not fish. We came after to a rapid, that makes the separation of the lake of the Hurons, that we call Superior or Upper, for that the wildmen hold it to be longer and broader besides a great many islands, which makes appear in a bigger extent. This rapid was formerly the dwelling of those with whom we were, and consequently we must not ask them if they knew where the hare laid.[1] We made cottages at our advantages, and found the truth of what those men had often said, that if once we could come to that place, we should make good cheer of a fish that they call *assickmack* which signifieth a white fish. The bear, the castors, and the *oriniack* [moose] showed themselves often but to their loss. Indeed it was to us like a terrestrial paradise after so long fasting, after so great pains that we had taken, to find ourselves so well, by choosing our diet, and resting when we had a mind to it. Tis here that we must taste with pleasure a sweet bit, we do not ask for a good swace [sauce]; it's better to have it natu-

rally it is the way to distinguish the sweet from the bitter.

But the season was far spent, and we use diligence and leave that place so wished, which we shall bewail to the cursed Iroquois; What hath that poor nation done to thee and being so far from thy country? Yet if they had the same liberty that in former days they have had, we poor French should not go further with our heads, except we had a strong army, those great lakes had not so soon come to our knowledge if it had not been for those brutish people; two men had not found out the truth of these seas so cheap; the interest and the glory could not do what terror doth at the end. We are a little better come to ourselves and furnished; we left that inn without reckoning with our host. It is cheap when we are not to put the hand to the purse, nevertheless we must pay out of civility: the one gives thanks to the woods, the other to the river, the third to the earth, the other to the rocks that stays the fish, in a word, there is nothing but *kinekoiur* of all sorts;[2] the incense of our incense is not spared. The weather was agreeable when we began to navigate upon that great extent of water. Finding it so calm and the air so clear we thwarted in a pretty broad place,[3] came to an isle most delightful for the diversity of its fruits; we called it the isle of the four beggars. We arrived about five of the clock in the afternoon that we came there, we suddenly put the kettle to the fire, we reside there a while, and seeing all this while the fair weather and calm, we went from thence at ten of the clock the same night to gain the firm land, which was six leagues from us, where we arrived before day. Here we found a small river, I was so curious that I inquired my dearest friends the name of that stream, they named me it *pauabickkomesibs*, which signifieth a small river of copper. I asked him the

---

[1] His companions were the Saulteur, who had fled west in the early 1650s as a result of the Huron-Iroquois wars. "Where the hare laid" was a proverbial expression meaning "where the secret is"; Radisson appears unwilling to ask the Saulteur for information about their former territory.

[2] *kinekoiur* meaning unknown; possibly a scribal misreading.

[3] *thwarted* crossed over (*OED* thwart 1).

reason, he told me, Come, and I shall show thee the reason why. I was in a place which was not two hundred paces in the wood, where many pieces of copper were uncovered, further he told me that the mountain I saw was of nothing else. Seeing it so fair and pure, I had a mind to take a piece of it, but they hindered me, telling my brother, there was more where we were to go....

From this place we went along the coasts, which are most delightful, and wondrous for its nature that made it so pleasant to the eye, the spirit, and the belly. As we went along we saw banks of sand so high, that one of our wildmen went up for our curiosity, being there, did show no more than a crow. That place is most dangerous when that there is any storm, being no landing place so long as the sandy banks are under water, and when the wind blows, that sand doth rise by a strange kind of whirling that are able to choke the passengers [travellers], one day you will see fifty small mountains at one side, and the next day, if the wind changes, on the other side. This puts me in mind of the great and vast wildernesses of Turkey land, as the Turks makes their pilgrimages....[1]

After this we came to a remarkable place. It's a bank of rocks that the wildmen made a sacrifice to, they call it *Nauitoucksinagoit* which signifies the likeness of the Devil, they fling much tobacco and other things in its veneration. It is a thing most incredible that that lake should be so boisterous, that the waves of it should have the strength to do what I have to say by this my discourse, first that it's so high and so deep that it's impossible to claim up to the point. There comes many sort of birds that makes their nest here, the *goilants* which is a white sea bird, of the bigness of pigeon, which makes me believe what the wildmen told me concerning the sea to be near directly to the point; it's like a great portal, by reason of the beating of the

waves, the lower part of that opening is as big as a tower, and grows bigger; in the going up there is I believe six acres of land; above it a ship of five hundred tons could pass by so big is the arch. I gave it the name of the portal of St. Peter, because my name is so called, and that I was the first Christian that ever saw it. There is in that place caves very deep, caused by the same violence. We must look to ourselves, and take time with our small boats, the coast of rocks is five or six leagues and there scarce a place to put a boat in assurance from the waves. When the lake is agitated the waves goeth in these concavities with force, and make a most horrible noise, most like the shooting of great guns. Some days afterwards we arrived to a very beautiful point of sand, where there are three beautiful islands, that we called of the Trinity, there be three in triangle. From this place we discovered a bay very deep, where a river empties itself with a noise for the quantity and depth of the water. We must stay there three days to wait for fair weather to make the carriage which was about six leagues wide, so done, we came to the mouth of a small river, where we killed some *oriniacks*. We found meadows that were squared, and ten leagues as smooth as a board; we went up some five leagues further, where we found some pools made by the castors, we must break them that we might pass. The sluice being broken what a wonderful thing to see the industry of that animal, which had drowned more than twenty leagues in the grounds, and cut all the trees, having left none to make a fire if the country should be dried up. Being come to the height, we must drag our boats over a trembling ground for the space of an hour. The ground became trembling by this means, the castor drowning great soils with dead water, herein grows moss which is two foot thick or thereabouts, and when you think to go safe and dry, if you take not great care you sink down to your head or to the middle of your body, when you are out of one hole you find yourself in another. This I

---

[1] Radisson is most likely referring to his memories of reading travel books rather than to personal experience of travelling in Turkey.

speak by experience for I myself have been catched often. But the wildmen warned me which saved me, that is that when the moss should break under me I should cast my whole body into the water on sudden. I must with my hands hold the moss, and go so like a frog, then to draw my boat after me there was no danger.…

The fort on Chequamegon Bay

…we went on half a day before we could come to the landing place, and were forced to make another carriage a point of two leagues long and some sixty paces broad. As we came to the other side we were in a bay of ten leagues about, if we had gone in. By going about that same point we passed a strait, for that point was very nigh the other side, which is a cape very much elevated like pyramids. That point should be very fit to build and advantageous for the building of a fort, as we did the spring following. In that bay there is a channel where we take great store of fishes, sturgeons of a vast bigness, and pikes of seven foot long. At the end of this bay we landed. The wildmen gave thanks to that which they worship, we to God of Gods to see ourselves in a place where we must leave our navigation and forsake our boats to undertake a harder piece of work in hand, to which we are forced. The men told us that we had five great days' journeys before we should arrive where their wives were. We foresee the hard task that we were to undergo by carrying our bundles upon our backs. They were used to it. Here everyone for himself and God for all.

We finding ourselves not able to perform such a task, and they could not well tell where to find their wives, fearing least the Nadoueceronons had wars against their nation and forced them from their appointed place, my brother and I we consulted what was best to do, and declared our will to them, which was thus: Brethren, we resolve to stay here, being not accustomed to make any carriage on our backs as ye are wont. Go ye and look for your wives; we will build us a fort here. And seeing that you are not able to carry all your merchandise at once, we will keep them for you, and will stay for you fourteen days. Before the time expired you will send to us if your wives be alive, and if you find them they will fetch what you leave here and what we have. For their pains they shall receive gifts of us. So you will see us in your country. If they be dead, we will spend all, to be revenged, and will gather up the whole country for the next spring, for that purpose to destroy those that were the causers of their death, and you shall see our strength and valour. Although there are seven thousand fighting men in one village, you'll see we will make them run away, and you shall kill them to your best liking by the very noise of our arms and our presence, who are the Gods of the earth among those people.

They wondered very much at our resolution. The next day they went their way and we stay, for our assurance in the midst of many nations, being but two almost starved for want of food. We went about to make a fort of stakes, which was in this manner. Suppose that the water side had been in one end; at the same end there should be murderers, and at need we made a bastion in a triangle to defend us from an assault. The door was near the water side, our fire was in the middle, and our bed on the right hand covered. There were boughs of trees all about our fort laid across, one upon another. Besides these boughs we had a long cord tied with some small bells, which were sentries, finally, we made an end of that fort in two days time.…

The 12th day we perceived a far off some fifty young men coming towards us, with some of our former companions. We gave them leave to come into our fort, but they are astonied calling us every foot devils to have made such a machine. They brought us victuals, thinking we were half starved, but were mightily mistaken, for we had more for them than they were able to eat, having three score bustards and many sticks where was meat hanged plentifully. They offered to carry our baggage being come a purpose, but we had not so much merchandise as when they went from us, because we hid some of them that they might not have suspicion of us. We told them that for fear of the daily multitude of people that came to see us for to have our goods would kill us. We therefore took a boat and put into it our merchandises, this we brought far into the bay, where we sunk them, bidding our devil not to let them to be wet nor rusted, nor suffer them to be taken away, which he promised faithless that we should return and take them out of his hands; at which they were astonished, believing it to be true as the Christians the Gospel.[1] We hid them in the ground on the other side of the river in a piece of ground. We told them that lie, that they should not have suspicion of us. We made good cheer. They stayed there three days, during which time many of their wives came thither, and we treated them well, for they eat not fowl at all scarce because they know not how to catch them except with their arrows. We put a great many rind about our fort, and broke all the boats that we could have, for the frost would have broken them or wildmen had stolen them away. That rind was tied all in length to put the fire in it, to frighten the more these people for they could not approach it without being discovered. If they ventured at the going out we put the fire to all the torches, showing them how we would have defended ourselves. We were Caesars, being nobody to contradict us, we went away free from any burden, whilst those poor miserables thought themselves happy to carry our equipage, for the hope that they had that we should give them a brass ring, or an awl or an needle.

A CEREMONIAL MEETING WITH THE NATIVES

There came above four hundred persons to see us go away from that place, which admired more our actions [than] the fools of Paris to see enter their King and the infanta of Spain, his spouse, for they cry out, God save the King and Queen.[2] Those made horrid noise, and called Gods and Devils of the earth and heavens. We marched four days through the woods. The country is beautiful, with very few mountains, the woods clear. At last we came within a league of the cabins where we laid that the next day might be for our entry. We two poor adventurers for the honour of our country, or of those that shall deserve it from that day. The nimblest and stoutest went before to warn before the people that we should make our entry tomorrow. Everyone prepares to see what they never before have seen. We were in cottages which were near a little lake some eight leagues in circuit. At the water side there were abundance of little boats made of trees that they have hollowed, and of rind.

The next day we were to embark in them, and arrived at the village by water, which was composed of a hundred cabins without pallasados.[3] There is nothing but cries, the women throw themselves backwards upon the ground thinking to give us tokens of friendship and of welcome. We destinated three presents, one for the men one for the women, and the other for the children, to the end that they should remember that journey, that we should be spoken of a hundred years after, if other Europeans should not come in those quarters and be liberal to them, which will hardly come to pass. The first present was a kettle, two hatchets, and six knives and a blade for a sword, the kettles was to call all nations that were their friends to a feast which is

---

[1] *our devil* Radisson and Des Groseilliers pretend they have a spirit under their control who guards their possessions.

[2] The royal entry of Louis XIV and his bride, Maria Theresa of Spain, took place in Paris in 1660; Radisson could only have heard about the procession second-hand.

[3] *pallasados* palisades; surrounding fences.

made for the remembrance of the death. That is, they make it once in seven years; it's a renewing of friendship.[1] I will talk further of it in the following discourse. The hatchets were to encourage the young people to strengthen themselves in all places, to preserve their wives, and show themselves men by knocking the heads of their enemies with the said hatchets, the knives were to show that the French were great and mighty and their confederates and friends. The sword was to signify that we would be masters both of peace and wars, being willing to help and relieve them, and to destroy our enemies with our arms. The second gift was of two and twenty awls, fifty needles, two graters of castors,[2] two ivory combs and two wooden ones, with red paint, six looking glasses of tin. The awls signifieth to take good courage, that we should keep their lives, and that they with their husbands should come down to the French when time and season should permit, the needles for to make them robes of castor, because the French loved them. The two graters were to dress the skins; the combs, the paint, to make themselves beautiful; the looking-glasses to admire themselves. The third gift was of brass rings, of small bells, and rasades of divers colours,[3] and given in this manner. We sent a man to make all the children come together. When we were there we throw these things over their heads. You would admire what a beat was among them, everyone striving to have the best. This was done upon this consideration that they should be always under our protection, giving them wherewithal to make them merry and remember us when they should be men.

This done, we are called to the council of welcome and to the feast of friendship, afterwards to the dancing of the heads. But before the dancing, we must mourn for the deceased, and then, for to forget all sorrow to the dance. We gave them four small gifts that they should continue such ceremonies, which they took willingly, and did us good, that gave us authority among the whole nation. We knew their councils, and made them do whatsoever we thought best. This was a great advantage for us, you must think. Amongst such a rawish kind of people a gift is much, and well bestowed, and liberality much esteemed, but prodigality is not in esteem, for they abuse it being brutish. We have been using such ceremonies three whole days, and were lodged in the cabin of the chiefest captains who came with us from the French. We liked not the company of that blind, therefore left him; he wondered at this, but durst not speak because we were demigods. We came to a cottage of an ancient witty man, that had had a great family and many children, his wife old nevertheless handsome. They were of a nation called Malhonmines, that is, the nation of oats, grain that is much in that country. I took this man for my father and the woman for my mother, so the children consequently brothers and sisters; They adopted me. I gave everyone a gift, and they to me.

FAMINE IN THE FOREST (WINTER 1659–60)

Having so disposed of our business: The winter comes on, that warns us the snow begins to fall, so we must retire from this place to seek our living in the woods. Everyone gets his equipage ready, so away we go, but not all to the same place. Two, three at the most, went one way, and so of another. They have so done because victuals were scant for all in a place but let us where we will, we cannot escape the mighty hand of God that disposes as he pleases, and who chastens us as a good and a common loving father and not as our sins do deserve. Finally we depart one from another. As many as we were in number, we are reduced to a small company. We appointed a rendezvous after two months

---

[1]   the Feast of the Dead; he provides an account below.

[2]   *graters*   scrapers for dressing beaver ("castor") skins (*OED* grater 2).

[3]   *rasades*   glass beads (French).

and a half, to take a new road, and an advice what we should do. During the said term we sent messengers everywhere to give special notice to all manner of persons and nation that within five moons the feast of death was to be celebrated, and that we should appear together, and explain what the devil should command us to say, and then present them presents of peace and union; now we must live on what God sends, and war against the bears in the meantime, for we could aim at nothing else, which was the cause that we had no great cheer....

...so the famine was among great many that had not provided before hand, and live upon what they get that day, never thinking for the next. It grows worse and worse daily.

To augment our misery we receive news of the Octauaks, who were about a hundred and fifty with their families. They had a quarrel with the Hurons in the isle where we had come from some years before in the Lake of the stairing hairs,[1] and came purposely to make wars against them the next summer. But let us see if they brought us anything to subsist withal. But are worst provided than we; having no huntsmen, they are reduced to famine. But, O cursed covetousness, what art thou going to do. It should be far better to see a company of rogues perish than see ourselves in danger to perish, by that scourge so cruel. Hearing that they have had knives and hatchets the victuals of their poor children is taken away from them yea what ever they have those dogs must have their share. They are the cursedest, unablest the unfamous and cowardliest people that I have seen amongst four score nations that I have frequented. O ye poor people, you shall have their booty, but you shall pay dearly for it. Everyone cries out for hunger; the women become barren, and dry like wood. You men must eat the cord, being you have no more strength to make use

of the bow, children, you must die. French, you called yourselves Gods of the earth that you should be feared, for your interest; notwithstanding you shall taste of the bitterness, and too happy if you escape. Where is the time past? Where is the plentiness that ye had in all places and countries? Here comes a new family of these poor people daily to us, half dead for they have but the skin and bones. How shall we have strength to make a hole in the snow to lay us down seeing we have it not to hale our rackets [snowshoes] after us nor to cut a little wood to make a fire to keep us from the rigour of the cold which is extreme in those countries in its season. Oh! if the music that we hear could give us recreation. We wanted not any lamentable music nor sad spectacle. In the morning the husband looks upon his wife, the brother his sister, the cousin the cousin, the uncle the nephew that were for the most part found dead. They languish with cries and hideous noise that it was able to make the hair stare on the heads that have any apprehension. Good God have mercy on so many poor innocent people, and of us that acknowledge thee, that having offended thee punishes us. But we are not free of that cruel executioner. Those that have any life seeketh out for roots which could not be done without great difficulty, the earth being frozen two or three foot deep and the snow five or six above it. The greatest subsistence that we can have is of rind tree which grows like ivy about the trees,[2] but to swallow it, we cut the stick some two foot long, tying it in faggot [bundles] and boil it, and when it boils one hour or two the rind or skin comes off with ease, which we take and dry it in the smoke and then reduce it into powder betwixt two grainstones, and putting the kettle with the same water upon the fire, we make it a kind of broth, which nourished us, but became thirstier and drier than the wood we eat.

---

[1] *the isle* Rock Island, at the entrance of Green Bay in Lake Michigan, which Des Groseilliers had visited in 1654.

[2] *rind tree* possibly wild grape.

The two first weeks we did eat our dogs. As we went back upon our steps for to get anything to fill our bellies, we were glad to get the bones and carcasses of the beasts that we killed; and happy was he, that could get what the other did throw away after it had been boiled three or four times to get the substance out of it. We contrived to another plot, to reduce to powder those bones, the rest of crows and dogs. So put all that together half foot within ground, and so makes a fire upon it. We covered all that very well with earth, so feeling the heat, and boiled them again and gave more froth than before. In the next place, the skins that were reserved to make us shoes, cloth, and stockings, yea, most of the skins of our cottages, the castors' skins, where the children beshit them above a hundred times, we burned the hair on the coals. The rest goes down throats eating heartily these things most abhorred. We went so eagerly to it that our gums did bleed like one newly wounded. The wood was our food the rest of sorrowful time. Finally we became the very images of death. We mistook ourselves very often taking the living for the dead and the dead for the living. We wanted strength to draw the living out of the cabins, or if we did when we could, it was to put them four paces in the snow. At the end the wrath of God begins to appease itself, and pities his poor creatures. If I should express all that befell us in that strange accidents, a great volume would not contain it. Here are above five hundred dead, men, women, and children. It's time to come out of such miseries. Our bodies are not able to hold out any further.

After the storm, calm comes. But storms favoured us, being that calm kills us. Here comes a wind and rain, that puts a new life in us, the snow falls, the forest clears itself, at which sight, those that had strings left in their bows take courage to use it. The weather continued so three days that we needed no rackets more, for the snow hardened much. The small stags are as if they were stakes in it after they made seven or eight capers.[1] It's an easy matter for us to take them and cut their throats with our knives. Now we see ourselves a little furnished, but yet have not paid, for it cost many their lives. Our guts became very straight by our long fasting, that they could not contain the quantity that some put in them. I cannot omit the pleasant thoughts of some of them wildmen. Seeing my brother always in the same condition, they said that some devil brought him wherewithal to eat, but if they had seen his body they should be of another opinion. The beard that covered his face made as if he had not altered his face. For me that had no beard they said I loved them, because I lived as well as they. From the second day we began to walk.

There came two men from a strange country who had a dog, the business was how to catch him cunningly, knowing well those people love their beasts. Nevertheless we offered gifts: but they would not, which made me stubborn. That dog was very lean, and as hungry as we were, but the masters have not suffered so much. I went one night near that same cottage to do what discretion permits me not to speak. Those men were Nadoueserous. They were much respected that nobody durst not offend them: being that we were upon their land with their leave. The dog comes out, not by any smell, but by good likes. I take him and bring him a little way. I stabbed him with my dagger. I brought him to the cottage, where he was broiled like a pig and cut in pieces guts and all, so everyone of the family had his share. The snow where he was killed was not lost, for one of our company, went and got it to season the kettle. We began to look better daily. We gave the rendezvous to the convenientest place to celebrate that great feast....

---

[1] *as if they were stakes* as if they were stuck fast in the snow.

THE FEAST OF THE DEAD

The time was nigh that we must go to the rendezvous. This was betwixt a small lake and a meadow. Being arrived most of ours were already in their cottages. In three days time, there arrived eighteen several nations, and came privately to have done the sooner. As we became to the number of five hundred we held a council; then the shouts and cries and the encouragements were proclaimed, that a fort should be builded. They went about the work and made a large fort; it was about six hundred and three score paces in length and six hundred in breadth: so that it was a square. There we had a brook that came from the lake and emptied itself in those meadows which had more than four leagues in length. Our fort might be seen afar off, and on that side most delightful: for the great many stags that took the boldness to be carried by quarters where at other times they made good cheer.[1]

In two days this was finished. Soon thirty young men of the nation of the beef arrived there, having nothing but bows and arrows, with very short garments, to be the nimbler in chasing the stags. The iron of their arrows were made of stag's pointed horns very neatly. They were all proper men, and dressed with paint. They were the discoverers and the foreguard. We kept a round place in the middle of our cabin, and covered it with long poles with skins over them that we might have a shelter to keep us from the snow. The cottages were all in good order in each ten, twelve companies or families. That company was brought to that place where there was wood laid for the fires. The snow was taken away, and the earth covered with deal tree boughs.[2] Several kettles were brought there full of meat. They rested and eat above five hours without speaking one to another. The considerablest of our companies went and made speeches to them. After one takes his bow and shoots an arrow, and then cries aloud, there speaks some few words, saying that they were to let them know the elders of their village were to come the morrow to renew the friendship and to make it with the French. And that a great many of their young people came and brought them some part of their ways to take their advice for they had a mind to go against the Christinos who were ready for them:[3] and they in like manner to save their wives and children. They were scattered in many cabins that night expecting those that were to come. To that purpose there was a vast large place prepared some hundred paces from the fort, where every thing was ready for the receiving of those persons. They were to set their tents that they bring upon their backs. The perches [poles or stakes] were put out and planted as we received the news. The snow put aside, and the boughs of trees covered the ground.

The day following they arrived with an incredible pomp. This made me think of the entrance that the Polanders did in Paris:[4] saving that they had not so many jewels, but instead of them they had so many feathers. The first were young people with their bows and arrows and buckler on their shoulders, upon which were represented all manner of figures: according to their knowledge, as of the sun and moon, of terrestrial beasts, about its feathers very artificially [artfully] painted. Most of the men their faces were all over dabbed with several colours. Their hair turned up, like a crown: and were cut very even, but rather so burned for the fire is their scissors. They leave a tuft of hair upon their crown of their heads, tie it, and put at the end of it some small pearls or some turkey stones to bind their

---

[1] that is, the stags were butchered and carried in pieces to a meal held at a place where the travellers had previously eaten.

[2] *deal tree* pine or fir.

[3] *Christinos* the Nahathaway, whom the French called the Cristinaux, hence "Cree." They are the "wandering nation" mentioned below.

[4] In 1573 Prince Albertus Laski came to France with a delegation of Polish ambassadors to offer the throne of Poland to Henri III.

heads.[1] They have a roll commonly made of a snake's skin where they tie several bear's paws, or give a form to some bits of buff's [buffalo] horns, and put it about the said roll. They grease themselves with very thick grease and mingle it in reddish earth, which they burn, as we our breeks:[2] With this stuff they get their hair to stand up. They cut some down of swan or other fowl that hath a white feather and cover with it the crown of their heads. Their ears are pierced in five places. The holes are so big that your little finger might pass through. They have yellow ware that they made with copper, made like a star or a half moon, and there hang it. Many have turkeys. They are clothed with *oriniack* and stag's skins, but very light. Every one had the skin of a crow hanging at their girdles. Their stockings all embroidered with pearls and with their own porkepick work.[3] They have very handsome shoes laced very thick all over with a piece sewn at the side of the heel, which was of a hair of buff, which trailed above half a foot upon the earth, or rather on the snow. They had swords and knives of a foot and a half long, and hatchets very ingeniously done, and clubs of wood made like backswords, some made of a round head that I admired it. When they kill their enemy they cut off the tuft of hair and tie it about their arms. After [over] all, they have a white robe made of castors' skins painted. Those having passed through the middle of ours that were ranged at every side of the way. The elders came with great gravity and modesty covered with buff coats which hung down to the ground. Everyone had in his hand a pipe of council set with precious jewels. They had a sack on their shoulders, and that that holds it grows in the middle of their stomachs, and on their shoulders. In

this sack all the world is enclosed.[4] Their face is not painted, but their heads dressed as the foremost. Then the women laden like unto so many mules, their burdens made a greater show than they themselves, but I suppose the weight was not equivalent to its bigness. They were conducted to the appointed place, where the women unfolded their bundles, and flang their skins whereof their tents are made, so that they had houses in less than half an hour.

After they rested, they came to the biggest cabin constituted for that purpose. There were fires kindled. Our captain made a speech of thanksgiving, which should be long to writ it. We are called to the council of new come Chiefs: where we came in great pomp, as you shall hear. First they come to make a sacrifice to the French, being Gods and masters of all things as of peace as wars, making the knives the hatchets, and the kettles rattle, etc. That they came purposely to put themselves under their protection: moreover, that they came to bring them back again to their country, having by their means destroyed their enemies abroad and near. So said, they present us with gifts of castors' skins, assuring us that the mountains were elevated, the valleys risen, the ways very smooth, the boughs of trees cut down to go with more ease, and bridges erected over rivers, for not to wet our feet. That the doors of their villages, cottages of their wives and daughters, were upon at any time to receive us, being we kept them alive by our merchandises. The second gift was, that they should die in their alliance, and that to certify to all nations by continuing the peace, and were willing to receive and assist them in their country, being well satisfied they were come to celebrate the feast of the dead. The third gift was for to have one of the doors of the fort

---

[1] *turkey stones* native turquoise.

[2] *breeks* breeches, greased so they would shed water (*OED* breek 1).

[3] *porkepick* porcupine quill embroidery.

[4] *sack* a medicine bag, containing totems and other objects sacred to the wearer.

opened, if need required, to receive and keep them from the Christinos that come to destroy them. Being always men, and the heavens made them so, that they were obliged to go before to defend their country and their wives, which is the dearest thing they had in the world, and in all times they were esteemed stout and true soldiers, and that yet they would make it appear, by going to meet them, and that they would not degenerate, but show by their actions that they were as valiant as their forefathers. The fourth gift was presented to us, which was of buff skins, to desire our assistance, for being the masters of their lives, and could dispose of them as we would, as well of the peace as of the wars, and that we might very well see that they did well to go defend their own country that the true means to get the victory was to have a thunder. They meant a gun, calling it *miniskoick*.

The speech being finished, they entreated us to be at the feast. We go presently back again to furnish us with wooden bowls. We made four men to carry our guns afore us, that we charged of powder alone, because of their unskillfulness that they might have killed their fathers. We each of us had a pair of pistols and sword, a dagger; we had a roll of porkepick about our heads, which was as a crown, and two little boys that carried the vessels that we had most need of: this was our dishes and our spoons. They made a place higher and most elevate knowing our customs, in the middle for us to sit where we had the men lay our arms. Presently comes four elders, with the calumet kindled in their hands; they present the candles to us to smoke, and four beautiful maids that went before us carrying bears' skins to put under us. When we were together, an old man rises and throws our calumet at our feet, and bids them, take of the kettles from of the fire, and spoke, that he thanked the sun, that never was a day to him so happy as when he saw those terrible men, whose words made the earth quake, and sang a while, having ended, came and

covers us with his vestment and all naked except his feet and legs, he saith, ye are masters over us dead or alive you have the power over us: and may dispose of us as your pleasure. So done, takes the calumet of the feast, and brings it; so a maiden brings us a coal of fire to kindle it. So done, we rose and [one? some?] of us begins to sing: we had the interpreter to tell them we should save and keep their lives, taking them for our brethren, and to testify that, we shot of all our artillery which was of twelve guns. We draw our swords and long knives to our defence if need should require, which put the men in such a terror that they knew not what was best to run or stay. We throw a handful of powder in the fire to make a greater noise, and smoke.

Our songs being finished, we begin our teeth to work. We had there a kind of rice, much like oats.[1] It grows in the water in three or four foot deep. There is a God that shows himself in every country almighty full of goodness and the preservation of those poor people who knoweth him not. They have a particular way to gather up that grain. Two takes a boat and two sticks, by which they get the ear down and get the corn out of it. Their boat being full, they bring it to a fit place to dry it, and that is their food for the most part of the winter, and do dress it thus. For each man a handful of that they put in the pot. That swells so much that it can suffice a man. After the feast was over, there comes two maidens bringing wherewithal to smoke the one the pipes, the other the fire. They offered first to one of the elders, that sat down by us. When he had smoked, he bids them give it us. This being done, we went back to our fort as we came.

The day following, we made the principal persons come together to answer to their gifts. Being come with great solemnity there we made our interpreter tell them, that we were come from the other side of the great salted lake, not to kill them

---

[1] *a kind of rice* wild rice.

700

but to make you live, acknowledging you for our brethren and children whom we will love henceforth as our own. Then we gave them a kettle. The second gift, was to encourage them in all their undertakings, telling them that we liked men that generously defended themselves against all their enemies, and as we were masters of peace and wars we are to dispose the affairs. That we would see an universal peace all over the earth and that this time we could not go and force the nations that were yet further to condescend and submit to our will, but that we would see the neighbouring countries in peace and union. That the Christinos were our brethren, and have frequented them many winters; that we adopted them for our children and took them under our protection; that we should send them ambassadors, that I myself should make them come, and conclude a general peace; that we were sure of their obedience to us; that the first that should break the peace, we would be their enemies, and would reduce them to powder with our heavenly fire. That we had the word of the Christinos as well as theirs, and our thunders should serve us to make wars against those that would not submit to our will and desire, which was to see them good friends to go and make wars against the upper nations, that doth not know us as yet. The gift was of six hatchets. The third was to oblige them to receive our propositions, likewise the Christinos to lead them to the dance of union which was to be celebrated at the death's feast, and banquet of kindred. If they would continue the wars, that was not the means to see us again in their country. The fourth was that we thanked them, for making us a free passage through their countries. The gift was of two dozen of knives; the last was of smaller trifles, six graters, two dozen of awls, two dozen of needles, six dozen of looking-glasses made of tin, a dozen of little bells, six ivory combs with a little vermilion. But for to make a recompense to the good old man that spake so favourably we gave him a hatchet and

to the elders each a blade for a sword, and to the two maidens that served us two necklaces, which put about their necks, and two bracelets for their arms. The last gift was in general for all the women to love us, and give us to eat when we should come to their cottages. The company gave us great *hohoho* that is thanks. Our wildmen made others for their interest.[1]

A company of about fifty were dispatched to warn the Christinos of what we have done: I went myself where we arrived the third day early in the morning. I was received with great demonstration of friendship; all that day we feasted danced and sing. I compared that place before to the Buttery of Paris,[2] for the great quantity of meat that they use to have there, but now will compare it to that of London. There I received gifts of all sorts of meat, of grease more than twenty men could carry. The custom is not to deface anything that they present.[3] There were above six hundred men in a fort with a great deal of baggage on their shoulders, and did draw it upon light sleds made very neatly. I have not seen them at their entrance for the snow blinded me. Coming back, we passed a lake hardly frozen [frozen hard], and the sun [shone upon it?] for the most part, for I looked a while steadfastly on it so I was troubled with this seven or eight days.

The meanwhile that we are there, arrived above a thousand, that had not been therein but for those two redoubted nations that were to see them do what they never before had, a difference:[4] which was executed with a great deal of mirth. I for fear of being envied I will admit, only that there were plays mirths, and bataills for sport, going and coming with cries, each played his part. In the public place

---

[1] perhaps meaning that the natives accompanying the travellers gave their own gifts.

[2] *Buttery of Paris* possibly *boucherie*, stockyards.

[3] *deface* discredit (French).

[4] *a difference* an arranged contest between two parties.

the women danced with melody. The young men that endeavoured to get a prize, endeavoured to climb up a great post very smooth and greased with oil of bear and *oriniack* grease. The stake was at least of fifteen foot high. The prize was a knife or other thing. We laid the stake there, but whoso could catch it should have it. The feast was made to eat all up. To honour the feast many men and women did burst. Those of that place coming back, came in sight of those of the village or fort made postures in similitude of wars. This was to discover the enemy by signs any that should do so we gave orders to take him or kill him and take his head off; the prisoner to be tied, to fight in retreating; to pull an arrow out of the body. To exercise and strike with a club, a buckler to their feet, and take it if need requireth, and defend himself if need requires from the enemy. Being in sentry to hark the enemy that comes near and to hear the better lay him down on the side. These postures are played while the drum beat. This was a serious thing, without speaking, except by nodding or gestures. Their drums were earthen pots full of water, covered with stag's skin. The sticks like hammers for the purpose. The elders have bomkins to the end of the staves, full of small stones, which makes a rattle, to which young men and women go in a cadence. The elders are about these pots beating them and singing. The women also by having a nosegay in their hands, and dance very modestly, not lifting much their feet from the ground, keeping their heads downwards making a sweet harmony. We made gifts for that while fourteen days' time. Everyone brings the most exquisite things to show what his country affords. The renewing of their alliances, the marriages according to their country customs are made; also the visit of the bones of their deceased friends for they keep them and bestow them upon one another. We sang in our language as they in theirs, to which they gave great attention. We gave them several gifts, and received many. They bestowed upon us

above 3 hundred robes of castors out of which we brought not five to the French being too far in the country. This feast ended, everyone returns to his country well satisfied....

RADISSON ALLEGES THAT HE HAS VISITED HUDSON BAY[1]

We went from isle to isle all that summer. We plucked abundance of ducks as of all other sort of fowls; we wanted nor fish nor fresh meat. We were well beloved, and were overjoyed that we promised them to come with such ships as we invented. This place hath a great store of cows [caribou]. The wildmen kill them not except for necessary use. We went further in the bay to see the place that they were to pass that summer. That river comes from the lake and empties itself in the River of Sagnes, called Tadousack, which is a hundred leagues in the great river of Canada, as where we were in the Bay of the North. We left in this place our marks and rendezvous. The wildmen that brought us defended us above all things, if we would come directly to them that we should be no means land, and to go to the river to the other side that is to the north towards the sea, telling us that those people were very treacherous. Now whether they told us this out of policy, lest we should not come to them first, and so be deprived of what they thought to get from us I know not. In that you may see that the envy and envy reigns everywhere amongst poor barbarous wild people as at courts. They made us a map of what we could not see, because the time was nigh to reap among the bustards and ducks....

This is a wandering nation, and containeth a vast country. In winter they live in the land for the hunting sake, and in summer by the water for

---

[1] Most scholars think that Radisson and Des Groseilliers did not have the time to make this journey, which involved crossing Lake Superior, making their way to the Albany river and following it to James Bay. He is likely retailing second-hand information.

fishing. They never are many together, for fear of wronging one another. They are of a good nature, and not great whore masters, having but one wife, and are more satisfied than any others that I knew. They clothe themselves all over with castors' skins in winter, in summer of stags' skins. They are the best huntsmen of all America, and scorns to catch a castor in a trap. The circumjacent nations go all naked, when the season permits it. But this have more modesty, for they put a piece of copper made like a finger of a glove, which they use before their nature. They have the same tenets as the nation of the beef, and their apparel from top to toe. The women are tender and delicate, and takes as much pains as slaves. They are of more acute wits than the men for the men are fools, but diligent about their work. They kill not the young castors, but leave them in the water, being that they are sure that they will take him again, which no other nation doth. They burn not their prisoners, but knock them in the head, or slay them with arrows, saying it's not decent for men to be so cruel. They have a stone of turquoise from the nation of the buff and beef, with whom they had wars. They polish them and give them the form of pearl long flat round, and hang them at their nose. They find green stones, very fine, at the side of the same bay of the sea to the northwest. There is a nation called among themselves neuter, they speak the beef and Christinos' speech, being friends to both. Those poor people could not tell what to give us, they were overjoyed when we said, we should bring them commodities. We went up on another river, to the upper lake....

...All the circumjacent neighbours do encourage us, saying that they would venture their lives with us, for which we were much overjoyed to see them so freely disposed to go along with us. Here nothing but courage. Brother, do not lie for the French will not believe thee. All men of courage and valour, let them fetch commodities, and not stand lazing and

be a beggar in the cabin. It is the way to be beloved of women, to go and bring them withal to be joyful. We present gifts to one and to another for to warn them to that end that we should make the earth quake, and give terror to the Iroquois if they were so bold as to show themselves....

THE EXPLORERS RETURN TO QUÉBEC

The Governor, seeing us come back with a considerable sum for our own particular [share] and seeing that his time was expired, and that he was to go away, made use of that excuse to do us wrong, and to enrich himself with the goods that we had so dearly bought. And by our means we made the country to subsist, that without us had been I believe oftentimes quite undone and ruined, and the better to say at his last breading, no castors no ship, and what to do without necessary commodities.[1] He made also my brother prisoner for not having observed his orders and to be gone without his leave although one of his letters made him blush for shame not knowing what to say, but that he would have some of them at what price soever, that he might the better maintain his coach and horses at Paris. He fined us four thousand pounds to make a fort at the three rivers, telling us for all manner of satisfaction that he would give us leave to put our coat of arms upon it, and moreover six thousand pounds for the country, saying that we should not take it so strangely and so bad, being we were inhabitants and did intend to finish our days in the same country with our relations and friends.[2] But the bougre did grease his chops with it,[3] and more made us pay a custom which was the 4th part which

---

[1] *the better to say...commodities* the reading in the manuscript, but the sense is obscure.

[2] Radisson is offended because the governor assumes they will stay in Canada. While Des Groseilliers likely did remain, Radisson would die in London.

[3] *bougre* scoundrel.

came to fourteen thousand pounds, so that we had left but forty-six thousand pounds, and took away £24000. Was not he a tyrant to deal so with us after we had so hazarded our lives and having brought in less than two years by that voyage as the factors of the said country said, between forty and fifty thousand pistols.[1] For they spoke to me in this manner, in which country have you been? from whence do you come? For we never saw the like. From whence did come such excellent castors, since your arrival is come into our magazine very near six hundred thousand pounds Tournois,[2] of that filthy stinking merchandise which will be prized like gold in France. And them were the very words that they said to me.

— (CA. 1659–60)

---

[1] *pistols* A pistol was a French coin, valued at about 16–18 shillings.

[2] a very large sum; approximately £46,000 in the 1660s.

Bishop Gilbert Burnet
1643 – 1715

The son of a prominent Edinburgh lawyer, Burnet attended Marischal College, Aberdeen, mastered Hebrew in Amsterdam, and became professor of divinity at Glasgow at the age of twenty-six; he refused the offer of several bishoprics—three times before he was thirty years old—before accepting that of Salisbury in 1689. A Whig and a latitudinarian who spoke out against the persecution of Catholics during the Popish Plot, Burnet had influence at both the Scottish and English royal courts and played a significant role in the religious and political life of the nation throughout the Restoration and during the Revolution of 1688. In the early 1670s Burnet was appointed chaplain to Charles II but was dismissed for criticizing the King's profligacy; he could claim better success with the Earl of Rochester,

publishing an account of the deathbed repentance Rochester made while Burnet was in attendance (1680). In addition to sermons, religious treatises, biography, and polemical works, Burnet published a three-volume *History of the Reformation in England* (1679, 1681, 1715); his best-known work, the autobiographical *History of My Own Time*, was published posthumously in two volumes (1724, 1734). While the *History* is not always historically accurate, it is an invaluable source for the personalities of the period.

For another account of the Restoration, see the selections from John Evelyn and Anthony à Wood; for another character of the King, see the Marquis of Halifax's *Character of Charles II*.

❧❧❧

History of My Own Time

THE RESTORATION

Upon the dispersing Lambert's army, Monk marched southward, and was now the object of all men's hope.[1] At London all sorts of people began to cabal together, royalists, presbyterians, and republicans. Holles told me,[2] the presbyterians pressed the royalists to be quiet, and to leave the game in their hands; for their appearing would give jealousy, and hurt that which they meant to promote. He and Ashley Cooper, Grimston and An-

nesley, met often with Manchester, Robarts, and the rest of the presbyterian party:[3] and the ministers of London were very active in the city: so that when Monk came up, he was pressed to declare himself. At first he would only declare for the parliament that Lambert had forced. But there was then a great fermentation all over the nation. Monk and the parliament grew jealous of one another, even while they tried who could give the best words, and express their confidence in the highest terms of one another. I will pursue the relation of this transaction no further: for this matter is well known.

The king had gone in autumn 1659 to the meeting at the Pyrenees, where Cardinal Mazarin

---

[1] *Lambert's army, Monk* John Lambert (1619–1683), Major-General of the army sent unsuccessfully to oppose the march south from Scotland of the army led by George Monck (or Monk), first Duke of Albemarle (1608–1670). For more on these events, see the account of the Restoration in John Evelyn's diary.

[2] *Holles* Denzil Holles, first Baron Holles of Ifield (1599–1680), statesman; sided with Parliament until the mid-1640s; made a peer and a member of the Council of State at the Restoration.

[3] Anthony Ashley Cooper, first Earl of Shaftesbury (1621–1683); Sir Harbottle Grimston (1603–1685); Arthur Annesley, first Earl of Anglesey (1614–1686); Edward Montagu, second Earl of Manchester (1602–1671); Sir John Robartes (1606–1685).

and Don Louis de Haro were negotiating a peace.[1] He applied himself to both sides, to try what assistance he might expect upon their concluding the peace. It was then known that he went to Mass sometimes, that so he might recommend himself the more effectually to both courts; yet this was carried secretly, and was confidently denied. Mazarin still talked to Lockhart upon the foot of the old confidence:[2] for he went thither to watch over the treaty; though England was now in such convulsions, that no minister from thence could be much considered, unless it was upon his own account. But matters were ripening so fast towards a revolution in England, that the king came back to Flanders in all haste, and went from thence to Breda. Lockhart had it in his power to have made a great fortune, if he had begun first, and had brought the king to Dunkirk. As soon as the peace of the Pyrenees was made, he came over and found Monk at London, and took all the pains he could to penetrate into his designs. But Monk continued still to protest to him in the solemnest manner possible that he would be true to the commonwealth, and against the royal family. Lockhart went away, persuaded that matters would continue still in that state: so that when his old friend Middleton writ to him desiring him to make his own terms,[3] if he would invite the king to Dunkirk, he said, he was trusted by the commonwealth, and could not betray them.

The house of commons put Monk on breaking the gates of the city of London, not doubting but that would render him so odious to them, that it would force him to depend wholly on themselves.

He did it: and soon after he saw how odious he was become by it. So conceiving a high indignation at those who had put him on such an ungracious piece of service, he sent about all that night to the ministers and other active citizens, assuring them that he would quickly repair that error, if they would forgive it. So the turn was sudden: for the city sent and invited him to dine the next day at Guildhall: and there he declared for the members whom the army had forced away in 1647 and 1648, who were known by the name of "the secluded members." And some happening to call the body that then sat at Westminster, the "Rump of a Parliament," a sudden humour run like a madness through the whole city of roasting the rump of all sorts of animals; and thus the city expressed themselves sufficiently. Those at Westminster had now no support: so they fell unpitied and unregarded. The secluded members came, and sat down among them; but all they would do was to give orders for the summoning a new parliament to meet the first of May: and so they declared themselves dissolved.[4]

There was still a murmuring in the army; so great care was taken to scatter them in wide quarters, and not to suffer too many of those who were still for the old cause to lie near one another.[5] The well and the ill affected were so mixed, that in case of any insurrection some might be ready at hand to resist them. They changed the officers that were ill affected, who were not thought fit to be trusted with the commanding those of their own stamp: and so created a mistrust between the officers and the soldiery. And above all they took care to have no more troops than was necessary about the city: and these were the best affected. This was managed with great diligence and skill: and by this conduct was that great turn brought about without the least tumult or any bloodshed; which was beyond what

---

[1] Cardinal Jules Mazarin (1602–1661), first minister of France, and Luis Méndez de Haro (1598–1661), chief minister of Spain, negotiated a peace between their two countries in November 1659.

[2] *Lockhart* Sir William Lockhart (1621–1676) began the civil wars on the Royalist side, but served as Cromwell's Ambassador to Paris during the second half of the 1650s.

[3] *Middleton* John Middleton, first Earl of Middleton (1619–1674).

[4] This was the formal ending of the "Long Parliament" after twenty years (November 1640–February 1660).

[5] *old cause* republicanism.

any person could have imagined. Of all this Monk had both the praise and the reward; though I have been told a very small share of it belonged to him. Admiral Montague was then in the chief command at sea, newly returned from the Sound, where he and De Ruyter, upon the orders they received from their masters, had brought the two northern kings to a peace;[1] the king of Sweden dying as it was a making up. He was soon gained to be for the king; and he dealt so effectually with the whole fleet, that the turn there was as silently brought about, without any revolt or opposition, as it had been in the army. The republicans went about as madmen, to rouse up their party; but their time was past. All were either as men amazed or asleep: they had neither the skill nor the courage to make any opposition. The elections of parliament men ran all the other way. So they saw their business was quite lost, and they felt themselves struck as with a spirit of giddiness; and then every man thought only how to save or secure himself. And now they saw how deceitful the argument was from success, which they had used so oft, and triumphed so much upon. For whereas success in the field, which was the foundation of their argument, depended much upon the conduct and courage of armies, in which the will of man had a large share, here was a thing of another nature. Their union was broke, and their courage sank, without any visible reason for either; and a nation that had run on long in such a fierce opposition to the royal family was now turned as one man to call home the king.

The nation had one great happiness during the long course of the civil wars, that no foreigners had got footing among them. Spain was sinking to nothing: France was under a base spirited minister:[2] and both were in war all the while. Now a peace was made between them, and very probably, according to what is in Mazarin's letters, they would have joined forces to have restored the king. The nation was by this means entirely in its own hands: and now, returning to its wits, was in a condition to put every thing in joint again: whereas, if foreigners had been possessed of any important place, they might have had a large share of the management, and would have been sure to have taken care of themselves. Enthusiasm was now languid: for that, owing its mechanical force to the liveliness of the blood and spirits, men in disorder and depressed could not raise in themselves those heats with which they were formerly wont to transport both themselves and others.[3] Chancellor Hyde was all this while very busy:[4] he sent over Dr. Morley,[5] who talked with the presbyterians much of great moderation in general, but would enter into no particulars: only he took care to let them know he was a Calvinist: and they had the best opinion of such of the Church of England as were of that persuasion. Hyde wrote in the king's name to all the leading men, and got the king himself to write a great many letters in a very obliging manner. Some that had been faulty sent over considerable presents, with assurances that they would redeem all that was past with their zeal for the future. These were all accepted of: their money was also very welcome; for the king needed money when his matters were on that crisis, and he had many tools at work, the management of which was

---

[1] Edward Montagu, first Earl of Sandwich (1625–1672) and the patron of Samuel Pepys; Michiel Adriaanszoon de Ruyter (1607–1676), the brilliant Dutch admiral who would lead his navy against the English during the Anglo-Dutch wars of the 1660s and 1670s. The treaty of Copenhagen (1660) confirmed the peace between Sweden and Denmark, the two "northern kings." The Sound or Ørsund is the narrow strait separating Denmark and Sweden.

[2] *a base spirited minister* Cardinal Mazarin.

[3] *Enthusiasm* religious enthusiasm, specifically the more "inspired" devotional practices that arose during the Interregnum; see the discussion by John Locke.

[4] *Hyde* Edward Hyde, later made the first Earl of Clarendon (1609–1674), Lord Chancellor (since 1658) and Charles II's chief advisor.

[5] *Morley* George Morley (1597–1684), later made Bishop of Winchester; he would preach Charles II's coronation sermon.

so entirely the chancellor's single performance that there was scarce any other that had so much as a share in it with him. He kept a register of all the king's promises, and of his own; and did all that lay in his power afterwards to get them all to be performed. He was also all that while giving the king many wise and good advices; but he did it too much with the air of a governor, or of a lawyer. Yet then the king was wholly in his hands.

I need not open the scene of the new parliament, or convention, as it came afterwards to be called, because it was not summoned by the king's writ. Such an unanimity appeared in their proceedings, that there was not the least dispute among them, but upon one single point: yet that was a very important one. Hale, afterwards the famous chief justice,[1] moved that a committee might be appointed to look into the propositions that had been made, and the concessions that had been offered by the late king during the war, particularly at the treaty of Newport,[2] that from thence they might digest such propositions as they should think fit to be sent over to the king. This was well seconded, but I do not remember by whom. It was foreseen that such a motion might be set on foot: so Monk was instructed how to answer it, whensoever it should be proposed. He told the house, that there was yet, beyond all men's hopes, an universal quiet all over the nation; but there were many incendiaries still at work, trying where they could first raise the flame. He said, he had such copious informations sent him of these things, that it was not fit they should be generally known: he could not answer for the peace, either of the nation or of the army, if any delay was put to the sending for the king: what need was there of sending propositions to him? Might they not as well prepare them, and

offer them to him, when he should come over? He was to bring neither army nor treasure with him, either to fright them or to corrupt them. So he moved, that they would immediately send commissioners to bring over the king: and said, that he must lay the blame of all the blood or mischief that might follow on the heads of those that should still insist on any motion that might delay the present settlement of the nation. This was echoed with such a shout over the house, that the motion was no more insisted on.

This was indeed the great service that Monk did. It was chiefly owing to the post he was in, and to the credit he had gained: for as to the restoration itself, the tide made so strong that he only went into it so dexterously as to get much fame and great rewards for that which will have still a great appearance in history. If he had died soon after, he might have been more justly admired, because less known, and seen only in one advantageous light: but he lived long enough to have his stupidity and his other ill qualities be well known: so false a judgment are men apt to make upon outward appearances. To the king's coming in without conditions may be well imputed all the errors of his reign: and therefore when the earl of Southampton came to see and feel what he was like to prove,[3] he said once in great wrath to chancellor Hyde, it was to him they owed all they either felt or feared; for if he had not possessed them in all his letters with such an opinion of the king, they would have taken care to have put it out of his power either to do himself or them that mischief that was like to be the effect of their trusting him so entirely. Hyde answered, that he thought he had so true a judgment, and so much good nature, that when the age of pleasure should be over, and the idleness of his exile, which made him seek new pleasures for want of other employment, was turned to an obligation to mind affairs,

---

[1] *Hale* Sir Matthew Hale (1609–1676), made Lord Chief Justice in 1671.

[2] *the treaty of Newport* negotiated between Charles I and the Parliamentary "peace" party in 1648.

[3] *Southampton* Thomas Wriothesley, fourth Earl of Southampton (1607–1667), Lord High Treasurer (1660–1667).

then he would have shaken off those unhappy entanglements. I must often put my reader in mind, that I leave all common transactions to ordinary books. If at any time I say things that occur in other books, it is partly to keep the thread of the narration in an unintangled method, and partly because I either have not read these things in books, or, at least, I do not remember to have read them so clearly and particularly as I have related them. I now leave a mad and confused scene, to open a more august and splendid one....

REIGN OF KING CHARLES II

With the restoration of the king a spirit of extravagant joy being spread over the nation, that brought on with it the throwing off the very professions of virtue and piety: all ended in entertainments and drunkenness, which overran the three kingdoms to such a degree, that it very much corrupted all their morals. Under the colour of drinking the king's health, there were great disorders and much riot everywhere: and the pretences to religion, both in those of the hypocritical sort, and of the more honest but no less pernicious enthusiasts, gave great advantages, as well as they furnished much matter, to the profane mockers at all true piety. Those who had been concerned in the former transactions thought they could not redeem themselves from the censures and jealousies that these brought on them by any method that was more sure and more easy, than by going in to the stream, and laughing at all religion, telling or making stories to expose both themselves and their party as impious and ridiculous.

The king was then thirty years of age, and, as might have been supposed, past the levities of youth and the extravagance of pleasure. He had a very good understanding: he knew well the state of affairs both at home and abroad. He had a softness of temper, that charmed all who came near him, till they found how little they could depend on good looks, kind words, and fair promises, in which he was liberal to excess, because he intended nothing by them but to get rid of importunity, and to silence all further pressing upon him. He seemed to have no sense of religion: both at prayers and sacrament he, as it were, took care to satisfy people that he was in no sort concerned in that about which he was employed: so that he was very far from being an hypocrite, unless his assisting at those performances was a sort of hypocrisy, as no doubt it was; but he was sure not to increase that by any the least appearance of devotion. He said once to my self, he was no atheist, but he could not think God would make a man miserable only for taking a little pleasure out of the way. He disguised his popery to the last: but when he talked freely, he could not help letting himself out against the liberty that under the Reformation all men took of inquiring into matters: for from their inquiring into matters of religion, they carried the humour further, to inquire into matters of state. He said often, he thought government was a much safer and easier thing where the authority was believed infallible, and the faith and submission of the people was implicit: about which I had once much discourse with him. He was affable and easy, and loved to be made so by all about him. The great art of keeping him long was, the being easy, and the making every thing easy to him. He had made such observations on the French government, that he thought a king who might be checked, or have his ministers called to an account by a parliament, was but a king in name. He had a great compass of knowledge, though he was never capable of great application or study. He understood the mechanics and physic: and was a good chemist, and much set on several preparations of mercury, chiefly the fixing it. He understood navigation well: but above all he knew the architecture of ships so perfectly, that in that respect he was exact rather more than became a prince. His apprehension was quick, and his memory good; and he was an everlasting talker. He told his stories with a good grace: but they came in his way too often. He had a very ill opinion both of men and women; and did not think there was either sincerity or chastity in the world out of principle, but that some had either the one or the other out of humour or vanity. He thought that nobody served him out of love: and so he was quits with all the world, and loved others as little as he thought they loved him. He hated business, and could not be easily brought to mind any: but when it was necessary, and he was set to it, he would stay as long as his ministers had work for him. The ruin of his reign, and of all his affairs, was occasioned chiefly by his delivering himself up at his first coming over to a mad range of pleasure. One of the race of the Villiers, then married to Palmer, a papist, soon after made earl of Castlemaine, who afterwards, being separated from him, was advanced to be duchess of Cleveland, was his first and longest mistress, by whom he had five children.[1] She was a woman of great beauty, but most enormously vicious and ravenous, foolish but imperious, ever uneasy to the king, and always carrying on intrigues with other men, while yet she pretended she was jealous of him. His passion for her, and her strange behaviour towards him, did so disorder him, that often he was not master of himself, nor capable of minding business, which, in so critical a time, required great application: but he did then so entirely trust the earl of Clarendon that he left all to his care, and submitted to his advices as to so many oracles.

—1724

---

[1] Barbara Villiers, Countess of Castlemaine and Duchess of Cleveland (1641–1709); her complaisant husband was Roger Palmer, created Earl of Castlemaine in 1661 to propitiate his wife's jealousy over Charles' marriage to Catharine of Braganza. The King was not her only lover. In 1667 she played a significant role in the campaign that led to the downfall of the Earl of Clarendon.

Elinor James
pub. 1675 – 1715

The polemical pamphleteer Elinor James was the working partner of her husband Thomas James, a successful London printer. Described by her contemporary John Dunton as a "she-state-politician," James wrote and self-published over twenty-three polemical broadsheets and pamphlets dedicated, for the most part, to the defence of the Anglican Church and conservative politics. Her staunch support of James II and her resistance to the settlement of the Glorious Revolution resulted in a conviction for "dispersing scandalous and reflective papers"; as a result, she was briefly committed to Newgate in December, 1689. While James's publications frequently offer religious and political advice to monarchs and Parliament alike, the substance of her corpus is more varied than is often acknowledged. James offers her opinion on a range of civic matters: taxation, public firework displays and apprenticeship. After her husband's death in 1711, James carried on the printing business. The date of her death is unknown.

⁂

Mrs. James's Vindication of the Church of England, in an answer to a pamphlet entitled A New Test of the Church of England's Loyalty [1]
(excerpts)

Sir,
I am very sorry to think that you should be always such a subtle adversary, but you say, you never had an opportunity to show your spite and malice until now. You say you could never find a *convincing reason*, and what was the cause? Is it not because it doth not consist with your interest;[2] for that is all that you aim at, for that is the god of this world, and he hath blinded your eyes, and stupefied your understanding, and thickened your skull, so that if an angel came to instruct you, you would not be able to receive it, if it did not agree with your interest.[3] I thought *liberty of conscience* might have changed your disposition,[4] seeing that the king's intention is so gracious, as thinking it is the best way to unite our differences, and to heal our breaches, and you know it was the care of the king and parliament, to prevent scandalous pamphlets against the king and government, and therefore it is strange to me how you can print your paper *with allowance*, when it is of such a pernicious nature, and its whole aim is against the government: surely those gentlemen that had the care of the government, are very negligent, or else you dare not say,

---

[1] written in response to the anonymous work *A New Test of the Church of England's Loyalty* (London, 1687). *A New Test* indicts the Church of England as an institution disloyal to English monarchy, offering as evidence: the attempted exclusion of Mary Tudor from the throne, the crowning of Elizabeth I, the murder of Mary Queen of Scots, the imposition of "universal uniformity" in "liturgy and discipline," the attempted exclusion of James II from the throne, and the failure to support James II in the "repeal of the sanguinary penal laws and the late impious tests." The author desires that the penal laws, the Corporation Act (1661) and the Test Acts (1673, 1678) be repealed so that English Catholics can worship without persecution and participate in English politics.

[2] *consist* agree (*OED* consist *v* 3).

[3] *thickened* emended from "thickens."

[4] *liberty of conscience* On April 4, 1687, James II announced a Declaration of Indulgence which suspended the penal laws, the Test Acts and the Corporation Act. Earlier in this pamphlet, Elinor James expresses dissatisfaction with "liberty of conscience": "As for conscience, I do not count it a sufficient guide, because it is not so infallible, but it is subject to err, and therefore it ought to be guided by the Word of God....And therefore I am not so much for liberty of conscience. But since it is the king's pleasure, I rest satisfied."

with allowance; certainly none that is in authority would grant it you, and if they did, they must be treacherous to their trust, and are no friend to the king and government: for can there be anything of a more pernicious consequence than this, that would destroy the very foundation? How do you think I can bear it, when God hath filled my heart full of love and loyalty, and I know you abuse them, for you have no cause to call their loyalty into question, for I know their loyalty, and have been a labourer with them, therefore I have the greater reason to plead for them: but I know you will say I am a woman, and why should I trouble myself? Why was I not always so, when I pleaded with the parliament about the right of succession, and with Shaftesbury, and Monmouth, and at Guild Hall, and elsewhere;[1]

.   .   .   .   .   .

I am sure my sovereign will not allow you to vilify and abuse us; for he is a prince of justice as well as mercy, and hath promised, that he will defend us, and not only so, but will venture as far as any in our vindication, and the king was satisfied with our loyalty, and declared it to the world, and how dare you condemn the king's judgment, and scandalize the Church; for all that knows her, knows her to be the only Church for loyalty: for doth any of you own the king to be supreme head and governor but she? And for your part, all the world knows what you own; so that my sovereign cannot be your supreme governor, and therefore is no comparison to be made, I myself can weigh you all down for loyalty; and if I can do so much for that am but one, what shall we all do? Therefore I know the king will not be angry with me if I vindicate the Church of England, for in [the] vindicating

of her, I vindicate His Majesty, which I have always done; for when the peer's speech abused my sovereign, I answered him for I hate rebellion, and the Church doth not hinder anyone from that singular gift of loyalty, for her desire is, *That all should fear God and honour the king*;[2] and she is the spouse of Christ, and He will own her for His mystical body, and everyone that truly believes in Christ, is a member of that body, and all the members make the whole, and her doctrine is holy:[3] I wish those that own her, would live according to her doctrines, for then they would be safe and happy: She hath been infallible in her duty to her king, which her discontented brethren know full well,[4] for that was the only thing that they laid to her charge, that she would not be treacherous to her prince, nor side with his enemies; for if she had, you would not have been so great as you are now, though she was not for Popery as some thought, for indeed she hath always been the bulwark against it; and that makes you envy her so: for you think if you can but bring her down, you shall do well enough with the brats whom you begot, though your infallible belief in them may deceive you; for though you made them enemies to the Church of England, yet I find they will prove no friends to the Church of Rome; for indeed every good soul will rather endure anything than to be enslaved with Popery: And as for the Church of England, she never lived under the slavish fear of it, as the dissenters did, but doth trust God withal, and desires nothing else but to serve God truly, and the king rightly: And as for her revelations, as you say are *peculiar to herself*, is a clear mistake, and yet her Lord and Head hath promised, *That the gates of hell shall not prevail*

---

[1] *Shaftesbury* Anthony Ashley Cooper, first Earl of Shaftesbury (1621–1683); *Monmouth* James Scott, first Duke of Monmouth and Buccleuch (1649–1685), was the natural son of Charles II by Lucy Walter. He plotted against his father and led an armed rebellion against James II, for which he was executed.

[2] *That all…the king* "Honour all men. Love the brotherhood. Fear God. Honour the King" (I Peter 2:17).

[3] *make* emended from "makes"; *mystical body…the whole* In I Corinthians 12, Paul argues that the Church, like the body, is a single entity made up of many members with different functions.

[4] *know* emended from "knows."

against her.[1] And what is the gates of hell? But all those things that lead us to darkness and ignorance, and to fling down God's holy will, and to set up the will of men, and secretly make us to be an enemy to Christ, and a friend to Anti-Christ?[2] But Christ is able to save HIS OWN, and that you shall know, for He hath His chosen people amongst all, and I really do believe He hath His saints and servants in the Church of Rome as well as any other and I hope (out of His infinite mercy) He will reconcile our differences, and make us happy: And as for those that envy our happiness, they shall not be able to stand before the Almighty in the day of His anger, for His power is able to disperse them, and to blow them away in a minute, as his divine power did the locusts.[3] Therefore I would advise all the enemies of the Church of England to be quiet and amend for the time to come, for while we are contriving the ruin of one another, God may justly destroy us all, and bring in the heathens, who may bring forth better fruits than we: And for your *allowing our loyalty* to King Charles I, I do not thank you, for it is well known, or else you would not have owned it;[4] for that destruction of three kingdoms, and the death of the best of princes, is writ in God's book, and who shall be called to an account for it, God Almighty knows, but I am sure you cannot be acquitted....[5] And for your loyalty to King Charles I, was it not for your own protection? For the wrath of God was so upon you for your sins and iniquities, that you might very well have the fear of Cain upon you: And as for the liturgy and discipline, what made it so hateful, but because we had complied as near as we could to you for unity's sake. And the occasion of the war, and of that good prince losing his life and crown, might be (for ought I know) for sheltering such unfortunate men as you are, for you were not so sensible nor so honest as Jonah was, for he declared the truth, that he was the man that had offended, and by his counsel the ship was saved;[6] but you are of a contrary nature, for you do not care if you perish yourselves, for others perish with you; but the saints and servants of God are not of that nature, as Abraham, Moses, David, and Christ Himself; for He undertook death that we might live; and poverty, that through Him we might be made rich; but you are an enemy, for you would have none rich but yourselves, thinking thereby to enslave us and triumph over us. Therefore I find you have the nature of Cain, who envied his brother, because his own deeds were evil. For my part, I can call God to witness I have been always for the peace of the king and kingdom, and there is nothing in the world that is dearer to me than the king's life and happiness; and if I had a thousand lives, I could sacrifice them all in vindication of His Sacred Majesty, without the hope of rewards of gain; and there is none of my enemies can object anything against me, but being overzealous for my sovereign lord: For my blessed Saviour hath taught me, *That I cannot serve two masters*, and the primitive Christians were always obliged to be for the interest of the prince in whose

---

[1] *are peculiar* emended from "is peculiar"; *gates of hell... against her* "And I say also unto thee, That thou are Peter, and upon this rock I will build my church; and the gates of hell shall not prevail against it" (Matthew 16:18).

[2] *make* emended from "makes."

[3] *envy* emended from "envies"; *They shall...His anger* "who can stand before his indignation? and who can abide in the fierceness of his anger?" (Nahum 1:6); *as his divine...locusts* "And the Lord turned a mighty strong west wind, which took away the locusts, and cast them into the Red sea" (Exodus 10:19).

[4] *And for...owned it* "We will allow them, however (and that's the only thing in my opinion, they can value themselves upon), that most of the members of this communion have been faithful and serviceable to K. Ch. I. during the unhappy commotions in his reign" (*A New Test* 3).

[5] *three kingdoms* England, Scotland and Ireland.

[6] *honest as Jonah* Jonah resisted the divine call by fleeing on a ship to Tarshish. When the ship was battered by winds, he admitted that his disobedience caused the storm and told the mariners to cast him into the sea (Jonah 1).

dominions they lived;[1] so that it is our Christian duty to love and pray for our own prince, but we have nothing to do with any other; and whoever is for the interest of another, cannot be a true subject to their own: Therefore my resolution is, that I will be true to my God, my king, and my country, and I am resolved (by the blessing of Almighty God) never to change if I were to suffer a thousand deaths, because God hath instructed me in that way from my infancy, and I find it most agreeable to the Word of God and my temper, for I am naturally inclined to love kingly authority: And as for my faith, it is to believe sincerely in Christ, and there is no other faith whereby anyone can be saved; for I am sure He is the infallible rock, and I have always kept to that from the beginning, and I hope I will continue so to the end:[2] And as for *the changes of religious worship*, that is not anything as to matter of faith, for prayers may be altered according to people's occasions, for they were never designed to be infallible and if the common prayer hath been altered, I did not care if it had been altered again, and again, rather than it should be a stumbling block to any (though there is not anything but what I like and love) and I think there is no good Christian but may say *Amen* to them, and I could wish our hearts were as holy as the prayers are good, then I am sure there is nobody would be weary of them: But hath not such as you put the people out of love with them, in saying, they came out of your mass book, and this you did to wound the Church of England, for her good will towards you;

. . . .

Sir, I wonder how you dare condemn the Church of England (I mean that part of it, which is for the king, common prayer and bishops) for her faith teaches her piety to her God, and loyalty to her prince; therefore she may appropriate to herself alone, *The principles of true loyalty* above all; for her doctrine is true, and exhorts all to repentance and good works, and teaches a true faith in Christ, and doth not judge any heretics that differs with her, but owns that whoever truly believes in Christ and works righteousness, may be in a state of salvation: and she is Christ's beloved spouse, and He will own her, and I doubt not but her faith is great enough (with God's help) to stand against all her opposers, for Christ will beautify her for His Word's sake; for though she doth not teach us that presumption as to think that any man is infallible, yet she owns God's Word to be infallible, and eternal, and a perfect guide to salvation. I wonder how anyone can be her enemy, but why should I? Was it not so from the beginning, for was not Cain envious against Abel, and were not brave and renowned men in their generations enemies to Moses,[3] and did not the high priests plot against my blessed Saviour? And did not Christ tell his disciples, *That the time would come, that they should think they did God good service to destroy them?*[4] They were not heathens that did it, but those mistaken Christians that thought they should merit by it; for I find all along that Satan hath made use of those that ought to be the greatest friends, to be the most inveterate enemies, as when he made use of a disciple to betray his Lord, and that great disciple that declared most love to his Lord, was the first that disowned Him.[5] This

---

[1] *That I...two masters* "No man can serve two masters: for either he will hate the one, and love the other; or else he will hold to the one, and despise the other" (Matthew 6:24).

[2] *He is the infallible rock* In the Old Testament, God is figured as a rock (e.g. Psalm 18:2, 62:2, 71:3), as is Christ in the New (e.g. I Corinthians 10:4). Christ is also figured as a stone (e.g. I Peter 2:4–8).

[3] *were* emended from "was."

[4] *That the...destroy them?* "They shall put you out of the synagogues: yea, the time cometh, that whosoever killeth you will think that he doeth God service" (John 16:2).

[5] *a disciple...his Lord* Judas Iscariot; for thirty pieces of silver, he led a band of Roman soldiers to arrest Jesus (Matthew 26:15), *great discipline...disowned Him* Simon Peter adamantly declared his love to Jesus only to renounce him three times after Jesus's capture (Matthew 26:69–75).

is the spite of our spiritual adversary; and the wisdom of God suffered it so to be, that we should not trust in anything, but in the most high God, that always takes care of them that trust in Him, and none can prevent the providential care that God takes of His; and Christ's Church must look to be persecuted by the enemies of her Lord, but through Him she shall be more than a conqueror.[1] Who is he that is so presumptuous to brand her with *killing of kings*? She abhors such doctrines, for she is a preserver of kings and princes, and makes more of her word than the enemies doth of their infallible promise, and I doubt not but it will pass current.[2] Hath not you been angry with her kings for her sake, and for what reason, only because she owned the Word of God in sincerity: And out of envy you sent men to divide her members, and destroy her government, and have you not been contriving her ruin all along, and transforming yourselves into all shapes to bring it to pass? And who begins all quarrels but you? And do you say, *That the Church is a viper?* No, no, it is such as you are; for you envy our happiness, and would hurry us into a confusion, because you think the king loves us too well, and stands in the gap to hinder your intentions, and is like an angel to keep peace amongst us, that every man should enjoy his right and property: But this is contrary to your temper, for you long to enjoy what other men have; and therefore the Church of England is the great eyesore: And since the king hath been so gracious to give *liberty of conscience*, you think that all the dissenters should be against the Church to devour her: but God knows it was for your sakes that the laws were put against dissenters, and how many good souls were against it, but dare not speak for fear of being counted Whigs;[3] but for my part, I made application to the late king, that the laws should not be put against them, not that I loved them so well, but I knew their nature, and don't delight that any should be afflicted; no not the Roman Catholics:

.   .   .   .

I know you would unthrone my sovereign, for to make yourselves lords and princes over us, but I hope God will never suffer it: for I know you are like the wheedling dissenters, that would not trust the king with his own power, but pretended they would employ it, and make him a glorious prince; but it was to destroy him: so you would wheedle the Church to take away her power, and then you think to do well enough with my sovereign, when you have got the power, and then you'll show your loyalty: but I hope the king will keep his power, and trust to none of you; for you will all prove treacherous if you can but make any advantage of it; for you cannot but know the sinking condition of your kingdom, and that makes you so busy; therefore you don't care who sinks, so you swim: But what is it that can hinder God's intentions, but repentance and amendment of life, for that is the glory that God desires; for that end Christ came into the world, that God *might be all in all*, and there is no doubt but God makes the angels ministering spirits, but they cannot do anything of themselves, for they continually wait upon the Almighty;[4] for when He moves they flee, and what injury can it be to you to pray to God that moves all things? I think it is the greatest favour that can be given to mortals, but you say, you are not worthy; and pray what is the reason of that? For did not Christ die for all that would lay hold of Him? But I find you have not attained to

---

[1] *more than a conqueror* "Nay, in all these things we are more than conquerors through him that loved us" (Romans 8:37).

[2] *pass current* pass for authentic currency.

[3] *were against* emended from "was against."

[4] *That God…in all* "And when all things shall be subdued unto him, then shall the Son also himself be subject unto him that put all things under him, that God may be all in all" (I Corinthians 15:28).

that excellent perfection to have a true faith in Christ, for if you had, you would never have brought your false accusations against us; for what do we do, that you find so much fault with us? for I am sure all condemn us for doing so much.[1] And as for the Dissenting Parliament, I was as much against them as any, but I wondered that they did do no more, when the late king said, he would establish the Protestant religion to the end of the world; but they were so factious they could not agree; for there was a duke stood in their way; but did not we stand for him, and overthrow all their doings? And did not we value the king's life (that now is) above our own: We could not adhere to their fair pretences, to do evil that good might come of it, neither to hurt him in the least, but trusted God with all; and if he was a king (as he is) we would lie at his mercy: And what made the dissenters to be so much against us, but because we were so much for His Majesty? And how dare any to abuse us? I have not patience to bear it, for if I let it alone, the very stones would speak in vindication of us.[2] And as for the parliament that now is, it is a very honest parliament, and I love them, and wish them all well, and they are knaves and fools that speak against them;[3] for they have established the king in his throne, and beat down his enemies, and have supplied his wants; and what is it we have not done for our sovereign? For we love him above all things in this world, for we acknowledge him to be Christ's vice-gerent, and therefore we own none (for our governor on earth) but he; and I do not doubt but our loyalty will outdo all upstart loyalty: for ours doth not proceed from Shaftesbury, but it proceeds from God: Therefore the Church of England needs not change her loyalty, neither will the king doubt it; for he is assured of her fidelity long ago; *therefore she need not learn of her Catholic neighbours,* for she is able to teach the world loyalty to princes. And as for the king's persuasions, he hath manifested to the world, he is a Christian Catholic and no Roman Catholic; for he doth not tie up conscience in such a narrow compass, as to think none are Christians but those that own Rome; and he hath declared, that it hath always been his opinion, and that His Majesty calls God to witness:[4]

.   .   .   .

Do not disturb the king's peace, but rest contented, lest God clips your wings, and if you fall, I hope you will have no more resurrections in this part of the world. And though others may prompt you, to be an enemy to the Church of England, yet their fall would be your ruin. But God be thanked we have no need to fear, for the king will not withdraw his favour from us, neither shall men or devils prevent it.

And so GOD save the KING.

—1687

---

[1] *condemn* emended from "condemns."

[2] *the very stones...of us* When the Pharisees tell Jesus to rebuke his disciples for calling him "the King that cometh in the name of the Lord," Jesus replies: "I tell you that, if these should hold their peace, the stones would immediately cry out" (Luke 19:40).

[3] *speak* emended from "speaks."

[4] *own* emended from "owns."

Cotton Mather
1663 – 1728

Born in Boston, where he would live his entire life, and educated at Harvard, Mather was a third-generation member of a prominent New England family of preachers and intellectuals. Mather began preaching in 1680 and was ordained formally in 1685; he shared the pulpit of Boston's Old North Church with his father, the minister and Harvard president Increase Mather. Mather published over four hundred books in his lifetime and left extensive work in manuscript, including his *Diary* and a translation of the entire Bible, the "Biblia Americana." Like his father, Mather believed in the reality of witches and in the necessity of punishing witchcraft, but he opposed the use of certain kinds of evidence instrumental in trials of the time. A life-long interest in science, which led him to correspond with Robert Boyle and argue on behalf of inoculation against smallpox, would win him membership in The Royal Society of London in 1713. His works include *Memorable Providences Relating to Witchcrafts and Possessions* (1689); *The Wonders of the Invisible World* (1693); an ecclesiastical history of New England, *Magnalia Christi Americana* (1702); and a blank verse translation of the Psalms, the *Psalterium Americanum* (1718).

Mather began his *Diary* in 1681 at the age of eighteen, and kept it until 1725; twenty-six manuscript volumes, each covering a single year, are extant, the rest being either lost or destroyed. Mather described his life as "a continual conversation with Heaven"; his diary is a record less of daily events than of the faith and sense of purpose that sustained him through a life of spiritual leadership and personal losses (only two of his fifteen children by three wives would survive him). Mather's *Diary* therefore shares more with John Bunyan's spiritual autobiography *Grace Abounding* than it does with other seventeenth-century diaries such as those by Samuel Pepys, John Evelyn, William Laud, or Lady Margaret Hoby.

ભૂ

Diary of Cotton Mather
(excerpts)

1681   1 d. 8 m. [October.][1]   After my rising thoughts had been employed on Psal. 126:5,[2] I spent this day in sowing the tears of repentance and supplication; with desires to humble myself before God for my old sins, and for my late ones; especially my exceeding sluggishness and laziness, and woeful dulness, in the service of God, and obtain his mercy in the pardoning and subduing of my sins, and my enjoyment of his presence with me, in my ministry.

My spirit was in agonies this day, when after my confession of sin I found my heart yet unbroken. I cried unto God, that he would embitter sin to me, and give me a just sorrow for my being so sinfully sorrowless as I am. I concluded,

"And, Lord, I hope thou hast now taken away my delight in sin. My heart would abhor it, and resist it. My soul does not like it. I think it is thus with me. If it be not thus, Lord, let me know it. Search me, try me, see if there be any way of wickedness in me. If I have done iniquity, or if I delight in doing it, show it me, and I will do so no more. I would give thee my heart and love, and soul, and all that I have, or am, or can. I am, like the man with a withered hand, essaying to do it. O my Lord, help me, in this my resignation."

---

[1]   Mather began each year's record on his birthday in February; March was therefore the first month.

[2]   "They that sow in tears shall reap in joy."

Afterwards, I made these attempts at closing with the Lord Jesus Christ.

"I have plunged my soul down into an horrible pit of sin and woe; but I cannot think of lying there. Salvation, I must, I must be made partaker of. And what shall I do? I am utterly unable to save myself. But there is one mighty to save, one whom God has laid help upon; him, him would I look unto. O my Lord Jesus Christ! Tho' I may be still as wretched and sinful as ever, yet is it not, is it not, as much my duty to come unto thee as ever! Art thou not able to save me? Lord, I will never dispute that; I know thou art, be my sins never so many, and never so horrid, and be my heart never so hard, and my state never so sad. And art thou not willing to save me? Indeed, I am unworthy; and I have nothing in me to move thee unto any saving notice of me. Yea, I have rejected thee, and therefore thou mayst reject me; and then I am in a forlorn condition indeed! But, Lord, it repents me that I have rejected thee, I will never, never, never do so again. My soul now followeth hard after thee. I see my need of thee; and an excellent beauty in thee. Oh! Surely thou art willing to undertake in the work of my salvation. Didst thou put away those that came unto thee, for the healing of their bodily diseases, when thou wast visibly incarnate here in this lower world? Art not those things recorded, as an intimation of what method I should use, and what success I should find, in my addressing of thee for the healing of my soul? Yea, which is a word full of life and Heaven! Tis one thing in the faith required of me, to believe thy willingness to accept of miserable sinners when they come unto thee; so that if I doubt thy willingness, I shall be guilty of a very criminal unbelief. Oh! therefore I look up unto thee. Wilt thou pass by me, now thou seest me in my blood; and shall it not be a time of love? Wilt thou not say unto me, live? O, let me now, believing, rejoice with joy unspeakable and full of glory! The Lord Jesus Christ, will be my priest, prophet,

king. He will engage for my good. He will take away my sins. He will bring me safe home to his father's house forever!"

☞ Towards the close of the day, I could not but use these words; "Lord, I know thou wilt be with me. Lord, I know thou wilt improve me in eminent services for thy name. Lord, I know thou will signalize me, as thou hast my father, my grandfathers, and my uncles before me. Hallelujah."

.   .   .   .

1683 5 d. 3 m. [May.] Upon many calls thereunto I spent this day in secret prayer with fasting, before the Lord.

And I will, to give one instructive instance unto my few friends, with whom I leave these papers, particularly recite the method of my proceedings, from the beginning, to the conclusion, of the day.

1. I began the day with expressing before the Lord my belief of his being a rewarder of them which diligently seek him, and my request that he would now strengthen me to seek him.

2. I then read the chapters of the Bible, which occurred unto me in my course of reading; and those chapters, I largely turned into prayers before the Lord.

3. Afterwards, I essayed in meditation to affect my own heart with a sense of the manifold vileness wherewith I have provoked God: My old sins, and my late sins; especially my woeful unfruitfulness, under my marvellous enjoyments, privileges and advantages.

All which, I then confessed, and bewailed, upon my knees, before God.

4. This done; I sang unto the Lord, that hymn of Barton's, which is called, *Confession of Sin*.[1]

5. Hereupon, I spent some time in pondering of a profitable and a seasonable question; and then in forming of some occasional reflections.

---

[1] *Barton's* William Barton, author of a popular verse translation of the Psalms first published in 1645.

6. I then went again unto my supplications; wherein I considered, that after all my vileness, the Lord is willing to deal with me in the way of the covenant of grace; and for that end, offered unto me such a surety and a saviour, as the blessed Jesus. Wherefore, I now stirred up myself to take hold of him, earnestly putting my soul into the hands of the mediator, and crying to him that he would convey unto me, not only pardon of sin, but also power against it, and make me an happy subject of all his redeeming works.

7. Now, I sang unto the Lord that hymn in Barton's which is entitled, *Humble Confessions and Supplications*. And I set myself, by further meditation, to establish myself in the use of such rules of speech as might render me a perfect man.

8. From which, I betook myself unto prayer. And my prayer now was, especially for such a door of utterance, as from time to time in my ministry I might have occasion for. ☞ And I had a full assurance that I was heard in this petition.

9. I then sang part of the 51st Psalm.

And so proceeded unto another prayer, wherein I presented before the Lord the desire of Solomon for wisdom; and for the presence of God with me, in all the concerns of my ministry.

10. Which being finished, I sang part of the 103d. Psalm. And then I examined myself by the signs of a state of nature, and a state of grace, given in Mr N. Vincent's, *True Touchstone;*[1] and found joyful cause to hope.

11. In the next place, I made another prayer; to recommend unto the blessing of God my particular friends, and all his people.

12. So I went unto a meeting of Christians, that were preparing for the Communion tomorrow and prayed and preached with them.

13. Leaving them I visited a sick neighbour and prayed with him.

14. And last of all, I shut up the day, renouncing all apprehension of merit in my duties, and relying upon the Lord Jesus Christ alone for acceptance and salvation.

.   .   .   .

1692 [May.] In the spring of this year, I preached, on the lecture, to the country, a sermon upon temptations; and now, behold my poor country entered quickly into temptation.

The rest of the summer was a very doleful time, unto the whole country.

The devils, after a most preternatural manner, by the dreadful judgment of Heaven took a bodily possession of many people in Salem, and the adjacent places; and the houses of the poor people began to be filled with the horrid cries of persons tormented by evil spirits. There seemed an execrable witchcraft in the foundation of this wonderful affliction, and many persons of diverse characters were accused, apprehended, prosecuted, upon the visions of the afflicted.

For my own part, I was always afraid of proceeding to convict and condemn any person as a confederate with afflicting demons, upon so feeble an evidence as a spectral representation.[2] Accordingly, I ever testified against it, both publicly and privately; and in my letters to the judges, I particularly besought them that they would by no means admit it; and when a considerable assembly of ministers gave in their advice about that matter, I not only concurred with their advice, but it was I who drew it up.

Nevertheless, on the other side, I saw in most of the judges a most charming instance of prudence and patience, and I knew their exemplary piety, and the agony of soul with which they sought the direction of Heaven; above most other people,

---

[1] Nathaniel Vincent (?1639–1697), a London minister ejected for Nonconformity, published *The True Touchstone* in 1681.

[2] *spectral representation* the testimony of a victim who claimed to have been attacked by a spectre bearing the appearance of a person he or she knew.

whom I generally saw enchanted into a raging, railing, scandalous and unreasonable disposition, as the distress increased upon us: For this cause tho' I could not allow the principles that some of the judges had espoused, yet I could not but speak honourably of their persons on all occasions; and my compassion, upon the sight of their difficulties, raised by my journeys to Salem, the chief seat of these diabolical vexations, caused me yet more to do so. And merely, as far as I can learn, for this reason, the mad people thro' the country, under a fascination on their spirits, equal to what our energumens had on their bodies,[1] reviled me, as if I had been the doer of all the hard things that were done in the prosecution of the witchcraft.

In this evil time, I offered, at the beginning, that if the possessed people might be scattered far asunder, I would singly provide for six of them; and we would see whether without more bitter methods, prayer with fasting would not put an end unto these heavy trials: But my offer (which none of my revilers would have been so courageous or so charitable as to have made) was not accepted.

.   .   .   .   .   .

1693 On March 28, Tuesday, between 4 and 5 a.m. God gave to my wife a safe deliverance of a son. It was a child of a most comely and hearty look, and all my friends entertained his birth with very singular expressions of satisfaction. But the child was attended with a very strange disaster; for it had such an obstruction in the bowels, as utterly hindered the passage of its ordure from it. We used all the methods that could be devised for its ease; but nothing we did could save the child from death. It languished, in its agonies, till Saturday, April 1, about 10 p.m. and so died, unbaptised. There was a conjunction of many and heavy trials in this

dispensation of God; but God enabled me to bear them all with an unexpected measure of resignation unto his holy will. I did not suffer such a discomposure in my thoughts, as to hinder me from preaching both parts of the day following; in the forenoon on Heb. 11:17; in the afternoon, on Job. 2:10, and to exemplify unto my congregation, a little of the faith, patience, thankfulness, which I then preached unto them.[2] On the Monday, the child was buried, with a very numerous and honourable attendance of my neighbours; and on one of the gravestones, I wrote only that Epitaph, RESERVED FOR A GLORIOUS RESURRECTION.

When the body of the child was opened, we found that the lower end of the *rectum intestinum*, instead of being musculus, as it should have been, was membranous, and altogether closed up. I had great reason to suspect a witchcraft in this preternatural accident; because my wife, a few weeks before her deliverance, was affrighted with an horrible spectre in our porch, which fright caused her bowels to turn within her; and the spectres which both before and after tormented a young woman in our neighbourhood bragged of their giving my wife that fright, in hopes, they said, of doing mischief unto her infant at least, if not unto the mother: and besides all this, the child was no sooner born, but a suspected woman sent unto my father a letter full of railing against myself, wherein she told him, *He little knew, what might quickly befall some of his posterity.* However I made little use of, and laid little stress on, this conjecture; desiring to submit unto the will of my heavenly Father without which, not a sparrow falls unto the ground.

.   .   .   .   .   .

[October 1693.] Among other things which entertained me at Salem, one was a discourse with one

---

[1] *energumens* people possessed by a spirit or devil (*OED*). Mather is saying that the "mad people" who criticized him for approving of the trials seemed to him as irrational mentally as those he believed were possessed physically.

[2] The biblical passages he preached on are, respectively, "By faith Abraham, when he was tried, offered up Isaac: and he that had received the promises offered up his only begotten son"; "Shall we receive good at the hand of God, and shall we not receive evil?"

Mrs. Carver, who had been strangely visited with some shining spirits, which were good angels, in her opinion of them.

She intimated several things unto me whereof some were to be kept secret. She also told me that a new storm of witchcraft would fall upon the country; to chastise the iniquity that was used in the wilful smothering and covering of the last; and that many fierce opposites to the discovery of that witchcraft would be thereby convinced.

Unto my surprise, when I came home, I found one of my neighbours horribly arrested by evil spirits. I then begged of God, that he would help me wisely to discharge my duty upon this occasion, and avoid gratifying of the evil angels in any of their expectations. I did then concern myself to use and get as much prayer as I could for the afflicted young woman; and at the same time, to forbid either her from accusing any of her neighbours, or others from enquiring any thing of her. Nevertheless, a wicked man wrote a most lying libel to revile my conduct in these matters; which drove me to the blessed God, with my supplications that he would wonderfully protect me, as well from unreasonable men acted by the devils, as from the devils themselves. I did at first it may be too much resent the injuries of that libel; but God brought good out of it; it occasioned the multiplication of my prayers before him; it very much promoted the works of humiliation and mortification in my soul. Indeed, the devil made that libel an occasion of those paroxysms in the town, that would have exceedingly gratified him, if God had not helped me to forgive and forget the injuries done unto me, and to be deaf unto the solicitations of those that would have had me so to have resented the injuries of some few persons, as to have deserted the lecture at the old meeting house.

When the afflicted young woman had undergone six weeks of preternatural calamities and when God had helped me to keep just three days of prayer

on her behalf, I had the pleasure of seeing the same success, which I used to have, on my third fast, for such possessed people as have been cast into my cares. God gave her a glorious deliverance; the remarkable circumstances whereof, I have more fully related in an history of the whole business.[1]

As for my missing notes,[2] the possessed young woman, of her own accord, enquired whether I missed them not? She told me, the spectres bragged in her hearing, that they had robbed me of them; she added, "Be not concerned; for they confess, they can't keep them always from you; you shall have them all brought you again." (They were notes on Ps. 119:9 and Ps. 90:12 and Hag. 1:7–9. I was tender of them and often prayed unto God, that they might be returned.) On the fifth of October following, every leaf of my notes again came into my hands, tho' they were in eighteen separate quarters of sheets. They were found dropped here and there, about the streets of Lynn; but how they came to be so dropped I cannot imagine; and I as much wonder at the exactness of their preservation.

It pleased God, that on October 3 my daughter Mary was taken very dangerously sick of a fever, with a vomiting, and with worms. I was by a stranger diversion upon my spirit hindered from importunate prayers for the life of the sick child; but at length, on October 5 in the evening, I had my heart wonderfully melted in prayers at my father[-in-law] Philip's where the child lay sick: I demanded not the life of the child, but I resigned it unto the mercy of God, in Jesus Christ; with such rapturous assurances of the divine love unto me and mine, as would richly have made amends for the death of more children, if God had then called for

---

[1] The young woman's name was Margaret Rule. The account was pirated and printed in Robert Calef, *More Wonders of the Invisible World* (1700), a book hostile to Mather.

[2] Notes for sermons he had intended to preach at Salem, "stolen from me, with such circumstances, that I am somewhat satisfied the spectres, or agents in the *invisible world*, were the robbers."

them. ☞ I was unaccountably assured, not only that this child shall be happy forever, but that I never should have any child, except what should be an everlasting temple to the spirit of God: Yea, that I and mine should be together in the Kingdom of God, world without end.

About six o'clock in the morning following, it being the sixth day of the month, and the sixth day of the week, the child near a month short of two years old, expired.

The next day it was buried in Boston, with an honourable attendance at the funeral.

On one of the gravestones, I wrote, GONE, BUT NOT LOST.

[October 10, 1693.] On this day, I also visited a possessed young woman in the neighbourhood,[1] whose distresses were not the least occasion of my being thus before the Lord. I wrestled with God for her: and among other things, I pleaded that God had made it my office and business to engage my neighbours in the service of the Lord Jesus Christ; and that this young woman had expressed her compliance with my invitations unto that service; only that the evil spirits now hindered her from doing what she had vowed: and therefore that I had a sort of right to demand her deliverance from these invading devils, and to demand such a liberty for her as might make her capable of glorifying my glorious Lord; which I did accordingly. In the close of this day, a wonderful spirit, in white and bright raiment, with a face unseen, appeared unto this young woman, and bid her, count me her father, and regard me and obey me as her father; for he said, the Lord had given her to me; and she should now within a few days be delivered. It proved, accordingly.

1696 *Memorandum.* About fifteen years ago, I bought a Spanish Indian, and bestowed him for a

servant on my father. About three years ago, Sir William Phips, our Governor, bestowed a Spanish Indian for a servant on myself. My servant affecting the sea, I permitted him to go to sea; and being an ingenuous fellow, I gave him an instrument for his freedom, if he served me till the end of the year 1697. Two years ago, the French took him, and I lost him. The loss occasioned me to make a cheerful resignation, unto the will of God. But I was hereupon persuaded and often expressed my persuasion, that my servant would be returned unto me. In the beginning of the year, an English man of war, by taking the vessel wherein my servant was, retook him. Nevertheless, the captain of the man of war being a fellow that had no principles of honour or honesty in him, I could by no means recover my servant out of his hands, who intended to make a perpetual slave of him. So, I gave over my endeavours to recover him; chiefly troubled for the condition of the poor servant. But then a strange conjunction of circumstances fell out, that the churlish captain was compelled without any consideration, but what I should please, to restore him. And my servant being so strangely returned, I set myself to make him a servant of the Lord.

1698 [June.] I have again, and again, received assurances from the Lord, which I have sometimes also in a convenient manner uttered, that the Lord was going to do an astonishing work in France, for the reviving of his holy religion there.[2] Behold, the whole principality of Orange, which is in the bowels of France, has had an astonishing work done upon it:[3] Its pastors being restored, the holy religion of Christ is restored with them, and the poor Pro-

[1] Margaret Rule again.

[2] *holy religion* Protestantism.

[3] as a consequence of the Treaty of Ryswick (see note below). Louis XIV had conquered the principality of Orange, located in present-day Provence, in the 1670s. The Princes of Orange, however, had long been based in the Netherlands.

testants, who had been dragooned into a sad apostasy,[1] are all, with transports of joy, recovered.

Briefly, I have many years ago published it, as my opinion, that the antichrist entered his last half-time at the half-Reformation in the former century, and that about an hundred and eighty years from thence would bring us to a new Reformation, vastly exceeding the former. Now, I live to see in 1697 greater tendencies to the new Reformation, than there were to be seen in 1517 for the half-Reformation, then begun.

O my Lord Jesus Christ, accept of me, the vilest of men, to do some great things for thee, in the approaching Reformation. Thou wilt accept of me! But, oh! make me a very holy, prayerful, watchful, and prudent man, that I may be fit for my master's use.

This day, both in my study, and in the public, I did, in imitation of the angels, in the first chapter of Zechariah, present this report before the Lord; that much of the earth sits still, and is at rest; thro' the peace lately ratified among the nations of Europe;[2] only Jerusalem is yet in its ruins; the French churches are dissipated, the Hungarian churches are desolated, the Piemontese churches are again afflicted: and I cried unto Heaven, for a marvellous redemption to be wrought for them. It will be done! It will shortly and surely be done!....

[July.] This day, when I was pouring out my prayers unto the Lord, I mentioned the prolongation of my life, to enjoy and improve more opportunities of glorifying him. In my prayers, I humbly represented unto the Lord that there were two objections against dying, which flesh would be ready to make; but thro' his grace I had conquered them. First, my flesh pleaded that the comforts of earth were too agreeable things to be easily forsaken. But my faith is persuaded and satisfied that the delights of Heaven are sweeter than the comforts of earth; and I can freely leave all the entertainments of this evil world, that I may be with Christ, where to be is by far the best of all. Secondly, my flesh pleaded, what will become of my poor offspring, when I am gone? But my faith is persuaded and satisfied, that God will be a father to my fatherless offspring; and my Lord Jesus Christ, whom I have served, without seeking, as many others would have done, to enrich myself with a portion for my children, will marvellously become such a guardian to my orphans, that they shall never want any good thing. My mind being on these two accounts thus easy, and ready to die, I then besought of the Lord, nevertheless, that he would yet spare my life, to work for him, a little more, among his people.

.   .   .   .

1699 [January.] About this time, understanding that the way for our communication with the Spanish Indies opens more and more, I set myself to learn the Spanish language. The Lord wonderfully prospered me in this undertaking; a few leisure minutes in the evening of every day, in about a fortnight, or three weeks time, so accomplished me, I could write very good Spanish. Accordingly, I composed a little body of the Protestant religion, in certain articles, backed with irresistible sentences of Scripture. This I turned into the Spanish tongue; and am now printing it, with a design to send it by all the ways that I can into the several parts of the Spanish America; as not knowing, how great a matter a little fire may kindle, or, whether the time for our Lord Jesus Christ to have glorious churches in America, be not at hand. The title of my compo-

---

[1] *dragooned* a policy directed by Louis XIV against the French Protestants in which Catholic soldiers were quartered in Protestant houses.

[2] The Treaty of Ryswick (October 1697) ended the War of the Grand Alliance (1689–1697), which had pitted England, Spain, the Dutch Republic, and the Holy Roman Empire against France.

sure is, *La Religion Pura, En Doze palabras Fieles, dignas de ser recebidas de Todos.*[1]

Oh! how happy shall I be, if the God of Heaven will prosper this my poor endeavour to glorify my Lord Jesus Christ.

But these my studies, in conjunction with some other inconveniences, raised the vapours of my spleen into my head. A grievous, painful, wasting headache seized me. In a few days, I was enfeebled with it into deplorable circumstances. I cried, unto the Lord, that for the sake of what my Lord Jesus Christ endured in his holy head, I might receive some ease of the pains in my sinful one. He heard my cry; and by the method of cupping,[2] he sent me relief. I was disabled from going abroad on the Lord's-day, 22 d. 11 m. [January.] But according to my poor strength, I spent part of it at home, on my knees, in prayers, with tears, lamenting my horrible filthiness, unthankfulness, and unfruitfulness, and imploring pardon, thro' the blood of Jesus.

I was able, on the Wednesday following, to discourse unto a great company of Christians at my house, above an hour, on the apostle's thorn in the flesh;[3] which I find some of the ancients, expound of a troublesome headache.

Nevertheless, my health is overthrown, and my spleen especially so disordered, that Satan gets into it: And now my mind is horribly buffeted with temptations, which tell me, that being unable to do any further service, and unworthy that God should help me to do any, I shall fall into an unserviceable old age, before I am forty years old. It is impossible for me to express the sad thoughts which now distress me, and confound me, and how much I am unhinged with them. Lord, pity thy poor servant; and tho' I am exceedingly vile, yet, O let me not be a cast away!

Under these grievous buffetings, I had no remedy, but earnest cries to Heaven. I had not health and strength enough in my frail body, to set apart whole days for prayer with fasting, as otherwise I would have done. But I took only my daily opportunities to plead the righteousness of my Lord Jesus Christ, who suffered wonderful temptation from Satan, without being betrayed into any sin, for the pardon of all the sin, which I discover under my temptation; and for my obtaining from heaven assistance against all temptation, and at length deliverance from temptation.

Some light, at last, began to appear unto me; and I begun to consider, whether these buffetings from Satan may not be permitted by Heaven to annoy me, because I am about a special piece of work, whereby the Kingdom of Satan may receive a more than ordinary blow; or, that so I may be prepared for some special mercy or service near unto me!

—(1681–99)

---

[1] "Pure religion, in twelve true articles, worthy of being received by all." Published with another Spanish text by Mather, *La Fe del Christiano* (Boston, 1699).

[2] *cupping*   a procedure for drawing blood by applying a heated cup to the skin.

[3] *apostle's thorn*   Paul, in II Corinthians 12:7.

Elizabeth Johnson
dates unknown

The following essay, prefaced to Elizabeth Singer Rowe's *Poems on Several Occasions. Written by Philomela* (1696), is remarkable for its radical, if brief, defence of women. Nothing is known of its author Elizabeth Johnson, who identifies herself as a friend to Rowe and her publisher John Dunton (*Philaret*). We know only that she wrote the Preface in Harding-Rents, May 10, 1696. Like Bathsua Makin and Margaret Fell, Johnson challenges the construction of the female as cognitively inferior and spiritually inadequate. This Preface is, in fact, a declaration of female constitutional independence in the face of attempts to dispossess women of mind and soul.

❦❦

Preface to the Reader

The occasion of this preface is, to give the world some account of the author of these *Poems*, as far as I'm permitted to do it: an employment I the more willingly choose, because our sex has some excuse for a little vanity, when they have so good reason for't, and such a champion among themselves, as not many of the other can boast of. We are not unwilling to allow mankind the brutal advantages of strength, they are superior to ours in force, they have custom on their side, and have ruled, and are like to do so, and may freely do it without disturbance or envy; at least they should have none from us, if they could but keep quiet among themselves. But when they would monopolize sense too, when neither that, nor learning, nor so much as wit must be allowed us, but all overruled by the tyranny of the prouder sex; nay, when some of 'em won't let us say our souls are our own, but would persuade us we are no more reasonable creatures than themselves, or their fellow animals; we then must ask their pardons if we are not yet so completely passive as to bear all without so much as a murmur. We complain, and we think with reason, that our fundamental constitutions are destroyed; that here's a plain and an open design to render us mere slaves, perfect Turkish wives, without properties, or sense, or souls; and are forced to protest against it, and appeal to all the world, whether these are not notorious violations on the liberties of freeborn Englishwomen? This makes the meekest worm amongst us all, ready to turn again when we are thus trampled on. But alas! What can we do to right ourselves? Stingless and harmless as we are, we can only kiss the foot that hurts us. However, sometimes it pleases heaven to raise up some brighter genius then ordained to succour a distressed people: an Epaminondas in Thebes; a Timoleon for Corinth (for you must know we read Plutarch now 'tis translated); and a Nassau for all the world.[1] Nor is our defenceless sex forgotten—we have not only Bunducas and Zenobias, but Sapphos, and Behns, and Schurmans, and Orindas, who have humbled the most haughty of our antagonists, and made 'em do homage to our wit, as well as our beauty.[2] 'Tis

---

[1] *Epaminondas...Corinth* Epaminondas (d. 362 B.C.E.) co-operated in the restoration of Theban power (379–371) and was celebrated for defeating the Spartan army at Leuctra. Timoleon (d. ca. 334 B.C.E.), a Corinthian, liberated Greek Sicily from military dictators and Carthaginian invaders; *Plutarch...translated* Plutarch's *Parallel Lives of Greeks and Romans* was translated into English by Thomas North in 1579. John Dryden headed a company of translators of the *Lives* and completed the task in 1683. Johnson likely refers to Dryden's translation; *Nassau* William III (1650–1702), King of England.

[2] *Bunducas...Orindas* Bunduca is another name for Boadicea (first century C.E.), the queen of ancient Britain who led a revolt against the Roman army, sacking and destroying Verulamium. Zenobia (third century C.E.), the wife of Odaenathus, secured power for herself in the name of her infant son after her husband's death. She controlled Syria,

true, their mischievous and envious sex have made it their utmost endeavours to deal with us, as Hannibal was served at Capua, and to corrupt that virtue which they can no otherwise overcome: and sometimes they prevailed:[1] But, if some angels fell, others remained in their innocence and perfection, if there were not also some addition made to their happiness and glory, by their continuing steadfast. Angels love, but they love virtuously and reasonably, and neither err in the object, nor the manner: And if all our poetesses had done the same, I wonder what our enemies could have found out to have objected against us. However, here they are silenced; and I dare be bold to say, that whoever does not come extremely prejudiced to these *Poems*, will find in 'em that vivacity of thought, that purity of language, that softness and delicacy in the love-part, that strength and majesty of numbers almost everywhere, especially on heroical subjects, and that clear and unaffected love to virtue; that height of piety and warmth of devotion in the Canticles, and other religious pieces; which they will hardly find exceeded in the best authors on those different kinds of writing, much less equalled by any single writer.

And now I have nothing more, I think, lies upon my hands, but to assure the reader, that they were actually writ by a young lady (all, but some of the "Answers," as is well-known to some persons of quality and worth), whose name had been prefixed, had not her own modesty absolutely forbidden it.

The way of thinking and writing is all along the same, only varying with the subject; and the whole so very agreeable a mixture, that unless *Philaret* and myself, who have the honour to be her friends, and who persuaded her to publish this first volume, are very partial, 'tis more than probable, they will meet with so favourable a reception with the pious and ingenious reader, that we may ere long prevail with her to oblige the world with a second part, no way inferior to the former.[2]

Hardings-Rents,
MAY 10TH 1696.

Elizabeth Johnson

---

devastated Bostra, conquered Egypt and overran Asia Minor. Sappho, born in Lesbos (b. ca. 612 B.C.E.), was a Greek poet whose work was collected in nine books. Aphra Behn (1640–1689) was a dramatist, novelist and poet. Anna Maria van Schurman (1607–1678) was a Dutch theologian, philosopher, and educational reformer. Orinda was the pseudonym of Katherine Philips (1632–1664), the poet and translator.

[1] *Hannibal was served at Capua* Hannibal (247–183/2 B.C.E.) was the great Carthaginian general of the Second Punic War between Rome and Carthage. In Plutarch's *Lives*, he and his men are described as a "great horde of robbers" who managed to bring almost all of Italy under their sway. The people of Capua were persuaded to come over to him "of their own accord" and to attach themselves firmly to his cause.

[2] *Philaret* John Dunton, the friend and publisher of Elizabeth Singer Rowe.

A MISCELLANY

Letters

ॐ

Oliver Cromwell
to Colonel Valentine Walton
(July 5, 1644)

Writing from his field camp at York, Oliver Cromwell sends his brother-in-law Valentine Walton news of a Parliamentary victory and condolences for the death in battle of Walton's eldest son, also named Valentine. At the time Governor of King's Lynn, Walton (1594–1661?) was a member of the Long Parliament, the Colonel of a regiment of foot, and was later one of the regicides. The battle of Marston Moor, fought near York on July 2, 1644, was one of the major Parliamentary victories of the wars. The Royalist forces were commanded by Prince Rupert, the King's nephew (see the letter following).

D ear Sir,
It's our duty to sympathize in all mercies; that we may praise the Lord together in chastisements or trials, that so we may sorrow together.

Truly England and the Church of God hath had a great favour from the Lord, in this great victory given unto us, such as the like never was since this war began. It had all the evidences of an absolute victory obtained by the Lord's blessing upon the godly party principally. We never charged but we routed the enemy. The left wing, which I commanded, being our own horse, saving a few Scots in our rear, beat all the Prince's horse. God made them as stubble to our swords, we charged their regiments of foot with our horse, routed all we charged. The particulars I cannot relate now, but I believe, of twenty-thousand the Prince hath not four-thousand

left.[1] Give glory, all the glory, to God.

Sir, God hath taken away your eldest son by a cannon-shot. It brake his leg. We were necessitated to have it cut off, whereof he died.

Sir, you know my trials this way:[2] but the Lord supported me with this, That the Lord took him into the happiness we all pant after and live for. There is your precious child full of glory, to know sin nor sorrow any more. He was a gallant young man, exceeding gracious. God give you his comfort. Before his death he was so full of comfort that to Frank Russel and myself he could not express it, it was so great above his pain. This he said to us. Indeed it was admirable. A little after, he said, one thing lay upon his spirit. I asked him, what that was. He told me that it was, that God had not suffered him to be no more the executioner of his [God's] enemies. At his fall, his horse being killed with the bullet, and as I am informed three horses more, I am told he bid them open to the right and left, that he might see the rogues run. Truly he was exceedingly beloved in the Army, of all that knew him. But few knew him, for he was a precious young man, fit for God. You have cause to bless the Lord. He is a glorious saint in heaven, wherein you ought exceedingly to rejoice. Let this drink up your sorrow; seeing these are not feigned words to comfort you, but the thing is so real and undoubted a

---

[1] Marston Moor was the bloodiest battle of the civil wars: about 4000 Royalists and 2000 Parliamentarians were killed; another 1500 men were captured. Cromwell is likely referring not only to casualties but also to the number of men he thought Rupert would be able to regroup after they had been dispersed by the rout.

[2] Cromwell's eldest surviving son, also named Oliver and like Walton's son a young soldier fighting in the Parliamentary army, had died of smallpox in March 1644.

truth. You may do all things by the strength of Christ. Seek that, and you shall easily bear your trial. Let this public mercy to the Church of God make you to forget your private sorrow. The Lord be your strength: so prays

Your truly faithful and loving brother,
OLIVER CROMWELL

My love to your daughter, and to my Cousin Percevall, Sister Desbrowe and all friends with you.

Charles I to Prince Rupert
(September 14, 1645)

The King, writing from Hereford, strongly reproves his nephew Rupert for surrendering Bristol to Thomas Fairfax and the New Model Army. Bristol was the last important city remaining in Royalist hands, particularly because it was the King's only valuable seaport; its loss marked the end of Royalist hopes in the south of England. Rupert had promised to hold the town for four months, but his position was untenable. Fairfax began the siege on September 4, and stormed through to capture one of the town's main forts six days later on September 10; Rupert had little choice but to surrender that day, but his uncle saw this decision as bordering on treachery. The King's spelling has not been modernized.

Hereford 14: Sep. 1645

Nepueu/though the losse of Bristol be a great blow to me, yet your surrendering it as you did, is of so much Affliction to me, that it makes me forget, not only, the consideration of that place, but is lykewais the greatest tryall of my constancy that hath yet befalen me; for, what is to be done? after one, that is so neer me as you ar, both in Blood & Friendship, submits himselfe to so meane an Action (I give it the easiest Terme) such; I have so much to say, that I will say no more of it; only, least rasheness of Judgement be layed to my Charge, I must remember you of your letter of the 12: of

Aug: wherby you asseured me, (that if no Muteny hapned) you would keepe Bristol for fower Monthes; did you keepe it fower Dayes? was there anything lyke a Muteny? more Questions might be asked but now, I confesse, to litle purpose: my Conclusion is, to desyre you to seeke your subsistance (untill it shall please God to determine of my Condition) somewhere beyond Sease, to which end, I send you heerewith a Passe, & I pray God to make you sencible, of your present Condition, & give you meanes, to redime what you have lost; for I shall have no greater Joy in a Victory, then a just occasion, without blushing, to asseure you of my being

Your loving Oncle & most faithfull frend
CHARLES R

Eleanor Gwynne to Laurence Hyde
(1678, probably May or June)

Nell Gwynne or Gwyn (1650–1687), a well-known actress and mistress to the King, writes a "Mr. Hyde" with the latest news and gossip from court. The recipient is almost certainly Laurence Hyde, second son of the Earl of Clarendon; the letter was likely sent while Hyde was in The Hague on diplomatic business. Gilbert Burnet described the popular and vivacious Gwynne as "the indiscreetest and wildest creature that ever was in a court." The people she mentions were all fixtures of the Restoration court: Sir Carr Scrope (1649–1680), minor poet, man of fashion, and one of the King's witty companions; Mrs. Moll Knight, "the famous singer" (in the words of John Evelyn), and one of Gwynne's rivals for the King's attentions; Catherine Pegge, Lady Green ("Lady grin" in the letter), a former royal mistress; John Wilmot, Earl of Rochester (1647–1680), the poet (see the introduction to the selection of his works); Henry Savile (1642–1687), diplomat and soon to be Vice-Chamberlain; Charles Sackville, Earl of Dorset (1638–1706), poet and Gwynne's former lover (see the introduction to the selection from his work); Thomas Shadwell (1642?–1692), the dramatist and poet whom Dryden targeted in "MacFlecknoe"; Joseph Harris (fl. 1661–1681), a celebrated actor; her two children by the King,

Charles Beauclerk, at the time Earl of Burford and later Duke of St. Albans (1670–1726), and James, Lord Beauclerk (1671–1680); and Lady Elizabeth Harvey, an organizer of court intrigue. The letter was likely dictated, as Gwynne implies near its end ("I cant make her write um"); the spelling (including the occasional doubled word) of the original has been retained.

Pray Deare Mr. Hide forgive me for not writeing to you before now for the reasone is I have bin sick thre months & sinse I recoverd I have had nothing to intertaine you withall nor have nothing now worth writing but that I can holde no longer to let you know I never have ben in any companie wethout drinking your health for I loue you with all my soule. the pel mel is now to me a dismale plase[1] sinse I have uterly lost S[r] Car Scrope never to be recoverd agane for he tould me he could not live allwayes at this rate & so begune to be a littel uncivil, which I could not sufer from an uglye *baux garscon*.[1] M[s] Knights Lady mothers dead & she has put up a scutchin no beiger then my Lady grins scunchis.[2] My lord Rochester is gon in the cuntrei. M[r] Savil has got a misfortune, but is upon recovery & is to mary an hairres,[3] who I thinke wont wont have an ill time ont if he holds up his thumb. My lord of Dorscit apiers wonse in thre munths, for he drinkes aile with Shadwell & M[r] Haris at the Dukes house all day long. my Lord Burford remimbers his sarvis to you. my Lord Bauclaire is is goeing into france. we are a goeing to supe with the king at whithall & my lady Harvie. the King remember his sarvis to you. now lets talke of state affairs, for we never caried things so cunningly as now for we dont

know whether we shall have pesce or war, but I am for war and for no other reason but that you may come home. I have a thousand merry conseets, but I cant make her write um & therfore you must take the will for the deed. god bye. your most loveing obedunt faithfull & humbel

sarvant
E.G.

John Evelyn to Sir Christopher Wren
(April 4, 1665)

John Evelyn (1620–1706), diarist, writer, and virtuoso, to Sir Christopher Wren (1632–1723), architect. Evelyn's son, also named John, was born in 1655, making him ten years old when this letter was written. Ralph Bohun, a Fellow of New College, Oxford, was appointed his tutor in 1665. Bohun had scientific interests: he would publish *A Discourse Concerning the Origin and Properties of Wind* in 1671. For more on Evelyn, see the introduction to the selection from his *Diary*.

Sir,
You may please to remember that some time since I begged a favour of you in behalf of my little boy: he is now susceptible of instruction, a pleasant, and (though I speak it) a most ingenious and pregnant child.[4] My design is to give him good education; he is past many initial difficulties, and conquers all things with incredible industry: do me that eternal obligation, as to enquire out and recommend me some young man for a preceptor. I will give him £20 per annum salary, and such other accommodations as shall be no ways disagreeable to an ingenious spirit; and possibly I may do him other advantages: in all cases he will find his condition with us easy, his scholar a delight, and the conversation not to be despised: this obliges me to wish he may not be a morose, or severe person, but

---

[1] *pel mel* Pall Mall, the highly fashionable street on which Gwynne lived (spelled as it is pronounced).

[2] *scutchin...scunchis* scutcheon; a heraldic panel mounted to display the coat of arms of a recently deceased person (the final "s" in the second instance of the word is a slip for "n").

[3] The projected marriage did not take place.

[4] *pregnant* imaginative, inventive, teeming with ideas.

of an agreeable temper. The qualities I require are, that he be a perfect Grecian, and if more than vulgarly mathematical, so much the more accomplished for my design: mine own defects in the Greek tongue and knowledge of its usefulness, obliges me to mention that particular with an extraordinary note: in sum I would have him as well furnished as might be for the laying of a permanent and solid foundation: the boy is capable beyond his years; and if you encounter one thus qualified, I shall receive it amongst the great good fortunes of my life that I obtained it by the benefit of your friendship,[1] for which I have ever had so perfect an esteem. There is no more to be said, but that when you have found the person, you direct him immediately to me, that I may receive, and value him.

Sir, I am told by Sir John Denham that you look towards France this summer:[2] be assured I will charge you with some addresses to friends of mine there, that shall exceedingly cherish you; and though you will stand in no need of my recommendations, yet I am confident you will not refuse the offer of those civilities which I shall bespeak you.

There has lain at Dr. Needham's a copy of the *Parallel* bound up for you,[3] and long since designed you, which I shall entreat you to accept; not as a recompense of your many favours to me, much less a thing in the least assistant to you (who are yourself a master), but as a token of my respect, as the book itself is of the affection I bear to an art which you so happily cultivate.

Dear Sir, I am
Yr &c.

Says-Court, 4 Apr. 1665

---

[1] The tutor Evelyn eventually hired was recommended not by Wren but by Dr. John Wilkins, Bishop of Chester.

[2] *Denham* Sir John Denham (1615–1669), the poet; see the introduction to the selection from his works.

[3] *a copy of the Parallel* a book by Evelyn, *A Parallel of the Antient Architecture with the Modern* (1664), a translation of a treatise by Roland Fréart, sieur de Chambray. Dr. Jasper Needham (d. 1679) was an eminent physician and close friend of Evelyn's.

Information from the Scottish Nation
1640

The following text, printed originally as a broadsheet, was published in August 1640, just before the Scottish army entered England to take Newcastle. Scottish agents and sympathizers circulated copies among the soldiers of the English army and the citizens of northern towns. Its purpose was to allay fears about the invasion, and to attempt to convince English readers that they shared with the Scots common grievances and a common enemy—the powers in London that sought, the Scots argued, to undermine the religious and political liberties of British subjects. The second Bishops' War ended with the occupation of Newcastle (which gave the Scots control over much of England's coal supply). Charles was compelled to summon Parliament in November 1640, and the public debate over the sources and boundaries of royal authority initiated by the Scottish pamphlet campaign would soon be continued by Parliamentary writers in England. For the King's response to this and other texts the Scots published to justify their actions, see his *Proclamation* against the Scots.

❧

Information from the Scottish Nation, to all the True English, Concerning the Present Expedition

Our distresses in our religion and liberties being of late more pressing than we were able to bear; our supplications and commissions, which were the remedies used by us for our relief, were after many delays and repulses, answered at last with the terrors of an army coming to our borders; a peace was concluded,[1] but not observed: And when we did complain of the breach, and supplicate for the performance, our commissioners were hardly entreated; new and great preparations were made for war; and many acts of hostility done against us, both by sea and land. In this case to send new commissioners or supplications, were against experience, and hopeless; to maintain an army on the borders is above our strength, and cannot be a safety unto us by sea: To retire homeward, were to call on our enemies to follow us, and to make ourselves and our country, a prey by land, as our ships and goods are made at sea. We are therefore constrained at this time to come into England, not to make war, but for seeking our relief and preservation.

Duty obliges us to love England as ourselves: Your grievances are ours; the preservation or ruin of religion and liberties, is common to both nations: We must now stand or fall together. Suffer not therefore malice and calumny to prevail so far as to persuade, that we come to make war, we call Heaven and Earth to witness, that we are far from such intentions, and that we have no purpose to fight, except we be forced, and in our own defence (as we have more fully expressed in our large Declaration)[2] we come to get assurance of the enjoying of our religion and liberties in peace against invasion: and that the authors of all our grievances and yours being tried in Parliament,[3] and our wrongs redressed, the two kingdoms may live in greater love and unity than ever before, which to our common

---

[1] *a peace* The Pacification of Berwick (June 18, 1639) concluded the first Bishops' War, but proved a compromise that satisfied neither the Scots nor the English.

[2] *The Intentions of the Army of the Kingdome of Scotland, Declared to their Brethren of England* (Edinburgh, 1640).

[3] *the authors of all our grievances* referring particularly to Archbishop Laud, who would be executed in 1645. See the selections from Laud's *Diary*.

rejoicing, we may confidently expect from the goodness of God, if the wicked counsels of papists, prelates and other fire-brands their adherents be not more harkened unto, than our true and honest Declarations.

And where it may be conceived, that an army cannot come into England but they will waste and spoil; we declare, that no soldiers shall be allowed to commit any outrage, or do the smallest wrong, but shall be punished with severity:[1] That we shall take neither meat nor drink, nor anything else, but for our moneys: and when our moneys are spent; for sufficient surety, which by public order shall be given to all such as shall furnish us things necessary. We neither have spared, nor will we spare our pains, fortunes, and lives in this cause of our assurance and your deliverance: and therefore cannot look from any well-affected to truth and peace, to be either opposed by force and unjust violence in our peaceable passage, or to be discouraged by wilful or uncharitable with-holding of means for our sustentation on our way. We are brethren: Your worthy predecessors at the time of Reformation, vouchsafed us their help and assistance.[2] We have for many years lived in love: we have common desires of the purity of religion and quietness of both Kingdoms: our hopes are to see better days in this island: our enemies also are common: Let us not upon their suggestions or our own apprehensions, be friends to them, and enemies to ourselves: We desire nothing but what in the like extremity (which we pray God your nation never find) we would most gladly upon the like Declaration grant unto you, coming with your supplications to the King's Majesty, were he living amongst us, and what ye would we should do unto you, we trust ye will be moved to do even so unto us, that the blessing of God may rest upon both.

—1640

---

[1] Alexander Leslie (ca. 1580–1661), the Scottish general, published *Articles* of behaviour for his soldiers that stressed the importance of maintaining good relations with the English population.

[2] English intervention helped ensure the victory of the Protestant cause in 1560, the year the Scottish Parliament ended all links with Rome and ushered in the Scottish Reformation.

The Putney Debates
1647

By autumn 1647, the New Model Army was the dominant power in the country, occupying London and holding the King prisoner at Hampton Court. Army, Parliament, and King, each one distrusting the other two, began to negotiate a political and religious settlement. At this point, a new group entered the discussion by publishing its demands: the Levellers. A well-organized party of political radicals, the Levellers asked the Council of the Army to sponsor public debates about the various solutions and plans that had been proposed; the Council agreed, recognizing that the Levellers enjoyed the support of many sympathizers in both the army and the civilian population. Held in Putney church in late October and early November 1647, these debates were recorded by William Clarke, secretary to the Council; the (contemporary) transcription of his shorthand notes constitutes one of the most extraordinary documents to survive from the era. That these debates were held at all is remarkable: for the moment at least, the Levellers were serious participants in the political process, and their rethinking of fundamental political and social principles exemplifies how far radical theory had gone in five years of war. In addition, the Putney debates let us hear the sound of seventeenth-century political discussion.

The following text is the record of the second day of debates, held on October 29. On one side are the army "grandees" Oliver Cromwell, Lieutenant-General of the Army, and Henry Ireton, the Commissary-General of Horse and Cromwell's son-in-law. On the other side are various Leveller spokesmen, army and civilian. The basis of the discussion was the first of several versions of the Leveller *Agreement of the People* (1647), the earliest attempt in England at a written constitution. Ireton begins the debate by pointing out that the first clause (reproduced below) might imply universal manhood suffrage, and that such an act could lead to an attack on private property and eventually to anarchy. The Levellers, the most influential of whom was Colonel Thomas Rainsborough, respond with a "natural right" argument that all men who live under a political system ought to have a voice in the election of that system's representatives. (It did not seem to occur to even the most radical to extend the vote to women.)

A committee would later agree on a form of the compromise franchise proposed here by Maximilian Petty, which would exclude servants, apprentices, and those living off charity, because their dependence on others made it possible for their vote to be misused. Rainsborough's call for a general rendezvous of the army was also agreed on. But just as the Levellers seemed poised to assume a measure of real influence, Cromwell and Ireton reasserted their control over the army by splitting the rendezvous into three groups. Two regiments attempted to mutiny by attending the first meeting without orders and wearing copies of the *Agreement of the People* in their hatbands as a sign of allegiance; they were reduced to obedience. Within a week, these struggles for power within the army were overshadowed by the King's escape from Hampton Court, an event that presaged the Second Civil War: political and social revolution was made secondary once more to military considerations.

❦❦❦

The Putney Debates:
The Debate on the Franchise

The Paper called the Agreement read.
Afterwards the first Article read by itself.

[From *An Agreement of the People* (1647): 1. That the people of England, being at this day very unequally distributed by counties, cities, and boroughs for the election of their deputies in Parliament, ought to be more indifferently proportioned, according to the number of the inhabitants; the circumstances whereof, for number, place, and manner, are to be set down before the end of this present Parliament.]

Commissary Ireton:[1] The exception that lies in it is this: it is said, they [votes] are to be distributed according to the number of the inhabitants, "The people of England," etc. And this does make me think, that the meaning is that every man that is an inhabitant is to be equally considered,[2] and to have an equal voice in the election of those representers, the persons that are for the general representative, and if that be the meaning then I have something to say against it. But if it be only that those people that by the civil constitution of this kingdom, which is original and fundamental, and beyond which I am sure no memory of record does go—

[Interjection] Not before the Conquest.

But before the Conquest it was so. If it be intended, that those that by that constitution that was before the Conquest, that has been beyond memory, such persons that have been [the electors] under that constitution should be the electors [still], I have no more to say against it.

Colonel Rainsborough:[3] Moved, that others might have given their hands to it.

Captain Denne:[4] Denied, that those that were set of their regiment, that they were their hands.

Ireton: Whether those men whose hands are to it, or those that brought it, do know so much of the matter as that they mean that all that had a former right of election, or those that had no right before are to come in?

Commissary Cowling:[5] In the time before the Conquest, and since the Conquest, the greatest part of the kingdom was in vassalage.

Mr Pettus [Petty]:[6] We judge that all inhabitants that have not lost their birthright should have an equal voice in elections.

Rainsborough: I desired that those that had engaged in it [might be included], for really I think that the poorest he that is in England has a life to live as the

---

[1] Henry Ireton (1611–1651), Commissary-General of Horse and a leader in the negotiations among the army, the King, and the Parliament in the later 1640s.

[2] *every man* referring to men only when used by speakers on either side of the debate. Captain John Clarke asks later if "every individual person in the kingdom" was to have a vote, but nobody responds in such a way as to imply he has suggested giving the vote to women.

[3] Thomas Rainsborough (d. 1648), Leveller and officer in both the navy and army; he was the most prominent officer to side consistently with radical political and religious causes. His death in October 1648 during a Royalist raid would significantly weaken the Leveller cause in the army.

[4] Probably Henry Denne (d. 1660?), a Baptist clergyman and army officer who would write against the Levellers after being pardoned for his role in the Leveller mutiny in 1649.

[5] Nicholas Cowling, Commissary-General (for Victuals) in the New Model Army. He is referring to the Norman Conquest of 1066. One foundation of Leveller arguments for political change was belief in the "Norman yoke," that is, the post-Conquest legal system that had usurped a (largely mythical) Anglo-Saxon tradition of democracy and freedom.

[6] Maximilian Petty (1617- d. after 1660), Leveller, one of two civilian spokesmen at the debates; he helped write the first two *Agreements of the People*.

greatest he; and therefore truly, sir, I think it's clear, that every man that is to live under a government ought first by his own consent to put himself under that government; and I do think that the poorest man in England is not at all bound in a strict sense to that government that he has not had a voice to put himself under; and I am confident that, when I have heard the reasons against it, that something will be said to answer those reasons, insomuch that I should doubt whether he was an Englishman or no, that should doubt of these things.

Ireton: That's this [the meaning of the phrase "according to the number of the inhabitants"?]:

Give me leave to tell you, that if you make this the rule, I think you must fly for refuge to an absolute natural right, and you must deny all civil right; and I am sure it will come to that in the consequence. This, I perceive, is pressed as that which is so essential and due, the right of the people of this kingdom, and as they are the people of this kingdom, distinct and divided from other people, as that we must for this right lay aside all other considerations. This is so just; this is so due; this is so right to them; and those that they do thus choose, must have such a power of binding all, and loosing all, according to those limitations. This is pressed as so due, and so just, as is argued that it is an engagement paramount all others, and you must for it lay aside all others; if you have engaged any others, you must break it; so look upon these as thus held out to us; so it was held out by the gentlemen that brought it yesterday.

For my part, I think it is no right at all. I think that no person has a right to an interest or share in the disposing of the affairs of the kingdom, and in determining or choosing those that shall determine what laws we shall be ruled by here, no person has a right to this that has not a permanent fixed interest in this kingdom, and those persons together are properly the represented of this kingdom, and consequently are to make up the representers of this kingdom; who, taken together, do comprehend whatsoever is of real or permanent interest in the kingdom, and I am sure (otherwise I cannot tell what), any man can say why a foreigner coming in amongst us, or as many as will coming in amongst us, or by force or otherwise settling themselves here, or at least by our permission having a being here, why they should not as well lay claim to it as any other.

We talk of birthright. Truly, [by] birthright there is thus much claim: men may justly have by birthright, by their very being born in England, that we should not seclude them out of England. That we should not refuse to give them air and place and ground, and the freedom of the highways and other things, to live amongst us, not any man that is born here, though he in birth or by his birth there come nothing at all that is part of the permanent interest of this kingdom to him. That I think is due to a man by birth. But that by a man's being born here he shall have a share in that power that shall dispose of the lands here, and of all things here, I do not think it a sufficient ground.

But I am sure if we look upon that which is the utmost, within man's view, of what was originally the constitution of this kingdom, upon that which is most radical and fundamental, and which if you take away, there is no man has any land, any goods, you take away any civil interest, and that is this: that those that choose the representers for the making of laws by which this state and kingdom are to be governed are the persons who, taken together, do comprehend the local interest of this kingdom; that is, the persons in whom all land lies, and those in corporations in whom all trading lies. This is the most fundamental constitution of this kingdom, and which if you do not allow, you allow none at all. This constitution has limited and determined it, that only those shall have voices in elections.

It is true, as was said by a gentleman [Rainsborough] near me, "The meanest man in England ought to have [a voice in the election of the government he lives under]." I say this: that those that have the meanest local interest, that man that has but forty shillings a year, he has as great [a] voice in the election of a knight for the shire as he that has ten thousand a year or more, if he had never so much, and therefore there is that regard had to it. But this still the constitution of this government has had an eye to, and what other government has not an eye to this. It does not relate to the interest of the kingdom if it do not lay the foundation of the power that's given to the representers, in those who have a permanent and a local interest in the kingdom, and who, taken altogether, do comprehend the whole, and if we shall go to take away this, we shall plainly go to take away all property and interest that any man has, either in land by inheritance, or in estate by possession, or anything else, if you take away this fundamental part of the civil constitution.

There is all the reason and justice that can be: if I will come to live in a kingdom, being a foreigner to it, or live in a kingdom, having no permanent interest in it, if I will desire as a stranger, or claim as one freeborn here, the air, the free passage of highways, the protection of laws, and all such things, and if I will either desire them or claim them, I (if I have no permanent interest in that kingdom) must submit to those laws and those rules, who taken together do comprehend the whole interest of the kingdom.

Rainsborough: Truly, sir, I am of the same opinion I was, and am resolved to keep it till I know reason why I should not. I confess my memory is bad, and therefore I am fain to make use of my pen. I remember that in a former speech this gentleman brought before this [meeting], he was saying that in some cases he should not value "whether [there were] a king or no king, whether lords or no lords, whether a property or no property." For my part I differ in that. I do very much care whether a king or no king, lords or no lords, property or no property; and I think, if we do not all take care, we shall all have none of these very shortly.

But as to this present business, I do hear nothing at all that can convince me why any man that is born in England ought not to have his voice in election of burgesses.[1] It is said that if a man have not a permanent interest, he can have no claim; and we must be no freer than the laws will let us to be, and that there is no [law in any] chronicle will let us be freer than that we [now] enjoy. Something was said to this yesterday, and I do think that the main cause why Almighty God gave men reason, it was that they should make use of that reason, and that they should improve it for that end and purpose that God gave it them, and truly I think that half a loaf is better than none if a man be an-hungry, yet I think there is nothing that God has given a man that any else can take from him, and therefore I say, that either it must be the law of God or the law of man that must prohibit the meanest man in the kingdom to have this benefit as well as the greatest. I do not find anything in the law of God, that a lord shall choose twenty burgesses, and a gentleman but two, or a poor man shall choose none: I find no such thing in the law of nature, nor in the law of nations. But I do find that all Englishmen must be subject to English laws, and I do verily believe that there is no man but will say that the foundation of all law lies in the people. And if in the people, I am to seek for this exemption.

And truly I have thought something: in what a miserable distressed condition would many a man that has fought for the Parliament in this quarrel be? I will be bound to say that many a man whose zeal and affection to God and this kingdom has

---

[1] *burgesses* members of Parliament for a borough, corporate town, or university.

carried him forth in this cause, has so spent his estate that, in the way the state, the army are going this way, he shall not hold up his head, and when his estate is lost, and not worth forty shillings a year,[1] a man shall not have any interest. And there are many other ways by which men have estates [which] (if that be the rule which God in his providence does use) do fall to decay; a man, when he has an estate, he has an interest in making laws; when he has none, he has no power in it. So that a man cannot lose that which he has for the maintenance of his family, but he must [also] lose that which God and nature have given him. And therefore I do, and am still of the same opinion, that every man born in England cannot, ought not, neither by the law of God nor the law of nature, to be exempted from the choice of those who are to make laws and for him to live under, and for him (for aught I know) to lose his life under, and therefore I think there can be no great stick in this.

Truly, I think that there is not this day reigning in England a greater fruit or effect of tyranny than this very thing would produce. Truly I know nothing free but only the knight of the shire, nor do I know anything in a parliamentary way that is clear from the height and fullness of tyranny. But as for this of corporations, it is as contrary to freedom as may be. For, sir, what is it? The king he grants a patent under the Broad-Seal of England to such a corporation to send burgesses. He grants to a city to send burgesses. When a poor base corporation from the king shall send two burgesses, when five hundred men of estate shall not send one, when those that are to make their laws are called by the king, or cannot act by [i.e. without] such a call, truly I think that the people of England have little freedom.

Ireton: I think there was nothing that I said to give you occasion to think that I did contend for this,

that such a corporation should have the electing of a man to the parliament. I think I agreed to this matter, that all should be equally distributed, but the question is whether it should be distributed to all persons, or whether the same persons that are the electors should be the electors still, and it equally distributed amongst them. I do not see anybody else that makes this objection; and if nobody else be sensible of it I shall soon have done. Only I shall a little crave your leave to represent the consequences of it, and clear myself from one misrepresentation of the thing that was misrepresented by the gentleman that sat next me. I think, if the gentleman remember himself, he cannot but remember that what I said was to this effect: that if I saw the hand of God leading so far as to destroy king, and destroy lords, and destroy property, and no such thing at all amongst us, I should acquiesce in it; and so I did not care, if no king, no lords, or no property, how in comparison of the tender care that I have of the honour of God, and of the people of God, whose name is so much concerned in this army. This I did deliver, and not absolutely.

All the main thing that I speak for, is because I would have an eye to property. I hope we do not come to contend for victory, but let every man consider with himself that he do not go that way to take away all property; for here is the case of the most fundamental part of the constitution of the kingdom, which if you take away, you take away all by that. Here are men of this and this quality are determined to be the electors of men to the parliament, and they are all those who have any permanent interest in the kingdom, and who, taken together, do comprehend the whole interest of the kingdom. I mean by permanent, local, that is not anywhere else. As for instance, he that has a freehold, and that freehold cannot be removed out of the kingdom. And so there's a corporation, a place which has the privilege of a market and trading, which if you should allow to all places equally, I do

---

[1] *forty shillings* the traditional minimum income from land necessary to be eligible to vote.

not see how you could preserve any peace in the kingdom, and that is the reason why in the constitution we have but some few market towns. Now those people by the former constitution were looked upon to comprehend the permanent interest of the kingdom, and those are the freemen of corporations; for he that has his livelihood by his trade, and by his freedom of trading in such a corporation, which he cannot exercise in another, he is tied to that place, his livelihood depends upon it; and secondly, that man has an interest, has a permanent interest there, upon which he may live, and live a freeman without dependence. These constitutions this kingdom has looked at.

Now I wish we may all consider of what right you will challenge, that all the people should have right to elections. Is it by the right of nature? If you will hold forth that as your ground, then I think you must deny all property too, and this is my reason. For thus: by that same right of nature, whatever it be that you pretend, by which you can say a man has an equal right with another to the choosing of him that shall govern him, by the same right of nature he has the same right in any goods he sees: meat, drink, clothes, to take and use them for his sustenance; he has a freedom to the land, the ground, to exercise it, till it.[1] He has the freedom to anything that anyone does account himself to have any property in. Why now I say, then, if you will, against the most fundamental part of civil constitution (which I have now declared), will plead the law of nature, that a man should, paramount this, and contrary to this, have a power of choosing those men that shall determine what shall be law in the state, though he himself have no permanent interest in the state, whatever interest he has he may carry about with him, if this be allowed, we are free, we are equal, one man must have as much voice as another. Then show me what step or difference, why, by the same right of necessity to sustain nature, it is for my better being. And possibly not for it neither: possibly I may not have so real a regard to the peace of the kingdom as that man who has a permanent interest in it; but he that has no permanent interest, that is here today and gone tomorrow, I do not see that he has such a permanent interest. Since you cannot plead to it by anything but the law of nature, but for the end of better being, and that better being is not certain, and more destructive to another; upon these grounds, if you do, paramount all constitutions, hold up this law of nature, I would fain have any man show me their bounds, where you will end, and take away all property?

Rainsborough: I shall now be a little more free and open with you than I was before. I wish we were all true-hearted, and that we did all carry ourselves with integrity; if I did mistrust you, I would [not] use such asseverations. I think it does go on mistrust, and things are thought too matters of reflection that were never intended. For my part, as I think, you forgot something that was in my speech, and you do not only yourselves believe that men are inclining to anarchy, but you would make all men believe that; and, sir, to say because a man pleads that every man has a voice, that therefore it destroys [by] the same [argument all property]. That there's a property, the law of God says it, else why God made that law, thou shalt not steal? I am a poor man, therefore I must be pressed; if I have no interest in the kingdom, I must suffer by all their laws, be they right or wrong. Nay thus, a gentleman lives in a county and has three or four lordships, as some men have, God knows how they got them, and when a parliament is called, he must be a parliament-man; and it may be he sees some poor men they live near, this man he can crush them. I have known an evasion to make sure he has turned

---

[1] Ireton is extrapolating, but this is an argument that Diggers such as Gerrard Winstanley would soon make, at least with respect to commons land; see the selection from Winstanley's work.

the poor man out of doors, and I would fain know whether the potency of men do not this, and so keep them under the greatest tyranny that was thought of in the world; and therefore I think that to that it is fully answered. God has set down that thing as to property with this law of his, thou shalt not steal. And for my part I am against any such thought, and I wish you would not make the world believe that we are for anarchy, as for yourselves.

Lieutenant-General [Cromwell]:[1] I know nothing but this, that they that are the most yielding have the greatest wisdom; but really, Sir, this is not right as it should be. No man says that you have a mind to anarchy, but the consequence of this rule tends to anarchy, must end in anarchy; for where is there any bound or limit set, if you take away this, that men that have no interest but the interest of breathing [should have no voice in elections]. Therefore I am confident on't, we should not be so hot one with another.

Rainsborough: I know that some particular men we debate with [claim we] are for anarchy.

Ireton: I profess I must clear myself as to that point; I would not desire, I cannot allow myself, to lay the least scandal upon any body. And truly, for that gentleman that did take so much offence, I do not know why he should take it so: we speak to the paper, not to persons, and to the matter of the paper, and I hope that no man is so much engaged to the matter of the paper. I hope our persons, and our hearts, and judgements are not pinned to papers, but that we are ready to hear what good or ill consequence will flow from it.

---

[1] Oliver Cromwell (1599–1658), at the time Lieutenant-General of the army and therefore the highest ranking officer present. In the absence of Thomas Fairfax, the Commander-in-Chief, Cromwell is presiding over the meeting, though he lets Ireton manage the discussion.

I have, with as much plainness and clearness of reason as I could, showed you how I did conceive the doing of this takes away that which is the most original, the most fundamental civil constitution of this kingdom, and which is, above all, that constitution by which I have any property. And if you will take away that and set up whatever a man may claim as a thing paramount that by the law of nature, though it be not a thing of necessity to him for the sustenance of nature, if you do make this your rule, I desire clearly to understand where then remains property.

Now then, the answer (I would misrepresent nothing) which had anything of matter in it, the great and main answer upon which that which has been said against this rests, seemed to be: that it will not make the breach of property, [because] there is a law, thou shalt not steal. The same law says, honour thy father, and mother: and that law does likewise hold out that it does extend to all that, in that place where we are in, are our governors, so that by that there is a forbidding of breaking a civil law when we may live quietly under it, and a divine law; and again it is said, indeed before, that there is no law, no divine law, that tells us that such a corporation must have the election of burgesses, of such a shire or the like. Divine law extends not to particular things; and so on the other side, if a man were to demonstrate his property by divine law, it would be very remote, but our property descends from other things, as well as our right of sending burgesses; that divine law does not determine particulars but generals, in relation to man and man, and to property, and all things else. And we should be as far to seek if we should go to prove a property in divine law as to prove that I have an interest in choosing burgesses of the parliament by divine law; and truly under favour I refer it to all whether these be anything of solution to that objection that I made, if it be understood. I submit it to any man's judgement.

Rainsborough: To the thing itself—property—I would fain know how it [the vote] comes to be the property [of some men, and not of others]: as for estates, and those kind of things and other things that belong to men, it will be granted that it is property, but I deny that that is a property, to a lord, to a gentleman, to any man more than another in the kingdom of England. If it be a property, it is a property by a law; neither do I think that there is very little property in this thing by the law of the land, because I think that the law of the land in that thing is the most tyrannical law under heaven, and I would fain know what we have fought for; and this is the old law of England and that which enslaves the people of England, that they should be bound by laws in which they have no voice at all. So the great dispute is who is a right father and a right mother. I am bound to know who is my father and mother, and I take it in the same sense you do. I would have a distinction, a character whereby God commands me to honour. And for my part, I look upon the people of England so, that wherein they have not voices in the choosing of their fathers and mothers, they are not bound to that commandment.[1]

Petty: I desire to add one word, concerning the word property. It is for something that anarchy is so much talked of. For my own part I cannot believe in the least, that it can be clearly derived from that paper. 'Tis true, that somewhat may be derived in the paper against the king, the power of the king, and somewhat against the power of the lords; and the truth is when I shall see God going about to throw down king and lords and property, then I shall be contented; but I hope that they may live to

see the power of the king and the lords thrown down, that yet may live to see property preserved. And for this of changing the representative of the nation, of changing those that choose the representative, making of them more full, taking more into the number than formerly, I had verily thought we had all agreed in it, that more should have chosen, all that had desired a more equal representation than now we have. For now those only choose who have forty shillings freehold. A man may have a lease for one hundred pounds a year, a man may have a lease for three lives; but for this, that it destroys all right that every Englishman that is an inhabitant of England should choose and have a voice in the representatives. I suppose it is the only means to preserve all property. For I judge every man is naturally free; and I judge the reason why men [chose representatives] when they are in so great numbers that every man could not give his voice [directly], was that they who were chosen might preserve property; and therefore men agreed to come into some form of government that they might preserve property, and I would fain know, if we were to begin a government [you would say]: "you have not forty shillings a year, therefore you shall not have a voice." Whereas, before there was a government every man had such a voice, and afterwards, and for this very cause, they did choose representatives, and put themselves into forms of government that they may preserve property, and therefore it [giving every man a voice] is not to destroy it.

Ireton: I think we shall not be so apt to come to a right understanding in this business if one man, and another man, and another man do speak their several thoughts and conceptions to the same purpose, as if we do consider what the objection is, and where the answer lies to which it is made; and therefore I desire we may do so too. That which this gentleman spoke last, the main thing that he seemed

---

[1] *that commandment* The injunction in the fifth commandment to "Honour thy father and thy mother" was generally interpreted as referring to "not only natural parents, but all superiors in age and gifts; and especially such as, by God's ordinance, are over us in place of authority, whether in family, church, or commonwealth" (from the Westminster Assembly's *Larger Catechism* of 1648).

to answer was this, that he would make it appear that the going about to establish this government, such a government, is not a destruction of property, nor does not tend to the destruction of property, because the people's falling into a government is for the preservation of property. What weight there [is] lies in this: since there is a falling into a government, and government is to preserve property, therefore this cannot be against property. The objection does not lie in that, the making of it more equal, but the introducing of men into an equality of interest in this government who have no property in this kingdom, or who have no local permanent interest in it. For if I had said that I would not wish at all that we should have any enlargement of the bounds of those that are to be the electors, then you might have excepted against it, but that I would not go to enlarge it beyond all bounds, so that upon the same ground you may admit of so many men from foreign states as would outvote you: the objection lies still in this, that I do not mean that I would have it restrained to that proportion, but to restrain it still to men who have a local, a permanent interest in the kingdom, who have such an interest that they may live upon it as free men, and who have such an interest as is fixed upon a place, and is not the same equally everywhere. If a man be an inhabitant upon a rack-rent for a year, for two years, or twenty years, you cannot think that man has any fixed permanent interest;[1] that man, if he pay the rent that his land is worth, and he has no advantage but what he has by his land, that man is as good a man, may have as much interest, in another kingdom. But here I do not speak of an enlarging this at all, but of keeping this to the most fundamental constitution in this kingdom. That is, that no person that has not a local and permanent interest in the kingdom should have an equal dependence in election; but if you go beyond this law, if you admit any man that has a breath and being, I did show you how this will destroy property. It may come to destroy property thus: you may have a major part, you may have such men chosen, or at least the major part of them, why those men may not vote against all property. You may admit strangers by this rule, if you admit them once to inhabit, and those that have interest in the land may be voted out of their land; it may destroy property that way. But here is the rule that you go by: for that by which you infer this to be the right of the people, of every inhabitant, and that because this man has such a right in nature, though it be not of necessity for the preserving of his being; therefore you are to overthrow the most fundamental constitution for this. By the same rule, show me why you will not, by the same right of nature, make use of anything that any man has for the necessary sustenance of me. Show me what you will stop at, wherein you will fence any man in a property by this rule.

Rainsborough: I desire to know how this comes to be a property in some men, and not in others.

Colonel Rich:[2] I confess that objection that the Commissary-General last insisted upon; for you have five to one in this kingdom that have no permanent interest. Some men [have] ten, some twenty servants, some more, some less; if the master and servant shall be equal electors, then clearly those that have no interest in the kingdom will make it their interest to choose those that have no interest. It may happen, that the majority may by law, not in a confusion, destroy property. There may be a law enacted, that there shall be an equality of goods and estate[s]. I think that either of the extremes may be urged to inconveniency; that is, men that have no interest as to estate should have no interest as to

---

[1] *rack-rent* a property whose rent was nearly equal to the annual income the tenant could obtain from it (*OED*).

[2] Nathaniel Rich (d. 1701), New Model Army officer; he would spend the later years of the Protectorate in and out of jail for opposition to Cromwell.

election. But there may be a more equal division and distribution than that he that has nothing should have an equal voice; and certainly there may be some other way thought of, that there may be a representative of the poor as well as the rich, and not to exclude all. I remember there were many workings and revolutions, as we have heard, in the Roman senate; and there was never a confusion that did appear, and that indeed was come to, till the state came to know this kind of distribution of election: that is how the people's voices were bought and sold, and that by the poor; and thence it came that he that was the richest man, and of some considerable power among the soldiers, and one they resolved on, made himself a perpetual dictator. And if we strain too far to avoid monarchy in kings, [beware] that we do not call for emperors to deliver us from more than one tyrant.

Rainsborough: I should not have spoken again. I think it is a fine gilded pill, but there is much danger, and it may seem to some that there is some kind of remedy. I think that we are better as we are, that the poor shall choose many; still the people be in the same case, be over-voted still. And therefore truly, sir, I should desire to go close to the business; and the thing that I am unsatisfied in is how it comes about that there is such a property in some freeborn Englishmen, and not others.

Cowling: Whether the younger son have not as much right to the inheritance as the eldest?

Ireton: Will you decide it by the light of nature?

Cowling: Why election was only forty shillings a year, which was more than forty pounds a year now, the reason was: that the commons of England were overpowered by the lords, who had abundance of vassals. But that still they might make their laws good against encroaching prerogatives; therefore

they did exclude all slaves. Now the case is not so; all slaves have bought their freedoms. They are more free that in the commonwealth are more beneficial. [Yet] there are men [of substance] in the country [with no voice in elections]: there is a tanner in Staines worth three thousand pounds, and another in Reading worth three horseskins.[1]

Ireton: In the beginning of your speech you seem to acknowledge by law, by civil constitution, the property of having voices in election was fixed in certain persons. So then your exception of your argument does not prove that by civil constitution they have no such property, but your argument does acknowledge by civil property. You argue against this law, that this law is not good.

Mr Wildman:[2] Unless I be very much mistaken we are very much deviated from the first question. And instead of following the first proposition to inquire what is just, I conceive we look to prophecies, and look to what may be the event, and judge of the justness of a thing by the consequence. I desire we may recall whether it be right or no. I conceive all that has been said against it will be reduced to this, that it is against a fundamental law; and another reason that every person ought to have a permanent interest: because it is not fit that those should choose parliaments that have no lands to be disposed of by parliament.

Ireton: If you will take it by the way, it is not fit that the representees should choose the representers, or the persons who shall make the law in the kingdom, who have not a permanent fixed interest in the kingdom.

---

[1] Staines is a town in Surrey just outside London, a few miles up the Thames from Putney; Reading is in Berkshire.

[2] John Wildman (1623–1693), a civilian Leveller who appears to have had some legal training. He made a fortune speculating in confiscated Royalist estates, and remained a life-long republican.

Wildman: Sir, I do so take it; and I conceive that that is brought in for the same reason, that foreigners might come as well to have a notice in our elections as well as the native inhabitants.

Ireton: That is upon supposition, that these should be all inhabitants.

Wildman: I shall begin with the last first. The case is different from the native inhabitant and foreigner. If a foreigner shall be admitted to be an inhabitant in the nation, he may, so he will submit to that form of government as the natives do; he has the same right as the natives but in this particular. Our case is to be considered thus: that we have been under slavery, that's acknowledged by all. Our very laws were made by our conquerors;[1] and whereas it's spoken much of chronicles, I conceive there is no credit to be given to any of them; and the reason is because those that were our lords, and make us their vassals, would suffer nothing else to be chronicled. We are now engaged for our freedom; that's the end of parliaments, not to constitute what is already, according to the just rules of government. Every person in England has as clear a right to elect his representative as the greatest person in England. I conceive that's the undeniable maxim of government: that all government is in the free consent of the people. If then upon that account, there is no person that is under a just government, or has justly his own, unless he by his own free consent be put under that government. This he cannot be unless he be consenting to it, and therefore, according to this maxim, there is never a person in England [but ought to have a voice in elections]; if, as that gentleman says be true, there are no laws that, in this strictness and rigour of justice, that are not made by those who he does consent to. And therefore I should humbly move, that if the question be stated,

which would soonest bring things to an issue, it might rather be this: whether any person can justly be bound by law not by his own consent, who does not give his consent that such persons shall make laws for him.

Ireton: Let the question be so: whether a man can be bound to any law that he does not consent to? And I shall tell you, that he may and ought to be, [despite the fact] that he does not give a consent to, nor does not choose any; and I will make it clear. If a foreigner come within this kingdom, if that stranger will have liberty who has no local interest here: he is a man, it's true, has air, that, by nature, we must not expel our coasts, give him no being amongst us, nor kill him because he comes upon our land, comes up our stream, arrives at our shore. It is a piece of hospitality, of humanity, to receive that man amongst us. But if that man be received to a being amongst us, I think that man may very well be content to submit himself to the law of the land; that is, the law that is made by those people that have a property, a fixed property in the land. I think, if any man will receive protection from this people, though he nor his ancestors, not any between him and Adam, did ever give concurrence to this constitution, I think this man ought to be subject to those laws, and to be bound by those laws, so long as he continues amongst them; that is my opinion. A man ought to be subject to a law, that did not give his consent. But with this reservation, that if this man do think himself unsatisfied to be subject to this law, he may go into another kingdom; and so the same reason does extend in my understanding, that a man that has no permanent interest in the kingdom, if he has money, his money is as good in another place as here; he has nothing that does locally fix him to this kingdom. If that man will live in this kingdom, or trade amongst us, that man ought to subject himself to the law made by the people who have the interest of this kingdom

---

[1] *our conquerors* the Normans.

in us. And yet I do acknowledge that which you take to be so general a maxim, that in every kingdom, within every land, the original of power, of making laws, of determining what shall be law in the land, does lie in the people that are possessed in the permanent interest in the land. But whoever is extraneous to this, that is, as good a man in another land, that man ought to give such a respect to the property of men that live in the land. They do not determine, why should I [i.e. they] have any interest of determining, what shall be the law of this land.

Major [William] Rainsborough:[1] I think if it can be made to appear that it is a just and reasonable thing, and that it is for the preservation of all the freeborn men, I think it ought to be made good unto them; and the reason is, that the chief end of this government is to preserve persons as well as estates, and if any law shall take hold of my person, it is more dear than my estate.

Colonel Rainsborough: I do very well remember that the gentleman in the window [said] that if it were so, there were no property to be had, because a fifth [five?] part[s] of the poor people are now excluded and would then come in.[2] So one on the other side said, if otherwise, then rich men shall be chosen; then, I say, the one part shall make hewers of wood and drawers of water of the other five, and so the greatest part of the nation be enslaved. And truly I think we are where we were still; and I do not hear any argument given but only that it is the present law of the kingdom. I say what shall become still of those many that have laid out themselves for the

Parliament of England in this present war, that have ruined themselves by fighting, by hazarding all they had. They are Englishmen. They have now nothing to say for themselves.

Rich: I should be very sorry to speak anything here that should give offence, or that may occasion personal reflection that we spoke against just now. I did not urge any thing so far as was represented, and I did not at all urge that there should be a consideration [of rich men], and that man that is [poor], shall be without consideration, [or that] he deserves to be made poor and not to live at all. But all that I urged was this: that I think it worthy consideration, whether they should have an equality in their interest. But however, I think we have been a great while upon this point, and if we be as long upon all the rest, it were well if there were no greater difference than this.

Mr Peters:[3] I think that this may be easily agreed on, that is, there may be a way thought of; but I would fain know whether that will answer the work of your meeting. I think you should do well to sit up all night, but I think that three or four might be thought of in this company. You will be forced to put characters upon electors or elected. Therefore I do suppose that if there be any here that can make up a representative to your mind, the thing is gained. But the question is, whether you can state any one question for the present danger of the kingdom, if any one question or no will dispatch the work.

Sir, I desire, that some question may be stated to finish the present work, to cement us wherein lies the distance; and if the thoughts [be] of the commonwealth, the people's freedom, I think that's

---

[1] William Rainsborough (fl. 1638–1673), younger brother of Thomas Rainsborough; an army officer and later a Ranter sympathizer connected with Lawrence Clarkson.

[2] Colonel Rich had said that "you have five to one in this kingdom that have no permanent interest," that is, five without permanent interest to every one that has. The confusion here is likely the transcriber's rather than Rainsborough's.

[3] Hugh Peter or Peters (1598–1660), Independent minister and army chaplain, famous for sermons of revolutionary zeal; in the 1630s, he had spent some time in New England as pastor of the congregation in Salem, Massachusetts.

soon cured. But I desire that all manner of plainness may be used, that we may not go on with the lapwing and carry one another off the nest. There is something else in that, must cement us where the awkwardness of our spirits lies.

Rainsborough: For my part, I think we cannot engage one way or other in the army if we do not think of the people's liberties; if we can agree where the liberty and freedom of the people lies, that will do all.

Ireton: I cannot consent so far before. As I said before, when I see the hand of God destroying king, and lords, and commons too, any foundation of human constitution, when I see God has done it, I shall, I hope, comfortably acquiesce in it; but first, I cannot give my consent to it, because it is not good, and secondly, as I desire that this army should have regard to engagements, wherever they are lawful, so would I have them have regard to this: that they should not bring that scandal upon the name of God, that those that call themselves by that name, those whom God has owned and appeared with, that we should not represent ourselves to the world as men so far from being of that peaceable spirit which is suitable to the Gospel, as we would have bought peace of the world upon such terms. We would not have peace in the world but upon such terms as should destroy all property, if the principle upon which you move this alteration, or the ground upon which you press that we should make this alteration, do destroy all kind of property or whatsoever a man has by human constitution. The law of God does not give me property, nor the law of nature, but property is of human constitution. I have a property and this I shall enjoy. Constitution founds property. If either the thing itself that you press or the consequence that you press [abolishes property], though I shall acquiesce in having no property, yet I cannot give my heart or

hand to it; because it is a thing evil in itself, and scandalous to the world, and I desire this army may be free from both.

Mr Sexby:[1] I see that though it [liberty?] were our end, there is a degeneration from it. We have engaged in this kingdom and ventured our lives, and it was all for this: to recover our birthrights and privileges as Englishmen; and by the arguments urged there is none. There are many thousands of us soldiers that have ventured our lives; we have had little property in the kingdom as to our estates, yet we have had a birthright; but it seems now, except a man has a fixed estate in this kingdom, he has no right in this kingdom. I wonder we were so much deceived. If we had not a right to the kingdom, we were mere mercenary soldiers. There are many in my condition, that have as good a condition; it may be little estate they have at present, and yet they have as much a right as those too who are their lawgivers, as any in this place. I shall tell you in a word my resolution. I am resolved to give my birthright to none, whatsoever may come in the way; and be thought that I will give it to none, if this thing that with so much pressing after [be denied]. There was one thing spoken to this effect: "that if the poor and those in low condition [...]". I think this was but a distrust of providence. I do think the poor and meaner of this kingdom, I speak as in that relation in which we are, have been the means of the preservation of this kingdom. I say, in their stations, and really I think that to their utmost possibility; and their lives have not been dear for purchasing the good of the kingdom. Those that act to this end are as free from anarchy or confusion as those that oppose it, and they have the law of God

---

[1] Edward Sexby (ca. 1616–1658), soldier, Leveller, and secret agent, one of the most outspoken and active Leveller spokesmen. He would spend two years in France (1651–52), publicizing Leveller ideas (and translating the *Agreement of the People* into French); in the later 1650s he was involved in various plots to assassinate Cromwell, and published *Killing Noe Murder* (1657) to justify these plans.

and the law of their conscience. But truly, I shall only sum up this in all: I desire that we may not spend so much time upon these things. We must be plain. When men come to understand these things, they will not lose that which they have contended for. That which I shall beseech you is to come to a determination of this question.

Ireton: I am very sorry we are come to this point, that from reasoning one to another we should come to express our resolutions. I profess for my part what I see is good for the kingdom, and becoming a Christian to contend for. I hope through God I shall have strength and resolution to do my part towards it, and yet I will profess direct contrary in some kind to what that gentleman said. For my part, rather than I will make a disturbance to a good constitution of a kingdom wherein I may live in godliness and honesty, and peace and quietness, I will part with a great deal of my birthright. I will part with my own property rather than I will be the man that shall make a disturbance in the kingdom for my property; and therefore if all the people in this kingdom, or representative[s] of them all together, should meet and should give away my property, I would submit to it, I would give it away. But that gentleman, and I think every Christian spirit, ought to bear that, to carry that in him, that he will not make a public disturbance upon a private prejudice.

Now let us consider where our difference lies. We all agree that you should have a representative to govern, but this representative to be as equal as you can; but the question is, whether this distribution can be made to all persons equally, or whether amongst those equals that have the interest of England in them? That which I have declared my opinion, I think we ought to keep to; that, both because it is a civil constitution, it is the most fundamental constitution that we have, and there is so much justice and reason and prudence, as I dare

confidently undertake to demonstrate, as that there are many more evils that will follow in case you do alter than there can in the standing of it. But I say but this in the general, that I do wish that they that talk of birthrights, we any of us when we talk of birthrights, would consider what really our birthright is. If a man mean by birthright whatsoever he can challenge by the law of nature, suppose there were no constitution at all, supposing no civil law and civil constitution, that that I am to contend for against constitution, [then] you leave no property, nor no foundation for any man to enjoy anything. But if you call that your birthright which is the most fundamental part of your constitution, then let him perish that goes about to hinder you or any man of the least part of your birthright, or will do it. But if you will lay aside the most fundamental constitution, and I will give you consequence for consequence, of [i.e. as] good upon constitution as you for your birthright, which is as good for aught you can discern as anything you can propose. At least it is a constitution; and if you were merely upon pretence of a birthright, of the right of nature, which is only true as for your better being, if you will upon that ground pretend that this constitution, the most fundamental constitution, the thing that has reason and equity in it, shall not stand in your way, is the same principle to me (say I), but for your better satisfaction you shall take hold of anything that a man calls his own.

Rainsborough: Sir, I see that it is impossible to have liberty but all property must be taken away. If it be laid down for a rule, and if you will say it, it must be so, but I would fain know what the soldiers have fought for all this while; he has fought to enslave himself, to give power to men of riches, men of estates, to make him a perpetual slave. We do find in all presses that go forth none must be pressed that are freehold men.[1] When these gentlemen fall out among themselves, they shall press the poor shrubs to come and kill them.[2]

Ireton: I must confess I see so much right in the business that I am not easily satisfied with flourishes. If you will lay the stress of the business upon the consideration of reason, or right relating to anything of human constitution, or anything of that nature, but will put it upon consequences, I will show you greater ill consequences; I see enough to say that, to my apprehensions, I can show you greater ill consequences to follow upon that alteration which you would have, by extending to all that have a being in this kingdom, than that by this a great deal. This is a particular ill consequence. This is a general ill consequence, and that is as great as this or any else, though I think you will see that the validity of that argument must lie, that for one ill lies upon that which now is, and I can show you a thousand upon this.

Give me leave but this one word. I tell you what the soldier of the kingdom has fought for. First, the danger that we stood in was that one man's will must be a law. The people of the kingdom must have this right at least, that they should not be concluded [but] by the representative of those that had the interest of the kingdom. So men fought in this because they were immediately concerned and engaged in it; other men who had no other interest in the kingdom but this, that they should have the benefit of those laws made by the representative, yet that they should have the benefit of this representative. They thought it was better to be concluded by the common consent of those that were fixed men, and settled men, that had the interest of this kingdom, and from that way I shall know a law and have a certainty. And every man that was born in it,

that has a freedom, is a denizen; he was capable of trading to get money, and to get estates by; and therefore this man, I think, had a great deal of reason to build up such a foundation of interest to himself; that is, that the will of one man should not be a law, but that the law of this kingdom should be by a choice of persons to represent, and that choice to be made by the generality of the kingdom. Here was a right that induced men to fight, and those men that had not this interest, and though this be not the utmost interest that other men have, yet they had some interest.

Now why we should go to plead whatsoever we can challenge by the right of nature against whatsoever any man can challenge by constitution; I do not see where that man will stop, as to point of property, that he shall not use that right he has by the law of nature against that constitution. I desire any man to show me where there is a difference. I have been answered: "Now we see liberty cannot stand without property." Liberty may be had and property not be destroyed; first, the liberty of all those that have the permanent interest in the kingdom, that is provided for. And [i.e. but] in a general sense liberty cannot be provided for if property be preserved. For, if property be preserved, that I am not to meddle with such a man's estate, his meat, his drink, his apparel, or other goods, then the right of nature destroys liberty. By the right of nature I am to have sustenance rather than perish; yet property destroys it for a man to have by the light of nature, suppose there be no human constitution.

Peters: I will mind you of one thing, that "upon the will of one man abusing us," and so forth. So that I profess to you, for my part I hope it is not denied by any man, that any wise, discreet man that has preserved England or the government of it [should have the vote]. I do say still under favour there is a way to cure all this debate. I think they will desire no more liberty if there were time to dispute it. I

---

[1] *presses* the impressment of men for compulsory military service.

[2] *shrubs* inferior or insignificant persons (*OED* shrub sb[1] 3).

think he will be satisfied and all will be satisfied, and if the safety of the army be in danger, for my part I am clear it should be amended, the point of election should be mended.

Cromwell: I confess I was most dissatisfied with that I heard Mr. Sexby speak of any man here, because it did savour so much of will. But I desire that all of us may decline that, and if we meet here really to agree to that which is for the safety of the kingdom, let us not spend so much time in such debates as these are, but let us apply ourselves to such things as are conclusive, and that shall be this: everybody here would be willing that the representative might be mended, that is, it might be better than it is. Perhaps it may be offered in that paper too lamely, if the thing be insisted upon too limited; why perhaps there are a very considerable part of copyholders by inheritance that ought to have a voice; and there may be somewhat too reflects upon the generality of the people. I know our debates are endless if we think to bring it to an issue this way. If we may but resolve upon a committee. If I cannot be satisfied to go so far as these gentlemen that bring this paper, I say it again, I profess it, I shall freely and willingly withdraw myself, and I hope to do it in such a manner that the army shall see that I shall by my withdrawing satisfying [satisfy] the interest of the army, the public interest of the kingdom, and those ends these men aim at. And I think if you do bring this to a result it were well.

Rainsborough: If these men must be advanced, and other men set under foot, I am not satisfied; if their rules must be observed, and other men, that are in authority, do not know how this can stand together, I wonder how that should be thought wilfulness in one man that is reason in another; for I confess I have not heard anything that does satisfy me, and though I have not so much wisdom or notions in my head, but I have so many that I could tell an

hundred to the ruin of my people. I am not at all against a committee's meeting; and as you say, and I think every Christian ought to do the same, for my part I shall be ready, if I see the way that I am going, and the thing that I would insist on, will destroy the kingdom, I shall withdraw it as soon as any. And therefore, till I see that, I shall use all the means, and I think it is no fault in any man to [refuse to] sell that which is his birthright.

Sexby: I desire to speak a few words. I am sorry that my zeal to what I apprehend is good should be so ill resented. I am not sorry to see that which I apprehend is truth, but I am sorry the Lord has darkened some so much as not to see it, and that is in short. Do you think it were a sad and miserable condition, that we have fought all this time for nothing? All here, both great and small, do think that we fought for something. I confess, many of us fought for those ends which, we since saw, were not that which caused us to go through difficulties and straits to venture all in the ship with you; it had been good in you to have advertised us of it, and I believe you would have fewer under your command to have commanded. But if this be the business, that an estate does make men capable, it is no matter which way they get it, they are capable, to choose those that shall represent them; but I think there are many that have not estates that in honesty have as much right in the freedom, their choice as free, as any that have great estates. Truly, sir, your putting off this question and coming to some other, I dare say, and I dare appeal to all of them, that they cannot settle upon any other until this be done; it was the ground that we took up arms, and it is the ground which we shall maintain. Concerning my making rents and divisions in this way, as to a particular, if I were but so, I could lie down and be trodden there. Truly I am sent by a regiment; if I should not speak, guilt shall lie upon me, and I think I were a covenant-breaker. And I do not know how we have

[been] answered in our arguments, and I conceive we shall not accomplish them to the kingdom when we deny them to ourselves. For my part, I shall be loath to make a rent and division, but for my own part unless I see this put to a question, I despair of an issue.

Captain Clarke:[1] The first thing that I shall desire was, and is, this: that there might be a temperature and moderation of spirit within us; that we should speak with moderation, not with such reflection as was boulted one from another,[2] but so speak and so hear as that which may be the droppings of love from one another to another's hearts.

Another word I have to say is: the grand question of all is, whether or no it be the property of every individual person in the kingdom to have a vote in election? And the ground is the law of nature, which, for my part, I think to be that law which is the ground of all constitutions. Yet really properties are the foundation of constitutions; for if so be there were no property, that the law of nature does give a principle to have a property of what he has, or may have, which is not another man's: this property is the ground of *meum* and *tuum* [mine and thine]. Now there may be inconveniences on both hands, but not so great freedom. The greater freedom, as I conceive, that all may have whatsoever. And if it come to pass that there be a difference, and that the one does oppose the other, then nothing can decide it but the sword, which is the wrath of God.

Captain Audley:[3] I see you have a long dispute, that you do intend to dispute here till the tenth of March.[4] You have brought us into a fair pass, and the kingdom into a fair pass, for if your reasons are not satisfied, and we do not fetch all our waters from your wells, you threaten to withdraw yourselves. I could wish, according to our several protestations, we might sit down quietly, and there throw down ourselves where we see reason. I could wish we might all rise, and go to our duties, and see our work in hand. I see both at a stand, and if we dispute here both are lost.

Cromwell: Really, for my own part I must needs say, while we say we would not make reflections, we do make reflections; and if I had not come hither with a free heart, to do that that I was persuaded in my conscience is my duty, I should a thousand times rather have kept myself away; for I do think I had brought upon myself the greatest sin that I was guilty of, if I should have come to have stood before God in that former duty which is before you, and if that my saying [that] which I did say, and shall persevere to say, that I should not, I cannot against my conscience do anything. They that have stood so much for liberty of conscience, if they will not grant that liberty to every man but say it is a deserting I know no what. If that be denied me, I think there is not that equality that I professed to be amongst us. I said this, and I say no more, that make your businesses as well as you can, we might bring things to an understanding; it was to be brought to a fair composure. And when you have said: if you should put this paper to the question without any qualification, I doubt whether it would pass so freely; if we would have no difference, we ought to put it. And let me speak clearly and freely; I have heard other gentlemen do the like. I have not heard the Commissary-General [Ireton] answered, not in a part to my knowledge, not in a tittle; if therefore, when I see there is an extremity of difference be-

---

[1] John Clarke (fl. 1645–1660), army officer; he later sat as an MP in every Parliament from 1653 to the end of the Protectorate.

[2] *boulted* bolted; probably in the contemporary sense meaning to blurt, to speak hastily or ill-advisedly (*OED* bolt v^2 5).

[3] Lewis Audley, an officer agitator.

[4] probably referring simply to a date months away, rather than to a specific event in the future.

tween you, to the end it may be brought nearer to a general satisfaction; and if this be thought a deserting of that interest, if there can be anything more sharply said, I will not give it an ill word. Though we should be satisfied in our consciences in what we do, we are told we purpose to leave the army, or to leave our commands, as if we took upon us to do it in matter of will. I did hear some gentlemen speak more of will than anything that was spoken for this way, for more was spoken by way of will than of satisfaction; and if there be not a more equality in our minds, I can but grieve for it. I must do no more.

Ireton: I should not speak, but reflections do necessitate, do call upon us to vindicate ourselves, as if we who have led men into engagements and services, had divided [from them] because we did not concur with them. I will ask that gentleman [Rainsborough] whom I love in my heart that spoke, whether when they drew out to serve the Parliament in the beginning, whether when they engaged with the army at Newmarket,[1] whether then they thought of any more interest or right in the kingdom than this, whether they did think that they should have as great interest in parliament-men as freeholders had, or whether from the beginning we did not engage for the liberty of parliaments, and that we should be concluded by the laws that such did make. Unless somebody did make you believe before now that you should have an equal interest in the kingdom; unless somebody do make that to be believed, there is no reason to blame men for leading so far as they have done; and if any man was far enough from such an apprehension, that man has not been deceived.

---

[1] a general rendezvous of the New Model Army, held in Newmarket June 4–5, 1647; the officers and soldiers agreed to a Solemn Engagement in which they vowed not to disband until various grievances had been redressed. It was the Solemn Engagement that formalized the system of choosing two "agitators" or representatives from each regiment.

And truly I shall say but this word more for myself in this business, because the whole objection seems to be pressed to me and maintained by me. I will not arrogate that I was the first man that put the army upon the thought either of successive parliaments or more equal parliaments. Yet there are some here that know who they were put us upon that foundation of liberty, of putting a period to this Parliament, that we might have successive parliaments, and that there might be a more equal distribution of elections. There are many here that know who were the first movers of that business in the army. I shall not arrogate that but I can argue this with a clear conscience: that no man has prosecuted that with more earnestness, and that will stand to that interest more than I do, of having parliaments successive and not perpetual, and the distributions of it; but, notwithstanding, my opinion stands good, that it ought to be a distribution amongst the fixed and settled people of this nation; it's more prudent and safe, and more upon this ground of right for it. Now it is the fundamental constitution of this kingdom; and that which you take away for matter of wilfulness, notwithstanding this universal conclusion, that "all inhabitants" as it stands. Though I must declare that I cannot yet be satisfied, yet for my part I shall acquiesce; I will not make a distraction in this army, though I have a property in being one of those that should be an elector; though I have an interest in the birthright, yet I will rather lose that birthright, and that interest, than I will make it my business, if I see but the generality of those whom I have reason to think honest men, and conscientious men, and godly men, to carry them another way. I will not oppose, though I be not satisfied to join with them. And I desire [to say:] I am agreed with you, if you insist upon a more equal distribution of elections; I will agree with you, not only to dispute for it, but to fight for it, and contend for it. Thus far I shall agree with you. On the other hand, those who differ their terms, I will not agree with you except you go further. Thus far I can go with you; I will go with you as far as I can. If you will appoint a committee to consider of some of that, so as you preserve the equitable part of that constitution, who are like to be freemen, and men not given up to the wills of others, keeping to the latitude which is the equity of constitutions, I will go with you as far as I can. I will sit down. I will not make any disturbance among you.

Rainsborough: If I do not speak my soul and conscience, I do think that there is not an objection made, but that it has been answered; but the speeches are so long. I am sorry for some passion and some reflections, and I could wish where it is most taken the cause had not been given. It is a fundamental constitution of the kingdom; there I would fain know, whether the choice of burgesses in corporations should not be altered.

The end wherefore I speak is only this: you think we shall be worse than we are, if we come to a conclusion by a vote. If it be put to the question, we shall all know one another's mind; if it be determined, and the resolutions known, we shall take such a course as to put it in execution. This gentleman says, if he cannot go he will sit still. He thinks he has a full liberty; we think we have not. There is a great deal of difference between us two. If a man has all he does desire, but I think I have nothing at all of what I fought for, I do not think the argument holds that I must desist as well as he.

Petty: The rich would very unwillingly be concluded by the poor. And there is as much reason, and indeed no reason, that the rich should conclude the poor as the poor the rich; but there should be an equal share in both. I understood your engagement was that you would use all your endeavours for the liberties of the people, that they should be secured. If there is a constitution, that the people are not

free, that should be annulled. That constitution which is now set up is a constitution of forty shillings a year, but this constitution does not make people free.

Cromwell: Here's the mistake: whether that's the better constitution in that paper, or that which is. But if you will go upon such a ground as that is, although a better constitution was offered for the removing of the worse, yet some gentlemen are resolved to stick to the worse. There might be a great deal of prejudice upon such an apprehension. I think you are by this time satisfied, that it is a clear mistake; for it is a dispute whether or not this be better, nay, whether it be not destructive to the kingdom.

Petty: I desire to speak one word to this business, because I do not know whether my occasions will suffer me to attend it any longer. The great reason that I have heard is the constitution of the kingdom, the utmost constitution of it; and if we destroy this constitution, there is no property. I suppose that if constitutions should tie up all men in this nature, it were very dangerous.

Ireton: First, the thing itself were dangerous, if it were settled to destroy property. But I say the principle that leads to this is destructive to property; for by the same reason that you will alter this constitution, merely that there's a greater constitution by nature, by the same reason, by the law of nature, there is a greater liberty to the use of other men's goods, which that property bars you of. And I would fain have any man show me why I should destroy that liberty which the freeholders and burghers in corporations have in choosing burgesses, that which if you take away, you leave no constitution; and this because there is a greater freedom due to me from some men by the law of nature. More than that, I should take another man's goods because the law of nature does allow me.

Rainsborough: I would grant something that the Commissary-General says. But whether this be a just property, the property says that forty shillings a year enables a man to elect; if it were stated to that, nothing would conduce so much whether some men do agree or no.

Captain Rolfe:[1] I conceive that, as we are met here, there are one or two things mainly to be prosecuted by us; that is especially unity, preservation of unity in the army, and so likewise to put ourselves into a capacity thereby to do good to the kingdom. And therefore I shall desire that there may be a tender consideration had of that which is so much urged, in that of an equal, as well as of a free representative. I shall desire that a medium, or some thoughts of a composure in relation to servants, or to foreigners, or such others such as shall be agreed upon. I say then, I conceive, excepting those, there may be a very equitable sense [p]resented to us from that offer in our own declarations wherein we do offer the common good of all, unless they have made any shipwreck or loss of it.

[Lieutenant] Chillenden:[2] In the beginning of this discourse there were overtures made of imminent danger. This way we have taken this afternoon is not the way to prevent it. I should humbly move that we should put a speedy end to this business, and that not only to this main question of the paper, but also according to the Lieutenant-General's motion, that a committee may be chosen seriously to consider the things in that paper, and

compare them with divers things in our declarations and engagements. That so as we have all professed, to lay down ourselves before God, if we take this course of debating upon one question a whole afternoon, if the danger be so near as it is supposed, it were the ready way to bring us into it. That things may be put into a speedy dispatch.

Clarke: I presume that the great stick here is this: that if every one shall have his property, it does bereave the kingdom of its principal fundamental constitution, that it [now] has. I presume that all people and all nations whatsoever have a liberty and power to alter and change their constitutions, if they find them to be weak and infirm. Now if the people of England shall find this weakness in their constitution, they may change it if they please. Another thing is this: if the light of nature be only in this, it may destroy the property which every man can call his own. The reason is this, because this principle and light of nature does give all men their own: as for example the clothes upon my back because they are not another man's. If every man has this property of election to choose those whom you fear may beget inconveniencies, I do not conceive that anything may be so nicely and precisely done, but that it may admit of inconveniency. If it be in that wherein it is now, there may those inconveniences rise from them. For my part I know nothing but the want of love in it, and the sword must decide it. I shall desire before the question be stated, it may be moderated as for foreigners.

Sir Hardress Waller:[3] This was that I was saying: I confess I have not spoken yet, and I was willing to be silent, having heard so many speak, that I might learn to. But it is not easy for us to say when this dispute will have an end; but I think it is easy to say

---

[1] Edmund Rolfe (fl. 1643–1656), an officer agitator. In June 1648 he would be accused, but acquitted, of plotting to assassinate the King.

[2] Edmund Chillenden (fl. 1638–1678), an officer agitator; later a General Baptist minister and Fifth Monarchist; after the Restoration he opened a coffee house.

[3] Sir Hardress Waller (ca. 1604–ca. 1666), commander of a New Model Army regiment; subsequently one of the regicides and active in Cromwell's Irish campaigns.

when the kingdom will have an end. But if we do not breathe out ourselves, we shall be kicked and spurned of all the world. I would fain know how far the question will decide it; for certainly we must not expect, while we have tabernacles here,[1] to be all of one mind. If it be to be decided by a question, and that all parties are satisfied in that, I think the sooner you hasten to it the better. If otherwise, we shall needlessly discover our dividing opinion, which as long as it may be avoided I desire it may. Therefore I desire to have a period.

Audley: I chanced to speak a word or two. Truly there was more offence taken at it. For my part I spoke against every man living, not only against yourself and the Commissary, but every man that would dispute till we have our throats cut. I profess, if so be there were none but you and the Commissary-General alone to maintain that argument, I would die in any place in England, in asserting that it is the right of every free-born man to elect, according to the rule, *quod omnibus spectat, ab omnibus tractari debet,* that which concerns all ought to be debated by all. He knew no reason why that law should oblige when he himself had no finger in appointing the lawgiver, and therefore I desire I may not lie in any prejudice before your persons.

Captain Bishop:[2] You have met here this day to see if God would show you any way wherein you might jointly preserve the kingdom from its destruction, which you all apprehend to be at the door. God is pleased not to come in to you. There is a gentleman, Mr Saltmarsh,[3] did desire what he has wrote may be read to the General Council. If God do manifest anything by him, I think it ought to be heard.

Ireton: That you will alter that constitution from a better to a worse, from a just to a thing that is less just is my apprehension; and I will not repeat the reasons of that, but refer to what I have declared before. To me, if there were nothing but this, that there is a constitution, and that constitution which is the very last constitution, which if you take away you leave nothing of constitution, and consequently nothing of right or property. I would not go to alter that, though a man could propound that which in some respects might be better, unless it could be demonstrated to me that this were unlawful, or that this were destructive. Truly, therefore, I say for my part, to go on a sudden to make such a limitation as that in general, if you do extend the latitude that any man shall have a voice in election who has not that interest in this kingdom that is permanent and fixed, who has not that interest upon which he may have his freedom in this kingdom without dependence, you will put it into the hands of men to choose, of men to preserve their liberty who will give it away.

I have a thing put into my heart which I cannot but speak. I profess I am afraid, that if we from such apprehensions as these are, of an imaginable right of nature, opposite to constitution, if we will contend and hazard the breaking of peace upon this enlargement of that business, I am confident our discontent and dissatisfaction, in that if ever they do well they do in this, if there be anything at all that is a foundation of liberty, it is this: that those who shall

---

[1] *while we have tabernacles* seems to mean to have debates like those held in religious meetings, though this is not a usage recorded in the *OED* for the period. Possibly also a figurative use of the recorded sense of occupying a temporary building, of living somewhere for a limited time (*OED* tabernacle *sb* 1); Waller is concerned about the usefulness of occupying time in theoretical debate when the military and political situation was still in flux.

[2] possibly George Bishop (d. 1668), a captain in the Parliamentary army, later a Quaker.

[3] John Saltmarsh (ca. 1612–1647), army chaplain; he had sent the Council of War a letter of reproof for breaking their promises, and warning them to heed the opinion of all speakers in these discussions, "from the highest to the meanest."

choose the lawmakers shall be men freed from dependence upon others. I think if we, from imaginations and conceits, will go about to hazard the peace of the kingdom, to alter the constitution in such a point, I am afraid we shall find the hand of God will follow it; we shall see that that liberty, which we so much talk of and contended for, shall be nothing at all by this our contending for it, by putting it into the hands of those men that will give it away when they have it.

Cromwell: If we should go about to alter these things, I do not think that we are bound to fight for every particular proposition. Servants, while servants, are not included. Then you agree that he that receives alms is to be excluded.

Lieutenant-Colonel Reade:[1] I suppose it's concluded by all, that the choosing of representatives is a privilege; now I see no reason why any man that is a native ought to be excluded that privilege, unless from voluntary servitude.

Petty: I conceive the reason why we would exclude apprentices, or servants, or those that take alms, it is because they depend upon the will of other men and should be afraid to displease. For servants and apprentices, they are included in their masters, and so for those that receive alms from door to door; but if there be any general way taken for those that are not bound, it would do well.

[Mr.] Everard:[2] I being sent from the agents of five regiments with an answer unto a writing, the committee was very desirous to inquire into the depth of our intentions. Those things that they had

there manifested in the paper, I declared it was the Lieutenant-General's desire for an understanding with us, and what I did understand as a particular person, I did declare, and were presuming those things I did declare did tend to unity. And if so, you will let it appear by coming unto us. We have gone thus far: we have had two or three meetings to declare and hold forth what it is we stand upon, the principles of unity and freedom. We have declared in what we conceive these principles do lie: I shall not name them all because they are known unto you. Now in the progress of these disputes and debates we find that the time spends, and no question but our adversaries are harder at work than we are. I heard that there were meetings (but I had no such testimony as I could take hold of), that there are meetings daily and contrivances against us. Now for our parts I hope you will not say all is yours, but we have nakedly and freely unbosomed ourselves unto you. Though these things have startled many at the first view, yet we find there is good hopes; we have fixed our resolutions, and we are determined, and we want nothing but that only God will direct us to what is just and right. But I understand that all these debates, if we shall agree upon any one thing: this is our freedom; this is our liberty; this liberty and freedom we are debarred of, and we are bereaved of all those comforts. In case we should find half a hundred of these, yet the main business is how we should find them, and how we should come by them. Is there any liberty that we find ourselves deprived of? If we have grievances let us see who are the hindrances, and when we have pitched upon that way. I conceive I speak humbly in this one thing as a particular person, that I conceive myself, that these delays, these disputes, will prove little encouragement. As it was told me by [one of] these gentlemen, that he had great jealousies that we would not come to the trial of our spirits and that perhaps there might happen another design in hand. I said to his Honour again, if they

---

[1] Thomas Reade, Lieutenant-Colonel in Colonel William Herbert's regiment.

[2] Robert Everard (fl. 1647–1664), soldier in Cromwell's regiment, a signatory of *The Case of the Army* (1647) and the first *Agreement of the People*.

would not come to the light, I would judge they had the works of darkness in hand. Now as they told me again on the other hand, when it was questioned by Colonel Hewson, they told me: "These gentlemen, not naming any particular persons, they will hold you in hand, and keep you in debate and dispute till you and we come all to ruin." Now I stood as a moderator between these things. When I heard the Lieutenant-General speak I was marvellously taken up with the plainness of the carriage. I said, I will bring them to you. You shall see if their hearts be so; for my part I see nothing but plainness and uprightness of heart made manifest unto you. I will not judge, nor draw any long discourses upon our disputes this day. We may differ in one thing, that you conceive this debating and disputation will do the work; we must put ourselves into the former privileges which we want.

Waller: I think this gentleman has dealt very ingenuously and plainly with us. I pray God we may do so too, and for one I will do it. I think our disputings will not do the thing. I think if we do make it our resolution that we do hold it forth to all powers, Parliament or King, or whoever they are, to let them know that these are our rights, and if we have them not we must get them the best way we can.

Cromwell: I think you say very well; and my friend at my back, he tells me that [there] are great fears abroad; and they talk of some things such as are not only specious to take a great many people with, but real and substantial, and such as are comprehensive of that that has the good of the kingdom in it. And truly if there be never so much desire of carrying on these things, never so much desire of conjunction, yet if there be not liberty of speech to come to a right understanding of things, I think it shall be all one as if there were no desire at all to meet. And I may say it with truth, that I verily believe there is as

much reality and heartiness amongst us, to come to a right understanding, and to accord with that that has the settlement of the kingdom in it, though when it comes to particulars we may differ in the way. Yet I know nothing but that every honest man will go as far as his conscience will let him; and he that will go farther, I think he will fall back. And I think, when that principle is written in the hearts of us, and when there is not hypocrisy in our dealings, we must all of us resolve upon this, that 'tis God that persuades the heart. If there be a doubt of sincerity, it's the devil that created that effect; and 'tis God that gives uprightness. And I hope with such an heart that we have all met withal; if we have not, God find him out that came without it; for my part I do it.

Ireton: When you have done this according to the number of inhabitants, do you think it is not very variable? I would have us fall to something that is practicable, with as little pains and dissatisfaction as may be. I remember that in the proposals that went out in the name of the army, it is propounded as a rule to be distributed according to the rates that the counties bear in the kingdom. And remember then you have a rule, and though this be not a rule of exactness, for the number will change every day; yet there was something of equality in it, and it was a certain rule, where all are agreed; and therefore we should come to some settling. Now I do not understand wherein the advantage does lie from a sudden danger upon a thing that will continue so long, and will continue so uncertain as this is.

Waller: 'Tis thought there's imminent danger; I hope to God we shall be so ready to agree for the future that we shall all agree for the present to rise as one man if the danger be such, for it is an impossibility to have a remedy in this. The paper says that this Parliament is to continue a year, but will the great burden of the people be ever satisfied with papers

[while] you eat and feed upon them? I shall be glad
that there be not any present danger; if not that you
will think of some way to ease the burden, that we
may take a course, and [deal with this] when we
have satisfied the people that we do really intend the
good of the kingdom. Otherwise, if the four Evan-
gelists were here, and lay free quarter upon them,[1]
they will not believe you.

Colonel Rainsborough: Moved, that the army might
be called to a rendezvous, and things settled....
—1647

---

[1] *free-quarter* the obligation to provide free room and board for
soldiers; the implication is that even the most fair-minded people will
cease eventually to support the army if the army cannot demonstrate
its good intentions.

The Trial of King Charles I
1649

By September 1648, any real chance of military victory for the King had ended. In the spring of that year, Parliamentary armies had quelled scattered Royalist uprisings (events usually known as the Second Civil War); and in August at Preston Oliver Cromwell defeated a Scottish army that had been promised the temporary establishment of Presbyterianism in return for the restoration of Royal prerogatives. In September an alliance of Parliamentary moderates sent commissioners to Newport on the Isle of Wight to discuss a peace settlement with the King. But some members of Parliament envisioned a settlement in which the King no longer played a role. With backing from the army, a radical minority in Parliament purged the House of Commons of its moderate majority in early December, and in January 1649 this "Rump" Parliament put the King on trial. The central charge was that Charles had "traitorously and maliciously" levied war against Parliament and the people they represented.

The trial began on January 20 and lasted eight days. Throughout the proceedings, Charles refused to acknowledge the jurisdiction of the court that had been created for the occasion. The first of the two texts below is the text he wrote to justify his refusal; he was not allowed to read this statement at the trial, but it was secretly printed shortly after the King was executed on January 30. For the political philosophy that underlies his argument, particularly the belief that a king cannot be subject to laws for which he himself provides the authority, see the 1610 speech to Parliament by King James VI/I. For another refusal to recognize the authority of a judicial body headed by John Bradshaw (though one motivated by a very different political philosophy), see Richard Overton's narrative, "The Proceedings of the Council of State." The second text here is the court's sentence. Fifty-nine judges (of the one hundred and thirty originally appointed) signed the death warrant; of these, twenty-nine were tried and convicted of treason in 1660, and thirteen were executed. In addition, the bodies of Oliver Cromwell, Henry Ireton, and Bradshaw (the president of the court) were exhumed for ceremonial hanging and quartering.

❧❧❧

The Trial of King Charles I

THE KING'S REASONS FOR DECLINING THE JURISDICTION OF THE HIGH COURT OF JUSTICE

Having already made my protestations, not only against the illegality of this pretended Court, but also, that no earthly power can justly call me (who am your King) in question as a delinquent, I would not any more open my mouth upon this occasion, more than to refer myself to what I have spoken, were I in this case alone concerned: but the duty I owe to God in the preservation of the true liberty of my people will not suffer me at this time to be silent: for, how can any free-born subject of England call life or anything he possesseth his own, if power without right daily make new, and abrogate the old fundamental laws of the land which I now take to be the present case? Wherefore when I came hither, I expected that you would have endeavoured to have satisfied me concerning these grounds which hinder me to answer to your pretended impeachment. But since I see that nothing I can say will move you to it (though negatives are not so naturally proved as affirmatives) yet I will show you the reason why I am confident you cannot judge me, nor indeed the meanest man in

England: for I will not (like you) without showing a reason, seek to impose a belief upon my subjects.

There is no proceeding just against any man, but what is warranted, either by God's laws or the municipal laws of the country where he lives. Now I am most confident this day's proceeding cannot be warranted by God's laws; for, on the contrary, the authority of obedience unto Kings is clearly warranted, and strictly commanded in both the Old and New Testament, which, if denied, I am ready instantly to prove.

And for the question now in hand, there it is said, that "where the word of a King is, there is power; and who may say unto him, what dost thou?" Eccles. 8:4. Then for the law of this land, I am no less confident, that no learned lawyer will affirm that an impeachment can lie against the King, they all going in his name:[1] and one of their maxims is, that the King can do no wrong. Besides, the law upon which you ground your proceedings, must either be old or new: if old, show it; if new, tell what authority, warranted by the fundamental laws of the land, hath made it, and when. But how the House of Commons can erect a Court of Judicature, which was never one itself (as is well known to all lawyers) I leave to God and the world to judge. And it were full as strange, that they should pretend to make laws without King or Lords' House, to any that have heard speak of the laws of England.

And admitting, but not granting, that the people of England's commission could grant your pretended power, I see nothing you can show for that; for certainly you never asked the question of the tenth man in the kingdom, and in this way you manifestly wrong even the poorest ploughman, if you demand not his free consent; nor can you pretend any colour for this your pretended commission, without the consent at least of the major part

of every man in England of whatsoever quality or condition, which I am sure you never went about to seek, so far are you from having it. Thus you see that I speak not for my own right alone, as I am your King, but also for the true liberty of all my subjects, which consists not in the power of government, but in living under such laws, such a government, as may give themselves the best assurance of their lives, and property of their goods; nor in this must or do I forget the privileges of both Houses of Parliament, which this day's proceedings do not only violate, but likewise occasion the greatest breach of their public faith that (I believe) ever was heard of, with which I am far from charging the two Houses; for all the pretended crimes laid against me bear date long before this Treaty at Newport, in which I having concluded as much as in me lay,[2] and hopefully expecting the Houses' agreement thereunto, I was suddenly surprised and hurried from thence as a prisoner;[3] upon which account I am against my will brought hither, where since I am come, I cannot but to my power defend the ancient laws and liberties of this kingdom, together with my own just right. Then for anything I can see, the higher House is totally excluded;[4] and for the House of Commons, it is too well known that the major part of them are detained or deterred from sitting;[5] so as if I had no other, this were sufficient for me to protest against the lawfulness of

---

[1] Since the monarch is the source of legal authority, lawyers in effect act in his name.

[2] Newport, on the Isle of Wight, was the site of negotiations (Sept.-Oct. 1648) between Charles and an alliance of moderate Parliamentarians. The King made concessions on religion and the militia, but admitted privately that he did so "merely in order to my escape."

[3] The army removed Charles from the Isle of Wight to the mainland on December 2.

[4] *the higher House*   the House of Lords.

[5] On December 6, the army either turned away or arrested all members of Parliament—a majority of the House of Commons—willing to continue negotiations with the King. In effect a military coup, "Pride's Purge" (named for the colonel who guarded the door) left only a radicalized "Rump" Parliament willing to put the King on trial.

your pretended Court. Besides all this, the peace of the kingdom is not the least in my thoughts; and what hope of settlement is there, so long as power reigns without rule or law, changing the whole frame of that government under which this kingdom hath flourished for many hundred years? (nor will I say what will fall out in case this lawless, unjust proceeding against me do go on) and believe it, the Commons of England will not thank you for this change; for they will remember how happy they have been of late years under the reigns of Queen Elizabeth, the King my father, and myself, until the beginning of these unhappy troubles, and will have cause to doubt, that they shall never be so happy under any new: and by this time it will be too sensibly evident, that the arms I took up were only to defend the fundamental laws of this kingdom against those who have supposed my power hath totally changed the ancient government.

Thus, having showed you briefly the reasons why I cannot submit to your pretended authority, without violating the trust which I have from God for the welfare and liberty of my people, I expect from you either clear reasons to convince my judgment, showing me that I am in an error (and then truly I will answer) or that you will withdraw your proceedings.

This I intended to speak in Westminster Hall, on Monday, January 22, but against reason was hindered to show my reasons.

THE SENTENCE OF THE HIGH COURT OF JUSTICE UPON THE KING

Whereas the Commons of England assembled in Parliament, have by their late Act intituled an Act of the Commons of England assembled in Parliament, for erecting an High Court of Justice for the trying and judging of Charles Stuart, King of England, authorised and constituted us an High Court of Justice for the trying and judging of the said Charles Stuart for the crimes and treasons in the said Act mentioned; by virtue whereof the same Charles Stuart hath been three several times convented before this High Court,[1] where the first day, being Saturday, the 20th of January instant, in pursuance of the said Act, a charge of high treason and other high crimes was, in the behalf of the people of England, exhibited against him, and read openly unto him, wherein he was charged, that he, the said Charles Stuart, being admitted King of England, and therein trusted with a limited power to govern by, and according to the law of the land, and not otherwise; and by his trust, oath, and office, being obliged to use the power committed to him for the good and benefit of the people, and for the preservation of their rights and liberties; yet, nevertheless, out of a wicked design to erect and uphold in himself an unlimited and tyrannical power to rule according to his will, and to overthrow the rights and liberties of the people, and to take away and make void the foundations thereof, and of all redress and remedy of misgovernment, which by the fundamental constitutions of this kingdom were reserved on the people's behalf in the right and power of frequent and successive Parliaments, or national meetings in Council; he, the said Charles Stuart, for accomplishment of such his designs, and for the protecting of himself and his adherents in his and their wicked practices, to the same end hath traitorously and maliciously levied war against the present Parliament, and people therein represented, as with the circumstances of time and place is in the said charge more particularly set forth; and that he hath thereby caused and procured many thousands of the free people of this nation to be slain; and by divisions, parties, and insurrections within this land, by invasions from foreign parts, endeavoured

---

[1] *convented* summoned (*OED* convent *v* 3b).

and procured by him,[1] and by many other evil ways and means, he, the said Charles Stuart, hath not only maintained and carried on the said war both by sea and land, but also hath renewed, or caused to be renewed, the said war against the Parliament and good people of this nation in this present year 1648;[2] in several counties and places in this kingdom in the charge specified; and that he hath for that purpose given his commission to his son the Prince, and others, whereby, besides multitudes of other persons, many such as were by the Parliament entrusted and employed for the safety of this nation, being by him or his agents corrupted to the betraying of their trust, and revolting from the Parliament, have had entertainment and commission for the continuing and renewing of the war and hostility against the said Parliament and people: and that by the said cruel and unnatural war so levied, continued and renewed, much innocent blood of the free people of this nation hath been spilt, many families undone, the public treasure wasted, trade obstructed and miserably decayed, vast expense and damage to the nation incurred, and many parts of the land spoiled, some of them even to desolation; and that he still continues his commission to his said son, and other rebels and revolters, both English and foreigners, and to the Earl of Ormond,[3] and to the Irish rebels and revolters associated with him, from whom further invasions of this land are threatened by his procurement and on his behalf; and that all the said wicked designs, wars, and evil practices of him, the said Charles Stuart, were still carried on for the advance-

ment and upholding of the personal interest of will, power, and pretended prerogative to himself and his family, against the public interest, common right, liberty, justice, and peace of the people of this nation; and that he thereby hath been and is the occasioner, author, and continuer of the said unnatural, cruel, and bloody wars, and therein guilty of all the treasons, murders, rapines, burnings, spoils, desolations, damage, and mischief to this nation, acted and committed in the said wars, or occasioned thereby; whereupon the proceedings and judgment of this Court were prayed against him, as a tyrant, traitor, and murderer, and public enemy to the Commonwealth, as by the said charge more fully appeareth. To which charge, being read unto him as aforesaid, he, the said Charles Stuart, was required to give his answer; but he refused so to do, and upon Monday, the 22nd day of January instant, being again brought before this Court, and there required to answer directly to the said charge, he still refused so to do;[4] whereupon his default and contumacy was entered;[5] and the next day, being the third time brought before the Court, judgment was then prayed against him on the behalf of the people of England for his contumacy, and for the matters contained against him in the said charge, as taking the same for confessed, in regard of his refusing to answer thereto: yet notwithstanding this Court (not willing to take advantage of his contempt) did once more require him to answer to the said charge; but he again refused so to do; upon which his several defaults, this Court might justly have proceeded to judgment against him, both for his contumacy and the matters of the charge, taking the same for confessed as aforesaid.

Yet nevertheless this Court, for its own clearer information and further satisfaction, have thought fit to examine witnesses upon oath, and take notice

---

[1] *invasions from foreign parts* referring to Irish Catholic forces, from whom Charles sought military support throughout the civil wars (see the reference to the Earl of Ormond below).

[2] Royalist risings in southeast England and Wales in the spring of 1648 were quashed by Fairfax and Cromwell in what is usually known as the Second Civil War.

[3] James Butler, twelfth Earl and subsequently first Duke of Ormond (1610–1688), the King's commander in Ireland.

[4] This was the day the King sought to read his reasons for refusing their jurisdiction, but was not allowed to do so.

[5] *contumacy* here, wilful disobedience of a court (*OED* contumacy 3).

of other evidences, touching the matters ordained in the said charge, which accordingly they have done.

Now, therefore, upon serious and mature deliberation of the premises, and consideration had of the notoriety of the matters of fact charged upon him as aforesaid, this Court is in judgment and conscience satisfied that he, the said Charles Stuart, is guilty of levying war against the said Parliament and people, and maintaining and continuing the same; for which in the said charge he stands accused, and by the general course of his government, counsels, and practices, before and since this Parliament began (which have been and are notorious and public, and the effects whereof remain abundantly upon record) this Court is fully satisfied in their judgments and consciences, that he has been and is guilty of the wicked design and endeavours in the said charge set forth; and that the said war hath been levied, maintained, and continued by him as aforesaid, in prosecution, and for accomplishment of the said designs; and that he hath been and is the occasioner, author, and continuer of the said unnatural, cruel, and bloody wars, and therein guilty of high treason, and of the murders, rapines, burnings, spoils, desolations, damage, and mischief to this nation acted and committed in the said war, and occasioned thereby. For all which treasons and crimes this Court doth adjudge that he, the said Charles Stuart, as a tyrant, traitor, murderer, and public enemy to the good people of this nation, shall be put to death by the severing of his head from his body.

—1649

A True Relation

1672

While English merchants had occasionally traded in slaves since the sixteenth century, a 1663 charter for the "Company of Royal Adventurers of England Trading in Africa" is the earliest document to list slaves as an officially recognized branch of English commerce. The slave trade grew in conjunction with the establishment in mid-century of sugar plantations in the West Indies; it is estimated that by the end of the century Dutch and English ships were carrying about 5000 slaves per year from the West African coast to labour in the plantations. After September 1672, the English trade was controlled by the Royal African Company. The following narrative was published in the same year the new company was given its charter, and its appearance reflects the growing importance of and interest in the African trade.

A True Relation purports to tell the story of John Watts (as told to his uncle, Richard Watts), held captive in the city of Old Calabar, a major trading port in what is now Nigeria. Old Calabar was founded by the Efik, a branch of the Ibibio-speaking peoples who still comprise one of the largest population groups in southeastern Nigeria. Efik traders played an important role in the slave trade through to the nineteenth century. Watt's geographical and much of his cultural detail accords with other (scattered) sources for the period: there seems no reason to doubt that the writer served on one of the English ships that did business in the port. But other details in his narrative, like the language Watts cites as native and the story of cannibalism (unattested by any other source or tradition for the area), have led some historians to deduce that his captivity narrative is likely fictitious, either entirely or at least in important details.[1] Whatever its status as an historical document, *A True Relation* should also be read as drawing on the conventions not only of the captivity narrative but also of travel writing and romance. For another captivity narrative, see the selection from Mary Rowlandson; for other accounts of native populations, see the selections from Edward Winslow and Pierre-Esprit Radisson.

⁂

A True Relation, of the Inhumane and Unparallel'd Actions and Barbarous Murders of Negroes or Moors: Committed on three English-men in Old Calabar in Guinny[2]

Among the variety of cruelties and murders, which history and experience daily inform us of, this, which I now intend to relate, is none of the least. And the story you shall have verbatim, from one of the sufferers' own mouth; who arrived lately in the Downs,[3] and is now in His Majesty's fleet.

In June 1668, the *Peach-tree* of London, a small vessel of the burthen of about sixty tons, Edward Dixon master, came into the Downs bound for Guinny, intending there to take in Negroes, and to transport them to the Barbados, and from thence to

---

[1] David Northrup, *Trade Without Rulers: Pre-Colonial Economic Development in South-Eastern Nigeria* (Oxford: Clarendon, 1978), p. 38; Monday Efiong Noah, *Old Calabar: The City-States and the Europeans* (Uyo, Nigeria: Scholars' Press, 1980), pp. 38–39.

[2] *Guinny* Guinea, the general name applied by Europeans to much of the Western coast of equatorial Africa. The city of Calabar, known until this century as Old Calabar, is a seaport in what is now southeastern Nigeria.

[3] *the Downs* a famous roadstead, or sheltered area of water near a shore where ships may rest at anchor; in the English Channel off the town of Deal, in Kent.

come for London,[1] where John Watts, the son of John Watts, of Elham, in the County of Kent, Chirurgion, shipped himself with the consent of Richard Watts, public notary of Deal;[2] little dreading that he, being not above eighteen years old, should meet with such a calamitous accident. The ship had not been long in the Downs, but a fair gale presenting, they suddenly hoisted sail, God's providence seeming to fill their sails with prosperous success; the first place they touched at was the Gold Coast,[3] where they stayed not long, but sailed to old Calabar in the Bith of Guinny.[4] They entered a river called the Cross River into Parrot Island.[5] After they had taken in their Negroes, and ready to sail, their anchor being a peek,[6] the Master calls up the boatswain and three men more, whereof the relator was one, and commands them to look out the copper bars that were left, and carry them on shore to try if they could sell them:[7] the boatswain with his small company desired that they might have arms with them, not believing the report of some, that informed them they were a harmless, and innocent people: they took with them three muskets and a pistol, and so rowed towards the shore, but not far from it unhappily our match fell into the water,[8] and the ship being fallen down from that narrow part of the river, nearer the sea, quite out of

our sight, we were consulting what would be safest for us to do: we were not willing to precipitate our own ruin, and we were also ashamed to return to our ship before we had dispatched what we were commanded to: at length the boatswain commanded the relator John Watts on shore, to the first house to light our match, which we recovered out of the water, after it was extinct; which he readily obeyed: but before he was twenty rods from the water side,[9] he was seized on by two blacks (or rather tawny Moors),[10] and by them haled above half a mile up into the country, and thrown with great violence upon his belly, and so compelled to lie till they stripped him; and more company coming to them, they were so eager for his poor canvas apparel, that some they tore off, others they cut off, and with that several pieces of his flesh, to his intolerable pain: with these rags they made little children aprons to cover their privities: linen and woolen being very scarce there.

The boatswain seeing this John Watts was thus carried away, was resolved with his other two companions to have him again, or else to venture all their lives for him. They arm themselves; but whilst they were consulting what to do, whether to venture on shore, or not, of a sudden they were beset with about a dozen men in several canoes, but they valiantly maintained their boat about the space of three hours, for after two of their three muskets were discharged, they defended themselves with their oars, and boat hooks. The boatswain received a mortal wound in his groin, and fell down in the boat; the other two adventured in the river, endeavouring by swimming to escape the merciless hands of cruel infidels; but the Negroes with their swift

---

[1] the infamous "triangle trade" route: the ships transported slaves from West Africa to work on the plantations of the West Indies, then carried sugar and other commodities back to London.

[2] Richard Watts appears to be the boy's guardian; he indicates at the end of the narrative that he is the one who has prepared the pamphlet for the press.

[3] *Gold Coast* present-day Ghana.

[4] *Bith of Guinny* now the Bight of Biafra, in the Gulf of Guinea.

[5] *Cross River...Parrot Island* The geography is accurate.

[6] *a peek* usually "a peak"; still anchored, but with the anchor cable wound in sufficiently so that it forms a straight line with the forestay.

[7] Finger-sized copper bars were the standard currency in that area at the time.

[8] *match* for lighting the muskets.

[9] *twenty rods* 110 yards, or about 100 metres.

[10] *blacks...tawny Moors* The two terms were not clearly distinguished in the period (a confusion evident in debates about the race of Shakespeare's Othello). But while Moors did control much of the slave trade in the interior, the local population in Old Calabar were Efik, the Ibibio-speaking people who still inhabit southeastern Nigeria.

canoes soon overtook them, and brought them on shore to the place where the relator was. The Negroes took the boatswain out of the ship's boat; and instead of endeavouring at all to preserve life which remained in him, immediately they robbed him of it; one of them with a keen weapon cutting off his head before his companions' faces; and then they prepare for their rare banquet, while he was yet reeking in his blood: they in a barbarous manner cut off pieces of flesh from off his buttocks and his thighs and his arms and shoulders, and broiled them on the coals, and with a great deal of impatience eagerly eat it before their faces to our great astonishment.[1] About fourteen days after, one of the company fell sick, and instead of being physicians to cure him, they were his butchers to murther him. They served him as they did the boatswain, cut off his head, and broiled and eat up his flesh and rejoiced exceedingly at this rich banquet. About ten days after the third fell sick, whom they served in the same manner.

This was no small cause of sorrow to the relator: the thoughts of their inhumane and barbarous actions sometimes surrounded him with fears and sorrows, hourly expecting to taste of the said cruelty. Death did not seem so terrible to him as the violent manner of it; being left now alone in a strange country, destitute of friends or acquaintance, or anything that might keep up his spirits: die he would fain, but not by the hand of infidels and barbarous monsters. But the great God that is most compassionate in the greatest extremities had pity on him, and notwithstanding the alteration of the climate and the want of clothes, and the strangeness of his food which was only herbs, he continued

in good health, and had time enough to lament this direful providence.

The natives who were daily expecting another banquet, met with a disappointment: either their customs or the over-ruling power of God would not suffer them to destroy him; he continuing still in health. Therefore they resolve to sell him: his *Arauna* or Master was pretty free to discourse him, which the relator was capable of, being about three years before in the West Indies, where he had learned the *Tata* language, which is easily attained being comprehended in a very few words, and all the Negroes speak of it.[2] He began to discourse his master to know the reason of their cruelty, who told him that he should rest himself contented, who if he were not sick, should not have his head cut off. In the boat which in the beginning they took with them, was a musket saved of the three which was not discharged; which his master some time after he had been with him, brought to him to know the use of it: he endeavoured as much as he could to make him apprehend the use of it, but still they professed their ignorance: but they commanded and threatened him to show the use of it. The fear of his master's displeasure and their inhumanity caused him to shoot it off; but the Negroes which expected some delightful thing were frustrated, and at the sudden noise and flash of fire (which they very much dread) ran from him, and were greatly affrighted; but quickly after hearing no more of that noise they came up to him again, and commanded him to do the like: he told them he had not powder which was the cause of the noise; but this would not satisfy these barbarians. He not being able to answer

---

[1] While the practice of human sacrifice is well attested on this part of the African coast up to the nineteenth century, there is no other record or tradition of cannibalism; Watt's story here seems unlikely; *Their... our* an example of the use of both third and first person narration within the same sentence.

[2] *Tata* not identified. While most of the languages spoken in Western Africa belong to the Niger-Congo language family, this family comprises several sub-families which themselves contain numerous highly distinct languages. Watts seems to be referring to a kind of widely understood patois, though the ethnographic appendix (perhaps added by an editor) states that Tata is *the* language of Old Calabar. However, none of the words Watts provides can be associated with *any* language spoken in the Old Calabar region.

their expectation, they concluded he was not willing, they proceed to threaten him, and were about to murder him, had not his master rescued him. Upon discourse after with this *Arauna* or Master he began to understand the reason of their barbarous dealing with him and his friends, he telling him that naturally the people were civil and simply honest, but if provoked, full of revenge; and that this cruelty was occasioned by some unhandsome action of carrying a native away without their leave about a year before; they resolving if any came ashore they should never go off alive.

He had not been above seven weeks in the country, but his master presented him to his King,[1] whose name was *E-fn-me* King of the *Buckamores*, who immediately gave him to his daughter, whose name was *Om-jah*, and when the King went abroad he attended him also as his page, throughout the whole circuit of his dominions, which was not above twelve miles, yet boasting extremely of his power and strength, but glorying exceedingly that he had a white to attend him, whom he employed to carry his bow and arrows at several places remote from the seaside; the people would run away from him for fear, others would fall down and seem to worship him, and use those actions as they do to their God. Their progress was never so long but they could return home at night, but never without a handsome load of a cup of the creature. During all the time of the relator's servitude there, he never knew him [the King] go abroad and come home sober. They drink of the best palm wine, and another sort of strong liquor, called *Penrore*. The relator quickly knew how to humour this profound Prince, and if any of the natives abused him, upon his complaint he had redress, as once by striving

with a negro his arm was broke, which by providence more than skill was set again.

After some months, the King of *Ca-la-nanch* whose name was *E-fn-man-cha*, hearing of this beautiful white, courted his neighbour Prince, that he would sell him to him; at length they struck a bargain, and the relator was sold for a cow and a goat; this King was a very sober and moderate person, free from treacheries and mischiefs, that the other was subject unto; and he would often discourse the relator, and ask him of his King and country, and if his kingdoms and dominions were as big as his, which were not above twenty-five miles in length and fifteen in breadth. He told him as much as his understanding and years made him capable of, keeping still in the bounds of modesty, and yet relating as much as possible to the honour and dignity of his sovereign; first informing him of the greatness of one of his kingdoms, the several shires and counties it contained, with number of its cities and towns and castles, and the strength of each, the infinite inhabitants, and valour of his subjects. One of these kingdoms was enough to amaze sufficiently this petty governor, that he need not to mention any more of his Majesty's glory and dignity. It put him into such a profound consternation, that he resolved to find out some way to tender his respects to this mighty prince, and no way could he find so convenient, as to tell the relator, that if he could find but a passage, he would let him go to England, to tell his Majesty of the great favour and respect he had for him. This did not a little rejoice our English man. Withal the King told him, that he would send him a present, which should be two cabareets or goats, which they do value at a very high rate; the King having not above 16 or 18. He tells the King, that the King of England had many thousands of his subjects, that were under the degree of gentlemen, which had a thousand of sheep apiece; the flesh of which, they valued at a very much higher rate than goats.

---

[1] *his King* As the narrative later describes, this and the other local kingdoms were small-scale: unlike the Ashanti, Fon and Yoruba west of the Niger river, most of the peoples of southeastern Nigeria, such as the Igbo and Ibibio, did not create large-scale kingdoms or federations.

Though our English man lived very handsomely with this *E-fn-man-cha* King of the *Ca-la-nanch*, yet his desires and his hopes were still for his native country: at length he obtained a promise from his King, that the first English ship that came into the road,[1] should have liberty to release or purchase him; this very much rejoiced his heart: now he thought every day a year, till he could hear of, or see some English ship arrived. Many times when he was alone, his heart would be oppressed with sighs and sobbings, when he thought of his relations, and the comfortable society that they had together; that it should be his unhappy fate to be captivated amongst barbarous infidels. Oftentimes did he walk down to the seaside, sometimes with hopes, sometimes with fear, earnestly expecting the winds of God's providence to blow in some English ship thither: his often recourse to the seaside was discerned by one *Ja-ga* a wizard, and the chiefest in three or four kingdoms thereabouts; they are persons that the natives give very much credit to, and on any difficult occasion run to them for satisfaction. That famous Delphean Oracle was never had in greater adoration,[2] than the prophetical speeches of these Moorish wizards. Though they have infinite numbers of them in every place, yet this *Ja-ga* had the most renown amongst them; and one day he comes to him, and very kindly asked him, why he so very often frequented that place; he told him, to see if he could discover any English vessel to come in there; but he being not unacquainted with his great fame, asked him when he did believe there would one come in, not that he was willing to give credit to any of their divinations, but supposing that he thereby should please him and answer his expectation. *Ja-ga* immediately told him that the fifteenth day after an English ship should come into

the road. Then he asked him whether that ship should carry him away. To this he answered doubtfully, but told him that he should be offered to the master of the ship, and if they could not agree, but that he should come to shore again, he should not be sold, and that in a very short time after he should die for grief.

These fifteen days seemed very long and tedious; many a look did he cast on the sea with an aching heart: the fourteenth day he went to the highest hill thereabout, but to no purpose, for he could discover no ship: next morning he went again two or three times, but saw none: about two or three hours after came running into *E-fn-man-cha*, some of the Moors, and told him there was a canoe coming, so they called our ships, at which our English man heartily rejoiced, hoping then to be released forthwith, yet durst not show his joy for fear of punishment or of death; for though he lived better now than with his first master, yet his service was far worse than the slaves in Turkey, and their diet worse than dog's meat; therefore had he cause enough of inward joy; the ship came immediately in, and he hies away presently to *Ja-ga*, to know if it were an English ship, who resolved him that it was; it happened to be the *St. Maloes,* merchant, Captain Royden commander, who hastened to dispatch his business, took in his Negroes, and was ready to sail, and our English man heard never a word what should become of him, the King never offering to sell him; this put him on a resolution to endeavour to make an escape, and to that end had prepared a piece of timber which he had drawn near the water side, on which he intended to paddle to the ship, which then lay about a league from the shore. Just by the seaside, as he was about to launch his little floating stick, he espied a great alligator, which will devour a man at a mouthful; so this made him alter his resolution, and resolve rather to live with inhumane infidels than to throw himself into so imminent a danger, which would have been

---

[1] *road* roadstead (see note above).

[2] *Delphean Oracle* the oracle in the temple of Apollo at Delphi in ancient Greece, the most famous in the classical world.

little less than self-murther. But the next day, which I may call a day of jubilee, Almighty God opened the heart of the King to let the poor English man go: he sent him in a canoe, placed between a negro's legs, with some others to guide this small vessel, for fear he should leap over-board, and swim to the ship. At a distance from the ship he hailed her in the English tongue, which was no small cause of admiration to those on board to hear an English tongue out of their canoes: the Negroes gave him leave to stand up and show himself to the Captain, to whom he gave an account how four were left there, and only he preserved. It was a pretty while before they could strike a bargain, though the Captain was resolved not to leave him behind. Several times the Negroes paddled away with their canoe, resolving not to part with him; but what with his entreaties and promises he persuaded them to the ship again, and they delivered him on board for forty-five copper bars and iron bars, each copper bar being about the bigness of a youth's little finger, the iron bars a little bigger.

Now were his joys completed, he thought himself, as it were caught up into the third heavens;[1] he could hardly persuade himself but it was a dream or vision, and that he did not really see English faces or embrace English bodies. It was some time before he could throw himself at the Captain's feet, and acknowledge his infinite cause of joy in himself, and thankfulness to him for his deliverance from such a severe captivity; that he that lately was a slave to infidels, that worship they know not what, should now see the faces of Christians, and join with them in worshipping the true God; and to him first he offered up the sacrifice of hearty thanksgiving, that had sent his angel to redeem him from so cruel a bondage. When he came on board, his hair was very long, and his skin tawny (Mulatto like) having gone naked all the time he was there,

and frequently anointing himself with palm oil, he looked like a tawny-Moor; but immediately the seamen aboard with Christian-like hearts apparelled him. The master commanded to hoist sail, and having a fair wind, they sailed to Barbados, where Captain Royden was to tarry some time; but the relator earnestly desiring to go to his native country, and his relations, got passage to the Downs, in the *Catharine* of London, Captain South commander, which through God's goodness in a few weeks arrived in the Downs, where the relator was put on shore, to his uncle, Mr. Richard Watts of Deal, his great joy and satisfaction, who took this relation from his own mouth.

Having showed you how he was captivated, and some part of his trials and troubles, and also his deliverance and freedom; we will now speak of the People, and of their Country, as it was taken from his own mouth, which is no more than others have spoken formerly, who have been in the same Country.[2]

The People: The People are very careless, idle, sluggish, given wholly to ease; going stark naked (only some of their chiefest having a little apron to cover their nakedness), not exercising themselves either in work or play; free from having any tillage whatsoever (a small part only for tobacco, for their own use, excepted), having no thought for tomorrow. Their stature and bigness not near so big as our English.

Language: Their language is called the *Tata* language; it is contained in very few words, only so much as barely discovers their intentions: and is in part understood of all Negroes.

---

[1] *third heavens* Paradise; see II Corinthians 12:2.

[2] While several earlier writers provide brief accounts of the Guinea coast, the most detailed seventeenth-century English source is later: John Barbot's *A Description of the Coasts of North and South Guinea* (1732), a record of his travels there between 1678 and 1682.

The Country: The Country seems to be very fertile, overgrown with wood: sugar canes naturally grow there. He has been in most parts of the West Indies, yet he says, he never saw bigger nor more juicy than is there: the people lie secure as they think, but indeed lie very open, & are a prey to a handful of men. There are many bears (which are very good meat) which they often eat of, when they take pains to catch them. They have also hogs, beefs, deer and buffaloes, divers sort of good eating fowls, as cocks and hens, parrots, parakeets, & roots and several sorts of herbs, also palm-wine, which they have by cutting a top of a tree, then issues forth the wine: sap of wood, when 'tis burning. There is also very good fish; there is plenty of many things, they only want laborious persons to catch provision (for all are wild) and to cut down the woods: John Watts being much in the West Indies, and understanding the way to make sugar, invited them to learn, having such excellent juicy canes. But idleness would not hearken to so reasonable a request.

Their Provisions: Their provisions is *Ebung*, a root like a turnip, and as good and hearty as a potato; yams, plantains, palm oil, water and palm wine for drink; their flesh is elephants, wild boars, sows and pigs, deer, monkeys, baboons, dogs, &c; their fish is sea-cows and bulls, alligators, albacores, the catfish &c.

Their Weapons: Bows, arrows, and swords, they make of a piece of iron they steal from the English, and beat out with stones, which they neatly engrave: also they have a lance, which is also tipped at end with a piece of iron, and cut and engraved with flints, as they do their swords: very few of them have either lance or sword, many of them have swords of iron-wood, so called there. Their bow is about four foot long: their arrows about two foot and a quarter: their lance is about five foot long.

These are the weapons they fight with, and with them do much mischief.

Of their Houses: Their houses are bigger or lesser, according to the family and number of wives every man enjoys (for every one hath liberty to have as many wives as he pleases; the ordinary men have two, three, or four; but the rich men and the King have many wives), set on scratches or posts covered with the leaves of a *Membo* (alias a Palm-wine) tree: the going in is very low (not above three foot high) and within, it is not six foot high: in this room is their fire kept day and night, their lodgings joining to this room: every wife hath her several house or lodging for her self and children, but all make use of this common fire, which is only for dressing of victuals; they have no occasion for a fire of any other use.

Of their Habit: The King and some great men have clouts as big as a sheet of large paper to cover their nakedness: so likewise the King's wives and great men's wives have a pilch or clout; but for the common people, they go stark naked, and are no more ashamed than brute beasts.

Of their God: They have no particular place of worship, neither do they congregate themselves, nor are there ministers, or in the least a talk of their God (but of fear of being beat by him) but like beasts rise out of their little lodgings, eat, drink and take their pleasures, and at night sleep again. He hath oftentimes heard them say, their God (which is the Devil) oftentimes appears to them in the likeness of a man, about two foot and a half high, as black as they are, whom they call *Ajah* (which is very strange that the Devil should give himself such a name, which is compounded of *A* and *Jah*, which is one of the names of God, as in Exodus: *Jah* is my name,[1] so *Ajah* being joined together, is as much as if the Devil should call himself without God, or against God. But for that the learned will tell you at ease, that with much study cannot be resolved by my pen). When any of them are sick, they go to the picture of their *Ajah*, and speak to it, then suddenly after he appears, as at other times: for when he appears in a human shape, he hath many copper bars about his loins, legs, neck, and arms, as the chief of them go with; then all presently worship him: then presently they kill dogs, goats, or chickens (but most commonly dogs) according as he commands, cutting off their heads, throwing the blood on the sick person, burning the bodies, and burying the heads and legs for a sacrifice to *Ajah*. If he recover, he takes three or four chickens and other things, and hangs them up alive by the legs over where he was sick, until they are dead; and when they are dead, he hangs them without his house at the top of a high pole, who that night are eaten up by the buzzards, and other wild fowl. If the sick man recover not, and if he be rich, they take several of his slaves before his face and behead them, and throw their blood on their master. These poor creatures think it a great honour that they may lose their lives for the recovery of their master's health.

If they die: If ordinary people be sick and like to die, they cut off their heads, and keep them above ground five days. But if a rich man be sick, they cut not off his head, but let him die naturally. And when five days are expired, they bury him with his copper bars about his neck, waist, arms, and legs, as they usually go, burying with him every sort of that household stuff they have, as a stool, an earthen pot, a calabash, a gourd, etc. and with him some of his servants' heads, sometimes three or four, sometimes ten or twelve, and this is a credit for the master, and

an honour to the servant.[2] Into the grave is killed and thrown in several goats, chickens, and other provisions, according to the number of the persons therein; for their *Ajah* persuades them they go into a far country, where there is all necessaries and all riches, and that this provision is to eat by the way for the gentleman and his men that are buried. But when once they come there, they shall have all whatever they desire.

Of their king: He knows not whether the King be hereditary or elective. This he observed in both Kingdoms, that every morning the young maidens of the town where the King lives, wait for the King's rising at his house or palace, which is larger and handsomer than any of theirs, because he has more wives; when he comes out they keep continual bowing with their heads and bodies to him for the space of eight or ten minutes, saying, *Aa, eera*, and clap their hands; which words, *Aa* is how do you, and *eera* is thanks for his health; he all the time saying *Aa*, or how do you. The whole people are as serviceable to their King, as we are to our Sovereign.

Slaves: The slaves they sell to the English are prisoners taken in war: the Kings war much against one another.[3] They have no holds, castles, nor prisons; but for keeping those they have taken, until the next ship comes in, with withes[4] they fasten them to a

---

[1] *one of the names of God* See Exodus 6:3, Psalm 68:4.

[2] a custom still practised in the area until the mid nineteenth century, when the Efik abolished it.

[3] *The slaves they sell to the English* European traders rarely collected slaves themselves (it was not worth their time), and did not even travel inland beyond the coast until long after the overseas trade had ended. Internal wars, raids, and kidnaping by other natives were likely the most common sources of slaves, though there is considerable evidence for later periods that enslavement also served as a judicial punishment, as Watts claims later in this section. Watts might also be making a distinction between "the slaves they sell to the English" and those who remained as part of the domestic slave trade, which continued in the area through to the early twentieth century.

[4] *withes* strong, supple twigs, like willow (*OED* withe *sb* 1).

pole, that they cannot untie themselves, and get home. They are also persuaded that they go to help that King to fight against his enemy, and that they shall live idly, and eat good victuals, drink good liquor, and have clothes, and that the King will give them great rewards. But if half were performed that is promised, they would be more ready to go, than we to fetch them.

How Ajah uses them: He oftentimes heard them cry out in the night, making a very great screeching noise, and lamentable cry, three or four hours together; and that is when they do not please *Ajah*, or he takes an occasion against them, for he keeps them as slaves. Next day they bemoan themselves to themselves, for if they complain one to another, then he beats and pinches them worse than before. They told him oftentimes that *Ajah* appears to them in several shapes, and very oftentimes fears them, he comes so ugly; but most times he comes in their own shape, with copper bars, as aforesaid.

Their Birth: There is no more compassion, nor care taken on them, or for them that are big with child, than there is England for their sows, cows, sheep, &c. (no nor so much), and when delivered, they take as little care of their children; for as soon as they are born, their mother fetches water, and with her hand puts it in their nostrils till they are almost strangled, then they take them up by the heels, their head downwards, for the water to run away; then they lay them on the ground, where after they have cried their fill, they fall asleep: this is all they have the first four and twenty hours. If they be poor women, they tie their children at their backs, and go to work.

Their Marriages: If a man and a maid agree, and resolve to be betrothed (for 'tis certainly reported, widows there never marry) they go before several persons, one whereof is the King, or a great man,

and cut each other's wrist with a flint stone, and suck each other's blood, and this is their marriage, and that knot there with them cannot be broken.

Of a Whore: If a woman be taken in whoredom, they carry her to an ants' nest (which there is bigger than a bushel, and hang in trees in a bunch like bees): under the ants they tie her fast with withes, then with a pole shake down the nest on her; where they keep her about half an hour, in which time she is almost stung to death: then they carry her to a fire, and heat her back, and also cut at least ten gashes in it, that she may be known: then for the next fault her husband sells her.[1]

A Scold: If a wife scold with any of her neighbours, or with her husband's other wives, and she be abusive, especially if she strikes, and he see it or have good evidence, he takes the scold, and cuts a cross in her shoulder about four inches long, and if she commit the like fault, he sells her. Thus they take occasion to sell their wives, children, and servants.

A Thief: Though they generally are thieves themselves when they come into our ships, yet they are severer against thieves in their own country by blows, and for the second fault sell them.

Wounds: If any be wounded, they knock the wound, and cut round about it, and that is all the remedy.

Rain: The rains come every full moon, which they call a year (for the moon is their governor for almost everything), but once in three or four moons it happens that so much water comes from the hills that it comes close to their towns, and oftentimes does mischief.

---

[1] Evidence from later periods indicates that slavery did function as a form of judicial punishment.

A Canoe: A canoe is their boat, which is the body of a tree, which they cut hollow, somewhat like unto one of our hog troughs.

Dressing of Victuals: They are very subject to their own humour, and will not be taught; he would have showed them how to dress their victuals, but they would not learn, saying, as for flesh, if it were little more than hot through, it were enough: so also they eat their herbs and fish: as for salt, he never saw any there.

—1672

The Gentlewoman's Companion
1673

*T*he Gentlewoman's Companion, a domestic advice manual and an early example of conduct literature, was first published in 1673. Hannah Woolley was identified on the title page and in subsequent pages as its author. Little is known of Hannah Woolley's parentage or early life. In 1647, she was married to Benjamin Woolley, master of the free school at Newport, and resided in Essex. The couple had four sons. When the family moved to Hackney in 1655, she managed the domestic affairs of her husband's boarding school. Widowed by Woolley, Hannah married Francis Challinor of St. Margaret's, Westminster in 1666.

Woolley published a series of books of recipes and domestic advice manuals, among them *The Lady's Directory* (1661), *The Cook's Guide* (1664), *The Queen-like Closet* (1671), and *The Lady's Delight* (1672). However, in *A Supplement To the Queen-like Closet*, Woolley objects to a book which has been published under her name, a work which she claims contains a false biography. She likely refers to *The Gentlewoman's Companion* which sets forth an account of her supposed early life.

The Gentlewoman's Companion not only includes principles of domestic management and a series of recipes as do her earlier works, but contains substantial counsel on social deportment and conduct. In the Epistle Dedicatory, the book is promoted as "a universal companion and guide to the female sex, in all relations, companies, conditions, and state of life even from childhood down to old age; and from the lady at the Court to the cook-maid in the country." *The Gentlewoman's Companion* seeks to define for its readers the proper role of gentlewomen in English society. Regardless of its authorship, *The Gentlewoman's Companion* is an entertaining account of the education and occupations of middle-class women in Restoration England. The date of Woolley's death is unknown.

❧❧❧

The Gentlewoman's Companion; Or, a Guide to the Female Sex:

THE INTRODUCTION

*T*he right education of the female sex, as it is in a manner everywhere neglected, so it ought to be generally lamented. Most in this depraved later age think a woman learned and wise enough if she can distinguish her husband's bed from another's. Certainly man's soul cannot boast of a more sublime original than ours; they had equally their efflux from the same eternal immensity, and therefore capable of the same improvement by good educa-tion.[1] Vain man is apt to think we were merely intended for the world's propagation, and to keep its human inhabitants sweet and clean; but, by their leaves, had we the same literature, he would find our brains as fruitful as our bodies. Hence I am induced to believe, we are debarred from the knowledge of human learning, lest our pregnant wits

---

[1] *they had equally...eternal immensity* Their souls emanated from the same divine source (*OED* efflux *sb* 4 *concr*). Compare Henry More's "all our souls are free effluxes from his essence" (*Psychozoia* Pref.). Likely it is an allusion to Agrippa's *De nobilitate et praecellentia foeminei sexus*: "God the Creator of all things, in whom the plenitude of both sexes dwells, both made man like himself: male and female created he them...Therefore there is no preeminence of nobility (between man and women, by the essence of the soul)" (trans. Edward Fleetwood, 1652).

should rival the towering conceits of our insulting lords and masters.[1]

Pardon the severity of this expression, since I intend not thereby to infuse bitter rebellion into the sweet blood of females; for know, I would have all such as are entered into the honourable state of matrimony to be loyal and loving subjects to their lawful (though lording) husbands. I cannot but complain of, and must condemn the great negligence of parents in letting the fertile ground of their daughters lie fallow, yet send the barren noddles of their sons to the university where they stay for no other purpose than to fill their empty sconces with idle notions to make a noise in the country.[2]

. . . .

WHAT QUALIFICATIONS BEST BECOME AND ARE MOST SUITABLE TO A GENTLEWOMAN

I have already endeavoured to prove, that though nature hath differed mankind into sexes, yet she never intended any great difference in the intellect. This will evidently appear not only from those many arguments learned Cornelius Agrippa hath laid down in a particular treatise for the vindication of the excellency of the female-sex, but likewise from the many learned and incomparable writings of famous women, ancient and modern, particularly Anna Comnena, who wrote the Eastern History in Greek, a large folio.[3] Nor can we without great ingratitude forget the memory of that most ingenious Dutch lady Anna Maria Schurman, who was so much admired by the greatest scholars in Europe

for her unparalleled, natural and acquired parts, that there were very few (as the great Salmasius, etc.) who did not frequently correspond with her by letters.[4] Her *Opuscula* or smaller works are now extant, printed in Holland in Latin, Greek, and Hebrew, in which there is a small tract, proving that a woman's capacity is no way inferior to man's in the reception of any sort of learning; and therefore exhorts all parents who are not much necessitated, not to let their children spin away their precious time, or pore on a sampler, till they have pricked out the date of their life;[5] but rather instruct them in the principles of those learned tongues, whereby they may at pleasure pick-lock the treasuries of knowledge contained in those languages, and adapt them for the conversation and discourse of most nations.

I need not go out of our native country to produce you examples of our own sex for your imitation and encouragement in treading the paths of learning. I shall forbear to speak of the incomparable worth and pregnant parts of some gentlewomen lately deceased, as Mrs. Philips the ingenious translatress of Pompey, etc. find what is extant of hers;[6] or her contemporaries will more at large express their matchless merit; nor shall I eulogize or praise the living, nominating any person, lest I be thought one partially addicted to flattery: Yet give me leave to say, I could instance

---

[1] *pregnant* fertile, inventive (*OED* pregnant *a*[2] II.3a,b).

[2] *noddles* heads as the seat of the mind, with a playful suggestion of dullness or emptiness (*OED* noddle *sb*[1] 3); *sconces* a jocular term for the head, especially the crown of the head (*OED* sconce *sb*[2] arch).

[3] *Cornelius Agrippa* as cited above; *Anna Comnena* (1083–1153 C.E.), the daughter of Alexius I, Emperor of Constantinople, is considered the first female historian. Her work *Alexias* (ca. 1148) is a fifteen-volume history of her family, the Comneni.

[4] *Anna Maria Schurman* also referred to as Anna Maria van Schurman (1607–1678). She was a Dutch scholar of international reputation. *Opuscula* (1648) is the collection of her theological and philosophical works. Schurman defended the education of women in *A Friendly Discourse Between Anna Maria Schurman and A. Rivetus Concerning the Capacity of Women for Scholarly Pursuits* (1638), as she did in *The Learned Maid; or, Whether a Maid may be a Scholar?* (1641), translated into English by Clement Barksdale in 1659.

[5] *sampler* a piece of canvas embroidered by a girl as a specimen of her skill (*OED* sampler *sb*[1] 3b).

[6] *Mrs. Philips…Pompey* Katherine Philips (1632–1664) translated Corneille's *La Mort de Pompée* into English verse and adapted it for the stage in 1663. Her poems and translations were published in 1667.

not a few, who (to the glory of our sex, and the place of their nativity if occasion modestly required) would not blush to answer a capricious *virtuoso* in three of the most useful tongues spoken or understood, that is Latin, French, and Italian.

I desire not to hyperbolize; it is probable they may not be so expert in the anatomizing an insect, or the discovery of some monstrous production, as these Academical Wits are; yet for ought I know, may find out many monstrosities in their brain, whilst they are subtly plumbing the depth of their self-admired understanding.

Now since it may hence appear, ladies, that you have no Pygmean souls, but as capable of gigantic growth as of your male opponents; apply yourself to your grammar by time, and let your endeavours be indefatigable, and not to be tired in apprehending the first principles of the Latin tongue. I shall forbear to give you rules for attaining the perfect knowledge thereof, but leave you to that method your tutor or skillful governess shall propound for your observation.

I need not tell you the vast advantages that will accrue hereby, your own experience will better inform you hereafter. However, I shall hint some, as first, your understanding the Latin tongue will enable you to write and speak true and good English; next it will accommodate you with an eloquent style in speaking, and afford you matter for any discourse: lastly, you will be freed from the fear of rencountering such who make it their business to ransack a new world of words to find out what are long and obscure;[1] not regarding how insignificant they carry a rattling sound with them. Thus these fops of rhetoric, spawns of non-intelligency, will venture the spraining of their tongues, and splay-

footing of their own mouths, if they can but cramp a young gentlewoman's intellect.[2]

. . . .

OF THE GOVERNMENT OF THE EYE

As prudence is the eye of the soul, so discretion is the apple of that eye but as for the natural eyes, they are the casements of the soul, the windows of reason: as they are the inlets of understanding, so they are the outlets or discoverers of many inward corruptions. A wanton eye is the truest evidence of a wandering and distracted mind. As by them you ought not to betray to others' view, your imperfections within; so be not betrayed by their means, by vain objects without: This made the princely prophet pray so earnestly, *Lord turn away my eyes from vanity.*[3] And hence appears our misery, that those eyes which should be the cisterns of sorrow, limbecks of contrition, should become the lodges of lust, and portals of our perdition.[4] That those which were given us for our assistants, should become our assassinates.

An unclean eye, is the messenger of an unclean heart; wherefore confine the one, and it will be a means to rectify the other. There are many objects a wandering eye finds out, whereon to vent the disposition of her corrupt heart.

The ambitious eye makes honour her object, wherewith she torments herself, both in aspiring to what she cannot enjoy; as likewise, in seeing another enjoy that whereto herself did aspire. The covetous makes wealth her object; which she obtains with toil, enjoys with fear, foregoes with grief; for being got, they load her; loved, they foil her; lost, they gall her. The envious makes her neighbour's flourishing

---

[1] *rencountering* encountering a person in a hostile fashion (*OED* rencounter *v* 1 *trans*).

[2] *fops* pretenders to wit, wisdom or accomplishments (*OED* fop *sb* 2); *splay-footing* slanting or sprawling (*OED* splay *adv* Aa,Bb; splay-foot 3).

[3] *Lord turn…from vanity* Psalm 119:37.

[4] *limbecks* apparatus formerly used in distilling (*OED* alembic).

condition her object; she cannot but look on it; looking, pine and repine at it; and by repining, with envy, murders her quiet and contentment. The loose or lascivious makes beauty her object; and with a leering look, or wanton glance, while she throweth out her lure to catch others, she becomes caught herself.

Gentlewomen, I am not insensible, that you frequent places of eminency for resort, which cannot but offer to your view variety of pleasing objects. Nay, there where nothing but chaste thoughts, staid looks, and modest desires, should harbour, are too commonly loose thoughts, light looks, and licentious desires in especial honour. The means to prevent this malady, which like a spreading canker disperseth itself in all societies, is to abate your esteem for any earthly object. Do you admire the comeliness of any creature? Remove your eye from thence, and bestow it on the contemplation of the super-excellency of your Creator.

Put a check to the straggling disposition of your eyes, lest Dinah-like, by straying abroad you are in danger of ravishing.[1] Now to preserve purity of heart, you must observe a vigilancy over every sense; where, if the eye which is the light of the body be not well disposed, the rest of the senses cannot choose but be much darkened. Be assured, there is no one sense that more distempers the harmony of the mind, nor prospect of the soul, than this window of the body. It may be said to open ever to the raven, but seldom to the dove.[2] Roving affections, it easily conveys to the heart; but dove-like innocence, it rarely retains in the breast. The very frame

of your eyes may sufficiently inform you how to govern and guide them. For it is observed by the most curious occultists, that whereas all irrational creatures have but four muscles to turn their eyes round about; man alone hath a fifth to draw his eyes up to heaven. Do not then depress your eyes, as if earth were the center of their happiness, but on heaven the haven of their bliss after earth. To conclude, so order and dispose your looks, that censure may not tax them with lightness, nor an amorous glance impeach you of wantonness. Send not forth a tempting eye to take another; nor entertain a tempting look darting from another. Take not; nor be taken. To become a prey to others, will enslave you, to make a prey of others will transport you. Look then upward, where the more you look, you shall like; the longer you live, you shall love. From the management of the eyes let us next proceed to speech.

OF SPEECH AND COMPLEMENT

The eye entertains itself not with more objects than the invention furnishes the tongue with subjects; and as without speech, no society can subsist; so by it we express what we are; as vessels discover themselves best by the sound. Let discretion make opportunity her anvil, whereon to fashion a seasonable discourse; otherwise, though you speak much, you discourse little.

It is true (ladies) your tongues are held your defensive armour, but you never detract more from your honour than when you give too much liberty to that slippery glib member. That ivory guard or garrison, which impales your tongue, doth caution and instruct you, to put a restraint on your speech. In much talk you must of necessity commit much error, as least it leaves some tincture of vain-glory, which proclaims the proud heart from whence it proceeded, or some taste of scurrility, which dis-

---

[1] *Dinah-like* When Dinah, the only named sister of the twelve sons of Jacob, "went out to see the daughters of the land" (Shalem), she was raped by Shechem, a Hivite, who then sought to marry her. To avenge the rape, her brothers Simeon and Levi killed Shechem and all the males residents of Shalem (Genesis 34:1–31).

[2] *raven...dove* The raven, believed mischievous and thievish, was popularly regarded as a bird of evil omen and mysterious character (*OED*). In biblical tradition, the dove symbolizes purity, peace and reconciliation. It is often identified with the Holy Spirit.

plays the wanton heart from whence it streamed.[1]

A well-disposed mind will not deliver anything till it hath rightly conceived; but its expressions are always prepared by a well-seasoned deliberation. Think not I would have you altogether silent (ladies) in company, for that is misbecoming error on the other side; but I would have you when you do speak, to do it knowingly and opportunely.

A saying of a philosopher will not be unworthy of your commemoration, who seeing a silent guest at a public feast, used the words, *If thou beest wise, thou art a fool; if a fool, thou art wise in holding thy peace*. For as propriety of speech affords no less profit than delight to the hearer, so it argues discretion in the speaker.

By the way, let me advise you never to tie yourself so strictly to elegancy, or ornament; as by outward trimming, the internal worth of right understanding should be altogether forgotten, and so your expressions savour of some absurd impertinency. This were to prefer the rind before the pith, and the sound of words before solid reason.[2]

That excellent precept of Ecclesiasticus, though it was spoken in general yet I know not to whom it is more particularly useful than to young women.[3] Thou that art young, speak, if need be, and yet scarcely when thou art twice asked. *Comprehend much in few words; in many, be as one that is ignorant; be as one that understandeth, and yet hold thy tongue.*

Volubility of tongue in these, argues either rudeness of breeding, or boldness of expression.

Gentlewomen, it will best become ye, whose generous education hath estranged ye from the first, and whose modest disposition hath weaned ye from the last, in public society to observe, rather than discourse; especially among elderly matrons to whom you owe a civil reverence, and therefore ought to tip your tongue with silence.

Silence in a woman is a moving-rhetoric, winning most, when in words it wooeth least. If opportunity give your sex argument of discourse, let it neither taste of affectation, for that were servile;[4] nor touch upon any wanton relation, for that were uncivil; nor anything above the sphere of your proper concern, for that were unequal. This will make your discourse generally acceptable, and free you from prejudicate censure.[5]

OF WANTON SONGS, AND IDLE BALLADS

Let your prudence renounce a little pleasure for a great deal of danger. To take delight in an idle vain song without staining yourself with the obscenity of it, is a thing in my mind almost impossible; for wickedness enters insensibly by the ear into the soul, and what care soever we take to guard and defend ourselves, yet still it is a difficult task not to be tainted with the pleasing and alluring poison thereof.

Physicians endeavour to persuade the wiser sort of men, as well as ignorant and credulous women, that a mother fixing steadfastly her eye on a picture, she will secretly convey the complexion, or some other mark on the infant; from hence we may be induced to believe, that the lascivious and wanton expressions contained in some songs and ballads may have the same effect in our imagination, and do most frequently leave behind them some foul impressions in our spirits.

---

[1] *tincture* trace; *fig.* a stain or blemish (*OED* tincture *sb* 5b,3b); *scurrility* coarseness or indecency of language, esp. in invective and jesting.

[2] *pith* the central or inward part; hence, the essential part (*OED* pith *sb* 4).

[3] *That excellent precept...to young women* "The stroke of the whip maketh marks in the flesh; but the stroke of the tongue breaketh the bones. Many have fallen by the edge of the sword: But not so many as have fallen by the tongue" (Ecclesiasticus 28:17–18).

[4] *affectation* artificiality; hollow or false display (*OED* affectation 4,5).

[5] *prejudicate censure* being judged or condemned in advance.

The reading [of] these wanton things do heat by little and little; it insensibly takes away the horror and repugnancy you ought to have to evil; by this means you acquaint yourself so thoroughly with the image of vice, that afterwards you fear it not though you meet with vice itself.

Licentiousness is not bred in a moment, at one and the same instant; so the contagion of loose songs seizeth by degrees on the heart; they may be said to work on the minds of youth as seed in the ground, it first appears only above the surface of the earth, but every day afterwards adds to its growth till it be fit for the sickle.

Nay more, these songs of wantonness will breed in you a more fitting boldness, which will put you on the confidence of practicing what you read or sing. Assure yourself, if you admit of a familiarity with these things, your innocency will be in daily danger.

You may easily believe this to be truth, if you consider the multiplicity of vanity and trumpery which stuff these ballads; how an amorous or rather foolishly-fond virgin forsook kindred and country, to run after a stranger and her lover. In another you find how craftily two lovers had plotted their private meetings to prosecute their unlawful enjoyments; and the letters that pass between for the continuation of their affection; which straight-ways makes the reader up to the ears in love. In the one is expressed the constancy of two fools one to the other; in the other, what trouble, what hazard, and what not, they run into, to ruin themselves, distract their parents, and leave a stain on their own reputations, never to be washed out.

These are the things which contain cunning lessons to learn the younger sort to sin more wittily;[1] and therefore no judicious person can comprehend with what reason these dangerous songs and sonnets be justified.

WHAT RECREATIONS AND PLEASURES ARE MOST FITTING AND PROPER FOR YOUNG GENTLEWOMEN

Recreations which are most proper and suitable to ladies, may be ranked under four principle heads, music, dancing, limning and reading.[2] Of dancing I have already lightly treated on in the directions for your deportment at balls; however, this I will say further on it, that though the Romans had no very great esteem for it, as it may appear by Sallust's speaking of Sempronia, *she danced better than became a virtuous lady*;[3] yet the mode and humour of these times look upon it not only as a generous and becoming property, but look upon gentility ill-bred if not thoroughly acquainted therewith;[4] and to speak the truth it is the best and readiest way to put the body into graceful posture; behaviour must of necessity halt without it; and how will you blush when you come into a mixed society, where each person strives to show her utmost art and skill in dancing, and you for the want thereof must stand still and appear like one whose body was well framed but wanted motion, or a soul to actuate it.[5]

In the next place, music is without doubt an excellent quality; the ancient philosophers were of the opinion, that souls were made of harmony and that that man or woman could not be virtuously

---

[2] *limning* painting, especially in water-colour or tempera (*OED* limning *vbl sb* 2).

[3] *Salust's speaking of Sempronia* Gaius Sallustius Crispus (ca. 86–35 B.C.E.) writes that though Sempronia was favoured with fortune, beauty and "a high degree of wit and charm," she was "able to play the lyre and dance more skillfully than an honest women need" and readily engaged in fraud, murder and sexual abandonment (*Bellum Catilinae* xxiiii–xxv).

[4] *property* attribute (*OED* property *sb* 5).

[5] *want* lack (*OED* want *sb²* 2); *actuate* perform (*OED* actuate *v* 1).

---

[1] *learn* teach (*OED* learn *v* II.4).

inclined who loved not music;[1] wherefore without it a lady or gentlewoman can hardly be said to be absolutely accomplished.

Limning is an excellent qualification for a gentlewoman to exercise and please her fancy therein. There are many foreign ladies that are excellent artists herein; neither are there wanting examples enough in his majesty's three kingdoms of such gentlewomen, whose indefatigable industry in this laudable and ingenious art, may run parallel with such as make it their profession.

Some may add stage-plays as a proper recreation for gentlewomen; as to that (provided they have the consent of parents or governess) I shall leave them to make use of their own liberty, as they shall think convenient.

I am not ignorant that stage-plays have been much envied at,[2] and not without just cause, yet most certain it is, that by a wise use, and a right application of manythings we hear and see contained therein, we may meet with many excellent precepts for instruction, and sundry great examples for caution, and such notable passages, which being well applied (as what may not be perverted) will confer no small profit to the cautious and judicious hearers.[3] Edward the Sixth the reformer of the English Church, did so much approve of plays, that he appointed a courtier eminent for wit and fancy to be the chief officer in supervising, ordering and disposing what should be acted or represented before his majesty, which office at this time retains the name of Master of the Revels. Queen Elizabeth,

that incomparable virtuous princess was pleased to term plays the harmless spenders of time, and largely contributed to the maintenance of the authors and actors of them.

But if the moderate recourse of gentlewomen to plays may be excused, certainly the daily and constant frequenting [of] them, is as much to be condemned.

There are an hundred divertisements harmless enough, which a young lady may find out, suitable to her inclination;[4] but give me leave to find out one for her which hath the attendance of profit as well as pleasure and that is reading.

Mistake me not; I mean the reading of books whose subjects are noble and honourable. There are some in these later days so stoical, that they will not allow any books to womankind, but such as may teach them to read, and the Bible. The most severe of them do willingly permit young gentlewomen to converse with wise and learned men; I know not then by what strange nicety they would keep them from reading their works. There are a sort of religious men in foreign parts, who do not debar the people from knowing there is a Bible; yet they prohibit them from looking into it.

I would fain ask these sour stoics what can be desired for the ornament of the mind, which is not largely contained and expressed in books? where virtue is to be seen in all her lovely and glorious dresses, and truth discovered in what manner soever it is desired. We may behold it in all its force, in the philosophers, with all its purity in faithful historians; with all its beauty and ornaments in golden-tongued orators, and ingenious poets.

In this pleasing variety (whatsoever your humour be) you may find matter for delectation and information.[5] Reading is of most exquisite and requisite use if for nothing but this, that these

---

[1] *souls were made of harmony* In Plato's *Timaeus*, the Demiurge brought the conflicting elements of Chaos into a harmony, proportion and unity modeled on his Idea of perfection. Into this body, circular in form and motion, he placed an invisible Soul, also circular in motion and numerically proportioned, which partook of reason and harmony.

[2] *envied at* disapproved of (*OED* envy *v* 2).

[3] *I am not ignorant...judicious hearers* In Renaissance anti-theatrical literature, stage-plays are considered socially disruptive and spiritually damning.

[4] *divertisements* diversions (*OED* divertisement *arch* 2).

[5] *delectation* delight (*OED* delectation).

dumb teachers instruct impartially. Beauty, as well as royalty, is constantly attended with more flatterers than true informers. To discover and acknowledge their faults, it is necessary that they sometimes learn of the dead what the living either dare not or are loth to tell them. Books are the true discoverers of the mind's imperfections, as a glass the faults of their face, herein shall they find judges that cannot be corrupted with love or hate. The fair and the foul are both alike treated, having to do with such who have no other eyes but to put a difference between virtue and vice. In persuading you to read, I do not advise you should read all books; advise with persons of understanding in your choice of books, and fancy not their quantity but quality. For why should ye seek that in many which you may find in one? The sun, whilst in our hemisphere needs no other light but its own to illuminate the world. One book may serve for a library. The reading of few books, is not to be less knowing, but to be the less troubled.

—1675

The Judgment and Decree of the University of Oxford
July 21, 1683

⌘

The Judgment and Decree of the University of Oxford, Passed in Their Convocation, July 21, 1683, against Certain Pernicious Books and Damnable Doctrines, Destructive to the Sacred Persons of Princes, Their State and Government, and of All Humane Society [1]

Although the barbarous assassination lately enterprised against the person of his sacred majesty and his royal brother engage all our thoughts to reflect with utmost detestation and abhorrence of that execrable villainy, hateful to God and man, and pay our due acknowledgements to the divine providence which, by extraordinary methods, brought it to pass that the breath of our nostrils, the anointed of the Lord,[2] is not taken in the pit which was prepared for him, and that under his shadow we continue to live and enjoy the blessings of his government; yet, notwithstanding, we find it to be a necessary duty at this time to search into and lay open those impious doctrines which, having of late been studiously disseminated, gave rise and growth to these nefarious attempts, and pass upon them our solemn public censure and decree of condemnation.

Therefore, to the honour of the holy and undivided Trinity, the preservation of catholic truth in the church, and that the king's majesty may be secured from the attempts of open and bloody enemies and machinations of treacherous heretics and schismatics, we, the vice-chancellor, doctors, proctors and masters regent and not regent,[3] met in convocation in the accustomed manner, time and place, on Saturday, the 21 of July, in the year 1683, concerning certain propositions contained in divers books and writings, published in English and also in the Latin tongue, repugnant to the Holy Scriptures, decrees of councils, writings of the fathers, the faith and profession of the primitive church, and also destructive of the kingly government, the safety of His Majesty's person, the public peace, the laws of nature and bonds of human society, by our unanimous assent and consent have decreed and determined in manner and form following:

THE FIRST PROPOSITION
All civil authority is derived originally from the people.

THE SECOND
There is a mutual compact, tacit or express, between a prince and his subjects, and that if he perform not his duty, they are discharged from theirs.

---

[1] With this work compare Sir Roger L'Estrange, *Considerations and Proposals in Order to the Regulation of the Press*, 1663. The present work might be held to illustrate the truth of the description of Oxford as the home of lost causes; it also shows that fears occasioned by memories of the Civil War took a long time to die, not unnaturally in view of political history between 1660 and 1688. The citations in the document are not explained; they are not necessary to its understanding, and most are easily tracked down by anyone who has learned to do library research. A highly readable account of the relevant background history is the chapter "The Reigns of Terror, 1678–85" in G.M. Trevelyan, *England under the Stuarts* (London: Methuen, 1904 and many reprints).

[2] *the breath of our nostrils*   See the headnote to Lancelot Andrewes.

[3] *masters regent and not regent*   The masters regent are those with the status of M.A., holding university appointments, who normally have a voice in decision making; masters not regent are M.A.s who are privileged to vote on certain special occasions.

THE THIRD

That if lawful governors become tyrants, or govern otherwise than by the laws of God and man they ought to do, they forfeit the right they had unto their government.

Lex Rex; Buchanan, *de Iure Regni; Vindiciae contra Tyrannos;* Bellarmine, *de Conciliis, de Pontifice;* Milton; Goodwin; Baxter, *H.C.* [*Holy Commonwealth*].

*

THE FOURTH

The sovereignty of England is in the three estates, viz. king, lords and commons. The king has but a coordinate power, and may be overruled by the other two.

Lex Rex; Hunton, *Of a Limited and Mixed Monarchy;* Baxter, *H.C.; Polit. Catechis.*

*

THE FIFTH [1]

Birthright and proximity of blood give no title to rule or government, and it is lawful to preclude the next heir from his right of succession to the crown.

Lex Rex; Hunt's *Postscript;* Doleman's *History of the Succession; Julian the Apostate; Mene Tekel.*

*

THE SIXTH

It is lawful for subjects, without the consent and against the command of the supreme magistrate, to enter into leagues, covenants and associations for defence of themselves and their religion.

Solemn League and Covenant; Late Association.

*

THE SEVENTH

Self-preservation is the fundamental law of nature, and supersedes the obligation of all others whenever they stand in competition with it.

Hobbes, *de Cive, Leviathan.*

*

THE EIGHTH [2]

The doctrine of the Gospel concerning patient suffering of injuries is not inconsistent with violent resisting of the higher powers in case of persecution for religion.

Lex Rex; Julian Apostate; Apolog. Relat.

*

THE NINTH

There lies no obligations upon Christians to passive obedience when the prince commands anything against the laws of our country; and the primitive Christians chose rather to die than to resist because Christianity was not yet settled by the laws of the empire.

Julian Apostate.

*

THE TENTH

Possession and strength give a right to govern, and success in a cause or enterprise proclaims it to be lawful and just; to pursue it is to comply with the will of God, because it is to follow the conduct of his providence.

Hobbes; Owen's sermon before the regicides, Jan. 331, 1648[/9]; Baxter; Jenkins' *Petition,* Oct. 1651.

*

THE ELEVENTH

In the state of nature there is no difference between good and evil, right and wrong; the state of nature is a state of war in which every man has a right to all things.

THE TWELFTH

The foundation of civil authority is this natural right, which is not given but left [i.e. *lent*] to the supreme magistrate upon men's entering into societies; and not only a foreign invader but a domestic rebel puts himself again into a state of nature to be proceeded against, not as a subject, but an enemy, and consequently acquires by his rebel-

---

[1] This is clearly aimed at those who wished to exclude Charles I's brother James from the throne on account of his Roman Catholicism.

[2] This takes aim at a doctrine which foreshadows the "liberation theology" of the twentieth century.

lion the same right over the life of his prince as the prince for the most heinous crimes has over the life of his own subjects.

THE THIRTEENTH
Every man, after his entering into a society, retains a right of defending himself against force, and cannot transfer that right to the commonwealth when he consents to that union whereby a commonwealth is made; and in case a great many men together have already resisted the commonwealth, for which every one of them expects death, they have liberty then to join together to assist and defend one another. Their bearing of arms subsequent to the first breach of their duty, though it be to maintain what they have done, is no new unjust act, and if it be only to defend their persons is not unjust at all.

THE FOURTEENTH
An oath superadds no obligation to [a] pact, and a pact obliges no farther than it is credited; and consequently if a prince gives any indication that he does not believe the promises of fealty and allegiance made by any of his subjects, they are thereby freed from their subjection; and, notwithstanding their pacts and oaths, may lawfully rebel against and destroy their sovereign.
Hobbes, *de Cive, Leviathan.*

*

THE FIFTEENTH
If a people that by oath and duty are obliged to a sovereign shall sinfully dispossess [him], and contrary to their covenants choose and covenant with another, they may be obliged by their later covenant, notwithstanding their former.
Baxter, *H.C.*

*

THE SIXTEENTH
All oaths are unlawful and contrary to the word of God.
Quakers.

*

THE SEVENTEENTH
An oath obliges not in the sense of the imposer, but the takers.
Sheriff's case.

*

THE EIGHTEENTH
Dominion is founded in grace.

THE NINETEENTH
The powers of this world are usurpations upon the prerogative of Jesus Christ; and it is the duty of God's people to destroy them in order to the setting Christ upon his throne.
Fifth-Monarchy Men.

*

THE TWENTIETH
The presbyterian government is the sceptre of Christ's kingdom, to which kings as well as others are bound to submit; and the king's supremacy in ecclesiastical affairs, asserted by the church of England, is injurious to Christ, the sole king and head of his church.
Altare Damascenum; Apolog. Relat.; Hist. Indulg.; Cartwright; Travers.

*

THE TWENTY-FIRST
It is not lawful for superiors to impose anything in the worship of God that is not antecedently necessary.

THE TWENTY-SECOND
The duty of not offending a weak brother is inconsistent with all human authority of making laws concerning indifferent things.
Protestant Reconciler.

*

THE TWENTY-THIRD
Wicked kings and tyrants ought to be put to death; and if the judges and inferior magistrates will not do their office, the power of the sword devolves to

the people. If the major part of the people refuse to exercise this power, then the ministers may excommunicate such a king; after which it is lawful for any of the subjects to kill him, as the people did Athaliah and Jehu Jezebel.
Buchanan; Knox; Goodman; Gilby; Jesuits.

*

THE TWENTY-FOURTH

After the sealing of the scripture-canon, the people of God in all ages are to expect new revelations for the rule of their actions (a); and it is lawful for a private man, having an inward motion from God, to kill a tyrant (b).[1]
(a) Quakers and other enthusiasts; (b) Goodman.

*

THE TWENTY-FIFTH

The example of Phineas is to us instead of a command, for what God has commanded or approved in one age must needs oblige in all.[2]
Goodman; Knox; Napthali.

*

THE TWENTY-SIXTH

King Charles the first was lawfully put to death, and his murderers were the blessed instruments of God's glory in their generation.
Milton; Goodwin; Owen.

*

THE TWENTY-SEVENTH

King Charles the first made war upon his parliament; and in such a case the king may not only be resisted, but ceases to be a king.
Baxter.

*

We decree, judge and declare all and every of these propositions to be false, seditious and impious; and most of them to be also heretical and blasphemous, infamous to Christian religion, and destruction of all government in church and state.

We further decree that the books which contain the aforesaid propositions and impious doctrines are fitted to deprave good manners, corrupt the minds of unwary men, stir up seditions and tumults, overthrow states and kingdoms, and lead to rebellion, murder of princes, and atheism itself. And therefore we interdict all members of the university from the reading [of] the said books, under the penalties in the statutes expressed. We also order the before-recited books to be publicly burnt by the hand of our marshal in the court of our schools.

Likewise we order that, in perpetual memory hereof, these our decrees shall be entered into the registry of our convocation; and that copies of them being communicated to the several colleges and halls within this university, they be there publicly affixed in the libraries, refectories, or other fit places, where they may be seen and read of all.

Lastly, we command and strictly enjoin all and singular readers, tutors, catechists, and others to whom the care and trust of institution of youth is committed that they diligently instruct and ground their scholars in that most necessary doctrine which, in a manner, is the badge and character of the church of England, of submitting to every ordinance of man for the Lord's sake,[3] whether it be to the king as supreme, or unto governors as unto them that are sent by him for the punishment of evil doers, and for the praise of them that do well; teaching that this submission and obedience is to be clear, absolute, and without exception of any state or order of men. Also that all supplications, prayers, intercessions and giving of thanks be made for all men, for the king, and all that are in authority, that we may lead a quiet and peaceable life in all god-

---

[1] This is relevant to our understanding of *Samson Agonistes*.

[2] For Phineas, see Numbers 25; and Norman T. Burns, "'Then stood up Phinehas': Milton's Antinomianism, and Samson's," in *Milton Studies 33: The Miltonic Samson*, 1996.

[3] This is based on Romans 13:1: "Let every soul be subject to the higher powers. For there is no power but of God: the powers that be are ordained of God." This is a favourite text in the Elizabethan Homilies, designed to obtain civil obedience.

liness and honesty, for this is good and acceptable in the sight of God our Saviour. And in especial manner that they press and oblige them humbly to offer their most ardent and daily prayers at the throne of grace for the preservation of our sovereign lord King Charles from the attempts of open violence and secret machinations of perfidious traitors, that he, the Defender of the Faith, being safe under the defence of the Most High, may continue his reign on earth till he exchange it for that of a late and happy immortality.

—1683

Index of Authors and Titles